Lecture Notes in Information Systems and Organisation

Volume 48

Lecture Notes in Information Systems and Organization—LNISO—is a series of scientific books that explore the current scenario of information systems, in particular IS and organization. The focus on the relationship between IT, IS and organization is the common thread of this collection, which aspires to provide scholars across the world with a point of reference and comparison in the study and research of information systems and organization. LNISO is the publication forum for the community of scholars investigating behavioral and design aspects of IS and organization. The series offers an integrated publication platform for high-quality conferences, symposia and workshops in this field. Materials are published upon a strictly controlled double blind peer review evaluation made by selected reviewers.

LNISO is abstracted/indexed in Scopus

More information about this series at http://www.springer.com/series/11237

Frederik Ahlemann · Reinhard Schütte ·
Stefan Stieglitz
Editors

Innovation Through Information Systems

Volume III: A Collection of Latest Research
on Management Issues

 Springer

Editors
Frederik Ahlemann
Faculty of Business Administration
and Economics
University of Duisburg-Essen
Essen, Germany

Reinhard Schütte
Faculty of Business Administration
and Economics
University of Duisburg-Essen
Essen, Germany

Stefan Stieglitz
Department of Computer Science
and Applied Cognitive Science
University of Duisburg-Essen
Duisburg, Germany

ISSN 2195-4968   ISSN 2195-4976   (electronic)
Lecture Notes in Information Systems and Organisation
ISBN 978-3-030-86799-7   ISBN 978-3-030-86800-0   (eBook)
https://doi.org/10.1007/978-3-030-86800-0

This Springer imprint is published by the registered company Springer Nature Switzerland AG
The registered company address is: Gewerbestrasse 11, 6330 Cham, Switzerland

Preface

Business Information Systems Engineering is a vital scientific discipline, which has objects of investigation that can hardly be more timely: the design, use, and management of information systems (IS). The discipline's wide range of topics is impressive, which is also documented through the contributions submitted to the 16th International Conference on Business Information Systems Engineering (WI21). Innovation through IS has been the guiding theme for the conference, representing both the present and the future. The coronavirus pandemic has made it clear to individuals, companies, and society as a whole that the digitalization trend will not lose its power for a long time to come. Areas of society long known for their slowness to adopt digital technologies, such as health, education, and government services, are opening up to the use of modern digital IS. The massive expansion of online shopping and the increased acceptance of digital customer touchpoints will stay even when the pandemic has ended. Moreover, virtual teamwork and working from home concepts are now implemented in many companies that were reluctant to embrace these trends before the pandemic started. Altogether, the past year has enabled a new level of digitalization and is driving companies to take further steps to digitalize products, services, and business models.

Digitalization is changing our world faster than ever, and Business Information Systems Engineering as a discipline has the potential to play a major role in understanding and shaping this development. Not only does Business Information Systems Engineering combine technical and economic knowledge in its origins, but also its intrinsic interdisciplinary nature gives it a great position to continue and extend collaboration with other disciplines, such as business economics, informatics, communication science, and psychology. In recent years, it has become clear that addressing complex organizational and societal problems requires theoretical and methodological approaches used in different disciplines. Making visible how rich, wide-ranging, and practically relevant the outcomes of our discipline are is a major goal besides contributing to the academic discourse of our community.

Business Information Systems Engineering as an established discipline gains its profile from three constituent aspects. *First*, Business Information Systems Engineering research presupposes an *information technology artifact*. This technical artifact is at least fundamentally understood (and not merely represented as a black box). This implies an understanding of the design process as well as the context of use. *Second*, the use of the technical artifact *takes place in a system that has social elements*. The integration of socio-organizational aspects is necessary because the appropriation and use of the artifact by people influences its mode of action. *Third, resource constraints can be observed in all actions in organizations.* Economic considerations are required if an organization's goal is to be achieved in the best possible way. This implies the need for economical design, use, and management of information technology (IT) artifacts as well as the question of added value that arises from their use. For example, Business Information Systems Engineering is not just about the issue of developing software according to user requirements but also about the successful use of software in organizations, which is reflected in economic dimensions.

It is a mark of great success that our discipline actively addresses a wide range of urgent research fields by submitting so many research articles to WI21. In these proceedings, we have structured the accepted papers in the areas of *domain, technology,* and *management* and a *general* area on innovative, emerging, and interdisciplinary topics and methods, theories, and ethics in Business Information Systems Engineering. The high number of papers submitted has made it necessary to publish several volumes. We have used the conference structure to divide the conference proceedings into three volumes. The first volume contains the domain-related tracks, supplemented by the two general tracks. In the second volume, the tracks on technology are summarized, and the third volume contains the management tracks. A total of 267 full papers and 80 short papers were submitted for the conference, of which 93 were accepted as full papers and 28 as short papers, resulting in an acceptance rate of 35% for the full papers and for the short papers. All the accepted papers passed a double-blind peer-review process.

The details of the short papers can be found in the table of contents and the brief introductions to the tracks; they are not detailed in this preface. The student track's interesting and diverse contributions, a clear indicator of the discipline's attractiveness for students, have also been included in the conference proceedings.

In the following, we briefly summarize the articles submitted for the different domains. In doing so, we aim to highlight the wide range and diverse nature of the contributions that characterize our academic community.

Volume I: Domain

Domain represents that part of the discourse that is of scientific interest, which has become highly differentiated due to problem specificity in research. This structure largely follows the divisions in management consultancies, standard software manufacturers, the software product-related organization of IT in companies or, in the area of research, also the call for applications-oriented research programs by the Federal Ministry of Economics in Germany. The domains contain their own "language games" with deviating application architectures and economical problem definitions. The five tracks on creating value through digital innovation in health-care, retail, digital services and smart product service systems, and smart city and e-Government examine a broad spectrum of current technology use in specific domains.

At the time of the conference, hardly any area is more present from the point of view of the digitization discussion than *Digital innovation in healthcare*. This is also documented by the contributions accepted in this track. The role of patients in the value creation of digital innovations often depends on the patients. One paper focuses on their attitudes toward apps for chronic disease management and another discusses in an empirical study how satisfied elderly people are with telemedical remote diagnostic applications. In the third paper, the evidence about patient engagement tools and their integration in patient pathways is analyzed. The transformation path from research to clinical practice for data-driven services is the subject of the last paper in this section, which analyzes how a third party can take part in less digitalized domains like health care.

The *Retail* domain is subject to two requirements as a result of digitalization: the improvement of internal and network-like value creation processes and the implementation of omnichannel customer requirements, including diverse customer touchpoints. The customer interface capabilities are essential for companies, especially after the pandemic experiences of the past year. The three selected contributions are dedicated to this topic. In the first contribution, the impact of the coronavirus pandemic on local retailers and local retailer shopping platforms was investigated with interviews. The role of personality traits and gender roles in choosing a consumer channel was investigated in a laboratory experiment with the result of significant differences in channel evaluation. The third paper discusses digitalization of luxury retail by assessing customers' quality perception of a digital sales desk for jewelry stores.

In a sense, a symbiosis of old material and new informational worlds is explored in the track *Digital services and smart product service systems*: A maturity model for manufacturers with five areas (strategy, culture, structure, practice, and IT) is used to show the stages from a pure product to a product service system provider, existing methods for the design of a digital service in operational practice are evaluated, a conceptual framework for tools for the development of digital services is designed, and requirements for augmented reality solutions for safety-critical services are formulated.

The *Digitalization and society—even in times of corona* track discusses societal challenges and the role and usage of information technologies. An empirical paper on an online survey conducted in March 2020 examines if willingness to release private data increases if fear of the crisis exists. The role of trust in government also has an impact on voluntary data provision, as shown in the paper. The perceived stress of knowledge workers working at home in COVID-19 times is investigated in another empirical study. The third paper reviews online platforms for cultural participation and education and develops a taxonomy. The differences in the challenges of digital transformations between industrial and non-profit organizations in the areas of business processes, business models, and customer experience are investigated using a grounded theory approach. The fourth paper discusses the success factors of pandemic dashboards and the development of dashboards for the specific requirements of COVID-19 data. The last paper in this section discusses the impact of digitizing social networks on refugee decision making in Germany.

The *Smart city and government track* contains both conceptual and empirical contributions. An empirical paper on competence requirements for the digitalization of public administration analyzes job advertisements, while a literature review on requirements for blockchain-based e-government services represents the status of the scientific debate on e-government blockchain approaches. The future of cities in the South Westphalia region in Germany is the subject of a scenario-based paper that examines how we can prepare cities against uncertain future circumstances. The potential uses of smart city data in smart city projects are explored through a taxonomy of such projects that provides guidance for real-world projects. The focus on sustainable urban logistic operations is directed in a contribution that offers a design-oriented strategic decision support approach. In the last contribution of the track, an explicable artificial intelligence approach is demonstrated as a support for public administration processes.

The two general tracks on innovative, emerging, and interdisciplinary topics and methods, theories, and ethics in Business Information Systems Engineering and the students' track conclude the first volume.

The track *Innovative, emerging, and interdisciplinary topics* includes five papers that address the influence of organizational culture on idea platform implementation, a taxonomy for data strategy tools and methodologies in the economy, the design of an adaptive empathy learning tool, an empirical study of secondary school students' openness to study Business Information Systems Engineering, and the altered role of 3D models in the product development process for physical and virtual consumer goods.

The track *Methods, theories, and ethics in Business Information Systems Engineering* includes three full papers on ethical design of conversational agents, a framework for structuring literature search strategies in information systems, and the design of goal-oriented artifacts from morphological taxonomies.

The *Student* track, which has been part of WI conferences since 2016, comprises 16 selected full papers and another 13 contributions accepted for the poster session. These contributions are listed in the table of contents. The program chairs consider the strong involvement of students as a distinguishing feature of Business Information Systems Engineering. For this reason, the student challenge became part of the WI2021 in Essen to bring students and companies together and to emphasize the application orientation as a further strength of Business Information Systems Engineering.

Volume II: Technology

The second volume is dedicated to the core of change in organizations, information *technology*. The five tracks of the second volume are data science and business analytics, design, management, and impact of AI-based systems, human–computer interaction, information security, privacy, and blockchain, and social media and digital work, which represent the wide range of technologies investigated in Business Information Systems Engineering.

The first track in the technology section is dedicated to the perspectives of *Data science and business analytics*. Hardly any area is associated with as much expectation in operational practice as the possibilities for using as much data as possible. A wide variety of contributions were selected that report on managing bias in machine learning projects and the design of hybrid recommender systems for next purchase prediction based on optimal combination weights, present a holistic framework for AI systems in industrial applications, use natural language processing to analyze scientific content and knowledge sharing in digital platform ecosystems demonstrated for the SAP developer community, and realize information extraction from invoices based on a graph neural network approach for datasets with high layout variety.

The second technology track, *Design, management, and impact of AI-based systems,* also covered a wide range of topics. The first paper presents a socio-technical analysis of predictive maintenance. The evaluation of the black box problem for AI-based recommendations is empirically investigated on the basis of interviews in the second paper, and the role of influencing factors and the challenges of chatbots at digital workplaces is the subject of the third contribution. Another empirical work examines the relationships of AI characteristics, project management challenges, and organizational change. The challenges for conversational agent usage through user-specific determinants and the potential for future research are the subject of the fourth paper in this track. A design science perspective is used for an augmented reality object labeling application for crowd-sourcing communities and also to construct an artificial neural network-based approach to predict traffic volume. A hybrid approach is used at a German bank by combining leveraging text classification with co-training with bidirectional language models. The eighth and final paper in this track contributes to explaining suspicion by designing an XAI-based user-focused anti-phishing measure.

One research direction that has been established in Computer Science longer than in Business Information Systems Engineering is *Human–computer interaction*. Four contributions were accepted, which deal with the influence of the human-like design of conversational agents on donation behavior, state-of-the-art research on persuasive design for smart personal assistants, a conversational agent for adaptive argumentation feedback, and insights from an experiment with conversational agents on the relation of anthropomorphic design and dialog support.

The five papers accepted in the *Information security, privacy, and blockchain* track consider data protection challenges and their solutions with regard to blockchain technologies from the perspective of German companies and organizations, a survey of private German users about the relationship between IT privacy and security behavior, cyber security challenges for software developer awareness training in industrial environments, the hidden value of using design patterns to whitebox technology development in legal assessments, and an analysis of the user motivations driving peer-to-peer personal data exchange.

The last technology track focuses on *Social media and digital work*. In the first accepted contribution, the design principles for digital upskilling in organizations are analyzed. A comparative study on content and analyst opinion, crowd- or institutionally oriented, is the subject of the second contribution. The third paper is dedicated to a no-code platform for tie prediction analysis in social media networks. The track on social media and digital work is rounded off with problems and solutions in digital work, exploring measures for team identification in virtual teams.

Volume III: Management

The third volume of the conference covers *Management* aspects and has the largest number of tracks. The volume includes tracks on data management and data ecosystems, digital education and capabilities, digital transformation and business models, digital innovations and entrepreneurship, enterprise modeling and information systems development, the future of digital markets and platforms, IT strategy, management, and transformation and, finally, management of digital processes and architecture.

Data management and data ecosystems form the starting point for value creation processes, which are expressed, among other things, in data-as-a-service considerations. In the first paper of this track, the authors design a data provenance system supporting e-science workflows. A taxonomy for assessing and selecting data sources is designed in the second paper, which also discusses aspects of the efforts for data integration in a big data context. Another literature-based paper develops four types of hybrid sensing systems as a combination of high-quality and mobile crowd sensing systems.

The *Digital education and capabilities* track includes four papers. In the first paper, a literature review about digital credentials in higher education institutions is presented. The interplay between digital workplace and organizational culture is investigated using a multi-case study in the second paper. The current performance of digital study assistants and future research fields are subject to state-of-the-art investigations in the last paper of this track.

The track *Digital transformation and business models* has been particularly topical and not only since the coronavirus pandemic. The first article takes a long-term look at which strategic orientations are identifiable, and digital business model patterns are investigated. In the second article, digital leadership is analyzed through a literature review. The path from the producer to the holistic solutions provider is an empirically oriented investigation of digital service development in an automotive environment, while the fourth contribution focuses on the success of digital transformation and asks, using the notion in IS literature, what is meant by digital transformation success. The last article in this track explores IT artifacts in people analytics and reviews tools to understand this emerging topic.

Digital innovation and entrepreneurship, the fourth management track, comprises four papers, which deal with the impact of business models on early stage financing, structuring the different capabilities in the field of digital innovation, structuring the digital innovation culture using a systematic literature review, and the question of how to recombine layers of digital technology to create digital innovation.

The track *Enterprise modeling and information systems development* as a traditional research field of our community includes three papers this year. The first is devoted to language-independent modeling of subprocesses for adaptive case management. Challenges of reference modeling are investigated in the second contribution by comparing conventional and multi-level language architectures. The last contribution is dedicated to how dimensions of supply chains are represented in digital twins by presenting a state-of-the-art survey.

With eight contributions, the *Future of digital markets and platforms* track indicates the enormous interest that our community is showing in this topic. This track also presents systematizing literature work in the form of literature reviews, taxonomies, and empirical work. The first paper undertakes a literature-based review of 23 digital platform concepts, leading to eight research focus areas. The second paper develops a taxonomy of industrial Internet of Things (IIoT) platforms with architectural features and archetypes. The third paper explains that existing reviews matter for future reviewing efforts. The reviewing effort, measured by the willingness to write an evaluation and how long the textual explanations are, is negatively correlated to the number of existing reviews. In an experiment with 339 participants, it was investigated how different evaluations are between anonymous crowds and student crowds in terms of their information processing, attention, and selection performance. The role of complementors in platform ecosystems is the subject of a literature-based review. In another paper, an empirical examination from social media analytics about IIoT platforms describes currently discussed topics regarding IIoT platforms. The principles for designing IIoT platforms are presented, analyzing an emerging platform and its ecosystem of stakeholders with a focus on their requirements. The track is rounded off with a contribution on how data-driven competitive advantages can be achieved in digital markets, which provides an overview of data value and facilitating factors.

Strategic IT management, which forms the core of the *Information technology strategy, management, and transformation* track, is also one of the traditional pillars of Business Information Systems Engineering at the interface with business administration. The first contribution considers the problem of how the design of IS for the future of leadership should be structured. The role of open source software in respect to how to govern open-source contributions is a case study-oriented research contribution of the second paper. The third paper analyzes feedback exchange in an organization and discusses the question of whether more feedback is

always better. The impacts of obsolescence in IT work and the causes, consequences, and counter-measures of obsolescence are the subject of the fourth paper
in this track. Chief digital officers, a significant role in the organization in times of
digitalization, are reviewed, and a suggestion for a research agenda is presented in
the fifth contribution. An empirical investigation of the relationship between digital
business strategy and firm performance is presented in paper six, and the role of IT
outside the IT department is discussed in paper seven of the track. The last paper
analyzes the requirements for performance measurement systems in digital innovation units.

The final track, *Management of digital processes and architectures*, concerns the
connection of digital processes and architectures. Consequently, the first contribution to the track asks the empirically motivated question: How does enterprise
architecture support the design and realization of data-driven business models?
Event-driven process controls, which are important in business reality, are related to
the Internet of Things (IoT) in the second contribution. This combination of the
technical possibilities of IoT systems with the event-driven approach defines the
purpose and attractiveness of IoT architectures and scenarios. Based on a literature
review, an outlook on a future research agenda is given, and the final contribution in
this track is dedicated to the status quo of process mining in the industrial sector and
thus addresses the use of an important method of Business Information Systems
Engineering in industry as a domain.

Due to the restrictions of the coronavirus pandemic, the International Conference
on Wirtschaftsinformatik 2021 will be held as a purely virtual event for the first
time. This is clearly a drawback, because meeting colleagues and getting into face-
to-face discussions is one of the highest benefits of this conference. Also, we are
sadly missing the chance to present the University of Duisburg-Essen and the
vibrant Ruhr area to our community. However, the conference's virtual design has
huge potential for the whole community to use and reflect on digital communication
and collaboration and to invent new concepts of interaction for the future.

The Conference Chairs would like to thank our sponsors who made the WI2021
possible and gave valuable input for innovative ways of virtual interaction and
collaboration. Furthermore, we want to thank the Rectorate of the University of
Duisburg-Essen for supporting the event. Moreover, we want to thank all those
researchers who contributed to WI2021 as authors, those colleagues who organized
conference tracks and workshops, and those who supported the track chairs as
associate editors, session chairs, and reviewers. We are aware that all these services
for the community are time-consuming and mean substantial efforts to make such a
conference a successful event. We are especially grateful for the support of the
scientific staff involved. In particular, we would like to thank Jennifer Fromm, Dr.
Erik Heimann, Lennart Hofeditz, Anika Nissen, Erik Karger, and Anna Y.
Khodijah.

In these special times, we would like to close the preface with the words of Friedrich Schiller (in German):

Einstweilen bis den Bau der Welt
Philosophie zusammenhält
Erhält sich das Getriebe
Durch Hunger und durch Liebe

April 2021

Frederik Ahlemann
Reinhard Schütte
Stefan Stieglitz
Conference Chairs WI 2021

Contents

Management of Digital Processes and Architectures

Data Management and Data Ecosystems

Introduction to the WI2021 Track: Data Management and Data Ecosystems

Christine Legner[1], Boris Otto[2], and Dirk Stelzer[3]

[1] University of Lausanne, Faculty of Business and Economics (HEC), Lausanne, Switzerland
christine.legner@unil.ch
[2] Fraunhofer Institute for Software and Systems Engineering (ISST), Dortmund, Germany
boris.otto@ isst.fraunhofer.de
[3] TU Ilmenau, Ilmenau, Germany
dirk.stelzer@tu-ilmenau.de

1 Track Description

Value creation in the digital economy is decisively dependent on the quality of data and the efficiency of their planning, processing, management and control. Triggered by the Internet of Things and emergent smart connected devices, data is also becoming a core component of business models or new services ("Data-as-a-Service"). Data is increasingly being monetized directly, and in this way new types of data ecosystems are emerging. The recently published data strategies of the German Federal Government and the European Commission underline the importance that data is attributed to the future competitiveness of companies and social prosperity.

Data management comprises all activities necessary for the management of data in companies and value creation networks. This includes in particular organizational tasks and data governance as well as data/information modeling and architectures. Digitalization and the Internet of Things have given rise to a wide range of research needs: Data management approaches need to be extended to new data classes, especially unstructured data, and data storage for heterogeneous data. In addition, data ecosystems require data sharing while at the same time ensuring the data sovereignty of the data provider and the protection of the data recipient's trust. There is also a need for research on the institutional, organizational, and technical design of data infrastructures that allow for the linking of internal with external and open data sets ("open data").

The research presented in this track shed light on these developments and can be categorized in two streams: The **first stream** comprises three papers that address the **challenges in data-driven organizations** related to the **integration of (external) data sources**. Research results comprise a taxonomy for data source selection, approaches for high-quality sensing of crowd-sourced data as well as a microservice architecture for data integration. The **second stream** extends the perspective to **data ecosystems** and tackles questions related to the design of **platforms for decentralized data sharing and processing**. It comprises two papers, one designing a blockchain-based data provenance system for e-science, and one outlining a research agenda for federated AI ecosystems in the context of edge intelligence.

2   Research Articles

2.1   DataData Source Selection Support in the Big Data Integration Process - Towards a Taxonomy (Felix Kruse, Christoph Schröer, and Jorge Marx Gómez)

Kruse, Schröer, and Gómez present a taxonomy for assessing and selecting data sources and thereby minimizing big data integration effort. The taxonomy may support data scientists in assessing feasibility of technical integration and decision-makers in comparing data providers and making a purchase decision.

2.2   Permissioned Blockchain for Data Provenance in Scientific Data Management (Julius Möller, Sibylle Fröschle, and Axel Hahn)

Möller, Fröschle, and Hahn design a data provenance system supporting e-science workflows and integrate it into an existing data space, the e-Maritime Integrated Reference Platform (eMIR). They elaborate on the architecture and blockchain design, present performance evaluation results and illustrate scientific workflows between two participating organizations that have an interest in keeping their data sets confidential.

2.3   Quantity over Quality? – A Framework for Combining Mobile Crowd Sensing and High Quality Sensing (Barbara Stöckel, Simon Kloker, Christof Weinhardt, and David Dann)

The paper by Stöckel et al. examines the combination of traditional High Quality Sensing methods and Mobile Crowd Sensing in Hybrid Sensing (HS) system. Based on a structured literature review, they identify four types of HS approaches and derive a framework that informs HS-related projects on the required process steps.

2.4   Dezentrale und Microservice-Orientierte Datenintegration am Beispiel Externer Datenquellen (Christoph Schröer and Jonas Frischkorn)

Schröer and Frischkorn's short paper presents research on management and governance of decentralized data sources for integration in federated data lakes. They propose using a microservice architecture and apply principles of domain-driven design.

2.5   Leveraging the Potentials of Federated AI Ecosystems (Marco Röder, Peter Kowalczyk, and Frédéric Thiesse)

This short paper by Röder, Kowalczyk, and Thiesse suggests combining federated learning and edge intelligence to build more sophisticated deep learning models in intra- or inter-company collaboration. The authors develop a research agenda to foster the potentials of value co-creation within federated AI ecosystems.

Data Source Selection Support in the Big Data Integration Process – Towards a Taxonomy

Felix Kruse[1]([⊠]), Christoph Schröer[2], and Jorge Marx Gómez[1]

[1] Department for Business Informatics (VLBA), Carl Von Ossietzky Universität Oldenburg,
Oldenburg, Germany
{felix.kruse,jorge.marx.gomez}@uni-oldenburg.de
[2] Volkswagen AG, Corporate Foresight, Wolfsburg, Germany
christoph.schroeer@volkswagen.de

Abstract. Selecting data sources is a crucial step in providing a useful information base to support decision-makers. While any data source can represent a potential added value in decision making, it's integration always implies a representative effort. For decision-makers, data sources must contain relevant information in an appropriate scope. The data scientist must assess whether the integration of the data sources is technically possible and how much effort is required. Therefore, a taxonomy was developed to identify the relevant data sources for the decision-maker and minimize the data integration effort. The taxonomy was developed and evaluated with real data sources and six companies from different industries. The final taxonomy consists of sixteen dimensions that support the data scientist and decision-maker in selecting data sources for the big data integration process. An efficient and effective big data integration process can be carried out with a minimum of data sources to be integrated.

Keywords: Data source selection · Big data integration · Taxonomy · Record linkage · Data science

1 Introduction

More and more information about real-world entities is digitized and stored in databases. This information can be company-related information such as new product releases, company acquisitions, patent applications, or person-related information such as their employer, published papers, or which competences they have. Many of this information is available in various internal and external databases. These data sources with complementary, additional, or different valuable information are rarely combined, which is why they can be called data silos [1]. There is often a lack of information about the existence and a lack of transparency about the content of the data sources [1]. The reduction of data silos leads to an increase in information value when several data sources are combined [2]. Decision-makers in companies and research need this added information value from combined data sources to make a decision that results in a successful action. This sequence can be described by the big data information value chain [3]. It describes the

F. Ahlemann et al. (Eds.): WI 2021, LNISO 48, pp. 5–21, 2021.
https://doi.org/10.1007/978-3-030-86800-0_1

sequence of (1) data, to (2) information, to (3) knowledge, which is used in a (4) decision, and results in an (5) action. It is crucial to select the data sources with the required information that is relevant for the decision-making. Since the required information can be located in different data sources, they must first be integrated. The data integration aims to enable uniform access to data, which are located in several independent data sources [2]. The Big Data Integration (BDI) technical challenges such as semantic, syntactic, and technical heterogeneity between data sources must be overcome to enable data integration [2, 4]. Figure 1 shows the BDI process extended by the process step of data source *selection*. First, the relevant external and internal data sources must be selected. Then the process steps *schema matching, record linkage,* and *data fusion* must be completed to finally obtain the integrated data source [2, 5].

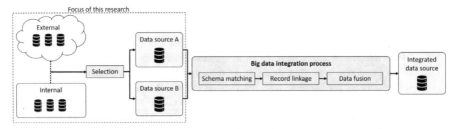

Fig. 1. Extended big data integration process to include data source selection [6]

The integrated database is used to develop a data product that supports business decisions. The data product can be a descriptive, predictive, or prescriptive analysis result. The Cross-Industry Standard Process for Data Mining (CRISP-DM) is widely used to develop a data product [6, 7]. In the first CRISP-DM phases business and data understanding, the data product's goal is defined, and the data sources are selected. These tasks are often performed by data scientists and decision-makers from the respective application departments, such as marketing or sales.

With the available number of data sources, there is often the problem that neither the data scientist nor the decision-maker is aware of all of them. The decision-maker cannot judge which data source contains the relevant information. The data scientist cannot estimate the technical effort required to receive and integrate the data sources. It is generally difficult to track the number of data sources, compare them with each other from the point of view of the data scientist and the decision-maker, and ultimately select the most suitable ones. The selection of data sources is a crucial task for carrying out an efficient and effective BDI process [4]. The goal should be to integrate as few data sources as possible to obtain the most appropriate information base. Because the more data sources have to be integrated, the more complex the BDI process is. At this point, the following research question arises, which is to be answered in this paper: *"How can the data source selection be supported in the big data integration process?"* To answer the research question, we used the qualitative research method to develop a taxonomy by Nickerson et al. [8]. Our research approach is inductive, since we obtain generalizing insights from concrete data sources and domain knowledge. The paper is structured as follows. In Sect. 2 the theoretical background is presented. In Sect. 3 the development and evaluation of the taxonomy is described. The final taxonomy is described in Sect. 4. Afterwards, the use of the taxonomy is described in Sect. 5. Finally, a summary and future research directions are presented in Sect. 6.

2   Background

Many research papers exist along the BDI process. The literature review of Kruse et al. [9] describes the current state of research in the field of entity linking and record linkage. Entity linking tries to extract relevant entities such as persons or companies from unstructured texts. Record linkage identifies records that refer to the same real-world entity, such as a person or a company. Furthermore, there are record linkage systems like Magellan[1] or the framework BigGorilla,[2] which are technically supporting the complete BDI process [10–12]. All these papers focus only on the three process steps *schema matching*, *record linkage*, and *data fusion*.

We conducted a literature search for the relevant topics *data source selection* and *creation of taxonomies to describe data sources*. The relevant research papers from both areas are presented below.

Data Source Selection Research: For the data source selection in the context of big data, papers such as that of Safhi et al. [13] exist. This paper develops an algorithm to identify the subset of relevant and reliable sources with the lowest cost from an existing set of data sources [13]. A prerequisite for the procedure is that all data sources are available and accessible to calculate the developed metrics. Safhi et al. [13] summarize the problem of data source selection as a compromise between the contribution of the source, its quality, and the associated costs.

Assaf et al. [14] developed a framework for assessing the quality of Linked Open Data. They developed a tool that profiles the data sources and evaluates them based on objectively measurable indicators. Nevertheless, the reference to the BDI process is missing in this paper.

Lin et al. [4] develop an algorithm for the evaluation of data quality. The algorithm calculates the number of expected correct values per attribute for a data source (truth discovery). With this single criterion, the data sources with the truest attributes can be selected [4]. The procedure requires full access to the data source to execute the algorithms. It also targets only the truth content criterion and helps to select the data sources with the highest truth content. A reference to the BDI process is missing.

Dong et al. [15] aim to support the selection of data sources before the BDI process starts so that the quality of the data and the data integration effort can be balanced. However, first, the authors focus on the last step of the BDI process, the data fusion, in which the conflicts of the already integrated data sources must be solved [15]. Building on this, Rekatsinas et al. [16] go further into detail by extending the approach of Dong et al. [15] for changing data sources.

---

[1] https://sites.google.com/site/anhaidgroup/projects/magellan.

[2] https://www.biggorilla.org/.

Data Source Taxonomy Research: There also exists research work to classify data sources with the help of a taxonomy. In the paper of Zrenner et al. [17] a data source taxonomy for the visibility of the supply chain network structure is developed. The taxonomy goal is to increase the knowledge of practitioners and researchers about data sources for supply chain network structures. According to Zrenner et al. [17], the taxonomy should support the initial data source selection. However, the taxonomy is limited to supply chain data sources and does not reference the BDI process.

Li et al. [18] present a rule-based taxonomy of dirty data. The taxonomy is designed to support companies in better monitoring, analyzing, and cleansing dirty data. The authors present a method to solve the problem of dirty data selection, since often not all data cleansing procedures can be performed due to limited computing capacity [18]. This taxonomy focuses on the support of the general data preparation and not the BDI process.

Roeder et al. [19] present a taxonomy to classify the heterogeneity of data sources and help researchers and professionals explore data sources. The authors consider the 5 V definition of big data (volume, velocity, variety, value, and veracity) when developing the taxonomy. However, the value and the veracity of the data sources are not taken into account. From the author's perspective, the added value of the data is challenging to measure objectively [19]. The taxonomy is evaluated by applying it to five other data sources. The paper lacks an evaluation with practitioners or researchers who were not involved in taxonomy development [19].

The presented papers show that research in the areas is conducted separately. No paper considers the creation of a taxonomy for data source selection. Also, no paper in both areas consider the BDI process. This research gap is investigated in our paper.

3   Development Process of the Data Source Taxonomy

The classification of objects of a domain into a taxonomy is a problem in many disciplines, such as information systems research. A taxonomy supports structuring and organizing knowledge of a defined domain. A taxonomy enables researchers to describe and investigate the relationships between the concepts captured in the taxonomy. Taxonomies as structure-giving artifacts play a key role in the exploration of new fields of research in Information Systems (IS) [8, 20]. A taxonomy T is defined as a set of n dimensions. Each of these dimensions contains mutually exclusive and overall complete characteristics [8]. Nickerson et al. [8] define that only one characteristic from each dimension may be assigned to an object [8, 19]. The taxonomy we have created allows for multiple selections of characteristics to increase the taxonomy's usefulness.

For the development of a taxonomy Nickerson et al. [8] have developed a widely used process. The process supports researchers in developing a taxonomy [8]. The process is shown in Fig. 2 and is described in the next section.

3.1 Development of the Taxonomy

In the first process step, *determine meta-characteristics*, the goal of the taxonomy should be defined. Based on the defined goal, the dimensions and characteristics can be determined in a targeted manner. Nickerson et al. [8] recommend deriving the goal from the potential users and the related use cases of the taxonomy [8].

Meta-characteristic: The taxonomy is intended to support a data scientist and a decision-maker in selecting data sources in the BDI process. The content of the data source should be described to estimate the added value of the information. Also, technical characteristics should be described in order to be able to estimate the possibilities and the effort required for data integration.

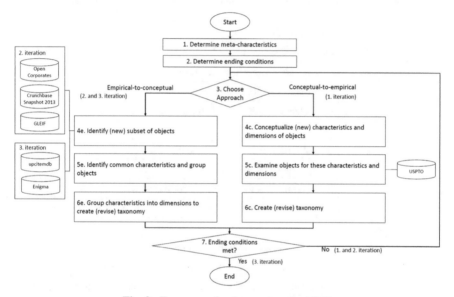

Fig. 2. Taxonomy development method [21]

In the second process step, *determine ending conditions*, objective and subjective ending conditions for the process are defined. These ending conditions are necessary to stop the iterative process [8]. This paper adopts the eight objective and five subjective ending conditions proposed by Nickerson et al. [8] (see Table 1). After each iteration, the ending conditions are checked (process step 7 *ending conditions met?*). The process stops when all conditions are met.

The iterative process begins in step three *choose approach*. In this process step, a decision is made between the empirical-to-conceptual and the conceptual-to-empirical approach. The choice of the approach is determined by the domain knowledge and the available objects. In our taxonomy development process, the data sources represent the objects.

The conceptual-to-empirical approach is recommended if a few data sources, but significant domain knowledge is available. The empirical-to-conceptual approach is recommended if little domain knowledge but many data sources are available [8, 19].

For the first iteration, we could decide between both approaches since the authors have domain knowledge and six relevant data sources. We decided to use the conceptual-to-empirical approach in the first iteration.

For this purpose, the dimensions and characteristics are first derived from existing theories (process step 4c *conceptualize (new) characteristics and dimensions of objects*).

For the initial creation of the taxonomy, we refer to the paper by Zrenner et al. [17], who developed a data source taxonomy for the field of supply chain management without reference to the BDI process. Their created taxonomy was first generalized so that the taxonomy can be used for any application area.

Table 1. Final conditions fulfilled per iteration of the taxonomy development [8]

Iteration			Ending condition
1	2	3	Objective condition
		x	All relevant objects have been examined
x	x	x	No merge or split of objects
	x	x	Each characteristic of each dimension was selected by one object
		x	No new dimension or characteristic was added
		x	No dimension was merged or split
x	x	x	Every dimension is unique
x	x	x	Every characteristic is unique within its dimension
x	x	x	Each combination of characteristics is unique and is not repeated
Subjective condition			
	x	x	Concise: meaningful without being unwieldy or overwhelming
	x	x	Robust: significant and informative characteristics
		x	Comprehensive: all objects or a sample of objects can be classified
x	x	x	Extendible: dimensions and characteristics can be easily added
x	x	x	Explanatory: the dimensions and characteristics explain the objects

The information quality of the data sources is crucial for the selection for integration [2]. Therefore, we take into account the widely used 15 information quality (IQ) dimensions of Wang et al. [21]. The IQ dimensions are divided into the superordinate categories, (1) intrinsic data quality, (2) contextual data quality, (3) representational data quality, and (4) accessibility data quality. The criteria give an overview of relevant evaluation dimensions of data sources [21], which are valid until today.

Furthermore, the taxonomy of Roeder et al. [19] is included in the development in order to consider the 5V (volume, velocity, variety, value, and veracity) of big data in the development of the taxonomy. In contrast to Roeder et al. [19], we objectively describe the value of a data source with our taxonomy. We will also try to describe the veracity property of big data objectively to a certain extent. The trustworthiness of a data source is a difficult criterion to measure. We think that this can only be reliably estimated by working with the data and independently checking the data and that only a rough tendency can be made when selecting data sources that have not yet been worked with in detail. In the next process step, *5c examine objects for these characteristics and dimensions*, the data source of the United States Patent and Trademark Office (USPTO)[3] was applied to the taxonomy. Then the process step *6c create(revise) taxonomy* was performed and it was determined that not all ending conditions were met (see Table 2). For the second iteration, we have chosen the empirical-to-conceptual method. First, in step *4c identify (new) subset of objects* we used the data sources OpenCorporates,[4] Crunchbase Open Data Map,[5] Crunchbase 2013 Snapshot[6] and Level-1 dataset from the Global Legal Entity Identifier (GLEIF) Foundation.[7]

With these data sources, the taxonomy was further developed in the process steps *5e identify common characteristics and group objects* and *6e group characteristics into dimensions to create (revise) taxonomy*. Even after the second iteration, not all ending conditions were fulfilled. The third iteration was performed with the empirical-to-conceptual method. The data sources upcitemdb[8] and a dataset of the Enigma platform[9] were used for further development. After the third iteration, all final conditions were met and the taxonomy development process was finished.

3.2   Evaluation of the Taxonomy

The iterative taxonomy development process and the subjective and objective ending conditions lead to an ex-ante evaluation [20]. The main goal of a taxonomy is to be useful and suitable for the defined use case (meta-characteristics). Since usefulness is a criterion that is difficult to measure, the taxonomy should be presented to and used by the addressed target group [8, 20]. The target group consists of data scientists and decision-makers in our case.

Szopinski et al. [20] presents a framework for the ex-post evaluation of a taxonomy, which is applied in this paper. The framework is divided into the following three sections.

1. Who, Subject of Evaluation?   The evaluation of a taxonomy can be performed by persons who have already been involved in the development of the taxonomy or who are new to the research project for evaluation. These persons can be researchers or practitioners [20]. For the evaluation, we were able to draw on researchers from the University of Oldenburg and Goettingen (see Table 2), who are experienced in both the development of a taxonomy and the selection of data sources. Furthermore, we were able to win over data scientists and decision-makers from different sectors like automotive

---

[3] https://developer.uspto.gov/product/patent-grant-bibliographic-dataxml.

[4] https://opencorporates.com/.

[5] Powered by Crunchbase: https://data.crunchbase.com/docs/open-data-map.

[6] Crunchbase 2013 Snapshot ©, Creative Commons Attribution License [CC-BY], https://data.crunchbase.com/docs/2013-snapshot.

[7] https://www.gleif.org/de/lei-data/gleif-concatenated-file/download-the-concatenated-file.

[8] https://www.upcitemdb.com/.

[9] At the time of access still freely available: https://public.enigma.com/browse/collection/stock-exchanges-company-listings/50a2457d-6407-4581-8f14-5d37a9410fa9.

OEM, software development, photo and online print service, energy utility, energy sales, and financial services to evaluate the taxonomy. With this evaluation partners, the target group of the taxonomy is covered.

2. What, Object of Evaluation? The evaluation can be performed directly with data sources (objects) or indirectly with papers reporting on data sources (research on the objects). Therefore data sources can be used, which have already been used for the development of the taxonomy or completely new data sources [20]. The evaluation in this paper was done in one case (ID 1) with data sources that have already been used for the development of the taxonomy (see Table 2). The evaluation runs with the IDs 3, 6, 7, and 9 based on the participating persons' expertise. The remaining evaluation runs were performed with new data sources.

Table 2. Overview of the evaluation of the taxonomy

Who			What	How		
ID	Sector	Role	Object (data source)	Focus group	Expert interview	Illustrative interview
1	University Oldenburg	Researcher	OpenCorporates, Crunchbase			x
2	Automotive OEM	Decision-maker	Internal data sources	x		x
3	University Goettingen	Researcher	About real-world		x	
4	Software Development	Data Scientist	Covid, Natural Earth, Wiki		x	x
5	Photo and online print service	Data Scientist	Weather data source	x		x
6	Energy Utility	Decision-maker	About real-world		x	
7	Energy Sales	Decision-maker	About real-world		x	
8	University Oldenburg	Researcher	UTKFace, IMDB-WIKI	x		x
9	Energy Utility	Data Scientist	About real-world		x	
10	Financial Services	Data Scientist	Internal data sources	x		x

3. How, Method of Evaluation? The evaluation can be carried out with different methods, which are described in the paper by Szopinski et al. [20]. We have chosen the methods expert interview, focus group, and illustrative scenario (with real data sources). The expert interview was used when one person out of the target group was available for evaluation (see Table 2 ID's 3, 4, 6, 7, and 9). The focus group was used if more than one person out of the target group was available (see Table 2 IDs 2, 5, 8, and 10). In both methods, we first introduced the taxonomy to the persons and then asked the following open questions recommended by [20]: (1) Is the taxonomy understandable and complete? (2) Have all relevant objects been considered in the taxonomy? (3) Which dimensions or characteristics should be changed, added or deleted?

In the evaluation method illustrative scenario (see Table 2 ID's 1, 2, 4, 5, 8, 10) the taxonomy was applied by the respective evaluation partners to data sources such as weather data (ID 5), Covid,[10] Natural Earth,[11] Wiki[12] data (ID 4), UTKFace,[13] IMDB-Wiki[14] (ID 8) or to internal company data (ID 2 and 10).

The feedback from the evaluation runs has led to adjustments to the taxonomy, so that it has been iteratively developed further (see Table 1). The subjective and objective ending conditions from Table 1 were used again to determine the end of the evaluation runs. After ten evaluation runs, all ending conditions were met, so that the final taxonomy was developed to assist in selecting data sources.

4   The Final Taxonomy

This section describes the final taxonomy (see Fig. 3). The taxonomy is intended to be used by data scientists and decision-makers who select data sources for the BDI process. We think that the selection of data sources depends strongly on the data product. The data source taxonomy should capture as objective criteria as possible to support an optimal decision for individual data products.

D1: Accessibility The dimension accessibility was taken over from the taxonomy of [17] and at the same time addresses the IQ dimension 7 accessibility [21]. The dimension has the characteristics $C_{1j} = \{$*Internal, external(open), external(closed)*$\}$. A distinction is made between internal and external data sources from the perspective of the user of the taxonomy. For external data sources, there is also a distinction between whether login data is required for access (*external(closed)*) or whether it is accessible without barriers (*external(open)*).

D2: Licensing The dimension License was created during the three development iterations. It has the characteristics $C_{2j} = \{$*Specification open-source license, provider own license, not available*$\}$. Under the characteristic *specification open source license* the existing open source license should be specified such as MIT or BSD-3-Clause. Commercial data source providers often conclude individual license agreements. Then the characteristic *provider own license* should be selected. If nothing is known about the license, select *not available*.

---

[10] https://www.kaggle.com/sudalairajkumar/novel-corona-virus-2019-dataset.

[11] http://www.naturalearthdata.com/downloads/10m-cultural-vectors/.

[12] https://www.kaggle.com/juanumusic/countries-iso-codes.

[13] https://susanqq.github.io/UTKFace/.

[14] https://data.vision.ee.ethz.ch/cvl/rrothe/imdb-wiki/.

Dimension	Characteristics					
D1: Accessibility	Internal		External (open)		External (closed)	
D2: Licensing	Specification Open Source License		Provider own license		Not available	
D3: Use after license expiry	Data can be further used		Data may no longer be used and must be deleted		Not available	
D4: Price model	Quantity-controlled	Time-controlled	One time costs		Free of charge	Data owner
D5: Interface	API		GUI	Manual download		Data medium
D6: Data structure	Strucutred		Semistructured		Unstructured	
D7: Reported point in time or period	Period of time		Point in time		Not available	
D8: Update	Real-time		Regular interval		Not available	
D9: Language	Source language(s)		Translated into language(s)		Not available	
D10: Scope of the data source	Complete		Self-selected extract		Provided extract	
D11: Preprocessing of the data	Schema created		Metadata generated	Metadata from the data provider		Keep original data format
D12: Current data status	Specification of the data status (date or version)					
D13: Real-world entity	Company	Person	Product	Patent	Geographical location	[...]
D13a: Number of records	Specification of the number			Not available		
D13b: Data volume	Specification of the volume			Not available		
D13c: Number of describing attributes	Specification of the number of descriptive attributes			Not available		
D14: Total data volume	Specification of the total volume			Not available		
D15: Number of tables or files	Specifying the number of tables or files			Not available		
D16: Added Information Value	Balance sheet data	Mergers and acquisitions information	Product information	Financing and stock exchange data	Corporate structures	Pantet applications, patent grants [...]

Fig. 3. Final data source taxonomy to support the data source selection

D3: Use after License Expiry The dimension use after license expiry was created by the evaluation with the practitioners. It has the characteristics $C_{3j} = \{$ *Data can be further used, data may no longer be used and must be deleted, not available*$\}$. The dimension is intended to describe the data sources in terms of how to deal with data after the license expires.

D4: Price Model The dimension price model is taken from the taxonomy of Zrenner et al. [17]. It has the characteristics $C_{4j} = \{$ *Quantity-controlled, time-controlled, one time costs, free of charge, data owner*$\}$. This dimension should describe the pricing model of the data source. In this dimension, multiple selections are possible, since, for example, a combination of a *quantity-controlled* and *time-controlled* pricing model is possible. The base account of OpenCorporates with 20000 requests per month is an example for such pricing models. If an internal data source is classified, the characteristic *data owner* should be selected.

D5: Interface The Interface dimension was created during the development-iterations and is intended to describe the user's access options to the data source. The characteristics $C_{5j} = \{$ *API, GUI, manual download, data medium*$\}$ serve this purpose. Multiple selections are possible. When selecting the characteristics, it is best to specify which data formats such as XML, JSON, or CSV are offered. The characteristic *data medium* is selected if the data source is provided e.g., via a hard disk or USB stick.

D6: Data Structure The dimension data structure is described by the characteristics $C_{6j} = \{$ *Schema(structured), schemeless(semi-structured or unstructured)*$\}$ whether the data source is structured, semi-structured or unstructured. The dimension was created during the development process.

D7: Reported Point in Time or Period The dimension reported point in time or period was created during the evaluation. The characteristics $C_{7j} = \{Period\ of\ time,\ point\ in\ time,\ not\ available\}$ are intended to describe the point in time or period covered by the data in the data source. For example, patent data from the USPTO exists since 1976, whereas an overview of AI start-ups only exists for the point in time July 2019.

D8: Update Frequency The dimension update frequency describes the update of the current data source with the characteristics $C_{8j} = \{Real\text{-}time,\ regular\ interval,\ not\ available\}$. The data source can be updated continuously in real-time or at a certain frequency, which should be specified if possible. If nothing is known about updating the data source, *not available* is selected. This dimension was created during the development process and address IQ Dimension 9 (timeliness) of Wang et al. [21].

D9: Language The Language dimension describes the language used in the data source. The dimension was created during the development process and was extended during the evaluation. The dimension has the characteristics $C_{9j} = \{Source\ language(s),\ translated\ into\ language(s),\ not\ available\}$. The languages that appear in the data source should be specified, such as German or English. During the evaluation, a data source was classified, which was translated into a common language by the data provider, for which the characteristic *translated into language(s)* was included. If the data source does not contain a language, but consists, for example, only of numerical values, *not available* is selected. This characteristic also arose during the evaluation of a practice partner who classified a sensor data source.

D10: Scope of the Data Source This dimension should describe the scope of the data source for classification into this taxonomy. The characteristics $C_{10j} = \{Complete,\ self\text{-}selected\ extract\ of\ data,\ provided\ extract\ of\ the\ data\}$ should be used for this purpose. If the data source is not complete, it is necessary to specify the user's criteria to make a selection or by the data provider. The dimension has been defined during the development-iterations. For example, Crunchbase provides an extract of the data from 2013.

D11: Preprocessing of the Data With the dimension preprocessing of the data, it is to be described whether the data source has already been preprocessed and on this basis the classification with the taxonomy is carried out. The characteristics $C_{11j} = \{Schema\ created\ or\ metadata\ generated\ (structured),\ structured\ metadata\ from\ the\ data\ provider,\ keep\ original\ data\ format\}$ are to be used for this. For example, JSON files will be preprocessed and converted to a structured format to get a first overview of the data source. Data providers of unstructured data, such as news data, often provide structured metadata for them. If a structured data structure already exists, the data structure is often not changed. This dimension was created during the evaluation process with the practice partners.

D12: Current Data Status The dimension current data status has one characteristic $C_{12j} = \{Specification\ of\ the\ data\ status\ (date\ or\ version)\}$ with which the current content status of the data source is to be indicated. The dimension was created during the development process.

D13: Real-World Entity This dimension is used to describe which real-world entities are represented in the data source. In the taxonomy in Fig. 3, the last cell (*[...]*) indicates that the characteristics should and may be supplemented by further entities. From the development and evaluation process the characteristics $C_{13j} = \{$*Company, person, product, patent, geographical location*$\}$ have emerged. This dimension is crucial for the BDI process since it is possible to identify whether and via which entity the data sources could potentially be connected. The goal of the process step record linkage is to identify records that belong to the same real-world entity [5].

D13a: Number of Records; D13b: Data Volume; 13c Number of Describing Attributes The dimensions 13a, 13b, and 13c should be filled in for each real-world entity, if possible. The specification of how many unique data records, how large the data volume, and how many describing attributes exist for each real-world entity should help evaluate the value and veracity of the data source. The objective, quantifiable criteria allow the assessment of whether the data source is potentially useful or not for the data product. Also, the number of descriptive attributes serves as a first indication for the execution of the BDI process steps schema matching and record linkage. Since it can be estimated how many attributes a comparison of the data records can be carried out. The unique number of data records and attributes correlated with the data volume can be used to estimate how complete the data source is.

Furthermore, whether the data source offers an appropriate scope (IQ dimension 19) and thus also relevance (IQ dimension 2) for the respective data product [21]. Other taxonomies like the one from Zrenner et al. [17] or Roeder et al. [19] use characteristics like high, medium, low, which are very subjective. This subjective criteria are difficult to use to compare different data sources. Our chosen objective numerical criteria can be used to compare different data sources.

D14: Total Data Volume This dimension should cover the entire data volume of the data source. If this is not available, the characteristic *not available* is used. This objective criterion also serves to evaluate the appropriate scope of the data source in comparison to other data sources.

D15: Number of Tables or Files This dimension should describe the number of existing tables or files of the data source. This objective criterion is intended to provide a first assessment of whether the scope is appropriate (IQ dimension 19) and the information can be relevant (IQ dimension 2) [21].

D16: Added Information Value This dimension was created during the development process and has been further extended during the evaluation process. With this dimension and its characteristics, the practitioners and researchers had the greatest difficulties understanding and applying it during the evaluation. This dimension should serve to objectively capture the big data characteristics value and the IQ-Dimension 2 value-added for the data source. The final taxonomy (see Fig. 3) shows some characteristics. Multiple selections are possible and the characteristics should be expandable if further data sources with new added information values are captured.

On the one hand, the characteristics must not be recorded in too much detail, as the effort to apply the taxonomy could become too high. On the other hand, the characteristics must not be recorded too roughly, so that the added value of the data source is adequately captured. An important requirement for the operationalization of the taxonomy is that the characteristics of this dimension are maintained and extended centrally so that the instances of the characteristics remain disjunctive.

5 Application of the Taxonomy in the Data Source Selection

We applied the final taxonomy to the Crunchbase (see Footnote 6), USPTO Patent Grants (see Footnote 3) and AI Startups[15] data sources to demonstrate the applicability and utility (Fig. 4). In the taxonomy meta-characteristic, it has been defined that the taxonomy users are data scientists and decision-makers. The users should be supported in the process steps business understanding and data understanding when designing a data product. Since the crucial data source selection for the data product development takes place in these phases. To demonstrate the utility of the taxonomy, Sect. 5.1 describes the data integration perspective and Sect. 5.2 the decision-maker perspective of the taxonomy.

Dimension	Crunchbase[6]				USPTO Patent Grants[3]				AI Startups[15]		
D1: Accessibility	External (closed)				External (open)				External (open)		
D2: Licensing	Provider own license				Provider own license				Not available		
D3: Use after license expiry	Not available				Data can be further used				Not available		
D4: Price model	Time-controlled				Free of charge				Free of charge		
D5: Interface	API	GUI	Manual download		API	GUI	Manual download (XML)		Manual download (Image, PDF, PowerPoint)		
D6: Data structure	Structured (MySql Dump)				Semistructured (XML)				Semistructured (PDF)		Unstructured (Image, PowerPoint)
D7: Reported point in time or period	Not available				1976 until today				July 2019		
D8: Update	Real-time				Regular interval				Not available		
D9: Language	english				english				deutsch		
D10: Scope of the data source	Provided extract (Crunchbase 2013 Snapshot)				Self-selected extract (One week 20.08 - 27.08.19)				Complete		
D11: Preprocessing of the data	Keep original data format				Schema created				Schema created		
D12: Current data status	2013				August 2019				Not available		
D13: Real-world entity	Company	Person	Product	Geographical location	Company	Person	Patent	Geographical location	Company		Geographical location
D13a: Number of records	118.342	117.318	25.059	7.976	34.409	209.123	114.138	24.682	279		47
D13b: Data volume	166 MB				12 MB	25 MB	14 MB	12 MB	32 KB		
D13c: Number of describing attributes	40				10	8	7	3	4		1
D14: Total data volume	300 MB				200 MB				32 KB		
D15: Number of tables or files	10 tables				9 tables				1 tables		
D16: Added Information Value	Worldwide				Patent applications in america				German ai-startups		
	Financing and stock exchange data		Corporate structures		Patent applications, patent grants				Funding and investor information		
	Relationships between Company, Person, Product				Relationships between Company, Person, Patent				Branch and application focus		
	Graduation of persons		Mergers and acquisitions information		Technology classification				Strategic startup orientation		

Fig. 4. Application of the taxonomy on the data sources Crunchbase, USPTO and AI Startups

5.1 Data Integration Perspective

From the data integration point of view the following questions could be answered for example:

[15] https://de.appanion.com/startups.

- Q1: Which real-world entity(ies) can be used to link the data sources?
- Q2: How many attributes are available for comparison?
- Q3: How is the data source structured?
- Q4: What is the data volume of the entities?
- Q5: How can the data source be accessed?

(Q1) The dimension D13 provides the information that the three data sources could be integrated via the entity company or geographical location. Integration via the patent entity of the USPTO Patent Grants data source is not possible because no other data source contains this entity.

(Q2) The dimension 13a contains the number of attributes for each real-world entity. This information is used for a first estimation of how successful and sophisticated the integration could be since the attributes that can be compared are identified in the BDI process step schema matching [5]. All Crunchbase entities are stored in a common table consisting of 40 attributes. The USPTO Patent Grants contains ten attributes for the entity company. The AI Startups contains four attributes for the entity company. For the integration of the AI startups with one of the other data sources, the four attributes must be mapped to the 10 or 40 attributes (schema matching). We assume that more attributes improve the quality of the BDI process result, but also increase complexity.

(Q3) The structure of the data source can be read from D6. The BDI process's effort increases if semi-structured or unstructured data sources are available because the BDI process requires structured data.

(Q4) If there is only a part of the data source available (D10) and data integration is to be carried out with this part, dimension 11 is relevant. Dimension 11 documents whether the original data structure has been retained or preprocessed. For example, the original XML structure (D6) of the USPTO Patent Grants was converted into a structured form (D11) with nine tables (D15). The number of data records (D13a) and the data volume (D13b) can be used to estimate the computing capacity required for data integration. If the data sources Crunchbase and AI Startups are to be integrated via the entity company, 33.017.418 (279 × 118.342) data records would have to be compared. At this point, the data scientist can get a first assessment of a suitable blocking algorithm to reduce the number of comparisons in the record linkage process.

(Q5) The dimension D5 provides the information on how to access the data source. The data source AI Startups only offers a manual download of the AI Startup Report in the data formats Image, PDF, and PowerPoint. This dimension is essential for determining the degree of automation of the subsequent operationalization of the data product.

5.2 Decision-Maker Perspective

We think that the choice of decision-makers data sources depends on the goal of the data product. Therefore, the taxonomy provides objective and comparable criteria that can be individually evaluated and prioritized for each data product.

The taxonomy allows the decision-maker to answer the following questions:

- Q1: Do the data sources contain useful information, added value, and appropriate scope for the data product?

- Q2: Are the data sources sufficiently reliable?
- Q3: Is the data current enough and goes back far enough into the past?
- Q4: What is the licensing model of the data sources?
- Q5: How expensive is the data source?

(Q1) The added value of the information provided by the data source can be taken from the dimension D16. If, for example, AI startups are required for a data product, the AI startup's data source is suitable. Patent information for the data product should also be used. The dimension D16 indicates the decision-maker that the AI startups data source does not provide this information and that the USPTO Patent Grants data source should be used. However, this data source only provides patent grants from America. These value-added information categories can thus be used to select an initial selection of data sources that are suitable for the data product. Via the dimension D10, the decision-maker can see the basis on which the descriptions of D11–D16 have been collected. With the dimensions D13, D13a, D13b, D13c, decision-makers can also estimate whether the data sources contain a sufficient scope for the data product. If, for example, german AI companies are to be analyzed and the decision-maker knows that about 1000 of such companies, the decision-maker recognizes that the AI Startups data source does not include all german AI companies.

(Q2) The trustworthiness of a data source is a difficult criterion to measure and we think that this can only be reliably estimated by working with the data and independently checking the data. The IQ dimensions believability (1), completeness (10), accuracy (4), and interpretability (5) [21] are covered by the big data characteristic veracity. We think that by specifying the data provider name, the license model (D2), the pricing model (D4), and the dimensions D13a, b, and c, the first estimation of the veracity of the data source can be supported.

(Q3) The up-to-dateness of the data source information can be read from D7 and D8. In D7, it is indicated whether the data source only represents a point in time, like the AI Startup data source, or whether it represents a period, like the USPTO Patent Grants from 1976 until today. In D8, it is indicated whether and how the data source is updated. For example, the USPTO Patent Grants data source is updated weekly. The update frequency of the data source is essential for the operationalization of the data product. Since a decision that has to be made daily, often requires a data source with information that is updated daily. Therefore, the update frequency is a knock-out criterion for the feasibility of a data product.

(Q4) With the dimension licensing (D2) and use after license expiry (D3), the decision-maker gets the information about the license model of the data source. It is equally important to consider the use of the data after the license expires. The reason for this is that any data products developed with this data may no longer be used after the license expires.

(Q5) With the dimension pricing model (D4), the decision-maker can estimate the cost of the data source and put it into a cost-benefit relation when evaluating his data product.

6   Conclusion and Further Research

The data source selection is a crucial step to develop a useful data product. Therefore, we have extended the BDI process to include the data source selection process step. We have shown that research exists in data source selection, taxonomy development for data sources, and the BDI process. However, these research areas have so far been considered mainly in isolation. With this paper, we try to link the research areas and defined the following research question: *How can data source selection be supported in the big data integration process?* To answer this research question, we developed a data source taxonomy according to the methodical approach of Nickerson et al. [8]. The taxonomy was evaluated according to the evaluation framework of Szopinski et al. [20] with data scientists and decision-makers from two universities and six companies from different sectors. For the development and evaluation of the taxonomy, real data sources such as OpenCorporates, Crunchbase 2013 Snapshot, Upcitemdb, or GLEIF were used.

The final taxonomy consists of sixteen dimensions and describes a data source in terms of content and technical criteria to support data scientists and decision-makers in selecting data sources in the BDI process. For example, the taxonomy provides an overview of the added information value of a data source in the form of categories. It also provides the real-world entities it contains, which can be used to integrate other data sources.

The data source taxonomy developed by us for selection support directly influences theory and practice. Our evaluation shows that companies see taxonomy as support.

Also, decision-makers can use the taxonomy to compare data providers and support a purchase decision based on the completed taxonomies. The taxonomy could be filled out by the data providers to reduce the decision-makers effort. The decision-maker can obtain an overview of the data sources that could potentially be purchased. Our research shows that the big data integration process, defined by [2], should be extended to include the process step data source selection. Our research shows that a taxonomy is suitable to structure and organize the many important aspects of data sources. At the same time, there are some limitations to our work. With the developed taxonomy, we have taken the first step into researching a data source taxonomy. There are many more data source relevant aspects that we have not considered, like security, privacy, compliance, GDPR, data anonymization, or company-specific organizational challenges. All these limitations offer the potential for future research and further development of the data source taxonomy. Also, the taxonomy should be evaluated and further developed in other companies and with other data sources. Especially dimension 16 (added information value) should be researched in more detail.

References

1. Stonebraker, M., Ilyas, I.: Data integration: the current status and the way forward. IEEE Data Eng. Bull. **41**, 3–9 (2018)
2. Dong, X.L., Srivastava, D.: Big data integration. Synth. Lect. Data Manag. **7**, 1–198 (2015)
3. Abbasi, A., Sarker, S., Chiang, R.: Big data research in information systems: toward an inclusive research agenda. J. Assoc. Inf. Syst. **17**(2), I–XXXII (2016). https://doi.org/10.17705/1jais.00423

4. Lin, Y., Wang, H., Li, J., Gao, H.: Data Source Selection for Information Integration in Big Data Era (2016)
5. Christen, P.: Data linkage: the big picture. Harvard Data Sci. Rev. (2019). https://doi.org/10.1162/99608f92.84deb5c4
6. Wirth, R.: CRISP-DM: towards a standard process model for data mining. In: Proceedings of the Fourth International Conference on the Practical Application of Knowledge Discovery and Data Mining, pp. 29–39 (2000)
7. Kruse, F., Dmitriyev, V., Marx Gómez, J.: Building a connection between decision maker and data-driven decision process. Archives of Data Science, Series A (Online First) 4, 16 S. online (2018)
8. Nickerson, R.C., Varshney, U., Muntermann, J.: A method for taxonomy development and its application in information systems. Eur. J. Inf. Syst. **22**, 336–359 (2013)
9. Kruse, F., Hassan, A.P., Awick, J.-P., Marx Gómez, J.: A qualitative literature review on linkage techniques for data integration. In: Bui, T. (ed.) 53rd Hawaii International Conference on System Sciences, HICSS 2020, Grand Wailea, Maui, Hawaii, USA, January 7–10, 2020, pp. 1063–1073. ScholarSpace/AIS Electronic Library (AISeL) (2020)
10. Konda, P., et al.: Magellan: toward building entity matching management systems. Proc. VLDB Endow. **9**(12), 1197–1208 (2016). https://doi.org/10.14778/2994509.2994535
11. Konda, P., Subramanian Seshadri, S., Segarra, E., Hueth, B., Doan, A.: Executing entity matching end to end: a case study. In: Herschel, M., Galhardas, H., Reinwald, B., Fundulaki, I., Binnig, C., Kaoudi, Z. (eds.) Advances in Database Technology – 22nd International Conference on Extending Database Technology, EDBT 2019, pp. 489–500. OpenProceedings.org, Lisbon, Portugal, 26–29 March 2019 (2019)
12. Govind, Y., et al.: Entity Matching Meets Data Science: A Progress Report from the Magellan Project (2019)
13. Safhi, H.M., Frikh, B., Ouhbi, B.: Data source selection in big data context. In: Indrawan-Santiago, M., Pardede, E., Salvadori, I.L., Steinbauer, M., Khalil, I., Anderst-Kotsis, G. (eds.) Proceedings of the 21st International Conference on Information Integration and Web-based Applications and Services, pp. 611–616. ACM, New York, NY, USA (2019)
14. Assaf, A., Senart, A., Troncy, R.: Towards an objective assessment framework for linked data quality. Int. J. Semant. Web Inf. Syst. **12**, 111–133 (2016)
15. Dong, X.L., Saha, B., Srivastava, D.: Less is more: selecting sources wisely for integration. Proc. VLDB Endow. **6**(2), 37–48 (2012). https://doi.org/10.14778/2535568.2448938
16. Rekatsinas, T., Dong, X.L., Srivastava, D.: Characterizing and selecting fresh data sources. In: Dyreson, C., Li, F., Özsu, M.T. (eds.) Proceedings of the 2014 ACM SIGMOD international conference on Management of data – SIGMOD '14, pp. 919–930. ACM Press, New York, New York, USA (2014)
17. Zrenner, J., Hassan, A.P., Otto, B., Marx Gómez, J.C.: Data source taxonomy for supply network structure visibility. Epubli (2017)
18. Li, L., Peng, T., Kennedy, J.: A rule based taxonomy of dirty data. GSTF Int. J. Comput. **1** (2011)
19. Roeder, J., Muntermann, J., Kneib, T.: Towards a taxonomy of data heterogeneity. In: Gronau, N., Heine, M., Poustcchi, K., Krasnova, H. (eds.) WI2020 Zentrale Tracks, pp. 293–308. GITO Verlag (2020)
20. Szopinski, D., Schoormann, T., Kundisch, D.: Because your taxonomy is worth it: towards a framework for taxonomy evaluation. In: Proceedings of the Twenty-Seventh European Conference on Information Systems (ECIS) (2019)
21. Wang, R.Y., Strong, D.M.: Beyond accuracy: what data quality means to data consumers. J. Manag. Inf. Syst. **12**, 5–33 (1996)

Permissioned Blockchain for Data Provenance in Scientific Data Management

Julius Möller$^{(\boxtimes)}$, Sibylle Fröschle, and Axel Hahn

University of Oldenburg, Ammerländer Heerstraße 114-118, 26129 Oldenburg, Germany
`{julius.moeller,sibylle.froeschle,axel.hahn}@uni-oldenburg.de`

Abstract. In the age of Big Data, the amount of data-driven research activities has increased significantly. However, when it comes to collaborative data processing in scientific workflows, provenance information of the used data is not always accessible. Especially in complex data ecosystems with multiple decentralized data sources, it is hard to keep track of the processing operations once they are completed. When sharing such data between different researchers and other involved parties, poor traceability of processing steps may also obstruct this process. In this paper, we introduce a blockchain based data provenance information system, which enables decentralized sharing of this information. We then integrate this system into the decentralized data sources context and address trust and traceability issues in the network with an identity-based solution. Furthermore, the system's performance is evaluated, and the concept is examined in a case study on the e-Maritime Integrated Reference Platform (eMIR).

Keywords: Data provenance · Blockchain · Scientific data management

1 Introduction

The automated recording and storage of huge amounts of data is increasingly important in both research and industry. The management of such *big data* data sets has long since ceased to be trivial and has become a major challenge for research and industry [1]. Additionally, the growing need for high-quality data assets in nearly any branch of industry has led to a new awareness of the actual value of data. In a data ecosystem controlled by different Data Producers, Data Owners, Data Consumers and Data Miners all represented by different physical entities, there is a need for tracking the production, transformation, and provision of data [2]. Also, it is a common scenario in industry and research that project partners agree on a specific objective and work together with different sets of data and data transformation nodes in shared networks. While this often happens in private networks, there are also emerging concepts for the usage of potentially public *data spaces* (cf. [3] for a general description or [4] for a reference architecture). Especially in research, specific data often must be selected, pre-processed, transformed and analyzed from a multitude of data. This digital process known as *e-Science workflow* has been discussed in a great number of publications (see e.g. [5] for an introduction to the topic, [6] for a taxonomy of e-Science workflow systems, and [7] for a more extensive

© The Author(s), under exclusive license to Springer Nature Switzerland AG 2021
F. Ahlemann et al. (Eds.): WI 2021, LNISO 48, pp. 22–38, 2021.
https://doi.org/10.1007/978-3-030-86800-0_2

overview). It is really important to be able to track every process step in the e-Science workflow to guarantee a high-quality data-driven research methodology [8]. Moreover, other researchers must be able to verify the authenticity and non-repudiation of the workflow metadata thus created to fully understand the process from which research findings have been made. The enormous value of scientific data for further processing in industrial applications, such as the training of decision-supporting machine learning models cannot be denied. Currently, many of the challenges of collaborative data processing are being addressed by upcoming cloud-based platform solutions [9]. While the cloud platform provider may be trustworthy and reliable, different parties providing, preparing, and transforming the data may not. Keeping track of the creation, the changes and the provision of data is a challenge in platform supported data spaces. Most of these problems can be observed in research activities involving industrial partners with economic interests: For instance, how could shipping companies provide data on vessel movement and fuel consumption as a basis for a collaborative research project on traffic optimization? Also, areas in which multiple partners need to cooperate, as it is done for example in the logistics industry, face similar problems: For instance, how could data from independent storage and transportation companies be securely made available, be processed and analyzed by other companies to gather knowledge about influence factors that can affect efficiency? The goal of this paper is to provide a decentral solution that closes these gaps and fits into the scientific data ecosystem. Our contributions are as follows: Firstly, we describe the setting of data provenance in e-Science. Secondly, with the assumption of an existing data space setup, we elicit the requirements a decentral solution needs to satisfy and motivate how the use of blockchain with an identity-based consensus method is best suited to this purpose. Thirdly, we present the architecture of our system. Finally, a prototypical implementation is evaluated in an example with an existing maritime data space.

2 Scientific Data Management in a Decentralized Context

2.1 Scientific Workflows and Data Provenance

The activity of scientific data management is often presented in cycles or processes. In general, this includes the steps from the import of source data to the extraction of knowledge from the processed data. This procedure is an important element of e-Science (electronic science), which deals with the generation of knowledge using digital infrastructures [10]. A well-founded and detailed model for the scientific data management process is provided by Crowston and Qin [11]. In a comparison of nine data management cycles/process models by Ball [12], the model of Crowston and Qin is identified as one of the most comprehensive models. Figure 1 shows a *summary* of the model. For workflow-oriented e-Science, data provenance is a very relevant topic: As a large number of publications with data-driven approaches for problem analysis and solving is emerging, the insufficient availability of trustworthy traceability measures is increasingly becoming a problem [13]. In the case of a poorly documented data processing workflow, other researchers would not be able to reproduce the author's results. Buneman et al. [14] define *data provenance* as follows: *"Data provenance – is the description of the origins of a piece of data and the process by which it arrived in a database"*.

The work of Simmhan et al. [2] provides a taxonomy of data provenance in e-Science: The application of provenance is subdivided into the sections of *data quality, audit trail, replication recipes, attribution,* and *informational purposes.* It also can be distinguished if the provenance information is related to the *data product* or *the process of its creation.* In this work, we will keep the focus on the audit trail for the whole process from data creation to the final data product.

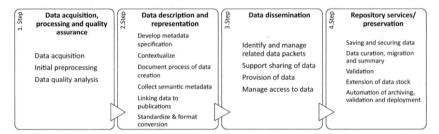

Fig. 1. Summary of the scientific data management process as described by [11].

2.2 Decentralized Data in Data Spaces

The term "data space" is widely used in different contexts. In the scope of this paper, we use the definition of data spaces given by Franklin et al. [3] who define a data space as a co-existent amount of data which is linked by a "data space support system" (or specifically a "data space support platform (DSSP)"). This system must fulfil a set of requirements to be recognized as such. Firstly, it must support a wide range of data types and formats covering all data in the data space. Secondly, it must offer means of searching, querying, updating, and administrating the data space. Data space queries are not required to result in a complete result of available data, an approximation is sufficient. And lastly, it must support tools to create a tighter integration of the data in the data space.

Data spaces can be found in situations where partial control over or knowledge of several data sources is available to a central entity. This central entity, however, is not able to maintain full control over the data sources and therefore tasks like data ingestion and harmonization are not trivial. Additionally, data spaces typically contain sets of syntactically and semantically different data [15].

Data space architectures have already been realized in several publications, e.g. as a vehicular data space [16], IoT data space [17] or maritime data space [18].

2.3 Identity-Based Blockchain

The blockchain concept has increasingly been applied in a large number of cases for enhancing cyber security and decentralizing control structures and has also been investigated for usage in a scientific research context e.g. in [19]. A blockchain typically works like a distributed database with some special functional principles, such as finding a network consensus on adding new information to the blockchain. Most consensus algorithms for blockchain applications require the cooperation of a vast number of nodes in the blockchain network. This often leads to slow performance when a new block needs to be accepted. Assuming that a smaller group of nodes with trusted identities, and only these nodes are used to determine a consensus, the performance can be improved significantly. Consensus algorithms utilizing this assumption are called Proof-of-Authority consensus [20]. Another important factor in the application of blockchain technology is the permission policy of the network. Common policies for blockchain are public, consortium-based, and private. These approaches mainly differ in the degree of centralization. Furthermore, permissions for reading data from and writing data to the blockchain may also be restricted depending on the permission policy of the blockchain [21].

2.4   Related Work

For the literature review, we analyze work in the area of data provenance in scientific data management with special regards to security, architecture, and workflow models. Additionally, we discuss work that uses blockchain technology in the context of storing data provenance information. The importance of data provenance for scientific data processing has already been discussed in a significant number of publications (see e.g. [22] for an overview, and [23, 24] for applications). Additional work on the security of data provenance has also been conducted in the past years. The work of Bertino et al. [25] gives a good overview of this topic and presents an architecture framework and methods for the secure exchange of data provenance. However, collaborative editing of this information is not considered. Hasan et al. [26] introduce a formal model for a secure provenance chain, in which document editing steps are cryptographically signed by their originators. In addition to that, hashes of the changed data are appended to the blocks of the editing chain. The model relies on public key cryptography and provides a good baseline for the secure provenance documentation. A framework for finding a consensus on a valid edit in a network of editing users is not discussed. Closely related to the work in this paper are the approaches of Ramachandran et al. [27] and Liang et al. [28], which both use a blockchain-based approach for securely organizing data provenance information. Ramachandran et al. use the Ethereum blockchain and smart contracts with the Open Provenance Model (see [29]) as their base. The consensus on a change of a document is determined by voting with all nodes or by randomized threshold voting and therefore seems very comprehensible for participants. The approach is evaluated with two real-world use-cases and the performance is considered applicable by the authors of the paper. Liang et al. also propose a blockchain based architecture, which, however, aims at integrating a *central* cloud-provider that stores the data that is being edited. An action-based method for tracking the changes in documents is utilized for creating the data provenance information. The blockchain is used to carry a distributed database which includes the tracked changes of the documents. Both works do not solve the problem of unidentifiable entities and only partially discuss the challenges of decentralized data sources. Apart from these papers, there are some others that *partly* address some of the discussed problems. Chen et al. [30] present a formal model for a blockchain data structure for efficient sharing of scientific workflow provenance data. Neisse et al. [31] discuss different design choices of a blockchain-based data provenance approach and their compliance with the GDPR. Finally, Tosh et al. [32] compare different consensus methods for cloud-based data provenance and come to the conclusion, that a Proof-of-Stake consensus seems to be the best method in such a setup.

2.5   Research Objective

There is an increasing need for data provenance solutions for scientific data management. Especially in data space environments, solutions with the ability to handle a high degree of decentralization of data need to be developed. In existing work, the problem of permissions to edit provenance information or having the right to vote for appending new data provenance information is not solved entirely. An identity-based permission system could possibly solve this issue and establish trust in a system of different editing parties. Also, the existing architectures cannot address the decentrality of the actual data in a data space setup. Requirements for scientific data processing are also only being discussed partially. Therefore, a permissioned, identity-based blockchain seems to be a candidate technology for establishing a data provenance information system. This seems to fit best to the presented scenario, as a central ledger infrastructure may not be able to establish overall trust. Moreover, it would require an independent organization to govern the ledger and protect it against security risks. While it is still possible to have authenticated and authorized entities, a central party would need to take the responsibility for the system, which would be a problem with several parties that may have conflicting interests that would have to be resolved for each workflow individually. A data provenance information system must be able to ensure the secure documentation of data provenance information and its consistency with the actual data in a trustworthy and reliable way for authorized entities. Additionally, it should be visible to researchers who authored the data provenance information. The system should be adapted to the needs of a data-driven science process, being able to track single workflow steps of data processing.

3   Design of the Data Provenance Blockchain with Identifiable Entities

3.1   Architectural Components

To introduce a secure documentation of data provenance in scientific workflows, several architectural components are required. Figure 2 gives an overview of the involved entities and components and their interactions. We assume, that an existing data space is present and has a DSSP as the corresponding support system (cf. Sect. 2.2) as this setup is one of the most common solutions.

The architectural components can be described as follows:

- **Identity Provider:** The Identity Provider is assumed to be a trusted entity with the function of providing cryptographic key-pairs linked to legal entities. Prerequisite for this is the existence of a Public-Key Infrastructure (PKI). The Identity Provider is needed for the identity-based consensus in our blockchain setup.

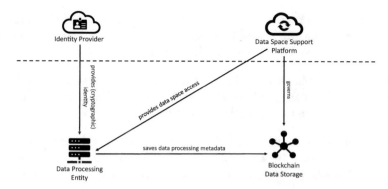

Fig. 2. Architecture overview of the data provenance management concept.

- **Data Space Support Platform (DSSP):** The Data Space Support Platform is the access point for data space access requests. It may also fulfil the functions of a Data Processing Entity as workflow steps of the e-Science Workflow may also be executed on the platform.
- **Data Processing Entity:** The Data Processing Entity is processing data from or provides data to the data space, which it accesses via the DSSP. Several Data Processing Entities can be involved in the processing of a single data set.
- **Blockchain Data Storage:** The Blockchain Data Storage contains the actual data provenance information and may also be used to organize data space access rights via smart contracts.

When a dataset is created, the originator, i.e. the first Data Processing Entity, provides first information on the data and makes the data available to the data space via the DSSP. The metadata of the data creation is then stored in the blockchain and can be retrieved by the next Data Processing Entity in the workflow. The data is then again processed, made available to the data space and the metadata is stored in the blockchain. Access to the blockchain always requires a cryptographic identity, provided by the Identity Provider.

3.2 Data Provenance Model

The classes and attributes of a data provenance model always depend on their use-case and the domain they are applied to. The data provenance model in our approach should describe the creation and processing of scientific data in e-Science workflows. We assume, that every transformation of the data can be partitioned into a chain of single processing steps. As a proof of concept, we use a simple workflow-oriented model whose steps are derived from the tasks of Crowston and Qin's model (see Sect. 2.1). We design this model in such a way that it can act as a template and can be extended further easily. Hence, we deliberately keep the attributes in our model general. We generalize the steps of the e-Science workflow to the following tasks: *Data Acquisition Process, Anonymization* (to comply with data protection regulations), *Data Quality Analysis, Preprocessing and Transformation* and *Conversion and Validation*. A formalized model of the proposed tasks is used to represent the data provenance information. Instances of this model for workflow steps can be serialized and then stored in the body of a blockchain block. The stakeholders in the processing of scientific data in our data space set-up can be modelled through the following roles (cf. [4]):

Data Owner. The Data Owner is considered possessing the actual data. This can be interpreted in a legal or technical sense and is not further specified for our approach. The Data Owner determines the access rights to the data.

Data Provider. The Data Provider is an entity which provides the technical means to access a specific data set. The Data Provider must be authorized by the Data Owner and only provide the data to other entities with access rights granted by the Data Owner.

Data Consumer. The Data Consumer is accessing a data set as a client of the Data Provider.

Physical entities in this model can also have multiple roles at the same time. Refer to Sect. 4.1 for an example.

3.3 Blockchain Architecture

Identities. In a collaborative research scenario, the anonymity (as e.g. found in cryptocurrency blockchains) of Data Processing Entities would lead to less traceability and trust between different parties as manipulations of the data would not cause any negative reputation for the guilty parties. Furthermore, the research community would benefit from a secure and transparent documentation of data processing workflows as investigations become easier reproducible. In our context, it is not a given that the transformations on a data set always can be reproduced and verified (against a hash) by any participant. Hence, for our system we require technological measures to be in place so that an entity that has processed data cannot repudiate their processing step and can be held responsible for the result. These considerations lead to the conclusion that a blockchain, applied to this problem would only fulfil its purpose if Data Processing Entities in a scientific workflow can be identified. We assume that physical identities are bound to cryptographic key pairs. To obtain such a key pair, Data Processing entities must fulfil several requirements, which are defined through the Identity Provider. These could be for example the evidence that a Data Processing Entity is part of a legally registered organization. After obtaining a key pair and a certificate stating its validity from the Identity Provider, the Data Processing Entity can participate in the blockchain network (see Fig. 2). Every transaction in the network that is committed by a Data Processing Entity must be signed with its private key, so that other entities can trace his interactions with the processed data.

Transactions. Storing data provenance information in the blockchain can be achieved in several different ways. Nevertheless, it must be kept in mind that any data, which is stored in a conventional blockchain is replicated by every node in the network and therefore causes traffic. Typically, data that is stored in a blockchain can be represented as transactions. From the perspective of a data space entity, the smallest monitorable change of a data set in our model is a single workflow step. For an entity who is executing a workflow step, there may be smaller processing steps as parts of its implementation of the workflow step, but these are normally not visible to any other entities. Hence, it is appropriate to define a workflow step as a transaction in the blockchain. Transactions also must contain a hash of the processed data to later enable other entities to verify that a transaction was related to a specific workflow step. This binds the data provenance information in the blockchain to the actual data set. In addition to the hash, meta-information (see Sect. 3.2) for processing the data by the system is also stored. However, this information cannot always be expected to include exact descriptions of used processes, as they may contain proprietary algorithms.

Blockchain Structure. It must be kept in mind, that in a data space, there is not only a single data set, that is being processed by its entities. Thus, there are several chains of transactions that must be stored in the blockchain network. For this reason, we propose to use multiple shorter chains, each representing a workflow for a single source data set (see Fig. 3).

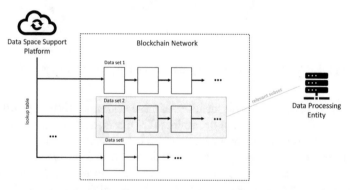

Fig. 3. Data set specific blockchain setup with multiple chains.

This has some advantages over a conventional, single blockchain: First, permissions can easily be set for every data set separately. Also, entities do not need to keep track of data sets, which they are not permissioned to access or not interested in. This reduces the locally used storage of the blockchain instance and prevents entities from wasting their computational resources to track transactions, in which they do not have any interests. To keep track of the different chains in the network, the DSSP can provide a central lookup table or any other means for optimizing access to the blockchain network. This task falls directly within the remit of such a platform. The permission model and deployment of the blockchain should follow a standardized process. In a more proprietary setup, Data Owner, Provider and Consumer may also have problems on finding a consensus on a process, even in a small group due to conflicting interests or because data exchange setups can also be dynamic or even fully automated. Standardization will largely prevent the occurrence of these problems and support the balance between administrative burden and benefits of the proposed method. Standardized procedures can also be supported by the DSSP.

Consensus and Smart Contracts. In the defined setup, the stakeholders in the process of data processing in the data space have been clearly identified. The existence of an Identity Provider now makes it possible to use a Proof-of-Authority (or identity-based) consensus method. The Data Owner of a source data set has been defined as the entity which holds the rights to distribute and modify the data set. We propose that the Data Owner nominates a subset of entities in the network that are authorized to vote on data provenance auditing for the data provenance information related to the specific data set (see Fig. 4).

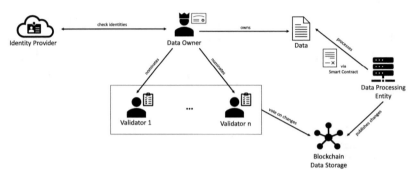

Fig. 4. Conceptual overview of proof-of-authority consensus mechanism.

The Data Owner can verify the identities of these *validators* via the Identity Provider. It is left open how the Data Owner determines this subset, as there can be several legal, organizational, or technical requirements which will be specific to the case. For example, the authorization of being a validator may include contractual agreements, which require validators to pay penalties, if agreements are violated. In return, a Data Owner may provide access to its data or act as a validator for the other party. Also, for scenarios with a stronger need to protect data, entities may also consider paying an independent organization to provide validation facilities. However, in the case of working with highly sensitive data, validators must be included in the process of the data processing and may be selected from the set of existent and authorized Data Processing Entities for validating the data processing steps of other authorized Data Processing Entities. Also, in less critical workflows, validators may also base their decisions on data processing metadata, without requiring access to the actual data sets.

Anytime a new block will be added to the blockchain, only the validators vote on the changes included in this block. In this way, our setup fulfils the definition of a consortium blockchain. Consensus algorithms like e.g. Aura or Clique can be used to implement the building of a consensus [20].

In the near past and with the approach of the Ethereum blockchain, so-called smart contracts have been in the focus of blockchain researchers and developers [33]. Smart contracts are pieces of code, which run on the blockchain and execute contract terms that have been defined in the code [34]. In the arrangement in Fig. 4, the Data Processing Entity accesses and processes the data, provided by the Data Owner via the data space. We propose to use the data provenance blockchain to deploy smart contracts between the

Data Owner and Data Processing Entities for the determination of access, modification, and distribution rights of data sets. The smart contracts will be deployed on the blockchain that is linked to the corresponding workflow. The DSSP can then subscribe to these smart contracts and manage data space access accordingly. Additionally, the nomination of validators may also be carried out via a smart contract. This formalizes the processes of data and right management and makes it decentrally available to all authorized parties. This completes our system design.

3.4 Security Analysis

The proposed system stores data provenance information without giving unauthorized parties the possibility to tamper with this information or its consistency with the data sets it relates to. Moreover, the system provides traceability (transactions can be traced to a legal identity) and non-repudiation (a participant cannot deny having carried out a transaction on the data set): this is implemented via the signatures within the blockchain structure and the binding of the access control to the data sets to the permissions given through the blockchain structure. We analyze what can happen when an unauthorized or authorized entity is compromised as well as blockchain specific attacks:

Threat 1: Unauthorized entities. When an unauthorized entity tries to add false information to the data provenance blockchain, this will be detected by the validators of the blockchain and the transaction will be discarded due to invalid signatures. Similarly, unauthorized entities will not have access rights to tamper with the data set.

Threat 2: Compromised validators. In general, there must be a significant amount of compromised validators [20], which is relatively unlikely in a data space setup with independent validators. However, if the Data Owner nominates a set of highly dependent validators this can become a security issue if he does not ensure that they are highly trustworthy at the same time. Also, conspiring validators will suffer a loss of reputation and possibly legal consequences if this attack is detected.

Threat 3: Compromised Data Owner. If a Data Owner is compromised, then he will perhaps be able to provide fake data within the original data set. However, since he must sign the data provenance information in the blockchain it cannot be denied having made the claim that it is real data later. Hence, when someone discovers that the data is not authentic, the compromised Data Owner risks his repudiation as Data Provider or could even be made liable if damage is caused. If a compromised Data Owner tries to tamper with the transactions or adds transactions, he is not authorized for then this will be spotted by the validators. Even though as the Data Owner he could nominate conspirator validators this is unlikely (cf. Threat 2). The case of a compromised Data Processing Entity is analogous.

Threat 4: Compromised DSSP lookup table. If the lookup table would contain false information, this would only lead to false access in the blockchain, which would be detected by any entity verifying the signatures or hash-values in the blockchain by cross checking with the identities of the expected entities with the help of the Identity Provider. The attacker might still duplicate a chain or prefix of a chain. However, this will not cause any harm as each block (describing data transactions) contains the hash of the actual data, and this data hash is cryptographically bound together with the metadata by the signature of the processing party. Moreover, if a regular party or the attacker tries to add blocks to a duplicated blockchain or prefix in a way that would lead to a fork of the workflow with respect to the respective blockchain then this will not pass the consensus algorithm as usual. If the attacker tries to add a new block with an inconsistent match between metadata and an existing data set, then this will be detected by the validating nodes as usual. At most, if the attacker duplicates a prefix of a chain the information that a data set was deleted might be lost, and a regular party who follows the corresponding link will not be able to access the data set as expected. In general, duplication is less of a problem here than in currency blockchains since the data sets and their provenance records are not "consumed" but rather a derived data set has to be deleted explicitly.

Threat 5: General blockchain attack scenario. There are a few general attack scenarios against a blockchain instance [35]. Attacks in which single nodes flood the blockchain with transactions are possible. Not all these attacks are always applicable. Since we deploy multiple chains with different permissions this will typically affect only a small section of our proposed blockchain network.

Threat 6: Compromised Identity Provider. A compromised Identity Provider would have fatal consequences for the proposed system. An attacker could invalidate the identities of authorized nodes, masquerade as an existing identity, and create new, malicious identities. A countermeasure for this attack would be the utilization of an identity provider with decentralized structures (see also Sect. 4.1).

This high-level analysis is only meant to show that the presented system is also promising with respect to security. We will provide a detailed design and state-of-the-art verification of the cryptographic architecture together with a resilience analysis in case of key compromises in future work.

4   Evaluation

4.1   Case Study: AIS Data Processing in a Maritime Data Space

In 2002 The Automatic Identification System (AIS) was introduced by the IMO SOLAS Agreement. It facilitates the submission of dynamic and static vessel properties (such as position, speed, destination, size, etc.) by vessels via VHF. Several publications make use of historical AIS data in their research process (see e.g. [36] for AIS-based collision risk analysis, [37] for anomaly detection or [38] for route prediction). Even though AIS is not encrypted and theoretically can be recorded by anyone, it requires powerful equipment to record it for larger areas. For this reason, it is often the case, that AIS data for a specific area needs to be exchanged between the recorder and users of the data, which is a typical business case in the maritime data domain (see e.g. MarineTraffic[1]). As a representative scientific workflow for a maritime data space, we use the process of

---

[1] https://www.marinetraffic.com/en/p/ais-historical-data.

creating a heat map for vessel traffic density for the German Bight from raw AIS data (in the NMEA0183 format, see [39]). Traffic density heat maps can especially be useful for traffic optimization and could, for instance, be used as a data source by Vessel Traffic Services (VTS) for optimizing traffic efficiency. For implementing this process, the e-Maritime Integrated Reference Platform (eMIR) [40], which offers an open modular research and test environment used for scientific analysis of maritime systems and data generation with a variety of maritime data sources, is utilized. The workflow is illustrated in Fig. 5: eMIR[2] uses a network of distributed sensors to continuously record the raw AIS messages from vessels in the German Bight (approx. 2.700.000 messages per day). This data is persisted in a PostgreSQL database. As AIS data contains public, unique ship identifiers (MMSI and IMO numbers), which must be treated as personal information, the data is anonymized by replacing the MMSI and IMO with a hashed value. All of this is done by an arbitrary Organization A (Data Owner/Data Provider) to create the source data set, which is distributed via the data space. In our example, Organization B (Data Consumer/Data Provider) uses this data set as a starting point for enhancing the data for further processing: Faulty entries are removed, and unnecessary attributes are filtered. A data science researcher from Organization C (Data Consumer) can then use the prepared data set to create a heat map for his research project.

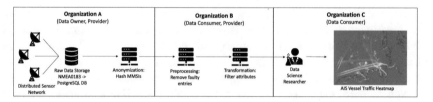

Fig. 5. Workflow for creating a Vessel Traffic Heatmap in a maritime data space.

For the realization, we instantiated the proposed concept in Sect. 3 in the eMIR data space setup to operate with its available resources. Figure 6 illustrates a technical overview of the realization for this case study: The Maritime Connectivity Platform[3] (MCP) is a platform to support the implementation of digital services for supporting the maritime industry and was selected as an identity provider as it features a decentralized management of identities (cf. Threat 6 in Sect. 3.4). For the realization of the blockchain network, R3's Corda Open Source[4] was selected as it provides interfaces to model real-world relations independently from crypto-currency features. Furthermore, it was optimized to run as a permissioned blockchain network and allows easy integration of blockchain peers and data processing logic. The process for creating the heatmap is completely automated and can for example be executed daily for tracking changes in traffic. In our case, we worked with data sets of 1.000.000 AIS data points. The documentation of the workflow in our system starts with the internal data acquisition,

---

[2] https://www.emaritime.de/.

[3] https://maritimeconnectivity.net/.

[4] https://www.corda.net/.

conversion, and anonymization of the data by Organization A. The data set is then made available to the data space for further processing by Organization B and C.

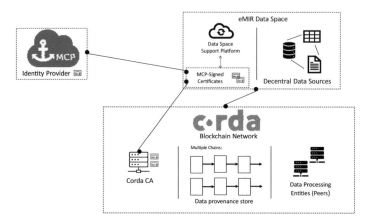

Fig. 6. Realization of the data provenance information system with Corda OS and the MCP.

Note, that the data acquisition, conversion, and anonymization cannot be observed by other participants of the data space. However, as the data is bound to the transactions by its hashes and the transactions are signed by their originator, the data and their processing could be revealed later in case of discrepancies to proof the validity of the data provenance information. For a single instance of the workflow, a total of six workflow steps were added to the data provenance system adding ~3KB of provenance data to the blockchain (per million AIS data points). Assuming ~2.7 million AIS data points are recorded per day, this would create ~9KB of provenance data in the blockchain per day, for the presented workflow. Finally, the case study successfully showed the applicability of the proposed concept. It could be seen that our concept can be integrated into existing workflows and the workflow model can be used to represent typical data processing steps. However, the integration of existing infrastructure, such as external identity providers is not always trivial. In our example, MIR keys could not directly be integrated into to the Corda OS framework, as they did not match the cryptographic requirements. For this reason, we authorized the Corda CA certificates making use of the MIR keys for each entity and made this information available via the DSSP for validation of signatures (as shown in Fig. 6). Finally, it could be shown that the system can be used to support typical data exchange problems that can be found in the maritime data domain and close the gaps of existing work. Gaining global data coverage for larger areas is very important to the international maritime industry. As this task is often not achievable for a single entity, data needs to be exchanged and analyzed collaboratively.

4.2 Performance Evaluation

We have implemented and evaluated a network of nodes that allows us to consider complete workflows and several validators. We used a typical windows machine (AMD

Ryzen 7 1700 @ 3 GHz, 16 GB RAM) for performance testing. Our focus in this evaluation is on changes in the node-setup, to derive implementation/setup-independent performance insights. Therefore, we mainly used a network of 10 nodes with different workflows and role set-ups (as shown in Table 1).

Table 1. Performance evaluation results.[5]

Number of nodes	Workflow setup	Avg. time per transaction
10	1 workflow, 1 validator	1860 ms
10	1 workflow, 2 validators	2366 ms
10	1 workflow, 4 validators	2801 ms
10	1 workflow, 6 validators	3379 ms
10	2 workflows, 2 validators each	1364 ms
10	3 workflows, 1 validator each	790 ms
5	1 workflow, 2 validators	1195 ms

In the first four trials we set up a single workflow and constantly raised the number of validators for that workflow. Consequently, the average time per transaction also significantly increased. This is obviously due to the higher number of nodes that need to communicate to find a consensus on adding a new workflow step. As stated in Sect. 3.4, a higher number of validators increases the security of the system. Finding the right balance of security and performance in terms of validators therefore can be identified as a challenge of the proposed system and could lead to poorly configured systems. Secondly, we investigated how parallel-running workflows affect the performance of the system. With the same number of nodes and validators (cf. rows 3 and 5 of Table 1), we already have a 52% faster transaction speed with two parallel workflows. Additionally, we conducted a test with 5 nodes and 2 validators in a single workflow. It was seen that two parallel running workflows almost have the same performance as a single workflow (cf. rows 5 and 7 of Table 1). We interpret this as a result of our permissioned approach with multiple chains. Lastly, it could be seen that the 'time per transaction'-measurements for our case study were already relatively high. According to R3 Ltd. [41], this seems to be a general problem of the open source implementation of Corda and is probably not related to our consensus mechanism. Also, due to our blockchain architecture, we do not expect scenarios in which thousands of participants issue transactions at a single blockchain instance. For an increasing number workflows, the system can easily and efficiently be scaled horizontally by adding additional blockchain instances as the results of the performance evaluation could show.

---

[5] Our implementation is available under: https://doi.org/10.5281/zenodo.3960262.

4.3   Extended Example: Setting with Confidential Data Sets

We now extend our case study to illustrate how our design can handle a setting where two participating organizations are competitors and have therefore an interest in keeping some of their data sets confidential. Assume there are three more participating organizations D, E, and F: both, D and E, are companies that specialize in algorithms to optimize AIS data sets for use in ship navigation systems; F is a company that develops ship navigation systems (potential client of both D and E). Moreover, E wishes to provide a demo service, where F could view up to three results of their latest algorithm run on data sets selected by F from the data space. Naturally, E does not wish that competitors such as D have access to the resulting data sets. With many demo data sets publicly available a competitor could at some point be able to reengineer the algorithm. The participants in this example will choose a legal contract (from a set of standardized templates) where every industrial participant is allowed to restrict access to data sets that result from one of their processing steps to other industrial participants of their choice. These in turn are then also bound to confidentiality (by the legal contract). Technically, E will establish a secret key K with F, encrypt the confidential data set under K, and only store it in encrypted form on the data space. The data hash for the provenance blockchain can be computed over the encrypted data set. Hence, the workings of the blockchain system are as usual. Naturally, this is also an example for the case when the validators will neither be able to nor obliged to verify that the processed data set is indeed the result of the transformation described in the data provenance information. Other scenarios where confidential data must be accessed by several participants can make use of multi-party key establishment schemes.

5   Discussion and Conclusion

In this work, we designed a blockchain-based data provenance system and integrated it into an existing data space setup. For this purpose, a scientific workflow-based model was utilized to track each data processing step of an e-Science approach. We used an external Identity Provider and a Proof-of-Authority-like consensus method to secure the blockchain against attacks and make the process of data provenance for scientific workflows more transparent and verifiable. Our multi-chain concept for separating data provenance information by their belonging workflows improved security and performance of the system. However, we identified the need to carefully consider certificate and performance requirements for implementations of our system. Also, the cases of several data sets being merged by a processing step or forks on the chain of data processing need to be evaluated further. We expect that our framework can easily be extended to these cases since it seems the best strategy to generate a new data set in such cases. The scenario of continuously changing data processing entities as permissioned users also should be investigated further as transactions in a blockchain-setup are immutable. In general, we aim to further integrate our concept into the data architecture of the eMIR Platform to provide an overall architecture for collaborative data science and integrated data provenance tracking. As the volume, variety and velocity of available data is increasing continuously, we cannot deny that data provenance management will play an equally important role. Collaborative e-Science has a big impact on today's research methodologies and needs solutions for trust issues and the problem of decentralized data. We expect concepts like ours to fill these gaps in the future and provide a secure and efficient possibility to track data provenance.

References

1. McAfee, A., Brynjolfsson, E., Davenport, T.H., Patil, D., Barton, D.: Big data: the management revolution. Harv. Bus. Rev. **90**, 60–68 (2012)
2. Simmhan, Y.L., Plale, B., Gannon, D.: A survey of data provenance in e-science. ACM SIGMOD Rec. **34**, 31–36 (2005)
3. Franklin, M., Halevy, A., Maier, D.: From databases to dataspaces: a new abstraction for information management. ACM SIGMOD Rec. **34**, 27–33 (2005)
4. Otto, B., et al.: International Data Space – Reference Architecture Model. https://www.intern ationaldataspaces.org/ressource-hub/publications-ids/ (2019)
5. Belloum, A., et al.: Collaborative e-science experiments and scientific workflows. IEEE Internet Comput. **15**, 39–47 (2011)
6. Deelman, E., Gannon, D., Shields, M., Taylor, I.: Workflows and e-Science: an overview of workflow system features and capabilities. Futur. Gener. Comput. Syst. **25**, 528–540 (2009)
7. Taylor, Ian J., Deelman, Ewa, Gannon, Dennis B., Shields, Matthew (eds.): Workflows for e-Science. Springer London, London (2007). https://doi.org/10.1007/978-1-84628-757-2
8. Rousidis, D., Garoufallou, E., Balatsoukas, P., Sicilia, M.-A.: Metadata for big data: a preliminary investigation of metadata quality issues in research data repositories. Inf. Serv. Use **34**, 279–286 (2014)
9. Jayaraman, P.P., Perera, C., Georgakopoulos, D., Dustdar, S., Thakker, D., Ranjan, R.: Analytics-as-a-service in a multi-cloud environment through semantically-enabled hierarchical data processing. Softw. Pract. Experience **47**(3), 1139–1156 (2017)
10. Humphrey, C.: E-Science and the Life Cycle of Research (2006)
11. Crowston, K., Qin, J.: A capability maturity model for scientific data management: evidence from the literature. Proc. Am. Soc. Inform. Sci. Technol. **48**, 1–9 (2011)
12. Ball, A.: Review of Data Management Lifecycle Models. University of Bath, IDMRC (2012)
13. Verbert, K., Manouselis, N., Drachsler, H., Duval, E.: Dataset-driven research to support learning and knowledge analytics. J. Educ. Technol. Soc. **15**, 133–148 (2012)
14. Buneman, P., Khanna, S., Wang-Chiew, T.: Why and where: A characterization of data provenance. In: Bussche, J., Vianu, V. (eds.) ICDT 2001. LNCS, vol. 1973, pp. 316–330. Springer, Heidelberg (2001). https://doi.org/10.1007/3-540-44503-X_20
15. Halevy, A., Franklin, M., Maier, D.: Principles of dataspace systems. Presented at the Proceedings of the Twenty-fifth ACM SIGMOD-SIGACT-SIGART Symposium on Principles of Database Systems (2006)
16. Rettore, P.H., Maia, G., Villas, L.A., Loureiro, A.A.: vehicular data space: the data point of view. IEEE Commun. Surv. Tutorials **21**, 2392–2418 (2019)
17. Curry, E., Derguech, W., Hasan, S., Kouroupetroglou, C., ul Hassan, U.: A real-time linked dataspace for the internet of things: enabling "pay-as-you-go" data management in smart environments. Future Gen. Comput. Syst. **90**, 405–422 (2019). https://doi.org/10.1016/j.fut ure.2018.07.019
18. Berre, A., Rødseth, Ø.: From digital twin to maritime data space: transparent ownership and use of ship information. Presented at the September 27 (2018)
19. Shrestha, A., Vassileva, J.: Blockchain-based research data sharing framework for incentivizing the data owners. In: Chen, S., Wang, H., Zhang, L.-J. (eds.) ICBC 2018. LNCS, vol. 10974, pp. 259–266. Springer, Cham (2018). https://doi.org/10.1007/978-3-319-94478-4_19

20. De Angelis, S., Aniello, L., Baldoni, R., Lombardi, F., Margheri, A., Sassone, V.: PBFT vs Proof-of-Authority: Applying the CAP Theorem to Permissioned Blockchain (2018)
21. Zheng, Z., Xie, S., Dai, H., Chen, X., Wang, H.: An overview of blockchain technology: architecture, consensus, and future trends. Presented at the 2017 IEEE International Congress on Big Data (BigData Congress) (2017)
22. Bowers, S.: Scientific Workflow, Provenance, and Data Modeling Challenges and Approaches. Springer (2012)
23. Chen, P., Plale, B., Aktas, M.S.: Temporal representation for scientific data provenance. In: 2012 IEEE 8th International Conference on E-Science, pp. 1–8. IEEE (2012)
24. Bowers, S., McPhillips, T., Ludäscher, B., Cohen, S., Davidson, S.: A model for user-oriented data provenance in pipelined scientific workflows. In: Moreau, L., Foster, I. (eds.) IPAW 2006. LNCS, vol. 4145, pp. 133–147. Springer, Heidelberg (2006). https://doi.org/10.1007/118908 50_15
25. Bertino, E., et al.: A roadmap for privacy-enhanced secure data provenance. J. Intell. Inf. Syst. **43**, 481–501 (2014). https://doi.org/10.1007/s10844-014-0322-7
26. Hasan, R., Sion, R., Winslett, M.: The Case of the Fake Picasso: Preventing History Forgery with Secure Provenance (2009)
27. Ramachandran, A., Kantarcioglu, D.: Using blockchain and smart contracts for secure data provenance management. arXiv preprint arXiv:1709.10000 (2017)
28. Liang, X., Shetty, S., Tosh, D., Kamhoua, C., Kwiat, K., Njilla, L.: ProvChain: a blockchain-based data provenance architecture in cloud environment with enhanced privacy and availability. Presented at the 16 May (2017)
29. Moreau, L., et al.: The open provenance model core specification (v1.1). Future Gener. Comput. Syst. **27**(6), 743–756 (2011). https://doi.org/10.1016/j.future.2010.07.005
30. Chen, W., Liang, X., Li, J., Qin, H., Mu, Y., Wang, J.: Blockchain based provenance sharing of scientific workflows. In: 2018 IEEE International Conference on Big Data (Big Data), pp. 3814–3820 (2018). https://doi.org/10.1109/BigData.2018.8622237
31. Neisse, R., Steri, G., Nai-Fovino, I.: A blockchain-based approach for data accountability and provenance tracking. In: Proceedings of the 12th International Conference on Availability, Reliability and Security, pp. 1–10 (2017)
32. Tosh, D., Shetty, S., Liang, X., Kamhoua, C., Njilla, L.: Consensus protocols for blockchain-based data provenance: Challenges and opportunities. Presented at the 1 October (2017). https://doi.org/10.1109/UEMCON.2017.8249088
33. Alharby, M., van Moorsel, A.: Blockchain based smart contracts : a systematic mapping study. Presented at the 26 August (2017). https://doi.org/10.5121/csit.2017.71011
34. Zheng, Z., Xie, S., Dai, H.-N., Chen, X., Wang, H.: Blockchain challenges and opportunities: a survey. Int. J. Web Grid Serv. **14**, 352–375 (2018)
35. Xu, J.J.: Are blockchains immune to all malicious attacks? Finan. Innov. **2**(1), 1–9 (2016). https://doi.org/10.1186/s40854-016-0046-5
36. Silveira, P., Teixeira, A., Soares, C.G.: Use of AIS data to characterise marine traffic patterns and ship collision risk off the coast of Portugal. J. Navig. **66**, 879–898 (2013)
37. Ristic, B., La Scala, B., Morelande, M., Gordon, N.: Statistical analysis of motion patterns in AIS data: anomaly detection and motion prediction. In: 2008 11th International Conference on Information Fusion, pp. 1–7. IEEE (2008)
38. Pallotta, G., Vespe, M., Bryan, K.: Vessel pattern knowledge discovery from AIS data: a framework for anomaly detection and route prediction. Entropy **15**, 2218–2245 (2013)
39. Langley, R.B.: NMEA 0183: A GPS Receiver Interface Standard. GPS World. 6, (1995)
40. Rüssmeier, N., Lamm, A., Hahn, A.: A Generic Testbed for Simulation and Physical Based Testing of Maritime Cyber-Physical System of Systems. Presented at the 14 November (2019)
41. R3 Ltd.: Corda – Sizing and performance, https://docs.corda.net/docs/corda-enterprise/3.3/sizing-and-performance.html. Accessed 5 Nov 2020

Quantity Over Quality? – A Framework for Combining Mobile Crowd Sensing and High Quality Sensing

Barbara Stöckel[1](✉), Simon Kloker[2], Christof Weinhardt[2], and David Dann[2]

[1] FZI Forschungszentrum Informatik, Karlsruhe, Germany
stoeckel@fzi.de
[2] Karlsruhe Institute of Technology, Karlsruhe, Germany
{simon.kloker,christof.weinhardt,david.dann}@kit.edu

Abstract. Mobile Crowd Sensing is a widespread sensing paradigm, successful through the ever-growing availability of mobile devices and their increasing sensor quality. Mobile Crowd Sensing offers low-cost data collection, scalability, and mobility, but faces downsides like unknown or low sensing quality and uncertainty about user behavior and movement. We examine the combination of traditional High Quality Sensing methods and Mobile Crowd Sensing in a Hybrid Sensing system in order to build a value-creating overall system, aiming to use both sensing methods to ensure high quality of data, yet also benefiting from the advantages Mobile Crowd Sensing has to offer such as mobility, scalability, and low deployment cost. We conduct a structured literature review on the current state and derive a classification matrix for Hybrid Sensing applications.

Keywords: Mobile Crowd Sensing · High quality sensing · Data combination · Hybrid sensing · Design science

1 Introduction

By now, *Mobile Crowd Sensing (MCS)* is a widespread large-scaled sensing paradigm. However, some of the most prominent applications, building on information gathered via MCS, like the traffic prediction service embedded in Google Maps, which counts more than one billion active users per month [1], belong to the subcategory of "opportunistic crowdsensing" [2]. This means data is shared without active user intervention and, consequently, is often not perceived as MCS by the user. MCS approaches belonging to the other subcategory of "participatory crowdsensing" [3], where users actively contribute data or information via mobile devices, have received more scientific attention so far. Although these applications do not generate revenue on the same scale as Google, many of them still have a notable number of active users. The user-generated database of Pl@ntnet [4], for instance, contains almost 1.8 million images covering nearly 28 thousand species [5] and does not only help plant enthusiasts to identify their uploaded plant photos automatically, but also makes an active contribution to preserve protected areas [6].

F. Ahlemann et al. (Eds.): WI 2021, LNISO 48, pp. 39–54, 2021.
https://doi.org/10.1007/978-3-030-86800-0_3

The spread of MCS is predominantly driven by the increasing presence of mobile devices (e.g., smartphones) as well as improved integrated sensor technology and their increasing performance (e.g., accuracy, battery life). In addition, the expansion of advanced mobile internet technologies (e.g., 4G, 5G) enables a variety of innovative new MCS applications, especially those depending on real-time processing, as large amounts of data can be transferred to the cloud with virtually no time delay.

In contrast, *High Quality Sensing (HQS)* describes traditional methods to collect data (or information), guaranteeing an almost error-free recording of the variable to be surveyed (e.g., via sensor, expert observation). These professional measurements, sometimes gathered within industrial contexts, are of high quality and verified. However, as they are disadvantageous in terms of mobility, scalability, deployment, and maintenance, they face the problem of being expensive and lacking in spatial and temporal coverage [7].

As MCS and HQS have, to a certain extent, complementary strengths and weaknesses, combining both methods in a *Hybrid Sensing (HS)* system offers the possibility to exploit the strengths of each method in order to compensate for the weaknesses of the other. While MCS comes with advantages in terms of mobility, causing improved spatial-temporal coverage and low-cost scalability [7, 8], as well as the ability to provide additional information for better context awareness through human input [9], HQS can provide reliable, high-quality data [10, 11] available for quality improvement of the overall system, for instance via sensor calibration or training of prediction models applicable on MCS data. Additionally, a cost-reduction may be achieved through optimal resource allocation in terms of energy consumption [12], maintenance or sensor deployment [13], when combining both sensing methods.

Against this backdrop, there is a variety of scientific literature that focuses on the combination of MCS and HQS. However, existing approaches differ substantially with regard to different aspects (e.g., strategic focus, data type) and there is no structured overview or general approach, resulting in a lack of knowledge transfer to other application areas.

Consequently, we argue it is time to take a step back and assess the current state of affairs by structuring existing approaches, methods and results. Our research question is therefore:

RQ_1: How can existing approaches on the value-creating combination of MCS and HQS be classified?

We approach this RQ by conducting a structured literature review, in which we condense the insights of 23 papers, which feature (prototypically) implemented and theoretical HS approaches. Since the results show that a structured approach towards building an HS system is still missing, we decided to address this striking research gap as well. Therefore, our second research question is:

RQ_2: What are the essential components when designing a HS system that combines MCS and HQS in value-adding way?

In a parallel and dependent process to deriving a classification for existing HS approaches (answering RQ_1), we iteratively develop a HS framework (answering RQ_2). These two tasks represent the main work of the first of three cycles in our overarching Design Science (DS) project [14], within which we aim to build a generic value-creating process for combining MCS and HQS. Whilst the focus of this paper lies on the results of the first cycle, in future work we will build a prototypical implementation of our HS framework (cycle two), for which we have chosen the context of road condition monitoring (RCM). We will leverage the prototype's evaluation results to further refine and generalize our approach later on (cycle three).

RCM is a suitable context for our research endeavour in so far, as the HS applications and theoretical approaches that we identified in literature primarily focus on stationary high-quality sensors (e.g., [10, 11]), leaving the application of mobile high-quality sensors, such as necessary in RCM, as a clear research gap. Conventional high-quality approaches on RCM include scanning the road profile with a high-quality Lidar sensor and determining the International Roughness Index (IRI), a global measurement for longitudinal evenness. This sensing method is expensive, due to the needed equipment and personnel expenses, and, therefore, not feasible for ensuring a high spatial-temporal coverage. The road condition on German federal motorways, for instance, is only recorded at fixed intervals of four years [15]. Moreover, roads in the federal states, districts, and municipalities are excluded and thus subject to individual local maintenance plans, leading to inconsistent road assessment. In recent years, various smartphone-based solutions [16] were implemented using data collected via smartphone sensors (e.g., accelerator, gyroscope) to predict the road quality (e.g., RoadSense [17], Roadroid [18]). Although they help to increase the spatial-temporal coverage, they cannot guarantee a reliable high quality. They do not attempt to include the structured and continuous combination of both MCS and HQS data in a HS system, which we therefore address as a novelty in our RCM use case (in cycle two), in order to solve the quality deficit.

The contribution of this paper is three-fold. First, with our structured literature review, we identify and structure existing approaches, methods, and findings. To the best of our knowledge, our paper represents the first structured literature review on this timely and important topic. Second, we introduce a novel HS classification matrix, which logically groups approaches with similar major tasks and challenges, enabling the classification of HS applications and consequently facilitating the transferability of knowledge. Third, we present the first version of a HS framework, which we will further refine in DS cycle two and three, which aims to provide a generalized approach to building a HS system for fellow researchers and practitioners.

The remainder of this paper is structured as follows. In the next section, we describe our research project and the DS methodology used. Section 3 reports on our results from the structured literature review on combining MCS and HQS. Based on the structured literature review, we then derive two interim artifacts (HS classification matrix and HS framework) in Sect. 4, providing more insight into our RCM use case. Section 5 discusses our results and paths for future research.

2 Design Science Research Methodology

In our research project, we employ a Design Science Research Methodology following the guidelines of Kuechler and Vaishnavi [14], which excels by its strong emphasis on an iterative procedure in rapid iterating cycles, making the development of the artifact flexible in its ability to react to re-evaluated requirements. Although several quick iterations are conducted, we define three main cycles for providing a contextual structure. In these three main cycles, we aim to build a HS framework, for value-creating combination of MCS and HQS, with a prototype implementation in a RCM use case using mobile high-quality sensors, which represents a novelty in the domain. With our DS project, we seek to solve the lack of a structured cross-disciplinary approach when it comes to the combination of MCS and HQS, due to which the potential offered by HS is not fully exploited and the transfer of derived knowledge to other applications is restrained. Our HS framework aims to help fellow researchers and practitioners to design HS applications and improve the knowledge transfer to their respective fields of application.

In the *first cycle*, we aim to clarify the problem space and classify different types of HS applications. Based on the knowledge deducted from literature, we draft an overall HS framework, according to whose design we will implement a prototype RCM application in the second and third cycle. Since the literature gives only incomplete information about the required components of the HS framework, the implementation in the following two cycles serves for evaluation and further refinement based on the results. The first cycle is already fully completed, the results of which are the main focus of this paper. In the *second cycle*, the operational infrastructure for the RCM application is set up, a crowd app is developed and extensively tested. An exploratory data analysis, data cleaning, and pre-processing steps for the MCS and HQS data are performed as a basis for the following data combination and model training. The working steps described up to this point have already been carried out following the first results of cycle one. Building on this, we will implement and evaluate a combination approach based on our HS framework in future work. This will comprise the geospatial data fusion (Data Combination), model

General DS Cycle	Design Cycle One HS classification and framework	Design Cycle Two RCM instantiation	Design Cycle Three Refinement and generalisation
Awareness of Problem	Structured literature review on combining MCS and HQS to identify problem and research gaps	Refinement of problem identification RCM problem identification	(Refinement of problem identification)
Suggestion	Derivation of meta-requirements (relevant components) for HS framework	Revision of meta-requirements for HS framework	Revision of meta-requirements for HS framework
Development	Derivation of HS classification matrix Development of HS framework	Instantiation of HS system in RCM application	Revision and generalisation of HS framework Revision of RCM implementation
Evaluation	HS classification matrix and HS framework draft are iteratively deducted from literature and continuously revised	Evaluation of HS framework based on RCM instantiation Expert testing to evaluate functionality of RCM application	Field test for quantitative evaluation Expert workshop to evaluate utility and derive Design Principles
Conclusion	Result: Hybrid Sensing Classification Matrix	Result: Initial applicable RCM HS system	Result: Design Theory (HS Framework)

Fig. 1. Design Science Research Methodology by Kuechler and Vaishnavi [14] applied to our project with three main cycles (executed tasks are highlighted in color, development in cycle two is currently in process) (Color figure online)

training for predicting the road quality based on sensor data (Data Processing) and system quality assessment (Quality Evaluation). The HS framework drafted in the first cycle and continuously refined in the second will be evaluated and discussed in the light our specific use case. In the *third cycle*, we want to use the results from cycle one and two to revise the overall HS framework and its instantiation in the RCM use case. We will further use the enhanced RCM application to derive specific conclusions, which we aim to generalize, regarding the overall HS framework including the topics of spatial-temporal coverage and quality measures, as well as identifying relevant quality enrichment tasks (e.g., task allocation, incentives) for improving the HS system (Fig. 1).

3 Literature Review

In the following section, we present the results of our structured literature review, which we conduct as a central task of the first design cycle. We thereby raise awareness of the problem and create the basis for the derivation of the preliminary artifacts described in more detail in Sect. 4.

3.1 Approach to Literature Review

We conduct a structured literature review following the methodological suggestions by Webster and Watson [19] and vom Brocke et al. [20]. In an explorative search, we identify an initial pool of literature for extracting relevant keywords, based on which we build a search term[1] for our structured literature search. We query a set of interdisciplinary databases (i.e., ACM Digital Library, AIS eLibrary, Emerald Insight, IEEE Xplore Digital Library, ProQuest, ScienceDirect/Scopus, Web of Science) for matching our search term in title, abstract, or keywords [20]. After removing duplicates, this results in 134 publications for further review. Since there is no commonly used term for what we refer to as HQS, we use describing and closely related terms for it in our search query resulting in 118 irrelevant findings, that are not concerned with the combination of MCS and HQS, which we identify by analyzing title and abstract. With the remaining 16 papers as our initial pool of literature, we conduct a successive backward and forward search, which result in further seven relevant publications, yielding a total of 23 articles. The identified articles both contain theoretical approaches, focusing on architecture or simulated models, and practical approaches with concrete or prototype implementations. We consider the paper [7] to be relevant as it adequately outlines opportunities and challenges of HS, but does not contain a HS approach. We present the results of our literature review grouped into classes, the derivation of which we explain in detail in Sect. 4.1, in the context of the development of the HS classification matrix.

In the following two subsections, we first clarify the terms MCS and HQS and then present an overview over existing HS approaches grouped in classes, highlighting the focus of the work.

---

[1] ("mobile crowdsensing" OR "mobile crowd sensing" OR "participatory sensing") AND ("industrial sens*" OR "traditional sens*" OR "stationary sens*" OR "static sens*" OR "special* sens*" OR "sensor node*" OR "expert contribut*" OR "industrial data" OR "hybrid" OR "industrial IOT" OR "industrial Internet of Things") *Note:* * represents one or more wildcard characters.

3.2 MCS and HQS: Clarification of Terms

Guo et al. [21] defines MCS as "a new sensing paradigm that empowers ordinary citizens to contribute data sensed or generated from their mobile devices, aggregates and fuses the data in the cloud for crowd intelligence extraction and people-centric service delivery". Participants in MCS can either collect "hard" data, stemming from physical internal or external sensors connected to the mobile device, or "soft" data, which refer to human-added information (e.g., annotations, human observations) [22].

We define HQS as a sensing method that collects data or information in high quality trustworthily, which means that the accuracy can be considered error-free and the recording of the data is reliable without failures (like e.g. sensor down times).

MCS can either be used to gather data (or information derived therefrom), that is also professionally measurable by HQS, or aim for gathering data or information that cannot be collected feasibly using professional measurement methods.

3.3 Literature Review on Combining MCS and HQS

We start by presenting the most frequent approach on HS, in which both sensing methods collect the same kind of data and focus on accumulating a large amount of data in order to improve the spatial-temporal coverage and/or data quality. For more clarity, we present them divided further into approaches that add HQ sensors on top of MCS and vice versa, that is adding MCS to an existing HQ sensor network. We address both in the following two paragraphs.

Aiming to overcome limitations of MCS and thus ensuring a stable sensing quality and spatial-temporal coverage, the following approaches add static sensor nodes on top of a MCS system. In order for incentive mechanisms to work in MCS applications, a sufficiently large user base is needed, yet MCS faces the problem that crowd participants do not provide sufficient data at all times (e.g., at night). The hybrid framework (HySense) presented in [23] offers a solution by adding stationary sensor nodes to an environmental monitoring MCS application to ensure spatial-temporal coverage. Users' mobility restrictions can be another source for unreliable sensing quality in MCS, which a HS network, containing both static and uncontrolled mobile nodes, seeks to solve in [24] and [11]. The authors formulate criteria for measuring the sensing service quality in HS, identify relevant influencing factors and develop a theoretical grid-based coverage strategy. In [25] missing sensory data from areas less covered by MCS is also compensated by additional static sensors, which are combined together by means of an interpolation strategy. Evaluation shows that a combining interpolation with a mix of static and mobile sensors yields better results over a simpler solution where interpolation is based only on data from static sensors.

In the following approaches, the situation is reversed, making MCS the means to improve a static sensor network, aiming to enrich by achieving an improved spatial-temporal coverage with the benefits of low costs and scalability. Four of the identified applications are (prototypically) implemented in an environmental context and one each in a smart city, smart factory and military setting. In [10] the authors introduce a hybrid sensor calibration scheme for MCS applications, to enable more accurate and dense measurements of natural phenomena adding mobile sensing to an existing sensing infrastructure (e.g., weather stations). The proposed scheme was applied to an environmental use case, in which a temperature map of a city was created, resulting in more detailed information than only the infrastructure-based measurements could provide. Another environmental use case (pollution monitoring) is portrayed in [26], in which MCS is presented as an opportunity to ensure better spatial-temporal coverage for stationary sensory networks in a flexible and cost-efficient manner. The authors focus on solving the resulting scheduling problem that faces the challenge of multiple sensor types generating heterogeneous data at different levels of granularity. In order to receive more accurate noise pollution maps with a better spatial-temporal coverage, a middleware solution is introduced in [27], providing a data assimilation technique to estimate noise pollution based on simulation and noise levels measured over both static and uncontrolled mobile sensor, that are added additionally. In [28] the authors examine the potential benefits of combining static and mobile sensors as a participatory sensor network in a use case of measuring the emission of a substance (e.g., pollutant), evaluating their results using mobility models for simulation. Turning away from environmental monitoring towards a smart city context, [12] presents a prototype for enriching stationary infrastructure sensors with smartphone data in order to improve the situation awareness in cities (public safety and sustainability). The authors aim to develop a dynamic sensing platform that intelligently assigns sensing tasks, not covered by static sensors, to smartphone users in a resource-efficient manner. In the context of smart factories a blockchain-based approach for integrating MCS into a static sensing network is introduced in [8], in order to improve the spatial coverage in a scalable and cost-effective manner. The work focuses on resolving the three main challenges, reliability, security and sensory data quality, arising when integrating MCS into a factory. The G-Sense (Global-Sense) architecture [29], prototypically implemented in a military context, integrates mobile sensors into static wireless sensor networks, featuring an algorithm for optimizing the timing for measuring and sending updated data from the mobile device to the server, while meeting the application requirements.

Having presented HS applications aiming to combine MCS and HQS by collecting the some kind of data or information in an accumulating manner, we now list approaches in which both methods are not equally prioritized. They aim to minimize resource input (e.g., sensor deployment, energy consumption) by cost-efficient replacement of the more expensive method, under the condition of a guaranteed minimum sensing quality. In order to improve the sensing quality and eliminate uncertainties resulting from mobility and varying sensing quality of individuals a collaborative sensing approach is presented in [30] and [31] using both mobile phones and stationary sensors in form of Wireless Sensor Networks (WSN). While [30] introduces an activation scheme for WSN, only enabling stationary sensors when the required sensing quality is not sufficient, [31] focuses on finding optimal locations for wireless sensors in order to minimize the required number of sensors. By solving an optimization problem, the authors in [13] determine the minimal amount of needed additional static sensors and their optimal locations to ensure stable sensing quality and availability, while simultaneously minimize the deployment costs. Trying to overcome limitations of both MCS and static WSN, like network latency, limited lifetime of WSN, costly mobile internet connection, and high battery consumption in the case of MCS, the authors in [32] and [33] introduce a RPL-routing protocol, enabling interaction between MCS and static WSN in a smart city context. In order to optimize activities between data utility (e.g., accuracy) and operational costs (e.g., sensor deployment), a comprehensive planning-based approach with prototype implementation for the combination of mobile devices and in-situ sensors in urban environmental sensing is presented in [34], addressing data generation, upload, and sensor calibration. The authors in [35] introduce a greedy algorithm to solve the dynamic sensor selection problem in a heterogeneous sensor network composed of both mobile sensors and stationary sensors, in terms of location, mobility pattern, energy constraint, and sensing cost.

All approaches listed above use MCS and HQS to obtain the same kind of measurement, for either data replacement or complement. Yet MCS can also be used to generate additional information, which cannot be collected feasibly via HQS methods. Especially all non-physiological measurements fall under additional information (e.g., context information, human perception), as they are difficult or impossible to monitor using traditional sensing networks. A lack of standardisation on data, service and method, uncertainty regarding the measurement of quality, and privacy concerns are common challenges arising when working with "soft" human data [36]. In the following paragraph we present the three applications we have found that use MCS to gain additional information to enrich HQS data.

The integration of spatial-temporal contextual information with human and technical sensor information from a geospatial perspective, which is yet another challenge, is discussed in [9], introducing a model of interactions between humans, the environment and technology in a smart city environment. The MCS application Allergymap [37] is developed in the field of public health monitoring and aims to help people with allergic diseases (e.g., by identification of allergens season, monitoring of treatment process etc.). It combines subjective user input and objective environmental data from fixed stations in a privacy aware manner, outputting a data visualisation in form of a map. The environmental monitoring network introduced in [38] differs from all previously mentioned cases in the fact that it is based on both stationary and mobile high quality sensor nodes. The crowd is used for further data enrichment via a mobile participatory sensing platform, which allows citizens to subjectively report and comment on situations with possible influence on environmental conditions.

The literature review shows, that several approaches on combining MCS and HQS and using its potential already exist, but there is no uniformly structured approach. Most prototypes are implemented in an environmental or smart city context. Our findings therefore lack in diversity of application, as well as the integration of mobile high-quality sensors.

4   Artifact Description

With the results of our structured literature review at hand, we now continue with the description of our two derived artifacts: The HS classification matrix and the HS framework.

4.1   Hybrid Sensing Classification Matrix

Based on the use cases identified in literature on combing both MCS and HQS we derive a Hybrid Sensing Classification Matrix (Fig. 2). We start the development of the

HS classification matrix by identifying the features, displayed on the horizontal and vertical axis in Fig. 2. For this, we first structure the found literature based on the main aspects of each paper (e.g., minimizing energy consumption, spatial-temporal coverage). In the same process, we extract relevant tasks and requirements for the creation of a first draft of a generic HS framework, which maps the overall process for the value-creating combining of both sensing methods. Based on those two parallel tasks, which are mutually dependent, we inductively derive superordinate distinguishing features for classifying HS systems. While doing so, we have our attention on two aspects. On the one hand, we aim for gaining distinguishing features that help to group the identified approaches into classes, which have similar relevant activities and challenges when concretely applying the HS framework. On the other hand, our features should help to divide the approaches into classes that separate as clearly as possible between approaches, that are most challenging to incorporate into one single framework, due to their varying relevant processing tasks. By inductively testing different distinguishing features we conclude that the overall goal of the data combination (vertical feature: strategic focus) answers the first mentioned aspect well and the used data basis (horizontal feature: data/information) answers the second. Note that other classification features (or more than two) are conceivable, but these have proven to be suitable for the development of the HS framework.

To summarize, while the characteristic depicted on the horizontal axis states whether the data or information collected using both methods is the same or different, the vertical characteristic differentiates between the strategic focus lying on data aggregation or substitution, thus resulting in an equal or unequal prioritization of both methods. This leads to the following four HS classes:

- **Complement:** Both methods collect the same data/information and both methods have equal priority, i.e. the methods do not aim to replace each other, but are combined in order to aggregate a large amount of data to achieve better spatial-temporal coverage, object coverage, or a quality improvement.
- **Direct Replacement:** Both methods collect the same data/information, but not both collection methods are equally prioritized, as they aim to minimize resource input (e.g., stationary sensors, energy consumption) by cost-efficient replacement of the more expensive method, under the condition of a guaranteed minimum sensing quality.
- **Supplement:** MCS and HQS gather a different kind of data/ information and both methods have equal priority, aiming to enrich each other by adding additional unknown data/ information.
- **Indirect Replacement:** MCS and HQS collect different types of data/information and not both methods are equality prioritized, as they aim for substitution, not aggregation. Although both methods collect a different type of data/information (e.g., sensor data vs. human subjective input), the data/information from one method can be used to approximate the data/information of the other method, thus making it able to replace the measurement.

Note that, whereas the horizontal differentiation between same and different data is clearly assignable, determining the strategical approach is in some cases not equally unambiguous. The overall goal of HS is the combination of both collection methods

		Information/ Data	
		Same	**Different**
Strategic Focus	**Aggregation**	**Complement** *Aim: Spatial-temporal coverage,* *object-based coverage, quality*	**Supplement** *Aim: Additional information (e.g.,* *context, subjective perception)*
	Substitution	**Direct Replacement** *Aim: Cost-efficient resource* *allocation*	**Indirect Replacement** *Aim: Cost-efficient resource* *allocation*

Fig. 2. Hybrid sensing classification matrix

in a way which maximizes the overall value (which has to be defined individually for each application, as it depends crucially on the strategic focus and could thus target e.g., data quality, coverage or, deployment costs), not replacing one method altogether. Consequently, a complementary component will always play a partial role in the system, even when the strategical approach aims for substitution. This circumstance makes it difficult to assign applications whose combination goal is not clearly communicated in the literature. Due to the fact that HS approaches featured in literature are often not described in full detail, as the research focus may lie on one very specific aspect and not the system as a whole, this is a situation that occurs occasionally. Although this makes a clear assignment difficult in some cases, we have tried to assign the identified approaches consistently to the best of our knowledge, based on the provided information in the respective papers. Table 1 features example HS systems found in literature with type assignment and main target. We found no applications aiming for Indirect Replacement, which leaves its relevance open for discussion, but also possible opportunities open for future research.

4.2 Hybrid Sensing Framework

In the following section, we describe the derivation of the Hybrid Sensing Framework, which aims to generalize the process of combining MCS and HQS in a value-create manner, and present our first draft, illustrated in Fig. 3. It visualizes the generalized processing steps in a HS system, including data collection, data combination, data processing, quality evaluation, and quality enhancement tasks for optional system improvement.

As mentioned in the previous section, we build our first draft of the HS framework based on the results of our literature review. For this purpose, we derive essential tasks, requirements and general recurring components from the literature on existing HS applications, yet as stated before the information provided is often incomplete. Therefore we will develop and evaluate an instantiation in a RCM use case (cycle 2), the evaluation results of which we will use for further refining the framework (cycle 3). As we do so, we will continuously check with the literature and the identified HS classes to ensure that all revisions maintain the universal validity of the HS framework.

The final HS framework should include all possible applications combining MCS and HQS, yet up to now, there is a lack of research on the combination of MCS and high-quality data gathered by mobile sensors, making it not possible to extract knowledge

Table 1. Example HS systems with classification

Ref.	Main aim	Context	Type
[10]	High quality through sensor calibration	Environmental monitoring (temperature map)	Complement
[23]	Spatial-temporal coverage	Environmental monitoring (ozone concentration)	Complement
[26]	Spatial-temporal coverage	Environmental monitoring (pollution mapping)	Complement
[30, 31]	Cost-efficient resource allocation (energy consumption, senor deployment)	Theoretical approach; evaluation via simulation	Direct Replacement
[34]	Optimization between data utility and operational costs	Community IoT systems in urban sensing	Direct Replacement
[38]	Additional information through subjective user input	Environmental monitoring (air quality)	Supplement
[37]	Additional information through subjective user input for personalized services	Allergy map	Supplement
	Spatial-temporal coverage	RCM (our project)	Complement

on this scenario from literature. We will therefore build a prototype application in our RCM use case to extract further knowledge, which we will use to refine and validate our framework draft in terms of generalization.

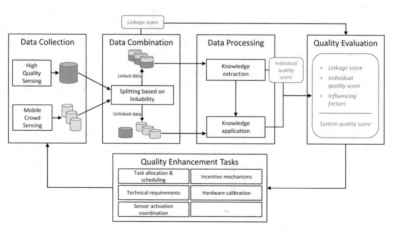

Fig. 3. Hybrid sensing framework illustrating the processing steps when combining MCS and HQS

Data Collection. MCS gathers human-generated data via mobile devices or connectable sensors [39]. HQS data is collected by either stationary sensor networks (e.g., [10, 11, 23, 24]), mobile high-quality sensors [38] or possibly expert observations. For our RCM application, we developed a crowd app for android phones, making it possible to gather relevant sensor data (e.g., acceleration, gyroscope, GPS) and upload it to our server. The high-quality data is collected, as described in the introduction, by a project partner specialized in RCM, providing us with IRI measurements. We tested both data collection methods extensively, making our operative infrastructure ready to use for large-scale data collection as a basis for the development of data combination methods.

Data Combination. Regardless of whether both methods collect the same or different data, in order to perform a value-creating processing, it must be combined by some kind of link characteristic, which is done in the Data Combination step. In the literature one finds mainly a spatial-temporal link (e.g., in [9, 23, 26]), but it would also be possible to link data, for example, over identical objects featured in images or data connected to a similar situation. In our use case, we have to answer questions on how to define geospatial coverage and how to deal with measurements taken at different times. Aim of this step is to have a data fusion method, merging both data types by geo-coordinates with respect to time and a linkage score (e.g., percentage geospatial coverage within a certain time interval).

Data Processing. From the linked MCS and HQS, data knowledge is extracted (e.g., in the form of a prediction [37], interpolation [25], assimilation [27] or calibration model [10]), which is subsequently used to enhance the unlinked data. When extracting knowledge based on the linked data (which can also be referred to as labeled data) an individual quality score for the specific knowledge extraction is derived, which serves to estimate the quality of the knowledge application on the unlinked data. We will use smartphone data collected via the crowd app, which can be linked to specialist data with respect to space and time, to extract knowledge in form of training an individual IRI prediction model for every crowd driver. This knowledge, in our case the individual model, will be used to predict the road quality based on data collected by the same driver. Every model has a known accuracy, which is the individual quality score for every driver. Data from crowd workers with no spatial-temporal coverage with high-quality data will be processed with a more generalized model, thus resulting in a greater prediction quality uncertainty.

Quality Evaluation. The creation of suitable and meaningful evaluation scores and identification of influencing factors [11] on the overall system quality, is a core task in the design of a HS system, as they serve as optimization target values when improving the system. We propose to evaluate the quality of the overall system based on the individual quality score, which describes the performance of the Data Processing, and the linkage score, which evaluates the Data Combination, also taking into account potential influencing factors. We will use the linkage score, that has yet to be defined, and the model accuracies as individual quality scores to determine the quality of our RCM system. We will also search for influencing factors in the evaluation.

Quality Enhancement Tasks. Apart from improving the individual quality score (Data Processing) and the linkage score (Data Combination), the overall system quality can also be improved by working on the relevant influencing factors. This can be achieved by means of subtasks which comprise topics like task scheduling and sensor coordination [26, 40], incentive mechanisms and data security [8], or simply stating technical requirements, to name a few. Research on "traditional" standalone MCS already offers extensive research in those domains, yet through changing the initial situation by combining MCS and HQS in a value-creating manner, it will be necessary to revise and extend some already well-researched approaches. Based on the results of our quality evaluation, we will derive and implement possible solutions for quality improvement. If there is too little crowd data available, for example, the development of incentive mechanisms could be of help. If poor prediction model results are based on insufficient linkable data, task allocation mechanisms, which assign crowd workers or specialists to specific sensing tasks, may be beneficial. The quality of smartphone data could be improved by defining a minimal technical standard.

5   Discussion and Outlook

HS gives us new opportunities to fully exploit the possibilities that the spread of mobile devices, and thus MCS, has to offer in a wider field of application. Alongside technical improvements (e.g., sensor quality), the flexibility of approaches is further extended by the possibility of connecting external sensors and integrating smart gadgets. This allows to create new cost-efficient industrial solutions, but also build services for participants, aiming for an improvement in quality of life in general. With the expansion of 5G networks, opportunities also arise for applications based on real-time information and high-speed cloud processing, enabling applications requiring computing power, mobile devices cannot provide (e.g., intelligent hazard detection in traffic based on smartphone image processing). However, involving people into the data collection process not only creates opportunities like improved spatial-temporal coverage, but also raises problems (e.g., security/privacy issues, data trustworthiness, incentive techniques) [7]. While most resulting challenges have been comprehensively discussed in literature in the domain of MCS, including high-quality sensors and the corresponding effect is so far not dealt with extensively. We now summarize frequently mentioned issues that present challenges for HS applications but also offer opportunities for improved solutions.

– Reliable high-quality data can contribute to enhanced *incentive techniques* by the development of more attractive crowd services. Furthermore, incentives can, when needed, promote the generation of overlapping data by both collection methods.
– Malicious misuse can be detected and prevented more easily, thus improving *data trustworthiness,* through the availability of verified high-quality measurements.
– Subjective human input offers opportunities for various new applications, yet represents a challenge due to the *lack of standardization* when combined with physiological sensor measurements.

- Some HS approaches will require a modified optimal *task allocation* for participants, when including high-quality sensors, and *sensor coordination* strategies, when aiming for a cost-efficient resource allocation.
- Finding suitable *quality and coverage metrics* and relevant influencing factors is crucial and has to be solved individually depending on the field of application, yet the definition of generalized requirements could help practitioners and researches.

We did not find any applications falling into the category of indirect replacement, but we see potential for this HS class when it comes to applications providing public benefit yet facing limited financial resources (e.g., crowd sourcing projects).

6 Conclusion

We conducted a structured literature review on the systematic combination of MCS and HQS (i.e., Hybrid Sensing). This is the first of three cycles in our DS project for creating a generic process for HS systems. We classified existing approaches by their data or information gathered and the strategical approach regarding the sensing method prioritization. This resulted in four main types, differentiating HS approaches: Complement, supplement, direct replacement, and indirect replacement. This categorization contributes a structure to open opportunities and challenges to address in the field of HS. We also presented a HS framework for the structured combination of MCS and HQS and identified the usage of mobile high-quality sensors in HS systems as research gap. Researchers and practitioners may use the framework to structure HS-related projects. The introduction of Quality Enhancement Tasks may be of high relevance for related fields (e.g., Citizen Science) that suffer from data quality issues [41]. We also discussed both contributions in the light of our RCM use case. After having set up the operational infrastructure, we will develop and evaluate an initial combination procedure in cycle two, answering questions regarding temporal-spatial coverage and quality assessment. In the third cycle, we will use the evaluation results to revise the HS framework and improve the RCM application to enable low-cost road maintenance, contributing to road safety by near real time damage detection.

References

1. Roy, S.: How Google Maps is positioned to become the next big content platform. https://www.financialexpress.com/industry/technology/how-google-maps-is-positioned-to-become-the-next-big-content-platform/2087251/. Accessed 28 Nov 2020
2. Kapadia, A., Kotz, D., Triandopoulos, N.: Opportunistic sensing: security challenges for the new paradigm. In: First International Conference on Communication Systems and Networks and workshops, pp. 1–10. IEEE (2009)
3. Burke, J.A., et al.: Participatory sensing. In: Workshop on World-Sensor-Web (WSW): Mobile Device Centric Sensor Networks and Applications (2006)
4. Joly, A., et al.: A look inside the Pl@ntNet experience. Multimedia Syst. **22**(6), 751–766 (2015). https://doi.org/10.1007/s00530-015-0462-9
5. Pl@ntnet Website: https://plantnet.org/en/. Accessed 28 Nov 2020

6. Bonnet, P., et al.: How citizen scientists contribute to monitor protected areas thanks to automatic plant identification tools. Ecol. Solut. Evidence **1** (2020)
7. Shu, L., Chen, Y., Huo, Z., Bergmann, N., Wang, L.: When mobile crowd sensing meets traditional industry. IEEE Access **5**, 15300–15307 (2017)
8. Huang, J., et al.: Blockchain-based mobile crowd sensing in industrial systems. IEEE Trans. Industr. Inf. **16**, 6553–6563 (2020)
9. Sagl, G., Resch, B., Blaschke, T.: Contextual sensing: integrating contextual information with human and technical geo-sensor information for smart cities. Sensors **15**, 17013–17035 (2015)
10. Son, S.-C., Lee, B.-T., Ko, S.K., Kang, K.: Hybrid sensor calibration scheme for mobile crowdsensing-based city-scale environmental measurements. ETRI J. **38**, 551–559 (2016)
11. Ding, S., He, X., Wang, J., Qiao, B., Gai, K.: Static node center opportunistic coverage and hexagonal deployment in hybrid crowd sensing. J. Signal Process. Syst. **86**, 251–267 (2017)
12. Liao, C.-C., et al.: SAIS: Smartphone augmented infrastructure sensing for public safety and sustainability in smart cities. In: Proceedings of the 1st International Workshop on Emerging Multimedia Applications and Services for Smart Cities, pp. 3–8 (2014)
13. Bijarbooneh, F.H., Flener, P., Ngai, E.C.-H., Pearson, J.: An optimisation-based approach for wireless sensor deployment in mobile sensing environments. In: 2012 IEEE Wireless Communications and Networking Conference (WCNC), pp. 2108–2112 (2012)
14. Kuechler, B., Vaishnavi, V.: On theory development in design science research: anatomy of a research project. Eur. J. Inf. Syst. **17**, 489–504 (2008)
15. Zustandserfassung und-bewertung (ZEB) auf Bundesfernstraßen: https://www.bmvi.de/Sha redDocs/DE/Artikel/StB/zustandserfassung-und-bewertung.html. Accessed 28 Nov 2020
16. Klopfenstein, L.C., et al.: Mobile crowdsensing for road sustainability: exploitability of publicly-sourced data. Int. Rev. Appl. Econ. **34**, 650–671 (2020)
17. Allouch, A., Koubâa, A., Abbes, T., Ammar, A.: Roadsense: smartphone application to estimate road conditions using accelerometer and gyroscope. IEEE Sens. J. **17**, 4231–4238 (2017)
18. Forslöf, L., Jones, H.: Roadroid: continuous road condition monitoring with smart phones. J. Civil Eng. Architec. **9**, 485–496 (2015)
19. Webster, J., Watson, R.T.: Analyzing the past to prepare for the future: writing a literature review. MIS Quarterly, xiii–xxiii (2002)
20. vom Brocke, J., et al.: Reconstructing the giant: on the importance of rigour in documenting the literature search process. In: ECIS 2009 Proceedings (2009)
21. Guo, B., Yu, Z., Zhou, X., Zhang, D.: From participatory sensing to Mobile Crowd Sensing. In: 2014 IEEE International Conference on Pervasive Computing and Communication Workshops, PERCOM WORKSHOPS 2014 (2014)
22. Rimland, J.C., Hall, D.L., Graham, J.L.: Human cognitive and perceptual factors in JDL level 4 hard/soft data fusion. In: Proceedings of SPIE – The International Society for Optical Engineering (2012)
23. Han, G., Liu, L., Chan, S., Yu, R., Yang, Y.: HySense: a hybrid mobile CrowdSensing framework for sensing opportunities compensation under dynamic coverage constraint. IEEE Commun. Mag. **55**, 93–99 (2017)
24. Ding, S., He, X., Wang, J., Dai, W., Wang, X.: Static node center hexagonal deployment in hybrid crowd sensing. In: 2015 IEEE 17th International Conference on High Performance Computing and Communications, 2015 IEEE 7th International Symposium on Cyberspace Safety and Security and 2015 IEEE 12th International Conference on Embedded Software and Systems, HPCC-CSS-ICESS 2015 (2015)
25. Girolami, M., Chessa, S., Adami, G., Dragone, M., Foschini, L.: Sensing interpolation strategies for a mobile crowdsensing platform. In: 5th IEEE International Conference on Mobile Cloud Computing, Services, and Engineering, MobileCloud 2017, pp. 102–108. IEEE (2017)

26. Zhu, Q., Uddin, M.Y.S., Venkatasubramanian, N., Hsu, C.-H.: Spatiotemporal scheduling for crowd augmented urban sensing. In: IEEE Conference on Computer Communications, IEEE INFOCOM 2018, pp. 1997–2005 (2018)
27. Hachem, S., et al.: Monitoring noise pollution using the urban civics middleware. In: IEEE First International Conference on Big Data Computing Service and Applications, BigDataService 2015, pp. 52–61. IEEE (2015)
28. Lent, R., Minero, M., North, R., Barria, J.: Evaluating mobility models in participatory sensing. In: Proceedings of the Annual International Conference on Mobile Computing and Networking, MOBICOM (2012)
29. Perez, A.J.: An Architecture for Global Ubiquitous Sensing (2011)
30. Ngai, E.C.-H., Xiong, J.: Adaptive collaborative sensing using mobile phones and stationary sensors. In: Proceedings of the International Conference on Dependable Systems and Networks (2011)
31. Ruan, Z., Ngai, E.C.-H., Liu, J.: Wireless sensor network deployment in mobile phones assisted environment. In: 2010 IEEE 18th International Workshop on Quality of Service (IWQoS), pp. 1–9 (2010)
32. Al Sawafi, Y., Touzene, A., Day, K., Alzeidi, N.: Toward hybrid RPL based IoT sensing for smart city. In: 2018 International Conference on Information Networking (ICOIN), pp. 599–604 (2018)
33. Sawafi, Y.A., Touzene, A., Day, K., Alzeidi, N.: Hybrid RPL-based sensing and routing protocol for smart city. Int. J. Pervasive Comput. Commun. 16, 279–306 (2020)
34. Zhu, Q.: Exploiting Mobile Plus In-Situ Deployments in Community IoT Systems (2019)
35. Ma, Y., Hou, F., Ma, S., Liu, D.: Dynamic sensor selection in heterogeneous sensor network. In: 2016 IEEE 83rd Vehicular Technology Conference (VTC Spring), pp. 1–5 (2016)
36. Resch, B., Blaschke, T.: Fusing human and technical sensor data: concepts and challenges. SIGSPATIAL Special 7, 29–35 (2015)
37. Kalogiros, L.A., Lagouvardos, K., Nikoletseas, S., Papadopoulos, N., Tzamalis, P.: Allergymap: a hybrid mhealth mobile crowdsensing system for allergic diseases epidemiology: multidisciplinary case study. In: 2018 IEEE International Conference on Pervasive Computing and Communications Workshops, PerCom Workshops 2018 (2018)
38. Bacco, M., Delmastro, F., Ferro, E., Gotta, A.: Environmental monitoring for smart cities. IEEE Sens. J. 17, 7767–7774 (2017)
39. Resch, B.: People as sensors and collective sensing-contextual observations complementing geo-sensor network measurements. In: Progress in Location-based Services, pp. 391–406. Springer (2013)
40. Ngai, E.C.-H., Xiong, J.: Adaptive collaborative sensing using mobile phones and stationary sensors. In: 2011 IEEE/IFIP 41st International Conference on Dependable Systems and Networks Workshops (DSN-W), pp. 280–285 (2011)
41. Weinhardt, C., Kloker, S., Hinz, O., van der Aalst, W.M.P.: Citizen science in information systems research. Bus. Inf. Syst. Eng. 62(4), 273–277 (2020). https://doi.org/10.1007/s12599-020-00663-y

Decentralized and Microservice-Oriented Data Integration for External Data Sources

Christoph Schröer[1,2(✉)] and Jonas Frischkorn[1]

[1] Volkswagen AG, Corporate Foresight, Wolfsburg, Germany
{christoph.schroeer,jonas.frischkorn}@volkswagen.de
[2] Very Large Business Applications (VLBA), Carl Von Ossietzky University Oldenburg, Oldenburg, Germany

Summary. Data lakes offer good opportunities to centrally use heterogeneous data for analytical questions in companies. However, there are also challenges and risks regarding missing reference architectures, accessibility or usability. By using modern architecture patterns such as microservices, data can alternatively be managed in a technically and organizationally decentralized manner. Easily accessible interfaces and microservice architecture patterns can maintain important data lake characteristics, such as accessibility and the provision of metadata. Thus, costs can be saved, data can be held accountable in the respective domains, and at the same time interfaces for analytical questions can be provided. The paper illustrates the idea in the form of a work-in-progress paper using the integration of external data sources as an example.

Keywords: Data lake · Microservice · External data sources

1 Introduction

Digitization and the associated digital transformation open up access to new information, reorganize processes, reduce costs and create market opportunities [1]. In the context of digital, strategically relevant decision-making processes, company-external, heterogeneous data sources can support a holistic overview of market events, innovations and competitors. The integration of many and various data sources can result in centralized, schema-less data lakes [2, 3], which result into monolithic data architectures in enterprises [4]. To collect, store, and process data and information in a powerful and context-aware manner, efficient information processing architectures are needed.

Regarding the complication, we are going to answer the following research question: *How can microservices support data integration with respect to the described challenges?*

In the second section, we first present the concept and explain the need for further research on how companies can integrate external data sources in decentralized, domain-specific data lake microservices and thus make platform solutions more efficient. Crucial here is the idea of avoiding a centralized data lake and considering analytical issues in the

F. Ahlemann et al. (Eds.): WI 2021, LNISO 48, pp. 55–60, 2021.
https://doi.org/10.1007/978-3-030-86800-0_4

architecture based directly on the domain data. In the third section, we illustrate the positive effects for companies and the scientific implications of microservice architectures. This paper ends with an outlook for further research.

2   Problem Statement and Challenges

Sawadogo (2020) defines data lakes as a scalable storage and analysis platform based on raw data for statisticians, data scientists or analysts. In addition to storage capabilities, essential concepts are a metadata system, data integration components, and data governance. Characteristics are accessibility, logical and physical organization, and scalability in storage and computational capacities [5]. A data lake represents the state of the data at any point in time [5–8]. A full overview of the state-of-the-art of data lakes is described for example, in the paper by [1].

Challenges in the implementation of data lakes are, for example, the lack of reference architectures [4, 5]. Specific characteristics such as metadata management and data governance are not trivially achievable. A data lake not only technically represents a central data store but is also organizationally managed by a central data team. This breaks the flow of data across multiple organizational entities, complicating data lineage [9]. Hadoop as a technology is often used together with the term data lake [6]. However, data lakes consist of different storage technologies suitable for structured, semi-structured, and unstructured data. The challenge here is to enable data retrieval across heterogeneous storage systems [5].

If external data sources continue to be integrated for analytical issues, architectural decisions have to be made. Due to the external generation, these cannot be directly assigned to an organizational, operational unit. There are various options for defining the functional area of responsibility:

- with the requesting department, which recognizes the need for an external data source,
- with a central data team that wants to draw on external data for strategically relevant projects,
- with a specialized department of that domain, which can be assigned to the external data sources. For example, the communications department can take responsibility for external news data.

Assigning external data to internal experts can harden the domain reference and understanding. At the same time, the latter can also benefit from analysis results. The integration of external data within the domain context (see Sect. 3) represents a success factor that we will investigate further.

3   Microservice-Oriented Data Integration

This paper shows an alternative approach to the technically and organizationally centralized data lake architecture. The Domain Driven Design (DDD) approach has been established in software development since 2003. DDD bases on software models through a ubiquitous language [10]. Data are always to be assigned to a domain and organizationally to a specialist department, that has a subject-specific understanding of the data. A central data team hast to gain this domain knowledge first to select and evaluate the right data for answering analytical questions. A central storage platform is not necessarily required to fulfill the characteristics of a data lake regarding data integration.

Microservices have been established themselves since 2014 as an architectural approach to develop applications as a set of cohesive, loosely coupled services [11]. Figure 1 gives an architectural proposal for microservice-oriented data integration, which is described in more detail in the following paragraphs. The proposal combines technical aspects of microservices with functional aspects of data lakes. We technically use the architecture prototypically for integrating and processing external data sources from the news, company, policy, and patent domains. This architectural proposal was derived using DDD approach, in that the external data sources each form their own bounded context.

The architecture proposes dedicated bounded contexts and thus **microservices** for the integration and storage of external data for each data source and domain. The Fig. 1 shows an example of a *data source A from domain 1*. Another data source could also originate from domain 1 but has other concepts and its own technical language. For example, the entity "company" can be defined by the terms "company", "enterprise" or "organization".

To be able to track states over time, *event stores* are used to map data changes in the form of events. For this purpose, we use the microservice architecture pattern of event sourcing [12]. In addition to this domain-specific provision of external data, one or more *microservices* can be implemented with *query-optimized access* for analytical use cases and accessed by interfaces. For this purpose, we are testing the Command Query Responsible Separation (CQRS) microservice architecture pattern [12] to update data via event sourcing.

Interfaces (API) of the microservices follow a uniform convention. The interface documentations are stored in the metadata system or *data source catalog*. Table 1 shows important characteristics of the interface methods. These were derived in internal workshops and are based on integrating of four external data sources and conducting of a practical case study.

The *data platform* shown in Fig. 1 implements well-known data lake architecture patterns and components [1] for data processing. A *data source catalog* helps to query information about data and data sources. The metadata system is not new with respect to the microservice-oriented approach but needs to be adapted for it. Interfaces can be used to query metadata of individual data sources and store the metadata in the *data source catalog* [13]. Interface documentation can also supplement the data source catalog. Semantic descriptions or knowledge graphs can supplement the *semantic layer.* Knowledge graphs can be used to query across microservices and data without knowing exactly which microservices need to be requested technically [14, 15].

The microservice-oriented approach differs from data marts in that dedicated microservices enable full access via interfaces and thus not just access in aggregated form to the dataset. Aggregated data and analysis results can be found in Fig. 1 in the form of *data products*.

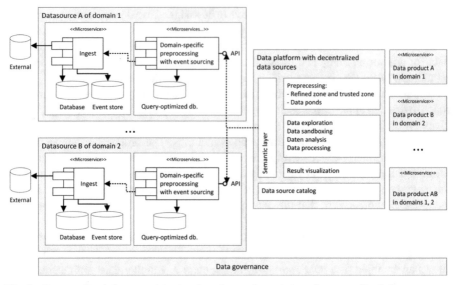

Fig. 1. Decentralized data provisioning based on microservices for centralized data teams to address analytical issues.

Data governance can be strengthened by the organizational responsibility of microservices in the specialist departments. The latter can check which data may be released, for example, complying with the rules of the EU General Data Protection Regulation. Furthermore, data quality aspects can also be evaluated here by domain experts, especially for external data sources. Figure 1 illustrates this aspect in that *data governance* already begins with data integration.

Table 1. Characteristics of the interface methods.

Characteristic	Description
Accessibility	Through an API method, access can be requested for each user
Metadata	An API method is to be used to provide metadata that includes, for example, descriptive statistics
Semantics	An API method is to be used to query semantic concepts that are represented, for example, in the form of a data model
Data retrieval	A data query should be able to retrieve raw data that can then be used for analytical questions
Scalability	Not all data can always be provided via an interface due to the volume. Since microservices are technology-open, query-optimized technologies as well as direct database access and Hadoop can be used

4   Summary and Outlook

To sum up, the paper demonstrates the concept of integrating data using DDD principles and decentralized microservices. Existing microservice architecture patterns and semantic concepts of data integration are combined to a new, technically, and organizationally decentralized integration approach.

Further research is needed to evaluate the extent to which other quality characteristics and legal frame conditions can be considered, such as performance or data privacy protection respectively. There is also a need for further research into the questions of whether the characteristics of data lakes can be retained and whether the domain reference can actually support the answering of analytical questions.

A currently known limitation is due to the microservice architecture itself since it initially entails increased complexity. If the microservice architecture is widely established in companies both organizationally and technically, our presented approach can expand and support data integration by means of microservices and thus analytical issues.

Disclaimer: The results, opinions and conclusions expressed in this publication are not necessarily those of Volkswagen Aktiengesellschaft.

References

1. Giebler, C., Gröger, C., Hoos, E., Eichler, R., Schwarz, H., Mitschang, B.: Data lakes auf den Grund gegangen. Datenbank-Spektrum **20**(1), 57–69 (2020). https://doi.org/10.1007/s13 222-020-00332-0
2. Mehmood, H., et al.: Implementing big data lake for heterogeneous data sources. In: 2019 IEEE 35th International Conference on Data Engineering Workshops (ICDEW) (2019). https://doi.org/10.1109/ICDEW.2019.00-3
3. Dixon, J.: Pentaho, Hadoop, and Data Lakes. https://jamesdixon.wordpress.com/2010/10/14/pentaho-hadoop-and-data-lakes/ (2010). Accessed 14 July 2020
4. Hai, R., Geisler, S., Quix, C.: Constance. An Intelligent Data Lake System. In: Proceedings of the 2016 International Conference on Management of Data (SIGMOD) (2016). https://doi.org/10.1145/2882903.2899389
5. Sawadogo, P., Darmont, J.: On data lake architectures and metadata management. J. Intell. Inf. Syst. **56**(1), 97–120 (2020). https://doi.org/10.1007/s10844-020-00608-7
6. Gupta, S., Giri, V.: Practical Enterprise Data Lake Insights. Handle Data-Driven Challenges in an Enterprise Big Data Lake. Apress, Berkeley, CA (2018)
7. Kim, J., Ha, H., Chun, B., Yoon, S., Cha, K.: Collaborative analytics for data silos. In: International Conference on Data Engineering (ICDE) (2016). https://doi.org/10.1109/ICDE.2016.7498286
8. Terrizzano, I., Schwarz, P., Roth, M., Colino, J.E.: Data wrangling: the challenging journey from the wild to the lake. In: 7th Biennial Conference on Innovative Data Systems Research (2015)
9. Janssen, M., Brous, P., Estevez, E., Barbosa, L., Janowski, T.: Data governance: organizing data for trustworthy artificial intelligence. Gov. Inf. Q. **37**(3), 101493 (2020). https://doi.org/10.1016/j.giq.2020.101493
10. Evans, E.: Domain-driven design. Tackling Complexity in the Heart of Software. Addison-Wesley, Upper Saddle River, NJ (2011)

11. Lewis, J., Fowler, M.: Microservices. A definition of this new architectural term. https://mar tinfowler.com/articles/microservices.html (2014). Accessed 30 April 2018
12. Richardson, C.: Microservice Patterns. With Examples in Java. Manning, Shelter Island, NY (2019)
13. Samourkasidis, A., Athanasiadis, I.N.: A semantic approach for timeseries data fusion. Computers and Electronics in Agriculture (2020). https://doi.org/10.1016/j.compag.2019.105171
14. Schmid, S., Henson, C., Tran, T.: Using Knowledge Graphs to Search an Enterprise Data Lake. In: Hitzler, P., et al. (eds.) ESWC 2019. LNCS, vol. 11762, pp. 262–266. Springer, Cham (2019). https://doi.org/10.1007/978-3-030-32327-1_46
15. Galkin, M., Auer, S., Vidal, M.-E., Scerri, S.: Enterprise Knowledge Graphs: A Semantic Approach for Knowledge Management in the Next Generation of Enterprise Information Systems (2017). https://doi.org/10.5220/0006325200880098

Leveraging the Potentials of Federated AI Ecosystems

Marco Röder[(⊠)], Peter Kowalczyk, and Frédéric Thiesse

Chair of Information Systems Engineering, University of Würzburg, Würzburg, Germany
{marco.roeder,peter.kowalczyk,frederic.thiesse}@uni-wuerzburg.de

Abstract. Deep learning increasingly receives attention due to its ability to efficiently solve various complex prediction tasks in organizations. It is therefore not surprising that more and more business processes are supported by deep learning. With the proliferation of edge intelligence, this trend will continue and, in parallel, new forms of internal and external cooperation are provided through federated learning. Hence, companies must deal with the potentials and pitfalls of these technologies and decide whether to deploy them or not and how. However, there currently is no domain-spanning decision framework to guide the efficient adoption of these technologies. To this end, the present paper sheds light on this research gap and proposes a research agenda to foster the potentials of value co-creation within federated AI ecosystems.

Keywords: Edge intelligence · Federated learning · AI ecosystem

1 Introduction

The umbrella term "deep learning" (DL) denotes algorithms from the broader field of artificial intelligence (AI) that seek to train complex artificial neural networks, which typically consist of numerous layers between the model input and output [1, 2]. Such deep neural networks (DNN) are particularly suited to process vast amounts of data effectively to solve prediction tasks [3]. Thus, DL holds the potential to drive a wide range of processes in important corporate areas, such as fraud detection, decision support, automation, and more [2, 4, 5]. However, the application of DL is also accompanied by challenges like learning from sparse data, model bias, poor model performance, or maintaining data privacy [4, 6, 7].

In light of the advances in cloud-based systems, DL components are increasingly used for business tasks as mentioned before [8, 9]. Moreover, a study by Deloitte from 2019 indicates that Internet of Things (IoT) projects using AI technologies will increase by 70 percent until 2022 [10]. With the proliferation of edge intelligence (EI) technologies, which push DL towards the edge of the network (e.g., IoT-devices, and edge servers), this distribution trend of DNN is continued [11]. Additionally, EI enables new collaboration potentials at various organizational stages by utilizing federated learning (FL) [12]. The objective of FL is to train a shared global DNN with the insights gained from decentral DNNs instantiated by locally dispersed clients [13, 14].

© The Author(s), under exclusive license to Springer Nature Switzerland AG 2021
F. Ahlemann et al. (Eds.): WI 2021, LNISO 48, pp. 61–68, 2021.
https://doi.org/10.1007/978-3-030-86800-0_5

For example, by deploying EI, an electronic article surveillance (EAS) system in retail (e.g., as proposed by Hauser et al. [15]), could be extended to facilitate DNNs on local EI devices such as, for example, RFID gates in stores. If FL is applied additionally, the local DNN could be trained collaboratively with insights gathered from other RFID gates located in the same store, with those from EAS systems in a larger retail store network, or even jointly with company-external sources.

Drawing on recent literature on ecosystems further substantiates the idea of such an interwoven application of EI and FL to build more sophisticated DL models. The term ecosystem originates from biology and is generally referred to as the fusion of multiple units that interact with each other and the environment [16, 17]. As far as data ecosystems are concerned, the ecosystem units share data either intra- or inter-organizational [18]. With regard to a federated AI ecosystem, shared insights from the EI instances (i.e., the entities of the ecosystem) can be either related to a specific task or even to integrated processes. The more entities involved in such a federated AI ecosystem, the greater the chance and possible magnitude of benefit for each of them [19, 20]. Thus, we leverage these possible effects by taking the ecosystem perspective [21] and loosely following the service-dominant (SD) logic put forward by Vargo and Lusch [22, 23], which emphasizes services (i.e., intangibles) rather than goods (i.e., tangibles) as the resources of exchange to co-create value [22, 24–26].

Combining EI and FL holds the potential to enhance the system's performance, generalizability and robustness, and thus assist to overcome current challenges associated with AI in practice (i.e., model bias, sparse data, data privacy, poor model performance) [27–31]. However, while current research endeavors are already directed towards the development of specific systems deploying FL [32, 33]—to the best of our knowledge— there is no guidance on how to identify and enhance suitable processes to leverage the potentials of EI and FL for value co-creation in ecosystems. To this end, we propose our research question as follows: *How can FL be used to empower AI ecosystems for value co-creation?*

In the following sections, we first elaborate on the technological background of EI and FL. We then present a corresponding research agenda to serve as a blueprint to assist and motivate researchers as well as practitioners to engage with this promising topic. Subsequently, we conclude the present paper by applying the design-oriented research methodology (DSRM) as proposed by Peffers et al. [34] to the research agenda and briefly outline the expected contributions.

2   Theoretical Background

2.1   Edge Intelligence

EI follows the edge computing (EC) paradigm [11]. EC can be described as a distributed and decentralized computing concept [35] which enables data processing to happen directly or in proximity to the data source [36]. More specifically, EC includes all nodes along the path from the end devices (e.g., sensors), over edge servers (e.g., micro-data centers) to the cloud data center [36]. For the sake of simplicity, we generally refer to these points as "edge nodes" (EN). Now, EI (cf. Fig. 1) can be regarded as the migration of traditionally cloud-based DNN to these ENs [33, 37]. Therefore, EI can overcome the specific issues associated with cloud computing (e.g., latency, data privacy, or communication inefficiency) [11, 36, 38–40]. Furthermore, shifting data processing to the edge of the network makes transferring all raw data to a central cloud unit obsolete [41]. Instead, data processing can take place in closer proximity to its origin, and thus preprocessed data are transferred [11, 41]. Each EN in this EI hierarchy is capable of consuming and producing data (e.g., by inferencing) [11]. Following the definitions of Zhou et al. and Xu et al., we refer to EI as the usage of AI algorithms locally on any of the ENs to enhance model training and inferencing, while simultaneously protecting the privacy and security of data [11, 41]. According to the idea of EC, each EN in this hierarchy is capable of collaborating with other nodes vertically or horizontally [11].

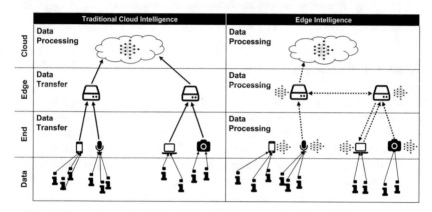

Fig. 1. Comparison of traditional cloud intelligence and edge intelligence [11, 41]

2.2 Federated Learning

In order to facilitate vertical or horizontal collaborative training of distributed DNNs, FL poses a promising solution [11]. The objective of FL is to train a shared global DL model provided by a high-level instance (model owner) by successively feeding insights gained from decentral DNNs which are instantiated by locally dispersed clients (data owners) [11–13, 33]. Therefore, the local DNN iteratively updates the global model [13]. Here it should be emphasized that private data are treated confidentially in the sense that they are not forwarded but rather remain with the data owner [11, 13]. Instead, only the parameter values of the local DNNs are used to update the global DNN, ideally making plausible data protection concerns obsolete [11, 33]. The training procedure of FL (cf. Table 1) can be divided into three steps: (1) task initialization, (2) local model training and updating, (3) global model aggregation and updating [33].

Although this decentralized learning approach is rich in potential (i.e., privacy protection, reduction of model bias), FL may also come along with downsides—namely algorithmic or practical challenges [27]. While the former may emerge by the difficulty to design an appropriate model averaging policy that is fast and robust despite limited availability of model updates or malicious contributors, the latter results from practical issues such as the restorability of private data by another client [27, 32, 42].

Table 1. Steps of federated learning [33]

Step		Description
	(1)	The model owner decides upon the training task and necessary data, initializes model hyperparameters, and shares the initialized model (G_i) with the data owners
Repeat	(2)	Each data owner applies G_i (or G_{i+j} respectively) as a local model and optimizes this model with private data. Finally, the data owner sends the updated local model parameters back to the model owner
	(3)	The model owner receives the updated parameters from the data owners and aggregates these updates effectively to a new global model (G_{i+j}). G_{i+j} is then sent back to the data owners

3 Research Agenda

As illustrated in section two, EI can lead to a reduction in latency, improves communication efficiency, and increases data security [11, 36, 38–40]. Additionally, FL may potentially help to overcome some of the hurdles in the context of AI deployment (i.e., model bias, sparse data, model performance) [27–31]. By combining both technologies we merge advantages and opt for a system which delivers a secure and efficient communication of the necessary information to build more sophisticated DL models in terms of performance, generalizability, and robustness. Now, by taking the SD logic perspective, we argue that building service ecosystems, which incorporate these technologies and additionally connect multiple entities, resembles a promising research field to be investigated further. Therefore, we encourage researchers and practitioners to engage with federated AI ecosystems by working on the following questions:

- Which processes can be enhanced by EI technologies and provide the potential for value co-creation based on FL through the exchange of insights?
- How to design and operate an effective SD platform with a reasonable modular FL architecture at company level?
- How to configure, monitor, and manage a federated AI ecosystem at an inter-company level to leverage the full potentials of value co-creation?
- How to maintain data security and prevent the recovery of original data in federated AI ecosystems?

4 Future Work and Expected Contribution

In the light of the identified research gap and our proposed agenda, we encourage researchers and practitioners to engage with this topic. Against this backdrop, we propose three possible follow-up studies that are directly associated with the aforementioned research agenda. Here, we especially focus on the first study and outline its backbone in depth (cf. Table 2). To this end, we follow the DSRM approach put forward by Peffers et al. [34]. Briefly summarized, design science research—besides behavioral research—as one of the two pillars of IS research offers a methodological toolset to create useful artifacts which are often directed towards business contexts [43–46].

Table 2. Overview on study 1, in line with the DSRM [34]

Identify problem and motivate	Configuring FL models to facilitate value co-creation in business networks and therefore outperform local instantiations due to generalizability and robustness remains an unexplored potential for a wide range of business applications. These circumstances determine the entry point of this first study
Define objectives and solution	We attribute this lack of practical value co-creation solutions to the absence of a corresponding decision framework that determines a suitable configuration of EI and FL for the specific task under consideration
Design and development	Hence, an artifact is designed to (i) identify processes to be enhanced with EI and FL, and (ii) to guide the effective implementation of such technologies to leverage the potentials of value co-creation. The decision framework is therefore not restricted to specific application domains, edge devices nor DNN configurations
Demonstration	Given a real-world application scenario with its corresponding environment of stakeholders, we aim for a first demonstration of the novel artifacts' utility
Evaluation	The evaluation is carried out in a formative and naturalistic manner [47]. More precisely, we aim for a stepwise assessment of the artifact's effectiveness in a real-world application scenario
Communication	The core of this first study is the development of a decision framework for the identification and enhancement of processes with EI and FL. The research findings are communicated via journals and conference proceedings

Drawing on the results of the first study (i.e., the decision framework), a consecutive study aims to assist companies with regard to the adoption of suitable FL models. To this end, we develop a service platform with the capability to accumulate insights from locally dispersed entities in a FL model to empower multiple corporate-specific processes with DL. Again, we plan to opt for a design-oriented research approach to develop the platform solution while considering its stakeholder's requirements.

A third and last proposed study extends the idea of a service platform by taking the inter-company perspective. Thus, the participating clients form a service ecosystem to share and therefore improve the robustness and generalizability of the FL model across multiple companies. Additionally, new ecosystem attendees benefit from the guided adoption of sophisticated DL models. For the purpose of control and enhancement, suitable metrics and components to real-time monitor and benchmark such a service ecosystem (e.g., in terms of latency or performance) are incorporated.

This article set out to propose the idea of federated AI ecosystems by merging both technologies EI and FL and by taking the ecosystems perspective. Furthermore, we elaborated a research agenda to boost the discussion in the IS community. Ultimately, we sketched out three possible follow-up studies at the nexus between EI, FL, and the SD logic perspective by applying the DSRM. However, as the research agenda shows, more research is yet to be conducted in this area.

References

1. Schmidhuber, J.: Deep learning in neural networks: an overview. Neural Netw. **61**, 85–117 (2015)
2. Lecun, Y., Bengio, Y., Hinton, G.: Deep learning. Nature **521**, 436–444 (2015)
3. Lv, Y., Duan, Y., Kang, W., Li, Z., Wang, F.: Traffic flow prediction with big data: a deep learning approach. IEEE Trans. Intell. Transp. Syst. **16**, 865–873 (2015)
4. Najafabadi, M.M., Villanustre, F., Khoshgoftaar, T.M., Seliya, N., Wald, R., Muharemagic, E.: Deep learning applications and challenges in big data analytics. J. Big Data **2**(1), 1–21 (2015). https://doi.org/10.1186/s40537-014-0007-7
5. Roy, A., Sun, J., Mahoney, R., Alonzi, L., Adams, S., Beling, P.: Deep learning detecting fraud in credit card transactions. In: 2018 Systems and Information Engineering Design Symposium (SIEDS), pp. 129–134. IEEE, Charlottesville, VA (2018)
6. van der Aalst, W.M.P., Bichler, M., Heinzl, A.: Responsible data science. Bus. Inf. Syst. Eng. **59**(5), 311–313 (2017). https://doi.org/10.1007/s12599-017-0487-z
7. Martin, K.E.: Ethical issues in the big data industry. MIS Q. Exec. **14**, 67–85 (2015)
8. Li, H., Ota, K., Dong, M.: Learning IoT in edge: deep learning for the internet of things with edge computing. IEEE Netw. **32**, 96–101 (2018)
9. Huang, Y., Ma, X., Fan, X., Liu, J., Gong, W.: When deep learning meets edge computing. In: Proceedings of the 25th International Conference on Network Protocols (ICNP), pp. 1–2. IEEE (2017)
10. Deloitte: Bringing AI to the device: Edge AI chips come into their own. (2019)
11. Zhou, Z., Chen, X., Li, E., Zeng, L., Luo, K., Zhang, J.: Edge intelligence: paving the last mile of artificial intelligence with edge computing. Proc. IEEE. **107**, 1738–1762 (2019)
12. Yang, Q., Liu, Y., Chen, T., Tong, Y.: Federated machine learning : concept and applications. ACM Trans. Intell. Syst. Technol. **10**, 1–19 (2019)
13. Brendan McMahan, H., Moore, E., Ramage, D., Hampson, S., Agüera y Arcas, B.: Communication-efficient learning of deep networks from decentralized data. Proc. 20th Int. Conf. Artif. Intell. Stat. AISTATS 2017, 54 (2017)
14. Konečný, J., McMahan, H.B., Yu, F.X., Richtárik, P., Suresh, A.T., Bacon, D.: Federated Learning: Strategies for Improving Communication Efficiency, 1–10 (2016).
15. Hauser, M., Zügner, D., Flath, C., Thiesse, F.: Pushing the limits of RFID: Empowering RFID-based electronic article surveillance with data analytics techniques. In: Proceedings of the International Conference on Information Systems (ICIS) (2015)
16. Moore, J.F.: The Death of Competition: Leadership and Strategy in the Age of Business Ecosystems. (1996)
17. Chapin, F.S., Matson, P.A., Mooney, H.A.: Principles of Terrestrial Ecosystem Ecology (2002)
18. Lis, D., Otto, B.: Data Governance in Data Ecosystems - Insights from Organizations. In: Proceedings of Americas' Conference on Information Systems (AMCIS) (2020)

19. Jarke, M., Otto, B., Ram, S.: Data sovereignty and data space ecosystems. Bus. Inf. Syst. Eng. **61**(5), 549–550 (2019). https://doi.org/10.1007/s12599-019-00614-2
20. Gelhaar, J., Otto, B.: Challenges in the emergence of data ecosystems. In: Proceedings of the 24th Pacific Asia Conference on Information Systems (PACIS) (2020)
21. Shipilov, A., Gawer, A.: Integrating research on interorganizational networks and ecosystems. Acad. Manag. Ann. (2020)
22. Vargo, S.L., Lusch, R.F.: Evolving to a New Dominant Logic for Marketing. J. Mark. (2004)
23. Vargo, S.L., Lusch, R.F.: Service-dominant logic: continuing the evolution. J. Acad. Mark. Sci. **36**, 1–10 (2008)
24. Akaka, M.A., Vargo, S.L., Lusch, R.F.: The complexity of context: a service ecosystems approach for international marketing. J. Int. Mark. **21**, 1–20 (2013)
25. Lusch, R.F., Nambisan, S.: Service innovation: A service-dominant logic perspective. MIS Q. Manag. Inf. Syst. (2015)
26. Vargo, S.L., Lusch, R.F.: Service-dominant logic 2025. Int. J. Res. Mark. (2017)
27. Kairouz, P., et al.: Advances and open problems in federated learning, (2019)
28. McMahan, H.B., Ramage, D., Talwar, K., Zhang, L.: Learning differentially private recurrent language models. In: Proceedings of the 6th International Conference on Learning Representations (ICLR) (2018)
29. Bagdasaryan, E., Veit, A., Hua, Y., Estrin, D., Shmatikov, V.: How to backdoor federated learning. arXiv (2018)
30. Greenland, S., Mansournia, M.A., Altman, D.G.: Sparse data bias: A problem hiding in plain sight. BMJ. (2016)
31. Wang, X., Han, Y., Wang, C., Zhao, Q., Chen, X., Chen, M.: In-edge AI: Intelligentizing mobile edge computing, caching and communication by federated learning. IEEE Netw. (2019)
32. Bonawitz, K., et al.: Towards federated learning at scale: System design (2019)
33. Lim, W.Y.B., et al.: Federated learning in mobile edge networks: a comprehensive survey. IEEE Commun. Surv. Tutorials. **22**, 2031–2063 (2019)
34. Peffers, K., Tuunanen, T., Rothenberger, M.A., Chatterjee, S.: A design science research methodology for information systems research. J. Manag. Inf. Syst. **24**, 45–77 (2007)
35. Deng, S., Zhao, H., Fang, W., Yin, J., Dustdar, S., Zomaya, A.Y.: Edge intelligence: the confluence of edge computing and artificial intelligence. IEEE Internet Things J. **4662**, 1 (2020)
36. Shi, W., Cao, J., Zhang, Q., Li, Y., Xu, L.: Edge computing: vision and challenges. IEEE Internet Things J. **3**, 637–646 (2016)
37. Zhang, X., Wang, Y., Lu, S., Liu, L., Xu, L., Shi, W.: OpenEI: An open framework for edge intelligence. In: Proceedings of the International Conference on Distributed Computing Systems, pp. 1840–1851. IEEE (2019)
38. Mach, P., Becvar, Z.: Mobile edge computing: a survey on architecture and computation offloading. IEEE Commun. Surv. Tutorials. **19**, 1628–1656 (2017)
39. Porambage, P., Okwuibe, J., Liyanage, M., Ylianttila, M., Taleb, T.: Survey on multi-access edge computing for internet of things realization. IEEE Commun. Surv. Tutorials. **20**, 2961–2991 (2018)
40. Greengard, S.: AI on edge. Commun. ACM. **63**, 18–20 (2020)
41. Xu, D., et al.: Edge Intelligence: Architectures, Challenges, and Applications. (2020)
42. Li, T., Sahu, A.K., Talwalkar, A., Smith, V.: Federated Learning: Challenges, Methods, and Future Directions. IEEE Signal Process. Mag. (2020)
43. March, S.T., Smith, G.F.: Design and natural science research on information technology. Decis. Support Syst. **15**, 251–266 (1995)
44. Hevner, A.R., March, S.T., Park, J., Ram, S.: Design science in information systems research. Mis Q. Manag. Inf. Syst. **28**, 75–105 (2004)

45. Gregor, S., Hevner, A.R.: Positioning and presenting design science research for maximum impact. MIS Q. Manag. Inf. Syst. **37**, 337–356 (2013)
46. Gregor, S., Jones, D.: The anatomy of a design theory. J. Assoc. Inf. Syst. **8**, 312–335 (2007)
47. Venable, J., Pries-Heje, J., Baskerville, R.: FEDS: a framework for evaluation in design science research. Eur. J. Inf. Syst. **25**, 77–89 (2016)

Digital Education and Capabilities

Introduction to the WI2021 Track: Digital Education and Capabilities

Isabella Seeber[1], Matthias Söllner[2], and Stefan Thalmann[3]

[1] Grenoble Ecole de Management, Grenoble, France
isabella.seeber@grenoble-em.com
[2] University of Kassel, Kassel, Germany
soellner@uni-kassel.de
[3] University of Graz, Graz, Austria
stefan.thalmann@uni-graz.at

1 Track Description

Digitisation is changing the way we learn and develop our skills and competences at the workplace. It also requires organisations to build up the necessary digital capabilities to meet ever changing demands. Consequently, there is a need to advance our understanding of "Digital Education" and "Digital Capabilities".

Digital Education deals with the influence of digitalization on (higher) education as well as informal or workplace learning in organisations (e.g., blended learning solutions, flipped classroom, MOOCs). In addition, digital education is also about the systematic development of competences and skills that learners in the digital age need in order to be successful on the job market as well as on the job in organisations.

Digital capabilities of an organization address the abilities necessary to utilize the opportunities offered by digitisation, building up resilience and appropriate organizational skills and adapting business processes and business models. Digital workplaces become essential places of knowledge exchange and learning, not only within organisations but also in cross-organisational settings. Organisations must therefore build up capabilities to deal with the challenges and opportunities of digitization and utilize disruptive technologies.

2 Research Articles

This year, the track received 24 submission from which seven were accepted.

2.1 Playing (Government) Seriously: Design Principles for E-Government Simulation Game Platforms (Sebastian Halsbenning, Marco Niemann, Bettina Distel, and Jörg Becker)

This full paper explores the design of a platform for serious simulation games in the domain of public administration and evaluates the platform in a public administration context. Various design principles for serious game platforms are offered.

2.2 New Workplace, New Mindset: Empirical Case Studies on the Interplay between Digital Workplace and Organizational Culture (Caterina Baumgartner, Eva Hartl, and Thomas Hess)

This full paper examines the interplay between organizational culture and digital workplaces through a multi-case study design and offers best practices. The study offers best practices for an efficient design of digital workplaces.

2.3 Individual Digital Study Assistant for Higher Education Institutions: Status Quo Analysis and Further Research Agenda (Christin Karrenbauer, Claudia M. König, and Michael H. Breitner)

This full paper focuses on digital study assistants (DSA) and reports the results of a literature review. The paper contributes a morphological box and research agenda for the development, adaption, introduction, and success of DSAs.

2.4 Digital Credentials in Higher Education Institutions: A Literature Review (Elena Wolz, Matthias Gottlieb, and Hans Pongratz)

This full paper explores digitizing of graduation certificates and digital credentials in higher education by conducting a literature review in the context of digital credentials. The findings open up promising research gaps for future research.

2.5 A Theory-Driven Design Science Research Approach Towards Gamified Videos in Digital Learning (Dennis Benner and Sofia Schöbel)

This short paper seeks to address the challenge of oftentimes low engagement in online trainings. To address this issue, the authors outline an overarching approach for developing meaningful gamified learning videos.

2.6 A Methodology to enhance Learning Processes with Augmented Reality Glasses (Tobias Dreesbach, Matthias Berg, Henning Gösling, Tobias Walter, Oliver Thomas, and Julia Knopf)

This short paper proposes a five-step methodology for the integration of Augmented Reality (AR) into learning processes for students. The authors further describe how the methodology helped to enrich an electro engineering lesson with AR elements.

2.7 Digitalization Mindset and Capabilities: Preliminary Results of an Action Research Study (Ralf Plattfaut and Vincent Borghoff)

Based on a nine-month in-depth action research study, this short paper contributes to our understanding of (changing) dynamic capabilities and individual employee mindsets and skills based on action research.

Playing (Government) Seriously: Design Principles for e-Government Simulation Game Platforms

Sebastian Halsbenning[✉], Marco Niemann, Bettina Distel, and Jörg Becker

University of Münster, ERCIS, Münster, Germany
{halsbenning,niemann,distel,becker}@ercis.de

Abstract. The digital transformation of the public sector is progressing but regularly not at the desired pace. Here, the digitalization skills of public officials are one important resource to cope with the demanding digital shift and rise of e-government. As there is still a lack of those competences, alternative educational approaches are needed. Promising and flexible methods are simulation games—although not widely used in the public sector. As a resolve, we are developing on a corresponding simulation game platform for about two years. In addition to sharing the artifact, this manuscript shall provide a set of design principles helping to create and facilitate the adoption of related platforms for the public sector.

Keywords: Simulation game platform · Digitalization skills · e-Government · Design principles · Competences

1 Introduction

Digitalization changes the service delivery and the internal organization of public administrations. In the public sector, this technological shift has become an important means to raise citizen-centricity and efficiency [1], for example, through digitalized services or reorganized workflows. Moreover, in research and practice, decent progress in technologies and concepts can be observed that take digital opportunities to enhance the performance of the public sector by, e.g., instantiating one-stop governments [2], offering proactive service delivery [3], or open-government initiatives [4]. The constantly increasing application and use of these new concepts and technological innovations are accompanied by a need for corresponding digitalization competences for public officials [5]. Those *e-competences* refer to one's ability to cope with digitalization and have to be constantly trained early on. Considering the strong influence of e-government on daily routines, adequate digitalization skills have become a success factor for e-government projects [6, 7]. Although this need has already been specified, e-competences are still a bottleneck to the digitalization of the public sector. One crucial reason for the shortage of e-competences in the public sector can be rooted back to education. As the education of future public officials primarily concentrates on legal, economic, and management aspects, a lack of a broad institutional penetration of e-competence is the result. Consequently, there is a need to focus more on teaching the required competences and IT

F. Ahlemann et al. (Eds.): WI 2021, LNISO 48, pp. 73–90, 2021.
https://doi.org/10.1007/978-3-030-86800-0_6

skills not only on the job but already in educational programs. This article addresses this gap in research and practice by focusing on the development of e-competences among public sector students.

As a solution for this problem, a growing number of recommendations of serious gaming or simulation games can be found in research [8, 9] including application scenarios in the area of information systems [10] and e-government [11, 12]. Especially for university programs in the field of public sector, simulation games are a suitable means for getting the learners used to the complex mesh of stakeholders in the political and administrative environment. Therefore, simulation games for teaching e-government settings have been established, the one by [12] being both comparatively recent and positively evaluated. We abstracted from the exact contents and setting of the presented game in order to create a simulation game platform (SGP) that is capable of hosting a series of structurally similar to equivalent setups. Looking at the overall lack of e-government competences in the public sector [13, 14], as well as the many competence areas [15] and the diversity of public administrations, it appears to be mandatory to be able to provide—over time—a series of similar simulations to account for the different educational needs. Further need for flexibility regarding the exact setup arises from the educational setting of the game—to keep it interesting for multiple iterations of students, changes must be easily possible, as otherwise inter-student exchange will lead to boredom. Hence, we build upon this research to further develop the idea by addressing the following two research goals:

(1) Design and evaluation of a configurable platform for simulation games tailored to the public administration domain.
(2) Development of design principles for e-government SGPs.

Therefore, we use a classical design science approach to pursue our research goals. We combine our prior, initial research on a simulation game *platform* with the simulation game *scenario* by [12] to derive design principles for e-government SGPs. The paper is structured as follows. In Sect. 2, we outline the background of our research on e-government competences and SGPs. Then, in Sects. 3–5, we explain the research design, the platform, and the setting in which our research has been conducted. This is followed by the presentation of our artifacts and the evaluation in Sect. 6. The paper is closed by a discussion of our findings as well as extant implications for further research.

2 Research Background

2.1 e-Competences and e-Government Simulation Games

The use of information and communication technologies to deliver public services (e-government) still concerns public administrations around the world. It is less the technical dimension that continues to challenge public organizations. Rather, practitioners and researchers alike point to the need of the workforce to adapt to and, eventually, design the digital transformation [12, 16]. The pace these technologies evolve at creates a substantial challenge insofar as the public workforce has to adapt to the changes accordingly. Even more, formerly valuable competences tend to become less important or even obsolete, while completely new competences, such as digital literacy, programming skills, and data science knowledge, need to be acquired [17, 18]. It is noteworthy that digital transformation not only requires the acquisition of technical competences. In contrast, researchers tend to identify more non-technical than technical competences as important such as business competences [18], project management competences [17], and socio-technical competences [15]. To ensure that future administrative staff is able to adapt quickly to changing conditions and to actively design the digital transformation, the necessary competences must be trained during their education.

The question remains how students can acquire these competences. Traditional programs and teaching formats need to be adapted with both new content (imparting new competences) and new learning strategies (imparting competences with new formats). Gamification and simulation games in particular have been proposed as one meaningful way to impart competences [19–21]. Simulation games not only train competences in a risk-free environment [12] but can also convey the complexities and oftentimes opaque structures in which public organizations act [11].

This article is based on a fairly recent simulation game in the domain of e-government that aims at imparting non-technical competences for public sector students [12]. Through this game, students train "[...] competences that cannot be taught through rather classic formats of instruction, such as cooperation, strategy development, and decision making" [12:3089]. This simulation game evolves around the (so far) fictitious overall scenario of the nation-wide introduction of service accounts in Germany. It consists of sixteen different roles the students are assigned to. The roles cover *functions in the public sector*, such as state governments and municipal administrations, *private sector companies* and *lobby groups, political parties*, and *public IT providers.* Each role is assigned to one student and has a 'secret' goal concerning the introduction of service accounts. These goals are designed as conflicts among the players. For example, one party is designed as techno-averse and aims at impeding the digital transformation. One of the state governments, however, wants to become the digital frontrunner and pushes digital innovations such as service accounts. Throughout the game, five events happen that challenge each role and define the further course of the game (conference on digital transformation, data leakage at the federal level, the bankruptcy of a municipality, state elections and change in government, national digital summit). One of these events, for example, is a *data leakage at the Federal Ministry of the Interior.* Millions of data sets of both businesses and citizens are leaked and this data breach changes the public opinion on the introduction of service accounts. As an example of the effects on particular roles and the overall course of the game, consider the following situations: The techno-averse party profits from this opinion swing as it questions digitalization in general, whereas the digital-oriented roles in this game (states, municipalities, businesses) need to address the public's concerns regarding data security and face difficulties in justifying their techno-friendly policies. The overall support for the service accounts is eroded and all roles involved need to take measures either to use this situation for their benefit or to prevent further damage. In total, five of these events shape the course of the simulation game [cf. for further details 12].

The students have to participate both in formal meetings, such as a simulated press conference and the simulated digital summit, and more informal meetings such as backroom talks either presenting and debating their positions or discussing the course of action with potential allies. The formal meetings are mainly organized by the teachers who act, for example, as conference chairs. The informal meetings have to be organized by the students themselves and the teachers are involved only upon request, for example, as negotiators.

Initially, the game was designed in a hybrid format, i.e., with both analogue and digital elements. The meetings—both formal and informal—were held in person, whereas press releases or comments could be posted via the university's Moodle platform (first iteration) or the SGP (second iteration). Furthermore, the game management was done digitally, i.e., announcements on the events and individual tasks were released via the platforms. However, reacting to the COVID-19 pandemic, the third iteration of the simulation game was executed as an online-only format using the SGP to its full extent as meetings in presence were not possible. Using both analogue and digital elements for this simulation game aims at mimicking the hybrid nature of real-life situations. Thereby, the simulation game trains competences that are otherwise hard to acquire through traditional teaching formats: *soft skills* such as leadership or conflict management, *socio-technical competences* such as politics of e-government, *organizational* and *managerial competences* such as process and change management, and finally, *political-administrative competences* such as legal framework knowledge [12].

2.2 Design of Simulation Game Platforms

Beyond the scenario as the abstract setting of a simulation game, the medium for its execution can be seen as a second layer or perspective on a simulation game, also referred to as the *game interface design* [22]. While simulation gaming and gamification have grown to separate fields of research during the last decade [23, 24], a research focus has primarily been given to its educational impact and its contribution to the learning success [25, 26]. In general, the results are oftentimes mixed and depend on the application context and circumstances of the simulation game under investigation [22, 27]. However, the learning outcomes of games applying (web-based) platforms are being positively evaluated [e.g., 28–31] but, here, the insights regarding platform design are limited to the individual implementation setting. Also, most of the related research does not divide the development process between the story and the implemented platform or piece of software.

Hence, research provides little guidance on the specifics of platform development or the choice of appropriate media for executing simulation games. This might be rooted back to the heterogeneity of simulation games, e.g., regarding applied game-design elements, degree and type of interaction among participants, and also the domain of application. Typically, the derivation of game-design elements is conducted independent of and prior to any platform development, as simulation games are also often used in offline or blended settings before being digitalized. They are subdivided into game mechanics and game dynamics, whereby game mechanics define the 'building blocks' of a game and game dynamics the consequential effects, e.g., competition, collaboration, and challenge [24]. Thus, the type of user interaction depends on both types of game-design elements but also the use of the general teaching setting, i.e., online, offline, or blended learning. In addition, for each domain of application different types of game-design elements might be preferable as this also depends on the learning objective [e.g., 27, 28, 32].

Table 1. Proposed design principles by [23:5–7]

1	Educational games must be purposefully built on game platforms that can adapt to various educational purposes
2	Educational games must be purposefully built on game platforms that can scale to achieve the desired level of complexity
3	Educational games platforms must be highly configurable to allow educators to design the workflow of the game relatively fast
4	Educational platforms must allow educators to enable and disable features of ⁓ personification (avatar), game rewards, student reputation/ranking
5	Educational platforms must allow educators to create games at varying degrees of interaction between students (competitiveness, cooperation)
6	Educational platforms must allow educators to define the level of ludic loops (pleasurable feedback loops between the game and the student)
7	Educational platforms must keep students in a state of arousal by continuously maintaining the games' challenge levels one grain higher than the students' skill levels

Given all these aspects that affect the digital representation of the game scenario, only a few attempts exist to translate these requirements into general design recommendations, i.e. reference models [33] or design principles [23]. The reference models for SGPs can be used as a starting point for conceptualizing a platform. As such reference models contain a strong processual view on the implementation of a serious game platform. In contrast, design principles extend design theory and aim at providing general design knowledge [34, 35]. By introducing (preliminary) design principles for SGPs, [23] address a research gap by providing a broad view on the needed actions for setting up an SGP (cf. Table 1). Their principles are designed to overcome the adoption barriers to using simulation games. However, the design principles are not yet evaluated or tested and lack positioning regarding application domains.

3   Research Design

Our research aims at both, the development of an innovative platform to host simulation games supporting competence education efforts in e-government as well as the derivation of design principles that can guide the development of similar platforms. Hence, we follow the Design Science paradigm as postulated by [36, 37]. Given our work on applicable (IT) artifacts our research can best be located in the genres design science research methodology (DSRM) and design-oriented IS research (DOIS) as presented by [38].

Hence, the design process follows the steps proposed by [37] (cf. Figure 1). First, an existing problem has been identified (*the lack of e-competences in administrative personnel*; cf. Sections 1 and 2 and [12]). Subsequently, the first objectives were defined by [12]—primarily regarding the creation of simulation games to enhance e-competences. It should be noted that the work of [12] in itself represents a full iteration through the DSR cycle depicted in Fig. 1. However, the artifact to be created was a different one, i.e., the simulation game as a concept, which was the conceptual baseline for the development of the configurable SGP. Hence, for this research, it is only linked as an informative publication to the first two phases.

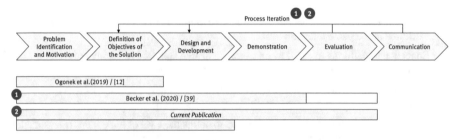

Fig. 1. Design science research-based approach based on [37]

However, the game was taken as the initial template for designing the platform but a previous step for our endeavor was to make the game as such scalable. Therefore, we first transferred the whole game setting into a digital counterpart including the structure with 16 roles and five events. As student groups are of different size and we are consequently aiming at a configurable platform, we extended the set of game roles while keeping the overall simulation game story. For example, we added the roles *Green and Sustainable* or *IT Planning Council* that were similarly integrated into the overall scenario as the initial set of roles.

Beyond these conceptual objectives, [39] identified that teaching digital competences based on pen and paper is a problematic endeavor (*back to Step 1 in* Fig. 1)—sketching first solution objectives for a digital SGP to support such competence-enhancing serious games. This contribution includes but is not limited to proposals for the enhanced execution or better support of remote teaching. Being a construction-oriented research approach [40], a first software artifact of the Game of Competences (GoC) was developed—which can be considered an "instantiation" artifact type [36] and a contribution of "Level 1" [41], respectively. The derived IT artifact was subsequently demonstrated to be functional through real-world use in a Master-level lecture. After completion of this initial, platform-supported iteration of the simulation game, unstructured feedback was collected from the participants through feedback discussions. This feedback rounds off our first DSR iteration (published in [39]) and has been used to refine the extant objectives and the associated IT artifact. Since the feedback revealed considerable improvement potential, the platform was revised accordingly to be of better value for upcoming iterations (*back to Step 3 in* Fig. 1). Based on the now revised platform another demonstration round was initiated, again including the now structured collection of feedback.

Over our iterations, we gathered considerable insights into how to improve the design of SGPs in the domain of e-competences. Among others, we aimed on gaining general insights into the usability of the platform interface, the closeness to reality, and the educational purpose. Hence, we decided to change the objectives that are addressed in the next DSR iteration and reported in this article. The core focus of our research is less on the IT artifact itself, but rather on deriving appropriate design principles that could guide similar research efforts [35] ("Level 2"-contribution [41]). For the derivation of the design principles, we use primarily the evaluation of the latest version of the platform (cf. Section 6.1) and compile the generated insights based on the guidelines outlined by [35]. As depicted in Fig. 1, the demonstration and evaluation of the designed principles will not be part of this manuscript.

4   Platform Design

We formalized and structured our goal of creating a configurable SGP for e-competences by putting them into an Entity Relationship Model (ERM) to identify the necessary entities and their relationships. This is visualized in Fig. 2.

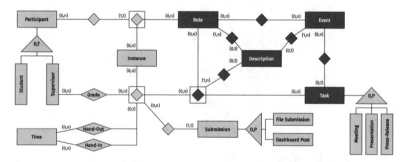

Fig. 2. Data model of the "Game of Competences" [39]

In this figure, the red parts denote the components of competence-aimed simulation games as proposed by [12]. After breaking down the game, it consists of a set of roles, events, and tasks associated with the individual events—each typically accompanied by a description providing further details on each of these elements. As different roles have to fulfill different tasks throughout events, the role-specific tasks (RSTs) have been introduced (*indicated through the re-interpreted relationship type*)—again linked to a description providing further information. These elements suffice to map the desired simulation game to the virtual world. However, to carry out the simulation game the additional management "layer" is required—which in Fig. 2 is depicted in gray. As indicated above, one of the major requirements is to host multiple parallel instances of each potential simulation game to cater to different courses throughout a given semester. Hence, both roles as well as RSTs are linked to participants, timeslots, and associated (graded) tasks only through instances (*again using the reinterpreted relationship type*). From an implementation perspective, the platform is realized as a traditional three-tier architecture separating client interfaces, business logic, and data storage [42]. To ensure stability, shareability, and ongoing of our work we consistently used established open-source technologies.

The current version of the Game of Competences has two different interfaces for its two primary user groups: participants (learners) and administrators (teachers), small parts of which are depicted in Fig. 3 and Fig. 4, respectively. In Fig. 3, we see the so-called Dashboard, which is the landing page participants see after logging into the platform. In the screenshot, we see an exemplary post of the role *The Hacker Group* (*the participants' names are intentionally omitted to enhance the immersion with the game*) warning another partaking role of a security vulnerability in its tax systems. Aside from texts, participants can also attach images to support their message (we replaced an existing picture with the logo of the partaking student's university for copyright reasons). The dashboard serves as the communication center of the GoC, representing a chronological timeline of the ongoing events. Participants have further menu items that allow them to get an overview of pending assignments and the next tasks and events to be attended. By clicking on their role name in the top-right corner of the menu bar they can also review their role-related information.

Fig. 3. Participants' view of the GoC/the dashboard [39]

As depicted in the menu bar at the top of Fig. 4, game administrators also have access to the dashboard—simply as they can also interact with the participants there, but also need the access to assess and grade participants contributions there. The view almost fully corresponds to the view of the participants, with the distinction that the administrator can see and access all available posts—also those invisible to certain participants (*parts of the game require communication between individual participants only*). Aside from that, the menu bar contains two additional entries not available to the participants: The *Session Management* and the *Game Management*. At this point, the red and gray elements in Fig. 2 become relevant again: The *Game Management* basically covers all elements depicted in red. Hence, a game in the terminology of the GoC is an abstract entity containing sets of roles, tasks, and events.

In the screenshot, you can see three tabs below the menu bar—one containing the simulation game proposed by [12] whereas the other one serves for development purposes. The third tab allows the creation of additional games. Within the tabs, the components of each game can be adjusted. To play a game with learners a so-called *Session* has to be instantiated (see the *Instance*-entity in Fig. 2), which can then be administered through the *Session Management*. Through the *Session Management* the administrators can invite and manage the participants, schedule events, and assign tasks to the learners.

Fig. 4. Administrators' view of the GoC/Game Management [39]

Furthermore, in case the session is part of a graded teaching unit, the *Session Management* also offers functionalities to check timely submissions of tasks and to grade participants (GUI is structurally equivalent to *Game Management*).

5 Setting

Last year the platform was first used to carry out the simulation game proposed by [12]. In that iteration, 25 international Master students enrolled in an e-government-oriented Master program participated in the simulation game. The simulation was embedded in a tech-oriented e-government lecture and the students were offered bonus points for continuous and constructive participation. That iteration has helped us to validate that having platform-support for carrying out such simulation games is both desirable and helpful [cf. 39]. Furthermore, we collected feedback on bugs and problems to improve the platform to a more smoothly working artifact.

Table 2. Overview of the student groups

Semester	# Students	Platform	Execution mode	Evaluation
Summer Term 2018	17	No	Mainly offline; use of digital means (Moodle, different submission types, meetings)	Feedback session; individual reflections; survey
Summer Term 2019	25	Yes	Blended learning; platform prototype; submissions to platform, meetings	Feedback session; unstructured bug reports
Summer Term 2020	27	Yes	Online; enhanced platform; platform submissions, communication via platform, online meetings	Feedback session; unstructured bug reports; survey

In this paper, we focus on the second platform's iteration that was conducted in the summer term 2020[1] with 27 international students of the same international Master's program as those of the first test iteration (cf. Table 2). The group consisted of students from different nationalities, having backgrounds primarily in social or political sciences but some also in more technical fields (e.g., computer science). While some students—through work-experience—already had interactions with public administrations, the majority of the participants had no insights into the setup and interactions of public administrations (especially not the German ones which are the simulation case). The required background information was continuously delivered in the form of accompanying traditional lectures, providing background knowledge about e-government in general as well as the German administrative system in particular. The further setup can be summarized as follows:

- to kick off the simulation game a one-hour introductory session was held, introducing the overall context, roles, and rules
- subsequently, each participant was assigned an individual role
- the role assignment was carried out at random
- role information was provided within the GoC platform and the initial invitation mail sent to the participants
- the platform itself only refers to the participants by their role names
- participants were encouraged to follow this pattern to enhance immersion
- to access the platforms the students could use whatever device they preferred
- the only restriction is that the platform could only be accessed through the university's VPN tunnel
- the game was subdivided into seven distinct events—each typically taking up two weeks of time where participants have to fulfill tasks
- typically, each participant has to fulfill up to two individual tasks (e.g., negotiations with another party, campaigning for elections) per event
- the average workload per week was about one hour strongly varying during the term
- the task schedule was not communicated to the students upfront—tasks were communicated through the game administrators or tasked participants
- to ensure that participants were notified about required actions, they received a mail-notification for each assigned task
- all in-game communication (incl. additional information from the game administrators or participant questions) the internal dashboard was used

At the end of the term, all participants were administered a link to a LimeSurvey, in which 17 out of 27 students participated. The survey was conducted anonymously and participants were given four weeks to fill in all questions. The survey took approx. 10–15 min—with the option to pause and resume the survey. We split the survey into two larger parts. In the first part, we asked about the student's general perceptions regarding SGPs, notifications, and usability. The second part was about the instantiated platform the students used during the simulation game. In the survey, we presented statements (cf.

---

[1] Due to the COVID-19 pandemic, the originally blended approach was carried out digital-only on the platform, supported by individual Zoom sessions to ensure "personal" interaction.

Table 3 and Table 4) with the option to rate them according to a five-point Likert scale. In some questions, the participants had also the option to prioritize special features or to provide further thoughts or feedback.

Additionally, we carried out a feedback session with the participants. Throughout this session, they could provide us with all feedback that they could not fit into the structured survey administered earlier. As a further means, we implemented a so-called "Impersonate" feature into the platform, similar to the "Impersonate User" functionality known from the Drupal CMS. It allows administrators to view the platform "through the eyes" of the participants to track issues.

6   Results

6.1   Evaluation

Given the first overall positive evaluation of the Game of Competences as an instantiation in the summer term 2019, in the second evaluation, we additionally gained insights on how to design e-government SGPs in general.

Table 3. General perceptions on simulation game platforms

Question/statement	+	O	–
A digital platform is suitable for playing simulation games	75%	12.5%	12.5%
A simulation game platform is suitable for teaching e-government settings	62.5%	25%	12.5%
Executing simulation games via digital platforms is superior to less digital options (e.g., pen and paper, only by email)	35.3%	29.4%	35.3%
Digital platforms contribute to make simulation games more real	31.25%	31.25%	37.5%

+: (completely) agree | O: indifferent | –: (completely) disagree

The presented evaluation results are based on the survey. Again, the majority of the participants rated the approach of using an SGP positive (cf. Table 3). Notably, this agreement decreases for e-government settings and disappears in comparison to other less digital options. This finding is supplemented by the preferences regarding task types, where the participants rated presentations and personal meetings as the most valuable means for a task. This indicates that a platform is not the one and unique solution for simulation games and, hence, has to be considered rather as a supporting tool for their execution.

Although, the reality aspect is important for a fruitful simulation game, a digital platform as such is not perceived as imitating real-world phenomena. Here, it turned out that notifications are seen as proper means to make a game more real (cf. Table 4). The initial purpose of notifications was simply to inform participants about tasks or events, which is unexceptionally rated as an important property. Beyond that, notifications also fulfill the function to convey a feeling of reality, e.g., a sense for pressure and urgency.

Table 4. Perceptions on functions of simulation game platforms

Question/statement	+	O	–
Notifications are important for simulation game platforms	100%	0%	0%
Notifications contribute to make a game setting more real	93.8%	0%	6.2%
For me, the notifications were important for playing the simulation game	93.3%	6.6%	0%
I would like to receive notifications for every action or event that affects my role	86.7%	13.3%	0%
I would have appreciated additional help functions on the platform	60%	20%	20%

+: (completely) agree | O: indifferent | –: (completely) disagree

Consequently, the evaluation revealed that notifications are more important for an SGP than anticipated. This finding influenced the formulation of design principle 3.

A further aspect to keep track of when developing SGPs are help functions. Even though exhaustive documentation was provided before the game started which was read by all players beforehand except of one, the evaluation revealed additional relevance of help functions. The majority of players expects additional help functions. Specifically, FAQs (75%) and tooltips (45%) were rated as the most compelling alternatives, whereas no one rated for personal tutorials (0%). This finding especially influenced the formulation of design principle 5.

In addition, the survey results gave meaningful insights for the design principles regarding communication, workload transparency, and training of competences. The participants argued for an expansion of the current communication channel since the platform should "allow actual interaction between characters, (...) to form groups (...) and share stuff in between". "Discussion threads or chat/email function" were also mentioned. Other participants pointed out that an overview "of the work done and events that happened until the present moment" and a "scoring system which assigns points for every task [immediately]" would be beneficial to reach more transparency about the workload. Lastly, the evaluation showed, on the one hand, that the participants had a good understanding of the targeted competences of the game and, on the other hand, that this aim was not met for all these target competences.

6.2 Design Principles

Based on the evaluation results and the learnings gathered throughout the platform development and implementation, we set forth with shaping and formulating the design principles. Finally, the iterative development process revealed seven design principles for the successful implementation and application of e-government simulation games:

1. *Build the platform scalable to different numbers of game roles, events, and tasks in order to ensure applicability to varying group sizes and equal shares of workload for users.*

This principle aims at the uncomplicated scalability of the platform. Learner groups vary in their size and game settings vary in their scope implicating an adjustment of the task distribution. For instance, with a rising number of game roles, the interaction possibilities among these roles increase disproportionally. Thus, adherence to the first principle ensures that varying group sizes are possible and do not affect the individual workload or competences to be trained. Here, scalability considers two distinct perspectives. First, the ordinary, usual purpose to cope with varying group size. Second, in a simulation game, scaling involves the further implication of keeping the workload on the same level since the game dynamics need also to scale up. Other platforms that only provide content or the possibility for interactions—without a dedicated workload for users—only need to adhere to the first aspect. So, the principle is primarily designed for learners' convenience as it allows a consistent game execution irrespective of the number of game roles, i.e., participants.

2. *Build the platform configurable to different numbers of game roles, events, and tasks in order to ensure quick game customization for teachers.*

This principle aims at the adaptability of the platform to different game scenarios. The structure, scope, complexity, and duration of simulation games can be different according to the application setting. For instance, a simulation game used to train public officials might have fewer events and tasks compared to using it as a supporting supplement to an e-government lecture, in order to account for time and other resource-related constraints in public administrations. Furthermore, the application on different federal levels will require different setups to accommodate the different tasks and responsibilities in the different administrative layers. In contrast to configurability in its usual fashion, an e-government SGP needs technical and content-related configurability. The platform needs to adapt to a plethora of different game scenarios (content-related) but also to various application scenarios (technical), in which teachers/learners might have different administrative/access rights or the default communication channels/notifications need adaptations. Thus, adherence to the second principle ensures that teachers can customize the number of game roles, events, and tasks according to the needs of the learner group and also to different game scenarios. The principle ensures to add or delete roles, events, and tasks as needed.

3. *Build the platform with real-time notifications and interaction channels in order to convey a feeling of reality for the users.*

This principle aims at the actual simulation of real-world phenomena. Beyond the game scenario as such, especially interaction mechanisms contribute to making simulation games more realistic. For instance, sudden events like data leakages or bankruptcies require immediate responses and prior arrangements among affected parties—in the real and in the fictitious setting. Thus, adherence to the third guideline ensures that the game becomes a constant companion while playing it. On the one hand, participants are faced with unforeseen happenings and need to react appropriately. On the other hand, participants also receive simple information about the happenings or actions of the other players, which keep them permanently updated.

4. *Build the platform with a distinct communication channel for learner-teacher interaction in order to install channels for providing confidential feedback.*

This principle aims at integrating the organizational context of the game into the platform. The execution of simulation games also comes along with conventional learners' problems or uncertainties. For instance, during the game, questions of understanding arise or participants provide and receive feedback on tasks. Thus, the adherence to the fourth principle ensures the embedding of real-world supervision into the platform and that no switching to other media is necessary. This requirement is of increased importance in cases of non-blended setups.

5. *Build the platform with different help functions in order to ensure that users are able to use every available functionality.*

This principle aims at keeping the flow of play by mitigating problems while using the platform. An SGP contains many features for uploads, posts, overviews, feedbacks, etc. For instance, a simple dashboard post may contain several options each for addressee selection, attachments, text formatting, or figures, which might be overwhelming for certain user groups. Thus, the adherence to the fifth principle ensures that in case of issues with platform functions, first, no interruption of the current game action is needed and, second, teachers and learners find immediate support when making changes to the game.

6. *Build the platform with a role's workload overview in order to inform participants on remaining time for submission and lower the uncertainty level regarding game organization given that providing this information does not affect the game.*

This principle aims at providing the participants with reasonable transparency regarding game execution. When playing a simulation game, the participants' time constraints regarding work, studies, or private affairs must be considered. Thus, adherence to the sixth principle ensures that the participants always have a general overview of upcoming tasks when entering the platform. Furthermore, such an overview helps game administrators to fairly distribute tasks and events among participants even in larger and complex setups. This reduces potential time conflicts and needs to be balanced with principle 3.

7. *Build the platform with competence-specific task templates in order to use appropriate task types that are dedicated to train certain competences.*

This principle aims at a targeted training of e-government competences. The wide range of different task types can be structured according to their contribution to building up certain competences. For instance, to gain *political-administrative competences* it is recommended to use tasks that yield background knowledge and domain understanding of the public sector. Thus, adherence to the seventh principle allows training for certain competence profiles.

7   Discussion and Conclusion

The evaluation goes beyond a classical artifact evaluation and revealed important additional aspects to be considered in e-government SGPs. Together with the learnings gained in the development process, the evaluation strongly contributed to shaping and refining the design principles. Based on the well-documented research process, the developed design principles constitute a transfer channel from how to educate e-government competence to its implementation in SGPs.

However, the design principles strongly differ in their domain orientation. For instance, design principles 3 and 7 take up specifics of the public sector, e.g. required interaction in a complex mesh of stakeholders and a focus on educating e-government competences. In contrast, principles 1 and 2 aiming at scalability, equal workload, and quick customization, may have to be considered also in other application domains. However, both principles ensure the flexible application into different curricula or the consideration of different educational levels of students. Although these two principles are similarly proposed by [23], up to now, our findings cannot confirm a transferability to other domains since targeted competences may be different from those of public administration. Recently, the simulation game has been adapted as an employee version, i.e., as a variant of the game that can be used to train public sector official's e-competences [43]. Normally, public servants can only participate in training programs to a limited extent. As such not only the content of the game needs to be modularized but also the gaming platform needs to adequately address the requirements of high scalability and workload transparency.

The evaluations of both the simulation game and the according platform indicate that neither a complete analogue nor a completely digital setup are appropriate means to convey e-competences. Rather, the students' evaluations indicate a preference for blended learning, i.e., the combination of analogue and digital formats. The SGP proposed in this article is designed as a solution for this requirement as it is conceptualized as a supportive instrument for the execution of the game rather than as the central element of the game.

Even though digitalization is not new, many public authorities and administrations are only recently catching up and identified lacking digital competences as a major hindrance [13, 44]. To catch up on a competent workforce, new study courses are created by individual administrations [45], with *Qualifica Digitalis* an overall qualification requirement assessment was started [44], and the IT planning council in Germany is establishing an online qualification program [46]. There, simulation games are explicitly mentioned as one means to avoid merely conveying theory but giving students practical experiences, which is crucial for these practice-oriented educational programs [44]. The usability of the platform was not explicitly considered during our evaluation and the derivation of our design principles. While usability is known to be a central feature of IT artifacts to ensure their adoption, there is already a plethora of usability related research available that addresses usability in general [47] and even for e-learning platforms [48]. To avoid unnecessary lengths and duplicated effort, corresponding design requirements were omitted.

The goal of our research was two-fold. First, we developed an SGP tailored to the public domain based on the simulation game proposed by [12]. The platform was iteratively designed and tested in a study group of international students. Second, we used the platform and the associated development and evaluation processes as vehicles to derive seven design principles for e-government SGPs following an extensive and well-documented research process. The design principles are a step towards theoretical guidance for the implementation of SGPs for e-government. These outcomes entail implications for research and practice. Our research extends the research on SGPs to the e-government area. Now, the research community can further test the design principles and investigate their generalizability and fit other domains. In addition, practitioners may use our results as a blueprint and guideline to the development of SGPs, thus, facilitating the diffusion and use of digitally supported simulation games for public sector education.

Limitations of the research comprise the sample of students. Although, the students who participated in (both) evaluations were very engaged and a critical audience, these groups are not a representative sample. Of course, they had a suitable lens for the public sector but, for example, public officials might have different preferences. Also, the design principles are not applicable to every kind of simulation game as they focus on games with interactions. All in all, our research is a contribution to the theoretical embedding of SGP development in the public sector domain.

Acknowledgements. The platform was developed for the ERASMUS Mundus Master of Science in Public Sector Innovation and eGovernance (PIONEER) at the University of Münster and was evaluated with the students. We express our thanks for their valuable contributions.

References

1. Persson, A., Goldkuhl, G.: Government value paradigms – bureaucracy, new public management, and e-Government. Commun. Assoc. Inf. Syst. **27**, 45–62 (2010)
2. Wimmer, M.A.: Integrated service modelling for online one-stop government. Electron. Mark. **12**, 149–156 (2002)
3. Scholta, H., Mertens, W., Kowalkiewicz, M., Becker, J.: From one-stop shop to no-stop shop: an e-government stage model. Gov. Inf. Q. **36**, 11–26 (2019)
4. Janssen, M., Charalabidis, Y., Zuiderwijk, A.: Benefits, adoption barriers and myths of open data and open government. Inf. Syst. Manage. **29**, 258–268 (2012)
5. Ogonek, N., Hofmann, S.: Governments' need for digitization skills: understanding and shaping vocational training in the public sector. Int. J. Public Adm. Digit. Age **5**, 61–75 (2018)
6. Müller, S.D., Skau, S.A.: Success factors influencing implementation of e-government at different stages of maturity: a literature review. Int. J. Electron. Gov. **7**, 136 (2015)
7. Stefanovic, D., Marjanovic, U., Delić, M., Culibrk, D., Lalic, B.: Assessing the success of e-government systems: an employee perspective. Inf. Manage. **53**, 717–726 (2016)
8. Freitas, S.D., Liarokapis, F.: Serious games and edutainment applications. In: Ma, M., Oikonomou, A., Jain, L.C. (eds.) Serious Games and Edutainment Applications, pp. 9–23. Springer-Verlag, London (2011)
9. Sanina, A., Kutergina, E., Balashov, A.: The Co-Creative approach to digital simulation games in social science education. Comput. Educ. **149**, 103813 (2020)
10. Löffler, A., Levkovskyi, B., Prifti, L., Kienegger, H.: Teaching the digital transformation of business processes : design of a simulation game for information systems education. In: 14th Int. Conf. Wirtschaftsinformatik, pp. 315–329 (2019)

11. Klievink, B., Janssen, M.: Simulation games for collaborative development in e-Government. In: Proceedings of the 43rd Hawaii International Conference on System Sciences (HICSS), pp. 1–9 (2010)
12. Ogonek, N., Distel, B., Becker, J.: Let's Play ... eGovernment! A simulation game for competence development among public administration students. In: Proc. 52nd Hawaii Int. Conf. Syst. Sci., pp. 3087–3096 (2019)
13. Ogonek, N.: Imparting Electronic Government Competences (2019)
14. Heeks, R.: Most eGovernment-for-Development Projects Fail: How Can Risks be Reduced? Manchester, UK (2003)
15. Hunnius, S., Paulowitsch, B., Schuppan, T.: Does E-government education meet competency requirements? An analysis of the German university system from international perspective. In: Proceedings of the Annual Hawaii International Conference on System Sciences, pp. 2116–2123 (2015)
16. European Commission: eGovernment Benchmark 2016. A Turning Point for eGovernment Development in Europe? Luxembourg (2016)
17. Mergel, I.: Kompetenzen für die digitale Transformation der Verwaltung. Innov. Verwaltung. **4**, 34–36 (2020)
18. Distel, B., Ogonek, N., Becker, J.: eGovernment competences revisited – a literature review on necessary competences in a digitalized public sector. In: 14th International Conference on Wirtschaftsinformatik, pp. 286–300. Siegen, Germany (2019)
19. Lean, J., Moizer, J., Towler, M., Abbey, C.: Simulations and games: use and barriers in higher education. Act. Learn. High. Educ. **7**, 227–242 (2006)
20. Mayer, I., Veeneman, W.: Games in a world of infrastructures simulation-games for research, learning and intervention, Delft (2002)
21. Mayer, I., Bekebrede, G., Warmelink, H., Zhou, Q.: A brief methodology for researching and evaluating serious games and game-based learning. In: Connolly, T.M., Hainey, T., Boyle, E., Baxter, G., Moreno-Ger, P. (eds.) Psychology, Pedagogy, and Assessment in Serious Games, pp. 357–393. IG (2013)
22. Deterding, S., Dixon, D., Khaled, R., Nacke, L.: From game design elements to gamefulness: defining "gamification". In: Proceedings of the 15th International Academic MindTrek Conference: Envisioning Future Media Environments, pp. 9–15 (2011)
23. El-Masri, M., Tarhini, A.: A design science approach to gamify education: from games to platforms. In: 23rd European Conference on Information Systems (ECIS), pp. 1–10. Münster, Germany (2015)
24. Blohm, I., Leimeister, J.M.: Gamification: design of IT-based enhancing services for motivational support and behavioral change. Bus. Inf. Syst. Eng. **5**, 275–278 (2013)
25. Hamari, J., Koivisto, J., Sarsa, H.: Does gamification work? A literature review of empirical studies on gamification. In: Proc. Annu. Hawaii Int. Conf. Syst. Sci., pp. 3025–3034 (2014)
26. Connolly, T.M., Boyle, E.A., MacArthur, E., Hainey, T., Boyle, J.M.: A systematic literature review of empirical evidence on computer games and serious games. Comput. Educ. **59**, 661–686 (2012)
27. Liu, C.C., Cheng, Y.B., Huang, C.W.: The effect of simulation games on the learning of computational problem solving. Comput. Educ. **57**, 1907–1918 (2011)
28. Cook, N.F., McAloon, T., O'Neill, P., Beggs, R.: Impact of a web based interactive simulation game (PULSE) on nursing students' experience and performance in life support training – a pilot study. Nurse Educ. Today **32**, 714–720 (2012)
29. Chang, Y.C., Chen, W.C., Yang, Y.N., Chao, H.C.: A flexible web-based simulation game for production and logistics management courses. Simul. Model. Pract. Theory **17**, 1241–1253 (2009)

30. Herranz, E., Colomo-Palacios, R., de Seco, A.A.: Gamiware: a gamification platform for software process improvement. In: Communications in Computer and Information Science (2015)
31. Simões, J., Redondo, R.D., Vilas, A.F.: A social gamification framework for a K-6 learning platform. Comput. Human Behav. **29**, 345–353 (2013)
32. Pasin, F., Giroux, H.: The impact of a simulation game on operations management education. Comput. Educ. **57**, 1240–1254 (2011)
33. Grabka, T.: Referenzmodelle für Planspielplattformen – Ein fachkonzeptioneller Ansatz zur Senkung der Konstruktions- und Nutzungskosten computergestützter Planspiele (2006)
34. Gregor, S., Hevner, A.R.: Positioning and presenting design science. MIS Q. (2013)
35. Chandra, L., Seidel, S., Gregor, S.: Prescriptive knowledge in IS research: conceptualizing design principles in terms of materiality, action, and boundary conditions. In: Proc. Annu. Hawaii Int. Conf. Syst. Sci. 2015, pp. 4039–4048. March (2015)
36. Hevner, A.R., March, S.T., Park, J., Ram, S.: Design science in information systems research. MIS Q. **28**, 75–105 (2004)
37. Peffers, K., Tuunanen, T., Rothenberger, M.A., Chatterjee, S.: A design science research methodology for information systems research. J. Manage. Inf. Syst. **24**, 45–77 (2008)
38. Peffers, K., Tuunanen, T., Niehaves, B.: Design science research genres: introduction to the special issue on exemplars and criteria for applicable design science research. Eur. J. Inf. Syst. **27**, 129–139 (2018)
39. Becker, J., Niemann, M., Halsbenning, S.: (Playing) government beyond pen & paper: conceptualization, implementation, and outlook. In: Proceedings of the 15th International Conference on Wirtschaftsinformatik, pp. 493–498 (2020)
40. Iivari, J.: A paradigmatic analysis of information systems as a design science a paradigmatic analysis of information systems as a design science. Scand. J. Inf. Syst. **19**, 39–64 (2007)
41. Gregor, S., Hevner, A.R.: Positioning and presenting design science research for maximum impact. MIS Q. **37**, 337–355 (2013)
42. Eckerson, W.W.: Three tier client/server architecture: achieving scalability, performance, and efficiency in client server applications. Open Inf. Syst. **10** (1995)
43. Ogonek, N., Distel, B., Hofmann, S.: Kompetenzvermittlung im öffentlichen Sektor neu gedacht (2020)
44. Schmeling, J., Bruns, L.: Kompetenzen, Perspektiven und Lernmethoden im Digitalisierten Öffentlichen Sektor, Berlin, Germany (2020)
45. land.nrw: Neuer Studiengang zum Verwaltungsinformatiker.
46. IT-Planungsrat: Entscheidung 2019/62 – Bildungs- und Weiterbildungsplattform E-Government
47. Nielsen, J.: Usability inspection methods. In: Conference Companion on Human Factors in Computing Systems – CHI '94, pp. 413–414. Boston, Massachusetts (1994)
48. Harrati, N., Bouchrika, I., Tari, A., Ladjailia, A.: Exploring user satisfaction for e-learning systems via usage-based metrics and system usability scale analysis. Comput. Human Behav. **61**, 463–471 (2016)

New Workplace, New Mindset: Empirical Case Studies on the Interplay Between Digital Workplace and Organizational Culture

Caterina Baumgartner(✉), Eva Hartl, and Thomas Hess

LMU Munich, Munich, Germany
{hartl,thess}@bwl.lmu.de

Abstract. Recently, firms have been observed to implement digital workplaces as strategic management tool to support their digital transformation. With this redesign of working environments, firms hope to foster their transformation by changing the organization's culture. With only little known on the impact of digital workplaces on cultural transformation, our study addresses this question and aims to disentangle the interplay of workplace redesign and culture. Based on the transformational journeys of four established firms, our study provides insights on the design of digital workplaces and derives a framework on the impact of digital workplaces on culture. Our results showcase best practices for an efficient design of digital workplaces and contribute to a better understanding of how digital workplaces foster cultural transformation.

Keywords: Digital workplace · Workplace transformation · Organizational culture · Strategic workplace redesign

1   Introduction

"We shape our buildings, thereafter they shape us" – Winston Churchill, 1943.

The redesign of workplaces as strategic management tool for steering organizational development has a long tradition [1]. However, in recent years in the context of digital transformation, new forms of strategic office redesign can be observed: Around the globe, firms have started to tear down walls and transform their workplaces into smart and agile work environments for knowledge workers [e.g. 2]. These so called "digital workplaces" are characterized by an increasingly digitized work environment that causes significant shifts in how work is conducted in organizations [3, 4], as well as an overall shift in organizational logics towards autonomy and creativity influenced by the New Ways of Working movement [5].

In the context of organizational digital transformation, firms were observed to experiment with the implementation of digital workplaces as strategic tool to support their organizational and cultural transformation [3, 6–9]. Within their digital transformation, firms essentially need to build capabilities for digital innovation in order to leverage value from new technologies [10]. However, recent research has emphasized the crucial importance of also considering transformations in organizations' socially constructed realities such as its identity [e.g. 11] or culture [e.g. 12, 13] and practitioners repeatedly stating culture as major hurdle for digital transformation [e.g. 14] support this claim. As one approach to steer an organization's culture change efforts towards a more fast-paced, agile, try-and-error and customer-centric culture, firms have been found to increasingly implement digital workplaces in the hope that the redesigning of work environments will alter an organization's culture [6, 15]. While first anecdotal narratives indeed suggest that digital workplaces can trigger cultural changes in form of increased employee connectedness, collaboration, and creativity [9, 16], only little is known on the impact of digital workplaces on cultural transformation. Prior research in the just emerging literature stream of digital workplaces predominantly took a technology-centric approach focusing on the promoted use of digital technologies and thereby covering only behavioral impacts of digital workplaces [4, 17]. Indeed, workplace design research has been criticized for a general disregard of effects on organizational culture [18]. We aim to close this research gap by disentangling the interplay between physical workplace redesign and its impact on a social level, i.e. organizational culture. We therefore investigate digital workplaces under a holistic approach as the composition of place, technology and people and follow IS research in adopting a value-centric understanding of organizational culture. Specifically, our study addresses the question: *How does the redesign of workplaces into digital workplaces impact cultural transformation?*

We conducted qualitative case studies and investigated four firms, which had recently implemented new workplaces as part of their digital transformation, in order to identify common underlying characteristics of digital workplace designs and their impact on organizational culture. Our findings are presented in form of a comprehensive framework disentangling the interplay between digital workplaces and culture via identifying four impact paths. With our research, we pick up a recent research call on the future of work and digital transformation in organizations [19]. Our findings contribute to strategic workplace design research by shedding light on its impact on organizational culture and expand the body of knowledge on the micro-level of digital transformation [3] by exploring the impact of an individual's workplace environment on organizational culture change endeavors in the context of digital transformation. From a practitioner's point of view we manage to provide insights on actual workplace design and highlight the substantial role of culture in the context of workplace redesign.

2 Theoretical Background

2.1 Digital Workplaces as Strategic Management Tool

Workplace design has a long-standing tradition in ergonomics and human-oriented computer science [4]. However, with workplaces being at the center of an organization's cost savings strategy and the organization's visual representation, workplaces have also drawn interest in the fields of environmental psychology, corporate real estate, facility management and strategic management [1]. Research on organizational spaces as a strategic management tool has evolved since the early 20th century, however with contemporary workplace strategies gaining more and more attention, practitioners and researchers alike have started to emphasize workplaces as a tool for steering organizational change and development [1]. Thus, it is hardly surprising that we see organizations experimenting with workplace redesign and transformation as a strategic tool to support their digital transformation [3, 6–8].

These recent developments in workplace strategic design are often termed as "digital workplaces" and are the results of two mega-trends. First, digital workplaces are heavily influenced by the New Ways of Working movement that led to a shift in organizational logics from control and function to autonomy and creativity [5]. In terms of organizational spaces, this implies that the future workplace "focuses on how and what work is done, not where and when it is done" [20, p. 1]. Second, this shift in the nature of work has been enabled and pushed by today's work environment becoming predominantly digital [4]. The adoption of digital technologies facilitated communication and collaboration in novel and flexible ways and thereby caused significant shifts in how work is conducted in organizations [3, 4].

However, recent research emphasizes that the concept of digital workplaces requires a holistic approach, as the fundamentally different way of working induced by digital workplaces not only stems from the employment of digital technologies, but also the designing of physical spaces and behavioral norms that lead to new approaches to get things done [9]. Under this holistic approach that complement existing concepts of remote working or home office, digital workplaces constitute an intertwining of physical spaces, social systems and technology [21]. Recent digital workplace literature thus aligns with the concept of "Bricks, Bytes, and Behavior" from the new ways of working literature [16]. Following these triad-conceptualizations, we define digital workplaces as *"the physical, technological and people-related arrangements that allow more flexible and collaborative ways of working to help organizations to cope with digital transformation."* [9, p. 136], as illustrated in Fig. 1. That is, we understand **place** as "all aspects concerning the physical work environment, spaces, and facilities" [e.g. 16]. This component of digital workplaces is often designed in form of flexible and task-oriented office spaces with the aim to support employees best possible with the task at hand and include quiet areas, community areas, telephone boxes or recreational areas [2, 16]. In this context, employees are also encouraged to work in different locations also outside the organization, e.g. at home or at the client. Secondly, **technology** refers to "all aspects of information technology usage within the company's digital ecosystem: Software, hardware, platforms, data and knowledge sharing" [e.g. 16]. The technology component of digital workplaces often contains tools and systems that shall drive a specific workstyle, e.g. innovation or knowledge sharing [9, 22]. Without the technology and respective infrastructure, it would not be possible to achieve high levels of flexibility or collaboration at the workplace. In this context, cloud infrastructure and the rise of mobile devices can be seen as key enablers for digital workplaces [2]. Lastly, the **people** component comprises "all aspects of employee behavior, their skill set, or relation to each other" [e.g. 16] and becomes particularly important as firms require their employees to develop particular digital capabilities in order to succeed in dynamic environments. Consequently, this component is aimed to be designed in a way that shall drive employees' digital competences in form of new leadership styles, technical skills or collaboration forms [9, 22].

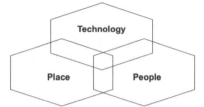

Fig. 1. Conceptualization of digital workplace and its components

2.2 Digital Workplaces and Culture Change

An organization's digital transformation entails its strategic response to disruptions triggered by digital technologies that encompasses the alteration of an organization's value creation paths. Central to this transformation are digital innovations, i.e. leveraging digital technologies to alter an organization's portfolio of products, processes, and business models [10, 23]. Next to digital innovations, recent research emphasizes that also transformations in organizations' socially constructed realities such as its identity [e.g. 11] or culture [e.g. 12, 13] are of crucial importance for a successful digital transformation. Especially for the latter, organizations have rated culture as a major hurdle for digital transformation [e.g. 14]. Especially large pre-digital organizations built on long success roads that legitimize firm cultures of stability, operational excellence and organizational hierarchy, now struggle with the demands of digital innovation that require a more fast-paced, agile, try-and-error and customer-centric approach [7, 8, 12, 13]. As part of this digital culture change, firms have been observed to increasingly establish digital workplaces [6] in the hope that by redesigning work environments for knowledge workers also employees' mindset and thereby the organization's culture is altered [15].

The notion that changes in workplace design may lead to organizational changes is in line with Lefebvre´s [24] view that social change is dependent on spatial change. However, a more moderate view is prevailing in recent workplace design research. This stream regards workplace redesigns as not necessarily creating organizational changes by themselves, but they may function as accelerator or reinforcement for the desired change [e.g. 25]. Consequently, also the implementation of digital workplaces has been found to lead to organizational changes in form of increased motivation and creativity of employees [16, 26], increased productivity, effectiveness, and engagement [7, 8]. Overall, digital workplaces were found to help firms succeed in the digital area by establishing the necessary capabilities and competences [9, 22]. However, most studies in the just emerging research stream on digital workplaces are technology-centric and focus on the promoted use of digital technologies [4, 17], thereby mostly covering the visible and behavioral impacts of digital workplaces. Despite the implementation of digital workplaces being found to be a common tool in digital transformation efforts to enable culture change [6], only little is known about the impact of digital workplaces on a firm's culture. Indeed, the exact nature of the induced organizational changes by digital workplaces is still unclear [27].

This stands representative for an overall lacking focus of workplace design research on organizational culture, which is criticized for having for most parts disregarded the effect of workplace redesign on organizational culture [18]. Only few studies have examined this effect. For example, studies investigating the move to open offices found that such open office layouts led to an autonomous and less formal culture [28], increased cross-departmental collaboration and increased culture of learning [29]. While these studies illustrate ways in which office layouts can influence organizational culture, they solely focus on physical design elements of the workplace, omitting the increased importance of technologies.

Given the importance of organizational culture change for digital transformation and the observed efforts of firms to support this change via implementing digital workplaces, we aim to close this research gap and to shed light on the effects of digital workplace redesign on organizational culture. While definitions of organizational culture differ, it is generally understood to cover the shared meaning and understanding of organizational members of what is considered as norm [e.g. 30, 31]. This understanding of culture puts symbolic and implicit elements in the center of investigation. We follow the within IS discipline prevailing value-centric focus on organizational culture [32, 33] and investigate workplace induced changes in organizational culture in form of values. Values are defined as the shared beliefs of organizational members about what is considered as desirable, e.g. norms and ideals that impact the members' actions by setting expectations and boundaries for appropriate behavior [31, 34]. We perceive this conceptualization of culture as necessary in order to be able to investigate the impacts of the physical (i.e. changes in workplace design in form of place, tools, and people) on the social (i.e. changes in cultural values). Some models of organizational culture like the three-layer pyramid model by Schein [31] comprise culture as both explicit and visible elements (e.g. artifacts such as behavior, language, symbols) as well as implicit aspects of culture (values and basic assumptions, which refer to the underlying belief system of unconscious, taken-for-granted beliefs). While we share their ontological view that the explicit and physical elements are representations of implicit elements and via realization become manifested as such, it is exactly these relations and influences that we aim to investigate and thus a clear-cut distinction between physical and social constructs is essential for our research.

3 Methodological Approach

Since digital workplaces are a rather new area of research and limited previous research is available, our study follows an exploratory approach. We chose a case study design, as case-study research allows for the investigation of recent phenomena in real-life context where boundaries are not clear. This approach further enables us to investigate both formal and informal processes. Specifically, we chose a multiple-case design which enables cross-case comparison, or more precisely results from one case can be compared and contrasted with the results of other cases [35]. To foster rigor, we followed common guidelines and recommendations for case study research [35, 36] to ensure the validity and reliability of our study.

3.1   Case Selection and Data Collection

For our multiple-case study, we studied four German firms that had recently undergone workplace transformation including physical and technological changes. The cases were sampled purposefully [37], with the aim to maximize diversity to allow for contrasting findings. We identified suitable research subjects by initial desk research on digital workplace implementation and further filtered for those that matched with our initial conceptualization of digital workplaces to end up with a final case selection that spans across different industries, firm sizes and business models.

Table 1. Overview on surveyed firms and data sources

	Auto_Com	Auto_Club	Financial Services_Com	Software Com
Industry	Automotive	Transport and mobility	Financial services	Software firm
Business activity	Automobile manufacturer	Mobility association	Asset manager for investments in tangible assets	Technology company with focus on hard- and software
Founded	1909	1903	2007	1975
Headquarter	Germany	Germany	Germany	USA
Legal form	Stock corporation	Registered association	Stock corporation	Corporation
Turnover 2019	57 billion €	0,21 billion €	0,16 billion € (2018)	125 billion $
# employees	91.000	2900	730	135.000/GER: 2700
# interviews	3	5	3	3
Interviewees by position	Head of IT for Employee, Project Lead HR IT, 2× Manager Planning Department	Chief Digital Office, Project Lead Smart Workplace, 3× Referent Digital Workplaces	Head of IT, Head of Digitalization, Transformation Manager	IT Director, Experience Lead, Digital Marketing Manager
Secondary data	30 pages	13 pages	8 pages	72 pages

Overall, the acquired sample includes four firms located in the same geographical region that differ in size, industry, organizational context. To ensure construct validity and for the purpose of triangulation [35], we collected data on the cases in form of semi-structured interviews and secondary data. Table 1 provides an overview of the cases and collected data. In order to obtain insights from different perspectives, we interviewed multiple experts per case with different professional backgrounds to avoid biases [38].

The interviews followed a semi-structured interview guideline [39] with sections on the firm's implementation of the digital workplace, its components and their design, as well as observed changes in organizational culture. Initial open questions allowed participants to openly share their experiences, with further sub-questions addressing themes and concepts identified in literature or that had emerged in the course of the first interviews. Overall, 14 interviews with 15 experts in both managerial and non-managerial positions were conducted via telephone or in person between Mai and July 2019. Our expert panel span across referents for digital workplaces without staff responsibility up to more senior team leads or C-level staff. The interviews ranged from 20 to 60 min, with an average interview length of 44 min. All interviews were conducted in German, were recorded – with permission of interviewees - and later transcribed, yielding 169 pages of verbatim reports. For triangulation purposes, we further collected secondary data in the form of company website information, blog and newspaper articles, press releases, and whitepaper on the digital workplaces of the case firms, resulting in an overall of 123 pages of secondary data. We obtained an initial understanding of the case firms' digital workplace design via secondary data and validated and extended these insights in the course of conducting interviews.

3.2 Data Analysis

The collected data was comprised within a case database [35] and stored as well as analyzed by using atlas.ti. The data was consequently coded in a combined deductive and inductive approach, considering themes and codes derived from literature findings and/or emerging from the data in the course of analysis [40]. First, our coding focused on a descriptive approach in order to derive insights on the design of digital workplace components, e.g. the quote: "From the very beginning we said very clearly that we no longer have any allocated workstations." was coded as "Place_ Desk sharing concept". Further on, we drew on grounded theory [41] and iteratively went through our data to uncover interactions of digital workplaces and organizational culture as well as cultural changes. In refining our codes, we combed through our data at least three times and matched our codes with themes from literature [39]. For example, we drew from the organizational culture profile [34] as orientation to define cultural values.

The analysis of our coded data followed a two-step approach. First, we conducted within-case analysis to gain familiarity with data, identified constructs or relations within one firm and derived a detailed description of the firms' digital workplace and the associated cultural changes. In the subsequent cross-case analysis, we compared and contrasted findings from the cases to reveal similar constructs and relationships across the four firms – also referred to as pattern searching [42] and thereby derived a holistic framework on the interaction of digital workplaces and culture. The analysis was performed by two researchers and emerging differences were discussed bilaterally and resolved consensually [35]. Following triangulation principles, we reflected on our initial understanding of the case firms' workplace redesign from secondary data with additional information obtained from the interviews, and vice versa validated the insights gained in the course of conducting interviews with secondary data.

4   Results

4.1   Within-Case Results

In this section we present the results of our multiple-case study by outlining the introductions of digital workplaces in the four studied firms and describing the respective induced cultural changes.

Automotive_Com: Started their digital workplace initiative in 2011 by launching a series of digital innovations, amongst them "Enterprise 2.0" – their version of a collaborative software to simplify collaboration and enhance employee connectedness, which ensures consistent experience across multiple employee-led initiatives and consists of team workspaces, wikis, social networking and document sharing. Part of their digitalization strategy was also the implementation of flexible work arrangements such as home office regulations. Later on, a new office building was completed in 2016 in which modern office design came into place that features new rooms flooded with light, open space offices and communication areas. However, everyone still has assigned desks and home office regulations depend on respective departments due to company regulations. With regard to people, employees' attitude towards the modern workplace is two-fold with some leaders that prefer the presence of employees and do not encourage them to work remotely. The present hierarchical structures and leadership change slowly towards a supportive style as mutual trust is not always present. Hence, some employees do not participate in this new workstyle and some leaders still decide on extent and modalities of home office, whereas in some departments work is carried out more hierarchy- and organization-independent now, resulting in a culture with partially more openness and transparency.

Auto_Club: With the completion of their new headquarters in 2014, Auto_Club started their flex-office concept, which includes desk-sharing concept, clean desk policies, co-working spaces, a creative space and various home bases – in other words meeting rooms with writable walls. At the same time a "smart workplace" concept was introduced after having identified that hardware was not competitive for new ways of working. Subsequently, everyone across the firm was equipped with new laptops and a platform based on Microsoft Sharepoint for knowledge exchange and collaborative teamwork was established before finally launching Office365 in 2019 to enable flexible working. People at Auto_Club are either very open or reluctant to the new workplace concept. Some stick with their fixed desks and thus hamper overall adoption of tools and facilities. Also, the perception of leadership has changed as more managers take on a more enabling role as "people managers". As a result, the firm culture benefits from higher levels of cooperation, innovation and trust. But due to opponents of the smart workplace concept, a divided firm culture can be observed, and beneficial cultural values occur slower.

Financial Services_Com: Quite recently at the beginning of 2019 they opened their "digital factory" – an innovation lab for a small fraction of employees from digital units and blueprint for future workplace transformation across the overall firm. For this purpose, an innovative room concept with group and quiet zones, open and closed meeting rooms, telephone boxes or lounge corners, where employees do not have assigned desks and rather choose the working environment that suits their task at hand, was established. Meeting rooms are equipped with touch screens and writable walls and innovative sensors monitor occupancy of rooms. Next to individual laptops and screens on every table, Microsoft 365 builds the foundation for collaborative teamwork and allows them to work jointly on documents or schedule project work. In accordance with new possibilities, members of the digital lab adopted an even more agile and flexible workstyle including daily standups or design thinking methodology. Leaders now have less administrative tasks and report faster decision making due to more proximity to employees. In this context also hierarchies have fully vanished, and the head of the digital unit says they even see themselves as a kind of "flatshare". As a consequence, employees are more confident and feel motivated. Even though a rather open mindset was already noticed before, cultural values such as innovation, mutual trust, flexibility and a culture where failure is seen as a chance have further evolved.

Software_Com: Introduced their "smart workspace" concept in 2016 with the move into their new headquarters. Trust-based working hours and home office had already been introduced at this point. The overall goal is the achievement of a work-life-flow – in other words a self-determined design of daily tasks with flowing transitions between work and private life. Next to desk-sharing and clean desk policies, four zones to think, accomplish, share and discuss are part of the initiative and further telephone booths, coffee lounges and recreational areas complement the new room concept. Employees were equipped with latest collaborative tools and additional cloud technology or interactive whiteboard technology in meeting rooms allows them to work collaboratively. Hereby, dozens of applications are part of an ecosystem that also ensures compatibility. Regarding hardware, employees can decide whether to use firm or own devices. Moreover, being an American tech firm, culture has developed evolutionarily and has since ever been based on values such as trust and innovation. This fact and employee involvement during the planning phase led to high identification, satisfaction and acceptance with the new workspace. Even though employees can work from home any time, people tend to work at the new office because they benefit from the office surrounding and from both formal and informal exchange with colleagues, resulting in a more efficient workstyle where coordination and alignment happens faster. At the same time the leadership role has shifted towards an enabling style, where managers support by providing the right resources. All in all, the already existent values of openness, innovation and high levels of trust and teamwork were further reinforced through workplace transformation, as well as increased satisfaction and faster coordination could be observed in this course.

4.2   Cross-Case Results

From our cross-case analysis, similarities and differences between the workplace designs of the cases and induced cultural changes emerge, as summarized in Table 2. With regard to workplace components, case firms introduced similar physical and technical advancements with the aim to support employees best possibly with their task at hand and encourage creativity, as Software_Com's Experience Lead underlines: "[…] only if the needs and requirements of people, space and technology are individually considered, the new work concept can unfold its full potential and enable innovation." However, different manifestations become visible, as physical office space and desk-sharing is less advanced at Auto_Com and Auto_Club and usage intensity of technical infrastructure differs from Software_Com and FS_Com. Nevertheless, interviews demonstrate that workstyles across all firms got more flexible with people switching locations, and more efficient as knowledge exchange and collaboration takes place more easily now which also facilitates organizational learning. Overall, despite different manifestations and approaches of digital workplaces among our case firms, cross-case results reveal that the firms approached their digital workplace design quite similarly.

With regard to our research question, cross-case analysis reveals that the introduction of digital workplaces induced cultural changes within the studied firms – particularly such concerning values of innovativeness, cooperation, and openness. Both, by introducing technological tools where employees simultaneously work together and by establishing a collaborative office environment, work processes and results become more transparent and knowledge sharing is facilitated, putting more emphasis on values like openness and transparency as we observed across all firms. More precisely, employees across our case firms now frequently encounter each other by switching workstations during the day, exchanging latest project insights and working within the same document. This also happens across hierarchies and consequently results in an increase of trust levels and openness. In this context, also Auto_Com mentions that integrity and transparency were fostered by transparent workstyles due to open office layout and document sharing: "We set great store […] above all transparency […]. I have to talk if something does not fit". These workplace advancements also lead to more exchange across hierarchies as "one speaks to each other independent of hierarchies and positions." [Project Lead HR IT, Auto_Com]. Overall, leaders particularly at Software_Com and FS_Com have high confidence in their team members and empower them. At Software_Com employees are encouraged to "[…] have more crazy ideas, ask more stupid questions." [Experience Lead]. Software_Com, which signals employees that risk-taking and failure is accepted and encouraged, observed increased trust levels and a cooperative teamwork culture: "Through this high sense of belonging […] that of course everyone feels safe here and at eye level." [Digital Marketing Manager, FS_Com]. Since employees can now decide where, when and how they want to work e.g. by using creativity rooms and trying out new things, increased values of flexibility but also risk-taking and openness which are beneficial for development of new skills and in the long run innovations become visible. In contrast, the fact that people can now also work from the coffee bar at Auto_Com led to prejudices among reluctant employees: "They are just sitting around drinking coffee and "working" a little bit" [Project Lead HR IT]. Consequently, values associated with trust or flexibility are to some extent lower because of some reluctant members within Auto_Com or Auto_Club. All in all, our cases demonstrate that the individual components and particularly their interaction induce changes in cultural values. Additionally, it was noted that cultural changes are an ongoing process and might not yet be visible in some cases as the Chief Digital Officer at Auto_Club mentioned that they are "still far from being finished" with changing their culture.

However, while having identified similar organizational values across our firms, we found that these values were impacted in varying degrees. The differences in the intensity

Table 2. Cross-case results

	Auto_Com	Auto_Club	Financial Services_Com	Software Com
Place	-Group offices and few private offices -Coffee bar and creative rooms -Fixed desks	-Group offices and few private offices -Creative space and zones -Desk sharing but resistance	-Open office -Open and closed meeting rooms, lounge areas -Desk sharing	-Open office, creative and recreational spaces -Dedicated work zones -Desk sharing
Technology				
Software	-Enterprise 2.0	-Office 365	-Office 365	-Office 365
Hardware	-Laptops for majority of staff	-Laptops for majority of staff	-Firm-wide laptops and phones	-Firm-wide laptops -Bring your own device
Equipment	-Screens and click share in meeting rooms	-Screens, whiteboards, click share technology	-Sensors for room utilization, writable walls	-Surface Hubs, writable walls
People				
Acceptance	-Partially accepted	-Partially accepted	-Positive attitude	-Positive attitude
Behavior and Skills	-Increased collaboration & communication	-Increased collaboration & communication	-Firm-wide collaboration -Self-organized learning -Adoption of agile methods	-Firm-wide collaboration -Self-organized learning -Employment of agile methods
Workstyle	-Partially flexible and agile workstyle -Partially increased autonomy	-Partially flexible and agile workstyle -Partially increased autonomy	-Flexible and agile workstyle across digital factory -Increased autonomy & decision making	-Flexible and agile workstyle across firm -Autonomy & decision making
Leadership	-Slowly blurring hierarchies	-Slowly blurring hierarchies	-Enabling leadership role	-Enabling leadership role

(continued)

Table 2. (*continued*)

	Auto_Com	Auto_Club	Financial Services_Com	Software Com
Cultural Values	-Openness -Transparency -Mutual trust -Teamwork Incremental change	-Flexibility -Cooperation -Participation -Tolerance of opponents Incremental change	-Flexibility -Risk taking -Mutual trust -Cooperation Promotion of existing values and occurrence of new values	-Flexibility -Mutual trust -Failure & learning culture Promotion of existing values and occurrence of new values

of cultural changes may be traced back to the firms' initial organizational culture and people-related elements. The cases of Auto_Com and Auto_Club, which were characterized by hierarchical structures, traditional workstyles, long tenure of employees and a leadership style that focuses on presence and expression of status: "[…] my house, my car, my horse, my private office" [Project Lead HR IT, Auto_Com] resulted in members showing resistance towards the digital workplace and thus a divided culture of opponents and supporters. In contrast Software_Com´s culture has always been based on values such as trust, innovation and risk-taking – which is why they "probably have less hurdles than an established German carmaker" [IT Director, Software_Com]. Next to this initial effect of implemented digital workplaces on organizational culture, we observed a later-stage reverse effect of the newly induced culture on the digital workplaces – particularly within the people dimension. As a consequence of the increased levels of mutual trust and appreciation that are present now at Software_Com and FS_Com, interviewees report that employees are more satisfied and motivated as they can now self-determine the modalities of their work, as the following quote reflects: "So it definitely makes me more satisfied and I think the majority of employees […] as well." [IT Director, Software_Com]. At this point it should also be mentioned that interviewees emphasized the role of management commitment and change management initiatives for adoption and success of workplace transformation.

5   Discussion

Our results not only provide a detailed overview of digital workplace design and its components, but also highlight the importance of taking on a comprehensive approach towards digital workplaces as we found many elements of digital workplaces to be heavily interrelated. Our cases demonstrate that collaboration was facilitated by new technical introductions and a change in people's workstyle came along that however also required a new skillset. As one example, the availability of white boards or document sharing on the one hand requires a certain technical skillset and on the other hand supports employees in working collaboratively within one document or project and affects their workstyle in terms of transparency and collaboration. Furthermore, the new technologies are reconciled with the physical surrounding itself as FS_Com and

Software_Com demonstrate with smart tables that can be controlled via smartphone. Our results further show that interrelations and dependencies amongst digital workplace components impact workplace effectiveness. In this context, the fact that remote working at Auto_Com depends on respective leaders, led to a rather immature version of digital workplaces.

With regard to the impact of digital workplaces on organizational culture, our results show that the implementation of digital workplaces triggers changes in an organization's values (a), but that the maturity of digital workplaces and resulting intensity of cultural changes is dependent on the prevailing underlying assumptions within organizations (b), and the organization's capability to overcome them, e.g. by supporting change management efforts (c). In turn, the resulting cultural changes from digital workplace implementation may again impact especially the people-related aspects of digital workplaces (d). These relations between digital workplace implementation and organizational culture are summarized in Fig. 2.

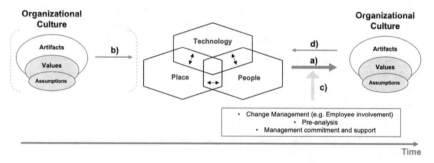

Fig. 2. Holistic framework on digital workplaces and organizational culture

First of all, our cases confirm that digital workplaces and their components indeed affect organizational culture (depicted as effect a). One could argue that physical and technical changes in context of digital workplaces happen on an artifact level as they are rather visible and then affect implicit values. More precisely, the new possibilities enabled by technical and spatial aspects on artifact level, have impact on cultural values in several ways: Employees can now autonomously decide on work location inside and outside the office and they have a variety of technical tools and work environments that support them, which also affects their workstyle and skillset. Not only will their workstyle become more independent, they will feel empowered because they are granted confidence and have room for creativity. However, if people appreciate this flexibility and if mutual trust among leaders and employees exists, the organizational culture can benefit from increased flexibility and openness (on value level). In our cases, values associated with flexibility (e.g. openness), teamwork and cooperation could be increased with the implementation of digital workplaces. These results support earlier research findings [15] that in line with our results also found digital workplaces to promote creativity and innovation [e.g. 43].

However, despite similarities in workplace design and overall identified cultural values, intensity level and manifestation of values differ between firms. A phenomenon which was also noted by previous research findings [44]. One could argue that basic assumptions such as mutual trust, high esteem and benevolent relations, which were present at Software_Com and FS_Com, are a reason why we have observed higher levels of flexibility and teamwork compared to other cases. Consequently, we observed leaders who support employees regarding goal achievement and work organization, strong team spirit as well as high overall adoption and identification with digital workplaces. In contrast, the reason for high resistance among leaders and employees at Auto_Com and Auto_Club could lie in prevailing basic assumptions that are more dedicated to control mechanisms and hierarchical relationships. In summary, our results point to three suggestions regarding the role of initial firm culture (depicted as effect b). The larger the gap between initial culture and pursued beneficial culture of innovation and flexibility, 1) the longer it takes until favorable outcomes in values are observed and/or 2) the lower the intensity level of cultural values after transformation and/or 3) the more likely the resistance of employees. In any event, these proposed effects require further research.

Moreover, our interview partners pointed out several moderating factors that support the cultural impact of digital workplace implementation (depicted as effect c). Especially when prevailing basic assumptions are misaligned with the implemented digital work-places and their targeted values, change management initiatives are required to bridge this cultural divide. A participative approach present at Software_Com with employees "co-creating" the new workplace, has therefore been found to be beneficial in manag-ing resistance and thus employees should be integrated in change initiatives as early as possible [45]. Furthermore, our results confirm previous findings on the importance of leadership for employee commitment: A transformational leadership style increases commitment of followers [46].

Lastly, our analysis also reveals that cultural values, induced by digital workplaces again interact with digital workplace components (depicted as effect d). As one exam-ple, the promoted participative leadership style again reinforces mutual trust within the firm. This reiterative interaction and longitudinal adjustment process between digital workplace and culture also is in line with Dery et al.´s [9] call for systemic learning and continuous feedback as essential elements for a successful implementation of digital workplaces.

6 Implications, Limitations and Future Research

The results of our multiple-case study show that the implementation of digital workplaces indeed lead to changes in organizational culture and foster values of flexibility, openness, teamwork and cooperation, creativity, and innovation. However, the maturity of digital workplaces and resulting intensity of cultural changes is dependent upon the prevailing underlying assumptions within organizations and their capability to overcome them. Our results further suggest a continuous adaptation between digital workplaces and culture, as induced cultural changes again support the people-component of digital workplaces.

By disentangling the complex interplay between digital workplaces and cultural transformation, our results contribute to strategic workplace design research by closing the existing research gap on the impact of workplace redesign on culture. Further, we contribute to the body of knowledge on the micro-level of digital transformation [3] by exploring the impact of individual workplace environments on organizational culture change endeavors in the context of digital transformation. The understanding of this relationship is crucial for impactful digital workplaces, as the success of digital workplace transformation is essentially dependent on culture. Moreover, our research sheds light on the actual design of digital workplaces thereby addressing the ongoing struggle of organizations in how to design their digital workplaces [17]. With our holistic approach, we enrich literature with a detailed account of four digital workplaces and their technological, physical and people-related components. From a practitioner's point of view, we manage to offer recommendations and best practices for practitioners in designing their digital workplace strategy. Further, our derived framework enables us to explain why similar arrangements in workplace initiatives lead to diverse cultural outcomes and might thus offer guidance for practitioners implementing digital workplaces. We further highlight the importance of change management, strategy development and employee integration for successful digital workplaces.

Next to these contributions, we need to point out some limitations of our study. While our qualitative approach allowed us to uncover interactions between digital workplaces and culture, it comes with the general limitation of qualitative research of lacking generalizability due to a small number of investigated cases. Future quantitative research might thus validate our results and also quantitatively assess the effect of digital workplace implementation on culture. Second, we studied firms that recently have implemented digital workplaces. To avoid biases from "honeymoon effects" [47], future research is encouraged to conduct longitudinal studies in order to assess long-term effects and to gain more detailed insights into how cultural changes evolve over time. Third, our study focused on the impacts of digital workplaces on culture. But as our results suggest, this interplay is more complex so future research might extend our framework by studying further moderating and mediating factors, as well as extend the scope of digital workplace impact. Lastly, our findings are based on interviews with rather managerial staff and may lack an employee perspective on cultural changes. While we are confident that our results also cover the employee perception as some of our interview partners were still on a lower seniority level without staff responsibility (thus can be considered as employees themselves), future research is encouraged to a stronger focus on non-executive levels when investigating the impacts of digital workplaces on culture.

Despite the mentioned limitations, we believe our holistic framework manages to enrich our understanding of the role culture plays in workplace transformation and gives valuable insights on actual digital workplace design. Importantly, it could be demonstrated that a new workplace does not necessarily change organizational culture but rather is a complex process of reciprocal changes that requires ongoing leadership and change management support.

References

1. Skogland, M.A.C., Hansen, G.K.: Change your space, change your culture: exploring spatial change management strategies. J. Corp. Real Estate **19**, 95–110 (2017)
2. Microsoft: The New World of Work. A Competitive Advantage for Irish Business (2005)

3. Meske, C., Junglas, I.: Investigating the elicitation of employees' support towards digital workplace transformation. Behav. Inf. Technol. **39**, 1–17 (2020)
4. Richter, A., Heinrich, P., Stocker, A., Schwabe, G.: Digital work design. Bus. Inf. Syst. Eng. **60**(3), 259–264 (2018). https://doi.org/10.1007/s12599-018-0534-4
5. Kingma, S.: New ways of working (NWW): work space and cultural change in virtualizing organizations. Cult. Organ. **25**, 383–406 (2019)
6. Hartl, E.: A characterization of culture change in the context of digital transformation. In: 25th Americas Conference on Information Systems, Cancún (2019)
7. Colbert, A., Yee, N., George, G.: The digital workforce and the workplace of the future. Acad. Manag. J. **59**, 731–739 (2016)
8. Kaarst-Brown, M.L., Quesenberry, J., Niederman, F., Weitzel, T.: Editors' comments: special issue editorial: new approaches to optimizing the digital workplace. MIS Q. Exec. **17**, 9–23 (2018)
9. Dery, K., Sebastian, I.M., van der Meulen, N.: The digital workplace is key to digital innovation. MIS Q. Exec. **16**, 135–152 (2017)
10. Vial, G.: Understanding digital transformation: a review and a research agenda. J. Strateg. Inf. Syst. **28**, 118–144 (2019)
11. Wessel, L., Baiyere, A., Ologeanu-Taddei, R., Cha, J., Jensen, T.: Unpacking the difference between digital transformation and IT-enabled organizational transformation. J. Assoc. Inf. Syst. **22**(1), 102–129 (2021). https://doi.org/10.17705/1jais.00655
12. Bilgeri, D., Wortmann, F., Fleisch, E.: How digital transformation affects large manufacturing companies' organization. In: Thirty Eighth International Conference on Information Systems, pp. 1–9. South Korea (2017)
13. Hartl, E., Hess, T.: The role of cultural values for digital transformation: insights from a Delphi study. In: Twenty-third Americas Conference on Information Systems, pp. 1–10. Boston (2017)
14. Capgemini: The Digital Culture Challenge: Closing the Employee-Leadership Gap. https://www.capgemini.com/fi-en/wp-content/uploads/sites/27/2018/09/dti-digitalculture_report_v2.pdf (2018)
15. van Heck, E., van Baalen, P., van der Meulen, N., van Oosterhout, M.: Achieving high performance in a mobile and green workplace: lessons from Microsoft Netherlands. MIS Q. Exec. **11**, 175–188 (2012)
16. de Kok, A.: The new way of working: bricks, bytes & behavior. In: Lee, J. (ed.) The Impact of ICT on Work, pp. 9–40. Springer, Singapore (2016)
17. Köffer, S.: Designing the digital workplace of the future – what scholars recommend to practitioners. In: Thirty Sixth International Conference on Information Systems, pp. 1–21. Fort Worth (2015)
18. Zerella, S., Von Treuer, K., Albrecht, S.L.: The Influence of office layout features on employee perception of organizational culture. J. Environ. Psychol. **54**, 1–10 (2017)
19. Baptista, J., Stein, M.-K., Lee, J., Watson-Manheim, M.B., Klein, S.: Call for papers: strategic perspectives on digital work and organizational transformation special issue. J. Strateg. Inf. Syst. (2017)
20. Dittes, S., Richter, S., Richter, A., Smolnik, S.: Toward the workplace of the future: how organizations can facilitate digital work. Bus. Horiz. **62**, 649–661 (2019)
21. Kane, G.: The workplace of the future: digital technology is transforming even our physical work spaces. MIT Sloan Manag. Rev. **56**, 1–8 (2015)
22. Kissmer, T., Knoll, J., Stieglitz, S., Groß, R.: Knowledge workers' expectations towards a digital workplace. In: Twenty-fourth Americas Conference on Information Systems, pp. 1–10. New Orleans (2018)
23. Hess, T., Matt, C., Benlian, A., Wiesböck, F.: Options for formulating a digital transformation strategy. MIS Q. Exec. **15**, 123–139 (2016)

24. Lefebvre, H., Nicholson-Smith, D.: The Production of Space. Oxford Blackwell (1991)
25. Tanis, J.: Workspace and behavior. In: Kuttner, P., Grech, C., Walters, D. (eds.) Future office Design Practice and Applied Research. Routledge, London (2008)
26. Amabile, T.M., Conti, R., Coon, H., Lazenby, J., Herron, M.: Assessing the work environment for creativity. Acad. Manag. J. **39**, 1154–1184 (1996)
27. Schwarzmüller, T., Brosi, P., Duman, D., Welpe, I.M.: How does the digital transformation affect organizations? Key themes of change in work design and leadership. Manage. Revue **29**, 114–138 (2018)
28. McElroy, J.C., Morrow, P.C.: Employee reactions to office redesign: a naturally occurring quasi-field experiment in a multi-generational setting. Hum. Relat. **63**, 609–636 (2010)
29. Hong, J.F., Easterby-Smith, M., Snell, R.S.: Transferring organizational learning systems to Japanese subsidiaries in China. J. Manage. Stud. **43**, 1027–1058 (2006)
30. Alvesson, M., Sveningsson, S.: Changing Organizational Culture: Cultural Change Work in Progress. Routledge (2015)
31. Schein, E.H.: Organizational culture. Am. Psychol. **45**, 109–119 (1990)
32. Tams, S.: Moving cultural information systems research toward maturity. Inf. Technol. People **26**, 383–400 (2013)
33. Leidner, D.E., Kayworth, T.: Review: a review of culture in information systems research: toward a theory of information technology conflict. MIS Q. **30**, 357–399 (2006)
34. O'Reilly, C.A., III., Chatman, J., Caldwell, D.F.: People and organizational culture: a profile comparison approach to assessing person-organization fit. Acad. Manag. J. **34**, 487–516 (1991)
35. Yin, R.K.: Case Study Research: Design and Methods. Sage, Thousand Oaks, CA (2014)
36. Koners, U., Goffin, K.: Learning from postproject reviews: a cross case analysis. J. Prod. Innov. Manag. **24**, 242–258 (2007)
37. Patton, M.Q.: Two decades of developments in qualitative inquiry: a personal, experiential perspective. Qual. Soc. Work **1**, 261–283 (2002)
38. Choudrie, J., Papazafeiropoulou, A., Lee, H.: A web of stakeholders and strategies: a case of broadband diffusion in South Korea. J. Inf. Technol. **18**, 281–290 (2003)
39. Myers, M.D.: Qualitative Research in Business and Management. Sage Publications, Thousand Oaks, CA (2009)
40. Ryan, G.W., Bernard, H.R.: Data management and analysis methods. In: Densin, N.K., Lincoln, Y.S. (eds.) Handbook of Qualitative Research, pp. 769–802. SAGE Publications, Thousand Oaks, CA (2000)
41. Glaser, B.G., Strauss, A.L.: Discovery of Grounded Theory: Strategies for Qualitative Research. Routledge, New York (1967)
42. Graebner, M.E., Eisenhardt, K.M.: The Seller's side of the story: acquisition as courtship and governance as syndicate in entrepreneurial firms. Adm. Sci. Q. **49**, 366–403 (2004)
43. Martins, E.C., Terblanche, F.: Building organisational culture that stimulates creativity and innovation. Eur. J. Innov. Manag. **6**, 64–74 (2003)
44. Klein, K.J., Sorra, J.S.: The challenge of innovation implementation. Acad. Manag. Rev. **21**, 1055–1080 (1996)
45. Waddell, D., Sohal, A.S.: Resistance: a constructive tool for change management. Manag. Decis. **36**, 543–548 (1998)
46. Abrell-Vogel, C., Rowold, J.: Leaders' commitment to change and their effectiveness in change – a multilevel investigation. J. Organ. Chang. Manag. **27**, 900–921 (2014)
47. Wohlers, C., Hertel, G.: Longitudinal effects of activity-based flexible office design on teamwork. Front. Psychol. **9**, 1–16 (2018)

Individual Digital Study Assistant for Higher Education Institutions: Status Quo Analysis and Further Research Agenda

Christin Karrenbauer[✉], Claudia M. König, and Michael H. Breitner

Leibniz Universität Hannover, Information Systems Institute, Hannover, Germany
{karrenbauer,koenig,breitner}@iwi.uni-hannover.de

Abstract. Today, digital assistants can support students during their studies. A quick and easily useable and accessible information transfer, individually tailored to the students' needs is required. Individual educational biographies and an increasing number of students require individual information provision and advice. Research on digital assistance systems has increased dramatically over the past decade. We focus on the individual digital study assistant (IDSA) field with its functionalities embedded in a typical student life cycle (SLC). In order to determine the status quo of DSA, we conduct a literature review with a focus on their functionalities. One research finding indicates that the DSA field generates a wide range of DSA functionalities. We structured them developing a morphological box. Finally, we discuss a further research agenda for the development, adaption, introduction, and success of IDSA.

Keywords: Literature review · Student life cycle · Individual digital study assistant · Morphological analysis · Further research agenda

1 Introduction

Students today have a wide variety of study courses and courses to choose from, partly due to the Bologna Process and the reforms that have taken place in higher education institutions (HEI). The Bradley Report in Australia initiated similar reorganizations that led to comparable effects. After the mentioned reforms, more students are able to begin their studies regardless of their social and educational background [1–3]. Thus, students' heterogeneity increased and corresponding individualized study needs, goals, and the need for individual support and counseling [4]. However, due to the increasing number of students [2] with a relatively constant number of lecturers [5, 6], personal advice alone is less feasible [7].

In addition, students prefer a quick and easy transfer of information [8]. One consequence of this is individually tailored alternatives that offer content for personal counseling or alternative options based on automation, such as a level support system. In periods of COVID-19, HEI is characterized by online lectures and seminars amongst others, in contrast to HEI routine before the pandemic. The need for regular presence lectures has

F. Ahlemann et al. (Eds.): WI 2021, LNISO 48, pp. 108–124, 2021.
https://doi.org/10.1007/978-3-030-86800-0_8

decreased. However, students currently face greater challenges regarding their intrinsic motivation in terms of studying. According to a nationwide study that deals with "Studying digitally in Corona times", more than 50% of the respondents state that, among other factors, self-organization is strongly difficult [9]. Following Wolters and Hussain [10] though, self-regulating abilities to self-study are considered key to completing HEI studies successfully. Self-regulatory competencies, such as self-organization, goal-oriented learning, etc., becomes increasingly important in context of individualized study. In order to overcome this challenge, the development and introduction of digital assistance systems, such as an individual digital study assistant (IDSA) [11] is a promising opportunity. The development aims to efficiently support students to formulate and achieve their individual educational goals. In this sense, an IDSA promotes self-regulating abilities by providing suitable functionalities. Promoting self-regulating skills is central to the development of an IDSA. Differentiated abilities are associated with helping students set their own goals [12] and to change these goals in a self-observation process [13]. In this way, students can determine whether strategies used serve to achieve goals in terms of a target-performance comparison [14]. This growing awareness of one's own competences, through target-performance comparisons and in interaction with (big) data and information, is another way to support the individuality of study programs. An IDSA can then take into account performance-related data (e.g., examination results and European Credit Transfer and Accumulation System (ECTS), other data (e.g., qualitative data from dialogues or feedback) from learning and campus management systems (LMS and CMS) and also data from external sources (e.g., from open educational resources (OER) platforms). By collecting information interactively, an IDSA can help students to organize and structure their studies. Situation-specific instructions, reminders, recommendations, and comparisons can enable individual, factual, and social reference norms and further standards. In this way and with growing self-regulating competencies, the increasing trend towards individualization, flexibility, internationalization, and networking can be countered. Accordingly, it is essential to understand the different phases students are going through during their study. A student life cycle (SLC) offers a clear structure in a HEI's diversity, shows all study phases, and merge them [15]. With the SLC, different needs can be better identified. It enables to meet functionalities appropriately. The combined analysis of DSA functionalities and SLC is therefore necessary for a successful, i.e., cost-efficient and accepted student-centered, IDSA development, introduction, and adaption.

DSA research has increased dramatically in the last decade. We focus on DSA functionalities and outline our body of knowledge. Thus, a literature and operated DSA review is performed, and the status quo of existing functionalities is analyzed. Based on our findings, we develop a morphological box with common DSA functionalities and further introduce a research agenda for an IDSA development, introduction, adaption, and success. In this respect, we concentrate on the following research questions:

RQ1: What is the status quo of typical DSA functionalities in HEI aligned to a SLC?
RQ2: What are further research topics for the development, adaption, introduction, and success of an IDSA in HEI considering a SLC?

First, we discuss the theoretical foundations of DSA and a typical SLC in HEI. Based on this, we describe our research design and methodology, followed by an elaboration of our results, including a morphological box. Afterwards, our results and findings are discussed, and implications and recommendations for research and practice are derived. A further research agenda, limitations, and conclusions complete our paper.

2   Theoretical Foundations

2.1   DSA in HEI

HEI structures and conditions have changed, e.g., because of HEI's digital transformation [16]. To address this, various digital systems have already been developed and used in the HEI context. Chatbots (also known as conversational agents, talkbots, chatterbots, artificial conversational entities, and virtual assistants) provide a natural language interface to process inputs from its users for an intelligent human-computer conversation. They usually are equipped with artificial intelligence and various data within, e.g., a knowledge base to react to the user's input and give answers [17–19]. Learning-oriented conversational agents used in the educational context are called pedagogical conversational agents (PCA) [20]. Different research and studies have been carried out in this emerging research stream. Meyer von Wolff et al. [17] conducted a quantitative survey and identified requirements for a HEI chatbot implementation and essential topics to cover. They were able to show that students are willing to use such a system and that it is reasonable in the HEI context. Winkler and Söllner [18] conducted a literature review in which they identified the individual student's diversity, a chatbot's building, and an educational process quality all influence a chatbot's effectiveness. In another literature review, Hobert and Meyer von Wolff [21] outlined that the amount of research in the field of PCA increased, with a trend for messenger-like PCA. The usage is mostly not restricted to a specific learning setting because of their mobile access and students can learn individually. More practically, Hobert [22], for example, introduced a learning system based on a chatbot that helps students to learn to program. According to Knote et al. [22] chatbot assistances are one out of five smart personal assistants (SPA) archetypes, besides adaptive voice (vision) assistants, embodied virtual assistants, passive pervasive assistants, and natural conversation assistants. Thereby, "SPAs are software agents that can automate and ease many of the daily tasks of their users by engaging with them via voice-based, natural language dialog […]. [They] comprise all types of voice-based software systems that enable humans to hold goal-oriented, natural conversations with computers […]" [24 p. 3].

A further opportunity to respond to the changes in the HEI is the implementation of an IDSA. In accordance with the previously introduced definitions, we define an IDSA as an efficient digital student support tool that helps to achieve individual educational goals through a connection of previously unrelated data and information, considering individual goals, interests, and the sensitization of own competencies. This interactive information gathering helps students to organize and structure their study with situation-specific guidance, reminders, and recommendations. Aligning with the introduced clusters for SPA by Knote et al. [23], an IDSA can have similar design characteristics to fit into the identified archetypes. It supports students in strengthening their self-organization and self-regulation skills, enabling them to organize and manage their studies individually. An IDSA does not support students in direct learning or training of content such as a PCA does with, e.g., learning for an exam. Instead, an IDSA offers tasks that deal with learning topics at a level of reflection.

2.2 Student Life Cycle

The SLC concept was initially introduced as a result of the need to professionalize administrative and IT-supported study processes. It enables efficient handling of interfaces to study organization and quality management systems [25]. SLC is also based on models of organizational research. In particular, theories of stakeholders and strategic management theories [26, 27], process-structured organizational systems, and functions of service and customer relations of a HEI are used [28, 29]. All relevant tasks and areas of students, lecturers, and HEI administrations in connection with courses are part of the SLC [15]. In general, the following phases can be highlighted [30]: (1) orientation, (2) application for a university place and enrollment, (3) participation in courses and examinations, (4) graduation and de-registration, as well as (5) alumni activities.

Structure and focus of SLC differ in teaching [25, 31], quality management [32], and cost of a CMS [15]. Bates and Hayes [33] note that students need more intensive support in the transition phase for important and sustainable decisions. Wymbs [34] emphasizes that much electronic data is already collected during the enrollment process. This data can be used for example to provide individual support for the decision-making process in the search for a suitable degree program by matching self-assessment data with artificial intelligence (AI) data. Overall, the focus is to act student-centered within the study phases. Therefore, different requirements for an IDSA can be concluded.

In the HEI environment, ongoing digital transformations lead to a broad spectrum of study programs, seminars, and lectures with various methodological-didactic and media-based designs. In this context, a SLC as an organizational structure offers a binding set of rules for students, lectures, and HEI administration, and thus provides stability in its diversity [25]. In particular, a dynamic SLC has the potential to divide the organization of studies into specific phases by defining support, information, and service activities for each phase [35]. Regarding the development of support and functionalities, we use the SLC by Sprenger et al. [15]. The following three stages encompass structured sub-dimensions that in turn provide orientation for developing and introducing DSA functionalities, see Table 1.

Table 1. Conceptualization based on SLC [15]

Before University Study	Recruitment	Application	Admission procedures	Enrollment/registration
During University Study	Examination procedures	Changing course of study	Preparation of performance reports	
	Organization of exams	Scheduling of classes, events, and rooms	Re-registration	
After University Study	Graduation		Alumni activities	

3   Research Design and Methodology

We conducted a literature review in the field of DSA and its functionalities to answer our research questions. We focused on scientific publications on DSA and followed Webster and Watson [36], Templier and Paré [37], and especially vom Brocke et al. [38, 39]. Vom Brocke et al. [38] propose guidelines for literature reviews to cope with today's literature overload. We followed these guidelines and shortly describe our research steps to ensure transferability and reproducibility. For a detailed overview of our review process, see our protocol available at https://seafile.cloud.uni-hannover.de/f/275bf02a8c03 4bffb35b/?dl=1.

Review Scope: We used Cooper's taxonomy [40] to extract the characteristics for our literature review. It aims to determine the status quo of DSA and its functionalities in HEI aligned with the SLC on a conceptual level and further identify existing research gaps for an IDSA development, introduction, adoption, and success. We therefore focused on research outcomes and research applications, however, rather from an espousal position. Our literature review and status quo analysis intended to identify a representative coverage of today's functionalities of DSA in scientific literature and operated by HEI. Results are helpful for practitioners as well as general and specialized scholars.

Conceptualization of the Topic: We relied on the introduced definition for an IDSA in the previous section. Based on Gumhold and Weber [41] and Fernandes et al. [42] we first investigated DSA in scientific publications in general to get an overview. However, as there already exist some DSA operated in HEI we also conducted a status quo analysis of startups without a scientific foundation. The outcome of this initial conceptualization formed our keywords for further analysis. We distinguished the identified papers and operated DSA in HEI regarding their functionalities for the different SLC phases. Here, we differed between functionalities for the phases before-, during-, and after finishing university study, see Table 1.

Literature and Operated DSA Search: First, we used a keyword search in IS databases to identify relevant literature and functionalities, as those databases include a great number of conferences and journals. Figure 1 shows the whole search process. In doing so, our initial search resulted in 1047 papers and 27 operated DSA in either English or German. To compromise our first findings, we reviewed the titles, abstracts, and keywords of the identified literature and excluded duplicates. This led us to take a closer look at 209 papers. Here, we defined inclusion and exclusion criteria to compromise the remaining papers and ensure their relevance [39]. We analyzed the papers in more detail to decide whether or not to define them as relevant and further tested running DSA. We additionally conducted forward-, backward-, author-, and similarity searches for the most important papers (Google Scholar). Through these processes, we identified 54 relevant papers and 23 operated DSA for a detailed analysis to determine the status quo of DSA functionalities for HEI aligned with the SLC, and to derive a research agenda.

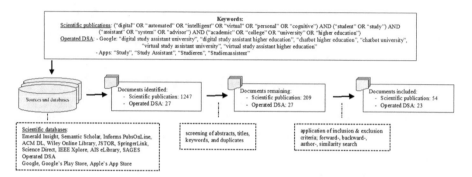

Fig. 1. Overview of our review process

Literature and Operated DSA Analysis and Synthesis: In the next phase, we analyzed and synthesized the identified literature focusing on the functionalities of a DSA. We used the SLC mentioned above to structure the results and categorized DSA functionalities into the phases before-, during-, and after university study. Based hereon, we derived a morphological box, which is an early output of a morphological analysis. The morphological analysis itself has its origin in the engineering sector but is now also used in numerous different areas, e.g., in energy informatics and social science, often as a systematic creativity technique to generate new ideas for occurring challenges, products, or artifacts. The first step of a morphological analysis is to identify and define dimensions to describe the analyzed system's generic aspects, followed by a definition of explicit design options (characteristics) in a next step. All information is stored in a matrix, the morphological box. It is possible to identify different design options (configurations) by selecting one characteristic for each dimension [42]. The morphological box enables a structured view of underlying features and challenges and allows a systematic perspective with numerous possible solutions [44]. Depending on the objectives and existing conditions of a DSA, we identified various functionalities. For our morphological box, we therefore used the SLC stages [15] as dimensions to structure the findings. Different functionalities then served as characteristics for the morphological box.

Further Research Agenda: In a last step, we used our results and findings, i.e., mainly the derived morphological box, to derive implications and recommendations for further research and derived a research agenda for an IDSA development, introduction, adaption, and success.

4   Results and Findings

Figure 2 shows the descriptive analysis of the identified publications regarding the number of publications per year from 2003 onwards. It shows that the yearly number increases in a long way. Except from 2003, initial research started in 2009, with most of the research published since 2017. We thus conclude that there is a rising interest in this research field.

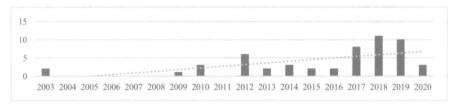

Fig. 2. Scientific publications per year regarding DSA in HEI

Based on the SLC [15], we structured our findings for DSA functionalities of our literature review and status quo analysis. Each of these SLC phases is further divided into specific activities. However, we excluded or merged some phases and selected those where a DSA application is possible and reasonable according to literature and/or running DSA. As the first step of the morphological analysis, the morphological box gives an overview of potential DSA functionalities in specific study phases. The aim is individual student support to promote self-regulating abilities in a demand-oriented way by digitally providing differentiated functionalities.

Before University Study: Through our literature review and status quo analysis, we were able to identify different functionalities of a DSA for the sub-dimension recruitment, application, and enrollment. However, none for the admission procedure, which is why we excluded it from further analysis and in the morphological box. For the recruitment sub-dimension, Page and Gehlbach [45] introduced a DSA "Pounce" that inter alia supports students in the transition from high school to college by providing personal guidance in this process. In case students are still unsure about field of study decisions, we identified different DSA functionalities. Some assistants provide a link with all faculties and fields of studies with detailed descriptions and study organization, e.g. [46]. On request, some DSA provide further information and links to related modules and credit points, e.g., [47]. Others additionally link to a self-assessment. Here interests are queried and a student's profile is generated. Based on this, individual suitable courses of study and information are then displayed (e.g., [48]). Some DSA are limited to functionalities for this sub-dimensions only. Jamil and Jarot [49] introduced a degree selection system to help students individually select the most suitable degree. "SAGES" is a further example [50]. It individually suggests majors and appropriates institutions for new and incoming students, based on, e.g., qualifications, competencies, interests, and city preferences.

The sub-dimension application includes admission and application-related functionalities [51]. Ravikumar et al. [52] introduced a DSA that guides students through the HEI application. Bani and Singh's [53] DSA is limited to this sub-dimension. They invented a chatbot that focuses explicitly on individual questions and problems that arise during and after the admission process and helps to solves them. Ranoliya et al. [54] presented a DSA that can answer FAQ, including those related to admission. "DINA" [55], as well as the DSA from Lalwani et al. [56] are dialog-oriented and directly answer questions related to, e.g., admission processes, requirements, and the HEI's ranking. Others rather provide links to these inquiries to give further information, e.g., [46]. In the case a DSA cannot answer questions or give information, it is either possible to chat with an agent or the DSA provides contact details for further information, e.g., [57].

Once introduced, some DSA provide functionalities for the sub-dimension of enrollment, e.g., [58]. The "KUSE Chatbot" [59] provides information on where to inform about this process and links to the page to do the enrollment. The DSA "Pounce" [45] supports students with activities related to enrollment. Once committed, it individually, proactively, and continually gets in touch with students until they express the intention to study at another HEI, which ultimately increased the enrollment rates. However, only a restricted number of DSA in literature as well as in practice addressed this sub-dimension.

During University Study: For this phase, we also focused on sources supported by our literature and status quo analysis. Therefore, we operated with these sub-dimensions in the morphological box: performance reports, organization of exams and assessments, distance learning, planning of examinations, changing course of studies, and scheduling of classes and events. Organization of exams and assessments provides a way for students to understand how they are learning through a learning self-test and individual evaluation. An individual checklist or an individual learning tip of the day offer an example of individual provision by linking data and functionalities [69, 70].

Scheduling is a function frequently found in the literature that supports students in organizing their individual daily routine of seminars and examinations [26, 60, 61]. Furthermore, Suvethan et al. [62] pursued the goal of supporting students with FAQ on administrative issues in 1st level support and also to provide them with a human advisor (2nd and 3rd level support). Another functionality is the feedback analysis required for each selected course and an automatic scheduler. Nwankwo [60] offered individual course registrations, course plans, assignments, scholarships, and regulations through the "AdvisorBot". Chen et al. [63] aimed to increase campus life's efficiency by using various campus resources, such as location-based messaging services, resource sharing, appointment management, and student social networking.

In addition, the sub-dimension of examination and enrollment is assigned different functionalities. Dibitonto et al. [58] provided with the DSA "LiSA" general and enrollment information supported by push function about individual deadlines and messages. In a double procedure, these are sent by e-mail and by the DSA at the same time. Henderson [64] focused with the developed DSA "AdviseMe" especially on the oral examination qualification. Gumhold and Weber [41] emphasized the attribute of interpreting the examination regulations.

A further sub-dimension describes the performance report. Muangnak et al. [59] worked with a dialogue-based system within their DSA that deals with applying scholarships and credit points for student activities. In addition to students, teachers are supported by operating with AI. Kamal [65] created a recommendation tool that can filter the information using the opinion of other people predicting a student's individual academic performance and interest for a course based on a collection of profiles of students who have similar interests and academic performance on prior courses. Nwankwo [60] developed a tool that records performance profiles from admission time and individually recommends exams based on the profile.

A next field is the function distance lecture. First experiments with transatlantic lectures are described by Herder et al. [66]. The DSA "Genius" [61] is used to provide OER or distance lectures. The recommendation mode offers lectures of individual interest to students.

A combination of functionalities described in the literature forms the activity of changing courses. The functionalities of the recruitment procedure can also be used here. Fernandes et al. [42] are developing a DSA that collects and evaluates personal data from students and provides individual feedback. Based on this, it makes recommendations, e.g., with regard to study programs. Jid Almahri et al. [67] also operated by means of machine learning (ML), designing a persona template for university students that supports the creation of data-driven personas. Among others, data is collected from students to evaluate cognitive engagement, performance expectations, and effort expectations. With this data, profiles can be created to help students learn to assess themselves better to make better study subjects choices.

After University Study: Graduation and alumni both are sub-dimensions of this phase. However, neither in the literature nor in the operated DSA we were able to identify functionalities for the sub-dimension of graduation. Thus, we excluded it from the morphological box. For the sub-dimension of alumni, some DSA provided a linkage to the alumni network's website with further information and possibilities [48, 57]. Others provided a list of alumni with their name and employer, accessible by a link [68]. These two functionalities were the only ones we were able to find during our research process.

Based on our literature review and operated DSA findings, we developed a morphological box, cf. Table 2. While we used the three different study phases mentioned above as dimensions with their specific activities as sub-dimensions, the identified functionalities serve as characteristics. Resulting, our morphological box consists of three dimensions, nine sub-dimensions, and various characteristics.

5   Discussion, Implications, and Recommendations

While the number of students has steadily increased [2], the amount of lecturers has remained almost constant [5, 6]. Due to the Bologna Process, diversity amongst students has equally inclined over the last 20 years. Thus, the proportion of individual counseling

Table 2. Morphological Box for DSA Functionalities

(Sub-)Dimension		Characteristic				Source
Before study	Recruitment	Personal guidance	Degree selection system		Link to faculty/field information	[45, 46, 48–50, 57]
		Link to self-assessment with recommendations		Majors and institution suggestion		
	Application	Guidance through application	Contact details		Questions & problems answering	[46], [51–57]
		Link for further information		FAQ admission		
	Enrollment	link for further information	information where to inform		proactive demand for status	[45, 58, 59]
During study	Exam procedures	Enrollment reminder & notification	Automated enrollment		Link to enrollment page	[52, 60, 62, 63]
	Scheduling of classes and exams	Manual entry in calendar	Automated entry in calendar		Schedule optimization	[26, 60, 61]
	Organization of exams/assessments	Self-test: learning strategies during studies	Individual checklist: learning strategies		Individual learning tips of the day	[69, 70]
	Performance report	Completed/open modules, grades, comparison to peers		SWOT analysis based on modules and grades with course suggestion		[59, 60], [65]
	Changing course of studies	Self-assessment with a persona template	Majors and institution suggestion		Link for further information	[42, 67]
	Distance lecture	Outside one´s own HEI with OER and other media	Within one's own HEI		Outside one´s own HEI with participation of different HEI	[61, 66]
After study	Alumni	Link to list of graduates			Link to alumni network	[48, 57, 68]

has also risen [4]. In addition, digital transformation processes have accelerated within the framework of HEI since the presence of COVID-19. This is especially obvious by drawing attention to the increasing online lectures and other offerings. In this connection, the study on "Online in Corona-times" [9] highlights that the topic of self-regulated study is becoming the focus of attention.

The majority of students is socialized in the digital environment which is reflected, for example, in changing information behavior. Especially today, students desire quick and easy information transfer [8]. We see this development as an opportunity to support students individually by dealing with the research topic IDSA, which we address by asking two research-questions. The first step here is to determine the status quo of DSA functionalities through a structured literature review, which is organized by the SLC. Our literature review has shown that while the first DSA developments took place in the 1990s [31], the majority was introduced in the last decade, see Fig. 1. The authors present different types and functionalities of a DSA, e.g., [62], but often without empirical evaluation. This includes studies that address both stakeholder requirements as well as the usefulness and relevance of DSA. This observation is also supported by the fact that DSA are increasingly found in status quo analysis but are often developed without any research before being introduced in HEI.

A critical point is that we deduced the requirements of potential users for a DSA within the SLC framework exclusively based on theory. From this systematic evaluation and our focus on designing individual support for students, a modification towards an IDSA is the next crucial step. To achieve this, we mapped our results in a morphological box. As a method of analysis and development, we designed functionality gradations. Thereby, more attention is paid to the variety of functionalities in the phase during study compared to the period before and after study. A functionality frequently described in literature is the organization of daily seminars and examination life in miscellaneous variations, see, e.g., [52]. This observation supports the increasing and diverse range of offers, whether in the context of seminars, working materials, or in the diversity of the study programs themselves. The question arises if the focus of functionality distribution follows a swarm research's core study, i.e., in research communities, this phase is considered relevant.

An IDSA development, introduction, and adaption in HEI structured along the SLC is the second research question, as further research topics become apparent with the focus on functionalities. For example, no stakeholder survey exists yet. The introduction of an IDSA is also linked to HEI's maturity as it determines whether an IDSA can be introduced and continued. For this study, we only considered the functionalities, whereas exploration of non-functionalities becomes equally important because in addition to maturity, it also decides whether an IDSA will be used. We developed a research agenda with additional topics and research questions, inspired by our findings, the morphological box, and theory-based, presented in Table 3 as an overview.

6   Conclusions and Limitations

With an increasing number and heterogeneity of students and the increasing availability of educational resources, an IDSA has the potential to individually support students in

Table 3. Overview of the Extracted Further Research Agenda

Topics for a further research agenda	Research questions
The IDSA development and potential functionalities are dependent on the IT maturity of an HEI. There is a need to develop such an IT maturity model for a IDSA development, introduction, and adoption cf. e.g., [3]	How does the IT maturity level of a HEI influence an IDSA development, adaption, introduction, and success?
Many stakeholders influence the IDSA development, introduction, and usage, but they have not yet been all identified, cf. e.g., [39, 51]	What are typical stakeholders for an IDSA development, introduction, adoption, and operation?
Many DSA in practice as well as in research are introduced. However, there often is a lack of foundations for developed functionalities and their usefulness. It requires more studies to firstly identify needs and requirements, and secondly an IDSA's usefulness and relevance, cf. e.g., [61, 62]	(1) What are typical requirements of all stakeholders for an IDSA development, introduction, adoption, and success? (2) How useful and relevant are operated IDSA?
We excluded some activities from the SLC in our morphological box, as there were no functionalities yet. For others, there only exist few functionalities yet, cf. e.g., [4]	(1) What are especially important activities for an IDSA operation? (2) How can IDSA functionalities be further developed to include all activities of a typical SLC?
We restricted the functionalities on those within the SLC. However, there are important activities students undergo, e.g., [71]	What are further important functionalities of an IDSA outside a typical SLC?
We focused on the functionalities of a DSA. There is a need to also identify non-functional requirements, cf. e.g., [56, 60]	What are non-functional requirements for an IDSA development, introduction, adoption, and success?
We focused on the functionalities for all phases of the SLC. However, different phases require an IDSA more than others, which has not yet been identified, cf. e.g., [45, 59]	Which phases within a typical SLC can be best supported by an IDSA?

getting information and advice quickly, easily, and automatically. Especially in times of COVID-19, an IDSA becomes even more important to support students in their digital semesters. We conducted a literature review and status quo analysis of existing DSA. As a result, we identified the status quo of typical DSA functionalities aligned to a SLC. Based on a morphological box, we structured the functionalities in the phases before-, during-, and after university study. While important functionalities for the before university study phase range from a degree selection system to application guidance, the visualization of completed and open modules with grades as well as the provision of OER are DSA functionalities during the study and a linkage to an alumni network after finishing study. Based on our results and findings, we additionally discussed an agenda for further research for an IDSA development, introduction, adoption, and success in this nascent field.

However, the literature selection and analysis are both influenced by our subjective perceptions, which might weaken our results. With the application of inclusion and exclusion criteria, we tried to minimize this subjective influence as much as possible. We further only identified a representative coverage of existing functionalities and these cannot be fully exhaustive. For the operated DSA, we limited our searches to Google, Google's Play Store, and Apple's App Store. There are more databases or platforms, e.g., LMS, to identify further DSA. Additionally, our morphological box resulted from our findings from the literature and status quo analysis, i.e., without expertise from different DSA stakeholders. It only discussed the status quo without evaluating the functionalities' relevance and usefulness for different stakeholders.

Our results and findings contribute to both research and practice. Researchers can build on the research agenda to close research gaps and address research needs. For HEI practitioners, the morphological box gives a structured overview of commonly used DSA functionalities. This is especially important for the development, introduction, adaption, and success of an IDSA.

Acknowledgement. Our research project "SIDDATA" is funded by the German Federal Ministry of Education and Research (FKZ 16DHB2123).

References

1. Brändle, T.: 10 Jahre Bologna-Prozess – Chancen, Herausforderungen und Problematiken. Springer, Wiesbaden (2010)
2. OECD.: Number of Students (Indicator). Tertiary 1995–2020, https://data.oecd.org/edures ource/number-of-students.htm. Accessed 28 August 2020
3. Clarke, J., Nelson, K., Stoodley, I.: The place of higher education institutions in assessing student engagement, success and retention: a maturity model to guide practice. In: Wyse, P., Billot, J., Frielick, S., Hallas J., Whitehead, E., Buissink-Smith, N. (eds.) Research and Development in Higher Education: The Place of Learning and Teaching, vol. 36, pp. 91–101 (2013)
4. Wong, B.T.M., Li, K.C.: Using open educational resources for teaching in higher education: a review of case studies. In: Proceedings of the International Symposium on Educational Technology (2019)

5. Klammer, U.: Diversity Management und Hochschulentwicklung. In: Kergel, D., Heidkamp, B. (eds.) Praxishandbuch Habitussensibilität und Diversität in der Hochschullehre. PES, pp. 45–68. Springer, Wiesbaden (2019). https://doi.org/10.1007/978-3-658-22400-4_3

6. Hornsby, D.J., Osman, R.: Massification in higher education: large classes and student learning. High. Educ. **67**, 711–719 (2014)

7. Marczok, Y.M.: Blended learning as a response to student heterogeneity. Managing innovation and diversity in knowledge society through turbulent time. In: Proceedings of the MakeLearn and TIIM Joint International Conference (2016)

8. Gikas, J., Grant, M.M.: Mobile computing devices in higher education: student perspectives on learning with cellphones, smartphones & social media. Internet High. Educ. **19**, 18–26 (2013)

9. Traus, A., Höffken, K., Thomas, S., Mangold, K., Schroer, W.: Stu.diCo. Studieren digital in zeiten von Corona. Universitätsverlag Hildesheim. https://doi.org/10.18442/150. Accessed 18 November 2020

10. Wolters, C.A., Hussain, M.: Investigating grit and its relations with college students' self-regulated learning and academic achievement. Metacogn. Learn. **10**, 293–311 (2015)

11. Murphy, M.P.A.: COVID-19 and emergency eLearning: consequences of the securitization of higher education for post-pandemic pedagogy. Contemp. Secur. Policy **41**(3), 492–505 (2020). https://doi.org/10.1080/13523260.2020.1761749

12. Zimmerman, B.: Goal setting: a key proactive source of academic self-regulation. In: Schunk, D.H., Zimmerman, B. (eds.), pp. 267–296. Taylor and Francis Group, New York (2012)

13. Vanslambrouk, S., Zhu, C., Lombaerts, K., Philipsen, B., Tondeur, J.: Students' motivation and subjective task value of participating in online and blended learning environments. Internet High. Educ. **36**, 33–40 (2018)

14. Schunk, D.H.: Self-regulated learning: the educational legacy of Paul R. Pintrich. Educ. Psychol. **40**, 85–94 (2015)

15. Sprenger, J., Klages, M., Breitner, M.H.: Cost-benefit analysis for the selection, migration, and operation of a campus management system. Bus. Inf. Syst. Eng. **2**, 219–231 (2010)

16. Bennett, S., Agostinho, S., Lockyer, L.: Technology tools to support learning design: implications derived from an investigation of university teachers' design practices. Comput. Educ. **81**, 211–220 (2015)

17. Meyer, R., von Wolff, J., Nörtemann, S.H., Schumann, M.: Chatbots for the information acquisition at universities – a student's view on the application area. In: Følstad, A., Araujo, T., Papadopoulos, S., Law, E.L.-C., Granmo, O.-C., Luger, E., Brandtzaeg, P.B. (eds.) CONVERSATIONS 2019. LNCS, vol. 11970, pp. 231–244. Springer, Cham (2020). https://doi.org/10.1007/978-3-030-39540-7_16

18. Winkler, R., Söllner, M.: Unleashing the potential of chatbots in education: a state-of-the-art analysis. In: Academy of Management Proceedings (2018)

19. Mikic, F.A., Burguillo, J.C., Llamas, M., Rodriguez, D.A., Rodriguez, E.: CHARLIE: an AIML-based chatterbot which works as an interface among INES and humans. In: EAEEIE Annual Conference (2009)

20. Wellnhammer, N., Dolata, M., Steigler, S., Schwabe, G.: Studying with the help of digital tutors: design aspects of conversational agents that influence the learning process. In: Hawaii International Conference on System Sciences (2020)

21. Hobert, S.; Meyer von Wolff, R.: Say Hello to your new automated tutor – a structured literature review on pedagogical conversational agents. Internationale Tagung Wirtschaftsinformatik (2019)

22. Hobert, S.: Say Hello to 'Coding Tutor'! Design and evaluation of a chatbot-based learning system supporting students to learn to program. In: International Conference on Information Systems (2019)

23. Knote, R., Janson, A., Söllner, M., Leimeister, J.M.: Classifying smart personal assistants: an empirical cluster analysis. In: Hawaii International Conference on System Sciences (2019)
24. Winkler, R., Neuweiler, M.L., Bittner, E., Söllner, M.: Hey Alexa, Please help us solve this problem! How interactions with smart personal assistants improve group performance. In: International Conference on Information Systems (2019)
25. Schulmeister, R.: Der "Student Lifecycle" als Organisationsprinzip für E-Learning. In: Keil, R., Kerres, M., Schulmeister, R. (eds.) eUniversity Update Bologna, pp. 45–78. Waxmann, Münster (2007)
26. Sjöström, J., Aghaee, N., Dahlin, M., Agerfalk, P.: Designing chatbots for higher education practice. In: Proceedings of the International Conference on Information Systems Education and Research (2019)
27. Porter, M.E.: Competitive Strategy: Techniques for Analyzing Industries and Competitors. The Free Press, New York (1980)
28. Donabedian, A.: The Definition of Quality and Approaches to Its Assessment – Explorations in Quality Assessment and Monitoring Chicago. Health Administration Press (1980)
29. Sursock, A.: Examining Quality Culture Part II: Processes and Tools – Participation, Ownership and Bureaucracy. European University Association, Brussels (2011)
30. Lizzio, A., Wilson, K.: Student Lifecycle, Transition and Orientation. In: Facilitating Commencing Student Success Across the Lifecycle: Strategic Student Orientation. Griffith University, Brisbane (2012)
31. Harlan, R.M.: The automated student advisor: a large project for expert systems courses. ACM SIGCSE Bull. 26(1), 31–35 (1994). https://doi.org/10.1145/191033.191046
32. Pohlenz, P., Mitterauer, L., Harris-Huemmert, S.: Qualitätssicherung im Student Life Cycle. Waxmann, Münster (2020)
33. Bates, L., Hayes, H.: Using the student lifecycle approach to enhance employability: an example from criminology and criminal justice. Asia-Pac. J. Cooper. Educ. Spec. Issue 18, 141–151 (2017)
34. Wymbs, C.: Make better use of data across the student life cycle. Enroll. Manage. Rep. 20, 8 (2016)
35. Gaisch, M., Aichinger, R.: Pathways for the establishment of an inclusive higher education governance system: an innovative approach for diversity management. In: Proposal for the EAIR Forum Birmingham (2016)
36. Webster, J., Watson, R.T.: Analyzing the past to prepare for the future: writing a literature review. MIS Q. 26, xiii–xxiiii (2002)
37. Templier, M., Paré, G.: A framework for guiding and evaluating literature reviews. Commun. Assoc. Inf. Syst. 37 (2015)
38. Vom Brocke, J., Simons, A., Niehaves, B., Reimer, K., Plattfaut, R., Cleven, A.: Reconstructing the giant: on the importance of rigour in documenting the literature search process. In: Proceedings of the European Conference on Information Systems (2009)
39. Vom Brocke, J., Simons, A., Riemer, K., Niehaves, B., Plattfaut, R., Cleven, A.: Standing on the shoulders of giants: challenges and recommendations of literature search in information systems research. Commun. Assoc. Inf. Syst. 37, 205–224 (2015)
40. Cooper, H.M.: Organizing knowledge syntheses. A taxonomy of literature reviews. Knowl. Soc. 1, 104–126 (1988)
41. Gumhold, M., Weber, M.: SASy – a study assistance system. In: Proceedings of the International Conference on New Educational Environments (2003)
42. Fernandes, J., Raposo, D., Armando, N., Sinche, S., Sá Silva, J., Rodrigues, A., et al.: ISABELA – a socially-aware human-in-the-loop advisor system. J. Online Soc. Netw. Media 16, 100063 (2020)
43. Ritchey, T.: Modeling alternative futures with general morphological analysis. World Fut. Rev. 3, 83–94 (2011)

44. Jantsch, E.: Technological Forecasting in Perspective. OECD, Paris (1976)
45. Page, L., Gehlbach, H.: How an artificially intelligent virtual assistant helps students navigate the road to college. AERA Open **3**, 1–12 (2017)
46. Universität Wien. https://ucard.univie.ac.at/studierende/. Accessed 28 August 2020
47. Technische Universität Berlin. https://alex.qu.tu-berlin.de/. Accessed 28 August 2020
48. Universität Innsbruck. https://www.uibk.ac.at/studium/. Accessed 28 August 2020
49. Jamil, R., Jarot, S.P.W.: Intelligent decision support system for degree selection using AHP technique. In: Proceedings of the International Conference on Computer and Communication Engineering (2012)
50. Bouaiachi, Y., Khaldi, M., Azmani, A.: A prototype expert system for academic orientation and student major selection. Int. J. Sci. Eng. Res. **5**, 25–28 (2014)
51. Patel, N.P., Parikh, D.R., Patel, D.A., Patel, R.R.: AI and web-based human-like interactive university chatbot (UNIBOT). In: Proceedings of the International Conference on Electronics Communication and Aerospace Technology (2019)
52. Ravikumar, R., Rajan, A.V., Abdulla, A., Ahamed, J.: A proposal for introducing virtual reality assistant at Dubai Women's College. In: Proceedings of the HCT Information Technology Trends (2017)
53. Bani, B.S., Singh, P.: College enquiry chatbot using A.L.I.C.E. Int. J. New Technol. Res. **3**, 64–65 (2017)
54. Ranoliya, B.R., Raghuwanshi, N., Singh, S.: Chatbot for university related FAQs. In: Proceedings of the International Conference on Advances in Computing, Communications and Informatics (2017)
55. Santoso, H.A., Winarsih, N.A.S., Mulyanto, E., Saraswati, G.W., Sukmana, S.E., Rustad, S., et al.: Dinus Intelligent Assistance (DINA) chatbot for university admission service. In: Proceedings of the International Seminar on Application for Technology of Information and Communication (2018)
56. Lalwani, T., Bhalotia, S., Pal, A., Bisen, S., Rathod, V.: Implementation of a chatbot system using AI and NLP. Int. J. Innov. Res. Comput. Sci. Technol. **6**, 26–30 (2018)
57. Creighton University. https://doit.creighton.edu/services-provided-doit/ask-iggy. Accessed 28 August 2020
58. Dibitonto, M., Leszczynska, K., Tazzi, F., Medaglia, C.M.: Chatbot in a campus environment: design of LiSA, a virtual assistant to help students in their university life. In: Kurosu, M. (ed.) HCI 2018. LNCS, vol. 10903, pp. 103–116. Springer, Cham (2018). https://doi.org/10.1007/978-3-319-91250-9_9
59. Muangnak, N., Thasnas, N., Hengsanunkul, T., Yotapakdee, J.: The neural network conversation model enables the commonly asked student query agents. Int. J. Adv. Comput. Sci. Appl. **11**, 154–164 (2020)
60. Nwankwo, W.: Interactive advising with bots: improving academic excellence in educational establishments. Am. J. Oper. Manage. Inf. Syst. **3**, 6–21 (2018)
61. Scheepers, R., Lacity, M.C., Willcocks, L.P.: Cognitive automation as part of Deakin. MIS Q. Exec. **17**, 89–107 (2018)
62. Suvethan, N., Avenash, K., Huzaim, M.A.Q., Mathusagar, R., Gamage, M.P.A.W., Imbulpitiya, A.: Virtual student advisor using NLP and automatic appointment scheduler and feedback analyser. Int. J. Sci. Eng. Res. **7**, 155–160 (2019)
63. Chen, Z., Xia, F., Cheng, R., Kang, J., Li, C.: OnCampus: a mobile personal assistant for college students. In: International Conference on Computers in Education (2012)
64. Henderson, K.L., Goodridge, W.: AdviseMe: an intelligent web-based application for academic advising. Int. J. Adv. Comput. Sci. Appl. **6**, 233–243 (2015)
65. Kamal, T.: Automatic academic advisor. In: International Conference on Collaborative Computing: Networking, Applications and Worksharing (2012)

66. Herder, P.M., Subrahmanian, E., Talukdar, S., Turk, A.L., Westerberg, A.W.: The use of video-taped lectures and web-based communications in teaching: a distance-teaching and cross-Atlantic collaboration experiment. Eur. J. Eng. Educ. **27**, 39–48 (2002)
67. Jid Almahri, F.A.A., Bell, D., Arzoky, M.: Personas design for conversational systems in education. Informatics **6**, 1–26 (2019)
68. Technische Universität Darmstadt. https://hermine-winf.de/. Accessed 28 August 2020
69. Klingsieck, K.: Kurz und knapp – die Kurzskala des Fragebogens "Lernstrategien im Studium" (LIST). Zeitschrift für pädagogische Psychologie **32**, 249–259 (2018)
70. Roth, A., Orgin, S., Schmitzl, B.: assessing self-regulated learning in higher education: a systematic literature review of self-report instruments. Educ. Assess. Eval. Account. **28**, 225–250 (2016)
71. Université Paris-Saclay. https://www.universite-paris-saclay.fr/en/campus-life/international-welcome-desk. Accessed 28 August 2020

Digital Credentials in Higher Education Institutions: A Literature Review

Elena Wolz[✉], Matthias Gottlieb, and Hans Pongratz

IT Service Center (ITSZ), Technical University of Munich, Munich, Germany
{elena.wolz,matthias.gottlieb,pongratz}@tum.de

Abstract. Digitalization is an essential driver for change, also influencing universities in their operation. However, the graduation certificate is still paper-based and does not fit employers' digitized recruitment processes. Digitizing the graduation certificate is overdue to align with the digitized processes of employers and universities. However, there is only a few research on that issue. This paper aims to conduct a systematic literature analysis. Therefore, we investigated 147 articles in the context of research on digital credentials. The results show that, although there is an increasing interest in this research area, the research community lacks an unique understanding of digital credentials. The paper gives an overview of research made so far and contributes to identifying research gaps in the context of digital credentials.

Keywords: Digital credentials · Digital badges · Higher education institutions

1 Introduction

Digitalization is changing almost every area of life. Also, it affects universities in their role as a teaching and researching organization [1]. Universities use new technologies to modify their processes; for example, developing simulated learning environments via virtual reality [2], video archives of lectures, and massive open online courses (MOOC) supporting the student's ability to learn independently regarding time and place [1]. The corona pandemic pushed the digitalization of education further. However, graduation certificates issued by German higher education institutions (HEI) are still paper-based leading to several inefficiencies. The paper-based graduation certificate does not fit the most digitized recruitment processes of employers, leading to the certificate owner's expenditures to digitalize the certificate, so automated processing of the contents is not possible by employers. Besides, the employer has to struggle with trust issues, as it is easy to falsify paper-based graduation certificates. Digitizing the graduation certificate could increase efficiency and is overdue to align with the digitized recruitment processes.

Digital credentials are "the digital equivalent of paper documents, plastic tokens, and other tangible objects issued by trusted parties" [3]. Additionally, for data protection and privacy, they provide the possibility to hide certain information for the accessing recipient [3]. We have two main reasons to analyze digital credentials in detail. First, using digital credentials for digitizing graduation certificates could solve the caused

© The Author(s), under exclusive license to Springer Nature Switzerland AG 2021
F. Ahlemann et al. (Eds.): WI 2021, LNISO 48, pp. 125–140, 2021.
https://doi.org/10.1007/978-3-030-86800-0_9

issues of paper-based certificates such as data protection and time for authentication and validation. Second, digital credentials in the context of HEIs are relatively new and little-discussed yet [4]. In addition to that, prior research lacks an overview of that research field, building the basis for further studies. The article provides a basis for further research on digital credentials in higher education. Thus, we follow the research question: *What is the current state of the art of research on digital credentials in the context of higher education institutions?*

The paper conducts a systematic literature review analyzing 147 papers in the context of digital credentials in higher education institutions. It contributes to evaluating the relevance of digital credentials as a research area in the context of higher education, the creation of a status quo of research in that field, and the identification of research gaps.

We structure the study as follows: In the section Terms and Related Work, we give a general understanding of digital credentials and their potential in the context of HEIs. Afterward, we describe the methodology approach and present in the section Results our findings. We discuss the findings in the section Discussion. Finally, we give an outlook for future research and state the paper's limitations in the section Conclusion.

2   Terms and Related Work

Digital credentials represent "the digital equivalent of paper documents, plastic tokens, and other tangible objects issued by trusted parties" [3]. In education, digital credentials enable the holder to decide which information when and how revealed to others. Additionally, digital credentials provide greater security than paper-based documents [3]. In conclusion, digital credentials can change the way of issuing and managing graduation certificates from paper-based to digitized.

Digital badges emerged in the educational area as another trend [5]. According to [6], a digital badge "is a representation of an accomplishment, interest or affiliation that is visual, available online, and contains metadata including links that help explain the context, meaning, process and result of an activity." Digital badges have their origin in games, where the user gets badges by reaching performance benchmarks. Within education, they tend to motivate learners by providing an incentive to identify the progress in learning and support credential management [6]. Digital badges contain metadata referring to the skills and knowledge earned, like information about the issuer, knowledge achieved, activities are undertaken to achieve the badge, and quality of the experiences and performances [6]. Digital badges are used for certification: formal, non-formal, and in-formal qualifications, but on a very granular level, not yet very widespread.

"**Micro-credentials** are a virtual, portable way of cashing in on acquired learning, especially granular skills" [7]. They are mini-certifications in study programs and enable students to represent the knowledge achieved through successfully participating in a module or course. To earn these micro-credentials, a student must submit evidence of their learning process, which is evaluated afterward. Employers can use this achievement accreditation for evaluating their new hires [8]. Therefore, the focus lies on the content and not the certificate replacement.

Alternative credentials represent learning certifications of non-credit programs and therefore are no digitization of traditional transcripts. These digital credentials describe an individual's skills and knowledge and complement the traditional transcript [9]. As a result, alternative credentials support the concept of lifelong learning.

Technical applications of digital credentials are found in the area of platforms. One application consists of a centralized server platform [10]; other platforms use the blockchain to manage digital credentials [11–15]. Platforms using the open-source Ethereum infrastructure have been implemented [12, 14] and solutions with the Bitcoin blockchain as the underlying infrastructure [11].

3 Methodological Approach

In order to assess the current state of the art on digital credentials in HEIs, we executed a systematic literature analysis based on [16] and [17]. The search for relevant literature covered the databases: Scopus, EBSCOHost, ACM Digital Library, ScienceDirect, IEEE Explore, and AISeL. To identify appropriate literature, we choose an iterative approach concerning the hit rate. As the goal is to derive the current status of research on digital credentials, we considered 'Digital Credentials' as a relevant keyword for the query in a five-step approach. Also, getting the newest word stem in this specific field [4]. Figure 1 illustrates the applied methodology.

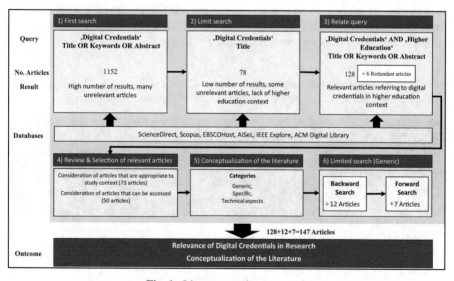

Fig. 1. Literature review approach

First, we searched for this within title, keywords, and abstract (result: hit rate 1152).

Second, to enclose the found literature, the keyword was searched only in the titles (result: hit rate 78). However, many of the found paper did not relate to the topic of digital credentials in HEIs. The fact that digital credentials are a general term used in different contexts causes less relevance. [3] defined digital credentials as "the digital equivalent of paper documents, plastic tokens, and other tangible objects issued by trusted parties."

Third, to further specify the query for this paper's research context, it was useful to add the keyword 'Higher Education' to the query. The search for 'Digital Credentials' and 'Higher Education' within title, keywords, and abstract resulted in 128 articles. We reviewed the articles and selected contributions that are relevant to the study. To define relevant articles, we elaborated if the studies are referring to the defined research context, resulting in 73 appropriate contributions. Among these 73 contributions, 23 could not be accessed. As a result, we included studies that could not be accessed in the literature's conceptualization but excluded them from further investigations.

Fourth, we categorized the digital credentials into generic, specific, technical aspects. Moreover, we documented the usage of terms in the context of digital credentials. To gather additional literature, we conducted a forward and backward search focusing on the category digital credentials generic, according to [16]. The forward and backward search revealed 19 additional contributions for investigation. In total, we reviewed 147 articles, whereby we used 73 articles for the conceptualization of the literature and further investigated 69 contributions according to their contents.

4   Results

We conceptualized 73 studies, and most contributions discuss digital badges (61). The other categories occur with similar frequency: generic (11), alternative credentials (4), micro-credentials (6), and technical application (6). Table 1 presents the identified papers and the number of papers assigned to a specific category.

Table 1. Conceptualization of contributions, Gen = Generic, DBa = Digital Badges, ACr = Alternative Credentials, MCr = Micro-Credentials, Tap = Technical Application

Author(s)	Gen	Digital Credentials Specific			Tap
		DBa	ACr	MCr	
AACSB [18], Bull [19]			X		
Matkin [9], Farmer and West [20]		X	X		
Swan [21]					X
Jirgensons and Kapenieks [22]		X			X
Kamišalić, Turkanović, Mrdović and Heričko [23], Hölbl, Kamisalić, Turkanović, Kompara, Podgorelec and Herićko [12], Arenas and Fernandez [24], Newswire [25], Newswire [26]	X				X
Connolly [27]	X	X			
Rimland and Raish [7], Lim, Nair, Keppell, Hassan and Ayub [8], Lewis and Lodge [28], [29], LaMagna [30]		X		X	

(*continued*)

Table 1. (*continued*)

Author(s)	Digital Credentials				TAp
	Gen	Specific			
		DBa	ACr	MCr	
Friedler [31]				X	
Parks, Parrish and Taylor [32], Newswire [33], Newswire [34], Norman [35]	X				
Newby and Cheng [36], Cheng, Richardson and Newby [37], Borras-Gene [38], Lim, Nair, Keppell, Hassan and Ayub [8], Friedler [31], Carey and Stefaniak [39], Cheng, Watson and Newby [40], Beattie and Jones [41], Hartnett [42], Shields and Chugh [43], Crafford and Matthee [44], Abramovich [45], Hickey [46], Wilson, Gasell, Ozyer and Scrogan [47], Hamson-Utley and Heyman [48], Olneck [49], McDaniel and Fanfarelli [50], Gamrat and Zimmerman [51], Elliott, Clayton and Iwata [52], Ahn, Pellicone and Butler [53], Rughinis [54], Newswire [55], Rimland and Raish [56], Bradley [57], Alliance for Excellent Education and Mozilla [58], Eaton, Rennie Center for Education and Policy [59], Newswire [60], Hartman and Andzulis [61], DiSalvio [62], Sullivan [63], Watters [5], Fanfarelli, Vie and McDaniel [64], Buchem [65], Gibson, Coleman and Irving [66], Brauer and Siklander [67], Virkus [68], LaMagna [30], Peck, Bowen, Rimland and Oberdick [69], Fedock, Kebritchi, Sanders and Holland [70], Ellis, Nunn and Avella [71], Ifenthaler, West, Flintoff, Lodge, Gibson, Beattie, Irving, Lewis, Coleman and Lockley [72], Mah, Bellin-Mularski and Ifenthaler [73], Diamond and Gonzalez [74], Carey [75], Balci, Secaur and Morris [76]		X			
Sum of Articles	**10**	**60**	**4**	**6**	**7**

4.1 Technical Application

The found contributions discuss technical applications referring to blockchain implementations in the context of digital credentials, digital badges, and higher education in general. [12, 22–24] Blockchain characteristics, features, and implementation challenges of the EduCTX project are described [12, 23]. A categorization stated by [23] assigns blockchain applications into institution-centric approaches and student-centric

approaches. While institution-centric applications focus on simplifying the higher education institution's processes, the student-centric category creates benefits from the
'student's perspective [23].

4.2 Specific Digital Credentials

Digital Badges

The usage of the specific term Digital Credentials relates to the mass of found articles
in the context of Digital Badges. However, there are several different understandings of
the characteristics and specifications of digital badges:

(1)   as micro-credentials [7, 8, 22, 36, 47, 51, 52, 57, 59],
(2)   as micro-credentials and micro-learning platform [37],
(3)   as a type of digital credentials [38, 58, 63],
(4)   as an alternative credential [9, 36, 53, 62],
(5)   as "a representation of an accomplishment, interest or affiliation that is visual,
       available online, and contains metadata including links that help explain the
       context, meaning, process, and result of an activity" [6],
(6)   as a graduation certificate [31],
(7)   as "a flexible format to allow educational programs to credential the learning that
       can sit alongside the curriculum" [41],
(8)   as "an online record of achievements, tracking the 'recipient's communities of
       interaction that issued the badge and the work completed to get it" [62],
(9)   as a nano-degree [57], and
(10)   as "an online image that tells people about a new skill that 'you've learned" [64].

Micro-credentials

Micro-credentials have been investigated in research very little so far [7, 8]. All authors
synonymize micro-credentials and digital badges. According to [7], "Digital badges or
micro-credentials are virtual representations of skill or knowledge, typically a granular
one." [8] define micro-credentials and digital badges for being the same as the individual
will get a digital badge when fulfilling the micro-credentials requirement. The research
focused on possibilities to implement micro-credentials in HEIs via design principles and
platform ecosystems [8]. Furthermore, potential benefits and existing vendors have been
described and the importance of design choices in that context concerning the convenience and success of implementation and aspects regarding deployment and evaluation
of micro-credentials [7].

Alternative Credentials

Alternative credentials are little discussed in research yet [9, 18, 19]. They represent
learning outcomes of individuals earned through informal learning that are based on
non-degree activities. These competencies refer to timely needs in professional life. [9,
18] refers to badges in the context of alternative credentials and states that they will affect

the relationship between higher education and society by representing skills achieved at the workplace instead of study programs. The found literature demonstrates the relevance of alternative credentials by providing a possibility to individuals choosing not to study [18, 19]. [19] points out that a "college diploma is not the only way to the good life, the intellectual life, the cultured life, or the American dream, and it is elitist to push for an educational ecosystem in which college is the only route." Furthermore, several aspects of establishing alternative digital credentials have been discussed, like the design of icons and to represent alternative digital credentials and the represented content, implementation methods, impacts of blockchain technology on alternative digital credentials, and requirements for issuing alternative digital credentials [9].

4.3 Generic Digital Credentials

Term Understanding of Digital Credentials
The conceptualization of the found articles focusing on the category of digital credentials generic in education together with the forward and backward search reveals that the usage of the generic term Digital Credential also has different associations in the found literature:

(1) as academic credentials [24, 25],
(2) as "Credentials are a means by which learners can signal important information about their knowledge, skills, and aptitudes." [32]
(3) as digital badges [38, 58, 63],
(4) as micro-credentials [8], and
(5) as a "digital record of their lifelong learning achievements. Include badges, internships, boot camps, certificates, MicroMasters, and stackable combinations, as well as traditional degrees. They are shareable with employers or other institutions. Institutions can record and manage the achievements of their learners in a way that is easy, safe, and inexpensive, and minimizes the risk of identity fraud" [33].

Technical Aspects of Digital Credentials
Most publications (15) elaborate applications of digital credentials in HEIs using blockchain. News articles have a prevalence of eight, and only one publication analyzes requirements and guidelines for implementing digital credentials.

The authors focusing on blockchain applications for implementing digital credentials in education investigated several aspects:

(1) technical characteristics of the blockchain [12, 15, 24, 77–80],
(2) challenges [23, 77, 78, 81, 82],
(3) benefits [15, 24, 32, 77, 82],
(4) enablers/requirements of using the blockchain [77, 82], as well as
(5) use cases of blockchain-based digital credential implementations [11, 12, 14, 15, 23, 24, 77, 79, 80],

The technical characteristics refer to the aspects such as how to guarantee security within the blockchain, consensus mechanisms in blockchain, different architectures, scalability, and network performance of blockchain technology [78].

The news articles found in the literature give superficial information on digital credentials, referring to the usage of digital credentials in higher education and implementation projects [25–27, 33, 34, 83, 84].

One of the found articles refers to the category requirements and guidelines for implementing digital credentials in HEIs. The publication describes requirements in the context of implementing digital credentials in higher education institutions by proposing a digital credential strategy [32].

5 Discussion

The results of our thematic analysis confirm an increasing interest in digital credentials for HEIs [1]. The number of identified publications per year shows a significant increasing trend in publications from 2015 on.

Further, the topic is of raising interest in the area of HEIs [4] and in the field of Information Systems (IS), which underlies the increasing numbers of publications per year found through the literature search in the context of digital credentials in higher education. The proportion of source categories illustrates that the topic is new in research, as there are only a few book nominations but many conference and journal publications.

Delimitation of Terms
To our surprise, using the terms digital credentials, digital badges, micro-credentials, alternative credentials, and digital academic credentials is not precisely distinct. A more precise specification will follow. Many contributions use digital badges referring to other terms like nano-degrees [57], micro-credentials [8, 22, 36, 47], graduation certificate [31], alternative credentials [36, 53, 62] or digital credentials [38, 58, 63]. Also, there is no unique understanding and usage of the terms *'Digital Credentials'* and *'Digital Badges'* within the research.

The results reveal *digital badges* as a generic term referring to several terms within that context to cover single courses like micro-credentials, alternative credentials, or a credential for a course within a study program. Further, a combination of several courses refers to nano-degrees, graduation certificates, and digital credentials [57]. Table 2 represents the hierarchical conceptualization of digital badges in higher education institutions.

Table 2. Conceptualization digital badges as morphologic box

Characteristics	Categories						
Degree of Coverage	Single Courses				Combination of Several Courses, Degree		
Content	Digital Credentials	Alternative Credentials	Credentials for a Course within a Study Program	Micro-Credentials	MicroMasters/ Nano-Degrees / MasterTrack / etc.	Graduation Certificate	Record of Achievement/ Learning
Further Specification	Micro-Learning Platform						

The term *digital credential* is in the discussion of the literature partially used for the term digital badges [8, 58]. The keywords of the query on the databases were Digital Credentials and Higher Education but resulted in a high number of contributions referring to digital badges (61 contributions). In conclusion, we consider that digital credentials and digital badges belong somehow together. Consequently, precision in the term of digital credentials is necessary. We understand the term digital credential from a verifier perspective regarding higher education as an umbrella term based on all other terms. The IS literature does not specify verifiable credentials in education but is used in the W3C-context [4]. Due to our focus, we do not further discuss this point.

Subsequently, we confirm the findings [33]. The degree of coverage distinguishes between single courses and a combination of achievements. Single courses refer to digital badges or micro-credentials, while the combination of achievements refers to certificates or digital academic credentials as well as MicroMasters. MicroMasters means that a student completes several MOOCs bundled for this purpose at edX for money and then spends 1–2 semesters at a cooperating university for a full Master's degree [85]. Summing up, a digital badge is always a digital credential, while a digital credential must not necessarily be a digital badge. Table 3 represents the hierarchical conceptualization of the terms in the context of digital credentials in higher education.

Table 3. Conceptualization digital credentials as morphologic box

Characteristics	Categories				
Degree of Coverage	Single Courses			Combination of Lifelong Learning Achievements	
Content	Digital Badges	Micro-Credentials	Certificates	Digital Academic Credentials or Traditional Degrees	MicroMasters / NanoDegrees / MasterTrack / etc.

In conclusion, a digital credential is a general term for digitized versions of a certificate or document representing achieved learning. A digital badge is a sub-term in that context, referring to the reveal of executed learning by specific certificate types like alternative credentials or credentials for a course within a study program. Thus, a digital badge is, in our way, understand as a distinct sign, emblem, token, or mark for a specific learning outcome within the curricula, while a digital credential can be for a whole curriculum such as a Bachelor's degree. Summarizing the study's findings, micro-credentials are mini-certifications within study programs referring to successfully participated courses, while alternative credentials are skill achievements outside the study program. Figure 2 illustrates the delimitation of the relevant terms in the context of HEI study programs.

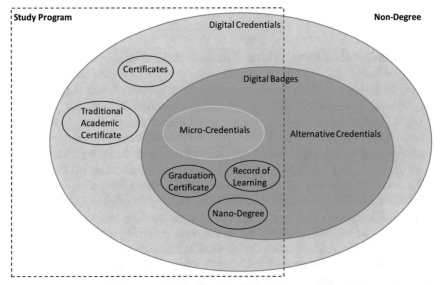

Fig. 2. Delimitation of digital credentials, digital badges, micro-credentials, alternative credentials

Research Spectrum

Moreover, the research spectrums of the research field of digital credentials in higher education vary between the different areas: research on *digital badges* and *micro-credentials* covers a broad research spectrum, while the spectrum of *alternative digital credentials*, *digital credentials*, and *technical applications* is in comparison to these smaller. The category *technical application* includes studies focusing on the usage of digital credentials and their methodological application. Table 4 demonstrates the research contents of the respective areas.

Table 4. Investigated Topics, Gen = Generic, DBa = Digital Badges, ACr = Alternative Credentials, MCr = Micro-Credentials, Tap = Technical Application

Category					
	Gen	**DBa**	**ACr**	**MCr**	**TAp**
Contents	Strategy /Guidelines	Implementation (Open Badges)	Relevance	Implementation	Blockchain Applications
		Use cases		Benefits	
		Benefits (Open Badges)		Provider Overview	
	Blockchain Applications	Implementation Challenges	Implementation	Design Options	Blockchain Applications (Digital Credentials)
	Relevance	Influence on Learning Progress		Application & Evaluation	Blockchain Applications (Digital Badges)

The conceptualization of literature referring to digital credentials in education yields that many contributions refer to digital credentials applications using blockchain, and only a few references to requirements for implementing digital credentials and common knowledge within that context. As a result, a research gap exists referring to shared knowledge and digital credentials requirements.

6   Conclusion, Limitation, and Future Research

Our literature review shows that higher education institutions' digital credentials play a role in several IS research areas, namely blockchain technology, environmental such as ecosystems and platforms, and e-government. Ideas regarding digital credentials are still in the early stages of research. However, digital credentials in higher education have been examined in diverse ways, leaving its broader role ambiguous and underutilized in the IS community. We shed light on the claim of different use of names and build a fundament with a more precise definition for the distinction of digital credentials and digital badges in the IS research field.

Our findings underlie limitations such as the applied databases' regulations and, therefore, the capturing only until august 2019. There may be further contributions referring to digital credentials not covered in our literature review approach. However, our focus was the first exploration of the topic, and in the increasing new stage of the topic *'digital credential',* we will look for whitepapers to analyze this foundation in more detail. In September 2019, the W3C working group "Verifiable claims" renamed to "Verifiable credentials" [86], so in future research, we will focus on the term verifiable credentials in higher education, too.

This study provides a basis for future research on digital credentials in HEIs, as an overview of the status quo in research is still missing. We hope that this collection of studies will provoke IS researchers and strategic management researchers to step up their collaborative efforts and will provide a fruitful foundation to support the next generation of insights around digital credentials in HEIs. The future of digital credentials in higher education is already possible with today's technology; it has to be applicably discovered.

References

1. Jaakkola, H., Aramo-Immonen, H., Henno, J., Mäkelä, J.: The digitalization push in universities. In: 2016 39th International Convention on Information and Communication Technology, Electronics and Microelectronics (MIPRO), pp. 1025–1031 (2016)
2. Hanna, D.E.: Higher education in an era of digital competition: emerging organizational models. J. Asynchron. Learn. Netw. **2**, 66–95 (1998)
3. Brands, S.: A Technical Overview of Digital Credentials (2002)
4. Duffy, K.H., Pongratz, H., Schmidt, J.P.: https://digitalcredentials.mit.edu/wp-content/upl oads/2020/02/white-paper-building-digital-credential-infrastructure-future.pdf
5. Watters, A.: Show me your badge. Campus Technol. Mag. **26**, 8–12 (2012)
6. Gibson, D., Ostashewski, N., Flintoff, K., Grant, S., Knight, E.: Digital badges in education. Educ. Inf. Technol. **20**(2), 403–410 (2013). https://doi.org/10.1007/s10639-013-9291-7
7. Rimland, E., Raish, V.: Micro-credentials and digital badges. Libr. Technol. Rep. **55**, 1–34 (2019)
8. Lim, C.L., Nair, P.K., Keppell, M.J., Hassan, N., Ayub, E.: Developing a framework for the university-wide implementation of micro-credentials and digital badges: a case study from a Malaysian Private University. In: 2018 IEEE 4th International Conference on Computer and Communications (ICCC), pp. 1715–1719 (2018)
9. Matkin, G.W.: Alternative Digital Credentials: An Imperative of Higher Education. Center for Studies in Higher Education, University of California, Berkeley (2018)
10. Mercury, M.T., Schmidt, K.J.: Generation, management, and tracking of digital credentials. In: Office, U.S.P.a.T. (ed.), vol. US 2017/0279614 A1, p. 16. United States (2017)
11. Colle, C., De Capitani, A., Lindroos, K., Maris, A., Virgl, T., Zylka, K.: Gradbase Decentralised Academic Record Verification Using the Bitcoin Blockchain. Imperial College London, London (2015)
12. Hölbl, M., Kamisalić, A., Turkanović, M., Kompara, M., Podgorelec, B., Heričko, M.: EduCTX: an ecosystem for managing digital micro-credentials. In: 2018 28th EAEEIE Annual Conference (EAEEIE), pp. 1–9 (2018)
13. Hope, J.: Issue secure digital credentials using technology behind bitcoin. Success. Regist. **17**, 1–4 (2018)
14. Sharples, M., Domingue, J.: The blockchain and kudos: a distributed system for educational record, reputation and reward. In: Verbert, K., Sharples, M., Klobučar, T. (eds.) EC-TEL 2016. LNCS, vol. 9891, pp. 490–496. Springer, Cham (2016). https://doi.org/10.1007/978-3-319-45153-4_48
15. Turkanović, M., Hölbl, M., Košič, K., Heričko, M., Kamišalić, A.: EduCTX: a blockchain-based higher education credit platform. IEEE Access **6**, 5112–5127 (2018)
16. Webster, J., Watson, R.T.: Analyzing the past to prepare for the future: writing a literature review. MIS Q. **26**, xiii–xxiii (2002)
17. Brocke, J.V., Simons, A., Niehaves, B., Riemer, K., Plattfaut, R., Cleven, A.: Reconstructing the giant: on the importance of rigour in documenting the literature search process. In: ECIS (2009)

18. AACSB: The Disruptive Power of Digital Credentials. BizEd **18**, 11–11 (2019)
19. Bull, B.: Why colleges should support alternative credentials. Chronicle High. Educ. **62**, 12 (2015)
20. Farmer, T., West, R.E.: Opportunities and challenges with digital open badges. Educ. Technol. **56**, 45–48 (2016)
21. Swan, M.: Chapter five – blockchain for business: next-generation enterprise artificial intelligence systems. In: Raj, P., Deka, G.C. (eds.) Advances in Computers, vol. 111, pp. 121–162. Elsevier, New York (2018)
22. Jirgensons, M., Kapenieks, J.: Blockchain and the future of digital learning credential assessment and management. J. Teach. Educ. Sustainability **20**, 145–156 (2018)
23. Kamišalić, A., Turkanović, M., Mrdović, S., Heričko, M.: A preliminary review of blockchain-based solutions in higher education. In: Uden, L., Liberona, D., Sanchez, G., Rodríguez-González, S. (eds.) LTEC 2019. CCIS, vol. 1011, pp. 114–124. Springer, Cham (2019). https://doi.org/10.1007/978-3-030-20798-4_11
24. Arenas, R., Fernandez, P.: CredenceLedger: a permissioned blockchain for verifiable academic credentials. In: 2018 IEEE International Conference on Engineering, Technology and Innovation (ICE/ITMC), pp. 1–6 (2018)
25. Newswire, P.R.: ODEM Issues Blockchain Certificates for Canadian Polytechnic. ODEM.IO-Certificates (2018)
26. Newswire, P.R.: Using Blockchain, New Mexico Community College Becomes First Community College to Issue Student-Owned Digital Diplomas. CNM-BlockchainDiploma (2017)
27. Connolly, B.: Credentials the new 'currency for careers'. CIO (13284045) 1–1 (2015)
28. Lewis, M.J., Lodge, J.M.: Keep calm and credential on: linking learning, life and work practices in a complex world. In: Foundation of Digital Badges and Micro-Credentials: Demonstrating and Recognizing Knowledge and Competencies, pp. 41–54 (2016)
29. Micro-credentials and digital badges. Libr. Technol. Rep. **55**, 1–34 (2019)
30. LaMagna, M.: Placing digital badges and micro-credentials in context. J. Electron. Resour. Librariansh. **29**, 206–210 (2017)
31. Friedler, A.: Teachers training micro-learning innovative model: opportunities and challenges. In: 2018 Learning with MOOCS, LWMOOCS 2018, pp. 63–65 (2018)
32. Parks, R., Parrish, J., Taylor, A.: Creating a digital credential strategy. Coll. Univ. **93**, 71–76 (2018)
33. Newswire, P.R.: Nine universities team up to create global infrastructure for digital academic credentials. MIT-Infrastructure (2019)
34. Newswire, P.R.: Popular digital credentialing platform raises $11.1 million. CREDLY-Funding (2019)
35. Norman, M.: Accessing services with client digital certificates: a short report from the DCOCE project. New Rev. Inf. Netw. **10**, 193–207 (2004)
36. Newby, T.J., Cheng, Z.: Instructional digital badges: effective learning tools. Educ. Tech. Res. Dev. **68**(3), 1053–1067 (2019). https://doi.org/10.1007/s11423-019-09719-7
37. Cheng, Z., Richardson, J.C., Newby, T.J.: Using digital badges as goal-setting facilitators: a multiple case study. J. Comput. High. Educ. **32**(2), 406–428 (2019). https://doi.org/10.1007/s12528-019-09240-z
38. Borras-Gene, O.: Use of digital badges for training in digital skills within higher education (2018)
39. Carey, K.L., Stefaniak, J.E.: An exploration of the utility of digital badging in higher education settings. Educ. Tech. Res. Dev. **66**(5), 1211–1229 (2018). https://doi.org/10.1007/s11423-018-9602-1
40. Cheng, Z., Watson, S.L., Newby, T.J.: Goal setting and open digital badges in higher education. TechTrends **62**(2), 190–196 (2018). https://doi.org/10.1007/s11528-018-0249-x

41. Beattie, S., Jones, W.: The momentum program: digital badges for law students, pp. 45–52 (2018)
42. Hartnett, M.: Digital badges - what is the state of play within the New Zealand Higher Education sector? In: ASCILITE 2018 Conference Proceedings, pp. 390–395 (2018)
43. Shields, R., Chugh, R.: Digital badges – rewards for learning? Educ. Inf. Technol. **22**(4), 1817–1824 (2016). https://doi.org/10.1007/s10639-016-9521-x
44. Crafford, R., Matthee, M.: Implementing open badges for recognition of learning achievements in South African Organization (2016)
45. Abramovich, S.: Understanding digital badges in higher education through assessment. On the Horizon **24**, 126–131 (2016)
46. Hickey, D.T.: Competency-based digital badges and credentials: cautions and potential solutions from the field. In: ICLS (2016)
47. Wilson, B.G., Gasell, C., Ozyer, A., Scrogan, L.: Adopting digital badges in higher education: scoping the territory. In: Foundation of Digital Badges and Micro-Credentials: Demonstrating and Recognizing Knowledge and Competencies, pp. 163–177 (2016)
48. Hamson-Utley, J., Heyman, E.: Implementing a badging system faculty development. In: Foundation of Digital Badges and Micro-Credentials: Demonstrating and Recognizing Knowledge and Competencies, pp. 237–258 (2016)
49. Olneck, M.R.: Whom will digital badges empower? Sociological perspectives on digital badges, pp. 5–11 (2015)
50. McDaniel, R., Fanfarelli, J.R.: How to design experimental research studies around digital badges, pp. 30–35 (2015)
51. Gamrat, C., Zimmerman, H.T.: An online badging system supporting 'educators' STEM learning. In: CEUR Workshop, pp. 12–23 (2015)
52. Elliott, R., Clayton, J., Iwata, J.: Exploring the use of micro-credentialing and digital badges in learning environments to encourage motivation to learn and achieve, pp. 703–707 (2014)
53. Ahn, J., Pellicone, A., Butler, B.S.: Open badges for education: what are the implications at the intersection of open systems and badging? Res. Learn. Technol. **22** (2014)
54. Rughinis, R.: Talkative objects in need of interpretation. Re-thinking digital badges in education. In: CHI 2013 Extended Abstracts on Human Factors in Computing Systems, pp. 2099–2108. ACM, Paris, France (2013)
55. Newswire, P.R.: Blackboard Partners with Mozilla to Support Use of Digital Badges. Blackboard-&-Mozilla (2013)
56. Rimland, E., Raish, V.: Chapter 2: overview, definitions, and benefits. Libr. Technol. Rep. **55**, 7–8 (2019)
57. Bradley, P.: Digital badging is growing, but employers remain wary. Commun. Coll. Week **28**, 39–40 (2016)
58. Alliance for Excellent Education, Mozilla, F.: Expanding Education and Workforce Opportunities through Digital Badges. Alliance for Excellent Education (2013)
59. Eaton, A., Rennie Center for Education, R., Policy: Expanding the Boundaries of Education: Two 'Cities' Efforts to Credential Real-World Skills through Digital Badges. Rennie Center for Education Research & Policy (2019)
60. Newswire, P.R.: IACET Announces Partnership with Badgr for the Open Digital Badge Experience Course. IACET-Badgr-Course (2019)
61. Hartman, K.B., Andzulis, J.: Industry-based certificates: student perceptions of benefits. Res. High. Educ. J. **36** (2019)
62. DiSalvio, P.: New pathways to credentialing: the digital badge. New Engl. J. High. Educ. (2016)
63. Sullivan, A.L.: Open Badges and Student Motivation: A Study of Their Relationship to Student Assessment Scores. ProQuest LLC (2018)

64. Fanfarelli, J., Vie, S., McDaniel, R.: Understanding digital badges through feedback, reward, and narrative: a multidisciplinary approach to building better badges in social environments. Commun. Des. Q. Rev. **3**, 56–60 (2015)
65. Buchem, I.: Design patterns for digital competency credentials based on open badges in the context of virtual mobility In: DeLFI Workshops 2018 (2018)
66. Gibson, D., Coleman, K., Irving, L.: Badging digital pathways of learning. In: ASCILITE-Australasian Society for Computers in Learning and Tertiary Education, Conference Proceedings 2019, pp. 440–444 (2019)
67. Brauer, S., Siklander, P.: Competence-based assessment and digital badging as guidance in vocational teacher education, pp. 191–196 (2019)
68. Virkus, S.: The use of Open Badges in library and information science education in Estonia. Educ. Inf. **35**, 155–172 (2019)
69. Peck, K., Bowen, K., Rimland, E., Oberdick, J.: Badging as micro-credentialing in formal education and informal education. In: Digital Badges in Education: Trends, Issues, and Cases, pp. 82–92 (2016)
70. Fedock, B., Kebritchi, M., Sanders, R., Holland, A.: Digital badges and micro-credentials: digital age classroom practices, design strategies, and issues. In: Foundation of Digital Badges and Micro-Credentials: Demonstrating and Recognizing Knowledge and Competencies, pp. 273–286 (2016)
71. Ellis, L.E., Nunn, S.G., Avella, J.T.: Digital badges and micro-credentials: Historical overview, motivational aspects, issues, and challenges. In: Foundation of Digital Badges and Micro-Credentials: Demonstrating and Recognizing Knowledge and Competencies, pp. 3–21 (2016)
72. Ifenthaler, D., West, D., Flintoff, K., Lodge, J., Gibson, D., Beattie, S., et al.: Moving forward with digital badges. In: ASCILITE 2016, pp. 275–277 (2016)
73. Mah, D.K., Bellin-Mularski, N., Ifenthaler, D.: Foundation of digital badges and micro-credentials: demonstrating and recognizing knowledge and competencies (2016)
74. Diamond, J., Gonzalez, P.C.: Digital badges for professional development: Teachers' perceptions of the value of a new credentialing currency. In: Foundation of Digital Badges and Micro-Credentials: Demonstrating and Recognizing Knowledge and Competencies, pp. 391–409 (2016)
75. Carey, K.: Show me your badge. N.Y. Times **162**, 28 (2012)
76. Balci, S., Secaur, J.M., Morris, B.J.: The effectiveness of gamification tools in enhancing academic performance and motivation of students in fully vs. partially gamified grading system of online classes. In: Proceedings of the Technology, Mind, and Society, p. 1. ACM, Washington, DC, USA (2018)
77. Grech, A., Camilleri, A.F.: Blockchain in Education. Publications Office of the European Union, Luxembourg (2017)
78. Kazakzeh, S., Ayoubi, E., Muslmani, B.K., Qasaimeh, M., Al-Fayoumi, M.: Framework for blockchain deployment: the case of educational systems. In: 2019 2nd International Conference on new Trends in Computing Sciences (ICTCS), pp. 1–9 (2019)
79. Oyelere, S., Tomczyk, Ł., Bouali, N., Joseph, A.F.: Blockchain technology and gamification – conditions and opportunities for education. In: Proceedings of the 8th International Adult Education Conference, Prague (2019)
80. Yeasmin, S., Baig, A.: Unblocking the potential of blockchain. In: 2019 International Conference on Electrical and Computing Technologies and Applications (ICECTA), pp. 1–5 (2019)
81. Haugsbakken, H., Langseth, I.: The blockchain challenge for higher education institutions. Eur. J. Educ. **2**, 41–46 (2019)
82. Alammary, A., Alhazmi, S., Almasri, M., Gillani, S.: Blockchain-based applications in education: a systematic review. Appl. Sci. **9**(12), 2400 (2019). https://doi.org/10.3390/app912 2400

83. Bitcoin   Magazine.   https://www.nasdaq.com/articles/cardano-blockchains-first-use-case-proof-university-diplomas-greece-2018-01-02
84. Campus Technology. https://campustechnology.com/articles/2018/06/11/southern-new-ham pshire-u-issues-blockchain-credentials-to-college-for-america-grads.aspx
85. edx: MicroMasters Trademark Guidelines. edx (2019)
86. W3C. https://www.w3.org/2017/vc/WG/

A Theory-Driven Design Science Research Approach Towards Gamified Videos in Digital Learning

Dennis Benner[(✉)] and Sofia Schöbel

University of Kassel, Information Systems, Kassel, Germany
{dennis.benner,sofia.schoebel}@uni-kassel.de

Abstract. Digitalization has opened new opportunities but also brought new challenges such as lower engagement of students in online training. Especially learning videos need to be changed in their design and structure to make them more engaging for users. So far, overarching design principles are missing that support the development of gamified learning videos. In our research-in-progress paper, we present an overarching approach on how to develop meaningful gamified learning videos. With our design science research approach, we plan to derive design principles and design features from our state-of-the-art design requirements. Additionally, we will conduct a field experiment to put our theoretical contributions to test and gather practical insights. Our research contributes to theory by clarifying how and why gamified videos can support better learning. In the long run, practical contributions can be given to developers about how to construct gamified learning videos.

Keywords: Gamified videos · Design · Learning · Engagement · Motivation

1 Introduction

Adapting learning techniques for the digital age is a challenge for individuals and organizations. This challenge may emerge due to technological changes, new policies or other disruptive factors. For students and universities this poses significant problems that need to be overcome. Technology-mediated learning (TML) offers tools that potentially can solve those issues [1, 2]. TML combines the advantages of synchronous (i.e., face-to-face) and asynchronous (i.e., technology-based) learning approaches [3]. Videos are one technology-based component of TML for educational purposes. Designing learning videos is a challenge on its own since bad design can demotivate students. Nowadays, videos are a well-established instrument in education [4] and have proven to be an effective tool [5]. In fact, studies have shown that many students prefer videos as learning material [6] and 47% of students use platforms like YouTube for their learning activities [7]. Because of the high effectiveness and acceptance of learning videos, continuous growth in learning videos can be observed [8]. Especially in the current times of the global COVID-19 crisis, online learning applications including the use of video content may become even more popular and offer the means to overcome the disruption in the educational systems [9].

Regardless, videos in learning most often fail to engage and motivate students if they are designed badly [10]. A prime example of this are long-winded and pre-recorded classroom lectures that effectively fail to engage and motivate students [10]. Therefore, it is important to address this potential issue by design to support the engagement and motivation of students, as both are critical factors for the learning success and well-being of students [11, 12]. Engaging and motivating students to pay more attention to videos they are learning with can happen by referring to gamification [13]. Gamification has been implemented successfully in many learning contexts before (i.e., [14, 15]). One successful example of gamified learning includes distance learning (e.g., e-learning), where gamification improves student interaction and learning experience [16, 17]. While both gamification and videos have been successfully used in e-learning applications on their own, details about applying gamification directly to learning videos remains yet to be explored as literature on this topic is virtually nonexistent. In order to create a first gamified video prototype and study its effects on student engagement, motivation and learning success, some guidance is recommended. Therefore, we use a DSR approach and start with formulating requirements on which we will base our DSR artifact [18]. Accordingly, gamified videos offer a twofold research opportunity regarding the design requirements as well as the potential effects on digitalized learning. Consequently, with this research-in-progress paper we demonstrate an approach of how we will develop and evaluate gamified learning videos and formulate the following research questions (RQ):

RQ1: What are design requirements for designing gamified videos in learning?
RQ2: What are the challenges of using gamification concepts for this type of media?

To answer the research questions, we propose a research approach based on Design Science Research (DSR) [19, 20]. We start by conducting a systematic literature analysis. Next, we derive design requirements from the literature, which refer to theories found in the literature. To support theory, we plan to conduct focus groups and workshops with stakeholders (e.g., students and tutors) at a university to gain practical insights. Using both theoretical knowledge and practical insights, we then plan to develop a first gamified video prototype that we plan to deploy in a real-world setting (i.e., university course with approximately 300 bachelor students). The main contribution of this research-in-progress paper is to provide an overview about our overall research approach for the development, analysis and evaluation of gamified learning videos. Overall, we hope that both theoretical researchers and practitioners will be able to draw from our planned contribution as we will demonstrate requirements about how to design gamified learning videos.

2   Theoretical Background

2.1   Gamified Learning

Learning with technology enables learning from anywhere and at any time, thus providing higher autonomy [21]. The increasing number of interdisciplinary programs leads to different kinds of learning situations that can be handled more effectively by using gamification [21]. Hence, gamification is a possible approach to motivate and engage users to use systems more regularly and conduct more in-depth learning by supporting their motivation. Hence, gamified learning and the use of gamified videos in learning has two purposes. The first is to encourage desired learning behavior. The second is to engage the users in learning using learning materials such as tutorials, digital documents or learning videos. Therefore, engagement has been proven to be positively correlated with the outcomes of user success, such as user satisfaction and academic achievements [22, 23]. Accordingly, gamification increases the motivation of users by providing different game design elements [24], by making an activity or task more fun and engaging and by encouraging exchange between users.

2.2 Fundamentals for Gamified Learning Videos

In general, gamification is an umbrella term that can be considered as the application of game design elements to a non-game context in order to motivate and engage users [25, 26]. However, the term can also be defined as a process of enhancing services, like learning videos, with motivational affordances to invoke gameful experiences and support desired behavioral outcomes [26]. Gamification essentially contains three components, namely motivational affordances, psychological outcomes and behavioral outcomes [26]. To combine the definitions stated above and to align them to the use of learning videos, we define gamification as the use of game design elements in learning contexts with the intention to increase a student's motivation and engagement.

All along one component is important when designing a gamified application and creating gamified videos for learning – game design elements. Generally, game design elements can be divided into certain groups by referring to the MDA Framework [27]. This framework suggests that game elements can be categorized as mechanics, dynamics or aesthetics, whereas game mechanics are those that can be worked with and designed for a gamified video [27]. Mechanics are the functioning components of a game that grant the designer ultimate control over the levers of the game so that the designer is able to guide the actions of the user [28]. Dynamics, on the other hand, are described as the player's interactions with mechanics. They determine what each player is doing in response to the mechanics of the system. Finally, aesthetics describes the emotional responses evoked in the individual while interacting with the game system.

To implement gamification, game design elements are used. In our study we refer to the taxonomy of game design elements introduced by Schöbel et al. [24]. The taxonomy classifies game design elements (attributes) like points, badges and levels according to the general categories representing the mechanic behind each game design element. For example, the mechanic *progress* refers to the game design elements *level* and *progress bar*, whereas *points* and *badges* represent *rewards*. Schöbel et al. [24] present the *feedback* game design element, which refers to *guidance* including visual cues. However, we also include non-visual representations in our study, as visual implementations like avatars may distract students from already visual media (i.e., videos). Instead, we will focus on easy to implement elements like, for example, points, badges, levels or textual feedback, depending on the findings of our literature review. Game design elements like time manipulation can be a difficult game mechanic to integrate. Because our intended content is of educational nature, the content itself can already introduce a significant cognitive load on the users [29]. Thus, introducing time manipulation can cause cognitive overload and create a negative experience.

Because gamified videos are a novel concept, there is no literature that we can directly derive integrations or applications of game mechanics from. Therefore, we refer to common uses of game mechanics that are not necessarily academic. For example, the learning platform Duolingo employs user-set goals to motivate students to follow their learning schedule. Another example is the popular streaming platform Twitch.tv, where viewers gain points for view time.

3   Methodology and Status Quo

This research-in-progress paper presents a DSR [19, 20] approach towards gamified videos. We base our research design on a well-regarded framework for DSR projects in the information systems research domain [30, 31], as illustrated in Fig. 1. Part of our research is the review of literature. Therefore, we adopt the literature review methods as suggested by Cooper [32] as well as Webster and Watson [33].

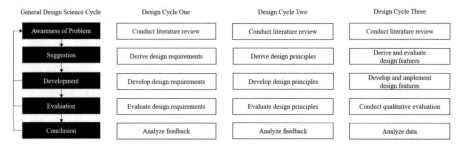

Fig. 1. DSR agenda towards gamified learning videos

Because of the nature of our approach, we focus on the applied theories or practices and applications (i.e., implementations) of gamified video material or environments, as the study closely relates gamification and video content. The goal of our review is to integrate the findings into our design requirements, which we then translate into design principles and eventually a feature that we will implement in our artifact. Since our gamified video approach is novel, we chose an exhaustive coverage for our literature review to gather as much input material as possible and provide overview that is as comprehensive as possible. Lastly, the organization of our literature review focuses on the concepts and methods used in the considered studies. As for the search process, we search ACM, AISeL, IEEEXplore, JSTOR, SSRN, ScienceDirect and SpringerLink, where we consider only peer-reviewed articles. For the database search we used a combination of the following keywords: gamification, learning videos, education and videos. We used wildcards whenever possible and adapted our search to the properties of each database. We then conduct a forward and backward search as introduced by Webster and Watson [33] with no restrictions, which allows us to expand our horizon and include non-scientific sources. Overall, we identified 1569 potentially relevant papers during the database search. After analyzing abstract and title, we kept 35 papers which we then examined in detail. The preliminary results of the literature analysis suggest a research gap for gamified learning videos. We can observe that literature about learning videos and gamification in learning focuses on three major theories: Self-Determination Theory [34, 35], the MDA framework [27] and the ARCS model [36, 37]. Moreover, all studies have in common that they try to support either the motivation or the engagement of students, some address both factors. As for the gamification elements, we find an array of elements being used, with points (e.g., [38–40]) and feedback (e.g., [15, 41, 42]) being used the most. However, we did not find a single study that included time constraint as a game element. Consequently, we will base our design requirements on these three major theories and focus on feedback and points as game design elements. Interestingly, the latter is already being used in real-world applications such as Twitch.tv, which gives points to users based on the amount of content consumed. Nevertheless, we have to acknowledge that due to the nature of the media (i.e., video content) some gamification elements may be hard or impossible to apply. We therefore will conduct a workshop with stakeholders including tutors and students at a university during future DSR cycles to find viable design elements that can be translated to a practical artifact.

4   Next Steps and Expected Contributions

For the next DSR cycle we plan to extend our literature review into neighboring disciplines and also include a more comprehensive media survey. Thereto we will extend our literature scope to interactive learning videos and studies that focus on gamifying the environment. Additionally, we plan to conduct focus groups and workshops with relevant stakeholders using design thinking [43, 44] methods to further support our theory-derived design requirements. In the second design cycle we then translate our developed design requirements into design principles that we will evaluate with relevant stakeholders. The third design cycle then aims to implement our developed design principles into a first prototype artifact of a gamified learning video that we will integrate in an online learning course at a university. The course will be targeted at a large audience of bachelor students; participation will be voluntary to prevent utilitarian motives behind using our gamified learning videos from the students' perspective. Results will be evaluated with quantitative methods to measure the effects of gamified learning videos on the academic success via a short examination, while motivation and engagement as well as the well-being of students are tested using a questionnaire. The field experiment will be designed as an A/B test. Overall, our research contributes to the design knowledge of digital learning by determining how and why gamified learning videos can support better learning outcomes. In this regard, we also highlight potential difficulties that are rooted in the nature of the media that we will address in-depth in future research. We hope researchers and practitioners will draw on our contributions to improve learning in the digital age by designing and developing gamified learning videos. Nevertheless, we also acknowledge the challenges we face due to the nature of video as media and the limitations rooted in our context (university online course) as well as our chosen methods and literature review.

References

1. Ally, M., Tsinakos, A.: Increasing access through mobile learning. Commonwealth Learn. (2014)
2. Gupta, S., Bostrom, R.: Technology-mediated learning: a comprehensive theoretical model. J. Assoc. Inf. Syst. **10**, 686–714 (2009)
3. Bitzer, P., Janson, A.: Towards a holistic understanding of technology-mediated learning services – a state-of-the-art analysis. In: European Conference on Information Systems (ECIS) (2014)
4. Brame, C.J.: Effective educational videos: principles and guidelines for maximizing student learning from video content. CBE Life Sci. Educ. **15**(4), es6 (2016). https://doi.org/10.1187/cbe.16-03-0125
5. Kay, R.H.: Exploring the use of video podcasts in education: a comprehensive review of the literature. Comput. Hum. Behav. **28**, 820–831 (2012)
6. Steinbeck, H., Matthiessen, J., Vladova, G.: Student learning behaviour in the digital age. In: International Conference on Information Systems (ICIS) (2019)
7. RfkB: Jugend/YouTube/Kulturelle Bildung. Horizont 2019. Studie: Eine repräsentative Umfrage unter 12- bis 19-jährigen zur Nutzung kultureller Bildungsangebote an digitalen Kulturorten
8. Hefter, M.H., Berthold, K.: Preparing learners to self-explain video examples: text or video introduction? Comput. Hum. Behav. **110**, 106404 (2020). https://doi.org/10.1016/j.chb.2020.106404
9. European Commission: Coronavirus: Online Learning Resources – Education and Training – European Commission. https://ec.europa.eu/education/resources-and-tools/coronavirus-online-learning-resources_en
10. Guo, P.J., Kim, J., Rubin, R.: How video production affects student engagement. In: Sahami, M. (ed.) Proceedings of the First ACM Conference on Learning Scale Conference, pp. 41–50. ACM, New York (2014)
11. Ryan, R.M., Deci, E.L.: Facilitating and hindering motivation, learning, and well-being in schools. Research and observation from self-determination theory. In: Wentzel, K.R., Wigfield, A. (eds.) Handbook of Motivation at School, vol. 2, pp. 96–117. Routledge, New York, London (2016)
12. de Barba, P.G., Kennedy, G.E., Ainley, M.D.: The role of students' motivation and participation in predicting performance in a MOOC. J. Comput. Assist. Learn. **32**, 218–231 (2016)
13. Thiebes, S., Lins, S., Basten, D.: Gamifying information systems – a synthesis of gamification mechanics and dynamics. In: Proceedings of the European Conference on Information Systems (ECIS) (2014)
14. Schöbel, S., Janson, A., Ernst, S.-J., Leimeister, J.M.: How to gamify a mobile learning application – a modularization approach. In: Thirty Eighth International Conference on Information Systems, pp. 1–12 (2017)
15. Schneider, T., Janson, A., Schöbel, S.: Understanding the effects of gamified feedback in mobile learning – an experimental investigation. In: Thirty Ninth International Conference on Information Systems (2018)
16. Ferianda, R., Herdiani, A., Sardi, I.L.: Increasing students interaction in distance education using gamification. In: 2018 6th International Conference on Information and Communication Technology (ICoICT), pp. 125–129 (2018)
17. Domínguez, A., Saenz-de-Navarrete, J., de-Marcos, L., Fernández-Sanz, L., Pagés, C., Martínez-Herráiz, J.-J.: Gamifying learning experiences. Practical implications and outcomes. Comput. Educ. **63** 380–392 (2013)

18. Hevner, A.R., March, S.T., Park, J., Ram, S.: Design science in information systems research. MIS Q. **28**, 75–105 (2004)
19. Hevner, A.R.: A three cycle view of design science research. Scand. J. Inf. Syst. **19**, 87–92 (2007)
20. Peffers, K., Tuunanen, T., Rothenberger, M.A., Chatterjee, S.: A design science research methodology for information systems research. J. Manag. Inf. Syst. **24**, 45–77 (2007)
21. Urh, M., Vukovic, G., Jereb, E., Pintar, R.: The model for introduction of gamification into e-learning in higher education. Procedia Soc. Behav. Sci. **197**, 388–397 (2015)
22. Ibanez, M.-B., Di-Serio, A., Delgado-Kloos, C.: Gamification for engaging computer science students in learning activities: a case study. IEEE Trans. Learning Technol. **7**, 291–301 (2014)
23. Hanus, M.D., Fox, J.: Assessing the effects of gamification in the classroom: a longitudinal study on intrinsic motivation, social comparison, satisfaction, effort, and academic performance. Comput. Educ. **80**, 152–161 (2015)
24. Schöbel, S., Ernst, S.-J., Söllner, M., Leimeister, J.M.: More than the sum of its parts – towards identifying preferred game design element combinations in learning management systems. Short paper. In: International Conference on Information Systems (2017)
25. Deterding, S., Dixon, D., Khaled, R., Nacke, L.: From game design elements to gamefulness: defining "gamification". In: Proceedings of the 15th International Academic MindTrek Conference Envisioning Future Media Environments, pp. 9–15 (2011)
26. Hamari, J., Koivisto, J., Sarsa, H.: Does gamification work? A literature review of empirical studies on gamification. In: 2014 47th Hawaii International Conference on System Sciences, pp. 3025–3034. IEEE (2014)
27. Hunicke, R., LeBlanc, M., Zubek, R.: MDA: A formal approach to game design and game research. In: Proceedings of the AAAI Workshop on Challenges in Game AI, 4, pp. 1722–1726 (2004)
28. Zichermann, G., Cunningham, C.: Gamification by design. Implementing Game Mechanics In Web And Mobile Apps. O'Reilly, Beijing (2011)
29. Chandler, P., Sweller, J.: Cognitive load theory and the format of instruction. Cogn. Instr. **8**, 293–332 (1991)
30. Kuechler, W., Vaishnavi, V.: The emergence of design research in information systems in North America. JDR **7**, 1–16 (2008)
31. Kuechler, B., Vaishnavi, V.: On theory development in design science research: anatomy of a research project. Eur. J. Inf. Syst. **17**, 489–504 (2008)
32. Cooper, H.M.: Organizing knowledge syntheses: a taxonomy of literature reviews. Knowl. Soc. **1**, 104–126 (1988)
33. Webster, J., Watson, R.T.: Analyzing the past to prepare for the future: writing a literature review. MIS Q. 13–21 (2002)
34. Deci, E.L., Ryan, R.M.: Self-determination theory: a macrotheory of human motivation, development, and health. Can. Psychol. **49**, 182–185 (2008)
35. Deci, E.L., Ryan, R.M.: The general causality orientations scale: self-determination in personality. J. Res. Pers. **19**(2), 109–134 (1985). https://doi.org/10.1016/0092-6566(85)900 23-6
36. Keller, J.M.: Development and use of the ARCS model of instructional design. J. Instr. Dev. **10**, 2–10 (1987)
37. Li, K., Keller, J.M.: Use of the ARCS model in education: a literature review. Comput. Educ. **122**, 54–62 (2018)
38. Coccoli, M., Iacono, S., Vercelli, G.: Applying gamification techniques to enhance the effectiveness of video-lessons. J. e-Learn. Knowl. Soc. **11**, 73–84 (2015)
39. Kleftodimos, A., Evangelidis, G.: Augmenting educational videos with interactive exercises and knowledge testing games. In: Proceedings of 2018 IEEE Global Engineering Education Conference (EDUCON), pp. 872–877 (2018)

40. Lee, H., Doh, Y.Y.: A study on the relationship between educational achievement and emotional engagement in a gameful interface for video lecture systems. In: 2012 International Symposium on Ubiquitous Virtual Reality, pp. 34–37. IEEE (2012)
41. Zhu, Y., Pei, L., Shang, J.: Improving video engagement by gamification: a proposed design of MOOC videos. In: Cheung, S.K.S., Kwok, L.-F., Ma, W.W.K., Lee, L.-K., Yang, H. (eds.) ICBL 2017. LNCS, vol. 10309, pp. 433–444. Springer, Cham (2017). https://doi.org/10.1007/978-3-319-59360-9_38
42. Kokkinaki, A.I., Christoforos, A., Melanthiou, Y.: Integrating open educational resources to foster serious games and gamification design principles. In: Mediterranean Conference on Information Systems (MCIS) (2015)
43. The Field Guide to Human-Centered Design. Design Kit. IDEO, San Francisco, CA (2015)
44. Villegas, E., Labrador, E., Fonseca, D., Fernández-Guinea, S., Moreira, F.: Design thinking and gamification: user centered methodologies. In: Zaphiris, P., Ioannou, A. (eds.) HCII 2019. LNCS, vol. 11590, pp. 115–124. Springer, Cham (2019). https://doi.org/10.1007/978-3-030-21814-0_10

A Methodology to Enhance Learning Processes with Augmented Reality Glasses

Tobias Dreesbach[1]([⊠]), Matthias Berg[2], Henning Gösling[1], Tobias Walter[2], Oliver Thomas[1], and Julia Knopf[2]

[1] German Research Center for Artificial Intelligence (DFKI), Smart Enterprise Engineering, Osnabrück, Germany
{tobias.dreesbach,henning.goesling,oliver.thomas}@dfki.de
[2] Forschungsinstitut Bildung Digital (FoBiD), Saarland University, Saarbrücken, Germany
{matthias.berg,tobias.walter,julia.knopf}@fobid.org

Abstract. Although Augmented Reality (AR) encourages self-managed learning and enhances the learner's reflection only few companies and schools use AR glasses in vocational training. In our research project we aim to support the dissemination of AR and speed up the augmentation of existing learning processes. But we did not come across methodologies for transferring a conventional learning processes into learning processes for AR Glasses. Therefore, we developed a methodology to enhance conventional learning processes with AR glasses by supporting the creation of AR enrichments for the individual process steps. We describe a use case of an electro engineering lesson that is enriched with AR elements using our methodology.

Keywords: Augmented reality glasses · Learning process · Methodology

1 Introduction

With Augmented Reality (AR), virtual 3D objects are integrated into a real environment in real time [1]. AR learning experiences enhance learning gains as well as motivation and help students to perform learning activities [2, 3]. AR glasses capture the environment and integrate virtual elements in the user's field of view. Areas of application include a wide range of topics, target groups and academic levels [4]. Several research projects target the field of AR in vocational training, e.g. [5, 6]. AR in vocational training encourages self-managed learning for direct instructions and enhances the reflection of the learners in task-oriented settings [7]. However, just a small number of the surveyed companies in a recent study use AR glasses in their vocational training [8]. Main concerns according to [9] are social consequences, privacy, security and a missing added value. To spread the use of AR in vocational training, we propose a methodology for the conversion of conventional learning processes into AR-based learning processes that takes the technical limitations of AR glasses into account. More precisely, with our methodology we want to ease and speed up the conversion of learning processes to AR-based learning processes. We aim to encourage the didactical use of AR glasses in learning settings so that more students can experience AR glasses with their potentials [7]. Beyond that our research provides suggestions to people who are not familiar with the implementation of AR applications. A few methodologies for the integration of AR devices in specific domains can already be found in the literature. For example, for the integration of AR into an intralogistics context [10] and into an Industry 4.0 context [11]. In the field of education, [12] proposed a methodology consisting of three steps to integrate AR devices into practical learning processes in an industrial environment: (1) A process analysis using the Business Process Model and Notation (BPMN) as the modelling language for the documentation of the conventional learning process. (2) Definition of process types and their AR potential. (3) Identification of the suitable AR device (tablet, smartphone, smart glasses) for each process type and implementation of an application for the AR-based training. A methodology for how to use AR glasses to improve the vocational training is given by [13]. They provide a list of design elements to exploit AR and wearable sensors for training purposes, e.g. with augmented paths to guide the trainee's motions or interactive virtual objects. For some of the design elements the expert's performance is captured in a certain process step with sensors and the trainees use AR glasses to project the captured data into their field of view. As we did not come across an established methodology to enhance existing conventional learning processes with AR glasses, we examined our research with the following research question: *Which steps are necessary to enhance a conventional learning process with AR glasses?*

In our ongoing research project, we evaluate the methodology regarding four technical use cases – one of those from a metalworking company we present in this paper.

2 Development of the Methodology

In our research project we identified the problem of a missing structured approach to convert conventional learning processes into AR-based processes. Therefore we used the design science research methodology (DSRM) proposed by [14] to enhance learning processes with AR glasses by supporting the creation of AR enrichments for the individual process steps. We used the DSRM, because it provides well-established guidelines for research in information systems and helps us to insure the relevance and effectiveness of our research output. The DSRM includes six steps, as shown in Fig. 1. We identified the problem (step 1) when we documented four processes in a technical training with BPMN to convert them to AR-based learning processes: (1) the operation of a milling machine, (2) the assembly of a two-way circuit, (3) an air conditioner, and (4) the programming of a servomotor. We decided to (step 2) develop a methodology for creating and adapting AR elements to the individual process steps after we scrutinized the BPMN models. In a literature review we identified applicable methodologies for the integration of AR devices in educational processes. For the design and development (step 3), we interviewed nine teachers and trainers in the field of vocational training about the didactic theory behind the use cases. We created a didactical and technical concept out of the results and applied the concepts to the learning processes. We are now implementing a prototype for AR glasses (step 4) covering the elicited use cases. During the evaluation (step 5), we will iterate back to compare our initial objectives to the actual observed results and to improve the effectiveness of our knowledge contribution [14]. We will evaluate our methodology by conducting a summative test [15] where we will measure the effects of the AR-based learning processes. A case study with students will be performed as well as expert interviews with teachers and trainers.

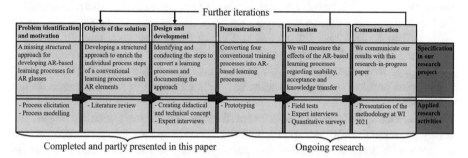

Fig. 1. Applied design science research method adopted from [14]

We divided our methodology in five consecutive steps:

1. Process analysis. An analysis of the problem statement is recommended. The inspection of the actual process and its environment provides an uniform understanding of the process [10]. Involved participants depend on the learning process and can have multiple roles which are the process owners (like teachers, trainers, foremen), didactic experts, students, trainees, AR experts, developers, and a project manager. The process owners make suggestions for the process selection and explain the process activities. All teaching materials are reviewed by the participants, and a shadowing approach is used during a learning session to observe possible failures and deviations regarding the optimal process. A process model is prepared to document the recorded process and its subprocesses. We suggest BPMN as the modelling language similar to [10] and [12]. Finally, the documented BPMN process is discussed with the process owners to confirm the correctness and completeness.

2. AR element selection. If the BPMN model is complete and consistent, all process steps in the BPMN model are evaluated regarding their potential for an AR enrichment. AR elements can be bound to the world to stay at the same position as the user moves around. They can also be bound to the user's device so that they are persistently available but not in a distracting manner. A wide range of AR elements to enrich a process is already discussed in the literature. Some examples for generic elements are: pictures, videos, explosion diagrams, X-ray visuals to uncover hidden structures and assisting visual aids like arrows as well as guideline and highlight elements [16]. For a wide range of AR elements [13] present how to use them for industrial training. Sometimes markers are needed to anchor the position of virtual objects to the real world. Moreover, a combination of the AR elements can increase the context sensitivity. While the AR experts present suggestions for possible AR elements, the process owners and didactic experts including the teachers and trainers express their demands and evaluate the AR element's didactical value for the individual process steps. The role of the developers is to give feedback regarding the technical feasibility based on a shortlist of AR devices.

If all participants agree to the selection, the project manager adds the AR elements as comments to the BPMN process steps. When the elements are not sufficient to support the process step new elements must be created.

3. Creation of new AR elements. When the process requires the development of new AR elements, the need of improvement for a process step and the underlying didactical concept is discussed between all participants and requirements are defined. Ideas for suitable realizations can also be suggested from all participants. In consideration of the didactical concept, the AR experts and the developers propose technical feasible and context-sensitive AR elements to enrich the process step and get feedback for it. If possible, a generic structure of the AR elements is preferred to reduce the effort. Generic elements can be reused with new content and combined with other AR elements in further process steps.

4. Clarification of the process concept. If all process steps are enriched, the project manager transfers the BPMN model with the AR enrichments into a detailed process concept which is provided to all participants. The concept contains a list of all process steps and their AR enrichment. It documents the demands of all participants and summarizes the results of the technical feasibility. A visual mock-up for the AR elements can be added to the concept.

5. Effort and feasibility review. In the last stage of our methodology the results are evaluated in a group discussion between all project participants. If problems in the concept are detected or demands are not fulfilled the process concept is adapted. The AR experts and developers select AR glasses based on the requirements and the predefined shortlist. After the successful evaluation, the implementation begins.

3   Methodology Application for a Technical Learning Session

In one of our use cases, recorded in a metalworking company, basic knowledge and skills in the field of electrical engineering are imparted during the construction of a multiway switching with one light bulb and two light switches. First, the trainees receive an instruction and theoretical background in the field of electrical engineering and must draw a circuit diagram. In a following practical part, they assemble the circuit based on their plan and check its functionality on a test stand. The assembly sequence is not prescribed. By acting independently in an authentic situation, new knowledge structures are supported which, according to the principles of situated learning, prevent inert knowledge [17]. For the application of our methodology we documented the process using a BPMN model, reviewed all teaching materials, and used a shadowing approach during a session to observe deviations regarding the optimal process. Since our documented BPMN process was discussed with the process owners we continued with the second step of our methodology. The AR experts of our project suggested AR enrichments for most steps of the process model by combining AR elements that were known from the literature and presented it to the process owners and didactical experts. The AR elements included text elements, pictures, and videos for the explanation of the process steps, checklists to support the self-management of the students and trainees, buttons to select working tasks and confirm their completion, a progress bar, a timer, and three-dimensional arrows to highlight physical artifacts within the physical location. QR codes were suggested to anchor the AR elements within a workplace like in other AR applications [18]. In the following discussion among all participants of our multidisciplinary team we worked out that the AR elements are sufficient for most process steps but additionally individual AR elements are required to support situated learning scenarios in the respective learning occupations – basically when a step was interactive, context-sensitive, collaborative, or strongly domain specific. In the third methodology step the required individual elements were developed. A challenging task was to check the accurate setup of the electrical parts and the wiring because the AR devices cannot interpret human actions during the assembly. The participants discussed the technical limitations of object detection and pattern recognition and, as a result, the process steps were enhanced with multiple choice queries, drag-and-drop matching tasks, and a questionnaire for the self-reflection if a task was successfully performed. During our fourth methodology step the enriched process was continuously updated in our process concept and reviewed by the process owners. We suggest adding value to the process concept by using mock-ups, which, in our use case, helped all participants to achieve a common understanding of the AR elements. A positive indicator of our methodology is that in the last step, the effort and feasibility review, no serious complications were detected.

4   Conclusion and Outlook

In this paper we present a methodology to enhance conventional learning processes with AR glasses by supporting the creation of AR enrichments for the individual process steps. Our methodology is based on five steps: process analysis, AR element selection, creation of new AR elements, clarification of the process concept, and effort and feasibility review. We present the application of the methodology for a learning process in an electrical engineering lesson. Due to the domain of our four use cases the methodology is so far limited to vocational training processes. In the current section of our research project we are implementing the AR elements for the use cases. We are in the first iteration of the DSRM and the evaluation of our implemented AR elements will start soon by measuring the didactical effects of our AR-based learning processes. A case study will be conducted to test the effectiveness of our methodology where two groups of trainees perform the learning process either with or without the AR Glasses while we measure their learning outcomes. Moreover, we will enrich more learning processes with our project partners to validate the efficiency of our methodology.

Acknowledgements. This Paper is accrued as part of the research project AdEPT (FKZ: 01PV18008E). The project is fostered from Federal Ministry of Education and Research (BMBF). We thank for the support enabled through that project.

References

1. Azuma, R.T.: A survey of augmented reality. Teleoperators Virtual Environ. **6**, 355–385 (1997)
2. Thomas, O., Metzger, D., Niegemann, H..: Digitalisierung in der Aus- und Weiterbildung. Springer Gabler, Berlin (2018)

3. Ibáñez, M.-B., Delgado-Kloos, C.: Augmented reality for STEM learning: a systematic review. Comput. Educ. **123**, 109–123 (2018)
4. Garzón, J., Pavón, J., Baldiris, S.: Systematic review and meta-analysis of augmented reality in educational settings. Virtual Real. **23**(4), 447–459 (2019). https://doi.org/10.1007/s10055-019-00379-9
5. Limbu, B.: WEKIT Framework & Training Methodology. Technical report (2019)
6. Utzig, S., Kaps, R., Azeem, S.M., Gerndt, A.: Augmented reality for remote collaboration in aircraft maintenance tasks. In: IEEE Aerospace Conference, pp. 1–10 (2019)
7. Lester, S., Hofmann, J.: Some pedagogical observations on using augmented reality in a vocational practicum. Br. J. Educ. Technol. **51**, 645–656 (2020)
8. Siepmann, F., Fleig, M.: eLearning BENCHMARING Studie 2020. Siepmann Media, Hagen im Bremischen (2020)
9. Harborth, D.: Unfolding concerns about augmented reality technologies: a qualitative analysis of user perceptions. Wirtschaftsinformatik, 1262–1276 (2019)
10. Berkemeier, L., Zobel, B., Werning, S., Ickerott, I., Thomas, O.: Engineering of augmented reality-based information systems: design and implementation for intralogistics services. Bus. Inf. Syst. Eng. **61**, 67–89 (2019)
11. Gattullo, M., Scurati, G.W., Fiorentino, M., Uva, A.E., Ferrise, F., Bordegoni, M.: Towards augmented reality manuals for industry 4.0: a methodology. Robot. Comput. Integr. Manuf. **56**, 276–286 (2019)
12. Sorko, S.R., Brunnhofer, M.: Potentials of augmented reality in training. Procedia Manuf. **31**, 85–90 (2019)
13. Limbu, B., Fominykh, M., Klemke, R., Specht, M., Wild, F.: Supporting training of expertise with wearable technologies: the WEKIT reference framework. In: Yu, S., Ally, M., Tsinakos, A. (eds.) Mobile and Ubiquitous Learning. PRRE, pp. 157–175. Springer, Singapore (2018). https://doi.org/10.1007/978-981-10-6144-8_10
14. Peffers, K., Tuunanen, T., Rothenberger, M.A., Chatterjee, S.: A design science research methodology for information systems research. J. Manag. Inf. Syst. **24**, 45–77 (2007)
15. Gregor, S., Hevner, A.R.: Positioning and presenting design science research for maximum impact. MIS Q. **37**, 337–355 (2013)
16. Keil, J., Schmitt, F., Engelke, T., Graf, H., Manuel, O.: Augmented reality views: discussing the utility of visual elements by mediation means in industrial AR from a design perspective. In: Chen, J., Fragomeni, G. (eds.) Virtual, Augmented and Mixed Reality: Applications in Health, Cultural Heritage, and Industry. VAMR 2018. Lecture Notes in Computer Science, vol. 10910. Springer, Cham. https://doi.org/10.1007/978-3-319-91584-5_24
17. Mandl, H., Kopp, B., Dvorak, S.: Aktuelle theoretische Ansätze und empirische Befunde im Bereich der Lehr-Lern-Forschung – Schwerpunkt Erwachsenenbildung –. Technical Report, Deutsches Institut für Erwachsenenbildung (2004)
18. Bacca, J., Baldiris, S., Fabregat, R., Graf, S.: Kinshuk: international forum of educational technology & society augmented reality trends in education: a systematic review of research and applications. Educ. Technol. **17**, 133–149 (2014)

Developing Digitalization Mindset and Capabilities: Preliminary Results of an Action Research Study

Ralf Plattfaut[✉] and Vincent Borghoff

Fachhochschule Südwestfalen, Process Innovation and Automation Lab, Soest, Germany
{plattfaut.ralf,borghoff.vincent}@fh-swf.de

Abstract. Organizations around the globe are faced with the digital transformation. However, many of these organizations, lack the corresponding individual skills and mindsets as well as the organizational capabilities to drive digital transformation. This short paper reports on preliminary results of an action research study. We conceptualize organizational digitalization capabilities as dynamic capabilities and create a theoretical understanding of these capabilities with their corresponding microfoundations, i.e., the individual employee's skills and mindset. Based on an in-depth nine months' action research study we aim to show in how far outside consulting support will change individuals' mindsets and skills as well as organizational capabilities. We thus contribute to both theory on organizational capability-building as well as dynamic capability theory.

Keywords: Digitalization · Skills · Mindset · Dynamic capabilities

1 Introduction

Virtually all organizations around the world are currently dealing with the digital transformation. However, organizations often lack capabilities to drive this digitalization on their own. Academic literature as well as general media has reported on many cases where companies and organizations seek outside help to transform themselves [1, 2], especially as individual skills and mindsets of employees with regards to digitalization are missing, too. Exemplarily, current employees "may have a […] less tech-savvy mindset and may lack the required technological capabilities to cope with the upcoming changes" [3]. Other authors agree that the digital transformation requires different skill-sets: Domain experts need to be able to navigate the digitalized world and technical specialists need to have a digital mindset [4].

This is especially true for Small to Medium-Sized Enterprises (SME). They also face an increasing importance of digitalization, a lack of corresponding capabilities, and a need for improvement in employees' skills and mindsets and rely on external support from consultants or software vendors. In this study, *we aim at deepening our understanding of the impact of external digitalization consulting on individual skills, individual mindset, and organizational capabilities.* We employ the dynamic capability

F. Ahlemann et al. (Eds.): WI 2021, LNISO 48, pp. 155–161, 2021.
https://doi.org/10.1007/978-3-030-86800-0_12

theory as a theoretical frame and aim at contributing a deeper understanding of micro-foundations of dynamic capabilities. To achieve this research objective, we conduct a nine month qualitative action research (AR) study [5]. In this short paper we describe the results of the first phase (diagnoses and action planning) and give an outlook on the later phases of our research.

2 Theoretical Background: Organizational Digitalization Capabilities and Individual Mindset and Skills

Like individual members, organizations also have specific capabilities to achieve an intended outcome. Especially in fast changing environments, the necessity of adaptation and innovation is urgent. Organizational capabilities are the ability to address these necessities and to achieve competitive advantages [6]. They can be understood as dynamic capabilities [7, 8], which are defined as *"the firm's ability to integrate, build, and reconfigure internal and external competences to address rapidly changing environments"* [9]. These organizational dynamic capabilities can be disaggregated into sensing, seizing and transforming [10–12]. Sensing represents the ability to recognize opportunities and threats, seizing the ability to address sensed opportunities, and transforming the process of modifying the resource base accordingly.

Sensing, seizing, and transforming require in turn abilities on an individual level [13–16], e.g., executives' cognitive capabilities.

Prior research showed that the motivation, skills, and expertise of managers are crucial for sensing and seizing in volatile environments [13]. Blyler and Coff [17] argued that social capital is a necessary (though not sufficient) condition for the existence of a dynamic capability, as only through social interaction resources are connected and recombined. The importance of this social factor becomes more apparent when considering heterogeneous individual knowledge, mindsets and skills between individuals and organizational positions [18]. This emphasizes a more individual view on the foundations of dynamic capabilities, as routines and organizational attitudes arise out of mindset and skill of individuals [14].

The concept of mindset bases in the field of cognitive psychology [19]. We define the mindset of an individual as their *set of beliefs, norms, rules, values* [20, 21]. Mindsets act as filters for external influences. Their foundations lie in past experiences. When facing new impressions or actions, those may be rejected or lead to an adaption in mindset [19, 22]. The individual and organizational mindset plays a big role in achieving successful digital transformation [3, 20]. Especially flexibility and change-orientation in mindset is seen as a key factor for success [4, 23]. Solberg et al. distinguish four different types of digital mindsets of individual employees and argue that more digital-positive mindsets need to flourish [20]. We see the individual mindset as one important microfoundation of organizational digitalization capabilities.

The second microfoundation of organizational digitalization capability is formed through the individual digitalization skill of employees and management [24]. On individual level, where the capabilities are grounded, one can distinguish between expertise and managerial skills [24]. With regards to IT and digitalization, expertise includes technical skills, like knowledge of programming languages, operational systems or databases.

In addition knowledge in technology management, as well as interpersonal skills and business functional knowledge is also shown to be important [25].

3   Research Approach

Action research (AR) first appeared in the 1940s. The concept was coined by the social psychologist Kurt Lewin [26], who was studying how social change can be facilitated [5]. The method itself spread broadly into other research fields and became popular in Information Systems research in the beginning 1980s. It follows an interventionist approach on gathering knowledge. AR as a method is also ideal for creating and analyzing change in organizations, which is a main focus of this study [27].

The study follows a linear, one-cyclic, AR approach [5, 28] with three phases of data collection [28], encapsulating the five steps of diagnosing, action planning, action taking, evaluation, and specifying learning [29] (Fig. 1). In this study we focus on SMEs as these allow studying both individual skills and mindset of a larger proportion of the workforce and organizational capabilities in detail. In such setting, the planned intervention will be more visible and thus the results appear to be magnified. Moreover, the organization needed to be in close proximity to the main researchers to ensure good availability of data. For these reasons, we selected GROW as our case study organization. GROW is a regional business development agency. Although GROW is organized as a private company, it is owned by the local and regional administrations from the corresponding region. The main goals for GROW are to attract new firms to the region and help the existing firms to prosper. GROW has 15 employees who work in the corresponding knowledge-intensive processes.

The first of the three phases covers the diagnosing and action planning phases. Here, we are able to observe employees, gather information from informal CEO discussions, and conduct four semi-structured interviews with employees (referenced as [11] to [14] below). The interviewees were one internal project manager and three employees who work with existing firms to enable their growth (two focused on production companies, one on healthcare). Each interview lasted between 38 and 56 min. The interviews were transcribed (between 10 to 13 pages of transcript) and carefully read by both authors and the interviewee.

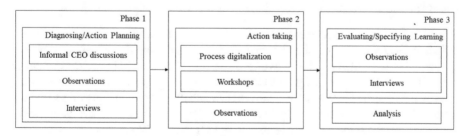

Fig. 1. Research and data collection approach

The second phase (action taking) includes the digitalization of three business processes as well as the conduction of topic specific workshops. We use light-weight IT, e.g.,

Robotic Process Automation, to redesign and automate administrative tasks identified in coordination with the management. Additionally, we will create meeting notes from every interaction with employees. These notes will concentrate on the content of the interaction and on potential observations regarding skills and mindset. During the third phase we collect further data through interviews. All qualitative date will be analyzed by a team of (then) four researchers. Two of these researchers will not be involved in data collection and the intervention to prevent researcher's bias and ensure fresh perspectives on the data at hand as well as potential alternative explanations [30].

4   Preliminary Results and Concluding Discussion

In the following we present our preliminary results from the first phase of our research. We have identified seven themes concerning the current state of the organization with regards to digitalization (Themes 1 and 2), organizational capabilities (Themes 3 and 4) and employees' individual mindset and skills Themes 5–7).

Theme 1: Share of Administrative Routines. All interviewed employees describe a relatively big amount of administrative work. These activities are considered to be non-value adding and take time and focus away from the original task, i.e., to attract new firms to the region and help existing firms develop. As one employee put it: "In the area of administrative tasks, I would say, they have a share of 40 to 50% of total" [13]. These administrative activities originate either from internal inefficiencies due to a lack of process digitalization or from complex interactions with external parties such as the shareholders (local district authority) or funding organizations on state or federal level.

Theme 2: Front Runner Among the Public Organizations in the Region. Although the high share of administrative routines could be reduced through additional internal digitalization, GROW can be seen as a frontrunner in digitalization when compared to the main shareholder, i.e., the district authority. This becomes especially visible as for some processes the district authority acts as a service provider. "Everything that has to do with the district authority is, in fact, more likely to have paper-based interface." [11] In contrast to this, GROW has started to digitalize their internal processes to a greater extent. Exemplarily, the organization switched to a modern full-fledged Office 365 environment and is currently migrating to a cloud-based CRM solution.

Theme 3: Low Internal Technical Digitalization Capabilities. Two observations highlight that GROW has very limited internal digitalization capabilities. Firstly, GROW has no internal IT department but depends on external providers. These IT providers are either part of the district authority, e.g., for telephone services, or are sourced on the external market, e.g., for the CRM system. This reliance on different external providers hinders further digitalization. Exemplarily, "because the [telephone] switchboard is currently still in the district authority, there is no call register in our CRM system" [13].

Theme 4: Digitalization Skills or Capabilities are No Recruiting Criteria. In addition, GROW does not include digitalization skills in their recruitment criteria. Both interviews and analyzed job advertisements show that specific IT or digitalization knowledge is not required from potential applicants.

Theme 5: Mindset of Passenger and not of Driver. Employees see themselves as pure users of digital technologies. There is no impetus for self-driven digitalization. Exemplarily, one employee sees himself as "one of those who use digital solutions with pleasure, when they are offered. But I do not start, conceptualize or develop something myself or make any innovations in that field" [12]. There is a strong understanding that someone should digitalize GROW, as long as these digital solutions are easy to use.

Theme 6: Innovation is Driven Bottom-up as well as Top-Down. Building on the fifth theme, we could also observe that innovation is mainly driven by the top management. There are rare instances when ideas also are generated by employees, but only in specific domains. Digital innovations "which affect the entire GROW workforce are ultimately initiated by the management. So the individual ideas may come from different people, but the actual impulse comes from the management" [14].

Theme 7: Low Individual IT Development Skills. As already mentioned, the individual IT development skills are fairly low. Most interviewees see themselves as interested users, but have no, or nearly no capability in terms of development (I1, I2 and I4). I3 has some basic IT background, but is no real programmer. Guided, less code-heavy development is possible for him, "but in general, when it comes to programming skills, I would say that I am still scratching the surface" [14].

Our preliminary results indicate that the dynamic digitalization capabilities of GROW are on intermediate levels. While with regards to sensing of new opportunities, some abilities exist, the contrary is true for the seizing and transforming abilities. Here, GROW heavily relies on external parties. In line with our conceptualization, the preliminary results also suggest that the individual mindset and capabilities of the employees with regards to digitalization is, at least in parts, on a level that can be improved. The mindset of employees regarding digital change at GROW is not active.

Based on these findings we aspire to reach a deeper understanding of the development of organizational capabilities through the underlying microfoundations of individual skills and mindsets. The next step in our research process is the intervention phase. This includes the active analysis of selected processes and the corresponding development of digital automation solution. During the intervention, qualitative data on the development of mindsets and skills will be collected continuously. The third data collection phase is scheduled after the implementation of the solutions. The used interview guideline will be adapted to cover planned future developments within the organizations IT and process landscape. The collected data will be aggregated and analyzed regarding changes in mindset and capabilities on both the individual and the organizational level. Moreover, we will regularly revisit GROW to understand the development of organizational capabilities.

Both intermediate and final results will be limited to a certain extent. Firstly, there is the risk of residual researcher's bias. We hope to overcome this bias to a large extent through a delineation between researchers actively involved in the intervention phase and researchers focusing on data analysis. Secondly, as the results are and will be generated from a single organization, generalizability needs to be further discussed.

References

1. Plattfaut, R.: Robotic process automation - process optimization on steroids? In: Krcmar, H., Fedorowicz, J., Boh, W.F., Leimeister, J.M., Wattal, S. (eds.) Proceedings of the 40th International Conference on Information Systems, ICIS 2019 . Association for Information Systems (2019)
2. Smith, H.A., Watson, R.T.: Digital transformation at carestream health. MIS Q. Executive **18**(1), 8 (2019)
3. Matt, C., Hess, T., Benlian, A.: Digital transformation strategies. Bus. Inf. Syst. Eng. **57**(5), 339–343 (2015). https://doi.org/10.1007/s12599-015-0401-5
4. Kane, G.C., Palmer, D., Nguyen Phillips, A., Kiron, D., Buckley, N.: Achieving digital maturity: adapting your company to a changing world. MIT Sloan Manage. Rev. **59**(1) (2017)
5. Baskerville, R.L., Wood-Harper, A.T.: A critical perspective on action research as a method for information systems research. J. Inf. Technol. **11**, 235–246 (1996)
6. Dosi, G., Nelson, R.R., Winter, S.G.: Introduction: the nature and dynamics of organizational capabilities. In: Dosi, G., Nelson, R.R., Winter, S.G. (eds.) The Nature and Dynamics of Organizational Capabilities. Oxford Univ. Press, Oxford (2009)
7. Priem, R.L., Butler, J.E.: Is the resource-based view a useful perspective for strategic management research? AMR **26**, 22–40 (2001)
8. Helfat, C.E., Peteraf, M.A.: The dynamic resource-based view: capability lifecycles. Strat. Mgmt. J. **24**, 997–1010 (2003)
9. Teece, D.J., Pisano, G., Shuen, A.: Dynamic capabilities and strategic management. Strat. Mgmt. J. **18**, 509–533 (1997)
10. Teece, D.J.: Explicating dynamic capabilities: the nature and microfoundations of (sustainable) enterprise performance. Strat. Mgmt. J. **28**, 1319–1350 (2007)
11. Plattfaut, R., Niehaves, B., Voigt, M., Malsbender, A., Ortbach, K., Poeppelbuss, J.: Service innovation performance and information technology: an empirical analysis from the dynamic capability perspective. Int. J. Innov. Mgt. **19**, 1550038 (2015)
12. Barreto, I.: Dynamic capabilities: a review of past research and an agenda for the future. J. Manag. **36**, 256–280 (2010)
13. Zahra, S.A., Sapienza, H.J., Davidsson, P.: Entrepreneurship and dynamic capabilities: a review, model and research agenda*. J. Manag. Stud. **43**, 917–955 (2006)
14. Felin, T., Foss, N.J.: Strategic organization: a field in search of micro-foundations. Strateg. Organ. **3**, 441–455 (2005)
15. Eisenhardt, K.M., Furr, N.R., Bingham, C.B.: CROSSROADS—microfoundations of performance: balancing efficiency and flexibility in dynamic environments. Organ. Sci. **21**, 1263–1273 (2010)
16. Helfat, C.E., Peteraf, M.A.: Managerial cognitive capabilities and the microfoundations of dynamic capabilities. Strat. Mgmt. J. **36**, 831–850 (2015)
17. Blyler, M., Coff, R.W.: Dynamic capabilities, social capital, and rent appropriation: ties that split pies. Strat. Mgmt. J. **24**, 677–686 (2003)
18. Felin, T., Powell, T.C.: Designing organizations for dynamic capabilities. Calif. Manag. Rev. **58**, 78–96 (2016)
19. Gupta, A.K., Govindarajan, V.: Cultivating a global mindset. AMP **16**, 116–126 (2002)
20. Solberg, E., Traavik, L.E.M., Wong, S.I.: Digital mindsets: recognizing and leveraging individual beliefs for digital transformation. Calif. Manag. Rev. **62**, 105–124 (2020)
21. Töytäri, P., Turunen, T., Klein, M., Eloranta, V., Biehl, S., Rajala, R.: Aligning the mindset and capabilities within a business network for successful adoption of smart services. J. Prod. Innov. Manag. **35**, 763–779 (2018)

22. Walsh, J.P., Charalambides, L.C.: Individual and social origins of belief structure change. J. Soc. Psychol. **130**, 517–532 (1990)
23. Hartl, E., Hess, T.: The role of cultural values for digital transformation: insights from a Delphi study. In: Twenty-third Americas Conference on Information Systems, AMCIS 2017, pp. 1–10. Boston, USA (2017)
24. Aral, S., Weill, P.: IT assets, organizational capabilities, and firm performance: how resource allocations and organizational differences explain performance variation. Organ. Sci. **18**, 763–780 (2007)
25. Kim, G., Shin, B., Kim, K., Lee, H.: IT capabilities, process-oriented dynamic capabilities, and firm financial performance. JAIS **12**, 487–517 (2011)
26. Lewin, K.: Action research and minority problems. J. Soc. Issues **2**, 34–46 (1946)
27. Baskerville, R., Myers, M.D.: Special issue on action research in information systems: making IS research relevant to practice: foreword. MIS Q. **28**, 329 (2004)
28. Baskerville, R., Wood-Harper, A.T.: Diversity in information systems action research methods. Eur. J. Inf. Syst. **7**, 90–107 (1998)
29. Susman, G.I.: Action research: a sociotechnical systems perspective. In: Morgan, G. (ed.) Beyond Method. Strategies for Social Research. Sage, Beverly Hills, Calif. (1985)
30. Levin, M.: Academic integrity in action research. Action Res. **10**, 133–149 (2012)

Digital Transformation and Business Models

Introduction to the WI2021 Track:
Digital Transformation and Business Models

Daniel Beverungen[1], Christiane Lehrer[2], Thomas Hess[2,3], and Martin Adam[4]

[1] University of Paderborn, Business Information Systems, Paderborn, Germany
daniel.beverungen@uni-paderborn.de
[2] Copenhagen Business School, Department of Digitalization,
Copenhagen, Denmark
cl.digi@cbs.dk
[3] Ludwig-Maximilians-Universität Munich, Institute for Information
Systems and Digital Media, Munich, Germany
thess@bwl.lmu.de
[4] Technical University of Darmstadt, Information Systems and E-Services,
Darmstadt, Germany
adam@ise.tu-darmstadt.de

1 Track Description

Information and communication technologies permeate all areas of our society. Objects become "smart" by adding information technology to them. Increasingly large and diverse data sets are available to document, analyze and predict events. Newer methods of artificial intelligence make it possible to transfer tasks previously reserved for humans to machines and information systems, but also create completely new tasks.

Such changes can have many implications. Customers and employees can change their behaviour. Organisations are rethinking their market position, adapting their structures and establishing new roles, such as that of a Chief Digital Officer. In particular, companies have to critically review their business models or develop new lines of business in parallel in order to be able to compete. On the one hand, a successful digital transformation can, among other things, lead to more economic growth; on the other hand, it is important to counteract or avoid unintended risks.

This conference track provides a framework for the presentation, discussion and development of innovative ideas on digital transformation from the perspective of individuals, (working) groups, organizations, networks, industries and society as a whole. As such, this track supports a broad spectrum of epistemological positions and research methods for the development of novel theories and IT artifacts.

2 Research Articles

2.1 What is Meant by Digital Transformation Success? Investigating the Notion in IS Literature (Philipp Barthel)

This systematic literature review investigates the current notions of digital transformation success, outlines new avenues for information systems research, and informs practitioners on how to assess digital transformation success.

2.2 Exploring Strategic Orientations in the Age of Digital Transformation: A Longitudinal Analysis of Digital Business Model Patterns (Hannes Kurtz, Andre Hanelt, Lutz Maria Kolbe)

This study the evolution of digital business models of 40 companies from 2007 until 2017. The article finds that four strategic orientations predominate, but that there are contextual dependencies in their application.

2.3 Untangling the Open Data Paradox: How Organizations Benefit from Revealing Data (Tobias Enders, Carina Benz, Gerhard Satzger)

This paper presents a set of expert interviews to elicit potential benefits that may originate from engaging in open data in the private sector. Thus, the paper showcases a novel path to extract value from data and to monetize it.

2.4 How Challenging is the Development of Digital Services in an Automotive Environment? An Empirical Study of the Incongruences between Business and IT Experts (Mirheta Omerovic Smajlovic, Nihal Islam, Peter Buxmann)

This case study analyzes the development of a digital service in an automotive environment with a focus on the collaboration of business and IT experts.

2.5 Digital Leadership – Mountain or Molehill? A Literature Review (Julia Katharina Ebert, Paul Drews)

This article develops a new definition of digital leadership based on a structured literature review. Thus, the article provides conceptual clarity of the term digital leadership and presents an inductively developed nomological network.

2.6 The IT Artifact in People Analytics: Reviewing Tools to Understand a Nascent Field (Joschka Andreas Hüllmann, Simone Krebber, Patrick Troglauer)

This paper investigates people analytics and the role of information technology by conducting a literature search. This research enhances the understanding of the implicit assumptions underlying people analytics and elucidates the role of IT.

What is Meant by Digital Transformation Success? Investigating the Notion in IS Literature

Philipp Barthel[(✉)]

Institute for Information Systems and New Media, LMU Munich, Munich, Germany
barthel@bwl.lmu.de

Abstract. Companies across all industries currently strive to successfully master their digital transformation. While information systems research to date has strongly emphasized identification of how companies achieve digital transformation success, the literature is still strikingly vague regarding the notion of digital transformation success itself and approaches to measure it. Therefore, we have conducted a systematic literature review to investigate how information systems studies discuss the concept of digital transformation success and which approaches to success measurement they propose and apply. Based on our analysis, we identify four clusters that represent different understandings of digital transformation success and 20 success dimensions that concretize success measurement. This study clarifies the notions of digital transformation success currently in use and outlines new avenues for information systems research. Further, the results inform practitioners regarding different options and approaches to assess digital transformation success.

Keywords: Digital transformation · Success · Literature review

1 Introduction

In recent years, digital transformation (DT) has emerged as one of the central topics in both research and practice [1]. In the course of the DT process, organizations can fundamentally redefine their established value propositions and value creation logics [2]. Consequently, organizations across nearly all industries have to rethink their processes, products, services, and business models [3]. To accomplish this task, changes to different organizational properties are often necessary [1, 4, 5]. Unsurprisingly, there is a rich body of literature on factors that have to be fulfilled in order to reach successful DT in an organization [6–8]. However, extant literature is often vague in referring to the concept of DT success itself. This could be because DT is an on-going, open-ended process, with high complexity, multidimensionality, and an extensive scope [5, 6]. Nevertheless, while "if you can't measure it, you can't manage it" might be an overstretched adage, prior research stresses how important identifying and evaluating the value contribution of DT efforts is in order to prioritize relevant issues and steer the DT process [9, 10].

© The Author(s), under exclusive license to Springer Nature Switzerland AG 2021
F. Ahlemann et al. (Eds.): WI 2021, LNISO 48, pp. 167–182, 2021.
https://doi.org/10.1007/978-3-030-86800-0_13

Determining and clarifying information systems (IS) success has a longstanding research history (e.g., [11, 12]). More recently, research has addressed the matter of DT success from different perspectives and with different foci. Several studies have identified and analyzed DT success factors (e.g., [7, 8, 13]). This literature primarily addresses the factors that bring about DT success, not necessarily the factors that are part of success itself. Another type of study discusses potential DT outcomes, such as financial improvement or increased market share (e.g., [14, 15]), but either focuses on a specific area of DT, or only marginally addresses DT outcomes. In all, the underlying understanding of DT success is rarely touched on in extant research. There are a few exceptions, which discuss DT success more thoroughly and in-depth (e.g., [6, 10, 16]). However, none of these papers claims to cover the current discourse in its entirety, and each investigates a different paradigm of DT success. Due to the topic's complexity, we require a comprehensive and systematic overview of what is meant by the term *DT success*. Therefore, we aim to capture the different notions of DT success in the present academic debate, including approaches to measure such success. IS research and practice can strongly benefit from a clearer and more comprehensively structured picture of how DT success is conceptualized, discussed, and measured. The research question we address is: *How is DT success conceptualized in IS literature?*

To answer this research question, we conducted a systematic literature review. We have derived different success dimensions from the identified literature and clustered them according to the underlying notions of DT success. Based on this analysis, we formulated an agenda for further research that can serve as a starting point for future research in this field. This study contributes to the literature by providing a structured and systematic overview of the different notions of DT success and gives insight on related approaches to success measurement. Especially, we want to create a basis for discussing DT success, adding to precision and transparency in the debate. Also, we lay a foundation for researchers that aim to investigate DT success evaluation as applied in practice, or that operationalize DT success measurement themselves. Additionally, this study can support practitioners in clarifying their expectations regarding the benefits DT holds for organizations and in selecting suitable measurement approaches.

2   Underlying Research Foundations

In the following section, we give a brief overview of the research on IS success and then elaborate on the underlying concept of DT, which guides our literature analysis.

IS Success. Research on IS success is an established and comprehensive strand within IS research, covering a range of different concepts, such as IS (business) value (e.g., [12, 17]) and IS impact (e.g., [18]). Demonstrating the value of information technology (IT) is an essential component of IS research that confirms its legitimacy [12, 17]. However, this research strand is not based on a uniform understanding of the various concepts, and there is no broad clarity on what IS success is and how it should be measured [12, 16]. Disagreement mainly arises regarding the assessment of "hard" vs. "soft" criteria and "macro" vs. "micro" level measurements [19]. There is, however, general consensus that IS success is a multidimensional and interdependent phenomenon that becomes manifest on different levels (e.g., market, firm, individual) [11, 18]. Many scholars find capturing IT's latent and intangible value and causally linking it to a given outcome such as firm performance [12, 17], as main challenges. This becomes even more difficult when value is created not only within an organization, but also across company boundaries, on an interorganizational level [20, 21]. The complexity related to determining IS' overall success sometimes results in the arbitrary selection of single items, neglecting the multidimensionality and interdependence of success categories [11]. These issues have often led to IS evaluation being inefficient, ineffective, or entirely ignored [19]. Thus, decisions on investment in IS are often based on opaque and incomprehensible grounds, which result in poor selection and management of investments [22]. Overall, research on IS success seeks to resolve these issues, improving measurement of IS success for both academic and practical purposes, thus enabling better understanding and decision making.

IS success research offers an important theoretical foundation for analyzing different notions of DT success. While IS success primarily deals with IT applications' and systems' value, often focused on process improvement [12, 20], DT success goes beyond implementing technology, involving elements of business innovation and transformation. Therefore, the latter requires dedicated consideration.

Digital Transformation. DT can be defined as "a process that aims to improve an entity by triggering significant changes to its properties through combinations of information, computing, communication, and connectivity technologies" [5, p. 118]. This process goes beyond the digitization of resources and can involve the transformation of processes, products, services, and business models [3]. There is an ongoing discussion on whether and how DT and digital innovation are connected. The line of argumentation we follow in this paper is that DT should be considered as an innovation process based on digital innovations [4, 7, 23]. These digital innovations are achieved by combining an innovative digital business concept and an innovative digital (technological) solution [3]. Digital innovations can drastically change an organization's value proposition and thus its entire identity [24]. In this regard, DT differs from other forms of IT-enabled organizational transformation that rather reinforce an organization's established value propositions and identity [2].

The potential outcomes and benefits of digital innovation processes, and therefore also DT can be manifold and become manifest on various organizational levels [24, 25]. Accordingly, organizations can pursue different objectives with altered foci regarding their DT activities [26, 27]. However, measuring and evaluating whether these objectives have been achieved turns out to be challenging, e.g., due to the transformation activities' objectives being vaguely stated, unpredictable, or open-ended [4, 28]. This can lead to situations in which organizations have no clear overview of their DT activities' value contribution and thus are struggling to prioritize high value activities and terminate low value activities [29]. While companies can apply practices like digital value assurance to improve oversight [9], there is still high demand for approaches that will clarify and measure the success of DT activities [10]. Otherwise, the risk is that DT activities will experience a legitimacy crisis [23, 30]. To lay a basis for these advancements, we believe a systematic literature review targeting current notions of DT success will provide a valuable starting point.

3 Research Method

To answer the research question, we conducted a systematic literature review. Literature reviews aim to critically examine and synthesize the current state of knowledge on
a specific topic, to identify potential knowledge gaps and biases in the literature and
to provide a basis for future research [31]. To ensure systematicity and transparency
of the literature review, we followed the guidelines Paré et al. [32] proposed. These
include documenting the research process in a comprehensive review protocol. To build
the literature sample, we followed a two-phased search process [33]. In the first phase,
we conducted a keyword search in the titles, abstracts, and keywords of the eight journals comprising the AIS Senior Scholars' Basket. In doing so, we aimed to capture
high quality research in the IS field. In order to also find contemporary research, we
included the proceedings of the major IS conferences ICIS, ECIS, WI, PACIS, HICSS,
and AMCIS. The search terms consisted of combinations of two elements. First, to find
papers addressing **digital transformation** success, the search terms "digital transfor-
mation"/"digital innovation" /"digitali(s|z)ation" were selected. As argued, we included
digital innovation because it is considered to be a core element of DT (e.g., [3, 4, 23]).
Further, we included the term digitalization because it is regularly applied to describe
processes that fit the definition of DT applied here (e.g., [10, 34, 35]). We excluded
any papers in which the phenomenon addressed did not fit the applied DT definition
[5]. Second, to find papers addressing digital transformation **success**, we applied the
terms "success"/"impact"/"performance"/"outcome"/"result"/"benefit"/"value". These
keywords were selected in accordance with practices followed in prior research [10, 16].
The keyword search yielded 399 results, which we screened to remove all papers that
discussed DT success only marginally, as well as all editor's comments, book reviews
and research-in-progress papers. Finally, 76 papers remained to be considered for further
analysis.

In the second phase, we conducted a forward and backward search following Webster and Watson [33]. With this search, we extended the sample by 45 papers from IS
outlets. The resulting 121 papers were then further assessed regarding their relevance
for answering the research question at hand. We excluded papers that do not allow conclusions to be drawn about their underlying understanding of DT success, that do not
name any success dimensions, or do not offer any indication of possibilities for success measurement. This resulted in the final literature sample of 39 papers (see Table
1). The final sample included no study published prior to 2014, and more than half of
the studies (24) were published after 2017. To analyze the literature, we followed an
inductive logic in an iterative process, deriving and coding the success dimensions the
papers alluded to. From some papers we derived only a single success dimension, while
others contained several dimensions. Success dimensions we found in the papers constructed out of multiple distinct sub-dimensions were disaggregated. For instance, we
would disaggregate "mature people & culture" [36] to its elements "structure", "leadership", and "competencies". We derived a total of 115 dimensions across all papers.
Next, during three iteration cycles, we aggregated identical or highly similar and related
dimensions. For instance, "leadership", "mindset", and "culture" were aggregated to
the dimension "culture & leadership". This procedure resulted in a final set of 20 distinct success dimensions. These success dimensions were then clustered according to

their underlying notion of DT success, resulting in four clusters. To test the consistency, plausibility, and differentiation of the success dimensions and clusters, we conducted a validation process in two workshops with two researchers, who had not been involved in the coding process, after which we made a few minor alterations.

Table 1. Literature sample

Journals (*No. of papers in final sample, TOTAL: 15*)
European Journal of Information Systems (*2*), Journal of Strategic Information Systems (*2*), MIS Quarterly (*2*), MIS Quarterly Executive (*3*), Other Journals (*6*)
Conferences (*No. of papers in final sample, TOTAL: 24*)
AMCIS (*3*), ECIS (*5*), HICSS (*3*), ICIS (*7*), PACIS (*2*), WI (*3*), Other Conferences (*1*)

4 Results

In the following section we present the resulting DT success dimensions and group them into four clusters. The different clusters reflect different underlying notions (or philosophies) of what DT success is. Importantly, these clusters are not mutually exclusive, nor without overlap. Also, the identified dimensions within the clusters are not independent of each other, nor are they collectively exhaustive.

Cluster I - Overall Company Value and Performance. Cluster I comprises all the success dimensions that directly relate to the entire company's success (see Table 2). The underlying premise here is that DT activities need to contribute directly to such overall success. The first dimension in this cluster, the *company value*, can already be considered as the most comprehensive success dimension. Potentially, all activities in the company have an effect on this dimension. If it were possible to show that a DT activity has a positive effect on company value, there would probably be no need to assess further success dimensions. However, the actual value of a company is difficult to determine, which is why the identified papers used stock market figures [37, 38]. *Efficiency & profitability* is similarly measured primarily by means of stock market figures and accounting figures, such as earnings per share (e.g., [39]), return on assets (ROA) (e.g., [38]), or abnormal stock returns (e.g., [40]). The next dimension, *sales volume & customer base*, primarily reflects growth, based on sales revenue (e.g., [41, 42]) and the customer base (e.g., [43, 44]). However, there are also non-financial dimensions in cluster I. *Company reputation & customer satisfaction* reflects the public perception of the company and its standing among customers, e.g., by measuring brand key performance indicators (KPIs) [45, 46] or customer satisfaction scores [47]. *Workplace quality* assesses employees' satisfaction (e.g., [16, 47]) and the resulting turnover rates (e.g., [42]).

In general, success dimensions in cluster I measure the fulfillment of overarching company goals on a macro level. However, it is not always possible to identify how a specific activity contributes to these encompassing macro objectives. This makes the direct use of many of these success dimensions for the operational evaluation of DT activities particularly challenging. Further, some of the dimensions rely heavily on stock market figures, which can only be determined for publicly listed companies. In this cluster, most dimensions can be financially calculated and therefore also measured quantitatively; however, there are also qualitative, non-financial and intangible dimensions included. Cluster I contains dimensions that are used as standalone measures (e.g., [37, 40]).

Table 2. Overview cluster I - overall company value and performance

Success dimension	Exemplary measurement approaches	Sources
Company value	Market cap; market-to-book ratio	[37, 38]
Efficiency & profitability	Earnings per share; operating margin; ROA	[38–40, 47–50]
Sales volume & customer base	Total turnover; market share growth; growth of customer base	[26, 41–44, 48, 49]
Company reputation & customer satisfaction	Online brand KPIs; brand index score; customer satisfaction score	[42, 45–47]
Workplace quality	Employee turnover and satisfaction	[16, 42, 47]

Cluster II - Digital Business Performance. The second cluster follows the premise that successful DT primarily involves creating and exploiting digital business areas, i.e., the profitable marketing of digital products, services, and business models (see Table 3). More abstractly, this is referred to as generating revenue through the deployment of digital technologies [30]. However, sales of physical products via digital channels is also included here [46]. This is reflected very directly in the dimension *revenue from digital business*, which assesses the growth of digital business. Also, the *profitability of digital business* is occasionally used as a success criterion. Another dimension in this cluster, reflecting a slightly different notion of DT success, is the *relative importance of digital business*. Here, scholars consider success to be reflected in digital business growth relative to other business areas, i.e., within the company the digital business share increases. The underlying premise here is that the digital business should become an important pillar of the overall business, possibly even replacing the prevalent core business. Not surprisingly, we also found reference to this success dimension in two papers in the media industry context. They explicitly mentioned that digital business will at least partially replace the traditional business [26, 51].

Cluster II can be closely related to cluster I, since successful digital business has an impact on the overall performance of the company and thus on its value [26, 46]. However, this does not always have to be the case, e.g., if digital business fields cannibalize companies' traditional fields it is conceivable that the effects overall will be neutral or negative. This is particularly evident with the *relative importance of digital business*, which could also be increased, if the core business shrinks, while digital business revenue remains the same. Accordingly, we distinguish clusters I and II, since cluster I measures whether the entire company is performing better through DT, while cluster II is exclusively oriented toward a company's digital business. Overall, the dimensions in this cluster are quantitative, financial, and tangible, thus relatively precise and continuously measurable.

Table 3. Overview cluster II - digital business performance

Success dimension	Exemplary measurement approaches	Sources
Revenue from digital business	Revenue from digital products and services; sales from online channels	[30, 46, 52–55]
Relative importance of digital business	Share of new digital business revenue relative to total revenue; share of revenue from all online sources	[26, 51, 52]
Profitability of digital business	Digital products' and services' profitability; online sales profitability	[46, 55]

Cluster III - Degree of Realized External Transformation. One condition for generating revenue with digital business is the availability of corresponding digital market offerings. In cluster III, DT success is defined as the realized transformation of market offerings (products and services), customer interaction (channels and touchpoints), partner networks, and overall business models (see Table 4). In contrast to cluster II, the focus here is more on evaluating the progress of the transformation and innovation process itself, not the economic output resulting from the process. Most dimensions in the cluster directly reflect how far an organization's value creation has been transformed, which is argued to be a central specific of DT [2, 34]. A significant number of dimensions in this cluster is derived from maturity models that aim to assess an organizations DT progress along multiple dimensions (e.g., [35, 36, 56]). The two most dominant dimensions in this cluster are *digital business model innovation* and *new digital products & service innovation*. These dimensions are considered as core aspects of transforming the value creation and they reflect a firm's ability to create new digital market offerings. For example, scholars assess whether the company has digital business models (e.g., [34, 39]) and if so, how advanced they are (e.g., [28, 36]), or they determine how many digital products and services (e.g., [51, 57]), digital patents (e.g., [38]), or product innovation projects (e.g., [52]) there are. These two dimensions prompt the distinction of a third dimension: *digitalization of existing products & services*, which indicates how far the existing offering is transformed, i.e., it reflects a different aspect of DT (e.g., [29]). However, further dimensions included in cluster III are not directly connected to digital products and services. The externally oriented DT's success can also be determined by assessing the *digitalization of customer interaction*, e.g., by the number of digital customer channels (e.g., [57]), the maturity of digital customer experience (e.g., [36, 56]), or the *partner network* area, e.g., by evaluating the cooperative value creation maturity (e.g., [6]).

To summarize, the dimensions in this cluster primarily assess the extent of externally oriented DT activities, but not their economic results. The measures we found can be both, qualitative and quantitative, as well as both tangible and intangible, but they are specifically non-financial. Consequently, taking purely quantitative measurement approaches to capture data (e.g., calculating numbers of products and patents, etc.) appears to be relatively easy. However, to increase their meaningfulness, quantitative measures often are combined with qualifying dimensions (e.g., the quality and responsiveness of development).

Table 4. Overview cluster III - degree of realized external transformation

Success dimension	Exemplary measurement approaches	Sources
Digital business model innovation	Number of realized digital business model innovations	[2, 13, 28, 34, 36, 39, 58–61]
New digital products & service innovation	Number of digital products and services; number of innovation projects; quality, continuity and responsiveness of digital products development	[27, 29, 35, 36, 38, 41, 48, 51, 52, 55–57, 59]
Digitalization of existing products & services	Existence and number of digitally enriched core products	[26, 29, 35]
Digitalization of customer interaction	Number and degree of digital customer channels utilized; maturity of digital customer touchpoints	[36, 52, 56, 57]
Partner network	Maturity of partner network, hybrid value creation	[6, 56]

Cluster IV - Degree of Realized Internal Transformation. All three previously discussed clusters are based on the fact that the organization itself is also changing, although these clusters' dimensions do not directly evaluate the progress of this internal transformation (see Table 5). Thus, cluster IV focuses on realized DT of the organization's structures, processes, and employees. The underlying premise is that successfully realized DT leads to a transformed internal organization. Similar to cluster III, many of the dimensions clustered here are derived from maturity models (e.g., [35, 36, 56]). Also similar to cluster III, literature contributing to this cluster follows multi-dimensional approaches to assess DT success, i.e., researchers measure success along multiple dimensions. The dimension *strategy* expresses the extent to which a digital strategy, vision, and agenda are present, mature, and continuously being developed (e.g., [35, 56]). It also indicates the extent to which the employees and management understand and accept this strategy (e.g., [52]). The dimension *structure, collaboration, & governance* reflects a range of changes to the organizational structure that are often seen as relevant successful DT outcomes, such as organizational agility (e.g., [56]) or self-organized teams (e.g., [36]). The dimension *processes* assesses the extent to which process innovations have been realized (e.g., [28, 41]) and to which they contribute to quality improvements (e.g., [47]). This is one of the few dimensions in the cluster that is directly quantifiable, e.g., measuring the cost reduction brought on by process improvements (e.g., [53, 55]). Next, the company's *IT* transformation is regularly assessed to determine the DT progress. This dimension considers the extent to which the IT infrastructure matures and develops further on a technological level (e.g., [6, 56]), but also the extent to which the IT department assumes its role as a DT driver (e.g., [36]). The next two dimensions primarily deal with the aspect of people in DT. *Culture & leadership* assesses the presence and maturity of organizational features such as innovative culture, mindset, and leadership style, while *competencies & knowledge* targets the maturity of digital skill, competence, and knowledge management. Lastly, *partner management* corresponds to the dimension *partner network* in cluster III, but focuses more on the maturity of the internal procedures to facilitate cooperating with partners.

Overall, many of the dimensions found in this cluster can and also are considered DT enablers or success factors. However, as they are also used to measure the success of DT activities and the progress of the DT process (e.g., [16, 47, 52]), we have included them here. The dimensions in this cluster reflect the most profound aspects of organizational transformation. Regarding measurability, most of the dimensions in this cluster are obviously qualitative, non-financial, and intangible, which largely impedes their direct, objective measurement. Maturity models try to remedy this situation by providing concrete criteria, which can be used to estimate the progress in a dimension (e.g., [35, 36, 56]). However, these models often require a specific understanding or DT focus [62].

Table 5. Overview cluster IV - Degree of realized internal transformation

Success dimension	Exemplary measurement approaches	Sources
Strategy	Maturity, acceptance, and transparency of digital vision, agenda, and strategy	[28, 35, 52, 56]

(continued)

Table 5. (*continued*)

Success dimension	Exemplary measurement approaches	Sources
Structure, collaboration & governance	Maturity of organizational structure, agility, digital team set-up, teamwork, management support	[6, 28, 35, 36, 56, 58]
Processes	Maturity of processes, process effectiveness, process efficiency, number of process innovations	[27, 28, 35, 36, 41, 47, 55, 56, 59, 63]
IT	Maturity of IT infrastructure; reliability, availability, and performance of IT	[6, 16, 35, 36, 56],
Culture & leadership	Maturity of innovation culture, digital affinity, digital mindset, leadership	[6, 35, 36, 52, 56],
Competencies & knowledge	Maturity of digital skills, competencies, knowledge management	[6, 35, 36, 47, 56],
Partner management	Maturity of procedures for cooperating with partners	[6, 56]

5   Implications for Research on DT Success

Looking at the clusters in relation to one another, there is a systemization along two axes (see Fig. 1). First, a distinction along two main paradigms becomes visible: *achievement of company's core objectives* and *progress of company's DT process*. The former defines DT success in terms of its effect on the overall firm success, i.e., success is determined by DT activities' direct contribution to the ultimate company objectives (e.g., [37, 38]). This paradigm is mainly reflected in clusters I and II, where an outcome-centric, macro-level perspective prevails. The latter defines DT success in terms of progressing the DT process, i.e., success is determined by the extent DT activities contribute to the company's desired state of becoming more digitally transformed (e.g., [29, 36]). This paradigm is mainly reflected in clusters III and IV, where a process-centric, micro-level perspective prevails. Second, a distinction can be made along the orientation of the clusters: *internally* (transformation of the organization) and *externally* (transformation of the market offering). Cluster III and IV can be classified quite clearly as externally (III) and internally (IV) oriented. Cluster I covers the entire company with its overarching objectives and thus spans both the internal and external perspectives. Cluster II has proven to be primarily externally oriented, since all dimensions relate to the digital business offerings' market success. We find that some articles can be located exclusively in one cluster and thus take a clear position on the notion of DT success (e.g., [37, 40,

43]). Other articles include success dimensions of several different clusters and thus emphasize the multi-faceted nature of DT success (e.g., [35, 36, 52]). Further, some researchers clearly aim to quantify DT outcomes (e.g., [38, 41]), while others strive to refine purely qualitative assessments (e.g., [36, 56]). Based on this comparison and the overall literature analysis, we consider three fields to be particularly important for research in the area of DT success.

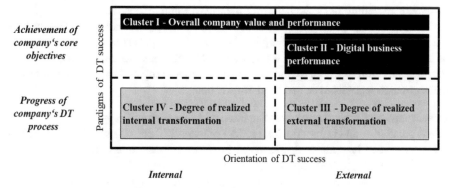

Fig. 1. Overview of DT success clusters

Concretization of DT Success. We have recognized different paradigms and orientations of DT success, therefore it is important for researchers to be aware of where they are located and on what premises they are built. Of the 121 papers that were short-listed, i.e., those dealing with DT success generally, we included only 39 in the final analysis because they were, at least to a reasonable degree, specific about the notion of DT success. Given the large variety of possible DT outcomes, the premises underlying DT success can be highly dependent on the vision an organization or industry pursues regarding DT (e.g., *relative importance of digital business* for the media industry). Thus, different organizations in different contexts measure different dimensions to capture DT success. It is therefore understandable that literature often remains unspecific regarding the DT success notion. Nevertheless, this lack of specificity also risks that the DT success concept remains elusive. This can then lead to the impression that DT success is fundamentally indeterminable and therefore cannot be measured. However, this is not a satisfactory circumstance in IS research and does not meet the requirements existing in reality [9, 10]. Thus, future research should further assist in making DT success concrete and be clear when referring to DT success. For instance, research on DT success factors should include the underlying premise of DT success. In addition, research could examine the latent expectations organizations have of DT to make the implicit notions of success more tangible.

Investigating DT Success Notions in Real-World Contexts. Across   all   clusters, there are only a few evaluation approaches that are actually applied in an organizational context. The papers we analyzed primarily report on DT success dimensions either still in a conceptual state or ones only used for scientific studies. Several of the measures we came across are not necessarily applicable in practice, as, for example, they require a company to be publicly listed (e.g., [37, 38]). We rarely found any approaches actually utilized in practice to operationally measure DT activities' success that can also support actual managerial decision making. The exceptions were mostly either focused on one specific DT area (e.g., [46]) or on a very top-down, strategic level (e.g., [26, 30]). Ryan et al. present a holistic approach, covering multiple dimensions as they were measured in the real-world context; however, the approach is also very specific to a health management setting [47]. Seeher et al. identify a range of metrics that are applied in practice; however, not linked to one specific case, as they were based on a Delphi study [52]. Besides what these articles report, there currently appears to be a knowledge gap on how companies in practice measure their DT activities' success. Thus, we highly recommend future research to find relevant cases, to identify and investigate DT success measurement approaches in their real-world context.

Development of Holistic but Concise Success Measurement Approaches. The different paradigms and orientations all reflect relevant DT outcomes and also show how DT success can be measured. There are however reasons to assume that companies are still struggling to find appropriate approaches for measuring their DT success [9]. Accordingly, future research could take up this challenge and contribute to developing new measurement approaches. The dimensions and clusters identified in this study could provide a basis for this. Since the dimensions are often interdependent, it could also be useful to consider them in combination. We propose aligning the dimensions in a way that combines strengths and mitigates weaknesses. For example, an attempt could be made to link the dimensions of clusters III and IV directly to clusters I and II in order to identify how implementation DT activities affects the overall objectives. It is also important to clarify the question of where to measure. We have found different approaches here, e.g., those at the level of the chief digital officer (e.g., [52]), in individual projects or project portfolios (e.g., [55]), in the digital business division (e.g., [54]), or at the level of the overall organization (e.g., [37]). We argue that it is important to be able to evaluate the overall success of the organizational DT. However, for the operational management of DT, it is also important to evaluate individual activities regarding their contribution to the overall DT success [9].

6   Conclusion, Limitations and Outlook

This study investigated the notion of DT success and related success measurement approaches in current IS literature. Therefore, we conducted a systematic literature search that yielded 39 papers. Analyzing these papers, we derived 20 individual success dimensions and assigned them to four clusters. The identified dimensions were analyzed within and between the clusters in order to learn how DT success is conceptualized in IS literature and to find out which measurement approaches are applied in practice and research. Finally, to support further attempts to improve our understanding of DT success, we have presented three recommendations for future research in this area.

With these results, we enrich the existing IS success literature by providing a first comprehensive overview of DT success, thus extending this established IS research strand from a primarily technology-centric perspective, to the more holistic perspective of digital innovation and transformation. We show that many topics already dealt with in the IS success literature (e.g., "hard" vs. "soft" criteria, "macro" vs. "micro" level measuring) are also relevant for DT success. However, with a few exceptions (e.g., [10, 16]), DT success measures have, to date, hardly been critically discussed. Further, we contribute to DT literature by discussing and systematizing various concurrent notions of DT success. By uncovering different DT success perspectives and paradigms, we hope to foster understanding of what DT success entails and to link the assumptions of what constitutes such success to specific success dimensions. Further, we demonstrate, how DT success can be measured on different levels, be it in the overall organization (macro) or regarding single transformation activities (micro). By discussing different approaches, we hope to support future research that will clarify the notion of DT success, identify and investigate applied measurement approaches in their real-world context, or even contribute to developing new measurement approaches. Overall, our study aims to reduce the elusiveness of DT success, as we consider this an important factor in maintaining and increasing the legitimacy of research in the DT field.

This study intends to motivate practitioners to deal extensively with the matter of DT success and consequently to assess their own DT activities. For this, they receive indications on which success dimensions and specific measurement approaches can be suitable for which type of DT objective. This study is subject to a set of limitations. The results depend partly on the underlying understanding of DT. Researchers with different assumptions might come up with different results. We therefore strived to make our assumptions and premises, as well as our overall review process, transparent. Further, this study's results do not provide a complete framework of all the success dimensions relevant in reality; they only reflect what we found in the analyzed literature. It is likely that there are other relevant dimensions. Thus, we want to encourage researchers to take up on these suggestions regarding areas of possible improvement, to further clarify the DT success concept and to investigate and advance measurement approaches applied in practice.

References

1. Hanelt, A., Bohnsack, R., Marz, D., Antunes Marante, C.: A Systematic review of the literature on digital transformation: insights and implications for strategy and organizational change. J. Manag. Stud. 1–39 (2020)
2. Wessel, L., Baiyere, A., Ologeanu-Taddei, R., Cha, J., Jensen, T.: Unpacking the difference between digital transformation and IT-enabled organizational transformation. J. AIS **22**, 102–129 (2021)
3. Wiesböck, F., Hess, T.: Digital innovations - embedding in organizations. Electron. Mark. **30**, 75–86 (2020)
4. Berghaus, S., Back, A.: Disentangling the fuzzy front end of digital transformation: activities and approaches. In: Proceedings of the 38th International Conference on Information Systems (ICIS), pp. 1–17 (2017)
5. Vial, G.: Understanding digital transformation: a review and a research agenda. J. Strateg. Inf. Syst. **28**, 118–144 (2019)
6. Vogelsang, K., Liere-Netheler, K., Packmohr, S., Hoppe, U.: Success factors for fostering a digital transformation in manufacturing companies. J. Enterp. Transform. 1–22 (2019)

7. Osmundsen, K., Iden, J., Bygstad, B.: Digital transformation: drivers, success factors, and implications. In: Proceedings of the 12th Mediterranean Conference on Information Systems (MCIS), pp. 1–15 (2018)
8. Morakanyane, R., O'Reilly, P., McAvoy, J., Grace, A.: Determining digital transformation success factors. In: Proceedings of the 53rd Hawaii International Conference on System Sciences (HICSS), pp. 4356–4365 (2020)
9. Gimpel, H., Hosseini, S., Huber, R., Probst, L., Röglinger, M., Faisst, U.: Structuring digital transformation: a framework of action fields and its application at ZEISS. J. Inf. Technol. Theor. Appl. **19**, 31–54 (2018)
10. Neumeier, A., Wolf, T., Oesterle, S.: The manifold fruits of digitalization - determining the literal value behind. In: Proceedings of the 13th Internationale Tagung Wirtschaftsinformatik (WI), pp. 484–498 (2017)
11. DeLone, W.H., McLean, E.R.: The DeLone and McLean model of information systems success: a ten-year update. J. Manag. Inf. Syst. **19**, 9–30 (2003)
12. Schryen, G.: Revisiting is business value research: what we already know, what we still need to know, and how we can get there. Eur. J. Inf. Syst. **22**, 139–169 (2013)
13. Holotiuk, F., Beimborn, D.: Critical success factors of digital business strategy. In: Proceedings of the 13th Internationale Tagung Wirtschaftsinformatik (WI), pp. 991–1005 (2017)
14. Böttcher, T.P., Weking, J.: Identifying antecedents and outcomes of digital business model innovation. In: Proceedings of the 28th European Conference on Information Systems (ECIS), pp. 1–14 (2020)
15. Bordeleau, F.-È., Felden, C.: Digitally transforming organisations: a review of change models of industry 4.0. In: Proceedings of the 27th European Conference on Information Systems (ECIS), pp. 1–14 (2019)
16. Liere-Netheler, K., Vogelsang, K., Packmohr, S., Hoppe, U.A.: Towards a framework for digital transformation success in manufacturing. In: Proceedings of the 26th European Conference on Information Systems (ECIS), pp. 1–19 (2018)
17. Kohli, R., Grover, V.: Business value of IT: an essay on expanding research directions to keep up with the times. J. AIS **9**, 23–39 (2008)
18. Gable, G.G., Sedera, D., Chan, T.: Re-Conceptualizing information system success: the is-impact measurement model. J. AIS **9**, 377–408 (2008)
19. Irani, Z., Love, P.E.: Developing a frame of reference for Ex-Ante IT/IS investment evaluation. Eur. J. Inf. Syst. **11**, 74–82 (2002)
20. Melville, N., Kraemer, K., Gurbaxani, V.: Information technology and organizational performance: an integrative model of IT business value. MIS Q. **28**, 283–322 (2004)
21. Mandrella, M., Trang, S., Kolbe, L.M.: Synthesizing and integrating research on IT-based value cocreation: a meta-analysis. J. AIS **21**, 388–427 (2020)
22. Farbey, B., Land, F., Targett, D.: Moving IS evaluation forward: learning themes and research issues. J. Strateg. Inf. Syst. **8**, 189–207 (1999)
23. Hinings, B., Gegenhuber, T., Greenwood, R.: Digital innovation and transformation: an institutional perspective. Inf. Organ. **28**, 52–61 (2018)
24. Kohli, R., Melville, N.P.: Digital innovation: a review and synthesis. Inf. Syst. J. **29**, 200–223 (2019)
25. Frey, J., Holotiuk, F., Beimborn, D.: Debating digital innovation: a literature review on realizing value from digital innovation. In: Procceedings of the 15th Internationale Tagung Wirtschaftsinformatik (WI), pp. 1–16 (2020)
26. Hess, T., Matt, C., Benlian, A., Wiesböck, F.: Options for formulating a digital transformation strategy. MIS Q. Exec. **15**, 125–139 (2016)

27. Barthel, P., Fuchs, C., Birner, B., Hess, T.: Embedding digital innovations in organizations: a typology for digital innovation units. In: Procceedings of the 15th Internationale Tagung Wirtschaftsinformatik (WI), pp. 1–15 (2020)

28. Arvidsson, V., Mønsted, T.: Generating innovation potential: how digital entrepreneurs conceal, sequence, anchor, and propagate new technology. J. Strateg. Inf. Syst. **27**, 369–383 (2018)

29. Chanias, S., Myers, M.D., Hess, T.: Digital transformation strategy making in pre-digital organizations: the case of a financial services provider. J. Strateg. Inf. Syst. **28**, 17–33 (2019)

30. Tumbas, S., Berente, N., vom Brocke, J.: Digital innovation and institutional entrepreneurship: chief digital officer perspectives of their emerging role. J. Inf. Technol. **33**, 188–202 (2018)

31. Rowe, F.: What literature review is not: diversity, boundaries and recommendations. Eur. J. Inf. Syst. **23**, 241–255 (2014)

32. Paré, G., Trudel, M., Jaana, M., Kitsiou, S.: Synthesizing information systems knowledge: a typology of literature reviews. Inf. Manag. **52**, 183–199 (2015)

33. Webster, J., Watson, R.T.: Analyzing the past to prepare for the future: writing a literature review. MIS Q. **26**, xiii-xxiii (2002)

34. Gierlich, M., Schüritz, R., Volkwein, M., Hess, T.: SMEs' Approaches for digitalization in platform ecosystems. In: Proceedings of the 23rd Pacific Asia Conference on Information Systems (PACIS), pp. 1–14 (2019)

35. Klötzer, C., Pflaum, A.: Toward the development of a maturity model for digitalization within the manufacturing industry's supply chain. In: Proceedings of the 50th Hawaii International Conference on System Sciences (HICSS), pp. 4210–4219 (2017)

36. Berger, S., Bitzer, M., Häckel, B., Voit, C.: Approaching digital transformation-development of a multi-dimensional maturity model. In: Proceedings of the 28th European Conference on Information Systems (ECIS), pp. 1–18 (2020)

37. Moker, A., Brosi, P., Welpe, I.: It Depends on the size: how firm strategic emphasis on digital transformation predicts market capitalization. In: Proceedings of the 53rd Hawaii International Conference on System Sciences (HICSS), pp. 5472–5481 (2020)

38. Hanelt, A., Firk, S., Hildebrandt, B., Kolbe, L.M.: Digital M&A, digital innovation, and firm performance: an empirical investigation. Euro. J. Inf. Syst. forthcoming, 1–24 (2020)

39. Hildebrandt, B., Hanelt, A., Firk, S., Kolbe, L.: Entering the digital Era – the impact of digital technology-related M&As on business model innovations of automobile OEMs. In: Proceedings of the 36th International Conference on Information Systems (ICIS), pp. 1–21 (2015)

40. Drechsler, K., Wagner, H.-T., Reibenspiess, V.A.: Risk and return of chief digital officers' appointment – an event study. In: Proceedings of the 40th International Conference on Information Systems (ICIS), pp. 1–17 (2019)

41. Ferreira, J.J., Fernandes, C.I., Ferreira, F.A.: To be or not to be digital, that is the question: firm innovation and performance. J. Bus. Res. **101**, 583–590 (2019)

42. Khin, S., Ho, T.C.: Digital technology, digital capability and organizational performance. Int. J. Innov. Sci. **11**, 177–195 (2019)

43. Huang, J., Henfridsson, O., Liu, M.J., Newell, S.: Growing on steroids: rapidly scaling the user base of digital ventures through digital innovation. MIS Q. **41**, 301–314 (2017)

44. Leischnig, A., Wölfl, S., Ivens, B., Hein, D.: From digital business strategy to market performance: insights into key concepts and processes. In: Proceedings of the 38th International Conference on Information Systems (ICIS), pp. 1–16 (2017)

45. Beutel, S., Bendig, D., Brettel, M.: The intangible value of digitalization - assessing the relationship of digital orientation and intangible value drivers. In: Proceedings of the 40th International Conference on Information Systems (ICIS), pp. 1–17 (2019)

46. Hansen, R., Sia, S.K.: Hummel's digital transformation toward omnichannel retailing: key lessons learned. MIS Q. Exec. **14**, 51–66 (2015)

47. Ryan, J., Doster, B., Daily, S., Lewis, C.: Targeting perioperative performance aligned to hospital strategy via DT. In: Proceedings of the 53rd Hawaii International Conference on System Sciences (HICSS), pp. 3628–3637 (2020)
48. Nwankpa, J.K., Roumani, Y.: IT Capability and digital transformation: a firm performance perspective. In: Proceedings of the 37th International Conference on Information Systems (ICIS), pp. 1–16 (2016)
49. Nwankpa, J.K., Datta, P.: Balancing exploration and exploitation of IT resources: the influence of digital business intensity on perceived organizational performance. Eur. J. Inf. Syst. **26**, 469–488 (2017)
50. Murawski, M., Bühler, J., Martensen, M., Rademacher, C., Bick, M.: How digital business strategy affects profitability: opening the 'black box' of performance. In: Proceedings of the 24th Americas Conference on Information Systems (AMCIS), pp. 1–10 (2018)
51. Karimi, J., Walter, Z.: The role of dynamic capabilities in responding to digital disruption: a factor-based study of the newspaper industry. J. Manag. Inf. Syst. **32**, 39–81 (2015)
52. Seeher, V., Beimborn, D., Holotiuk, F.: How to evaluate the performance of the CDO - a Delphi study on KPIs for CDOs. In: Proceedings of the 28th European Conference on Information Systems (ECIS), pp. 1–15 (2020)
53. Fichman, R.G., Dos Santos, B., Zheng, Z.: Digital innovation as a fundamental and powerful concept in the information systems curriculum. MIS Q. **38**, 329–353 (2014)
54. Freitas Junior, J.C.d.S., Maçada, A.C.G., Brinkhues, R.A.: Digital capabilities as key to digital business performance. In: Proceedings of the 23rd Americas Conference on Information Systems (AMCIS), pp. 1–10 (2017)
55. Wiesböck, F.: Innovating in a digital world – the role of digital product innovation capabilities. In: Proceedings of the 27th European Conference on Information Systems (ECIS), pp. 1–16 (2019)
56. Berghaus, S., Back, A.: Stages in digital business transformation: results of an empirical maturity study. In: Proceedings of the 10th Mediterranean Conference on Information Systems (MCIS), pp. 1–17 (2016)
57. Leonhardt, D., Hanelt, A., Huang, P., Mithas, S.: Does one size fit all? theorizing governance configurations for digital innovation. In: Proceedings of the 39th International Conference on Information Systems (ICIS), pp. 1–17 (2018)
58. Muehlburger, M., Rueckel, D., Koch, S.: A framework of factors enabling digital transformation. In: Proceedings of the 25th Americas Conference on Information Systems (AMCIS), pp. 1–10 (2019)
59. Sebastian, I., Ross, J., Beath, C., Mocker, M., Moloney, K., Fonstad, N.: How Big old companies navigate digital transformation. MIS Q. Exec. **16**, 197–213 (2017)
60. Jöhnk, J., Oesterle, S., Ollig, P., Riedel, L.-N.: The complexity of digital transformation – conceptualizing multiple concurrent initiatives. In: Proceedings of the 15th Internationale Tagung Wirtschaftsinformatik (WI), pp. 1–15 (2020)
61. Soto Setzke, D., Opderbeck, L., Böhm, M., Krcmar, H.: Pathways to successful business model innovation in the context of digital transformation. In: Proceedings of the 24th Pacific Asia Conference on Information Systems (PACIS), pp. 1–14 (2020)
62. Remane, G., Hanelt, A., Wiesboeck, F., Kolbe, L.: Digital maturity in traditional industries – an exploratory analysis. In: Proceedings of the 25th European Conference on Information Systems (ECIS), pp. 143–157 (2017)
63. Soh, C., Yeow, A., Goh, Q., Hansen, R.: Digital transformation: of paradoxical tensions and managerial responses. In: Proceedings of the 40th International Conference on Information Systems (ICIS), pp. 1–17 (2019)

Exploring Strategic Orientations in the Age of Digital Transformation: A Longitudinal Analysis of Digital Business Model Patterns

Hannes Kurtz[1]([⊠]), Andre Hanelt[2], and Lutz M. Kolbe[1]

[1] Information Management, Georg-August-University Göttingen, Göttingen, Germany
hannes.kurtz01@stud.uni-goettingen.de,
lutz.kolbe@wiwi.uni-goettingen.de
[2] Digital Transformation Management, University of Kassel, Kassel, Germany
hanelt@uni-kassel.de

Abstract. In the course of digitalization, fundamental mechanisms according to which companies operate are changing. Companies are forced to develop new, digital capabilities, which in turn, alter a company's set of competitive moves and thus its business strategy. While much effort is undertaken to examine digital business strategy through several theoretical lenses, there has never been empirical research on archetypical strategic orientations regarding companies' adoption mechanisms to environmental changes in a digital context. This study fills named research gap by investigating if the established framework of Miles and Snow (1978) is still applicable in the digital age. In doing so, it examines the evolution of digital business models of 40 companies from 2007 until 2017. We found that all four orientations predominate, but that there are contextual dependencies in their application or change.

Keywords: Digital business strategy · Strategic orientations · Digital business model · Cluster analysis

1 Introduction

In the era of proliferating digitalization across societies, digital technologies are fundamentally reshaping traditional business [1]. A reason for this is, that they enable firms to develop and allocate different sets of capabilities and thus alter the company's set of possible competitive moves [2, 3]. This led to firms in almost every industry conduct a vast amount of initiatives to exploit new digital technologies in order to gain advantage over their competitors [4, 5]. With this ongoing digital transformation, therefore, conventional wisdom about scale, scope, design, and execution of business strategy is changing. This leads to a new concept named digital business strategy, defined as "organizational strategy formulated and executed by leveraging digital resources to create differential value" [4]. Consequently and given the importance of the topic for contemporary managerial practice, increasingly more researchers set out to advance our understanding of digital business strategy by using different approaches [6].

F. Ahlemann et al. (Eds.): WI 2021, LNISO 48, pp. 183–199, 2021.
https://doi.org/10.1007/978-3-030-86800-0_14

Nevertheless, as Bharadwaj et al. [4] state, many questions remain unanswered and theoretical findings have not been empirically proven yet. For example, in the context of digital transformation, unlike as in classical strategy research, there is a lack of knowledge regarding archetypical strategic orientations concerning organizations' adaption behavior. Here a framework derived by Miles and Snow [7] enables one to classify companies according to their adaption behavior in order to cope with changes in their environment. However, filling this gap is of great importance, as aforementioned digital transformation of nearly every industry creates "both game-changing opportunities for – and existential threats to – companies" [8]. In order to remain competitive, companies, thus, have to adapt their business models and business strategies, but can come up with different strategic responses to these challenges [4, 6].

To examine whether the existing strategic orientations of Miles and Snow [7] still apply in the age of digital transformation may, therefore, aid in advancing our knowledge about digital business strategy and its influence on business practice and digital transformation. Accordingly, we investigate the following research question: *Are the predominant types of strategic orientation still valid in a digital context, and do companies change their strategic orientation over time?* In order to derive an answer to this question, we analyzed the business models of 40 companies from 2007 until 2017. We thus investigated 240 digital business model pattern configurations using the taxonomy developed by Remane et al. [9]. Employing a two-step cluster analysis, we determine group membership and allocate companies to the four strategic orientations derived by Miles and Snow [7]. This procedure enables us to point out possible changes in the strategic orientation of individual companies. It further allows us to investigate antecedents and reasons for changes in more detail. By analyzing the clusters, we found out that all four strategic orientations prevail in the context of digital business model innovation. Furthermore, we were able to detect changes in the strategic orientations of companies over time.

Our work provides important contributions to information systems (IS) research. To the best of our knowledge, we are the first to set out an empirical examination of strategic orientations from different companies stemming from different industries within a digital context. We, thus, contribute to a better understanding of digital business strategy and digital transformation. Furthermore, we analyzed strategic orientations in the digital age using the construct of digital business model patterns and therefore contributed to a better integration of the concepts business strategy and business models as well as IS and strategic management research.

2   Background

2.1   Digital Business Strategy and Strategic Orientations

Strategy is often defined as a set of committed choices made by management and a contingent plan of actions and activities designed to achieve a particular goal [10]. These choices relate to topics such as resource investments or the set of a firm's dynamic capabilities needed to deploy these resources [11]. The digital transformation of nearly every industry is fundamentally reshaping traditional business practice and, therefore, business strategy. The pervasiveness of digital technology, for instance, leads to a radical change of product architecture, making it difficult to disentangle digital products and services from their underlying IT infrastructure. Besides, increasing digitization of operations and processes within organizations can be seen [12, 13]. As a consequence, scholars such as Drnevich and Croson [11] argue that information technology enhances current non-digital capabilities and enables new digital capabilities. In doing so, it directly affects the mechanisms by which value is created and captured in order to make a profit. It thus alters the business-level strategic alternatives to value creation and capturing. Furthermore, IT-based capabilities determine how much of the value from these opportunities can be captured and help to defend named value against competitors. As a result, information technology matters to business success as well as to business strategy [11]. This leads to a fusion of these two concepts into an overarching phenomenon called digital business strategy [4, 14].

An inherent part of the strategy is the adoption mechanism of a company's strategy formulation process in response to its environment. As a consequence, many scholars view strategy as immutable in the way that over time, companies progress habitual mechanisms to respond to their environmental influences [15, 16]. Since companies face different environmental influences, they develop different habitual mechanisms resulting in different manifestations of strategy. IS research provides much knowledge about different aspects of digital business strategy. On the other hand, there is no framework for the categorization of strategic orientations with respect to a company's adoption mechanism to environmental changes, as is the case in general management research. In this research domain, a framework developed by Miles and Snow [7] is well established. Because of its attributed longevity, industry-independent nature, and its correspondence with the strategic posture of firms across multiple industries and countries [17], their typology has been the subject of considerable research attention over time [18]. Thereby, the framework condenses, among others, central elements of the resource-based view and dynamic capabilities [19] and postulates four generic types of strategy: First, the *Prospectors*, present the one extreme of the typology. These companies are first movers, in market/product innovation, creators of change and uncertainty, and flourish in volatile markets [16, 20]. Furthermore, they can be characterized by risk-taking behavior, loose resource control, and less focus on cost efficiencies [21]. Second, the other extreme, are called *Defenders* and are characterized as companies offering a stable portfolio of products and exhibiting no or little engagement in market/product innovation [15, 18]. In addition, companies following this strategic orientation are risk-averse [21]. *Analyzers*, the third type, represent an intermediate type due to balancing a unique combination of characteristics from the two extremes. These companies are often characterized as being second movers and having a selective approach, only imitating prospectors' new products and market opportunities that have successful returns [16]. Lastly, *Reactors*, are companies that lack a clear strategic orientation resulting from a short-term emphasis [18]. Casadesus-Masanell and Ricart [10] point out, that strategy is a set of a company's committed choices and actions. Miles and Snow [7], in turn, state that these choices and activities, over time, result in habitual mechanisms which can be classified into archetypical strategy types. Concurrently, it is important to point out that strategy is not the set of activities itself. The set of activities, in contrast, is represented by the business model. The next section briefly characterizes the link between the concepts strategy and business model and shows how business model patterns can be used to evaluate a firm's realized business strategy.

2.2 Digital Business Model Patterns

Simply put, a business model describes the general way in which companies create and capture value [22, 23]. Furthermore, the business model in its firm-specific conception allows us to describe and design specific components as well as the interactions between these [23]. With this, the business model consists of different, recurring components. First, the *value proposition*, which depicts the value as product and service content that is brought to the customer and target segment. Second, the *value network*, which describes how the value is created and delivered to the customer. Third, the *revenue/cost* model, which specifies how the value is captured [24, 25]. The firm-specific conception simultaneously implies that a firm can gain a competitive advantage by making unique choices or linking components differently [10, 26]. Therefore, the business model concept is a useful lens for understanding a company's underlying logic [26, 27]. Coming back to the link between business strategy and business model, both concepts intersect, but are not the same. The definition of business strategy above implies that a company has a vision or an idea of how it will position itself or work in the future [28]. The available strategic actions of a company thus are choices that constitute the configuration of the company's business model. More specifically, strategy refers to the contingent plan about which business model a company should use [29]. Hence, the business model concept can be understood as a representation of lower-level instantiations of a company's realized strategy [10, 30].

The majority of business model components are often quite transparent [26]. This is because they usually consist of a recombination of already existing solutions i.e. patterns [31]. Alexander's definition of patterns is that "each pattern describes a problem which occurs over and over again in our environment, and then describes the core of the solution to that problem, in such a way that you can use this solution a million times over, without ever doing it the same way twice" [32]. Business model patterns, thus, are commonly used, and proven configurations of specific components of a business model [33, 34]. As a consequence, the concept of business model patterns can be used to systematically analyze a company's business model [35]. In their study, Remane et al. [9] classified a database of patterns into *purely digital, digitally enabled,* and *not necessarily digital.* They also classified patterns according to their hierarchical impact. *Prototypical* patterns describe holistic business models of which a company may well use simultaneously such as Apple applying *[IT] equipment/component manufacturers* as well as *Multi-sided platforms.* In contrast *Solution* patterns representing specific building blocks of business models such as *Channel maximization.* Furthermore, patterns are classified by four meta-components. The *value proposition* gives an overall view of a company's products and services. *Value delivery* describes the customer segments, channels for delivering the value proposition and the company's customer relationship. *Value creation* explains the key resources, key activities and key partnerships of a company. Finally, *value capture* describes the company's revenue streams and cost structure [9].

3   Methodology, Data Sample and Analysis

In order to answer the proposed research question mentioned above, we used a longitudinal data set to assess the evolution of digital business model patterns over time and identify within and across companies and industry sectors [36]. We did this by using a cluster analysis to allocate business model pattern configurations to the four strategic orientations derived by Miles and Snow [7] and are thus in line with earlier IS research [e.g. 37].

The object of the first phase was to create a database containing business model descriptions of companies for the years 2007, 2009, 2011, 2013, 2015, and 2017. Beginning in 2007, it was ensured that the introduction of the iPhone was covered. This can be seen as a breakthrough mobile device leading to more people than ever being connected to the internet. It was necessary to only include companies in the sample for which we could draw on the same source of information to ensure a certain degree of objectivity. We therefore decided to include only publicly traded companies. Accordingly, we used the index "NASDAQ Composite" as a starting point for data collection. The "NASDAQ Composite" lists the largest stocks traded on the NASDAQ (National Association of Securities Dealers Automated Quotation). The index is a price index primarily containing tech-savvy companies. By an API to "Thomson Reuters Datastream," we compiled lists of all index constituents, including their ISIN-Number, SIC-Codes, and stock prices on 31.06. for their respective years. To include smaller companies such as start-ups in the sample, we decided to use the stock price rather than market capitalization as an indicator. Accordingly, we sorted the lists of constituents referring to their price in descending order. For reasons of manageability, the lists were cut to the top 250 companies. It is essential to have company data for the entire period. As a consequence, we reduced the sample to those companies that were in the top 250 for the entire period resulting in a sample of 51 companies to be analyzed. Since a company's business model is the underlying research object, we used Item 1, which is included in the Form 10-K as the description of a company's business model. This document, which is required by the SEC (United States Securities and Exchange Commission), represents annual financial statements in a highly standardized form that companies using the American financial market are obliged to prepare annually. Having Item 1 included in Form 10-K contains a detailed description of each companies' business and thus forms the most accurate, comparable, and comprehensive description possible for this study. According to the rules, not all companies in our sample had to provide the Form 10-K. Therefore, we were only able to download the document for 45 companies for all years. Next, we downloaded the companies' financials for the period from 2007–2017. Not all companies provided data for the whole period resulting in 5 more companies being dropped from the sample. This results in a sample of 40 companies and a database of 240 business model descriptions for the period.

To investigate business model patterns within the companies' business model descriptions, we used the taxonomy developed by Remane et al. [9]. In order to analyze the business models within the Form 10-K, we generated a matrix for each year. These matrices consist of the individual companies and the business model patterns identified by Remane et al. [9]. In the following, the companies' business descriptions were compared with the descriptions of the individual patterns. For the sake of verifiability, statements matching the patterns have been marked within Item 1 of Form 10-Ks with the corresponding designation. At the same time, the corresponding business model patterns were assigned to the respective company in the matrix. Thereby, companies could apply several *prototypical* as well as *solution* patterns simultaneously.

In order to avoid mistakes, encode as accurately as possible, and to grant verifiability, we followed the proven deductive approach of qualitative content analysis developed by Mayring [38]. The following Table 1 shows typical patterns included in the database, their descriptions, and a corresponding reference to these patterns we found in the business description within the Item 1 of Apple's Form 10-K 2013.

Table 1. Exemplary quote within companies' Form 10-K's

Pattern Name	Characteristics according to Remané et al. (2017)	Description of Pattern by Remané et al. (2017)	Company's quote in Form 10-K
(IT) equipment/ component manufacturers	Prototypical Digitally enabled Value proposition Value creation	Produce IT equipment and components	"The Company designs, manufactures, and markets mobile communication and media devices, personal computers, and portable digital music players." (Form 10-K 2013 – Apple Inc.)
Multi-sided platforms	Prototypical Purely digital Value Proposition	Bring together two or more distinct but interdependent groups of customers, where the presence of each group creates value for the other groups	"The Company continues to expand its platform for the discovery and delivery of third-party digital content and applications through the iTunes Store." (Form 10-K 2013 – Apple Inc.)
Channel maximization	Prototypical Digitally enabled Value delivery Value capture	Leverage as many channels as possible to maximize revenues	"The Company sells its products worldwide through its online stores, its retail stores, its direct sales force, and third-party wholesalers, resellers, and value-added resellers." (Form 10-K 2013 – Apple Inc.)

The target of the third phase was the empirical determination of group membership by conducting a cluster analysis. In doing so, we performed a two-step cluster analysis in SPSS. By using the Log-likelihood distance, this approach can cluster continuous as well as categorical variables [39]. We divided our period of investigation into three separate periods to control for possible time lacks in strategic decisions to investigate the evolution of constituents and characteristics for the specific clusters. Thereby each cluster represents a strategic orientation of the Miles and Snow's [7] typology. We used three variables to characterize the derived clusters which the following Table 2 shows.

In the last phase, we qualitatively analyzed each cluster by using the taxonomy derived by Remane et al. [9], the matrices per year, and the statistics from the cluster analysis. First, we examined the clusters by the number of companies within the cluster, the industrial affiliation of these companies, and the focus of their business. In the next step, we analyzed the configurations within the clusters and their evolution over the period using the predefined *variables prototypical* vs. *solution-oriented, fully digital* vs.

Table 2. Expected value of variables for each strategic orientation

Variable	Controls for	Defender	Reactor	Analyzer	Prospector
ø Number of patterns	Diversity of configurations	Low	No	Medium	High
ø Change of pattern	Changes within configurations	No/Low	No	Low/Moderate	Moderate/High
Variance of pattern change	Continuity of change within configurations	No/Low	No	Low	Moderate/High

digitally-enabled, *value proposition*, *value delivery*, *value creation*, and *value capture* originating from the meta-components and dimensions of the taxonomy.

4   Findings

4.1   Strategic Orientations in the Digital Age

Table 3 illustrates the results of the two-way clustering. It shows a distance silhouette coefficient of 0.8 for the first period and 0.7 for the second and third period. Besides, the ratio of cluster shrinks from 16 to 2.67 over the course of time. Reasons for this is that the cluster representing *Analyzers* levels down over time, while the cluster representing *Prospectors* increases by two in the second, and by three companies in the third period. The clusters representing *Defenders* and *Reactors*, in contrast, are stable over time.

Table 3. Overview of clustering

Period	Distance of silhouettes coefficient	Number of companies within the cluster	Ratio cluster
T1 (2007 & 2009)	0.8	Defender (7)*, Reactor (16), Analyzer (16), Prospector (1)	16
T2 (2011 & 2013)	0.7	Defender (7), Reactor (16), Analyzer (14), Prospector (3)	5.33
T3 (2015 & 2017)	0.7	Defender (7), Reactor (16), Analyzer (11), Prospector (6)	2.67

*Number of companies included in a cluster within brackets

Table 4 lists the companies and their industry affiliation included in the clusters within the individual periods. Especially companies stemming from a rather asset-heavy industry such as *(20) Food and Kindred Products, (53) General Merchandise Store* or *(13) Oil and Gas Extraction or Mining* can be assigned to the cluster *Defender*. The strategic orientation *Reactor*, in turn, merely represents companies from the B2B sector such as *(28)*

Chemicals and Allied Products, (35) Industrial and Commercial Machinery and Computer Equipment. Companies of both clusters do not change their strategic orientation within our period of investigation. In contrast, the cluster representing the strategic orientation of *Analyzers* includes companies from a variety of industries. Within this cluster, the companies Amazon and Apple changed their strategic orientations from the first to the second period. From then on they can be considered as *Prospectors.* Both companies already had a strong digital background and can be described as tech-savvy. From the second to the third period, the companies Booking Holdings, Costar and Morningstar also changed their strategic orientations from being *Analyzers* to being *Prospectors.* Interesting to note is, that in contrast to the first two companies mentioned, these companies exhibit asset-light business models. The last cluster, representing *Prospectors*, at the beginning only contained Alphabet, stemming from the industry *(73) Business Services.* Over the course of time it increases by integrating aforementioned five companies.

With respect to the characteristics of the individual DBMP configurations of the respective strategic orientations, significant differences can be identified, which are typical for the respective strategic orientations. The strategic orientation *Defender* exhibits the smallest number of digital business model pattern. With 3.39 digital business model pattern, the cluster representing *Analyzers* shows the average value. In contrast, *Prospectors* have by far the highest number of digital business model patterns. Simultaneously, *Prospectors* are the only companies that exhibit changes within their configurations in the first period. Taking a look at the evolution of configuration characteristics, in contrast to *Analyzers* and *Prospectors*, the configuration characteristics of *Defenders* do not change over time. The first two strategic orientations, however, both exhibit a higher amount of digital business model patterns in the second period, which decreases again in the third. The same trend can be seen with the exchange of patterns. Regarding the hierarchical impact, *Defenders* clearly show a solution-oriented configuration. With an amount of 90%, they further apply a mostly digital business model pattern. The configurations of *Analyzers* and *Prospectors* share to a large extend the same characteristics and exhibit more prototypical-oriented and thus holistic digital business model pattern configurations. At the same time, they have less purely digital configurations and thus exhibit much digital business model pattern which are digitally enabled. Consequently, they have a strong physical component in their digital business model pattern configuration. Furthermore, the orientation of the configurations of both strategic orientations is only slightly changing throughout the investigation. However, it can be stated that the orientation towards prototypical as well as towards digitally enriched business model pattern is increasing from period one to period three. Concerning the dimensions the individual strategic orientations target, it is striking that the strategic orientation *Defender* has a focus on the dimension *value proposition* and *value capture.* Concurrently, with only 10%, it neglects the dimension *value creation.* This fits exceptionally well with the very solution-oriented approach of *Defenders.* It further leads to the picture that companies following this strategic orientation enrich their already existing, physical business with fully digital and solution-oriented business model patterns such as *Channel maximization* or *Online advertising and public relations.* The value creation continues to take place primarily in the traditional business. Coming to *Analyzers* and *Prospectors,* we find different configurations. The configurations of both strategic orientations are

Table 4. Overview of companies within clusters for each period

Company (Sic)	T1	T2	T3
Alphabet (737)	P	P	P
Amazon (591)	A	P	P
Amerco (421)	A	A	A
Amgen (282)	R	R	R
Apple (357)	A	P	P
Atrion (384)	R	R	R
Biogen (283)	R	R	R
Bio-Techne (283)	R	R	R
BOK Financial (602)	R	R	R
Booking Holdings (738)	A	A	P
Cerner (737)	A	A	A
CH Robinson Worldwide (473)	A	A	A
Churchill Downs (794)	A	A	A
Coca Cola (208)	D	D	D
Costar (738)	A	A	P
Costco Wholesale (533)	A	A	A
Dollar Tree (533)	D	D	D
Equinix (481)	A	A	A
Erie Indemnity (641)	R	R	R
F5 Networks (737)	A	A	A
Fiserv (737)	A	A	A
Henry Schein (504)	A	A	A
Iberiabank (602)	R	R	R
ICU Medical (384)	R	R	R
Idexx Laboratories (283)	A	A	A
Isramco (131)	D	D	D
Landstar System (421)	D	D	D
Magellan Health (801)	R	R	R
Medicinova (283)	R	R	R
Microstrategy (737)	A	A	A
Middleby (358)	R	R	R
Morningstar (628)	A	A	P
National Western Life (631)	R	R	R
Nordson (356)	R	R	R
Northern Trust (602)	R	R	R
Paccar (371)	R	R	R
Sanderson Farms (201)	D	D	D
Stericycle (495)	R	R	R
T Rowe Price (628)	D	D	D
Wynn Resorts (701)	D	D	D

*D = Defender; R = Reactor; A = Analyzer; P = Prospector; ** T1 = (2007–2009); T2 = (2011–2013); T = 3 (2015–2017); *** Sic Codes in brackets; **** Companies which change their strategic orientations in the following period in bold

*D = Defender; R = Reactor; A = Analyzer; P = Prospector; ** T1 = (2007–2009); T2 = (2011–2013); T = 3 (2015–2017); *** Sic Codes in brackets;
**** Companies which change their strategic orientations in the following period in bold

comparatively balanced but differentiate from each other in nuances. Thus, with 82% of the applied patterns, prospectors have a much stronger focus on the business model dimensions *value creation*, whereas this focus is lower regarding the strategic orientation of *Analyzers*. At the same time, it is noticeable that the weighting of the patterns of *Prospectors* changes more strongly from the second to the third period than it does regarding the configuration of *Analyzers*. This may be due to a stronger exchange of patterns or the change in the strategic orientation of three companies from an approach of an *Analyzer* to one of a *Prospector*. The following Table 5 shows the characteristics of digital business model configurations of all strategic orientations for all periods in more detail.

Table 5. Overview of cluster characteristics over all periods

Strategic Orientation	∅ Amount of Pattern	∅ Change of Pattern	Continuity of Change	∅ Proto-typical	∅ Purely Digital	∅ Value Proposition	∅ Value Delivery	∅ Value Creation	∅ Value Capture
T1									
Defender	2.29	0.00	0.00	10%*	90%	69%	31%	10%	62%
Reactor	0.00	0.00	0.00	–	–	–	–	–	–
Analyzer	3.93	0.00	0.89	64%	36%	50%	50%	62%	42%
Prospector	15.0	4.00	5.20	64%	36%	68%	32%	79%	47%
T2									
Defender	2.29	0.00	0.00	10%	90%	69%	31%	10%	62%
Reactor	0.00	0.00	0.00	–	–	–	–	–	–
Analyzer	4.61	0.71	0.74	69%	31%	56%	44%	69%	39%
Prospector	16.8	2.67	3.03	63%	37%	55%	45%	82%	41%
T3									
Defender	2.29	0.00	0.00	10%	90%	69%	31%	10%	62%
Reactor	0.00	0.00	0.00	–	–	–	–	–	–
Analyzer	4.09	0.27	0.51	67%	33%	49%	51%	69%	34%
Prospector	10.7	2.75	2.30	68%	32%	69%	31%	76%	51%

*Percentages indicate the average of digital business model patterns, which can, according to Remane et al., (2017), be assigned to a particular business model dimension. Thereby, patterns can target more than one dimension

4.2 Evolution of Digital Business Model Configurations and Changes in Strategic Orientations

The number of companies in clusters is not consistent throughout the period of investigation. Hence, it is evident that several companies had changed group membership throughout the investigation, suggesting fundamental changes in their strategic orientation. The following Tables 6, 7, and 8 show exemplary evolutions of digital business model pattern configurations of three companies. Firstly, Apple as an example of a company changing its strategic orientation from being an *Analyzer* to being a *Prospector*.

Secondly, F5 Networks as a company following the strategic orientation of an *Analyzer* over the whole period. Lastly, Coca Cola which clearly can be assigned to the strategic orientation of a *Defender.*

Apple's core configuration consists of prototypical business model patterns such as *Marketplace exchange,* or *Multi-sided platforms.* These patterns, as well as few others, build a stable core over the course of time. Other prototypical, as well as solution-oriented patterns, are placed and exchanged around these core patterns. Thereby they either take on a supporting function or act as own independent businesses. For example, patterns such as *E-shop* or *Bricks + clicks* appear in the wake of time and disappear again if necessary. Both patterns, as well as patterns such as *Channel maximization,* clearly pursue the objective to sell the products produced by Apple and to open up various distribution channels. Other patterns, such as *Trust intermediary,* in turn, represent independent businesses with their revenue streams. An important role in Apple's configuration and its evolution is played by the digitally enabled patterns *(IT) equipment/component manufacturer* and *Digitally charged products.* In the second period, the company makes the most changes and builds up many patterns. Taking a closer look, one can see that most of the patterns adapted in this period, such as *Digital add-on, Product as point of sales,* or *Remote usage and condition monitoring,* closely related to Apple's hardware products.

Table 6. Evolution of Apple's digital business model pattern configuration

Year	Applied Patterns
2007	**(IT) equipment/component manufacturers***, Channel maximization, **Digitally charged products**, Digitization, IP trader, **Marketplace exchange, Multi-sided platforms, Software firms,**
2009	**(IT) equipment/component manufacturers**, Channel maximization, **Digitally charged products**, Digitization, E-Shop, IP trader, **Marketplace exchange, Multi-sided platforms, Software firms,**
2011	**(IT) equipment/component manufacturers**, Channel maximization, Digital add-on, Digital lock-in, **Digitally charged products**, Digitization, E-Shop, Infrastructure services firms, IP trader, **Marketplace exchange, Multi-sided platforms, Software firms,**
2013	**(IT) equipment/component manufacturers**, Bricks + clicks, Business intelligence, Channel maximization, Digital add-on, Digital lock-in, **Digitally charged products**, Digitization, E-Shop, Inventor, Licensing, **Marketplace exchange, Multi-sided platforms**, Physical freemium, Product as point of sales, Remote usage and condition monitoring, Selling online services, **Software firms**, Trust intermediary,
2015	**(IT) equipment/component manufacturers**, Channel maximization, **Digitally charged products**, Digitization, E-Shop, Infrastructure services firms, **Marketplace exchange, Multi-sided platforms, Software firms**, Trust intermediary,
2017	**(IT) equipment/component manufacturers**, Channel maximization, **Digitally charged products**, Digitization, E-Shop, **Marketplace exchange, Multi-sided platforms**, Selling online services, **Software firms**, Trust intermediary,

* Digital business model patterns in bold represent the core configuration

Taking a look at the digital business model pattern configuration of another *Analyzer*, F5 Networks, the two prototypical patterns *Infrastructure service firm* and *Software firm* build the core of the configuration. Interesting to note is that the pattern *Customer supplier of hardware* was exchanged for the pattern *(IT) equipment/component manufacturer* in the second period. Furthermore, the company adds the pattern *Application service providers* in the third period. This pattern promises ongoing revenue through continues service fees and hence represents a modification of the traditional software business F5 Networks already was in. Accordingly, the company has primarily adapted patterns that represent a further development or superior solution to the previous core business. This showcases the behavior of an *Analyzer* who assess possibilities and is more wait-and-see in its actions.

Table 7. Evolution of F5 Networks' digital business model pattern configuration

Year	Applied Patterns
2007	Custom suppliers of hardware, **Infrastructure services firms***, **Software firms**,
2009	Custom suppliers of hardware, **Infrastructure services firms**, **Software firms**,
2011	Custom suppliers of hardware, **Infrastructure services firms**, **Software firms**,
2013	(IT) equipment/component manufacturers, **Infrastructure services firms, Software firms**,
2015	(IT) equipment/component manufacturers, Application service providers, **Infrastructure services firms, Software firms**,
2017	(IT) equipment/component manufacturers, Application service providers, **Infrastructure services firms, Software firms**,

* Digital business model patterns in bold represent the core configuration

In contrast, the company Coca Cola represents the approach of a *Defender*. Its business can be described as asset-heavy and physical. Nevertheless, the company exhibits the digital business model patterns *Channel maximization,* and *Online advertising, and public relations.* These solution-oriented and fully digital business model patterns are clearly pursuing the goal of strengthening the core business and increasing sales of produced beverages. At the same time, the evolution of business model patterns does not change over time, suggesting that the company sees digital technology as an enabler rather than a direct source of value creation and delivery. There is also evidence for this shown by the lack of mention of business model patterns such as *Enterprise resource planning*, which usually is the standard in such a business model.

5 Discussion and Conclusion

5.1 Discussion of Findings

Our findings reveal important new perspectives. All strategic orientations derived by Miles and Snow [7] are present within our sample. At the same time, we can see contextual dependencies with regard to the application of specific strategic orientations and

Table 8. Evolution of Coca Cola's digital business model pattern configuration

Year	Applied Patterns
2007	**Channel maximization, Online advertising and public relations,**
2009	**Channel maximization, Online advertising and public relations,**
2011	**Channel maximization, Online advertising and public relations,**
2013	**Channel maximization, Online advertising and public relations,**
2015	**Channel maximization, Online advertising and public relations,**
2017	**Channel maximization, Online advertising and public relations,**

* Digital business model patterns in bold represent the core configuration

changes to new ones. These refer to the industry a company is in and to the materiality of its core product or service.

Companies applying the strategic orientation of a *Reactor* either do not have a clear digital business strategy or fail to communicate it. Both may indicate that they consider the formulation and execution of a digital business strategy to be less promising. At the same time, these companies mainly stem from B2B industries with strong engineering foci as well as high tech and knowledge-intensive products in niche markets. Reasons may be, that the industry characteristics simply do not call for a digital business strategy or the technology is not yet mature enough to provide a significant benefit. At the same time, our study raises two further explanations. Our study shows that certain business model patterns are communicated less strongly than patterns that appeal to a company's value proposition. Prominent example are patterns such as *Enterprise resource planning* or *Supply chain management* which are not communicated even if they are central to specific companies' business models. While Coca Cola, for instance, is traditionally viewed as a brand-driven company, there is no doubt about the influence of Coca Cola's supply chain on the company's success [40]. Companies such as Coca Cola can perceive these patterns as commodities and, hence, communicate them less strongly than other patterns leading to our second explanation. *Defenders* often stem from asset-heavy industries but, as opposed to *Reactors*, have a stronger customer interface. Accordingly, these companies communicate their digital business model pattern much stronger. Concurrently, these patterns are often solution-oriented, digital patterns which are easy to implement. Furthermore, these patterns create direct value to the customers or support the actual value proposition of a physical product, such as the pattern *Channel maximization* does. This may be an indication that many companies and entire industries still do not understand the importance of digital technologies for creating differential value and competitive advantages in nuances. Accordingly, they underestimate the effect of digital technology on the actual success of a company. Therefore, they may tend to consider IT strategy to be subordinate to business strategy and still do not assign them any strategic relevance at the business level.

With regard to the context of product materiality, our study shows that purely digital business models, such as those of software firms, do not necessarily result in more strategic flexibility and increased option space of competitive moves. Hence, our findings are in contrast to statements from other studies that say that characteristics of digital technology per se lead to more freedom and flexibility [41]. Many software firms within our sample follow the strategic orientation of an *Analyzer* and show a certain homogeneity of the applied and exchanged patterns. In addition, their configurations exhibit a strong specialization. All of these company's adopted the prototypical pattern *Application service provider* at the same time. The pattern is very similar to the pattern named *Software firm* and only refines the way value is created. Apart from these "punctual" improvements, most pure software companies did not undertake any far-reaching innovations. Rather, the companies which combined different technologies (e.g. physical and digital) showed the most volatile business model configuration and were engaged in different initiatives, even at the same time. This leads to platforms which often base on physical devices. Apple for instance, digitally enriched their hardware products and, thus, was able to establish a digital platform. This increased Apple's option space and enabled the company to experiment with different patterns and enter new businesses. Here we can see links to the work of Nambisan et al. [42, 43], which describe a general shift from in-house innovation to innovation networks in business ecosystems based on digital platforms. This reinforces the statement made by Yoo et al. [44] that says that one of the key imperatives of innovation is the question of how to design, build and sustain a vibrant platform that enables different actors to settle their products on it.

5.2   Implications for iS Research and Business Practice

Our study unravels important insights by shedding light on the nature of strategic orientations in a digital context. Many studies have examined the concept of digital business strategy through several theoretical lenses. To the best of our knowledge, we are the first to empirically examine established generic types of strategic behavior, derived by Miles and Snow [7], in the context of an ongoing digital transformation. First of all, we were able to show that the framework of Miles and Snow [7] is still applicable in the digital age. Nevertheless, while all strategic orientations prevail, we were able to show contextual differences with regard to the application of the individual strategy types. These are reflected in the dimensions of industrial environment and materiality of the product or service. Thus, in contrast to other studies, we can show that the digital transformation in individual industries seems to be proceeding differently, or that digital strategies in the industries have a different status. Furthermore, we were able to show that digital business model configurations do not per se lead to increased freedom.

Furthermore, we show that (digital) business model patterns are a useful tool to analyze a company's (digital) business model and draw conclusions about its (digital) business strategy. Practitioners can use this tool to counteract uncertainties in the analysis, formulation and implementation of digital business strategies, since digitization is often the subject of strong hype cycles and the use of digital technologies and digital business models is often very unreflective. A wait-and-see attitude and the adaptation of business models at the right time, as Apple shows in our example, is often much more promising than simply trying out all business models at once. At the same time, however, it must be pointed out that digital technologies influence firm performance and underestimating them can be problematic for companies. A strategic consideration of digital issues on the business level is therefore indispensable.

5.3   Limitations and Future Research

Our study has three limitations. First, the creation of our database. Here we only included publicly traded companies. Thus, it remains to be questioned whether the inclusion of non-publicly traded companies would change our results and how feasible our findings are, for instance, with regard to different company sizes. Furthermore, due to using the *NASDAQ Composite,* we limited our study to companies based and traded in the United States of America. Furthermore, the index is known for listing highly tech-savvy companies. Using this index was necessary in order ensure a consistent and stable foundation as well as the availability of the Form 10-K. At the same time, taking a broader sample from companies all over the world would have enriched our study, as it would have included several perspectives and different approaches of companies from other cultural and environmental contexts. Second, survivorship bias can significantly influence the results of a study. Since we only observed companies within the top 250 of the *NASDAQ Composite* according to their closing price it is possible to draw wrong conclusions. The index is perceived as very volatile and it can be misleading to exclude companies and their adaption behavior, which had a different closing price at that specific time. However, switching to the *NASDAQ-100* would not have been beneficial as we also wanted to give smaller companies known to experiment with new business models, such as start-ups, the opportunity to get into sample. Third, the accuracy of the Form 10-Ks can be questioned. Other scholars such as Weill et al. [45] also have used this document as a source for analyzing a company's business model. The document consequently can be perceived as a reliable source. In addition, companies are subject to strict regulations when filling it. Concurrently, they are free to decide which part of their business models they want to describe. Therefore, it cannot be completely guaranteed that all business model patterns are contained in the Form 10-K and whether all nuances of digital business strategy were thus examined. This makes further research necessary to counter these limitations. It is also important to empirically evaluate the four strategic orientations in a digital context and gain more insights concerning moderating variables such as industry characteristics or management decisions. At the same time, a qualitative approach could be useful to obtain in-depth information about companies and applied digital business strategies and their nuances. Furthermore, the strategic orientations also have to be linked more closely to already existing theoretical concepts such as path dependency, design capital, or digital posture. In addition, future research with a qualitative approach can help to solve aforementioned problems and limitations by using interviews or case studies, for example.

References

1. Tilson, D., Lyytinen, K., Sørensen, C.: Digital infrastructures: the missing is research agenda. Inf. Syst. Res. **21**, 748–759 (2010)
2. Mithas, S., Tafti, A., Mitchell, W.: How a firm's competitive environment and digital strategic posture influence digital business strategy. MIS Q. **37**, 511–536 (2013)
3. Pavlou, P.A., El Sawy, O.A.: From IT leveraging competence to competitive 16th international conference on Wirtschaftsinformatik, march 2021, Essen, Germany advantage in turbulent environments: the case of new product development. Inf. Syst. Res. **17**, 198–227 (2006)

4. Bharadwaj, A., El Sawy, O.A., Pavlou, P.A., Venkatraman, N.: Digital business strategy: toward a next generation of insights. MIS Q. **37**, 471–482 (2013)
5. Matt, C., Hess, T., Benlian, A.: Digital transformation strategies. Bus. Inf. Syst. Eng. **57**(5), 339–343 (2015). https://doi.org/10.1007/s12599-015-0401-5
6. Vial, G.: Understanding digital transformation: a review and a research agenda. J. Strateg. Inf. Syst. **28**, 118–144 (2019)
7. Miles, R., Snow, C.: Organizational strategy, structure, and process. Acad. Manag. Rev. **3**, 546–562 (1978)
8. Sebastian, I.M., Ross, J.W., Beath, C., Mocker, M., Moloney, K.G., Fonstad, N.O.: How big old companies navigate digital transformation. MIS Q. Exec. **16**, 197–213 (2017)
9. Remane, G., Hanelt, A., Tesch, J.F., Kolbe, L.M.: The business model pattern database — a tool for systematic business model innovation. Int. J. Innov. Manag. **21**, 1–61 (2017)
10. Casadesus-Masanell, R., Ricart, J.E.: From strategy to business models and onto tactics. Long Range Plann. **43**, 195–215 (2010)
11. Drnevich, P.L., Croson, D.C.: Information technology and business -level strategy : toward an integrated theoretical perspective. MIS Q. **37**, 483–509 (2013)
12. El Sawy, O.A.: The IS core IX: The 3 faces of information system identity: connection, immersion, and fusion. Commun. Assoc. Inf. Syst. **12**, 588–598 (2003)
13. Yoo, Y., Henfridsson, O., Lyytinen, K.: The new organizing logic of digital innovation: an agenda for information systems research. Inf. Syst. Res. **21**, 724–735 (2010)
14. Coltman, T., Tallon, P.P., Sharma, R., Queiroz, M.: Strategic IT alignment: twenty-five years on. J. Inf. Technol. **30**, 91–100 (2015)
15. Hambrick, D.C.: Some tests of the effectiveness and functional attributes of Miles and Snow's strategic types. Acad. Manag. J. **26**, 5–26 (1983)
16. Haj Youssef, M.S., Christodoulou, I.: Assessing miles and snow typology through the lens of managerial discretion: how national-level discretion impact firms strategic orientation. Manag. Organ. Stud. **4**, 67–73 (2017)
17. Hambrick, D.C.: On the staying power of defenders, analyzers, and prospectors. Acad. Manag. Exec. **17**, 115–118 (2003)
18. Desarbo, W.S., Di Benedetto, C.A., Song, M., Sinha, I.: Revisiting the miles and snow strategic framework: uncovering interrelationships between strategic types, capabilities, environmental uncertainty, and firm performance. Strateg. Manag. J. **26**, 47–74 (2005)
19. Shortell, S.M., Zajac, E.J.: Perceptual and archival measures of miles and snow ' s strategic types : a comprehensive assessment of reliability and validity. Acad. Manag. J. **33**, 817–833 (1990)
20. Walker, O., Boyd, H., Mullin, J.: Marketing Strategy: Planning and Implementation. Irwin/MCGraw-Hill, Homewood (2003)
21. Segars, A.H., Grover, V., Kettinger, W.J.: Strategic users of information technology: a longitudinal analysis of organizational strategy and performance. J. Strateg. Inf. Syst. **3**, 261–288 (1994)
22. Chesbrough, H.: Business model innovation: It's not just about technology anymore. Strateg. Leadersh. **35**, 12–17 (2007)
23. Demil, B., Lecocq, X.: Business model evolution: in search of dynamic consistency. Long Range Plann. **43**, 227–246 (2010)
24. Bohnsack, R., Pinkse, J., Kolk, A.: Business models for sustainable technologies: exploring business model evolution in the case of electric vehicles. Res. Policy. In: 16th International Conference on Wirtschaftsinformatik, March 2021, Essen, Germany, vol. 43, pp. 284–300 (2014)
25. Morris, M., Schindehutte, M., Allen, J.: The entrepreneur's business model: toward a unified perspective. J. Bus. Res. **58**, 726–735 (2005)

26. Teece, D.J.: Business models, business strategy and innovation. Long Range Plann. **43**, 172–194 (2010)
27. Osterwalder, A., Pigneur, Y., Tucci, C.L.: Clarifying business models: origins, present, and future of the concept. Commun. Assoc. Inf. Syst. **16**, 1–25 (2005)
28. Wirtz, B.W., Pistoia, A., Ullrich, S., Göttel, V.: Business models: origin, development and future research perspectives. Long Range Plann. **49**, 36–54 (2016)
29. Casadesus-Masanell, R., Ricart, J.E.: How to design a winning. Harv. Bus. Rev. **89**, 3–9 (2011)
30. Al-Debei, M.M., Avison, D.: Developing a unified framework of the business model concept. Eur. J. Inf. Syst. **19**, 359–376 (2010)
31. Gassmann, O., Frankenberger, K., Cisk, M.: The Business Model Navigator: 55 Models that will Revolutionise your Business. UK: Pearson, Harlow (2014)
32. Alexander, C., Ishikawa, S., Silverstein, M.: A Pattern Language: Towns, Buildings. Constructions. Oxford University Press, New York, USA (1977)
33. Lüttgens, D., Diener, K.: Business model patterns used as a tool for creating (new) innovative business models. J. Bus. Model. **4**, 19–36 (2016)
34. Rudtsch, V., Gausemeier, J., Gesing, J., Mittag, T., Peter, S.: Pattern-based business model development for cyber-physical production systems. Procedia CIRP. **25**, 313–319 (2014)
35. Abdelkafi, N., Makhotin, S., Posselt, T.: Business model innovations for electric mobility: What can be learned from existing business model patterns? Int. J. Innov. Manag. **17**, 1–41 (2013)
36. Yin, R.K.: Discovering the future of the case study. method in evaluation research. Eval. Pract. **15**, 283–290 (1994)
37. Haas, P., Blohm, I., Leimeister, J.M.: An empirical taxanomy of crowdfunding intermediaries. In: Thirty Fifth International Conference Information System, pp. 1–18 (2014)
38. Mayring, P.: Qualitative content analysis: theoretical foundation, basic procedures and software solution (2014)
39. Řezanková, H.: Cluster analysis and categorical data. Statistika **46**, 216–232 (2009)
40. Evans, R., Danks, A.: Strategic supply chain management: creating shareholder value by aligning supply chain strategy with business strategy. In: Gattorna, J., and Jones, T., (eds.) Strategic Supply Chain Alignment: Best Practice in Supply Chain Management, pp. 32–52, Routledge (1998)
41. Huang, J., Henfridsson, O., Liu, M.J., Newell, S.: Growing on steroids: rapidly scaling the user base of digital ventures through digital innovation. MIS Q. **41**, 301–314 (2017)
42. Nambisan, S.: Architecture vs. ecosystem perspectives: Reflections on digital innovation. Inf. Organ. **28**(2), 104–106 (2018)
43. Nambisan, S., Lyytinen, K., Majchrzak, A., Song, M.: Digital innovation management: reinventing innovation management research in a digital world. MIS Q. **41**, 239–253 (2017)
44. Yoo, Y., Boland, R.J., Lyytinen, K., Majchrzak, A.: Organizing for innovation in the digitized world. Organ. Sci. **23**, 1398–1408 (2012)
45. Weill, P., Vitale, M.: Place to Space: Migrating to E-Business Models, Boston, USA (2001)

Untangling the Open Data Value Paradox: How Organizations Benefit from Revealing Data

Tobias Enders[✉], Carina Benz, and Gerhard Satzger

Karlsruhe Institute of Technology, IISM and KSRI, Karlsruhe, Germany
{tobias.enders,carina.benz,gerhard.satzger}@kit.edu

Abstract. Inspired by governmental institutions publishing data for more than a decade, also private sector organizations have started engaging in open data initiatives in recent years. While monetary expenses to engage in open data are tangible, its benefits remain vague, thus fueling the open data paradox. We conduct a set of expert interviews to untangle this paradox to elicit potential benefits that may originate from engaging in open data in the private sector. Our preliminary results show three distinct groups of benefits: internal improvements, innovation driver, and external visibility. With this paper, we lay the foundation for a comprehensive model on exploring open data benefits. For practitioners, we showcase a novel path to extract value from data and to monetize it.

Keywords: Open data · Benefits · Data value · Data monetization

1 Introduction

By now, most organizations acknowledge the role of data as a strategic asset that carries implicit value [1]. Inspired by contemporary trends towards openness and social responsibility, firms let their organizational boundaries become permeable to enable collaboration and innovation [2]. In recent years, private sector firms have started sharing their data with the general public as open data. Given a high level of uncertainty of its benefits, investments are still scarce and fuel the open data paradox [3].

The paradox describes a setting between data provider and data consumer: While data consumers refrain from building services or business models based on open data given its uncertain perpetuity, data providers hesitate to make investments given a lack of evidence of innovation and added value [3]. This paper aims to untangle one side of the paradox by showcasing benefits and thus calling for more investments into open data. Our overall objective of this study is the development of a comprehensive model on the benefits of open data in private sector organizations. This paper represents the first pillar, which is based upon expert interviews.

Given that extant literature offers little insight into benefits of engaging in open data in private sector organizations, our initial data collection is based upon a set of expert interviews. This approach allows obtaining first-hand knowledge from firms that have been active in open data. Hence, we pursue the following research questions: *"What are the benefits from engaging in open data in private sector organizations?"* To

F. Ahlemann et al. (Eds.): WI 2021, LNISO 48, pp. 200–205, 2021.
https://doi.org/10.1007/978-3-030-86800-0_15

address this question, we conduct ten semi-structured interviews across multiple industry sectors. Preliminary results show that there are three distinct groups of benefits: internal improvements, innovation driver, and external visibility.

The paper is structured as follows: Sect. 2 introduces the fundamentals of open data followed by the research design in Sect. 3. Section 4 discusses the preliminary results of our study before closing with a conclusion and research outlook in Sect. 5.

2   Fundamentals of Open Data

Over the years, literature has produced various understandings and conceptualizations of what is meant by openness [4]. Open data – representing an open resource in the universe of openness – makes no exception: A multitude of definition of what open data entails has emerged. We follow the concept that defines open data as a form of content that can be freely used, modified, and shared by anyone and for any purpose [5]. Despite this notion, organizations oftentimes restrict data reuse and re-distribution and thereby dilute the meaning of data being truly open.

Given the ambiguity in research on "openness", it is crucial to contextualize open data towards adjacent research fields. Schlagwein et al. [6] suggest a framework to conceptualize different research streams: Openness as higher order concept, open sources, open process and open effects. In line with the proposed framework, we understand open data to be an open resource similar to open API [7] and open source software [8]. In contrast, open processes include open innovation [2, 9] and crowdsourcing [10]. While open resources may represent an input to open processes, we must clearly distinguish between those fields of research and their contributions.

While the phenomenon of open data is just gaining momentum in the private sector [11], open government data (OGD) has already proven to enable value creation [12]. Driven by changes in legislation, such as in the European Union [13] and Unites States [14], the public sector has been a role model on open data initiatives for almost two decades. Whilst research into expected benefits of OGD provides initial insights, little is known about potential benefits in the private sector. As for OGD, institutions strive, for instance, for a higher level of transparency [15, 16], democratic accountability and improved citizen services [17]. Furthermore, there is a hope that open data promotes collaboration activities between citizens and government [18, 19]. From an economic perspective, OGD has also proven to enable the formation of new business models [20]. Given that public and private organizations operate towards different objectives - maximization of social welfare versus maximization of profits -, additional research is needed to capture and contrast those benefits.

3   Research Design

To explore benefits derived from open data, we conduct a set of semi-structured expert interviews across multiple industry sectors [21]. For the selection of interview participants, we follow a criterion-i purposeful sampling approach [22]. The criteria are defined as such that all interviewees must have direct knowledge of working with open data in private sector organizations, hence, provide first-hand information. Both, technical and business roles of the interviewees are in focus to explore different perspectives. An overview of the experts is provided in Table 1. In total, ten interviews are conducted; either over the phone or in-person. Each interview lasts between 45 min and one hour and is recorded and transcribed for further analysis.

The interviews are analyzed by conducting two distinct coding cycles [23]. To account for the explorative nature of the study, an open coding cycle with no pre-defined list of codes is used for the first iteration. The second coding cycle consists of an axial coding to resemble codes and to ensure that categories and subcategories relate to each other accordingly. To verify the results, we ask a second, independent researcher to re-code all interviews. Discrepancies between the coding of the researchers are discussed until a mutual agreement is reached. The software MAXQDA supports this work.

Table 1. Overview of interviewees

Interviewee	Job role	Industry
1	Team Lead IT & Engineering	Chemicals
2	Chief Data Officer	Energy
3	Head Big Data Strategy	Energy
4	Chief Data Officer	Banking
5	Head Data-Based Business Models	Automotive
6	Head Data Strategy	Automotive
7	IT Architect	Travel & Transport
8	IT Architect	Travel & Transport
9	Business Data Manager	Logistics
10	IT Enterprise Architect	Travel & Transport

4 Preliminary Results

Uncertainty about open data benefits keeps organizations from investing in these initiatives. Our preliminary results show that firms experience benefits across multiple domains: Open data contributes to internal improvements, acts as an innovation driver and improves the firm's visibility towards external stakeholders. A visual representation is shown in Fig. 1 followed by an explanation of each category.

Internal Improvements. Despite open data being an initiative primarily targeting external stakeholders, it offers multiple internal benefits to the data provider itself. We separate those benefits into *culture*, *process* and *data*. We observe that the workforce (*culture*) experiences a mindset shift towards a sharing and collaborative behavior. Driven by the role model of sharing data with external parties, there is an increased awareness of employees to value and foster sharing activities within the organization itself. Furthermore, employees are intrinsically motivated to acquire new skills on data management,

Internal Improvements	Innovation Driver	External Visibility
Culture *Process* *Data*	*External Resources* *Service Offerings* *Business Models*	*Transparency* *Brand Reputation* *Community-Building*

Fig. 1. Open data benefits

which can be transferred to subsequent projects. The IT Architect of Travel & Transport company recalls: "(…) the employees from our department that participated [in the open data project] learnt a lot, especially how to handle the data". As for *process*es, we observe that open data supports efforts to standardize processes across the organization. For instance, access management processes are streamlined across departments to enable all employees to have access to a common data repository. Also, having access to a structured open data interface expedites internal software development cycles, which directly translates into cost savings. In a particular case, a travel & transport firm shortened their application development cycle times by up to 50%. As for a *data* focus, we find that engaging in open data leads to the creation of central data repositories (e.g., data lake), which serve as a one-stop data shop for the entire organization. Also, open data promotes automation efforts given pre-curated data for automated report generation. In summary, we observe that open data contributes to a de-silofication across the organizations; i.e., organizational silos fade away in favor of shared repositories, processes and mindsets.

Innovation Driver. Revealing data to the outside can reinforce a company's innovation potential. It offers *access to external resources* and reflects an option to combat internal capacity constrains: Through open data, companies can profit from time, knowledge, skills and ideas of externals engaging with the data sets. Being intrinsically motivated, external problem solvers invest their personal resources free of charge and contribute to idea generation and problem solving. This creative potential may even translate into *new service offerings* being implemented by the organization itself (e.g., through IP purchasing or licensing) or complementing their business when being offered by the external innovator. In fact, we find external innovators to develop solutions to previously unknown problems, e.g. by addressing issues of minority customer groups. In a concrete use case, a train and rail operator made information about available cargo spaces on their passenger trains available as open data. Inspired by the idea to reduce CO_2 emissions for transporting parcels, a Swiss-based startup used this data to develop a service that allowed same-day parcel delivery by train. For the last mile, the startup uses cargo bikes. Through the use of open data, a win-win situation for both sides emerged: For the startup, the data enabled the service and hence their business model as a whole. For the train & rail operator, additional cargo transported meant additional revenue. Interestingly, open data can *enable new business models* for the data provider as well: While open data is revealed free of charge, organizations start implementing freemium payment models. We find that firms allow access to limited or aggregated open data as a trigger for interested parties to pay for more granular data. Thus, companies establish new business models and thereby monetize their data assets. While extant literature discusses the emergence of new business models in connection with open government data [12], it represents a novel perspective for private sector organizations. In summary, we observe open data to spark innovation by leveraging resources outside the company and opening potential for novel business models and services.

External Visibility. Open data offers benefits related to an enhanced external visibility of the firm. Publishing data creates *transparency* by allowing insights into the company's operations. As a consequence, the interviewees confirm a positive impact on the *brands' reputation*. This is further accelerated by press releases, spreading the word via online and offline media such as blogs, business journals and newspapers. We find that this leads to positive outcomes. For instance, firms experience a spike in the number of applicants for open job positions - especially from recent university graduates. The Chief Data Officer from an Energy company notes: "[open data] is an opportunity for us to present the company and get to know university graduates (…) that we might have the opportunity to hire at a later point in time". Similarly, other external entities take notice of the company, such as investors in pursuit of new investment opportunities. Moreover, we observe *community-building* activities between the firm, creative minds and developers. Establishing a relationship with the community is of utmost importance to enable feedback mechanisms and learn about data needs. Summarizing, open data enhances transparency, brand reputation and community-building, resulting in improved visibility towards external stakeholders.

## 5	Conclusion and Outlook

This paper investigates how private sector organizations engaging in open data benefit from these initiatives. As a first step towards a holistic model on open data benefits, we conduct expert interviews to reveal insights on the companies' experience. We find open data to contribute to internal improvements, to act as an innovation driver and to enhance the firm's visibility towards external stakeholders. For organizations, we illustrate that engaging in open data represents a novel path to extract value from data and to benefit in monetary and non-monetary ways. By providing evidence of value created through open data, we disentangle one side of the open data value paradox. Most notably, open data creates an opportunity for firms to obtain access to skills, time and ideas at no additional charge to co-create value and boost innovation.

While this study's findings are limited given that only single observations were made for each of the organizations, we plan on extending our knowledge base to arrive at a comprehensive model of open data benefits. In particular, we aim to deepen our insights by drawing on in-depth case studies with firms that have been practicing open data for several years. This allows us to observe benefits as they evolve over a longer period of time and hence, we are not dependent on retrospective considerations of individuals. Those findings will be complemented by and contrasted with a structured literature review on open data benefits across multiple domains. In addition to extending our data base, we intend to further analyze organizational change implications of engaging in open data. For instance, open data enables new business models that need to be aligned and integrated with existing ones. While this work has a strong focus on potential benefits of open data, future research needs to critically reflect on the drawbacks and risks that may occur when revealing open data in a digital ecosystem.

References

1. Wixom, B.H., Ross, J.W.: How to monetize your data? MIT Sloan Manag. Rev. **58** (2017)
2. Chesbrough, H.: The future of open innovation. Res. Manag. **60**, 35–38 (2017)
3. Jetzek, T.: Innovation in the open data ecosystem: exploring the role of real options thinking and multi-sided platforms for sustainable value generation through open data. In: Carayannis, E.G., Sindakis, S. (eds.) Analytics, Innovation, and Excellence-Driven Enterprise Sustainability. Palgrave Studies in Democracy, Innovation, and Entrepreneurship for Growth, pp. 137–168. Palgrave Macmillan US, New York (2017)
4. Dahlander, L., Gann, D.M.: How open is innovation? Res. Policy. **39**, 699–709 (2010)
5. Open Knowledge Foundation: The Open Definition. https://opendefinition.org/. Accessed 01 July 2020
6. Schlagwein, D., Conboy, K., Feller, J., Leimeister, J.M., Morgan, L.: Openness with and without Information technology: a framework and a brief history. J. Inf. Technol. **32**, 297–305 (2017)
7. Benlian, A., Hilkert, D., Hess, T.: How open is this platform? the meaning and measurement of platform openness from the complementers' perspective. J. Inf. Technol. **30**, 209–228 (2015)
8. Henkel, J.: Selective revealing in open innovation processes: the case of embedded Linux. Res. Policy. **35**, 953–969 (2006)
9. West, J., Salter, A., Vanhaverbeke, W., Chesbrough, H.: Open innovation: the next decade. Res. Policy. **43**, 805–811 (2014)
10. Howe, J.: Crowdsourcing: How the Power of the Crowd is Driving the Future of Business. Random House (2008)
11. Enders, T., Benz, C., Schüritz, R., Lujan, P.: How to implement an open data strategy ? analyzing organizational change processes to enable value creation by revealing data. In: Proceedings of 28th European Conference on Information Systems (2020)
12. Ahmadi Zeleti, F., Ojo, A., Curry, E.: Exploring the economic value of open government data. Gov. Inf. Q. **33**, 535–551 (2016)
13. European Parliament: Directive 2003/98/EC on the re-use of public sector information. https://eur-lex.europa.eu/LexUriServ/LexUriServ.do?uri=OJ:L:2003:345:0090:0096: en:PDF. Accessed 05 Sept 2020
14. Obama, B.: Transparency and Open Government. https://obamawhitehouse.archives.gov/the-press-office/transparency-and-open-government. Accessed 15 May 2020
15. Bertot, J.C., Jaeger, P.T., Grimes, J.M.: Using ICTs to create a culture of transparency: E-government and social media as openness and anti-corruption tools for societies. Gov. Inf. Q. **27**, 264–271 (2010)
16. McDermott, P.: Building open government. Gov. Inf. Q. **27**, 401–413 (2010)
17. Janssen, M., Charalabidis, Y., Zuiderwijk, A.: Benefits, adoption barriers and myths of open data and open government. Inf. Syst. Manag. **29**, 258–268 (2012)
18. Kassen, M.: A promising phenomenon of open data: a case study of the Chicago open data project. Gov. Inf. Q. **30**, 508–513 (2013)
19. Johnson, P., Robinson, P.: Civic hackathons: innovation, procurement, or civic engagement? Rev. Policy Res. **31**, 349–357 (2014)
20. Janssen, M., Zuiderwijk, A.: Infomediary business models for connecting open data providers and users. Soc. Sci. Comput. Rev. **32**, 694–711 (2014)
21. King, N.: Using interviews in qualitative research. In: Cassell, C., Symon, G., (eds.) Essential Guide to Qualitative Methods in Organizational Research, pp. 11–22. SAGE (2004)
22. Palinkas, L.A., Horwitz, S.M., Green, C.A., Wisdom, J.P., Duan, N., Hoagwood, K.: Purposeful sampling for qualitative data collection and analysis in mixed method implementation research. Admin. Policy Ment. Health Ment. Health Serv. Res. **42**(5), 533–544 (2013)
23. Saldaña, J.: The Coding Manual for Qualitative Researchers. SAGE, London (2009)

How Challenging is the Development of Digital Services in an Automotive Environment? An Empirical Study of the Incongruences Between Business and IT Experts

Mirheta Omerovic Smajlovic[(✉)], Nihal Islam, and Peter Buxmann

Technische Universität Darmstadt, Darmstadt, Germany
{omerovic,islam,buxmann}@is.tu-darmstadt.de

Abstract. The ongoing digitalization empowers incumbent firms on their path from mere producers into providers of holistic digital service solutions. Although digitalization offers a wide range of opportunities such as improved internal processes or new business models, it also leads to managerial and organizational challenges. To identify the cause of specific challenges in an automotive environment, we analyze the development of a digital service with a focus on the collaboration of business and IT experts in this process. Within the scope of a case study in an automotive environment and by consideration of the technological frames of references (TFR) theory as a framework, our results present relevant frame domains in which dominate incongruences between business and IT experts that consequently lead to related challenges. Our key findings and insights extend the existing research and practice related to the development of digital services in an automotive environment.

Keywords: Digital service · Automotive environment · Technological frames of reference theory · Case study

1 Introduction

Information systems (IS) development in general and especially innovative digital services enable firms to create new business values [21] but also require them to revisit their entire organizing and managerial logic [12, 20, 36]. This particularly holds for incumbent firms, as the embedment of digital technologies forces firms to break away from established innovation paths [32, 33] without jeopardizing existing product innovation practices [80, 82]. We find the automotive environment particularly interesting as the new technologies enable a wide variety of digitalization possibilities within the world of vehicles. It is now becoming possible that vehicles can communicate between themselves and with the surrounding digital environment [6, 7], enabling a platform for delivering digital services [25, 70, 83]. Moreover, new competitor landscapes motivate the growing emphasis on digital transformation within the automotive industry [4]. For instance, the launch of the open car communications platform enabling third-party

© The Author(s), under exclusive license to Springer Nature Switzerland AG 2021
F. Ahlemann et al. (Eds.): WI 2021, LNISO 48, pp. 206–222, 2021.
https://doi.org/10.1007/978-3-030-86800-0_16

developers' access to multiple sensors in the vehicle was a big hit for automotive circles breaking the institutionalized tradition of in-house development [32]. In this regard, to keep the market position and compete against existing and novel digital competitors, car manufacturers are increasingly penetrating the world of software development to provide digital services in-house [45, 68, 82]. Such an insourcing process requires significant managerial and organizational changes [32, 33]. For instance, a collaboration between business and IT experts acquires completely new dimensions and modes of an organization requiring "the mutual accommodation and blending of business and IT interests" [29].

The collaboration between business and IT experts is a widely discussed topic within IS research. However, most of the previous studies focus on a company-wide strategic level of alignment and as noted in Vermerris et al. (2014) [84] "it largely ignores the operational practices that help achieve alignment in IT projects". And, while there are multiple studies of IT and business collaboration and alignment at the macro strategic and structural levels [76], only a few studies are tackling the project level of analysis (e.g. [9] and [13]). Moreover, there has been an expansion in identifying and analyzing diverse aspects of the development of digital services in multiple industries (e.g. [75, 80, 88]), but there are no insights related to the specific challenges of the business and IT experts' collaboration in this new digital landscape of an established automotive environment. Since a collaboration between business and IT experts is essential for exploiting the potentials of digitalization [80], it is important to understand the challenges of the development of digital services from their perspectives. Against this background, we aim to answer the research question of *what are the incongruences between business and IT experts that lead to related challenges in the development of digital services in an automotive environment*. To answer this, we have analyzed the development of a digital service in the context of a case study within a globally operating car manufacturer and interviewed business and IT experts collaborating on the project. By conducting interviews (N = 18) and data handling we sort our findings in the technological frames of reference theory (TFR) [66], which represents our theoretical lens for the data analysis. This framework helps us to investigate how the project participants perceive the project requirements [16, 26] and analyze the human sense-making processes [10, 14] as it represents a systematic approach to examine assumptions, expectations, and knowledge people have about the technology [66].

2   Theoretical Background

Many studies simultaneously use expressions related to digitalization. While "digitization" describes the transition from analog to digital through technology, "digitalization" includes further changes in processes. Finally, the term "digital transformation" includes all transformational processes and impacts that go beyond the business perspective, such as organizational and cultural changes [61]. In the existing literature, there are a variety of expansions in identifying and analyzing diverse facets of digital services and digital transformation. For instance, the literature on personal information disclosure [2], technology and innovation [17], governance of intellectual property [30], ecosystems [75], incumbent environments [80], and supply chain [88] show the increased interest in specific aspects related to the development of digital services. Considering these facets, the term digital service refers to utility obtained or arranged through a digital transaction [3, 87] where the bundling of diverse resources and IT artifacts leads to new value experiences [54, 63].

Prior researchers have dealt extensively with aspects around the business and IT collaboration and their alignment. Chan and Reich (2007) [11] provide a review of the alignment literature in IT. Gerow et al. (2014) [24] report on the development of definitions and measure six types of alignment including alignment between IT and business strategies, infrastructures, and processes, while also examining the strategies across these two domains that are linked with infrastructures and processes. Haffke and Benlian (2013) [35] demonstrate the importance of interpersonal understanding for the business and IT partnership, while Preston and Karahanna (2009) [72] draw attention to the necessity to align the organizations' IS strategy with its business strategy. Finally, Sledgianowski and Luftman (2005) [79] describe the use of a management process and assessment tool that can help to promote long-term IT-business strategic alignment. Recent studies also show that IT strategies generally focus on the internal processes and have a rather limited impact on driving innovations in business development [59, 83]. However, the role of IT is no longer to merely ensure efficient processes but also to lead innovativeness and new digital services development [37]. For decades, digitalization has led to different organizational transformations [78], but the product-centric nature of the vehicle manufacturers [42, 55] still requires major structural changes to accommodate both business and IT interests [19, 29]. IT is becoming a leading part of the business model [9, 52, 67], where different approaches to development processes of digital services and vehicle production have to integrate [71]. In order to build up such digital service competencies, vehicle manufacturers are establishing new ways of collaboration between business and IT in their value creation processes [58, 69]. Therefore, within this research work, we aim to extend and shed light on the business and IT collaboration under such new conditions. The literature on alignment has strong parallels with the TFR theory since it provides a useful analytic lens to investigate how the project participants perceive the project requirements. This theory acknowledges that different groups in a development process have different interpretations, so-called "technological frames", of the usefulness, importance, and significance of technologies. This research approach has been introduced within the IS research by Orlikowski and Gash (1994) [66] who identified three frame domains: "nature of technology", referring to the understanding of the technology's capability and functionality; "technology in use", describing the actual conditions and consequences of technology usage; and "technology strategy", which takes into account the vision of the technology value for the organization. Using the results of the empirical study where they interviewed technologists and users about the "Notes technology", Orlikowski and Gash (1994) [66] claim that the differing perspectives of these two groups onto the technology create difficulties and conflicts in the usage of the "Notes technology". The core finding of the TFR theory shows that if key groups have different perceptions within the frames the organization might experience incongruence of the frames. The incongruence leads to organizational inefficiencies. These variable "dimensions" of the TFR theory facilitate an analysis of the perspectives of business and IT experts, which are dynamic in nature [1, 53]. Many empirical studies supported the findings of Orlikowski and Gash (1994) (e.g. [38, 51, 57, 87]), while only a few researchers pointed out contrasting effects as well (e.g. [15, 46]). Building on the negative effects of the incongruity between the frames, many studies suggested mechanisms to overcome the misalignment between different groups such as power [14], politics [44], interaction and communication [77], exchange of knowledge [73], understanding of technology [37], tool support, and the clear defining of procedures [34].

3 Methodology

To address our research question about the cause of the challenges related to the development of a digital service from the business and IT experts' perspectives, we conducted an interpretive case study [90] which is well suited to explore cognitive processes behind judgments of technology [62] as well as the overall topic in-depth [23, 40, 43]. Cognitive research relies on the fundamental principle that an individual's knowledge is structured through experience and interaction [22, 28]. As a basis of an iterative process of data collection and analysis, we used the TFR theory as a framework to investigate the preconditions of challenges in a collaboration between business and IT experts [66]. In the following, the research setting and the data analysis are described in detail.

3.1 Research Setting

In the case study, we investigated the collaboration between business and IT experts in the development of a digital service within a large German car manufacturer (CAR AG; a pseudonym). The rationale underlying our selection of the CAR AG was influenced by the following factors: the ability to take advantage of the opportunities offered by digitalization, the rich context of related challenges due to the first-time development of a digital service, and finally the availability of information. CAR AG employs almost 300,000 employees and is one of the world's biggest manufacturers of commercial vehicles with a global reach. Their focus lies on different areas of digitalization, whose goal is to steer the change in transforming a manufacturing entity into the provider of holistic digital services and solutions. The case study we investigated focuses on the development of a digital service comprising both hardware and software in the vehicle. The hardware component acts as a host for software and services in the vehicle. The digital service acts as an open platform and can host software and services from both the CAR AG and third parties. The development of this digital service started in 2015. In the course of 2018, many other business units/departments of the CAR AG became involved in the project. The roles of the experts within each business unit/department were different, but their expertise could broadly be divided into business and IT areas. The communication between them mostly occurred on a non-regular basis. This situation and the previously described research gap inspired us to interview business and IT experts who were intensively involved in this project to see what their interpretations and perspectives related to the development of a digital service are, in order to get insights about the cause of specific challenges.

3.2 Data Collection and Analysis

Our research work is based on the interpretive case study that follows the principles of planning, designing, preparing, collecting, analyzing, and sharing of data, as described in Yin (2009) [89]. The units of analysis are the business and IT experts who closely collaborate on the development of a digital service in the CAR AG. Business experts are responsible for business development (e.g. customer requirements, pricing), while IT experts take care of software and hardware development of a digital service (e.g. coding, testing). Generally, an expert is a person with special knowledge in a subject area [5]. Our primary data sources are interviews which were conducted face-to-face throughout May and June of 2019. We used a semi-structured interview guideline to minimize the bias and unstructured discussions by providing the same introductions and encouragements to each interviewee [27]. As suggested in Yin (2017) [91], the interviewee selection followed a heterogeneous purposive sample approach applying three predefined criteria: (1) interviewees are well informed; (2) their field of activity is either in a business unit or in an IT department; (3) at least three years of experience in the respective roles. In total, we carried out 18 interviews (see Table 1). Business (BU) and Information Technology (IT) experts received the same questions.

Table 1. Interviewed experts

ID	Y	Function|*Expertise*	ID	Y	Function|*Expertise*
BU1	4	Business Developer *Use Case Development*	IT1	3	Software Developer *Diagnosis and Flashing*
BU2	5	Strategy Expert *Migration of Data*	IT2	3	Software Architecture Expert *Device Management*
BU3	3	Sales Manager Customer Acquisition	IT3	4	Software Developer Prototyping
BU4	3	Business Developer *Use Case Development*	IT4	5	Software Developer *Prototyping*
BU5	3	Sales Expert Use Case Development	IT5	5	Software Architecture Expert *Testing*
BU6	6	Service Product Owner *Substitution Use Case*	IT6	3	IT Project Manager *Defining IT Requirements*
BU7	4	Sales Expert *Customer Requirements*	IT7	6	Platform Development *Expert Technological Fit*
BU8	3	Business Developer *Use Case Development*	IT8	4	IT Security Manager *Security Testing*
BU9	5	Strategy Expert *Strategy Development*	IT9	4	IT Project Manager *Technological Feasibility*

Table 1 shows the ID-number of the interviewees (ID), their organizational function and expertise, and years of experience (Y). Interviews lasted roughly sixty minutes and were audio-recorded. The interview guide consisted of three parts. In the first part, we collected information about the individual involvement within the project and the personal experiences of interviewees. The second part was about the business value and technological functionality of a digital service. In the final part, we surveyed the perceived success of the development of a digital service and influencing factors. For the conduct of the study, we took care to adhere to the seven principles of interpretive field research described by Klein and Myers (1999) [47]. In detail, our understanding of business and IT experts' perspectives as a whole is achieved through the iteration of their individual opinions, a reflection of the context of the automotive organization, and our interaction with the experts. Moreover, throughout the entire process of data analysis, we were sensitive to possible differences between theoretical preconceptions and actual findings, as well as to possible interpretation differences among experts. For the process of data analysis, we used a content data analysis [49] so that we were able to assume a broad perspective [85, 86] and allow for the emergence of frame domains, but at the same time be able to identify the relations between the codes within frames and assimilations with the TFR theory. To sort and refine data categories, we first followed the open coding instructions as described in Miles et al. (1994) [60], while for the theory fit we used the TFR framework presented in Orlikowski and Gash (1994) [66]. In the first phase, we coded all statements reflecting knowledge, expectations, and assumptions creating the frame domains. Using separate code categories, we coded all statements concerning frame incongruence. Frame incongruence describes the issues arising from the existing different perspectives within the frame domains [66]. In a second phase, we integrated codes into aspects, assigned the aspects to business and IT experts, and finally compared the findings. We conducted a pattern coding where we established relations between the aspects and clustered them into the frame content domains. Although there are different views also within IT and business expert groups, for simplification reasons we represent only the homogenous views. Two coders using the qualitative data transcription and analysis software "f4" have done the coding. For each transcribed interview, codes were assigned to the opinions that were found to be most common amongst the participants by both persons separately. After a discussion between the coders, all categories are combined and marked only those that were coded by all.

4 Empirical Results

Since the frame domains are time and context-dependent, we followed the encouragement from Orlikowski and Gash (1994) [66] to examine them in situ, rather than priori. By coding all statements reflecting knowledge, assumptions, and expectation of business and IT experts about the development of a digital service, three frame domains emerged that led to the experts' frame incongruity:

(1) *Business Values of a Digital Service* refers to the business and IT experts' perspective of the digital service business potential and value;
(2) *Technological Functionalities of a Digital Service* refers to the perspective of the business and IT experts about its technological functionalities and;

(3) *Strategy for the Development Process of a Digital Service* refers to the perspective of the business and IT experts about the successful execution of the development process of a digital service.

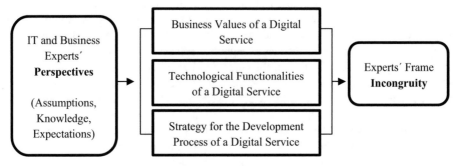

Fig. 1. Frame domains related to the development of a digital service

Figure 1 illustrates the frame domains of our findings. In the following sub-chapters, we briefly describe each frame domain and list the content characteristics that were most repeated by either IT or business experts. For instance, for the frame domain "business values of a digital service", we listed the business values often mentioned by either business or IT experts. Based on how often certain aspects were mentioned, we placed the values accordingly, which were then illustrated through tables and box symbols. The white box (□) demonstrates that none of the IT or business experts mentioned a certain aspect. The white box with a little black dot inside (▫) symbolizes that less than three experts mentioned the aspect. The black box within the white one (▣) shows that between three and six of the experts mentioned it, while the black box (■) shows that more than six of the business or IT experts mentioned it. If the values for identified characteristics are found to be different within these frame domains, we can conclude that business and IT experts possess distinct frames [66].

4.1 Business Values of a Digital Service

The business values of the digital service refer to the assumptions, expectations, and knowledge of the business and IT experts about the potential of the digital service to win over customers and provide positive returns for the CAR AG. Table 2 shows the identified business values of the digital service. As can be seen in Table 2, both business and IT experts agree that a great benefit of this digital service is the possibility to provide customers a platform to develop their own solutions. The following citation of one business expert exemplifies this finding: *"Digital service helps us provide new innovative products or services that are beyond [the] classic automotive environment"* (BU3). An IT expert also emphasized this aspect through the comment that: *"Digital service has the potential to offer customized and individualized specific software adaptations"* (IT4). The remaining aspects consistently differ. IT experts see prominent business value in establishing the recurring long-term payments for the digital service itself and a possibility to save on costs through the use of only one hardware for multiple digital services: *"[...] we make some money by selling the hardware and then by establishing recurring payments for the service"* (IT8).

Table 2. Business vlues of a digital service

Business Experts	Business Values of a Digital Service	IT Experts
☐	The digital nature of the service ensures recurring payments	◙
■	Digital service enables the customers to develop customized digital solutions	■
⊡	Cost efficiencies	■
■	Digital service enables the upselling power for the vehicles	⊡

On the other hand, business experts rather focus on the short-term benefits and upselling potential for vehicles. Namely, they do not observe the digital service as a stand-alone business, but rather as the additional benefit for the vehicle customers, which will result in an increase in vehicle sales: *"If we can fix this (digital) solution and the customer is satisfied, we will sell more vehicles"* (BU4). These differing perspectives on the business values of the digital service relate to several issues between business and IT experts. IT experts complained about vague requirements from the business side due to different expectations related to the real value that the final service should have: *"Mostly, there is a gap in how the business describes the business solution. It is never as detailed as IT needs it and this gap is huge"* (IT9). On the other hand, business experts pointed out the problem of trust: *"If I say that the customer is not willing to give out so much money, I would expect IT colleagues to understand this."* (BU4).

4.2 Technological Functionalities of a Digital Service

Digital service technological functionalities refer to the perceived technological potential of a digital service regarding its software and hardware components. As Table 3 shows, IT experts seem very enthusiastic about the general-purpose nature of the digital service that allows easier development and fast prototyping. The following IT expert´s quotation exemplifies this finding: *"Digital service has one feature that enables me to easily make function prototypes without reinventing the new hardware platform"* (IT6). Business experts, on the other hand, rather praise the customer context offered by the digital service technology. As the following quotation shows, they appreciate the power of the digital service to combine data and automate the processes for the customers: *"[The] combination of the driver information, vehicle and sensors are creating the main added value for the customer"* (BU2). Moreover, business experts agreed that the real capability of the digital service lies in its ability to connect different customers onto one platform, creating the ecosystem for services and customers.

Table 3. Technological functionalities of a digital service

Business Experts	Technological Functionalities of a Digital Service	IT Experts
▣	Decoupling car and software development	■
⊡	General-purpose platform nature	■
⊡	Fast prototyping	■
■	Flexibility to combine data	⊡
▣	Digital service as the ecosystem enabler	⊡

According to both groups of experts, these differing perspectives cause the following issues between the two groups. Business experts criticize the classical structure: *"Classical set-up within the CAR AG is that you have business and IT as separate organizations and therefore it is always difficult to come to the same level of understanding about requirements and how they could be implemented"* (BU6). IT experts mostly agreed on this point as summarized with the following quote: *"A lot of times it is difficult to see the client behind all of it, it is abstract because that is more of a job for business experts and for us it is more technical oriented"* (IT3).

4.3 Strategy for the Development Process of a Digital Service

This frame domain encompasses the generalized assumptions, knowledge, and expectations from the business and IT experts about how the digital service should be developed from the organizational and project management context. Table 4 shows that the business and IT experts also here have different perspectives on what might make the development of a digital service successful. Business experts believe that the following factors will make the process successful: finding the paying customer who would like to invest in the digital service and create their services, clearly defined deadlines and timelines, as well as a good strategy to overcome legal and political issues. The following business expert's quotation exemplifies some of these findings: *"What matters is customer acceptance and how many devices you can bring to the field and how many paying customers you connect [with]"* (BU5). In contrast to this, IT experts rather assume that the proper software development documentation and IT security of a digital service are the main issues that they have to tackle to make the process successful. The following quotation exemplifies this finding: *"The security is the most critical part of the digital service because it is [...] to open up the intellectual property of the car"* (IT5).

However, both business and IT experts agree that the technological stability of a digital service is a crucial prerequisite for the successful execution of the process. Differing perspectives of business and IT experts about the strategy relate to the lack of communication in the process. As the following quotations show, both business and IT experts feel there is miscommunication between them: *"There is a big language barrier [...] and therefore, there is a lack of communication"* (IT8). In another interview, we noted a similar view: *"These IT experts [...] have been recently hired and they define*

Table 4. Strategy for the development process of a digital service

Business Experts	Strategy for the Development Process of a Digital Service	IT Experts
■	Ensuring the technological stability of the digital service	■
■	Finding paying customers	⊡
⊡	Design a proper software development documentation	■
■	Formulating clear and aligned timelines of the process	⊡
▣	Exploring the tactics to overcome legal and political issues	⊡
■	Overcoming conflicting political environments	⊡
□	Ensuring the IT security of the digital service	■

their own processes, but they do not fit into the processes of CAR AG and therefore, there is the lack of understanding" (BU9).

5 Discussion

Based on the approach of the TFR theory, we illustrate that business and IT experts hold different perspectives on (1) business values, (2) technological functionalities, as well as the (3) strategy for the development process of a digital service.

Firstly, when it comes to the "business values of a digital service" frame domain, we found that IT experts perceive a digital service as a completely new business model, which might enable recurring payments and a long-term relationship with a customer (e.g. *"[…] we make some money by selling the hardware and then by establishing recurring payments for the service"* (IT8)). On the other hand, business experts appreciate the upselling value for vehicles that the digital service might provide (e.g. *"If we can fix this (digital) solution and the customer is satisfied, we will sell more vehicles"* (BU4)). This key finding shows the orientation of IT experts towards a digital service as a business per-se, while business experts still observe it as an additional service that comes on top of vehicle sales. In particular, while IT experts would like to focus on the long-term benefits of the new digital service, business stakeholders rather appreciate short-term positive returns through the increased number of sold vehicles. This sort of different practice philosophies and ambidexterity of a development process cause particular challenges between IT and business experts in the development of digital services within automotive organizations (e.g. lack of trust, vague requirements) [74, 92]. Therefore, there is a necessity to balance between the long-term and short-term demands of a market by providing digital services that enable both recurring payments and short-term upselling power for the vehicles.

Secondly, regarding the "technological functionalities of a digital service" frame domain, IT experts perceive the general-purpose nature as one of the most compelling technological functionalities of the digital service (e.g. *"Digital service has one feature that enables me to easily make function prototypes without reinventing the new hardware platform"* (IT6)). In contrast, business experts put a stronger emphasis on the flexibility to combine data (e.g. *"[The] combination of the driver information, vehicle and sensors is creating the main added value for the customer"* (BU2)). This key finding is in line with existing research, which confirms that IT experts have a more engineering perspective [56, 65] while business experts have rather a strategic understanding of technology [39, 66]. Further key findings in this frame domain show that such differing perspectives relate to the classical divisional structure between business and IT, which still exist within incumbent automotive environments. Such separation leads to a vague definition of requirements for the development process. However, for the progress and success in developing a digital service, it is necessary that all stakeholders previously agree on what needs to be accomplished and how [31]. In our view, incumbent firms in an automotive environment must rethink their existing organizational structures of business and IT departments where research could play a crucial role in providing suitable options and possibilities. Against this background, in IS research we need more studies that investigate the organizational setups suitable to incorporate 'old' and 'new' functionalities into their structure in a complementary and not impeding way [48, 50]. For this purpose, incumbent firms in an automotive environment need to reflect on the talents and skills of experts because such a new environment seeks employees who are able to integrate digital technology expertise with business knowledge and vice versa [71].

Thirdly, the "strategy for the development process of a digital service" frame domain shows that IT experts put a great emphasis on the existence of good software development documentation and IT security of the digital service (e.g. *"The IT security is the most critical part of a digital service because it is a very big challenge to open up the intellectual property of the car"* (IT5)). Yet, business experts see the challenges related to the politics and legal issues, as well as the necessity to find a paying customer as crucial factors to succeed in this project (e.g. *"What matters is customer acceptance and how many devices you can bring to the field and how many paying customers you connect [with]"* (BU5)). To align these perspectives, existing IS research has shown that business and IT planning must integrate to ensure the implementation of business objectives in both IT and business planning and operations [8, 39]. The differences here relate to the fact that business experts believe that recently employed IT experts should adhere to existing processes and structures within a long-existing automotive environment. The expectation that IT experts should simply integrate into existing processes and structures is an interesting finding. In our view, for the successful process execution, there is a need for both sides to compromise. As the findings of Sklyar et al. 2019 [81] have recently shown, the development of digital services cannot rely on the old-fashioned centralized style of the organization, but requires greater integration between central structure and units implementing the projects.

6 Conclusion

Our study aimed to identify incongruences between business and IT experts in order to be able to create clarity on the specific challenges in the development of digital services. Against this background, we investigated the collaboration between business and IT experts working on the development of a digital service within the automotive manufacturer. Based on the TFR theory, we have found three frame domains that lead to incongruence on the part of business and IT experts. Thereby, the business and IT experts' misalignments represent a real challenge in successfully developing digital services. For instance, we previously described how business and IT experts perceive the business model behind a digital service differently. While IT experts see it as a business per se with possible long-term recurring payments, business experts rather emphasize the potential to improve the sales of the vehicles. This incongruence might lead to multiple issues such as a lack of trust or misunderstanding. Therefore, in practice, when managers are in charge of projects where both business and IT expertise are needed, we highly recommend these managers to understand the framing logic and to examine if business and IT experts have similar views on the vision, objectives, and values of a digital service. Moreover, since both expert groups relate the existence of different perspectives in the technological functionalities of a digital service mostly to the existing traditional structures of automotive organizations, the current organization and the division of the business and IT units should be challenged. The identified frame incongruences between business and IT experts might help automotive organizations to organize their business and IT teams more effectively.

Regarding the implications for research, we extended the knowledge about specific challenges based on the TFR theory. Many studies used the concept of the TFR theory as a framework, but to the best of our knowledge, all of the empirically studied technologies applied for the improvement of internal processes and organization (e.g. [14, 51, 57]). With our study, we firstly introduced novel technological frames related to the development of a digital service within an incumbent firm in an automotive environment, and secondly, showed the applicability of the theory for the technologies meant for the external customers of the organization [64]. Thereby, we focused on the business-centric perspective where the scope lies within the digital service at the interface of customers and not the improvement of internal processes [59]. Thus, we were able to specify and extend the knowledge on framing processes applying the TFR theory in the context of internal development for external customers. We, therefore, demonstrated the usability of this theory for any organizational environment operating in similar circumstances. Furthermore, as IT becomes the leading part of the business model and strategy [18, 41], digital transformation in incumbent firms requires the establishment of new ways of collaboration between business and IT in their value creation processes [58]. To meet the challenges of digitalization, IT functions search for new modes of organizations and forms of collaboration and alignment with the business departments [51]. Given the increasing relevance of digitalization in firms, research on success factors and identifying organizational and managerial challenges of the digital services development within traditional structures is of great importance for IS research and practice.

However, our study comes with certain limitations. Due to the interpretive nature of the research, results represent the sense-making process of the researchers. Moreover, our study focused on the development of digital service from the perspective of the business and IT experts while investigating the process of digital product development from the top management level. This could have given different results because they have a cross-process view. Finally, the case study and interpretive research are limited in generalizability. Since the identified aspects related to the frame domains of our case study are based on an automotive environment, the findings might be too specific. Nevertheless, the framing structure is of a more general nature that facilitates the formations of judgments for the research. For future research, a longitudinal analysis of framing processes could be useful in order to figure out the details and to extend the identified effects.

References

1. Allen, J.P., Kim, J.: IT and the video game industry: tensions and mutual shaping. J. Inf. Technol. **20**(4), 234–244 (2005)
2. Anderson, C.L., Agarwal, R.: The digitization of healthcare: boundary risks, emotion, and consumer willingness to disclose personal health information. Inf. Syst. Res. **22**(3), 469–490 (2011)
3. Athanasopoulou, A., Bouwman, W.A.G.A., Nikayin, F.A., de Reuver, G.A.: The disruptive impact of digitalization on the automotive ecosystem: a research agenda on business models, platforms and consumer issues. In: The 29th Bled eConference: Digital Economy (2016)
4. Battleson, D.A., West, B.C., Kim, J., Ramesh, B., Robinson, P.S.: Achieving dynamic capabilities with cloud computing: an empirical investigation. Eur. J. Inf. Syst. **25**(3), 209–230 (2016)
5. Bogner, A., Littig, B., Menz, W., (eds.): Interviewing Experts. Springer, London (2009). https://doi.org/10.1057/9780230244276
6. Brookes, R., Patricio, P.: What becomes a car. Proposed Paper for: BIT 2014 Conference Workshop-Technology Enabled Business Models: Platforms, Analytics and Performance (2014)
7. Broy, M., Kruger, I.H., Pretschner, A., Salzmann, C.: Engineering automotive software. Proc. IEEE **95**(2), 356–373 (2007)
8. Birchmeier, Z.P.: Exploring the conditional benefits of team diversity: the interaction of task requirements and team composition on tacit coordination efficiency (Doctoral dissertation) (2004)
9. Campbell, B.R.: Alignment: Resolving ambiguity within bounded choices. In: Pacific Asia Conference on Information Systems. University of Hong Kong (2005)
10. Cenfetelli, R.: Inhibitors and enablers as dual factor concepts in technology usage. JAIS **5**(11), 472–492 (2004). https://doi.org/10.17705/1jais.00059
11. Chan, Y.E., Reich, B.H.: IT alignment: what have we learned? J. Inf. Technol. **22**(4), 297–315 (2007)
12. Chanias, S., Hess, T.: Understanding digital transformation strategy formation: insights from Europe's automotive industry. In: PACIS (2016)
13. Cragg, P., King, M., Hussin, H.: IT alignment and firm performance in small manufacturing firms. J. Strateg. Inf. Syst. **11**(2), 109–132 (2002)
14. Davidson, E.J.: Technology frames and framing: a socio-cognitive investigation of requirements determination. MIS Q. **26**, 329–358 (2002)
15. Davidson, R.J.: Affective style, psychopathology, and resilience: brain mechanisms and plasticity. Am. Psychol. **55**(11), 1196 (2000)
16. Davidson, E.: A technological frames perspective on information technology and organizational change. J. Appl. Behav. Sci. **42**(1), 23–39 (2006)
17. Dougherty, D., Dunne, D.D.: Digital science and knowledge boundaries in complex innovation. Organ. Sci. **23**(5), 1467–1484 (2012)

18. Dijkman, R.M., Sprenkels, B., Peeters, T., Janssen, A.: Business models for the Internet of Things. Int. J. Inf. Manage. **35**(6), 672–678 (2015)
19. Delaney, K., Levy, E.: Internet of Things: Challenges, Breakthroughs and Best Practices. Cisco Report (2017)
20. Firnkorn, J., Müller, M.: Selling mobility instead of cars: new business strategies of automakers and the impact on private vehicle holding. Bus. Strat. Environ. **21**(4), 264–280 (2012)
21. Fichman, R.G., Dos Santos, B.L., Zheng, Z.E.: Digital innovation as a fundamental and powerful concept in the information systems curriculum. MIS Q. **38**(2), 329–343 (2014)
22. Fiol, C.: Consensus, diversity, and learning in organizations. Organ. Sci. **5**(3), 403–420 (1994)
23. Flynn, D., Du, Y.: A case study of the legitimation process undertaken to gain support for an information system in a Chinese university. Eur. J. Inf. Syst. **21**(3), 212–228 (2012)
24. Gerow, J.E., Thatcher, J.B., Grover, V.: Six types of IT-business strategic alignment: An investigation of the constructs and their measurement. Eur. J. Inf. Syst. **24**(3), 1–27 (2014)
25. Golestan, K., Sattar, F., Karray, F., Kamel, M., Seifzadeh, S.: Localization in vehicular ad hoc networks using data fusion and V2V communication. Comput. Commun. **71**, 61–72 (2015)
26. Goes, P.: Editor's comments: information systems research and behavioral economics. MIS Q. **37**(3), iii–viii (2013)
27. Gibbert, M., Ruigrok, W., Wicki, B.: What passes as a rigorous case study? Strateg. Manag. J. **29**(13), 1465–1474 (2008)
28. Griffith, T.L.: Technology features as triggers for sensemaking. Acad. Manag. Rev. **24**(3), 472–488 (1999)
29. Gregory, R.W., Keil, M., Muntermann, J., Mähring, M.: Paradoxes and the nature of ambidexterity in IT transformation programs. Inf. Syst. Res. **26**(1), 57–80 (2015)
30. Greenstein, S., Lerner, J., Stern, S.: Digitization, innovation, and copyright: what is the agenda? Strateg. Organ. **11**(1), 110–121 (2013)
31. Gilchrist, A., Burton-Jones, A., Green, P.: The process of social alignment and misalignment within a complex IT project. Int. J. Project Manage. **36**(6), 845–860 (2018)
32. Henfridsson, O., Mathiassen, L., Svahn, F.: Managing technological change in the digital age: the role of architectural frames. J. Inf. Technol. **29**, 27–43 (2014)
33. Henfridsson, O., Yoo, Y.: The liminality of trajectory shifts in institutional entrepreneurship. Organ. Sci. **25**(3), 932–950 (2014)
34. Harnisch, S., Kaiser, J., Buxmann, P.: Technological Frames of Reference in Software Acquisition Decisions: Results of a multiple case study (2013)
35. Haffke, I., Benlian, A.: To understand or to be understood? A dyadic analysis of perceptual congruence and interdependence between CEOs and CIOs. Darmstadt Technical University, Department of Business Administration, Economics and Law (2013)
36. Hanelt, A., Piccinini, E. Gregory, R. Hildebrandt, B., Kolbe, L.: Digital Transformation of preliminary Industries. Exploring the impact of Digital trends on business Models of Automobile Manufacturers. Proceedings of the 12th Internationalen Tagung Wirtschaftsinformatik. Osnabrück (2015
37. Horlach, B., Drews, P., Schirmer, I.: Bimodal IT: Business-IT alignment in the age of digital transformation. Multikonferenz Wirtschaftsinformatik (MKWI) (2016)
38. Hsu, C.W.: Frame misalignment: interpreting the implementation of information systems security certification in an organization. Eur. J. Inf. Syst. **18**, 140–150 (2009)
39. Huang, C.D., Hu, Q.: Achieving business - IT strategic alignment via enterprise-wide implementation of balanced scorecards. Inf. Syst. Manage. **24**(2), 173–184 (2007)
40. Huang, P.Y., Pan, S.L., Ouyang, T.H.: Developing information processing capability for operational agility: implications from a Chinese manufacturer. Eur. J. Inf. Syst. **23**(4), 462–480 (2014)

41. Islam, N., Buxmann, P., Eling, N.: Why should Incumbent Firms jump on the Start-up Bandwagon in the Digital Era? - A Qualitative Study. In: Leimeister, J.M.; Brenner, W. (Hrsg.): Proceedings der 13. Internationalen Tagung Wirtschaftsinformatik (WI 2017), St. Gallen, S. 1378–1392 (2017)
42. Juehling, E., Torney, M., Herrmann, C., Droeder, K.: Integration of automotive service and technology strategies. CIRP J. Manuf. Sci. Technol. **3**, 98–106 (2010)
43. Kaiser, J., Buxmann, P.: Organizational design of IT supplier relationship management: a multiple case study of five client companies. J. Inf. Technol. **27**(1), 57–73 (2012)
44. Kandathil, G., Wagner, E.L., Newell, S.: Translating es-embedded institutional logics through technological framing: an Indian-based case example. In: ECIS, p. 47 (2011)
45. Kyriazis, D., Varvarigou, T.: Smart, autonomous and reliable Internet of Things. Procedia Comput. Sci. **21**, 442–448 (2013)
46. Kilduff, M., Angelmar, R., Mehra, A.: Top management-team diversity and firm performance: examining the role of cognitions. Organ. Sci. **11**(1), 21–34 (2000)
47. Klein, H.K., Myers, M.D.: A set of principles for conducting and evaluating interpretive field studies in information systems. MIS Q. **23**(1), 67–94 (1999)
48. Kohli, R., Melville, N.P.: Digital innovation: a review and synthesis. Inf. Syst. J. **29**(1), 200–223 (2020)
49. Lacity, M.C., Janson, M.A.: Understanding qualitative data: a framework of text analysis methods. J. Manag. Inf. Syst. **11**(2), 137–155 (1994)
50. Legner, C., et al.: Digitalization: opportunity and challenge for the business and information systems engineering community. Bus. Inf. Syst. Eng. **51**, 301–308 (2017)
51. Lin, A., Silva, L.: The social and political construction of technological frames. Eur. J. Inf. Syst. **14**(1), 49–59 (2005)
52. Lindgren, R., Andersson, M., Henfridsson, O.: Multi-contextuality in boundary-spanning practices. Inf. Syst. J. **18**(6), 641–661 (2008)
53. Luftman, J., Brier, T.: Achieving and sustaining business - IT alignment. Calif. Manage. Rev. **42**(1), 109–122 (1999)
54. Lusch, R.F., Nambisan, S.: Service innovation: a service-dominant logic perspective. MIS Q. **39**(1), 155–176 (2015)
55. Mahut, F., Daaboul, J., Bricogne, M., Eynard, B.: Survey on Product-Service System applications in the automotive industry. IFAC-PapersOnLine **48**(3), 840–847 (2015)
56. Markus, M.L., Bjørn-Andersen, N.: Power over users: its exercise by system professionals. Commun. ACM **30**(6), 498–504 (1987)
57. Mathieu, J.E., Heffner, T.S., Goodwin, G.F., Salas, E., Cannon-Bowers, J.A.: The influence of shared mental models on team process and performance. J. Appl. Psychol. **85**, 273–283 (2000)
58. Matthies, B.D., et al.: An ecosystem service-dominant logic - integrating the ecosystem service approach and the service-dominant logic. J. Clean. Prod. **124**, 51–64 (2016)
59. Matt, C., Hess, T., Benlian, A.: Digital transformation strategies. Bus. Inf. Syst. Eng. **57**, 339–343 (2015)
60. Miles, M.B., Huberman, A.M., Huberman, M.A., Huberman, M.: Qualitative data analysis: an expanded sourcebook (1994)
61. Mergel, I., Edelmann, N., Haug, N.: Defining digital transformation: results from expert interviews. Govern. Inf. Q. **36**(4), 101385 (2019)
62. Nardon, L., Aten, K.: Valuing virtual worlds: The role of categorization in technology assessment. J. Assoc. Inf. Syst. **13**(10), 4 (2012)
63. Nambisan, S., Lyytinen, K., Majchrzak, A., Song, M.: Digital Innovation Management: reinventing innovation management research in a digital world. MIS Q. **41**(1), 223–238 (2017)
64. Nambisan, S.: Information technology and product/service innovation: a brief assessment and some suggestions for future research. J. Assoc. Inf. Syst. **14**(4), 215–226 (2013)

65. Orlikowski, W.J.: Computer technology in organizations: some critical notes. In New Technology and the Labour Process, pp. 20–49. Palgrave Macmillan, London (1988)
66. Orlikowski, W.J., Gash, D.C.: Technological frames: making sense of information technology in organizations. ACM Trans. Inf. Syst. **12**(2), 174–207 (1994)
67. Omerović M., Islam N., Buxmann P.: Unlashing the next wave of business models in the internet of things era: a systematic literature review and new perspectives for a research agenda. In: Proceedings of the 53rd Hawaii International Conference on System Sciences (2020)
68. Porter, M.E., Heppelmann, J.E.: How smart, connected products are transforming competition. Harv. Bus. Rev. **92**(11), 64–88 (2014)
69. Pagoropoulos, A., Maier, A., McAloone, T.C.: Assessing transformational change from institutionalizing digital capabilities on implementation and development of Product-Service Systems: Learnings from the maritime industry. J. Clean. Prod. **166** (2017)
70. Pillmann, J., Wietfeld, C., Zarcula, A., Raugust, T., Alonso, D.C.: Novel common vehicle information model (cvim) for future automotive vehicle big data marketplaces. In: 2017 IEEE Intelligent Vehicles Symposium (IV) (2017)
71. Piccinini, E., Hanelt, A., Gregory, R., Kolbe, L.: Transforming industrial business: the impact of digital transformation on automotive organizations. In: Thirty-Sixth International Conference on Information Systems, Fort Worth 2015 (2015)
72. Preston, D., Karahanna, E.: How to develop a shared vision: the key to IS strategic alignment. MIS Q. Exec. **8**(1) (2009)
73. Robey, D., Sahay, S.: Transforming work through information technology: A comparative case study of geographic information systems in county government. Inf. Syst. Res. **7**, 93–110 (1996)
74. Reich, B.H., Benbasat, I.: Factors that influence the social dimension of alignment between business and information technology objectives. MIS Q. 81–113 (2000)
75. Riasanow, T., Galic, G., Böhm, M.: Digital transformation in the automotive industry: towards a generic value network. In: 25th European Conference on Information Systems (ECIS) (2017)
76. Reynolds, P., Yetton, P.: Aligning business and IT strategies in multi-business organizations. J. Inf. Technol. **30**(2), 101–118 (2015)
77. Sarker, N.D.B., Joshi, K.D.: Knowledge transfer in virtual systems development teams: An exploratory study of four key enablers. IEEE Trans. Prof. Commun. **48**(2), 201–218 (2005)
78. Scott Morton, M.S.: The corporation of the 1990s: Information technology and organizational transformation. Oxford University Press, Sloan School of Management (1991)
79. Sledgianowski, D., Luftman, J.: Business - IT strategic alignment maturity: a case study. J. Cases Inf. Technol. **7**(2), 102–120 (2005)
80. Svahn, F., Mathiassen, L., Lindgren, R.: Embracing digital innovation in incumbent firms: how volvo cars managed competing concerns. MIS Q. **41**(1), 239–253 (2017)
81. Sklyar, A., Kowalkowski, C., Tronvoll, B., Sörhammar, D.: Organizing for digital servitization: a service ecosystem perspective. J. Bus. Res. **104**, 450–460 (2019)
82. Tiwana, A., Konsynski, B., Bush, A.: Platform evolution: coevolution of platform architecture, governance, and environmental dynamics. Inf. Syst. Res. **21**(4), 675–687 (2010)
83. Venkatesh, V., Thong, J., Xu, X.: Consumer acceptance and use of information technology: extending the unified theory of acceptance and use of technology. MIS Q. **36**(1), 157–178 (2012)
84. Vermerris, A., Mocker, M., Van Heck, E.: No time to waste: the role of timing and complementarity of alignment practices in creating business value in IT projects. Eur. J. Inf. Syst. **23**(6), 629–654 (2014)
85. Walsham, G.: Doing interpretive research. Eur. J. Inf. Syst. **15**, 320–330 (2006)
86. Walsham, G.: Interpretive case studies in IS research: nature and method. Eur. J. Inf. Syst. **4**(2), 74–81 (1995)

87. Williams, K., Chatterjee, S., Rossi, M.: Design of emerging digital services: a taxonomy. Eur. J. Inf. Syst. **17**(5), 505–517 (2008)
88. Xue, L., Zhang, C., Ling, H., Zhao, X.: Risk Mitigation in supply chain digitization: system modularity and information technology governance. J. Manag. Inf. Syst. **30**(1), 325–352 (2013)
89. Yin, R.K.: Case study research: design and methods. In: Essential Guide to Qualitative Methods in Organizational Research, vol. 24 (2009)
90. Yin, R.K.: Research design issues in using the case study method to study management information systems. Inf. Syst. Res. Chall.: Qual. Res. Meth. **1**, 1–6 (1989)
91. Yin, R.K.: Case study research and applications: Design and methods. Sage publications (2047)
92. Yoo, Y.J., Henfridsson, O., Lyytinen, K.: The new organizing logic of digital innovation: an agenda for information systems research. Inf. Syst. Res. **21**, 724–735 (2010)

Digital Leadership – Mountain or Molehill?
A Literature Review

Julia K. Eberl[✉] and Paul Drews

Institute of Information Systems, Leuphana University Lüneburg, Lüneburg, Germany
Julia.Eberl@stud.leuphana.de, Paul.Drews@leuphana.de

Abstract. Despite the high relevance of digital leadership (DL) in practitioner outlets, its definition and determinants remain fuzzy, resulting in impeded DL theory development. Based on a structured literature review grounded in 96 publications, we developed a new definition of DL and a nomological determinant network. First, we provide conceptual clarity by differentiating DL from E-leadership with a definition of the former. Second, we present an inductively developed nomological network that specifies 13 DL determinants structured per the categories organizational level, individual level, and digital leader. Based on this network, we propose six future research areas, which are (1) theoretical clarity of DL as a concept, (2) measurement systems, (3) DL's impact on output variables, (4) empirical evidence about determinants of the nomological network, (5) research design extensions through further perspectives and instruments, and (6) approaches to adopt DL.

Keywords: Digital leadership · Digital transformation · Literature review · Organizational transformation · Leadership 4.0

1 Introduction

The year 2020 has turned out to be an unplanned milestone in the progress of digital transformation. Due to required social distancing to avoid the distribution of the Corona virus disease 2019, companies have enabled employees to work from home and adjust their business models to the resultant new demands. Automotive companies started to produce medical components, authority visits were digitalized, schools initiated remote education, and doctors offered virtual consultation hours [1, 2]. Microsoft CEO Satya Nadella summarizes the situation with, "We've seen two years' worth of digital transformation in two months" [3]. But how were these changes possible in such a short time? According to Breuer and Szillat [4], the challenge to digital transformation is not the availability of technology, but developing new leadership competencies [5]. Most companies are now evaluating and planning the adoption of digital leadership (DL) as a leadership approach aiming at supporting the realization of digitally enabled business models by changing the behavior of leaders, organizational structures and employee management [6, 7]. Although DL receives great attention in practitioner outlets [8–10], there are only a few companies reporting details about methods and strategies summarized under the buzzword DL [11]. Further, in contrast to companies' high interest in adopting DL in practice, DL seems to be a rarely discussed phenomenon in leadership research. A 12-year analysis by Dinh et al. [12] of the 10 top-tier academic outlets of leadership theory in 2012 characterizes E-leadership with less than 1% representation as a nascent discipline [12]. This analysis does not thematize DL at all. From a research perspective, one could state that DL is rather a molehill than a mountain at the moment. This article seeks to address this theory-practice gap by the following research question: How is DL currently defined and conceptualized in the literature, and which research gaps can be identified?

To answer this question, we analyzed 96 contributions from the current DL literature from an inductive approach, following the recommendations by Wolfswinkel et al. [13]. Based on this analysis, we developed a definition of DL and identified its determinants in a nomological network. Moreover, we identified six future DL research areas to create a research agenda for future investigations in the field of DL.

2   Methodology

Our concept-based DL literature review follows the approaches of Wolfswinkel et al. [13] and Webster and Watson [14]. To avoid a lack of documentation and ensure reliability, an additional step from Ogawa and Malen's [15] framework was added as first step resulting in the following steps for the literature review: (1) create an audit trail documenting the reviewers' steps, (2) define the research scope, (3) search for literature, (4) select appropriate publications based on step (2), (5) analyze the selected literature, and (6) present the results. The remainder of this section describes this approach's application in this DL literature review.

First, an audit trail was initiated in a digital notebook. The purpose of this documentation is to provide evidence for all steps and thereby increase traceability [16]. The audit trail consists of the above-mentioned steps and documents the results. Moreover, it reflects decisions that were taken, such as inclusion and exclusion criteria, databases, and papers.

The literature review's purpose, as structured by Cooper's taxonomy [17], is to identify the central issues in DL research by focusing on research outcomes in the commercial sector by analyzing representative contributions. As such, the authors took a neutral perspective to conceptually organize the literature review for a general scholarly audience.

Based on that purpose, we gained an initial overview of the current state of the literature from March 2020 to the end of May 2020. This overview showed that DL is highly thematized in practical papers, as well as in Information Systems (IS) research. Hence, the literature search included general databases (Google Scholar, Emerald Insights, Science Direct) in addition to specialist sources focusing on IS (Association for Information Systems (AIS) Library), leadership (Elsevier, PsycINFO, Web of Science), and business administration (Business Source Premier via EBSCO, ABI/INFORM). To integrate a practical perspective, the database searches included non-peer-reviewed articles, and forward and backward searches were conducted. Furthermore, pertinent journals (*The Leadership Quarterly, Journal of Management, Information & Organization, Journal of MIS*) were manually examined for the latest publications to locate DL in overall leadership and IS research. The search was based on the keywords "digital leadership," "digital leader," "digitalization AND leadership," "leadership 4.0," and "leader 4.0," filtering out work not mainly focusing on DL in the title or abstract. The resulting initial sample size of n = 287 papers from 1997 to 2020 (37 of the 287 papers stemmed from the forward and backward search [14]) was reduced by applying exclusion criteria as shown in Table 1. In this way, we gathered a literature collection of n = 96 works from 2000 to 2020.

Table 1. Exclusion criteria and sample size

Exclusion criteria	Sample size (n) after applying exclusion criteria
Non-commercial context (e.g. public sector, education)	n = 192
Missing DL focus in the body of the text	n = 146
No detailed description of DL aspects or outcomes	n = 127
Artifacts of similar content, research type, and references were scanned and consolidated to the most relevant papers	n = 96

The review process was conducted in four steps, starting with a template to collect general information about the articles, such as publishing outlet, date, industry and context, paper type (practitioner outlet/research paper), research question, and design (observational, experimental, quantitative/qualitative), as well as a summary of the central statements and methods. Second, we inductively created codes about DL and added these codes to every paper in the review. We evaluated the created literature database regarding the used codes and reflected outcomes. Third, we developed determinants and their relationships based on the collection of codes. Lastly, we summarized the determinants by their influence on the categories digital leader, organizational level, and individual level.

3   Findings

In the following Sect. 3.1, we increase clarity on DL based on the current state of the literature by analyzing the concept's definition and creating a nomological network of 13 DL determinants divided into three categories. Afterward, we thematize the determinants (Sects. 3.2–3.4) and identify six future research areas (Sect. 3.5).

3.1   DL Definition and Nomological Network

The analysis shows that within the 36 publications that explicitly discuss the definition of DL, definitional fuzziness exists in the following three aspects.

First, the relation between E-leadership and DL is unclear in the current literature state. Avolio, Kahai, and Dodge [18] define E-leadership as "a social influence process mediated by advanced information technologies (AIT) to produce a change in attitudes, feelings, thinking, behavior and/or performance of individuals, groups, and/or organizations" [19]. Therefore, E-leadership will not change the fundamentals of business but the execution of business as supported by technology [20]. Klus and Müller [21], meanwhile, use E-leadership and DL as synonyms.

Second, the analyzed literature provides abstract definitions of DL [11, 19–21] that impede the differentiation between E-leadership and DL. For example, Meffert and Swaminathan [22] define DL as an approach suitable for the digital age, which is similar to El Sawy [11], who understands "doing the right things for the strategic success of digitalization for the enterprise and its business ecosystem" as DL.

The third finding speaks against using E-leadership and DL as synonyms, as DL is more extensive than E-leadership. While E-leadership uses technology to support existing business [20], DL is an instrument to achieve the target of digitally enabled business models [6, 7], digital organization [6, 23], and employee management [9, 24]. To influence these dimensions, DL adjusts different determinants in the company [11, 25, 26].

We seek to overcome the current lack of a comprehensive DL definition by providing our own, which is grounded in the literature review's results and the three aspects discussed above:

Digital leadership is a complex construct aiming for a customer-centered, digitally enabled, leading-edge business model by (1) transforming the role, skills, and style of the digital leader, (2) realizing a digital organization, including governance, vision, values, structure, culture, and decision processes, and (3) adjusting people management, virtual teams, knowledge, and communication and collaboration on the individual level.

This definition includes three important parts. First, it specifies DL's purpose, which is establishing customer-centric business models by using technology. In contrast to E-leadership, which uses technology as a mediator, DL's outcome is the usage of digitally enabled business models. Second, the definition identifies the determinants influenced by DL to meet the objective. Third, it concerns the digital leader, who steers the different determinants to serve the purpose.

Based on the literature analysis, we created a DL nomological network that provides an overview of the concept's determinants (see Fig. 1). The network is structured per the categories of influence on the organization, the individual, and the digital leader, such as people management influences the individual. The network is comprised of determinants and adds relations based on the codes identified in the review process.

3.2 Digital Leader

The current state of the literature mentions skills, roles, and leadership styles as important characteristics of a digital leader. Most of the reviewed literature (53%) focuses on skills, whereas roles and leadership styles are only represented in 27% of the analyzed papers.

Role. Several articles (n = 33) describe the changed role of the leader, even though unclarity exists about who this leader is. This lack of clarity impedes defining DL. Most articles focus on digital leaders in disciplinary roles [27–31]. For instance, according

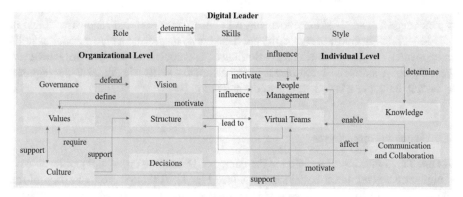

Fig. 1. Determinants of DL

to a study by Deloitte Digital GmbH [32], 70% of companies that meet digital transformation's success criteria have a single responsible person in place: the Chief Digital Officer (CDO). However, the CDO role harbors the danger of a disconnected digital unit. Therefore, LEGO emphasizes the importance of a CDO by suggesting a digital leader as CDO in every business unit [11]. Nevertheless, it needs to be questioned if one Digital Leader in the role of the CDO per company or per business unit is capable to achieve the goal of DL. Yet, a minority of the analyzed papers point out that every employee must act as a digital leader, as followers take over entrepreneurial responsibilities for the company [27, 33]. However, this change is rarely thematized in the analyzed literature (n = 2). Still, the publications show that in contrast to traditional leaders who act from a command and control perspective [34] and as the lone decision-makers with hierarchical distance from their followers [35], a digital leader connects with a team as a mentor, coach, talent builder, and learning guide who does not require disciplinary power [24, 34, 36, 37]. The digital leader needs the skills to be a visionary [38] who acts as a role model for employees [25, 28–30].

Style. The leadership style of a digital leader is rarely discussed in the literature (n = 5). Because of the relevance of authentic, transformational, and transactional leadership styles in DL, Prince [39] comes to the theoretical conclusion that DL overlaps with authentic, transactional, and transformational leadership. Therefore, transactional and transformational leadership have a direct influence on digital skills and digital strategy, whereas authentic leadership's impact is limited to digital skills [39]. The authentic leadership style of a digital leader drives employees to develop innovations [39] and engage in participative decision-making [40]. However, a transactional approach provides processes to meet organizational requirements, as employees are motivated to be digitally savvy and adopt new technologies with rewards [41]. A digital leader's transformational leadership style is a consultative and delegating approach [42] that inspires followers to be innovative [43].

Skills. Visionary, digitally savvy, collaborative, adaptable, and motivating are the most mentioned skills of a digital leader [21, 23, 44–46] in the literature. These five skills result from two types of digital leader skillsets existing in the literature: (1) empirical papers suggest a small skillset focusing on agility, openness and innovative thinking [23, 44, 45]. (2) In contrast to that, the published reviews present a high amount of skills categorized as digital business, general mindset, and social attitude [21, 46]. However, these extensive skillsets blur the focus on the distinctive skills of a digital leader required to flexibly adjust to a broad variety of digitalization tasks.

3.3 Organizational Level

Vision. The definition of a vision is the center of DL on the organizational level, as it is highly connected to other determinants (see Fig. 1). Although the realization of the vision is formulated in the strategy, which is mentioned in the analyzed literature, neither strategy nor the relation between strategy and vision are described [47]. As the digital world is constantly changing, agility could have replaced the need for long-term plans as summarized in a strategy. However, the analyzed literature does not give evidence on why strategy is not a DL determinant.

Still, there is evidence that digitally successful companies more often have a digital vision than others [48]. A vision should be clearly formulated, aspiring, holistic, sustainable, inspiring, convincing [22, 45], and define the company's value and purpose [49, 50]. Inconsistency exists about the creation of a vision by a leader or staff as a living artifact [49, 51]. A vision serves four purposes: (1) to act as a roadmap and define the direction of change [52, 53] and the knowledge required for that [29], (2) to motivate employees, (3) to orient which digital trends are relevant to serving the vision [4, 24, 29, 35, 42, 54, 55], and (4) to lead an agile organization when strict processes are not in place, as collaboration is supported by employees' strongly identifying with the vision [56].

Governance. Although corporate governance is well known to prevent innovations and slow down decisions in practice [34, 50], 13% of the analyzed literature includes governance as part of DL to define a boundary in which the digital vision can be realized [57]. Therefore, governance defends the vision by evaluating investments and activities according to their contribution to the vision [48, 58]. Even though the frequency is unclear, the analyzed literature emphasizes two different governance functions: (1) DL requires governance for data privacy [59, 60] and information quality [61], and (2) innovation committees are staffed with the most innovative employees to drive and align strategic innovations [7, 62]. However, a knowledge gap regarding technology governance, values, and risk exists within governance board members [63].

Values. The existing literature mentions the following values in the context of DL:

However, the impact of values on a company's vision, as common guidance for globally distributed teams [64, 72] and to motivate employees when the companies' values match their employees' values [53] is not analyzed. When it comes to the definition of values, Bolte et al. [53] show that within start-ups, the values of openness, transparency, trust, and employee focus are more frequently represented than in other companies. Meanwhile, especially older companies focus on traditional values, such as thoroughness and precision [8]. Moreover, the question arises if all values mentioned

Table 2. Values in the context of DL

Values	References
Diversity and inclusion	[8, 34, 64, 65]
Sustainability	[33, 39, 50, 66, 67]
Trust	[11, 19, 33, 34, 42, 45, 51, 56, 61, 66, 68–71]
Freedom to experiment	[53, 64]
Openness	[11, 19, 24, 33, 44, 51, 54, 64, 69, 72–74]
Transparency	[6, 33, 42, 49, 51, 57, 64, 73, 75]
Employee focus	[6, 11, 33, 35, 48, 49, 52, 57, 59, 65, 76, 77]
Customer centricity	[4, 33, 36, 45, 49, 51, 54, 56, 59, 76–83]

have dependencies to DL (like freedom to experiment) or if they are general values of companies like sustainability.

Culture. As culture is a norm that transports companies' philosophies and policies to employees and customers, culture is discussed in 51% of the analyzed literature in the context of supporting network structures and virtual teams, as well as being aligned with values [84]. As such, DL has the objective to create an innovative [23, 30, 42, 52, 57, 79, 81, 85], positive [84], and collaborative [23, 29, 86] culture. Culture sets technology first, not legacy, [52, 80], and encourages employees to take risks [23, 39, 50, 56] and fail [19, 53, 57, 87, 88]. Although some papers in the literature declare culture as a mandatory determinant of DL, the dependency of DL on culture is disputed as 49% of the literature does not cover culture at all. Another important aspect of culture is the mindset of digital leaders and employees. DL emphasizes a digital [24, 33, 52, 82], experimental [11, 54], and growth-centered mindset that encourages employees to be curious, think differently, and continuously expand their knowledge [39, 89] resulting in the employees feeling more empowered and committed [19]. Yet, the literature does not mention how this culture and the mindset can be realized.

Decisions. DL requires decision processes that enable the company to act nimbly and fast [4, 27, 28, 72]. Therefore, decisions can be made with incomplete information [34, 52, 88], including new types of data, such as unstructured and social media data, to obtain a predictive perspective and minimize uncertainty by taking into account predictive simulations, virtual reality, and big data correlations [33, 34, 52, 54, 55, 59, 81, 90–92]. Besides these rational, data-based decisions [54], papers also report that the final decision is influenced by intuition [34, 51, 59, 72].

Moreover, the literature focuses on people who have the authority to make decisions. Because of the complexity and required knowledge for decision-making, authority frequently shifts from the leader to employees and cross-functional teams [11, 24, 46, 48, 65, 73, 88, 91, 93, 94]. As such, employees are more motivated by the empowerment to participate in decisions and expect more success [7]. This authority emphasizes the dependency to the role of the digital leader as every employee needs to act as a digital leader. Notwithstanding the positive impacts on motivation, agility, and potential success, the literature also reports that the final decision is usually made by the leader [34, 35, 69].

Structure. There is a consensus in the literature that digital leaders need to reduce existing hierarchical structures [35, 39, 53, 56, 59, 72–74, 83] to increase employees' motivation [53, 92], innovations [65], and agility when reacting to changing customer demands. People work in highly connected, dynamic, and temporary networks that are established for a specific purpose and time [19, 22, 23, 31, 33, 50, 51, 65, 71, 72, 74, 83, 84, 88, 89, 95, 96]. Accordingly, work in networks needs to be supported by agile methods and approaches, such as design thinking and prototyping [8, 10, 24, 26, 55, 83, 93].

In contrast to the consensus regarding hierarchy and agile methods, the reviewed literature presents different opinions when it comes to DL's organizational positioning. A digital unit within the organization is implemented to drive innovation, whereas classical IT is responsible for operating legacy systems [7, 31, 97]. This concept leads to a disconnected digital unit and does not drive change in the overall company [33, 56, 98]. Therefore, Trompenaars & Woolliams [81] recommend harmonizing the strengths of traditional and digital units.

3.4   Individual Level

People Management. People management, employee motivation, and rewards are highly influenced by flexible network structures, vision, and employee empowerment to make decisions [7, 31, 34, 93]. Digital leaders support employees in self-management and career development [26, 33, 53, 55]. As such, digital leaders act as coaches and give feedback independent from formal authority [89]. Furthermore, DL needs to promote employees' intrinsic motivation by supporting their identification with the company's values [7, 46, 51, 56, 62], improving the alignment of life and work [65], and contributing to personal well-being [77]. In addition, extrinsic motivation can be triggered by supporting standardized tasks with gamification [7] and performance indicators [60]. The literature also reports targets for teamwork [93], democratized salary definition, and employee hiring and evaluation [66].

Knowledge. Because of technology's high rate of change, companies have to constantly adjust their workforce's capabilities, as manifested by Lego with the mantra "Hire for a Career, not a Job" [11]. Moreover, knowledge is an essential factor in providing digital business models [74]. That is why DL establishes a culture of life-long learning [33, 38, 50, 53, 57, 72, 88, 94, 99], including professional and soft skills [50]. To support learners and motivate employees, formats need to change to user-centric, mobile experience, including gamification [94]. Further, motivation is created by a digital leader who acts as an idol for learning [76]. Besides these learning methods, according to Bolte et al. [53], the coaching format is not as successful in large companies as in start-ups. Overall, learning has a significant impact on DL's success [100] although the used learning formats and their impact is not thematized.

Virtual Teams. Working in networks leads to the demand for creating virtual teams for specific projects [65]. Furthermore, increased employer attractiveness, motivation, agility, and creativity can be achieved by enabling employees to work where, when, and how they want [65, 101]. Hence, leading virtual teams is an important determinant of DL. The digital leader needs to coach employees regarding cultural and ethical sensibility to enable teamwork in globally distributed and heterogenous teams [24, 51, 57, 60, 64, 68, 72, 95]. However, leading individuals in a virtual team is rarely mentioned in the reviewed literature. Meetings between leaders and employees are important to discussing feedback and addressing employees' situations [10, 72, 102]. Especially more passive employees need coaching on participating in virtual teams and written communication to avoid isolation [19, 34].

Collaboration and Communication. Another DL determinant is collaboration and communication, which enables a collaborative culture, virtual team, and network structure [50, 59, 64]. For this reason, extended collaboration brings agile network structures to life when people are motivated to collaborate across functions and organizations to find the right knowledge to work together [48, 50, 54, 56, 57, 96, 97, 99, 103]. In addition, digital leaders use social media platforms to engage across companies [24] with customers, partners, employees, and other stakeholders [4, 20, 33, 53, 54, 73, 75, 101, 103]. Compared to other determinants of DL as described in this paper, the impact of collaboration and communication on faster reaction to customer requests [38, 56], higher managerial effectiveness [64], quantitative productivity improvements [64], and increased digital leader organizational legitimacy is non-controversial. However, the success of communication does not only depend on quantity but also on the content which has not been studied so far. Moreover, Bolte et al. [53] show in a survey-based study that the leader's and the follower's perspectives on communication highly diverge, as the leader observes more communication activities than the follower receives.

3.5 Future Research

This literature review contributes to the understanding of the determinants of DL, including the digital leader, the organizational level, and individual level. We can see that initial steps in practice and research have been taken, though we now identify six areas that require further attention in upcoming research.

First, a common understanding of DL and its comparison to other leadership styles should be developed, as the relevant skills of a digital leader can also be found in other leadership approaches [44, 46]. Hence, theoretical advancements can be made by defining DL and advancing its characteristic features. Moreover, DL's differentiation from and overlap with authentic, transformative, and transformational leadership should be analyzed [39].

Second, these theoretical advancements should be supported by developing a DL measurement system. Based on a questionnaire, different facets of DL and adoption stages can help leaders identify their DL status.

Third, besides measuring DL's status in a company, DL's impact on output variables is unclear. Although Weill & Wörner [80], Valentine and Steward [63] and Rüth and Netzer

[104] identify DL's positive impact on agility, innovativeness, and customer experience, the determinants of DL leading to these and other outcomes need to be further analyzed.

Fourth, missing evidence also exists in this paper's nomological network. More empirical research is required to evaluate and improve the set of determinants and the impact of DL on a company's intended outcome.

Fifth, to get the above-mentioned results, higher variation in research and stronger survey designs are needed. This starts with the research participants. The current state of the literature is based on quantitative surveys and interviews with digital leaders, as in the analyzed literature, only Bolte et al. [53] includes followers' perspectives. To avoid the influence of context variables, further research instruments, such as online panels or student samples, can be used to extend the understanding of DL.

Sixth, in addition to endeavors that seek to improve the understanding of DL, additional research is required regarding DL's adoption. To accomplish this, three approaches can be combined: First is conducting a longitudinal survey and interviews within the same research group during their transition to DL. Second, two independent units of the same company, with one unit transitioning to DL, can be compared regarding the differences in their determinants and outcomes. Third, a pioneering industry can be identified to analyze the realization, impact, and lessons learned along the DL journey.

4 Conclusion and Limitations

Is DL a molehill or a mountain? The journey to finding the answer to this question led us through a review of DL's different definitions, resulting in the development of a new definition for the term. Although Prince [39], Valentine [58], and Klus and Müller [21] analyze single determinants of DL, this literature review extracted the 13 most relevant determinants from the 96 reviewed articles and summarized the relationships of these determinants in a nomological network for the first time. The determinants in this network are structured per (1) the digital leader's skills, roles, and leadership style, (2) DL's organizational level, including company vision, values, culture, governance, decisions, and structure, and (3) DL's individual level, consisting of people management, knowledge, virtual teams, as well as collaboration and communication.

Based on these results, we conclude that DL is more than a molehill, as the analyzed literature describes companies' requirements for DL and its determinants. However, to become a mountain, DL's fuzzy definition and implementation, as well as its determinants, need to be clarified by further research, as identified in Sect. 3.5.

This article has three limitations: (1) Despite the systematic research approach to increase objectivity, the analysis was conducted by one researcher; (2) DL research is present internationally; the current literature review only covers the most relevant German and English publications, other languages are not considered; and (3) DL is quickly evolving; because of that, further papers could have been published during the publication process of this literature review.

Although DL is important in practice, it is at an early research stage and requires further investigations, as described in Sect. 3.5.

References

1. Wuest, T., Kusiak, A., Dai, T., Tayur, S.R.: Impact of COVID-19. ORMS Today **47**, 1–16 (2020)
2. Greenhalgh, T., Wherton, J., Shaw, S., Morrison, C.: Video consultations for covid-19. BMJ **368**, 1–2 (2020)
3. Spataro, J.: 2 years of digital transformation in 2 months. https://www.microsoft.com/en-us/microsoft-365/blog/2020/04/30/2-years-digital-transformation-2-months/. Accessed on 12 July 2020
4. Breuer, S., Szillat, P.: Leadership and digitalization contemporary approaches towards leading in the modern day workplace. Dialogue **1**, 24–36 (2019)
5. Horlacher, A., Hess, T.: What does a chief digital officer do? managerial tasks and roles of a new c-level position in the context of digital transformation. 49th Hawaii International Conference on System Sciences, Waikoloa Beach, pp. 5126–5135 (2016)
6. Oberer, B., Erkollar, A.: Leadership 4.0: digital leaders in the age of industry 4.0. Int. J. Organ. Leadersh. **7**, 404–412 (2018)
7. Petry, T.: Digital Leadership – Unternehmens-und Personalführung in der Digital Economy. In: Petry, T. (ed.) Digital Leadership, pp. 21–82. Haufe Lexware GmbH, Freiburg im Breisgau (2016)
8. Buhse, W.: Digital Leadership bei der Robert Bosch GmbH. Wissensmanagement **6**, 14–15 (2014)
9. Jenewein, T.: Digital leadership bei SAP. In: Petry, T. (ed.) Digital Leadership, pp. 373–384. Haufe Lexware GmbH, Freiburg im Breisgau (2016)
10. Neun, W.: Digitale Transformation und Agilität in der Praxis. Springer, Wiesbaden (2020). https://doi.org/10.1007/978-3-658-19624-0
11. El Sawy, O.A., Kræmmergaard, P., Amsinck, H., Lerbeck Vinther, A.: How LEGO built the foundations and enterprise capabilities for digital leadership. MIS Q. Executive **15**, 141–166 (2016)
12. Dinh, J.E., Lord, R.G., Gardner, W.L., Meuser, J.D., Liden, R.C., Hu, J.: Leadership theory and research in the new millennium: Current theoretical trends and changing perspectives. Leadersh. Q. **25**, 36–62 (2014)
13. Wolfswinkel, J.F., Furtmueller, E., Wilderom, C.P.: Using grounded theory as a method for rigorously reviewing literature. Eur. J. Inform Syst. **22**, 45–55 (2013)
14. Webster, J., Watson, R.T.: Analyzing the past to prepare for the future: writing a literature review. MIS Q. **26**, xiii–xxiii (2002)
15. Ogawa, R.T., Malen, B.: Towards rigor in reviews of multivocal literature: applying the exploratory case method. Rev. Educ. Res. **61**, 265–286 (1991)
16. Randolph, J.: A guide to writing the dissertation literature review. Res. Eval. **14**, 1–13 (2009)
17. Cooper, H.M.: Organizing knowledge syntheses: a taxonomy of literature reviews. Knowl. Soc. **1**, 104–126 (1988)
18. Avolio, B.J., Kahai, S., Dodge, G.E.: E-Leadership: implications for theory, research and practice. Leadersh. Q. **11**, 615–668 (2001)
19. Balan, A.C., Cavendish, K.: Leadership in the Digital and Social Era-A Theoretical Review and Digital Gamification for Employee Development. School of Economics and Management, Lund University
20. DasGupta, P.: Literature review: e-Leadership. ELJ **4**, 1–36 (2011)
21. Klus, M.F., Müller, J.: Identifying leadership skills required in the digital age. Westfälische Wilhelms-Universität, Münster (2018)
22. Meffert, J., Swaminathan, A.: Leadership and the urgency for digital transformation. Lead. Lead. **88**, 44–49 (2018)

23. Kane, G.C., Nguyen Phillips, A., Copulsky, J., Andrus, G.: How digital different is(n't) different. MIT Sloan Manag. Rev. **60**, 34–39 (2019)
24. Eggers, B., Hollmann, S.: Digital Leadership - Anforderungen, Aufgaben und Skills von Führungskräften in der "Arbeitswelt 4.0". In: Keuper, F., Schomann, M., Sikora, L.L., Wassef, R. (ed.) Disruption and Transformation Management, pp. 43–68. Springer Fachmedien, Wiesbaden (2018). DasGupta, P.: Literature Review: e-Leadership. ELJ 4, 1–36 (2011)
25. Van Dick, R., Helfritz, K.H., Stickling, E., Gross, M., Holz, F.: Digital leadership. Personalwirtschaft **8**, 1–23 (2016)
26. Buhse, W.: Changing the Mindset: Die Bedeutung des Digital Leadership für die Enterprise 2.0-Strategieentwicklung. In: Lembke, G., Soyez, N. (ed.) Digitale Medien im Unternehmen, pp. 237–252. Springer, Berlin Heidelberg (2012). https://doi.org/10.1007/978-3-642-29906-3_13
27. Rassek, A.: Digital Leadership: Was zeichnet einen Digital Leader aus?. https://karriereb ibel.de/digital-leadership/. Accessed on 11 July 2020
28. Wade, M., Obwegeser, N.: How to choose the right digital leader for your company. MIT Sloan Manag. Rev. **60**, 1–4 (2019)
29. Gouveia, L.B.: Emerging alternatives to leadership and governance for a digital ecosystem. In: 15th European Conference on Management Leadership and Governance, pp. 1–43. Porto (2019)
30. Underwood, C.: Developing leadership roles for a digital age. Strateg. HR Rev. **18**, 233–234 (2019)
31. Zeichhardt, R.: E-Leader, CDOs & Digital Fools - eine Führungstypologie für den digitalen Wandel. In: Keuper, F., Schomann, M., Sikora, L.I., Wassef, R. (eds.) Disruption and Transformation Management, pp. 3–21. Springer Fachmedien, Wiesbaden (2018)
32. Deloitte Digital GmbH: Überlebensstrategie "Digital Leadership". https://www2.deloitte.com/de/de/pages/technology/articles/survival-through-digital-leadership.html. Accessed on 27 June 2020
33. Borowska, G.: Digital leadership for digital transformation. Contemp. Econ. Electron. Sci. J. **10**, 11–19 (2019)
34. April, K., Dalwai, A.: Leadership styles required to lead digital transformation. Effect. Executive **22**, 14–45 (2019)
35. Ehmann, B.: Quick Guide Agile Methoden für Personaler. Springer Fachmedien, Wiesbaden (2019). https://doi.org/10.1007/978-3-658-27345-3
36. Bosch, U., Hentschel, S., Kramer, S.: Digital Offroad: Erfolgsstrategien für die digitale Transformation. Haufe-Lexware, Freiburg im Breisgau (2018)
37. Zupancic, T., Verbeke, J., Achten, H., Herneoja, A.: Digital leadership. In: 34th eCAADe Conference, vol. 1, pp. 63–68. Oulu (2016)
38. Krug, P., Weiß, M., Lang, J.: Digital Leadership: Führung im Zuge der digitalen Transformation. Wirtschaftsinformatik Manage. **10**(6), 48–59 (2018). https://doi.org/10.1007/s35764-018-0106-x
39. Prince, K.A.: Digital Leadership: Transitioning into the Digital Age. James Cook University, Queensland (2018)
40. Anderson, H.J., Baur, J.E., Griffith, J.A., Buckley, M.R.: What works for you may not work for the (Gen) Me: Limitations of present leadership theories for the new generation. Leadersh. Q. **28**, 245–260 (2017)
41. Akinbode, A.I., Shuhumi, S.R.A.: Change management process and leadership approaches. Int. J. Soc. Sci. **4**, 609–618 (2018)
42. Kieser, H.: The Influence of Digital Leadership, Innovation and Organisational Learning on the Digital Maturity of an Organisation. University of Pretoria, Pretoria (2017)

43. Judge, T.A., Bono, J.E.: Five-factor model of personality and transformational leadership. J. Appl. Psychol. **85**, 751–765 (2000)
44. Pabst von Ohain, B.: Leader Attributes for Successful Digital Transformation. Fortieth International Conference on Information Systems, pp. 1–17. Munich (2019)
45. Promsri, C.: The developing model of digital leadership for a successful digital transformation. GPH - Int. J. Bus. Manag. **2**, 1–8 (2019)
46. Klein, M.: Leadership characteristics in the era of digital transformation. Bus. Manage. Stud. **8**, 883–902 (2020)
47. Mintzberg, H.: The strategy concept I: five Ps for strategy. Calif. Manage. Rev. **30**, 11–24 (1987)
48. Westerman, G., Bonnet, D., McAfee, A.: Leading Digital: Turning Technology into Business Transformation. Harvard Business Press, Cambridge (2014)
49. Fisk, P.: The making of a digital leader. BSR **13**, 43–50 (2002)
50. Tiekam, A.: Digital Leadership Skills that South African Leaders Need for Successful Digital Transformation. University of Pretoria, Pretoria (2019)
51. Khan, S.: Leadership in the Digital Age: A Study on the Effects of Digitalisation on Top Management Leadership. Stockholm University, Stockholm (2016)
52. Aron, D., Waller, G., Weldon, L.: Flipping to Digital Leadership: The 2015 CIO Agenda. https://www.gartner.com/en/documents/2864717/flipping-to-digital-leadership-the-2015-cio-agenda. Accessed on 04 March 2020)
53. Bolte, S., Dehmer, J., Niemann, J.: Digital Leadership 4.0. Acta Technica Napocensis **61**, 637–646 (2018)
54. Chadha, S.: Digital leadership - leveraging the uniqueness of digital. Hum. Capital **3**, 24–31 (2019)
55. Afandi, W.: The role of strategic leadership in digital transformation process. Int. J. Recent Res. Appl. Stud. **33**, 19–22 (2017)
56. Petry, T.: Digital leadership. In: North, K., Maier, R., Haas, O. (eds.) Knowledge Management in Digital Change. PI, pp. 209–218. Springer, Cham (2018). https://doi.org/10.1007/978-3-319-73546-7_12
57. Crummenerl, C., Kemmer, K.: Digital Leadership - Führungskräfteentwicklung im digitalen Zeitalter. https://www.capgemini.com/consulting-de/wp-content/uploads/sites/32/2017/08/14-10-16_digital_leadership_v11_web_17102016.pdf. Accessed on 12 July 2020
58. Valentine, E.: Enterprise Business Technology Governance: New Core Competencies for Boards of Directors in Digital Leadership. Queensland University of Technology, Brisbane (2016)
59. Sahyaja, C., Sekhara Rao, K.S.: New Leadership in the digital era - a conceptual study on emotional dimensions in relation with intellectual dimensions. Int. J. Civ. Eng. Technol. **9**, 738–747 (2018)
60. Antoni, C.H., Syrek, C.: Digitalisierung der Arbeit: Konsequenzen für Führung und Zusammenarbeit. Gr. Interakt. Org. **48**, 247–258 (2017)
61. Outvorst, F., Visker, C., de Waal, B.M.E.: Digital leadership - as the only way to survive a changing digital world? In: 14th European Conference on Management, Leadership and Governance, Utrecht, pp. 300–306 (2018)
62. Doyé, T.: Digital leadership. In: Fend, L., Hofmann, J. (eds.) Digitalisierung in Industrie-, Handels- und Dienstleistungsunternehmen, pp. 207–224. Springer, Wiesbaden (2020). https://doi.org/10.1007/978-3-658-26964-7_11
63. Valentine, E., Stewart, G.: Enterprise business technology governance: three competencies to build board digital leadership capability. In: Proceedings of the 48th Annual Hawaii International Conference on System Sciences, pp. 4513–4522. Waikoloa Beach (2015)
64. Kraft, M.H.G.: How to lead with digital media effectively? a literature-based analysis of media in a E-leadership context. J. Eco. Dev. Environ. People **8**, 42–53 (2019)

65. Kolzuniak, J.: Digital Leadership - Entwicklung eines Führungsmodells für effizientes Agieren in einer digital vernetzten Arbeitsumgebung im Vertrieb der Geschäftsbanken. Deutsches Institut für Bankwirtschaft - Schriftenreihe Band 14b, pp. 1–52 (2017)
66. Lenz, U., Grützmacher, P.: Was bin ich (noch), und was sollte ich sein? Die Auswirkungen der Digitalisierung auf die Rolle der Führungskraft. In: von Au, C. (ed.) Führen in der vernetzten virtuellen und realen Welt. LAP, pp. 1–18. Springer, Wiesbaden (2018). https://doi.org/10.1007/978-3-658-18688-3_1
67. Asri, A.A.S.M.A.N., Darma, G.S.: Revealing the digital leadership spurs in 4.0 industrial revolution. Int. J. Bus. Eco. Manag. 3, 93–100 (2020)
68. Lindner, D.: Studie 3: digital leadership in KMU – Was sagen Führungskräfte? In: KMU im digitalen Wandel. essentials, pp. 29–36. Springer, Wiesbaden (2019). https://doi.org/10.1007/978-3-658-24399-9_7
69. Meier, C., Sachs, S., Stutz, C., McSorley, V.: Establishing a digital leadership barometer for small and medium enterprises (SME). In: Proceedings of the MKL and TIIM International Conference, pp. 103–109. Lubin (2017)
70. Sievert, H., Scholz, C.: Engaging employees in (at least partly) disengaged companies. Results of an interview survey within about 500 German corporations on the growing importance of digital engagement via internal social media. Public Relations Rev. 43, 894–903 (2017)
71. Bersin, J.: Digital leadership is not an optional part of being CEO. Harv. Bus. Rev. 12, 2–4 (2016)
72. Schwarzmüller, T., Brosi, P., Duman, D., Welpe, I.M.: How does the digital transformation affect organizations? Key themes of change in work design and leadership. Manage. Revue 29, 113–137 (2018)
73. Yücebalkan, B.: Digital leadership in the context of digitalization and digital transformations. Curr. Acad. Stud. Soc. Sci. 1, 489–505 (2018)
74. Goethals, G.R., Sorenson, G., Burns, J.: Leadership in the Digital Age. Sage Publications, London (2004)
75. Bennis, W.: Leadership in a digital world embracing transparency and adaptive capacity. MIS Q. 37, 635–636 (2013)
76. Reinhardt, K., Lueken, S.: Digital leadership Exzellenz- Kompetenzmodell für erfolgreiche Führung im digitalen Zeitalter. In: Hartmann, M. (ed.) Impulse für digitale Lösungen: Empfehlungen für Kleine und Mittlere Unternehmen, pp. 35–45. Berliner Wissenschafts-Verlag, Berlin (2018)
77. Zeike, S., Bradbury, K., Lindert, L., Pfaff, H.: Digital leadership skills and associations with psychological well-being. Int. J. Environ. Res. Public Health 16, 1–12 (2019)
78. Sultan, Y.H., Suhail, K.S.: The impact of significant factors of digital leadership on gamification marketing strategy. Int. J. Adv. Res. Dev. 4, 29–33 (2019)
79. Weisman, R.: A Leadership Approach to Successful Digital Transformation Using Enterprise Architecture. University of Ottawa, Ottawa (2019)
80. Weill, P., Wörner, S.L., González, F.: Is your company a digital leader or a digital laggard? MIT Sloan CISR XVII, 1–4 (2017)
81. Trompenaars, F., Woolliams, P.: Going digital internationally. Organ. Dev. J. 34, 11–35 (2016)
82. Mangelmann, R.: Digitale Transformation in der Finanzbranche - Auswirkungen neuer Technologien und eines veränderten Kundenverhaltens auf Geschäftsmodell und Unternehmensführung. In: Petry, T. (ed.) Digital Leadership, pp. 129–150. Haufe Lexware GmbH, Freiburg im Breisgau (2016)
83. Jesse, N.: Organizational evolution - how digital disruption enforces organizational agility. IFAC-PapersOnLine 51, 486–491 (2018)

84. Wang, C., Cardon, P.W.: The networked enterprise and legitimacy judgments: why digital platforms need leadership. J. Bus. Strat. **40**, 33–39 (2019)
85. Hearsum, S.: How to develop digital leadership capability. Strateg. HR Rev. **14**, 208–210 (2015)
86. Schirmer, H.: Entwicklung von Digitalkompetenzen und Führungskultur im Zeitalter der Digitalen (r)Evolution - Darstellung am Beispiel Continental. In: Petry, T. (ed.) Digital Leadership, pp. 355–372. Haufe Lexware GmbH, Freiburg im Breisgau (2016)
87. Citrin, J., Neff, T.: Digital leadership. Organ. People **18**, 42–50 (2000)
88. Bohlen, W.: Digital leadership – Wie verändert die Digitalisierung die Mitarbeiterführung und was müssen Personalmanager bereits heute tun? In: Fürst, R.A. (ed.) Gestaltung und Management der digitalen Transformation, pp. 277–292. Springer, Wiesbaden (2019)
89. Petrucci, T., Rivera, M.: Leading growth through the digital leader. J. Leadersh. Stud. **12**, 53–56 (2018)
90. Tanniru, M.: Digital Leadership. Oakland University, Rochester (2017)
91. Temelkova, M.: Skills for digital leadership-Prerequisite for developing high-tech economy. Int. J. Adv. Manag. Soc. Sci. **7**, 50–74 (2018)
92. Weiner, J., Tanniru, M., Khuntia, J., Bobryk, D., Naik, M., LePage, K.: Digital leadership in action in a hospital through a real time dashboard system implementation and experience. J. Hosp. Adm. **5**, 34 (2016)
93. Bäuchle, R.: Digital Leadership–inwiefern können Objectives and Key Results die bestehenden Herausforderungen der Unternehmensführung bewältigen? Ostfalia Hochschule für angewandte Wissenschaft, Wolfenbüttel (2019)
94. Dorozalla, F., Klus, M.F.: Digital leadership – Status quo der digitalen Führung. In: Groß, M., Müller-Wiegand, M., Pinnow, D.F. (eds.) Zukunftsfähige Unternehmensführung, pp. 89–103. Springer, Heidelberg (2019). https://doi.org/10.1007/978-3-662-59527-5_5
95. Lorenz, M.: Digitale Führungskompetenz. Springer, Wiesbaden (2018). https://doi.org/10.1007/978-3-658-22673-2
96. Borins, S., Brown, D.: Digital leadership: the human face of IT. In: Borins, S., Kernaghan, K., Brown, D., Bontis, N. (eds.) Digital State of the Leading Edge, pp. 277–301. University of Toronto Press, Toronto (2007)
97. Creusen, U., Gall, B., Hackl, O.: Digital Leadership. Springer, Wiesbaden (2017)
98. Hensellek, S.: Digital leadership – Ein Rahmenwerk zur erfolgreichen Führung im digitalen Zeitalter. In: Kollmann, T. (ed.) Handbuch Digitale Wirtschaft, pp. 1189–1207. Springer, Wiesbaden (2020). https://doi.org/10.1007/978-3-658-17291-6_81
99. Dückert, S.: Leitbild der digitalen Führungskraft. In: Petry, T. (ed.) Digital Leadership, pp. 115–128. Haufe Lexware GmbH, Freiburg im Breisgau (2016)
100. Mihardjo, L.W.W., Rukmana, R.A.N.: Does digital leadership impact directly or indirectly on dynamic capability: case on indonesia telecommunication industry in digital transformation? J. Soc. Sci. Res. **4**, 832–841 (2018)
101. Tardieu, H., Daly, D., Esteban-Lauzán, J., Hall, J., Miller, G.: Leadership—what is required of leaders and leadership to achieve digital success? In: Deliberately Digital. FBF, pp. 95–105. Springer, Cham (2020). https://doi.org/10.1007/978-3-030-37955-1_11
102. Banks, G.C., Dionne, S.D., Sayama, H., Schmid Mast, M.: Leadership in the digital era: social media, big data, virtual reality, computational methods, and deep learning. Leadersh. Q. **30**, I–II (2019)
103. Crummenerl, C., Seebode, R.O.: Das Geheimnis erfolgreicher digitaler Transformationen - Warum Führung, Befähigung und Kultur den Unterschied machen. In: Petry, T. (ed.) Digital Leadership, pp. 151–186. Haufe Lexware GmbH, Freiburg im Breisgau (2016)
104. Rüth, R., Netzer, T.: The key elements of cultural intelligence as a driver for digital leadership success. Leader. Educ. Person.: Interdisc. J. **2**(1), 3–8 (2019). https://doi.org/10.1365/s42681-019-00005-x

The IT Artifact in People Analytics: Reviewing Tools to Understand a Nascent Field

Joschka A. Hüllmann[1,2(✉)], Simone Krebber[1,2], and Patrick Troglauer[1,2]

[1] European Research Center for Information Systems, Competence Center Smarter Work, Münster, Germany
{huellmann,s_kreb01,ptroglau}@uni-muenster.de
[2] School of Business and Economics, Department of Information Systems, Interorganisational Systems Group, University of Münster, Münster, Germany

Abstract. Despite people analytics being a hype topic and attracting attention from both academia and practice, we find only few academic studies on the topic, with practitioners driving discussions and the development of the field. To better understand people analytics and the role of information technology, we perform a thorough evaluation of the available software tools. We monitored social media to identify and analyze 41 people analytics tools. Afterward, we sort these tools by employing a coding scheme focused on five dimensions: methods, stakeholders, outcomes, data sources, and ethical issues. Based on these dimensions, we classify the tools into five archetypes, namely *employee surveillance*, *technical platforms*, *social network analytics*, *human resources analytics*, and *technical monitoring*. Our research enhances the understanding of implicit assumptions underlying people analytics in practice, elucidates the role of information technology, and links this novel topic to established research in the information systems discipline.

Keywords: People analytics · IT artifact · Archetypes · Social network analytics · Human resources analytics

1 Introduction

People analytics is gaining momentum. Defined as "socio-technical systems and associated processes that enable data-driven (or algorithmic) decision-making to improve people-related organizational outcomes" [1], people analytics seeks to provide actionable insights on the link between people behaviors and performance grounded in the collection and analysis of quantifiable behavioral constructs [2].

Applications of people analytics are found in the digitization of the human resources function, which seeks to substitute intuition-based decisions through data-driven solutions. For example, Amazon tried to complement their hiring process with an AI solution, resulting in considerable controversy[1]; and HireVue offers an AI solution to analyze

---

[1] https://www.reuters.com/article/us-amazon-com-jobs-automation-insight-idUSKCN1M K08G (accessed 2020–12–30).

F. Ahlemann et al. (Eds.): WI 2021, LNISO 48, pp. 238–254, 2021.
https://doi.org/10.1007/978-3-030-86800-0_18

video interviews[2]. However, the application of people analytics is not limited to the human resources function. Swoop offers social insights on engagement and collaboration for employees and managers alike[3]; and Humanyze hands out sociometric badges to employees to measure and analyze any part of business operations, meticulously[4].

Defying the growing concerns about algorithmic decision making and privacy [3, 4], while sidelining questions about the validity of the computational approaches amidst issues of algorithmic discrimination and bias [5], people analytics gathers a growing interest in academic and professional communities. Tursunbayeva et al. [6] attest the topic a continuously growing popularity based on a Google Trends query and depict an increasing number of publications in recent years. In 2017, people analytics made a first appearance on the main stage of the information systems discipline with a publication at the premier International Conference on Information Systems [4], before being problematized at further outlets (e.g., [3, 7]).

Despite growing interest, there is considerable controversy surrounding the topic. Being termed a "hype topic" [1], or a "hype more than substance" [8], multiple authors complain about the lack of academic inquiry. For example, we miss a conceptual foundation of the topic, leading to ambiguity and blurry definitions of core constructs [1]. Marler and Boudreau [9] review the literature on people analytics and criticize the scarcity of empirical research. Other studies focus on privacy, algorithmic discrimination, and bias [3], or the validity of the underlying approaches and their theoretical coherence [1].

While academia is looking to build a solid conceptual foundation of people analytics by synthesizing and structuring the field, practitioners focus on practical recommendations and selling professional advice. Subsuming the corpus of both academic and practitioners' literature, we find that information technology plays a seminal role in how people analytics is understood and presented. This is expected, given the definition of people analytics as a socio-technical system, which is enabled by big data and advances in computational approaches [4]. Surprising, however, is the lack of inquiry into the actual IT artifacts of people analytics. From the perspective of the information systems discipline, people analytics is a nascent phenomenon that would benefit from reviewing the IT artifacts and linking them to the established discourse.

Back in 2001, Orlikowski and Iacono [10] reprimanded the information systems discipline that it left defining the IT artifact to commercial vendors. Nowadays, we find the nascent topic of people analytics in an analogous situation. The topic of people analytics is driven by vendors and practitioners with only little research. Different tools are offered under the term people analytics, leading to confusion and conceptual ambiguity [1]. Therefore, we ask the following research questions:

RQ1: What is people analytics as understood by reviewing existing tools in terms of methods, data, information technology use, and stakeholders?

RQ2: What established discourse in the information systems discipline provides insights for inquiring people analytics?

---

[2] https://www.hirevue.com/ (accessed 2020–12-30).

[3] https://www.swoopanalytics.com/ (accessed 2020–12-30).

[4] https://www.humanyze.com/ (accesses 2020–12-30).

In our study, we addressed these questions by looking at the IT artifact and reviewing available people analytics tools. To this end, we monitored social media, mailing lists, and influencers for five months in 2019 to collect a sample of 41 people analytics tools. Two researchers coded the tools based on a coding scheme developed in an earlier work [1].

Our goal was to enhance the understanding of people analytics by shining light into the available IT artifacts. By clarifying what solutions are being sold as "people analytics", we sought to understand better what people analytics is. Since people analytics is a novel topic for the information systems discipline, we related our results to the established discourse. We hope to provide a basis for information systems scholars to make sense of people analytics, and guide subsequent conversations and research into the topic.

The remainder of this manuscript is structured as follows: First, we provide some background for people analytics. Then, we explain the benefits of looking at the IT artifact, before describing our methods. Afterward, we depict our results, closing with a discussion and relating the archetypes to the established discourse in the information systems discipline.

2   People Analytics

People analytics appears under different terms such as *human resources analytics* [9], *workplace* or *workforce analytics* [11, 12], or *people analytics* [3]. Tursunbayeva et al. [6] provide an overview of the different terms. People analytics depicts "*socio-technical systems and associated processes that enable data-driven (or algorithmic) decision-making to improve people-related organizational outcomes*" [1]. Typically, the means include predictive modeling, enabled by information technology, that makes use of descriptive and inferential statistical techniques. For example, Rasmussen and Ulrich [13] report on an analysis that links crew competence and safety to customer satisfaction and operational performance.

Some authors understand people analytics as an exclusively quantitative approach, analyzing big data, behavioral data, and digital traces [1, 14]. Examples include machine learning of video interviews to identify new hires[5]; or linear regression of pulse surveys to improve leadership skills[6]. Other definitions include qualitative data and focus on the scientific approach of hypothetic-deductive inquiry and reasoning. For example, Levenson [12] as well as Simon and Ferreiro [15] argue that people analytics should combine quantitative and qualitative methods to improve the outcomes of an organization.

The nucleus of people analytics is found in the human resources (HR) discipline, enriching traditional HR controlling and key performance indicators with insights from big data and computational analyses. As a result, people analytics has been described as the modern HR function that makes the move to data-driven decisions over intuition for informing traditional HR processes such as recruiting, hiring, firing, staffing, or talent development [9]. Despite the nucleus in HR, other researchers see it as reflecting a

---

[5] https://www.hirevue.com/ (accessed 2020–12-30).

[6] https://cultivate.com/platform/ (accessed 2020–12-30).

transformation of the general business, involving all kinds of business operations that affect people [4, 12]. Here, the underlying premise is that data is more objective, leads to better decisions, and, ultimately, guides managers to achieve higher organizational performance [4].

Big data, computational algorithms, and information technology provide the basis for people analytics according to the dominant perceptions in the literature [1]. Information technology enables computational analyses that inform people-related decision-making. For example, data warehouses collect, aggregate, and transform data for subsequent analysis, platforms visualize the data and enable interactive analytics, and machine learning algorithms and applications of artificial intelligence are programmed and embedded into the information technology infrastructure. Subsequently, various authors see information technology artifacts playing a focal role in people analytics [4, 12]. However, despite the seemingly high importance of information technology in people analytics endeavors, the actual tools seldom play a role in the manuscripts we reviewed. Both academics and practitioners rarely paint a concise picture of the tools when discussing people analytics. This fact is surprising given the variety of roles, functions, and purposes of information technology in the context of people analytics and the blurry conceptual boundaries of the topic [1]. It is unclear how to characterize and understand what is at the core of information technology for people analytics.

3 The IT Artifact

3.1 Enhanced Understanding Through IT Artifacts

Since people analytics is a nascent topic, there is a lack of basic or fundamental information about it—neither academia nor consultancies provide a concise and exhaustive definition of the topic [6]. However, there is a market for people analytics tools with solutions being offered to practitioners. These software tools are what we mean by the term "IT artifacts". Looking into them, we seek to enhance our understanding of people analytics.

Formally, we understand the "IT artifact" as an information system, emphasizing that the focal point of view lies on computer systems, but without dismissing the links to the social organization. Therefore, the IT artifact is a socio-technical system and comprises computer hardware and software. It is designed, developed, and deployed by humans imbued with their assumptions, norms, and intentions, and embedded into an organizational context [10].

How does a look into the IT artifact help? In 2010, Schellhammer [16] has recalled repeated requests over the years to put the IT artifact back into the center of research, inter alia, Orlikowski and Iacono [10], Alter [17], Benbasat and Zmud [18], and Weber [19]. It has been criticized that the IT artifact is "taken for granted" [10] as a black box, and treated as an unequivocal and non-ambiguous object [18]. However, the IT artifact is far from a stable and independent object. It is a dynamic socio-technical system that evolves over time, embedded into the organization, and linked to people and processes. IT artifacts come in many shapes and forms. Not inquiring the variety of the IT artifact and acknowledging its peculiarities means missing out and not understanding the implications and contingencies of the IT artifact for individuals and organizations [10]. Corollary, making sense of the IT artifact helps to inform our understanding of technology-related organizational processes and phenomena. Furthermore, understanding the implications of IT artifacts helps to build better technology in the future [10].

However, already 20 years ago, Orlikowski and Iacono [10] have claimed that defining the IT artifact is being left to practitioners and vendors, and we see an analogous situation with the nascent field of people analytics, today. People analytics is driven by practitioners and vendors, who propagate their understanding through their tools and services. They offer different tools varying in purpose and functionality under the term "people analytics", leading to conceptual ambiguity and confusion. Little academic research has sought to clear up and provide a consistent theoretical foundation [1]. This is crucial as the plurality of IT artifacts in people analytics yields different organizational implications depending on context, situation, and environmental factors. For example, legal issues depend on the country where people analytics is deployed, and privacy issues depend on the data being collected and aggregated. Anonymized analyses may be allowed, while personalized data collection may be prohibited. Depending on the organizational culture, different IT artifacts in people analytics might be welcomed or met with resistance [17]. The implications do not only refer to intended outcomes of implementing people analytics but also the unintended and side effects [1, 10]. One example is algorithmic bias and discrimination, where algorithms trained on historical data reproduce existing stereotypes [4]. A deep understanding of the IT artifact in people analytics allows judgement of the associated risk of running it [17]. Especially, since people analytics is a topic of utmost sensitivity due to data protection and privacy concerns.

3.2 The IT Artifact in People Analytics

Motivated by the lack of basic information about people analytics, exacerbated by the ambiguity in definition and the plurality of solutions offered, we seek to address this repeated call in the context of people analytics. We look at the IT artifact in people analytics to enhance our understanding of the topic.

Implicit assumptions of the IT artifact in people analytics presume a tool view of technology with an intended design [10] and focus on enhancing the performance of people-related organizational processes and optimizing their outcomes [12]. At the same time, the manuscripts we reviewed in the literature show an absence of explicitly depicting the IT artifact and its underlying assumptions. So far, practitioners' literature primarily focuses on maturity frameworks and high-level recommendations, while the scholarly literature provides commentaries and overviews [9]. There is a lack of deep dive into the design and the underlying assumptions of IT artifacts by scholars and consultancies alike. It is unclear how IT artifacts fulfill the proclaimed promises of people analytics to improve people-related organizational outcomes, and what the implications of different IT artifacts in people analytics are on organizational processes. Alter [17] encourages to pop the hype bubble: How do people analytics tools actually change the organization in a meaningful way and deliver business impact?

Understanding and organizing what we know about the IT artifacts in people analytics helps to address this knowledge gap [17]. To this end, Alter [17] suggests investigating different types of IT artifacts. Through learning about IT artifacts, we seek insights into the underlying assumptions and mental conceptions that practitioners hold on how people analytics functions in practice. Therefore, our study aims to distinguish IT artifacts of people analytics into five archetypes to capture the diverging conceptions in the field.

We refer to the use of the word "archetype" by Rai [20]. In our understanding, an archetype is a prototype of a particular system that emphasizes the dominant structures and patterns of said system. The archetype depicts the "standard best example" of a particular conception of people analytics. We refrained from using the word "categories" because the differences between archetypes are neither exhaustive nor distinct. Instead, Fig. 1 demonstrates the overlaps between the archetypes.

4 Methods

4.1 Identifying the Tools—Monitoring Social Media

We identified a long list of people analytics software vendors. The list was curated by monitoring influencers (e.g., David Green, the People Analytics and Future of Work Conference), mailings lists (insight222, myhrfuture, Gartner), and posts tagged with people analytics on social media platforms (LinkedIn, Twitter) in the period from August to December 2019. While monitoring, we continuously updated a list with all the mentioned tools in the context of people analytics. We tried to be as inclusive as possible. For the long list, we included all platforms which have been labelled as people analytics, because we sought to describe what the practitioners understand as people analytics—not our understanding. Accordingly, our list contained general-purpose platforms. Although these platforms are reported in the results section for completeness sake, we dismissed them for the discussion, as learning about people analytics from general-purpose platforms is limited. For example, we included PowerBI but did not discuss it further.

We cleansed the long list by filtering vendors who did not provide sufficient information. We ended up with a shortlist of 41 vendors. Most of them are small enterprises specialized in people analytics and only offer one particular tool, but the list also includes Microsoft, SAP, and Oracle (see Fig. 1).

To gather information about the IT artifacts, we screened the vendors' websites employing three search strategies based on keywords. Primarily, we tried to use (1) *the search function of the website*. Because the majority of websites did not have a search function, we included (2) *Google's site search function* (e.g., "site: http://exa mple.com/ HR "analytics"). Since a Google search provides many irrelevant results (similar to Google Scholar), we also (3) *manually navigated the websites and looked for relevant information based on keywords*. The keywords were "People Analytics", "HR/Human Resources Analytics", "Workplace Analytics", "Workforce Analytics", and "Social Analytics Workplace". Following hyperlinks was conducted ad-hoc and based on intuition, because each vendor named or positioned the relevant sections of the websites differently.

4.2 Analysis and Coding Scheme

We sorted the people analytics IT artifacts into five archetypes based on a coding scheme adapted from a previous study [1]. The coding scheme is agnostic to the search approach and can be used for a web search or a traditional literature review. We used only five of the nine dimensions because the remaining four dimensions were irrelevant to our study. They referenced meta information (e.g., what term is being used), or did not apply to our type of material (e.g., authors and journal are not helpful for analyzing vendors' websites). The five dimensions we used are: *methods, stakeholders, outcomes, data sources,* and *ethical issues.* These five dimensions elucidate the mental conception underlying people analytics tools, highlighting the implicit assumptions about people analytics and the role of IT held by the vendors.

The *methods* dimension describes what procedures and computational algorithms are implemented in the people analytics IT artifacts. The *stakeholders* address the driving sponsors, primary users, and affected people (= the people from whom data is collected). The *outcomes* depict the purpose of the IT artifact (i.e., what organizational processes or decisions are informed). The *data sources* refer to the kind of data that is collected for the analysis (e.g., quantitative digital traces, surveys, or qualitative observations). The *ethical issues* expose what and how unintended effects and ethical issues of privacy, fairness, and transparency are discussed by the vendors and dealt with in the software.

While the coding scheme provides the dimensions, it does not include concrete codes within each dimension. As a result, we sorted IT artifacts into five archetypes based on an explorative two-cycle coding approach (following [21]). During the first cycle, two researchers independently generated codes from the software descriptions inductively. The first cycle yielded a diverging set of codes that differed in syntax (the words being used as the codes) and semantics (what was meant by the codes). During the second cycle, the same two researchers jointly resolved all non-matching codes to generate the final set of codes. From the final set of codes, we derived the archetypes intuitively.

5   Results

We identified 41 relevant vendors for people analytics software, sorted them into the dimensions, and derived five archetypes: *technical monitoring, technical platform, employee surveillance, social network analytics* (SNA), and *human resources analytics* (HRA). The latter two categories are overlapping, with tools that provide both human resources and social network analytic capabilities. Additionally, HRA tools fall in either of two subcategories, *individual self-service and improvement* or *managerial HR* tools.

The results in this manuscript aggregate the prevalent and shared characteristics of the archetypes, but do not go into fine-granular details about each tool. However, we provide an accompanying wiki-esque website that provides the full details for each software tool[7].

---

[7] The website is available at: https://johuellm.github.io/people-analytics-wiki/.

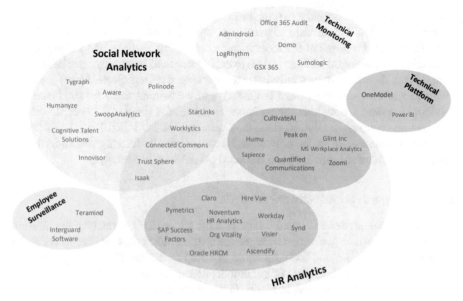

Fig. 1. Surveyed people analytics tools and archetypes

5.1 Archetype 1: Employee Surveillance

"Interguard Software" and "Teramind" fall into the first archetype *employee surveillance* (N = 2). Both are based on the concept of monitoring employees by invasive data collection and reporting, going as far as continuously tracking the employees' desktop screen. The IT artifact comprises two components: first, a local sensor that is deployed on each device to be tracked [14]. Such sensors collect fine granular activity data, enabling complete digital surveillance of the device and its user. The second component is an admin dashboard, which is provided as a web-based application. Such an application offers visualization and benchmarking capabilities to compare employees based on selected performance metrics. The espoused goals of employee surveillance are not only the improvement of performance outcomes but also ensuring employee compliance with company policies. For example, "Teramind" offers notifications to prevent data theft and data loss. Qua definition, the tools target and affect the individual employees who are being monitored. There is a lack of discussion on potential side and unintentional effects. Severe privacy issues, infringements and violations of the European Union General Data Protection Regulation (GDPR) [22], as well as negative effects of surveillance and invasive monitoring of employees are not discussed [3, 4].

5.2 Archetype 2: Technical Platforms

"Power BI" and "One Model" are *technical platforms* (N = 2), offering the tools and infrastructure needed to conduct analyses without providing predefined ones. Users can conduct analyses of any kind on these platforms, including people analytics. Addressed users are analysts and developers implementing analyses based on visualizations, dashboards, connecting various data sources (e.g., human resources information systems), or digital traces. Promises of the tools include supporting analyses and facilitating the generation of meaningful insights related to the business and its employees. The tools are general and, therefore, do not only cater to people analytics projects. Hence, learning about people analytics from them is limited, and we dismiss them for the discussion section. However, we included these tools in the results despite the lack of specific information on people analytics, since they were part of our initial long list of people analytics software vendors. We only cleansed the long list by filtering vendors, who did not provide sufficient information to be coded (as outlined in Sect. 4.1).

5.3   Archetype 3: Social Network Analytics

The overall goal of *social network analytics* tools (N = 12) is to analyze the informal social network in the organization by highlighting the dyadic collaboration practices that are effective and improving those practices that are ineffective. The espoused goals by the vendors are the optimization of communication processes to increase productivity, and identifying key employees to retain. Other goals range from monitoring communication for legal compliance to creating usage reports for data governance. A subset of tools allows managers to identify the informal leaders and knowledge flows in the organization, accelerating change, collaboration, and engagement, promising a better alignment and coherence in the leadership team. All SNA tools apply quantitative social network analysis, computing graph metrics over dyadic communication actions. Herein, the communication actions are considered edges, whereas the employees are represented by nodes. Further means include the analysis of content data by natural language processing such as sentiment analysis, or topic modeling, and other machine learning approaches. Besides, traditional null hypothesis significance testing (NHST) is applied on the social network data to illuminate causal effects in the dyadic collaboration data. As data sources, digital traces from communication and collaboration system logs, surveys, master data, network data, and Microsoft365 data are used to perform analyses that can be conducted on individual, group, and organizational levels. In the context of SNA tools, especially security and privacy issues as well as GDPR violations emerge as ethical issues, since sensitive communication data is being investigated.

5.4   Archetype 4: Human Resources Analytics

Human resources analytics tools (N = 24) generally fall in either of two subcategories, (1) *individual self-service and improvement* or (2) *managerial HR* tools.

Eight HRA tools are categorized as *individual self-service and improvement*. These tools are used by employees or leaders and managers for evaluating and improving their current habits, (collaboration) practices, leadership, functional or business processes, and skills, increasing productivity, effectiveness, engagement, and wellbeing, handling organizational complexity and change, and reducing software costs. To reach their goals, *individual self-service and improvement* tools use pulse surveys, nudges, dashboards, reports, partially enriched with data from devices across the organization (e.g., work time, effort, patterns, processes), machine learning, visualization, logs from communication and collaboration systems, video recordings (not video surveillance), learning management systems, and Microsoft365 data. Afterward, analyses can be conducted on the individual and/or group level.

Eleven HRA tools fall in the second category *managerial HR*. These tools are concerned with the management of human assets, including talent management and hiring, general decisions on workforce planning, and the management of organizational change and are provided by the HR department. Their level of analysis can be the individual, group, and organizational level and methods range from machine learning to predictive analyses, voice analyses, as well as reporting, surveys, and visualizations. Data sources come from multiple systems and range from HR (information systems), financial, survey, and psychometric data, to cognitive and emotional traits as well as videos and voice recordings (not surveillance). Moreover, as outlined in Fig. 1, five tools exist which we classify as both, SNA and HRA tools, since they provide social network as well as human resources analytics capabilities. The goals of these tools range from decision-making around people at work, gathering insights (e.g., collaboration patterns, engagement, and burnout) to drive organizational change, developing and improving performance and wellbeing of high performers in the organization, and deriving insights to enhance employees' experiences and satisfaction. To provide insights, all SNA-HRA tools apply social network analyses which are based on logs from communication and collaboration systems, and, additionally, some of the tools make use of pulse surveys. The analyses are performed on individual, group, and organizational levels. Typically, the stakeholder is only the HR department, although some tools target general management.

Like in SNA, security and privacy issues as well as GDPR non-conformity result as ethical issues for all (SNA-)HRA tools. As people analytics as human resources analytics are designed and implemented by humans, discrimination, bias, and fairness (e.g., in hiring, firing, and compensation), as well as the violation of individual freedom and autonomy, and the stifling of innovation are additional issues.

5.5   Archetype 5: Technical Monitoring

Technical monitoring tools (N = 6) aim for reducing IT spending, timesaving by employing prebuild dashboards, anticipating and decreasing technical performance issues (e.g., latency, uptime, routing), reducing time2repair, identifying cyber threats, ensuring security and compliance, increasing productivity, and troubleshooting. Insights are generated by visualization (as a dominant method), machine learning, descriptive analyses, nudges, and the evaluation of sensors which are deployed to different physical locations or network access endpoints. The level of analysis mostly concerns technical components but the individual, organizational, and group level can be considered as well. Stakeholders range from IT managers, system admins, data science experts, and analysts to security professionals. As data sources, custom connectors, as well as sensor, log, and Microsoft365 data are employed. Security and privacy concerns emerge as ethical issues, because employees' behaviours can be tracked through monitoring physical devices.

6 Discussing Two Archetypes of People Analytics

Discussing people analytics against the theoretical backdrop of the topic in the information systems literature is futile, because there is not a coherent conception available [1, 6]. Instead, we relate the two main archetypes to the established discourse on social network and human resources analytics, respectively. Comparing people analytics with the two research areas enables us to understand two different facets of the phenomenon and opens avenues for future research. Vice versa, the insights from our discipline can inform people analytics in practice.

We cannot learn about the contingencies and mental conceptions of people analytics from the three archetypes *technical monitoring* (N = 6), *technical platform* (N = 2), and *employee surveillance* (N = 2), as they are too general to provide relevant insights. They account for less than 25% (N = 10) of all tools which we examined. Instead, we focus on the two archetypes *social network analytics* (N = 12) and *human resources analytics* (N = 24) tools and their implications for people analytics to contribute to a better understanding of the topic. We map our results to the five dimensions of the coding scheme (methods, stakeholders, outcomes, data sources, ethical issues), which we adopted. Apart from the ethical issues, we elaborate on further concerns that occur in the field of SNA and HRA.

6.1 People Analytics as Social Network Analytics

Social network analytics is a prominent topic in the information systems discipline, with multiple authors providing comprehensive literature overviews [23–26]. Central questions are shared with *people analytics as social network analytics* and include, inter alia, knowledge sharing [27, 28], social influence, identification of influencers, key users and leaders [29, 30], social onboarding [31], social capital, shared norms and values [32], and informal social structures (see Table 1). Methods employed include sentiment analysis and natural language processing [33, 34], qualitative content analysis [35], and calculation of descriptive social network analysis measures—Stieglitz et al. provide an overview of the methods [36, 37]. Contrary, *people analytics tools* focus exclusively on quantitative approaches. In social network analytics research, privacy is a rare concern, since data is often publicly available in the organization (for enterprise social networks and public chats), and sensitive private data is often excluded in favor of deidentified metadata such as the network structure. Validity concerns are seldom discussed by the vendors of people analytics tools, whereas it presents an active topic in the information systems discipline.

In *people analytics as social network analytics*, the relevant data sources are digital traces from communication and collaboration systems [14, 24], as well as tracking sensors such as Humanyze sociometric badge [38, 39]—the same as in research.

The methods, data sources, and goals of the analysis are shared among practice and academia. However, the lack of discussion on the side effects is standing out, in particular the missing transparency about the validity of the tools' analyses. This reflects the question of whether people analytics tools fulfill the vendors' promises.

With digital traces we only observe actions that are electronically logged [14]. The traces represent raw data, basic measures on a technical level which are later linked to

Table 1. Comparing people analytics as social network analytics to information systems

Dimension	People analytics as social network analytics	Social network analytics in information systems
Methods	Social Network Analysis, Natural Language Processing (Sentiment Analysis, Topic Modelling), Null Hypothesis Significance Testing	Social Network Analysis, Natural Language Processing (Sentiment Analysis, Topic Modeling) [33, 34], Qualitative Content Analysis [35]
Stakeholders	Managers, Employees	Managers (e.g., [40])
Outcomes	Productivity, Key Employees, Informal Leaders, Knowledge Flows, Compliance	Knowledge Sharing [27, 28], Influencers, Informal Leaders [29, 30], Onboarding [31], Social Capital, Shared Norms [32]
Data Sources	Digital Traces	Digital Traces, Surveys [14, 24]
Ethical Issues and Concerns	Privacy	Privacy [3], Validity [14, 41]

higher-level theoretical constructs [42]. Hence, they only provide a lens or partial perspective on reality [43]. Digital traces only count basic actions as they do not include any context [14, 40]. The data is decoupled from meta-information such as motivation, tasks, or goals, and often only includes the specific action as well as the acting subject [44]. As digital traces are generated from routine use of a particular software or device [14], different (1) usage behaviors, (2) individual affordances, or (3) organizational environments affect the interpretation and meaning of digital traces [41, 43]. For example, the estimation of working hours based on emails is only feasible if sending emails constitutes a major part of the workday [40].

Furthermore, from digital traces being technical logs also follows that they "do not reflect people or things with inherent characteristics" [43]. Instead, digital traces should be considered as indicators pertaining to particular higher-level theoretical constructs [32, 45]. However, drawing theoretical inferences without substantiating the validity and reliability of digital traces as the measurement construct is worrisome [45]. Operationalization through digital traces still remains a mystery in the field of people analytics and conclusions about organizational outcomes should be met with skepticism and caution. In contrast to social network analytics, despite the collected data typically being deidentified, the problem of reidentification does exist [46] and privacy is, therefore, a severe concern for people analytics. Besides, security and informational self-determination issues [4, 22], surveillance capitalism [47], labor surveillance [48], the unintentional use of data, as well as infringements and violations of the GDPR are central concerns.

6.2 People Analytics as Human Resources Analytics

Human resources analytics has been dubbed the next step for the human resources function [9], promising more strategic influence [12]. The surveyed tools focus on machine learning, multivariate null hypothesis significance testing, descriptive reporting, and visualizations of key performance indicators. Similar topics are being discussed in the scholarly literature on human resources analytics [12, 49]. Typical stakeholders include human resources professionals as the driving force behind people analytics and the employees—or potential recruits—as the subjects being analyzed. Promised outcomes by the IT artifact vendors include productivity benefits, engagement, and wellbeing of employees, as well as improving the fundamental processes of the human resources function. The vendors advertise a vision of empowered human resources units that gain a competitive advantage through the application of people analytics [12]. Contrary, the academic literature on human resources analytics sticks to the focus on improving the fundamental human resources processes [9, 49].

Unintended effects are seldom addressed by the vendors, whereas they pose a prominent topic in the pertinent discussions around people analytics. Some vendors remark their compliance with the European Union's general data protection regulation but are not transparent about their algorithms, potential discrimination, and bias, as well as validity issues [1, 3, 4]. Conversely, these topics pose shared concerns to scholars in the information systems discipline (see Table 2).

Algorithms and tools are designed and implemented by humans and, as a result, bias may be included in the design or imbued in the implemented software [4]. Machine learning algorithms that learn from historical data, may reproduce existing stereotypes and biases [4, 5] (e.g., the amazon hiring algorithm[8]). The target metrics and values are defined by the managers and their underlying values and norms, and may lead to the dehumanization of work, only relying on numbers that matter [50]. Privacy is paramount when digital traces are concerned [48]. An increasing volume of data may lead to increased privacy concerns. Secondary, non-intended use of the data for analysis purposes that were unknown at the time of data collection increases privacy concerns [51, 52]. In general, people analytics is subject to legal scrutiny [22].

Table 2. Comparing people analytics as human resources analytics to information systems

Dimension	People analytics as human resources analytics	Human resources analytics in information systems
Methods	Null Hypothesis Significance Testing, Descriptive Reporting, Visualizations, Predictive Analytics	Multivariate Statistics, Visualizations, Descriptive Metrics, Predictive Analytics [2, 12, 49]
Stakeholders	Human Resources Managers, Employees	Managers, Business Units [12]

(continued)

---

[8] https://www.reuters.com/article/us-amazon-com-jobs-automation-insight-idUSKCN1M
K08G (accessed 2020–12-30).

Table 2. (*continued*)

Dimension	People analytics as human resources analytics	Human resources analytics in information systems
Outcomes	Productivity, Engagement, Wellbeing, Improvement of Human Resources Processes	Strategy Execution, Competitive Advantage [12], Human Resources Processes (Recruiting, Training, Staffing), Effectiveness, Efficiency, Engagement [9, 12, 27, 49]
Data Sources	(Pulse) Surveys, Psychometrics, Human Resources Information Systems, Digital Traces	Surveys, Interviews [12], Digital Traces [6, 40]
Ethical Issues and Concerns	Privacy	Privacy [4, 6], Discrimination and Bias [3, 5, 50], Validity [9, 40]

7 Conclusion

We monitored social media to identify and analyze 41 people analytics IT artifacts by focusing on the five dimensions methods, stakeholders, outcomes, data sources, and ethical issues. The dimensions were adapted from a coding scheme of a previous work [1]. We coded the tools based on the dimensions and derived five archetypes, namely *employee surveillance*, *technical platforms*, *social network analytics*, *human resources analytics*, and *technical monitoring*, and outlined their specific properties for each dimension. These archetypes contribute to understanding people analytics in practice.

We elaborated on the two main archetypes *social network analytics* and *human resources analytics* by illuminating people analytics through a research-oriented perspective, which enabled us to better comprehend the core of people analytics and the underlying role of information technology. Vice versa, the insights from these research areas can inform people analytics professionals. These comparisons offered us a critical view on potential issues with people analytics, popping the hype bubble and addressing validity, privacy, and other issues underlying the promises of the vendors. To this end, we explained which established discourse in the information systems discipline provides relevant knowledge for practitioners.

Despite having conducted a thorough research approach, our study is subject to limitations. First, we only looked at 41 vendors in a dynamic field, where new vendors may come to life every other month. Second, we only analyzed the publicly available documents and information provided by the vendors. Third, although the coding was performed by two independent researchers, it is still a subjective matter.

Our study makes an important contribution toward establishing a mutual understanding of people analytics between practitioners and academics. The derived archetypes can act as a starting point for stimulating future projects in research and practice. Based on the derived archetypes, the inquiry can be extended into selected topics of validity and privacy among others. Vendors should be transparent about the methods and how the pro-claimed goals are supposed to be achieved. They should clearly address unintended side effects and potential issues with privacy and validity. Consequently, a critical assessment of whether people analytics tools deliver the value that they promise is required.

Acknowledgements. We thank Laura Schümchen and Silvia Jácome for their support in analyzing the data and Oliver Lahrmann for programming the first version of the website.

References

1. Hüllmann, J.A., Mattern, J.: Three issues with the state of people and workplace analytics. In: Proceedings of the 33rd Bled eConference, pp. 1–14 (2020)
2. Levenson, A., Pillans, G.: Strategic Workforce Analytics (2017)
3. Gal, U., Jensen, T.B., Stein, M.-K.: Breaking the vicious cycle of algorithmic management: a virtue ethics approach to people analytics. Inf. Organ. **30**, 2–15 (2020)
4. Gal, U., Jensen, T.B., Stein, M.-K.: People analytics in the age of big data: an Agenda for IS Research. In: Proceedings of the 38th International Conference on Information Systems (2017)
5. Zarsky, T.: The trouble with algorithmic decisions: an analytic road map to examine efficiency and fairness in automated and opaque decision making. Sci. Technol. Hum. Values. **41**, 118–132 (2016)
6. Tursunbayeva, A., Di Lauro, S., Pagliari, C.: People analytics—a scoping review of conceptual boundaries and value propositions. Int. J. Inf. Manage. **43**, 224–247 (2018)
7. Leonardi, P.M., Contractor, N.: Better People Analytics: Measure Who They Know, Not Just Who They Are Harvard Business Review (2018)
8. van der Togt, J., Rasmussen, T.H.: Toward evidence-based HR. J. Organ. Eff. People Perform. **4**, 127–132 (2017)
9. Marler, J.H., Boudreau, J.W.: An evidence-based review of HR analytics. Int. J. Hum. Resour. Manag. **28**, 3–26 (2017)
10. Orlikowski, W.J., Iacono, C.S.: Research commentary: desperately seeking the "IT" in IT research—a call to theorizing the IT artifact. Inf. Syst. Res. **12**, 121–134 (2001)
11. Guenole, N., Feinzig, S., Ferrar, J., Allden, J.: Starting the workforce analytics journey (2015)
12. Levenson, A.: Using workforce analytics to improve strategy execution. Hum. Resour. Manage. **57**, 685–700 (2018)
13. Rasmussen, T., Ulrich, D.: learning from practice: how HR analytics avoids being a management fad. Organ. Dyn. **44**, 236–242 (2015)
14. Hüllmann, J.A.: The construction of meaning through digital traces. In: Proceedings of the Pre-ICIS 2019, International Workshop on The Changing Nature of Work, pp. 1–5 (2019)
15. Simón, C., Ferreiro, E.: Workforce analytics: a case study of scholar – practitioner collaboration. Hum. Resour. Manage. **57**, 781–793 (2018)
16. Schellhammer, S.: Theorizing the IT-artifact in inter-organizational information systems: an identity perspective. Sprouts Work. Pap. Inf. Syst. **10**, 2–23 (2010)
17. Alter, S.: 18 reasons why IT-reliant work systems should replace "The IT Artifact" as the core subject matter of the IS field. Commun. Assoc. Inf. Syst. **12**, 2–32 (2003)
18. Benbasat, I., Zmud, R.W.: The identity crisis within the IS discipline: defining and communicating the discipline's core properties. MIS Q. **27**, 183–194 (2003)
19. Weber, R.: Still desperately seeking the IT artifact. MIS Q. **27**, iii–xi (2003)

20. Rai, A.: Avoiding type III errors: formulating IS research problems that matter. MIS Q. **41**, iii–vii (2017)
21. Saldana, J.: The Coding Manual for Qualitative Reseachers. SAGE Publications Ltd, London, UK (2009)
22. Bodie, M.T., Cherry, M.A., McCormick, M.L., Tang, J.: The law and policy of people analytics. Univ. Color. Law Rev. **961**, 961–1042 (2017)
23. Högberg, K.: Organizational social media: a literature review and research Agenda. Proc. 51st Hawaii Int. Conf. Syst. Sci. **9**, 1864–1873 (2018)
24. Schwade, F., Schubert, P.: Social Collaboration Analytics for Enterprise Collaboration Systems: Providing Business Intelligence on Collaboration Activities, pp. 401–410 (2017)
25. Viol, J., Hess, J.: Information Systems Research on Enterprise Social Networks – A State-of-the-Art Analysis. Multikonferenz Wirtschaftsinformatik, pp. 351–362 (2016)
26. Wehner, B., Ritter, C., Leist, S.: Enterprise social networks: a literature review and research agenda. Comput. Networks. **114**, 125–142 (2017)
27. Riemer, K., Finke, J., Hovorka, D.S.: Bridging or bonding: do individuals gain social capital from participation in enterprise social networks? In: Proceedings of the 36th International Conference on Information Systems, pp. 1–20 (2015)
28. Mäntymäki, M., Riemer, K.: Enterprise social networking: a knowledge management perspective. Int. J. Inf. Manage. **36**, 1042–1052 (2016)
29. Berger, K., Klier, J., Klier, M., Richter, A.: Who is Key...? characterizing value adding users in enterprise social networks. In: Proceedings of the 22nd European Conference on Information Systems, pp. 1–16 (2014)
30. Richter, A., Riemer, K.: Malleable end-user software. Bus. Inf. Syst. Eng. **5**, 195–197 (2013)
31. Hüllmann, J.A., Kroll, T.: the impact of user behaviours on the socialisation process in enterprise social networks. In: Proceedings of the 29th Australasian Conference on Information Systems, pp. 1–11, Sydney, Australia (2018)
32. Hüllmann, J.A.: Measurement of Social Capital in Enterprise Social Networks: Identification and Visualisation of Group Metrics, Master Thesis at University of Münster (2017)
33. Cetto, A., Klier, M., Richter, A., Zolitschka, J.F.: "Thanks for sharing"—Identifying users' roles based on knowledge contribution in Enterprise Social Networks. Comput. Netw. **135**, 275–288 (2018)
34. Behrendt, S., Richter, A., Trier, M.: Mixed methods analysis of enterprise social networks. Comput. Netw. **75**, 560–577 (2014)
35. Thapa, R., Vidolov, S.: Evaluating distributed leadership in open source software communities. In: Proceedings of the 28th European Conference on Information Systems (2020)
36. Stieglitz, S., Dang-Xuan, L., Bruns, A., Neuberger, C.: Wirtschaftsinformatik **56**(2), 101–109 (2014). https://doi.org/10.1007/s11576-014-0407-5
37. Stieglitz, S., Mirbabaie, M., Ross, B., Neuberger, C.: Social media analytics – challenges in topic discovery, data collection, and data preparation. Int. J. Inf. Manage. **39**, 156–168 (2018)
38. Waber, B.: People Analytics: How Social Sensing Technology Will Transform Business and What It Tells Us about the Future of Work. FT Press, Upper Saddle, New Jersy, USA (2013)
39. Oz, T.: People Analytics to the Rescue: Digital Trails of Work Stressors. OSF Prepr (2019)
40. Hüllmann, J.A., Krebber, S.: Identifying temporal rhythms using email traces. In: Proccedings of the America's Conference of Information Systems, pp. 1–10 (2020)
41. Howison, J., Wiggins, A., Crowston, K.: Validity issues in the use of social network analysis for the study of online communities. J. Assoc. Inf. Syst. 1–28 (2010)
42. Chaffin, D., et al.: The promise and perils of wearable sensors in organizational research. Organ. Res. Methods. **20**, 3–31 (2017)

43. Østerlund, C., Crowston, K., Jackson, C.: Building an apparatus: refractive, reflective and diffractive readings of trace data. J. Assoc. Inf. Syst. 1–43 (2020). https://doi.org/10.17705/1jais.00590

44. Pentland, B., Recker, J., Wyner, G.M.: Bringing context inside process research with digital trace data. Commun. Assoc. Inf. Syst. (2020)

45. Freelon, D.: On the interpretation of digital trace data in communication and social computing research. J. Broadcast. Electron. Media. **58**, 59–75 (2014)

46. Rocher, L., Hendrickx, J.M., de Montjoye, Y.A.: Estimating the success of re-identifications in incomplete datasets using generative models. Nat. Commun. **10**, 1–9 (2019)

47. Zuboff, S.: Big other: surveillance capitalism and the prospects of an information civilization. J. Inf. Technol. **30**, 75–89 (2015)

48. Ball, K.: Workplace surveillance: an overview. Labor Hist. **51**, 87–106 (2010)

49. van den Heuvel, S., Bondarouk, T.: The rise (and fall?) of HR analytics. J. Organ. Eff. People Perform. **4**, 157–178 (2017)

50. Ebrahimi, S., Ghasemaghaei, M., Hassanein, K.: Understanding the role of data analytics in driving discriminatory managerial decisions. In: Proceedings of the 37th International Conference on Information Systems (2016)

51. Bélanger, F., Crossler, R.E.: Privacy in the digital age a review of information privacy research in information systems. MIS Q. **35**, 1017–1041 (2011)

52. Bhave, D.P., Teo, L.H., Dalal, R.S.: Privacy at work: a review and a research Agenda for a contested terrain. J. Manage. **46**, 127–164 (2020)

Digitale Innovationen and Entrepreneurship

Introduction to the WI2021 Track: Digital Innovation and Entrepreneurship

Peter Buxmann[1] and Ferdinand Thies[2]

[1] Technische Universität Darmstadt, Software and Digital Business Group,
Darmstadt, Germany
`peter.buxmann@tu-darmstadt.de`
[2] University of Liechtenstein, Institute for Entrepreneurship,
Vaduz, Liechtenstein
`Ferdinand.thies@uni.li`

1 Track Description

Information and communication technologies (ICT) have become an increasingly important driver of novel and often disruptive innovations. Digital innovations are changing products, services, and entire business models.

Thereby, various technological developments like the Internet of Things (IoT) or Artificial Intelligence (AI) have the potential to sustainably change how value is created. These developments affect all sectors, as they are not limited to IT-related industries anymore, but by now touch traditional product- and service industries both within the business-to-business and the business-to-consumer sector.

Due to new and emerging ecosystems and new technological opportunities, traditional companies need to regularly question and possibly adapt their business models or build new business branches to survive. Corporate Entrepreneurship and the possibility to foster digital innovation within traditional companies receive growing attention. At the same time, digital innovations also offer the opportunity to develop new solutions as a foundation of new companies and to challenge existing companies and business norms.

This track will therefore examine the impact of digital innovations on the design and behavior of existing and new businesses.

2 Research Articles

2.1 Recombining Layers of Digital Technology: How Users Create and Capture Value (Axel Hund, Viktoria Diel, Heinz-Theo Wagner)

The paper investigates how users can create innovation by re-combining existing elements of digital technology. For this purpose, empirical data from a study are evaluated and recommendations for producers and possibilities for more in-depth research are derived.

2.2   Enter the Shark Tank: The Impact of Business Models on Early Stage Financing (Timo Phillip Böttcher, Valentin Bootz, Tetiana Zubko, Jörg Weking, Markus Böhm, Helmut Krcmar)

The study analyzes the business model of 72 startups and the amount of received seed investment. A Pearson's product-moment correlation test is applied to calculate the correlation between these variables. The research shows a correlation between the business model and the amount of received seed investment. We identify the patterns Two-Sided Market, Layer Player, and Freemium to have a significant positive effect on the investment sum. This research guides entrepreneurs in business model design and contributes to the discussion of success factors for startup success.

2.3   Structuring the Jungle of Capabilities Fostering Digital Innovation (Christoph Buck, Timo Gruenke, Katharina Stelzl)

Based on a structured literature review and a qualitative analysis of existing capabilities, the paper presents a Digital Innovation Capability Model. By structuring layers, areas and associated capabilities, the model provides the first holistic view in the literature. It can serve as a basis for a targeted scientific discourse and a valuable orientation model for the development of a capability composition to foster Digital Innovation in organizations.

2.4   Digital Innovation Culture: A Systematic Literature Review (Daniel Kiefer, Clemens Van Dinther, Julian Spitzmüller)

The purpose of this paper is to identify the characteristics of organizational culture that foster digital innovations. Based on a systematic literature review on three scholarly databases, we initially found 778 articles that were then narrowed down to a total number of 23 relevant articles. After analyzing these articles, we determine nine characteristics of organizational culture that foster digital innovations: corporate entrepreneurship, digital awareness and necessity of innovations, digital skills and resources, ecosystem orientation, employee participation, agility and organizational structures, error culture and risk-taking, internal knowledge sharing and collaboration, customer and market orientation as well as open-mindedness and willingness to learn.

Recombining Layers of Digital Technology: How Users Create and Capture Value

Axel Hund[1]([⊠]), Viktoria Diel[1], and Heinz-Theo Wagner[2]

[1] Chair of Information Systems and Services, University of Bamberg, Bamberg, Germany
axel.hund@uni-bamberg.de
[2] Neu-Ulm University of Applied Sciences, Neu-Ulm, Germany
heinz-theo.wagner@hnu.de

Abstract. Recombination is central to the creation of innovation. Since digital innovation is product and use agnostic, not only producers and firms can carry out recombination, but users themselves can select and recombine different digital resources. We investigate why users select and recombine digital resources from different layers (content, service, network, device) of the layered modular architecture in a personal context. Our results allow us to make three key contributions: (1) We underscore the importance to distinguish between intra-layer and inter-layer recombination and uncover different reasons to carry out intra- or inter-layer recombination. (2) We show that the network layer appears to be invisible to users when recombining digital resources in a personal context. (3) We outline recommendations and research questions for future research, based on our findings.

Keywords: Digital innovation · Recombination · Use recombination · Design recombination

1 Introduction

The concept of recombination is central to innovation research since the seminal writings of Schumpeter: "To produce means to combine materials and forces within our reach [...] To produce other things [...] means to combine these materials and forces differently" [1, p.65]. Since then, the perspective that innovation is created by combining already existing materials and forces in new ways is enduring across disciplines (e.g., [2, 3]). By applying the concept of combination and recombination to different environments, research has found that not only the physical components of a product can be recombined to generate innovation, but also knowledge (e.g., [4]) and organizational units (e.g., [5]).

Drawing on the recombination perspective, extant research notes that digital innovation comes about by recombining digital and physical components and exhibits a new form of architecture distinct form traditional non-digital products. Digital innovation is now characterized by the layered modular architecture, which "[...] extends the modular architecture of physical products by incorporating four loosely coupled layers of devices, networks, services, and contents created by digital technology" [6, p. 724].

Within and across these four different layers resources can be recombined in unforeseen ways leading to digital innovation [6, 7]. Moreover, this recombination can be performed by users. Until recently, recombination was implicitly considered to be only carried out by producers (e.g., [8–11]) since recombining different components in order to produce value required product-specific expertise and an overview of the product design [6]. In that respect, Henfridsson et al. [11] argue that traditional innovation research focuses almost exclusively on recombination carried out by producers, yet the malleability of digital resources enables users to perform recombination themselves. This is possible, because digital resources, which are "entities that serve as building blocks in the creation and capture of value from information" [11, p. 90] are highly malleable and allow flexible recombination with other digital resources across different layers. Therefore, it is necessary to distinguish between design recombination and use recombination to better understand how recombination can lead to digital innovation. *Design recombination* is carried out by producers who define how a certain set of digital resources is connected in order to create a value offering for users. *Use recombination*, on the other hand, is performed by the users of such value offerings and describes the activity of recombining different parts of an offering with parts of another offering [11].

However, extant studies' exclusive focus on design recombination undercuts insights from the cocreation literature that show "how value is created in use by many actors, suggesting that digital innovation is a collaborative effort of integrating resources" [11, p. 91]. Until now, we have very limited insights into what prompts users to select different digital resources and recombine them across and within the four different layers of device, network, services, and contents. Thus, we put forward the following research questions:

RQ1: *Which specific digital resources from the four layers of content, service, network, and device are selected by users and why?*
RQ2: *How and why do users recombine digital resources within and across the four layers of devices, networks, services, and contents?*

To answer the research question, we conducted 21 exploratory interviews in which we asked about the digital resources selected by the respondents. We then categorized these digital resources along the four layers of device, network, service, and content to determine how and why users select and recombine digital resources from different layers. In the next section, we review the relevant literature before describing our methodology. We then present our findings and discuss their theoretical and practical implications. We conclude with an outlook on future research and a short conclusion.

2   Related Literature

"Recombination is at the heart of innovation" [11, p. 89]. This is also true for digital innovation, which is defined as the process of creating new products by recombining physical and digital components in novel ways [6]. Doing so leads to new market offerings and business processes, which already transformed entire industries [12] and initiated the rapid decline of previous market leaders such as Kodak [13]. By recombining physical components with digital components, previously analog products become digitized and acquire the properties of digital technologies such as reprogrammability [14], and editability [15]. These properties are central to digital innovation and require firms to organize within innovation networks [16, 17] and change the way innovation is managed [12, 18]. Furthermore, while purely physical products typically have a modular architecture, recombining digital and physical components leads to a *layered* modular architecture, which consists out of four loosely coupled layers (content, service, network, device) [6]. These four layers lead to fluid product boundaries and allow the recombination of components across different layers for different purposes. The fluid product boundaries make the components in a layered modular architecture product agnostic since they can be recombined with other components independently of a specific design hierarchy and the envisioned final product [6].

While research already distinguishes between different types of recombination that focus on either tangible components, organizational structures or knowledge [19], recombination is predominantly regarded as an activity carried out by the producer-side (e.g., firms) to create value offerings to consumers and users [e.g., 8, 20]. Henfridsson et al. [11] call recombination carried out by producers *design recombination* and note that design recombination is only one side of the coin. The other side is recombination carried out by users while using different value offerings, which is called *use recombination*. Importantly, users can be individuals, firms or even algorithms [11]. By combining and recombining parts of various value offerings in use, users make use of the agnostic nature of digital resources [6, 21]. Doing so, users contribute to the "increasingly amorphous agency as well as vaguely determined initial outcomes, resulting from a continuous flow of augmenting, expanding, and integrating new digital technologies into infrastructure and broader ecosystems" [22, p. 5]. Hence, the traditional distinction between central and peripheral stakeholders is increasingly obsolete, since players take different roles in different networks. "Instead there are many formal and informal networks, with relatively little overlap, each for its own different and often temporary purpose" [23, p. 17].

Following this line of thought, Henfridsson et al. [11] argue that the unit of analyses must shift from products and components to the notion of digital resources. Digital resources, which enable capturing value from information and serve as building blocks for digital innovation, can manifest on each of the four layers (content, service, network, device). This shift towards digital resources also underlines the malleability and agnosticism associated with the layered modular architecture, which enables users themselves to recombine different value offerings from firms in unforeseen ways [11]. While users have more influence, it is only by considering design recombination and use recombination together we obtain a full picture about recombination [24].

Figure 1 illustrates how for each layer, there exists a value space, which is a network of interlinked digital resources, which are created and dissolved by various actors for differing purposes. Each digital resource "(1) belongs to a specific value space, (2) hosts the potential to simultaneously be part of multiple value paths, and (3) is typically product-agnostic" [11, p. 92]. Producers conduct design recombination by connecting digital resources to create value paths, which serve as value offering to users, whereas users carry out use recombination by selecting a specific digital resource from such value offerings and connecting them to digital resources from other value offerings. By connecting digital resources in unforeseen ways across and within layers, users create individual value connections [11].

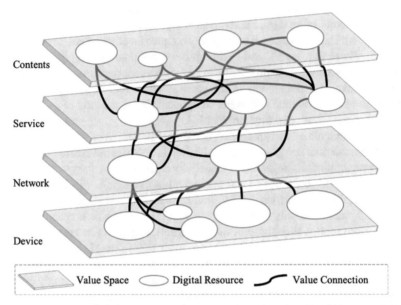

Fig. 1. Value spaces, digital resources, value connections (based on Henfridsson et al. [11])

3 Method

Qualitative, explorative research methods are perfectly suited for open research questions as they are able to provide initial information about a topic and to create a basic understanding of the research subject [25]. While recombination itself is a well-researched subject across various fields (e.g., [1, 4, 6]), use recombination is a newly established area in the field of recombination and innovation research [11]. Thus, we chose an explorative research approach to examine which specific digital resources from the four layers of content, service, network, and device are selected by users and why? Furthermore, we want to understand how and why users recombine digital resources within and across the four layers of devices, networks, services, and contents to create digital innovation. To identify suitable interview partners, we established various rules such as the interest in digital services and devices and the regular use of digital services and devices as selection criteria. Furthermore, to gain better insights into use recombination in a personal context, we focused on users with different educational and professional backgrounds that recombine digital resources in a predominantly personal context. In total 21 interviews were conducted, as listed in Table 1.

The interviews were conducted on site between August and October 2019 using a semi-structured interview guide and were based on the following structure: First, the participants were asked about their attitudes towards digital resources and their expertise in dealing with them. Then they were asked which digital resources they use and how often they use them. Following up, the focus shifted towards the reasons and motivation for selecting and recombining various resources. Afterwards, the participants were asked to describe how exactly they go about selecting, combining and recombining different digital resources. The interviews were recorded with the consent of the interviewees and subsequently transcribed.

Table 1. Overview interview partners

ID	Educational level	Field of education and training	Current occupation
IP01	Bachelor	Business Administration	Student
IP02	Bachelor	Business Administration	Student
IP03	A-Levels	Mechanical Engineering	Student
IP04	Bachelor	Mechanical Engineering	Student
IP05	Master	Business Education	Teacher
IP06	Bachelor	Health Care Management	Assistance to Management
IP07	Professional Training	Bike Mechanic	Paramedic
IP08	Professional Training	Office Clerk	Administrative Employee
IP09	Master	Electrical Engineering	Research Assistant
IP10	Master	Business Administration	Project Engineer
IP11	Master	Business Administration	Institutional Sales Manager
IPI2	Bachelor	Robotics	Student
IP13	Master	Innovation Management	Digital Innovation Manager
IP14	Bachelor	Educational Sciences	Student
IPI5	Professional Training	Electrical Engineering	Electrical Engineer
IPI6	Master	Business Administration	Human Ressource Manager
IP17	Master	Physics	Research Assistant
IP18	Doctorate	Mechanical Engineering	Speaker Business IT
IP19	Professional Training	Industrial Clerk	Commercial Clerk
IP20	Master	Business Administration	Senior Associate Consulting
IP21	Professional Training	Wholesale Merchant	Commercial Clerk

Data analysis was carried out after transcription according to the guidelines for qualitative content analysis by Mayring [25]. To do so, we defined clear research questions and then identified a framework in the literature to guide our data analysis. The layered modular architecture of digital technology, which is central to the field of digital innovation research in general and use recombination in specific [6, 11], was chosen. Following best practices in the literature [25, 26], we deductively coded each interview according to our coding guidelines. Table 2 provides an overview of the characteristics of each layer and the respective coding rule. After categorizing relevant codings along the four layers of the layered modular architecture, we inductively coded within each category, searching for patterns and emerging subcategories. Any unclear codings were discussed among the authors until an agreement was reached.

Table 2. Coding guidelines based on Yoo et al. [6] and Henfridsson et al. [11]

Layer	Layer characteristic	Coding rule
Content	**Definition**: The content layer includes digital data **Example**: Maps, music, video, pictures	Statements about information of any kind in a digital format, which can be stored, shared, watched, read, etc
Service	**Definition**: The services layer is software based and consists of functional applications enabling the interaction with contents **Example**: Social media Applications, smart lightning	Statements about any application that is selected by the user for its specific functionality and/or enables the processing of contents
Network	**Definition**: The network layer consists of logical transmission software and the physical transport resources **Example**: Transmitters, network standards	Statements about the selection of digital and non-digital resources that enable the transmission of signals
Device	**Definition**: The device layer contains hardware and software resources for storing and processing **Example**: Computer, operating system	Statements about any kind of hardware and/or the software needed to use the hardware

4 Analysis Part 1: Digital Resource Categories and Reasons for Selection

To answer our first research question *"Which specific digital resources from the four layers of content, service, network, and device are selected by users and why?"* we now present our results regarding specific digital resources. We first show which digital resources our interview partners mentioned and then go on to highlight reason for users to select a specific digital resource.

4.1   Digital Resources Selected by Users – An Overview

For the content layer we coded statements about information in any kind of digital format, which can be stored, shared, watched, read etc. Examples are contents such as music, podcasts, books, videos and maps. During our analysis three subcategories emerged, which help structuring the identified digital resources in the content layer even further. The subcategories are audible, visual, and written and describe the nature of the content.

Table 3. Types of digital resources

Layer	Subcategory	Examples
Content	Audible	Podcast, music, voice message
	Visual	Pictures, video, video telephony, series, movies, maps
	Written	Books, notes, links, written messages
Service	Messaging	WhatsApp, Skype, e-mail client (e.g., Outlook), Telegram, iMessage, Facebook Messenger
	Streaming	Netflix, Amazon Prime Video, Spotify, Apple Music, YouTube
	Navigation	Google Maps, Apple Maps, Open Street Maps
	Socializing	Facebook, Snapchat, Xing, LinkedIn
	Storage	OneDrive, Dropbox, Google Drive, iCloud, Own Cloud
	Voice Assistance	Siri, Google Assistant, Alexa
	Payment	PayPal, Apple Pay, Google Pay
	Online Shopping	AirBnB, Booking.com, Amazon, H&M, Zalando, eBay, Lieferando, Check24
	Smart Home	Smart lightening, smart heating, smart shutters
	Browser	Opera, Internet Explorer, Google Chrome
	Mobility	DB-Navigator, Uber, car sharing
Device	Immobile	Beamer, printer, PlayStation, smart TV
	Mobile	Smart board, smartphone, tablet, laptop, e-book reader, smart watch, Bluetooth box, headphones, e-scooter, car

The service layer is defined as software based functional applications, which enable the interaction with contents. Examples include services such as WhatsApp, Netflix, Spotify etc. Each of the identified services enables users to access and interact with content and the service layer is also the most frequently mentioned layer within our data set. Analyzing the way, the interviewees referred to a respective service allows inductively deriving subcategories based on the functionality the mentioned applications offer. By following this logic, a total of eleven subcategories emerged, which are categorized by what kind of service they provide. For example, applications such as Netflix and Spotify, which offer the service of streaming series or music, are both categorized as "Streaming" services. While they enable access to and interaction with different types of contents (Spotify/audible content, Netflix/visual content) they nonetheless provide the same type of service (streaming). Similarly, "Messaging" includes services, which enable access to and interaction with any kind of digital messages, even if the nature of the content differs significantly such as in the case of e-mail providers and Skype.

One of the key findings in this step of analysis was the absence of any mentions of the network layer. The network layer is about digital and non-digital resources that enable the transfer of signals or how Henfridsson et al. [11, p. 94] put it: the "logical transmission software and the physical transport resources". While the network layer plays an important role by providing network standards (e.g., TCP/IP) [6], it appears that users do not consider different networks. This might hold interesting implications for design recombination, which we will address in the discussion.

The device layer is defined as hard- or software which is needed to be able to use digitalized hardware. Examples include laptops, beamers, smartphones etc. During the analysis two subcategories emerged, which allow to distinguish between "immobile" and "mobile" devices. Immobile devices can only be used at the location they were installed at whereas mobile devices can be used at any place. Table 3 provides an overview of the identified digital resources.

4.2 Reasons for Selecting Digital Resources

After the identification of different digital resources across the layers of content, service and device, we now turn to the reasons for selecting a specific digital resource. Besides the obvious reasons for selecting a digital resource (such as perceived usefulness and perceived ease of use [e.g., 27]), we discover that integration, compatibility, and network effects are particularly important in the context of digital resources.

Integration is about tight linkings between different digital resources. By tightly integrating different digital resources with each other, it is possible to ensure better synchronization between certain digital resources, which can lead to a better performance and less problems arising when combining digital resources that are intended to be linked with each other. This can help saving time, which was mentioned frequently and appears to be a general reason for the selection of digital resources. Or how IP13 put it: "[…] the inherent promise of technology is to save time". Similarly, a tight integration can also increase the overall experienced convenience. "I am very open-minded, […] I am actually often looking for things that simplify life in general" (IP17). Convenience plays an important role when deciding between similar value offerings from different companies. For example, the level of integration between different digital resources offered by a company plays an important role. "[I] am a dedicated apple user, so I really like the fact that it's all integrated, synchronized and yes, it makes my life easier in many ways" (IP02). Similarly, payment services, which are tightly integrated with a specific device also help saving time and increase convenience in daily life. "I use payment services such as ApplePay, because it is much, much more convenient to pay with it, it is faster at the checkout, you briefly hold your smartphone up to the front of the device for the cards and you don't have to enter a pin, you confirm with your fingerprint or with FaceID. It is simply much faster and more convenient than paying by card or cash" (IP04). Time saving and convenience are the most common reasons for selecting voice assistance. "Very, very open, because I think it simply makes everyday life easier, perhaps to save time or in situations where you shouldn't be distracted by typing something somewhere that can be done with a voice assistant." (IP07) However, data protection also plays a role in connection with voice assistance. The factors convenience and time-saving are important when choosing a navigation service. "Both Apple [maps] and Google [maps] […], […], to avoid traffic jam, so I usually let both navigate in parallel to see where I can save time, who wants to be in a traffic jam, right?" (IP07). While a tight integration of certain digital resources can increase convenience and simplify life, it typically reduces the overall compatibility with other digital resources, which is another frequently mentioned reason for selecting a digital resource.

Compatibility with other digital resources is another major reasons for selecting a digital resource. In this context, storage services are noteworthy, with several respondents saying that they select a storage solution, because it is compatible with their own devices or with other users' operating systems. This is summed up in the statement of IP04: "iCloud for example is much more compatible with Apple devices than Dropbox, so I use iCloud for internal sharing and Google Drive is of course much more compatible with Windows products and Android products, so my friends probably use it and to share documents with them as easy as possible I use it as well". Additionally, the availability of materials independently of a device and also the provision of free storage capacity by a storage service is an advantage for IPs. IP02 stated: "meanwhile I like the cloud services very much, because you can easily access them from all kinds of devices" and IP04 pointed out: "in the past I used Dropbox a lot, because I had free storage there and my friends also used it". In addition, storage services are being selected for the improved collaboration, e.g. in group work. "With Dropbox you had the possibility […] to edit things online, but also to exchange with other people, […] which was extremely practical especially for the university, also for presentations or other group projects" (IP11). Further, the number of users a service has was mentioned to be an important factor for selection, particularly for social and messenger services (e.g., IP07). Here, compatibility with other digital resources influences how many users can access and use a specific service. For example, IP07 states "So, WhatsApp […] started, because there are just so many people". Similarly, social recommendations play an important role, yet users can only follow recommendations from their social circle if the respective digital resource is compatible with the digital resources they are using.

Network Effects. In addition, the number of users a service has was frequently mentioned as an important factor for selection, particularly in the case of social and messenger services. Some services are almost exclusively selected because they already have a high number of users and are, therefore, more useful for other users. For example, IP07 states: "Well, WhatsApp […] started because there are just so many people". But other services whose value proposition is not about social contacts or the promise that many other people will use the service also benefit from higher user numbers, as social recommendations play an important role. For example, IP03 states: "I came to Spotify or Netflix mainly through friends who used it before and recommended it to me".

5   Analysis Part 2: How and Why Do Users Recombine Different Digital Resources Within and Across Layers?

Building upon the identified categories of digital resources and why users select them, we now turn to our second research question: *How and why do users recombine digital resources within and across the four layers of devices, networks, services, and contents?* In total, we identify five different paths that users take to recombine digital resources. One key insight is the importance of distinguishing between recombining digital resources within the same layer, which we term intra-layer recombination and recombining digital resources across different layers, which we term inter-layer recombination. Furthermore, we identify different paths that users take to carry out intra-layer recombination (Path 1–4) and inter-layer recombination (Path 5). Figure 2 depicts an overview of the different paths of recombination in use.

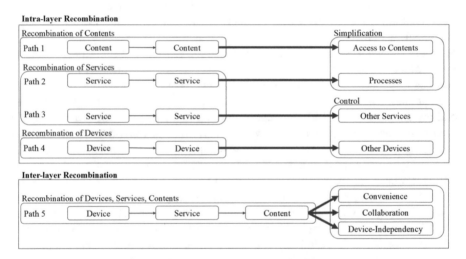

Fig. 2.   Different paths of use recombination

5.1   Intra-layer Recombination

Path 1: Content Layer. The first path for use recombination takes places on the content layer. Users typically recombine different digital resources at the content level to facilitate access by embedding a piece of content such as a link or file in a message or other document to make the content available to others. For example, IP05 describes an intra-layer recombination on the content level by integrating links on exercise sheets for students, which facilitates accessing the content.

Path 2: Service Layer.   The second path for use recombination takes place on the service layer. Users typically recombine digital resources at the service level to simplify a process and benefit from several services simultaneously. For example, the process of buying something online is oftentimes carried out by using multiple services simultaneously. Typically, the service of an online shopping service is combined with a payment service. IP03 stated for instance: " Well, […] the most common example is actually shopping over the smartphone, e.g. at Amazon or Zalando, I always pick out things that I would like to have and then I am transferred from the shopping cart to e.g. Paypal and can pay my purchase directly with the Paypal app." In this context IP05 mentioned that the payment process is significantly simplified by the recombination of the services. Hence, intra-layer recombination within the content or service layer is carried out to simplify a process or simplify access to content.

Path 3: Service Layer. The second path within the service layer, is initiated by a voice assistant. Voice assistants appear to have a specific role in use recombination since they are typically used to control various other digital resources. Examples from the interviews include among others the use of the voice assistant to set a timer "I use voice assistance to set a timer" (IP09), to add things to note applications, to start streaming services "I'll tell Siri to open up Spotify" (IP06), to control smart home applications as smart lightening or smart heating "I can control my smart home products via voice assistance" (IP03) or to start the navigation in navigation services. It was noticeable that voice assistance was always used to control the other service. Hence, intra-layer recombination on the service layer that includes the use of a voice assistant is carried out to control other services.

Path 4: Device Layer. The fourth path for use recombination takes place on the device layer. The intra-layer recombination on the device layer is carried to control other devices – similar to the reason stated for Path 3. For example, on the device layer users state that the combination of mobile devices with other mobile devices (e.g., smartphone and Bluetooth box) is mentioned since it allows to conveniently add more functionalities. Furthermore, they recombine mobile devices such as a smartphone with immobile devices such as smart TVs, to facilitate remote control. For example, IP10 states: "I can control my TV with my smartphone" (IP10). Hence, intra-layer recombination within the device layer is carried out by recombining mobile and immobile devices to enable remote control.

5.2   Inter-layer Recombination

Path 5: Device, Service, and Content Layer. The fifth path for use recombination takes place across the device, service, and content layer. Path 5 depicts how users select one or several digital resources on the device layer to use one or several digital resource on the service layer, which then enables access to one or several digital resources on the content layer. Typically, Path 5 leads to more convenience when using specific offerings. IP04 provides an example of Path 5 which starts by connecting the smartphone (device) with a car (device) via a car communication application (service) and goes on with accessing a navigation service (service) by using voice assistance (service) of the smartphone and the map (content). The interview partner highlights how recombining various digital resources from different layers increases the convenience of the navigating process immensely. IP09 complements this path by adding streaming services (service) and the music (content) they provide. This again contributes to the convenience the recombination of devices, services and contents offers to the user. Thus, inter-layer recombination across the device, service, and content layer can include one or several digital resources from each layer and is carried out to increase the overall convenience of using specific offerings.

Furthermore, users recombine digital resources across the device, service, and content layer to enable collaboration and become independent from specific physical devices. For example, IP06 describes recombining a laptop (device) with a document (content), which is then uploaded into a cloud (service) folder to be shared via a link (content) with other people by sending the link in a message (content) via a messenger (service) or to be downloaded on a different device (e.g. tablet or smartphone). Doing so facilitates collaborating with multiple people (IP06) and also decreases dependency on a specific physical device by accessing documents "from the laptop I share via iCloud with my iPad and with my smartphone so that I can use it on all devices" (IP04). Hence, inter-layer recombination across the device, service, and content layer can facilitate collaboration and reduce the dependency on a specific device.

6 Discussion and Conclusion

To better understand the interplay of various actors pursuing different purposes, we set out to examine how and why users select and recombine digital resources from the layered modular architecture [6].

As stated in the introduction, our research questions are:

RQ1: *Which specific digital resources from the four layers of content, service, network, and device are selected by users and why?*
RQ2: *How and why do users recombine digital resources within and across the four layers of devices, networks, services, and contents to create digital innovation?*

Regarding RQ1, we found that users only select digital resources from the content, service, and device layer, while not considering the network layer. Additionally, we identify 16 subcategories across the three layers of content (3 subcategories), service (11 subcategories), and device (2 subcategories). Moreover, our results show that users select digital resources depending on the level of integration and compatibility, as well as network effects. While a tight integration of digital resources can increase convenience and simplify life, it reduces the overall compatibility with other digital resources. These contradicting reasons to select a digital resource underscore the oftentimes paradoxical nature of digital innovation [28, 29] and highlight that digital innovation also creates paradoxical circumstances for individuals in a non-professional context.

Regarding RQ2, we identify five different paths that users take to recombine different digital resources. More specifically, we show the importance to distinguish between intra-layer and inter-layer recombination [11] since there are different reasons for carrying out intra- or inter-layer recombination. While intra-layer recombination aims mainly at facilitation (e.g., access to contents/processes) and controlling other services or devices, inter-layer recombination appears to enable collaboration and increasing independency from specific physical devices. Moreover, our results demonstrate that use recombination in a non-professional context is oftentimes not primarily focused on the creation of novelty as is the case in design recombination (e.g., [6, 30]) but provides a way for users to generate an individual value path that addresses a personal problem and, thereby, create and capture value [11].

Before discussing the implications of our findings, we want to highlight some limitations that have to be considered. Methodologically, our research is limited since we only included users in a non-professional context from German-speaking countries in the data collection, i.e. the results of this study allow only limited conclusions to be drawn about the behavior pattern during recombination and the reasons behind the use of digital innovations by people from other cultures or in a professional context. Furthermore, particularly young participants (<20 years) and persons older than 39 years were not included in the study, which is why no statement can be made about their user behavior. Beyond this, a distortion of the results of the study can be assumed due to the subjective selection of the experts who were interviewed on the topic and it cannot be assumed that these experts represent the entire population. Moreover, the answers cannot be checked for completeness or accuracy, which is why it must be trusted that the respondents answered the questions honestly and completely. However, Helfferich [31] notes that if someone takes part in an interview, it can be assumed that this person will not lie openly.

Despite these limitations, our findings allow us to make some suggestions for practitioners: producers who want to expand their user base need to consider the reasons behind a user's choice, as users actively weigh the pros and cons of different digital resources. In particular, the degree of integration and compatibility that each digital resource exhibits appear to be deciding factors for users. Considering these factors will enable producers to actively promote more valuable links with the digital resources they offer. In addition, although digital innovation by definition includes a network layer that enables the transmission of signals, users do not seem to consider the network layer when selecting digital resources. Therefore, the network layer seems not to be a crucial argument for users in a non-professional context to select or recombine a digital resource.

Building upon our findings, we derive valuable avenues for future research. Table 4 highlights three key considerations and puts forward questions for future research.

To conclude, this paper examines the reasons behind the selection and recombination process carried out by users. Our findings allow us to make three key contributions to extant literature: (1) We underscore the importance to distinguish between intra-layer and inter-layer recombination and uncover different reasons for users to carry out intra- or inter-layer recombination. (2) We show that the network layer appears to be invisible to users in a personal context. (3) We outline recommendations and research questions for future research, based on our findings.

Table 4. Key considerations and future research

Key considerations	Research questions for future research
Distinction between **intra-layer** recombination and **inter-layer** recombination	• Which role does the product-agnostic nature of digital resources play for users when carrying out either intra-layer or inter-layer recombinations? • Are there generally different motivations to consider intra-layer or inter-layer recombinations? • How, if at all, does the distinction between intra-layer and inter-layer recombination influence the firm's strategy to appropriate value?
Network layer appears to not be considered by users when selecting and recombining digital resources	• Under what circumstances (e.g., privacy concerns), if at all, do users consider the network layer when selecting and recombining digital resources? • Which role does the network layer play for firms when recombining digital resources with the aim to produce new, digital value offerings to users? • How can firms leverage the network layer, which appears to not be considered by users, to communicate value to users and, thereby, channel value paths through the digital resources offered by them?
Influence between use and design recombination appears not to be considered by users	• Under which circumstances, if at all, do users consider their influence on design recombination and their power to shape digital innovation? • How can firms promote path channeling by fostering more use recombination with digital resources they control? • How can firms develop mechanisms that promote path channeling by allowing users to appropriate a part of the created value?

References

1. Schumpeter, J.A.: The Theory of Economic Development. Interest, and the Business Cycle. Harvard University Press, Cambridge, Mass, An Inquiry into Profits, Capital, Credit (1934)
2. Fleming, L.: Recombinant uncertainty in technological search. Manage. Sci. **47**, 117–132 (2001)
3. Kogut, B., Zander, U.: Knowledge of the firm, combinative capabilities, and the replication of technology. Organ. Sci. **3**, 383–397 (1992)
4. Galunic, D.C., Rodan, S.: Resource recombinations in the firm. knowledge structures and the potential for schumpeterian innovation. SMJ **19**, 1193–1201 (1998)
5. Karim, S., Kaul, A.: Structural recombination and innovation. unlocking intraorganizational knowledge synergy through structural change. Organ. Sci. **26**, 439–455 (2015)
6. Yoo, Y., Henfridsson, O., Lyytinen, K.: The new organizing logic of digital innovation. an agenda for information systems research. ISR **21**, 724–735 (2010)
7. Yoo, Y., Boland, R.J., Lyytinen, K., Majchrzak, A.: Organizing for innovation in the digitized world. Organ. Sci. **23**, 1398–1408 (2012)
8. Henfridsson, O., Mathiassen, L., Svahn, F.: Managing technological change in the digital age. Role Archi. Frames. JIT **29**, 27–43 (2014)
9. Sambamurthy, V., Bharadwaj A., Grover, V.: Shaping agility through digital options. reconceptualizing the role of information technology in contemporary firms. MISQ **27**, 237 (2003)
10. Lee, J., Berente, N.: Digital innovation and the division of innovative labor: digital controls in the automotive industry. Organ. Sci. **23**, 1428–1447 (2012)
11. Henfridsson, O., Nandhakumar, J., Scarbrough, H., Panourgias, N.: Recombination in the open-ended value landscape of digital innovation. Inf. Organ. **28**, 89–100 (2018)
12. Nambisan, S., Lyytinen, K., Majchrzak, A., Song, M.: digital innovation management: reinventing innovation management research in a digital world. MISQ **41**, 223–238 (2017)
13. Lucas, H.C., Goh, J.M.: Disruptive technology: how kodak missed the digital photography revolution. JSIS **18**, 46–55 (2009)
14. Yoo, Y.: Computing in everyday life. a call for research on experiential computing. MISQ **34**, 213–232 (2010)
15. Kallinikos, J., Aaltonen, A., Marton, A.: The Ambivalent ontology of digital artifacts. MISQ **37**, 357–370 (2013)
16. Hund, A., Wagner, H.-T.: Innovation networks and digital innovation. how organizations use innovation networks in a digitized environment. In: Proceedings of the 14th International Conference on Wirtschaftsinformatik (IS) Siegen, pp. 1–15. Germany (2019)
17. Lyytinen, K., Yoo, Y., Boland, R.J., Jr.: Digital product innovation within four classes of innovation networks. ISJ **26**, 47–75 (2016)
18. Hund, A., Wagner, H.-T., Gewald, H.: The impact of digitization on contemporary innovation management. In: Proceedings of the 25th Americas Conference on Information Systems (AMCIS) Cancún, pp. 1–9. Mexico (2019)
19. Hund, A.: Recombination in times of pervasive digitalization: a review. Proceedings of the 41st International Conference on Information Systems (ICIS) India, pp. 1–17 (2020)
20. Hund, A., Holotiuk, F., Wagner, H.-T., Beimborn, D.: Knowledge management in the digital era. how digital innovation labs facilitate knowledge recombination. In: Proceedings of the 27th European Conference on Information Systems (ECIS) Stockholm-Uppsala, pp. 1–15. Sweden (2019)
21. DeLanda, M.: A new philosophy of society. Assemblage Theory and Social Complexity. Continuum, London (2006)

22. Nambisan, S., Lyytinen, K., Yoo, Y. (eds.): Handbook of Digital Innovation. Edward Elgar Publishing, Cheltenham, UK, Northampton, MA (2020)
23. Majchrzak, A., Griffith, T.L.: The new wave of digital innovation: the need for a theory of sociotechnical self-orchestration. In: Nambisan, S., Lyytinen, K., Yoo, Y. (eds.) Handbook of digital innovation, pp. 17–40. Edward Elgar Publishing, Cheltenham, UK, Northampton, MA (2020)
24. Monteiro, E.: Reflections on digital innovation. Inf. Organ. **28**, 101–103 (2018)
25. Mayring, P.: Qualitative Content Analysis: Theoretical Foundation, Basic Procedures and Software Solution. Klagenfurt (2014)
26. Creswell, J.W., Creswell, J.D.: Research Design. Qualitative, Quantitative, and Mixed Methods Approaches. SAGE, Los Angeles (2018)
27. Davis, F.D., Bagozzi, R.P., Warshaw, P.R.: User acceptance of computer technology: a comparison of two theoretical models. Manage. Sci. **35**, 982–1003 (1989)
28. Svahn, F., Mathiassen, L., Lindgren, R., Kane, G.C.: Mastering the digital innovation challenge. MIT Sloan Manag. Rev. **58**, 14–16 (2017)
29. Ciriello, R.F., Richter, A., Schwabe, G.: The paradoxical effects of digital artefacts on innovation practices. EJIS **28**, 149–172 (2019)
30. Carnabuci, G., Operti, E.: Where do firms' recombinant capabilities come from? intraorganizational networks, knowledge, and firms' ability to innovate through technological recombination. SMJ **34**, 1591–1613 (2013)
31. Helfferich, C.: Leitfaden- und Experteninterviews. In: Baur, N., Blasius, J. (eds.) Handbuch Methoden der empirischen Sozialforschung, pp. 559–574. Springer, Wiesbaden (2014). https://doi.org/10.1007/978-3-531-18939-0_39

Enter the Shark Tank: The Impact of Business Models on Early Stage Financing

Timo Phillip Böttcher[(✉)], Valentin Bootz, Tetiana Zubko, Jörg Weking, Markus Böhm, and Helmut Krcmar

Chair for Information Systems and Business Process Management, Technical University of Munich, Garching, Germany

{timo.boettcher,v.bootz,tetiana.zubko,joerg.weking,markus.boehm, helmut.krcmar}@tum.de

Abstract. Investments are the necessary fuel for startup development. However, new ventures face difficulties in obtaining financial investments. The investors aim to invest in startups with high success chances and quick return on investment. The business model (BM) of a startup was proven to be a determinant of its success. However, there is a lack of research on the influence of the BM on the amount of received seed funding. This study analyzes the BMs of 72 startups and the amount of received seed investment. We applied Pearson's product-moment correlation tests to calculate the correlation between these variables. Our research shows a correlation between the BM and the amount of received seed investment. We identify the patterns Two-Sided Market, Layer Player, and Freemium to have a significant positive effect on the investment sum. This research guides entrepreneurs in BM design and contributes to the discussion of success factors for startup success.

Keywords: Business model · Startup · Financing

1 Introduction

"It's a unique idea there's no question, the question is it a good idea, and if the Sharks hear a good idea, they'll fight each other for a piece of it." - Phil Crowley on Shark Tank [1].

Entrepreneurs face a chicken-egg-problem in the early stages of founding a new startup: They need money to finance their early-stage tasks of market evaluation, product development, and market entry. The chances of success depend heavily on this initial funding [2], since they do not qualify for bank loans. However, as they do not have much to present to potential investors but their value proposition and the plan on how to create and capture this value, which is articulated in the business model [3], getting this early-stage financing is a tough task [4, 5]. On the other side, investors take significant risks when investing in early-stage startups. They cannot rely on early market success, sales figures, or other prominent investors' involvement. They need to evaluate the potential success based on the entrepreneurs' business model [6, 7]. Consequentially

F. Ahlemann et al. (Eds.): WI 2021, LNISO 48, pp. 275–289, 2021.
https://doi.org/10.1007/978-3-030-86800-0_20

the available capital for such investments is also scarce [6]. Thus, identifying a good, success-promising business model is crucial for either side.

Considering that 90% of the new startup ventures fail, investing in startups comes with very high risk [8]. Thus, investors seek ways to evaluate the quality of startups to reduce these risks and increase their chances of receiving a return on investment [8]. However, screening early-stage ventures is a highly noisy process, and evidence on the plausibility of their methods from empirical studies is inconclusive [9]. Due to a variety of challenges, such as limited data at the time of founding and a comparatively small number of successful ventures, the question about the prediction of a startup success remains an open topic of the research [10].

Both sides, entrepreneurs and investors, spend much effort in finding each other and maximize their profit. To evaluate this fit, the business model has emerged recently [11]. It represents a formal, conceptual model of the firm's strategy in terms of its value proposition, value creation, and value capture [12]. For startups, it captures the business idea and the set of activities to create value [13], that can be presented to potential investors [14].

A growing body of scholars has studied the correlation between startup performance and its selected business model [15–18]. The startup performance was measured by outcomes such as startup survival [17] or growth against revenue [15]. Both qualitative and quantitative research show that there is a correlation between a startup's business model and its performance. While research on established firms shows, that unique business models are a source of competitive advantage and even disruption [12, 19, 20], and research on startups in later stages shows that it is a critical factor for survival and success [21–23], research lacks acks investigations in startups' early stages. Even though the early stages of a startup are characterized by ideation and business planning, the influence of the business model on seed investment in startups' early stages is unknown [4]. Therefore, we analyze the relationship between applied business model patterns and the amount of seed investment received by startups. We address the following research question:

RQ: How important is the business model for startups to receive seed investment?

This paper performs statistical analysis about how the amount of startup seed investments correlates with the applied business model pattern. Our research provides an analysis of specific business model patterns and targets whether some business model patterns receive higher or lower levels of seed investment. For this purpose, we use an industry-independent dataset of 72 startups from the USA. The startups are categorized according to the 55 business model patterns developed by Gassmann, Frankenberger and Csik [24]. We performed a point-biserial correlation to test whether the applied business model pattern influences the seed funding amount.

We contribute to the business model and entrepreneurship research by showing that the applied business model patterns influence the seed investment received by startups. For entrepreneurs, this provides guidance for business model design. For investors, the results help guide their investment decisions.

The remainder of this paper is structured as follows. The second chapter describes related work, including relevant BM literature. The third chapter details the methodology to create and analyze the dataset. In the fourth chapter, we present the results of the statistical analysis, followed by the discussion and implications of these results in chapter five. The final chapter concludes with the contributions of the paper and avenues for future research.

2 Related Work and Hypothesis Development

In recent years, both academics and practitioners paid much attention to the concept of the business model. Originating in the emergence of e-commerce, digitalization, and digital transformation are key drivers of the concept's popularity. As a formal, conceptual representation of strategy it presents the firm's proposition on how to achieve its goals [14]. It describes how the firm interacts with its environment to create, capture, and deliver value to the customer [12]. Therefore, the business model can be used as a unit of analysis for explaining how firms plan and execute their strategy [25].

Based on the firm's resource-based view, strategy aligns resources and capabilities to achieve a competitive advantage and superior firm performance [26]. Business model scholars build upon this theory to argue the business model, as an articulation of strategy, influences firm performance [27]. A unique business model imposes a superior value creation and capture strategy. It may even be more influential on the created value than the offered product itself, and the business model's innovations provide greater opportunities than innovations of the product [12, 28]. For example, as we can observe in the platform economy, firms can create a differentiating value proposition and competitive advantage by creating a unique and innovative business model. Still, scholars point out that the business model is no holy grail, and no guarantees of success can be given only based on the business model [29]. However, it provides a mean for strategic planning in complex and digital ecosystems as it illustrates the strategy and forces management to question their options [25].

As these findings mainly rely on qualitative research approaches, recent reviews of the field call for more quantitative research to strengthen and validate the existing findings. Most influential are two studies by Zott and Amit [22, 23] analyzing the effect of efficient and novel business model designs on firm performance. These independent constructs were applied in subsequent studies, e. g. Brettel, Strese and Flatten [30] and Kulins, Leonardy and Weber [31]. In the context of entrepreneurship, the business model was shown to influence startup survival [17, 32]. [33] showed that the novelty of business model designs influences startup investors' decisions. Kulins, Leonardy and Weber [31] revealed how business model design influences entrepreneurial firms' market value after they went public.

Based on the qualitative and quantitative researches on the business models, there is a connection between the selected business model and the probability of a startup's success. We argue that the business model of a startup is already influential in its initial phases. Considering that investors need to rely partly on the presented business model and aim to invest in companies with higher success chances and survival rates, to earn a high rate of return from their investments [34], we put forward the hypothesis that the applied business model pattern influences the amount of seed investment a startup receives, visualized in Fig. 1.

Hypothesis: The applied business model pattern influences the amount of seed investment received by a startup.

| Applied Business Model Pattern | *influences* → | Amount of Seed Funding |

Fig. 1. Theoretical model

3   Dataset and Research Method

Our dataset is based on data from Crunchbase (www.crunchbase.com). This platform provides company insights, including early-stage funding data of startups and their value proposition [35]. To ensure recency, yet avoid any effects linked to the expected decline in venture capital due to the COVID-19 pandemic [36], we looked at seed funding rounds in the fourth quarter of 2019. To obviate inconsistency with investment levels among different countries, we only selected startups founded in the US. A total of 593 startups matched our selection criteria.

Out of these, we randomly selected a sample of 100 startups. Following Böhm, Weking, Fortunat, Mueller, Welpe and Krcmar [15], we coded 55 binary values representing the 55 business model patterns developed by Gassmann, Frankenberger and Csik [24]. The binary values indicate whether a pattern was applied (1) or not (0). This coding resulted in a vector, as illustrated in Table 1, for each startup.

Table 1. Example of encoding table of business model pattern applied by startup

BMP	1	2	3	4	...	52	53	54	55
Appl.	0	0	0	1	...	0	1	1	0

The business model patterns are labeled 1 to 55 in alphabetical order. To gather the required information for coding, we analyzed the startups based on their Crunchbase profile, their website, and other publicly available information such as news, press reports, and founders' interviews. To ensure reliability, the encoding was performed by 2 of the authors in regular meetings. The coding was done between May and June 2020. During the coding process, 28 of the 100 sampled startups had to be removed from the sample, since the applied business model patterns could not be confidently identified based on the available data.

Figure 1 visualizes the coverage of business model patterns in our dataset of the remaining 72 startups. Out of 55 patterns, 48 were applied by at least one of the startups in the dataset. The five most frequently applied patterns were #11 *Digitalization* (73,6%), #48 *Subscription* (47,2%), #15 *Flat Rate* (43,1%), #32 *Open Business Models* (40,3%) and #18 *Freemium* (38,9%). Overall, the dataset shows a bias towards patterns linked to digital products and services despite being unbiased with regards to the industry (Fig. 2).

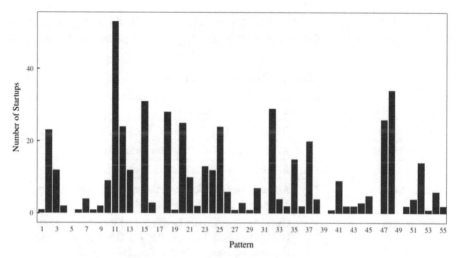

Fig. 2. Coverage of business model patterns

To test our hypothesis that the applied business model patterns influence seed funding, we performed point-biserial correlation tests. This equals Pearson's product-moment correlation with one variable represented as interval/ratio data and one dichotomous variable on a nominal/categorical scale [37]. The point-biserial correlation tests provide a coefficient as a measure of strength and direction of the correlation. In our case, the received seed funding (in US dollar) provides our ratio data, while the dichotomous variable indicates the use of the analyzed business model pattern. This allows us to analyze the seed funding received by startups that applied the business model pattern under investigation and compare it with those startups that did not apply it. We have minimized outlier effects caused by small sample sizes by limiting our analysis to these business model patterns where both comparison groups (pattern applied/not applied) contained at least 10 startups. This reduced the number of analyzed patterns from 55 to 17.

After analyzing the impact of all 55 patterns, we used the hierarchical taxonomy by [38] that identifies the following high-level business model patterns: *merchant odel* groups wholesalers and retailers of goods and services [39]. *Multi-Sided Platforms* serve two or more interdependent customer segments, where both segments are required to make the business model work [38]. Besides, we generalize focus on a particular *Customer Group* or market segment and use of a specific *Pricing Model* or *Revenue Stream* and group pattern that change the *Value Network* or the way it is interacted with and ones that offer certain products or services (*Value Proposition*) or develop an offering in a certain way (*Value Proposition Development*) [17].

Table 2 shows the mapping of the original pattern to the high-level generalization. Whenever the original patterns were not as frequent, we grouped startups that applied at least one of them to analyze the high-level pattern's impact. For example, the patterns *Orchestrator* (2,8% of the total sample) and *Self Service* (6,9% of the total sample) were rather infrequent individually. However, we used them when analyzing startups that applied at least one *Value Network* pattern (45,8% of the total sample). Besides, the high-level patterns enabled in-group comparisons (e.g., *Subscription* and *Pay-per-Use*).

Table 2. High-level pattern mapping

High-level pattern	Business model pattern
Merchant Model	Direct Selling, E-Commerce, Shop-in-Shop, Supermarket
Multi-Sided Platform	Affiliation, Peer-to-Peer, Two-Sided Market
Customer Group	Aikido, Long Tail, Target the Poor, Ultimate Luxury
Pricing Model	Add-on, Auction, Barter, Fractional Ownership, Freemium, No Frills, Pay What You Want, Robin Hood
Revenue Stream	Cash Machine, Crowd Funding, Flat Rate, Franchising, Hidden Revenue, License, Pay-per-Use, Performance-based Contracting, Rent Instead of Buy, Subscription
Value Network	Integrator, Layer Player, Orchestrator, Revenue Sharing, Self Service
Value Proposition	Cross Selling, Customer Loyalty, Experience Selling, Guaranteed Availability, Ingredient Branding, Leverage Customer Data, Lock-In, Make More Of It, Mass Customization, Razor and Blade, Reverse Innovation, Solution Provider, Whitelabel
Value Proposition Development	Crowdsourcing, Digitalization, From Push to Pull, Open Business Models, Open Source, Reverse Engineering, Trash to Cash, User Designed

4   Results

The results from Pearson's product-moment correlation tests on our original patterns, where our analysis indicates the effects of applying individual patterns on seed funding, are shown in Table 3. Positive and negative correlation coefficients (r_{pb}) respectively indicate an increase or decrease in received funding when the specific pattern is applied, while a coefficient of zero indicates no correlation. The p-values serve as indicators for statistical significance, representing the probability of observing the data seen in our analysis if applying a particular pattern does not affect seed funding [40].

Out of the 17 patterns that were applied by at least n = 10 startups in our dataset, nine revealed a correlation coefficient with a magnitude larger than 0.1. For *Two-Sided Market*, *Layer Player*, and *Freemium*, our data indicated the strongest correlations with larger than 0.2 correlation coefficients. *Direct Selling* and *Aikido* were the only patterns that showed negative correlations. However, only the patterns *Two-Sided Market* and *Layer Player* resulted in a p-value < 0.05 indicating significance. Since the p-value for the Freemium pattern is only slightly above this 0.05 threshold with a $p = 0.0592$, but below the $p = 0.1$ threshold, we consider this correlation significant.

Table 3. Pearson's product-moment correlations

Business model pattern	N	r_{pb}	p-value
Two-Sided Market (*)	14	0.2657	0.0241
Layer Player (*)	12	0.2464	0.0370
Freemium (+)	28	0.2234	0.0592
Integrator	13	0.1566	0.1890
Direct Selling	24	-0.1309	0.2731
Open Business Model	29	0.1251	0.2952
Pay Per Use	15	0.1203	0.3141
Aikido	12	-0.1054	0.3782
Digitization	53	0.1034	0.3875

$+p < 0.10$; $*p < 0.05$; $**p < 0.01$

Exemplary, Fig. 3 visualizes how the correlation effects of the *Freemium* pattern ($r_{pb} = 0.2234$) are manifested in our data. The interquartile range for the received seed funding of startups that applied the *Freemium* pattern (n = 28) begins at \$1M and ends at \$4.23M with a median of \$2.46M. For startups that did not apply the pattern (n = 44), the 25th percentile is \$0.67M, and the 75th percentile is \$2.84M, with a median of \$1.58M.

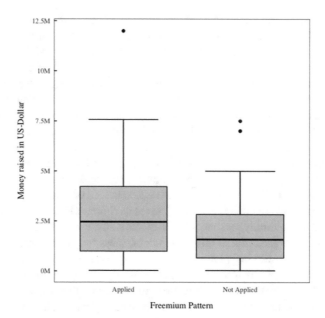

Fig. 3. Boxplot for freemium pattern

Table 4 shows the results of our correlation analysis for high-level patterns. The data indicate that specifying a *Value Network* pattern correlates with higher seed funding at $r = 0.3149$, yet with a low p-value of 0.007. Applying *Pricing Model, Revenue Stream, Multi-Sided Platform,* or *Value Proposition* pattern also correlates with a slight increase in seed funding. Conversely, using *the Merchant Model* pattern correlates with a slight decrease.

Table 4. Pearson's product-moment correlations for high-level patterns

Business model pattern	n	r_{pb}	p-value
Value Network (**)	33	0.3149	0.0071
Pricing Model	35	0.1769	0.1370
Revenue Stream	59	0.1269	0.2880
Multi-Sided Platform	33	0.1264	0.2900
Merchant Model	25	−0.1198	0.3161
Value Proposition	53	0.1117	0.3504

$+p < 0.10$; $*p < 0.05$; $**p < 0.01$

5   Discussion

Business model research argues that the business model has its share of influence on firm performance. By applying the concept of business model patterns on a sample of 72 US-startups, we analyzed the correlation between seed funding and business models. First, we showed the effects of 55 patterns elaborated by Gassmann, Frankenberger and Csik [24]. Second, we grouped our original patterns to analyze eight high-level patterns based on research from Weking, Hein, Böhm and Krcmar [38]. We identified three business model patterns (*Two-Sided Market, Layer Player & Freemium*) and one higher-level pattern (*Value Network*) that lead to significantly higher seed funding.

Multiple other studies have investigated the impact of the business model in various economic contexts and for different types of firms [22, 41–44]. However, in organizational research, many factors interrelate and emerge towards firm performance [45, 46]. Researchers' difficulty is to account for these interrelations of complex business ecosystems [47, 48]. Unlike other fields, e. g. medical research, experiments where these factors can be isolated are seldomly persuadable. With this study, we chose the context of early-stage startups. We argued that in this stage the business model is of higher importance since it highlights the startups' plans about their unique value proposition, value creation and capture mechanisms as well as their in this stage activities to implement them [3]. Even though this does not isolate the business model from other influences such as personality traits of founders or previous entrepreneurial experience, it increases its impact on the outcome.

We found the strongest correlational effect for the business model pattern of two-sided markets. This pattern is also known as the platform business model that became increasingly popular through digital innovation, created the so-called "platform econo-my" and disrupted many industries such as mobility, retail, and sports. This popularity, caused by several highly successful startups such as Uber, Amazon, and Urban Sports Club, leads to investors' high expectations. As we noted earlier, early stage investors need to rely on the idea of the startup. Applying a business model that has been success-ful in other industry contexts provides an opportunity for a successful startup. However, research on digital platforms finds that such markets are often characterized by winner-takes-all markets and first-mover advantages [49]. A startup trying to establish its digital platform either in a new market or as a competition to another platform needs to scale fast. The network effects that can and need to be achieved in these markets require the early investment and early success of the platform. If this success is not achieved, it is more likely for the startup to fail. In their study on startups' chances for survival Weking, Böttcher, Hermes and Hein [17] found this negative correlation between the two-sided market pattern and startup survival. Also noting the relatively low number of startups applying this pattern in our analysis, we see the high-risk early-stage investors take when investing in a two-sided market startup. Hence, if they do so, they invest more to increase the chances that the startup can leverage network effects and gain early market success.

Similarly, the Layer Player pattern profits from economies of scale. The pattern describes companies that add single activities to the value creation in a value chain. Therefore, they engage in multiple ecosystems. Just like a digital platform, that needs to leverage network effects and grow fast, a Layer Player needs to establish its service in multiple industries quickly and scale its operations. As seed investors often supply more than just money, e. g. their network, the startups profit from the investment to use the money and the network to establish their services. Connecting the startup in their network shows the trust an investor has in the idea. This trust then manifests in the amount of investment. In their study Weking, Böttcher, Hermes and Hein [17], found that this pattern correlates with startup failure. They argue that it is difficult to establish the service in different industries, as they are often dominated by established players. As their study did not account for the role of investors for startup survival, our findings may propose future research on the influence of seed investment on survival after a specific time.

For the Freemium pattern, we found that the median investment is nearly one mil-lion US$ higher for startups applying this pattern. Like the previously discussed patterns, the Freemium pattern also has gained popularity through the digital transformation. We observe this pattern in almost all areas of digital services such as media (e. g. Spotify), cloud storage (e. g. Dropbox), cloud computing (e. g. AWS) or productivity (e. g. End-note). The idea behind this pattern is to provide free basic and paid premium services, where the premium customers cross-finance the free offering. Unlike the previous two patterns, this pattern is not centrally related to the value proposition but the value cap-ture. Based on previous research, users are more likely to buy a service or product after being able to test it for free. The challenge for startups applying this pattern is to convert as many users to the premium service as possible. The seed funding helps to create an appealing premium service early, e. g. by providing the most popular music, and to establish the customer base. If the startup succeeds with this, research indicates a higher chance of survival, thus a return on investment for the investors [17].

One may assume that high funding results in higher chances for startup success. However, for the patterns *two-sided market* and *layer player*, our results and the results of Weking, Böttcher, Hermes and Hein [17] do not support this assumption. While our results show higher seed funding for these patterns, their research indicates lower chances of survival of startups. As argued above, the two patterns engage in highly competitive ecosystems. The funding is needed to establish the startup and capture its share of the value. The popularity and success of connected and integrated business models like digital platforms, e. g. Uber, Amazon, and Urban Sports Club lead to high expectations, thus high investments. However, the lower chances of survival indicate that high early-stage funding does not correlate with startup survival in these ecosystems. Investments in such business models take a high risk in the hope that they will also yield a high reward.

On a higher level, patterns related to the value network are of particular interest for investors. These patterns describe business models that add value-creating activities to a network, participate in the value capture, and generally have close interaction with other business models in their network [38]. For example, we observe such close interactions in digital platform ecosystems, where platform owners, sponsors, complementors, and customers have close interaction. The platform owner is especially interested in keeping his network connected to create lock-in effects to avoid users switching to other platforms. For investors, startups participating in such an interacting network seem worth an investment as they often integrate into existing profitable networks.

5.1 Contributions to Research

Our paper makes three theoretical contributions. First, we contribute to business model research. As an articulation of a firm's strategy and the planned activities to implement this strategy, the business model provides a novel lens to analyze different strategies' performance. Our results show that the business model influences the amount of seed funding received by a startup. The findings contribute to acknowledging that the business model is a source of competitive advantage and superior firm performance [50–53]. We address several calls for research [16, 54, 55]. We provide quantitative, industry-independent results to demonstrate business model performance, thus achieve generalizability. The identification of specific, tangible business model patterns supports the understanding that the business model is a source of competitive advantage.

Second, we contribute to entrepreneurship research by providing further explanations of startup performance. Our results show how startups with different business models receive different amounts of seed investment. In particular, we identify three business model patterns (*two-sided market, layer player*, and *freemium*) that significantly increase the investment sum. As funding is an essential factor for startup success [2], this contributes to the discussion about the influence of the business model on startup success [56].

Third, we contribute to research on ecosystems. Driven by the rapid development of digital technologies, today's business environment is characterized by complexity and uncertainty [47]. Firms become more and more intertwined, and value is created by firm networks rather than value chains [57]. For these networks, the theory of the ecosystem has emerged recently [58]. We show that investors invest more money in platform business models (two-sided market) that try to create a new platform ecosystem and in layer players that add services to complex firm networks. This supports the business model as a unit of analysis to analyze how firms create and capture value in ecosystems [59, 60].

5.2 Contributions to Practice

For practice, we provide insights from both the startup and the investor perspective. Our research provides indications for entrepreneurs when designing their business models. The knowledge that some business models receive higher startup funding than others highlights the importance of business model design. We argue that the identified patterns two-sided market, layer player, and freemium also require a higher investment, in the beginning, to get the business started and establish the startup's value proposition in the respective market. For investors, we observe a preference for business models integrated into their ecosystem. The results provide guidance for investment decisions. Depending on their risk aversion, different patterns, that we showed to receive more funding, provide higher chances of receiving a return on investment. As we discuss that the identified patterns require more capital to become successful and full commitment of the investor is needed in the early stages of the startup, early-stage investors can decide whether they can provide this investment and commitment.

5.3 Limitations

While this paper provides first insights on the effects of business model patterns on early-stage financing, it is subject to some limitations. First, the identified patterns are not the perfect way to receive seed investment. As earlier research highlights, there is no one successful business model [51, 61]. Designing a business model is as much art as systematic [12], so creativity and innovativeness play an essential part for startups to succeed. Second, the business model is a dynamic construct, thus changes over time [62]. Our research only provides a static snapshot of the business model at the time of our coding. Thus, the result may only be valid for a specific time frame, and the successful patterns in different macro-economic context may change. Third, our sample size of 72 startups limits generalizability. Even though we were able to identify significant correlations, the analysis should be repeated on a larger sample. We also focused on US startups only to account for differences in the available capital for seed investment. Thus, our results may be limited to US firms and may be compared with analysis for different markets.

6 Conclusion and Future Research

The importance of startups for an economy is often highlighted in entrepreneurship research. Startups produce innovations, create jobs, and drive economic growth. However, only a few startups survive. Seed investment is crucial for many startups, as capital is a valuable but missing resource. Also, startups can profit from the knowledge and network of their investors. This research provides an analysis of the influence of the business model on the received early-stage investments. Based on a sample of 72 US-startups, we identify three business model patterns that lead to higher seed investments: *two-sided market, layer player,* and *freemium.*

Further research should elaborate on the relationship between business models, startup funding, and startup survival [7]. The business model, need for external financing, and related firm performance change during the different stages of business development [56]. To cope with the challenge of startup success, time-series data, and control variables that account for ecosystem complexity may provide insights into this relationship and its development in different stages of the startup. Through longitudinal time-series, the evolution, adaptions, and various influences of the business model may become observable and provide a better understanding of the success and failure of startups and clarify the paradoxes in research.

Acknowledgement. The authors would like to thank the track chairs, editors and all anonymous reviewers for their helpful comments and suggestions. We thank the German Federal Ministry for Economic Affairs and Energy for funding this research as part of the project 01MK20001B (Knowledge4Retail).

References

1. Burnett, M.: Shark Tank. Sony Pictures Television, USA (2009)
2. Amara, N., Halilem, N., Traoré, N.: Adding value to companies' value chain: role of business schools scholars. J. Bus. Res. **69**, 1661–1668 (2016)
3. Doganova, L., Eyquem, M.: What do business models do? innovation devices in technology entrepreneurship. Res. Policy **38**, 1559–1570 (2009)
4. Fisher, G., Kotha, S., Lahiri, A.: Changing with the times: an integrated view of identity, legitimacy, and new venture life cycles. Acad. Manag. Rev. **41**, 383–409 (2016)
5. Islam, M., Fremeth, A., Marcus, A.: Signaling by early stage startups: US government research grants and venture capital funding. J. Bus. Ventur. **33**, 35–51 (2018)
6. Bachher, J.S.G., Paul D.: Financing Early Stage Technology Based Companies: Investment Criteria Used By Investors (1996)
7. Antretter, T., Blohm, I., Grichnik, D.: Predicting Startup Survival from Digital Traces: Towards a Procedure for Early Stage Investors. In: International Conference on Information Systems (ICIS) (Year)
8. Amar, K.A., Agrawal; Alok, Choudhary: Predicting the Outcome of Startups: Less Failure, More Success (2016)
9. Scott, E.L., Shu, P., Lubynsky, R.M.: Are 'Better' Ideas More Likely to Succeed? An Empirical Analysis of Startup Evaluation. Harvard Business School Working Papers (2015)
10. Saini, A.: Picking Winners: A Big Data Approach To Evaluating Startups And Making Venture Capital Investments. Massachusetts Institute of Technology (2018)
11. Susan C., Davidson, L.R.A.: Applications of the business model in studies of enterprise success, innovation and classification: an analysis of empirical research from 1996 to 2010 (2012)
12. Teece, D.J.: Business models, business strategy and innovation. Long Range Plan. **43**, 172–194 (2010)
13. Zott, C., Amit, R.: Business model design: an activity system perspective. Long Range Plan. **43**, 216–226 (2010)

14. Massa, L., Tucci, C.L., Afuah, A.: A critical assessment of business model research. Acad. Manag. Ann. **11**, 73–104 (2017)
15. Böhm, M., Weking, J., Fortunat, F., Mueller, S., Welpe, I., Krcmar, H.: The business model DNA: towards an approach for predicting business model success. In: 13. Internationale Tagung Wirtschaftsinformatik (WI 2017), p. 1006–1020
16. Zott, C., Amit, R., Massa, L.: The business model: recent developments and future research. J. Manag. **37**, 1019–1042 (2011)
17. Weking, J., Böttcher, T., Hermes, S., Hein, A.: does business model matter for startup success? a quantitative analysis. In: 27th European Conference on Information Systems
18. Haddad, H., Weking, J., Hermes, S., Böhm, M., Krcmar, H.: Business Model Choice Matters: How Business Models Impact Different Performance Measures of Startups, pp. 828–843 (2020)
19. Magretta, J.: Why business models matter. Harv. Bus. Rev. **80**, 86+ (2002)
20. Alberti-Alhtaybat, L., Al-Htaybat, K., Hutaibat, K.: A knowledge management and sharing business model for dealing with disruption: the case of Aramex. J. Bus. Res. **94**, 400–407 (2019)
21. Osiyevskyy, O., Dewald, J.: Inducements, impediments, and immediacy: exploring the cognitive drivers of small business managers' intentions to adopt business model change. J. Small Bus. Manage. **53**, 1011–1032 (2015)
22. Zott, C., Amit, R.: Business model design and the performance of entrepreneurial firms. Organ. Sci. **18**, 181–199 (2007)
23. Zott, C., Amit, R.: The fit between product market strategy and business model: implications for firm performance. Strateg. Manag. J. **29**, 1–26 (2008)
24. Gassmann, O., Frankenberger, K., Csik, M.: The Business Model Navigator: 55 Models That Will Revolutionise Your Business. Pearson, Harlow (2014)
25. Lanzolla, G., Markides, C.: A business model view of strategy. J. Manage. Stud. Press **14**, 540–553 (2020)
26. Hedman, J., Kalling, T.: The business model concept: theoretical underpinnings and empirical illustrations. Eur. J. Inf. Syst. **12**, 49–59 (2003)
27. Teece, D.J.: Business models and dynamic capabilities. Long Range Plan. **51**, 40–49 (2018)
28. Chesbrough, H.: Business model innovation: opportunities and barriers. Long Range Plan. **43**, 354–363 (2010)
29. Shafer, S.M., Smith, H.J., Linder, J.C.: The power of business models. Bus. Horiz. **48**, 199–207 (2005)
30. Brettel, M., Strese, S., Flatten, T.C.: Improving the performance of business models with relationship marketing efforts – an entrepreneurial perspective. Eur. Manag. J. **30**, 85–98 (2012)
31. Kulins, C., Leonardy, H., Weber, C.: A configurational approach in business model design. J. Bus. Res. **69**, 1437–1441 (2016)
32. Andries, P., Debackere, K.: Adaptation and performance in new businesses: understanding the moderating effects of independence and industry. Small Bus. Econ. **29**, 81–99 (2006)
33. Fu, Y., Tietz, M.A.: When do investors prefer copycats? conditions influencing the evaluation of innovative and imitative ventures. Strateg. Entrep. J. **13**, 529–551 (2019)
34. Cavallo, A., Ghezzi, A., Dell'era, C. and Pellizzoni, E.: Fostering Digital Entrepreneurship from startup to scaleup: The role of Venture Capital funds and Angel Groups (2019)
35. Marra, A., Antonelli, P., Dell'Anna, L., Pozzi, C.: A network analysis using metadata to investigate innovation in clean-tech – implications for energy policy. Energy Policy **86**, 17 (2015)
36. Sheskin, D.: Handbook of Parametric and Nonparametric Statistical Procedures. CRC Press, Boca Raton (2004)

37. Remane, G., Hanelt, A., Tesch, J., Kolbe, L.: The Business model pattern database—a tool for systematic business model innovation. Int. J. Innov. Manage. **21**, 1750004+ (2017)
38. Weking, J., Hein, A., Böhm, M., Krcmar, H.: A hierarchical taxonomy of business model patterns. Electron. Mark. **30**(3), 447–468 (2018). https://doi.org/10.1007/s12525-018-0322-5
39. Osterwalder, A., Pigneur, Y.: Business Model Generation: A Handbook for Visionaries, Game Changers, and Challengers. Osterwalder & Pigneur, Amsterdam (2010)
40. Althouse, A.D., Soman, P.: Understanding the true significance of a P value. J. Nucl. Cardiol. **24**, 191–194 (2017)
41. Pati, R.K., Nandakumar, M.K., Ghobadian, A., Ireland, R.D., O'Regan, N.: Business model design–performance relationship under external and internal contingencies: evidence from SMEs in an emerging economy. Long Range Plan. **51**, 750–769 (2018)
42. Kim, S.K., Min, S.: Business model innovation performance: when does adding a new business model benefit an incumbent? Strateg. Entrep. J. **9**, 34–57 (2015)
43. Morris, M.H., Shirokova, G., Shatalov, A.: The business model and firm performance: the case of russian food service ventures. J. Small Bus. Manage. **51**, 46–65 (2013)
44. Tavassoli, S.A.M., Bengtsson, L.: The role of business model innovation for product innovation performance. Int. J. Innov. Manage. **22**,1850061 (2018)
45. Park, Y., Mithas, S.: Organized complexity of digital business strategy: a configurational perspective. MIS Q. **44**, 85–127 (2020)
46. Zhang, M., Chen, H., Lyytinen, K.: Principles of organizational co-evolution of business and it: a complexity perspectivE. In: 27th European Conference on Information Systems (ECIS), Stockholm & Uppsala, Sweden (2019)
47. Benbya, H., Nan, N., Tanriverdi, H., Yoo, Y.: Complexity and information systems research in the emerging digital world. MIS Q. (2020)
48. Tanriverdi, H., Rai, A., Venkatraman, N.: Research commentary—reframing the dominant quests of information systems strategy research for complex adaptive business systems. Inf. Syst. Res. **21**, 822–834 (2010)
49. Schilling, M.A.: Technology success and failure in winner-take-all markets: the impact of learning orientation, timing, and network externalities. Acad. Manag. J. **45**, 387–398 (2002)
50. Amit, R., Zott, C.: Value creation in E-business. Strateg. Manag. J. **22**, 493–520 (2001)
51. Brea-Solís, H., Casadesus-Masanell, R., Grifell-Tatjé, E.: Business model evaluation: quantifying walmart's sources of advantage. Strateg. Entrep. J. **9**, 12–33 (2015)
52. Casadesus-Masanell, R., Zhu, F.: Business model innovation and competitive imitation: the case of sponsor-based business models. Strateg. Manag. J. **34**, 464–482 (2013)
53. Böttcher, T., Weking, J.: Identifying antecedents and outcomes of digital business model innovation. In: 28th European Conference on Information Systems, Marrakesh (2020)
54. Lambert, S., Davidson, R.: Applications of the business model in studies of enterprise success, innovation and classification: an analysis of empirical research from 1996 to 2010. Eur. Manag. J. **31**, 668–681 (2013)
55. Al-Debei, M.M., Avison, D.: Developing a unified framework of the business model concept. Eur. J. Inf. Syst. **19**, 359–376 (2010)
56. George, G., Bock, A.J.: The business model in practice and its implications for entrepreneurship research. Entrep. Theory Pract. **35**, 83–111 (2011)
57. Coltman, T., Tallon, P., Sharma, R., Queiroz, M.: Strategic IT alignment: twenty-five years on. J. Inf. Technol. **30**, 91–100 (2015)
58. Jacobides, M.G., Cennamo, C., Gawer, A.: Towards a theory of ecosystems. Strateg. Manag. J. **39**, 2255–2276 (2018)
59. Vial, G.: Understanding digital transformation: a review and a research agenda. J. Strateg. Inf. Syst. **28**, 118–144 (2019)
60. Fitzgerald, M., Kruschwitz, N., Bonnet, D., Welch, M.: Embracing digital technology: a new strategic imperative. Sloan Management Review **55**, 1–13 (2013)

61. Weill, P., Malone, T., Apel, T.: The business models investors Prefer. MIT Sloan Manag. Rev. **52**, 17–19 (2011)
62. Demil, B., Lecocq, X.: Business model evolution: in search of dynamic consistency. Long Range Plan. **43**, 227–246 (2010)

Structuring the Jungle of Capabilities Fostering Digital Innovation

Christoph Buck[1,2(✉)], Timo Grüneke[3,4], and Katharina Stelzl[3,4]

[1] Centre for Future Enterprise, QUT Business School, Queensland University of Technology, Brisbane, Australia
christoph.buck@qut.edu.au
[2] Philipps-Universität Marburg, Marburg, Germany
christoph.buck@wiwi.uni-marburg.de
[3] FIM Research Center, University of Bayreuth, Bayreuth, Germany
{timo.grueneke,katharina.stelzl}@fim-rc.de
[4] Project Group Business and Information Systems Engineering of Fraunhofer FIT, Bayreuth, Germany
{timo.grueneke,katharina.stelzl}@fit.fraunhofer.de

Abstract. Driven by digitalization, the business environment is changing at an increasing pace. To be able to react to this, organizations must gain competitive advantages through Digital Innovation (DI). This special form of innovation requires a reorganization and further development of the resource and capability base of an organization. The existing literature shows a proliferation of definitions and a jungle of individual capabilities with regard to DI. Based on a structured literature review and a qualitative analysis of existing capabilities, the paper presents a DI Capability Model. By structuring layers, areas and associated capabilities, the model provides the first holistic view in the literature. It will serve as a basis for a targeted scientific discourse and a valuable orientation model for the development of a capability composition to foster DI in organizations.

Keywords: Capability Model · Digital innovation · Digital innovation capability · Systematic literature review · Dynamic capability

1 Motivation

Advancements in digital technology are transforming businesses and society at a furious pace as they become an inherent part of our daily routines and fundamentally change the way people work, communicate, and consume [1]. These changes create both, completely new markets and satisfy changed customer needs what makes them inherently disruptive. Therefore, incumbent organizations are facing rapid market dynamics and constant change within an intensive and competitive environment [2].

To withstand these rapid developments in a digital world and continue to establish competitive advantages, organizations must increasingly reinvent themselves and drive digital innovation (DI) [1, 3]. Early studies on DI focused on the digitalization of internal processes [1, 4], while upcoming Information Systems (IS) research investigates digital technologies and their transformative effect on products, services, and business models [5–7], e.g., by adding digital capabilities to physical products [7]. However, the convergence of several domains, new processes, methods, and conditions as well as speeds of innovation in the digital era, require various developments of resources, processes, and capabilities for DI [8–10].

Although there is a consensus in the literature that DI requires new capabilities and, if necessary, a reorganization of existing capabilities [11], the scientific discourse lacks a holistic view. Different disciplines view innovation induced by digital technologies from very limited perspectives. IS research, for example, distinguishes between information technology (IT) assets and IT capabilities and refers to the latter as capabilities with a potential creation of competitive advantage [12, 13], as they are firm-specific and difficult to imitate [14]. Various authors emphasize that digital capabilities are the skills and routines needed to leverage digital assets to create value [13, 15, 16]. This brings in a digital flavor to the broader perspective of management research which postulates the concept of dynamic capabilities [17–20].

Despite a broad body of literature on dynamic capabilities and innovation capabilities, the scientific discourse has not yet been able to identify and link the necessary capabilities for DI by mapping them holistically. Due to the high relevance of DI and a jungle of perspectives and partial considerations of capabilities being relevant to foster DI, we pose the following research question: *What capabilities do organizations need to foster digital innovation?*

To answer this research question, we conducted a structured literature review (SLR) to identify relevant capabilities. Based on a qualitative analysis, we were able to condense the identified capabilities and developed a DI Capability Model representing a comprehensive, qualified, and structured state of the current scientific discourse. The DI Capability Model comprises nine capability layers, 26 capability areas, and 58 capabilities that are discussed in 74 high-quality scientific articles.

The paper is structured as following. In the next chapter, we show the relationship between DI and organizational capabilities. In Sect. 3, we describe the structured literature review and the applied analysis. Section 4 presents the DI Capability Model. The article concludes with a conclusion, discussion, and ideas for further research.

2 Theoretical Background

2.1 Digital Innovation

In dynamic business environments characterized by technological advancements, blurred markets, short product life cycles, and changing customer needs, DI is crucial for organisations to sense, seize, and transform upcoming opportunities (and threats) to maintain competitive advantage [1, 12, 21]. Hence, *DI* is defined as the 'use of digital technology during the process of innovating' [22] as a means or an end [6]. Digital technologies extract, create, analyse, communicate, or use information in specific contexts [23]. Thereby, we refer to the term 'innovative' as something that is perceived as new by the respective organization, where "it matters little […] whether or not an idea is objectively new as measured by the lapse of time" [24].

To transfer upcoming opportunities into DI initiatives, the *DI process* comprises four phases: the initiation, development, implementation, and exploitation phase [3]. Moreover, recent research underpins the importance of capabilities to foster DI [1, 3]. However, a holistic view on what capabilities are required is missing. To better understand capabilities and related concepts in general, we provide insights on the role of capabilities to gain competitive advantage in Sect. 2.2.

2.2 Organizational Capabilities

According to the *resource-based view* (RBV), organizations achieve competitive advantage by the composition of its resources for the generation of value [25]. Following [26], this is "the match an organization makes between its internal resources and skills and the opportunities and risks created by its external environment." Taking account for dynamic environments and the emergence of digital technologies, the *dynamic capabilities view* (DCV) has extended the RBV [18]. Accordingly, *resources* are divided into assets and capabilities [27]. *Assets* can be either tangible or intangible and are (in-) permanently at the power of disposition by the organization [20]. Intangible assets further split into intellectual and cultural assets [28]. *Capabilities* are tacit resources located in people and developed through learning [29]. Hence, capabilities are about the ease of performing an action that is required in a given situation [30].

More precise, *organizational capabilities* are "the capacity of an organization to purposefully create, extend, or modify its resource base" [31]. Hence, they are "socially complex routines that determine the efficiency with which organizations physically transform inputs into outputs" [32]. According to the DCV, an organization possesses both ordinary and dynamic capabilities [33]. Ordinary capabilities relate to "the performance of administrative, operational, and governance-related functions that are (technically) necessary to accomplish tasks" [34]. Dynamic capabilities emerge from organizational learning [35] and change over time [17].

A similar, but more detailed classification of capabilities differentiates between capabilities that contribute to gaining competitive advantages and therefore introduce the modes 'off' and 'on' or, in a figurative sense, the states 0 and 1. According to [33], the notation of 'zero-order' describes "how we earn a living now capabilities". These capabilities are the ability to perform the essential operational activities of the organization in the day-to-day business [32, 33] and, thus, do not necessarily further the course of its overall performance. By contrast, 'first-order' capabilities are dynamic in their nature and contribute somewhat to the performance of the organization and enable competitive advantages to be obtained. They are allocated to a continuum, starting from a lower to a higher level. First-order lower capabilities constitute change and directly influence an organizations' outcome by using existing capabilities to their advantage. First-order higher capabilities create new capabilities through learning. These capabilities thus not only take advantage of all three dynamic components (sensing, seizing, and transforming) but act on this basis herein creating a competitive advantage.

3 Research Method

To answer the research question, we used the methodology of a SLR to derive a type two theory for the IS discipline [36]. A SLR allows us to structure and to assess the current state of research in the field of capabilities. Furthermore, reviewing the literature is crucial to advancing any scientific discipline [37, 38]. In our case, we were able to identify reviews trying to unite and illuminate different literature directions on capabilities. To the best of our knowledge, no review has yet been able to compile a multitude of definitions and relate them to DI. To close this gap, we follow [37] complemented by techniques of [39] to conduct our SLR. Subsequently, we derived four search strings (("organization* capabilit*" OR "organisation* capabilit*"); (dynamic capabilit*) AND (innovation capabilit*); ("digital* capabilit*"); ("information technology capabilit*" OR "information systems capabilit*" OR "IT capabilit*" OR "IS capabilit*")) from our research questions to be found within the topic (title, abstract, author keywords, and Keywords Plus) of the search engine Web of Science. By applying our search strings, we initially found (n = 6017) articles from Web of Science. We checked for duplets (n = 18) as we conducted every search separately resulting in (n = 5999). As stated above, research on capabilities is located at the intersection of several research streams, prompting us to identify high-quality research (relevance and citation performance) from journal publications. Thereupon we used the SCImago journal rank (SJR) indicator [32] as quality criteria and excluded journals and consequently articles with an SJR of less than 4.0 or none. For the remaining articles (n = 375) we adopted inclusion criteria to further narrow down our set. This was achieved by screening titles and abstracts and evaluating articles for their RQ relevance from 'low' (score = 1; no connection to the research question) to 'high' (score = 4; article deals with a capability and clear connection to the research question). Only articles scoring three or four were included into our final set (n = 115) and after full-text screening (n = 74) were included into our DI Capability Model.

For the analysis of the research contributions, we extended the method of a SLR by adding grounded theory techniques [39]. Thereby, we based our approach on the three coding steps of open coding, axial coding, and selective coding. As a first step, we identified relevant definitions of capabilities in each article. One author initially coded interesting sections and a second author then confirmed the coding in MAXQDA. Subsequently, from about 500 initial codes in 115 articles axial coding focused on identifying capability areas (CA) and overarching capability layers as well as the relationships between the originally coded capabilities. Furthermore, insufficient definitions and code refinement resulted in about 300 codings and 74 articles used. Finally, several iterative cycles of selective coding were performed to refine the CA and layers. The rearranging, merging of layers (e.g., learning-related and knowledge-related capability layer) and the assignment as zero- or first-order capabilities resulted in nine capability layers, 26 capability areas, and 58 capabilities.

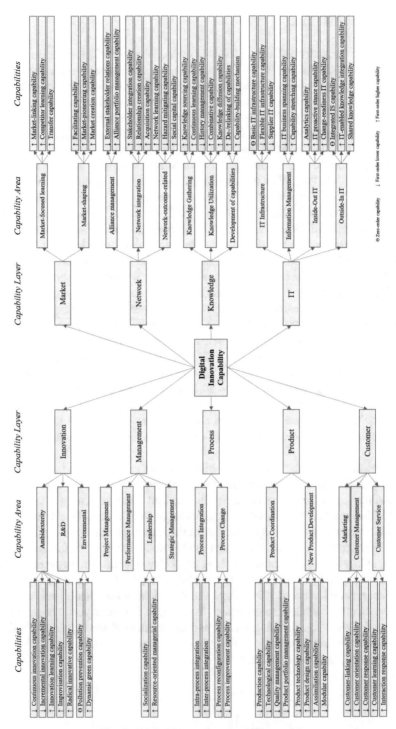

Fig. 1. Digital innovation capability model

4 Digital Innovation Capability Model

Structuring the jungle of capabilities required for DI, the DI Capability Model identifies and links capabilities nurturing DI. Therefore, it comprises layers including underlying CA and capabilities. It is important to note that all layers, CA, and capabilities are inter-related even though they are presented separated. Moreover, each capability is classified as a zero-order (ө), first-order lower (↓), or first-order higher (↑) capability. Figure 1 shows the DI Capability Model, detailed descriptions are provided below.

Innovation-Related Capability Layer: This layer comprises capabilities that foster innovation by adding value through offering a new product or service that, in turn, increases competitiveness. The CA of *Ambidexterity* emphasizes the ability to enhance or generate and nurture new ideas that lead to new product offerings through known patterns of action [40]. This can be achieved by structured evaluation of and exploit-ing the existing (↓ *Continuous innovation capability* [41, 42]) as well as in enhanc-ing products or services (↓ *Incremental innovation capability* [43]). By contrast, this CA also aims for exploring the new (↑ *Innovation learning capability*) and includes spontaneous actions to react to an unknown situation with novel solutions by drawing from existing knowledge (↑ *Improvisation capability*). If the exploration is conducted, transformational outcomes may occur changing products and enhancing organizational capabilities (↑ *Radical innovative capability* [10, 43]). *Research and Development* is a CA which resembles the ability to build new technologies by assembling new tech-nical resources and evaluating them. This can be achieved through the research ability to identify, understand, assess, and apply internal and external knowledge [19, 44–48]. Capabilities subject to the *Environmental* CA contribute towards aligning organiza-tion's operations in an environmentally friendly manner. On the one hand, it focuses on reducing pollution (ө *Pollution prevention capability*), on the other it aims to closely interact with stakeholders and reconfigure organizationally embedded resources to build complementary green capacities (↑ *Dynamic green capability*).

Management-Related Capability Layer: This layer focuses on capabilities being rel-evant for managing an organization. The *Project Management* CA describes the ability to understand the requirements a client desires as well as the design of products. More-over, it focuses on the budgeting of total time requirements and the efficient use of resources [49]. The *Performance Management* CA describes the ability to establish monitoring, evaluation, and control systems to oversee the organizational performance and steer management initiatives [50]. The *Strategic Management* CA defines the ability to direct resources appropriately to achieve organizational goals. By providing guidance on existing strategies, strategic management can also help to align activities with objec-tives or to assist in deciding on strategic goals and allocating appropriate resources [51]. The *Leadership* CA is connected to the ability to establish a shared believe system and organizational culture (↓ *Socialization capability* [52, 53]). Part of this is the ability to guide organizations systematically through the process of resource reconfiguration and transformation activities (↑ *Resource-oriented managerial capability* [54]).

Process-Related Capability Layer: This layer integrates capabilities related to the management of processes. They are not limited to one respective field but interact throughout organizational levels. The CA of *Process Integration* defines the ability to create and coordinate digital connections between entities and to coordinate them. Looking inside the organizations, entities resemble to resources or activities and are production oriented (↓ *Intrafirm process integration capability* [55]). Looking outside, entities lie outside and need coordination of transaction interdependencies (↑ *Interfirm process integration capability* [55]). The *Process Change* CA describes the ability to modify processes (e.g., routine processes) through targeted reorganization, improving existing processes, and learning new processes (↓ *Process reconfiguration capability* [56]). Change also occurs by systematic enhancement of existing processes to streamline activities (↓ *Process improvement capability* [57]).

Product-Related Capability Layer: This layer deals with capabilities that are related to the process of producing and changing products or activities [50, 58]. Capabilities to obtain a product are clustered in the CA *Product Coordination*. This CA deals with capabilities that enable organizations to convert multiple inputs into outputs (↓ *Production capability* [59]). To achieve this, it is necessary to use different technologies (↓ *Technological capability* [48, 60–62]). Furthermore, the conversion process must be monitored using quality criteria and requires the elimination of errors (↓ *Quality management capability*). At the same time, a product portfolio must manage the trade-off between short-term demands for performance and long-term development of capabilities (↓ *Product Portfolio Management* [56]). The *New Product Development* CA unites capabilities that support the creation of new products, thus changing the product portfolio offered by using technological components (↓ *Product technology capability* [63]). To create new products, design elements can be rearranged (↑ *Product design capability* [64]) and inputs for new product development or adaptation can be included (↑ *Assimilation capability* [65]). Therefore, an interplay between a problem-solving process and resulting performance criteria is required (↓ *Modular capability* [66]).

Customer-Related Capability Layer: All capabilities that help organizations to address or interact with the customer are gathered in this layer. It is not only dealing with CA that describe capabilities to serve current (e.g., latest needs and expectations) but also to create relationship with new customers. It is closely linked to the market-related capability layer and partly overlaps. The *Customer Management* CA focuses on fostering established relationships with customers but also to integrate them into innovation activities. This is achieved through the management of relationships (↓ *Customer-linking capability* [61, 63]), the monitoring of needs (↓ *Customer orientation capability* [67]), and the response to needs (↓ *Customer response capability* [49, 67]). The *Marketing* CA comprising marketing capabilities that are used in a broader sense to describe the two capability-layers customer and market [47, 48, 60–62, 68] but also just customers [44, 69] or just market [46]. In terms of *Customer Service*, this CA focuses on the activity of offering products to the customer [67]. The ability to learn and create knowhow (↑ *Customer learning capability* [42]) about the needs (e.g., customer orientation capability) allows for the integration into novel products through the interaction with the customer (↑ *Interaction response capability* [70]).

Market-Related Capability Layer: This layer comprises capabilities being relevant for markets, i.e., places where entities exchange goods and services subject to the influence of externalities [62]. The *Market Focused Learning* CA focuses in contrary to customer learning, additionally on other entities present in the market to integrate the respective knowledge [68]. This allows to monitor the market and reflect changes enabling timely measures of action (↑ *Market-linking capability* [61]). Such entities might be competitors to learn from (↑ *Competitor learning capability* [42]) in order to replicate product offerings or facilitate abilities to transfer the offerings to different markets (↑ *Transfer capability* [62, 65, 71]). The *Market Shaping* CA provides capabilities that make it possible to gather valuable information to discover new linkages of resources (↑ *Facilitating capability* [64, 72, 73]), propose them to the market, and thereby shaping its nature [72]. The discovery of new links provides organizations with a head start resulting in a higher learning curve and enables the creation of a new market (↑ *Market-pioneering capability* and ↑ *Market creation capability* [74]).

Network-Related Capability Layer: This layer allows organizations to connect with other organizations but also customers [68, 75]. The *Alliance Management* CA refers to the management of external linkages to exchange operation experience [76]. These linkages occur, e.g., with suppliers as stakeholders wanting information on their past performance (↓ *External stakeholder relations capability* [51]). Likewise, the supplier might share knowledge or information the organization seeks enabled through the relationship. These exchange processes are not limited to one stakeholder but to a portfolio that needs managing. This allows organizations to tap into different knowledge pools that can be absorbed for own use (↑ *Alliance portfolio management capability* [77]). The *Network Integration* CA goes one step further than the management of alliances. It actively integrates stakeholders into organizational activities (↑ *Stakeholder integration capability* [41, 61]). Managing linkages to external entities can also be focused on leading an innovation network. This network can either be closed aiming at a collective innovation effort or open. In the latter, the organization acts as a facilitator or incubator for other innovators thereby learning from the entity (↑ *Network orchestration* [78]). Thus, the ability to nurture the external relationship is the basis for integration. The extreme of integration is the actual acquisition of the network partner to absorb its resources to extend and mix them with own ones (↑ *Acquisition capability* [62, 65]). The *Network Outcome-related* CA subsumes capabilities that underpin the results from established linkages with stakeholders. This outlines the organization's learning and sense-making capabilities but also share knowledge e.g., with suppliers (↑ *Network learning capability* [42, 68, 79]). Besides, capabilities to reduce risk referring to collaborative agreements (↓ *Hazard mitigating capability* [80]) as well as capabilities to gain advantage of memberships in social networks are important (↑ *Social capital capability* [64]).

Knowledge-Related Capability Layer: When talking about organizational knowledge and its integration we tap into the research stream of absorptive capacity. This research stream is relevant in IS and DI due to its manifold contributions, constructs, and implications [52, 81]. This layer summarizes knowledge-based (focus on knowledge collection) and learning-related capabilities (focus on learning from knowledge). The *Knowledge Gathering* CA in its core captures the knowledge (e.g., technology trends) relevant to organizations to store in repositories. This knowledge then can be used to inform activities such as innovation (↑ *Knowledge sourcing capability* [82–85]). Activity outcomes from that utilization thus inform the knowledge repositories continuing the knowledge gathering (↑ *Continuous learning capability* [41]). The *Knowledge Utilization* CA compared to gathering makes use of the knowledge. One way is to draw on an organizations' history to control its perceptions and derive insights to guide actions (↓ *History management capability* [53, 83, 86]). Among this CA is the ability of organizations to not only build up knowledge from internal sources, but to integrate and (re-) combine knowledge to gain new insights (↑ *Combinative capability* [53, 68, 82, 85]). It is also important to be able to circulate knowledge within the organization (↑ *Knowledge diffusion capability* [52, 65, 84, 85]). Otherwise knowledge silos occur, so that knowledge is not used. The CA of *Development of Capabilities* delinks capabilities from areas they have already been applied to and relinks them to new areas (↑ *De-/relinking of capabilities* [62]). Eventually, the organization has the capacity to build new capabilities, which is not a matter of selecting new resources, but of adding value to existing (↑ *Capability-building mechanism* [47, 64, 73]).

IT-Related Capability Layer: This layer is defined "[…] as [the] ability to mobilize and deploy IT-based resources in combination or copresent with other resources and capabilities" [12] and is adapted by other authors [87–90]. The *IT Infrastructure* CA includes capabilities that enable generally usable systems to be provided, e.g., to communicate via suitable application systems (θ *Basic IT infrastructure capability* [91]). Environmental influences challenge IT to develop and implement quickly and, thus, gain importance to react to internal or external changes (↓ *Flexible IT infrastructure capability* [92]). Lastly, organizations can also use systems provided by a third party such as suppliers including complementary service offerings (↓ *Supplier IT capability* [93]). The CA *Information Management* incorporates capabilities that use IT infrastructure to serve users with data and information [50]. It enables the integration and transformation of knowledge as well as the use of its resources to improve the accomplishment of organizational goals (↓ *IT business spanning capability* [52, 91]). It also covers the ability to extend current capabilities to develop a new product requiring capabilities or knowledge not yet acquired (↑ *Capability stretching capability* [94]). Capabilities in the *Inside-out IT* CA help to make use of IT infrastructure and Information Management to increase knowledge application within the organization [52]. Insights are generated through the analysis and transformation of data (↓ *Analytics capability* [95]). Besides, the ability to create new business opportunities through searching for exploitation of IT resources or the embrace of novel IT innovations belongs into this CA (↑ *IT proactive stance capability* [91, 96]). To do so, the IT needs to be open for change to enable the delivery of competitive advantage through new product offerings (↑ *Change-readiness IT capability* [9, 97]). The *Outside-in IT* CA allows for external integration and identification of knowledge to redirect them into the organization [52]. This includes providing information and connecting to customers and supply chain partners (θ *Integrated IS capability* [83]) or alliance partners (↑ *IT-enabled knowledge integration capability* [98]). The codification of process knowledge and the strategic use for customer purposes are also part of this CA (↓ *Shared knowledge capability* [92]).

5 Conclusion, Discussion and Further Research

Due to the rapid development of digital technologies, the business environment is changing at an ever-faster pace [1]. Digitalization no longer only promotes innovations to increase operational efficiency, but changes customer needs, value creation processes, and entire markets. To respond to these changes, organizations must reconfigure and expand their resource and capability base to achieve DI [3]. However, capabilities being relevant for DI has not yet been holistically examined. The capability literature resembles a jungle of perspectives and partial considerations, which is characterized by a non-uniform world of terms and definitions. To identify relevant capabilities for DI and to name their interaction, a holistic approach is required. With the DI Capabilities Model presented, we introduce, to the best of our knowledge, the first holistic view of DI-relevant capabilities. The DI Capability Model comprises nine capability layers, 26 capability areas, and 58 capabilities that are associated with DI in high-quality scientific articles and, thus, represents a comprehensive, qualified, and structured state of the current scientific discourse. This is a valuable contribution to support further research and can be leveraged for goal-driven DI in organizations.

Our detailed analysis of different research domains on DI-relevant capabilities shows that first-order capabilities and entrepreneurial mindsets in particular are becoming increasingly important for the complex and interdisciplinary challenges of DI. It turns out that micro-foundations such as culture, work organization, and individual capabilities are important antecedents for the successful development of DI-relevant capabilities [11]. Interestingly, digital technology capabilities (e.g., artificial intelligence, machine learning, Big Data) are not very pronounced in the model presented. This may be due to the fact that relevant capabilities are more pronounced in terms of the application of and value creation by digital technologies and do not relate to individual digital technologies. It is also possible that such specific capabilities are not included in our data set due to their novelty and, thus, are not published so far.

Due to the nature of our research, this study comes up with some limitations. As we conducted a structured literature review, further research could widen the scope and more broadly define inclusion criteria to cover more literature. Thus, further research should investigate every capability layer with an in-depth analysis of literature and include, for example, conference publications to grasp latest research findings e.g., [99] who cleared up the space concerning business process management capabilities. Furthermore, our qualitative analysis of the capability definitions used as well as their consolidation and condensation into the presented DI Capability Model is not free of bias. Future research should investigate the identified layers, areas, and capabilities more thoroughly and empirically confirm their interaction.

References

1. Nambisan, S.: Digital entrepreneurship: toward a digital technology perspective of entrepreneurship. Entrep. Theory Pract. **41**, 1029–1055 (2017)
2. Loonam, J., Eaves, S., Kumar, V., Parry, G.: Towards digital transformation: lessons learned from traditional organizations. Strateg. Chang. **27**, 101–109 (2018)

3. Kohli, R., Melville, N.P.: Digital innovation: a review and synthesis. Inf. Syst. J. **29**, 200–223 (2018)
4. Fichman, R.: Going beyond the dominant paradigm for information technology innovation research: emerging concepts and methods. J. Assoc. Inf. Syst. **5**, 314–355 (2004)
5. Ciriello, R.F., Richter, A., Schwabe, G.: Digital Innovation. Bus. Inf. Syst. Eng. **60**, 563–569 (2018)
6. Vega, A., Chiasson, M.: A comprehensive framework to research digital innovation: the joint use of the systems of innovation and critical realism. J. Strateg. Inf. Syst. **28**, 242–256 (2019)
7. Yoo, Y., Henfridsson, O., Lyytinen, K.: Research commentary—the new organizing logic of digital innovation: an agenda for information systems research. Inf. Syst. Res. **21**, 724–735 (2010)
8. Gupta, M., George, J.F.: Toward the development of a big data analytics capability. Inf. Manag. **53**, 1049–1064 (2016)
9. Zhou, K.Z., Wu, F.: Technological capability, strategic flexibility, and product innovation. Strateg. Manag. J. **23** (2009)
10. Eggers, J.P., Kaul, A.: Motivation and ability? A behavioral perspective on the pursuit of radical invention in multi-technology incumbents. Acad. Manag. J. **61**, 67–93 (2018)
11. Wilden, R., Devinney, T.M., Dowling, G.R.: The architecture of dynamic capability research identifying the building blocks of a configurational approach. Acad. Manag. Ann. **10**, 997–1076 (2016)
12. Bharadwaj, A.S.: A resource-based perspective on information technology capability and firm performance: an empirical investigation. MIS Q. **24**, 169 (2000)
13. Lioukas, C.S., Reuer, J.J., Zollo, M.: Effects of information technology capabilities on strategic alliances: implications for the resource-based view. J. Manag. Stud. **53**, 161–183 (2016)
14. Bhatt, G.D., Grover, V.: Types of information technology capabilities and their role in competitive advantage: an empirical study. J. Manag. Inf. Syst **22**, 253–277 (2005)
15. Levallet, N., Chan, Y.E.: Role of digital capabilities in unleashing the power of managerial improvisation. MIS Q. Exec. **17**, 4–21 (2018)
16. Yoo, Y., Boland, R.J., Lyytinen, K., Majchrzak, A.: Organizing for innovation in the digitized world. Ind. Corp. Chang. **23**, 1398–1408 (2012)
17. Teece, D.J.: Dynamic capabilities: routines versus entrepreneurial action. J. Manag. Stud. **49**, 1395–1401 (2012)
18. Helfat, C.E., Raubitschek, R.S.: Dynamic and integrative capabilities for profiting from innovation in digital platform-based ecosystems. Res. Policy **47**, 1391–1399 (2018)
19. Rothaermel, F.T., Hess, A.M.: Building dynamic capabilities: innovation driven by individual-, firm-, & network-level effects. Ind. Corp. Chang. **18**, 898–921 (2007)
20. Helfat, C.E., Peteraf, M.A.: The dynamic resource-based view: capability lifecycles. Strateg. Manag. J. **24**, 997–1010 (2003)
21. Schryen, G.: Revisiting IS business value research: what we already know, what we still need to know, and how we can get there. Eur. J. Inf. Syst **22**, 139–169 (2013)
22. Nambisan, S., Lyytinen, K., Majchrzak, A., Song, M.: Digital innovation management: reinventing innovation management research in a digital world. MIS Q. **41**, 223–238 (2017)
23. Zuppo, C.M.: Defining ICT in a boundaryless world: the development of a working hierarchy. IJMIT **4**, 13–22 (2012)
24. Rogers, E.M.: Diffusion of Innovations. Free Press, New York (1983)
25. Powell, T.C.: Research notes and communications strategic planning as competitive advantage. Strateg. Manag. J. **13**, 551–558 (1992)
26. Grant, R.M.: The resource-based theory of competitive advantage: implications for strategy formulation. Calif. Manag. Rev. **33**, 114–135 (1991)

27. Amit, R., Schoemaker, P.J.H.: Strategic assets and organizational rent. Strateg. Manag. J. **14**, 33–46 (1993)
28. Hafeez, K., Zhang, Y., Malak, N.: Core competence for sustainable competitive advantage: a structured methodology for identifying core competence. IEEE Trans. Eng. Manag. **49**, 28–35 (2002)
29. Hine, D., Parker, R., Pregelj, L., Verreynne, M.-L.: Deconstructing and reconstructing the capability hierarchy. Ind. Corp. Chang. **23**, 1299–1325 (2014)
30. Paulhus, D.L., Martin, C.L.: The structure of personality capabilities. J. Pers. Soc. Psychol. **52**, 354–365 (1987)
31. Helfat, C.E., Peteraf, M.A.: Understanding dynamic capabilities: progress along a developmental path. Strateg. Organ. **7**, 91–102 (2009)
32. Collis, D.J.: Research note: how valuable are organizational capabilities? Strateg. Manag. J. **15**, 143–152 (1994)
33. Winter, S.G.: Understanding dynamic capabilities. Strateg. Manag. J. **24**, 991–995 (2003)
34. Teece, D.J.: A dynamic capabilities-based entrepreneurial theory of the multinational enterprise. J. Int. Bus. Stud. **45**, 8–37 (2014)
35. Zollo, M., Winter, S.G.: Deliberate learning and the evolution of dynamic capabilities. Ind. Corp. Chang. **13**, 339–351 (2002)
36. Gregor, S.: The nature of theory in information systems. MIS Q. **30**, 611 (2006)
37. Webster, J., Watson, R.T.: Analyzing the past to prepare for the future: writing a literature review. MIS Q. **26**, xiii–xxiii (2002)
38. Templier, M., Paré, G.: A framework for guiding and evaluating literature reviews. Commun. Assoc. Inf. Syst. **37** (2015)
39. Wolfswinkel, J.F., Furtmueller, E., Wilderom, C.P.M.: Using grounded theory as a method for rigorously reviewing literature. Eur. J. Inf. Syst. **22**, 45–55 (2013)
40. O'Reilly, C.A., Tushman, M.L.: Ambidexterity as a dynamic capability: resolving the innovator's dilemma. Res. Organ. Behav. **28**, 185–206 (2008)
41. Sharma, S., Vredenburg, H.: Proactive corporate environmental strategy and the development of competitively valuable organizational capabilities. Strateg. Manag. J. **19**, 729–753 (1998)
42. Voss, G.B., Voss, Z.G.: Competitive density and the customer acquisition-retention trade-off. J. Mark. **72**, 3–18 (2008)
43. Subramaniam, M., Youndt, M.A.: The influence of intellectual capital on the types of innovative capabilities. Acad. Manag. J. **48**, 450–463 (2005)
44. Krasnikov, A., Jayachandran, S.: The relative impact of marketing, research-and-development, and operations capabilities on firm performance. J. Mark. **72**, 1–11 (2008)
45. Rothaermel, F.T., Hill, C.W.L.: Technological discontinuities and complementary assets: a longitudinal study of industry and firm performance. Ind. Corp. Chang. **16**, 52–70 (2005)
46. Narasimhan, O., Rajiv, S., Dutta, S.: Absorptive capacity in high-technology markets: the competitive advantage of the haves. Mark. Sci. **25**, 510–524 (2006)
47. Danneels, E.: Organizational antecedents of second-order competences. Strateg. Manag. J. **29**, 519–543 (2008)
48. Danneels, E.: Survey measures of first- and second-order competences. Strateg. Manag. J. **37**, 2174–2188 (2016)
49. Ethiraj, S.K., Kale, P., Krishnan, M.S., Singh, J.V.: Where do capabilities come from and how do they matter? A study in the software services industry. Strateg. Manag. J. **26**, 25–45 (2005)
50. Mithas, R.: Sambamurthy: how information management capability influences firm performance. MIS Q. **35**, 237 (2011)
51. Koufteros, X., Verghese, A.J., Lucianetti, L.: The effect of performance measurement systems on firm performance: a cross-sectional and a longitudinal study. J. Oper. Manag. **32**, 313–336 (2014)

52. Roberts, G., Dinger, G.: Absorptive capacity and information systems research: review, synthesis, and directions for future research. MIS Q. **36**, 625 (2012)
53. Jansen, J.J.P., van den Bosch, F.A.J., Volberda, H.W.: Managing potential and realized absorptive capacity: how do organizational antecedents matter? Acad Manage. J. **48**, 999–1015 (2005)
54. Townsend, D.M., Busenitz, L.W.: Turning water into wine? Exploring the role of dynamic capabilities in early-stage capitalization processes. J. Bus. Ventur. **30**, 292–306 (2015)
55. Rai, A., Arikan, I., Pye, J., Tiwana, A.: Fit and misfit of plural sourcing strategies and IT-enabled process integration capabilities: consequences of firm performance in the U.S. electric utility industry. MIS Q. **39**, 865–885 (2015)
56. Eggers, J.P.: All experience is not created equal: learning, adapting, and focusing in product portfolio management. Strateg. Manag. J. **33**, 315–335 (2012)
57. Anand, G., Ward, P.T., Tatikonda, M.V., Schilling, D.A.: Dynamic capabilities through continuous improvement infrastructure. J. Manag. **27**, 444–461 (2009)
58. Benner, M.J., Tushman, M.L.: Exploitation, exploration, and process management: the productivity dilemma revisited. Acad. Manag. Rev. **28**, 238 (2003)
59. Ayabakan, S., Bardhan, I.R., Zheng, Z.: A data envelopment analysis approach to estimate IT-enabled production capability. MIS Q. **41**, 189–205 (2017)
60. Wilden, R., Gudergan, S.P.: The impact of dynamic capabilities on operational marketing and technological capabilities: investigating the role of environmental turbulence. J. Acad. Mark. Sci. **43**, 1–19 (2014). https://doi.org/10.1007/s11747-014-0380-y
61. Song, M., Di Benedetto, C.A., Nason, R.W.: Capabilities and financial performance: the moderating effect of strategic type. J. Acad. Mark. Sci. **35**, 18–34 (2007)
62. Danneels, E.: The dynamics of product innovation and firm competences. Strateg. Manag. J. **23**, 1095–1121 (2002)
63. Moorman, C., Slotegraaf, R.J.: The contingency value of complementary capabilities in product development. J. Mark. Res. **36**, 239 (1999)
64. Blyler, M., Coff, R.W.: Dynamic capabilities, social capital, and rent appropriation: ties that split pies. Strateg. Manag. J. **24**, 677–686 (2003)
65. Branzei, O., Vertinsky, I.: Strategic pathways to product innovation capabilities in SMEs. J. Bus. Ventur. **21**, 75–105 (2006)
66. Pil, F.K., Cohen, S.K.: Modularity: implications for imitation, innovation, and sustained advantage. Acad. Manag. Rev **31**, 995–1011 (2006)
67. Setia, P., Venkatesh, V., Joglekar, S.: leveraging digital technologies: how information quality leads to localized capabilities and customer service performance. MIS Q. **37**, 565–590 (2013)
68. Weerawardena, J., Mort, G.S., Salunke, S., Knight, G., Liesch, P.W.: The role of the market sub-system and the socio-technical sub-system in innovation and firm performance: a dynamic capabilities approach. J. Acad. Mark. Sci. **43**, 1–19 (2014). https://doi.org/10.1007/s11747-014-0382-9
69. Kor, Y.Y., Mahoney, J.T.: How dynamics, management, and governance of resource deployments influence firm-level performance. Strateg. Manag. J. **26**, 489–496 (2005)
70. Ramani, G., Kumar, V.: Interaction orientation and firm performance. J. Mark. **72**, 27–45 (2008)
71. Zott, C.: Dynamic capabilities and the emergence of intraindustry differential firm performance: insights from a simulation study. Strateg. Manag. J. **24**, 97–125 (2003)
72. Nenonen, S., Storbacka, K., Windahl, C.: Capabilities for market-shaping: triggering and facilitating increased value creation. J. Acad. Mark. Sci. **47**(4), 617–639 (2019). https://doi.org/10.1007/s11747-019-00643-z
73. Makadok, R.: Toward a synthesis of the resource-based and dynamic-capability views of rent creation. Strateg. Manag. J. **22**, 387–401 (2001)

74. Franco, A.M., Sarkar, M.B., Agarwal, R., Echambadi, R.: Swift and smart: the moderating effects of technological capabilities on the market pioneering-firm survival relationship. Manag. Sci. **55**, 1842–1860 (2009)
75. Walter, A., Auer, M., Ritter, T.: The impact of network capabilities & entrepreneurial orientation on university spin-off performance. J. Bus. Ventur. **21**, 541–567 (2006)
76. Leiblein, M.J., Madsen, T.L.: Unbundling competitive heterogeneity: incentive structures and capability influences on technological innovation. Strateg. Manag. J. **30**, 711–735 (2009)
77. Jiang, R.J., Tao, Q.T., Santoro, M.D.: Alliance portfolio diversity and firm performance. Strateg. Manag. J. **31**, 1136–1144 (2010)
78. Giudici, A., Reinmoeller, P., Ravasi, D.: Open-system orchestration as a relational source of sensing capabilities: evidence from a venture association. Acad. Manag. J. **61**, 1369–1402 (2018)
79. Lorenzoni, G., Lipparini, A.: The leveraging of interfirm relationships as a distinctive organizational capability: a longitudinal study. Strateg. Manag. J. **20**, 317–338 (1999)
80. Leiblein, M.J.: What do resource- and capability-based theories propose? J. Manag. **37**, 909–932 (2011)
81. Volberda, H.W., Foss, N.J., Lyles, M.A.: Perspective—absorbing the concept of absorptive capacity: how to realize its potential in the organization field. Ind. Corp. Chang. **21**, 931–951 (2010)
82. Phene, A., Almeida, P.: Innovation in multinational subsidiaries: the role of knowledge assimilation and subsidiary capabilities. J. Int. Bus. Stud. **39**, 901–919 (2008)
83. Setia, P., Patel, P.C.: How information systems help create OM capabilities: consequents and antecedents of operational absorptive capacity. J. Oper. Manag. **31**, 409–431 (2013)
84. Vera, D., Nemanich, L., Vélez-Castrillón, S., Werner, S.: Knowledge-based and contextual factors associated with R&D teams' improvisation capability. J. Manag. **42**, 1874–1903 (2016)
85. Lewin, A.Y., Massini, S., Peeters, C.: Microfoundations of internal and external absorptive capacity routines. Ind. Corp. Chang. **22**, 81–98 (2011)
86. Suddaby, R., Coraiola, D., Harvey, C., Foster, W.: History and the micro-foundations of dynamic capabilities. Strateg. Manag. J. **41**, 530–556 (2020)
87. Chae, H.-C., Koh, C.E., Prybutok, V.R.: Information technology capability and firm performance: contradictory findings & their possible causes. MIS Q. **38**, 305–326 (2014)
88. Drnevich, P.L., Croson, D.C.: Information technology and business-level strategy: toward an integrated theoretical perspective. MIS Q. **37**, 483–509 (2013)
89. Mishra, S., Modi, S.B., Animesh, A.: The relationship between information technology capability, inventory efficiency, and shareholder wealth: a firm-level empirical analysis. J. Oper. Manag. **31**, 298–312 (2013)
90. Aral, S., Weill, P.: IT assets, organizational capabilities, and firm performance: how resource allocations and organizational differences explain performance variation. Ind. Corp. Chang. **18**, 763–780 (2007)
91. Lu (Ramamurthy), K.: Understanding the link between information technology capability and organizational agility: an empirical examination. MIS Q. **35**, 931 (2011)
92. Ray, M.: Barney: information technology and the performance of the customer service process: a resource-based analysis. MIS Q. **29**, 625 (2005)
93. Weigelt, C.: Leveraging supplier capabilities: the role of locus of capability deployment. Strateg. Manag. J. **34**, 1–21 (2013)
94. Wang, T., Chen, Y.: Capability stretching in product innovation. J. Manag. **44**, 784–810 (2018)
95. Wu, L., Lou, B., Hitt, L.: Data analytics supports decentralized innovation. Manag. Sci. **65**, 4863–4877 (2019)
96. Eggers, J.P., Park, K.F.: Incumbent adaptation to technological change: the past, present, and future of research on heterogeneous incumbent response. Acad. Manag. Ann. **12**, 357–389 (2018)

97. Clark, C.E., Cavanaugh, N.C., Brown, C.V., Sambamurthy, V.: Building change-readiness capabilities in the IS organization: insights from the Bell Atlantic experience. MIS Q. **21**, 425 (1997)

98. Liu, Y., Ravichandran, T.: Alliance experience, it-enabled knowledge integration, and ex ante value gains. Ind. Corp. Chang. **26**, 511–530 (2015)

99. Kerpedzhiev, G.D., König, U.M., Röglinger, M., Rosemann, M.: An exploration into future business process management capabilities in view of digitalization. Bus. Inf. Syst. Eng. **63**(2), 83–96 (2020). https://doi.org/10.1007/s12599-020-00637-0

Digital Innovation Culture: A Systematic Literature Review

Daniel Kiefer[1][(✉)], Clemens van Dinther[1], and Julian Spitzmüller[2]

[1] ESB Business School, Reutlingen University, Reutlingen, Germany
{Daniel.Kiefer,Clemens.Van_Dinther}@Reutlingen-University.de
[2] Itdesign GmbH, Tübingen, Germany
Julian.Spitzmueller@itdesign.de

Abstract. Digitalization increases the pressure for companies to innovate. While current research on digital transformation mostly focuses on technological and management aspects, less attention has been paid to organizational culture and its influence on digital innovations. The purpose of this paper is to identify the characteristics of organizational culture that foster digital innovations. Based on a systematic literature review on three scholarly databases, we initially found 778 articles that were then narrowed down to a total number of 23 relevant articles through a methodical approach. After analyzing these articles, we determine nine characteristics of organizational culture that foster digital innovations: corporate entrepreneurship, digital awareness and necessity of innovations, digital skills and resources, ecosystem orientation, employee participation, agility and organizational structures, error culture and risk-taking, internal knowledge sharing and collaboration, customer and market orientation as well as open-mindedness and willingness to learn.

Keywords: Digital · Innovation · Culture · Organization · Transformation

1 Introduction

Many companies are still overwhelmed by digital transformation, in particular when it comes to proactive behavior and discussing its actual impact and potentials for companies [1]. Innovation has always played a crucial role for competitive advantage and corporate success [2, 3]. It can be used to adapt to changes in the business environment and to meet customer needs [4]. Likewise, the requirements for innovations have changed over the past few years: the increased intensity of competition, technological development and changing customer needs result in shortened product lifecycles [5]. Consequently, there is increased pressure to create innovations in companies in a more effective and efficient way.

Creating these innovations in the digital era is a serious challenge for companies that cannot be solved easily. Innovation culture is mentioned as a key driver to manage digital transformation [6]. New digital products, services, business models or ecosystems need an organizational culture that creates and fosters these digital innovations [7]. Therefore, many companies have already introduced new concepts and methods such as agile project management or design thinking in order to encourage digital innovations. However, in order to manage its digital transformation and to be successful and innovative in the digital age, a company might need much more than just a digital strategy and the usage of new technology and methods. Changing the organizational culture in favor of the digital transformation implies a radical change in the way people think, behave and collaborate in companies, how they generate ideas and how they make decisions.

Nevertheless, the concrete design of a digital innovation culture and its characteristics are still unclear [8–10]. Research on both organizational and innovation culture has a long tradition and offers a variety of definitions, models and studies [5, 11]. However, current research does not consider the changes due to digitalization that were mentioned in the beginning of this article. Moreover, most research of digital transformation focuses on the technological or economical aspects (such as business model innovation or ecosystems) and miss out on the cultural aspect [12]. But organizational culture has always been a high obstacle for business transformations and many sophisticated strategies have failed to overcome this obstacle.

Only [9] and [10] address the topic of digital innovation in the context of organizational culture. [9] conducted a Delphi study in where he interviewed participants from companies to identify cultural values for digital transformation. [10] collected data through exploratory case studies and pictured it on culture levels from [13] (e.g. artifacts). But both lack of general expressiveness regarding digital innovation culture. This is due to the limited method of the studies and the small frame of reference ([9] interviewed twenty five German employees from various industries and [10] analyzed German case studies). This shows that the topic has received little attention in the scientific community so far. [14] recently noted: *"that because of the shift in the locus of innovation and because some of our core organizing axioms may be challenged or fundamentally changed by the digital revolution, the nature of innovation and organizational scholarship may be at a transition point."*

This is why, we strongly believe that digitalization will change more than products, technologies, processes and strategies. To a greater extent and starting one step prior, we think that companies will nurture ongoing digital innovations by creating a suitable organizational culture. Consequently, we are exploring the characteristics of organizational culture that benefit digital innovations. This leads to the following research question:

RQ: What characteristics should an organizational culture have to foster digital innovations?

To answer this research question, we have conducted a systematic literature review. The structure of the paper is as follows: First, the theoretical context of innovation, organizational culture and digital transformation is explained. Second, the literature review, its methodology and its results are presented. Third, we discuss the results and limitations of the literature review as well as its implications for future research.

2 Theoretical Context and Boundaries

As outlined in the introduction, the three aspects "Innovation", "Digital Transformation" and "Organizational Culture" form the context of our research (Fig. 1). The innovation aspect deals with the question of how innovations can be fostered. Digital transformation determines the context in which these innovations happen. Organizational culture addresses the practiced patterns, approaches and values in form of characteristics. Finally, "Digital Innovation Culture" is the subject of our research. In the following section, we will briefly define these terms.

Fig. 1. Overall context of digital innovation culture

Innovation refers to the usage of novel ideas, products, services, processes that are new to the implementing organization and create an advantage for the organization [4].

Digital transformation describes the transformation of organizations that is based on the usage of digital technology and radically changes business operations and value creation [15]. According to [16], digital innovations are characterized as "the carrying out of new combinations of digital and physical components to produce novel products". As we do not see digital innovations limited to products only (e.g. services and business models), we define digital innovations as innovations that are enabled by digital technologies.

Following [13], organizational culture is "a pattern of shared basic assumptions that was learned by a group as it solved its problems of external adaptation and internal integration, that has worked well enough to be considered valid and, therefore, to be taught to new members as the correct way to perceive, think, and feel in relation to those problems". Moreover, [13] provides a model to describe and analyze organizational culture which consists of three levels: artifacts, espoused beliefs and values as well as underlying assumptions. Whereas artifacts are characterized as being observable (e.g. organizational structures, processes, clothing, and stories), espoused beliefs and values deal with the strategies, goals, norms and moral principles in an organization. Underlying assumptions are beliefs that are taken-for-granted and unconscious. They are widely accepted within an organization and people do not question them anymore.

These three aspects set our research boundaries for the literature review and explain the context of our search. By looking at the overlap of all three aspects (Fig. 1), we can clarify the construct "Digital Innovation Culture". Consequently, we define digital innovation culture as an organizational culture that fosters digital innovations.

3   Research Method

In order to identify how a digital innovation culture looks like, we followed the approach for literature reviews suggested by [17, 18]. Figure 2 illustrates the seven-step search process that was conducted as part of this literature review to identify characteristics that foster a digital innovation culture.

The actual literature search process was started after the framework conditions were set within the first and second step according to the defined research question from Sect. 1. The extraction log is the basis of the literature search. All necessary information is stored in it and which is used for the final matrix. The matrix consists of articles that are considered relevant. Based on these articles the research question is answered step by step. The keyword search process (step 3) consists of several iterations. The actual analysis and evaluation of the literature consists of the title and abstract analysis (step 4) as well as the full text analysis (step 5). The result is the final extraction log, which is used as the basis for the matrix. It should be emphasized that forward and backward searches were also part of the literature search strategy in this contribution (step 6). The results of the individual process steps as well as the number of identified articles after the various search iterations are presented in the following chapters.

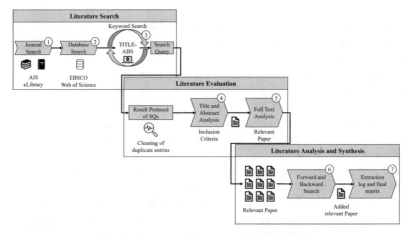

Fig. 2. Process of literature research [17, 18]

3.1   Literature Search

Based on the research question formulated in Sect. 1, first articles were collected in journals and databases to derive suitable keywords for the search query. The aspects from Fig. 1 were also used to derive relevant keywords for the comprehensive search. Digital innovation is an emerging research field, which is why we also included IS conference proceedings of the AIS eLibrary. Our search is limited to peer-reviewed articles[1].

We conducted our search in July and August 2020 on the scholarly databases EBSCO and Web of Science, which are recommended by [19–21]. The search was focused on the "title" and "abstract" fields. The language of the articles is limited to English and German. Our final search query is as follows:

$$(digit*) \; AND \; (innovat * \; OR \; creativ*) \; AND \; (cultur * \; OR \; organization) \; AND \\ (compan * \; or \; firm \; or \; business) \tag{1}$$

3.2 Literature Evaluation

By following these steps, our search resulted in an initial set of 778 contributions.

After removing duplicates (82) and articles in other languages than English and German (58), we had 683 remaining articles.

In the next phase the contributions were analyzed of their suitability based by their title. We were able to exclude most of these articles when we went through the titles. By analyzing their abstracts and conclusions we had a closer look whether they could help to answer our research question. After we went through the articles, a finding was that that many articles deal with the impact of digitalization on national culture or on culture industry. Another area was e-government. Those papers were excluded from the analysis because the focus lies on companies (see selection criteria 3.2).

After this stage, 123 potentially relevant articles remained which were then read carefully in the fourth phase of our selection (see literature analysis process in Fig. 3).

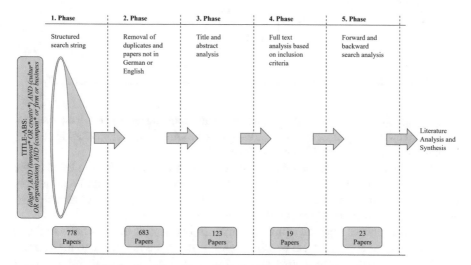

Fig. 3. Resulting papers from the literature analysis process

---

[1] As we received few results in the AIS eLibrary, we also included non-peer-reviewed articles of this database only.

For the selection of the encountered and remaining articles, we established the following inclusion criteria, whereby all three must be fulfilled:

1. Articles must have a focus on digital transformation.
2. Articles must address digital innovation.
3. Articles must deal with organizational culture in companies or at least parts of it.

Those inclusion criteria reduced the number of articles to 19. Finally, a forward and backward search lead to four additional articles which makes 23 relevant contributions in total.

3.3 Literature Analysis and Synthesis

The relevant 23 articles were analyzed with regard to our research question. Figure 4 illustrates the procedure based on the recommendations of [17].

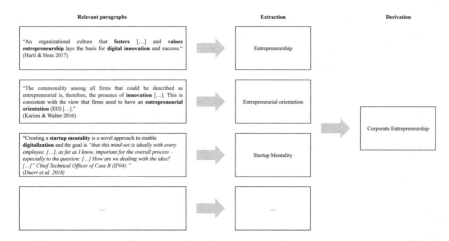

Fig. 4. Exemplary illustration of the literature analysis and synthesis based on [17]

As a first step, all 23 articles were carefully read again and the aspects or characteristics described or mentioned by the authors, which promote a digital innovation culture, were listed in a table[2] with 108 entries at the end.

In a second step the characteristics considered important, which were listed in the table, were compared with each other. It became apparent that the different authors use different names for the same relevant characteristics (e.g. entrepreneurship [9], entrepreneurial orientation [22] and startup mentality [10], etc.).

In a third iterative step, the equivalent entries – key aspects of the articles to foster digital innovation culture – were classified, clustered and unified in categories (characteristics). As an output nine characteristics of organizational culture that were in some way considered important for a digital innovation culture in the articles were derived.

---

[2] MS Excel, a spreadsheet application, was utilized for the literature analysis and synthesis process.

In a fourth step, a matrix was developed that shows which article mentions specific characteristics relevant to the fostering of a digital innovation culture (Table 1, Sect. 4). It should be taken into account that based on the sole frequency of naming a characteristic, no evaluation can be made with regard to its importance compared to the other characteristics. This is a core task for further research to conduct extensive studies to measure the relevance of the individual characteristics.

4   Results of the Literature Review

Table 1 compromise the results of the literature analysis and synthesis based on [17] and gives an overview of the unified characteristics as well as in which paper they are discussed (marked by "x" if mentioned in the respective article).

The following Fig. 5 visualizes the results from Table 1 graphically. Based on the number of entries and the sum of the relevant articles, a percentage of the frequency distribution of the respective organizational culture characteristic is calculated. This does not reflect the importance of the characteristic in the organization compared to the others, but shows which ones have been mentioned particularly frequently to foster digital innovation. The result could be used in assessments to benchmark and display the profile of the digital innovation culture of single organizations.

4.1   Corporate Entrepreneurship

Corporate Entrepreneurship was mentioned several times in the relevant articles. In order to stay ahead of competitors, to be first to market and to grow, companies must proactively identify new business opportunities [36]. Therefore, it is helpful to encourage employees to find these new business opportunities [22]. Ideally, all employees should become entrepreneurs [10, 23] This requires a shift of responsibilities towards employees and also giving them more freedom and foster a digital innovation culture [9, 34].

4.2   Digital Awareness and Necessity of Innovations

Another important characteristic is the awareness in the company regarding digital transformation, its impact, threats and opportunities as well as the need for innovations. This awareness begins at top management level [28, 33]. It is important that digital transformation is taken seriously and that a clear strategy and mission contribute to a common understanding within the company, stress the importance of digital transformation and encourage employees to come up with new ideas and business opportunities [27, 31, 32, 40] Putting that in one sentence: "True change needs true authenticity" [40]. So, using new technologies or setting up innovation labs as an alibi without a real purpose is not enough to become truly digital and innovative within the digital transformation [35]. The necessity of innovations should be anchored in the organizational culture of a company because innovation is one way for a company to grow and to make improvements [9].

Table 1. Result of the literature review: mentioned characteristic per paper

Paper	Corporate Entrepreneurship	Digital Awareness and Necessity of Innovations	Digital Skills and Resources	Ecosystem Orientation	Employee Participation, Agility and Organizational Structures	Error Culture and Risk-Taking	Internal Knowledge Sharing and Collaboration	Customer and Market Orientation	Open-Mindedness and Willingness to Learn	Sum
[8]		x	x	x		x	x	x	x	7
[9]	x	x		x	x	x	x	x	x	8
[10]	x	x	x	x	x	x	x	x		8
[22]	x				x	x			x	4
[23]	x	x	x		x	x			x	6
[24]		x	x	x				x		4
[25]								x		1
[26]		x			x		x			3
[27]		x		x	x		x	x	x	6
[28]		x	x	x				x	x	5
[29]			x		x	x	x		x	5
[30]			x		x			x	x	4
[31]		x		x	x		x			4
[32]	x	x	x	x	x	x				6
[33]		x	x		x	x	x		x	6
[34]	x		x		x		x	x	x	6
[35]		x	x		x	x		x	x	6
[36]	x	x		x		x	x	x	x	7
[37]			x		x	x			x	4
[38]	x		x	x	x				x	5
[39]		x	x		x		x	x		5
[40]		x	x		x	x	x	x	x	7
[41]			x	x	x	x	x	x	x	7
Sum	8	15	16	11	18	13	13	14	16	

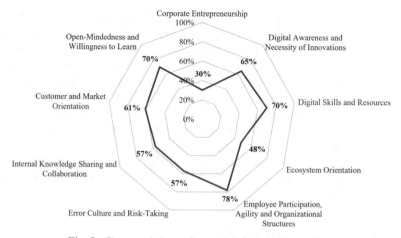

Fig. 5. Characteristics to foster digital innovation culture

4.3 Digital Skills and Resources

Creating digital innovations requires several skills and resources. Companies might want to evaluate employees' technological competencies and offer opportunities to enhance these competencies, develop completely new ones or hire new employees with the wanted skills. In this context, it should be noted that some companies overestimate their competencies, especially in the digital area. Missing resources and skills can also be obtained from external partners in an ecosystem [10, 29, 30, 34, 40].

Looking at hard skills, data management and data analytics as well as several associated domains (e.g. artificial intelligence, machine learning and statistical modelling) were mentioned very often in the relevant articles for a successful digital transformation [24, 38, 39, 41]. Besides these hard skills, soft skills are important, too. Especially change management skills are useful [23].

4.4 Ecosystem Orientation

Innovations sometimes need external partners [27]. As resources and knowledge of companies are limited [41], it might be useful to search for complementary capabilities outside the company [36]. For example, traditional manufacturing companies could therefore partner up with IT firms to equip products with digital components [10]. Digital platforms enable a value creation with other companies in digital ecosystems or networks [32]. Especially when building end-to-end solutions for customers, an open innovation approach is advantageous. Close collaboration with external partners increases knowledge and provides heterogeneous resources. Paired with digital awareness, this can lead to radical innovations [28]. For that reason, companies should be willing to collaborate and share their knowledge with external partners in a network that has a shared purpose [9, 31].

4.5 Employee Participation, Agility and Organizational Structures

A higher involvement of employees in decision making and more freedom might have a positive impact on the success of innovative projects [32]. Many others argue in the same way and say that employees should have more responsibilities, freedom and opportunities to participate in decision making [9, 10, 22, 26]. This requires transparency and an open discussion of innovation initiatives and possible solutions [26, 40]. Furthermore, the employees' involvement also helps to change their behavior. By empowering employees, companies can profit from enhanced innovation processes as well as from a faster ability to react to changes in the business environment. Additionally, mutual decision making helps to eliminate silos within the company [10].

According to [37], agility (defined as operational and strategic flexibility together with customer responsiveness) is crucial in order to adapt to changes in the business environment and to foster digital innovation culture.

4.6 Error Culture and Risk-Taking

In times of digital transformation, it is difficult to predict future changes in business environment. It needs courage to fight this uncertainty [9, 23].A willingness to take risks is essential for companies to explore new opportunities and to experiment in order to come up with new ideas [27, 40]. Without taking risks, companies might miss a chance to create new innovations or to deliver them to the market. When exploring new things and taking risks, some projects might go wrong and failure might occur but where a risk is taken there is also the chance of new innovation. Instead of wasting resources for too long on corrupted projects, failures should be admitted [35].

4.7 Internal Knowledge Sharing and Collaboration

The creation of new ideas and an increased participation of employees in innovation initiatives demand for knowledge sharing and a closer collaboration within the company across all business units and hierarchical levels [9, 10, 22, 40]. Therefore, the partly dominating silo mentality in companies must be abolished [26, 27, 39]. An integration of IT departments and business departments should especially be intended, as IT drives and enables digital transformation [10, 33, 35]. A close collaboration across business units also enables an identification of shared interests among employees and their special qualifications [26].

4.8 Customer and Market Orientation

Digital transformation might also have an impact on how companies create value. This characteristic addresses the customer orientation in value creation and companies' attention to changes in the market such as emerging technologies and competitors. Not reacting to market changes clearly makes digital transformation very difficult [35]. Some companies also fear losing their customers to competitors if they cannot offer the demanded digital products and services [10]. Therefore, customer centricity is crucial for businesses which means to address customer needs and align new products and services with them [9, 39]. Some articles even go one step further and talk about customer integration or value co-creation. This means that customers are directly involved in innovation processes and work together on new products and services [10, 25, 34].

4.9   Open-Mindedness and Willingness to Learn

Digital transformation might cause and require radical changes. Whether a company deals with those changes successfully also depends on the attitude of their employees and their willingness to change and learn as well as their acceptance of new ideas.

Emerging technologies require open-mindedness and, as mentioned before, sometimes it is necessary to question the existing business model, assumptions and competencies [22, 25, 28, 35, 36]. Companies should encourage lateral thinking, out-of-the-box thinking and curiosity [38, 40]. According to most articles in this literature review, it is highly crucial that employees are open to change and willing to learn and develop [8, 10, 23, 25, 26, 32, 34, 35].

5   Discussion and Implications for Future Research

The characteristics outlined for fostering a digital innovation culture were synthesized on the basis of established papers and explained in more detail. Most of the identified articles do not explicitly focus on organizational culture and how it can foster digital innovations and even fewer articles specifically talk about digital innovation culture. However, all articles had at least some aspects regarding organizational culture that are related to our research question and helped us to identify the characteristics above. A broad and comprehensive framework that explicitly addresses most of these characteristics in a holistic approach is nonexistent. First attempts were delivered by [9] and [10].When we reviewed the papers, one discovery was that many articles dealt with the impact of digitization on national culture, the culture industry, as well as e-government. Considerably fewer dealt directly about companies.

When comparing our derived characteristics to foster a digital innovation culture in organizations with relevant research on the culture of innovation in organizations, it is evident that they overlap in some areas.

For example, market orientation on the one hand and customer and market orientation on the other hand. At the same time, however [42] lacks a clear reference to corporate entrepreneurship, digital awareness, error culture and risk-taking as well as ecosystem orientation. All of which play a decisive role in the promotion of digital innovations. The following Table 2 compares [42] identified characteristics for fostering an Innovation Culture with our characteristics for fostering a digital innovation culture.

The following Table 3 gives a summary of the characteristics and why each of them should receive more attention in order to foster digital innovations in organizations. More questions regarding further research could address the concrete design of these characteristics and how they can be managed and implemented in corporate practice. Additionally, the correlation among the identified characteristics should be investigated. The importance of particular characteristics might vary and should be object of future research.

Table 2. Comparison of innovation culture and digital innovation culture characteristics

Innovation culture [42]	Digital innovation culture
Innovation propensity	Corporate entrepreneurship
Organizational constituency	Employee participation, agility and organizational structures
Creative and empowerment	Error culture and risk-taking
Organizational learning	Open-mindedness and willingness to learn
Market orientation	Customer and market orientation
Value orientation	Customer and market orientation
Implementation context	–
–	Ecosystem orientation
–	Digital awareness and necessity of innovations
–	Digital skills and resources
–	Internal knowledge sharing and collaboration

Companies from the "old world", whose current focus or core competences are not associated with digital innovation, might especially profit from a framework that helps to transform the organizational culture and foster digital innovations. This problem should be considered in future studies. Appropriate questions for each characteristic were developed as a first step towards creating such a framework (Table 3).

Table 3. Characteristics, digital relevance and future research questions

Characteristic	Digital relevance	Future Research questions
Corporate entrepreneurship	Enhance proactivity; foster idea generation and innovations	What skills should a corporate entrepreneur have to create digital innovations?
Digital awareness and necessity of innovations	Justifies upcoming changes and explains the need for innovations	How can companies achieve this awareness and create a common understanding?
Digital skills and resources	Especially IT related skills are required	How should companies evaluate their competencies and identify missing skills?
Ecosystem orientation	Necessary to create innovative end-to-end solutions for customer	How can a company find appropriate partners and integrate them in a digital ecosystem?

(*continued*)

Table 3. (*continued*)

Characteristic	Digital relevance	Future Research questions
Employee participation, agility and organizational structures	Fast changes in business environment require agility, flexibility and fast decision making	How should companies deal with radical innovations and disruptive technologies? Is it possible to avoid spin-offs?
Error culture and risk-taking	Enhance proactivity; promote learning; encourage experiments (e.g. with new technologies) and efficient innovations	What general conditions do companies have to meet in order to encourage experiments and change employees' minds as well as their behavior?
Internal knowledge sharing and collaboration	Cross-functional collaboration fosters digital innovations and creates synergies	How can companies abolish silos and create a collaborative climate across business units? How can this knowledge exchange be managed and recorded?
Customer and market orientation	Ensure customer value; data analytics enable new services and business models	How can companies manage the balancing act between market-pull and innovation-push?
Open-mindedness and willingness to learn	Learning is crucial for the success of digital transformation; new methods, skills and partners are needed which requires open-mindedness	This long-lasting and radical change in employees' minds is difficult to accomplish. How can companies establish this new way of thinking?

6 Conclusion and Limitations

Innovations are crucial for companies to manage digital transformation successfully. The organizational culture of a company has a great impact on the creation of these digital innovations. The contribution of this paper is novel and relevant for research and practice. The established research question has been answered by identifying and describing characteristics of organizational culture that foster digital innovations on the basis of established literature. At the same time, the term "Digital Innovation Culture" was introduced to emphasize the importance of such a cultural approach to digital transformation and innovation.

However, there are also limiting aspects regarding the results for several reasons. First, the findings are limited to the articles that were taken into account for this literature review. The selected scholarly databases as well as our key word search and literature selection restrict the list of articles in a certain and a subjective way that we are aware of. Second, it is possible to cluster the key aspects of the relevant articles in other ways. Therefore, our identified characteristics might neither be perfect nor do we claim their completeness.

Based on the insights of this paper, empirical research in companies can help to elaborate the characteristics, to conceptualize digital innovation culture and to identify management challenges in this area.

References

1. Bradley, J., Loucks, J., Macaulay, J., Noronha, A., Wade, M.: Digital Vortex. How Digital Disruption Is Redefining Industries. Global Center for Digital Business Transformation, Lausanne (2015)
2. Kao, J.J.: The art & discipline of business creativity. Strateg. Leadersh. **25**, 6–11 (1997)
3. Tushman, M.L.: Winning through innovation. Strateg. Leadersh. **25**, 14–19 (1997)
4. Rujirawanich, P., Addison, R., Smallman, C.: The effects of cultural factors on innovation in a Thai SME. Manag. Res. Rev. **34**, 1264–1279 (2011)
5. Tian, M., Deng, P., Zhang, Y., Salmador, M.P.: How does culture influence innovation? A systematic literature review. Manag. Decis. **56**, 1088–1107 (2018)
6. Fitzgerald, M., Kruschwitz, N., Bonnet, D., Welch, M.: Embracing digital technology. A new strategic imperative. MIT Sloan Manag. Rev. (2013)
7. Westerman, G., Bonnet, D., McAfee, A.: Leading Digital. Harvard Business Publishing, Boston (2014)
8. Nambisan, S., Lyytinen, K., Majchrzak, A., Song, M.: Digital innovation management: reinventing innovation management research in a digital world. Manag. Inf. Syst. Q. **41**, 223–238 (2017)
9. Hartl, E., Hess, T.: The role of cultural values for digital transformation. Insights from a Delphi study. In: 23rd Americas Conference on Information Systems. AMCIS 2017, pp. 1–10. Association for Information Systems, Atlanta (2017)
10. Duerr, S., Holotiuk, F., Wagner, H.-T., Beimborn, D., Weitzel, T.: What Is digital organizational culture? Insights from exploratory case studies. In: Bui, T. (ed.) 51st Hawaii International Conference on System Sciences. HICSS 2018, pp. 1–10. AIS Electronic Library, Hawaii (2018)

11. Wiedmann, K.-P., Lippold, A., Buxel, H.: Status quo der theoretischen und empirischen Innovationskulturforschung sowie Konstruktkonzeptualisierung des Phänomens Innovationskultur. der markt – Int. J. Mark. **47**, 43–60 (2008)
12. Wokurka, G., Banschbach, Y., Houlder, D., Jolly, R.: Digital culture: why strategy and culture should eat breakfast together. In: Oswald, G., Kleinemeier, M. (eds.) Shaping the Digital Enterprise, pp. 109–120. Springer, Cham (2017). https://doi.org/10.1007/978-3-319-409 67-2_5
13. Schein, E.H.: Organizational Culture and Leadership. Wiley, Hoboken (2004)
14. Benner, M.J., Tushman, M.L.: Reflections on the 2013 decade award—"exploitation, exploration, and process management: the productivity dilemma revisited" ten years later. AMR **40**, 497–514 (2015)
15. Libert, B., Beck, M., Wind, Y.: 7 questions to ask before your next digital transformation. Harvard Bus. Rev. (2016)
16. Yoo, Y., Lyytinen, K.J., Boland, R.J., Berente, N.: The next wave of digital innovation: opportunities and challenges. A report on the research workshop 'digital challenges in innovation research. SSRN J. 1–37 (2010)
17. vom Brocke, J., Cleven, A., Niehaves, B., Plattfaut, R., Riemer, K., Simons, A.: Reconstructing the giant. On the importance of rigour in documenting the literature search process. In: Newell, S., Whitley, E.A., Pouloudi, N., Wareham, J., Mathiassen, L. (eds.) 17th European Conference on Information Systems. ECIS 2009, pp. 2206–2217. Association for Information Systems, Atlanta (2009)
18. Frost, R., Lyons, K.: Service systems analysis methods and components. A systematic literature review. Serv. Sci. **9**, 219–234 (2017)
19. Wolfswinkel, J.F., Furtmueller, E., Wilderom, C.P.M.: Using grounded theory as a method for rigorously reviewing literature. Eur. J. Inf. Syst. **22**, 45–55 (2013)
20. Okoli, C., Schabram, K.: A Guide to conducting a systematic literature review of information systems research. SSRN Journal.(2010)
21. Bandara, W., Miskon, S., Fielt, E.: A systematic, tool-supported method for conducting literature reviews in information systems. In: 19th European Conference on Information Systems. ECIS 2011, p. 221. Association for Information Systems, Atlanta (2011)
22. Karimi, J., Walter, Z.: Corporate entrepreneurship, disruptive business model innovation adoption, and its performance. The case of the newspaper industry. Long Range Plann. **49**, 342–360 (2016)
23. Billington, M., Ellersgaard, B.: Unleashing disruptive leadership - teaching carpe diem! Bus. Educ. Innov. J. **9**, 133–138 (2017)
24. Bleicher, J., Stanley, H.: Digitization as a catalyst for business model innovation a three-step approach to facilitating economic success. J. Bus. Manag. 62–71 (2016)
25. da Rosa, S.C., Schreiber, D., Schmidt, S., Júnior, N.: Management practices that combine value cocreation and user experience. An analysis of the nubank startup in the Brazilian market. Revista de Gestão, Finanças e Contabilidade **7**, 22–43 (2017)
26. Dahl, A., Lawrence, J., Pierce, J.: Building an innovation community. Res. Technol. Manag. **54**, 19–27 (2011)
27. Frishammar, J., Richtnér, A., Brattström, A., Magnusson, M., Björk, J.: Opportunities and challenges in the new innovation landscape. Implications for innovation auditing and innovation management. Eur. Manag. J. **37**, 151–164 (2019)
28. Goduscheit, R.C., Faullant, R.: Paths toward radical service innovation in manufacturing companies. A service-dominant logic perspective. J. Prod. Innov. Manag. **35**, 701–719 (2018)
29. Govindarajan, V., Trimble, C.: Organizational DNA for strategic innovation. Calif. Manag. Rev. **47**, 47–76 (2005)
30. Ho, J.C., Chen, H.: Managing the disruptive and sustaining the disrupted. The case of Kodak and Fujifilm in the face of digital disruption. Rev. Policy Res. **35**, 352–371 (2018)

31. Igartua, I.J., Retegi, J., Ganzarain, J.: IM2, a maturity model for innovation in SMEs. Dirección y Organización, 42–49 (2018)
32. Karimi, J., Walter, Z.: The role of dynamic capabilities in responding to digital disruption. A factor-based study of the newspaper industry. J. Manag. Inf. Syst. **32**, 39–81 (2015)
33. Kayser, V., Nehrke, B., Zubovic, D.: Data science as an innovation challenge. from big data to value proposition. J. Technol. Manag. Innov. **8**, 16–25 (2018)
34. Luo, J., van de Ven, A., Jing, R., Jiang, Y.: Transitioning from a hierarchical product organization to an open platform organization. A Chinese case study. J. Organ. Des. **7**, 1–14 (2018)
35. Neus, A., Buder, F., Galdino, F.: Are you too successful to digitalize? How to fight innovation blindness. GfK-Mark. Intell. Rev. **9**, 31–35 (2017)
36. Quinton, S., Canhoto, A., Molinillo, S., Pera, R., Budhathoki, T.: Conceptualising a digital orientation. Antecedents of supporting SME performance in the digital economy. J. Strateg. Mark. **26**, 427–439 (2018)
37. Ravichandran, T.: Exploring the relationships between IT competence, innovation capacity and organizational agility. J. Strateg. Inf. Syst. **27**, 22–42 (2018)
38. Sousa, M.J., Wilks, D.: Sustainable skills for the world of work in the digital age. Syst. Res. Behav. Sci. **35**, 399–405 (2018)
39. Troilo, G., de Luca, L.M., Guenzi, P.: Linking data-rich environments with service innovation in incumbent firms. A conceptual framework and research propositions. J. Prod. Innov. Manag. **34**, 617–639 (2017)
40. Vey, K., Fandel-Meyer, T., Zipp, J.S., Schneider, C.: Learning & development in times of digital transformation. Facilitating a culture of change and innovation. Int. J. Adv. Corp. Learn. **10**, 22–32 (2017)
41. Zeng, J., Glaister, K.W.: Value creation from big data: looking inside the black box. Strateg. Organ. **16**, 105–140 (2018)
42. Dobni, C.B.: Measuring innovation culture in organizations. Eur. J. Innov. Manag. **11**, 539–559 (2008)

Enterprise Modelling and Information Systems Development

Introduction to the WI2021 Track: Enterprise Modelling and Information Systems Development

Peter Fettke[1,2] and Kristina Rosenthal[3]

[1] German Research Center for Artificial Intelligence (DFKI),
Saarbrücken, Germany
peter.fettke@dfki.de
[2] Saarland University, Saarbrücken, Germany
[3] Enterprise Modelling Research Group, University of Hagen, Hagen, Germany
kristina.rosenthal@fernuni-hagen.de

1 Track Description

The design and implementation of innovative information systems is a prerequisite for realizing new business models and represents an essential basis for the digital transformation. With a long tradition and undisputed contribution to the discipline of Business & Information Systems Engineering, enterprise modelling marks an important foundation as essential activity during information systems development and organizational analysis: Enterprise models are the central basis of methods of information system development and aim at the joint design of information systems and corresponding organizational action systems. In a world driven by digital technologies, enterprise modelling marks an essential expertise for understanding and shaping the digital enterprise.

The track *Enterprise Modelling and Information Systems Development* is a forum for current research results on conceptual modelling, enterprise modelling and information systems development. Current challenges in the corresponding fields of research are addressed, including in particular the use of conceptual models in the context of "innovative forms of organization, new business models, cooperation and interaction forms, which may reach considerable complexity and place high demands on the design of information systems" [1].

The Track Co-Chairs would like to thank the Associate Editors for their support and recommendations during the review process and the Reviewers who contributed their insights and advice.

2 Research Articles

The four accepted research articles in the track *Enterprise Modelling and Information Systems Development* (three full papers and one short paper) address current challenges in the corresponding research fields and take different methodical stances to advance our knowledge on enterprise modelling and information systems development.

2.1 How the Dimensions of Supply Chain are Reflected by Digital Twins: A State-of-the-Art Survey (Falk Freese, André Ludwig)

The first paper is motivated by the need for a higher level of transparency and visibility in supply chains. Building on the concept of digital twins, the paper follows a literature review approach to present a state of the art of digital twins for supply chains. The authors arrive at a classification scheme providing general dimensions for digital twins for supply chains and analyze the existing supply chain digital twinz accordingly.

2.2 Making a Case for Multi-level Reference Modeling – A Comparison of Conventional and Multi-level Language Architectures for Reference Modeling Challenges (Sybren de Kinderen, Monika Kaczmarek-Heß)

In the second paper, the authors aim to show the suitability of multi-level modeling for the challenges of reference modeling in comparison to conventional meta modeling approaches. As comparative scenario, a well-established reference model for smart grid cyber security is used. The authors conclude that multi-level modeling provides a natural candidate for the creation and use of reference models.

2.3 Notation-Agnostic Subprocess Modeling for Adaptive Case Management (Johannes Tenschert, Sebastian Dunzer, Martin Matzner)

The third paper proposes an approach combining structured process models for routine aspects of knowledge-intensive processes with ad-hoc activities and artifacts within the same context. The work is motivated by the requirements of knowledge workers who perform structured and ad-hoc activities requiring a single system of record. The approach has been implemented in the Adaptive Case Management System Pertuniti and is illustrated based on a scenario in the context of providing a lecture.

2.4 Capturing the Dynamics of Business Models: Towards the Integration of System Dynamics and Reference Modeling (Maren Stadtländer, Thorsten Schoormann, Ralf Knackstedt)

This short paper investigates the use of reference modeling for System Dynamics-based business model development. As first steps in a design science research project, the authors describe benefits and requirements, give a preliminary overview of existing System Dynamics models providing a basis for designing reference model components and present an outlook on their next steps.

Reference

1. Frank, U., Strecker, S., Fettke, P., vom Brocke, J., Becker, J., Sinz, E.: The research field "modeling business information systems": current challenges and elements of a future research agenda. Bus. Inf. Syst. Eng. **6**(1), 39–43 (2014)

How the Dimensions of Supply Chain are Reflected by Digital Twins: A State-of-the-Art Survey

Falk Freese[✉] and André Ludwig

Kuehne Logistics University, Hamburg, Germany
{falk.freese,andre.ludwig}@the-klu.org

Abstract. Transparency of supply chains is important. A more transparent supply chain would help to react in real-time by detecting and solving many issues e.g. production interruptions and delivery bottlenecks. A supply chain digital twin can help to increase the transparency and create an overall more robust and flexible supply chain. With real-time data streams from sensors, a digital twin allows simulation, monitoring, and controlling and provides information about its real-world counterpart. Based on a literature review approach, we analyze academic and industrial application and use cases to identify the current state-of-the-art of supply chain digital twins. Subsequently we develop a classification scheme for supply chain digital twins. The classification scheme provides six different dimensions like scope, actor, asset, flow reference object, performance measurement, and supply chain process that are relevant for digital twins in the context of supply chain.

Keywords: Digital twin · Supply chain · Literature review

1 Introduction

The Covid-19 global pandemic has shown how vulnerable supply chains are to external events. Industries are alarmed because of fears for their sensitive supply chains. Even a problem at a small supplier can cause issues for global corporations [1]. During the pandemic the supply of face masks became a problem. Within weeks, the Covid-19 global pandemic had turned an item that would otherwise cost just a few cents into one of the most sought-after goods worldwide. Countries around the world suddenly wanted to have many masks at the same time. The prices were climbing to astronomical heights, whether simple surgical masks or high-quality anti-virus masks, like N95 respirators. The same happened to medical ventilators that were needed for treating severe cases of the virus. Many more supply chains for all types of goods were interrupted [2]. A higher level of supply chain transparency and visibility would have helped to detect deviations faster and react on supply shortages in a shorter time frame. Also, predictions on consequences for downstream tiers and proactive countermeasures could be initiated earlier.

© The Author(s), under exclusive license to Springer Nature Switzerland AG 2021
F. Ahlemann et al. (Eds.): WI 2021, LNISO 48, pp. 325–341, 2021.
https://doi.org/10.1007/978-3-030-86800-0_23

Also beyond Covid-19 transparency is needed in supply chains in particular since they have become longer, larger, more dispersed and complex over the past 25 years [3]. Transparency provides a way to ensure that the supply chain reduces the risks to supply chain members and end users. These supply chain risks [4] include e.g. risk of community disruptions that impact supplier availability and productivity [3] or the risk of potential non-delivery loses [4]. In addition to reducing risk, transparency also enables members of the supply chain to trace products and to ensure accuracy [5]. An improved transparency and visibility enhance the supply chain performance. They allow high-quality supply chain information exchange resulting in high delivery quality [6]. The need for additional supply chain transparency has been identified and described in detail by numerous authors [7, 8]. They call for an investigation into how a company should use technology to enable greater visibility and transparency in the supply chain.

One of the most recent developments in providing increased transparency and visibility of products, services and processes is the concept of digital twins [9]. Digital twins have gained a lot of attention for multiple application areas [10]. Technologies like cyber physical systems with a large number of different sensors allow industrial Internet of Things devices connected to the internet to provide a constant stream of contextual data [11]. This data can be processed in real-time based on edge computing, in-memory databases as well as with particular algorithms and simulations [12]. Following Tao et al. [13], a digital twin describes a virtual replication of a product or process. The virtual replication as digital twin allows simulations and provides information about its real-world counterpart [13]. Companies adopt digital twins in order to gain transparency of their products and processes and in the end increase efficiency and effectivity of their business [14].

In this paper we take a look at the state-of-the-art of digital twins and their applications in the field of supply chain. Supply chain is an important application field for digital twins as transparency, prediction and coordination are urgently needed. While a number of companies have already started first implementations of digital twins for supply chains [15–17], the scientific literature of supply chain digital twins is currently scarce. A large amount of papers concerning the digital twin in general can already be found. Some papers focus on the manufacturing and production process of the supply chain [18–20]. However, to the best knowledge of the authors, none of them takes the whole supply chain into account. We address this research gap in our paper. We want to contribute to the understanding of opportunities and challenges of supply chain digital twins to guide future implementation decisions. Therefore, we answer the following research questions:

RQ1: What is the current state-of-the-art of supply chain digital twins?
RQ2: Which dimensions of supply chains should be reflected by digital twins?
RQ3: What are the existing implemented systems for supply chain digital twins?
RQ4: What are their design choices and technical characteristics?

In order to answer these questions, we follow a literature review approach. First, we review the existing scientific literature as well as industry publications about supply chain digital twins to investigate the type of research that has been conducted so far. Then, we analyze the different applications and use cases of supply chain digital twins. Based on the analyzed use cases we develop a classification scheme for supply chain digital twins. The classification scheme distinguishes between supply chain and digital twin dimensions. The supply chain dimensions are scope, actor, asset, flow reference object, performance measurement and supply chain process. The digital twin dimensions include purpose, creation time and connection. The classification scheme provides relevant implications for business and research. We contribute to the literature on digital transformation by analyzing the IT artifact of the digital twin. We contribute to research on the digital twin by analyzing the use of the digital twin in the specific context of the supply chain. Our study also contributes to practice by breaking down the relevant dimensions for digital twins in the supply chain.

The paper is structured as follows. First, the theoretical background of digital twins is outlined. Afterwards the methodical approach is described. Subsequently the articles and use cases from industry and academia are analyzed, followed by an outline of relevant dimensions of a classification scheme and a use case analysis. The paper ends with contributions including limitations and an outline for future research.

2 Theoretical Background

In the following chapter the theoretical background concerning digital twin is outlined. First, we look at definitions of supply chain and digital twin individually. Then we extract the state-of-the-art of supply chain digital twins from related surveys.

2.1 Supply Chain

A supply chain is a complex and dynamic system consisting of suppliers and customers. Companies depend on networks to satisfy customer needs [21, 22]. The company is a building block of this network. In the supply chain, companies are part of complex networks, because satisfying customer needs requires collaboration. The management of the supply chain entails the strategic coordination of traditional business functions and tactical decisions across these business functions. The goal is to improve the long-term performance of individual companies and the supply chain as a whole. In the simplest case the supply chain of a company only takes direct suppliers and direct customers into consideration. With increasing maturity of supply chain management, the scope is expanded up from raw material sourcing to different tiers of production, distribution, up to the final consumer. [23, 24]. The processes of the supply chain are described in the supply chain reference model (SCOR) [25]. It describes on a general level business processes that are performed within a company and between the players in a cross-company value chain. It includes the involved key processes of plan, source, make, deliver, (return) as well as flows of goods, information and payments.

2.2 Digital Twin

The idea of digital twins has been around since 1991 [26], but only the Internet of Things concept has promoted its implementation. In the historic context the concept of digital twins was coined first in the aviation industry. A twin is an identical manifestation of an object. Digital meaning that its twin is not an object of the real world but data saved in an information system. Glaessgen and Stargel [27] give the following definition: "A Digital Twin is an integrated multiphysics, multiscale, probabilistic simulation of an as-built vehicle or system that uses the best available physical models, sensor updates, fleet history, etc., to mirror the life of its corresponding flying twin." Ivanov et al. [9] define supply chain digital twin as a model that can represent the network state for any given moment in time and allow for complete end-to-end supply chain visibility to improve resilience and test contingency plans. The supply chain of digital twins covers the complete supply chain, from the supplier to production to customer including all intermediaries. The supply chain digital twin tracks all processes according to the SCOR model, as illustrated in Fig. 1. The first application was in product lifecycle management where the digital twin supported the product starting from its design phase till its usage phase [28]. The concept of digital twins was then extended for processes, like the manufacturing process [29].

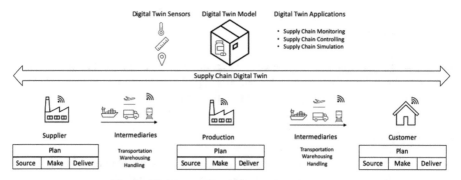

Fig. 1. SCOR model and supply chain digital twin

Digital twin technology has the potential of supporting different applications, such as providing real-time transparency (supply chain monitoring). Different technologies are part of a digital twin. A digital twin is using a combination of cyber physical systems, artificial intelligence and machine learning to create a digital copy of a product or process. The sensor data gathered from the physical products or processes, observed and analyzed in digital twins, can be connected and used for predictive maintenance [30]. Tao and Zhang [31] distinguish five aspects of key technologies. One aspect is the interconnection and interaction with the physical system. Multi-agent technologies and standardization technologies fall under this aspect. Another issue is the aspect of smart production and precious services based on the digital twin data. Service encapsulation and artificial intelligence are assigned to that aspect. Modeling, operation and verification form the third aspect of key technologies. The fourth aspect is operation and evolution of digital twins. Key technologies under this aspect are iterative optimization and real-time interaction and convergence. The last aspect is construction and management of digital twin data. All big data technologies fall under this aspect like data cluster storage, data cleaning, data integration and data fusion.

Digital twins are used in different areas of application from healthcare [32] to construction industry [33]. The area of supply chain for digital twins often focuses on the production part, like shop-floor digital twins [29]. Supply chain digital twins focus on the entire supply chain. They provide real-time data of products and processes in the supply chain and increase the transparency [34].

An example for a digital twin in the context of supply chain is a digital twin of shipments. Finnair Cargo, an air freight carrier, includes the contents of a package or container in its digital twin [35]. If an item is shipped a digital twin has already been created with by preexisting data with e.g. its geometry. Alternatively, the item data can be generated when preparing the shipment, using 3D scanning. The combination of product and packaging data could help companies improve efficiency by automating packaging selection and container packaging strategies to optimize usage and product protection. [35].

2.3 Related Surveys

The research that focuses specifically on supply chain digital twins is scare. Srai et al. [34] provide an overview by looking at three industry cases from pharmaceutical, organic food and precision agriculture. They derive possible attributes from those cases consisting of ambitions, scope, boundaries and infrastructure. The attribute scope is further divided in assets, unit ops, network configuration and multi-echelon inventory and service modelling. The attribute infrastructure is divided in platform technology, supply chain mapping tools and digital data acquisition management. In addition, they identify opportunities and challenges for the three industry cases. Opportunities include improved service quality, reliable authentication, digital platforms and resource efficiency. Challenges include end-to-end visibility, sensitivity of information, lack of agreed infrastructure, product-technology complexity and technology accessibility and skills [34]. The authors derive possible attributes of a supply chain digital twins from three industry cases. We include those industry cases in our analysis.

The literature focusing only on the manufacturing part of the supply chain for digital twins provides a larger variety of papers. Those papers focus on specific shop-floor digital twins. Tao and Zhang [31] provide in their paper "Digital Twin Shop-Floor: A New Shop-Floor Paradigm Towards Smart Manufacturing" a new concept for shop-floor digital twins. They identify five key technologies. The first key technology is the interconnection and interaction in the physical shop-floor and the second key technology the modeling, operation and verification of the virtual shop-floor. Another key technology is the construction and management of digital twin data as well as the operation and evolution of the digital twins. The fifth key technology is smart production and precious services based on the digital twin data. Tao and Zhang [31] subsequently identify challenges consisting of keeping adequate two-way connection between physical and virtual spaces. Another challenge is the need for high fidelity models on the digital twin side to provide a stable foundation for the physical object regards to variability, uncertainty and fuzziness. An additional challenge is the seamless integration of the digital twin in respect to the large amount of data [31].

Other research focuses on production and cyber physical systems [14, 18, 36]. Uhlemann et al. [37] develop a learning factory-based concept for digital twins demonstrating the potential of real time data acquisition in production systems. Ivanov et al. [9] focus on the ripple effect, resilience, and disruption risks by data-driven optimization, simulation, and visibility in the context of supply chain digital twins. In our paper we address the research gap for supply chain digital twins. Building on aforementioned literature we analyze applications and use cases from industry and academia and develop a classification scheme.

3 Methodology

In order to answer the question on the state-of-the-art of supply chain digital twin applications a literature study was conducted in the first quarter of 2020. First, we separated the technical approaches from the conceptual ones and analyzed the various applications and use cases. The results can be found in Sect. 4.1. A further objective of this study was to specify relevant supply chain dimensions and to develop a classification scheme upon existing supply chain digital twin research [9, 34, 38]. Two types of dimensions are relevant in our case, supply chain dimension and digital twin dimensions. They are summarized in Sects. 4.2. and 4.3. Finally, in Sect. 4.4 we assigned use cases to those dimensions and characteristics to identify the focus of the use cases.

We conducted our search in different steps to identify relevant peer-reviewed articles on supply chain digital twins. In the first step we conducted the snow-balling technique on the existing literature reviews on the subject. In the second step we searched in the following databases: Google Scholar, IEEE, ACM, ScienceDirect, Springer. We used combinations of the keywords: digital twin + supply chain. We extended the keywords by synonyms used for digital twins in industry: smart logistics, logistics intelligence. Both terms refer to similar technical concepts as supply chain digital twins and there is a large overlap between the different terms [39, 40]. In addition, we looked at similar concepts such as supply chain control tower and supply chain analytics. In the search for use cases from the industry we looked at university repositories, industry white papers and short technical descriptions on project landing pages. Many industry applications focus on specific digital twins features. We decided to include these articles as we consider that the information provided is a valuable use case.

In total, we obtained approximately 250 papers. To evaluate the search results, we defined inclusion and exclusion criteria for considering a paper or industry use case for our study. These criteria provide a broad foundation to select state-of-the-art papers and use cases. For a paper to be included in our result set, the title and abstract of the paper or the description of the use case must indicate that the work considers the application of digital twin technologies on some type of supply chain. Papers that were non-accessible or not available as full-paper documents were excluded from the result set. These criteria provide a broad foundation to select state-of-the-art papers and use cases. They comprise:

- Inclusion criteria 1: The paper should be published after 2010.
- Inclusion criteria 2: From the title and abstract of the paper or the description of the use case, it must be clear that the work considers the application of digital twin technologies on some type of supply chain.
- Exclusion criteria 1: Non-accessible paper or non-available full-paper document.

- Exclusion criteria 2: The length of paper is less than 4 pages.

There are possible limitations to our research methodology. However, we think that our approach has brought together the critical mass of applications and use cases on digital twins in supply chains that exists both in academia and industry, allowing us to carry out an in-depth analysis of the topic.

4 Analysis

First the applications and use cases are specified. Then the dimensions of supply chain and digital twin are described. Finally, the use cases are analyzed based on the dimensions.

4.1 Applications and Use Cases from Industry and Academia

In the following section we analyze the selected articles based on the research questions. We analyze 30 different applications from academia and industry that are outlined in Table 1.

Table 1. Supply chain digital twin applications and use cases

Authors	
Academia	Industry
Agostinho et al. 2016 [41]	Agility Insights, 2020 [42]
Arya, 2017 [43]	AnyLogistix, 2020 [44]
Glaessgen and Stargel 2012 [27]	Arm, 2020 [45]
Grabis et al. 2020 [46]	Bain & Company, 2020 [47]
Zhu et al. 2017 [48]	BearingPoint, 2020 [49]
Ivanov et al. 2019 [9]	Capgemini, 2020 [50]
Ivanov and Dolgui 2020 [51]	DB Schenker, 2020 [52]
Kunath and Winkler 2018 [53]	Deloitte, 2020 [54]
Lee et al. 2018 [55]	Deutsche Post DHL Group, 2019 [17]
Marmolejo-Saucedo 2020 [56]	Finnair Cargo, 2020 [35]
Moder et al. 2020 [57]	Kuehne + Nagel, 2016 [16]
Srai et al. 2019 [34]	LLamasoft, 2019 [58]
Trzuskawska-Grzesińska 2017 [59]	SAP, 2020 [60]
Zhuang et al. 2018 [36]	Solvoyo, 2020 [61]
Zsifkovits 2019 [62]	Team GmbH, 2020 [63]

The technology of the digital twin can have different development steps and different functionalities. Based on the focus of the application and the use case, different names for digital twin can be found in industry and academia, for example smart logistics or logistics intelligence [16].

4.2 Supply Chain Dimensions

Based on the use cases, we identify six supply chain dimensions that are relevant for digital twins to answer RQ2. The dimensions are derived from supply chain literature. We classify the different elements of the supply chain based on different dimensions and corresponding characteristics as outlined in Table 2. Based on the relevant dimensions of supply chain, we analyze the use cases accordingly.

Table 2. Classification scheme of supply chain in relation to digital twins

Dimension	Characteristics
Scope [64]	Internal supply chain, external supply chain
Actor [65]	Shippers, freight forwarders, manufacturers
Asset [66]	Assets at network nodes (i.e. warehouses, plants, handling equipment), assets at network links (i.e. vehicles, trucks, trains, containers)
Flow reference object [67]	Goods (i.e. stock), information (i.e. status data, stock levels), finances (i.e. credits, invoices), liabilities (i.e. bill of lading)
Performance measurement [68]	Costs, quality, resource utilization, flexibility, visibility, trust, innovativeness
Supply chain process [23]	Demand planning, procurement process, production planning, production, warehouse and distribution

Scope: Scope describes the different reach of the digital twin, if the digital twin is just for the internal supply chain of a company or if it is extended to external companies' supply chain. We observed that in most use cases, the focus is on the internal supply chain. With an internal supply chain, the focus is only within one company, therefore interfaces to other companies do not have to be considered. With external supply chains there exists a cross-company digital twin. The data from different companies must be integrated from different information systems. In addition, the companies must share their data with the other companies.

Actor: Actors in the supply chain are decision makers pursuing different objectives. In the analyzed use cases the different actors are not explicitly named. But based on different process steps different actors are involved. Actors include shippers who transport goods from one location to another. In addition, there are manufacturers who are responsible for the production of the goods.

Asset: Assets in the supply chain context describe inter alia products and vehicles. The asset dimension of supply chain digital twins refers to any kind of asset. They interact between the various supply chain processes. This dimension also includes other assets such as production plants and machinery. In the investigated use cases a lot of different assets are elaborated in detail with specific digital twin solutions for specific assets. For example, digital twins for ships were used to monitor their location [16].

Flow Reference Object: Flow reference objects describe objects like goods, information and financial values. Flow reference objects move along the process stages of the supply chain. Digital twins consist of physical objects and corresponding information. In the uses cases the flow reference objects goods and information were the main focus. Financial values were not part of the use cases.

Performance Measurement: The dimension of performance measurement describes the criteria to evaluate supply chain performance. The most common performance measurements are cost and quality. Other performance measures are resource utilization, flexibility, visibility, trust and innovativeness [68]. The analyzed use cases focus on cost, quality and visibility. Digital twin applications focus on cost-reduction targets. Digital twins can accelerate the quality [17]. Another important performance measurement for digital twins is visibility. The digital twin enhances the visibility of a process. Enhanced visibility helps in providing a better basis for decision-making and consequently making better short-, mid- and long-term decisions [17, 44].

Supply Chain Process: In the investigated use cases, different cases for specific supply chain processes were identified. There are supply chain digital twins specific for shipment processes or warehouse processes. The production process accounts for a large number of use cases. Supply chain digital twins for processes demand planning or procurement are non-existent.

4.3   Digital Twin Dimensions

We combine our findings with the digital twin dimensions of purpose, creation time and connection from Enders and Hoßbach [69] to assign design choices and technical characteristics to the analyzed use cases.

Purpose: The purpose of digital twins can be divided into three main characteristics: simulation, monitoring and control [69].

Simulation is a procedure for the analysis of systems that are too complex for theoretical or formulaic treatment. Real-time analytics analysis the data stream in real-time and allows fast reaction when deviations occur. In the simulation use case, the behavior of physical objects can be reproduced in a virtual space, therefore planning or optimizing products or processes are possible without having to rely on the physical object. Simulation can be used to calculate, when a product reaches an objective [69].

The monitoring use case includes all applications focusing on the representation of the current state and its interpretation of a physical object [69]. This use case describes the visibility aspect of supply chain digital twins and summarizes the different protection applications.

The control use case describes applications, where supply chain digital twins directly influence products or manufacturing assets [69]. One important and common use case is the traceability of different assets. Track and trace allow to know the exact position of a product in real-time through the flow of the supply chain. If the product deviates from predefined factors, appropriate measures can be taken. In the field of logistics, it can be used to track and trace the transportation of goods. It allows to know when a good will reach a customer. Containers on ships or airfreight on planes as well as items on trucks and trains can be tracked and traced [27]. The tracking of single packages or reusable containers provides a use case [17, 52].

Creation Time: Creation time of a digital twin describes if the digital twin was created before or after the corresponding physical object. Digital twins that are created before the physical twin are often used in the development of new products. They are called digital twin prototypes [70]. Digital twins that are created after the physical object are called digital twin instances. In the context of supply chain digital twins in all analyzed use cases the creation time of the digital twin is after the physical twin creation.

Connection: Enders and Hoßbach [69] divide digital twins based on the connection in no connection, one-directional or bi-directional digital twins. This equals the distinction from Kritzinger et al. [19] into digital models, digital shadows and digital twins. The analyzed use cases resemble the findings from Enders and Hoßbach [69]. Most applications that are available use one-directional connection.

4.4 Digital Twin Use Cases Analysis

We analyze the different use cases by dimensions to investigate the existing implemented systems for supply chain digital twins and analyze their design choices and technical characteristics. Figure 2 displays the dimensions and its characteristics. It shows the focus of the state-of-the-art use cases. The bubble size represents the number of use cases per characteristic, also given in brackets.

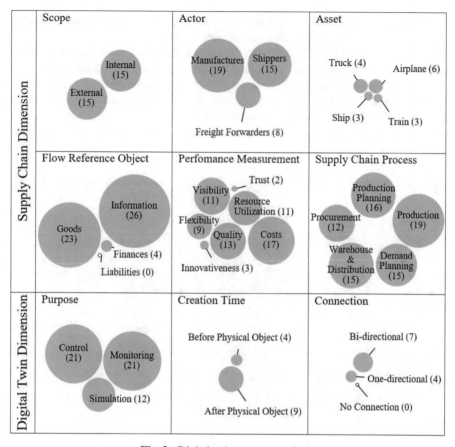

Fig. 2. Digital twin use case analysis

The main focus of the use cases are goods and information in the supply chain dimension flow reference object. This confirms that the information provided by sensors is the most important component of digital twins. Since these digital twins relate to specific goods in the supply chain, the connection between information and goods is usually covered in the use cases. Furthermore, this analysis shows that information and goods are the most important factors both in research for academic use cases as well as in industry use cases.

The digital twin dimension purpose with simulation, monitoring and control is mostly addressed in the use cases. An important reason for introducing digital twins in the supply chain context is the monitoring and controlling of processes. Our analysis shows that in addition, simulation remains an important reason, but is of less importance in the supply chain context. For example, containers along the supply chain are often monitored in relation to their GPS position or temperature. Rarely addressed are liabilities and responsibilities as characteristics of the supply chain digital twin. In particular elements of the bill of lading such as confirmation of loading, evidence of the terms of contract of carriage and documents of title to goods must be represented by supply chain digital twin as they constitute crucial responsibilities in international trade. They ensure that exporters receive payment and importers receive the goods.

So far, in supply chain digital twins, the focus is on information and goods. Financial flows are rarely considered and integrated into the digital twin. With regard to the digital twin dimension connection most use cases utilize bi-directional connections. The connection of digital twins is often not directly addressed in the use cases. On the one hand, sensors deliver data from the object to the digital twin, on the other hand, the digital twin delivers information back to the object. This bi-directional connection was only mentioned in few use cases.

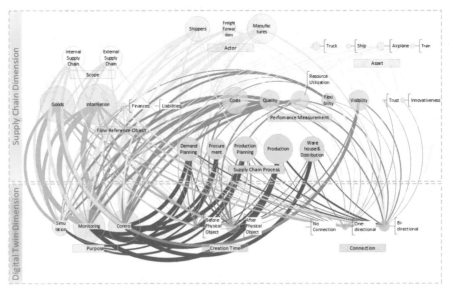

Fig. 3. Cross-dimension data map

Figure 3 shows the relationship between the different dimensions using a data map. The bubble size corresponds to the number of use cases. The link shows how often the different dimensions are connected to each other. This can be determined from the thickness of the links. The strongest links are between goods and information and monitoring and controlling. Currently, mainly observational aspects are being addressed with supply chain digital twins. There are hardly any use cases with simulation and planning aspects. The aspect of financial obligations and duties plays an important role in this context and is rarely considered.

Another strong link exists between the digital twin dimension purpose and the supply chain dimension supply chain processes. The individual supply chain processes such as demand planning, procurement, production planning, production and warehouse are often mentioned in connection with monitoring and controlling in the use cases. This shows the importance of the processes in relation to digital twins. The digital twins are integrated within the supply chain processes and provide its purpose.

5   Contribution, Limitation, and Future Research

Based on a systematic literature review, we identified and analyzed different applications and use cases for supply chain digital twins. We analyzed the existing research approaches on the subject of digital twins for supply chains. We developed a classification scheme with the relevant supply chain dimensions to answer the question which elements of the supply chain can be represented by digital twins. We analyzed in detail the existing supply chain digital twins. In addition, we analyzed their design choices and technical characteristics using dimensions of digital twin applications from Enders and Hoßbach [69].

Supply chain digital twins are just in their infancy. Although the concept of digital twins has been around for many years the use of supply chain digital twins is quite new. Only in the last year researchers and practitioners started to cultivate this topic. In our paper we provide an overview of these first approaches and categorize them based on relevant supply chain dimensions. Building on previous supply chain digital twin research [9, 34, 38] we provide general dimensions for digital twins in the context of supply chain. In addition, we contribute by providing an overview of different supply chain digital twin application and use cases and outline the characteristics that are frequently or rarely used.

This paper has limitations as the literature search was limited to Google Scholar, IEEE, ACM, ScienceDirect and Springer with defined keywords. Even though a vast number of use cases were identified, additional use cases that could not be found with the used search engines and keywords may exist. For example, specific terms which are only used in individual industries, i.e. food tracing in agriculture, may be a reason why use cases were not discovered. Furthermore, use cases may exist that have not yet been published in scientific papers or reported by companies.

Regarding the analysis of the use cases there is a threat of validity in the evaluation of the individual use cases. The assignment of the individual use cases to the dimensions was carried out by two independent domain experts, however there is still the risk of subjective assessments leading into a threat of validity.

The field of supply chain digital twin provides great opportunities for further research. Further research can build on theses dimension and identify and analyze design goals, interoperability and inter-organizational integration issues. We call for future work to deeper investigate the different supply chain digital twin dimension. Especially the under-represented characteristics need further investigation, e.g. how can the financial aspects be represented in supply chain digital twins.

References

1. Choi, T.Y., Rogers, D., Vakil, B.: Coronavirus is a wake-up call for supply chain management. https://hbr.org/2020/03/coronavirus-is-a-wake-up-call-for-supply-chain-management. Accessed 16 Apr 2020
2. Carter, S.L.: Sold-out coronavirus N95 face masks offer lesson in price gouging – Bloomberg. https://www.bloomberg.com/opinion/articles/2020-01-31/sold-out-coronavirus-n95-face-masks-offer-lesson-in-price-gouging. Accessed 16 Apr 2020

3. Kashmanian, R.M.: Building greater transparency in supply chains to advance sustainability. Environ. Qual. Manag. **26**, 73–104 (2017). https://doi.org/10.1002/tqem.21495
4. Wu, T., Blackhurst, J., Chidambaram, V.: A model for inbound supply risk analysis. Comput. Ind. **57**, 350–365 (2006). https://doi.org/10.1016/j.compind.2005.11.001
5. Zelbst, P.J., Green, K.W., Sower, V.E., Bond, P.L.: The impact of RFID, IIoT, and blockchain technologies on supply chain transparency. J. Manuf. Technol. Manag. **31**, 441–457 (2019). https://doi.org/10.1108/JMTM-03-2019-0118
6. Bartlett, P.A., Julien, D.M., Baines, T.S.: Improving supply chain performance through improved visibility. Int. J. Logist. Manag. **18**, 294–313 (2007). https://doi.org/10.1108/095 74090710816986
7. Sodhi, M.M.S., Tang, C.S.: Research opportunities in supply chain transparency. Prod. Oper. Manag. **28**, 2946–2959 (2019). https://doi.org/10.1111/poms.13115
8. Kache, F., Seuring, S.: Challenges and opportunities of digital information at the intersection of big data analytics and supply chain management. Int. J. Oper. Prod. Manag. **37**, 10–36 (2017). https://doi.org/10.1108/IJOPM-02-2015-0078
9. Ivanov, D., Dolgui, A., Das, A., Sokolov, B.: Digital supply chain twins: managing the ripple effect, resilience, and disruption risks by data-driven optimization, simulation, and visibility. In: Ivanov, D., Dolgui, A., Sokolov, B. (eds.) Handbook of Ripple Effects in the Supply Chain. ISORMS, vol. 276, pp. 309–332. Springer, Cham (2019). https://doi.org/10.1007/978-3-030-14302-2_15
10. Gartner: Gartner Top 10 strategic technology trends for 2018 - smarter with Gartner. https://www.gartner.com/smarterwithgartner/gartner-top-10-strategic-technology-trends-for-2020/. Accessed 11 Feb 2020
11. Rajkumar, R., Lee, I., Sha, L., Stankovic, J.: Cyber-physical systems: the next computing revolution. In: Proceeding - Design Automation Conference, pp. 731–736 (2010). https://doi.org/10.1145/1837274.1837461
12. Lasi, H., Fettke, P., Kemper, H.-G., Feld, T., Hoffmann, M.: Industry 4.0. Bus. Inf. Syst. Eng. **6**(4), 239–242 (2014). https://doi.org/10.1007/s12599-014-0334-4
13. Tao, F., Cheng, J., Qi, Q., Zhang, M., Zhang, H., Sui, F.: Digital twin-driven product design, manufacturing and service with big data. Int. J. Adv. Manuf. Technol. **94**(9–12), 3563–3576 (2017). https://doi.org/10.1007/s00170-017-0233-1
14. Negri, E., Fumagalli, L., Macchi, M.: A review of the roles of digital twin in CPS-based production systems. Procedia Manuf. **11**, 939–948 (2017). https://doi.org/10.1016/j.promfg.2017.07.198
15. McKinsey: Improving warehouse operations–digitally—McKinsey. https://www.mckinsey.com/business-functions/operations/our-insights/improving-warehouse-operations-digitally. Accessed 26 Feb 2020
16. Kuehne + Nagel: Kuehne + Nagel pioneers new application of logistics market intelligence as part of its digital evolution. https://newsroom.kuehne-nagel.com/kuehne--nagel-pioneers-new-application-of-logistics-market-intelligence-as-part-of-its-digital-evolution/. Accessed 26 Feb 2020
17. Deutsche Post DHL Group: Deutsche post DHL group—Jun 27, 2019: DHL trend report: implementation of digital twins to significantly improve logistics operations. https://www.dpdhl.com/en/media-relations/press-releases/2019/dhl-trend-report-implementation-digital-twins-significantly-improve-logistics-operations.html. Accessed 26 Feb 2020
18. Uhlemann, T.H.J., Schock, C., Lehmann, C., Freiberger, S., Steinhilper, R.: The digital twin: demonstrating the potential of real time data acquisition in production systems. Procedia Manuf. **9**, 113–120 (2017). https://doi.org/10.1016/j.promfg.2017.04.043

19. Kritzinger, W., Karner, M., Traar, G., Henjes, J., Sihn, W.: Digital twin in manufacturing: a categorical literature review and classification. IFAC-PapersOnLine **51**, 1016–1022 (2018). https://doi.org/10.1016/j.ifacol.2018.08.474

20. Lim, K.Y.H., Zheng, P., Chen, C.-H.: A state-of-the-art survey of digital twin: techniques, engineering product lifecycle management and business innovation perspectives. J. Intell. Manuf. **31**(6), 1313–1337 (2019). https://doi.org/10.1007/s10845-019-01512-w

21. Lummus, R.R., Vokurka, R.J.: Defining supply chain management: a historical perspective and practical guidelines Introduction to supply chain concepts definition of supply chain. Ind. Manag. Data Syst. **99**, 11–17 (1997)

22. Beamon, B.M.: Supply chain design and analysis: models and methods. Int. J. Prod. Econ. **55**, 281–294 (1998). https://doi.org/10.1016/S0925-5273(98)00079-6

23. Mentzer, J.T., Keebler, J.S., Nix, N.W., Smith, C.D., Zacharia, Z.G.: Defining supply chain management. J. Bus. **22**, 1–25 (2001)

24. Janvier-James, A.M.: A new introduction to supply chains and supply chain management: definitions and theories perspective. Int. Bus. Res. **5**, 194–208 (2011). https://doi.org/10.5539/ibr.v5n1p194

25. Huan, S.H., Sheoran, S.K., Wan, G.: A review and analysis of supply chain operations reference (SCOR) model. Supply Chain Manag. **9**, 23–29 (2004). https://doi.org/10.1108/135985 40410517557

26. Gelernter, D.H.: Mirror Worlds: Or, the Day Software Puts the Universe in a Shoebox… How It will Happen and What It will Mean. Oxford University Press, Oxford (1991)

27. Glaessgen, E.H., Stargel, D.S.: The digital twin paradigm for future NASA and U.S. Air force vehicles. In: Collection of Technical Papers - AIAA/ASME/ASCE/AHS/ASC Structures, Structural Dynamics and Materials Conference, pp. 1–14 (2012).https://doi.org/10.2514/6. 2012-1818.

28. Grieves, M.W.: Virtually intelligent product systems: digital and physical twins. (2019). https://doi.org/10.2514/5.9781624105654.0175.0200

29. Qi, Q., Tao, F., Zuo, Y., Zhao, D.: Digital twin service towards smart manufacturing. Procedia CIRP **72**, 237–242 (2018). https://doi.org/10.1016/j.procir.2018.03.103

30. Liu, Z., Meyendorf, N., Mrad, N.: The role of data fusion in predictive maintenance using digital twin. In: AIP Conference Proceedings, 1949 (2018). https://doi.org/10.1063/1.503 1520

31. Tao, F., Zhang, M.: Digital twin shop-floor: a new shop-floor paradigm towards smart manufacturing. IEEE Access **5**, 20418–20427 (2017). https://doi.org/10.1109/ACCESS.2017.275 6069

32. Feng, Y., Chen, X., Zhao, J.: Create the individualized digital twin for noninvasive precise pulmonary healthcare. Significances Bioeng. Biosci. **1**, 1–5 (2018). https://doi.org/10.31031/sbb.2018.01.000507

33. Kaewunruen, S., Rungskunroch, P., Welsh, J.: A digital-twin evaluation of net zero energy building for existing buildings. Sustainability **11**, 1–22 (2018). https://doi.org/10.3390/su1 1010159

34. Srai, J.S., Settanni, E., Tsolakis, N., Aulakh, P.K.: Supply chain digital twins : opportunities and challenges beyond the hype, 26–27 (2019)

35. FInnair Cargo: Data Sharing. https://cargo.finnair.com/en/finnair-cargo-is-helping-spearh ead-a-revolutionary-new-data-sharing-standard-called-one-record-1784328. Accessed 24 Aug 2020

36. Zhuang, C., Liu, J., Xiong, H.: Digital twin-based smart production management and control framework for the complex product assembly shop-floor. Int. J. Adv. Manuf. Technol. **96**(1–4), 1149–1163 (2018). https://doi.org/10.1007/s00170-018-1617-6

37. Uhlemann, T.H.J., Lehmann, C., Steinhilper, R.: The digital twin: realizing the cyber-physical production system for industry 4.0. Procedia CIRP **61**, 335–340 (2017). https://doi.org/10.1016/j.procir.2016.11.152

38. Ivanov, D., Dolgui, A.: New disruption risk management perspectives in supply chains: digital twins, the ripple effect, and resileanness. IFAC-PapersOnLine **52**, 337–342 (2019). https://doi.org/10.1016/j.ifacol.2019.11.138

39. Uckelmann, D.: A definition approach to smart logistics. In: Balandin, S., Moltchanov, D., Koucheryavy, Y. (eds.) NEW2AN 2008. LNCS, vol. 5174, pp. 273–284. Springer, Heidelberg (2008). https://doi.org/10.1007/978-3-540-85500-2_28

40. Wang, Y., Caron, F., Vanthienen, J., Huang, L., Guo, Y.: Acquiring logistics process intelligence: methodology and an application for a Chinese bulk port. Expert Syst. Appl. **41**, 195–209 (2014). https://doi.org/10.1016/j.eswa.2013.07.021

41. Agostinho, C., et al.: Towards a sustainable interoperability in networked enterprise information systems: trends of knowledge and model-driven technology. Comput. Ind. **79**, 64–76 (2016). https://doi.org/10.1016/j.compind.2015.07.001

42. Agility Insights: What is a Supply Chain Control Tower?. https://www.agility.com/insights/smart-shipping/what-is-a-supply-chain-control-tower/. Accessed 25 Aug 2020

43. Arya, V., Sharma, P., Singh, A.: An exploratory study on supply chain analytics applied to spare parts supply chain. **24**, 1571–1580 (2017). https://doi.org/10.1108/BIJ-04-2016-0053

44. AnyLogistix: Supply Chain Digital Twins. https://www.anylogistix.com. Accessed 02 Aug 2020

45. Logistics – Arm. https://www.arm.com/solutions/logistics. Accessed 25 Aug 2020

46. Grabis, J., Stirna, J., Zdravkovic, J.: Capability management in resilient ICT supply chain ecosystems. In: ICEIS 2020 – Proceedings of 22nd International Conference on Enterprise Information Systems, vol. 2, pp. 393–400 (2020). https://doi.org/10.5220/0009573603930400

47. Bain & Company: Supply chain control towers: getting to the promised land. https://www.bain.com/insights/supply-chain-control-towers-getting-to-the-promised-land/. Accessed 02 Aug 2020

48. Zhu, S., Song, J., Hazen, B.T., Lee, K., Cegielski, C.: How supply chain analytics enables operational supply chain transparency: an organizational information processing theory perspective. **48**, 47–68 (2017). https://doi.org/10.1108/IJPDLM-11-2017-0341

49. BearingPoint: Log360 – Der Digital Twin Ihrer Supply Chain—BearingPoint Deutschland. https://www.bearingpoint.com/de-de/unser-erfolg/insights/log360-digital-twin-supply-chain/. Accessed 23 Apr 2020

50. Capgemini: Global supply chain control towers achieving end-to-end supply chain visibility. https://www.capgemini.com/wp-content/uploads/2017/07/Global_Supply_Chain_Control_Towers.pdf. Accessed 25 Aug 2020

51. Ivanov, D., Dolgui, A.: A digital supply chain twin for managing the disruption risks and resilience in the era of Industry 4.0. Prod. Plan. Contr. (2020)

52. DB Schenker: Verpackungsberatung und –entwicklung. https://www.dbschenker.com/de-de/produkte/verpackungssysteme/verpackungsberatung-und--entwicklung. Accessed 02 Apr 2020

53. Kunath, M., Winkler, H.: Integrating the digital twin of the manufacturing system into a decision support system for improving the order management process. Procedia CIRP **72**, 225–231 (2018). https://doi.org/10.1016/j.procir.2018.03.192

54. Deloitte Deutschland: Supply chain control tower. https://www2.deloitte.com/de/de/pages/operations/articles/supply-chain-control-tower.html. Accessed 25 Aug 2020

55. Lee, C.K.M., Lv, Y., Ng, K.K.H., Ho, W., Choy, K.L.: Design and application of internet of things-based warehouse management system for smart logistics. Int. J. Prod. Res. **56**, 2753–2768 (2018). https://doi.org/10.1080/00207543.2017.1394592

56. Marmolejo-Saucedo, J.A.: Design and development of digital twins: a case study in supply chains. Mob. Netw. Appl. **25**(6), 2141–2160 (2020). https://doi.org/10.1007/s11036-020-015 57-9
57. Moder, P., Ehm, H., Ramzy, N.: Digital twin for plan and make using semantic web technologies – extending the JESSI/SEMATECH MIMAC standard to the digital reference. In: Keil, S., Lasch, R., Lindner, F., Lohmer, J. (eds.) EADTC 2018-2019. LNEE, vol. 670, pp. 24–32. Springer, Cham (2020). https://doi.org/10.1007/978-3-030-48602-0_3
58. LLamasoft: The digital supply chain twin – an emerging trend to reveal interconnected insights. https://llamasoft.com/the-digital-supply-chain-twin-an-emerging-trend-to-reveal-interconnected-insights/. Accessed 23 Apr 2020
59. Trzuskawska-Grzesińska, A.: Control towers in supply chain management – past and future. J. Econ. Manag. **27**, 114–133 (2017). https://doi.org/10.22367/jem.2017.27.07
60. SAP: Software und Technologie von SAP für digitale Zwillinge. https://www.sap.com/germany/products/digital-supply-chain/digital-twin.html. Accessed 23 Apr 2020
61. Solvoyo: Digital twin is an old idea - just new to supply chain—supply chain analytics, planning & optimization software. https://www.solvoyo.com/digital-twin-supply-chain/. Accessed 23 Apr 2020
62. Zsifkovits, H., Industrielogistik, L., Leoben, M.: Smart Logistics – Technologiekonzepte und Potentiale. **164**, 42–45 (2019). https://doi.org/10.1007/s00501-018-0806-9
63. TEAM GmbH: Logistics intelligence von TEAM - KPI: analyse von Daten, Kennzahlen-Generierung in der Intralogistik. https://www.team-pb.de/logistics-intelligence/. Accessed 25 Aug 2020
64. Barratt, M., Barratt, R.: Exploring internal and external supply chain linkages: evidence from the field. J. Oper. Manag. **29**, 514–528 (2011). https://doi.org/10.1016/j.jom.2010.11.006
65. Giannoccaro, I., Pontrandolfo, P.: Supply chain coordination by revenue sharing contracts. Int. J. Prod. Econ. **89**, 131–139 (2004). https://doi.org/10.1016/S0925-5273(03)00047-1
66. Mason, S.J., Ribera, P.M., Farris, J.A., Kirk, R.G.: Integrating the warehousing and transportation functions of the supply chain. Transp. Res. Part E Logist. Transp. Rev. **39**, 141–159 (2003). https://doi.org/10.1016/S1366-5545(02)00043-1
67. Pfohl, H.-C., Gomm, M.: Supply chain finance: optimizing financial flows in supply chains. Logist. Res. **1**(3–4), 149–161 (2009). https://doi.org/10.1007/s12159-009-0020-y
68. Chan, F.T.S.: Performance measurement in a supply chain. Int. J. Adv. Manuf. Technol. **21**, 534–548 (2003). https://doi.org/10.1109/INDIN.2008.4618224
69. Enders, M.R., Hoßbach, N.: Dimensions of digital twin applications-a literature review dimensions of digital twin applications-a literature review completed research. In: Twenty-Fifth Americas Conference on Information Systems, Cancun, pp. 1–10 (2019)
70. Kahlen, F.-J., Flumerfelt, S., Alves, A. (eds.): Transdisciplinary Perspectives on Complex Systems. Springer, Cham (2017). https://doi.org/10.1007/978-3-319-38756-7

Making a Case for Multi-level Reference Modeling – A Comparison of Conventional and Multi-level Language Architectures for Reference Modeling Challenges

Sybren de Kinderen[(✉)] and Monika Kaczmarek-Heß

Faculty of Business Administration and Economics, Research Group Information Systems and Enterprise Modelling, Institute for Computer Science and Business Information Systems (ICB), University of Duisburg-Essen, Essen, Germany
{sybren.dekinderen,monika.kaczmarek-hess}@uni-due.de

Abstract. As a continuation of our earlier work, in this paper we focus on the suitability of multi-level modeling for the creation and use of reference models. Specifically, we first discuss known challenges of reference modeling. Then, using the UML (for conventional meta modeling) and the FMML^X (for multi-level modeling) as language architectures of choice, we show how conventional meta modeling contributes to challenges of reference modeling, and how the added flexibility and expressiveness of multi-level modeling can address these. We use an excerpt of NISTIR 7628, a well-established reference model for smart grid cyber security, as an illustrative scenario.

Keywords: Reference modeling · Multi-level modeling · Comparison

1 Introduction

Reference models, being conceptual models, abstract away from one specific organization, and instead focus on characteristics common to many organizations, within or across one or more industries and/or application domains [1, 2]. Reference models are created to provide so-called best practices for particular domains/scenarios [3], and as such hold several promises, e.g., (1) fostering reuse, cf. [1, 4], meaning that instead developing models from scratch, one can capitalize on already encoded expertise, and (2) fostering a shared domain understanding, cf. [1, 5], by providing a common semantic reference system [1] to stakeholders.

Those promises express themselves in reference modeling still being a topic of active research, e.g., [6–9], and in particular, in the design and adoption of reference models for various domains, cf. [1]. A relatively recent example of such a domain is the electricity sector, where reference models such as NISTIR 7628 have been proposed, being a logical reference model for smart grid cyber security [10, 11]. Nevertheless, there are several challenges associated with, both, the design and use of a reference model. As we discuss in Sect. 2.1, these challenges include finding a balance between *generality* and *specificity*,

© The Author(s), under exclusive license to Springer Nature Switzerland AG 2021
F. Ahlemann et al. (Eds.): WI 2021, LNISO 48, pp. 342–358, 2021.
https://doi.org/10.1007/978-3-030-86800-0_24

supporting *variability*, and consistent *adaptation* of a reference model. As we discuss in our earlier work [12], while these challenges have been already reported a while ago, they still play a pertinent role in recent reference models, like the mentioned NISTIR 7628.

In this paper, we argue that the mentioned reference modeling challenges are partially related to the characteristics of the modeling languages used to create and disseminate reference models. Especially, we show how these challenges arise for reference models that rely on conventional meta modeling (next to the afore- mentioned NISTIR 7628, these include, e.g., UML-CI for critical infrastructure modeling [13], and E-MEMO for e-commerce scenarios [14]). Conventional meta modeling, of which UML class diagrams [15] are a prominent exemplar, has not been natively designed with classification levels in mind [16], and (in keeping with its basis in object-orientation) maintains a strict separation between types and instances. As such, as we show in Sect. 3.2, conventional meta modeling does not *naturally* lends itself well to expressing domain hierarchies with different levels of classification, while this is very much of importance to reference modeling. While mechanisms such as generalization/specialization, and specific to the UML, redefinition and default values, can be partly used, still redundancies and inconsistencies of reference models remain an issue. Also, in keeping with [16], using conventional meta modeling leads to accidental complexity of reference models, in the sense that their complexity increases not due to the complexity of the domain one is modeling, but rather due to the underlying language (architecture) that is being used. Especially, this expresses itself in the use of multiple abstraction mechanisms where one should suffice, like with the use of generalization/specialization within the abstraction level meant for language specification (and so, one is "overloading the level" [16]), or the use of redefinition plus default values, where in principle instantiation can suffice.

Additionally, we argue that the application of a relatively novel language architecture, namely a multi-level language architecture, contributes to addressing these challenges. Multi-level modeling is an emerging trend that accounts for multiple, i.e., more than one, levels of classification within one single body of model content [17, 18]. As we explain in more detail in Sect. 4.1, a multi-level modeling language architecture offers expressiveness and flexibility that naturally fit with the idea of reference models, by capitalizing on mechanisms such as a relaxed type/instance dichotomy, or deferred instantiation [18].

As such, the purpose of this paper is to make a case for multi-level reference modeling, with a focus on comparing a reference model as created with conventional meta modeling, with the same reference model as created through multi-level modeling. To this end we compare a reference model as created with conventional meta modeling (using UML), with the same reference model created using a multi-level language architecture (using Flexible Meta Modeling and Execution Language (FMML^x) [18]). We perform this comparison in the light of a set of well-established reference model challenges, as reported in [12]. As a running scenario, we use an excerpt of a smart cyber security reference model by [10, 11], and, building on our previous work, the multi-level cyber security reference model.

As already mentioned, this paper is a continuation of earlier work. In [12], we discussed typical challenges regarding the creation and use of reference models, and showed how multi-level modeling, as a language architecture, can help address these. However, for the presented challenges a systematic comparison of multi-level modeling to conventional meta-modeling is missing. This leads to unresolved issues like the possibility of using subtyping, or power types, to address reference model challenges while using conventional meta modeling. The paper at hand is meant to address this gap.

The paper is structured as follows. In Sect. 2 we provide a background on reference models, recap reference model challenges from earlier work, and introduce the smart grid cyber security reference model that is used for illustration purposes for the remainder of the paper. In Sect. 3 we subsequently discuss the extent to which conventional meta modeling can address reference modeling challenges and discuss its limitations. Subsequently, in Sect. 4, we introduce multi-level modeling, and show how it can be used to overcome the limitations of conventional meta modeling. Section 5 concludes with the final remarks.

2 Reference Modeling

2.1 Reference Models and Challenges in Their Creation and Usage

Although a common definition of a reference model has not been established yet, cf. [3, 6–8], it is usually understood as a special type of an information model. From the variety of reference model definitions, cf. [1, 5, 19, 20], in this paper we adopt the definition from Thomas [19, p. 1]: "[r]eference models are reusable representations of abstract know-how for a given application domain". This definition emphasizes (i) abstraction of a reference model, in the sense of moving beyond one particular application context [1], as well as (ii) a reference model targeting a class of problems in a given domain [2].

To create a reference model a modeling language is used, which provides a set of constructs and rules that dictate how modeling concepts can be combined. Here, typically traditional modeling languages such as Entity Relationship Model (ERM) [21], Unified Modeling Language (UML) [15], Event-Driven Process Chain (EPC) [22], or Business Process Model and Notation (BPMN) [23], cf. [20], are either directly used, or extended with additional constructs to increase their expressiveness [24, 25].

Reference models come with a variety of prospective uses [6–9]. By capitalizing upon the domain knowledge encoded in the reference model, reference models may serve as a blueprint, e.g., for designing an information system [26], or for business process management [5]. As such, one avoids the resource-intensive task of designing a domain model from scratch. Thus, reference models are seen to promote knowledge sharing, communication, and reference implementations [27].

While these are attractive prospects, as we point out in our earlier work [12], reference modeling comes with a set of challenges, which limit its full potential. In the following, we summarize a subset of challenges as relevant in the light of this paper.

Challenge 1: Expressing both general and specific domain information, i.e., addressing a conflict between reuse and productivity.

To ensure coverage of a class of problems, and thus, be applicable beyond a specific context/organization, a reference model should offer general concepts [26, 28]. At the same time, to meet the goals of a particular setting (e.g., for implementation purposes), and thus, to increase model productivity, a reference model should also provide specific concepts [28]. Therefore, a reference model needs to be detailed enough to be usable for an organization [28]. Unfortunately, current modeling languages provide only a limited set of mechanisms for expressing both generic and specific concepts [18, 24]. Especially for this paper, this holds for reference models based upon the UML [18]. As we detail in Sect. 3.2, while mechanisms like generalization/specialization can be used, they offer only a limited means for expressing both the generic and specific within a reference model.

Challenge 2: Expressing variability while avoiding redundancy, i.e., providing flexibility to users of reference models.

Partially overlapping with the call for specific concepts, reference models should account for variability. This means that a reference model should provide coverage of a range of specific requirements/constraints [26], e.g., to adapt a reference model to the processes of a specific industry, as done, e.g., in [24]. Thus, it is required to distinguish between those parts of the system that are invariant within the group of intended users, and other parts that may need individual adaptation. At the same time, redundancy in a reference model should typically be avoided (see, e.g., [24], who in their configurable reference modeling approach speak of "mutually exclusive alternatives"). Unfortunately, only a limited set of mechanisms is provided that can deal with both variability and redundancy. These mechanisms either extend an existing modeling language (like EPCs, as done in [24]), or, as we show specifically in Sect. 3.2, rely on mechanisms like the mentioned generalization/specialization, or instantiation [20].

Challenge 3: Supporting adaptation of reference models, while ensuring compliance and integrity of the system.

The reference modeling language as well as resulting reference models need to offer flexibility. By this we mean that reference model adaptation and extension should be possible, since reference models cannot contain all individual requirements of all potential users [28] (cf. also Challenge 2). While adapting a reference model to the needs of a specific organization (e.g., for implementation purposes), and vice versa, when adapting a reference model based upon its specific application, one should ensure consistency of the adaptation to the reference model. In the simplest case, this implies copying a reference model and adjusting it to the context at hand. However, in that case redundancies may arise, and potential inconsistencies as well [2]. One can envision adding extensions to the reference model, like in [29], but this can be cumbersome and importantly: such extensions are often designed for a one-way adaptation only. For instance, [29] is designed to ensure that an organization-specific model complies with the reference model, but it is not designed to check adaptations of the reference model itself.

2.2   A Reference Model for Smart Grid Cyber Security

The NIST reference model for cyber security, as encoded in NISTIR 7628 [10], offers concepts, cyber security requirements, and guidelines specific to the electricity sector. It follows that the NISTIR 7628 elements are specific for the energy sector in terms of, e.g., considered actors, and types of IT infrastructure. For example, it distinguishes between different equipment types like a smart meter or a customer gateway (also referred to as a home area network gateway in NISTIR 7628 [10, p. 18]). A customer gateway, being relevant for our running example in Sects. 3.2 and 4.2, is an (embedded) piece of equipment on the customer side, which acts as a communication interface towards other parts of the smart grid (like the service provider), and which can take care of computationally intensive tasks, like encrypting sensitive metering data prior to transmission.

The NISTIR 7628 has been widely touted for providing guidance on cyber security concerns in smart grid projects, cf. e.g., [30–33], but its adoption and maintenance is partially hampered by the above-mentioned challenges. In particular, [32] points out a lack of systematicy in relating the generic security requirements and guidelines to the concerns of specific smart grid projects, stating that this relation has to be established in an ad-hoc manner. While by no means we want to claim that these challenges are fully due to an underlying language architecture, further in the paper we explain why a language architecture based on conventional meta modeling does not provide a satisfactory solution, and we illustrate the potential that multi-level modeling has in addressing them. It is important to note that at the core of this paper stands a comparison between conventional meta modeling and multi-level modeling. As such, we use the NISTIR 7628 reference model only in as far as it illustrates this comparison, for which a relatively small subset of the larger model, presented in [12], suffices.

3   Challenges of Reference Modeling with Conventional Meta Modeling

3.1   Conventional Meta Modeling

As stated in Sect. 2.1, different languages, and potentially their accompanying language architectures, can underlie a reference model. In this paper, we focus on conventional meta modeling. We do so since, for reference models emphasizing a static perspective on an organizational action system (as opposed to a dynamic perspective, as done in, e.g., [5, 9, 25]), conventional meta modeling is often an underlying language (architecture) of choice, as among others visible in (i) a reference architecture for NISTIR 7628 [33], (ii) UML-CI, a reference model for critical infrastructure modeling [13], or (iii) E-MEMO [14], a family of reference models for e-commerce development.

Conventional meta modeling refers to language architectures that are based on the Meta Object Facility (MOF [34]). In MOF, one defines the abstract syntax of a language in terms of a meta model on the M_2 level, in terms of defining the key concepts of a language, their attributes and relations. Subsequently, this meta model can be instantiated into models, which reside on the M_1 level. In line with these two classification levels conventional meta modeling is also referred to as two-level meta modeling [35].

Conventional meta modeling exhibits a fundamental distinction between meta model elements residing on the M_2 level and model elements residing on the M_1 level. Instantiation is the only allowed, one-way, relation between these two levels, to instantiate a model element from a meta model element (but not vice versa). This distinction, also referred to as a type-instance dichotomy [16] is inherited from the object-oriented paradigm underlying conventional meta modeling, which makes a strict separation between classes and objects [16, 17].

As a result of the type-instance dichotomy classes cannot have a state. This is because they reside on the M_2 level, and thus, serve as language specification. Furthermore, the type-instance dichotomy leads to a separation between language specification and language application. Finally, in conventional meta modeling instantiation is only possible to directly proceeding classification levels, also referred to as "shallow instantiation" [17].

As we detail in Sect. 3.2, the above inherent characteristics of conventional meta modeling, i.e., classes not having a state, a separation between language specification and language application, and shallow instantiation, have a considerable impact on the creation and use of reference models.

3.2 Challenges with Conventional Meta Modeling

To showcase the challenges which arise from employing conventional meta modeling, in the following we focus on the UML, being standardized and widely used. In addition, UML is often the language of choice for contrasting conventional meta modeling with multi-level modeling, cf. e.g., [16, 17], hence it makes sense to proceed in a similar spirit for reference modeling challenges specifically.

Challenge 1: Expressing both general and specific domain information. *Rationale:* As stated in Sect. 2.1, we should be able to express both generic and specific domain concepts, while expressing domain information as soon as it becomes known, in order to avoid redundancy. When employing UML, we can partly deal with this challenge through a combined use of generalization/specialization, redefinition, and default values. Especially, generalization/specialization allows us to create abstraction hierarchies of concepts, whereas redefinition in combination with default values partially allows us to incorporate information in the reference model, as soon as it becomes known.

However, this would address the challenge only partially. In particular, redefinition in UML allows one to modify a data type and default value, while ensuring that the redefined element "[…] shall be consistent with the RedefinableElement it redefines" [15, p. 100]. However, while UML tracks the exact element being redefined (through a "redefinitionContext" [15, p. 100] what exactly "consistency" entails here, and what kinds of specific checks are necessary, remains ambiguous. This has resulted in calls for clear definitions of redefinition (e.g., [36], and a recently reported open issue for UML 2.5.1[1]), and calls for extensions, in the form of additional well-formedness rules, which enforce a consistent redefinition, cf. e.g., [37]. As a result, the inconsistent redefinition mechanism

---

[1] see https://issues.omg.org/issues/spec/UML/2.5#issue-47019. The issue has been reported on 21-7-2020. This open issue provides a minor indication that redefinition is still not well defined.

from UML may allow for violating monotonic model extensions, in the sense of catering for inconsistencies of specialized classes, which redefine attributes/association ends of their superclass. Finally, default values allow for assigning values to attributes as soon as they become known. However, this assignment happens on the type level, i.e., separate from the running data of the organization. So, any updates/modifications as it pertains to attribute values from the running organization would have to be separately mirrored in the default values. Finally, since within the UML one is creating the reference model on the M_2 level, and one uses the abstraction mechanism generalization/specialization at the same time, one is in principle using two abstraction mechanisms where one should suffice (in [16], this is also referred to as "overloading the level").

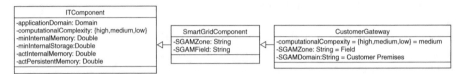

Fig. 1. An excerpt from the NISTIR cyber security reference model, reconstructed with the UML

Scenario: For our scenario, we focus on an excerpt of NISTIR 7628 dealing with smart grid components. Specifically, in Fig. 1 we see how generalization/specialization allows us express both general and specific concepts, starting with a general "ITComponent" whose attributes are inherited and specialized to the class "SmartGridComponent", and finally into the class "CustomerGateway". Equally, we can see how redefinition, combined with default values, allows us to assign values to attributes from the class "CustomerGateway", such as "computationalComplexity" being assigned the default value "medium", and the two SGAM-related attributes equally being assigned relevant values.

Nevertheless, for the same scenario we can also observe limitations that conventional meta modeling imposes, when it comes to expressing the general and specific at the same time. Firstly, since default values exist on the type level, an update, like the "computationalComplexity" of a "CustomerGateway" being changed to "high", which can be a reflection of a change in a class of technologies, needs to be made manually. Secondly, since (a) UML does not maintain a clear hierarchy of semantic richness among its primitive types (e.g., a Boolean type having less permissible instantiations than a type String), and (b) the question of what type of consistency should be kept remains at least partly open, one can in principle envision redefining the types of the attributes "minInternalMemory" and "minStorage" from the class "ITComponent" to "String" for its subclass "SmartGridComponent". However, for the sake of maintaining monotonic model extensions, this is not desired.

Challenge 2: Expressing variability while avoiding redundancy. *Rationale:* UML can partially ensure variability of a reference model, so that on the type level it can be "configured" according to the needs of a (class of) scenarios. Prominently, as with Challenge 1, the combination of generalization/specialization, redefinition and default values allows us to express domain information on a level of abstraction suitable for a range of application scenarios.

However, in line with core notions of conventional meta modeling, UML only allows for instantiation to the directly proceeding classification level. As a result of this, we cannot constrain on a high level of classification at what exact proceeding level of classification domain information should be added. This in turn limits the ability to account for variability.

Scenario: Consider again Fig. 1. Here variability and the avoidance of redundancy is partially supported by using generalization/specialization, e.g., to express for a range of scenarios a generic class "ITComponent" with attributes such as "computationalComplexity: high, medium, low", "minInternalMemory: Double", and "actInternalMemory: Double". However, importantly, we are not able to express *when* these attributes should be assigned a value, since in UML – like in conventional meta modeling – *abstraction level is not a first class* citizen. As such, when to assign values to attributes (and equally: when to specify association ends) is arbitrary in the UML. For example, using the UML in our scenario we cannot distinguish between when to assign a value for "minInternalMemory: Double", which for NISTIR 7628 is important for a *type* of smart grid component (e.g., a "CustomerGateway"), and when to assign a value for "actInternalMemory: Double", which is important for a specific smart grid component (e.g., "CustomerGateway9876").

Challenge 3: Supporting adaptation of reference models, while ensuring compliance. *Rationale:* As stated, it is desired that a reference model can be adapted, both in the sense of adaptation to a specific context, but also so that context-specific adaptations can become part of the reference model.

In the UML, one can adapt a reference model as follows. First, one can simply copy-paste the reference model and adapt it for the situation at hand, but as stated in Sect. 2.1 especially in the absence of added consistency checks, like in [29], this can be error-prone and can lead to inconsistencies. Note that the underspecified notion of redefinition, mentioned under Challenge 1, is also relevant here, since any adaptations that are made through redefinition may violate monotonicity.

Second, one can instantiate the reference model, and, with the use of constraints (as typically expressed in OCL [38]), one can check the well-formedness of any extensions. Yet, in that case, one has to essentially "duplicate" the reference model, leading to redundancies. Finally, power types are a candidate for model adaptation. A power type can be defined as a model pattern whereby the instances of a certain class are subclasses of another class [39], and has a dedicated notation in UML [40, p. 530]. As such, a power type in principle can be used to alleviate the strict separation between type and instance, avoiding the aforementioned duplication of model elements. Yet, power types are conceptual only, and as a result natively lack mechanisms for consistency checks. As such, if anything changes (in the power type class, or in either of the relevant subclasses), there is subsequently no means to ensure consistency.

Scenario: In the scenario, for illustration purposes, we focus on power types. Figure 2 presents the use of this modeling pattern for our scenario. In this case, "CustomerGateway" is a subclass of "SmartGridComponentType", and at the same time "Customer-Gateway" can be considered as an instance of "SmartGrid- Component", since the latter is a power type. However, as stated power types are a conceptual pattern only, meaning that consistency checks on the subclasses, which act also as instances, are lacking.

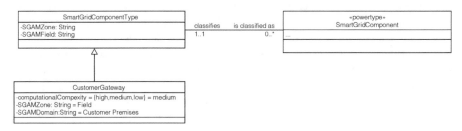

Fig. 2. Using power types as a workaround for the type-instance dichotomy

4   Multi-level Reference Modeling

To alleviate the discussed limitations of conventional meta modeling, we now introduce multi-level modeling (Sect. 4.1), and discuss its possibilities for reference modeling using the same excerpt of the smart grid cyber security reference model (Sect. 4.2).

4.1   Multi-level Modeling

Partly as a response to the limitations of conventional meta modeling [16, 17], multi-level modeling refers to modeling approaches which share the following core ideas, cf. [41]: (1) one can define an arbitrary number of classification levels in one and the same body of model. This means that one can employ as many classification levels as needed for expressing the domain knowledge at hand [16]. This is opposed to the two classification levels (M_2 and M_1) from conventional meta modeling; (2) one can defer instantiation, meaning that one can constrain the instantiation to a model element residing at a specific classification level [18]. This is opposed to shallow instantiation for conventional meta modeling, whereby one can instantiate only to the directly proceeding level; (3) one can relax the strict separation between type and instance [17], allowing one to populate and use a model with instance level data. This is again opposed to conventional meta modeling which adheres to a strict type-instance dichotomy.

Different multi-level modeling approaches exist, such as, among others, m-objects and m-relations [42], deep instantiation [16], and the Flexible Meta Modeling and Execution Language (FMML^x) [18]. As an exemplary multi-level modeling approach, for this paper we select FMML^x to show how multi-level modeling alleviates the limitations introduced by conventional meta modeling. One of the reasons for selecting the FMML^x is that, besides the expertise of the authors, it appears to be the only approach with a meta modeling editor (XModeler [18]) that has an integrated language execution engine. For future research this allows for, among others, computational analysis of reference models.

4.2 Addressing Challenges with Multi-level Modeling

Figure 3 shows an excerpt of cyber security reference model created with FMML^x, containing the same domain information captured earlier with UML (Sect. 3.2). When it comes to expressing both the generic and specific information (Challenge 1), with classification levels being a first class citizen in multi-level modeling, we can naturally model the domain hierarchy, as relevant for the smart grid reference model. Similar to the use of generalization/specialization in Sect. 3.2, we can thus express domain concepts both on a high level of abstraction (e.g. an "ITComponent" and its attributes), and on a lower level one (e.g., for "SmartGridComponent"). However, in addition, due to having a relaxed type-instance dichotomy, multi-level modeling allows us to express naturally domain information as soon as it is known. For example, to assign a particular value to "minInternalMemory" for a "Customer Gateway". Especially of note here, is that due to the relaxed type-instance dichotomy one can keep the attribute value up-to-date with the data of the running organization. This is in contrast to using default values in UML, which one needs to update separately on the type level on the basis of instance-level data. Also one can concisely express domain information on the basis of having a relaxed type-instance dichotomy only, instead of having to rely on two mechanisms specific to UML (default values and redefinition).

When it comes to coverage of different domain scenarios while avoiding redundancy (Challenge 2), the above multi-level modeling characteristics are equally important. For example, to express characteristics of different types of "IT Component" once, thus avoiding redundancy, while covering a wide range of different domain scenarios through the ability of expressing both the generic and the specific. However, of additional importance for Challenge 2 is the ability of multi-level modeling to defer instantiation of a model element to a particular level of classification. In FMML^x deferred instantiation is expressed through intrinsicness. Intrinsicness, which in Fig. 3 is depicted as a white number on a black background, expresses the classification level one instantiates the model element to (intrinsicness is depicted for attributes Fig. 3, but equally can be used for association ends). For our scenario, this intrinsicness allows us to constrain the initialization of values of attributes for "IT Component", which resides on level M_3. For example, for the abstraction hierarchy of "IT Component" we can express that "minInternalMemory: Double" shall be instantiated on level M_1, whereas "actInternalMemory: Double" is to be instantiated on level M_0. In a more general sense, this deferred instantiation through intrinsicness allows us to constrain already on a high level of abstraction when domain information becomes relevant. This in turn provides additional means for ensuring variability. Finally, when it comes to the adaptation of reference models (Challenge 3), multi-level modeling enforces a *monotonic* model extension [18]. As a result, extensions to a reference model are consistent with the domain rules already encoded into the multi-level model on a higher level of classification. So for example, arbitrarily changing the attribute type "minInternalMemory" from a "Double" to a "String" on a lower level of abstraction would not be allowed. As stated in Sect. 3.2, UML redefinition is at the very least not clearly defined and underspecified in how it maintains consistency, making it likely that one can violate monotonicity. In addition, as stated in Sect. 4.1 with multi-level modeling the different levels of classification are all part of one and the same model – conceptually speaking at least. As a result, no matter what adaptations are made, one is in principle adapting one and the same reference model. While this introduces new challenges in its own right, at the very least, it means avoiding redundancies during adaptation.

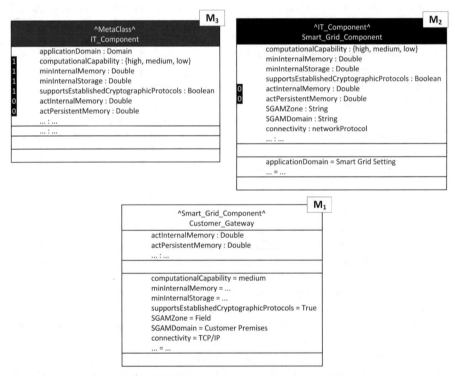

Fig. 3. An excerpt from the NISTIR cyber security reference model, reconstructed with the FMML$^\text{X}$

4.3 Summarizing Comparison

Table 1 provides a summarized comparison between using conventional meta modeling and multi-level modeling, as illustrated by their respective application to the same, smart grid cyber-security, reference model.

As can be observed, UML offers several mechanisms which at least partly address the challenges discussed so far. Especially, the combined use of generalization/specialization, redefinition, and default values allows us to account for both (a) general concepts and their relevant properties. For example, in our scenario an "IT Component" and its attributes cover a wide range of specific smart grid components, and (b) specific concepts and their properties, to cover specific scenarios. For example, a "Customer Gateway", as relevant for scenarios specifically involving customer premises. This addresses partly Challenges 1 and 2, in the sense of balancing the general and the specific, avoiding redundancy (by using generalization/specialization), and by allowing

Table 1. Comparing UML and FMML^X for addressing reference model challenges

Lang	Challenge 1	Challenge 2	Challenge 3
UML	+ creating hierarchies of concepts with generalization/specialization + assigning values using default values and redefinition − modification of default values restricted to type level − underspecified semantics of redefinition, violation of monotonic model extensions − overloading the level + mature tools and mechanisms	+ covering variability and redundancy partly using the abstraction mechanism mentioned in Challenge 1 − "shallow instantiation", no possibility to constrain model elements according to their classification level; − same issues as under Challenge 1, e.g., monotonic model extensions are likely not guaranteed + mature tools and mechanisms	− reference model adaptation either (1) needs additional consistency checking mechanisms, when simply duplicating it, or (2) leads to redundant model elements, when instantiating it (due to a strict separation between types & instances), or (3) lacks consistency checking mechanisms when using power types + mature tools and mechanisms
FMML^X	+ an arbitrary number of classification levels allowing to create hierarchies of concepts + relaxed type-instance dichotomy allowing to assign state to classes − immaturity of model management mechanisms	+ intrinsicness (deferred instantiation) + an arbitrary number of classification levels + relaxed type-instance dichotomy − immaturity of model management mechanisms	+ monotonic model extensions + adapting one and the same body of model − immaturity of model management mechanisms

for variability, in the sense of covering a wide range of constraints/application scenarios. Also, while using UML we can partially account for reference model adaptation (Challenge 3), in the three manners summarized in Table 1.

As pointed out above, UML provides notable capabilities to satisfy our purposes. In particular, this regards the design of domain hierarchies by using a combination of generalization/specialization, default values, and redefinition. However, UML also comes with a set of limitations. As we have seen these limitations are alleviated by FMML^x mainly since, being a multi-level modeling approach, FMML^x treats *classification levels as a first-class citizen* and relaxes the *strict separation between types and instances*. As such, as we have illustrated with our simplified example, FMML^x offers many features that fit naturally with the idea of reference modeling. Especially, having (1) an arbitrary number of classification levels, as well as (2) a relaxed type-instance dichotomy, allows one to naturally mirror hierarchies of domain information (which is important to Challenge 1 and Challenge 2). Importantly, compared to the UML in FMML^x such hierarchies can be created without redundancies or inconsistencies, and can also conceptually speaking be succinctly created (e.g., without the need to overload the level, or having to use both redefinition and default values as workarounds, when instantiation can suffice). In addition, the intrinsicness offered by FMML^x specifically, and the notion of deferred instantiation generally, allows us to specify at what level of classification a model element should be instantiated. For example, to express that "minInternalMemory: Double" must be instantiated on level M_1, whereas "actInternalMemory: Double" must be instantiated on level M_0. This contributes to expressing variability in the reference model (Challenge 2). In contrast, with the shallow instantiation of UML this kind of constraining ac- cording to level of classification is simply not possible. Finally, FMML^x lends itself naturally to model adaptations (Challenge 3), since it enforces monotonic model extensions, and at least conceptually speaking, one makes the adaptations in one and the same body of model.

However, while promising in terms of the underlying ideas, multi-level modeling, being a relatively novel language architecture, introduces also several challenges. Firstly, multi-level modeling approaches still need to mature in terms of model management. Especially, given that adaptations are made to one and the same body of model, additional mechanisms are needed in order to deal with the increased complexity [43, 44]. This directly impacts Challenge 1–3: while it can naturally mirror domain hierarchies (Challenge 1), deal with variability (Challenge 2) and can ensure consistent model adaptation (Challenge 3), the *usability* of multi-level modeling approaches in terms of typical model management mechanisms (navigating the models, viewpoints, etc.) is, as it currently stands, limited.

For example, returning to our cyber security reference model, beyond our small excerpt the NISTIR 7628 provides a comprehensive coverage of cyber security concerns, which requires an equally comprehensive reference model. It can be foreseen that managing such a comprehensive reference model is challenging to manage with the current state of multi-level modeling approaches. Taking also into consideration the rapid changes in the electricity sector and its according cyber security concerns, this motivates further the mechanisms to deal with the complexity of multi-level models.

Secondly, an additional concern is that basic multi-level modeling terms have not been properly defined, such as "level", cf. [45]. This in turn impacts the design of multi-level modeling features, such as deferred instantiation, being one of the unique features of multi-level modeling. Particularly, the question emerges to what extent we can assume levels to be absolute, or rather if they are relative to the problem at hand.

Finally, the creation of multi-level models requires a change in the users' mindset: they need to think in multiple levels of classification, and not only two. Assigning concepts to multiple classification levels is not a trivial task, and currently there is lack of guidelines and heuristics for designing such a multi-level model [44, 46].

5   Conclusions and Outlook

In this paper, we have shown how multi-level modeling provides a natural candidate for the creation and use of reference models, compared to reference models based on conventional meta modeling. Especially, as shown on the basis of a comparative scenario, as a language architecture multi-level modeling is a natural fit to address reference model challenges since (a) it treats the notion of a classification level as a first class citizen. As opposed to conventional meta modeling, which is restricted to two classification levels, this allows one to naturally mirror hierarchies of domain concepts inherent to reference modeling, (b) due to relaxing the difference between types and instances, it is easier to adapt and synchronize a reference model conformant to the data of a running organization. Finally, please note that modeling languages not subscribing to the MOF can also be used for the creation and use of reference models. For creating reference models with an emphasis on a static perspective such languages include the data modeling language ERM (as mentioned in Sect. 2.1), or the fact modeling language Object Role Modeling (ORM, [47]). These modeling languages provide abstraction mechanisms which differ from those in conventional meta modeling, like the different set-based generalization/specialization mechanisms inherent to ERM [48, pp. 92–94]. Yet, importantly, even when using an alternative language, these languages still do not treat abstraction levels as a first class citizen. And so, even while these languages may offer additional flexibility, when it comes expressing different abstraction levels, they are still expected to suffer similar fundamental limitations as in the MOF. Of course, still a comparison of non-MOF based to multi-level modeling languages may be warranted for future research.

References

1. Frank, U., Strecker, S.: Open reference models-community-driven collaboration to promote development and dissemination of reference models. EMISA **2**(2) (2007)
2. Fettke, P., Loos, P.: Perspectives on reference modeling. In: Fettke, P., Loos, P. (eds.) Reference Modeling for Business Systems Analysis, pp. 1–21 (2007)
3. Thomas, O.: Understanding the term reference model in information systems research: history, literature analysis and explanation. In: Bussler, C.J., Haller, A. (eds.) BPM 2005. LNCS, vol. 3812, pp. 484–496. Springer, Heidelberg (2006). https://doi.org/10.1007/11678564_45
4. Sonntag, A., Fettke, P., Loos, P.: Inductive reference modelling based on simulated social collaboration. In: Proceedings of the 2017 Wirtschaftsinformatik Conference, AIS (2017)

5. Rehse, J.-R., Fettke, P., Loos, P.: A graph-theoretic method for the inductive development of reference process models. Softw. Syst. Model. **16**(3), 833–873 (2015). https://doi.org/10. 1007/s10270-015-0490-0

6. Schütte, R.: Reference models for standard software—scientific myth instead of practical reality? In: Bergener, K., Räckers, M., Stein, A. (eds.) The Art of Structuring: Bridging the Gap Between Information Systems Research and Practice, pp. 125–136. Springer, Cham (2019). https://doi.org/10.1007/978-3-030-06234-7_12

7. Kraume, K., Voormanns, K., Zhong, J.: How a global customer service leader is using a reference model to structure its transformation while remaining fast and agile. In: Bergener, K., Räckers, M., Stein, A. (eds.) The Art of Structuring: Bridging the Gap Between Information Systems Research and Practice, pp. 101–111. Springer, Cham (2019). https://doi.org/10.1007/ 978-3-030-06234-7_10

8. Janiesch, C., Winkelmann, A.: The goat criteria—a structured assessment approach for reference models. In: Bergener, K., Räckers, M., Stein, A. (eds.) The Art of Structuring: Bridging the Gap Between Information Systems Research and Practice, pp. 63–74. Springer, Cham (2019). https://doi.org/10.1007/978-3-030-06234-7_7

9. Scholta, H., Niemann, M., Delfmann, P., Räckers, M., Becker, J.: Semi-automatic inductive construction of reference process models that represent best practices in public administrations: a method. Inf. Syst. **84**, 63–87 (2019)

10. NIST Smart Grid Cybersecurity Panel: NISTIR 7628-guidelines for smart grid cyber security, vol. 1–3 (2010)

11. Neureiter, C., Engel, D., Uslar, M.: Domain specific and model based systems engineering in the smart grid as prerequisite for security by design. Electronics **5**(2), 24 (2016)

12. de Kinderen, S., Kaczmarek-Heß, M.: Multi-level modeling as a language architecture for reference models: on the example of the smart grid domain. In: Becker, J., Novikov, D.A. (eds.) 21st IEEE Conference on Business Informatics, CBI, Volume 1 - Research Papers, Moscow, Russia, 15–17 July, pp. 174–183. IEEE (2019)

13. Bagheri, E., Ghorbani, A.A.: UML-CI: a reference model for profiling critical infrastructure systems. Inf. Syst. Front. **12**(2), 115–139 (2010)

14. Frank, U., Lange, C.: E-MEMO: a method to support the development of customized electronic commerce systems. ISeB **5**(2), 93–116 (2007)

15. OMG: The OMG unified modeling language (OMG UML), version 2.5.1. Technical report (2017)

16. Atkinson, C., Kühne, T.: Reducing accidental complexity in domain models. SoSyM **7**(3), 345–359 (2008)

17. Atkinson, C., Kühne, T.: The essence of multilevel metamodeling. In: Gogolla, M., Kobryn, C. (eds.) UML 2001. LNCS, vol. 2185, pp. 19–33. Springer, Heidelberg (2001). https://doi. org/10.1007/3-540-45441-1_3

18. Frank, U.: Multilevel modeling – toward a new paradigm of conceptual modeling and information systems design. BISE **6**(6), 319–337 (2014)

19. Thomas, O.: Version management for reference models: design and implementation. In: Becker, J., Delfmann, P. (eds.) Reference Modeling: Efficient Information Systems Design Through Reuse of Information Models, pp. 1–26. Physica-Verlag (2007)

20. vom Brocke, J.: Design principles for reference modeling: reusing information models by means of aggregation, specialisation, instantiation, and analogy. In: Reference Modeling for Business Systems Analysis, pp. 47–76. IGI Global, Hershey (2007)

21. Chen, P.P.: The entity-relationship model - toward a unified view of data. ACM Trans. Database Syst. **1**(1), 9–36 (1976)

22. Scheer, A.W.: ARIS – Modellierungsmethoden, Metamodelle, Anwendungen, 4th edn. Springer, Heidelberg (2001). https://doi.org/10.1007/978-3-642-56676-9

23. Dijkman, R., Hofstetter, J., Koehler, J. (eds.): BPMN 2011. LNBIP, vol. 95. Springer, Heidelberg (2011). https://doi.org/10.1007/978-3-642-25160-3
24. Rosemann, M., van der Aalst, W.: A configurable reference modelling language. Inf. Syst. **32**(1), 1–23 (2007)
25. Fettke, P., Loos, P., Zwicker, J.: Business process reference models: survey and classification. In: Bussler, C.J., Haller, A. (eds.) BPM 2005. LNCS, vol. 3812, pp. 469–483. Springer, Heidelberg (2006). https://doi.org/10.1007/11678564_44
26. Frank, U.: Evaluation of reference models. In: Reference Modeling for Business Systems Analysis, pp. 118–140. IGI Global, Hershey (2007)
27. Koch, S., Strecker, S., Frank, U.: Conceptual modelling as a new entry in the bazaar: the open model approach. In: Damiani, E., Fitzgerald, B., Scacchi, W., Scotto, M., Succi, G. (eds.) OSS 2006. IIFIP, vol. 203, pp. 9–20. Springer, Boston, MA (2006). https://doi.org/10.1007/0-387-34226-5_2
28. Matook, S., Indulska, M.: Improving the quality of process reference models: a quality function deployment-based approach. DSS **47**(1), 60–71 (2009)
29. Reinhartz-Berger, I., Soffer, P., Sturm, A.: Organisational reference models: supporting an adequate design of local business processes. Int. J. Bus. Process. Integr. Manag. **4**(2), 134–149 (2009)
30. Kotut, L., Wahsheh, L.A.: Survey of cyber security challenges and solutions in smart grids. In: 2016 Cybersecurity Symposium, pp. 32–37. IEEE (2016)
31. Abercrombie, R.K., Sheldon, F.T., Hauser, K.R., Lantz, M.W., Mili, A.: Risk assessment methodology based on the NISTIR 7628 guidelines. In: 2013 46th Hawaii International Conference on System Sciences (HICSS), pp. 1802–1811. IEEE (2013)
32. Chan, A., Zhou, J.: On smart grid cybersecurity standardization: issues of designing with NISTIR 7628. IEEE Commun. Mag. **51**(1), 58–65 (2013)
33. Neureiter, C., Uslar, M., Engel, D., Lastro, G.: A standards-based approach for domain specific modelling of smart grid system architectures. In: 2016 11th System of Systems Engineering Conference (SoSE), pp. 1–6. IEEE (2016)
34. OMG: Meta Object Facility (MOF) core specification (2016) Version 2.5.1
35. Atkinson, C., Gerbig, R.: Melanie: multi-level modeling and ontology engineering environment. In: Proceedings of the 2nd International Master Class on Model- Driven Engineering: Modeling Wizards, pp. 1–2 (2012)
36. Bildhauer, D.: On the relationships between subsetting, redefinition and association specialization. In: 9th Conference on Databases and Information Systems (2010)
37. Nieto, P., Costal, D., Gmez, C.: Enhancing the semantics of UML association redefinition. Data Knowl. Eng. **70**(2), 182–207 (2011)
38. Warmer, J.B., Kleppe, A.G.: The Object Constraint Language: Getting Your Models Ready for MDA. Addison-Wesley Professional, Boston (2003)
39. Odell, J.J.: Advanced Object-Oriented Analysis and Design Using UML, vol. 12. Cambridge University Press, Cambridge (1998)
40. Booch, G., Rumbaugh, J., Jacobson, I.: The Unified Modeling Language Reference Manual, 2nd edn. Addison-Wesley Reading, Boston (2005)
41. Neumayr, B., Schrefl, M., Thalheim, B.: Modeling techniques for multi-level abstraction. In: Kaschek, R., Delcambre, L. (eds.) The Evolution of Conceptual Modeling, pp. 68–92. Springer, Berlin (2011). https://doi.org/10.1007/978-3-642-17505-3
42. Neumayr, B., Grün, K., Schrefl, M.: Multi-level domain modeling with m-objects and m-relationships. In: Proceedings of the Sixth Asia-Pacific Conference on Conceptual Modeling, vol. 96, pp. 107–116. Australian Computer Society, Inc. (2009)
43. Töpel, D., Benner, B.: Maintenance of multi-level models – an analysis of elementary change operations. In: MULTI@MoDELS (2017)

44. Kaczmarek-Heß, M., Nolte, M., Fritsch, A., Betz, S.: Practical experiences with multi-level modeling using FMMLx: a hierarchy of domain-specific modeling languages in support of life-cycle assessment. In: Clark, T., Neumayr, B., Rutle, A. (eds.) Proceedings of the 5th Int. Workshop on Multi-Level Modelling 2018 (2018)
45. Kühne, T.: A story of levels. In: Hebig, R., Berger, T. (eds.) Proceedings of MODELS 2018 Workshops: ModComp, MRT, OCL, FlexMDE, EXE, COMMitMDE, MDETools, GEMOC, MORSE, MDE4IoT, MDEbug, MoDeVVa, ME, MULTI, HuFaMo, AMMoRe, PAINS co-located with ACM/IEEE 21st International Conference on Model Driven Engineering Languages and Systems (MODELS 2018), Copenhagen, Denmark, 14 October 2018, vol. 2245, pp. 673–682. CEUR Workshop Proceedings, CEUR-WS.org (2018)
46. Almeida, J.P.A., Frank, U., Kuehne, T.: Multi-level modelling (report from Dagstuhl seminar 17492). Dagstuhl Rep. **7**(12), 18–49 (2018)
47. Halpin, T.: ORM 2. In: Meersman, R., Tari, Z., Herrero, P. (eds.) OTM 2005. LNCS, vol. 3762, pp. 676–687. Springer, Heidelberg (2005). https://doi.org/10.1007/11575863_87
48. Elmasri, R.: Fundamentals of Database Systems. Pearson Education India, London (2004)

Notation-Agnostic Subprocess Modeling for Adaptive Case Management

Johannes Tenschert[(⊠)], Sebastian Dunzer, and Martin Matzner

Chair of Digital Industrial Service Systems,
University of Erlangen-Nürnberg, Nürnberg, Germany
{johannes.tenschert,sebastian.dunzer,martin.matzner}@fau.de

Abstract. Even though knowledge work comprises tasks that cannot be modeled a priori, some structure for routine work or an outlined course of action is often necessary. Knowledge workers perform structured and ad-hoc activities – and a wide range of requirements typically yields many tools. To avoid redundant and scattered process information, a single system of record capable of consolidating flexibility and modeling of different aspects of processes is desirable. For knowledge-intensive processes, we outline how to combine process models for structured routine aspects with the ad-hoc activities and flexibility of social software in the same context. Therefore, a case comprises modeled subprocesses as well as ad-hoc activities and artifacts. The shared context allows to transparently combine aspects and deviate from predefined models. We prototypically implement our approach and show that ad-hoc project management and different notations can be applied within the same case.

Keywords: Adaptive case management · Subprocess modeling ·
Knowledge-intensive business process · Process flexibility

1 Introduction

In recent years, the share of knowledge work in the workforce rapidly increased, and knowledge-intensive processes became customary. In the US, around 50% of the work can be attributed to knowledge work, and other countries show similar tendencies [1, 2]. Knowledge workers are responsible for their own contribution in terms of quantity and quality [3], and they perform emergent processes [4]. Flexibility requirements often yield multiple support systems for the same process, e. g. groupware, collaboration tools, and business process management (BPM) systems. These need to be integrated or manually kept consistent. Otherwise there is no clear system of record. Adaptive case management (ACM) systems aid within this realm.

Business process modeling typically entails capturing the whole process. This approach increases efficiency for predictable and frequent processes. For knowledge-intensive processes with a lot size of 1, and for unstructured work, this sort of process support is detrimental. Modeling scarcely executed processes often cannot be amortized with efficiency gains. Moreover, different processes of an organization might be appropriate for different modeling notations or paradigms. Current techniques only allow mixing paradigms to some degree.

This paper introduces an approach to combine structured process models for routine aspects of knowledge-intensive processes with ad-hoc activities and artifacts within the same context. Our approach is notation-agnostic and thereby permits mixing modeling languages within the same overall case. Knowledge workers can transparently deviate from predefined models or decide to not apply them at all, e. g. by creating and adapting tasks and other artifacts that have not been modeled in advance. The approach facilitates creating a single system of record. We apply cases as the context for all routine and ad-hoc work. Process models are applied as subprocess models using data from this context. Subprocess models can be combined as they are initiated on demand. All related case artifacts are stored or referenced within the same case. We prototypically implement our approach and a motivating example in the commercial ACMS Pertuniti.

The following sections introduce fundamentals in regard to ACM and process modeling paradigms, and a motivating example in the context of providing a lecture. Section 6 captures our approach on notation-agnostic subprocess modeling, and Sect. 7 outlines the implementation in the commercial ACMS Pertuniti. Afterwards, we discuss the approach and introduce related work. Finally, we conclude and outline further work.

2 Fundamentals

Since we combine structured process models with flexibility of ACM, our approach has to consider many existing techniques. Hence, we first introduce ACM and outline modeling paradigms we consider as applicable for subprocess models.

2.1 Adaptive Case Management

The term *adaptive case management* (ACM) has been introduced in *Mastering the Unpredictable* [5]. ACM systems support knowledge workers that perform emergent or unstructured work. The actions performed in these processes are typically not known in advance [4]. The focal point for organizing the work is the *case*. Typical artifacts are ad-hoc tasks and unstructured notes or documents. As design and execution are the same phase, an ACM system has to support knowledge workers in planning their emergent processes.

In contrast to process-driven applications, support systems in case management must consider flexibility and ad-hoc activities, the focus on documents and unstructured data, and empowering knowledge workers to deviate from predefined models to support new situations in emergent processes. Still, knowledge work also comprises some routine work that our approach intends to reduce.

2.2 Process Modeling Paradigms

Today, business process models can be created in a wide range of modeling paradigms that entail different benefits and limitations.

Declarative. Declarative process modeling became prevalent for ACM [6, 7]. It is an approach to create flexibility in processes to support less predictable courses of action [7–9]. Although knowledge work is inherently unpredictable, some aspects *can* contain predictable dependencies. Declarative notations focus on dependencies [10, 11]. Declarative models allow the execution of any modeled activity, unless a constraint prevents it [6]. They explicitly prohibit behavior and implicitly describe applicable paths. There is a wide range of declarative process modeling notations, e. g. Declare [12], CMMN [13], DCR graphs [14], and DPIL [15].

Imperative. In contrast, imperative approaches describe all permitted paths [16]. They implicitly prohibit behavior [17]. Imperative models focus on describing sequences of actions [8]. Subsequently, they can be considered detrimental for ACM [18]. Depending on the level of detail, such models enable process automation [16]. Even though process mining leveraged the generation of process models from data, imperative modeling is time- and resource-intensive [19]. Routine tasks that knowledge workers perform can be improved or even automated with imperative approaches. Prominent examples of imperative process modeling languages comprise BPMN [20], Petri nets [21], and eEPC [22].

Hybrid. Additionally, there are process modeling notations that combine imperative and declarative modeling [11]. While BPMN 2.0 allows modeling ad-hoc subprocesses [20], BPMN-D facilitates declarative sections in imperative BPMN models [10]. Van der Aalst suggests that accepting Petri nets [21] can include declarative semantics as well. The workflow engine Camunda facilitates interchangeability between CMMN, DMN and BPMN.[1]

3 Related Work

We classify our approach as a workflow execution system specifically designed for flexible processes which allows for modeling routine tasks as subprocesses and delivers a shared context for case data management. In the following, we distinguish our approach from existing ACMS, and BPMS which support knowledge work and routine tasks at the same time. For the identification of related work, we conducted a literature search on *Google Scholar* and examined pertinent conference proceedings, i. e. BPM, CAiSE, ECIS, ICIS, and WI.

Künzle and Reichert introduced PHILharmonicFlows [23, 24] as an object-aware process management framework that focuses on the *data object* as their primary process element. For example, HR processes have an open position and several applicants. Traditional BPM approaches typically have to focus on either the position or the applicant as the process instance, i. e. the primary focus. Here, each data object has its own state. PHILharmonicFlows differentiates micro and macro processes for object behavior and object interactions [23, 25]. For ad-hoc activities in knowledge work, process support is restricted to predefined (note) attributes to be filled with arbitrary values. Our approach

---

[1] https://www.camunda.com (visited on 2020–05-31).

is similar in regard to allowing to manage different subprocess instances that have their own state and can focus on different data objects – or stakeholders in the context of HR. In addition, we allow combining subprocesses with ad-hoc activities and subprocess models for different aspects of the work. Furthermore, we expect that knowledge workers may create their own subprocess models as they can capture single aspects of the work, i. e. they do not need to model the whole process.

Fragment-based production case management [26, 27] divides complex processes with many possible execution paths into shorter process fragments. These describe one particular aspect of the process and are linked with data objects and common activities. Pre and post conditions of activities describe the data flow of a process. The approach allows modeling the happy path, exceptions, and global procedures as individual fragments of a process. Users may choose different variants of fragments, e. g. in contract management, either pre-approved contracts can be applied, or new contracts have to be reviewed. The result of both fragments is an accepted contract that can be a precondition for other fragments. Even though individual fragments can be kept small, modelers have to consider the whole process, and ad-hoc activities and artifacts are not considered in the model. Unlike PHILharmonicFlows, "fragment instances" cannot focus on different data objects, at least not in the sense of multiple data objects of the same type. However, fragment-based modeling can be imported into our approach both as running subprocess instances, but also in regard to dependencies between subprocess instances.

Van der Aalst et al. [28] introduced Proclets, a framework for lightweight speech-act-based interacting workflow processes based on Petri nets. Proclets are Petri nets that are connected via ports and corresponding annotations in regard to cardinality and multiplicity. Individual proclets describe the life cycle of an instance. For the connection, they exchange performatives over channels like email that are stored in a traceable knowledge base. Similar to our approach, individual proclets can capture a different focus on entities as subprocess instances, e. g. for HR. However, all activities for a particular instance are modeled within the Proclet, i.e. it is not intended to further divide the process into smaller aspects of the work. Proclets could also be imported into our approach as a single notation for subprocess instances.

4 Methods

We intend to open adaptive case management to knowledge-intensive processes consisting of structured, semi-structured, and completely ad-hoc activities. Therefore, our approach revolves around two hypotheses:

H1. No predefined process schema is necessary to support traceability in knowledge work.
H2. Routine and ad-hoc activities that share the same context can be supported within the same system of record.

With a speech-act-based approach, Hypothesis H1 has already been investigated [29], and yielded the prototype Agora [30] as well as the spin-off Pertuniti [31, 32]. For Hypothesis H2, a focus on speech acts yielded first results that depend on explicit and implicit (e. g. annotations in process models) documentation of interactions. Here, we focus on H2 without requiring additional annotations. From H2, we can directly derive two research questions:

RQ1. Can routine and ad-hoc activities that share the same context be performed within the same system?
RQ2. Can different execution semantics of routine work be performed within the same system?

For communication-centric knowledge-intensive work, RQ1 can already be affirmed by the prototype Agora [30]. To derive a general answer, we want to extend an approach for process support for completely ad-hoc activities with process support for routine work. In the commercial ACMS Pertuniti[2], no process schema is necessary to perform collaborative work in a traceable way. Prior to our extensions, Pertuniti did not include any workflow engine, and automation was restricted to document generation as well as a REST interface to attach web services to. First, we extend Pertuniti with a workflow engine for a subset of BPMN that performs subprocesses within the same case as ad-hoc activities.

For RQ2, we add additional workflow engines and abstract execution commonalities and differences (see Sect. 6.5). We affirm RQ2 by providing a case and subprocess model that is not tailored to a specific process modeling notation, and that allows performing subprocess instances of different process modeling notations and execution semantics within the same shared context, i. e. in the same case.

We further evaluate RQ1 and RQ2 by applying this approach in the ACMS Pertuniti, and by demonstrating that it can fulfill the requirements of the following motivating example.

5 Motivating Example

We motivate subprocess modelling in ACM by applying the lecture module *Process Analytics* (PA) as a case, or rather, a set of cases. We consider every term of the lecture PA as one case. It shares a common context and consists of weekly lectures, an excursion, a project, a written examination and other ad-hoc tasks. Although the project differs every year, it comprises a mandatory excursion to an industry partner. The lecture-unit preparation is knowledge-intensive. Some lecture units require revision for the new term. Other units, such as fundamentals, might remain similar for years. Holding lectures is predictable up to a certain degree, but may vary depending on the students' number and participation. For these reasons, it seems unsuitable to model designing and holding lectures.

In contrast, exam preparations do not change over the years. They mainly rely on dependency-related information, i. e. we apply declarative modeling. Hence, we implemented a DCR graph to prepare exams (cf. Fig. 1). Examiners may decide to conduct the examination orally. In this case, they do not initiate the model. After an examiner

---

[2] https://www.pertuniti.com (visited on 2020–11-30).

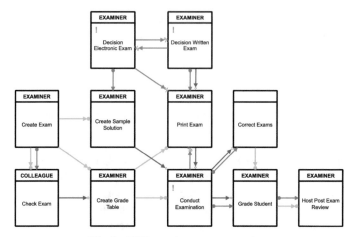

Fig. 1. DCR graph: exam preparation

has created an exam, it needs a review by a colleague. In declarative notations, case workers can execute activities multiple times when there is no related constraint. In most cases, the examiner creates more than one version of an exam. Before conducting the examination, the examiner must create a grade table. After the examination, the examiner, colleagues, and assistants correct the exams. Thereafter, the examiner enters the grade for each student. Last, examiners must host a post-exam review. The examiner has one decision of whether s/he conducts an electronic or written examination. While electronic exams must include the sample solution, written exams require printing prior to the examination. The single system of record aids in creating the sample solutions, since all lecture slides and transcripts are immediately available.

Planning an excursion is a predictable process. Thus, we modeled organizing it in BPMN (cf. Fig. 2). Depending on the industry partner, the responsible needs to enter the date and target location of the excursion in a form. Afterwards, the approval from the central university must be retrieved. If the trip is approved, all students in the project are automatically registered for the excursion. Meanwhile, the organizer compares travel options. If the excursion takes more than a day, the organizer has to search for accommodation. Capturing these options may result in unstructured documents. After the trip, all invoices and bills need to be captured to settle payment.

As we show with the lecture module, one case can comprise structured, semi-structured, and ad-hoc work. Hence, ACM can still benefit from modeled sub processes for routine aspects. We applied notations for routine work based on the process to be supported, which is not supported in available ACM systems.

While the motivating example is academic, this mode of work can be found in many – maybe unexpected – areas: In regulated domains, e. g. medical quality management, core processes have to be documented in advance, and traceability of process instances is mandatory.

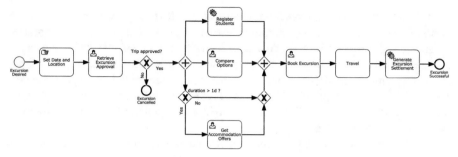

Fig. 2. BPMN model: lecture excursion

6 Notation-Agnostic Subprocess Modeling

Our approach to process support enables combining complete ad-hoc activities and modeled processes within the same context, a case. Our approach comprises a case model, dynamic case and process states, and a data dependency model. Furthermore, we outline how an ACMS could handle common and differentiating execution semantics.

6.1 Case Model

Since knowledge-intensive processes consist of ad-hoc and routine fragments, one process model typically cannot capture them. Nonetheless, they should be performed within one traceable context. While concrete artifacts may vary between domains, this section introduces a case model that allows execution of modeled routine subprocesses as well as ad-hoc activities.

Definition 1 (Case Instance). *A case instance $c = s, A, D, I, \sum$ consists of a state $s \in S$ of state types S, a set of master data attributes $A \in K \times V$ as key-value pairs with unique keys, a set of arbitrary artifact data D, a set of subprocess instances I, and a set of performed activities, i. e. an event log Σ.*

Optionally, a case should also contain an unique identifier, and depending on the domain, it may contain a case type of some sort. The set of arbitrary artifact data D substantially simplifies actual case management systems. In reality, D may contain artifacts of arbitrary types that are supported in different ways, e. g. a calendar for events, a Kanban board for task lists, or some file hierarchy for documents. As many case management systems provide functions to manage case master data, we apply key-value pairs. These can be further specified with e. g. case types. Σ is a consolidated event log of all modeled and ad-hoc activities performed within the case instance.

Definition 2 (Subprocess Instance). *A subprocess instance $i = \mathcal{M}, s, A, \psi_\mathcal{N}, \sum_i$ consists of a reference to a specific process model $\mathcal{M}$ of modeling notation $\mathcal{N}$, a state $s \in S_\mathcal{M}$, i. e. states that are applicable to process model $\mathcal{M}$, arbitrary attributes $A \in K \times V$ for an internal variable scope if necessary, a notation-specific execution state $\psi_\mathcal{N}$, and an instance-specific event log Σ_i.*

This definition contains three representations of states to capture a variety of requirements. Process states $s \in S_{\mathcal{M}}$ might be useful to derive the success of subprocess instances, e. g. labels on BPMN end events. Knowledge workers may derive the course of action based on states of past subprocess instances, i. e. ACM systems should depict this state prominently. As execution semantics of different notations require different data models, $\psi_{\mathcal{N}}$ can capture notation-specific execution states, e. g. tokens or included activities. Some arbitrary attributes $s \in A$ might be adaptable by end users, otherwise they could also be stored in $\psi_{\mathcal{N}}$.

A **subprocess model** may reference and adapt not only their instance state, but also the case state, e. g. for creating case artifacts or to use case master data at decision points. Hence, subprocess models could be applied as case templates.

6.2   Sketch

Based on the running example, the difference in the context of ACM becomes apparent. Figure 3 depicts the ad-hoc and routine activities involved in giving a lecture on process mining. The case contains many documents and groupware artifacts, e. g. lecture notes and test data, exercises, a course-specific calendar of the lecturer, ad-hoc tasks to improve the lecture over time, and important interactions with stakeholders. The tasks are not modeled in advance as in this case, planning is clearly part of the work and tasks of this granularity are performed once.

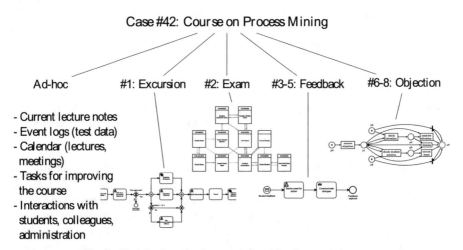

Fig. 3. Sketch of motivating example with subprocess instances

Each semester, and not only for this course, students attend excursions to partners of the chair for a guest lecture. Since this aspect is performed sufficiently often, it can be modeled as a structured subprocess model (cf. Fig. 2) to facilitate coordination and applying best practices. The same is true for preparing an exam (cf. Fig. 1). Processes for feedback and handling objections could also be automated in regard to their documentation and to trigger manual tasks.

The case provides a shared context for the whole lecture. Each modeled process actually is a subprocess, and no redundant data entry for capturing the context is necessary. If one subprocess instance finishes, the whole course may continue until the lecturer no longer expects feedback and objections. Moreover, models for excursions and feedback might be shared with case types for seminars, colloquia, or projects.

6.3 Case and Process State

For ACM, case state primarily coordinates knowledge workers, not workflow engines. Therefore, the typical distinction into [active, finished, aborted] [26], or synonyms like [running, closed, canceled] is neither necessary nor sufficient. Similar to BPMN, knowledge workers may require specific end states where the classification into regularly closing a case and canceling one is not always possible, and maybe additional active states for routing and prioritizing as well. Hence, in [29] and in Pertuniti, these are configurable and can be used for filtering.

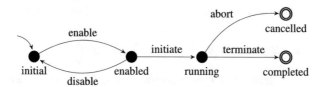

Fig. 4. Execution lifecycle of a subprocess instance

Process state coordinates both knowledge workers and workflow engines. Hence, the execution lifecycle is similar to process fragments in Chimera [26], as depicted in Fig. 4. If the applied modeling notation provides some sort of end state, e. g. BPMN end events or accepting nodes in Petri nets, the subprocess instance is annotated with this end state as well.

6.4 Data Dependencies

As introduced in Definition 1, the case contains all resulting data artifacts. A subprocess instance should reference external artifacts it depends on either in its attributes A, i. e. V may include reference types, or in the execution state $\psi_{\mathcal{N}}$. If artifacts are stored within the same context, other subprocess instances may use them. For example, in regulated branches, creating a document may trigger reviewing and approving it. In a shared context, the subprocess model does not necessarily have to know the reviewing process, i. e. this approach facilitates loose coupling.

If subprocess models of the same overall case do not know each other, they might impose redundant data entry on knowledge workers. For loose coupling, we can formulate user tasks that optionally request information if necessary: *require(type, scope, name)*, e. g. *require*("text", case, "location"). Types can be attributes or other artifacts available at the selected scope.

6.5 Common and Differentiating Execution Semantics

While implementing the approach, commonalities and differences between execution semantics become apparent. For typical paradigms, a workflow engine can provide an event log of all activities performed within the instance. Regardless of notation, a workflow engine can derive applicable next activities, e. g. current tokens in BPMN, available tasks in DCR graphs based on markings, and applicable transitions in Petri nets. Depending on the notation, some decisions are performed by the user, some by a workflow engine. Activities can be manual, i. e. the model supports in regard to coordination, or automated.

Differences arise in regard to decisions: Some notations entail that automated activities can be triggered without supervision, some notations require user input as decisions are non-deterministic. Obviously, declarative notations require more sophisticated internal states to capture intermediate results for dependencies. Even token-based notations can be implemented differently, as in BPMN it is relevant which incoming sequence flow has been passed by a token, while e. g. in Petri nets, the amount of tokens suffices. Obviously, these characteristics can be translated to some degree with additional nodes. All notations that we apply in Sect. 7 require different internal states for execution.

7 Demonstration: Lecture "Process Analytics"

We prototypically implemented the processes outlined in Sect. 5 and extended the ACMS Pertuniti in regard to offering subprocess workflow engines and enabling execution of multiple subprocesses of different notations. Pertuniti [31, 32] is an academic spin-off and the results of this paper were designed and implemented in close collaboration. It targets knowledge-intensive processes with an emphasis on ad-hoc processes, i. e. when the actual process unfolds as it is performed. No defined process model is the expected default. Pertuniti shows characteristics of groupware and social software, and implements process management as project and knowledge management.

Still, knowledge workers also perform routine work to some degree, and organizations of regulated domains, like healthcare, have to model some processes or aspects in advance. Process models in Pertuniti are implemented according to the outlined approach to combine flexibility of ACM with structure and automation. Processes can be modeled as a subset of BPMN, DCR graphs, and accepting Petri nets. While BPMN and DCR graphs are expected to be applied by customers, accepting Petri nets are primarily intended to show that the approach allows different types of imperative and declarative notations.

In Pertuniti, the whole sketch of Fig. 3 can be performed in practice. For ad-hoc activities, document management is available for current lecture notes, test data, or other files, and it does not require predefined process models. The course schedule and individual meetings with students and research assistants can be managed in a calendar. Ad-hoc tasks can be managed in categorized lists and a Kanban board. Similar to customer relationship management systems, all additional important communication, e. g. notes on conversations with the exam office or questions that might be good candidates for the exam, can be captured as typed interactions. As all case artifacts are stored within the same system of record, they can easily be directly referenced and commented. Each case

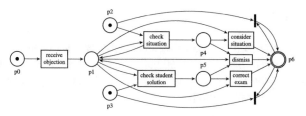

Fig. 5. Objections as accepting Petri nets

and artifact can be annotated with arbitrary attributes in an EAV schema. All activities performed within a case are captured within an "activity stream", i. e. an event log that is displayed to knowledge workers. Activity streams are available on case, subprocess and case artifact level to support traceability and coordination of case workers involved.

Figure 1 for conducting exams can be applied without any adaptations. It is primarily intended for coordination, i. e. the steps are not automated. The service task "Generate Excursion Settlement" of Fig. 2 has to be annotated with the appropriate document template and a variable mapping. Register students is currently a manual task. Figure 5 provides an example for an accepting Petri net for objections after the exam. It requires that objections that are dismissed are checked in regard to the situation and solution. For acceptable objections, checking what has been objected to suffices.

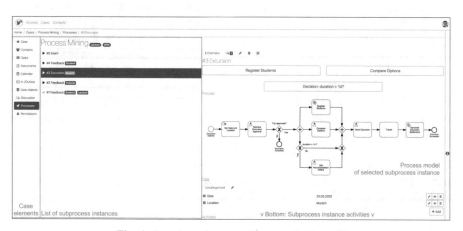

Fig. 6. Running subprocess instances in Pertuniti

All these process models of different notations can be applied as subprocesses within the same context. Figure 6 depicts how these subprocesses are integrated into a case: Each case has a list of subprocess instances. From this list, subprocess models can be initiated, and manual activities and decisions applicable for running instances can be performed. An instance overview depicts the corresponding model and provides an instance-level activity stream.

8 Discussion

We discuss our approach in regard to notions of the term adaptive case management, applicability of different modeling notations within the same system, roles and impact on execution semantics, a case as the shared context of all corresponding activities, and in regard to process mining techniques.

8.1 Adaptive Case Management

Due to the prevalence of model-based ACM systems, Keith Swenson wrote a position paper that postulated "any work support system that depends upon processes designed with BPMN (or BPMN-like languages) cannot be considered an ACM system" [18]. While his statement is intended to raise discussions, we need to show that our approach that combines ACM with BPMN-like languages can still be considered ACM. This question should first be divided into 1) what can be considered as adaptive case management, and 2) whether our approach still fits the definition.

To resolve 1), there are different opinions: CMMN [13] introduces the general concepts with "Any individual Case may be resolved in a completely ad-hoc manner, but as experience grows in resolving similar Cases over time, a set of common practices and responses can be defined for managing Cases in a more rigorous and repeatable manner. This becomes the practice of Case management [...]" [13, p. 5], i. e. that case work can be performed completely ad-hoc, but that they see case management only *after* introducing cases in a more rigorous and repeatable manner, or rather by being modeled. They emphasize this point with "A Case has two distinct phases, the design-time phase and the run-time phase" [13, p. 6]. For *adaptive* case management, even the actions to be performed in a case are typically not known in advance [4]. An ACMS has to support knowledge workers in *planning* their course of action, but also in changing the plan [4], and knowledge work unfolds [5]. In knowledge work, planning and performing work converge, i. e. the two *distinct* phases of design-time and run-time should no longer be distinct for *adaptive* case management.

Correspondingly, we apply the term "ad-hoc activity" as actually not being known in advance, even though notations like BPMN contain abstract "ad-hoc tasks". Analogous, modeled process fragments are either structured or semi-structured, but not unstructured work, i. e. we apply "unstructured" similar to "not (yet) modeled". By supporting unstructured work with these definitions, ACM systems could be interesting in project management situations as well.

To answer part 2), our approach does not rely on structured processes, and no process schema is necessary to perform work. Knowledge workers decide whether to apply a process model or perform activities manually. Our approach allows for user-defined routine subprocesses that do not need to be designed by experts, can initially be implemented with little investment and a varying degree of BPM experience, and the concrete implementation facilitates reducing tacit knowledge in process models. Subprocess models act as a support mechanism to reduce manual work and decision making. Work support systems may include means to simplify routine work, even in ACM. As Pertuniti (cf. Sect. 7) and Agora [29, 30] show, ACM systems can provide structured routine fragments of processes alongside ad-hoc activities.

8.2 Notation-Agnostic Process Modeling

Typically, deciding on which modeling notation to use, and whether to apply an imperative or declarative paradigm, entails the choice of the process support system. The appropriate notation highly depends on the process to be supported, and on previous experience of the modeler. Currently, we cannot identify a modeling notation or paradigm that fits every situation or requirement, and most likely, there is none. A notation-agnostic approach of subprocess models with a shared context facilitates modelers to apply the notation they know and want to use. Declarative and imperative paradigms and notations can be combined within the same process support system.

If knowledge workers want to use a subprocess model, they must explicitly invoke it. The knowledge worker decides which activities are necessary or whether a model should be used at all. Changes of the process do not require changing the model as knowledge workers can transparently deviate from it. Changing the model can be performed as soon as the manual effort of deviating from it would be more expensive. Further, in regulated domains, e. g. healthcare, certain processes must be modeled in advance [31]. Such models can be used as subprocess models in our approach. Knowledge workers can then invoke the model to automate particular activities, e. g. generating documents or entering attributes.

Our approach does not require modeling full processes: Routine aspects or fragments suffice to facilitate automation and traceability. By not requiring models for a complete process with all edge cases, end users are enabled to model small routine aspects of their work themselves, and can still continue to manually perform work in the same context. Routine fragments of different types of processes can be combined, e. g. approving and booking travel expenses. Fragments may range from document templates or forms to full process models. Additionally, we prevent modeling processes that may not be reasonable or even feasible for a lot size of 1. A first iteration of support, subsequently, requires only very little investment. As knowledge workers can instantly apply subprocesses, we facilitate them gaining experience and confidence in BPM, which yields better models with less effort.

8.3 Roles and Execution Semantics

Roles in actual knowledge-intensive processes are often fluid. Explicitly capturing them may only be necessary if projects become larger, or in regulated domains. In our approach, roles can be assigned on demand. For example, roles annotated in DCR graphs or BPMN swimlanes can be interpreted as a requirement to be filled. If no user is available for the role, the engine can ask which user should assume it. If knowledge workers want to perform a certain task with an annotated role, the engine can document assuming that role. Once a role is assigned, it is available for other subprocesses as well.

8.4 The Case as Shared Context

A case as the shared context of routine and ad-hoc activities allows reducing manual data entry since subprocess instances may use the same master data and case artifacts. For example, the location of participating at a conference, approving travel expenses and actually booking the trip is the same. Subprocesses may apply data of an instance scope, a case scope, or case artifacts, i. e. not all context is based on global variables. Still, capturing dependencies between context data and subprocesses is an open problem that, with current techniques, does require "programmer-like skills" to fully understand them. Solutions need to find an appropriate compromise that concerns ontologies for coordination, aspects of compiler construction and encapsulation for defining scopes, and a sensible effort for defining and modeling the scope appropriate to non-programming domain experts.

Dependencies between different process models might also become desirable, as subprocesses still *are* aspects of an overall process. As subprocess modeling allows for loose coupling between aspects, capturing dependencies between tasks and subprocesses could be extended to stay loose coupling for concrete artifacts. The speech-act-based approach of Agora [29, 33] is intended to allow just that by deriving inferences and applying rules based on interactions. For dependencies of activities of the same knowledge worker that do not require interactions, approaches like Chimera [26] could be generalized to our approach. This way, one could derive "aspect-oriented BPM" similar to aspect-oriented programming.

8.5   Towards Adaptive Case Mining

Finally, making activity streams explicit on different granularities could facilitate process mining techniques for routine aspects of a case. Currently, a happy path for ACM case instances is not very sensible as knowledge workers can assume a lot size of 1. However, discovery, conformance checking, and enhancement [34] of routine fragments of a case could facilitate automation and execution. For that, process mining techniques might need to be adapted in regard to record linkage and to better correlate and ignore ad-hoc activities and artifacts. Currently, the granularity of subprocess instance event logs allows applying process mining techniques, but not yet in the context of the whole case.

9   Conclusion

We introduced an approach to combine ad-hoc activities and automation in ACM via subprocess modeling. A case serves as the shared context all activities are performed in, and contains all routine and ad-hoc case artifacts. Knowledge workers can transparently deviate from predefined subprocess models. They may add additional tasks in a case, change any case artifacts or deciding if and which subprocess models to invoke. The support system implementing our approach serves as a system of record for the whole case.

We implemented the lecture module process analytics in the ACMS Pertuniti that applies our approach and enables executing subprocesses of cases modeled in BPMN, DCR graphs, and accepting Petri nets. Our motivating example uses all three notations and requires ad-hoc activities as well. The approach makes all ad-hoc and routine activities transparent by providing activity streams on case, subprocess instance, and case artifact level.

Still, some challenges remain. First of all, we plan to conduct an in-depth empirical evaluation of our approach. As it is prototypically implemented in the commercial ACMS Pertuniti, we are going to assess the quality of our approach in a real-world setting. Further topics are open for future research from a technical point of view. Due to the isolation of subprocess instances, dependencies between instances are only captured by the shared context. To remain loosely coupled, solutions might consider further abstractions of goals and tasks. Moreover, data dependencies between models currently are solved similar to global variables in programming languages, and do not consider ontologies and more sophisticated encapsulation. Finally, our focus on event logs of different granularity unveils that process mining for routine aspects of knowledge-intensive processes might become a viable option. Process mining techniques need to be adapted in regard record linkage and correlating ad-hoc artifacts to really make process mining a viable option in ACM.

References

1. Lund, S., Manyika, J., Ramaswamy, S.: Preparing for a new era of knowledge work. McKinsey Q. **4**, 103–110 (2012)
2. Swenson, K.D.: Robots don't innovate - innovation vs automation in BPM, May 2015
3. Drucker, P.F.: Knowledge-worker productivity: the biggest challenge. Calif. Manag. Rev. **41**(2), 79–94 (1999)
4. Swenson, K.D.: Innovative organizations act like systems, not machines. In: Fischer, L. (ed.) Empowering Knowledge Workers: New Ways to Leverage Case Management, pp. 31–42. Future Strategies Inc. (2014)
5. Swenson, K.D.: The nature of knowledge work. In: Mastering the Unpredictable: How Adaptive Case Management will Revolutionize the Way that Knowledge Workers Get Things Done. Meghan-Kiffer Press (2010)
6. Hildebrandt, T., Marquard, M., Mukkamala, R.R., Slaats, T.: Dynamic condition response graphs for trustworthy adaptive case management. In: Demey, Y.T., Panetto, H. (eds.) OTM 2013. LNCS, vol. 8186, pp. 166–171. Springer, Heidelberg (2013). https://doi.org/10.1007/978-3-642-41033-8_23
7. Pesic, M., van der Aalst, W. M. P.: A declarative approach for flexible business processes management. In: Eder, J., Dustdar, S. (eds.) BPM 2006. LNCS, vol. 4103, pp. 169–180. Springer, Heidelberg (2006). https://doi.org/10.1007/11837862_18
8. Haisjackl, C., et al.: Understanding declare models: strategies, pitfalls, empirical results. Softw. Syst. Model. **15**(2), 325–352 (2014). https://doi.org/10.1007/s10270-014-0435-z
9. Zugal, S., Soffer, P., Haisjackl, C., Pinggera, J., Reichert, M., Weber, B.: Investigating expressiveness and understandability of hierarchy in declarative business process models. Softw. Syst. Model. **14**(3), 1081–1103 (2013). https://doi.org/10.1007/s10270-013-0356-2
10. De Giacomo, G., Dumas, M., Maggi, F.M., Montali, M.: Declarative process modeling in BPMN. In: Zdravkovic, J., Kirikova, M., Johannesson, P. (eds.) CAiSE 2015. LNCS, vol. 9097, pp. 84–100. Springer, Cham (2015). https://doi.org/10.1007/978-3-319-19069-3_6
11. Schönig, S., Jablonski, S.: Comparing declarative process modelling languages from the organisational perspective. In: Reichert, M., Reijers, H.A. (eds.) BPM 2015. LNBIP, vol. 256, pp. 17–29. Springer, Cham (2016). https://doi.org/10.1007/978-3-319-42887-1_2
12. van der Aalst, W.M.P., Pesic, M., Schonenberg, H.: Declarative workflows: balancing between flexibility and support. Comput. Sci. Res. Dev. **23**(2), 99–113 (2009)

13. Object Management Group: Case Management Model and Notation (CMMN). Technical report (2016). https://www.omg.org/spec/CMMN/1.1/PDF

14. Mukkamala, R.R.: A formal model for declarative workflows. Ph.D, IT University of Copenhagen (2012)

15. Zeising, M., Schönig, S., Jablonski, S.: Towards a common platform for the support of routine and agile business processes. In: International Conference on Collaborative Computing: Networking, Applications and Worksharing, pp. 94–103 (2014)

16. de Leoni, M., Maggi, F.M., van der Aalst, W.M.P.: Aligning event logs and declarative process models for conformance checking. In: Barros, A., Gal, A., Kindler, E. (eds.) BPM 2012. LNCS, vol. 7481, pp. 82–97. Springer, Heidelberg (2012). https://doi.org/10.1007/978-3-642-32885-5_6

17. Fahland, D., et al.: Declarative versus imperative process modeling languages: the issue of understandability. In: Halpin, T., et al. (eds.) BPMDS/EMMSAD -2009. LNBIP, vol. 29, pp. 353–366. Springer, Heidelberg (2009). https://doi.org/10.1007/978-3-642-01862-6_29

18. Swenson, K.D.: Position: BPMN is incompatible with ACM. In: La Rosa, M., Soffer, P. (eds.) BPM 2012. LNBIP, vol. 132, pp. 55–58. Springer, Heidelberg (2013). https://doi.org/10.1007/978-3-642-36285-9_7

19. van der Aalst, W.M.P.: Process Mining: Data Science in Action, 2nd edn. Springer, Heidelberg (2016). https://doi.org/10.1007/978-3-662-49851-4

20. Object Management Group: Business Process Model and Notation (BPMN) (2011). http://www.omg.org/spec/BPMN/2.0

21. Aalst, W.M.P.: Everything you always wanted to know about Petri nets, but were afraid to ask. In: Hildebrandt, T., van Dongen, B.F., Röglinger, M., Mendling, J. (eds.) BPM 2019. LNCS, vol. 11675, pp. 3–9. Springer, Cham (2019). https://doi.org/10.1007/978-3-030-266 19-6_1

22. Scheer, A.W.: ARIS—vom Geschäftsprozess zum Anwendungssystem. Springer, Heidelberg (2013). https://doi.org/10.1007/978-3-642-56300-3

23. Künzle, V., Reichert, M.: Philharmonicflows: towards a framework for object-aware process management. J. Softw. Maint. Evol. Res. Pract. 23(4), 205–244 (2011)

24. Künzle, V., Reichert, M.: Philharmonicflows: research and design methodology. Universität Ulm (2012)

25. Künzle, V., Reichert, M.: A modeling paradigm for integrating processes and data at the micro level. In: Halpin, T., et al. (eds.) BPMDS/EMMSAD -2011. LNBIP, vol. 81, pp. 201–215. Springer, Heidelberg (2011). https://doi.org/10.1007/978-3-642-21759-3_15

26. Hewelt, M., Weske, M.: A hybrid approach for flexible case modeling and execution. In: La Rosa, M., Loos, P., Pastor, O. (eds.) BPM 2016. LNBIP, vol. 260, pp. 38–54. Springer, Cham (2016). https://doi.org/10.1007/978-3-319-45468-9_3

27. Meyer, A., Herzberg, N., Puhlmann, F., Weske, M.: Implementation framework for production case management: modeling and execution. In: Enterprise Distributed Object Computing Conference (EDOC), pp. 190–199 (9 2014)

28. van der Aalst, W.M.P., Barthelmess, P., Ellis, C.A., Wainer, J.: Proclets: a framework for lightweight interacting workflow processes. Int. J. Coop. Inf. Syst. 10(04), 443–481 (2001)

29. Tenschert, J.: Speech-act-based adaptive case management. Ph.D. thesis, Friedrich-Alexander-Universität Erlangen-Nürnberg, Erlangen (2019)

30. Tenschert, J., Lenz, R.: Agora - speech-act-based adaptive case management. In: Azevedo, L., Cabanillas, C. (eds.) Proceedings of the BPM Demo Track 2016 Co-located with the 14th International Conference on Business Process Management (BPM 2016), Rio de Janeiro, Brazil, 21 September 2016, vol. 1789, pp. 61–66. CEUR Workshop Proceedings (2016)

31. Tenschert, J., Hormesch, M.: Flexibility, adherence, and guidance for regulated processes with case management. In: BPM 2020 Industry Forum. CEUR Workshop Proceedings (2020)

32. Tenschert, J., Marmaridis, S.: Pertuniti: subprocess modeling and hierarchic case management. In: BPM 2020 Demo Track. CEUR Workshop Proceedings (2020)
33. Tenschert, J.C., Lenz, R.: Towards speech-act-based adaptive case management. In: AdaptiveCM 2016–5th International Workshop on Adaptive Case Management and Other Non-workflow Approaches to BPM (2016)
34. van der Aalst, W. M. P., et al.: Process mining manifesto. In: Daniel, F., Barkaoui, K., Dustdar, S. (eds.) BPM 2012. LNBIP, vol. 99, pp. 169–194. Springer, Heidelberg (2012). https://doi.org/10.1007/978-3-642-28108-2_19

Capturing the Dynamics of Business Models: Towards the Integration of System Dynamics and Reference Modeling

Maren Stadtländer[(⊠)], Thorsten Schoormann, and Ralf Knackstedt

Information Systems, University of Hildesheim, Hildesheim, Germany
{maren.stadtlaender,thorsten.schoormann,
ralf.knackstedt}@uni-hildesheim.de

Abstract. In face of the complexities of business models as well as their dynamic and uncertain environments, business model designers increasingly rely on a systemic view, for example by applying System Dynamics. Despite acceptance in research and practice, this approach comes however with several drawbacks such as high complexity of model construction and the models themselves. To overcome these challenges, we examine the potential of integrating reference modeling and System Dynamics. In this study, we describe the expected benefits and requirements of reference modeling for business models, give a preliminary overview of suitable reference model components, and outline promising directions of our ongoing and future research.

Keywords: Business modeling · System Dynamics · Reference models

1 Introduction and Problem Awareness

With the rising complexity, dynamics, and interconnectedness of today's businesses and the innovation of existing and introduction of entirely new business models, research increasingly understands a business model as "*a complex system of interrelated subcomponents [...] interacting with heterogenous internal and external influences leading to the evolution of its components and the system itself*" (p. 8) [1], with the notion that "*business models themselves are never static*" (p. 3) [2]. This requires firms to view their business model through a systemic lens across the entire lifecycle in order to prevent undesired consequences of their design choices or, in the worst case, the implementation of non-viable business ventures.

Visualization has been considered a promising approach to guide the development and assessment of business models [3]. Thus far, business model modeling languages (e.g., the Business Model Canvas (BMC) [4]) often take a static view of the components implemented to create and deliver value [2]. However, as the components of a business model such as its value proposition and revenue model are highly interdependent [5], business model development can benefit from considering these interrelations. In this line, the approach of System Dynamics (SD) [6] has started to be recognized with acceptance from scholars (e.g., [7, 8]) and practitioners (e.g., [9]) alike. Generally, SD offers

F. Ahlemann et al. (Eds.): WI 2021, LNISO 48, pp. 376–383, 2021.
https://doi.org/10.1007/978-3-030-86800-0_26

notations for depicting the causal relations in a system as well as diagrams examining its state with the goal of emulating a system's past behavior and identifying the root cause(s) for a behavior under examination. Studies using SD in the context of business models include modeling sustainability-oriented business models [10], case studies on benefits of SD for business model innovation [7, 9], and case studies adapting the BMC to create a causal loop diagram [11]. Also, SD is researched for assessing a business model's viability [12] and experimenting with business model alternatives [13]. However, even though SD is a useful tool for (re-)designing and assessing business models, the approach comes with several shortcomings: (a) business models captured with SD are often overwhelmingly large and complex [7, 9, 14], especially since (b) many users (e.g., practitioners or managers) lack experience with them, leading to low-quality models and dependence on external modeling expertise [9, 11, 15]. SD is (c) not easy to learn and apply [15], particularly whenever the stakeholders involved wrongly expect a quick and simple modeling experience [14], or when they thus far have embraced a static, linear mindset towards business models [11]. Lastly, (d) while it is generally desirable to include a diverse set of stakeholders at the business model design stage, this diversity of views has been observed to lead to a "*least common denominator consensus*" (p. 397), in which stakeholders resort to oversimplifying, modeling linear causal links between elements, or applying "*conventional business model logic*" (p. 400) [7]. This is detrimental because SD specifically aims to examine non-linear relationships between elements of a system.

Against this backdrop, this short paper reports on the first steps of an overarching Design Science Research (DSR; [16, 17]) project in which we explore how the reuse of model components or entire models can bridge these shortcomings and support business model designers. While approaches for model reuse exist in different fields such as software engineering (cf. [18] for an overview), we specifically suggest to build upon reference modeling (RM) (e.g., [19–22]). We find RM promising as this approach is not only established in Information Systems research and practice (for an overview see [23]; more recent studies apply RM to, e.g., business process management [24, 25], or data modeling [26] and management [27]) but has also been applied in the context of business models (e.g., [28–31]) and dynamic modeling (e.g., [32–34]) before. As overarching goal of our research, we therefore pose the following question: *How to make use of reference modeling to overcome the challenges when applying SD in business model development?* Overall, we bring together three different streams: business model development, System Dynamics, and reference modeling. In this paper, we present our first steps towards developing an artifact (a *reference model*) to respond to our research question by giving an *awareness of problems* arising through the use of SD for business model development (Sect. 1) and making a *suggestion* for addressing these challenges through reference modeling (Sect. 2). Next, we provide an overview of studies using SD for business model development. Thereby, we tentatively identify a starting point for reference model *development* in the form of potentially reusable model components, and thereby demonstrate the feasibility of reference modeling in this domain, while pointing out gaps requiring further examination (Sect. 3). Finally, we give an outlook next steps regarding the research question (Sect. 4).

2 Reference Modeling for System Dynamics-Based Business Model Development

Reference models can be defined as reusable "*generic conceptual models that formalize state-of-the-art or best practice knowledge of a certain domain*" (p. 2) [22], and reference modeling as the act of constructing and applying such models [19]. Through reference modeling, benefits such as time and cost reduction during model construction and increased model quality are expected to arise [21]—thus, promising avenues to address the aforementioned challenges of SD in terms of (re-)designing business models. Additionally, we expect reference models to provide a valuable basis for less experienced modelers because a pre-defined structure allows them to explore the complex interdependencies of a business model without the pitfall of (wrongly) assuming linear causal relations, and supports including only relevant variables for decreased model complexity. Research has already begun to explore the use of generic SD models in the context of business design and assessment (e.g., [11, 13, 35–37]). However, the majority has focused on describing cases in which a general model was used as a basis for constructing a specific one (e.g., [38], building upon the BMC), with limited elaboration on the benefits of model reuse (e.g., best practice knowledge) in the modeling process itself or how to derive such generic models. Hereby, the potential of reference modeling in supporting SD-driven business model design remains untapped. Moreover, we lack specific requirements for how a *reference model* and its corresponding *reference model components* (i.e., partial models or single elements that are then, for example, aggregated) should be designed and applied. Therefore, we base our suggestion particularly on requirements from reference modeling literature. For designing a purposeful solution in the form of a reference model for SD-based business model development, the following requirements need to be considered.

First, different criteria concerning reference model quality like generality, flexibility, completeness, usability, and understandability are stressed in literature [39]. In context of business model design this implies, for example, that a reference model should be generic enough to apply to different projects while remaining helpful to an individual designer, which also requires considering the tradeoff between generality and specificity [21]. Also, the reference model should contain all necessary business model components to be considered complete. Thus, as a first requirement, *a reference model for SD-based business model design must adhere to general RM quality criteria (RQ1)*.

Second, business model designers require support when applying the reference model to their project. Literature suggests, for example, methodical support, the use of model (component) repositories, or automated approaches for adaptation [21]. Hence, *support for business model designers in applying the reference model* is needed *(RQ2)*.

Third, RM research describes language-based requirements such as: adaptability of the language [40]; enabling placeholders, integrating interfaces or connectors for aggregating model components, and providing generic, adaptable elements [41]; highlighting components in need of adaptation [21]. While some, such as modules for aggregating several models, are already available for SD [42], others may require extending the SD notation or integrating further languages. Therefore, our solution should *make use of existing SD constructs and extend them where necessary (RQ3)*.

3   Reference Model Components in Related Literature

To identify a status quo and potential base for deriving reference model components, we conducted a preliminary literature survey on articles applying SD to business models. Following [43], we searched AISeL, Wiley Online Library, Science Direct, ACM, and JSTOR for "system dynamics" and terms related to business models and business model frameworks (e.g., "business model", "resources", "service provision"; 8 relevant studies). We extended this literature base through a forward and backward search [43] starting from two recent papers [7, 11], which yielded another 6 relevant articles, and analyzed the SD models using the framework by [44].

Table 1 gives an overview of the results, with each line describing an SD model and indicating the components of a business model included. We list both generic models (i.e., providing generalized SD elements) and non-generic models (i.e., capturing a specific case; marked with an asterisk). Studies containing a generic and a non-generic SD model mapping the same business model components [11, 36] have been grouped in the table. Through our analysis, we were able to examine for which business model components generic or non-generic models or model elements already exist that may serve as a basis for the subsequent development of reference model components.

Table 1. Potential reference model components per business model component [44].
(• model contains element for business model component, * generic model)

Source	Strategy	Resources	Network	Customers	Value proposition	Revenues	Service provision	Procurement	Finances
[11]/[11]*	–	•	•	•	•	•	•	–	•
[13]*	–	•	•	•	•	•	•	–	•
[35]*	–	•	•	•	•	•	•	–	•
[36]/[36]*	–	•	•	•	•	•	•	–	•
[37]	–	–	–	•	•	•	•	–	•
[38]*	–	–	–	–	–	•	–	–	•
[45]	–	–	–	–	–	–	–	–	•
[46]	•	•	–	–	–	•	•	–	•
[47]	–	–	–	–	•	–	–	–	–
[48]*	•	•	–	•	–	•	•	–	•
[49]	–	•	•	•	•	•	–	–	•
[50]	–	–	–	–	•	•	–	–	•
[51]	–	•	–	–	–	•	–	–	•
[52]*	–	•	•	•	•	•	–	•	•

The following five main observations emerge: First, those models describing the most components often use the BMC as a generic blueprint and for structuring the variables (e.g., [11, 13, 35, 37]). Second, monetary aspects (revenues and finances), which are relevant economic factors and easily quantified, are most represented across the models (e.g., maintenance spending [49], total salary [35]). Third, the strategy behind a company's business model (e.g., outsourcing policy [46]) is underrepresented in our sample. Fourth, some of the generic models provide examples of more specific variables to use in place of the generic ones (e.g., *"Resource_1 eg Raw materials"* [36]). Finally, in some cases, the SD elements mapping one business model component are not tightly interconnected, but instead individual elements for the specific component are dispersed across the entire model (e.g., [49]), which may hinder easy reuse.

4   Research-in-Progress and Outlook

In this paper, we have motivated reference modeling as a promising approach for overcoming challenges of using SD in business model development and assessment such as a high model complexity and difficulty of the construction process. Furthermore, we have derived an initial set of requirements, and given an overview of existing SD models providing a basis for designing reference model components. In line with the DSR methodology, several steps are necessary for developing and evaluating our artifact. First, most often generic components form the base for applying reference modeling [53]. These may be entirely generic or dedicated to, for example, a specific industry. Hence, we need to *elicit generic components* from existing research and practice. One of the advantages of SD is the opportunity to create models precisely capturing an individual system. Standardized reference model components can lower the cost (time, money) of modeling, while potentially limiting a precise match between the model and the real system. Therefore, in line with the requirements described in Sect. 2, we need to *identify a suitable level of standardization* for the reference model, considering model fit and modeling cost. Second, SD modeling and simulation can be applied during business model design (e.g., [35]), but also for assessment after its implementation (e.g., [49]). Therefore, it is necessary to *examine how SD modeling integrates into the business model lifecycle* and *adapt existing business model development methodologies or propose new ones*. Third, various researchers highlight the benefit of applying software tools for developing business models (e.g., [2, 54–56]). However, there is in general a lack of SD-driven tools to support developing business models with a systemic mindset [13], wherefore it is necessary to *examine requirements of tools for SD-driven business model development allowing for reference modeling support* and *how these may be instantiated* as a software prototype. Finally, our reference model must provide a satisfactory solution to the identified shortcomings, and ideally should be compared to other available reuse approaches. To ensure quality of the solution, guidelines for evaluating reference models (cf. [19]) should be considered.

Ultimately, we hope to extend existing research on model reuse in using SD for business model design through a reference model and its application in order to empower business model designers to capture the dynamics of business models and their uncertain environment.

Acknowledgement. This work was partially funded by the State of Lower Saxony under the project "Qualität Plus" (ID: 27-73724/15-4). We would like to thank for their support.

References

1. Schaffer, N., Pfaff, M., Kcrmar, H.: Dynamic business models: a comprehensive classification of literature. In: MCIS 2019 Proceedings (2019)
2. Bouwman, H., de Reuver, M., Heikkilä, M., Fielt, E.: Business model tooling: where research and practice meet. Electron. Mark. **30**(3), 413–419 (2020). https://doi.org/10.1007/s12525-020-00424-5
3. Täuscher, K., Abdelkafi, N.: Visual tools for business model innovation: recommendations from a cognitive perspective. Creat. Innov. Manag. **26**, 160–174 (2017)
4. Osterwalder, A., Pigneur, Y.: Business Model Generation: A Handbook for Visionaries, Game Changers, and Challengers. Wiley, Hoboken (2010)
5. Amit, R., Zott, C.: Creating value through business model innovation. MIT Sloan Manag. Rev. **53**, 36–44 (2012)
6. Forrester, J.W.: Industrial Dynamics. MIT Press, Cambridge (1961)
7. Moellers, T., von der Burg, L., Bansemir, B., Pretzl, M., Gassmann, O.: System dynamics for corporate business model innovation. Electron. Mark. **29**(3), 387–406 (2019). https://doi.org/10.1007/s12525-019-00329-y
8. John, T., Kundisch, D., Szopinski, D.: Visual languages for modeling business models: a critical review and future research directions. In: ICIS 2017 Proceedings (2017)
9. Groesser, S.N., Jovy, N.: Business model analysis using computational modeling: a strategy tool for exploration and decision-making. J. Manag. Contr. **27**(1), 61–88 (2015). https://doi.org/10.1007/s00187-015-0222-1
10. Abdelkafi, N., Täuscher, K.: Business models for sustainability from a system dynamics perspective. Organ. Environ. **29**, 74–96 (2016)
11. Cosenz, F., Noto, G.: A dynamic business modelling approach to design and experiment new business venture strategies. Long Range Plan. **51**, 127–140 (2018)
12. Köpp, S., Schwaninger, M.: Scrutinizing the Sustainability of Business Models: System Dynamics for Robust Strategies. University of St. Gallen, St. Gallen (2014)
13. Cosenz, F., Rodrigues, V.P., Rosati, F.: Dynamic business modeling for sustainability: exploring a system dynamics perspective to develop sustainable business models. Bus. Strateg. Environ. **29**, 651–664 (2020)
14. Cosenz, F.: Supporting start-up business model design through system dynamics modelling. Manag. Decis. **55**, 57–80 (2017)
15. Featherston, C.R., Doolan, M.: A critical review of the criticisms of system dynamics. In: 30th International Conference of the System Dynamics Society (2012)
16. Hevner, A.R., Ram, S., March, S.T.: Design science in information systems research. Manag. Inf. Syst. Q. **28**, 75–105 (2004)
17. Vaishnavi, V., Kuechler, B. and Petter, S.: Design science research in information systems. http://desrist.org/design-research-in-information-systems/. Accessed 26 Nov 2020
18. Frakes, W.B., Kang, K.: Software reuse research: status and future. IEEE Trans. Softw. Eng. **31**, 529–536 (2005)
19. Fettke, P., Loos, P.: Referenzmodellierungsforschung. Wirtschaftsinformatik **46**(5), 331–340 (2004). https://doi.org/10.1007/BF03250947
20. vom Brocke, J.: Referenzmodellierung. Gestaltung und Verteilung von Konstruktionsprozessen. Logos-Verlag, Berlin (2015)
21. Becker, J., Delfmann, P., Knackstedt, R.: Adaptive reference modeling: integrating configurative and generic adaptation techniques for information models. In: Becker, J., Delfmann, P. (eds.) Reference Modeling, pp. 27–58. Physica-Verlag, Heidelberg (2007)
22. Becker, J., Knackstedt, R., Pfeiffer, D., Janiesch, C.: Configurative method engineering - on the applicability of reference modeling mechanisms in method engineering. In: AMCIS 2007 Proceedings (2007)

23. Fettke, P., Loos, P.: Classification of reference models: a methodology and its application. IseB **1**, 35–53 (2003)
24. Scheer, A.-W., Nüttgens, M.: ARIS architecture and reference models for business process management. In: van der Aalst, W., Desel, J., Oberweis, A. (eds.) Business Process Management. LNCS, pp. 376–389. Springer, Heidelberg (2000). https://doi.org/10.1007/3-540-45594-9_24
25. Scheer, A.-W.: Business Process Engineering: Reference Models for Industrial Enterprises. Springer, Heidelberg (1998). https://doi.org/10.1007/978-3-642-79142-0
26. Fellmann, M., Koschmider, A., Laue, R., Schoknecht, A., Vetter, A.: Business process model patterns: state-of-the-art, research classification and taxonomy. Bus. Process. Manag. J. **25**, 972–994 (2019)
27. Legner, C., Pentek, T., Otto, B.: Accumulating design knowledge with reference models: insights from 12 years' research into data management. J. Assoc. Inf. Syst. **21**, 735–770 (2020)
28. Keller, R., König, C.: A reference model to support risk identification in cloud networks. In: Proceedings of the 35th International Conference on Information Systems (2014)
29. Han, E., Suh, B., Shin, S.K.: Developing a reference model for analyzing mobile platform business: from an ecosystem view. In: AMCIS 2016 Proceedings (2016)
30. Gilsing, R.A.M., Türetken, O., Grefen, P.W.P.J., Adali, O.E.: A reference model for the design of service-dominant business models in the smart mobility domain. In: Proceedings of the 39th International Conference on Information Systems (2018)
31. Schmid, B.F., Lindemann, M.A.: Elements of a reference model for electronic markets. In: Proceedings of the Thirty-First Hawaii International Conference on System Sciences, pp. 193–201 (1998)
32. Pundoor, G., Herrmann, J.W.: A hierarchical approach to supply chain simulation modelling using the supply chain operations reference model. Int. J. Simul. Process Model. **2**, 124–132 (2006)
33. Bagheri, E., Ghorbani, A.A.: UML-CI: a reference model for profiling critical infrastructure systems. Inf. Syst. Front. **12**, 115–139 (2010)
34. Xu, L., Tan, W., Zhen, H., Shen, W.: An approach to enterprise process dynamic modeling supporting enterprise process evolution. Inf. Syst. Front. **10**, 611–624 (2008)
35. Cosenz, F., Noto, G.: Fostering entrepreneurial learning processes through dynamic start-up business model simulators. Int. J. Manag. Educ. **16**, 468–482 (2018)
36. Cosenz, F., Bivona, E.: Fostering growth patterns of SMEs through business model innovation. A tailored dynamic business modelling approach. J. Bus. Res. (2020, in press)
37. Gomez Segura, M., Oleghe, O., Salonitis, K.: Analysis of lean manufacturing strategy using system dynamics modelling of a business model. Int. J. Lean Six Sigma (2019, ahead of print)
38. Bianchi, C.: Introducing SD modelling into planning and control systems to manage SMEs' growth: a learning-oriented perspective. Syst. Dyn. Rev. **18**, 315–338 (2002)
39. Matook, S., Indulska, M.: Improving the quality of process reference models: a quality function deployment-based approach. Decis. Support Syst. **47**, 60–71 (2009)
40. Rosemann, M., van der Aalst, W.: A configurable reference modelling language. Inf. Syst. **32**, 1–23 (2007)
41. vom Brocke, J.: Design principles for reference modeling: reusing information models by means of aggregation, specialisation, instantiation, and analogy. In: Fettke, P., Loos, P. (eds.) Reference Modeling for Business Systems Analysis, pp. 47–76. IGI Global, Hershey (2007)
42. Simantics: Simantics System Dynamics: Open Source Modelling and Simulation Tool for Simantics. http://sysdyn.simantics.org/
43. vom Brocke, J., Simons, A., Niehaves, B., Reimer, K., Plattfaut, R., Cleven, A.: Reconstructing the giant: on the importance of Rigour in documenting the literature search process. In: ECIS 2009 Proceedings (2009)

44. Wirtz, B.W., Pistoia, A., Ullrich, S., Göttel, V.: Business models: origin, development and future research perspectives. Long Range Plan. **49**, 36–54 (2016)
45. Auer, C., Follack, M.: Using action research for gaining competitive advantage out of the internet's impact on existing business models. In: BLED 2002 Proceedings (2002)
46. Bivona, E., Montemaggiore, G.B.: Understanding short- and long-term implications of "myopic" fleet maintenance policies: a system dynamics application to a city bus company. Syst. Dyn. Rev. **26**, 195–215 (2010)
47. Currie, W.L., Joyce, P., Winch, G.: Evaluating application service provisioning using system dynamics methodology. Br. J. Manag. **18**, 172–191 (2007)
48. Fang, Y., Davidsen, P.: Building business-to-consumer competence in Chinese fast-growing industries: a system dynamics model. In: AMCIS 2003 Proceedings (2003)
49. Mayo, D.D., Dalton, W.J., Callaghan, M.J.: Steering strategic decisions at London underground: evaluating management options with system dynamics. In: Proceedings of the 2003 International Conference on Machine Learning and Cybernetics, pp. 1578–1584. IEEE (2003)
50. Risch, J.D., Troyano-Bermúdez, L., Sterman, J.D.: Designing corporate strategy with system dynamics: a case study in the pulp and paper industry. Syst. Dyn. Rev. **11**, 249–274 (1995)
51. Strohhecker, J., Größler, A.: Implementing sustainable business strategies. Syst. Res. Behav. Sci. **29**, 547–570 (2012)
52. Hajiheydari, N., Zarei, B.: Developing and manipulating business models applying system dynamics approach. J. Model. Manag. **8**, 155–170 (2013)
53. vom Brocke, J., Buddendieck, C.: Konstruktionstechniken für die Referenzmodellierung - Systematisierung, Sprachgestaltung und Werkzeugunterstützung. In: Becker, J., Delfmann, P. (eds.) Referenzmodellierung, pp. 19–49. Physica-Verlag, Heidelberg (2004)
54. Schoormann, T., Behrens, D., Knackstedt, R.: The noblest way to learn wisdom is by reflection: designing software tools for reflecting sustainability in business models. In: ICIS 2018 Proceedings (2018)
55. Szopinski, D., Schoormann, T., John, T., Knackstedt, R., Kundisch, D.: Software tools for business model innovation: current state and future challenges. Electron. Mark. **30**(3), 469–494 (2019). https://doi.org/10.1007/s12525-018-0326-1
56. Osterwalder, A., Pigneur, Y.: Designing business models and similar strategic objects: the contribution of IS. J. Assoc. Inf. Syst. **14** (2013)

Future of Digital Markets and Platforms

Introduction to the WI2021 Track: Future of Digital Markets and Platforms

Rainer Alt[1], Armin Heinzl[,2], and Christof Weinhardt[3]

[1] Leipzig University, Information Systems Institute, Leipzig, Germany
rainer.alt@uni-leipzig.de
[2] University of Mannheim, Chair in General Management
and Information Systems, Mannheim, Germany
heinzl@uni-mannheim.de
[3] KIT - Karlsruhe Institute of Technology, Institute of Information Systems
and Marketing, Karlsruhe, Germany
christof.weinhardt@kit.edu

1 Track Description

Digital markets and digital platforms have gained importance in recent years. Today, the majority of the ten most valuable companies worldwide pursue a platform business model. Similarly, many established supply chain models are evolving into multi-sided platform models and change the competitive dynamics in many industries. Driven by strong technology change, the world of digital markets and platforms is evolving to comprise a variety of strategic, functional and technological design options. For example, we are seeing more and more decentralized marketplaces and platforms that are fully digitalized and replacing traditional intermediaries and existing value-added structures (Alt 2020). This concerns not only systems in the consumer-oriented area such as app stores and social media platforms, but also more technical interorganizational systems such as Industrial Internet-of-Things (IIoT) platforms or industry ecosystems. In this sense, also service industries such as banking are currently discussing the concepts of open banking and platform banking. In addition, an increasingly intense competition between platform providers on the one hand and a combination of different platforms on the other may be observed. At the same time, the concentration in American or Asian platform markets creates a high degree of dependencies and a lack of platform sovereignty, i.e. the market power of the dominating "very large platforms" has revealed negative consequences for consumers as well as for competition (van der Aalst et al. 2019). In view of these developments, our conference track aimed to discuss new developments in the field of digital markets and platforms.

2 Research Articles

The track attracted 22 papers, which were reviewed by an associated editor and by at least two reviewers. We would like to thank all who contributed and present the following eight full and two short papers, which were accepted after one review round:

- "A Systematic Literature Review of Digital Platform Business Models" by Dennis Mallon yields 23 digital platform concepts, which were related to 20 aggregated business model components and led to the formulation of eight research focus areas and three future research areas.
- "A Taxonomy of Industrial IoT Platforms' Architectural Features" by Laurin Arnold, Jan Jöhnk, Florian Vogt and Nils Urbach analyzes the technology stack of industrial IoT platforms and presents a taxonomy of IIoT platforms' architectural features and platform archetypes.
- "Explaining Reviewing Effort: Existing Reviews as Potential Driver" by Alexander Kupfer, Christoph Rohde and Steffen Zimmermann) identify that the reviewing effort and the difference between the reviews' and the own valence relates to the number of existing reviews.
- "A Comparison of Crowd Types: Idea Selection Performance of Students and Amazon Mechanical Turks" by Victoria Banken presents an experiment how anonymous workers attracted via crowdworking platforms perform compared to student teams, where members are known.
- "Data-driven Competitive Advantages in Digital Markets: An Overview of Data Value and Facilitating Factors" by Victoria Fast, Daniel Schnurr and Michael Wohlfarth collects empirical evidence on the business value and economic benefits that firms can derive from data-driven digital markets.
- "Tweeting in IIoT Ecosystems – Empirical Insights from Social Media Analytics about IIoT Platforms" by Dimitri Petrik, Katharina Pantow, Patrick Zschech and Georg Herzwurm reveal currently discussed topics in social media regarding digital platforms in the industrial IoT domain.
- "The Role of Complementors in Platform Ecosystems" by Marius Deilen and Manuel Wiesche conduct a literature review to understand the types of complementors. The heterogeneity and the individual evaluation of are derived as major findings to understand the role of complementors.
- "How to Design IIoT-Platforms your Partners are Eager to Join: Learnings from an Emerging Ecosystem" by Tobias Moritz Guggenberger, Fabian Hunke, Frederik Möller, Anne-Cathrine Eimer, Gerhard Satzger and Boris Otto derive principles for designing IIoT platforms.
- "What Goes Around, Comes Around: The Effects of 360-Degree Experiences on Peer-To-Peer Platform Behavior" by Anke Greif-Winzrieth, Christian Peukert and David Dann is a short paper that describes initial results on the impact of 360-degree pictures on consumer behavior.
- "Prominence-for-data schemes in digital platform ecosystems: Economic implications for platform bias and consumer data disclosure" by Marc Bourreau, Janina Hofmann and Jan Krämer is the second short paper and compares prominence-for-data against prominence-for-money schemes.

References

Alt, R.: Evolution and perspectives of electronic markets. Electron. Mark. **30**(1), 1–13 (2020). https://doi.org/10.1007/s12525-020-00413-8

Van der Aalst, W., Hinz, O., Weinhardt, C.: Big digital platforms. Bus. Inf. Syst. Eng. **61**(6), 645–648 (2019). https://doi.org/10.1007/s12599-019-00618-y

A Systematic Literature Review of Digital Platform Business Models

Dennis Mallon[(✉)]

Berlin Institute of Technology, Chair for Information and Communication
Management, Berlin, Germany
`dennis.mallon@campus.tu-berlin.de`

Abstract. Platforms and business models have been a subject of academic analysis and practical application for years. As digital platforms are significantly different due to an intervened and complex nature, typologies, fundamental concepts, and business models have been studied from separated perspectives. This paper reviews the platform and business model literature using a systematic literature review that identifies concepts underlying digital platforms. Henceforward, this research develops a working definition and links 109 business model components to 24 digital platform concepts to figure out what components constitute digital platforms' business models. Furthermore, the analysis shows that several digital platform concepts were deficient or not represented by business model components indicating the need for future research. The study concludes and discusses theoretical and practical implications, suggests future research areas, and marks its limitations.

Keywords: Digital platform · Business models · Business model components

1 Introduction

Digital platforms, as drivers for our time's technical infrastructure, change permanently the way people and socio-technical ecosystems communicate, socialize, interact, consume, and share with one another [1–4]. The emergence of these large-scale and multi-sided digital platforms disrupts numerous industries, such as transportation, banking, and retailing, and continue to change the traditional intermediation between supply and demand in our markets [5]. At its core, digital platforms coordinate and mediate between heterogeneous actors around a product, a resource, a service, or a technology based on direct or indirect network effects. The generated dynamics achieve growth by innovative and highly scalable business models that break familiar processes, intervene in exchange value chains, and gain exclusive access to customers [6, 7]. Digital platforms are embedded into more extensive digital infrastructures and compete on all technical and non-technical architecture levels while generating causal dynamics with users, internal resources, technical systems, complementors, and physical assets [8]. This generativity produces ecosystems that create research objects which surpass traditional information systems in size and scope [9]. The distributed internal structure and its intertwined connection to its environment pose massive research challenges and grow the scope and diversity of scientific discourse rapidly [1, 10].

As a unit of analysis and modeling for businesses, the concept of Business Models started to get attention in the 1990s [11–13]. Many definitions and interpretations of the business model concept were formed, leading to an inconsistent and even ambiguous state of research [7, 12, 14–16]. For instance, Osterwalder defined a Business Model as: "…conceptual tool that contains a set of elements and their relationships and allows expressing the business logic of a specific firm" [17, p. 3]. Schweiger et al. built on the research of Osterwalder and stated that business model components represent the smallest element of a business model and can therefore be used to examine specific parts of a business model in detail separately, such as the revenue model or the governance structure [18]. Nevertheless, a digital platform business model differs from traditional business models. Different models can be applied for sellers, buyers, complementors, and partners on various technical and non-technical architecture levels simultaneously [19]. The need for an accurate understanding of the digital platform business model and its components as a unit of analysis increases as aggregates such as industries, profit pools, or markets are no longer the ultimate references [5, 20]. Therefore, this research uses a systematic literature review methodology to answer the following research questions (RQ).

RQ: *What components constitute the business model of digital platforms and relate to the digital platforms' underlying concepts?*

First, this review presents the methodological approach used during this research in section two. Second, section three provides a theoretical background on digital platform business models and defines its term in a working definition. Third, this research identifies the underlying concepts the literature is currently referring to when corresponding to digital platforms and presents the findings in a concept matrix after Webster and Watson [21]. In this study, concepts can be understood as abstract ideas or general notions mentioned by other authors that summarize certain phenomena observed in digital platforms. Also, abstract description, classification of platform mechanisms, description of characteristics, and digital platforms' peculiarities are summarized under concepts. Fourth, after extracting business model components from the literature, this research links these components to the digital platforms' underlying concepts and presents its results in section four. Fifth, section five discusses the results, derives theoretical implications and practical implications, indicates avenues of research activities for the future, and points to this study's limitations.

2   Research Design and Methodology

The following research is based on a systematic literature review [22]. It seeks to uncover the sources relevant to the digital platform business model to contribute to the business model research stream's relevance and rigor, explaining how one research builds on what is already known [23, 24]. The following overview provides a summary of the literature research procedure.

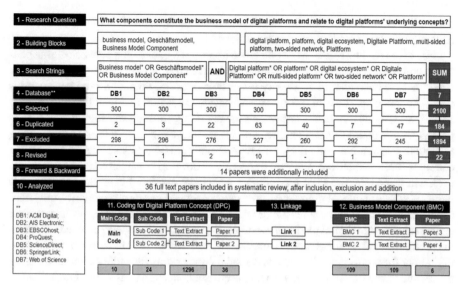

Fig. 1. The systematic literature research process

The author divided the research question from section one into equivalent term fields, which are linked independently of one another, and then with one another [25]. This approach is called the block building method [25]. As a result, a so-called term matrix creates subject blocks and search terms according to a scheme illustrated in Fig. 1, steps two and three. The aim is to identify different synonyms for the sub-terms. Rowley and Slack also stated that it is commonly recommended to use a set of search phrases to exclude irrelevant contributions [24, 26]. Based on the subject blocks, the author derived and applied the following search strings: (digital platform* OR platform* OR digital ecosystem* OR Digitale Plattform* OR multi-sided platform* OR two-sided network* OR Plattform*) AND (Business model* OR Geschäftsmodell* OR Business Model Component*) to collect literature on the subsequent search library databases: ACM Digital Library, AIS Electronic, EBSCOhost, ProQuest, ScienceDirect, SpringerLink, Web of Science. For selecting the literature, the author used the database functionality to sort the results concerning the relevance of a return in the database. This study selected the highest-ranking records that appear at the top of the list based on the library database ranking system considering the database fields abstract, title, and keywords. A limitation was set to the first 300 papers per database due to the high return on hits. After this threshold, the author conducted a title and abstract screening but did not identify additional new concepts, which is a sign of near completion. A specific time range, as an example, the last five years, was not applied in this research as this limitation would not have included fundamental research. For instance, the concept of network effects, which has been significant for digital platforms, has been broadly discussed at the beginning of 2000. Also, articles in English and German were selected to reduces language bias. Roughly 2% of the article were written in German. The author screened the title, abstract, and keywords of 2100 articles, removed 184 duplicates, and subsequently applied the inclusion and exclusion criteria. Excluded from this research are studies about application development, benchmarks, crowdfunding, cybersecurity, education, farming, and political communication.

Furthermore, this research only included articles if a connection between digital platforms and business model components were indicated or if underlying digital platform concepts have been identified. Twenty-two articles were eligible for this review after this step. The author performed a forward-and-backward search and included additionally 14 articles [21, 24]. A backward search means going through the sources' bibliographies, and a forward search identifies articles that have cited the relevant publications, to include relevant literature [21]. This review analyzed 36 articles using an explorative coding process, which was repeated iteratively to develop conclusive coding constructs [27]. More specifically, 1296 text phrases have been extracted from the literature and iteratively coding into 24 digital platform sub-concepts. For reasons of clarity, only concepts that were mentioned at least four times were considered. These sub-concepts were aggregated into ten digital platform concepts. Separately, this review screened the literature and extracted business model components, and further related these components to digital platform concepts. The business model components the author identified during the review of the literature, are given and used as a conceptual basis. The connection of business model components to digital platform concepts followed an iterative approach of linking a business model component by its description and definition. Henceforward, the results are presented and analyzed in Sect. 4.

3   Theoretical Background on Digital Platform Business Models

Over the last couple of decades, there has been an extensive research on business models centering around how firms create, deliver, and capture value [28, 29]. Several literature reviews and investigations of the business model concept led to various scientific literature definitions and practical understandings [16]. Often cited in the literature are Zott et al., which define that: "A business model depicts the content, structure, and governance of transactions designed so as to create value through the exploitation of business opportunities" [30, p. 493]. Henceforward Teece defines: "A business model articulates the logic and provides data and other evidence that demonstrates how a business creates and delivers value to customers. It also outlines the architecture of revenues, costs, and profits associated with the business enterprise delivering that value" [31, p. 173].

With the emergence of digital technology and the ever-increasing importance, availability, and usability of data, traditional, analog, or offline business models get often disrupted [5]. For digital platforms does the digital technologies in use imply homogenization of data, editability, reprogrammability, distributedness, and self-referentiality, which can lead to multiple inheritances in distributed settings, depending on the control mechanism and governance principles applied by the platform owner [4, 10, 32]. As all digital platforms build on a constantly evolving information technology, the digital infrastructure and its continually changing software base are vital drivers of dynamics and changes within the digital platform [3]. Therefore, Tiwana defines digital platforms to the extent that it: "…consists of an extensible codebase of a software-based system that provides core functionality shared by the modules that interoperate with it and the interfaces through which they interoperate" [33, p. 676]. As an extendible codebase enables third-party development of complementors via boundary resources, the integration of complementors is highly relevant for the digital platforms' design [34]. The boundary resource can exist on multiple digital platforms layers and often shift very rapidly [35]. Moreover, data as a boundary resource is gaining importance in practice. The users provide their data to the digital platform. The platform owner makes this data accessible via software tools, like Application Interfaces (API) and Software Development Kits (SDK) to complementors [1]. The platform and the complement often regulate this exchange by an arms' length relationships [1, 36]. The integration is an incremental part of digital platforms. Multiple external parties, like users, providers of services, digital products, and complements, are invited on the layered, modular architecture to create value [37, 38]. Recently, Abdelkafi noted that a platform architecture is: "...a modularization that partitions the system into (1) a set of components whose design is stable and (2) a complementary set of components which are allowed – indeed encouraged – to vary" [39, p. 554]. Henceforward, the adaption to changes creates an incredibly complex task because organizations and business environments continuously evolve. The paradox of change implies the need for digital platforms to remain stable simultaneously and form a solid foundation for further enrolment and be sufficiently flexible to support unbounded growth and innovation effects [1, 40–42]. This digital platform's behavior is necessary to obtain the generativity, which describes the: "...overall capacity to produce unprompted changes driven by large, varied, and uncoordinated audiences" [43, p. 1980]. Several researchers stated the importance of the right balance between central and decentral structures because the governance determines whether the layered, modular architecture will successfully lever the innovation [33, 38, 44, 45]. Tiwana defines governance regarding who decides what and stated that: "...architecture can reduce structural complexity, governance can reduce behavioral complexity..." [46, p. 118]. Based on the work of Wareham et al., Constantinides describes the development of platform governance as a challenge, as it is how: "...to establish governance mechanisms that appropriately bound participant behavior without excessively constraining the desired level of generativity..." [38, 47, pp. 1195–1196]. The decision about openness and control mechanism applies on various levels, ranging from open interfaces to open source as bounding participants affect value creation and capture [1, 39, 48]. Therefore, in a closed platform, the fear of losing control of the platform owner can keep industry players from joining in the first place [39]. More users can be attracted in an open platform, creating a greater pool of potential contributors, which can lead to more innovations, probably in a shorter time frame [39, 49].

Further research adds to the technical understanding and characterizes digital platforms as a socio-technical assemblage encompassing the technical elements and associated organizational processes and standards [40]. The organization is primarily incremental for digital platforms as the entire culture, like mental models, skills, experiences, traditions, and the organizational identity, needs to relate to the digital setup, the underlying concepts, and its dynamics [50]. Moreover, the organizational set up needs to absorb the architectural modularity, as the organization needs to provide the variety and flexibility to handle technological trajectories [51]. Furthermore, it is essential to add non-technical aspects of digital platforms, such as the utilization as a mediator between different actors to facilitate the multi-party exchange of goods, services, or information to create value between the user and capture the value [20]. At its core, digital platforms enable a sharing system among user groups, providing digital services to communicate, conduct transactions, collect, process, and share data related to their common interests or activities [50]. Balancing the quality and quantity of the exchange enables a repeatable user interaction that is often facilitated in consumers' online communities [1, 51]. Necessary for the transaction on platforms is the user's trust as it influences the platform's sales [52, 53]. Schreieck et al. found that most digital platforms use a rating or review system to establish trust and to decrease perceived risk as users are more likely to use the platform due to the protective mechanisms [52]. These platforms are often categorized as marketplaces or transaction platforms and are subsumed under the definition of digital platforms for this research [34].

Centrally significant for digital platforms are network externalities or network effects as an enabler of dynamics to increase the single participants' utility as the platform's size grows [50]. Network effects can either be direct or indirect [7]. Network effects are direct, if the value of a digital platform depends on the number of users in the same user group, meaning it becomes more attractive for users as the total number of users on the same side increases [1, 11]. Indirect network effects occur when the platform's value depends on the users' number in a different user group. It becomes more attractive for one group of users as the number of another group increases [11].

Additionally, digital platforms can apply economies of scale, meaning that the average cost declines as users' number increases [11]. The concept is not unique to digital platforms, but the effects are more evident as the marginal costs are often close to zero. The integration of user and complementors, initiate a constant innovation funnel whereby potential perspectives or ideas for innovations can be included, creating user acceptance [14, 54, 55]. Transactions, network effects, technical and non-technical adaption created various dynamics for digital platforms. Just recently, Abdelkafi et al. have shown that platform businesses' dynamics have been studied from three perspectives, the dynamics effects of digital platforms on markets and industry, the evolutionary dynamics of a platform, and competition effects among platforms [39]. The literature constitutes several delimiting and overlapping concepts and definitions depending on the author's perspectives and investigation area. Guggenberger et al. suggest subsuming digital platform business models under the definition and as a subtype of digital business models [34]. Also, Guggenberger et al. and Reuver et al. argue for the need to determine the subject of investigation. Therefore this research outlines a working definition based on the literature found during this review. Digital Platform Business Models are a conceptual extension of business models that operate on a continually evolving digital infrastructure, creating value while enabling interactions between user groups in the ecosystem, based on network effects [11, 34, 50]. The digital infrastructure and the continually changing and extensible codebase of the software-based systems provide core functionality that enables integration of multiple parties via boundary resources and fosters value creation [3, 33]. The digital platform business model incorporates the organizational needs to provide the variety and flexibility to handle technological trajectories to absorb the architectural modularity [51]. Digital platforms compete on all technical and non-technical architecture levels while generating causal dynamics and innovation funnels with users, internal resources, technical systems, complementors, and physical assets [8]. Overall, the focus lies on delivering digital offerings and digital experiences to customers building highly scalable business solutions in a socio-technical ecosystem [34, 39].

4   Results

This research identified 109 business model components found in the literature and linked them to 24 underlying digital platform concepts to answer the research question from section one. Figure 2 provides an overview of the results based on Webster and Watson [21].

Digital Platform Concepts				Linkage		Business Model Components		
Main Concept	Sub-Concept	# of paper	% of paper	#	in %	Components extracts found in literature	# of paper	% of paper
Adaption / Change	Adaption / Change	5	14%	3	3%	Growth; Platform Lifecycle; Product lifecycle	2	6%
Competitive behaviour	Co-operation	9	25%	4	4%	Co-opetition; Collaboration; Key Partners; Partner Network	3	8%
	Competition	7	19%	8	7%	Competition; Competitive enviorment; Focus on business unit; Focus on business web; Industry scope; Product and service market affected	3	8%
Complements	Complementor Behavior	5	14%	2	2%	Relationship complementor – platform owner; Single vs. multihoming	2	6%
	Complementor Innovation	5	14%	-	-%		-	-%
Digital Infrastructure	Technical Architecture + Modularization	12	33%	2	2%	Technical modularity; Technology design	2	6%
	Software	8	22%	3	3%	Compatibility; Software Interfaces; Software tools (API; SDK)	1	3%
	Technical Infrastructure	16	44%	5	5%	Curation/editorial of data; Data; External data and content usage; Internal data and content usage; Technology infrastructure	3	8%
	Technical Innovation	5	14%	-	-%		-	-%
Dynamics	Dynamics	9	25%	-	-%		-	-%
	Network Effects	15	42%	1	1%	Achieving network effects	1	3%
	Economics of Scale	5	14%	1	1%	Economics of scale	1	3%
Financials	Revenue, Pricing and Costs	5	14%	19	17%	Finance / Revenue (streams); Capital structure; Financial aspects; Pricing and revenue sharing; Profit; Revenue model	6	17%
Governance and Control	Boundary	10	28%	3	3%	Data as Boundary Resource; Documentation; Software tools as Boundary resource	1	3%
	Control	13	36%	5	5%	Control; Control mechanism; Formal control mechanisms; Giving up control over technology; Informal control mechanisms	3	8%
	Governance	12	33%	12	11%	Actors / Roles; Distribution of power; Relationship to stakeholders; Governance Rules; Information (streams); Legals aspects; Number of sides; Ownership; Relationship of Actors; Strategy / Vision / Objective	3	8%
	Integration	6	17%	4	4%	Horizontal/ Vertical integration; Link to physical assets; Relevance of national/local characteristics	2	6%
	Openness	12	33%	3	3%	Granting access to technology; Openness; Use of platform by other applications or platforms	3	8%
Organization	Organization + Culture	6	17%	7	6%	Focus on Organization; Key Resources; Leadership; Organizational Design; Organizational form; Processes / workflow; Resources	2	6%
Other	Other	-	-%	2	2%	Critical success factors; Utility	1	3%
User	Innovation	5	14%	1	1%	Innovation	1	3%
	Interaction	5	14%	4	4%	Channels; Customer Segments; Distribution Channel; Target Customer	2	6%
	Trust	4	11%	4	4%	Customer Relationship; Customer Relationship in a broader sends; Relationship end-user – platform; Review system	3	8%
Value	Transaction	11	31%	2	2%	Transaction content; Transaction type	1	3%
	Value Capture, Creation, Proposition	9	25%	14	13%	Key Activities; Marketplace; Product / Service (streams); Service Design; Value chain / Core competencies; Value Configuration; Value Creation; Value Proposition	5	14%
				109	100%			

Fig. 2. Matrix - business models components linked to digital platform concepts

The matrix above aggregates the extracted and coded literature into main and sub-concepts. The illustration shows the count of papers mentioned for the respective digital platform concept, in absolute and relative figures to the papers' total count. The listed business model components were linked according to the digital platform sub-concepts' alphabetical order. The count of papers mentioning business model components is shown in absolute and relative figures. Components with the same meaning are summarized in this matrix but are counted as occurred. The illustration shows the number of business model components linked to the digital platform sub concept under Linkage's headline. Afterward, the outcomes were indexed into a) the relevance of digital platform concept and b) the relevance of business model component towards digital platform concept. Furthermore, index a was subtracted from index b to determine the distance c, as shown in the following formula.

$$Index\ a - Index\ b = Distance\ c \tag{1}$$

Henceforward the distances between a and b were categorized into HR – high representation, MR - medium/equal representation, LR - Low representation, VLR – very low representation, NR – no representation. The results of the indexation are presented in Fig. 3.

Digital Platform Concept		Index a	Index b	Distance c	Category
Main Concept	Sub Concept				
Adaption / Change	Adaption / Change	0.31	0.16	0.15	MR
Competitive behaviour	Co-operation	0.56	0.21	0.35	LR
	Competition	0.44	0.42	0.02	MR
Complements	Complementor Behavior	0.31	0.11	0.21	MR
	Complementor Innovation	0.31	0.00	0.31	NR
Digital Infrastructure	Software	0.50	0.16	0.34	LR
	Technical Architecture + Modularization	0.75	0.11	0.64	VLR
	Technical Infrastructure	1.00	0.26	0.74	VLR
	Technical Innovation	0.31	0.00	0.31	NR
Dynamics	Dynamics	0.56	0.00	0.56	NR
	Network Effects	0.94	0.05	0.88	VLR
Financials	Economics of Scale	0.31	0.05	0.26	LR
	Revenue, Pricing and Costs	0.31	1.00	-0.69	HR
Governance and Control	Boundary	0.63	0.16	0.47	LR
	Control	0.81	0.26	0.55	LR
	Governance	0.75	0.63	0.12	MR
	Integration	0.38	0.21	0.16	MR
	Openess	0.75	0.16	0.59	VLR
Organization	Organization + Culture	0.38	0.37	0.01	MR
Other	Other	0.00	0.11	-0.11	-
User	Innovation	0.31	0.05	0.26	LR
	Interaction	0.31	0.21	0.10	MR
	Trust	0.25	0.21	0.04	MR
Value	Transaction	0.69	0.11	0.58	VLR
	Value Capture, Creation, Proposition	0.56	0.74	-0.17	HR

Fig. 3. Distance between the relevance of business model components in digital platforms

Business model components linking to the concept of Revenue, Pricing, and Costs (distance: −0.69) and the concept of Value Creation, Value Capturing, and Value Proposition (−0.17) show a high representation as well as a distance below zero. The distance below zero indicates an overrepresentation or a lower relevance of these business model components for digital platform business models than other components, like the technical infrastructure. A high representation results from an intense investigation in the literature [14, 18, 56].

The second category describes a distance between 0–0.2 and determines an equal or medium representation of the business model components toward the relevance as a digital platform concept. In this category, business model components linking to Adaption/Change (0.15), Competition (0.02), Complementor Behavior (0.21), Governance (0.12), Integration (0.16), Interaction (0.10), Organization + Culture (0.01) and Trust (0.04) showing a similar representation with its relevance to constitute the business model of digital platforms. Furthermore, an overlap of the description of business model components and digital platform concepts was identified [36, 56, 57].

A third category shows business model components with a distance between 0.2–0.5 towards the digital platform concepts. For instance, Boundary (0.47) as a digital platform concept was mentioned in ten articles indicating a relatively high relevance for digital platforms. Also, research on digital platforms has emphasized the need to focus on boundaries between digital platforms and their ecosystem, where independent actors pragmatically engage innovations utilizing the opportunities and limitations of the digital or layered-modular architecture [3, 4, 58]. While investigating the boundary as a business model component, a lower relevance than other components indicates a low consideration of this concept in business model components. Similar to the sub-concept Boundary, Co-operation (0.35), Control (0.55), Economics of Scale (0.26), Innovation (0.26), and Software (0.34) stipulate a relative underrepresentation toward other business model components, like the value creation.

As a fourth category, this research identified that concepts, specifically related to digital platforms, find a deficient representation in business model components. For instance, the concept of Network Effects (0.88), highly relevant as a fundamental concept for digital platforms' existence and operation, was linked to one business model component. Also, Openness (0.59), Technical Architecture + Modularization (0.64), Technical Infrastructure (0.74), Transaction (0.58) show a significantly lower representation as business model components than other components.

The fifth category presents digital platform concepts, where no business model components were relatable. Complementor Innovation (0.31), Dynamics (0.56), and Technical Innovation (0.31) found no consideration as a business model component. The category, Other, summarizes components like critical success factors and utility, which could not be related to platform concepts.

5   Discussion and Conclusion

This section concludes the theoretical and practical implications of this research, draws areas for future research based on the research findings, and states its limitations. Based on the findings, this research creates a working definition and relates 109 business model components to 24 digital platform concepts to figure out what components constitute digital platforms' business model. The results acknowledge that a strong research interest exists for business model components of non-digital platforms' as mainly technical and specifically platform concepts are relatively underrepresented by the components derived from the literature. A strong influence of economic and financial interest populates their relevance in the business model components. Also, Reuver et al. criticized the high interest in pricing strategies and financial dynamics rather than innovation dynamics within the economics literature [1].

5.1 Theoretical Implications

First, this review extends the definition of digital platform business models currently examined in the literature. It works on a more substantial connection of digital platform concepts and the business model research streams while integrating digital platform concepts to precisely define the subject of investigation. Therefore this research creates a working definition based on previous work and includes substantial aspects, like dynamics [1, 34]. Still, the difficulty to clearly distinguish between digital and analog and the reflection in business models and components will be a challenging research subject as the digitalization extends the scope of information technology in almost all areas of these socio-technical ecosystems [1].

Second, this study extracts underlying digital platform concepts and presents its relevance currently discussed in the literature. By analyzing the results, areas of the current research interest have been identified. Pointing out the complexity and unique aspects such as network effects helps to understand how digital platforms take over large parts of markets across industries [5]. Furthermore, this study includes user-centric platform business model components such as the users' trust and interactions and therefore adds to prior literature.

Third, this study elaborates business model components constituting digital platform business models. By comparing the relevance of the digital platform concept to the relevance of business model components linked to these concepts, this research identifies five categories. The relative underrepresentation of the digital platform concept, like network effects, technical innovation, and the platform dynamics, indicates the need to further investigate the role of business model components and their adaption through digitalization in digital platform business models.

5.2 Practical Implications

First, this study contributes to the analysis of digital platforms. Without an investigation of the underlying concepts necessary for digital platforms, a holistic understanding of digital platforms and their generative existence is lacking. This study elaborates and derives these platform concepts from the literature, helping practices to design digital platform business model. For instance, this study contributes to increase the awareness for practice to consider an ecosystemic viewpoint and integrate the dynamics created in digital platforms' intertwined nature. Therefore, this research further points out the importance of anticipating changes, adjusting business models, and aligning complementarities to sustain platform viability [44, 59].

Second, this research contributes to the application of the business model concepts. As business model components represent the smallest element of a business model that examines specific parts of a business model in detail, this research analyzes these components' relevance in digital platform business models. This investigation helps practices to consider additional components relevant in applying business model concepts. Without an adaption to the emergence of digital change around business models, Osterwalder's concept of nine blocks probably can be getting less useable in practice increases the risk of a more defective application [13, 60].

5.3 Future Research

Digital platforms make a difference to existing concepts due to their digital infrastructure, the modularization, the integration of complements, the applied governance and controls, the evolving causal relationship within the ecosystem, the innovation dynamics, and the internalization based on network effects [1, 3]. A clear distinction between business model components gets less accurate due to the emergence of information technology, like automation, machine learning, and artificial intelligence [1, 3, 39]. The need increases to anticipate the influence of digitalization and its effects on the business model components itself. This research proposes in **Research Area 1** that further research efforts enhance the business model concept holistically and include dynamics, the innovation, digitally, by users and complementors. Furthermore, it would be worth investigating other business model components, like the user interaction and their adaption to constant digital platforms changes.

Digital platforms use their technical architectures and organizational structures as a source of strategic opportunity to change their directions and relationships over time [39]. These underlying causal relationship should be known and govern carefully [38]. The integration into the associated ecosystems and, in turn, to other ecosystems increases the risk of unforeseen effects in case of unexpected and no manageable changes [53, 59]. Most platforms use the data gathered from transactions and enhance the causal grid as briefly described in the following: more users generate more data, which can be used to improve user experience, which attracts more users because the platform has more users and more data, it can deliver better advertisement campaigns and thereby attract more revenues, which in turn can be used to improve user experience, which attracts more users [11, 61]. This research proposes in **Research Area 2** to investigate digital platforms' causalities using an appropriate modeling language to enhance the mental model of decision-makers, users, complementors, and regulators [62, 63].

Furthermore, the digital platform replaces horizontal and vertical structures with an ecosystemic understanding. Most business model concepts to date still overlook the systemic participation of actors [5, 11, 64]. Digital platforms bring together multiple user groups on various levels of their architecture and create network externalities. This intersection between users, complementors regulators, and digital platforms requires a systematical understanding [1, 3, 35]. For instance, Beer compared business systems to biological systems, emphasizing that organizations as an organism respond to their environment [65]. This ecological perspective argues that the market economy is best understood as a living evolving ecosystem [7, 65, 66]. This research proposes in **Research Area 3** to increase the effort to analyze digital platforms from a system thinking viewpoint, applying system models to emphasize the impact on the socio-technical ecosystem we humans also belong.

5.4 Limitations

This study's limitation lies in the fact that this research was done by one reviewer, which implies a high researcher bias of applying inclusion and exclusion criteria. A structured approach, including a reiterated critical reflection on the decisions, has been chosen to reduce individual bias by the author. Nevertheless, a second and a third researcher would have been provided more objectivity. Additionally, the high amount of hits returned by one literature database opens the questions of this literature database's request. Also, the proposed systematic procedure was enhanced iteratively. During the research process, several studies were added due to the researcher's decision.

Acknowledgments. The author is grateful and wishes to thank the anonymous reviewers for their constructive comments. The Editors-in-Chief's significant encouragement and help in providing excellent feedback and advice are much appreciated and helped to improve the overall quality of this research endeavor.

References

1. de Reuver, M., Sørensen, C., Basole, R.C.: The digital platform: a research agenda. J. Inf. Technol. **33**, 124–135 (2018)
2. Hein, A., Scheiber, M., Böhm, M., Weking, J.: Toward a design framework for service-platform ecosystems. Res. Papers. **132** (2018)
3. Hein, A., Schreieck, M., Wiesche, M., Böhm, M., Krcmar, H.: Digital platform ecosystems. Electron Markets **30**, 87–98 (2020)
4. Yoo, Y., Henfridsson, O., Lyytinen, K.: The new organizing logic of digital innovation: an agenda for information systems research. Inf. Syst. Res. **21**, 724–735 (2010)
5. Demil, B., Lecocq, X., Warnier, V.: "Business model thinking", business ecosystems and platforms: the new perspective on the environment of the organization. M@n@gement, **21**(4), 1213–1228 (2018)
6. Bundesministerium für Wirtschaft und Energie: Weissbuch-Digitale Plattformen. Digitale Ordnungspolitik für Wachstum, Innovation, Wettbewerb und Teilhabe (2017)
7. Kim, J.: The platform business model and business ecosystem: quality management and revenue structures. Manchester (2016)
8. Pon, B., Seppälä, T., Kenney, M.: Android and the demise of operating system-based power: firm strategy and platform control in the post-PC world. Telecommun. Policy **38**, 979–991 (2014)
9. Sørensen, C., Landau, J.S.: Academic agility in digital innovation research: the case of mobile ICT publications within information systems 2000–2014. J. Strateg. Inf. Syst. **24**, 158–170 (2015)
10. Henfridsson, O., Mathiassen, L., Svahn, F.: Managing technological change in the digital age: the role of architectural frames. J. Inf. Technol. **29**, 27–43 (2014)
11. Fehrer, J.A., Woratschek, H., Brodie, R.J.: A systemic logic for platform business models. J. Serv. Manag. **29**, 546–568 (2018)
12. Amit, R.H., Zott, C.: Business model innovation: creating value in times of change. creating value in times of change. SSRN J. (2010)
13. Osterwalder, A., Pigneur, Y., Tucci, C.L.: Clarifying business models: origins, present, and future of the concept. Commun. Assoc. Inf. Syst. **16**, 1–25 (2005)
14. Krcmar, H., Friesike, S., Bohm, M., Schildhauer, T.: Innovation, society and business: internet-based business models and their implications. SSRN J. (2012)
15. Zott, C., Amit, R., Massa, L.: The business model: recent developments and future research. J. Manag. **37**, 1019–1042 (2011)
16. Teece, D.J.: Business models and dynamic capabilities. Long Range Plan. **51**(1), 40–49 (2018)
17. Yablonsky, S.: A multidimensional framework for digital platform innovation and management: from business to technological platforms. Syst. Res. Behav. Sci. **35**, 485–501 (2018)

18. Schweiger, A., Nagel, J., Böhm, M., Krcmar, H.: Platform business models. In: Project Consortium TUM Living Lab Connected Mobility (ed.) Digital Mobility Platforms and Ecosystems, pp. 66–77. mediaTUM (2016)
19. Täuscher, K.: Business models in the digital economy: an empirical classification of digital marketplaces
20. Sorri, K., Seppänen, M., Still, K., Valkokari, K.: Business model innovation with platform canvas. J. Bus. Models 7(2), 1–13 (2019)
21. Webster, J., Watson, R.T.: Analyzing the past to prepare for the future: writing a literature review. Manage. Inf. Syst. Q. 26, xiii–xxiii (2002)
22. Paré, G., Trudel, M.-C., Jaana, M., Kitsiou, S.: Synthesizing information systems knowledge: a typology of literature reviews. Inf. Manage. 52, 183–199 (2015)
23. Shaw, J.: A schema approach to the formal literature review in engineering theses. System 23, 325–335 (1995)
24. Vom Brocke, J., et al.: Reconstructing the giant: on the importance of rigour in documenting the literature search process, 2206–2217
25. Guba, B.: Systematische Literatursuche. Wiener medizinische Wochenschrift 158, 62–69 (2008)
26. Rowley, J., Slack, F.: Conducting a literature review. Manag. Res. News 27, 31–39 (2004)
27. Saldaña, J.: The coding manual for qualitative researchers. SAGE, Los Angeles, Calif., London, New Delhi, Singapore, Washington DC, 14 (2016)
28. Foss, N.J., Saebi, T.: Fifteen years of research on business model innovation. J. Manag. 43, 200–227 (2017)
29. Župič, I., Budler, M., Trkman, P.: Characterization of business model research. Bibliometric analysis and the future agenda. In: Digital Transformation – From Connecting Things to Transforming Our Lives, pp. 719–731. University of Maribor Press (2017)
30. Amit, R., Zott, C.: Value creation in E-business. Strateg. Manag. J. 22, 493–520 (2001)
31. Teece, D.J.: Business models, business strategy and innovation. Long Range Plan. 43, 172–194 (2010)
32. Kallinikos, J., Aaltonen, A., Marton, A.: The ambivalent ontology of digital artifacts. Manag. Inf. Syst. Q. 37, 357–370 (2013)
33. Tiwana, A., Konsynski, B., Bush, A.A.: Platform evolution: coevolution of platform architecture, governance, and environmental dynamics. Inf. Syst. Res. 21, 675–687 (2010)
34. Guggenberger, T., Möller, F., Boualouch, K., Otto, B.: Towards a unifying understanding of digital business models (2020)
35. Walton, N.: Ecosystems thinking and modern platform-based ecosystem theory. In: Walton, N. (ed.) The Internet as a Technology-Based Ecosystem, vol. 17, pp. 85–117. Palgrave Macmillan UK, London (2017)
36. Schreieck, M., Wiesche, M., Krcmar, H.: Design and governance of platform ecosystems. - key concepts and issues for future research. ECIS 2016 Proceedings Research Papers, 76 (2016)
37. Foerderer, J., Kude, T., Mithas, S., Heinzl, A.: Does platform owner's entry crowd out innovation? evidence from google photos. Inf. Syst. Res. 29, 444–460 (2018)
38. Constantinides, P., Henfridsson, O., Parker, G.G.: Introduction—platforms and infrastructures in the digital age. Inf. Syst. Res. 29, 381–400 (2018)
39. Abdelkafi, N., Raasch, C., Roth, A., Srinivasan, R.: Multi-sided platforms. Electron Markets 29, 553–559 (2019)
40. Tilson, D., Sorensen, C., Lyytinen, K.: Change and control paradoxes in mobile infrastructure innovation: the Android and iOS mobile operating systems cases. In: 2012 45th Hawaii International Conference on System Sciences, pp. 1324–1333. IEEE (2012)
41. Tilson, D., Lyytinen, K., Sørensen, C.: Digital infrastructures: the missing is research agenda. Inf. Syst. Res. 21, 748–759 (2010)

42. Resca, A., Za, S., Spagnoletti, P.: Digital platforms as sources for organizational and strategic transformation: a case study of the midblue project. J. Theor. Appl. Electron. Commer. Res. **8**, 11–12 (2013)
43. Zittrain, J.: The generative internet. Harv. Law Rev. **52**, 1974 (2006)
44. Parker, G., van Alstyne, M., Jiang, X.: Platform ecosystems: how developers invert the firm. How developers invert the firm. Manage. Inf. Syst. Q. **41**, 255–266 (2017)
45. Rochet, J.-C., Tirole, J.: Platform competition in two-sided markets. J. Eur. Econ. Assoc. **1**, 990–1029 (2003)
46. Tiwana, A.: Platform ecosystems. Aligning architecture, governance, and strategy. Morgan Kaufmann, Waltham, MA (2013)
47. Wareham, J.D., Fox, P.B., Cano Giner, J.L.: Technology ecosystem governance. Organ. Sci. **1195–1215**, 15 (2013)
48. Eisenmann, T.R.: Managing proprietary and shared platforms. Calif. Manage. Rev. **50**, 31–53 (2008)
49. Huber, T.L., Kude, T., Dibbern, J.: Governance practices in platform ecosystems: navigating tensions between cocreated value and governance costs. Inf. Syst. Res. **28**, 563–584 (2017)
50. Eferin, Y., Hohlov, Y., Rossotto, C.: Digital platforms in Russia: competition between national and foreign multi-sided platforms stimulates growth and innovation. Dig. Policy, Regul. Governance **21**, 129–145 (2019)
51. Spagnoletti, P., Resca, A., Lee, G.: A design theory for digital platforms supporting online communities: a multiple case study. J. Inf. Technol. **30**, 364–380 (2015)
52. Schreieck, M., Hein, A., Wiesche, M., Krcmar, H.: The challenge of governing digital platform ecosystems. In: Linnhoff-Popien, C., Schneider, R., Zaddach, M. (eds.) Digital Marketplaces Unleashed, pp. 527–538. Springer, Heidelberg (2018). https://doi.org/10.1007/978-3-662-49275-8_47
53. Yun, J.J., Won, D., Park, K., Yang, J., Zhao, X.: Growth of a platform business model as an entrepreneurial ecosystem and its effects on regional development. Eur. Plan. Stud. **25**, 805–826 (2017)
54. Chesbrough, H.: Business model innovation: opportunities and barriers. Long Range Plan. **43**, 354–363 (2010)
55. Surowiecki, J.: The Wisdom of Crowds. Why the many are smarter than the few and how collective wisdom shapes business, economies, societies, and nations. Knopf Doubleday Publishing Group, New York (2005)
56. Nooren, P., van Gorp, N., van Eijk, N., Fathaigh, R.Ó.: Should we regulate digital platforms? a new framework for evaluating policy options. Policy Internet **10**, 264–301 (2018)
57. Täuscher, K., Laudien, S.M.: Understanding platform business models: a mixed methods study of marketplaces. Eur. Manag. J. **36**, 319–329 (2018)
58. Eaton, B., Elaluf-Calderwood, S., Sørensen, C., Yoo, Y.: Distributed tuning of boundary resources: the case of apple's iOS service system. Manag. Inf. Syst. Q. **39**, 217–243 (2015)
59. Teece, D.J.: Dynamic capabilities and (digital) platform lifecycles. Adv. Strateg. Manag. **37**, 211–225 (2017)
60. Groesser, S.N., Jovy, N.: Business model analysis using computational modeling: a strategy tool for exploration and decision-making. J. Manag. Control. **27**(1), 61–88 (2015). https://doi.org/10.1007/s00187-015-0222-1
61. Prüfer, J., Schottmuller, C.: Competing with big data CentER discussion paper. SSRN J. (2017)
62. Forrester, J.W.: Industrial Dynamics. Martino Publ, Mansfield Centre, Conn (2013)
63. Groesser, S.N., Schaffernicht, M.: Mental models of dynamic systems: taking stock and looking ahead. Syst. Dyn. Rev. **28**, 46–68 (2012)

64. Wieland, H., Hartmann, N.N., Vargo, S.L.: Business models as service strategy. J. Acad. Mark. Sci. **45**(6), 925–943 (2017). https://doi.org/10.1007/s11747-017-0531-z
65. Beer, S.: Brain of the Firm. John Wiley & Sons, Chichester (1995)
66. Rothschild, M.L.: Bionomics Economy as Ecosystem. . Holt, New York (1992)

A Taxonomy of Industrial IoT Platforms' Architectural Features

Laurin Arnold[1,2(✉)], Jan Jöhnk[1,2], Florian Vogt[1], and Nils Urbach[1,2,3]

[1] FIM Research Center, University of Bayreuth, Bayreuth, Germany
{laurin.arnold,jan.joehnk,florian.vogt,nils.urbach}@fim-rc.de
[2] Project Group Business and Information Systems Engineering of the Fraunhofer FIT, Bayreuth, Germany
[3] Frankfurt University of Applied Sciences, Frankfurt, Germany

Abstract. In the industrial Internet of Things (IIoT), the concept of digital platforms has received significant attention. Although IIoT platforms revolve around similar business objectives, they address a variety of use cases and, thus, differ considerably in their architectural setup. While research has already investigated IIoT platforms from a business or design perspective, little is known about their underlying technology stack and its implications. To unveil different IIoT platform configurations and better understand their architectural design, we systematically develop and validate a taxonomy of IIoT platforms' architectural features based on related literature, real-world cases, and expert interviews. On this foundation, we identify and discuss four IIoT platform archetypes. Our findings contribute to the descriptive knowledge in this ambiguous research field, while also elucidating the interplay of IIoT platforms' architectural setup and their purpose. From a managerial viewpoint, our results may guide practitioners in comparing and selecting a suitable IIoT platform.

Keywords: Industrial Internet of Things · IIoT Platforms · Architecture · Taxonomy · Archetypes

1 Introduction

In recent years, a large number of digital platforms emerged across industries. Digital platforms and their surrounding ecosystem form complex socio-technical systems that build on developing and managing an appropriate IT architecture and governance regime [1]. In the uprising industrial Internet of Things (IIoT), the concept of digital platforms has received significant attention, leading to the emergence of more than 620 IIoT platforms by today [2] and building a market that is growing by more than 26% a year until 2024 [3]. Such IIoT platforms provide a digital infrastructure to connect industrial devices into digital networks to collect and process the generated data and consequently facilitate data-driven services [4]. Thus, Mineraud et al. [5] define IIoT platforms as middleware systems to support and integrate heterogeneous hardware, on top of which third parties can develop complementary applications. Such applications cover manifold solutions, such as production optimization through asset monitoring and advising, machine

F. Ahlemann et al. (Eds.): WI 2021, LNISO 48, pp. 404–421, 2021.
https://doi.org/10.1007/978-3-030-86800-0_28

health monitoring through anomaly detection, or customer transparency through better traceability.

Addressing a variety of use cases, IIoT platforms differ considerably in terms of their underlying technology stack and architectural setup [6]. This is partly due to the technical complexity in business-to-business environments and the lack of established standards in the IIoT leading to rather siloed development [6]. Consequently, the IIoT platform landscape, while revolving around similar business objectives, is scattered. On the one hand, this creates issues for companies that must understand the IIoT platform market to select a vendor that successfully integrates into their existing IT infrastructure. Companies lack a comprehensive scale to organize and guide decisions in the scattered IIoT platform landscape. On the other hand, it creates issues for researchers that seek to understand the interplay of IIoT platforms' architecture and business models, which are strongly interwoven in the context of digital technology. Research has already put effort into investigating IIoT platforms, focusing on their business model [7, 8], framework [9], or design criteria [10]. However, we still miss a unified classification of IIoT platforms' fundamental building blocks, which we subsume as architectural design options, to enable a transparent evaluation and comparison of existing IIoT platforms. Thus, we ask:

How can IIoT platforms be classified by their architectural features?

To answer this research question, we develop a taxonomy of IIoT platforms' architectural features following Nickerson et al.'s guidelines [11]. Taxonomies are well suited to lay the groundwork for emergent research fields and serve as a first step toward systematizing the fundamental design decisions [12]. For taxonomy development, we use both the literature and empirical knowledge from 22 IIoT platforms as well as seven semistructured expert interviews. For taxonomy evaluation, we classify 50 IIoT platforms and, thus, identify and conceptualize four archetypes of IIoT platforms.

Our taxonomy contributes to the descriptive knowledge in this ambiguous research field by explaining the architectural dimensions and prevalent manifestations of digital platforms in the IIoT. Further, we contribute to the prescriptive knowledge by elucidating the interplay between IIoT platforms' architectural setup and their purpose. Lastly, our results provide a comprehensive overview of architectural dimensions that may guide practitioners in comparing and selecting a suitable IIoT platform.

2   Foundations

2.1   Digital Platforms

Originally viewed as multi-sided markets that enable interactions between different actors, the digital platform concept increasingly captured innovation activities [13]. Today, digital platforms are a pivotal element for technological innovation as the examples of Apple, Facebook, or Microsoft show [1]. Capturing this essence, Tiwana et al. [14] define digital platforms as the "extensible codebase of a software-based system that provides core functionality shared by the modules that interoperate with it and the interfaces through which they interoperate". Adding to this view, the network of third-party providers (i.e., complementors) that builds around a digital platform is often referred to as a digital platform ecosystem [15]. We adopt this view and see a digital platform as an extensible technological foundation on top of which third parties can build platform-augmenting applications. Within this view, architecture plays a significant role in the overall design of a digital platform [16]. Tiwana et al. [14] define the architecture of a digital platform as the "conceptual blueprint that describes how the ecosystem is partitioned into a relatively stable platform and a complementary set of modules that are encouraged to vary, and the design rules binding on both". Digital platforms' varying architecture makes it possible to differentiate between them and determines their evolutionary paths [14].

Digital platforms bring together three important stakeholders: the platform owner, complementors, and users. The platform owner runs and governs the digital platform. Complementors build on the digital platform and broaden its functionality with applications. The users consume the functionalities provided by the digital platform [1].

2.2 (Industrial) Internet of Things

The Internet of Things (IoT) integrates technology-enabled physical objects into a global cyber-physical network [17]. It uses recent advances in digital technology such as ubiquitous communication, pervasive computing, or ambient intelligence to connect these objects based on standardized communication protocols. With the help of these technologies, everyday objects turn into so-called smart things [18].

Prior research examines the IoT in terms of its architecture, for example, as a layered reference model [19]. This often results in a multi-layer description of services offered at different architectural levels, depending on the business needs, technical requirements, and technologies. A common three-layer IoT architecture differentiates the perception, network, and application level [20]. The perception level controls objects and collects data, the network level enables information exchange of the data, and the application level supports business services by analyzing the data.

The application of the IoT concept in an industrial context received particular interest in recent years as it proved to be a prime example of the applicability and its underlying economic potential [21]. Current trends in the manufacturing industry point towards combining traditional production, automation, and computational intelligence into a complex system known as the industrial IoT. The literature describes the IIoT concept with different names such as Industry 4.0, Industrial Internet, or Internet of Production [21, 22]. The terms IoT and IIoT are occasionally also used synonymously [4]. Sisinni et al. [19] describe it as being about "connecting all the industrial assets, including machines and control systems, with the information systems and the business processes". Thus, IIoT leverages the mechanical engineering industry into the digital era [23]. Through extraction and utilization of machine data, it is a key enabler for the creation of digital networks in manufacturing processes and ultimately lays the foundation for a smart production system [4].

2.3 Industrial Internet of Things Platforms

IIoT platforms function as a middleware that orchestrates the heterogeneous device landscape in the IIoT and provides a technological infrastructure fostering connectivity and interoperability between the smart machines, control systems, and enterprise software systems [24]. On top of the technological infrastructure, applications provide data-driven services to the platforms' users [25]. These applications consequently extend the machines' functionality by collecting and processing the generated data, thus generating additional value [4]. IIoT platforms exclusively operate in a business-to-business environment, which entails higher technological complexity due to existing hardware, IT infrastructure, and processes, compared to business-to-consumer markets in which most digital platforms operate [4].

Even though IIoT platforms operate in the same industry, they specialize in different service offerings (e.g., equipping devices with digital technology and connecting them to the internet, managing the machinery for more flexible production, or deriving findings through analyzing data). To realize these services, they require different architectural features. As a result, the IIoT platform landscape is scattered among different manifestations, making it difficult to compare IIoT platforms with each other and understand the value they can create.

Research just recently began investigating IIoT platforms, covering different aspects such as their business model [8, 26], frameworks for classification [9], or their design criteria [10]. Regarding the business model, Hodapp et al. [8] focused on constituent elements of a business model and developed a taxonomy to understand the IoT platform market. Similarly, Endres et al. [26] explored IIoT business models to identify their IIoT specific components and overall business model archetypes. One of the archetypes they identified is the 'IIoT platform business model' which is characterized by data-driven analyses through platforms and the applications on them. Regarding IIoT frameworks, Moura et al. [9] proposed a framework that is divided into layers responsible for describing and accommodating key elements for IIoT implementation in an organization. Lastly, researchers investigated how IIoT platforms can be set up by elucidating their design criteria [10] or the concept of boundary resources [24].

However, we still miss a unified classification of architectural design options to enable a transparent evaluation and comparison of existing IIoT platforms. We deem this a practical approach to uncover underlying differences of IIoT platforms that research thus far has not been able to demonstrate.

3 Method

3.1 Taxonomy Development

According to Glass and Vessey [27], taxonomy development refers to a method of "assigning members to categories in a complete and unambiguous way". Taxonomies are schemes with which specific amounts of knowledge can be structured, analyzed, and organized, thus fostering the understanding of the phenomenon [27]. Embedded in the field of design science research, taxonomies can contain both descriptive and prescriptive knowledge and represent artifacts in the form of models [11]. In information systems research, taxonomy development is well received and has already been successfully applied in different contexts when exploring emerging research fields such as smart things [18] or agile IT setups [28]. In line with this exemplary work, we follow the iterative taxonomy development method proposed by Nickerson et al. [11]. This method integrates conceptual and empirical perspectives into one comprehensive method and, thus, fosters the iterative usage of both paradigms. The method follows a seven-step-structure: (1) determination of a meta-characteristic that reflects the purpose of the taxonomy and its target group, (2) determination of ending conditions, (3) choice of either an empirical-to-conceptual (E2C) or conceptual-to-empirical (C2E) approach, (4) conceptualization of characteristics and dimensions, (5) examination of objects, (6) initial design or revision of the taxonomy, and (7) testing of ending conditions. The taxonomy's purpose is reflected in its meta-characteristic, which the researcher defines, together with ending conditions, at the beginning of the development process. Several iterations of taxonomy design and revision, choosing either a C2E or an E2C approach, follow. After each approach, the research tests the resulting taxonomy against the ending conditions until they are met.

For step (1), we define our meta-characteristic as follows: *Architectural features of IIoT platforms*. Thus, our meta-characteristic reflects that we seek to guide both further research and practitioners. For step (2), we determine objective as well as subjective ending conditions of the taxonomy development process [11]. As for the formal correctness of the taxonomy development, we test against the following objective criteria after each iteration: (I) every dimension is unique, (II) every characteristic is unique within its dimension, and (III) at least one object is classified under each characteristic of every dimension. Following Nickerson et al. [11], we define our subjective ending conditions that taxonomy development is finished after the evaluation sees it to be concise, robust, comprehensive, extensible, and explanatory. Besides, we follow Jöhnk et al. [28] and Püschel et al. [18] in combining mutually exclusive (ME) and non-exclusive (NE) dimensions to allow for a parsimonious taxonomy.

For steps (3) to (7), we alternately conducted two C2E and two E2C iterations. In the first iteration (C2E), we searched relevant literature following the guidelines of Webster and Watson [29] and vom Brocke et al. [30]. We deliberately decided to start with a C2E iteration to account for the growing amount of literature as a means to initially structure the field. Thus, we considered research on IoT, IIoT, and digital platforms to gain a comprehensive perspective on the emerging phenomenon of IIoT platforms and to populate initial dimensions and characteristics in our taxonomy. We searched the scientific databases ACM Digital Library, AIS Electronic Library, IEEE Xplore Digital Library, and SpringerLink with the following search string: TITLE("IoT platform*" OR "IIoT platform*" OR "internet of things platform*" OR "industrial internet of things platform*" OR "digital platform*") AND ABSTRACT("architecture" OR "taxonomy" OR "classification"). This search string resulted in 281 publications which we subsequently screened regarding information on architectural features of digital or (I)IoT platforms. Screening the results' titles, abstracts, and – where necessary – full-texts, we reduced the results to 91 remaining relevant publications. We used this knowledge base and additional literature from a forward- and backward search to extract and consolidate architectural features in a table. Drawing on this list in joint discussions, we developed the first increment of our taxonomy consisting of 19 dimensions and related characteristics organized in four overarching layers. Considering that the literature only rarely focuses on IIoT's specifics compared to the IoT and most architectural features in the literature revolve around security aspects, we decided to continue the taxonomy development process.

In the second iteration (E2C), we sought to back the preliminary insights with empirical evidence. Thus, we examined 22 IIoT platforms for their architectural features. We selected platforms identified through market research (e.g., from Gartner's Magic Quadrant and practitioner reports) and those mentioned in literature from the first iteration. For instance, Guth et al. [6] describe architectural features for AWS IoT and Microsoft Azure IoT Hub, among others. Thus, the descriptions and analyses from previous work helped us to confront our emerging taxonomy with existing renowned IIoT platforms. We obtained relevant information for our taxonomy development from platform providers' technical documentation, websites, whitepapers, and relevant press releases. These insights helped us to identify new architectural dimensions and characteristics as well as to substantiate and improve the existing ones. By the end of the second iteration, our taxonomy consisted of 21 dimensions organized in four layers.

In the third iteration (C2E), we returned to the literature to ground the new observations in prior work. Thereby, we strengthened and verified the findings from the second iteration. Specifically, we searched for theoretical concepts describing our observations of IIoT platforms' architectural features and dropped or consolidated dimensions and characteristics in line with our meta-characteristic. For instance, while we found information on IIoT platforms' governance in the second iteration, it does not describe their architectural features in the narrower sense, which is why we removed them from the taxonomy. The third iteration resulted in a taxonomy of 13 dimensions and related characteristics that are organized in four overarching layers.

In the fourth iteration (E2C), we collected and analyzed additional primary data from seven expert interviews (see Table 1). We deemed this iteration necessary to account for IIoT platforms' novelty and peculiarities in developing and evaluating our taxonomy. Our interviews were semi-structured, following an interview guide to ensure coverage and comparability between the interviews [31]. Each interview consisted of four building blocks: introduction (participants, research project, taxonomy research, and clarification of focal terms and concepts), discussing the layers and dimensions of the taxonomy, discussing the characteristics for each dimension in the taxonomy, and overall feedback. We selected interviewees from our industry network (convenient sampling) according to their knowledge in the field of IIoT and/or IIoT platforms. Our experts contribute perspectives from different backgrounds and industries to offset potential biases. The interviews lasted between 55 and 78 min and at least two of the authors were present in each interview. We recorded all interviews with the experts' consent and analyzed them systematically. Thus, all authors engaged in discussing the experts' feedback and further developing the taxonomy. We incorporated the proposed changes between interviews to discuss the improved taxonomy iteratively.

3.2   Cluster Analysis and Archetype Identification

Based on our taxonomy, we seek to identify, conceptualize, and elucidate typical architectural setups of IIoT platforms (i.e., typical combinations of architectural features). This is to understand better the current IIoT platform landscape and guide scholars as well as practitioners in this field. We identified distinct IIoT platform archetypes using cluster analysis. This statistical technique groups objects with similar characteristics and aims for a high degree of homogeneity within each cluster group and a high degree of heterogeneity between cluster groups [32].

Table 1. Overview of the seven expert interviews

	Role of interviewee	Industry	Employees (2019)	Revenue (2019)	Duration
1	Customer engineer	Technology	119,000	141bn €	59 min
2	Software developer	Automotive	133,000	104bn €	58 min
3	Emerging tech. specialist	Automotive	133,000	104bn €	55 min
4	Software architect	Software Dev.	20	1m €	58 min
5	Head of AI/Data analytics	Manufacturing	20,000	3.3bn €	61 min
6	Founder/CEO	Technology	5	-	78 min
7	Data scientist	Automotive	90,000	55bn €	69 min

For this step, we collected data on 50 IIoT platforms that provided the real-world cases for cluster analysis. We used the publicly accessible IIoT supplier database of the market research company IoT One to obtain a comprehensive list of relevant IIoT platforms [33]. Following a structured selection process, this platform sampling approach helped us to gain a larger number of IIoT platforms for classification compared to the taxonomy development phase. At the same time, this approach was detached from any focus and platform selection choices in previous work to increase the transparency and comprehensibility of our cluster analysis. The IoT One database contained information on 3,063 companies at the time of the data collection. We narrowed down the search results using the databases' filter options to select 'platform-as-a-service' entries, resulting in a list of 591 elements. Subsequently, we filtered the list by the five available revenue categories (<$10m, $10m–$100m, $100m–$1bn, $1bn–$10bn, >$10bn) to cover IIoT platforms of different sizes, popularity levels, and with different value propositions. We then sorted the results by profile completeness and selected the first ten platforms from each revenue category that provided sufficient documentation to classify them in our taxonomy (the selected IIoT platforms are listed in Sect. 5).

One author classified the selected IIoT platforms, frequently discussing ambiguities within the research team. We choose agglomerative hierarchical clustering with the Ward algorithm and Manhattan distance function as our clustering approach. We coded every characteristic as binary (1: the IIoT platform offers this architectural feature; 0: the IIoT platform does not offer this architectural feature) and normalized the dimensions' distance as [0;1] to avoid overrating dimensions with more characteristics [18]. Agglomerative hierarchical clustering shows solutions for all possible number of clusters. Thus, we used triangulation to choose the optimal number of clusters based on different statistical measures, visual graph interpretation, as well as interpretability and meaningfulness based on our real-world observations [34]. Regarding the statistical measures, both the kl-index as well as the h-index indicated four clusters as optimal. Additionally, the Dindex and the Hubert index as visual graph interpretation methods support four clusters as the optimal number of clusters as they show a significant peak in their second differences plot, which corresponds to a significant increase in the measure's value. In joint discussions with all authors, we reviewed the four cluster solution and the edge solutions (three and five clusters) to eventually decide on the final four cluster solution. Subsequently, we conceptualized the archetypes' specifics and implications.

4 Taxonomy of Architectural Setups of Industrial IoT Platforms

In the following, we present our final taxonomy (see Fig. 1) and describe the dimensions and characteristics in detail. The taxonomy consists of 13 dimensions encompassing 38 characteristics that we defined according to the pre-specified meta-characteristic. To improve our taxonomy's comprehensibility and real-world fidelity, we structure the dimensions in four layers, i.e. infrastructure, network, middleware, and application layer [18].

4.1 Infrastructure Layer

Industrial IoT platforms are created and cultivated on top of digital infrastructures [35]. In the context of IIoT platforms, such digital infrastructure is represented by the smart things that are connected to the platform and the technical resources on which the platform operates. In this layer, we found three relevant dimensions.

Hardware Support. Regarding the devices that IIoT platforms allow to be connected to it, we found that some IIoT platforms constrain the connectivity to *certified hardware* (e.g., proprietary or selected third-party devices) which are approved by the platform owner, while others are *hardware-agnostic*, meaning they support any hardware as long as it fits the platforms' rough technical specifications.

Platform Hosting. Another differentiation of the infrastructure is how the IIoT platform is hosted. While defining requirements for IIoT platforms, Petrik and Herzwurm [7] name three ways of how IIoT platforms can be hosted: *on-premise*, in a *cloud*, or in a *hybrid* way using both approaches. We adopt these characteristics and extend them by differentiating between *public* and *private cloud* specifications as experts repeatedly pointed out the difference during the interviews.

Data Processing. Our taxonomy research process revealed that IIoT platforms process data on different boundaries of the platform. We found that most IIoT platforms process their data *on-platform*, meaning that depending on the level of platform hosting this happens on-premise or in the cloud. Many IIoT platforms though also offer to process data on the *edge*, meaning that processing happens in a local network or within the smart things without all generated data being sent to the IIoT platform. As some IIoT platforms offer a mixture of both approaches, we also included *fog* as a situation-based data processing characteristic.

	Dimension		Characteristics			
Infrastructure Layer	Hardware Support	ME	Certified Hardware		Hardware-Agnostic	
	Platform Hosting	NE	On-Premise	Public Cloud	Private Cloud	Hybrid
	Data Processing	NE	Edge	Fog		On-Platform
Network Layer	Physical Data Transportation	NE	Wired	Short-Range Wireless	Cellular	LPWAN
	Logical Data Transmission	NE	Internet Protocols	IoT-Specific Protocols		Industry-Specific Protocols
Middleware Layer	Data Structure	NE	Structured		Unstructured	
	Analytics Types	NE	Descriptive	Real-Time	Predictive	Prescriptive
	Analytics Technology	ME	Basic		Advanced	
	External Integration	NE	Business	Machine		Web Services
	Platform Source Code	ME	Open Source	Open Components		Closed Source
Application Layer	APIs	ME	Standardized APIs		Custom APIs	
	Application Deployment	NE	Platform-Native	Containerized		Off-Platform
	Marketplace	NE	Internal Marketplace	External Marketplace		No Marketplace

Fig. 1. Taxonomy of IIoT platforms' architectural features (ME: dimension is mutually exclusive; NE: dimension is non-exclusive)

4.2 Network Layer

As connectivity and interoperability of devices and applications are core capabilities of any IIoT platform, we defined a network layer to collect the respective dimensions. Generally, two prominent frameworks can be found in the literature to describe the structure of networks: OSI and TCP/IP model. We used these models to derive two dimensions that describe the network layer of an IIoT platform, similar to the proposed stack-lower and stack-upper layer of Sisinni et al. [19].

Physical Data Transportation. These options can be categorized into *wired*, meaning a cable-bound transmission, and wireless, therefore cable-unbound transmission. While the former represents a homogeneous group of transmission methods, the latter contains heterogeneous groupings of different wireless transmission methods. Therefore, we distinguish wireless transmission methods into three sub-categories: *short-range wireless*, which includes protocols with high performance but high power consumption and limited range (e.g., WiFi or Bluetooth), *cellular*, which have high performance, high power consumption, and long range (e.g., 5G or LTE), and *low power wide area networks (LPWAN)*, which have low performance, low power consumption and medium to high range (e.g., SigFox or LoRa).

Logical Data Transmission. Consequently, we found that IIoT platforms use different protocols to ensure a common data structure for information exchange. We distinguish between *internet protocols*, which emerged from the conventional internet (e.g., HTTP, XMPP, or Websockets), *IoT-specific protocols*, which meet specific requirements of the IoT and thus overcome many drawbacks of internet protocols (e.g., MQTT, AMQP, or CoAP), and *industry-specific protocols*, summarizing existing industry standards to connect machines (e.g., Modbus, CAN, or BACnet).

4.3 Middleware Layer

Integrating data with applications on the IIoT platform leads to different specifications, which we summarize in the middleware layer. It is responsible for the accumulation and further processing of collected data (e.g., to applications) and consists of all functionalities required by a cyber-physical system. Thus, the layer is integrating the connected hardware to the platform and the software built upon it [6].

Data Structure. When generating data in the IIoT, data can be collected and streamed in different formats and structures. Some IIoT platforms explicitly state that they can deal with *unstructured* data, while others can only process *structured* ones.

Analytics Types. Making use of generated data is a central feature of every IIoT platform. We distinguish four types of analytics methods in the domain of IIoT: *descriptive analytics*, which is the most basic form, and which analyzes historical data to reconstruct events, *real-time analytics* that focuses on current data to identify events, *predictive analytics*, which uses both historical and real-time data to predict future events, and *prescriptive analytics*, which takes the predictive approach even a step further to advise on how to deal with upcoming events.

Analytics Technology. Consequently, IIoT platforms use different kinds of technology to analyze data. We found that they can be categorized into *basic* technologies, such as statistical modeling, and *advanced* technologies such as machine learning and neural networks.

External Integration. IIoT platforms can not only analyze data collected from devices directly connected to the platforms but also include data from external sources. We found that platforms differ in their offerings to integrate other (enterprise) systems. *Business* integration includes systems that deal with business processes and data from

ERP, CRM, or SCM systems, *machine* integration includes legacy systems that are used in factories such as existing PLC or SCADA systems, and *web services* integration include internet-based data sources.

Platform Source Code. The examination of exemplary IIoT platforms revealed that they leverage different approaches to further develop their software. We distinguish between *open source*, meaning that platforms provide their complete source code to the public, *open components*, meaning that platforms release single modular parts of the platform source code to the public or leverage components already being open source, and *closed source*, meaning that platforms keep their source code proprietary.

4.4 Application Layer

Based on the collected data as well as functionalities provided within the middleware layer, IIoT platforms offer the possibility of integrating applications developed internally or by third parties [1]. We summarize the architectural specifics of this provision in the application layer.

APIs. To integrate not only external systems but also applications, IIoT platforms offer different APIs. While on some platforms we only found *standardized* APIs which are maintained by the platform owner, we found other cases where platforms offered possibilities to build *custom* APIs based on predefined syntax and specifications (e.g., via an API Manager).

Application Deployment. The empirical analysis of IIoT platforms revealed that platforms use different approaches to deploy applications built internally or by third-party contributors. In most cases, applications are *platform-native*, meaning that applications have been built with tools provided by and directly running on the platform (e.g., rules engines). In other cases, we found that applications were *containerized*, meaning that the applications have been developed in an external environment, but are deployed on the platform in a containerized environment (e.g., Docker), and in few cases we found that applications were deployed *off-platform*, meaning that the applications are developed and hosted on different infrastructure (e.g., Cloud Foundry).

Marketplace. For the provision of applications to platform users, we found that IIoT platforms use different approaches. They either run an *internal marketplace*, which can be understood like an app-store on a mobile phone, or they make use of an *external marketplace*, which integrates the app-store of another digital platform (e.g., Eclipse Kura Marketplace) into the IIoT platform, or they have *no marketplace* at all.

5   Industrial IoT Platform Archetypes

Drawing on our sample of 50 IIoT platforms, we demonstrate the applicability and usefulness of our taxonomy. Thus, we first derive overarching observations on IIoT platforms' architectural features. Overall, most platforms are hardware-agnostic (82%) and hosted via a public cloud service (96%), even though many platforms offer to choose other settings (on-premise 68%, private cloud 54%, hybrid 36%) as well. While almost all IIoT platforms can process data on-platform (96%) or on the edge (72%), we found that only a minority is capable of situation-based data processing (fog 22%). Most IIoT platforms rely on wired (96%) or short-range wireless (90%) data transportation technologies (cellular 50%, LPWAN 66%). Further, they use different combinations of protocols (internet 52%, IoT-specific 40%, industry-specific 76%). Note that we only considered this characteristic as existing if the IIoT platform offered more than one protocol to account for the diversity of data transmission. Regarding data analysis, most IIoT platforms can handle structured (90%) as well as unstructured (86%) data. Further, all IIoT platforms can analyze data descriptively (100%), with that number declining, the more complex analysis gets (real-time 88%, predictive 64%, and prescriptive 22%). Accordingly, our sample shows a fair split between basic analytics technology used (44%) and advanced methods (56%) used. For external integration of data, most IIoT platforms can integrate web services (90%, business 64%, machine 48%). As for source code openness, two thirds (64%) are closed source (open source 10%, open components 26%). Further, we found a majority of IIoT platforms offering standardized APIs (82%) and deploying applications on the platform (96%) (containerized 24%, off-platform 42%). Lastly, more than half (58%) of IIoT platforms do not offer a marketplace for applications.

Based on the cluster analysis among the IIoT platforms, we identified four archetypes, which we describe hereinafter. These archetypes indicate typical combinations of IIoT platforms' architectural features. We emphasize distinctive characteristics per cluster and conceptualize the archetypes with real-world insights.

5.1 Archetype 1: Allrounders (26%)

IIoT Platforms of this archetype typically have strong markedness in many (non-exclusive) characteristics (see Fig. 2). While they are strong in different platform hosting options, they also offer various network data transportation options and data transmission protocols. Further, they stand out for strong analytics capabilities and external system integration possibilities. As the only cluster, these IIoT platforms strongly leverage external innovations through open components and deploy applications through various ways on the platform, while also maintaining an internal marketplace. Allrounders are IIoT platforms that offer a full-stack solution to its users. Our data sample shows that these platforms provide comprehensive services and cover a wide range of application scenarios, ranging from device connectivity and monitoring, over data visualizations and prescriptive processes, to over-the-air updates or command execution.

5.2 Archetype 2: Purists (38%)

This archetype comprises IIoT platforms that typically have strong markedness in only a few characteristics (see Fig. 3). As they strongly focus on public cloud hosting, they also tend towards on-platform data processing. Further, they offer only selected data transportation options and transmission protocols. Most IIoT platforms in this cluster

Dimension	Characteristics			
Hardware Support	Certified Hardware 15%		Hardware-Agnostic 85%	
Platform Hosting	On-Premise 85%	Public Cloud 100%	Private Cloud 62%	Hybrid 70%
Data Processing	Edge 100%	Fog 15%	On-Platform 100%	
Physical Data Transportation	Wired 100%	Short-Range Wireless 100%	Cellular 38%	LPWAN 77%
Logical Data Transmission	Internet Protocols 85%	IoT-Specific Protocols 62%	Industry-Specific Protocols 77%	
Data Structure	Structured 100%		Unstructured 100%	
Analytics Types	Descriptive 100%	Real-Time 100%	Predictive 100%	Prescriptive 69%
Analytics Technology	Basic 15%		Advanced 85%	
External Integration	Business 85%	Machine 62%	Web Services 92%	
Platform Source Code	Open Source 15%	Open Components 70%	Closed Source 15%	
APIs	Standardized APIs 69%		Custom APIs 31%	
Application Deployment	Platform-Native 92%	Containerized 85%	Off-Platform 69%	
Marketplace	Internal Marketplace 69%	External Marketplace 0%	No Marketplace 31%	
Included IIoT Platforms (In Alphabetical Order)	AIP+, Bosch IoT Suite, GE Predix, Google IoT, IBM Watson, Informatica IoT Platform, Kaa IoT, Microsoft Azure, Onesait Platform, Oracle IoT, Redhat IoT Platform, Salesforce IoT Cloud, Siemens Mindsphere			
Scale	characteristic $c \geq 75\%$	$75\% > c \geq 50\%$	$50\% > c \geq 25\%$	$c < 25\%$

Fig. 2. Characteristics of the Allrounders archetype

utilize basic analytics technology, leading to less-developed data analysis. Lastly, most platforms of this archetype do not maintain a marketplace for applications. Purist IIoT platforms are focused on a narrow use and, thus, provide only necessary functionalities. They can be extended mostly through applications that are built with platform-native tools such as rules engines or low-code/no-code development environments.

Dimension	Characteristics			
Hardware Support	Certified Hardware 16%		Hardware-Agnostic 84%	
Platform Hosting	On-Premise 47%	Public Cloud 100%	Private Cloud 53%	Hybrid 21%
Data Processing	Edge 26%	Fog 0%	On-Platform 100%	
Physical Data Transportation	Wired 89%	Short-Range Wireless 74%	Cellular 58%	LPWAN 42%
Logical Data Transmission	Internet Protocols 42%	IoT-Specific Protocols 21%	Industry-Specific Protocols 53%	
Data Structure	Structured 89%		Unstructured 74%	
Analytics Types	Descriptive 100%	Real-Time 79%	Predictive 37%	Prescriptive 0%
Analytics Technology	Basic 68%		Advanced 32%	
External Integration	Business 42%	Machine 16%	Web Services 79%	
Platform Source Code	Open Source 11%	Open Components 11%	Closed Source 78%	
APIs	Standardized APIs 89%		Custom APIs 11%	
Application Deployment	Platform-Native 95%	Containerized 0%	Off-Platform 42%	
Marketplace	Internal Marketplace 16%	External Marketplace 11%	No Marketplace 73%	
Included IIoT Platforms	Aeris IoT, Asavie IoT, Ascalia IoT, AT&T M2X, Autodesk Fusion Connect, Ayla, Blackberry IoT, Blynk.io, Copa-Data Zenon, DeviceHive, EPLAN IoT, Eurotech Everyware, Exact IoT, Exosite Murano, Infor IoT, Teamviewer IoT, UBIQWEISE 2.0, Telia IoT, WolkAbout			

Fig. 3. Characteristics of the Purists archetype

5.3   Archetype 3: Analysts (24%)

IIoT platforms in this cluster show strong markedness in specific characteristics (see Fig. 4). They are characterized by specifications on data processing and analysis. Consequently, they focus not only on edge and on-platform but also on fog data processing. Their focus is on industry-specific protocols, while different data transportation options are offered. Regarding data analysis, these IIoT platforms provide strong analytics options, backed by advanced technologies and comprehensive integration of other company systems. Further, their source code is mostly closed, applications are deployed internally, and they don´t maintain a marketplace for applications. Analysts are IIoT platforms that place a specific focus on data-driven insights and decision-making using high-end analytics technology. A widespread use case for this archetype is the linkage of production lines and their optimization. We also found that many platforms offer their own sensors or edge devices in an as-a-service model to make better use of data-gathering.

Dimension	Characteristics			
Hardware Support	Certified Hardware 8%		Hardware-Agnostic 92%	
Platform Hosting	On-Premise 83%	Public Cloud 83%	Private Cloud 50%	Hybrid 33%
Data Processing	Edge 100%	Fog 42%		On-Platform 92%
Physical Data Transportation	Wired 100%	Short-Range Wireless 100%	Cellular 25%	LPWAN 75%
Logical Data Transmission	Internet Protocols 16%	IoT-Specific Protocols 16%	Industry-Specific Protocols 100%	
Data Structure	Structured 83%		Unstructured 92%	
Analytics Types	Descriptive 100%	Real-Time 92%	Predictive 75%	Prescriptive 17%
Analytics Technology	Basic 17%		Advanced 83%	
External Integration	Business 58%	Machine 67%	Web Services 100%	
Platform Source Code	Open Source 0%	Open Components 17%	Closed Source 83%	
APIs	Standardized APIs 75%		Custom APIs 25%	
Application Deployment	Platform-Native 100%	Containerized 0%	Off-Platform 8%	
Marketplace	Internal Marketplace 17%	External Marketplace 0%	No Marketplace 83%	
Included IIoT Platforms	Alibaba IoT Cloud, Altair SmartWorks, Altizon, AWS IoT, Foghorn, Foghub, Hitachi Vantara Lumada, Losant, Relayr.io, SE EcoStruxure, Synap IoT, XMPro IoT			

Fig. 4. Characteristics of the Analysts archetype

5.4 Archetype 4: Connectors (12%)

This archetype comprises IIoT platforms with strong markedness in the network layers' and middleware layers' characteristics (see Fig. 5). These IIoT platforms are more critical regarding the connected hardware, with every second platform only supporting certified hardware. Data processing is possible in multiple ways, with a strong focus on fog processing. Data transportation possibilities and logical transmission protocols are widely offered and are supplemented by rich external system integration options. Regarding data analysis, this archetype uses basic technologies and offers only limited analytics types. Applications can be deployed either on or off the platform while using mostly a marketplace.

Connectors are IIoT platforms that specialize in integrating devices into their platforms to extract and gather data. They put stronger restrictions on hardware support or only offer standardized APIs to comply with the technological complexity and provide a reliable basis for additional contributions of platform actors. As their focus is on these topics, they rely on other services and solutions to make use of the data and provide advanced analytics tools, which other users can adopt through the marketplace.

5.5 Discussion of the Cluster Results

While exploring the four archetypes and the associated IIoT platforms in detail, we unveiled some specialties that we discuss in the following. *Allrounders* represent the most holistic archetype, characterized by an extensive list of architectural features that enable a wide range of possible application scenarios. However, this entails increased technical

Dimension	Characteristics			
Hardware Support	Certified Hardware 50%		Hardware-Agnostic 50%	
Platform Hosting	On-Premise 67%	Public Cloud 100%	Private Cloud 50%	Hybrid 17%
Data Processing	Edge 100%	Fog 67%	On-Platform 83%	
Physical Data Transportation	Wired 100%	Short-Range Wireless 100%	Cellular 100%	LPWAN 100%
Logical Data Transmission	Internet Protocols 83%	IoT-Specific Protocols 100%	Industry-Specific Protocols 100%	
Data Structure	Structured 83%		Unstructured 83%	
Analytics Types	Descriptive 100%	Real-Time 83%	Predictive 50%	Prescriptive 0%
Analytics Technology	Basic 83%		Advanced 17%	
External Integration	Business 100%	Machine 83%	Web Services 100%	
Platform Source Code	Open Source 17%	Open Components 0%	Closed Source 83%	
APIs	Standardized APIs 100%		Custom APIs 0%	
Application Deployment	Platform-Native 100%	Containerized 17%	Off-Platform 50%	
Marketplace	Internal Marketplace 83%	External Marketplace 0%	No Marketplace 17%	
Included IIoT Platforms	Cisco Jasper, Cumulocity, Itron IoT, Particle.io, PTC Thingworx, Windriver&Telit DeviceWise			

Fig. 5. Characteristics of the Connectors archetype

complexity, resulting in higher initial investment for end-users owing to the necessity of external system integrators, which are usually already partnered with Allrounders. IIoT platforms of this archetype are suitable for end-users that pursue a comprehensive approach to their IIoT strategy and require an end-to-end solution. *Purists*, in contrast, are defined by a lower technical complexity and selection of architectural features, which reduces the number of possible application scenarios but fosters a user-friendly experience and faster implementation. Thus, they are also suitable for smaller companies and applications where the available resources are scarce. Considering the different revenue categories in our data sample, we find that Allrounders are typically rather big (almost 80% of our Allrounders make at least $1bn), while Purists are rather small (start-up) IIoT platforms. This raises thrilling questions regarding IIoT platforms' evolution [36], for instance, whether Purists are a predecessor to developing into Allrounders or if they focus on specific functionalities. *Analysts* are specialized IIoT platforms focusing on advanced data analysis through high-end technology (e.g., artificial intelligence). They often rely on users to provide adequate infrastructure to enable data transmission to the platform and are, thus, particularly suitable for users that already have a multitude of data that they want to exploit. Lastly, *Connectors* focus on connecting heterogeneous devices to their IIoT platform. As they tend to have less developed analytics tools, they rely on third-party developers to provide (individual) solutions via the internal marketplace to the users. We leave it to further research to investigate how the four archetypes may complement each other and how their services can be jointly operated.

6   Conclusion and Outlook

Despite IIoT platforms' increasing importance for businesses, we still miss an understanding of different architectural setups and associated consequences of such digital platforms. Further, selecting the right IIoT platform in the heterogeneous solution landscape has become increasingly challenging for practitioners. To bridge this research gap and address the underlying practical problem, we developed a taxonomy of IIoT platforms' architectural features. In the development process, we built on empirical data from both analyzing IIoT platforms and conducting semi-structured expert interviews with practitioners involved with the IIoT, as well as conceptual data from the literature on

IoT, IIoT, and digital platforms. Our final taxonomy comprises 13 dimensions organized in four layers that help researchers and practitioners to better understand this emerging phenomenon. Further, we identify and conceptualize four IIoT platform archetypes from 50 real-world cases that help us to systematize the IIoT platform landscape and add an architectural perspective to recent discourse.

Thus, our theoretical contribution is threefold. First, our taxonomy adds to the descriptive knowledge in this relatively young research field by structuring and explaining what architectural features constitute prevalent manifestations of IIoT platforms. Thereby, we follow de Reuver et al.'s [15] recommendation to foster the development of contextualized theories on digital platforms as well as to conduct data-driven research. Second, we offer researchers and practitioners a mutual nomenclature that specifies IIoT platforms' architectural features. With this, we extend current research, which is largely limited to rather simple category lists built through vague development processes. Third, we elucidate typical architectural setups of IIoT platforms and how this shapes their business logic. We see this as the necessary foundations to better understand the reciprocal interplay of both aspects, i.e. how architectural design options enable IIoT platform business models and vice versa. From a managerial perspective, our taxonomy and the four archetypes help practitioners in comparing different IIoT platform solutions and enable them to select the one that not only fits the existing IT infrastructure but also provides desired solution capabilities.

We acknowledge some limitations in our research that open promising avenues for further research. Our taxonomy rests on the data used and the sequence of iterations. Although our dataset covers a fair amount of IIoT platforms of different sizes and with different foci in terms of their value proposition, we might have missed some instantiations. Future research may incorporate additional IIoT platforms and conduct further iterations to validate and update our proposed taxonomy and the resulting archetypes. Further, we did not address potential dependencies between dimensions and characteristics or the architectural success criteria of IIoT platforms. Investigating these aspects may help in the successful design and use of IIoT platforms. Lastly, future research may test our archetypes' external validity to ensure their generalizability and to explore their evolutionary paths (e.g., IIoT platform sizes within and across clusters).

References

1. Tiwana, A.: Platform Ecosystems. Morgan Kaufmann, Waltham, MA (2014)
2. Lueth, K.: IoT Platform Companies Landscape 2019/2020. IoT Analytics (2019)
3. Industry ARC: IIoT Platform Market - Analysis, Growth and Forecast 2019–2025, https://www.industryarc.com/Research/Iiot-Platform-Market-Research-500754
4. Pauli, T., Marx, E., Matzner, M.: Leveraging industrial IoT platform ecosystems. In: 28th European Conference on Information System (2020)
5. Mineraud, J., Mazhelis, O., Su, X., Tarkoma, S.: A gap analysis of Internet-of-Things platforms. Comput. Commun. 1–12 (2016)
6. Guth, J., et al.: A detailed analysis of iot platform architectures: concepts, similarities, and differences. In: Di Martino, B., Li, K.-C., Yang, L.T., Esposito, A. (eds.) Internet of Everything. IT, pp. 81–101. Springer, Singapore (2018). https://doi.org/10.1007/978-981-10-5861-5_4
7. Petrik, D., Herzwurm, G.: Platform ecosystems for the industrial Internet of Things. In: Int Workshop on Software-intensive Business (2018)

8. Hodapp, D., Remane, G., Hanelt, A., Kolbe, L.M.: Business models for IoT platforms: empirical development of a taxonomy and archetypes. In: 14. Int Tagung WI (2019)
9. Moura, R., Ceotto, L., Gonzalez, A., Toledo, R.: Industrial Internet of Things platforms - an evaluation model. In: Int Conf on Comp Sci and Comp Intel (2018)
10. Werner, P., Petrik, D.: Criteria catalog for industrial iot platforms from the perspective of the machine tool industry. In: 14. Int Tagung WI (2019)
11. Nickerson, R., Varshney, U., Muntermann, J.: A method for taxonomy development and its application in information systems. Eur. J. Inf. Syst. **22**, 336–359 (2013)
12. Williams, K., Chatterjee, S., Rossi, M.: Design of emerging digital services: a taxonomy. Eur. J. Inf. Syst. **17**, 505–517 (2008)
13. Gawer, A., Cusumano, M.A.: Industry platforms and ecosystem innovation. J. Prod. Innov. Manag. **31**, 417–433 (2014)
14. Tiwana, A., Konsynski, B., Bush, A.A.: Platform evolution: coevolution of platform architecture, governance, and environmental dynamics. Inf. Syst. Res. **21**, 675–687 (2010)
15. de Reuver, M., Sørensen, C., Basole, R.C.: The digital platform: a research agenda. J. Inf. Tech. **33**, 124–135 (2018)
16. Spagnoletti, P., Resca, A., Lee, G.: A design theory for digital platforms supporting online communities. J. Inf. Tech. **30**, 364–380 (2015)
17. Oberländer, A.M., Röglinger, M., Rosemann, M., Kees, A.: Conceptualizing business-to-thing interactions – a sociomaterial perspective on the Internet of Things. Eur. J. Inf. Syst. **27**, 486–502 (2018)
18. Püschel, L., Schlott, H., Röglinger, M.: What´s in a smart thing? development of a multi-layer taxonomy. In: 37th Int Conf on Inf Sys (2016)
19. Sisinni, E., Saifullah, A., Han, S., Jennehag, U., Gidlund, M.: Industrial Internet of Things: challenges, opportunities, and directions. IEEE Trans. Ind. Inf. **14**, 4724–4734 (2018)
20. Jing, Q., Vasilakos, A.V., Wan, J., Lu, J., Qiu, D.: Security of the Internet of Things: perspectives and challenges. Wireless Netw. **20**(8), 2481–2501 (2014). https://doi.org/10.1007/s11276-014-0761-7
21. Wortmann, F., Flüchter, K.: Internet of Things - technology and value added. Bus. Inf. Syst. Eng. **57**, 221–224 (2015)
22. Boyes, H., Hallaq, B., Cunningham, J., Watson, T.: The industrial Internet of Things (IIoT): an analysis framework. Comput. Ind. **101**, 1–12 (2018)
23. Kiel, D., Arnold, C., Voigt, K.-I.: The influence of the Industrial IoT on business models of established manufacturing companies. Technovation **68**, 4–19 (2017)
24. Petrik, D., Herzwurm, G.: Towards the IIoT ecosystem development - understanding the stakeholder perspective. In: 28th Eur Conf on Inf Sys (2020)
25. Hodapp, D., Gobrecht, L.: Towards a coherent perspective: a review on the inter-play of the Internet of Things and Ecosystems. In: 29th Eur Conf on Inf Sys (2019)
26. Endres, H., Induska, M., Ghosh, A., Baiyere, A., Broser, S.: Industrial Internet of Things (IIoT) Business model classification. In: 40th Int Conf on Inf Sys (2019)
27. Glass, R.L., Vessey, I.: Contemporary application-domain taxonomies. IEEE Softw. **12**, 63–76 (1995)
28. Jöhnk, J., Röglinger, M., Thimmel, M., Urbach, N.: How to implement Agile IT setups: a taxonomy of design options. In: 25th Eur Conf on Inf Sys (2017)
29. Webster, J., Watson, R.: Analyzing the past to prepare for the future: writing a literature review. MIS Q. **26**, xiii–xxiii (2002)
30. vom Brocke, J., Simons, A., Riemer, K., Niehaves, B., Plattfaut, R., Cleven, A.: Standing on the shoulders of Giants: challenges and recommendations of literature search in information systems research. Commun. Assoc. Inf. Syst. **37**, 205–224 (2015)
31. Myers, M., Newman, M.: The qualitative interview in IS research: examining the craft. Inf. Organ. **17**, 2–26 (2007)

32. Hair, J., Black, W., Babin, B.: Multivariate Data Analysis. Pearson Education (2010)
33. IoT One, https://www.iotone.com/suppliers. Accessed 26 Aug 2020
34. Jick, T.D.: Mixing qualitative and quantitative methods: triangulation in action. Admin. Sci. Q. **24**, 602–611 (1979)
35. Constantinides, P., Henfridsson, O., Parker, G.G.: Platforms and infrastructures in the digital age. Inf. Syst. Res. **29**, 381–400 (2018)
36. Henfridsson, O., Bygstad, B.: The generative mechanisms of digital infrastructure evolution. MIS Q. **37**, 907–931 (2013)

Explaining Reviewing Effort: Existing Reviews as Potential Driver

Christoph Rohde[1][(✉)], Alexander Kupfer[1], and Steffen Zimmermann[2]

[1] Department of Information Systems, Production and Logistics Management, University of Innsbruck, Innsbruck, Austria
{christoph.rohde,alexander.kupfer}@uibk.ac.at
[2] Institute of Business Analytics, Ulm University, Ulm, Germany
steffen.zimmermann@uni-ulm.de

Abstract. Online reviews systems try to motivate users to invest effort in writing a review since their success crucially depends on the reviews' helpfulness. However, other factors might influence future reviewing effort as well. We analyze whether existing reviews matter for future reviewing effort. Analyzing a dataset from Google Maps which covers 40 sights across Europe with over 37,000 reviews, we find that reviewing effort – measured by the propensity to additionally write a textual review and (textual) review length – is negatively related to the number of existing reviews. Further, also the rating distribution of existing reviews matters: If there is a large discrepancy between the existing ratings and the own rating, we observe more additional textual reviews. Our findings provide important implications for review system designers regarding the presentation of review metrics: changing or omitting the display of review metrics for potential reviewers might increase their reviewing effort.

Keywords: Online reviews · Reviewing effort · Online review platform · Existing reviews

1 Introduction

Consumer reviews are strongly influencing the purchase decisions of other consumers. About 80% of consumers agree that reviews directly influence their consumption decisions [1], and over 70% consider them as the most credible information source [2]. Reviews are particularly important in online markets which do not allow tangible experiences before consumption and thus come with substantial information asymmetry [3]. For such markets, the reduction of information asymmetries by increasing review helpfulness has been shown to impact future sales performance [4], and reduce costs associated with product returns [5]. However, only a minority of consumers submit an actual review [6]. Even when consumers write a review, they are typically short and lack helpful information [7, 8]. While reviewing effort is important since it can be directly related to review helpfulness [9], Cao et al. [10] argue that consumers do not invest enough effort into writing a review. An online review platform's success, however, strongly depends

F. Ahlemann et al. (Eds.): WI 2021, LNISO 48, pp. 422–436, 2021.
https://doi.org/10.1007/978-3-030-86800-0_29

on the helpfulness of its reviews and thus, review system designers want to create design features which increase the reviewing effort of their users.[1] One aspect to ensure the effectiveness of design features is to understand users' underlying cognitive mechanisms when they observe the already existing reviews before they review by themselves. Thus, being aware of these mechanisms can help to create design features that increase the effort that users invest into writing reviews and thus make reviews more helpful. This would help to reduce information asymmetries in online markets and increase social welfare by reducing costs from mismatching products.

While research has already analyzed the effect of existing reviews on the propensity to review at all [11], and on the rating valence [12, 13], there is – to the best of our knowledge – no study that has analyzed the effect of existing reviews on reviewing effort, which is the amount of effort that users invest into reviewing an object. Since reviewing effort, however, is an important factor for review helpfulness, we aim to examine the following research question:

How do previously existing reviews influence reviewing effort?

We focus on two main metrics for existing reviews, namely the number of existing reviews and the rating distribution of existing reviews. For the number of existing reviews, we develop our hypotheses based on the collective effort model and for the rating distribution of existing reviews, we apply the expectation disconfirmation theory and balance theory, respectively. We empirically test our hypotheses with online reviews from Google Maps and analyze 37,370 reviews over a period of 12 months. The review system of Google Maps represents a well-suited research environment since textual reviews are not mandatory (a star rating is sufficient) and we can thus use the propensity to additionally write a textual review as a proxy for reviewing effort. We further use the length of textual reviews as a second proxy for reviewing effort. Our findings confirm the hypotheses and suggest that existing reviews matter for future reviewing effort. In more detail, the number of existing reviews is negatively associated with both proxies for reviewing effort. For the rating distribution of existing reviews, we observe a statistically significant association with one proxy for reviewing effort: If the discrepancy between the existing rating distribution (i.e., very positive ratings) and the user's own rating (i.e., very low rating) is large, the user is more likely to additionally write a textual review.

This study has important theoretical and practical implications: First, for theoretical implications, our findings suggest that reviewing can be seen as a collective task by the users of a review system and, as described by the collective effort model, the phenomenon of social loafing is relevant in the online review setting as well: A high number of existing reviews is related to a lower propensity to additionally write a textual review and to shorter textual reviews. Additionally, we provide evidence that the expectation disconfirmation theory in combination with the balance theory not only helps to explain the tendency to submit a positive or negative rating (as shown by [13]) but also to explain reviewing effort.

---

[1] Note that for the remainder of this paper, we use the term "user" for persons who are actively contributing to the online review system (i.e., reviewing). On the contrary, we use the term "consumers" for those who read online reviews but do not necessarily write reviews.

Second, for practical implications, our results suggest that review system designers may reconsider the presentation of review metrics. For example, review system designers could specifically highlight the number of existing reviews if the number is low and not highlighting them if the number of existing reviews is high. Similarly, review system designers could segment users into subgroups (based on, e.g., age, language or purpose of purchase) to display the (lower) number of existing reviews for the subgroup than for the (higher) total number of existing reviews. Regarding the rating distribution of the existing reviews, review system designers could highlight the existing rating distribution in the case of a high discrepancy which could then motivate users to increase their reviewing effort.

2 Related Literature

Prior research on the reviewing behavior of users has mainly been focusing on different intrinsic motivations of users to write a review. Balasubramanian and Mahajan [14], for instance, provide a theoretical framework based on social interaction utility which postulates that users gain utility through the reviewing activity. The authors distinguish between different types of user utilities that can be obtained by writing online reviews. Hennig-Thurau et al. [15], extend this framework by including two additional utility types and derive particular motives for each user utility type.

While these frameworks are useful in explaining the initial motivation of a user to act as reviewer, the influence of the user environment is neglected. This includes, among other things, that users typically observe the already existing reviews, which might influence their own reviewing behavior. In this context, Dellarocas et al. [11], study the influence of the number of existing reviews on the propensity for users to review a product at all. Based on an archival dataset of online movie reviews, the authors find that users are more likely to contribute a review for products that are less available and less successful in the market (i.e., niche products). Muchnik et al. [12], analyze another aspect of the existing reviews which are the existing ratings. They find that prior ratings create a significant social influence bias in the form of asymmetric herding effects. Users are more likely to give a positive rating when prior ratings are positive but tend to correct prior negative ratings upwards. Similarly, Ho et al. [13] also study the influence of prior ratings on reviewing behavior. The authors use the expectation disconfirmation theory to hypothesize that the disconfirmation experienced (i.e., the discrepancy between the expectation built by existing reviews and the own experience) by a user influences whether to post a rating and what rating to post. Their results suggest that individuals are more likely to post a rating when the disconfirmation degree is higher and that disconfirmation amplifies the direction of rating.

All these studies have in common that they highlight the importance of the existing reviews for future reviewing behavior: Whether users submit a review at all [11], or whether users give a positive or negative rating [12, 13]. There is – to the best of our knowledge – no study, however, which analyzes the effect of existing reviews on reviewing effort. Considering the enormous economic relevance of online reviews and reviewing effort as an important factor for review helpfulness, this study aims to develop an understanding of the underlying cognitive mechanisms of existing reviews that influence reviewing effort.[2]

3 Theoretical Background and Hypotheses Development

To study the influence of the number of existing reviews on the propensity to review a product at all, Dellarocas et al. [11], draw on the collective effort model by Karau and Williams [16], as a theoretical framework. The difference to our analysis is, however, that we analyze the effect of existing reviews on reviewing effort, measured by (i) the propensity to additionally write a textual review and (ii) the review length. These variables are appropriate to measure the reviewing effort because users have the option to only submit a star-rating. If a user decides to additionally write a textual review, this requires additional effort from the user. Writing lengthier reviews also requires additional effort from the user and prior research already measured reviewing effort through measuring the length of textual reviews [17].

Nonetheless, we build on the collective effort model by Karau and Williams [16], for our hypotheses regarding the effect of the number of existing reviews. Reviewing an object can be seen as a collective task that is accomplished by many different individuals who provide their unique perspectives. The aim of this collective task is to provide a complete and informative picture of an object that could not be accomplished by one individual alone. Therefore, we expect the collective effort model to fit well for a mechanism that influences reviewing effort. Importantly, the collective effort model describes the underlying psychological mechanisms that leads individuals to invest less effort when working collectively than when working individually. This phenomenon – called social loafing – is especially relevant in situations when individuals have the feeling that their individual effort will not make a major impact on the outcome of the collective task [18], and that the evaluation potential of an individual's effort is diminished for a collective task [19]. Translating this to online reviews, it means on the one hand that the individual effort is clearly distinguishable from the effort of others since the review is directly attributed to a user by her name and/or her photo next to the review. On the other hand, however, individuals would feel that their own review has less impact on the total evaluation of the reviewed object if the number of existing reviews is high. Thus, even though the user can see her name and photo linked to the review, the individual review is less discoverable due to the high number of existing reviews and the user might have the feeling that her individual effort will not make a major impact on the outcome of the collective task. We therefore expect that the number of previously existing reviews reduces the individual's reviewing effort. As outlined above, users have the possibility to submit a star rating in our research environment, and to additionally write a (non-mandatory) textual review. Since writing an additional review implies a higher reviewing effort, we formulate our hypothesis H1 as follows.

---

[2] Note that Burtch et al. [17], study the influence of actively providing information about the number of previously written reviews to users on reviewing effort. Their setting, however, is very different to our setting since they directly send users the information about how many reviews have been submitted by other users to deliberately provide a social norm.

H1: *The number of existing reviews decreases the propensity to write a textual review.*

In the same vein, we further hypothesize that this psychological mechanism also influences the effort invested in case a textual review is submitted. Users have the option to freely choose the length of their textual review. Even though users can simply copy a text, prior research has argued that lengthier reviews require more effort [17], and the fact that a user decided to write a textual review at all does not imply that the user will write a lengthy and informative review. In fact, most textual reviews are short and lack useful information [10]. Thus, additionally measuring the review length is important to determine how much effort users invest into a review once they have decided to write a textual review. Using the analogous explanation as above, a user may decrease her efforts for writing a textual review if the number of already existing reviews is large. Thus, the large number of existing reviews increases the probability of social loafing since the evaluation potential of the reviewer´s effort decreases as the review is perceived as less discoverable. Thus, the user might also believe that the review will have less of an impact because of the large number of existing reviews. Therefore, we formulate our hypothesis H2 accordingly.

H2: *The number of existing reviews decreases the length of a textual review.*

Further, we expect that not only the number of existing reviews is a relevant review metric for users' reviewing effort, but also the rating distribution of existing reviews. Users typically develop an expectation about the object to review based on the rating distribution of the existing reviews they observe and then experience the object.[3] Thus, there exists an interaction between the observed rating distribution of the existing reviews and the user's own experience which is described by the expectation disconfirmation theory [20, 21]. This theory is a cognitive theory which explains the satisfaction of individuals after experiencing and evaluating an object as a function of the disconfirmation of previously generated expectations. The expectation disconfirmation theory states that individuals are more likely to experience a high level of dissatisfaction when disconfirmation (the discrepancy between their expectations and their own evaluation of the object) is large. Vice versa individuals will experience a higher level of satisfaction if the individual's original expectation gets outperformed. Thus, the disconfirmation experienced has a moderating effect on the relationship between expectations and satisfaction after evaluation of the object. Prior research has shown that disconfirmation effects increase the propensity to submit a rating at all and that the user´s rating tends to be biased in the direction of the disconfirmation [13]. In other words, if the expectation of a user before consumption is high but she is then having a poor experience, disconfirmation degree is high which will increase the propensity to submit a rating and lead a more negative rating, respectively. We expect that similar cognitive mechanisms underlie for the case of reviewing effort: Users that experience a high level of dissatisfaction which arises from a high disconfirmation degree might want to vent their

---

[3] The outlined process of developing an expectation is not necessarily true for all users as they might also use other information sources. However, we expect that the sentiment of these other information sources correlates with the rating distribution of the existing reviews.

negative feelings. We thereby draw on the balance theory which states that individuals try to restore balance after they have become unbalanced [22, 23]. In the case of online reviews, Hennig-Thurau et al. [15], already mentioned this mechanism as one motive to review. Thus, we argue that users who experience a high disconfirmation degree are more motivated to review and will therefore invest more effort: A user who observed, for instance, a positively skewed rating distribution of existing reviews but has a poor own evaluation, experiences a high disconfirmation degree and is more likely to additionally write a (non-mandatory) textual review. Therefore, our hypothesis H3 reads as follows:

H3: *The disconfirmation degree increases the propensity to write a textual review.*

Analogous to the argumentation above, we expect that users who are writing a textual review will invest more effort into writing the review if the degree of disconfirmation experienced is high. Users who experience a high disconfirmation degree will be less satisfied and thus will invest more effort into writing the review to restore balance. Consequently, we expect that the degree of disconfirmation experienced increases the length of textual reviews. We formulate our H4 accordingly:

H4: *The disconfirmation degree increases the length of textual reviews.*

4 Empirical Analysis

4.1 Research Environment

We use the review system of Google Maps as research environment for our empirical analysis. As mentioned before, textual reviews are not mandatory on Google Maps, which allows us to analyze not only the length of reviews (i.e., H2 and H4) but also the propensity to write a textual review (i.e., H1 and H3). On Google Maps, users can virtually review every location ranging from restaurants and hotels, over shops to sights. Since restaurants, hotels and shops are subject to personal taste and depend on individual experiences (e.g., noisy room, unfriendly staff etc.), we focus on sights like bridges or fountains which are less sensitive to these subjective issues. In fact, due to the lack of interpersonal experiences, motivational aspects to writing reviews for sights are even more relevant. Further, sights are typically less sensitive to time variability than restaurants (e.g., a new chef) or hotels (e.g., renovated rooms). We, therefore, select 10 bridges, 10 squares, 10 fountains, and 10 monuments across Europe as relevant locations. We checked that these sights do not charge visitors, are accessible to the public, and are reviewed on Google Maps. We extract data from the Google Maps website by scraping all existing reviews for each sight. Selected sights are located in 27 different cities across Europe and range from 25 de Abril Bridge in Lisbon to the Freedom Monument in Latvia.

Reviews on Google Maps do unfortunately not include a timestamp but rather relative date information (like, e.g., one week ago) which restricts our period of analysis. More specifically, for all reviews written in the last year, Google Maps provides monthly relative dates (like, e.g., 11 months ago). For all reviews that are older than one year, only yearly relative dates are provided (like, e.g., two years ago). We, therefore, focus on the period with monthly reviews for our analysis. Since the review data was downloaded at the end of November 2017, our relevant period of analysis ranges from December

2016 to November 2017. For each review, we retrieved the review date, the star rating, the textual review (if available), and the number of reviews the user has already written. Table 1 presents descriptive statistics of all available reviews for each sight group individually and all sights in aggregate. Note that the number of reviews used in our regression analysis is lower than the number of all existing reviews since there already existed reviews before the beginning of our analysis (i.e., before December 2016).

Table 1. Summary statistics.

	All Sites	Monuments	Squares	Fountains	Bridges
Avg. Rating	4.43	4,45	4.35	4.47	4.49
Std. Deviation Ratings	0.83	0.81	0.86	0.83	0.80
Minimum Avg. Rating	4.15	4.36	4.31	4.15	4.30
Maximum Avg Rating	4.73	4.61	4.73	4.55	4.72
Number of Reviews	56,794	10,466	19,394	8,804	18,130
Minimum Number of Reviews	237	380	237	978	318
Maximum Number of Reviews	3053	2931	1835	3035	2013
Number of Textual Reviews	24,035	4,542	7,611	4,065	7,817
Avg. Number of Characters	65	66	64	69	62
Std. Deviation Nr. of Characters	67	63	68	68	69
Minimum Avg. Nr. of Characters	53	53	62	57	53
Maximum Avg. Nr. of Characters	83	71	82	77	83

Notes: Minimum/Maximum Avg. Rating and Minimum/Maximum of Avg. Number of Characters refer to the average sight-level minimum/maximum of the respective location category. Minimum/Maximum of Number of Reviews refers to the absolute sight-level minimum/maximum of the respective category.

4.2 Data Preparation and Method Specification

To test our hypotheses empirically, we have to appropriately aggregate existing reviews. Since we obtain monthly review data, we aggregate existing reviews on a monthly basis as follows: When starting in month 1 with our analysis, we need to add up all existing reviews until month 1. When analyzing month 2, all existing reviews are added up until month 2, and so on.[4] Table 2 abstractly shows how our data structure looks like for one sight.

We then obtain specific existing review data for each sight and each month, respectively. For H1 and H2, we use the number of existing reviews as an independent variable

---

[4] As noted above, data restricts us to rely on monthly observations of the review environment. This implies that we have to neglect reviews that are previously written in the same month in our analysis.

Table 2. Abstracted data structure.

Individual review specific data							Existing review data	
Review ID	Month	Rating	Text review	Photo	Review length	User experience	Nr. of existing reviews	Rating skewness of existing reviews
1	12/2016	5	Yes	Yes	150	25	200	−1.60
2	12/2016	5	No	No	–	150	200	−1.60
3	01/2017	3	No	No	–	3	202	−1.65
4	01/2017	5	Yes	Yes	100	55	202	−1.65
5	01/2017	4	Yes	Yes	120	35	202	−1.65

Notes: We use the rating skewness rather than the rating average of existing reviews as "rating distribution of existing reviews" since this better captures whether the rating distribution is overall positive. E.g., while one 1-star and four 5-star ratings have an average rating of 4.2 and a skewness of –2.24, two 3-star and three 5-star ratings have the same average rating but a higher skewness (–0.61). Thus, the more negative the value for skewness, the more overall positive the rating distribution of existing reviews.

in our regression analysis. The dependent variables – proxies for reviewing effort – are given by the individual reviews and represent whether an additional textual review has been submitted (H1) and the length of the textual review (H2). We use review-specific and user-specific data as control variables.

We estimate a logit model for H1 as our dependent variable is binary and indicates whether the individual review includes a textual review or not:

$$Text_{i,t,j} = \alpha + \beta_1 \ln(Num\_Rev_{i,t-1}) + \beta_2 Controls_{i,t,j} + \epsilon_{i,t,j} \qquad (1)$$

where $Text_{i,t,j}$ represents a binary variable being 1 if a review includes a text and 0 otherwise. $\ln(Num\_Rev_{i,t-1})$ represents the natural log of the total number of existing reviews before month t (i.e., month $t - 1$). $Controls_{i,t,j}$ depicts user-specific data for review j that might affect the likelihood to write a review. More specifically, our control variables are the natural log of user experience, the actual rating, and whether the review includes an additional picture which we expect to influence the reviewing effort as well: First, more experienced users (measured by the total number of reviews submitted by this user) might feel more related to the platform and therefore show more commitment to the collective reviewing task. Second, we expect that users, which have a specific positive or negative experience, might also include a (more detailed) explanation for this experience. Finally, when users add a picture to the review, they might also be likely to describe it.

For H2, we estimate an OLS regression with the number of characters as the dependent variable. For this analysis, the number of observations is lower as we obviously only include textual reviews. The estimation equation is defined by

$$\ln(Length_{i,t,j}) = \alpha + \beta_1 \ln(Num\_Rev_{i,t-1}) + \beta_2 Controls_{i,t,j} + \epsilon_{i,t,j} \qquad (2)$$

where $\ln(Length_{i,t,j})$ represents the natural log of number of characters for review j. We use the same independent variables including control variables as in Eq. (1) above since we expect the same mechanism to work for writing longer reviews as for writing a review at all. Note that in both estimations, $\epsilon_{i,t,j}$ denotes the remaining error term. Robust standard errors are used in all models. For robustness, we additionally include month dummies to account for seasonal-specific like weather or holiday seasons.

To test H3 and H4, we additionally take the rating distribution of the existing reviews into account. For the underlying dataset, however, the rating distribution is highly skewed (i.e., most of the ratings have 4 stars or 5 stars). Thus, it is unlikely that a user experiences a high degree of disconfirmation in the way of an individual positive experience but a negative rating distribution of existing reviews. On the contrary, it is more likely to experience a high disconfirmation degree if the individual experience is negative since the previous ratings are outstandingly positive. Therefore, we focus our analysis on the latter case and proceed as follows: For each sight and month, we calculate the rating skewness for the existing review data as a measure for the rating distribution of existing reviews (see the note in Table 2 for an explanation why rating skewness is appropriate). We then sample each review in two groups based on the rating skewness of the existing review data. More specifically, one group represents an extremely positive rating (i.e., one third of the dataset) and the other group represents all other reviews with a less extreme but still positive rating (i.e., two third of the dataset). To finally test our hypotheses, we only pick 1-star ratings and 2-star ratings, since they imply a high degree of disconfirmation for the extremely positive rating group, and compare (i) the proportion of textual reviews for H3 and (ii) the length of textual reviews for H4 with the other group of reviews by using a one-sided t-test. Importantly, this focus on one direction of disconfirmation leads to the fact that we cannot analyze the entire scope (i.e., positive and negative disconfirmation) of Hypothesis 3 and Hypothesis 4, respectively.

4.3 Results

The results of our analysis for H1 and H2 are depicted in Table 3. For H1, Columns (i) and (ii) are relevant. The number of existing reviews is statistically significant and negative, implying that an increase in the number of reviews is negatively related to the propensity to write an additional text. This confirms our hypothesis H1 that the existing reviews in terms of the number of previously existing reviews are negatively associated with users' propensity to write a textual review. The result does not change after controlling for seasonal effects (i.e., Column (ii)). Interestingly, while the tendency is generally towards not submitting a textual review (i.e., negative and statistically significant constant), all control variables tend to increase the likelihood to submit a textual review. Since the marginal effects of a continuous and log-transformed variable are difficult to interpret, we created a new categorical variable which categorizes the number of reviews into ten bins. The first bin indicates the lowest number of existing reviews (i.e., an average of 240 reviews), the last bin indicates the highest number of existing reviews (i.e., an average of 2,325 reviews). We re-estimate Eq. (1) above but replace $\ln(Num\_Rev_{i,t-1})$ with this categorical variable. This allows a convenient interpretation of the marginal effect for each bin, separately. Figure 1 below shows the average marginal effects for each bin including their 95% confidence intervals. Remarkably, we observe that the higher the number of existing reviews (i.e., bins with a higher number), the more negative the marginal effect on the propensity of writing an additional text. This observation is in line with our theoretical framework suggesting that the higher the number of existing reviews, the lower the reviewing effort.

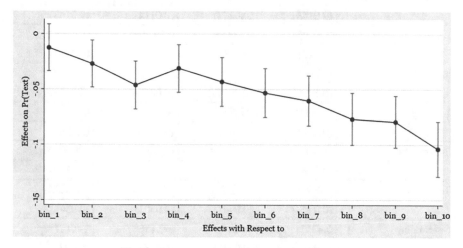

Fig. 1. Average marginal effects with 95% CIs.

For review length, Columns (iii) and (iv) of Table 3 are relevant. Similar as for a textual review, we observe a statistically significant negative relationship between review length and the number of existing reviews. The use of log-transformed data allows us to interpret the coefficients easily: A 1% increase in the number of existing reviews is associated with a decrease of review length by 6.7% (see Column (iii)). Controlling for seasonal effects by adding month dummies does not change the results qualitatively meaning that we find support for H2 as well. The coefficients of the control variables, however, provide some interesting findings: While both, the submission of a picture and user experience, is positively related to review length, the submission of a 5-star rating is associated with a decrease in review length by 15.6% compared to the base level of a 3-star rating. Contrarily, the submission of a 2-star rating is related to an increase of 20% compared to the base level. The insignificant coefficient of a 1-star rating might be related to the low number of 1-star ratings submitted in our dataset (only 1.4% of all ratings are 1-star ratings). To account for this issue, we generate a less granular rating variable which ranges from 1 to 3, where 1 includes 1- and 2-star ratings, 2 includes all 3-star ratings and 3 includes 4- and 5-star ratings. While the result for the number of reviews does not change, the revised rating variable exhibits the expected coefficients: rating category 1 is significantly positive and rating category 3 is significantly negative related to review length (results not tabulated).

The results of our analysis for H3 and H4 are depicted in Table 4. The first two columns indicate that users with a bad experience (i.e., 1-star rating or 2-star rating) are more likely to write a textual review if the existing review rating distribution is extremely positive. The difference is, based on a one-sided t-test, statistically significant

Table 3. Results for H1 and H2.

Dependent variable:	(i) Text (0/1)	(ii) Text (0/1)	(iii) ln(Length)	(iv) ln(Length)
ln(Nr. of reviews)	−0.123***	−0.215***	−0.0671***	−0.0829***
	(0.0183)	(0.0238)	(0.0114)	(0.0143)
Picture	0.549***	0.514***	0.284***	0.279***
	(0.112)	(0.113)	(0.0542)	(0.0543)
ln(User experience)	0.793***	0.800***	0.0512***	0.0526***
	(0.00950)	(0.00967)	(0.00580)	(0.00587)
1-star rating	0.880***	0.870***	0.120	0.119
	(0.131)	(0.131)	(0.0800)	(0.0801)
2-star rating	0.530***	0.533***	0.200***	0.202***
	(0.116)	(0.116)	(0.0719)	(0.0719)
4-star rating	0.0623	0.0622	−0.0236	−0.0226
	(0.0440)	(0.0441)	(0.0305)	(0.0306)
5-star rating	0.431***	0.427***	−0.156***	−0.157***
	(0.0410)	(0.0411)	(0.0284)	(0.0285)
Constant	−1.953***	−1.622***	3.997***	−0.0829***
	(0.137)	(0.159)	(0.0868)	(0.0143)
Month dummies	NO	YES	NO	YES
R-squared	0.21	0.21	0.02	0.02
Observations	37,370	37,370	17,058	17,058
Mean VIF	4.06	4.58	1.62	2.17

*Notes: We use the centered 3-star rating is the base of the (indicator variable) individual rating. Column (i) and (ii) represent the logit model in Eq. (1)above. The goodness of fit measure is therefore pseudo-R-squared. Column (iii) and (iv) represent the OLS regression in Eq. (2). Robust standard errors in parentheses. *** $p < 0.01$, ** $p < 0.05$, * $p < 0.1$.*

and partially supports our hypothesis H3 for the case of negative disconfirmation An extremely positive existing rating distribution increases the likelihood to write a textual review by nearly 10 percentage points in the case of a 1-star rating. For review length (i.e., H4), however, the difference between the extremely positive rating distribution and the less extreme rating distribution is not statistically significant. The length of 1-star ratings and 2-star ratings in the case of an extremely positive rating distribution are not statistically significant different to the group of reviews which include a less extreme existing rating distribution.

Table 4. Results for H3 and H4.

	Textual reviews (0/1)		Length (in characters)	
	1-star rating	2-star rating	1-star rating	2-star rating
Reviews with an extremely positive existing rating distribution	34,57% (n = 188)	41,94% (n = 155)	67 (n = 65)	61 (n = 65)
Reviews with a less extreme existing rating distribution	25,37% (n = 406)	35,82% (n = 455)	75 (n = 103)	90 (n = 163)
t-statistic	2,32**	1,36*	0,02	−1,12

Notes: For all columns, a one-sided t-test is applied. For testing the statistical difference of review length, the variable was log-transformed. $** p < 0.05$, $* p < 0.1$.

5   Discussion and Conclusion

This study emphasizes the importance of existing reviews for future reviewing effort. First, we observe that the sole number of existing reviews matters for reviewing effort: A high number of existing reviews is associated with both, a lower number of additional textual reviews (H1) and a shorter length of textual reviews (H2). Thus, both hypotheses, which are developed from the collective effort model by Karau and Williams [16], can be confirmed. If a potential reviewer observes that there exists already a large number of reviews, her individual contribution will not make a big impact on the collective task of reviewing. Consequently, her reviewing effort will be rather low. On the contrary, if the existing number of reviews is low, the individual review is much more visible and impactful which makes the reviewer to put more effort into the task.

Second, our study highlights the importance of the rating distribution of existing reviews as well: If the rating distribution of existing reviews differs strongly to the own experience (measured by the individual rating), the high disconfirmation degree results in a higher propensity to additionally write a textual review. While this partially supports our hypothesis H3 developed from the expectation disconfirmation theory, we do not find support for hypothesis H4 – the actual review length is independent from the disconfirmation degree. Notably, we examined the content of reviews with a high disconfirmation degree and, based on anecdotical evidence, their topics do not differ from the content of reviews with a lower disconfirmation degree. We do not find any evidence that these reviews argue against the other existing reviews and their ratings. Thus, it seems that users with a high disconfirmation degree are more likely to additionally write a textual review but when they write the actual review, the content seems very similar to other reviews with the same rating. In fact, reviews with a low rating typically focus on outlining the own (bad) experience.

5.1 Theoretical Implications

From a theoretical perspective, our results contribute to understand the determinants of reviewing effort invested by the users. So far – to the best of our knowledge – no study has analyzed the relationship between the existing reviews and reviewing effort. Existing studies that use existing reviews as an independent variable focus on the propensity to submit a review at all or on the existing ratings. We provide additional evidence that reviewing can be seen as a collective task and the underlying cognitive mechanisms that individuals undergo when performing this task are accurately described by the collective effort model. In fact, we observe the phenomenon of social loafing in our online review setting as well. Further, our results indicate that the number of existing reviews as a typical metric in review systems does not serve as a social norm and thus social comparison theory is not adequately describing the underlying psychological influence of the existing reviews on reviewing effort (see [17], for a discussion). Similarly, our results also support the hypothesis by Hennig-Thurau et al. [15], that, among other motives, users submit a review to vent negative feelings: The expectation disconfirmation theory by Oliver [21], states that a high disconfirmation degree results in an increase level of dissatisfaction and this, in turn, makes users to restore the balance of the existing review ratings [22, 23]. Thus, our findings indicate that observing the number and the rating distribution of existing reviews triggers multiple cognitive mechanisms.

5.2 Practical Implications

The practical implications of our study are that review system designs need not only to consider consumers (who are observing the existing reviews) but also potential reviewers. Thus, while providing detailed information about existing reviews is helpful for consumers, it might also bring potential reviewers to invest less effort. Thus, review system designers face an important trade-off because helpful reviews mainly depend on the effort invested. They might incorporate adjusted design features like, for instance, omitting information about the number of existing reviews or displaying only a few highlighted reviews at the first page to increase the users' feeling that they are might a significant contribution to the collective task of reviewing. With such a feature, the own review might be perceived as impactful and more discoverable. Similarly, review system designers could also segment users into subgroups so that each user only sees the existing reviews from other users of this subgroup, which is based on, e.g., age, language or purpose of purchase. Regarding the influence of the existing review rating distribution, review system designers could incorporate a design feature which highlights the existing rating distribution for early adopters of products to increase the disconfirmation experienced early on in a product lifecycle. Thus, the better a potential disconfirmation is observed, the more likely users will increase their reviewing effort.

5.3   Limitations and Future Research

Our research has some limitations which, however, offer fruitful possibilities for future research. First, the analysis is based on a dataset that consists of sights across Europe on Google Maps. It might be possible that the observed effects of the number of existing reviews and rating distribution are not generalizable across both, review platforms and review objects. Thus, future research could explore whether our findings can be confirmed, for instance, with other review objects on different review platforms. Furthermore, for sights that have no existing reviews yet, the underlying cognitive mechanism might again be different and could be addressed by future research.

Second, due to the nature of our data collection method, some contextual factors such as the average overall rating at the time, the most recent reviews or the top picture of the sight, might be missing. Thus, conducting a similar analysis with a different dataset may be appropriate.

Third, the rating distribution in our dataset is very positively skewed. This means that we could only test the effects of disconfirmation in one direction. Additionally, the ratings of users could be influenced by these positively skewed existing ratings and thus create significant herding effects. For future research, it is important to analyze whether the effects of disconfirmation influence the reviewing effort in both ways and whether herding effects are present.

Lastly, our findings suggest that the applied theories are accurately describing the underlying cognitive mechanisms that users undergo when reviewing an object and perceiving the existing reviews. Nonetheless, further research might solidify our insights regarding the applicability of these theories to this context. For example, experimental studies could be conducted to isolate the observed effects of the existing reviews on reviewing effort.

References

1. ChannelAdvisor. Consumer Survey: Global Consumer Shopping Habits, https://www.channeladvisor.com/blog/industry-trends/2011-global-consumer-shopping-habits-survey/. Accessed 27 Apr 2020
2. Nielson. Word-of-mouth recommendations remain the most credible, https://www.nielsen.com/id/en/press-releases/2015/word-of-mouth-recommendations-remain-the-most-credible/. Accessed 27 Apr 2020
3. Hong, Y., Pavlou, P.A.: Product fit uncertainty in online markets: nature, effects, and antecedents. Inf. Syst. Res. 25(2), 328–344 (2014)
4. Yu, X., Liu, Y., Huang, X., An, A.: Mining online reviews for predicting sales performance: a case study in the movie domain. IEEE Trans. Knowl. Data Eng. 24(4), 720–734 (2010)
5. Sahoo, N., Dellarocas, C., Srinivasan, S.: The impact of online product reviews on product returns. Inf. Syst. Res. 29(3), 723–738 (2018)
6. Hu, N., Zhang, J., and Pavlou, P.A.: Overcoming the J-shaped distribution of product reviews. In: Communications of the ACM, pp. 144–147 (2009)
7. Mudambi, S., and Schuff, D.: What makes a helpful online review? A study of customer reviews on Amazon.com. MIS Q. 34(1), 185–200 (2010)
8. Askalidis, G., Kim, S.J., Malthouse, E.C.: Understanding and overcoming biases in online review systems. Decis. Support Syst. 97(5), 23–30 (2017)

9. Wang, J., Ghoang, J., Ghose, A., and Ipeirotis, P.: Bonus, disclosure, and choice: What motivates the creation of high-quality paid reviews? In: Proceedings of the International Conference on Information Systems (ICIS 2012), Association for Information Systems (AIS), Atlanta (2012)

10. Cao, Q., Duan, W., Gan, Q.: Exploring determinants of voting for the helpfulness of online user reviews: a text mining approach. Decis. Support Syst. **50**(2), 511–521 (2011)

11. Dellarocas, C., Gao, G., Narayan, R.: Are consumers more likely to contribute online reviews for hit or niche products? J. Manag. Inf. Syst. **27**(2), 127–158 (2010)

12. Muchnik, L., Aral, S., Taylor, S.J.: Social influence bias: a randomized experiment. Science **341**(6146), 647–651 (2013)

13. Ho, Y.C., Wu, J., Tan, Y.: Disconfirmation effect on online rating behavior: a structural model. Inf. Syst. Res. **28**(3), 626–642 (2017)

14. Balasubramanian, S., Mahajan, V.: The economic leverage of the virtual community. Int. J. Electron. Commer. **5**(Spring), 103–138 (2001)

15. Hennig-Thurau, T., Gwinner, K.P., Walsh, G., Gremler, D.D.: Electronic word-of-mouth via consumer-opinion platforms: what motivates consumers to articulate themselves on the internet? J. Interact. Mark. **18**(1), 38–52 (2004)

16. Karau, S.J., Williams, K.D.: Understanding individual motivation in groups: the collective effort model. In: Turner, M.E. (ed.) Groups at work: Theory and research, pp. 113–141. Erlbaum, Mahwah, NJ (2001)

17. Burtch, G., Hong, Y., Bapna, R., Griskevicius, V.: Stimulating online reviews by combining financial incentives and social norms. Manage. Sci. **64**(5), 2065–2082 (2017)

18. Karau, S.J., Williams, K.D.: Social loafing: a meta-analytic review and theoretical integration. J. Personality Soc. Psychol. **65**(4), 681 (1993)

19. Harkins, S.G.: Social loafing and social facilitation. J. Exp. Soc. Psychol. **23**, 1–18 (1987)

20. Bhattacherjee, A.: Understanding information systems continuance: an expectation-confirmation model. MIS Q. 351–370 (2001)

21. Oliver, R.L.: Effect of expectation and disconfirmation on postexposure product evaluations: an alternative interpretation. J. Appl. Psychol. **62**(4), 480 (1977)

22. Heider, F.: Attitudes and cognitive organization. J. Psychol. **21**, 107–112 (1946)

23. Newcomb, T.M.: An approach to the study of communicative acts. Psychol. Rev. **60**, 393–404 (1953)

A Comparison of Crowd Types: Idea Selection Performance of Students and Amazon Mechanical Turks

Victoria Banken[✉]

Department of Information Systems, Production and Logistics Management, University of
Innsbruck, Innsbruck, Austria
Victoria.Banken@uibk.ac.at

Abstract. Crowdsourcing is an effective means to generate a multitude of ideas
in a very short amount of time. Therefore, companies and researchers increasingly
tap into the power of the crowd for the evaluation of these ideas. However, not
all types of crowds are the equally capable for complex decision-making tasks,
which might result in poor selection performance. This research aims to evaluate
differences in anonymous crowds and student crowds regarding their information processing, attention and selection performance. A web-experiment with 339
participants was conducted to reveal that 1) undergraduate Information Systems
students perform better in idea selection than crowd workers recruited from Amazon Mechanical Turk, 2) attention checks increase selection performance and 3)
while crowd workers indicate to process information more systematically, students
acquire more information for evaluation than crowd workers.

Keywords: Open Innovation · Crowdsourcing · Crowd types · Amazon
Mechanical Turk · Student sample · Attention

1 Introduction

Companies increasingly utilize online platforms to kick off innovation contests and
thereby tap into the creative power of the crowd to generate new business models, drive
innovativeness and enhance competitive advantage [1–4]. In such contests, the crowd
easily generates hundreds and sometimes thousands of potentially promising ideas [5, 6]
that are typically filtered by domain experts [6]. The complex decision making process, to
pick the few most original, unique, useful, and elaborated ideas [7], commonly requires
substantial amounts of resources [4]. Google received more than 150,000 ideas and 3,000
employees devoted their time to review the submissions to finally announce 16 winners[1].
Those who filter such large quantities of ideas are not only faced with the challenge of
an exceeding cognitive load imposed by this complex task [8], but also by the issue of
similar ideas occurring in substantial amounts [9].

---

[1] https://www.cnet.com/news/google-announces-project-10100-themes/.

F. Ahlemann et al. (Eds.): WI 2021, LNISO 48, pp. 437–453, 2021.
https://doi.org/10.1007/978-3-030-86800-0_30

In order to reduce cognitive load and to ease the idea selection process, organizations do not only rely on experts for evaluation, but also on small teams, the crowd or automated idea screening systems [10]. However, the crowd utilized in research tends to differ from the crowd relied upon in practice. In practice, the crowd often consists of internal employees or externals such as potential customers or the ideators themselves that can comment or vote on ideas on the ideation platform [5, 6]. In scientific research, the crowd commonly consist of anonymous crowd workers recruited via crowdsourcing platforms, such as Amazon Mechanical Turk (MTurk) or Figure Eight (formerly known Crowdflower) [11–13], or University students [14, 15] in addition to small expert teams or an internal crowd. Both types of crowds, anonymous crowd workers and students, are used as participant's source in various fields of research [16]. However, the different crowd types also perform disparate tasks. Typical tasks on a crowd working platform are image tagging, relevance feedback or document labeling [17] as well as surveys administered by top researchers [16]. However, crowd platforms rarely offer tasks that require more time and cognitive effort such as idea selection tasks. This is in line with the literature stating that crowd workers deliver high quality work as long as the tasks are not effort-responsive [16]. Students on the other side, are considered unique in terms of their reflective thought [16] and are long accepted as participant source. Multiple studies exist that use students as a proxy for the crowd for a variety of tasks including idea selection [14, 15]. However, a problem remains: How to identify good quality work in idea selection? For classification problems or programming there usually exists one truly good answer, but in innovation contests, it would be very time-consuming and expensive to examine which idea is the best, because essentially, they would all need to be implemented. Hence, researchers developed quality control mechanisms such as attention checks or gold questions for which one truly correct answer exists [18–20].

This paper investigates how crowd types differ in their attention, information processing style and performance when accomplishing complex decision-making tasks such as idea selection. An online experiment with a crowd recruited from Amazon Mechanical Turk and a crowd of European undergraduate students was conducted.

2   Theoretical Background

2.1   Crowd Tasks

Crowdsourcing means bringing people in from outside the company and involving them in a creative, collaborative process [21]. Crowdsourcing has been gaining increasing interest, because the "wisdom of the crowd", the independent judgements of a large and diverse group of individuals, has been proven to be relatively accurate [22]. Following that, a wide variety of tasks with different levels of complexity have been passed over to the crowd. These tasks cover activities in all phases of the value chain including but not limited to crowd testing, funding, ideation, logistics, production, promotion and support [23]. Cognitively less demanding tasks such as data annotation, image tagging, accessing content on the web or finding information online [24] were shown to be completed pretty accurately by the crowd [e.g., 25]. However, complex tasks that require strenuous effort like creating content, generating or evaluating ideas provide mixed results [4]. While many studies show that the crowd is able to quickly generate hundreds or thousands of ideas [5, 26], selection performance may not be considerably higher than chance [11, 12, 27, 28]. One reason is the high cognitive demand that is imposed by the task of comparing very similar ideas [26] and processing multiple idea attributes [29]. Another reason might be related to the characteristics of the crowd. Thus, to better understand this issue, this paper first investigates which types of crowd exist.

2.2 Crowd Types in Idea Selection

Specific tasks call for domain-specific or company internal knowledge, hence, companies do not only ask externals but also their employees to make suggestions. Consequently, the crowd can be distinguished into being either internal or external to the crowdsourcer [23]. In practice, the evaluation of ideas is done by three types of raters that are the crowd, a jury of experts, and self-assessments, which can also be used in combination [10, 30]. In research, the "crowd" is a widely used term and can refer to anonymous crowd workers from crowd platforms such as Amazon Mechanical Turk or FigureEight, but also a University student crowd, user crowd or an internal employee crowd. Student samples were used to compare different evaluation mechanisms [14, 31]. Related research suggests that students who are evaluating ideas based on a multi-criteria rating scales outperform students that were evaluating ideas in prediction markets [31]. Furthermore, a student sample was utilized to show that rating scales invoke higher ease of use than preference markets and that perceived ease of use mediates the role between the evaluation mechanism and decision quality [14]. Additionally, a study found that higher decomposition of information load (fewer ideas per screen) leads raters to acquire more information on ideas and to eliminate more ideas, which improved choice accuracy [28]. Online consumer panels were found to represent a better way to determine a "good" idea than are ratings by experts [33]. And significant agreement was found between theatre projects that were funded by the funding crowd and experts [34]. Anonymous crowd workers have been recruited, because a multitude of responses can be generated in a short time. The ratings for novelty of an anonymous crowd (MTurk) are highly correlated with those of experts [35]. The evaluations of an MTurk crowd were also used to develop an expertise prediction heuristic to automatically identify experts within the crowd [13]. Crowd workers of MTurk that evaluate sets with similar ideas have higher elimination performance and lower cognitive effort than those crowd workers that evaluated sets with random ideas [11]. Idea selection done by users was relatively successful when compared to expert assessments and even technically naïve users recruited from Amazon Mechanical Turk yielded satisficing results [36]. Contrary to previous studies of crowd evaluations for simple aesthetic tasks, one study also provides first evidence of the limitations of anonymous crowd evaluations (Crowdflower), and warns that crowd evaluations are not adept to the expert ratings when more complex submission such as business models are evaluated [12]. While crowds were frequently compared to experts, little is known about whether one crowd type might be better able at selecting high quality ideas than another. Hence, this research aims to evaluate differences in anonymous crowds and student crowds regarding their information processing, attention and selection performance.

2.3 Information Processing

It is important to understand how raters process the ideas and decide on their quality to better deal with challenges related to the complex and effort intensive selection process. When making decisions, people engage in disparate types of cognitive processes that can be distinguished into intuition [37] and reasoning [38], also referred to as System 1 and System 2. System 1 represents intuition and denotes fast, automatic, and effortless information processing. System 2 represents reasoning, being a slow, controlled, and effortful information processing [39]. System 1 thinking consists of subsystems which include autonomous behaviors and domain-specific knowledge obtained through domain-general learning mechanisms [40]. When utilizing System 1 cognitive processes to make decisions, individuals tend to use shortcuts in their decision making [41] and adopt rules of thumb stored in their long-term memory to process information [42]. System 2 information processing makes use of the central working memory system [40]. When individuals engage in System 2 cognitive processes, all available options are objectively compared until a decision is made. Usually, individuals are expected to make decisions as objectively as possible, since rational decision making is supposed to lead to accurate choices and, thus, good decisions [43]. However, as the information processing capacity of a human cognitive system is limited, it is impossible to evaluate all possible outcomes [44, 45]. Hence, due to their limited rationality choices lose objectivity.

2.4 Attention and Quality Control in Crowdsourcing

Crowdsourcing platforms such as Amazon Mechanical Turk or Figure Eight allow to collect large amount of responses in a very short amount of time. Unfortunately, the process of verifying the quality of submitted results is not that easy and often workers take the chance to submit low quality work [17]. Hence, quality control is essential for requesters of the crowdsourced tasks and it comes in various forms. First, requesters rely on redundant task assignment and ask multiple crowd workers the same questions [17, 46]. Further, financial incentives such as performance-based payments are used to increase the quality of submissions [46]. Next, over time attention check questions or gold questions were developed, which are a small set of tasks for which the requester knows the correct answer and, thus, is able to directly assess the quality of the submission [18]. These questions should be unique for each task or study in order to reduce the probability for a crowd worker to be familiar with the attention check questions and hence, to increase their effectiveness [16]. One type of these attention checks are instructional manipulation checks (IMC), where participants demonstrate that they were reading and following the instructions [19]. IMCs typically consist of a text in which the participants are instructed to answer in a specific way to a question that is posted below. When a participant does not read the text, s/he would answer the question incorrectly and hence, would fail the IMC. Factual manipulation checks are questions with an objective, matter-of-fact answer. The problem with factual manipulation checks is that participants can easily search the internet for the correct answer and they do so, if researchers do not intervene with the simple instruction to not look up the answers [16]. Another attention check is the affirmation form in which crowd workers indicate whether they paid attention and answered the questions honestly [47]. Keith et al. review crowd studies and identified that only 22.8% of the studies report on using attention checks, among which are direct, archival and statistical attention checks such as instructed items (e.g. "Please select strongly disagree, if you are paying attention.", bogus items (e.g., "My friends are all mermaids."), questions to recall information from the instructions or an article, or measuring the time spent on the task [48].

2.5   Research Model and Hypotheses Development

It is commonly noted that there are differences between various participant sources with respect to their attention, cognitive processing styles and task performance. The crowd in general was found to be a good proxy for experts' in idea evaluation [36]. This includes both, the student crowd as well as the anonymous crowd. However, one study found that crowd workers from Figure Eight were not as good as commonly assumed [12]. This is in line with the literature stating that crowd workers deliver high quality work as long as the tasks are not effort-responsive [16]. Students on the other side, are considered unique in terms of their reflective thought [16]. Hence, anonymous crowd workers are assumed to have lower selection performance than students.

> *H1: Crowd workers from anonymous crowd working platforms will have lower selection performance in terms of a) lower accuracy, b) higher false negative rate and c) higher false positive rate than a student crowd.*

Crowd workers have learned to be attentive to specific types of questions such as attention questions. They tend to search for information that help them to quickly come to a decision as some of the crowd workers make a living of these short and often ill paid crowd task. Whereas students like to engage in cognitively demanding tasks as they also selected to enroll in a University program. Hence, the following hypotheses regarding the crowd types' cognitive load and information processing styles can be formulated:

> *H2: Crowd workers from anonymous crowd working platforms will have lower cognitive load than a student crowd.*

> *H3: Crowd workers from anonymous crowd working platforms will process information a) more heuristically and b) less systematically than a student crowd.*

Combining the arguments mentioned above, a research model is proposed that compares the relationships between two crowd types (anonymous crowd and student crowd) and their selection performance, cognition and information processing (see Fig. 1).

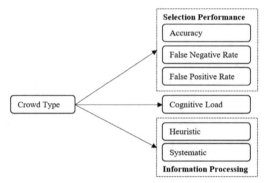

Fig. 1. Research model

3 Methodology

This study compares two different crowds, i.e., an anonymous crowd and a student crowd, with regards to their attentiveness, information processing styles and their resulting selection performance using a web-experiment consisting of a pre-survey, an idea selection task and a post-survey.

3.1 Idea Set

In the idea selection task, participants were presented with 35 ideas from the "Gratitude at the Workplace" Challenge hosted on openIDEO[2]. The contest was selected because the ideas covered a broad range of topics that did not require any technical or domain-specific knowledge. The ideas were accessible and easily comprehensible for individuals that have a basic understanding of appreciation and workplaces. The original ideas were adapted and shortened to control for the idea length and possible effects on the selection (e.g., shorter ideas are easier to comprehend and therefore selected). The ideas were randomly allocated to subsets. Ideas and subsets were allocated to participants in random sequence to control for order bias using the Smart Idea Allocation method [49]. Ideas were presented with their title, description and the number of likes they received on the platform.

3.2 Subjects

Data was collected from 284 crowd workers recruited from Amazon Mechanical Turk (using the platform cloudresearch.com) and 55 undergraduate students enrolled in an introductory course to Information Systems (IS) at a European University (via the online course forum). Participants that failed the reCaptcha on the first page (to identify bots or machines) or the first simple instructional attention check ("Click the radio button for strongly agree.") were excluded to ensure a representative sample. After eliminating all

---

[2] The original ideas of and information about the contest can be found on the following website: https://challenges.openideo.com/challenge/gratitude-in-the-workplace/brief.

participants that failed at least one attention check question, 87 MTurks and 49 students remained. The reward consisted of a fix and a variable, performance-based payment as recommended for effort-responsive tasks [46]. While MTurks received 2.50 USD, students received 3.6 points as course credit for successful completion of the whole task as a fixed reward. The variable amount consisted of a bonus for every good idea they selected (+0.30 USD for MTurks and + 0.3 points for students) minus a deduction for every bad idea they selected (−0.10 USD for MTurks and −0.1 points for students). The payment model for MTurks was chosen to comply with the minimum wage for the United States, as the expected duration to complete the task was about 20–30 min. The reward was special for both participant groups, while MTurks received an above average payment compared to other tasks on the platform, students had the chance to receive course credits. Participation was voluntary for students and MTurks. Furthermore, students had the opportunity to choose between two different tasks to receive course credit similar to MTurks who could move on to another Human Intelligence Task (HIT). Only MTurks that completed at least 100 HITs and had an approval rate of minimum 80% (i.e., 80% or more of that participant's previous submissions were approved by requesters) were allowed to participate in the task. MTurks were, with on average 38 years (SD = 10.8 years) about 16 years older than students that were on average 22 years old (SD = 2.9 years). Among the MTurks 56% indicated to be male, 43% female and 1% others; students indicated to be 45% male and 55% female. All participants graduated from high school. Additionally, the majority of MTurks (51.7%) and some students (4.1%) possess a Bachelor's degree. Undergraduate IS students are expected to have some basic understanding of human resources and workplace innovation. MTurks themselves have some form of employment relationship with the requesters of the HITs and more than 60% of the crowd workers in previous studies participate on MTurk to generate a second source of income [50]. Participants were also asked to rate to what extent they usually experience or express gratitude "while collaborating with colleagues", "by receiving or giving donations", "from your leader or as a leader", "via platforms and applications", "via e-mail", "during business trips and travels", "during meditation", "in or to specific groups of people (e.g., healthcare, farmers, police)", and "through handcrafted objects (e.g., handwritten notes, paintings, collages)" (7-point-Likert scale from 1 = "strongly disagree" to 7 = "strongly agree"). On average, MTurks and students indicated a level of experience with gratitude of 4.78 and 4.44 with a standard deviation of .98 and .72, respectively. Both crowd types more often experienced or expressed gratitude while collaborating with colleagues ($M_{crowd worker}$ = 5.38, $M_{students}$ = 5.24) and from their leader or as a leader ($M_{crowd worker}$ = 5.05, $M_{students}$ = 5.29). To conclude, students as well as MTurks should have sufficient experience with "Gratitude at the Workplace" to evaluate the ideas.

3.3 Experimental Procedure and Task Instructions

Once participants accepted the task on their specific platform (cloudresearch.com for MTurks and online course forum for students), they were redirected to the pre-survey. On the welcome screen, participants were informed about the task, the reward scheme and the approval criteria. Specifically, they were informed about the expected minimum work duration for the task to be 8 min with an average about 20–30 min. Furthermore, they were notified to pay attention to answer all attention questions correctly to receive the fixed reward (see Sect. 3.4 Attention Checks). Afterwards, participants answered some perception-based questions and were informed about the task setting: "Imagine you are a Human Resource (HR) Manager. The organization you work for wants to foster gratitude at the workplace. Research shows that too many people are feeling unappreciated and taken for granted at work. Gratitude strengthens our relationships, improves our health and motivates us. Hence, you organized an external innovation contest about gratitude at the workplace and received 39 ideas from the crowd. You know that you want to assess the ideas as objectively as possible and not according to your own preferences." Participants then selected categories of their interest and were further introduced to the selection environment: "Click the Select-Button if you deem an idea novel and feasible. Click the Read-more button to see the full idea description. You can select zero, one or multiple feasible and novel ideas from each set. The progress tracker bar shows you how far along you are in the task. Click the next button to get a new subset; there is no back button." The binary assessment can be understood as a holistic rating scale, which means that only one score with a single trait is collected [51]. The meaning of "feasible and novel" was further explained in order to guide the attention to relevant quality criteria: "An idea is feasible, if it can be easily implemented and is socially acceptable. An idea is novel, if it is new and original; not like anything seen before." Participants agreed that they have understood the task setting and the selection environment and were then directed to the selection platform. On each of the next seven screens (see Fig. 2), four to seven ideas were presented where participants could check boxes to select feasible and novel ideas indicated by check mark and "novel and feasible". Note that after three screens four Latin dummy text ideas were presented as attention check. The experiment ended with a survey that collected perception-based variables and demographic data. During the task, the author included seven different attention checks. When participants failed an attention check question they were notified and could not proceed with the task.

3.4 Measures and Operationalization

Performance Measures. The binary nature of the idea quality (low quality vs. high quality) allows to use performance metrics from the field of Information Retrieval (e.g., [11, 52]). The selection of each participant is compared to the gold standard in a confusion matrix (see Table 1). To assess selection performance in innovation contests, three particular measures are relevant, which are the selection accuracy, false negative rate and false positive rate. Selection accuracy (ACC) is the proportion of all correct predictions (true positives and true negatives) divided by all predictions [53]. The more ideas are correctly classified as being high or low quality, the higher is the measure. As contest managers might be concerned with fear of missing out [54], the false negative rate (FNR), which is the fraction of ideas that have been incorrectly classified as being low quality [53], should be low. Furthermore, having low quality ideas in the consideration set increases subsequent evaluation effort, which is at best avoided [55]. Hence, the false positive rate (FPR), which represents the fraction of ideas that have been incorrectly classified as being high quality [53], should be low.

In scientific research, the gold standard is usually established through multiple raters with domain knowledge (e.g., [9, 14]). Hence, seven Human Resources experts were

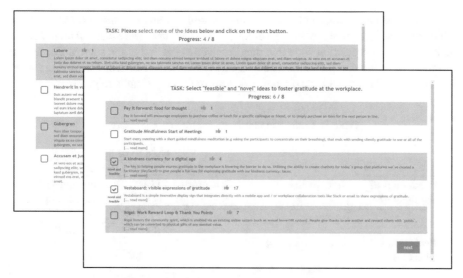

Fig. 2. Screenshots of Idea Selection Platform

asked to rate the ideas according to their feasibility and novelty. Based on the experts aggregated assessments, six ideas were defined as high quality ideas and the remaining 29 ideas as low quality. The ratio of 17% good ideas is in line with the literature, which states that 10–30% of user generated ideas are of high quality [31].

Attention Checks. Seven different attention check questions were included. Two simple instructional attention checks were included in the pre-survey and in the post-survey, where participants were asked to "Click the radio button for strongly agree/disagree." A memory attention check question was included that consisted of two question, one was asked in the pre-survey and one in the post-survey. Participants were supposed to select the same answers in both questions. In the first multiple-choice question, they were notified to remember their choice for a later stage of the task. Specifically, participants were asked "What would you like to have for your birthday?" and could choose among "Birthday cake", "Health for family and friends" and/ or "Laptop". Another memory attention check, this time without prompting, was included after the idea selection task in the post-survey and asked participants to "Please select those ideas that you have been presented with in the previous idea selection task." Five options were available in this idea recognition task from which four were self-invented ideas about Virtual Reality apps that were not presented before and one option said "None of the above". Participants were supposed to select "None of the above" as the other ideas were not related to the "Gratitude at the Workplace" topic of the contest. Furthermore, a task-related attention check was included during the idea selection task. After completing the first half of idea sets, participants were presented with four Latin dummy text ideas. One dummy text idea title was "Hendrerit in vulptate" and the corresponding short description "Duis autem vel eum iriure dolor in hendrerit in vulputate velit esse molestie consequat, vel illum dolore eu feugiat nulla facilisis at vero eros." As these ideas did not have any meaning, participants were supposed to not select any of the ideas. The last attention check question for both groups was the completion time, which was expected to be more than eight minutes. MTurks were also asked to submit their individual completion code that they received at the end of the survey. The author refrained from including attention checks that test factual knowledge as it was shown that crowd workers would use the internet to solve these questions (e.g., [16]).

Table 1. Confusion matrix and performance measures

		Gold Standard	
		High quality	Low quality
Prediction of	High quality	True positive (TP)	False positive (FP)
participant	Low quality	False negative (FN)	True negative (TN)
Performance Measures	Accuracy:	$ACC = \dfrac{\Sigma TP + \Sigma TN}{\Sigma TP + \Sigma FP + \Sigma TN + \Sigma FN}$	
	False Negative Rate:	$FNR = \dfrac{\Sigma FN}{\Sigma TP + \Sigma FN}$	
	False Positive Rate:	$FPR = \dfrac{\Sigma FP}{\Sigma FP + \Sigma TN}$	

Cognition and Information Processing Styles. All measurements to operationalize our research variables are based on previously validated operationalizations and have been adapted to the context of our study. Four items were used to deduce Extraneous Cognitive Load (ECL), that is the cognitive load imposed by the task presentation [56]. Finally, the items for heuristic (HEU) and systematic (SYS) information processing were adapted from Novak and Hoffman's experiential and rational situation-specific thinking style scales, defined as the experiential or rational thinking style or momentary thinking orientation adopted by a consumer in a specific situation. [57]. See Table 1 in Online Appendix[3] for the adapted survey items. All items were measured on a 7-point-Likert scale (from 1 = "strongly disagree" to 7 = "strongly agree").

4   Data Analysis and Results

This study investigates the differences between an anonymous crowd and a student crowd in terms of attention, information processing styles and selection performance when selecting ideas for an innovation contest.

Statistical Assumptions. First, data was checked against violation of statistical assumptions for analysis of variance. For normal distribution, data was visually inspected with Q-Q plots, boxplots and histograms as well as skewness and kurtosis statistics for each group. For the selection performance measures Accuracy, FNR and FPR and the perception-based variables systematic processing and heuristic processing, boxplots and histograms indicated a close to bell curve; skewness and kurtosis are mostly close to 0. Homogeneity of variance was tested with Levene's statistics, which turned out to be satisfactory for most variables (ACC: F = 1.784, p = .184; FNR: F = 0.943, p = .333;

---

[3] https://tinyurl.com/y2xl2rtv.

FPR: F = 0.639, p = .425; SYS: F = 2.486, p = .117; HEU F = .130, p = .719) as p-values should be greater than .05 [58]. For ECL, Levene's test was significant and hence, the assumptions of homogeneity of variance did not hold [58]. To conclude, the data are sufficiently normally distributed and homogeneity of variance is satisfactory, hence, multiple analysis of variance is conducted.

Reliability and Validity. To test convergent and discriminant validity, exploratory factor analysis with Promax (kappa = 4) rotation was performed. Most of the items of the perception-based constructs loaded well on three of the resulting four factor solutions with factor loadings higher than .5. One item (SYS7) loaded on the fourth additional factor. However, this was the only one and hence, it was kept for analysis. Cross-loadings were low and MSA-values higher than .5. All these values exceeded the recommended thresholds [59] and therefore convergent and discriminant validity are deemed satisfactory. Reliability analyses with Cronbach's Alpha were performed for extraneous cognitive load (Cronbach's α = .911), heuristic processing (Cronbach's α = .799) and rational processing (α = .762). All perception-based constructs reached the recommended threshold of .7 [59].

4.1 Attention

To start with, 284 MTurks and 55 students passed the first (reCaptcha) and second ("Click strongly agree") attention check (see Table 2). The task-related attention check followed and only 37.0% of MTurks answered it correctly, whereas 90.9% of the students were able to correctly not select any of the Latin dummy text ideas. From the remaining 105 MTurks and 50 students, 101 MTurks correctly answered the second simple instructional attention check ("Click strongly disagree") while all students followed that instruction correctly. The memory attention check with prompting (birthday present) was answered correctly by 99 of the remaining MTurks and again all students remembered their choice from the multiple-choice question from the pre-survey correctly. Whereas the memory attention check without prompting (idea recognition test) was answered correctly by 88 of the remaining MTurks and by 49 of the remaining students. The expected completion time of at least eight minutes was met by 87 of the remaining MTurks and 49 of the remaining students. The average completion time of the remaining MTurks is 23:08 min and is significantly shorter than the completion time of the students with 45:31 min, $F(1, 134) = 61.243, p < .001$, partial $\eta^2 = .314$. In total, 89.0% of the students and only 30.6% of the MTurks were able to successfully complete the complex selection task and all attention checks, indicating that students are more attentive to complex decision-making tasks.

Attention and Selection Performance. As crowd workers seem to be rather inattentive to the attention checks, the author analyzed whether there are differences in selection performance over time, i.e., before and after the task-related attention check. The performance measures accuracy, false negative rate and false positive rate were calculated for the first half and for the second half of idea sets. A within-subject MANOVA of all participants (N = 339) reveals statistically significant differences for all three performance measures over time, Wilks $\lambda = 0.769$, F (5, 130) = 7.822, p < .001. Specifically, selection accuracy was on average 55.4% for the first half and for the second half with 58.5% significantly higher (F (1, 338) = 19.040, p < .005). Furthermore, the false positive rate

Table 2. Exclusion of participants based on attention checks

	MTurks	Students	Total
Participants	284	55	339
Excluded from analysis	197	6	203
Failed task related AC	179	5	184
Failed simple instructional AC	4	0	4
Failed memory AC with prompting	2	0	2
Failed memory AC without prompting	11	1	12
Failed completion time	1	0	1
Included in analysis	87	49	136
(Success Rate)	(30.6%)	(89.0%)	(40.1%)

was 41.5% for the first half and significantly lower for the second half with 37.3% (F $(1, 338) = 19.040$, p < .005). These results indicate that the task-related attention check increased selection performance.

4.2 Selection Performance, Cognition and Information Processing

To examine the effect of the crowd type on selection performance, cognitive load and information processing styles, the author performed multiple analyses of variance. The crowd type had a significant effect on all tested variables, Wilks $\lambda = 0.769$, F $(3, 336) = 12.760$, p < .001, partial $\eta^2 = .231$. The mean values, standard deviation and median for each crowd type and each variable can be found in Table 3. The results of the MANOVA are presented in Table 4. The anonymous crowd worker have a lower selection accuracy (57.8%), indicating that they are not as good as the student crowd (64.7%) at identifying the truly good and truly bad ideas as suggested by the gold standard (F $(1, 134) = 9.529$, p < .005, partial $\eta^2 = .066$). While no significant effect was found for the false negative rate, MTurks have a higher false positive rate (38.3%) than students (29.4%) (F $(1, 134)$ $= 9.105$, p < .005, partial $\eta^2 = .064$), which means that MTurks define more ideas as high quality even though they are categorized as low quality by the experts, inducing higher subsequent evaluation effort.

The anonymous crowd experiences significantly lower extraneous cognitive load (Mean = 3.22) than the student crowd (Mean = 4.20) (F $(1, 134) = 15.034$, p < .005, partial $\eta^2 = .101$). With regards to information processing, MTurks reports significantly higher values for heuristic processing (Mean = 5.15) than the students (Mean = 4.61) (F $(1, 134) = 10.322$, p < .005, partial $\eta^2 = .072$). Interestingly, MTurks simultaneously report higher values for systematic processing (Mean = 5.29) than the students (Mean = 4.83) as well (F $(1, 134) = 10.727$, p < .005, partial $\eta^2 = .074$).

Due to the surprising finding that MTurks also outperformed students in terms of systematic processing, the author tested the extent of systematic processing with behavioral data gathered on the selection platform. Participants could click on the „read more" button to read the full idea description, which is an indicator of how much information was acquired to make the decision whether or not to select an idea. Hence, the variable information acquisition is the sum of clicks on the "read more" button. An ad-hoc analysis revealed that MTurks clicked on the read more button on average 20.1 times and students 26.0 times. This difference in information acquisition between MTurks and students was found to be significant, $F(1, 134) = 13.515$, $p = .000$, partial $\eta^2 = .092$. Interestingly, MTurks reported that they systematically processed the ideas, but they acquired less information about the idea than the students.

Table 3. Descriptive statistics for performance measures, cognition and information processing

	ACC		FNR		FPR		ECL		HEU		SYS	
	C	S	C	S	C	S	C	S	C	S	C	S
N	87	49	87	49	87	49	87	49	87	49	87	49
M	.578	.647	.609	.639	.383	.294	3.22	4.20	5.15	4.61	5.29	4.83
SD	.131	.111	.252	.234	.174	.149	1.56	1.06	0.95	0.95	0.85	0.67
Mdn	.600	.629	.667	.667	.345	.278	3.00	4.00	5.20	4.80	5.43	4.71

M = Mean, SD = Standard Deviation, Mdn = Median, C = Crowd, S = Student

Table 4. MANOVA for crowd type

Source	DF	Mean square	F	p-value	partial η^2
MANOVA Dependent variable: *Selection Accuracy*					
Treatment	1	0.148	9.529	**.002**	.066
Error	134	0.016			
MANOVA Dependent variable: *FNR*					
Treatment	1	0.029	0.474	.493	.004
Error	134	0.061			
MANOVA Dependent variable: *FPR*					
Treatment	1	0.249	9.105	**.003**	.064
Error	134	0.027			
MANOVA Dependent variable: *Extraneous Cognitive Load*					
Treatment	1	29.788	15.034	**.000**	.101
Error	134	1.981			
MANOVA Dependent variable: *Heuristic Processing*					
Treatment	1	9.340	10.322	**.002**	.072
Error	134	0.905			
MANOVA Dependent variable: *Systematic Processing*					
Treatment	1	6.662	10.727	**.001**	.074
Error	134	0.621			

5   Conclusion

This study compares two different crowds, i.e., an anonymous crowd and a student crowd, with regards to their attentiveness, information processing styles and their selection performance using a web-experiment. It was found that crowd workers recruited from Amazon Mechanical Turk have lower selection performance in terms of lower selection accuracy and higher false positive rate. Indicating that the student crowd is better at identifying high quality and low quality ideas correctly and produces less subsequent evaluation effort as fewer low quality ideas are included in the set for further consideration. Furthermore, MTurks experience lower extraneous cognitive load as they are more familiar with crowd tasks than undergraduate students from the Information Systems discipline. MTurks reported to process information more heuristically than students. Surprisingly, they also outperformed students in terms of systematic processing. Even though MTurks indicate to process information in depth, an ad-hoc analysis of their click behavior revealed that they acquire less information about the ideas. This study expands our understanding of two crowd types, examines their suitability for complex decision-making tasks and offers three main contributions. First, the IS student crowd selects ideas more accurately and with a lower false positive rate than the anonymous MTurk crowd. Second, this study confirms that crowd types process information differently in terms of heuristic and systematic processing as well as in terms of their actual processing behavior. Third, this study also provides a methodological contribution as it explores diverse attention checks and finds that using a task-related attention check increases selection performance of the crowd.

Like any other study, this study has its limitations, which, in turn, opens the door for future research. First, the crowd reported high levels of heuristic and systematic processing, which could not yet be fully explained. One attempted explanation could be that processing information, independent of whether heuristically or systematically, is socially desirable. Furthermore, heuristic and systematic processing are subjective perception variables and hence, do not necessarily reflect the participants' behavior. While the inclusion of mouse tracking behavior acts as a means to validate the information processing style, it does not yet suffice and further hard data would be desirable. Future research could examine potential biases and eye tracking could expand the existing database to better understand the crowds' information processing. Second, while this paper demonstrates that the student crowd performs better than the MTurks, our understanding of why is limited to students being more attentive. Future research could aim at identifying causal mechanisms that explain this effect. Third, while this study included only two external crowd types, namely undergraduate IS students and MTurks, future research could include contrasting crowds to enhance generalizability. An internal employee crowd, students from another discipline or anonymous crowd workers from crowd platform with a focus on more complex tasks might perform better in selecting ideas from a "Gratitude at the Workplace" contest. While all participants are expected to have a general understanding of human resources and workplace innovation, little is known about the participants' experience with the complex task of selecting good ideas from an innovation contest. Finally, students and MTurks received a different reward. MTurks received a financial reward whereas students received course credits, which might have had an impact on their motivation to accurately perform the task. Future research could consider the same incentive to rule out that there is an effect on information processing, attention and selection performance.

Acknowledgments. The research leading to the presented results was funded by the Austrian Science Fund (FWF): P 29765.

References

1. Chesbrough, H.W.: The Era of open innovation. MIT Sloan Manag. Rev. **127**(3), 34–41 (2003)
2. Du Plessis, M.: The role of knowledge management in innovation. J. Knowl. Manag. **11** (2007)
3. Gassmann, O., Enkel, E.: Towards a theory of open innovation: three core process archetypes. R&D Manag. Conf. (2004)
4. Nagar, Y., Boer, P., de, Garcia, A.C.B.: Accelerating the review of complex intellectual artifacts in crowdsourced innovation challenges. In: 37th International Conference on Information Systems (2016)
5. Bjelland, O.M., Wood, R.C.: An inside view of IBM's 'Innovation Jam.' MIT Sloan Manag. Rev. **50**(1). 32 (2008)
6. Jouret, G.: Inside Cisco' s search for the next big idea. Harv. Bus. Rev. **87**, 43–45 (2009)
7. Dean, D.L., Hender, J.M., Rodgers, T.L., Santanen, E.L.: Identifying good ideas: constructs and scales for idea evaluation. J. Assoc. Inf. Syst. **7**(10), 646–699 (2006)
8. Sweller, J.: Cognitive load during problem solving: effects on learning. Cogn. Sci. **12**(2), 257–285 (1988)
9. Kornish, L.J., Ulrich, K.T.: Opportunity spaces in innovation: empirical analysis of large samples of ideas. Manage. Sci. **57**(1), 107–128 (2011)
10. Merz, A.: Mechanisms to select ideas in crowdsourced innovation contests - a systematic literature review and research agenda. In: European Conference on Information Systems (2018)
11. Banken, V., Seeber, I., Maier, R.: Comparing pineapples with lilikois: an experimental analysis of the effects of idea similarity on evaluation performance in innovation contests. In: 52nd Hawaii International Conference on System Sciences (2019)
12. Görzen, T., Kundisch, D.: Can the crowd substitute experts in evaluating creative jobs? an experimental study using business models. In: 24th European Conference on Information Systems (2016)
13. Burnap, A., Gerth, R., Gonzalez, R., Papalambros, P.Y.: Identifying experts in the crowd for evaluation of engineering designs. J. Eng. Des. **28**(5), 317–337 (2017)
14. Blohm, I., Riedl, C., Füller, J., Leimeister, J.M.: Rate or Trade? identifying winning ideas in open idea sourcing. Inf. Syst. Res. **27**(1), 27–48 (2016)
15. Riedl, C., Blohm, I., Leimeister, J.M., Krcmar, H.: Rating scales for collective intelligence in innovation communities: Why quick and easy decision making does not get it righ. In: 31st International Conference on Information Systems (2010)
16. Goodman, J.K., Cryder, C.E., Cheema, A.: Data collection in a flat world: the strengths and weaknesses of mechanical Turk samples. J. Behav. Decis. Mak. **26**(3), 213–224 (2013)
17. Ipeirotis, P.G., Provost, F., Wang, J.: Quality management on Amazon Mechanical Turk. Work. Proc. - Hum. Comput. Work. 2010 (2010)
18. Checco, A., Bates, J., Demartini, G.: Adversarial attacks on crowdsourcing quality control. J. Artif. Intell. Res. **67**, 375–408 (2020)
19. Oppenheimer, D.M., Meyvis, T., Davidenko, N.: Instructional manipulation checks: detecting satisficing to increase statistical power. J. Exp. Soc. Psychol. **45**(4), 867–872 (2009)
20. Hauser, D.J., Schwarz, N.: Attentive Turkers: MTurk participants perform better on online attention checks than do subject pool participants. Behav. Res. Methods **48**(1), 400–407 (2015)
21. Howe, J.: The rise of crowdsourcing. Wired Mag. **14**(6), 1–4 (2006)
22. Surowiecki, J.: The Wisdom of the Crowds. Anchor Books, New York (2005)
23. Durward, D., Blohm, I., Leimeister, J.M.: Crowd work. Bus. Inf. Syst. Eng. **58**(4), 281–286 (2016)

24. Difallah, D.E., Catasta, M., Demartini, G., Ipeirotis, P.G., Cudré-Mauroux, P.: The dynamics of micro-task crowdsourcing. In: 24th International Conference on World Wide Web - WWW 2015 Companion (2015)

25. Bentivogli, L., Federico, M., Moretti, G., Paul, M.: Getting expert quality from the crowd for machine translation evaluation. In: 13th Machine Translation Summit (2011)

26. Di Gangi, P., Wasko, M., Hooker, R.: Getting customers' ideas to work for you: learning from Dell how to succeed with online user innovation communities. MIS Q. Exec. 9(4) (2010)

27. Rietzschel, E., Nijstad, B., Stroebe, W.: Productivity is not enough: a comparison of interactive and nominal brainstorming groups on idea generation and selection. J. Exp. Soc. Psychol. 42(2), 244–251 (2006)

28. Santiago Walser, R., Seeber, I., Maier, R.: The fewer, the better? Effects of decomposition of information load on the decision making process and outcome in idea selection. 27th Eur. Conf. Inf. Syst (2020)

29. Hoornaert, S., Ballings, M., Malthouse, E.C., Van den Poel, D.: Identifying new product ideas: waiting for the wisdom of the crowd or screening ideas in real time. J. Prod. Innov. Manag. 34(5), 580–597 (2017)

30. Bullinger, A.C., Moeslein, K.: Innovation contests – Where are we? In: AMCIS 2010 Proceedings. Americas Conference on Information Systems (2010)

31. Blohm, I., Riedl, C., Leimeister, J.M., Krcmar, H.: Idea evaluation mechanisms for collective intelligence in open innovation communities: do traders outperform raters? In: 32nd International Conference on Information Systems (2011)

32. Wibmer, A., Wiedmann, F.M., Seeber, I., Maier, R.: Why less is more: an Eye tracking study on idea presentation and attribute attendance in idea selection. In: 27th European Conference on Information Systems (2019)

33. Kornish, L.J., Ulrich, K.T.: The importance of the raw idea in innovation: testing the sow's ear hypothesis. J. Mark. Res. 51(1), 14–26 (2014)

34. Mollick, E.R., Nanda, R.: Wisdom or Madness? comparing crowds with expert evaluation in funding the arts. Manage. Sci. 62(6), 1533–1553 (2016)

35. Kudrowitz, B.M., Wallace, D.: Assessing the quality of ideas from prolific, early-stage product ideation. J. Eng. Des. 24(2), 120–139 (2013)

36. Magnusson, P.R., Wästlund, E., Netz, J.: Exploring users' appropriateness as a proxy for experts when screening new product/service ideas. J. Prod. Innov. Manag. 33(1), 4–18 (2016)

37. Magnusson, P.R., Netz, J., Wästlund, E.: Exploring holistic intuitive idea screening in the light of formal criteria. Technovation. 34(5–6), 315–326 (2014)

38. Riedl, C., Blohm, I., Leimeister, J.M., Krcmar, H.: Rating scales for collective intelligence in innovation communities: why quick and easy decision making does not get it right. In: 31st International Conference on Information Systems (2010)

39. Kahneman, D.: A perspective on judgment and choice. Am. Psychol. 58(9), 697 (2003)

40. Evans, J.: In two minds: dual-process accounts of reasoning. Trends Cogn. Sci. 7(10), 454–459(2003)

41. Croskerry, P., Singhal, G., Mamede, S.: Cognitive debiasing 1: origins of bias and theory of debiasing. BMJ Qual. Saf. 22 (2013)

42. Jahn, G., Chemnitz, D., Renkewitz, F., Kunze, S.: Heuristics in multi-attribute decision making: effects of representation format. CogSci. (2007)

43. Sadler-Smith, E., Shefy, E.: The intuitive executive: understanding and applying "Gut Feel" in decision-making. Acad. Manag. Exec. 18(4), 76–91 (2004)

44. Simon, H.: Rational choice and the structure of the environment. Psychol. Rev. 63(2), 129 (1956)

45. Miller, G.A.: The magical number seven, plus or minus two: some limites on out capacity for processing information. Psychol. Rev. 65(2), 81 (1956)

46. Ho, C.-J., Slivkins, A., Suri, S., Wortman Vaughan, J.: Incentivizing high quality crowdwork. In: International World Wide Web Conference Committee (2015)
47. Rouse, S.: A reliability analysis of Mechanical Turk data. Comput. Human Behav. **43**, 304–307 (2015)
48. Keith, M.G., Tay, L., Harms, P.D.: Systems perspective of amazon mechanical Turk for organizational research: review and recommendations. Front. Psychol. **8**, 1359 (2017)
49. Banken, V., Ilmer, Q., Seeber, I., Haeussler, S.: A method for Smart Idea Allocation in crowd-based idea selection. Decis. Support Syst. **124**, 113072 (2019)
50. Ipeirotis, P.: Demographics of Mechanical Turk, New York (2010)
51. Harsch, C., Martin, G.: Comparing holistic and analytic scoring methods: issues of validity and reliability. Assess. Educ. Princ. Policy Pract. **20**(3), 281–307 (2013)
52. Walter, T.P., Back, A.: A text mining approach to evaluate submissions to crowdsourcing contests. In: 46th Hawaii International Conference on System Sciences (2013)
53. Metz, C.E.: Basic principles of ROC analysis. Semin. Nucl. Med. **8**(4), 283–298 (1978)
54. Sarigianni, C., Banken, V., Santiago Walser, R., Wibmer, A., Wiedmann, F., Seeber, I.: Innovation contests: how to design for successful idea selection. In: 53rd Hawaii International Conference on System Sciences (2020)
55. Riedl, C., Blohm, I., Leimeister, J.M., Krcmar, H.: The effect of rating scales on decision quality and user attitudes in online innovation communities. Int. J. Electron. Commer. **17**(3), 7–36 (2013)
56. Chang, C.C., Liang, C., Chou, P.N., Lin, G.Y.: Is game-based learning better in flow experience and various types of cognitive load than non-game-based learning? Perspective from multimedia and media richness. Comput. Human Behav. **71**, 281–227 (2017)
57. Novak, T.P., Hoffman, D.L.: The fit of thinking style and situation: new measures of situation-specific experiential and rational cognition. J. Consum. Res. **36**(1), 56–72 (2009)
58. Hair, J.F., Black, W.C., Babin, B.J., Anderson, R.E.: Multivariate data analysis; a global perspective (2010)
59. Nunnally, J.C.: Psychometric Theory. McGraw-Hill, New York (1978)

Data-Driven Competitive Advantages in Digital Markets: An Overview of Data Value and Facilitating Factors

Victoria Fast[(✉)], Daniel Schnurr, and Michael Wohlfarth

School of Business, Economics and Information Systems, University of Passau, Passau,
Germany
{victoria.fast,daniel.schnurr,michael.wohlfarth}@uni-passau.de

Abstract. Recent high-profile merger and antitrust cases as well as policy debates worldwide have focused on the relationship between access to (big) data and firms' competitive advantages in digital markets. These discussions have brought forward numerous conceptual arguments for and against the conjecture that market power may be derived from a firm's access to big data. Based on a review of the economic, information systems and management literature, this paper presents an overview of the aggregate empirical evidence on the business value and economic benefits that firms can indeed create from big data in the Internet economy. Moreover, six facilitating factors for data-driven market power are proposed that enable a firm to establish a sustained competitive advantage based on the economic benefits from data. Finally, we point to policy measures which may address competitive concerns in data-driven digital markets and highlight opportunities for future information systems policy research.

Keywords: Big data · Data-driven business models · Competition in digital markets · Market power · Regulation · Policy · Online platforms · Internet economy

.

Acknowledgments. This project was funded by the Bavarian State Ministry of Science and the Arts and coordinated by the Bavarian Research Institute for Digital Transformation (bidt).

F. Ahlemann et al. (Eds.): WI 2021, LNISO 48, p. 454, 2021.
https://doi.org/10.1007/978-3-030-86800-0_31

Tweeting in IIoT Ecosystems – Empirical Insights from Social Media Analytics About IIoT Platforms

Dimitri Petrik[1,2(✉)], Katharina Pantow[2], Patrick Zschech[3], and Georg Herzwurm[2]

[1] Graduate School of Excellence Advanced Manufacturing Engineering (GSaME), Stuttgart, Germany
dimitri.petrik@gsame.uni-stuttgart.de
[2] Department of VIII: Information Systems II, University of Stuttgart, Stuttgart, Germany
{katharina.pantow,georg.herzwurm}@bwi.uni-stuttgart.de
[3] Intelligent Information Systems, Friedrich-Alexander University, Nuremberg, Germany
patrick.zschech@fau.de

Abstract. The market for the Industrial Internet of Things (IIoT) platforms remains highly dynamic and is rapidly evolving regarding the growth of the platform-based ecosystems. However, digital platforms, used in the industrial business-to-business setting, differ significantly from the established platforms in the business-to-consumer domains and remain little researched. In this study, we apply a data-driven approach and conduct bottom-up and top-down content analysis, exploring social media data on the current state of IIoT platforms. For a top-down analysis, we draw on the theoretical concept of platform boundary resources. Specifically, we apply descriptive analytics and topic modeling on the Twitter data regarding the market-ready IIoT platforms Adamos, Cumulocity, Watson IoT, MindSphere, Leonardo, and ThingWorx, thus conducting an exploratory multiple case study. Our findings generate descriptive insights on the currently discussed topics in the area of IIoT platforms, contributing to the knowledge of the current state of digital platforms used in IIoT.

Keywords: Industrial IoT · IoT platform · Platform strategy · Boundary resources · Twitter analytics

1 Introduction

Industrial Internet of Things (IIoT) platforms build an interoperable and modularly extendable digital infrastructure to connect heterogeneous industrial assets, enterprise information systems, and other networked objects across the borders of a single company [1, 2]. Industrial companies show a growing interest in IIoT platforms to capture value from the connected assets, either to make their production more efficient or to develop new business models. IIoT platforms, as a domain-specific type of digital platforms, foster generativity, and change the organization of traditional supply-chains. Thus, the platformization of manufacturing and mechanical engineering industries causes intense

© The Author(s), under exclusive license to Springer Nature Switzerland AG 2021
F. Ahlemann et al. (Eds.): WI 2021, LNISO 48, pp. 455–472, 2021.
https://doi.org/10.1007/978-3-030-86800-0_32

competition between incumbent enterprise software providers (e.g., Microsoft, SAP, Software AG, IBM) and industrial companies (e.g., Siemens, General Electric, Hitachi, Bosch, ABB). Both types of actors launch platforms and establish IIoT ecosystems, with the numbers of platform providers increasing year after year [3, 4]. Building upon the competitive advantages from their traditional business fields, such companies have become platform owners, offering extensible codebases to the heterogeneous types of third-party complementors through regulated access routines [5–7]. The complementors use the platform to contribute their unique capabilities and create platform-based IoT solutions. These complementary solutions rely on the network effects and increase the value of the platform and help the platform companies to manage the variety of use cases and to profit from the generativity [4, 5, 8, 9]. Therefore, IIoT platforms also act as an innovation architecture for complementors, fitting the concept of digital innovation platforms, and transforming the innovation processes [10, 11]. Accordingly, the possibilities to achieve platform-based growth and the collaboration in platform-based ecosystems determine the present research objectives within the platform research [12, 13]. One of the relevant concepts to explain the process of enabling third-party innovation are the platform boundary resources (BR), which define the interfaces between the platform provider and the complementors [14, 15]. Prior research recognized multiple aspects of benefit in the provision of BR, which range from the control to the attractiveness [14, 16, 17]. The concept of BR is even recognized as an appropriate research lens to study advanced topics of digital platforms [18].

Although previous research has already shown that digital platforms in business-to-consumer (B2C) differ in various aspects from platforms in the enterprise domains such as IIoT [9, 19, 20], and highlighted the multitude of existing BR in the IIoT domain, the is not much research work studying the IIoT platforms, the inherent ecosystems and the used BR in this domain. Even though digital platforms represent popular research directions in information systems (IS) research [13, 18], many existing papers study the transactional platforms and not the innovation platforms. Furthermore, most of the studies on innovation platforms set the software platforms in business-to-consumer (B2C) domains as the research object. Overall, the majority of the prior research articles do not entirely comply with the enterprise IIoT context that is for instance defined by the differences in the impact of network effects [20], the maturity of the platforms or the criticality of the data processed on the platform. Additionally, compared to the mature B2C platform-mediated markets, the competition-driven dynamics in the market for IIoT platforms remains high, despite the ongoing consolidation [21]. Accordingly, IIoT platforms represent an exciting research object in a rapidly changing enterprise environment, providing an under-researched application domain for digital platforms in a business-to-business (B2B) setting.

Against this background, our goal was to shed light on the current topics connected to IIoT platforms and the possible BR used to leverage ecosystem dynamics [6, 9]. Currently, only one IIoT ecosystem, based upon the Siemens MindSphere platform, has been closely analyzed, taking into account the BR offered and their potential to create attractiveness in the platform-based IIoT ecosystem [17]. Hence, to bring the research platform dynamics in IIoT ecosystems forward, we use social media data from Twitter that represents the voices of the ecosystem participants (i.e., platform providers and platform users), including multiple platform providers. This data helps to identify current topics in IIoT the practitioners talk about concerning the IIoT platforms. We utilize the BR as a theoretical framework [10, 22] since the projection of these platform-complementor interfaces on the gathered Twitter data helps to appraise the relevance of the concepts related to platform dynamics in the extensive set of raw data.

RQ1: *What are currently discussed topics in the domain of IIoT?*

RQ2: *What can we learn about the use of boundary resources in IIoT?*

In particular, we use social media data from Twitter and derive empirical insights from six popular IIoT platforms: MindSphere (Siemens), Adamos and Cumulocity (Software AG), Leonardo (SAP), Watson IoT (IBM), and ThingWorx (PTC). To address RQ2, we utilize the concept of boundary resources (BR) as a research lens to reduce the data noise and improve the understanding of social media data, supporting the interpretative analysis of the extracted tweets [18, 23]. Thus, by examining a large amount of Twitter data and applying BR as a research lens, and a theoretical framework, we complement the field with descriptive insights regarding BR-related strategies in IIoT ecosystems (e.g., which BR are present in corporate communication and how for instance influencers are used to promote specific IIoT topics) and therefore provide an additional perspective that distinguishes from current IS studies dealing with platform-based ecosystems [3, 4, 20, 24].

2 Theoretical Background and Related Work

2.1 Digital Platforms and the Industrial Internet of Things

To get a comprehensive understanding, IIoT platforms should be considered from the technical and economic perspectives. Adding the ecosystems, the organizational perspective completes the understanding of the concept. From the technical perspective, IIoT platforms provide scalable middleware, offering interfaces for the connected smart devices, cyber-physical systems, and enterprise software systems. Thus, IIoT platforms provide interoperability and help to overcome the connectivity-related challenges, which are grounded in the variety of used and incompatible industrial protocols.

Usually, IIoT platforms are understood as scalable multi-layered architectures. Supplemented by the modularity, the functionality of the platform core is connected with the periphery to extend its capabilities, matching the requirements for the vast amount of the industrial use cases [1, 2, 25]. Due to the usual complexity of the industrial use cases, companies are required to collaborate on the IoT solutions [8, 20]. Thus, offering a digital infrastructure, IIoT platforms bridge the distance between multiple solution providers. Acting as multi-sided markets, they leverage access to new industrial customers for the complementors [3, 13].

However, despite connecting heterogenous market-sides, due to the variety of the use cases, IIoT platforms are not generating strong indirect network effects, which argues against the application of the multi-sided platform definition, provided by Evans and Schmalensee [20, 26]. Nevertheless, IIoT platforms usually foster the building of ecosystems consisting of complementary and industrial companies. The IIoT platform provider is usually an incumbent company with a background either in industry or enterprise software. It can use its power to design the ecosystem in a way, to fuel generativity created upon its platform [27, 28]. Intermediating the various stakeholder types and increasing their collaboration, IIoT platforms may also foster generativity and create unforeseen value [29]. The value is achieved by interacting actors who depend on each other's activities and use the IoT platform to create IoT applications [1, 30]. In order to maximize the value of the whole platform-based ecosystem, the platform provider should also pay attention to the balancing effects achieved through BR to attract and foster third-party innovation [17]. Prior research already acknowledged that if the ecosystems are left ungoverned, the balance in the ecosystem can be disturbed by the dominance of certain complementors [31]. That is why we explain the concept of BR in the next section.

2.2 Platform Boundary Resources in the Internet of Things

BR represent a concept to explain how the platform providing companies can stay in control of the external innovation, contributed by the ecosystem participants, simultaneously sourcing the complementors with the required tools and routines [32]. Conceptualized by Ghazawneh and Henfridsson, the BR concept consists of technical (TBR) and non-technical or social (SBR) platform resources. Application programming interfaces (APIs) or development tools represent exemplary forms of TBR, while the platform documentation, the license agreements, or the platform-related events represent exemplary forms of SBR.

Prior research recognized how BR are used by the ecosystem to create the complements [32]. Platform providers usually shape the BR design after their initial release, while the ecosystem can exercise power to affect the BR design during the platform cycle [33]. Consequently, BR were conceptualized as a governance model for platform providers, which use alternating sourcing and restricting actions to tune the BR and change third-party innovation [32]. This view of BR comes primarily from the B2C perspective, where the aim is to guide the innovation focus in the desired direction with regard to the complements. Due to the criticality of the data to be processed on the IIoT platform, the control aspect of BR is a sensitive issue for platform users in IIoT and therefore, the sourcing aspect predominates in the industrial use of BR. Accordingly, different IIoT platform providers maintain various BR [19, 34] and use them, even more, to enable the complementors to contribute, instead of governing them, since the B2B complementors are much more sensitive to the dependencies caused by the platform provider's lock-in. Despite this fact, we do not know much about the perception of IIoT platforms by the enterprise complementors and especially about the effect of BR in IIoT on platform dynamics. The numerous BR types used in IIoT create even more complexity for the platform provider in an already highly competitive and fragmented market. The quality of the offered BR is valued by the complementors and affects the complementor satisfaction with the IIoT platform and the ecosystem [17, 19, 33]. Lastly, BR can be used in competition, e.g., for closing the gaps of new market entrants in platform-mediated markets [35].

Taken together, BR can be considered as mechanisms from the platform provider perspective, which in turn, also need to be communicated via different corporate channels, such as Twitter, Facebook, GitHub, etc. The perception of this communication by the ecosystem participants plays a crucial role to position the platform, including the promotion of BR for active complementary involvement. However, the mentioned social media platforms allow public discussions about the IoT, so a platform provider usually has little control over this public communication. Thus, different aspects are discussed and communicated by different ecosystem participants. Thus, in order to gain a better understanding about recently discussed topics and the strategic use of BR in IIoT ecosystems, the present research focuses on the analysis of a social media channel as a pre-dominant communication platform, where aspects related to TBR and SBR are frequently discussed in public.

3 Research Method

3.1 Twitter Analytics and Applied Methods

Social media platforms provide a rich, steadily growing, and valuable source of user-generated content and interaction data. Since the data is highly diverse and interdisciplinary, and it can readily be extracted from online platforms, it is of particular interest for research purposes [36, 37]. The social microblogging platform Twitter offers enormous amounts of publicly available data, which can be studied in different ways. Compared to the analysis of scientific literature, published tweets offer current data without much delay. The tweets may include key trends and moods of communities or offer insights on the corporate strategies if the official statements are being studied. In addition, Twitter offers various metrics, which can be included for analysis purposes as well [36–38].

Hence, social media and especially Twitter can be used by practitioners to support decision making, and likewise, it can be used successfully by researchers to enable studies of mass data [23]. Relevant techniques include descriptive analysis, content analysis, or network analysis, whereby the choice of the technique depends on the research goal. This paper presents the results of the descriptive metrics analysis and content analysis, incorporating bottom-up and top-down analysis techniques [36, 38].

With descriptive analysis, Twitter data can be analyzed concerning the users, their tweets, and related metrics such as the numbers of followers, tweets, and retweets. Tweets can be grouped by their hashtags, as these are used to mark tweets on a specific topic. Moreover, hashtags also allow tweets to reach a wider audience since they can be found more easily using hashtags as search terms. Descriptive analyses are suitable for obtaining a basic knowledge of the tweet data in the initial phase of the investigation. After becoming familiar with the basic properties of the tweets, a content analysis provides detailed results about specific topics. For this purpose, text categorization is a central element. With manual coding, one can choose between a bottom-up and a top-down approach. Top-down investigations are based on existing pre-defined categories, while bottom-up methods generate these categories during the analysis [23]. The bottom-up approach was chosen due to the open research questions of this paper. This procedure should guarantee a holistic examination of the platforms, discussed on Twitter. Concerning the topics that are known in advance (i.e., BR), a top-down approach was used to investigate IIoT platforms specifically through a specific lens to get a focus on the desired objects of investigation. To master the challenges posed by large amounts of text data, we rely on a topic modeling approach using the Latent Dirichlet Allocation (LDA) technique [23]. LDA is suitable for automated text categorization as a form of unsupervised machine learning. It is based on the theory that documents contain a random set of topics defined by a certain word combination. Overall, the use of LDA in the context of topic modeling was successfully used in IS research before, for instance, to analyze social media posts, job advertisements, mobile app stores, and many more [23].

3.2   Case Selection

Since the market for IIoT platforms is still highly fragmented, currently no platform provider has yet been able to significantly assert its platform in the competition and capture a dominant position. This situation is indicated by the steadily increasing numbers of platform companies in the domains of IoT and IIoT [39]. The latest market report on IIoT platforms was conducted by ForresterWave in Q4 2019. It contains a benchmark to define the research object and select suitable platforms. Thus, instead of focusing on a single platform, our case study selection includes six IIoT platforms of leading platform providers [40] summarized in Table 1.

We have specifically focused on leading platforms as it can be assumed that, due to their gained maturity within the field, they have already established various successful mechanisms in the sense of BR, and created ecosystems, thus provide valuable insights about their platform scope, the discussed topics and the possibly used BR in this particular B2B segment. All the platforms match the definition of platforms as "the extensible codebase of a software-based system that provides core functionality shared by apps that interoperate with it, and the interfaces through which they interoperate" [6]. Furthermore, all of the six platforms offer openly accessible documentation for third-party complementors to develop applications and provide extensive documentation on the connectivity of assets. Therefore, the six platforms represent attempts to create IIoT ecosystems and lead open communication on Twitter, also being represented on Twitter by specific hashtags.

3.3   Data Collection and Preparation

For our study, a python-based scraping and analytics program was developed and launched through a command-line interface of Anaconda, an open-source distribution for Python and R. Utilizing the Twitter scraping script, we crawled the tweets using the hashtags (see column #hashtag in Table 1) within a defined range and saved the extracted tweets and their metadata as a.csv file. As an interim step, we built word clouds to perform our LDA analysis. Our implementation was based on several libraries, such as twitterscraper, matplotlib.pyplot, sklearn, wordcloud. Our source code can be retrieved online: https://github.com/Kypez/Twitter-Scrap-IoT-Platform.

The tweets collected and analyzed were posted between 01-01-2015 and 31-08-2019. There is no limit to the number of tweets. Instead, start and end dates were used as a time limit. To ensure a comparable and uniform analysis of the terms, we included only tweets posted in English. During data cleansing, we deleted stop words (as they have no relevance to the context and distort the frequencies), retweets (as they are considered as duplicates), and irrelevant tweets that were scrapped mistakenly by the script (e.g., "How many of these have you ever been to?" or "Write in the comments which costume you like best"). Furthermore, the hashtags of the individual platforms were removed as

Table 1. Overview of the studies IIoT platforms

Platform	#hashtag	Platform characteristics
Adamos (Software AG, DMG Mori, Dürr, Zeiss, ASM PT)	#adamos	Availability: since 2017 Background of the platform provider: IT and mechanical engineering Software AG 2018 revenue: 865.7 million EUR
Cumulocity (Software AG)	#cumulocity	Availability: since 2012 Background of the platform provider: IT Software AG 2018 revenue: 865.7 million EUR
Watson IoT (IBM)	#IBMWatson	Availability: since 2014 Background of the platform provider: IT Turnover IBM 2018: 79.6 billion USD
MindSphere (Siemens)	#MindSphere	Availability: since 2016 Background of the platform provider: Manufacture/ Production Siemens 2018 sales: 83 billion EUR
Leonardo (SAP)	#SAPLeonardo	Availability: since 2017 Background of the platform provider: IT SAP 2018 revenue: 25.96 billion EUR
ThingWorx (PTC)	#Thingworx	Availability: since 2014 Background of the platform provider: IT PTC 2018 sales: USD 1.24 billion USD

they are the most common terms of the tweets. Table 2 depicts some descriptive statistics on the collected and analyzed data:

Table 2. Number of tweets after data collection and cleansing

Platform	# of the collected tweets	# of tweets after data cleansing
Adamos	415	201
Cumulocity	813	438
Watson IoT	136673	134677
MindSphere	12737	11416
Leonardo	8470	7330
ThingWorx	4922	3132
Sum	164030	157194

4 Results

4.1 Descriptive Analysis

In order to get an overview of general information of the data, descriptive analyses are first carried out using the bottom-up method. The cleansed files from the previous section are used. It is noticeable that the hashtag #IBMWatson with 134,677 (85.3%) of a total of 157,869 tweets has a significantly higher number of tweets than the other hashtags, suggesting a possible distortion of the results in further data analysis. Therefore, the tweets about this platform are not considered in further analyses, apart from the LDA analysis. Without the consideration of IBM Watson, it is evident that the MindSphere, the Leonardo, and the ThingWorx platforms were responsible for the generation of the most tweets. The MindSphere community on Twitter is responsible for 49% of the examined tweets. Almost one third (32%) of all tweets were published on the SAP Leonardo platform. In total, the ThingWorx, the Cumulocity IoT, and the Adamos platforms only share 6% of the remaining tweets.

The second descriptive evaluation tackles the frequency of tweets to show how used hashtags are distributed over the years, as shown in Table 3. Most of the tweets were published in 2018, whereas a continuous increase of tweets can be observed from 2015 to 2018. Since the study was conducted in August 2019, the figure from that year cannot be compared in absolute terms with the figures of the other years. If the platforms are examined individually, a similar distribution for Cumulocity IoT and MindSphere becomes evident. Adamos and ThingWorx show the most tweets for 2017, and later the numbers drop similarly as for the other platforms. The Leonardo platform has an equivalently high number of tweets in 2017 and 2018. However, one can expect a smaller number of tweets for 2019. It is also revealed that there are no tweets for Adamos and Leonardo for the years 2015 and 2016.

Table 3. Frequency distribution of tweets from January 2015 to August 2019

Platform	2015	2016	2017	2018	2019
Adamos	0	0	94	71	36
Cumulocity	9	15	76	232	106
MindSphere	10	617	3110	5299	2380
Leonardo	0	0	3094	3264	972
ThingWorx	550	769	862	588	363
Sum	569	1401	7236	9454	3857

If we look at the frequency of tweets over time, it becomes clear that the annual number will increase from 2015 to 2018. In this four-year period, the annual number of all tweets examined rises from 569 to 10010, i.e., the frequency increases by a factor of 17.59. Although on average, the number of Tweets of each platform increases over the years, the results suggest that the tweets of the MindSphere platform show the highest growth. By contrast, there are no tweets for the SAP Leonardo platform for the years 2015 and 2016. A high number of tweets was posted one year later, with only a slight increase in 2018, whereby a drop can be predicted for Leonardo in 2019. In total, no complete data was available for the year 2019, and the period under investigation contains only about 2/3 (3857) of the year. An extrapolated development for all platforms indicates a drop in the tweet intensity resulting in a total predicted number of 5785 tweets that would be posted in 2019. This figure is significantly lower than in the previous year's figure. This decline is more strongly reflected in the Leonardo, MindSphere, and Cumulocity IoT platforms. Extrapolated, the frequency of tweets on Adamos and ThingWorx would be only slightly below the previous year's figure.

The next descriptive analysis deals with the user profiles, investigating which types of user accounts publish the largest number of tweets. Table 4 provides a summarized overview. The results provide some insights into the activity within the ecosystems. A sufficient number of tweets posted by private accounts indicate the existence of an organic ecosystem. On the opposite, a majority of tweets posted by corporate accounts indicate a coordinated strategy for the ecosystem development, orchestrated by the platform provider. Among the top 10 users of the examined IIoT ecosystems, we observe an equal share of 25 private accounts and 25 corporate accounts. For #adamos and #Thingworx, the users with the most tweets are corporate ones. Private accounts show the highest activity for the other four ecosystems. In the case of the Adamos, there is only one private account among the top 10. For Cumulocity IoT, the list also includes more corporate accounts than private ones. With the platform ThingWorx, the number of private users and corporate accounts is equal.

Focusing on the top 10 users, we can see that with regard to SAP Leonardo, mainly private users publish a more significant number of tweets for the platform. There is only one official SAP account in the top 10 (i.e., "SAP Intelligent RPA"), ranking 8th position with 73 tweets in total. First, this indicates that the company is active on Twitter from 2017 onwards (cf. Table 3). Second, it indicates that a vibrant ecosystem of platform users was

Table 4. Number of private accounts and corporate accounts with the most tweets

Platform	Number of private accounts	Number of corporate accounts	Account type with the most tweets
Adamos	1	9	Corporate
Cumulocity	4	6	Private
MindSphere	7	3	Private
Leonardo	8	2	Private
ThingWorx	5	5	Corporate

created. It remains striking that the popularity of the platform without the development of the tweet frequencies, especially among private users, suddenly reaches a very high level, suggesting that SAP actively promoted the platform when it was launched. In contrast, the Adamos platform is mainly represented by the corporate accounts of the Adamos shareholders (e.g., Software AG, DMG, Duerr, and Carl Zeiss). The small number of 201 tweets for Adamos suggests that the platform is comparatively unknown and, therefore, only a few private users participate in the Twitter discussion regarding Adamos.

4.2 Content Analysis

The following tweet evaluations are part of the content analysis. In the run-up to the identification of topics, we study common words using word clouds to identify ten most frequent terms. This is followed by the evaluation of the terms using the LDA approach. For this purpose, the number of topics and terms must be determined. An initial test with five topics and ten terms revealed that this number of topics and terms is too high for platforms with few tweets, and therefore, the topics only differed by a few single terms. After adjustments, we decided to set three topics with ten or twelve terms each or four topics with twelve terms each, depending on the total number of tweets and the result of the test evaluation. Overall, the application of the LDA method shows that, in many cases, the tweets use specific terms to highlight a certain topic, as seen in Table 5, although not all terms are necessarily required to access a certain topic.

The identified topics, which are reflected by their respective terms, reveal a heterogeneous picture. For example, some topics primarily refer to specific domain orientations (e.g., IBM Watson topic 3 healthcare), while others refer to technological directions (e.g., Leonardo topic 1 data analytics). Moreover, the identified topics within a platform cannot be clearly distinguished from one another. However, between the various platforms, relatively clear topics can be identified.

The Adamos platform, for example, deals with hackathons in two out of three topics and mentions partners of the platform particularly often. In two of three topics of the platform Cumulocity IoT, the term "softwareaginfluencer" is included. MindSphere deals with terms such as "industrial", "manufacturing" or "industry40" in several topics. The SAP Leonardo topics contain the term "sapphirenow" in two of three cases. The tweets of the ThingWorx platform contain the term "Liveworx" in all three topics.

Table 5. Identified topics and related terms of the LDA analysis

Platform	Most probable terms	Topic
Adamos	new, iiot, machine, platform, duerrag, zeiss_group, softwareag, iot engineering, partners	Partnership
	softwareag, iiot, iot, platform, hackathon, duerrag, zeiss_group digital, team, adamosgroup	Shareholders
	hackathon, digitization, strongertogether, teams, industrial, iot, challenges, motto, crosscompany, interdisciplinary	Teamwork
Cumulocity	iot, softwareag, wire, business, build, solutions, test, team, solution, fast	Development
	iot, softwareag, free, iiot, 30, softwareaginfluencer, days, platform, trial, solution	Sales promotion
	ot, softwareag, platform, iiot, global, softwareaginfluencer, partnership, innovation, leading	Influencing
Watson IoT	ibm, cognitive, iot, help, ai, new, bluemix, services, using, apps	Portfolio
	ibm, ai, cognitive, new, bigdata, personality, analytics, machinelearning, similar, learning	Analytics
	ai, ibm, data, cancer, like, health, world, help, healthcare, care	Healthcare
MindSphere	siemens, iot, digitalization, business, iiot, atos, hm18, siemensindustry, use, new, digital, digitaltransformation	Digitilization
	siemens, iot, data, industrial, iiot, industry40, digital, new, lounge, partner, cloud, atos	Industry
	siemens, iot, iiot, platform, manufacturing, cloud, ai, aws, solutions, just, open, apps	Openness
	iot, iiot, siemens, bigdata, atos, industry40, siemensindustry, cyber security, digital, analytics, sps_live, siemensusa	Partner
Leonardo	iiot, blockchain, machinelearning, ai, sap, bigdata, cloud, analytics, s4hana, industry40, innovation, internetofthings	Data analytics
	sap, iot, digital, new business, intelligent, blog, erp, sapphirenow, post, innovation, iiot	Digitilization
	sap, iot, learning, sapphirenow, machine, learn, sapteched, help, join, data, ai, business	Portfolio
ThingWorx	Ptc, iot, iiot, tips, liveworx, platform, digitaltransformation, manufacturing, connectivity, free	Digitilization
	iot, ptc, liveworx, learn, new, data, platform, partner, solution, analytics	Unspecified

(*continued*)

Table 5. (*continued*)

Platform	Most probable terms	Topic
	iot, ptc, certification, ar, blog, training, things, liveworx, using, internet	Education

One of the topics deals with terms such as "manufacturing" and "connectivity", another with "training" and "certification". The evaluation indicates that especially tweets with the hashtag #IBMWatson refer less to the IIoT area than tweets from other platforms. Several terms in the word cloud refer to personality analyses (e.g., "personality similar", "personality insight") and health care (e.g., "treat patient", "doctors treat", "disease doctors", "patient care"). At least two topics contain the terms "ibm", "cognitive", "ai" and "new". It is noticeable that no topic contains terms related to IIoT, but instead analogous to the word cloud, terms such as "personality", "cancer", "health", "healthcare" and "care". It seems that the tweets on IBM Watson do not address specifically the industrial field of application of the platform, which is an interesting insight for practitioners to categorize the platform.

In addition to the above-described bottom-up procedure of content, we also applied a top-down approach, which specifically investigates to what extent TBR and SBR are mentioned in the tweets. For this purpose, two BR are selected for each category and their frequency in the tweets is examined. As TBR the terms "API" and "SDK" are examined, as SBR the terms "Hackathon" and "Documentation". We used the same preparation steps as for the LDA analysis, except for the creation of a "string". Since the term "API" is often part of other words, we defined it as an independent word in the analysis. The results of the top-down analysis of the selected BR show that the SBR "Hackathon" with 124 citations is the most frequently discussed BR. Hackathons are the most frequently mentioned BR for Adamos, Cumulocity IoT, and MindSphere. For Leonardo and ThingWorx APIs are mentioned most often. The results of the top-down analysis are presented in Table 6.

Table 6. Frequencies of mentions of selected BR in the analyzed tweets

Platform	API	SDK	Hackathon	Documentation	Sum
Adamos	0	0	45	0	45
Cumulocity	1	1	12	0	14
MindSphere	0	0	55	2	57
Leonardo	22	6	10	0	38
ThingWorx	10	6	2	0	18
Sum	33	13	124	2	172

5 Discussion

5.1 Descriptive Analysis

The first descriptive analysis examines the tweet frequencies and how the tweets are distributed over different platforms. The study shows that IIoT platforms have different levels of awareness among the Twitter community and potential customers. The data indicate that MindSphere is more popular than the other platforms, and the last three platforms are relatively unknown. There is no clear relationship to the platform providers' financial data, but the tweet frequencies go in line with the financial power of the respective platform providers. Siemens has the highest total revenue of €83 billion for the year 2018 of all the platforms examined, which is significantly higher than the revenue of a company like Software AG, which is only €865.7 million. The observed activity on Twitter indicates that the MindSphere platform attracts more platform users than financially smaller platforms (i.e., Adamos). The only surprise is the massive over-presence to IBM Watson IoT on Twitter, with IBM's revenue for 2018 being similar to that of Siemens. However, the observed frequencies do not allow any conclusions about the platform's actual penetration rate.

The declining tweet numbers indicate the overall fading of the IIoT hype. This initially surprising result goes hand in hand with the findings of the yearly Gartner hype cycle for emerging technologies. The hype cycle for 2018 shows that IoT platforms are then in reaching the peak of exaggerated expectations, i.e., expectations for IoT platforms are saturated, and attention is slightly decreasing. The reasons for the significant decrease in tweets about SAP Leonardo should be further investigated in order to derive possible reasons for activity stagnation, as observed in this single case. Currently, based upon the figures for SAP, a general recommendation for practitioners regarding the decrease in the ecosystem activity is to **actively promote the awareness of the platform** and the ecosystem activities in order not to fall behind the competition.

Furthermore, we investigated when the platforms were available and when tweets were posted for the platforms. It becomes clear that for most platforms, the first tweets were posted in the year of release or one year after. In terms of the development of frequencies, SAP Leonardo is an exception compared to the other platforms. While most platforms show a gradually increasing trend, the number of tweets for SAP Leonardo in the first year is above 3,000 tweets, which will hardly increase next year.

The analysis of the account types suggests that platforms with few tweets are more likely to be represented by involved corporates than by private accounts. On closer inspection of the users, four names, in particular, stand out: Ywan van Loon, Dean Anthony Gratton, and Sarah-Jayne Gratton. Further exploration revealed that these users are influencers in the area of IoT. Own statements on the website of Sarah-Jayne Gratton, according to her, she is a member of the Siemens Influencer Community. Her account is also among the top 10 of MindSphere on Twitter. In the typology of Twitter users, according to Tinati et al., influencers can play different roles, such as idea starters, amplifiers, or curators of certain contents [40]. These findings indicate that **platform providers are deliberately influencing the IIoT topics and use Twitter strategically to leverage the ecosystem activity and awareness**. The influencers' function is to facilitate communication of products and present specific opinions since influencers appear credible with regard to statements about the products [40]. PTC goes even further, installing for ThingWorx multiple accounts, while among the first two official accounts of PTC, the account "PTC University" takes the first place. The account was created to address academic user types with targeted information and educational opportunities and indicates **strategic efforts to attract a specific market-side**.

5.2   Bottom-Up Analysis

The LDA technique is intended to provide information on which topics are discussed in connection with the platforms. Thus, the ten most frequently used terms were examined. The term "iot" and the company name of the respective platform are the most often used terms. For Adamos, Cumulocity IoT, MindSphere, and ThingWorx, the term "iiot" is also frequently used, among the top five ranks for these platforms. These results validate that the **IoT and its industrial application are in the focus** of the Twitter-based strategies of four platforms out of six. We clearly see that the most frequent terms in the tweets of the SAP and IBM platforms have no explicit mention of the IIoT range. The top 10 terms describe general, current topics of IoT, such as "ai", "machinelearning", "blockchain", "cloud" or "bigdata". Thus, IBM obviously advertises domain-agnostic intelligent technologies. Additionally, this leads to the assumption that **SAP and IBM, in comparison to the other platforms, rather have IoT or other business processes in their scope, instead of the industrial instantiation of the platform**.

Regarding Adamos, the most frequently mentioned terms are also reflected in those used for topic formation. One of the three topics suggests that new partners of the IIoT platform are announced in the tweets, which are mostly from the mechanical engineering sector. The other two topics both contain the term "hackathon". This suggests that this specific SBR has a high value for the platform and therefore appears frequently in the Twitter discussion. One identified topic includes more general terms such as "team", while another topic provides more insight. We assume that this message focuses strongly on the interdisciplinarity of cross-company teams and emphasizes that companies are stronger when they join forces. These findings suggest that **small platforms, in particular, such as Adamos, form alliances with other companies and rely on less standardized relationships** with the complementors. At the same time, these partnerships are interdisciplinary. It is likely that joint events are used by Adamos to meet new potential partners or to deepen the relationship with existing partners. Certain tweets also indicate the cooperation between Adamos and Cumulocity IoT.

5.3   Top-Down Analysis

The top-down approach enables the specific analysis of the BR topic. As a clear result, it was identified that especially the technical BR "API" and "SDK" are hardly mentioned in the tweets. This contrasts with the scientific literature, which mainly focuses on TBR. The SBR "Documentation" is also a very rarely mentioned topic on Twitter. These are surprising results since the APIs, and the documentation are mentioned as the most important resources from the complementors' perspective [17, 33]. The most frequently mentioned BR is "Hackathon" with 124 mentions of 172. Judging the frequency solely, the tweets suggest that hackathons clearly represent an important BR in the IIoT domain. This result is consistent with the results of the conducted LDA analysis. Especially for Adamos, hackathons seem to build an essential part of the platform strategy, fueled by this type of SBR. For other platforms, social events such as trade fairs and conferences are also important for communication on Twitter. This insight offers potential for further research on corporate events and their influence on driving the platform dynamics. For the MindSphere-related tweets, we discovered some cloud-related terms, such as "cloud" and "aws", indicating at least some mentioning of the TBR (e.g., "How Siemens launched #MindSphere the open #IoT platform on AWS in just 8 weeks #unlockthepotential"). We assume this to be a **controlled strategy to advertise the platform's developer orientation**. Hence, advertising an effortless integration for IoT developers, this concrete example shows how platform companies can communicate certain platform features on Twitter. Surprisingly, SAP was the only platform provider to communicate the term "cloud" for Leonardo. From this, it can be assumed that IIoT platforms facilitate the provision of TBR without an appropriate advertisement, despite their relevance to implement IoT use cases. The results reveal a connection between SBR and the establishment of strategic partnerships. It can be seen that with regard to IIoT platforms, **strategic partners are more in focus than application developers**. Further, the data confirms that Twitter is largely used to communicate resourcing platform strategies. However, it is also apparent that some BR serve both resourcing and securing. An example of this is the controlled publishing of platform-related information. Hence, these measures can be used by the platform owner in a targeted manner to control the capabilities of complementors via shared information. This can also be considered as securing actions. The use of Twitter, in general, can be rather defined as a resourcing strategy since tweets serve as a communication medium. Targeted content can be published, either through official channels or even be promoted by influencers. These, in turn, can be strategically positioned to foster contact with users.

5.4   Limitations and Outlook

To sum up, the paper conducts exploratory research of different IIoT ecosystems, examining Twitter as a rich data source. Applying a data-driven approach to the domain-specific platform research, we extract knowledge on the BR-related strategies in IIoT. We could also identify different platform scopes (e.g., blockchain for SAP or academics for ThingWorx). After applying the BR concept as a research lens, we see that TBR-related activities are rarely communicated on Twitter compared to the SBR. A complementary analysis of the IIoT TBR discussions on portals such as GitHub could also provide valuable insights about the design and the impact of TBR on the developers' choice of IIoT platforms. It would also help get a more complete picture of the current challenges and problems in the use of BR in IIoT. Across platforms, the slightly decreasing number of IoT-related tweets is also interesting, and exploring the exact reasons for this offers exciting directions for future research. Following the analysis of the Twitter account types, a social network analysis of entire IIoT ecosystems and their connections with each other should be conducted in the future. We believe that the use of influencers and controlled communication by IIoT platform companies may be used to support the perceived rule adequacy within the respective ecosystem [7]. However, the influence of

Twitter on this construct has not yet been investigated and offers another research opportunity. In addition, the study reveals some evidence on the current alliancing strategy focus [24] across the relevant IIoT ecosystems, despite its lower degree of scaling [7]. Due to page limitations, further data analysis techniques such as sentiment analysis could not be applied and represent a limitation of the present study. Tweets in IIoT ecosystems can be converted into positive, neutral, or negative groups and sorted according to their emotion-based allocations, thus enabling opinion mining [41]. Furthermore, the derived findings are interpretative and, therefore, of limited validity. Our current results stay at a descriptive level in this course and should be regarded with caution as they do not allow any causal conclusions. Consequently, a future validation by investigations with additional data sources is necessary to bring forward the research on platform dynamics in the enterprise IIoT context.

References

1. Guth, J., et al.: A detailed analysis of IoT platform architectures: concepts, similarities and differences. In: Di Martino, B., Li, K.-C., Yang, L.T., Esposito, A. (eds.) Internet of Everything, pp. 81–101. Springer, Singapore (2018). https://doi.org/10.1007/978-981-10-5861-5_4
2. Boyes, H., Hallaq, B., Cunningham, J., Watson, T.: The industrial internet of things (IIoT): an analysis network. Comp. Ind. **101**, 1–12 (2018)
3. Pauli, T., Emanuel, M., Matzner, M.: Leveraging industrial IoT platform ecosystems: insights from the complementors' perspective. In: Proceedings of the 28th European Conference on Information Systems (2020)
4. Endres, H., Indulska, M., Ghosh, A., Baiyere, A., Broser, S.: Industrial internet of things (IIoT) business model classification. In: Proceedings of the 40th International Conference on Information Systems (2019)
5. Baldwin, C.Y., Woodard, C.J.: The architecture of platforms: a unified view. In: Gawer, A. (ed.) Platforms, Markets and Innovation, pp. 19–44 (2009)
6. Tiwana, A., Konsynski, B., Bush, A.A.: Platform evolution: coevolution of platform architecture, governance, and environmental dynamics. Inf. Syst. Res. **21**(4), 675–687 (2010)
7. Petrik, D., Herzwurm, G.: Towards the IIoT ecosystem development - understanding the stakeholder perspective. In: Proceedings of the 28th European Conference on Information Systems (2020)
8. Gawer, A.: Bridging differing perspectives on technological platforms: toward an integrative framework. Res. Pol. **43**(7), 1239–1249 (2014)
9. Marheine, C., Pauli, T.: Driving generativity in industrial IoT platform ecosystems. In: Proceedings of the 41st International Conference on Information Systems (2020)
10. Cusumano, M., Gawer, A., Yoffie, D.: The Business of Platforms: Strategy in the Age of Digital Competition, Innovation, and Power. Harper Business, New York (2019)
11. Parker, G., Van Alstyne, M.W., Jiang, X.: Platform ecosystems: how developers invert the firm. MIS Q. **41**(1), 255–266 (2017)
12. Schüler, F., Petrik, D.: Objectives of platform research: a co-citation and systematic literature review analysis. In: Seiter, M., Grünert, L., Steur, A. (eds.) Management Digitaler Plattformen. Springer, Wiesbaden (2021). https://doi.org/10.1007/978-3-658-31118-6_1
13. Hein, A., et al.: Digital platform ecosystems. Electron. Mark. **30**(1), 87–98 (2019). https://doi.org/10.1007/s12525-019-00377-4
14. Ghazawneh, A., Henfridsson, O.: Governing third-party development through platform boundary resources. In: Proceedings of the 31st International Conference on Information Systems, pp. 1–18 (2010)

15. Karhu, K., Gustafsson, R., Lyytinen, K.: Exploiting and defending open digital platforms with boundary resources: android's five platform forks. Inf. Syst. Res. **29**(2), 479–497 (2018)
16. Eaton, B.D., Elaluf-Calderwood, S., Sorensen, C., Yoo, Y.: Distributed tuning of boundary resources: the case of Apple's iOS service system. MIS Q. **39**(1), 217–243 (2015)
17. Petrik, D., Herzwurm, G.: Boundary resources for IIoT platforms – a complementor satisfaction study. In: Proceedings of the 41st International Conference on Information Systems (2020)
18. de Reuver, M., Sørensen, C., Basole, R.C.: The digital platform: a research agenda. J. Inf. Tech. **33**(2), 124–135 (2018)
19. Petrik, D., Herzwurm, G.: IIoT ecosystem development through boundary resources. A siemens mindsphere case study. In: Proceedings of the International Workshop on Software-Intensive Business, pp. 1–6. ACM, New York (2019)
20. Schermuly, L., Schreieck, M., Wiesche, M., Krcmar, H.: Developing an industrial IoT platform – trade-off between horizontal and vertical approaches. In: Proceedings of the 14th Conference on Wirtschaftsinformatik (2019)
21. Turck, M. https://mattturck.com/iot2018/. Accessed 01 Aug 2020
22. Myers, M.D.: Qualitative Research in Business & Management. Sage, London (2013)
23. Debortoli, S., Junglas, I., Müller, O., vom Brocke, J.: Text mining for information systems researchers: an annotated topic modeling tutorial. Comm. Assoc. Inf. Syst. **39**(7), 110–135 (2017)
24. Marheine, C.: Governance strategies to drive complementary innovation in IoT platforms: a multiple case study. In: Proceedings of the 15th Conference on Wirtschaftsinformatik (2020)
25. Porter, M.E., Heppelmann, J.E.: How smart connected products are transforming competition. Harvard Bus. Rev. **92**(11), 64–88 (2014)
26. Evans, D.S., Haigu, A., Schmalensee, R.: Invisible Engines How Software Platforms Drive Innovation and Transform Industries. The MIT Press, London (2006)
27. Iansiti, M., Levien, R.: The Keystone Advantage: What the New Dynamics of Business Ecosystems Mean for Strategy, Innovation, and Sustainability, pp. 1–10. Harvard Business School Press, Boston (2004)
28. Jacobides, M.G., Cennamo, C.: Gawer, A: Towards a theory of ecosystems. Strat. Man. J. **39**(8), 2255–2276 (2018)
29. Nambisan, S., Wright, M., Feldman, M.: The digital transformation of innovation and entrepreneurship: progress, challenges and key themes. Res. Pol. **48**(8), 103773 (2019)
30. Adner, R.: Match your innovation strategy to your innovation ecosystem. Harv. Bus. Rev. **84**(4), 98 (2006)
31. Saadatmand, F., Lindgren, R., Schultze, U.: Configurations of platform organizations: implications for complementor engagement. Res. Pol. **48**(8), 103770 (2019)
32. Ghazawneh, A., Henfridsson, O.: Balancing platform control and external contribution in third-party development: the boundary resources model. Inf. Syst. J. **23**(2), 173–192 (2013)
33. Petrik, D., Herzwurm, G.: Complementor satisfaction with boundary resources in IIoT ecosystems. In: Abramowicz, W., Klein, G. (eds.) BIS 2020. LNBIP, vol. 389, pp. 351–366. Springer, Cham (2020). https://doi.org/10.1007/978-3-030-53337-3_26
34. Schreieck, M., Hakes, C., Wiesche, M., Krcmar, H.: Governing platforms in the internet of things. In: Ojala, A., Holmström Olsson, H., Werder, K. (eds.) ICSOB 2017. LNBIP, vol. 304, pp. 32–46. Springer, Cham (2017). https://doi.org/10.1007/978-3-319-69191-6_3
35. Karhu, K., Rittala, P.: Slicing the cake without baking it: opportunistic platform entry strategies in digital markets. L. R. Plan. 101988 (2020)
36. Stieglitz, S., Dang-Xuan, L., Bruns, A., Neuberger, A.: Social media analytics. Wirtschaftsinformatik **56**(2), 101–109 (2014)
37. Atzmueller, M.: Mining social media: key players, sentiments, and communities. WIREs Data Min. Knowl. Discov. **2**, 411–419 (2012)

38. Joseph, N., Kar, A.K., Ilavarasan, P.V.: Review of discussion on internet of things (IoT): insights from twitter analytics. J. Glob. Inf. Manage. **25**(2), 38–51 (2017)
39. PTC. https://www.ptc.com/en/resources/iiot/report/forrester-wave. Accessed 02 Aug 2020
40. Tinati, R., Carr, L., Hall, W., Bentwood, J.: Identifying communicator roles on Twitter. In: Proceedings of the 21st International Conference on World Wide Web (2012)
41. Thelwall, M., Buckley, K., Paltoglou, G., Cai, D., Kappas, A.: Sentiment strength detection in short informal text. J. Am. Soc. Inf. Sci. Tech. **61**(12), 2544–2558 (2010)

The Role of Complementors in Platform Ecosystems

Marius Deilen[(⊠)] and Manuel Wiesche

Chair of Digital Transformation, Technical University of Dortmund, Dortmund, Germany
{marius.deilen,manuel.wiesche}@tu-dortmund.de

Abstract. Platform ecosystems have recently drawn considerable research attention to scholars in various disciplines, as the influence of platforms is increasingly relevant in the economy. However, most research focused on the technological- and business aspect of platforms taking the viewpoint of the platform owner. Little research has been conducted to understand and analyze heterogeneous types of complementors in platform ecosystem. To this end, we conduct a literature review of relevant journals and conferences on the view of complementors in platform ecosystems. Based on this analysis we derive two important topics for future research: the heterogeneity of complementors in platform ecosystems and the individual evaluation of complementors. This scientific article contributes to the understanding of complementors in platform ecosystems in the information systems literature by structuring the relevant research of the complementors with respect to their role and contributions to platform ecosystem and presenting possible avenues for future research.

Keywords: Platform · Ecosystem · Complementor · Innovation · Literature review

1 Introduction

Digital markets and digital platform ecosystems are becoming increasingly important in the economy. As of 2019, seven of the ten most valuable publicly listed companies measured by market capitalization, including Apple, Amazon, Alphabet, Facebook, Alibaba, Tencent and Microsoft rely on platform business models [1]. These companies managed to create a sustainable platform ecosystem in which the innovations are not generated by the platform provider itself, but by complementors[1] in the platform ecosystem [3–6]. The actors in a platform ecosystem involve typically a central actor (platform owner or hub firm) that orchestrates value creation and value appropriation by engaging complementors, to operate in the platform ecosystem [7–9]. These complementors provide complementary goods to the ecosystem defined as any other product or service, which

---

[1] In scientific literature, scholars use various synonyms for developers on platforms (see Table 1). In the following course of this paper, we use the expression "complementor" according to the definition of Brandenburger and Nalebuff [2] as an acronym for "the developer of a complementary product".

© The Author(s), under exclusive license to Springer Nature Switzerland AG 2021
F. Ahlemann et al. (Eds.): WI 2021, LNISO 48, pp. 473–488, 2021.
https://doi.org/10.1007/978-3-030-86800-0_33

enhances the attractiveness of the focal product or service such as add-ons, extensions or modules [2, 10, 11]. Hence, the success of a platform increasingly depends on active complementors who develop innovative complementary goods to stimulate user demand for the platform [12].

With low barriers to entry, little or no up-front costs for developing and publishing complementary goods and simultaneous direct market access to a large number of potential customers, platform ecosystems provide an interesting business environment for various complementors [3, 13, 14]. However, the lens through which the literature has focused on research with regard to complementors in platform ecosystems has been predominantly economic or technical in nature taking the viewpoint of platform providers [7, 15]. Although there is an academic consensus in research that complementors make a substantial contribution for enriching [7, 12, 16] and expanding platform ecosystems [8, 17, 18], much less attention has been devoted to investigate the organizational, social and economic aspects of the complementor community.

Towards this end, we conducted a literature review, focusing on the role of complementors in platform ecosystems. In a first step, we try to conceptualize the complementors in platform ecosystem, since existing literature often uses synonyms like "developer" [8, 19, 20], "partner" [21, 22] and "complementor" [7, 12, 20, 23, 24] homogenously without distinguishing socio- and demographic dimensions of a complementor. In a second step, we investigate how the existing literature investigates and classifies the contributions of complementors to platform ecosystems. In the last step, we investigate the relationship between platform owner and complementor on four different key dimensions. By showing the state-of-the-art literature, our review reveals open topics for scholars in IS and management with regard to the role of complementors in platform ecosystems. Addressing these open issues will significantly contribute to the understanding of heterogeneous complementor structures in platform ecosystems. The results are useful for both theory and practice, as we show that the role of the complementors and their heterogeneous structure has so far been largely overlooked in research, calling for further research in this area.

In the following, Sect. 2 starts with a description of the literature review process on complementors in platform ecosystems. Afterwards, we present the results by structuring the contributions according to different perspectives on the role of complementors in platform ecosystems. The paper concludes with a discussion of findings and limitations.

2 Design of the Literature Review

In this literature review, we looked for publications that (a) focus on the platform ecosystem as unit of analysis and (b) emphasis on the role of complementor in platform ecosystems. We examined relevant outlets following the guidelines of Webster and Watson [25] and vom Brocke et al. [26].

In the first step, since both platforms and complementors are associated with different terms in scientific literature, we compiled synonyms for both parameters "platform ecosystem" and "complementor" in order to ensure the highest possible coverage of all scientific writings as Table 1 shows. The internal linking of the terms via the OR operator for each search string and the subsequent linking via the AND operator ensured that all articles dealing with the complementor perspective in platform ecosystems are included.

Table 1. Summary of synonyms for platform and complementors.

Category A platform ecosystem		Category B complementors
platform		partner*
ecosystem		complementor*
platform ecosystem	**AND Connection**	developer*
digital platform		entrepreneur*
digital platform ecosystem		start-up*
platform-based ecosystem		entrepreneurship
		digital entrepreneurship
OR Connection		**OR Connection**

In the second step, we conducted a literature search based on the mentioned keywords in all journals included in the Senior Scholars' Basket of Journals of the Association for Information System and in the Financial Times 50.[2] Additionally, we focused on contributions published at the following conference to encompass the most current research topics in the field of platform economics: International Conference on Information Systems (ICIS), European Conference on Information Systems (ECIS), Americas' Conference on Information Systems (AMCIS), Hawaii International Conference on System Sciences (HICSS), and Wirtschaftsinformatik (WI). For all articles provided in the search results, the final selection process included an examination of the abstract of each article based on our search criteria (a) focus on the platform ecosystem as unit of analysis and (b) emphasis on the role of complementor in platform ecosystems. If the match with our search criteria was unclear after analyzing the abstract, the full text was read for the decision on inclusion in the final dataset.

Third, in line with the guideline of vom Brocke et al. [26] and based on the publications collected so far, we carried out a forward and backward search, resulting in additional five articles from a variety of sources. Among the additional sample, we found published textbooks and articles from several economic journals relating to the field of Information Systems and Management.

Based on our search process and the forward and backward search, we were able to find a total of 224 relevant articles. After analysis of these articles based on the unit of analysis (a) focus on the platform ecosystem and (b) emphasis on the role of complementor in platform ecosystems, we obtained a final literature data set of 60 relevant articles. Table 2 shows a summary of the literature search process and the selected relevant article per outlet category.

3   Empirical Results on Complementors in Platform Ecosystems

In this section, we summarize the findings and coded articles of the literature analysis on complementors in platform ecosystems based on the concept matrix illustrated in Table

---

[2] The VHB-JOURQUAL3 list for IS and the Financial Times' FT-50 list are available online at https://vhbonline.org/fileadmin/user_upload/JQ3_WI.pdf and https://www.ft.com/content/340 5a512-5cbb-11e1-8f1f-00144feabdc0.

Table 2. Summary of the literature search process

Outlet		Hits	Selected
IS journals	All Journals within the AIS Basket of Eight	49	12
Management journals	All journals within the Financial Times 50	135	32
IS conferences	ICIS, ECIS, AMCIS, HICSS, WI	40	11
Other	Other Journals, Conferences and Books	–	5
Total		**224**	**60**

3. Based on our analysis, we structure the concept matrix along three dimensions: 1) the conceptualization of complementors, 2) the contributions of complementors to platform ecosystems, and 3) the relationship between complementor and platform owner.

3.1 Conceptualization of Complementors in Platform Ecosystem Literature

The initial analysis of our iterative coding process literature revealed that literature consider complementors frequently, but almost exclusively in direct relation to other aspects of a platform ecosystem. Of the 60 identified and relevant outlets, only 18 articles look at the complementor in detail, while the other 42 articles examine in particular the interrelation between the complementor and different aspects of a platform. As Table 4 illustrates, articles dealing directly or indirectly with the role of the complementor in platform ecosystems show different criteria by which scholars conceptualize complementors.

The articles distinguish complementors in platform ecosystems especially according to their organization size. Benlian et al. [30], for example, examine how complementors perceive the openness of a platform from their perspective. In this context, Benlian et al. [30] distinguish complementors for their research objective strictly according to their organizational structure and derived the distinction between employed developers, entrepreneur, hobby developers and others. Boudreau et al. [29] use similar distinguishing features by deriving the heterogeneity between complementors in platform ecosystems based on the number of employees of the respective complementor to investigate the extent to which intellectual property rights protection mechanisms differ between small and large complementors on platforms.

Other studies distinguish between complementors in platform ecosystems in terms of their scope of remuneration. For example, Boudreau & Jeppesen [31] differentiate complementors in terms of their compensation structure in order to investigate whether complementors react to the growth of a platform in a competitive context despite the lack of compensation. Other studies link the remuneration of complementors to the degree of employment in order to take into account the heterogeneity of complementors in platform ecosystems. For example, Schaarschmidt et al. [32] classify complementors according to the degree of employment into *full-time paid developer*, *part-time paid developer* and *not paid developer* to investigate the relationship between lead userness and developers' innovative work behavior.

Another distinguishing feature is the nature of the incentive for the complementor to engage and provide value on the platform. In order to create a heterogeneity in the

Table 3. Concept matrix - role of complementors in platform ecosystems

Article	Conceptualization of complementors			Contribution of complementors			Relationship platform owner and complementor			
	Complementor direct observation	Complementor indirect observation	Differentiation of complementors	Driver of Innovation	Knowledge provision	Platform growth and network effects	Competitiveness	Strategy- & goal expectancy	Leadership and power asymmetries	Platform openness and governance
AIS basket of eight										
Anderson, Parker & Tian (2014)		x		x		x			x	x
Benlian, Hilkert & Hess (2015)		x	x							x
Bergvall-Kåreborn & Howcroft (2014)		x		x		x	x			x
Ghazawneh & Henfridsson (2015)		x					x			x
Ghazawneh & Henfridsson (2015)	x			x	x	x	x		x	x
Huber, Kude & Dibbern (2017)		x		x					x	x
Hurni et al. (2020)	x		x	x		x		x	x	
Oh et al. (2015)		x		x				x	x	
Parker, Van Alstyne & Jiang (2017)	x			x		x	x		x	x
Qiu, Gopal & Hann (2017)	x		x	x	x			x	x	x
Sarker et al. (2020)		x		x		x			x	x
Tiwana (2015)		x				x				x
Financial Times 50, Conferences and other										
48 articles	14	34	13	43	12	25	33	16	30	43
Total	**18**	**42**	**16**	**52**	**14**	**32**	**37**	**19**	**37**	**54**

Table 4. Conceptualization of Complementors in Platform Ecosystems

Differentiation criteria of complementor	Conceptualization of complementor type	Reference
(1) Complementor size Criterion differentiated in 13 studies Criterion not differentiated in 47 studies	Major developer Minor developer De novo complementors Small complementor Large complementor	[18, 27–31]
(2) Scope of remuneration Criterion differentiated in 2 studies Criterion not differentiated in 58 studies	Full-time paid developer Part-time paid developer Unpaid developer	[31, 32]
(3) Incentive of complementor Criterion differentiated in 4 studies Criterion not differentiated in 56 studies	Employed developers Entrepreneurs, Indies Hobby developers	[14, 19, 23, 27]
(4) Scope of contribution to platform ecosystem Criterion differentiated in 5 studies Criterion not differentiated in 55 studies	Small content suppliers Large content suppliers Developer with small user base Developer with large user base	[5, 19, 33–35]
(5) Organizational form Criterion differentiated in 7 studies Criterion not differentiated in 53 studies	Individual complementor perspective	[4, 5, 27, 29, 31, 36, 37]
Criterion differentiated in 3 studies Criterion not differentiated in 57 studies	Institutional complementor perspective	[5, 28, 29]

complementor structure, Hilkert et al. [14] conceptualize complementors as salaried programmer, freelancer, entrepreneur, hobby programmer and student with regard to their incentives for participation on a platform in order to examine motivation factors of complementors. The study indicate that the motives "external rewards" and "status and employment opportunity" were the predominant incentives for complementors on the Facebook platform [14]. Similarly, Hurni et al. [23] distinguish the complementors in their study of the interactions of governance mechanisms of a platform and the effect on complementor dedication. In the course of this research objective, the authors define complementor dedication as "the extent to which a complementor is devoted, faithful, and willing to invest in the partnership with a platform owner" [23], showing that there is a strong relationship between complementor dedication and the appropriate rule design of the platform ecosystem.

The fourth differentiation criterion based on the performed literature analysis is the scope of contribution of complementors and their complementary services to platform ecosystems [5, 19, 33–35]. For example, Parker et al. [19] differentiate three types of complementors, named core developers, extension developers and data aggregators with regard to their contribution to the platform ecosystem. According to Parker et al. [19], core developers are individuals employed by the platform owner to develop tools and applications that ensure effective use of the platform by users. Extension developers, on the other hand, are external parties or third-party developers who enhance the functionality of the platform through innovative complementary products, thereby increasing the value of the platform ecosystem. Data aggregators collect various interaction-based data according to platform governance and sell them to specific organizations, enabling them to target e.g. matching advertising to users.

The fifth and last differentiation criterion is the differentiation between complementors in platform ecosystems regarding their organizational form. The majority of scientific studies consider complementors as institutional organizations in the form of (entrepreneurial) business ventures [28, 29, 33]. Some articles consider complementors more as individual entrepreneurs engaged in platform ecosystems [4, 36]. A distinction between the two forms of consideration of the organizational structure and the respective available resources of the complementor is of crucial scientific importance since the strategic capabilities of complementors differ thereby significantly. For example, Miric et al. [29] investigates complementors' actions of capturing and protecting intellectual property in platform ecosystem. Based on the available resources of the complementor and its organizational structure, Miric et al. [29] conclude that many individual, small complementors protect their intellectual property through informal protecting mechanisms, whereas larger business ventures are able to protect their intellectual property through a combination of informal- and formal intellectual property rights mechanisms [29].

In the course of the analysis and interpretation of the analyzed literature, five core dimensions of differentiation between complementors in platform ecosystems emerged as shown in Table 4: the organizational size of the complementor (1), the level of remuneration (2), the motivational factors of participation on platforms (3), the level of contribution of complementors in platform ecosystems (4) and the underlying organizational form of the complementor (5). Thereby, scholars synthesize their differentiation based on the organizational characteristics of complementors (1, 2, 5) as well as their relation and reciprocal action with the platform ecosystem (3, 4).

3.2 Contribution of Complementors in Platform Ecosystem Literature

We found in addition that the reviewed articles consider the influence of complementors on the platform ecosystem from diverse perspectives as shown in Fig. 1. First, scholars find that complementors (a) create customer value through innovative complementary products and services [12, 13, 38]. The fundamental decision on the degree to open up the platform and outsource innovation to external parties depends both on the network effects and on the number of complementors [3, 39]. Companies open up their platform to an increasing extent once a certain threshold of complementors are achieved in the market [8]. As soon as companies decide to open the platform to external parties, the number of complementors on the platform itself becomes crucial for the innovation capabilities of the platform ecosystem [3, 8, 40]. An excessive increase of complementors in an ecosystem often leads to a reduction of innovation incentives, which the scientific literature often refers to as the crowding-out effect [13].

Second, researchers regard the contribution of the complementor in (b) providing knowledge to the platform ecosystem [20, 36]. The community of participants in a platform ecosystem generates different types of information, which complementors use to identify and exploit entrepreneurial opportunities [32, 39]. The generation and use of information stimulates thus further growth of the platform [12, 17]. Additionally, complementors develop knowledge-based information by recombining skills or technological resources with increasing participation in a platform ecosystem [39]. This information and capabilities expand the existing pool of routines, resulting in continuous performance improvement of products or services in a platform ecosystem [20].

A third perspective is (c) the growth of the platform ecosystem through the complementors' complementary products and the resulting customer satisfaction based on network effects [16, 41, 42]. Complementors significantly contribute to the generation of network externalities through their innovative complementary products, as they increase the value of the ecosystem and respond to the needs of heterogeneous user structures [16, 18]. However, the decision of complementors to interact on a given platform depends on the presence of the platform's network effects as a vast installed-base of users in turn increases the attractiveness of the platform for complementors to pursue entrepreneurial opportunities [42, 43].

The analyzed literature shows academic consensus that complementors contribute in an essential way to the existence and progress of the entire platform ecosystem. As Fig. 1 illustrates, researchers mainly focus on increased innovation capabilities of the platform ecosystem through complementors [3, 7, 39], the provision of external knowledge from complementors [12, 17, 20] and the growth potential of the platform by complementary products of complementors [16, 18, 44]. The contribution of complementors, however, is mainly analyzed from the perspective of the platform owner in order to examine the effects of participation on the platform ecosystem.

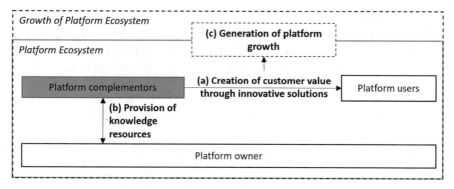

Fig. 1. Contribution of complementors in platform ecosystems

3.3 Relationship between Platform Owner and Complementor

Based on our literature analysis, we identified four key aspects focusing on the relationship between platform owner and complementor. We also focused in particular on areas of conflict between platform provider and complementor.

Competitive Pressure on Platforms: Of the 60 articles, 37 articles dealt directly or indirectly with the competition between complementors on platforms. Complementors are primarily independent entrepreneurs and autonomous parties who offer their knowledge and complementary products or services on the platform with significantly different capacities to generate competitive advantages [7, 14, 27]. The scientific literature largely omits that hobby developers, freelancers and developers in small start-ups represent the majority of app developers on mobile platforms [14]. Participating on platforms has significant advantages for complementors, since they have direct access to a large number of consumers without having to build these structures themselves. At the same time, however, the complementors face the challenge of immediately differentiating themselves in a cluster of similar products from other competitors [32]. In order to survive in the market in the long term, the visibility of their complementary products is of decisive importance for the complementors. Due to the strong competitive pressure and the increasing number of complementors on platforms, complementors attempt to place their complementary products on the market through faster development cycles or by entering relevant market niches [20, 27, 35]. This applies in particular to new complements in the market. Experienced and larger complementors succeed more easily in maintaining their superior market position in complex platform ecosystems and in generating sustainable value in the platform ecosystem because of their experience [20].

Besides the direct competition between complementors, three articles dealt with the phenomenon of platform owner entry and its effects on the competitive situation inside the platform ecosystem [28, 37]. In particular, researchers investigated the absorption mechanism, whereby the platform provider offers own complementary products or functionalities that were previously provided by complementors [45]. Accordingly, complementors respond comprehensively to the platform owner's entry into its market niche by adapting both value creation and value retention strategies [28]. If there is a threat of market entry by the platform operator, complementors reduce innovation efforts in the affected markets but increase the innovation efforts in the non-affected markets. During this transition, complementors focus more on generating short-term profits through price increases in the affected markets [37]. In addition, the entry of a platform supplier into its own market is perceived differently depending on the individual characteristics of the complementor. While larger, more diverse complementors perceive entry as an opportunity for innovation, smaller complementors increasingly view market entry by the platform provider as threatening to their own market position [28].

Strategy- and Goal Expectancy: When analyzing the relationship between platform owner and complementor, some studies within the literature analysis focus on the strategy- and goal expectancy. In contrast to other market environments, complementors on platforms have to pursue several, sometimes contradictory and externally stipulated business objectives [4, 23, 36]. On the one hand, the platform provider sets goals, visions and structures for the platform ecosystem, which the complementor, as an entrepreneur, has to follow. [36] On the other hand, the complementor must also ensure that his own company differentiates itself sufficiently from the competitors and can survive even if the platform fails [7, 17]. This dual-goal expectancy bears potential conflicts if the goals of the ecosystem operator and the goals of the individual complementor are in strong conflict [36, 41]. For example, the platform provider may wish to make its platform particularly attractive through pricing campaigns in order to make greater use of network effects, while the complementary complementor pursues the goal of increasing revenues, leading to considerable trade-offs between complementor and platform owner.

Platform Leadership and Power Asymmetries: In the context of platform economics, high power asymmetries can arise in the relationship between complementor and platform operator, as complementors have little or no influence on platform operators' decisions regarding their strategic choices [38]. In particular, tensions in pricing and the provision structure between platform owner and complementor illustrate the asymmetries in the negotiating power between platform provider and complementor [42, 46]. The imbalances and power asymmetries entail the risk of a loss of trust between platform provider and complementor. However, trust is a significant factor for the relationship between platform provider and complementor for the long-term success of the platform [47]. Platform owners can strengthen trust between complementors in the platform economy, especially through effective governance mechanisms such as intellectual property right protection. A fair and sustainable governance structure has a positive significant impact on the motivation of complementors to engage on the platform [36].

Platform Openness and Governance: The platform openness and governance is an important research topic since the value of a platform relies on its complementary products provided by the platform complementor [18, 40, 48]. However, research in this area mainly focused on the role of platform owners' decisions for strategically examining the optimal degree of openness and control of a platform [49, 50]. The governance and openness of a platform, in addition to income potential, technical skills and individual attitude, is a significant factor in the choice of complementors to engage on a platform [44]. Complementors' engagement is especially high in horizontal platform governance systems in which each complementor receives the same opportunities for value capture and value creation [10]. In addition to the governance structure of the platform and the distribution of decision-making rights, the degree of architectural openness also influences the extent of complementor engagement. Ceteris paribus, the higher the degree of openness of a platform, the lower the barrier for complementors to make asset-specific investments and thus to participate on the platform [4]. The maximum degree of openness of a platform ecosystem suggests that there are no restrictions on participation or use of the platform. Boudreau [3] shows that providing more open access to complementors lead to a significant increase in the development rate of new devices, illustrated by an inverse U-shape relationship between the open structure of a platform and the innovation performance in the platform ecosystem. Complementors show higher innovation incentives for more open platform ecosystem up to the point where the platform is too crowded, which in turn leads to financial constraints for complementors due to price competition, resulting in a loss of attractiveness of the platform [3, 7, 44].

4   Discussion

In this section, we discuss two central issues based on our literature analysis: the heterogeneity of complementors and the individual assessment of complementors in platform ecosystem. We suggest that future research on these issues deepens our understanding of complementors in platform ecosystems, allowing scholars to derive important recommendations for theory and practice.

4.1   Heterogeneity of Complementors in Platform Ecosystems

Despite a strong consensus among scholars from IS and management regarding complementors as particularly important in markets with network effects such as platforms [18, 42, 43, 50], the vast majority of studies with direct or indirect focus on the complementor role in the ecosystem consider complementors universally and homogeneously. As illustrated in Table 4, scholars differentiate complementors along different parameters. A scientific consensus how to distinguish and classify complementors is still lacking although complementors differ significantly in numerous dimensions, including size, experience, financial background, strategic orientation or motivation. It is essential for platform owners to understand the heterogeneous complementor structures in their ecosystem in order to be able to adapt their governance rules accordingly and ensure long-term success of the platform [7, 40]. Due to this research gap, existing studies show little insights how platform owners can strategically manage complementors or create incentives for them so far.

A first step could be to analyze the structure of complementors in demographic and economic terms and classify complementors according to these dimensions. For example, Wen et al. (2019) examined strategic reactions of complementors in case of platform-owner entry [37]. According to Wen et al. (2019) the entry of the platform provider leads to a reduction in the innovative capabilities of the complementors and generates a price increase for the applications affected by the entry of the platform owner. A differentiation of complementors in terms of their economic structure could reveal further interesting aspects regarding the response capabilities of complementors, since smaller complementors generally have fewer strategic resources than large complementors. Therefore, considering the heterogeneity of complementors in platform ecosystems might reveal whether and to what extent complementors in a platform ecosystem react differently to the platform provider's entry into their market [15, 44].

Distinctions between platform types can also be of central importance, as it can be assumed that the heterogeneous structures of complementors differ according to their openness and the hurdle of entry barriers. IS literature distinguishes mostly between transaction- and innovation platform typologies [51, 52]. A transaction platform is a technology, a product or a service, which facilitates the exchange between different users, buyers or providers as an intermediary (e.g. Uber or eBay), whereas an innovation platform refers to a technology, product or service that serves as a basis on which other organizations are able to develop complementary digital artefacts (e.g. Apple iOS Store, Google Android Platform) [51]. Since different platform typologies have different resource requirements, a differentiation regarding the structure of heterogeneous complementors based on different platform typologies would be of scientific interest. Individual complementors or small entrepreneurial ventures usually have limited resources, so their interactions are more likely to take place on platforms that either use few resources or have extensive resources provided by the platform provider (e.g. app development) [17, 23, 36, 51]. In contrast, institutional organizations with access to diverse resources are able to engage in platform ecosystems that require intensive resource utilization (e.g. videogame development) [23, 29, 51, 52]. For example, for small complementors publishing an application for an open source platform such as Linux is probably easier and cheaper to accomplish than publishing applications in the store of Microsoft Windows, resulting in a likely higher proportion of smaller complementors in Linux. This phenomenon might also affect the boundary objectives of platforms, which are often subject to research in IS literature. Due to limited resources, smaller complementors need to have access to simpler boundary objectives, while large complementors have the resources to handle complex boundary objectives.

4.2   Individual Evaluation of Complementors in Platform Ecosystems

Additionally, the literature research revealed that scientific literature omits the research dimension considering the complementor at the individual level. The perspective of the complementor is based on an abstract representation, seeing complementors as an important part of the ecosystem with regard to the innovation- and growth capabilities of a platform. In line with this argument, research largely omits the individual characteristics, the entrepreneurial needs and the underlying motivation of complementors although e.g. Bergvall-Kåreborn and Howcroft [38] already called for research regarding complementors on an individual level. In particular, small complementors are of great importance, as they represent an economically significant part of the complementor structure from the perspective of the platform provider [29]. The limited awareness of this research strand is surprising, since complementors and their different characteristics are an essential core component in platform ecosystems, having a direct impact on the long-term success of a platform [3, 8, 38]. Through a precise understanding of complementors with regard to their individual characteristics, their entrepreneurial structures and their motivational basis, owners can align their platform governance structure more efficiently and thus achieve significant long-term competitive advantages [4, 36].

First scientific articles show interesting approaches to gain a better understanding of complementors on an individual level. Nambisan et al. [36] analyze the self-regulation processes of complementors in platform ecosystems to successfully manage the dual goal expectancy between platform owner and complementor. Hilkert et al. [14] investigate the individual motivation factors of complementors and their influence on the intensity of platform participation. This line of research is, in contrast to research on the impact of complementors on platforms, largely unilluminated. The few scientific articles dealing with the individual consideration of complementors on platforms provide a basis for more scientific investigation [4, 14, 23, 36]. On this foundation, a promising approach to this research strand would be to examine the heterogeneous motivational factors of complementors on platforms with regard to their organizational structures and their reciprocal actions with the platform ecosystem.

4.3 Limitations

Despite the aforementioned valuable contributions, this literature review is subject to limitations. First, despite greatest care, this literature analysis may not encompass all relevant studies with the mentioned keywords. For instance, authors may have consistently used different synonyms for complementors or platform ecosystems, resulting in a missing coverage of these articles. Second, in order to make the results of this study comparable, we had to simplify and cluster the results of the studies during the coding process. As a result, some articles find no representation in the results as they may have been overlooked or lost during the process. The third and final limitation of this study is that the questions for future research based on the presented literature analysis could be influenced by the author's perspective. Hence, there may be additional open research topics for future research. Despite the mentioned and other limitations, this literature analysis offers one of the first explorations regarding the conceptualization of complementors in platform-based ecosystems.

5 Conclusion

In this scientific article, we summarized recent literature focusing on the role of complementors in platform ecosystem and derived open topics for future research based on the results of our literature analysis. We showed the different perspectives in current research regarding the conceptualization and the role of complementors in platform ecosystems and aggregated the contributions of the complementors in the platform economy. Furthermore, we identified and highlighted two major issues for future research: First, we suggest that future research must take a closer look at the heterogeneous structures of complementors on platforms. As in other competitive environments, complementors in platform ecosystems differ significantly from each other. So far, this aspect has hardly been taken into account although understanding heterogeneous complementor structures is particularly relevant for platform owners to ensure efficient platform functionality and consistent growth. Second, we recommend to analyze the complementors in the ecosystem of the platform on an individual level. An analysis on an individual level would significantly contribute to our understanding of the complementor and their incentives to interact on a platform. This improved understanding helps platforms to target their governance mechanisms in order to attract certain types of complementors to their platforms.

References

1. Biggest companies in the world 2019 | Statista. www.statista.com/statistics/263264/top-companies-in-the-world-by-market-value/
2. Brandenburger, A., Nalebuff, B.: Co-opetition. Doubleday, New York (1998)
3. Boudreau, K.: Open platform strategies and innovation: granting access vs devolving control. Manage. Sci. **56**, 1849–1872 (2010)
4. Nambisan, S., Siegel, D., Kenney, M.: On open innovation, platforms, and entrepreneurship. Strateg. Entrep. J. **12**, 354–368 (2018)
5. Wang, R.D., Miller, C.D.: Complementors' engagement in an ecosystem: a study of publishers' e-book offerings on Amazon Kindle. Strat. Manage. J **41**, 3–26 (2020)
6. Schreieck, M., Wiesche, M., Kude, T., Krcmar, H.: Shifting to the cloud – how SAP's Partners cope with the change. In: Proceedings of the 52nd Hawaii International Conference on System Sciences, pp. 6084–6093 (2019)
7. Wareham, J., Fox, P.B., Cano Giner, J.L.: Technology ecosystem governance. Organ. Sci. **25**, 1195–1215 (2014)
8. Parker, G., van Alstyne, M., Jiang, X.: Platform ecosystems: how developers invert the firm. MIS Q. **41**, 255–266 (2017)
9. Hein, A., Weking, J., Schreieck, M., Wiesche, M., Böhm, M., Krcmar, H.: Value co-creation practices in business-to-business platform ecosystems. Electron. Mark. **29**(3), 503–518 (2019). https://doi.org/10.1007/s12525-019-00337-y
10. Jacobides, M.G., Cennamo, C., Gawer, A.: Towards a theory of ecosystems. Strat. Manage. J **39**, 2255–2276 (2018)
11. Hein, A., Schreieck, M., Wiesche, M., Böhm, M., Krcmar, H.: The emergence of native multi-sided platforms and their influence on incumbents. Electron. Mark. **29**(4), 631–647 (2019). https://doi.org/10.1007/s12525-019-00350-1
12. Eckhardt, J.T., Ciuchta, M.P., Carpenter, M.: Open innovation, information, and entrepreneurship within platform ecosystems. Strateg. Entrep. J. **12**, 369–391 (2018)
13. Boudreau, K.J.: Let a thousand flowers bloom? An Early look at large numbers of software 'apps' developers and patterns of innovation. Organ. Sci. **23**, 1409–1427 (2012)
14. Hilkert, D., Benlian, A., Hess, T.: Motivational drivers to develop apps for social software-platforms: the example of Facebook. In: AMCIS 2010 Proceedings, p. 86 (2010)
15. Ghazawneh, A., Henfridsson, O.: A Paradigmatic analysis of digital application marketplaces. J. Inf. Technol. **30**, 198–208 (2015)
16. Anderson, E.G., Parker, G.G., Tan, B.: Platform performance investment in the presence of network externalities. Inf. Syst. Res. **25**, 152–172 (2014)
17. Srinivasan, A., Venkatraman, N.: Entrepreneurship in digital platforms: a network-centric view. Strateg. Entrep. J. **12**, 54–71 (2018)
18. Venkatraman, N.: Preferential linkage and network evolution: a conceptual model and empirical test in the U.S. video game sector. Acad. Manage. J. **47**, 876–892 (2004)
19. Parker, G., van Alstyne, M., Choudary, S.P.: Platform Revolution. How Networked Markets are Transforming the Economy - and How to Make Them Work for You. W.W. Norton & Company, New York, London (2017)

20. Kapoor, R., Agarwal, S.: Sustaining superior performance in business ecosystems: evidence from application software developers in the iOS and Android smartphone ecosystems. Organ. Sci. **28**, 531–551 (2017)
21. Davis, J.P.: The group dynamics of interorganizational relationships. Adm. Sci. Q. **61**, 621–661 (2016)
22. Sarker, S., Bjørn-Andersen, N.: Exploring value cocreation in relationships between an ERP vendor and its partners: a revelatory case study. MIS Q. **36**, 317–338 (2012)
23. Hurni, T., Huber, T.L., Dibbern, J., Krancher, O.: Complementor dedication in platform ecosystems: rule adequacy and the moderating role of flexible and benevolent practices. Eur. J. Inf. Syst. 1–24 (2020)
24. Cheng, K., Schreieck, M., Wiesche, M., Krcmar, H.: Emergence of a post-app era – an exploratory case study of the WeChat mini-program ecosystem. In: 15th International Conference on Wirtschaftsinformatik (2020)
25. Webster, J., Watson, R.: Analyzing the past to prepare for the future: writing a literature review. MIS Q. **26**, xiii–xxiii (2002)
26. vom Brocke, J., Simons, A., Niehaves, B., Riemer, K., Cleven, A.: Reconstructing the giant: on the importance of rigour in documenting the literature search process. In: Seventeenth European Conference on Information Systems, Verona
27. Qiu, Y., Gopal, A., Hann, I.-H.: Logic pluralism in mobile platform ecosystems: a study of indie app developers on the iOS app store. Inf. Syst. Res. **28**, 225–249 (2017)
28. Foerderer, J., Kude, T., Mithas, S., Heinzl, A.: Does platform owner's entry crowd out innovation? Evidence from Google photos. Inf. Syst. Res. **29**, 444–460 (2018)
29. Miric, M., Boudreau, K.J., Jeppesen, L.B.: Protecting their digital assets: the use of formal & informal appropriability strategies by App developers. Res. Policy **48**, 103738 (2019)
30. Benlian, A., Hilkert, D., Hess, T.: How open is this platform? The meaning and measurement of platform openness from the complementers' perspective. J. Inf. Technol. **30**, 209–228 (2015)
31. Boudreau, K.J., Jeppesen, L.B.: Unpaid crowd complementors: the platform network effect mirage. Strat. Manage. J. **36**, 1761–1777 (2015)
32. Schaarschmidt, M., Stol, K.-J., Walsh, G., Bertram, M.: Lead users' innovative work behavior in digital platform ecosystems: a large scale study of app developers. In: International Conference on Information Systems (ICIS 2019), Munich (2019)
33. Huang, P., Ceccagnoli, M., Forman, C., Wu, D.J.: When do ISVs join a platform ecosystem? Evidence from the enterprise software industry. In: Proceedings of the 30th International Conference on Information Systems, Phoenix, AZ, 15–18 December 2009
34. Barlow, M.A., Verhaal, J.C., Angus, R.W.: Optimal distinctiveness, strategic categorization, and product market entry on the Google Play app platform. Strat. Manage. J. **40**, 1219–1242 (2019)
35. Tian, J., Zhao, X., Ling, X.: Technological compatibility between platforms and multi-homing of third-party developers. In: International Conference on Information Systems (ICIS 2019), Munich (2019)
36. Nambisan, S., Baron, R.A.: Entrepreneurship in innovation ecosystems: entrepreneurs' self-regulatory processes and their implications for new venture success. Entrep. Theory Pract. **37**, 1071–1097 (2013)
37. Wen, W., Zhu, F.: Threat of platform-owner entry and complementor responses: evidence from the mobile app market. Strat. Manage. J. **40**, 1336–1367 (2019)
38. Bergvall-Kåreborn, B., Howcroft, D.: Persistent problems and practices in information systems development: a study of mobile applications development and distribution. Inf. Syst. J. **24**, 425–444 (2014)
39. Parker, G., van Alstyne, M.: Innovation, openness, and platform control. Manage. Sci. **64**, 3015–3032 (2018)

40. Ghazawneh, A., Henfridsson, O.: Balancing platform control and external contribution in third-party development: the boundary resources model. Inf. Syst. J. **23**, 173–192 (2013)
41. McIntyre, D.P., Srinivasan, A.: Networks, platforms, and strategy: emerging views and next steps. Strat. Manage. J. **38**, 141–160 (2017)
42. Eisenmann, T., Parker, G., van Alstyne, M.: Strategies for two-sided markets. Harv. Bus. Rev. **84**, 92–101+149 (2006)
43. Katz, M.L., Shapiro, C.: Systems competition and network effects. J. Econ. Perspect. **8**, 93–115 (1994)
44. Um, S., Kang, D., Hahn, J., Yoo, Y.: Popularity and competition in a digital platform ecosystem: a network perspective. In: International Conference on Information Systems (ICIS 2018), San Francisco (2018)
45. Schreieck, M., Wiesche, M., Krcmar, H.: The platform owner's challenge to capture value – insights from a business-to-business IT platform. In: Proceedings of the International Conference on Information Systems (ICIS 2017), Seoul, South Korea, 10–13 December 2017 (2017)
46. Oh, J., Koh, B., Raghunathan, S.: Value appropriation between the platform provider and app developers in mobile platform mediated networks. J. Inf. Technol. **30**, 245–259 (2015)
47. Perrons, R.K.: The open kimono: how Intel balances trust and power to maintain platform leadership. Res. Policy **38**, 1300–1312 (2009)
48. Schreieck, M., Wiesche, M., Krcmar, H.: Design and governance of platform ecosystems – key concepts and issues for future research. In: Twenty-Fourth European Conference on Information Systems (ECIS), İstanbul, Turkey (2016)
49. Eisenmann, T.R., Parker, G., van Alstyne, M.: Opening platforms: how, when and why? In: Gawer, A. (ed.) Platforms, Markets and Innovation, pp. 131–162. Edward Elgar Publishing, Cheltenham (2009)
50. Parker, G.G., van Alstyne, M.W.: Two-sided network effects: a theory of information product design. Manage. Sci. **51**, 1494–1504 (2005)
51. Gawer, A., Evans, P.C.: The rise of the platform enterprise: a global survey. In: The Emerging Platform Economy, no. 1 (2016)
52. de Reuver, M., Sørensen, C., Basole, R.: The digital platform: a research agenda. J. Inf. Technol. **33**, 124–135 (2018)

How to Design IIoT-Platforms Your Partners are Eager to Join: Learnings from an Emerging Ecosystem

Tobias Moritz Guggenberger[1,3]([✉]), Fabian Hunke[2], Frederik Möller[1,3],
Anne-Cathrine Eimer[2], Gerhard Satzger[2], and Boris Otto[1,3]

[1] Chair for Industrial Information Management, TU Dortmund University, Dortmund, Germany
{Tobias.Guggenberger,Frederik.Moeller,
Boris.Otto}@tu-dortmund.de, {Tobias.Moritz.Guggenberger,
Frederik.Moeller,Boris.Otto}@isst.fraunhofer.de
[2] Karlsruhe Institute of Technology, Karlsruhe, Germany
{Fabian.Hunke,Gerhard.Satzger}@kit.edu,
Anne-Cathrine.Eimer@student.kit.edu
[3] Fraunhofer ISST, Dortmund, Germany

Abstract. Building and sustaining a successful platform business remains one of the biggest challenges in the age of digitalization and platformization, particularly in the manufacturing industry. The art of managing the partner ecosystem to create and distribute mutual benefits depends on the design of the platform – thus, on the implemented mechanisms and functionalities, typically complemented by third-party applications. Therefore, it is eminently important to attract potential partners to enter the ecosystem. With this article, we provide substantial insight into the case of an emerging platform and its respective ecosystem of stakeholders. We analyze their individual requirements, abstract them into general key requirements, and finally develop design principles. Thus, our research, on the one hand, extends the current knowledge of platform literature with new, generalized knowledge about platform design, especially in the development phase. On the other hand, we contribute to the emerging field of participant attraction previously focusing on complementors.

Keywords: IIoT-platform · Platform ecosystems · Digital transformation · Case study · Design principles

1 Introduction

The diffusion of digital technology is changing society and, in addition to that, the economic organization and products, services, and business models [1, 2]. In the industrial context, the continuous digitization of manufacturing processes and assets leads to cyber-physical-systems, which are the root of the industrial Internet of Things (IIoT) [3]. IIoT refers to the industrial *things* (e.g., machines, trucks, or loading carriers) connected via

F. Ahlemann et al. (Eds.): WI 2021, LNISO 48, pp. 489–504, 2021.
https://doi.org/10.1007/978-3-030-86800-0_34

information and communication technologies [3, 4]. Platforms are an essential architectural component for the IIoT as they facilitate the control and, in addition to that, the optimization of these manufacturing systems [3–6]. Therefore, the design of IIoT-platforms is directly correlated to such systems' efficiency and effectiveness [3, 5], making the study attractive for both scholars and practitioners.

Platforms, which are internally used, focus on integrating innovative capabilities to create value through network externalities within and between different platform sides in the service network [7–9]. The set of agents related to a platform is referred to as the platform ecosystem [10–12]. Although the platform construct has been a subject of interest for the last decades, research specifically focused on IIoT-platforms is rare [13–15]. From an economic perspective, there are fundamental differences between the market characteristics of the prominent B2C platforms and IIoT-platforms in the manufacturing industry. The market size, fragmentation, and competition influence the necessary strategies and tactics for firms to establish successful platforms [13, 16].

Moreover, in contrast to consumer platforms, industrial platforms rely heavily on cross-side network effects and collaboration, which the platform owner needs to foster precisely [17, 18]. Additionally, since the actors and their resources are different, value co-creation processes occur that might be hard to understand from the incumbent's perspective [19]. Following this argumentation, IIoT-platform owners face a massive "chicken-and-egg problem" [7] that we define as the *scalability problem of industrial platforms*.

While growing the ecosystem, platform owners need to manage varying interests and boundary conditions and implement those in the platform's architecture and processes. For example, governance and orchestration are two significant issues for value creation and capturing [18, 20]. The latter is one of the strongest incentives for ecosystem participation and the primary focus when designing a platform. Beyond that, the integration of resources leads to value co-creation between service providers and consumers, which remains an unfamiliar issue for traditionally product-oriented firms [21]. The platform design is central for the development and economic success of such ecosystems. It is important to integrate both the technical and business perspective while studying and engineering digital platforms [22]. Our study contributes to this specific aspect, as we propose design principles for an artifact that meets these conditions.

Thus, manufacturing industries must develop high-performance platforms with functionalities that address customers' individual needs to be successful in digitization. In order to achieve this, the requirements of the respective groups must be identified and analyzed with regard to their integrability. For this purpose, we report on a case-that gives us an excellent, in-depth insight into the individual requirements of ecosystem participants. With the interview technique, we were able to overview both the static and dynamic components of the ecosystem regarding the interaction among the participants. To interpret our results reasonably, we used qualitative content analysis to structure our interpretative process using theoretical knowledge from different technical and managerial platform literature streams. Based on this, we can propose *design principles for IIoT-platforms*. We have, therefore, defined the following research question:

Research Question (RQ): How should an IIoT-platform be designed to deploy a stakeholder friendly environment?

The remainder of the article is structured as follows. First, we give an overview of the relevant theoretical background, which encompasses the digital transformation of the manufacturing industry, the role of platforms in the fourth industrial revolution, and the economic foundations of successful platform businesses. This is followed by an overview of the conducted research method. Subsequently, we present the study's findings, including generalized design principles we have derived from those findings. Lastly, we discuss our contributions and the limitations of our research and suggest possible further research endeavors.

2 Theoretical Background

2.1 Digitization of Manufacturing and the Role of IIoT-Platforms

Using modern technologies in industrial contexts to digitize assets aims at the cyber-physical integration of production sites, which scholars refer to as the fourth industrial revolution or Industry 4.0 [23]. Those digital factories are part of the industrial Internet of Things (IIoT) and require novel means for control that rely on digital platforms [4, 5]. A network layer connects the physical resources from an architectural viewpoint and makes them controllable and, thus, optimizable through digital platforms [3, 6].

Depending on the discipline, a *platform* can either refer to technological or economic models [22]. In information systems and management research, a platform is commonly defined as a technical architecture that facilitates the integration of capabilities and resources [12, 22, 24]. They connect different agents at different levels of analysis that result from the scope of the platform (internal, supply chain-, and industry-wide [22]). Digital platforms are modular technological systems that comprise a stable core and varying auxiliary modules, which enhance the potential usefulness of such systems [15, 24]. Integrating the core and periphery is realized through boundary resources, such as technological interfaces (e.g., APIs) or Software Development Kits (SDKs), which are opening the possibility for third-party developers to contribute such complementary modules, e.g., applications [25, 26]. Influenced by the success of prominent digital platforms, like Facebook and Amazon, their potential is evaluated in almost any sector [24, 27].

In manufacturing industries, IIoT-platforms are of particular interest for smart factories [15] since they are at the heart of these concepts [5]. The key functions of the IIoT-platforms are "event processing, event notification, and real-time analytics, to name a few" [4]. Furthermore, they allow integrating other systems, such as Enterprise Resource Management (ERP) or Manufacturing Execution Systems (MES). Besides that, data management, data analysis, and decision making are basic modules of the digital representation of such systems [6]. Compared to software platforms such as SAP, which are also opening themselves for external developers to an ecosystem, IIoT-Platforms focus on extending the range of functions and integrating digital assets as the core of the value proposition [5, 28].

2.2 Building Successful Digital Platform Ecosystems

From a business perspective, the opening of an internal or supply chain platform to other actors has several economic implications that rely on, simplified, the foundation of a multi-sided market around the platform [29]. The economic view of platforms as enablers of transactions is closely related to the engineering view, which focuses on technology [22, 30]. Indisputably, economic success can only be achieved through adequate technology. These multi-sided markets are characteristic of network externalities, which can be *direct* or *indirect* [7–9]. A growing number of agents in one market-side, commonly exemplified by the increasing value of communication technology (e.g., WhatsApp vs. Signal) when user numbers rise, generates the prior. The latter depends on the rise of agents in a different market-side. For example, the value of an Android phone increased when the number of applications exploded, and vice versa. The value of Nokia declined fast when the developers turned their backs on them. The most important result is that firms have to make sure to "get both sides on board" [7, p. 991]. Unfortunately, this is easier said than done because it requires specific actions to attract participants joining the ecosystem through incentives based on governance mechanisms [20, 31]. Thus, a growing number of complementors leads to increased customization potential.

Within platform ecosystems, *coopetition,* and value co-creation occur, making new strategies necessary [2, 10, 12, 21, 32]. Distinct types of ecosystems are distinguishable that differ in their specific structure and characteristics [11]. They have in common that positive network effects do not necessarily arise until specific actions are undertaken, e.g., developing a governance structure and orchestration [18, 20]. So does Hurni et al. [33] emphasize governance as a key for the dedication of complementors to attract them investing in the partnership with the platform owner. Vice versa, a platform will lose its importance for developers if their decision-making rights are very limited, and their coordination costs are high. Other scholars refer to the motivation of complementors to join a platform ecosystem as basically driven by the platform's "innovativeness and its commercial capital" [34].

Above that, it remains unclear for the potential participants how they contribute to the value co-creation and their benefits, respectively [22, 27]. Beyond the creation of value, the capturing of value remains an important issue for the platform leader and complementors [18].

In conclusion, the economic success of a platform relies on scaling their ecosystem, generating network effects to create value, and facilitating capturing the value for the platform leader and every other participant, respectively. Moreover, the technological perspective acts as an enabler for successful platforms. While the role of attracting the complementor as a source of innovative capabilities for the platform has been researched intensively, the overarching perspective of different perspectives on the attractiveness of a platform has so far been neglected. Thus, this research contributes to a better understanding of the platform design related to ecosystem participants needs and, foremost, the motivational interaction between the different needs that can be described as the first step towards an ecosystem tension management.

3   Research Method

3.1   Study Design

The design principles originate from a qualitative interview study with 15 experts from industry practice. The interview is an accepted research method to collect data engraved in industry practitioners' experiences and social settings [35, 36]. We selected interview partners based on various stakeholder roles (see Sect. 4) to inquire about the most comprehensive view on emerging ecosystems in IIoT-platforms. The stakeholders reflect the emerging ecosystem of an IIoT-platform established in 2015, a spin-off of an established incumbent machine manufacturer (see Sect. 4). A semi-structured interview guide guided each interview. It is the most goal-oriented option, contrary to the open interview (with no restrictions) and structured interviews as the research retain structure and comparability, yet leaves enough flexibility to adjust to *ad hoc* situations in the interview [39].

3.2 Data Collection and Analysis

We had the opportunity to study representative participants of the emerging platform ecosystem directly with multiple interviews (see Table 1) and indirectly through secondary data. The management of the platform owner and the machine manufacturer actively supported the project as sponsors and provided us with "legitimacy and credibility" [37, p. 588]. As a result, all participants greatly assisted us, especially with arranging interview dates and informal meetings, which was very valuable. In addition to collecting primary data, we had the opportunity to attend team meetings and analyze secondary data (e.g., current surveys and internal documents). For an appropriate study

Table 1. Interview details[1]

Stakeholder	Role	Duration (h)
Platform Owner	Pre-Sales Manager/Consultant	00:41
	Consultant	00:45
	Consultant	00:59
Machine Manufacturer	Partner Management	00:50
	Project Leader	00:35
	Product Manager Internal App Development	00:41
	Customer Guard	01:01
	Industry 4.0 Expert in Communication & Security	00:48
Complementor	Data Scientist, Predictive Maintenance	00:47
	Managing Director, Maintenance	00:50
	Managing Director, Digital Solutions	00:59
	Managing Director, Maintenance	00:46
Customer	Managing Director, Sheet Metal Processing	00:32
	Industry 4.0 Expert, Manufacturer	00:37
	Managing Director, Sheet Metal Processing	01:28

---

[1] All interviews were conducted in German and translated into English here. Verbatim quotes are coded as follows: 2 letters referring to the stakeholder + 4 letters referring to the role (e.g. PP.Cons for a consultant of the platform owner).

of the phenomenon, we conducted 15 formal interviews, which we recorded and transcribed. Also, we used the informal meetings and internal documents to understand the context further.

We conducted a qualitative content analysis to analyze the transcribed interviews using MaxQDA. Qualitative content analysis [38, 39] is a flexible [39] research technique that allows the analysis and interpretation of meanings from qualitative data [38, 40], e.g., interview transcripts, as it delivers "replicable and valid inferences from texts [...]" [38, p. 18]. The analytical process focuses on the coding of elements of the documents [40]. Central for every qualitative content analysis is the system of categories, which can either be deducted from theory, inductively derived from the text, or determined by a combined method [39].

To verify the quality of the entire coding process and determine its validity, we measured the intercoder reliability, which we calculated based on four counter coded interviews. The criterion of intercoder reliability verifies the correspondence between two coders. It is examined whether the assignment of the predefined codes between two different coders to non-segmented material finds an agreement. We use Cohen's kappa to measure the degree of the agreement following Brennan and Prediger's [41] model for its calculation and reached a value of **0.64** – suggesting a substantial agreement between the two coders [42].

In conclusio, the coding seemed valid regarding the four counter-coded interviews. Therefore, the analysis of the interviews is completed, and we present the results of the analysis in the next section.

3.3 Design Principle Generation

This research aims to derive design principles to generate prescriptive knowledge regarding the design of IIoT-platforms, i.e., codified and formalized design knowledge that guides practitioners to design artifacts more efficiently and, ultimately, successfully [43]. Thus, rather than describing artifact design descriptively, they explicitly intend to advise designers to achieve a pre-determined set of goals [44]. As there is no standard way to derive design principles, some use Action Design Research (ADR) (e.g., [45]) or follow established DSR methods (e.g., [46]). Following the recommendations of [47], we develop *supportive* design principles that we formulate by eliciting *meta-requirement* for each stakeholder in the IIoT-platform's ecosystem. Meta-requirements, in that regard, are general requirements that do not address a single instance of artifact implementation but rather a class of artifacts [48]. Subsequently, each design principle requires to address at least one meta-requirement, a relationship, which is usually termed *value grounding* [44]. Although there is a variety of formulation approaches (for an overview, see [49]), we chose to formulate our design principles according to the linguistic template of [43]. It demarcates constituent elements and, thus, provides excellent potential for rigorous formulation. We deviate from the exact linguistic wording if this would hinder comprehensibility. The template is as follows [43, p. 4045]:

"Provide the system with **[material property—in terms of form and function]** in order for users to **[activity of user/group of users—in terms of action]**, given that **[boundary conditions—user group's characteristics or implementation settings]**."

The template refers to material properties that explicate what the artifact should consist of to be able to execute the intended action. Lastly, as their environment demarcates design principle instantiation, they are only supposed to be valid in specific boundary conditions [43].

4 The Case of an Emerging IIoT-Platform: Requirements Towards the Platform Owner

4.1 Case Description

The platform under research connects several stakeholders we consider in our research. The groups are described below:

- *Platform owner:* Responsible for the provision of the infrastructure, both technically and organizationally. He assumes the role of the mediator and ensures that all platform members can achieve their goals.
- *Machine manufacturer:* The machine manufacturer, in this case, must be seen in close cooperation with the platform owner. The primary goal of the machine manufacturer is to offer its customers a better service and thus to increase customer satisfaction.
- *Complementor:* The complementor is a software company that supplements the platform with additional applications (Third-party Apps).
- *Customer*: Small-to-medium-sized manufacturing company (sheet metal processing), which is under pressure to increase its efficiency steadily. As a result, the customer is forced to have increasing competences in the field of digitalization.

From a technical perspective, the platform enables the vertical and horizontal integration of different systems through applications, e.g., for the horizontal level: ERP- and MES-System integration. Furthermore, applications allow functionalities to include the overview of machine utilization, material consumption, or the current machine program in real-time. Custom applications can extend those with more specific functions.

As the platform brings the stakeholders together and bundles their needs to create benefit for all of them, the definition of a multi-sided platform fits the above-described use case. A lack of technological maturity dominates the general environment in which the company operates due to the industry structure itself. For example, the direct connectivity of machines is currently not possible due to a high degree of heterogeneity. Therefore, it is necessary to develop alternative models to achieve these objectives. Nevertheless, the number of digital services provided by complementors is continuously increasing. Accordingly, a platform for the provision of digital solutions and data could be a suitable approach. Conflicts between the different stakeholders due to varying expectations of the platform are possible. For this reason, it is essential to identify the requirements and expectations to find out which potential conflict areas can arise. Finally, by elaborating on the guidelines, the core for developing the platforms can be defined.

4.2 Requirements Towards the Platform Owner

The case study provided in-depth insights into the mindset, problems, and requirements of the various stakeholders involved in an IIoT-platform. In this section, we first outline the industry-specific challenges for IIoT-platforms and then describe the key requirements derived from the qualitative content analysis, which form the basis for the design principles defined in the subsequent section.

We identified three deeply grounded challenges in the branch: First, many challenges of implementing IIoT-platforms result from the **traditional branch of mechanical engineering**. That leads to at least two obstacles. Cultivated over decades, the organizational blindness leads companies to oversee opportunities that digital innovations can offer:

"In many places, there are many doubts or I would sometimes say just not necessarily a lot of experience, and then something new is always abstract and in doubt a bit more difficult." (TP.DiSo).

Beyond that, the branch is diametrically opposed to the agile branch of the Software Industry, which can lead to communication issues and refusal of innovation, which may be perceived as risks, as a third-party manager confirms:

"It is a change, a service-related change, many say: "I'm not gonna take that risk. This is probably a general problem, which you will probably hear often in other industrial-software areas as well." (TP.DiSo).

Second, similar to the first challenge, the **digitally enabled business models** are unfamiliar to the traditional ones and require new perspectives on, e.g., cooperation or value propositions. Applying business models or constellations from other digital sectors are hardly imaginable:

"[...] I must never become dependent on a platform if there is no other way. With the 'Apple App Store', there is no other way, but anywhere else, we will always look for alternatives through our strategy. Unless we see that the benefit is so great, then I might do that, but until then, I don't see a problem with that." (MM.PaMa).

The third challenge is the **technical diversity of the industry**. IT infrastructure and technical systems, e.g., machinery, are very heterogeneous, which leads to increased effort for integrating the systems. That is apparent to the platform owner's consultants:

"What makes it difficult from my point of view at the moment is that we always operate in an environment in which other IT systems already exist. That can be an ERP that can be IT system XY [...]" (PP.Cons).

Based on the case findings, we formulated meta-requirements that we generalize and condense to key requirements [50]. Further, we clustered the key requirements into thematic categories that address *Technical, Organizational, Service,* or *Economic* issues. Table 2 shows the final list of key requirements.

Table 2. Meta-Requirements (MR) and Key-Requirement (KR) derived from the study.

MR	Key Requirement	Stakeholder	Description
Technical	Standards for Integration (KR1)	Customer	Refers to the necessity of standards for technical integration of platform actors.
	Provided data and interfaces (KR2)	Complementor	The platform must provide data and efficient interfaces for further development of products and services.
	Storage capacities (KR3)	Complementor	The platform should offer transactions, integration, and cloud storage.
Organizational	Strong customer involvement (KR4)	General	Further development and operation of the platform depends on a high level of customer involvement.
	Central cooperation in one place (KR5)	Complementor	The platform designed should enable users to manage operational processes cooperatively.
	Providing security and confidence (KR6)	Complementor	The platform must ensure a trusted and secure environment for the user.
Services	Partner Management (KR7)	Customer	The value of complementary services and products must constantly increase through active partner management.
	Provision of solutions for different business areas (KR8)	Customer	Refers to the need for a diversified service offering that covers diverse business needs.
	Personal Support (KR9)	Customer	Refers to personal and individual advice from qualified service personnel.
Economic	Cost reduction and service improvement as added value (KR10)	General	Refers to the main value proposition of the platform.
	Efficiency gain and cost savings (KR11)	Customer	Refers to the main requirement on the customer side.
	Attractive and cost-effective business model (KR12)	Customer	Refers to the business model of the platform owner. It is necessary to act in a particularly cost-effective manner in order to be competitive.
	Ensuring revenue from performance (KR13)	General	Using a performance-based approach so that the value of higher performance is shared with the platform owner.

5   Design Principles for IIoT-Platforms

Based on key requirements derived in Table 2, we formulated design principles as a response to them [47]. Following the example of [51], Table 3 lists seven design principles with short titles and corresponding key requirements that they address. In the following, we will elaborate on the design principles in more detail and provide explicatory rationales for their existence.

Table 3. Design principles and Key Requirements.

Short title of Design Principles (DP)	Addressed Key Requirements
DP1: Low Entry Barriers	1, 2
DP2: Focus on transactions and cloud-services	2, 3
DP3: Trusted collaboration between platform actors	4, 5, 6
DP4: Active ecosystem management	7
DP5: Customizable solutions and support	8, 9
DP6: Value proposition: Efficiency for cost savings	10, 11, 12
DP7: Gain-sharing approach	13

5.1   Technical Cluster

Design Principle 1: Provide the system with low entry barriers in order for users to switch easily to/from your platform at the lowest cost and effort-intensive technical adjustments or problems, given the technical design of platform integration components.

Rationale: In platform literature, switching costs refer to the effort one platform user must undertake (e.g., in installing new software) to change a utilized platform. For competing platforms, having low entry barriers to access platforms is key [52]. The design principle refers to two components. First, those entry barriers must be small in terms of technical effort. That means that the platform should provide commonly used technological standards and interfaces so that the actors can integrate quickly, rather than having to adopt new technologies (**KR1**). The second component addresses the attractiveness of the platform for complementors to contribute products and services. Thus, the platform should provide suitable interfaces (e.g., APIs and respective documentation) and rich data (**KR2**). The latter is of crucial importance for developers to create individualized products and services that rely on the needs of the customers. That will finally lead to a higher ecosystem value. The relevance of DP1 is also underpinned by the multi-homing literature, which indicates, on the one hand, that the quality of a complement is lower when ported onto a platform whose architecture is complex [53]. A reduction of complexity can be achieved by the use of standards and interfaces, as this prevents an adaptation of the complements. On the other hand, the absence of compatibility between different platforms weakens the competition and increases costs [54].

Additionally, research suggests that limiting access, which increases the probability of single-homing, damages at least one side of the market [55].

Design Principle 2: Provide the system with both transaction enablement and cloud-services in order for users to have an integrated platform for most common operations, given the design of the technical service structure of the platform.

Rationale: The platform should provide mechanisms for the transactional exchange of services and products on the platform that utilizes an underlying cloud-infrastructure. That is necessary to enable independent access to data and services and allows for modern technical integration **(KR3)**. These services must use commonly accepted interfaces and (anonymous) user data in order for developers to, e.g., train their Machine Learning Algorithms **(KR2)**.

5.2 Organizational Cluster

Design Principle 3: Provide the system with centralized collaboration capabilities between all user groups in order for users to interact easily with their customers or partners, given the design of the interaction mechanism of the platform.

Rationale: The third design principle addresses KR4, KR5, and KR6. First, the design principle prescribes that customers must be involved on the platform to facilitate goal-oriented integration into value-creating mechanisms **(KR4)**. Second, the actors should be able to work collaboratively on executing business processes to facilitate the collaborative generation of innovation and contributions **(KR5)**. Lastly, for collaboration to work, the platform must ensure secure exchanges between actors to have the necessary trust in the platform infrastructure to join the platform ecosystem and contribute to it **(KR6)**.

5.3 Services Cluster

Design Principle 4: Provide the system with the capability of active ecosystem management of partners, complementarities, and value sharing, in order for users to ensure the greatest possible benefit to users in the long term.

Rationale: Actor management is a vital issue in platform organization and requires tools for their active design [14, 56]. Thus, the design principle prescribes the integration of mechanisms for the active management of ecosystem actors. The overarching goal is to foster and make more convenient complementation of the core platform components with additional products and services. Finally, this will lead to the increased overall attractiveness of the ecosystem through high value delivered by strong partners **(KR7)**.

Design Principle 5: Provide the platform with customizable solutions and support functions in order to satisfy the needs of each user in the most effective manner and to avoid creating entry barriers given the design of platform service structures.

Rationale: The IIoT-platform should offer highly individualized and, thus, diversified products and services to different customer segments with shared requirements. In that, the degree of individualization must pay into tailoring offerings to customer demands so that they apply to a variety of business needs **(KR8)**. Additionally, the IIoT-platform should provide the customer with individualized support services, which cover all areas that could hinder customers from integrating into the platform ecosystem. Thus, these support services must cover a range from technical integration to working on the platform. Simply put, each actor must receive support services on each level of the integration process **(KR9)**.

5.4   Economical Cluster

Design Principle 6: Provide the platform with a focus on the value proposition on multiple layers to increase service efficiency and enable cost reductions for customers to give the design of the superordinate value proposition of the platform.

Rationale: Attractive value propositions are at the core of platform business models and contain multiple layers [2, 57]. First, the platform's value should clearly indicate for its users that using the platform results in reducing cost and improvement of services. That means that users should identify opportunities either for optimization or improve their service-level quality **(KR10)**. That requirement is mirrored by the customer side, which should be provided with a high degree of efficiency gains to decide to join and use the platform **(KR11)**. On the platform owner side, the platform should be run economically so that a clear cost-benefit advantage is identifiable and contributes to the platform's survival. This is of particular importance, as poor efficiency sets rigid limits to scalability **(KR12)**.

Design Principle 7: Provide the platform with a gain-sharing approach to strengthen the community in order for users to rely on a broad diversification of risks and to distribute the platform's benefit amongst all participants.

Rationale: The platform should pursue a gain-sharing logic that builds on performance-based mechanisms. In that, most performing stakeholders would gain a larger share of revenue generated in the platform ecosystem. Overall, if the gain of the platform ecosystem rises at large, there should be distribution mechanisms considering stakeholder contributions adequately. That approach also includes the platform owner. Finally, such mechanisms result not only in sharing value but also in decreasing the risk of high expenses or fees in low-performance periods **(KR13)**.

6   Discussion

6.1   Conclusion and Implications

The success of digitalization of the manufacturing industry lies in the usage of platforms that are used to connect, control, and optimize IIoT-systems. Although these systems' relevance is known, as they represent an important architectural component, we lack an understanding of how such platforms need to be designed for success and how to get "everyone on-board". Scholars already investigated single aspects, such as the attraction of complementors and launching strategies [58], but we lack in a comprehensive and overarching understanding of how to bring those economic issues together and how this will influence the design decisions of a particular platform.

We bridge the gap between different perspectives, at least the technological and economical, to offer a nascent design theory in the form of design principles derived from a specific case that is representative for the IIoT-platforms. Therefore, we have first identified several requirements from the platform's stakeholders and abstracted them to design principles that work for the class of IIoT-platforms. Furthermore, we defined four clusters of design decisions regarding technical, organizational, service, and economic decisions. Thus, this allows us to, on the first hand, contribute to the growing platform literature that deals with value creation, value capture, and, foremost, attracting participants. On the other hand, we provide substantial guidelines for practitioners, which are planning to develop an IIoT-platforms to extend their current value propositions. In the following, we present our scientific and managerial contributions in detail.

Our work provides prescriptive guidelines for designing an IIoT-platforms and considers multiple perspectives in terms of **scientific contributions**. Accumulating prescriptive knowledge is an issue of paramount importance in design science [59]. Thus, it extends the current knowledge base of platform literature with new, generalized knowledge about platform design, especially in the fast-growing field of platform design, which is of high importance. Also, our research may lead other researchers to complement, cross-validate, or extend our design principles, as to contribute to closing additional gaps in platform design literature.

In terms of **managerial contributions**, our work gives practitioners prescriptive guidelines, which assist (though, they do not guarantee) successful IIoT-platform design. Applying these principles enables the development of platforms that foster the emergence of an ecosystem that provides an attractive environment for all stakeholders. As the design principles follow established guidelines in their formulation, they, dedicatedly, prescribe pathways for action that should be easily instantiable. Furthermore, our analysis might help managers of ecosystem participants to better understand the complementors, customers, or the platform owner. This will help them align their activities, strategize, or negotiate more effectively.

6.2 Limitations and Outlook

Our work is subject to **limitations**. Firstly, design principles, rather than being a guarantee for success, are supporting guidelines that help designers in bringing about an artifact more efficiently. Yet, their instantiation requires stark contextualization with the designer's environment and personal experience [43, 47, 60]. Naturally, as the design principles are the product of a qualitative interview study, they, by their very design, can only cover a delimited spectrum of design areas that were perceived and interpreted as necessary by the authors. The case is fixed on a single firm that was selected based on theoretical considerations, which, even though the case is of high value in representativeness, implies stark borders in generalizability [61].

Lastly, our work is fertile soil for **further research**. Several requirements indicate that there are many tensions between the different stakeholder-groups in such IIoT-platform ecosystems, whereas their management seems to be of crucial importance. We suggest that future research should pay particular attention to this. It also favors more in-depth analysis, e.g., in the context of a multiple case study, that would span a sample of new firms. That would greatly benefit the generalizability of the results and contribute to painting a much more complete picture.

References

1. Yoo, Y., Boland, R., Lyytinen, K., Majchrzak, A.: Organizing for innovation in the digitized world. Organ. Sci. **23**, 1398–1408 (2012)
2. Guggenberger, T.M., Möller, F., Boualouch, K., Otto, B.: Towards a unifying understanding of digital business models. In: Proceedings of the Twenty-Third Pacific Asia Conference on Information Systems, Dubai, United Arab Emirates (2020)
3. Wan, J., et al.: Software-defined industrial internet of things in the context of industry 4.0. IEEE Sens J. 1 (2016)
4. Yaqoob, I., et al.: Internet of Things architecture: recent advances, taxonomy, requirements, and open challenges. IEEE Wirel. Commun. **24**, 10–16 (2017)
5. Boyes, H., Hallaq, B., Cunningham, J., Watson, T.: The Industrial Internet of Things (IIoT): an analysis framework. Comput. Ind. **101**, 1–12 (2018)
6. Chen, B., Wan, J., Shu, L., Li, P., Mukherjee, M., Yin, B.: Smart factory of industry 4.0: key technologies, application case, and challenges. IEEE Access **6**, 6505–6519 (2018)
7. Rochet, J.-C., Tirole, J.: Platform competition in two-sided markets. J. Eur. Econ. Assoc. **1**, 990–1029 (2003)
8. Eisenmann, T., Parker, G., van Alstyne, M.: Strategies for two-sided markets. Harvard Bus. Rev. **84**, 1–11 (2006)
9. Katz, M.L., Shapiro, C.: Network externalities, competition, and compatibility. Am. Econ. Rev. **75**, 424–440 (1985)
10. Jacobides, M., Cennamo, C., Gawer, A.: Towards a theory of ecosystems. Strateg. Manag. J. **39**, 2255–2276 (2018)
11. Guggenberger, T.M., Möller, F., Haarhaus, T., Gür, I., Otto, B.: Ecosystem types in information systems. In: Proceedings of the 28th European Conference on Information Systems, Marrakech, Morocco (2020)
12. Parker, G., van Alstyne, M., Jiang, X.: Platform ecosystems: how developers invert the firm. MIS Quart. **41**, 255–266 (2017)
13. Schermuly, L., Schreieck, M., Wiesche, M., Krcmar, H.: Developing an industrial IoT platform – trade-off between horizontal and vertical approaches. In: 14. Internationale Tagung Wirtschaftsinformatik (WI 2019) (2019)
14. Petrik, D., Herzwurm, G.: Towards the IIoT ecosystem development - understanding the stakeholder perspective. In: Proceedings of the 28th European Conference on Information Systems, Marrakesh, Morocco (2020)
15. Baldwin, C.Y., Woodard, C.J.: The architecture of platforms. A unified view. Harvard Bus. Sch. Finan. 1–31 (2008)
16. Schreieck, M., Wiesche, M., Krcmar, H.: Design and governance of platform ecosystems – key concepts and issues for future research. In: Proceedings of the 24th European Conference on Information Systems, Istanbul, Turkey (2016)

17. Aulkemeier, F., Iacob, M.-E., van Hillegersberg, J.: Platform-based collaboration in digital ecosystems. Electron. Mark. **29**(4), 597–608 (2019). https://doi.org/10.1007/s12525-019-003 41-2
18. Teece, D.J.: Profiting from innovation in the digital economy: enabling technologies, standards, and licensing models in the wireless world. Res. Policy **47**, 1367–1387 (2018)
19. Vargo, S.L., Lusch, R.F.: It's all B2B…and beyond: Toward a systems perspective of the market. Ind. Market Manag. **40**, 181–187 (2011)
20. Helfat, C.E., Raubitschek, R.S.: Dynamic and integrative capabilities for profiting from innovation in digital platform-based ecosystems. Res. Policy **47**, 1391–1399 (2018)
21. Lusch, R., Nambisan, S.: Service innovation: a service-dominant logic perspective. MIS Quart. **39**, 155–175 (2015)
22. Gawer, A.: Bridging differing perspectives on technological platforms: toward an integrative framework. Res. Policy 1239–1249 (2014)
23. Wang, S., Wan, J., Zhang, D., Li, D., Zhang, C.: Towards smart factory for industry 4.0: a self-organized multi-agent system with big data based feedback and coordination. Comput Netw. **101**, 158–168 (2016)
24. de Reuver, M., Sørensen, C., Basole, R.C.: The digital platform: a research agenda. J. Inf. Technol. **33**, 124–135 (2017)
25. Ghazawneh, A., Henfridsson, O.: Balancing platform control and external contribution in third-party development: the boundary resources model. Inform. Syst. J. **23**, 173–192 (2013)
26. Tiwana, A.: Evolutionary competition in platform ecosystems. Inform. Syst. Res. **26**, 266–281 (2015)
27. Van Alstyne, M.W., Parker, G., Paul Choudary, S.: Pipelines, platforms, and the new rules of strategy. Harvard Bus. Rev. **2016**, 54–62 (2016)
28. Petrik, D., Herzwurm, G.: Boundary resources for IIoT platforms–a complementor satisfaction study. In: Proceedings of the 41st International Conference on Information System (2020)
29. Gawer, A., Cusumano, M.A.: Industry platforms and ecosystem innovation. J. Prod. Innov. Manag. **31**, 417–433 (2013)
30. Adner, R.: Ecosystem as structure. J. Manag. **43**, 39–58 (2017)
31. Hagiu, A.: strategic decisions for multisided platforms. MIT Sloan Manag. Rev. **55** (2014)
32. Nalebuff, B.J., Brandenburger, A.M.: Co-opetition: competitive and cooperative business strategies for the digital economy. Strategy Leadersh. **25**, 28–33 (1997)
33. Hurni, T., Huber, T.L., Dibbern, J., Krancher, O.: Complementor dedication in platform ecosystems: rule adequacy and the moderating role of flexible and benevolent practices. Eur. J. Inf. Syst. **40**, 1–24 (2020)
34. Kude, T., Dibbern, J., Heinzl, A.: Why do complementors participate? An analysis of partnership networks in the enterprise software industry. IEEE Trans. Eng. Manag. **59**, 250–265 (2012)
35. Schultze, U., Avital, M.: Designing interviews to generate rich data for information systems research. Inf. Organ. **21**, 1–16 (2011)
36. Myers, M.D.: Qualitative research in information systems. MIS Q. Manag. Inf. Syst. **21**, 241 (1997)
37. Patton, M.Q.: Qualitative Research & Evaluation Methods. Integrating Theory and Practice. SAGE, Los Angeles (2015)
38. Krippendorff, K.: Content Analysis. An Introduction to its Methodology. SAGE, Los Angeles (2019)
39. Mayring, P.: Qualitative Content Analysis: Theoretical Foundation, Basic Procedures and Software Solution. Klagenfurt (2014)
40. Weber, R.P.: Basic Content Analysis. SAGE Publications, Newbury Park (1990)

41. Brennan, R.L., Prediger, D.J.: Coefficient kappa: some uses, misuses, and alternatives. Educ. Psychol. Meas. **41**, 687–699 (1981)
42. Landis, J.R., Koch, G.G.: The measurement of observer agreement for categorical data. Biometrics **33**, 159 (1977)
43. Chandra Kruse, L., Seidel, S., Gregor, S.: Prescriptive knowledge in IS research: conceptualizing design principles in terms of materiality, action, and boundary conditions. In: Proceedings of the 48th Hawaii International Conference, pp. 4039–4048 (2015)
44. Goldkuhl, G.: Design theories in information systems-a need for multi-grounding. JITTA: J. Inf. Technol. Theory Appl. **6**, 59–72 (2004)
45. Sein, M., Henfridsson, O., Purao, S., Rossi, M., Lindgren, R.: Action design research. MIS Quart. **35** (2011)
46. Peffers, K., Tuunanen, T., Rothenberger, M.A., Chatterjee, S.: A design science research methodology for information systems research. J. Manag. Inform. Syst. **24**, 45–77 (2007)
47. Möller, F., Guggenberger, T.M., Otto, B.: Towards a method for design principle development in information systems. In: Hofmann, S., Müller, O., Rossi, M. (eds.) DESRIST 2020. LNCS, vol. 12388, pp. 208–220. Springer, Cham (2020). https://doi.org/10.1007/978-3-030-64823-7_20
48. Walls, J.G., Widmeyer, G.R., El Sawy, O.A.: Building an information system design theory for vigilant EIS. Inform. Syst. Res. **3**, 36–59 (1992)
49. Cronholm, S., Göbel, H.: Guidelines supporting the formulation of design principles. In: Proceedings of the 29th Australasian Conference on Information Systems (2018)
50. Koppenhagen, N., Gaß, O., Müller, B.: Design science research in action - anatomy of success critical activities for rigor and relevance. In: Proceedings of the 20th European Conference on Information Systems, pp. 1–12 (2012)
51. Möller, F., Guggenberger, T., Otto, B.: Design principles for route-optimization business models: a grounded theory study of user feedback. In: Proceedings of the 15th International Conference on Wirtschaftsinformatik (2020)
52. Economides, N.: The economics of networks. Int. J. Ind. Organ. **14**, 673–699 (1996)
53. Cennamo, C., Ozalp, H., Kretschmer, T.: Platform architecture and quality trade-offs of multihoming complements. Inform. Syst. Res. **29**, 461–478 (2018)
54. Doganoglu, T., Wright, J.: Multihoming and compatibility. Int. J. Ind. Organ. **24**, 45–67 (2006)
55. Belleflamme, P., Peitz, M.: Platform competition: who benefits from multihoming? Int. J. Ind. Organ. **64**, 1–26 (2019)
56. Foerderer, J., Kude, T., Schuetz, S.W., Heinzl, A.: Knowledge boundaries in enterprise software platform development: antecedents and consequences for platform governance. Inf. Syst. J. **29**, 119–144 (2019)
57. Täuscher, K., Laudien, S.M.: Understanding platform business models: a mixed methods study of marketplaces. Eur. Manag. J. **36**, 319–329 (2018)
58. Reuver, M., de Nederstigt, B., Janssen, M.: Launch strategies for multi-sided data analytics platforms. In: ECIS 2018 (2018)
59. Simon, H.A.: The Sciences of the Artificial. MIT Press, Cambridge (1996)
60. Chandra Kruse, L., Seidel, S.: Tensions in design principle formulation and reuse. In: Proceedings of the 12th International Conference on Design Science Research in Information Systems and Technology (2017)
61. Eisenhardt, K.M.: Building theories from case study research. Acad. Manag. Rev. **14**, 532–550 (1989)

What Goes Around, Comes Around: The Effects of 360-degree Experiences on Peer-to-Peer Platform Behavior

Anke Greif-Winzrieth[✉], Christian Peukert, and David Dann

Karlsruhe Institute of Technology, Institute of Information Systems
and Marketing, Karlsruhe, Germany
{anke.greif-winzrieth,christian.peukert,david.dann}@kit.edu

Abstract. Platforms for peer-to-peer accommodation sharing are flourishing and changing the overall tourism industry. Ever since, providers on those platforms use photos to advertise their accommodation. Due to the advancement of virtual reality technology, nowadays, it is technologically feasible to provide 360-degree photos with reasonable effort. Yet, popular platforms do not offer the possibility of providing 360-degree photos. To explore what effect an implementation of 360-degree photos could have on consumer behavior, this article sets out to investigate how different presentation formats (ordinary photos, 360-degree desktop, virtual reality) influence consumer perception within a laboratory experiment. Testing these presentation formats in a pilot study ($N = 45$), we observe significant differences regarding consumers' diagnosticity, enjoyment, and transaction intention, while trust-related variables did not differ substantially. With the outlined research endeavor, we expect to contribute to a better understanding of virtual reality's potential in the platform economy.

Keywords: Virtual reality · Platform economy · 360-degree experiences

1 Introduction

The number of bookings on peer-to-peer (P2P) accommodation sharing platforms is ever increasing, so that such platforms have become an integral part of the tourism industry [1]. In contrast to ordinary B2C platforms, on P2P platforms, users are dealing with private individuals (peers) and, thereby, may face fraudulent offers or inappropriate conditions [2]. To bridge existing information asymmetry between the two peers (i.e., provider and consumer) and enable transactions, trust is a crucial prerequisite [3–6]. To engender trust, providers on P2P accommodation platforms usually substantiate their accommodation's actual quality by presenting (several) photos. Nowadays, it would also be feasible to provide 360-degree content, which allows for conveying a more complete illustration of the offerings (floor plan, layout, size). Similarly in recent years, virtual reality (VR) technology has advanced in a manner that it is now readily available to the broad consumer population (driven by falling prices and at the same time increasing system performance) and can thus be used to approach customers in a novel fashion

© The Author(s), under exclusive license to Springer Nature Switzerland AG 2021
F. Ahlemann et al. (Eds.): WI 2021, LNISO 48, pp. 505–511, 2021.
https://doi.org/10.1007/978-3-030-86800-0_35

[7, 8]. However, up to now, such a feature is not yet implemented on any major P2P platform, even though 360-degree photos can be created with virtually all contemporary mobile phones (e.g., using the Google Street View app). Within the tourism industry, several hotel chains and travel agencies (e.g., TUI) are already offering 360-degree experiences to provide customers with comprehensive pre-booking experiences on their potential travel destinations. Further, users' demand for 360-degree photos has already been expressed in forums of major P2P platforms [9]. Against this backdrop, our research endeavor's overarching research question is: *How do 360-degree views influence users' perceptions of P2P accommodation sharing platform offerings?*

Within this research in progress paper, we present results from an exploratory pilot study and propose an experimental design for further investigation of user behavior on P2P accommodation sharing platforms that provide 360-degree content. We compare three treatments where participants either see ordinary photos (*Desktop Plain*) or 360° photos presented either on a desktop screen (*Desktop 360*) or in a VR headset (*VR*).

2 Theoretical Background and Related Work

Since the rise of the platform economy, IS research has investigated various drivers and impediments of the use of P2P accommodation platforms [5, 10]. **Trust** is an essential factor that most studies agree on, rendering it a key influencing variable for platform usage [4]. Scholars started to break down trust into different facets, namely trust in the peer (provider or consumer), trust in the platform, and trust in the product (only relevant from a consumer perspective) [4]. Accordingly, platforms are particularly designed to support these trust relations and implement user interface artifacts to establish trust [6]. In this context, it is surprising that the potential of including 360-degree experiences into the design of P2P platforms has not yet received much attention – neither from a scientific perspective nor from the platform providers themselves.

A growing number of hotels provide 360-degree representations of the rooms on their websites, but there is still little research on how these new presentation formats influence actual booking behavior. In most cases, these 360-degree experiences consist of panoramic photos, that can be accessed via different devices, including smartphones, tablets, desktop computer screens, or VR headsets. The main difference between these devices lies in the degree of immersion that can be delivered. Immersion is system-specific [11] and has been defined as "the extent to which the computer displays are capable of delivering an inclusive, extensive, surrounding and vivid illusion of reality to the senses of a human participant" [10, pp. 604/605]. VR headsets thus deliver a higher degree of immersion than desktop screens, smartphones, or tablets based on the system specifications.

VR has emerged as a rapidly growing technology, and its implications, fields of usage, and possibilities are continually increasing. A related study by Suh and Lee [13] shows that providing VR access to web stores can increase customer learning about products and purchase intentions. In the tourism context, VR provides several opportunities, such as building an a priori sensory experience of a travel destination [14], which has been shown to increase the likelihood of visiting the destination itself in the future [15]. Overall, existing studies suggest that the presence of VR interfaces may enrich customer experiences during the booking process and thus influence **booking behavior**. Depending on the hardware used and the nature of a 360-degree experience, applications can be classified in different degrees of immersion [12], which, in turn, may affect the **telepresence** perception [16, 17]. Comparing behavior in 2D and 3D virtual worlds displayed on a desktop screen, Nah et al. found a significant effect on perceived telepresence and perceived **enjoyment** [18]. Similarly, Peukert et al. [19] revealed that a VR shopping experience significantly increases the perceived telepresence (and further telepresence positively affects enjoyment) compared to a desktop experience. Evaluating offers on P2P platforms, consumers must rely on the information provided by the supplying peer (e.g., the content transmitted via the presented images). Thereby, the presentation format may substantially influence their perceived **diagnosticity**. In this context, Jiang and Benbasat [20–22] already showed that different virtual product experiences increase the perceived diagnosticity compared to pallid picture presentation.

3 Pilot Study

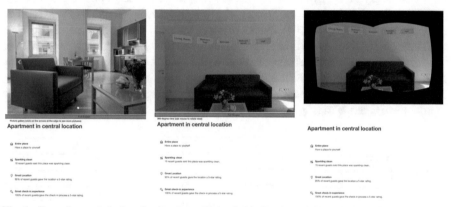

Fig. 1. Experimental design for Desktop Plain (left), Desktop 360 (middle), and VR (right) treatment. Exemplary visualization of the representation (top), general information about the accommodation (bottom).

Our pilot study investigates how different presentation formats influence several variables of interest related to user perceptions and behavior on P2P accommodation sharing platforms (variables printed in bold in Sect. 2). In the scenario-based lab experiment, participants take on a prospective guest's role on a P2P sharing platform evaluating an accommodation. They were instructed to imagine that they are looking for a place to stay in a foreign town for two nights and use an online platform such as Airbnb, 9flats, or Wimdu. We use a fully-furnished accommodation, presented in three different treatments (tested between subjects): Frist, the *Desktop Plain* treatment is aligned towards the presentation of accommodations on contemporary P2P accommodation sharing platforms. Participants can assess the accommodation by browsing several photos (taken by a professional photographer using a Canon EOS 5d Mark II). Second, the *Desktop 360*

treatment provides participants with an interactive 360 view of each room (using an
Insta360 ONE X placed in the middle of each room). Using drag & drop mouse ges-
tures, the angle of view can be rotated, and virtual buttons allow to navigate into all
other rooms. Third, in the *VR* treatment, participants are equipped with an Oculus Go
head-mounted display and a controller to assess the room in a VR environment. The
general information about the accommodation below the treatment is constant across
treatments. Figure 1 provides an overview of the three treatments.

Following the treatment, participants were asked to answer a set of survey items.
To ensure content validity, we use validated scales adapted to the context of our study
(telepresence [18, 23, 24], diagnosticity [25], trust in provider [26], trust in product
[4], enjoyment [27, 28], booking intention [29]). We recruited 68 participants from the
subject pool of the Karlsruhe Decision and Design Lab (KD^{2}Lab) using hroot [30]. Three
observations were excluded because participants failed an attention check, and we lost
20 survey responses due to technical issues[1]. This leads to a sample of 45 participants
(mean age 22.9 years, SD = 3.79; 36% female). The experiment is implemented in
oTree [31] and React 360 [32]. All scales meet the commonly applied Cronbach's alpha
cutoff value of >.70 [33], except *trust in product* for which one item had to be dropped
for further analysis. Significant differences in telepresence perceptions between groups
(ANOVA, $F_{(1,43)} = 7.97, p = .007$) and higher telepresence in VR than in Desktop Plain
(Wilcox rank-sum test, $p = .004$), but not between VR and Desktop 360 or Desktop Plain
and Desktop 360, indicate that our manipulation was partly successful. We evaluate the
treatment's effect on the variables of interest with a set of ANOVAs and post-hoc Wilcox
rank-sum tests and find significant differences between treatments for diagnosticity,
enjoyment, and intention to book. We find no significant differences between treatments
in trust-related variables (Fig. 2).

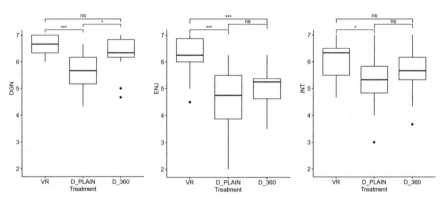

Fig. 2. ANOVA analysis for diagnosticity $F_{(1,43)} = 6.55, p = .014$), enjoyment ($F_{(1,43)} = 22.2$,
$p < .001$), and intention to book ($F_{(1,43)} = 3.72, p = .06$). ***: <.001, **: <.01, *: <.05.

[1] Due to a coding mistake, some items were not displayed to the participants, such that the data
for some constructs was incomplete. This was fixed after the first session, ensuring data quality
for the remaining sessions considered for analysis.

4 Expected Contribution and Future Work

Beyond important learnings for our main study, the results of the pilot study already provide valuable insights. First, we find significant differences between the perceptions of telepresence and diagnosticity among the VR and the Desktop Plain treatment groups. Nevertheless, the results of comparing these groups to the Desktop 360 group remain inconclusive. This indicates that VR and Desktop Plain may constitute two extrema with the Desktop 360 treatment somewhere in between. For the main study, we may consider reducing the set of treatments by omitting the Desktop 360 treatment in the first place. If we find support for the pilot study results suggesting that the effects of Desktop Plain and VR differ significantly, we could further investigate the spectrum between these two extrema by including the Desktop 360 treatment and further treatments like the presentation of 360-degree photos on mobile devices that allow for more interactive navigation (e.g., moving the device to change the perspective).

For the main study, we further expect valuable insights from the analysis of behavioral variables, including the time spent in each room or the areas of visual attention. We also consider enhancing the VR treatment by enabling participants to "walk" through the virtual representation (similar to Google Street View). Another interesting topic is to challenge our results' external validity by validating if the effects remain stable when replacing the Insta360 ONE X photos with 360-degree photos generated with common mobile phone applications. To further substantiate the main study's external validity, the overall experimental design follows a two-staged procedure. First, a booking-phase, in which participants inform themselves about an accommodation in a laboratory environment, and second, a visit-phase, in which participants visit the respective accommodation in the real world. From a theoretical perspective, the Expectation Confirmation Theory [34] may represent a suitable lens for our study's theoretical embedding.

We expect our main study's contribution to be twofold. First, to the best of our knowledge, our study represents the first to assess the effect of 360-degree experience on P2P platform behavior. Thereby, the study may demonstrate that 360-degree photos constitute a new kind of trust-building signal that has not yet received much attention in literature. Furthermore, uncovering mediators between different representation formats and transaction intentions may provide valuable theoretical insights for scholars and platform designers. Second, our results have implications for platform operators and users. Platform operators can use the results to evaluate whether the integration of 360-degree experiences makes sense for their platform and how it affects their users' behavior. Evaluating key economic indicators such as the booking intention shows if more profits can be generated through 360-degree experiences or if it is just a marketing gimmick. On the other hand, platform users can benefit on the providing side (i.e., the host) by leveraging 360-degree photos to acquire more transactions and, eventually, demand higher prices. On the consuming side (i.e., the guests), they may benefit by being able to evaluate offers in a more detailed manner, thereby having a better feeling when entering the transaction and ultimately seeing their expectations more fulfilled when arriving at the accommodation.

References

1. Dann, D., Teubner, T., Weinhardt, C.: Poster child and guinea pig—insights from a structured literature review on Airbnb. Int. J. Contemp. Hosp. Manag. **31** (2019). https://doi.org/10.1108/IJCHM-03-2018-0186
2. AirbnbHell: AirbnbHell: uncensored Airbnb stories from hosts and guests. https://www.airbnbhell.com/. Accessed 15 Feb 2019
3. Gebbia, J.: How Airbnb Designs for Trust (2016)
4. Hawlitschek, F., Teubner, T., Weinhardt, C.: Trust in the sharing economy. Die Unternehmung - Swiss J. Bus. Res. Pract. **70**, 26–44 (2016). https://doi.org/10.5771/0042-059X-2016-1-26
5. Möhlmann, M., Geissinger, A.: Trust in the sharing economy: platform-mediated peer trust. In: Handbook on the Law of the Sharing Economy. Cambridge University Press (2018). https://www.ted.com/talks/joe_gebbia_how_airbnb_designs_for_trust
6. Hesse, M., Dann, D., Braesemann, F., Teubner, T.: Understanding the platform economy: signals, trust, and social interaction. In: HICSS 2020 Proceedings, pp. 1–10 (2020). https://doi.org/10.24251/HICSS.2020.631
7. Yang, S., Xiong, G.: Try it on! contingency effects of virtual fitting rooms. J. Manag. Inf. Syst. **36**, 789–822 (2019). https://doi.org/10.1080/07421222.2019.1628894
8. Flavián, C., Ibáñez-Sánchez, S., Orús, C.: The impact of virtual, augmented and mixed reality technologies on the customer experience. J. Bus. Res. **100**, 547–560 (2019). https://doi.org/10.1016/j.jbusres.2018.10.050
9. Airbnb Community Center: How can I add a 360 Virtual Tour to my listing? https://community.withairbnb.com/t5/Hosting/How-can-I-add-a-360-Virtual-Tour-to-my-listing/td-p/30741/page/7. Accessed 09 Aug 2019
10. Hawlitschek, F., Teubner, T., Gimpel, H.: Understanding the sharing economy - drivers and impediments for participation in peer-to-peer rental. In: Proceedings of the 49th Hawaii International Conference on System Sciences, pp. 4782–4791 (2016). https://doi.org/10.1109/HICSS.2016.593
11. Bowman, D.A., McMahan, R.P.: Virtual reality: how much immersion is enough? Computer (Long. Beach. Calif) **40**, 36–43 (2007). https://doi.org/10.1109/MC.2007.257
12. Slater, M., Wilbur, S.: A framework for immersive virtual environments (FIVE): speculations on the role of presence in virtual environments. Presence Teleoperators Virtual Environ. **6**, 603–616 (1997). https://doi.org/10.1162/pres.1997.6.6.603
13. Suh, L.: The effects of virtual reality on consumer learning: an empirical investigation. MIS Q. **29**, 673 (2005). https://doi.org/10.2307/25148705
14. Guttentag, D.A.: Virtual reality: applications and implications for tourism. Tour. Manag. **31**, 637–651 (2010). https://doi.org/10.1016/j.tourman.2009.07.003
15. Gibson, A., O'Rawe, M.: Virtual reality as a travel promotional tool: insights from a consumer travel fair. In: Jung, T., tom Dieck, M.C. (eds.) Augmented Reality and Virtual Reality. PI, pp. 93–107. Springer, Cham (2018). https://doi.org/10.1007/978-3-319-64027-3_7
16. Schultze, U., Orlikowski, W.J.: Research commentary—virtual worlds: a performative perspective on globally distributed, immersive work. Inf. Syst. Res. **21**, 810–821 (2010). https://doi.org/10.1287/isre.1100.0321
17. Sharda, R., et al.: Foundation for the study of computer-supported collaborative learning requiring immersive presence. J. Manag. Inf. Syst. **20**, 31–64 (2004). https://doi.org/10.1080/07421222.2004.11045780
18. Nah, F.F.-H., Eschenbrenner, B., DeWester, D.: Enhancing brand equity through flow and telepresence: a comparison of 2D and 3D virtual worlds. MIS Q. **35**, 731–747 (2011). https://doi.org/10.2307/23042806

19. Peukert, C., Pfeiffer, J., Meißner, M., Pfeiffer, T., Weinhardt, C.: Shopping in virtual reality stores: the influence of immersion on system adoption. J. Manag. Inf. Syst. **36**, 755–788 (2019). https://doi.org/10.1080/07421222.2019.1628889

20. Jiang, Z., Benbasat, I.: Virtual product experience: effects of visual and functional control of products on perceived diagnosticity and flow in electronic shopping. J. Manag. Inf. Syst. **21**, 111–147 (2005). https://doi.org/10.2139/ssrn.1400827

21. Jiang, Z., Benbasat, I.: The effects of presentation formats and task complexity on online consumers' product understanding. MIS Q. **31**, 475–500 (2007). https://doi.org/10.2307/251 48804

22. Jiang, Z., Benbasat, I.: Investigating the influence of the functional mechanisms of online product presentations. Inf. Syst. Res. **18**, 454–470 (2007). https://doi.org/10.1287/isre.1070. 0124

23. Kim, T., Biocca, F.: Telepresence via television: two dimensions of telepresence may have different connections to memory and persuasion. J. Comput. Commun. **3** (1997). https://doi. org/10.1111/j.1083-6101.1997.tb00073.x

24. Klein, L.R.: Creating virtual product experiences: the role of telepresence. J. Interact. Mark. **17**, 41–55 (2003)

25. Xu, J.D., Benbasat, I., Cenfetelli, R.T.: The nature and consequences of trade-off transparency in the context of recommendation agents. MIS Q. **38**, 379–406 (2014). https://doi.org/10. 25300/MISQ/2014/38.2.03

26. Gefen, D., Karahanna, E., Straub, D.W.: Inexperience and experience with online stores: the importance of TAM and trust. IEEE Trans. Eng. Manag. **50**, 307–321 (2003). https://doi.org/ 10.1109/TEM.2003.817277

27. Koufaris, M.: Applying the technology acceptance model and flow theory to online consumer behavior. Inf. Syst. Res. **13**, 205–223 (2002). https://doi.org/10.1287/isre.13.2.205.83

28. Ghani, J.A., Supnick, R., Rooney, P.: The experience of flow in computer-mediated and in face-to-face groups. In: Proceedings of the International Conference on Information Systems, pp. 229–237 (1991). https://aisel.aisnet.org/icis1991/9

29. Gefen, D., Straub, D.W.: Managing user trust in B2C e-Services. e-Service J. **2**, 7–24 (2003). https://doi.org/10.2979/esj.2003.2.2.7

30. Bock, O., Baetge, I., Nicklisch, A.: hroot: Hamburg registration and organization online tool. Eur. Econ. Rev. **71**, 117–120 (2014). https://doi.org/10.1016/j.euroecorev.2014.07.003

31. Chen, D.L., Schonger, M., Wickens, C.: oTree—an open-source platform for laboratory, online, and field experiments. J. Behav. Exp. Financ. **9**, 88–97 (2016). https://doi.org/10. 1016/j.jbef.2015.12.001

32. Facebook Inc.: React 360

33. Bagozzi, R.P., Yi, Y.: On the evaluation of structural equation models. J. Acad. Mark. Sci. **16**, 74–94 (1988)

34. Oliver, R.L.: A cognitive model of the antecedents and consequences of satisfaction decisions. J. Mark. Res. **17**, 460–469 (1980). https://doi.org/10.1177/002224378001700405

Prominence-for-Data Schemes in Digital Platform Ecosystems: Economic Implications for Platform Bias and Consumer Data Collection

Marc Bourreau[1]([✉]), Janina Hofmann[2], and Jan Krämer[2]

[1] Department of Economics and Social Sciences, Telecom ParisTech, Paris, France
marc.bourreau@telecom-paristech.fr
[2] School of Business, Economics and Information Systems,
University of Passau, Passau, Germany
{janina.hofmann,jan.kraemer}@uni-passau.de

Abstract. It is crucial for content providers (CPs) to appear prominently on dominant online platforms in order to attract consumer demand. Apart from organic search results, content providers can obtain such prominence also in return for a monetary payment to the platform, e.g., in the form of sponsored search results. In this article, we investigate some of the economic consequences, if such payment can also be made with consumers' data instead of money. Since data is non-rivalrous, the economic effects of data sharing for prominence are more complex and differ from paying for prominence. In a game-theoretic model we show that more consumer data will be collected as soon as CPs can obtain prominence on the platform. Whether the platform is more biased under a prominence-for-money scheme or under a prominence-for-data scheme depends on the marginal value of shared (non-exclusive) data. If this value is high, prominence-for-data will yield a higher platform bias, lead to more data collection by the CPs, and ultimately lower consumer surplus. Our results therefore bear important insights for the regulation of data-rich online platforms.

Keywords: B2B data sharing · Prominence on platforms · Consumer data · Data collection

1 Introduction

The European Commission recognizes online platforms as the "key gatekeepers of the internet" (European Commission 2017, p. 7). For instance, 82% of small and medium enterprises (SMEs) state in a survey realized by the European Commission that they are reliant on search engines in order to favor their offered services and products (European Commission 2017). The main purpose of online platforms is to organize and present the available content in a way that facilitates the consumers' discovery process for content (Krämer and Schnurr 2018; Renda 2015). However, this also implies that online platforms have the ability to steer consumers towards a specific content provider (CP) by giving that CP more prominence on the platform. Prominence is commonly granted

© The Author(s), under exclusive license to Springer Nature Switzerland AG 2021
F. Ahlemann et al. (Eds.): WI 2021, LNISO 48, pp. 512–516, 2021.
https://doi.org/10.1007/978-3-030-86800-0_36

in return for monetary payments to the platform (e.g., sponsored search results), usually elicited in the course of a position auction. However, platforms have also been accused to extract data from CPs (e.g., on consumer behavior), which helps them to optimize their business and to increase their data-induced market power. Often platforms induce CPs to share some of their data by offering them benefits on the platform or through access to some additional services (e.g., a social login or fulfillment service). In this paper, we specifically consider the scenario where a CP is offered more prominence on the platform (e.g. by biasing the search results in favor of that CP) in return for access to the CP's data.

This scenario is exemplified by Google's accelerated mobile pages (AMP) project, whose main purpose is to speed up mobile websites by hosting the content directly on Google's services. However, this also has the (likely intended) effect that Google is able to attain the usage statistics of unaffiliated websites that are accessed via AMP. In return, AMP-enabled websites are placed more prominently in the mobile search results, e.g. by showing in the so-called carousel results or simply be being listed higher in the mobile search results page (because they load faster). Thus, in effect, AMP is a means to implement data for prominence (Jun et al. 2019).

This relatively new phenomenon of business-to-business (B2B) data sharing as an alternative currency for CPs to gain prominence on online platforms has not been considered in the economic literature so far, despite its practical and political relevance. B2B data sharing reveals certain characteristics and implications which differ strongly from monetary payment. Most importantly, data is non-rivalrous which means that it can be duplicated effortlessly. This implies that the welfare effects of payments in data are far more complex since welfare is not simply shifted from the sender to the recipient of the payment.

2 Related Literature

We contribute to the emerging literature on digital platform ecosystems, which is reviewed more generally by De Reuver et al. (2018) as well as Hein et al. (2020). More specifically, we consider how the value generated by data is distributed between the platform and the complementors (see Tiwana (2015)) for a review. Our paper especially contributes to two literature branches – payment for prominence and data-driven markets.

First, payment for prominence on online platforms has previously been considered in various contexts – i.e. usability, welfare effects and policy regulations. Receiving prominence on platforms is crucial for content providers to obtain consumer demand (Krämer and Zierke 2020). For instance, Ursu (2018) shows that a higher ranking and thus, more prominence significantly increases the consumers' click through rates. Krämer and Schnurr (2018) review the literature concerning both the strategic and the welfare effects of paying for prominence in order to investigate whether there is a need for a platform neutrality regulation. On the one hand, if CPs compete in prices, sponsored search on rankings results in increased prices and thus, a lower consumer surplus. Although the platform's and the CPs' profits increases, the CPs may end up in a prisoners' dilemma and hence, the total welfare is likely to be smaller under payment for prominence (Armstrong and Zhou 2011; Zhou 2011). On the other hand, if CPs compete in qualities, content providers which offer a higher quality also have an higher willingness-to-pay for prominence on the platform and hence, prominence serves as signals for the CPs' content quality and increases the consumer surplus and the total welfare (Athey and Ellison 2011; Chen and He 2011; de Cornière and Taylor 2020; Krämer and Zierke 2020). Therefore, consumers are not necessarily worse off under a prominence for data scheme. In particular, De Cornière and Taylor (2019) study the effects of biased intermediation for a, with the platform, integrated CP. Depending on whether the seller's and the consumers' payoffs are conflicting or congruent, a bias can be beneficial for consumers.

Second, several theoretical papers model competition in data-driven markets. For instance, Prüfer and Schottmüller (2017) analyze under which conditions duopolies are stable and when monopolies emerge in data-driven markets. De Cornière and Taylor (2020) examine under which conditions a firm with a better (worse) data set generates more (less) consumer utility in data-driven mergers or consumers privacy concerns regarding data disclosure. Gu et al. (2020) as well as Ichihashi (2019) model competition of data intermediaries explicitly. One of their main findings is that the economic profits of a firm are the greater, the more data is exclusively available to that firm. We built on their results and take these findings as input for our model. De Cornière and de Nijs (2016) analyze the impact of disclosing consumer information on product prices. In their model an online platform decides whether to give advertisers access to the platform's consumer information prior bidding on the platform's advertising slots but before learning the consumers' information. While there is a burgeoning literature on digital platforms, payment-for-prominence, and data-driven markets, respectively, to the best of our knowledge, the economic impacts of prominence-for-data schemes have not been studied in the literature so far.

3   Model

We develop a game-theoretic model in order to analyze the economic implications of data-for-prominence schemes in the platform economy. In our model, a monopolistic platform can decide to offer one of two CPs more prominence on the platform (e.g., by biasing the search results) in return for a share of the CP's data. The platform can steer consumers to one of the two CPs by giving it prominence on the platform, e.g., by ranking it systematically higher in the search results everything else being equal. In this case, we will say that the platform has a 'bias'.

Both CPs compete for the consumers' attention, and they offer their content for free, but collect data from the users that consume their content.

The consumers single-home and after entering the platform, they choose which of the two CPs they want to visit. The consumer demand of each CP depends on three main factors. Everything else being equal, consumers prefer the CP which (1) collects less data about them, and (2) which offers content that is closer to the consumer's individual preference; but (3) the CP's demand depends also on the platform's bias.

Moreover, the CPs compete with the platform on the data market (e.g., the market for targeted advertising, selling data analytics services or simply as a data broker) in which they can exploit the consumer data acquired by offering their consumer-facing service. While we abstract from modelling competition in the data market explicitly, we borrow the central insight from explicit models of competition data intermediaries (Gu et al. 2020; Ichihashi 2019) that the economic profits of a firm are the greater, the more of the firm's data is exclusively available to that firm. The platform and the CPs can reap higher profits in the data market, the more user data they possess. However, due to the non-rivalry of data, competition in the data market intensifies as more firms possess the same data sets. This enables us to examine the trade-offs the CPs face when sharing data in return for prominence, what impact the substitutability of the acquired data has on data sharing and the welfare effects.

We compare three scenarios. First, a baseline scenario where the platform can choose to bias the presentation in favor of one of the CPs, but does not receive a compensation in money or data in return. Second, a prominence-for-data scheme, where the platform offers to bias the presentation in favor of one CP in return for a share of that CP's data. Third, a counterfactual prominence-for-money scheme, where the platform offers to bias the presentation in return for a financial payment, but where the platform does not receive additional data from the CP.

We analyze the scenarios by backwards induction in order to determine the subgame-perfect equilibria. Thereby, the timing is as follows: In Stage 1, the platform chooses a prominence offer by selecting a level of bias and, depending on the scenario, a compensation in terms of data or money. In Stage 2, the CPs decide whether to accept the prominence offer. In Stage 3, the CPs choose their data collection level, and in Stage 4, the consumers decide which CP to access and demands are realized.

4 Findings

We find that the platform has no incentive to bias the presentation in favor of one CP, if it does not receive a compensation in return. An unbiased platform maintains the highest possible level of competition for consumers between the CPs, and induces the CPs to limit the amount of data that they collect from consumers. On the one hand, this is good for the platform itself, especially if the platform has already access to large consumer data sets, because it avoids that CPs can collect more data on consumers themselves, which would lower the average value of the platform's data set. On the other hand, an unbiased platform also preserves consumers' privacy in the best possible way, and avoids that some consumers may be steered away from the content that would offer them the highest utility. Therefore, an unbiased platform always provides the highest possible consumer surplus.

Introducing a bias would weaken the competition between CPs and allow them to collect more data from consumers. This in turn, intensifies the competition with the platform on the data market.

However, we can also show that if the platform can be compensated for giving prominence to a CP, either through a prominence-for-money or prominence-for-data scheme, then this provides the platform with additional incentives to introduce a bias. The bias can either be higher under a prominence-for-money scheme or a prominence-for-data scheme, depending in the marginal value of non-exclusive data.

If the value of shared (non-exclusive) data is low, the platform has a larger incentive to bias under a prominence-for-money scheme, and will also make larger profits under this scheme. However, if the marginal value of shared data is high, then a prominence-for-data scheme leads to a higher platform bias, and a higher platform profit. However, for consumers a larger platform bias is always welfare decreasing, because it weakens the competition between CPs, and leads to collection of more data, and hence higher privacy costs for consumers.

References

Armstrong, M., Zhou, J.: Paying for prominence. Econ. J. **121**(556), F368–F395 (2011)

Athey, S., Ellison, G.: Position auctions with consumer search. Q. J. Econ. **126**(3), 1213–1270 (2011)

Chen, Y., He, C.: Paid placement: advertising and search on the internet. Econ. J. **121**(556), F309–F328 (2011)

De Cornière, A., De Nijs, R.: Online advertising and privacy. RAND J. Econ. **47**(1), 48–72 (2016)

De Cornière, A., Taylor, G.: A model of biased intermediation. RAND J. Econ. **50**(4), 854–882 (2019)

De Cornière, A., Taylor, G.: Data and competition: a general framework with applications to mergers, market structure, and privacy policy. In: CEPR Discussion Paper, DP14446 (2020)

De Reuver, M., Sørensen, C., Basole, R.C.: The digital platform: a research agenda. J. Inf. Technol. **33**(2), 124–135 (2018)

European Commission: Communication from the commission on the mid-term review on the implementation of the digital single market strategy: A Connected Digital Single Market for All. COM (2017) 228, European Commission (2017)

Gu, Y., Madio, L., Reggiani, C.: Data brokers co-opetition. Working paper (2020)

Hein, A., et al.: Digital platform ecosystems. Electron Mark. **30**, 87–89 (2020)

Ichihashi, S.: Non-competing data intermediaries. Working paper (2019)

Jun, B., Bustamante, F.E., Whang, S.Y., Bischof, Z.S.: AMP up your mobile web experience: characterizing the impact of Google's accelerated mobile project. In: The 25th Annual International Conference on Mobile Computing and Networking, pp. 1–14 (2019)

Krämer J., Zierke O.: Paying for prominence: the effect of sponsored rankings on the incentives to invest in the quality of free content on dominant online platforms (2020)

Krämer, J., Schnurr, D.: Is there a need for platform neutrality regulation in the EU? Telecommun. Pol. **42**, 514–529 (2018)

Prüfer, J., Schottmüller, C.: Competing with big data. TILEC Discussion Paper, vol. 2017-006, CentER Discussion Paper, vol. 2017-007. (2017)

Renda: Antitrust, regulation and the neutrality trap: A plea for a smart, evidence-based internet policy (2015)

Tiwana, A.: Evolutionary competition in platform ecosystems. Inf. Syst. Res. **26**, 266–281 (2015)

Ursu, R.M., Aryotejo, G., Mufadhol, M.: The power of rankings: quantifying the effect of rankings on online consumer search and purchase decisions. Mark. Sci. **37**, 530–552 (2018)

Zhou, J.: Ordered search in differentiated markets. Int. J. Ind. Organ. **29**(2), 253–262 (2011)

IT Strategy, Management and Transformation

Introduction to the WI2021 Track: IT Strategy, Management and Transformation

Nils Urbach[1] and Paul Drews[2]

[1] FIM Research Center, Project Group BISE of Fraunhofer FIT,
Frankfurt University of Applied Sciences, Frankfurt, Germany
nils.urbach@fim-rc.de
[2] Leuphana University of Lüneburg, Institute of Information Systems,
Lüneburg, Germany
paul.drews@leuphana.de

1 Track Description

In the digital age, new developments in digital technologies lead to significant changes in the economy and society. A key feature of a digitized corporate world is that digital technologies are not only used to support business processes, but are increasingly becoming an inherent part of products, services and business models. While information technology has been an important production factor for most companies for a long time, digital innovations are now leading to a digital transformation of many industries [1]. On the one hand, digital business model innovations offer companies the opportunity to conquer established and new markets with fresh ideas. On the other hand, many companies are increasingly exposed to the risk of falling victim to the disruptive effects of digitalization.

In this context, the development and implementation of IT strategies and the management of the IT function are becoming more and more critical tasks for the company as a whole. Corporate IT has so far concentrated on translating the requirements of the business departments into high-quality IT services as effectively as possible and on managing operations. Today, the corporate IT function needs to engage in shaping the entire company [2]. As part of this transformation, the IT function has to deal with the requirements of customers and partners of the company, evaluate and introduce IT innovations and adapt the IT landscape to the changing needs. The development and implementation of innovative services increasingly require the integration of business and IT. In addition to participating in innovation processes, traditional IT management tasks are also changing: Developments such as cloud computing simplify the outsourcing of elements of the IT value chain.

These developments cause a gradual change in the roles and skills of today's IT functions, which is also reflected in changed structures, processes, methods and governance mechanisms [3]. Accordingly, many new and interesting questions arise on the social, organizational, technical and economic aspects of strategic IT management and organizational change. Previous knowledge as well as established models and theories of information systems should be questioned and advanced against the background of these developments.

2   Research Articles

We were happy to receive 29 paper submissions (23 full papers, 6 short papers) in total to our track. After a thorough review process, we selected the 7 most promising research articles for publication in the conference proceedings and presentation at the conference, resulting in an overall acceptance rate of about 24%.

The first paper by Fuchs et al. [4] analyzes organizational feedback exchange with an agent-based simulation model. The study shows that feedback length stays in an inverted U-shape relationship with ROI. Contrarily, feedback frequency is negatively correlated with ROI.

The second paper by Gierlich [5] aims at identifying the most important challenges organizational leaders are facing in the coming years regarding novel technologies as well as the strategies to overcome them by conducting a Delphi study and follow-up interviews. The findings emphasize the increasing role of employee empowerment, that organizational change is essential to overcome the challenges, and leadership-related IS can facilitate this transformation.

The third paper by Godefroid et al. [6] presents a systematic literature on the role of lightweight IT in times of shadow IT and IT consumerization. In their study, the authors assess pertinent publications regarding their contribution to the conceptualization of the interplay of heavyweight and lightweight IT and the benefits and corresponding risks of lightweight IT in practice.

The fourth paper by Gussek et al. [7] concentrates on the topic of obsolescence in IT work. The authors conducted a systematic literature review. Based on the synthesis of 115 research papers, causes for obsolescence, consequences of obsolescence, and countermeasures against obsolescence are presented as the three central dimensions of the topic.

The fifth paper by Haskamp et al. [8] presents an empirical analysis of requirements for performance measurement systems in digital innovation units (DIU). The study contributes to evaluating the performance of DIU more adequately and, thus, improving decision-making.

The sixth paper by Kurtz et al. [9] presents an empirical investigation of digital business strategy and firm performance based on a panel fixed effect regression. As a key result, they find that not all digital business strategy types achieve to result in a positive impact.

References

1. Legner, C., et al.: Digitalization: opportunity and challenge for the business and information systems engineering community. Bus. Inf. Syst. Eng. (bise) 59, 301–308 (2017). https://doi.org/10.1007/s12599-017-0484-2
2. Urbach, N., Drews, P., Ross, J.: Digital business transformation and the changing role of the IT function. MIS Q. Executive 16, ii–iv (2017)
3. Urbach, N., et al.: The Impact of digitalization on the IT department. Bus. Inf. Syst. En. (BISE) **61**, 123–131 (2019)

4. Fuchs, S., Rietsche, R., Aier, S., Rivera, M.: Is more always better? Simulating feedback exchange in organizations. In: Proceedings of the 16th International Conference on Wirtschaftsinformatik (WI 2021), Essen, Germany (2021)

5. Gierlich, M.: Designing future IS for Leadership: overcoming challenges in leadership with suitable IS. In: Proceedings of the 16th International Conference on Wirtschaftsinformatik (WI 2021), Essen, Germany (2021)

6. Godefroid, M., Plattfaut, R., Niehaves, B.: IT outside of the IT department: reviewing lightweight IT in times of Shadow IT and IT consumerization. In: Proceedings of the 16th International Conference on Wirtschaftsinformatik (WI 2021), Essen, Germany (2021)

7. Gussek, L., Schned, L., Wiesche, M.: Obsolescence in IT work: causes, consequences and counter-measures. In: Proceedings of the 16th International Conference on Wirtschaftsinformatik (WI 2021), Essen, Germany (2021)

8. Haskamp, T., Lorson, A., de Paula, D., Uebernickel, F.: Bridging the gap - an analysis of requirements for performance measurement systems in digital innovation units. In: Proceedings of the 16th International Conference on Wirtschaftsinformatik (WI 2021), Essen, Germany (2021)

9. Kurtz, H., Hanelt, A., Firk, S.: Digital business strategy and firm performance - an empirical investigation. In: Proceedings of the 16th International Conference on Wirtschaftsinformatik (WI 2021), Essen, Germany (2021)

Is More Always Better? Simulating Feedback Exchange in Organizations

Sacha Fuchs[1][(✉)], Roman Rietsche[1], Stephan Aier[1], and Michael Rivera[2]

[1] Institute of Information Management, University of St. Gallen, St. Gallen, Switzerland
{sacha.fuchs,roman.rietsche,stephan.aier}@unisg.ch
[2] Department of Strategic Management, Temple University, Philadelphia, PA, USA
rivera@temple.edu

Abstract. More and more employees request feedback from their organizations to develop and learn. This is reflected by a growing number of digital feedback apps which facilitate high-frequency feedback exchange. However, the effect of feedback has hardly been studied on an organizational level due to complexity. Therefore, we strive to analyze organizational feedback exchange with an agent-based simulation model. Concretely, we study the effect of feedback length and feedback frequency on the organizational return on investment (ROI) of feedback exchange. Our study shows that feedback length stays in an inverted U-shape relationship with ROI. Contrarily, feedback frequency is negatively correlated with ROI. When analyzed jointly, two sweet spots arise: one for medium-length, frequent feedback, and the other, for longer infrequent feedback.

Keywords: Organizational feedback exchange · Feedback app · Return on investment · Simulation · Agent-based modeling

1 Introduction

Employees and the generation Y request more and more feedback from their managers [1]. Additionally, they demand instant responses which they are used to from social media platforms [1]. This call for new forms of feedback is clearly reflected by the increasing number of digital feedback apps that facilitate more frequent feedback exchange [2]. For example, workstream collaboration solutions like Slack, Skype, MS Teams or standalone feedback apps like DevelapMe0F[1], Lattice1F[2], 15Five2F[3], offer a wide array of mechanisms that can be used to facilitate feedback in organizations [3].

But why are organizations concerned with providing feedback to their employees? Building upon the insight that employees can be a key component of competitive advantage [4], the improvement of existing work practices is of high relevance [5]. One method for helping employees to improve their work practices, is constructive and timely feedback. The existing body of knowledge highlights the strategic value of feedback as an

---

[1] https://www.develapme.com/.
[2] https://lattice.com/.
[3] https://www.15five.com/.

F. Ahlemann et al. (Eds.): WI 2021, LNISO 48, pp. 521–536, 2021.
https://doi.org/10.1007/978-3-030-86800-0_37

essential driver of employee motivation, learning and development [6, 7]. Feedback helps improve employees' performance, when they anticipate, seek, receive, process, react to, and finally use feedback to adjust their practices [8].

However, the effectiveness of feedback is dependent on its structure and content as it determines the receivers reaction [9]. A feedback message comprises the content [10], its timing [11] and the form of delivery [12]. The study at hand focuses on two of those components in the given context of digital feedback apps. First, the feedback content which is at the core of any feedback. Specific feedback helps employees improve, but if the message is too long, employees might ignore it [11]. Therefore, in this study we analyze the *feedback length* as a proxy for several content dimensions. Second, we explore the effect of *feedback frequency,* which is a highly discussed topic in literature and practice. In the past feedback was seen as an annual management process such as managers provide feedback to their employees once-a-year [13]. However, this approach has been criticized for a long time [2, 14, 15] as in "the world isn't really on an annual cycle anymore for anything" [16].

The trend of more and more feedback has hardly been challenged in the literature, since measuring this effect on an organizational level is highly complex and problematic as components of the feedback process are interdependent and depend on organizational characteristics [9]. Hence, the question arises as how much feedback is necessary and beneficial for organizations. Previous studies were predominantly focused on an individual level of analysis to build a comprehensive understanding around the concept of feedback. These efforts have led to an extensive body of literature that explains the processes, components, and advantages of feedback. For example, feedback characteristics [9], behavior reactions to feedback [6, 17, 18] and feedback efficiency [14].

In fact, the effects of feedback on an organizational level could only be studied within the constraints of empirical settings. However, the strong conceptual basis allows us to overcome those constraints and to explore the organizational effects of feedback through well-grounded computer simulation experiments. Specifically, agent-based modeling can be used to model emergent phenomena stemming from interactions among individuals [19]. This allows us to generate data on the organizational level from empirical insights gathered on the individual level. For that purpose, we strive for answering the following research question: What is the influence of feedback length and feedback frequency on organizational return of investment (ROI)?

We contribute to theory in several ways. First, we provide descriptive knowledge by shedding light on the aggregation logic of existing individual-level feedback concepts on the organizational level. Second, we are, best to our knowledge, the first studying the interrelationship of feedback length and feedback frequency on an organizational level analysis. Third, we propose that there is a combined sweet spot of rather short and frequent feedbacks, delivered via a feedback app, for maximizing the impact of feedback on the organizational ROI.

We contribute to practice by providing insights for the development of feedback trainings for managers. Furthermore, our study allows developers of feedback apps to derive design features from our findings. For example, an app may help feedback givers in achieving the optimal length for their message or send a reminder when the next feedback is due. These efforts enable organizations to enhance the ROI of their feedback exchange and ultimately build competitive advantage.

2 Conceptual Foundation

Our simulation model builds upon three research disciplines. First, feedback as a part of organizational science. Second, the evaluation of the ROI of corporate projects builds upon insights from accounting and finance. Third, research on socio-technical interactions with digital artifacts like feedback apps belong to the realm of information systems research.

2.1 Definition of Feedback

Feedback in the traditional world was conceptualized as information provided by an agent (e.g., manager, colleague, book) regarding aspects of one's performance or understanding. Thus, feedback is a "consequence" of performance [20]. Hence, the purpose of feedback is to assess a state and evaluate its strengths and weaknesses once at the end of the carried-out task [21]. Feedback was not seen as something given along the learning process to incrementally improve performance and support self-reflection over time [22]. Thus, this definition does not explicitly contain the idea that feedback can have multiple purposes, such as motivation, initiation of self-regulated processes or provision of suggestions for improvement in the future. The conceptualization of the purpose of feedback and how it should be provided has changed. Feedback is no longer seen as a one-time event but rather as a process in which employees have an active role to play [23]. Consequently, more recent definitions conceptualize feedback as a process through which employees make sense of information from various sources and use it to enhance their work or learning strategies. Hence, this conception goes beyond notions that feedback is principally about managers or human resources informing employees about strengths, weaknesses and how to improve, but it rather emphasizes the centrality of the employee's role in sense-making and processing the comments to improve subsequent work.

There is a broad body of research around feedback characteristics. For example, scholars distinguish between formal and informal feedback [9]. Furthermore, feedback differs for tasks which require skill or effort [24] and creativity or diligence [25]. Moreover, performance depends on the amount of ambiguity and uncertainty surrounding a particular task [26].

While feedback can be applied in many areas of life, we study it in the context of organizations. Organizations can shape their employees feedback orientation by fostering a feedback culture [8]. Furthermore, organizational feedback develops from a task-based approach to an organizational practice [5]. Therefore, several authors argue that feedback should be studied as a complex product of organizational culture [8, 9, 27]. One of the reasons organizations provide feedback to their employees to gain competitive advantage [5]. While this shows that feedback can bring positive returns if it is applied correctly, it still generates cost. Concretely, providing, reading, and reflecting upon feedback requires time resources from employees which could be used for other productive tasks. However, investments in human capital should be analyzed like any other corporate investment [28]. For this, the measure of ROI can be used as a widely accepted metric throughout business [28]. Phillips [29] proposes a calculation which sets net returns in relation to total investment cost. However, while the value of the investments in human resources can often be determined easily, the benefits are sometimes hard to monetize [30].

2.2 Characteristics of a Feedback Message in the Context of Feedback Apps

Feedback can either be provided verbally or in written form. Verbal feedback is mostly delivered face-to-face, which includes body language and intonation [31]. In contrast, written feedback is rather delayed and emotions are often hidden between the lines [32]. To facilitate written feedback, organizations have increasingly adopted feedback apps [33]. Feedback apps are digital work tools, enabling written feedback exchange [2, 33]. Such technological artifacts make it easier for organizations to provide the increased feedback frequency demanded by employees [34].

The length of a feedback is highly correlated with its specificity [34]. Therefore, insights about the relationship between specificity and performance can assumed to be existent for feedback length. While high specificity leads to enhanced performance [35], too lengthy feedbacks might not get read at all [11]. Especially, when feedback is provided frequently, high specificity is not effective [35]. This implies a sweet spot which optimizes specificity and makes sure that the message will be read.

Today's working world is characterized by a dynamically changing environment. Therefore, annual reviews do not fit in anymore [2]. Consequently, large international organizations such as Accenture, Adobe, Goldman Sachs or SAP implement regular check-ins and instant feedback tools [14, 15]. Similarly, scholars suggest that feedback should be provided more often and in an informal way. In particular, the feedback process should follow a continuous nature [36]. Frequent feedback is more effective in improving employee performance than infrequent feedback [35]. However, Holderness, Olsen and Thornock [37] claim that frequent feedback is only able to improve performance when employees consent to receiving high-frequency feedback. Hence, feedback frequency has a curvilinear, inverted-U relationship with task performance [38]. But if feedback is provided less frequently, it has to be more detailed to be effective [39]. Furthermore, the frequency base-rate depends on the underlying task that is performed by employees [39].

3 Research Method

3.1 Simulation

The basic idea behind the methodology of computer simulation is mimicking real-word constructs with software code [40]. To achieve this, researchers program connections and interactions between simplified theoretical concepts. This allows them to run experiments with various parameter settings and analyze different outcomes [41]. Agent-based modelling is one such simulation method, which enables quantitative theory development. As the name suggests, it consists of agents, which act upon the given situation by pre-defined behavior rules [19]. This method is particularly useful in conducting 'what-if' analyses by modifying inputs or processes [42]. Consequently, organizational science scholars have accepted the methodology and take advantage of simulation models in their research [43–45].

In developing the agent-based simulation model, this study follows the process proposed by Sargent [41, 45, 46]. First, the theoretical foundation is synthesized from the existing body of literature. These insights are used to build a conceptual model. Based on this conceptual model, the simulation is being implemented. This step includes the calibration and validation of the model. Lastly, experiments with the built model are conducted and the resulting data is being analyzed.

3.2   Conceptual Model Development

Next to the theoretical foundations presented in chapter two, the organizational context plays an important role for developing the simulation. Therefore, we collected and analyzed data in a US-bank's call center to build an empirical foundation for the simulation model. For this, we introduced a designated feedback app which was built into the agents' workflow. Whenever a ticket was resolved, the manager provided feedback. While it was not mandatory to use the app, the strong integration built a favorable foundation. Our data contains 4'076 feedbacks collected over the period of one year. Feedback exchange happened between 131 unique givers and 181 unique receivers.

This organizational setting makes sense, as the main task of call center agent is to solve tickets. First, solving a ticket can easily be priced by multiplying the required time with the hourly wage of a call center agent. This is often a hurdle in measuring return in organizational settings. Second, this task can be measured and recorded easily. Third, task outcomes are comparable among employees. This allows managers to identify inefficiencies and build feedback recommendations upon these insights. In conclusion, our organizational setting features a task which requires effort and diligence, and managers give informal feedback on it.

Concretely, three simulation model parameters stem from this data. First, to evaluate individual work performance, we use the daily number of solved tickets per call center agent. Second, we have information about the length of feedback messages measured in words. Third, the number of days between feedback interactions gives us the feedback frequency. We analyzed the distribution of these three measures with a kernel density estimation. From this, we derived a function that allows the simulation model to sample data that follow the empirical distribution. By feeding empirical data into the simulation model, our results can be grounded in a more realistic scenario, which safeguards the validity of simulation results.

3.3   Simulation Development and Validation

To develop the simulation model, this study utilizes NetLogo [47], a software tool specifically developed for agent-based modelling. This tool has been successfully utilized in previous studies [42] and is able to simulate organizational behavior [48].

Agents: The simulation consists of two types of agents. First, managers who are responsible of several subordinates and provide feedback to them. Second, call center agents solving support tickets. In doing so, they receive feedback from their managers.

Interactions: In the beginning of the simulation, all agents are created and configured according to model inputs. Managers are responsible to provide feedback to their assigned employees. This happens after a certain time interval, which is sampled from the empirical model described previously. For this job, they must perform two tasks. First, they need to monitor an employee's work. Second, they need to write the feedback message. Both tasks require a time investment from managers. The monitoring time is randomly drawn, and the writing time is calculated based on the number of words of a feedback and the average duration to write a word. When an employee receives a feedback, the model triggers three actions. First, the employee reads the feedback. Second, she needs to reflect upon the content [18]. Third, she reacts to the feedback [9]. The first two require a time investment by the employee, which follow the same logic as the writing and monitoring of the manager. The reaction is modeled according to the following logic. The first decision is whether the employee accepts the feedback [9]. If she accepts it, she decides whether she is willing to change or not [17]. The former leads to an improved performance in the form of an increased ticket solving speed, the latter implies an unchanged working speed. However, if the employee does not accept the feedback in the first place, she faces another decision. She can either react negatively and reduce her performance or ignore the message and stay at the same output level [17]. Employees' reactions are randomly assigned to them at the beginning of a simulation run. Afterwards, they change it based on assigned probabilities, which reflect different personalities and business events.

After the employee reacted to the feedback, the manager again reacts to the employee's behavior. If the manager recognizes that the employee is changing his or her behavior (both negatively or positively), increases the frequency and length of the feedback message. This implies a higher feedback perceived quality, which in turn leads to improved outcomes [9]. Table 1 summarizes the most important model parameters.

Organizational Setting: We set the number of employees in the simulation in such a way, that they represent a call center team. This allows us to optimize simulation speed while capturing sufficient interactions among workers. Furthermore, the obtained results can be scaled for larger organizations. To control the time dimensions, we set the number of working hours per day (8) and the working days per year (261) to US-standards. As we run the simulation for three years, this translates to 783 ticks.

To account for differences in the value of time for managers and employees, we set an individual hourly wage for each agent type. The validity of the simulation model was analyzed by applying three techniques [46]. First, internal validity tests ensure the consistency of results across different simulation runs with the same setting. The model was calibrated until there was low enough variance in the results across multiple simulation runs. However, some variance is expected, as the various random variables lead to different starting points. Second, degeneracy tests allowed us to set ranges for model parameters. For example, time ranges over more than five years do not produce

Table 1. Model parameters

Parameter	Description	Default Value	Justification
Ticket solving time	The amount of time it takes an employee to solve a ticket	Dist. from feedback app	Empirical data
Probability of behavior change per round	Determines the likelihood that an employee changes his behavior from the one a feedback back	Personality type: 1: 10% 2: 25% 3: 50%	Parameter testing
Feedback acceptance	Whether or not an employee accepts a feedback	TRUE or FALSE according to behavior change	[9]
Willingness to change	Whether or not an employee is willing to change	TRUE or FALSE according to behavior change	[9]
Negative reaction	Whether or not an employee shows a negative reaction	TRUE or FALSE according to behavior change	[49]
Feedback length	Length of the feedback message in words	Dist. from feedback app	Empirical data
Feedback frequency	The number of days between consecutive feedback	Dist. from feedback app	Empirical data
Positive change	Base rate of improvement (scaled with length, frequency and learning effect)	0.5	Empirical data
Negative change	Performance reduction occurring when employee reacts negatively	0.001	Parameter testing
Learning effect	Scales the improvement with a learning effect	Learning speed follows a sigmoid-curve	[50]
Feedback giver reaction	How a feedback giver reacts to recipient's behavior after receiving feedback	For positive and negative reactions increased frequency and length	[51]

(continued)

Table 1. (*continued*)

Parameter	Description	Default Value	Justification
Writing time per word	How long it takes to write a word (seconds)	Random: 1.5–4	Based on average of adults
Monitoring time	Time to check employee's work (minutes)	Random: 4–10	Parameter tests
Reading time per word	How long it takes to read a word (seconds)	Random: 0.4–1	Based on average of adults
Reflection time	Reflect upon the feedback content (minutes)	Random: 2–10	Parameter tests

valid results as the mechanisms of the simulated organization are different in the long run. Similarly, not all employees will ever be willing to change their behavior. Lastly, through sensitivity analysis the effects of the independent variables could be validated. We did this by changing one independent variable at the time ceteris paribus.

3.4   Simulation Experiments

All three experiments measure ROI of feedback exchange in the simulated organization. For this, we analyze the simulation results as follows. The measure of return is based on the additional ticket volume the agents solved thanks to the feedback they received. This volume is multiplied with the average ticket solving time. To calculate returns and investments in the same unit, the total time is multiplied by the wage of call center agents. The organization's feedback cost consists of the agent's and manager's time investments as specified in the previous section multiplied with each agent type's wage. This allows us to calculate ROI by subtracting the total costs from the total gains to receive the return and then dividing the result with the total costs.

Table 2. Simulation experiments (each simulation run comprised 783 time steps)

Experiments	Setup
Feedback length	We shifted the distribution of the feedback length from 0 to 800 words in steps of 10 and ran the simulation 50 times per setting. Thus, the analyses of individual effects were based on $n = 4,050 = 81 \times 50$ simulation runs. The feedback frequency was set to the baseline of the empiric data
Feedback frequency	We shifted the distribution of the feedback frequency from 0 to 125 in steps of 1 and ran the simulation 50 times per setting. Thus, the analyses of individual effects were based on $n = 6,300 = 126 \times 50$ simulation runs. The feedback length was set to the baseline of the empiric data

(*continued*)

Table 2. (*continued*)

Experiments	Setup
Joint effects	We shifted the distribution of the feedback length and feedback frequency simultaneously. The length from 0 to 800 in steps of 20 and the frequency from 0 to 125 in steps of 5. Then, we ran the simulation 30 times per setting. Thus, the analyses of individual effects were based on $n = 31{,}980 = 41 \times 26 \times 30$ simulation runs

This measure represents a ratio that shows how many times a monetary unit invested in feedback exchange is rising financial return from it.

The first experiment varies the independent variable feedback length. To do so, we move the distribution of the kernel density estimation. Therefore, the average sample will be either lower or higher than in the empirical distribution. This allows us to vary the length of feedback messages from managers. Second, we vary the frequency of the feedbacks by again moving the empirical distribution. Finally, we vary both variables simultaneously to study combined effects. Table 2 presents an overview of our experiments.

4 Simulation Results

To analyze the data generated by our simulation experiments, we conducted regression analyses. Hereby, the analysis of our R^2-values (Tables 3, 4 and 5) revealed that non-linear models were significantly better in explaining the relationship between our independent variables and ROI. Therefore, we present the results of our polynomial regression analysis. Due to the highly different magnitude of the independent variables and the dependent variable, coefficients are rather small. While we could normalize independent variables to scale the ratio, we prefer the intuitiveness of the operationalization of feedback length through the number of words and feedback frequency through the amount of days between feedbacks. Furthermore, even small changes in ROI have a significant impact for large organizations.

4.1 Individual Effects of Feedback Length

Figure 1 reveals a relationship between feedback length and ROI, which follows an inverted U-shape. Table 3 shows that the length of feedback messages has a significant (all parameters $p < 0.001$) impact on the ROI of feedback in organizations ($R^2 = 0.215$). Very short feedbacks (0–150 words) provide less return than medium ones (150–450 words). But the longer a feedback message is written, the lower the ROI gets after a tipping point. Hence, the ideal feedback length is medium.

Table 3. Regression models for the individual effects of feedback length

Model	Linear	Quadratic	Cubic
Intercept	1.098***	−0.087***	−0.035
FB-Length	0.0001	0.016***	0.024***
FB-Length^2		−2.279e−05***	−5.908e−05***
FB-Length^3			3.456e−08***
R^2	0.000	0.215	0.241
F-Statistic	4.627	4906	3807
AIC	1.830e+05	1.744e+05	1.731e+05

Notes: * $p < 0.01$; ** $p < 0.005$; *** $p < 0.001$

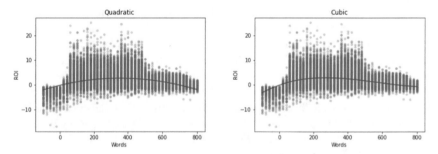

Fig. 1. Individual effects of feedback length

4.2 Individual Effects of Feedback Frequency

While the cubic model provides a better fit for the feedback length, Fig. 2 reveals that for feedback frequency, the quadratic and cubic model are very similar. Both show a falling ROI for larger delays between feedbacks. Therefore, Table 4 indicates that ROI is highest when organizations provide frequent feedback ($R^2 = 0.206$).

4.3 Joint Effects of Feedback Length and Feedback Frequency

The quadratic model (Table 5) suggests that frequent (0–21 days), medium-length feedback boosts the highest ROI potential for organizations ($R^2 = 0.343$). The effect of

Table 4. Regression models for the individual effects of feedback frequency

Model	Linear	Quadratic	Cubic
Intercept	1.313***	2.124***	2.253***
FB-Frequency	−0.023***	−0.063***	−0.075***
FB-Frequency^2		0.0003***	0.0006***
FB-Frequency^3			−1.361e-06
R^2	0.173	0.206	0.207
F-Statistic	1320	819.2	548.2
AIC	2.565e+04	2.540e+04	2.539e+04

Notes: * $p < 0.01$; ** $p < 0.005$; *** $p < 0.001$

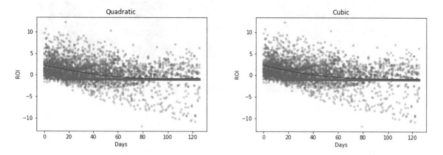

Fig. 2. Individual effects of feedback frequency

Table 5. Regression models for the joint effects of feedback length & frequency

Model	Linear	Quadratic	Cubic
Intercept	5.068***	5.938***	4.942***
FB-Length	−0.004***	0.003***	0.024***
FB-Length^2		−1.333e−05***	−7.494e−05***
FB-Length^3			4.631e-08***
FB-Frequency	−0.032***	−0.100***	−0.133***
FB-Frequency^2		0.0004***	0.0009***
FB-Frequency^3			−1.342e−06***
Length × Frequency		5.245e−05***	5.189e−05***
Length^2 × Frequency			9.643e−08***
Length × Frequency^2			−6.127e−07***
R^2	0.249	0.343	0.375
F-Statistic	5299	3345	2135
AIC	1.532e+05	1.489e+05	1.473e+05

Notes: * $p < 0.01$; ** $p < 0.005$; *** $p < 0.001$

feedback length is much stronger in shorter frequencies than for longer time-periods between feedbacks. The cubic model reveals another level of complexity. While the sweet spot is also for medium-length, frequent feedback, there is another high-point for infrequent feedback which is long (Fig. 3). Furthermore, the frequency shows a higher sensitivity than in the quadratic model. The low point is represented by long feedbacks that are sent very frequently.

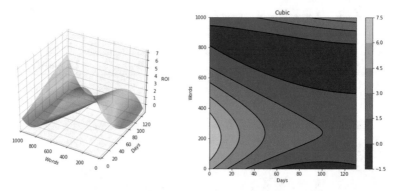

Fig. 3. Joint effects of feedback length & frequency

5 Discussion

In the past feedback was seen as an annual management process in which managers provide feedback to their employees for the entire year. However, the world isn't really on an annual cycle anymore for anything [16]. Employees and the generation Y request to receive more and timely feedback from their managers. Nevertheless, the trend of more and more feedback has hardly been challenged in the literature, since measuring this effect on an organizational level is highly complex and problematic. Hence, the question arises as how much feedback is necessary and beneficial for organizations. Therefore, we explored the organizational effects of feedback through well-grounded computer simulation experiments in a specific task setting. This limits the generalizability of our results to a subset of tasks and organizations.

Our study presents several findings. First, we show that the feedback length has a curve-linear relationship with ROI of feedback exchange that follows an inverse U-shape. This implies that there is a sweet spot for feedback length when optimizing ROI. While very short messages do not suffice in delivering enough specificity, too long feedbacks might not get read or overwhelm recipients. This is consistent with previous literature [39]. However, our findings extend the current knowledge as they measure the impact not only on performance but on ROI. This is important because the performance gain must be financially justified [28].

Second, feedback frequency has a negative relationship with ROI. The less frequent employees get feedback, the lower is the return for the organization. While the cost is low, the performance is not high either. This implies that if feedback cannot be provided frequently, the resources might not be worthwhile, and the investment should be rejected. Nevertheless, some of our findings are not consistent with literature. While Casas-Arce et al. [39] describe an inverted U-shape relationship between frequency and performance, we present a falling relationship. However, we analyze another dependent variable which is conceptualized as ROI. Furthermore, Casas-Arce et al. [39] acknowledged that the relationship may alter for different tasks.

Third, we analyzed the joint effects of feedback length and feedback frequency. Our analysis shows that when the days between consecutive feedbacks are low, the length of the feedback has a large effect. If the frequency is smaller, the impact of a change in length is much lower. Moreover, Fig. 3 shows two optimal points. One represents frequent, medium-length feedback. The other less frequent, but long feedback. This might seem contradictory as we have previously shown a negative relationship between ROI and feedback frequency when analyzed isolated. However, this second optimum can be understood as very resource effective. Because feedback is not given often, the associated costs are low. Hence, smaller improvements still have a positive ROI.

This study's findings have several theoretical and practical implications. First, it extends existing literature by studying individual level effects of feedback exchange on the organizational level. This allows us to challenge the assumption that more feedback is always better. Our study shows that organizations must analyze their investments in feedback apps to gain the expected benefits. Second, while past research revealed interactions of feedback length and feedback frequency on the individual level, our study is, best to our knowledge, the first to shed a light on joint effects of these two feedback characteristics. Third, we revealed that for maximizing ROI, organizations must motivate their employees to write rather short feedback and provide it frequently. While it requires more time resources than annual feedbacks, the return makes the investment worthwhile.

We contribute to practice in three ways. g Second, app developers can derive design choices from our insights. For example, a feedback app can highlight whether a feedback message contains enough words while it is written. Additionally, managers could receive push messages when the next feedback for an employee is due. Third, managers must closely analyze organizational feedback exchange and adjust their strategy by analyzing the ROI of their efforts. Our insights provide them guidance in doing so.

6 Conclusion and Limitations

No study comes without limitations. First, to operationalize the ROI we selected ticket solving speed as measure of return. While this allows us to overcome the hurdle of monetizing a cultural investment [30], we ignore other important factors. For example, the quality of the solved ticket plays an equally important role for long-term success. Further studies could analyze the ROI with a focus on quality. Second, as any model we had to abstract from the conceptual foundations. For instance, our simulation model assumes that all employees stay with the organization. This is not true in practice and might have an impact on ROI as organizations invest in resources they will not possess in the future and therefore, cannot profit from arising competitive advantages. Third, our results are only valid for a certain type of task. Solving tickets is a relatively easy and repetitive task. In contrast, tasks such as drug discovery, creative work or legal counselling are more complex and do not follow the same logic. Therefore, further studies need to analyze the impact of task type on the ROI of feedback.

In conclusion, our findings have significant implications for both theory and practice. We show that organizations can optimize ROI from feedback exchange by varying the feedback length and frequency. While feedback length shows an inverted U-shape relationship with ROI, feedback frequency is negatively correlated. When analyzed jointly, medium-length, frequent feedback and infrequent, longer feedback represent ROI sweet spots.

References

1. Barth, L.: Wie Unternehmen eine attraktive, aber anspruchsvolle neue Generation von Potenzialträgern begeistern und binden können. https://www.egonzehnder.com/de/insight/werben-um-die-generation-y
2. Levy, P.E., Tseng, S.T., Rosen, C.C., Lueke, S.B.: Performance management: a marriage between practice and science – Just Say "I do". In: Buckley, M.R., Wheeler, R.A., Halbesleben, R.B.J. (eds.) Research in Personnel and Human Resources Management, pp. 155–213. Emerald Publishing Limited (2017)
3. Lechler, R., Stoeckli, E., Rietsche, R., Uebernickel, F.: Looking beneath the tip of the iceberg: the two-sided nature of chatbots and their roles for digital feedback exchange. In: Proceedings of the 27th European Conference on Information Systems (ECIS 2019) (ed.) (2019)
4. Carmeli, A., Weisberg, J.: Exploring turnover intentions among three professional groups of employees. Hum. Resour. Dev. Int. **9**, 191–206 (2006)
5. Baker, N.: Employee feedback technologies in the human performance system. Hum. Resour. Dev. Int. **13**, 477–485 (2010)
6. Ilgen, D.R., Fisher, C.D., Taylor, M.S.: Consequences of individual feedback on behavior in organizations. J. Appl. Psychol. **64**, 349–371 (1979)
7. Ilgen, D.R., Barnes-Farrell, J.L., McKellin, D.B.: Performance appraisal process research in the 1980s: what has it contributed to appraisals in use? Organ. Behav. Hum. Decis. Process. **54**, 321–368 (1993)
8. London, M., Smither, J.W.: Feedback orientation, feedback culture, and the longitudinal performance management process. Hum. Resour. Manag. Rev. **12**, 81–100 (2002)
9. Mulder, R.H., Ellinger, A.D.: Perceptions of quality of feedback in organizations. Eur. J. Train. Dev. **37**, 4–23 (2013)
10. Narciss, S.: Feedback strategies for interactive learning tasks. In: Spector, J.M., Merrill, M.D., Elen, J., Bishop, M.J. (eds.) Handbook of Research on Educational Communications and Technology, pp. 125–144. Springer, New York (2008)
11. Shute, V.J.: Focus on formative feedback. Rev. Educ. Res. **78**, 153–189 (2008)
12. Tata, J.: The influence of managerial accounts on employees' reactions to negative feedback. Group Org. Manag. **27**, 480–503 (2002)
13. Buckingham, M., Goodall, A.: Reinventing performance management. Harv. Bus. Rev. **93**, 40–50 (2015)
14. Cappelli, P., Tavis, A.: The performance management revolution. Harv. Bus. Rev. **94**, 58–67 (2016)
15. Pulakos, E.D., Hanson, R.M., Arad, S., Moye, N.: Performance management can be fixed: an on-the-job experiential learning approach for complex behavior change. Ind. Organ. Psychol. **8**, 51–76 (2015)
16. Nisen, M.: The management cliche you really can't afford to ignore. Quartz (2015)

17. Raemdonck, I., Strijbos, J.-W.: Feedback perceptions and attribution by secretarial employees. Eur. J. Train. Dev. **37**, 24–48 (2013)

18. Anseel, F., Lievens, F., Schollaert, E.: Reflection as a strategy to enhance task performance after feedback. Organ. Behav. Hum. Decis. Process. **110**, 23–35 (2009)

19. Bonabeau, E.: Agent-based modeling: methods and techniques for simulating human systems. Proc. Natl. Acad. Sci. **99**, 7280–7287 (2002)

20. Hattie, J., Timperley, H.: The power of feedback. Rev. Educ. Res. **77**, 81–112 (2007)

21. Schleicher, D.J., Baumann, H.M., Sullivan, D.W., Levy, P.E., Hargrove, D.C., Barros-Rivera, B.A.: Putting the system into performance management systems: a review and agenda for performance management research. J. Manag. **44**, 2209–2245 (2018)

22. Ashford, S.J., Tsui, A.S.: Self-regulation for managerial effectiveness: the role of active feedback seeking. Acad. Manag. J. **34**, 251–280 (1991)

23. Dawson, P., et al.: What makes for effective feedback: staff and student perspectives. Assess. Eval. High. Educ. **44**, 25–36 (2019)

24. Baumeister, R.F., Hutton, D.G., Cairns, K.J.: Negative effects of praise on skilled performance. Basic Appl. Soc. Psychol. **11**, 131–148 (1990)

25. de Stobbeleir, K.E.M., Ashford, S.J., Buyens, D.: Self-regulation of creativity at work: the role of feedback-seeking behavior in creative performance. AMJ **54**, 811–831 (2011)

26. London, M., Mone, E.M.: Performance management: processes that reflect and shape organizational culture and climate. In: The Oxford Handbook of Organizational Climate and Culture, p. 79 (2014)

27. Dahling, J.J., O'Malley, A.L.: Supportive feedback environments can mend broken performance management systems. Ind. Organ. Psychol. **4**, 201–203 (2011)

28. Avolio, B.J., Avey, J.B., Quisenberry, D.: Estimating return on leadership development investment. Leadersh. Q. **21**, 633–644 (2010)

29. Phillips, J.J.: Return on Investment in Training and Performance Improvement Programs. Butterworth-Heinemann, Amsterdam (2003)

30. Murray, L.W., Efendioglu, A.M.: Valuing the investment in organizational training. Ind. Commer. Train. **39**, 372–379 (2007)

31. Kulik, J.A., Kulik, C.-L.C.: Timing of feedback and verbal learning. Rev. Educ. Res. **58**, 79 (1988)

32. Kulhavy, R.W.: Feedback in written instruction. Rev. Educ. Res. **47**, 211 (1977)

33. Stöckli, E., Uebernickel, F., Brenner, W., Weierich, A., Hess, S.: Digital feedback for digital work? affordances and constraints of a feedback app at insurcorp. In: Proceedings of the International Conference on Wirtschaftsinformatik (WI) (ed.) (2019)

34. Miller, J.S.: High tech and high performance: Managing appraisal in the information age. J. Lab. Res. **24**, 409–424 (2003). https://doi.org/10.1007/s12122-003-1004-3

35. Park, J.-A., Johnson, D.A., Moon, K., Lee, J.: The interaction effects of frequency and specificity of feedback on work performance. J. Organ. Behav. Manag. **39**, 164–178 (2019)

36. Pulakos, E.D., O'Leary, R.S.: Why is performance management broken? Ind. Organ. Psychol. **4**, 146–164 (2011)

37. Holderness, D.K., Olsen, K.J., Thornock, T.A.: Assigned versus chosen relative performance information: the effect of feedback frequency on performance. J. Manag. Account. Res. **32**, 137–158 (2020)

38. Lam, C.F., DeRue, D.S., Karam, E.P., Hollenbeck, J.R.: The impact of feedback frequency on learning and task performance: challenging the "more is better" assumption. Organ. Behav. Hum. Decis. Process. **116**, 217–228 (2011)

39. Casas-Arce, P., Lourenço, S.M., Martínez-Jerez, F.A.: The performance effect of feedback frequency and detail: evidence from a field experiment in customer satisfaction. J. Account. Res. **55**, 1051–1088 (2017)

40. Law, A.M., Kelton, W.D.: Simulation Modeling and Analysis. McGraw-Hill, New York (1991)
41. Davis, J.P., Eisenhardt, K.M., Bingham, C.B.: Developing Theory Through Simulation Methods. AMR **32**, 480–499 (2007)
42. Nan, N., Tanriverdi, H.: Unifying the role of IT in hyperturbulence and competitive advantage via a multilevel perspective of IS strategy. MIS Q. **41**, 937–958 (2017)
43. Burton, R.M., Obel, B.: Computational modeling for what-is, what-might-be, and what-should-be studies—and triangulation. Organ. Sci. **22**, 1195–1202 (2011)
44. Fioretti, G.: Agent-based simulation models in organization science. Organ. Res. Methods **16**, 227–242 (2013)
45. Haki, K., Beese, J., Aier, S., Winter, R.: The evolution of information systems architecture: an agent-based simulation model. MIS Q. **44**, 155–184 (2020)
46. Kuhl, M.E., Steiger, N.M., Armstrong, F.B., Jones, J.A. (eds.): Proceedings of the 2005 Winter Simulation Conference. IEEE, Piscataway (2005)
47. Wilensky, U.: NetLogo. Center for Connected Learning and Computer-Based Modeling, Northwestern University, Evanston (1999)
48. Abar, S., Theodoropoulos, G., Lemarinier, P., O'Hare, G.: Agent based modelling and Simulation tools: a review of the state-of-art software. Comput. Sci. Rev. **24**, 13–33 (2017)
49. Murphy, K.R.: Performance evaluation will not die, but it should. Hum. Resour. Manag. J. **30**, 13–31 (2020)
50. Leibowitz, N., Baum, B., Enden, G., Karniel, A.: The exponential learning equation as a function of successful trials results in sigmoid performance. J. Math. Psychol. **54**, 338–340 (2010)
51. Elicker, J.D., Levy, P.E., Hall, R.J.: The role of leader-member exchange in the performance appraisal process. J. Manag. **32**, 531–551 (2006)

Identifying and Overcoming Future Challenges in Leadership: The Role of IS in Facilitating Empowerment

Maren Gierlich-Joas[✉]

Institute for Information Systems and New Media, LMU Munich, Munich, Germany
gierlich@bwl.lmu.de

Abstract. As digital workplaces change due to innovative technologies, managers have to deal with novel expectations of leadership. In more concrete terms, employees tend to prefer enabling leadership styles over coercive approaches. At the same time, information systems (IS) for leadership get more powerful and are applied in support of leadership. In this study, we investigate both the challenges that arise for leadership because of the changes in framing conditions and how these challenges can be overcome. We carry out an explorative Delphi study to build on the experience of a carefully selected panel of experts. We also gain important insights by conducting qualitative follow-up interviews with specific experts from the panel. The findings emphasize the increasing role of employee empowerment. Organizational change is essential to overcome the challenges, and leadership-related IS can facilitate this transformation to a certain degree. In sum, this study contributes to research on leadership in the digital age.

Keywords: Digital transformation · Leadership · Empowerment · Delphi study

1 Introduction

"Upcoming challenges regarding leadership can only be overcome if managers empower their employees." (Consultant1).

Leadership is changing due to the spread of novel technologies and increasing amounts of data. Over the past few decades, leadership has shifted in a more data-centric and employee-focused direction [1]. The use of leadership-related information systems (LRIS)—IS tailored to manage employees on an interpersonal level and to exercise the authority to co-ordinate tasks—makes leadership decisions more objective [2, 3]. These systems have evolved, and their range of functions has drastically expanded [4]. Basic payroll systems from the 1950s evolved into early versions of decision support systems in the 1980s, and sophisticated people analytics solutions have recently been developed [4]. The first systems were mainly designed to facilitate operative tasks in HR, whereas today's solutions support strategic decision making and drive change in leadership [5]. The question is whether this new generation of LRIS helps to master future challenges in leadership.

F. Ahlemann et al. (Eds.): WI 2021, LNISO 48, pp. 537–553, 2021.
https://doi.org/10.1007/978-3-030-86800-0_38

The analysis of past research leads to two major areas of interest: On the one hand, prior research has examined leadership tasks and novel requirements. Scholars have identified employees' shifting values and remote work as triggers for leadership changes [1, 6]. On the other hand, research on LRIS has focused on existing solutions. To a large extent, some technologies already support leaders' tasks effectively. However, biases and information overloads are potential shortcomings hindering the successful transformation in leadership [3, 7]. The gap between the desired and the present system features might even widen due to the changes in organizations' framing conditions and the transformation in leadership styles.

From studying past contributions, we derive a lack of understanding of technologies' role in mastering future challenges for leadership. With this study, we aim to outline future challenges for leadership and approaches to overcome them. Thus, we propose the following research question:

RQ: *What are the most important challenges facing the leader of an organization in the coming years regarding novel technologies, and how can they be overcome?*

The remainder of the paper is organized as follows: Firstly, we outline the theoretical foundation for the study by introducing the concept of leadership (Sect. 2.1), deriving current trends and technological developments (Sect. 2.2) and presenting control theory as a theoretical lens (Sect. 2.3). Next, we describe the chosen methodological approach—a Delphi study design—by outlining the selection of the expert panel, data collection and data analysis (Sect. 3). The study's findings are presented in Sect. 4, followed by additional insights that we derived from semi-structured interviews with selected experts from the panel to deepen our understanding. We discuss our findings in Sect. 5. Finally, our theoretical and practical contributions are highlighted, limitations are pointed out, and suggestions for further research are listed in Sect. 6. The study offers insights for theory and practice as it contributes to the understanding of future challenges in leadership from a control theory point of view and sheds light on the opportunities to overcome them, partly by using LRIS.

2   Theoretical Foundation

2.1   Concept of Leadership

Leadership has a long history in the field of management, and definitions vary greatly. Following an extensive literature overview, "[l]eadership has been defined in terms of individual traits, leader behaviour, interaction patterns, role relationships, follower perceptions, influence over followers, influence on task goals, and influence on organizational culture" [8]. One similarity between the definitions relates to one party exerting influence on another party; apart from that, however, the meanings can differ significantly [8]. Most scholars distinguish between "management" and "leadership" by defining management as more task-oriented and leadership as more visionary [9], although the two concepts do overlap in some respects [8]. According to Mintzberg, the "leader" is a specific facet of a manager's roles consist of interpersonal, informational and decisional roles [10]. Leadership itself includes different functions, such as composing a team, setting objectives, defining KPIs and measuring progress, building a relationship with employees and managing organizational and cultural ambidexterity [11].

In the context of this work, we define leadership as the management of employee relations and the exercise of authority to co-ordinate tasks within a company to fulfil operative and strategic goals [12]. Leadership has been conceptualized in various leadership theories and leadership concepts. While leadership theories aim to offer explanations for leadership behaviour or to predict future developments, leadership concepts address the implementation of concrete guidelines.

2.2 Current Trends in Leadership and Leadership-Related Information Systems

In a digital work environment, leadership is subject to change. Driven by the use of novel technologies (technology-push) and the changing needs of employees (technology-pull), leadership approaches increasingly focus on collaboration, empowerment and participation [1].

Regarding the technology-push, the use of IS in HR and leadership has drastically escalated over the past few decades. The aim of IS is to collect, process, store, analyse and disseminate information for a specific purpose [13]—in this case, to support leadership. Hence, we define leadership-related IS (LRIS) as a specific class of IS that are used to support operative and strategic goals inside firms in order to manage employees on an interpersonal level and to exercise their authority to co-ordinate tasks [12]. Thus, we understand LRIS as a combination of strategic management information systems (MIS) and operational human resource information systems (HRIS). MIS are part of LRIS as their purpose is to aggregate and analyse leadership-related data in a data warehouse and to visualize important findings on dashboards so that managers can use data to improve their decision-making abilities [14]. In addition to these strategic planning and control systems, HRIS have emerged as "system[s] used to acquire, store, manipulate, analyse, retrieve, and distribute information regarding an organization's human resources to support HRM and managerial decisions" [15]. For both types of IS, the range of functionalities has been extended significantly since they were first introduced to the market, leading to the chance to facilitate controlling and strategic leadership activities [4]. Integrating insights from operative everyday observations in HR with long-term strategical predictions forms a basis for data-driven leadership approaches.

As for the technology-pull, there is a rising demand for empowerment, which creates a strong interest in LRIS supporting transparency and participation [16]. Once these novel digital solutions are applied in firms, they trigger a transformation on the business side [17]. In times of organizational or technological change, "[l]eadership becomes a very critical element of change management" [18]. Consequently, novel leadership concepts, like shared leadership, which emphasize the role of employees, replace static approaches that put managers in the foreground [6]. Furthermore, leadership has to be tailored to an increasingly digital organization, and digital capabilities have to be built up, which is referred to as "digital leadership" [19]. Similarly, the concept of e-leadership describes "leadership in a technology-enabled working environment, leader's competence and the requirements of tasks" [6]. Thus, digital leadership and e-leadership refer to leadership in an increasingly digital work setting, in contrast to IT leadership, which describes IT management and is not the focus of this study [20].

2.3 Leadership from a Control Theory Perspective

The highlighted trends in leadership change the traditional control styles, which leaders apply and can be examined from a control theory perspective. Control is "any attempt to align individual behaviours with organizational objectives" [21]. Control theory has been transferred from the field of management [22] to IS research and is often used in the context of software development [23]. However, because of its origins, the range of application is much broader and covers both organizational and leadership phenomena [24]. Control theory covers the who, when, why, what and how dimensions of the use of control in an organizational context [24].

The use of control is strongly connected to current leadership approaches. The how dimension, in particular, is of interest for the study, as it describes two distinct control styles: coercive and enabling [25]. Coercive control describes ways of leadership that aim to track employees during task execution [24]. By contrast, an enabling control style aims to "enable employees to better master their tasks" [24] by providing transparency on processes in a way that permits employees to work in a self-organized way. Thus, despite the negative connotation of "control", positive control styles can also be defined as employee-friendly.

Coercive and enabling control styles can be distinguished by four generic principles; repair, internal transparency, global transparency and flexibility [26] (see Table 1). An enabling control style is characterized by a high degree of repair, which helps with employee integration. Enabling control styles have high levels of internal transparency (the understandability of internal processes) and global transparency (employees' involvement in the broader organization). If a control style is flexible and designed to support individual skills, it is labelled as enabling; if flexibility is low, it can be classified as coercive [26].

Table 1. Features of enabling and coercive control styles (following Adler)

	Repair	Internal transparency	Global transparency	Flexibility
Coercive control	Low	Low	Low	Low
Enabling control	High	High	High	High

Both control styles are reflected in different styles of leadership. As prior research shows, employees clearly demand enabling control mechanisms [27]. Hence, modern leadership approaches should satisfy the request for maximal internal and global transparency, the integration of employees and flexible solutions tailored to every individual's needs. In sum, these novel trends in leadership can be interpreted using the various dimensions of control theory.

3 Methodological Approach

We apply a Delphi study to investigate future challenges in leadership from several experts' perspectives. The Delphi study seeks to build consensus between a group of experts on a specific question via a structured process of repetitive questionnaires with controlled feedback [28, 29]. In this study, a ranking-type Delphi study is applied to identify relevant factors and reach agreement on their relative importance [28, 29]. The structured and anonymous process is suitable to gain insights from the collective experience of experts while avoiding biases that might arise from direct confrontation [30]. Prior contributions demonstrate the fit between similar research questions and the methodology of Delphi studies [31].

The work follows the process established by Schmidt [32], which consists of brainstorming, selection and ranking. In total, four rounds were conducted on a weekly basis between June and July 2020. The study was designed, pre-tested and carried out via an online survey platform that can provide anonymity to the respondents [30]. Throughout the whole process, established quality criteria, were used to ensure the methodological rigour of the study (see Table 2).

Table 2. Attributes used to assess ranking-type Delphi studies (following [30])

Areas	Attributes	Fulfilled?
Research design	Follow explicit procedures for expert selection	(Search strategy)
	Use clear selection criteria	x
	Document expert demographics and profiles	x
	Ensure anonymity of participants	x
	Report response rate to initial call	x
	Report panel size	x
	Pretest task instructions and questionnaire	(Final design)
Brainstorming Narrowing down Ranking	Provide clear brainstorming instructions	x
	Ask experts to describe the meaning of items	x
	Have researchers consolidate list of items	x
	Have experts comment and validate list	x
	Report final number of items	x
	Provide clear narrowing down instructions	x
	Randomly order list of items	x
	Clearly specify item selection rule	x
	Apply a stopping rule	x
	Provide clear ranking instructions	x
	Randomly order items (in 1st round)	x
	Ask experts to justify their rankings	x
	Perform appropriate statistical analyses	x
	Apply a stopping rule	x
	Provide controlled feedback to experts	x

3.1 Panel Selection

The first step of a Delphi study is the panel selection. The procedure of selecting and inviting the experts was guided by Paré's recommendations for rigorous Delphi studies

[30], following principles like clearly defining the selection criteria, documenting the experts' demographics and ensuring the panellists' anonymity.

Firstly, we created a knowledge resource nomination worksheet (KRNW) to derive categories of experts [28]. The KRNW consisted of specialists from industry (suppliers and users of IS for leadership), academia and consultants. Experts from industry are senior-level HR personnel or the leaders of a highly specialized team, e.g. people analytics. They have worked at least two years at a company recently awarded for innovative leadership approaches and use LRIS. Owing to the company sample and the position of the experts within the organization, they are considered suitable for our study. Experts from academia are professors or senior-level researchers at renowned German universities or research institutes and have published research on digital leadership or LRIS in the past three years. Thus, they have a deep knowledge of relevant scientific trends. Consultants were nominated if they work in a consultancy firm specializing in leadership and digital transformation and have at least two years of experience. Because of the clear definition of selection criteria following Paré [30], we assume that we established a qualified panel representing a wide range of perspectives.

Next, the experts were listed and ranked by qualifications. A total of 88 individuals were invited to the study and 23 agreed to participate, which is in line with recommenddations for panel sizes and equals a response rate of 26% [33]. 17 of these experts (74%) are male, which we consider a representative distribution, given the background and the positions we sampled for. Furthermore, 61% of the panellists have an industry background, 17% do research in the field, and 22% are consultants (see Table 3).

Table 3. Profile of the expert panel

Characteristics	Panel profile	(n = 23)
Functional affiliation	Industry	14 (61%)
	Academia	4 (17%)
	Consulting	5 (22%)
Years of experience	Mean	9.8 years
	Min. value	2 years
	Max. value	20 years
Industry	IT	6
	Consulting	5
	Academia	4
	Pharmaceutics	2
	Mechanical engineering	1
	Electrical engineering	1
	Finance	1
	Telecommunications	1
	Construction	1
	Logistics	1

3.2   Data Collection and Analysis

In the following section we outline our data collection, consisting of the different phases of brainstorming, selection and ranking.

Brainstorming. The data collection process (see Table 4) starts with the brainstorming phase, which facilitates the unstructured collection of responses to one (or multiple) open question(s) introduced by the researchers [32]. We posed the initial question: "What are the most important challenges facing the leader of an organization in the coming years regarding the spread of novel technologies and the rising volume of data?".

The experts were asked to name at least five challenges and to describe them briefly in order to increase clarity of their meaning [32]. To achieve a diverse set of initial responses, the number of responses was not limited, in line with the recommendation by Schmidt [32]. The specialists named 114 challenges, which the researchers consolidated by following the guidelines by Paré [30]. The consolidated list of 24 challenges was handed back to the panel for validation to reduce noise and provide further opportunities to receive feedback from the experts [30].

Selection. The selection phase aims to narrow down the consolidated lists obtained via the brainstorming phase to a manageable number of items. The participants were instructed to choose the ten most relevant challenges from the lists, so a concrete number of items was stated [30]. The items were ordered randomly to avoid any biases [32]. Moreover, the validated explanations of the items were displayed during all phases when hovering over the items to create a mutual understanding and avoid noise. The selection was clear-cut, and the items were taken as inputs for the subsequent ranking phase if at least 50% of the experts had selected them.

Ranking. For the ranking phase, the participants received a fourth questionnaire, which instructed them to rank the shortened list of challenges. For each challenge, the percentage of panel experts who selected the respective value in the previous selection phase was indicated in an anonymous way to equip the panellists with controlled feedback of the panel's evaluation as suggested by Paré [30]. Additionally, we asked for a brief justification of the ranking of the challenges to increase the study's explanatory power [30].

After the first ranking, the mean rank for each item and the Kendall's W coefficient were calculated. Kendall's W is a measure for agreement ranging from 0 (no consensus) to 1 (perfect consensus) [28]. A value of W greater than 0.7 indicates strong agreement and is often applied as a stopping criterion for the iterative ranking phase [32]. However, before conducting a new round, the trade-off to increase the value of W and the risk of losing participants has to be considered carefully [32]. Dropout rates between 20 and 30% are considered normal for Delphi studies [34], but we did not want to endanger the study's findings by adding a fifth round. Thus, the study was closed when a Kendall's W of 0.22 was reached in the fourth round.

Table 4. Overview of the data collection process

	Brainstorming		Selection	Ranking
Round	1	2	3	4
Theme	Collection of initial items	Validation of consolidated lists	Selection of top ten items	Ranking of the final lists
Responses	23	20	20	19
Response rate	100%	87%	100%	95%

3.3 Additional Data Collection via Follow-Up Interviews

After completing the Delphi study, we followed the suggestion by Singh et al. to conduct follow-up interviews with selected panellists to add depth to our findings [31]. We approached five experts from the original panel: two male and three female experts; one was working in consultancy, one in academia and three in industry (see Table 6). Building on Myers and Newman, we prepared guidelines for the semi-structured interviews [35]. In the interviews, we asked the experts to elaborate on (1) the main challenges from the Delphi study, (2) ways to overcome them and, (3) more specifically, the role of LRIS in overcoming them. The interviews were conducted via video-conferencing tools between October and November 2020 and lasted between 25 and 40 min. The participants' anonymity was guaranteed during the whole process, and feedback from the earlier Delphi study was provided. The interviews were recorded, transcribed and then analysed with the software Atlas.ti following iterative rounds of coding as suggested by Miles et al. [36].

Table 6. Overview of panellists for follow-up interviews

Pseudonym	Industry	Experience (years)	Gender
Provider1	IT	10	Female
Provider2	IT	4	Male
User10	Mechanical engineering	5	Female
Consultant4	Consultancy	17	Female
Academic1	Academia	6	Male

4 Findings

4.1 Findings Regarding Leadership Challenges

In the brainstorming session, numerous leadership challenges were collected in connection with digital transformation. Table 5 illustrates the findings of the selection and ranking phase for the challenges ordered by their rank after the fourth round, including the experts' definitions.

Table 5. Findings of the selection and ranking phase for leadership challenges

Challenge	Selection share of experts who selected the challenge	Ranking mean rank	Rank
Empowerment of employees: hand responsibility to employees and refrain from strict hierarchies	65%	3.63	1
Digital transformation and organizational change: lead employees in times of digital transformation	75%	3.68	2
Innovation culture: foster a culture of learning that benefits from innovations in leadership in reverse	70%	4.21	3
Purposeful leadership: provide meaningful goals to employees	65%	4.84	4
Individual leadership: address individual needs instead of applying a "one-size-fits-all" approach	60%	5.21	5
Digital competences: build up knowledge on the use of novel technologies	60%	5.42	6
Remote leadership: lead and motivate teams from a distance	65%	6.58	7
Agile methods: lead teams with less clearly structured hierarchies and shift responsibilities	50%	7.05	8
Volatile environment: adapt leadership to a dynamically changing environment	50%	7.16	9
Ambidexterity: manage tensions between the core business and novel innovations in leadership	55%	7.21	10

When contrasting the different subgroups of the panel by academia vs. industry vs. consulting or by manager perspective vs. employee perspective, the mean ranks for the items do not differ much. However, managers ranked "digital transformation and organizational change" first and "empowerment of employees" third, whereas employees prioritized "empowerment". The Kendall's W values for the different subgroups do not differ greatly and range between 0.21 and 0.36, so the level of agree-ment is similar for the different groups. Below, the top three challenges are outlined.

Challenge #1 - Empowerment of Employees. The approach of handing responsibility to employees and refraining from strict hierarchies was ranked first. One panellist stated that "leadership should be a social participation process" (Academic1). Empowerment can lead to "an abolition of leaders in a traditional way [...] but it challenges employees as they need to take responsibility" (Academic2). Overall, empowerment is considered a key factor because "upcoming challenges [...] can only be overcome if managers empower their employees" (Consultant1).

Challenge #2 - Digital Transformation and Organizational Change. The panellists defined the challenge as "leading employees in times of digital transformation"; for this reason, they strongly refer to the concept of digital leadership. Since "business models change drastically, internal organizational change is a logical consequence" (User4). Therefore, "capabilities that did not exist before rise in importance" (User 2).

Challenge #3 – Innovation Culture. The third-placed challenge is "innovation cul-ture", meaning the ability to "foster a culture of learning that benefits from innovations in leadership in reverse". The definition highlights the understanding that innovations are enabled by a certain culture and leadership style. "Innovation culture is strongly related to individual leadership styles [...] that drive transformational change" (User 12). Since shaping an organization's culture is one of the tasks of its leaders [11], creating a culture of innovation is viewed as a crucial challenge to remain competitive.

4.2   Enhancing Findings with Results from Follow-Up Interviews

Guided by the insights from the follow up interviews, we derived more in-depth findings on empowerment as challenge and ways to overcome this obstacle.

Empowerment as a Challenge. Discussing the challenge of empowerment in depth led to insights regarding its perceived importance. The experts agreed: "codetermination is an important topic in many firms" (Provider2). "It sets the framing conditions for employees to master digital transformation as it provides opportunities to shape their environment" (Consultant4). Thus, while empowerment is seen as a game-changer for leadership in the digital age, it comes with certain challenges.

For example, defining empowerment in practice seems to raise questions, as "a major challenge is to develop a model of what empowerment actually is" (Provider2). The concept "seems to be too fuzzy and people understand different things" (Academic1). The scope of empowerment needs to be defied in terms of "who is empowered, when, for which reason and up to which degree?" (Academic1). Thus, starting initiatives for empowerment is difficult if clear objectives are lacking.

Once the term "empowerment" is clarified, its implementation has to be conducted thoroughly. Enforcing empowerment might lead to mistrust: "I was used to doing everything my way, and suddenly everything becomes transparent – I don't like that" (Consultant4). In this scenario, empowerment can be interpreted as control instead of a chance for self-organization, which "leads to great negative outcomes" (Academic1) and which has to be avoided to keep employee satisfaction high. And even if the goals for empowerment are clarified, "the organizational structure and culture can be burdens" (Academic1).

Overcoming the Challenge of Empowerment. Our selected experts outlined a few solutions to overcome the challenge of empowerment from a non-technical perspective (see Table 7). Firstly, establishing a culture of trust and a mindset of supportive leadership is considered crucial; otherwise, measures to increase empowerment might be interpreted as control. Employees need to have incentives to trust empowerment initiatives and related LRIS. The novel organizational mindset goes hand in hand with a changed understanding of leadership. As decision making can be supported by LRIS, "leaders can invest more time in caring for their employees, developing them" (Consultant4).

Secondly, organizations have to establish transparency to reach empowerment. "Transparency is key to empowering employees, as those who don't have access to data and don't see the big picture can't make decisions wisely" (Provider1). "By showing positive and negative use-case scenarios [of LRIS] in a transparent way, acceptance can be increased" (Provider2). Furthermore, companies have to "prove that tracking mechanisms are not applied" (Provider2). To increase trust, transparency needs to be implemented at all organizational levels, and experts are "mystified as to why employees should become fully transparent when companies aren't disclosing their data" (Provider1). They demand a reciprocal model of transparency that grants both managers and employees access to the data.

Lastly, digital capabilities need to be built up to facilitate the use of LRIS. "Employees in IT-related environments are happy with the systems, but for employees in production, […] the manager is in charge of using the tools" (Provider1). Employees need to be permitted to take over responsibility and use these systems independently.

The Role of LRIS in Overcoming the Challenge of Empowerment. Additionally, the experts outlined ways in which technology can facilitate empowerment, "as structures and data become visible" (Provider1). Some of the system functionalities were named that help to increase empowerment and transparency (see Table 7).

Firstly, LRIS help to define empowerment and measure the success of empowerment initiatives. As employee surveys can be conducted digitally every week, "they give leaders an important overview regarding mood, motivation and feedback" (Consultant4). Via structured feedback routines, KPIs for empowerment can be displayed on charts to illustrate their long-term development.

Secondly, LRIS assist in generating transparency as a basis for empowerment. Applying the "principles of user design controlling […] to visualize insights in comprehensive ways, e.g. by using traffic light notifications" (Provider2), facilitates overall transparency. Customized dashboards for each employee or manager should display the individuals' progress, as well as the teams' working status (User10). Performance measures can be documented and taken as a reference for staff appraisals.

Moreover, using training sessions of LRIS enhances employees' digital capabilities: "on-site trainings that are tailored to the individual stakeholder groups are essential", so employees can convert their opportunities for engagement into actual self-organized work routines (User10). Thus, technology can support the process of developing digital capabilities.

Last but not least, LRIS help to enforce data protection regulations by depicting different user roles with different degrees of data access. However, the experts disagreed on the conceptualization of the different user roles. While one stated that "management should be able to see and compare more data [than the employees]" (Provider10), another explained that "every team member and team leader should have access to all data, [following the principle of] reciprocal transparency" (Consultant4).

In sum, the panel mostly viewed the use of LRIS to overcome the challenge of empowerment in an optimistic light. One expert even stated: "Every task that does not require human intelligence can be undertaken or supported by technical systems" (Academic2). However, the panellists mostly agreed that the role of technology in overcoming the challenge of empowerment is limited. "Technology can also get in the way [of empowerment]" as the tools might replace talks between leader and employee but cannot fully cover the interpersonal level, which leads to misunderstandings (User10). Thus, LRIS drive empowerment initiatives but only to a certain degree. "Digital innovations in the HR context can help in overcoming certain challenges but often we expect too much […]. The way we empower employees is strongly driven by daily interactions which cannot be replaced by technologies" (Acadmic1). Along with the technological solution, the organizational side has to adapt as well which is highly context-specific: "Saying 'we have a great tool' is not enough." (Consultant4).

Table 7. Approaches for overcoming the challenge of empowerment

Overcoming the challenge	The role of LRIS
Define empowerment and set KPIs to track initiatives	– Introduce regular surveys & metrics to measure empowerment
Create transparency for work processes across all organizational levels	– Integrate customized dashboards to monitor work processes – Use LRIS for performance assessment
Build up digital capabilities to use LRIS	– Make use of training sessions for LRIS – Stick to intuitive user interfaces
Establish a culture of trust by redefining leadership	– Limited support by LRIS (as it mainly needs organizational change) – Define distinct user roles to ensure data protection and enhance trust

5   Discussion

The study's findings can be summarized in two major points:

Firstly, leadership's shift towards enabling styles entails novel challenges. Control theory is very suitable to investigate these challenges and we heeded previous calls to apply control theory at the interface of leadership to benefit from its wide span of application [23]. In light of control theory, the top-ranked challenges reflect an enabling leadership approach. The four principles of enabling control styles—namely, repair, internal transparency, global transparency and flexibility (see Table 1)—are present in the challenges cited by the panellists. By contrast, challenges that reveal a clearly coercive approach to leadership, like "transparency on performance measurement" or "monitoring of employees", were named in the brainstorming phase but not chosen in the selection phase. Thus, the experts agreed on the overall trend towards employee-centric, enabling leadership approaches. As recent studies in the field of control theory highlight, the novel degree of transparency in organizations can be used to either enable or track employees [25, 37]. Thus, the thorough implementation of transparency is of high importance as it lays the foundation to prevent mistrust and enables ways of successful empowerment [16]. By examining the challenge of empowerment in an explorative way, we add to the literature on leadership in the digital age and control theory [1, 24]. We find that enabling leadership styles can only be implemented successfully if challenges to organizational culture and the use of LRIS are overcome.

Secondly, novel LRIS assist in overcoming empowerment as a future challenge in leadership. As the systems provide transparency and offer ways to measure empowerment and employee performance, they strongly drive digital leadership. Scholars have investigated the evolution of IS in the field of HR, which depicts the change from supporting basic HR function to facilitating strategic decision making [4]. Many studies illustrate how HRIS can support recruiting processes, performance evaluation or workforce planning [38]. However, we suggest that novel systems reach even further and can support leadership. Unlike HRIS, LRIS have a strategic orientation and, thus, make it easier to overcome leadership challenges like empowerment.

However, standalone tools will not be sufficient to overcome the mentioned challenges and drive digital leadership approaches. Technological and organizational changes need to go hand in hand. This phenomenon has been investigated with the concept of "technochange"—the strategic use of IT to derive organizational benefits by integrating IT introduction and complementary organizational changes to manage digital culture change via the introduction of IT [39]. This concept supports our findings, as LRIS are implemented for the strategic purpose of changing leadership. However, complementary organizational change is essential to drive digital leadership.

6   Conclusion

6.1   Theoretical and Practical Contribution

In the study, we investigated future challenges in leadership through the lens of control theory. The Delphi study and the follow-up interviews with carefully selected experts shed light on the obstacles that can be expected, including empowerment, digital transformation and innovation culture. In addition, it is possible to map the challenges to enabling leadership styles. Implementing LRIS with a complementary change in organizational culture can help to overcome the particular challenges. In summary, the study serves as a stepping stone for research on digital innovation in leadership.

Firstly, the study contributes to an understanding of the emerging challenges for leadership in a digital work context. Coming from a management-oriented perspective, we outline challenges for leadership. Next, we provide solutions from a more technology-focused perspective and clarify the role of IS in overcoming the mentioned burdens. In this way, the study aims to bridge the gap between research on design-oriented IS and research on management-oriented HR [1].

Secondly, with our study, we emphasize the growing importance of LRIS in driving digital transformation in organizations. In contrast to previous studies [4], we highlight the systems' option to facilitate strategic leadership topics and not only operational HR processes. LRIS can democratize power by providing transparency for employees and are, therefore, key to creating empowerment.

Thirdly, the traditional way of conducting Delphi studies was extended as suggested by several scholars, e.g. Schmidt et al. [33] and Singh et al. [31]. Instead of limiting ourselves to collecting and prioritizing challenges (understanding the problem), we examine solutions through semi-structured interviews (solving the problem).

From a practical point of view, the study provides novel insights on upcoming leadership trends, related challenges and requirements for LRIS. We offer insights to managers regarding how leadership might change in the digital age and how using LRIS can facilitate this transformation. Moreover, following the outlined challenges, LRIS providers can develop their solutions according to the future needs of the market.

6.2 Limitations and Outlook

Although the study was very thorough, our research did have certain limitations. Some of these limitations concern the application of the Delphi study (1), while others involve the general research setting (2).

Firstly, concerning the panel, it is important to note that Delphi studies do not require a representative sample following statistical assumptions [30]. Nonetheless, it might be difficult to draw general assumptions from a relatively small sample that has a high degree of innovativeness. We tried to address this potential shortfall by investigating a diverse sample; however, it should be noted that leadership is highly related to external factors (e.g. culture) that could not be controlled. Furthermore, the level of consensus is relatively low (Kendall's W of 0.22), and a higher degree would have been favourable. Still, as Paré states, as long as appropriate stopping rules are applied, the study's validity does not necessarily suffer from a small degree of agreement [30].

Secondly, concerning the research setting, the Delphi study is a helpful tool to answer "what could/should be" questions, but the explanatory detail that can be expected in qualitative studies is limited. Multiple fields for open comments in the survey addressed this limitation, but only to a limited degree. Therefore, semi-structured qualitative interviews with selected experts from the panel added depth to the findings and helped to derive solutions for the listed challenges. However, specific design requirements for future LRIS remain a topic for further investigation. Moreover, the stated challenges and options to overcome them are highly subjective. Owing to the explorative approach, the items do not necessarily follow the mutually exclusive and collectively exhaustive principle. Thus, some challenges might overlap while there were other important factors that the panellists did not mention.

Despite these issues, we consider this study an important starting point for promising future research. Regarding the application of the method (1), adding more rounds of ranking might help to increase the value of the Kendall's W. Future researchers are encouraged to investigate larger samples and to contrast panels with different cultural backgrounds. In addition, we recommend enhancing the research setting (2). To structure the statements from the panellists and avoid missing out on relevant aspects, we suggest contrasting the empirical findings with existing literature. Adding insights from previous scholars after the initial brainstorming phase can be a solid approach to increase the robustness of the findings. Furthermore, we consider Delphi studies a promising foundation for design science research projects as they are an instrument to define the objectives of a solution and to derive design requirements for technical and organizational artefacts [40]. Thus, applying the learnings from this study to a design science research project can pave the way for design-oriented research on digital innovation in leadership.

References

1. Cortellazzo, L., Bruni, E., Zampieri, R.: The role of leadership in a digitized world: a review. Front. Psychol. **10**, 1–21 (2019)
2. Gierlich, M., Hess, T.: Towards an understanding on datas' influence on leadership. In: Internationale Tagung der Wirtschaftsinformatik (2020)
3. Tursunbayeva, A., Di Lauro, S., Pagliari, C.: People analytics—a scoping review of conceptual boundaries and value propositions. Int. J. Inf. Manag. **43**, 224–247 (2018)
4. Johnson, R.D., Lukaszewski, K.M., Stone, D.L.: The evolution of the field of human resource information systems: co-evolution of technology and HR processes. Commun. ACM **38**, 533–553 (2016)
5. Wirtky, T., Laumer, S., Eckhardt, A., Weitzel, T.: On the untapped value of e-HRM: a literature review. Commun. ACM **38**, 20–83 (2016)
6. Dinh, J.E., Lord, R.G., Gardner, W.L., Meuser, J.D., Liden, R.C., Hu, J.: Leadership theory and research in the new millennium: current theoretical trends and changing perspectives. Leadersh. Q. **25**, 36–62 (2014)
7. Gal, U., Blegind Jensen, T., Stein, M.-K.: Breaking the vicious cycle of algorithmic management: a virtue ethics approach to people analytics. Inf. Organ. **30**, 1–15 (2020)
8. Yukl, G.A.: Managerial leadership: a review of theory and research. J. Manag. **15**, 251–289 (1989)
9. Zaleznik, A.: Managers and leaders: are they different? Havard Bus. Rev. **82**, 74–81 (1977)
10. Mintzberg, H.: The manager's jobs: Folklore and fact. In: Vecchio, R.P. (ed.) Leadership, Notre Dame, Indiana, pp. 49–61. University of Notre Dame Press (2007)
11. Morgeson, F.P., DeRue, D.S., Karam, E.P.: Leadership in teams: a functional approach to understanding leadership structures and processes. J. Manag. **36**, 5–39 (2009)
12. Beare, H., Caldwell, B., Millikan, R.: Dimensions of leadership. In: Crawford, M., Kydd, L., Riches, C.R. (eds.) Leadership and Teams in Educational Management, pp. 24–39. Open University Press, Buckingham (1997)
13. Rainer, R.K., Potter, R. E.: Introduction to Information Systems. Wiley, Hoboken (2007)

14. Gorry, A.M., Michael S.S.: A framework for management information systems. Manag. Sloan Rev. **13, 4961** (1971)

15. Kavanagh, M.J., Johnson, R.D. (eds.): Human resource information systems: basics, applications, and future directions. Sage, Los Angeles (2018)

16. Gierlich-Joas, M., Hess, T., Neuburger, R.: More self-organization, more control – or even both? Inverse transparency as a new digital leadership concept. Bus. Res. Forthcoming **13**, 921-947 (2020)

17. Wiesböck, F., Hess, T.: Digital innovations - embedding in organizations. Electron. Mark. **30**, 75–86 (2020)

18. Nadler, D.A., Tushman, M.L.: Beyond the charismatic leader: leadership and organizational change. Calif. Manag. Rev. **32**, 77–97 (1990)

19. Legner, C., et al.: Digitalization: opportunity and challenge for the business and information systems engineering community. Bus. Inf. Syst. Eng. **59**, 301–308 (2017)

20. Hoving, R.: Information technology leadership challenges – past, present, and future. Inf. Syst. Manag. **24**, 147–153 (2007)

21. Kirsch, L.J.: The management of complex tasks in organizations: controlling the systems development process. Organ. Sci. **7**, 1–21 (1996)

22. Ouchi, W.G.: The relationship between organizational structure and organizational control. Adm. Sci. Q. **22**, 95–113 (1977)

23. Cram, W.A.: Information systems control: a review and framework for emerging information systems processes. J. Assoc. Inf. Syst. **17**, 216–266 (2016)

24. Cram, W.A., Wiener, M.: Technology-mediated control: case examples and research directions for the future of organizational control. Commun. Assoc. Inf. Syst. **46**, 70–91 (2020)

25. Heuman, J., Wiener, M., Remus, U., Mähring, M.: To coerce or to enable? Exercising formal control in a large information systems project. J. Inf. Technol. **30**, 337–351 (2015)

26. Adler, P.S., Borys, B.: Two types of bureaucracy: enabling and coercive. Admin. Sci. Q. **41**, 61–89 (1996)

27. Carasco-Saul, M., Kim, W., Kim, T.: Leadership and employee engagement: proposing research agendas through a review of literature. Hum. Resour. Dev. Rev. **14**, 38–63 (2015)

28. Okoli, C., Pawowski, S.D.: The Delphi method as a research tool: an example, design considerations and applications. Inf. Manag. **42**, 15–29 (2004)

29. Skinner, R., Nelson, R.R., Chin, W.W., Land, L.: The Delphi method research strategy in studies of information systems. Commun. ACM **37**, 31–63 (2015)

30. Paré, G., Cameron, A.-F., Poba-Nzaou, P., Templier, M.: A systematic assessment of rigor in information systems ranking-type Delphi studies. Inf. Manag **50**, 207–217 (2013)

31. Singh, R., Keil, M., Kasi, V.: Identifying and overcoming the challenges of implementing a project management office. Eur. J. Inf. Syst. **18**, 409–427 (2009)

32. Schmidt, R.C.: Managing Delphi surveys using nonparametric statistical techniques. Decis. Sci. **28**, 763–774 (1997)

33. Schmidt, R.C., Lyytinen, K., Keil, M., Cule, P.: Identifying software project risks: an international Delphi study. J. Manag. Inf. Syst. **17**, 5–36 (2001)

34. Bardecki, M.J.: Participants' response to the Delphi method: an attitudinal perspective. Technol. Forecast Soc. Change **25**, 281–292 (1984)

35. Myers, M.D., Newman, M.: The qualitative interview in IS research: examining the craft. Inf. Organ. **17**, 2–26 (2007)

36. Miles, B.M., Huberman, A.M., Saldana, J.: Qualitative Data Analysis: A Methods Sourcebook. SAGE Publications Ltd. (2013)

37. Liu, G.H., Chua, C.E.: The reinforcing effects of formal control enactment in complex IT projects. J. Assoc. Inf. Syst. **21**, 312–340 (2020)

38. Gal, U., Blegind Jensen,s T., Stein, M.-K.: People analytics in the age of Big Data: an agenda for IS research. In: Proceedings of the Annual International Conference on Information Systems, pp. 1–11. Association for Information Systems (2017)
39. Markus, M.L.: Technochange management: using IT to drive organizational change. J. Inf. Technol. **19**, 4–20 (2004)
40. Kloör, B., Monhof, M., Beverungen, D., Braäer, S.: Design and evaluation of a model-driven decision support system for repurposing electric vehicle batteries. Eur. J. Inf. Syst. **27**, 171–188 (2018)

IT Outside of the IT Department: Reviewing Lightweight IT in Times of Shadow IT and IT Consumerization

Marie-E. Godefroid[1,2(✉)], Ralf Plattfaut[2], and Björn Niehaves[1]

[1] Wirtschaftsinformatik, Universität Siegen, Siegen, Germany
{marie.godefroid,bjoern.niehaves}@uni-siegen.de
[2] Process Innovation & Automation Lab, Fachhochschule Südwestfalen, Soest, Germany
plattfaut.ralf@fh-swf.de

Abstract. A plethora of theoretical perspectives on the phenomenon of IT outside of the IT department exists. One recent perspective is lightweight IT as introduced by Bygstad [1]. It is interesting as it takes a positive view on this phenomenon and contrasts lightweight from heavyweight IT. To reflect on the current understanding of lightweight IT this paper presents a systematic literature review. Publications are assessed regarding their contribution to the conceptualization of the interplay of heavyweight and lightweight IT and the benefits and corresponding risks of lightweight IT in practice. Based on these insights, drivers, benefits, and risks of lightweight IT are derived. This allows a comparison with the parallel research streams of IT Consumerization and Shadow IT as the two other dominant perspectives on the phenomenon of IT outside of the IT department. The comparison shows significant overlap, but also conceptual differences. As a result, six questions for further research are derived.

Keywords: Lightweight IT · Literature review · IT consumerization · Shadow IT

1 Introduction

One of the main concerns in the discussion on the implications of digitalization for the IT department is the future integration of digitalization efforts outside of the Information Technology (IT) department – especially in the context of technologies such as Robotic Process Automation (RPA) or Mobile Applications [2]. To date there are different perspectives regarding the phenomenon of IT outside of the IT department - the dominant ones being the rather favorable view of IT Consumerization [3] and the more cautious view of Shadow IT [4]. Both perspectives look at slightly different aspects of the phenomenon: IT Consumerization focuses on the use of privately owned IT resources for business purposes [3] and Shadow IT describes the covert autonomous use of IT by business entities and the appropriate reactions of the IT department [4]. The overall judgment remains divided, but even the literature on Shadow IT sees desirable qualities like innovation potential and a source of creativity in this phenomenon [4, 5]. So the

F. Ahlemann et al. (Eds.): WI 2021, LNISO 48, pp. 554–571, 2021.
https://doi.org/10.1007/978-3-030-86800-0_39

question remains if organizations should allow IT outside of the IT department and how to integrate it into their overall IT efforts [2].

One of the concepts that tries to solve this problem is lightweight IT introduced by Bygstad in 2015 [1]. The main idea of the concept is that new "lightweight" technologies require a different knowledge regime and should therefore be developed and run outside of the IT department [1]. In the past 5 years, several research contributions have added to this concept and tested its practicability. But so far, no literature review on the topic exists and the concept has not been placed into the context of other parallel research streams. This paper therefore aims to close this gap and derive a better overview of the different perspectives on the phenomenon of IT outside of the IT department in the literature. Starting from the new concept of lightweight IT we ask the following research questions:

- RQ1: Which contributions have been made and which practical insights have been gained regarding the lightweight IT concept since its original introduction by Bygstad in 2015 [1]?
- RQ2: What are overlaps and differences of the lightweight IT concept and the parallel research streams IT Consumerization and Shadow IT already established in information systems (IS) literature?

To answer these questions, we first detail the lightweight IT concept. The concepts of IT Consumerization [3, 6] and Shadow IT [4, 7] have already been exhaustively described in the literature, therefore they will only presented briefly here. Next, we document our methodological approach to review the literature. Then we present the findings with regard to the initial questions. Finally, these results will be discussed together with a reflection on limitations and further research ideas.

2 Background

2.1 Lightweight IT

The concept of lightweight IT was developed based on two trends: The growing size and interconnectedness of IT systems and IT Consumerization. The effects of IT Consumerization – the use of privately owned resources (hardware or software) for business purposes – are understood to be a major driver in the redefinition of the relationship between the IT department and it's consumers, the employees [3].

Bygstad's case studies on Norwegian e-health innovation successes led him to postulate the need for "a socio-technical knowledge regime driven by competent users' need for IT services, enabled by the consumerization of digital technologies." [1, p. 2] To put it simply, Bygstad introduces the notion that new technologies (tablets, electronic whiteboards, mobile phones, etc.), i.e., lightweight IT, require a new knowledge regime with a development culture that focuses on innovation and experimentation. So, the focus is on business owned resources being used for business purposes. Bygstad builds here on the knowledge regime idea from sociology and political science that includes the connections between all actors involved from IT professionals to vendors, the work practices, and the collective conventions like the shared knowledge on development and use of technologies [1, 8, 9]. For this paper the shorter and more general definition of "the overall approach to how IT can be used in work practices, and the collective conventions on the appropriate use" [8, p. 185] later introduced in the same paper will be used.

Bygstad compares lightweight IT with heavyweight technologies which he defines as "[a] knowledge regime, driven by IT professionals, enabled by systematic specification and proven digital technology and realized through software engineering" [8, p. 182]. Examples include traditional ERP systems that are managed by the IT department. In contrast, lightweight IT is characterized as supporting frontend process work, being owned by the business side, and consisting of non-invasive solutions [8]. Due to these characteristics they require a loose coupling to heavyweight IT regarding technology, standards, and organization [1]. Examples for lightweight solutions are:

- Mobile apps used for information or simple acquisition processes in everyday life or as part of a work routine – e.g., a mobile application to support the treatment of patients with high blood pressure [10].
- RPA supporting work processes – e.g., a Norwegian bank using RPA for the entire accounts-opening process for young home buyers in their mobile bank [11].
- Whiteboards, tablets and sensors supporting welfare technology solutions, often from start-up firms - several cases report on the lightweight Imatis solution that introduces whiteboards and mobile phones into the work processes of hospitals [12].

2.2   Related Concepts Already Established in IS

In the following we briefly present the neighboring concepts IT Consumerization, Shadow IT, and Business IT with a focus to drivers, benefits and risks:

IT Consumerization. According to Niehaves et al. [3], IT Consumerization refers to the use of privately-owned IT resources for business purposes. An example is the employee who checks his business e-mail on a private phone [3]. The most current literature review on the topic defines it more broadly as the use of consumer IT for work purposes [6]. This phenomenon is driven by consumers and their individual needs, e.g., employees that are used to a certain degree of efficiency and enjoyability of consumer IT now demand it in their business environment. This is enabled through the increasing number of knowledge workers and more tech-savy staff. This comes in combination with a shift to a bottom up innovation approach in IT [3].

IT Consumerization has several benefits and risks. It has been shown to increase employee satisfaction. As employees are already well acquainted with the technology it has a very high speed of adoption. The example above indicates one of the reasons for increased employee availability and for the organization it is also beneficial, that the IT investment is done by the employee. Finally, this phenomenon has been shown to increase customer focus. At the same time IT Consumerization also carries specific risks. The use of private resources can lead to security issues, as these are not managed and monitored by the organization's IT department. Often it is also not clear how support should be organized and supporting every employee device can lead to a high level of complexity. As the organization doesn't control the complete IT used in the process anymore this can also lead to a loss of process control.

Shadow IT and Business IT. The autonomous deployment, procurement, and management of IT by business representatives without alignment with the IT department is a common phenomenon. If it happens covertly it is defined as Shadow IT and if it is overt as Business IT [4]. The business managed IT concept emerged in the context of Shadow IT research, but it is probably phenomenologically closer to lightweight IT in many instances. Therefore, we carve out this phenomenon from our comparison as it requires an in-depth discussion. The use of Shadow IT is driven by several factors. There is a set of drivers that are inherent to the business function. There is the technical accessibility and IT user competence e.g., businesspeople being more knowledgeable on IT topics than before. Then there is the employee motivation, impact orientation and the peer behavior e.g., the motivation of business representatives to use IT to further their own goals. Motivational factors can also occur on the business level i.e., business environment uncertainty and BU power loss. Another set of drivers stems from the business-IT relationship. Non overt use of technologies can also be caused by IT organization and BU non-alignment. This can be amplified by IT system shortcomings, IT organization slowness, competence lack, or resource scarcity in IT organization. Finally, drivers can also be lack of restriction or awareness as well as a beneficial cost structure anticipation [4].

Shadow IT has several benefits and risks. In line with the business representative's motivation a key benefit is productivity gain and innovation increase. This can facilitate agility and flexibility of business operations for example by enhancing collaboration. Better business operations can improve user or customer satisfaction. The lack of collaboration with the IT department comes with severe security risks and can lead to a lack of data privacy. Shadow IT solutions are typically not integrated with the other systems of the organization and thereby can cause data inconsistencies. This might also lead to architecture insufficiency. The co-existence of several solutions can also lead to loss of synergies and can create inefficiencies. Finally it can lead to loss of control and cause a lack of continuity [4].

3   Method

The literature review was conducted following a sequential process [13] with the aim to create synthesis of existing knowledge [14]. We selected a keyword based approach to retrieve relevant publications on the topic as this has been identified as the most established approach in IS [13]. In a first step, publications were identified based on a keyword-based search in the key IS outlets and then by a forward search on the identified publications. Based on the lightweight IT concept postulated by Bygstad [1] we searched for "lightweight IT" OR "lightweight information systems" OR "lightweight technologies" OR "heavyweight IT" OR "heavyweight information systems" OR "heavyweight technologies". We searched in the senior scholar basket of eight as well as in proceedings of the key AIS conferences focusing on title and abstract of the publications: European Journal of Information Systems (EJIS), Information Systems Journal (ISJ), Information Systems Research (ISR), Journal of Association of Information Systems (JAIS), Journal of Information Technology (JIT), Journal of Management Information

Systems (JMIS), Journal of Strategic Information Systems (JSIS), Management Information Systems Quarterly (MISQ), International Conference on Information Systems (ICIS), European Conference on Information Systems (ECIS), Pacific Asia Conference on Information Systems (PACIS), and Americas Conference on Information Systems (AMCIS). The identified publications were then manually screened for relevance. Next, a Google Scholar based forward search was conducted for those pertaining to the topic. In the three last steps, the identified 164 publications were manually screened for relevance [15]. Please refer to Fig. 1 for the review process. This allowed us to identify 33 publications for a more detailed analysis. Following the suggested procedure for qualitative literature reviews, the different mentions of lightweight IT in these publications were coded by the authors based on their use of the concept [15]. This was done in two iterations to ensure consistent use of the categories.

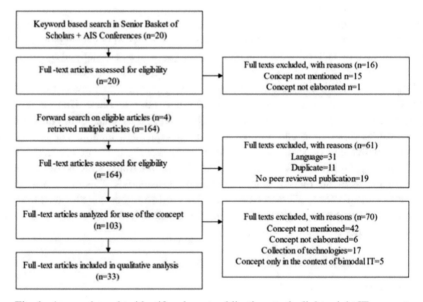

Fig. 1. Approach used to identify relevant publications to the lightweight IT concept.

The findings of the literature review and the subsequent comparison with IT Consumerization and Shadow IT are presented along the two research questions.[1]

4   Findings

In the following, we briefly present an overview of the results of our literature review in table format which we then discuss in more detail in the subsequent chapters. These were

---

[1] Details on the 33 papers that were considered for this literature review can be found at https://www.dropbox.com/s/xisnntihxqzf7j2/WI2021_Table%201_IT%20outside%20of%20the%20IT%20Department.pdf?dl=0. They are also marked with an (*) in the reference list.

analyzed regarding (1) industry area, (2) featured technology, (3) governance model (4) drivers, (5) benefits, and (6) risks. Due to limited space we present the results of the industry area (1) and featured technology (2) in textual format and therefore limit our table overview to those publications identifying governance aspects as well as drivers, benefits, or risks. The full table can, however, be found online (Table 1).

Table 1. Selection of results from the literature review on lightweight IT.

Publication	Governance model	Drivers	Benefits	Risks
Bygstad [1]	The governance of lightweight IT is unresolved	User needs, IT-Consumerization, vendor cooperation, need for a different knowledge regime	Low costs, innovation, time to market	Security, lack of integration, scalability
Bygstad [8]	-	User needs, IT Consumerization, vendor cooperation, need for a different knowledge regime	User satisfaction, low costs, innovation, time to market, non-invasive, organic growth	Scalability, security
Bygstad and Bergquist [16]	-	Vendor cooperation	Innovation, non-invasive	Security
Bygstad and Iden [17]	4 governance models (Central control, Bimodal IT, Laissez faire, and Platform model)	User needs IT-Consumerization	Easy to implement, Innovation	Security and data privacy issues
Bygstad and Øvrelid [12]	-	User needs IT-Consumerization	Innovation	Security, Lack of integration
Bygstad et al. [18]	-	User needs	Innovation, time to market	Lack of integration
Hallberg et al. [10]	Centralized IT governance for lightweight IT	-	User focus	Lack of integration

(*continued*)

Table 1. (*continued*)

Publication	Governance model	Drivers	Benefits	Risks
Hertzum and Simonsen [19]	-	-	User satisfaction, easy to implement	-
Hevner and Malgonde [20]	Governance model platform	-	Innovation	-
Kopper et al. [7]	Governance model platform	-	-	-
Mitrakis [21]	Governance model Bimodal IT	-	-	-
Osmundsen et al. [22]	2 governance strategies to mitigate lack of control mechanisms	User needs	Low costs, easy to implement, time to market, non-invasive	Synergy loss
Øvrelid [23]	-	User needs, IT-Consumerization, vendor cooperation	User focus, inno-vation, easy to implement, time to market	Security, lack of integration Scalability
Øvrelid and Bygstad [24]	-	User needs, IT-Consumerization	Low costs, innovation	Security, scalability
Øvrelid and Bygstad [25]	Decentralized IT governance for lightweight IT	-	Low costs, innovation	-
Øvrelid and Halvorsen [26]	-	-	Increased employee satisfaction, innovation	-
Øvrelid and Halvorsen [27]	-	-	Increased employee satisfaction, innovation	Lack of integration
Øvrelid et al. [28]	Governance model Bimodal IT	-	Innovation	-

(*continued*)

Table 1. (*continued*)

Publication	Governance model	Drivers	Benefits	Risks
Øvrelid et al. [29]	Governance model Bimodal IT	-	-	-
Øvrelid et al. [30]	-	-	Innovation	-
Øvrelid et al. [31]	-	User needs IT-Consumerization	Innovation	-
Øvrelid and Kempton [32]	-	IT Consumerization	Innovation, non-invasive	Lack of integration
Penttinen et al. [33]	-	IT Consumerization	Low costs, Innovation, non-invasive	Security, lack of integration
Stople et al. [11]	-	User needs	Low costs, easy to implement, Innovation, non-invasive	Lack of integration, support complexity
Torkil-sheyggi and Hertzum [34]	-	User needs	User focus, easy to implement, innovation	-
Urbach and Ahlemann [35]	Systematic separation of backend- and frontend development	-	-	-
Willcocks et al. [36]	Centralized IT governance for lightweight IT	User needs, vendor cooperation	Low costs, easy to implement, innovation	Security, scalability

The five publications Aanestad et al. [37], Asatiani et al. [38], Bygstad and Hanseth [39], Halvorsen et al. [40], Klotz et al. [4], and Urbach and Ahlemann [41] are not mentioned here as they do not detail the governance model, drivers, benefits, risks of lightweight IT. Please refer to the full table online. (see footnote 1).

4.1 General Application Areas and Industries

From the 33 publications reviewed in depth, two main contributions regarding the lightweight IT concept were identified: First, the interplay between lightweight and heavyweight IT was conceptualized further and, second, benefits and corresponding risks were explored through a number of case studies. These case studies focused mainly on the healthcare industry (22 out of 33) and a few others like financial services (3), telco (3), government services (2), utilities (2), electronics, engineering, IT services and retail. Five publications did not include a case study or a specific industry. Also, the case studies looked at different types of lightweight applications: Mobile phones (15), whiteboards (14), tablets (6), RPA (5), touch screens (3), other applications (3) and only one publication looked explicitly at the use of sensors (IoT).

4.2 Governance Models

Different contributions have dealt with the question how heavyweight and lightweight IT can be technically and organizationally integrated ranging from four proposed governance concepts to the special requirements of RPA. Firstly, four governance models are being proposed as a kind of repertoire, that can be mixed and used as needed: the Central Control, the Bimodal IT, the Laissez-fair and the Platform Model [17]:

- **Central Control Model:** Often used by heavyweight IT vendors that add mobile apps to their solutions. The (heavyweight) IT department decides over and prioritizes lightweight IT initiatives. This ensures a focus on integration and security, but constrains innovation [17].
- **Bimodal IT Model:** Following Gartner's notion a separate IT department is installed for lightweight IT. Heavyweight standards are enforced as soon as solutions are set into production, which can lead to the heavyweight IT departments resources being the constraining factor for innovation. This idea was for example discussed by Urbach and Ahlemann [41], who recommend a systematic separation of backend- and frontend development, because the later tends to be lightweight and thus demands for a more agile and user centric development approach. But they consider this as a transitionary solution. As no part of the organizations of the future is going to remain untouched from digitalization, they foresee a much closer integration of business and IT departments [41]. They assume that the organizational boundaries between business and IT might not remain as separate organizations: Application-related IT experts will work directly together with users in the specialist areas, which will lead to interdisciplinary teams [35]. This model is also favored in the context of modern IT Service Management (ITSM) to allow for digitalization [21]. The practical value of this approach was proven in the context of the Digital Renewal mega-program in the Norwegian healthcare sector where a special unit was able to start several lightweight projects and infuse innovation into the large-scale integration and standardization effort. Further research also highlighted the innovation discourse in such mega-programs [28, 29].
- **Laissez-fair Model:** Lightweight solutions are allowed to be developed as standalone solutions with the support of vendors or the heavyweight IT department. This optimally uses knowledge, abilities and monetary resources in the business for innovation, but can have drawbacks regarding security and scalability [17].

- **Platform Model:** The heavyweight solution becomes a platform for the lightweight solutions, which are typically integrated via application program interfaces (APIs). Several publications looked at the lightweight IT concept in this context ranging over different topics: The modular implementation of lightweight IT to be used to compliment a core infrastructure, which is grown as an extension of the existing base and designed and developed over its whole life cycle, [7] the usefulness of the concept in context of a new innovative development approach for applications on digital platforms, [20] its part in a platformization process [39] and its potential regarding platforms that embrace end-user IT development to enable Shadow IT becoming overt business IT [7].

Secondly, special attention has been placed on RPA as a lightweight solution, especially when compared with heavyweight backend automation [33]. For example a closer coupling of RPA initiatives to the central IT department [36] or a more decentralized approach [38] are being proposed. An in-depth study of the latter revealed building enthusiasm for digitization and local ownership as advantages and lack of control mechanisms and end-to-end process view as disadvantages. Two mitigation strategies were proposed: Tightening the loose coupling after an initial innovation period and introducing a central body for control coordination and prioritization [22]. The notion of a tighter coupling also appears regarding mobile phone systems [10].

4.3 Drivers, Benefits, and Risks of Lightweight IT

Drivers. The case studies detail several drivers for lightweight IT. User needs are mentioned as the main driver of lightweight IT across publications [1, 8, 11, 12, 17, 18, 22–24, 31, 34, 36]. Several publications also mention that this is enabled by IT Consumerization[2] e.g., the availability of consumer devices and applications for the use in work context as detailed above [1, 8, 12, 17, 23, 31–33]. Apparently, it is helpful if expert users cooperate with the vendors of these devices or applications [1, 8, 16, 23, 36]. Finally, Bygstad [1] explicitly mentions the need for a different knowledge regime for lightweight IT as a driver [1, 8].

Benefits and Corresponding Risks. The case studies also highlight several benefits and related risks of lightweight IT. These additional insights allow a better understanding of the concept:

- User focus, satisfaction improvement & lack of scalability – solutions focus on users' immediate needs (short-term usefulness of solutions) [23] and can even be deployed in a design-in-use approach, where the solution is initially incomplete by design and then developed further by the users [34]. It could even be shown that employee satisfaction with their work environment could be improved, for example when a new lightweight solution significantly reduced interruptions of work through telephone calls of other wards for nurses [18]. But this comes at a cost: Because solutions are so highly tailored to a particular environment and not built with scalability in mind, typically they do

---

[2] Explicitly mentioned by Bygstad [1], but has also differences later discussed in the comparison.

not scale well. Some solutions have to be reconfigured from scratch for additional users [8].

- Low costs, easy to implement & support complexity – Typically, lightweight solutions work with simple applications on cheap technology [1]. Moreover, their implementation is relatively cheap as they do not require specialized IT staff [19] and have limited training needs due to intuitive design and workflow focus [17]. But costs can arise later in the lifecycle, when changes in the underlying heavyweight infrastructure can lead to increased maintenance needs. For an RPA implementation team this was especially bitter as they were not always aware of changes in advance, which lead to unplanned downtime [11].
- Innovation increase, short time to market & lack of security – Several case studies looked at the application of lightweight IT solutions in the context of process innovation [12, 16, 18, 23, 26, 27, 30–32]. Three characteristics of lightweight IT were hereby identified to be especially helpful:

- Usability and implementation speed, which allows for a fast introduction of the new systems – also based on the ability to bypass the existing infrastructure [23].
- Availability of the solutions on the market and vendors' ability to support pilots, and implementations in an agile way including experimenting, prototyping and testing which leads to short development cycles [26].
- Modular structure and layered architecture that allows for a loose coupling to other system components [16].

But this approach has also drawbacks: nearly all studies found that security and data privacy issues arise, because they are not sufficiently covered in the initial iterations of solutions, as the focus is on fast and innovative solutions [17].

- Non-invasive, lack of integration, organic growth & synergy loss – solutions are often non-invasive as they only act as a presentation layer [8] like for example a BI solution that supports clinical processes across boundaries with data from different heavyweight systems [16]. But dependability on heavyweight IT and the necessary interfaces remain an issue [12]. Solutions can grow organically as users' needs change [1]. Such often decentralized efforts can lead to redundancies and local optimization as there is no central perspective on long-term synergy effects [22].

4.4 Comparison to IT Consumerization and Shadow IT

To facilitate the discussion of the differences we created a Venn diagram. As lightweight IT is, however, still a recently discovered concept we ask our readers to treat this rather as an indication then an absolute comparison (Fig. 2).

Bygstad and Iden refer explicitly to parallel research streams: "The responses from IT departments [to the arrival of smartphones and other technologies] have been mixed but have generally been negative. For instance, bring-your-own-device *(BYOD)* frequently creates unexpected problems, and parts of the IT industry have tried to stop the lightweight trend, naming it *shadow IT* […]. We believe that this approach is futile,

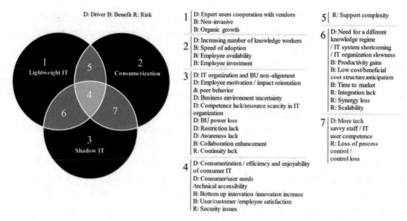

Fig. 2. Visualization of the lightweight IT, IT Consumerization and Shadow IT comparison.

mainly because user-driven IT is now an important source of business innovation." [17], p. 385][3] In the following IT Consumerization and Shadow IT as the two dominant other perspectives on IT outside of the IT department are compared to lightweight IT. Following Briel et al. [42] we now discuss each sector of the Venn diagram briefly:

(1) **Lightweight IT.** The drivers, benefits and risks explicitly mentioned for lightweight IT may not appear in the two other concepts due to different perspectives. IT Consumerization focuses rather on the effects of using existing consumer IT for work purposes [3]. In contrast lightweight IT focuses on building new solutions which leads to the focus on benefits like non-invasive, and organic growth [8]. Shadow IT focuses more on the relationship to the IT department [4] which might explain why expert user cooperation with external vendors is not a focus.

(2) **IT Consumerization.** For IT Consumerization the increased number of knowledge workers is mentioned as a driver. The literature on lightweight IT only mentions the (process) knowledge contributions and configuration efforts by the users [19]. This could be explained with the focus on (technical) vendor support instead of "more tech savvy" expert users, which depends largely on the lightweight solution in question. For example to implement RPA solutions inhouse employees need to acquire new (technical) skills [22]. The benefits speed of adoption, employee availability and employee investment cited for IT Consumerization [3] do not appear for lightweight IT as they are in part due to employees using private resources for business purposes, which is not the case for lightweight IT [8].

(3) **Shadow IT.** The drivers IT organization and BU non-alignment, employee motivation /impact orientation & peer behavior, business environment uncertainty, BU power loss, restriction lack, and awareness lack mentioned for Shadow IT do not appear for lightweight IT. One reason could be the positive focus on solutions and their innovation potential [1]. The benefit collaboration enhancement was not explicitly mentioned, as the focus was rather on organizational level process

---

[3] In this paper BYOD will be included in IT Consumerization to avoid conceptual overlaps.

improvement [26]. The risk lack of continuity appears only with the reverse interpretation that lightweight IT is only used as long as it is beneficial to users and that it grows organically [1].

(4) **Lightweight IT, IT Consumerization and Shadow IT.** Bygstad [1] even cites IT Consumerization as an enabler in his definition of lightweight IT and technical accessibility is also mentioned regarding Shadow IT [1, 4]. In combination with that *individual needs of consumers/users are mentioned for all three concepts* [1, 3, 4]. Therefore, it seems to be the same technical progress that drives all these phenomena. Typically this is mentioned in close proximity with enabling innovation that all three concepts also cite as a benefit [1, 3, 4]. Customer focus or customer satisfaction as both mentioned for IT Consumerization and Shadow IT was also shown to improve through internal process optimization. The same was found for making the lightweight solution directly available to customers. For example patients could self-check-in and avoid or at least manage queues with the Imatis solution in a Norwegian hospital [18]. The risks caused by security and privacy issues are also cited as one of the main concerns regarding lightweight IT. For example Medicloud's strategy for security and privacy was challenged by Microsoft and other heavyweight players [24].

(5) **Lightweight IT and IT Consumerization.** IT Consumerization looks at the use of private IT resources for business purposes [3]. In contrast, lightweight IT looks at the use of business resources for business purposes, the difference to the established IT research is the type of technologies used [1]. But here also lies the similarity as both concepts look at the use of new technologies like mobile services provided by 3rd party vendors for business. Some of the drivers, benefits, and risks described in the literature were also identified in the case studies on lightweight IT. *Regarding drivers the new technologies (*sensors, apps, tablets, etc.) lightweight IT focuses on also play a large role in consumer IT and IT Consumerization is mentioned as an explicit driver for lightweight IT [1]. *The e-health mega-program case in Norway clearly showed the shift to a bottom up innovation approach in IT as a starting point for lightweight IT [28]. The benefit of* increased employee satisfaction due to lightweight tool support was observed for example when nurses in a hospital reported an improved atmosphere as communication was done via the system instead of continuous phone calls [18]. The loose coupling of lightweight IT to the underlying infrastructure can lead to support complexity for example the maintenance of RPA robots at a Norwegian bank, that had to be changed in reaction to every change in the underlying systems, was perceived to require an ongoing and increasing effort [11].

(6) **Lightweight IT and Shadow IT.** The Shadow IT concept deals with IT run by business outside the IT-department [4]. Lightweight IT does the same, but focuses on specific solutions, that require a different knowledge regime and therefore should be developed outside the heavyweight IT department as Bygstad argues [1]. This differs significantly from Shadow IT, where the focus is on policy setup, awareness training and IT systems gap resolution [4]. In most cases lightweight IT is overt, but there are also cases where solutions are implemented without the prior knowledge of the IT department for example when RPA was deployed without prior knowledge of the IT department [43]. For Shadow and business-managed IT several causing

factors, benefits and risks have been identified, which show interesting overlaps to lightweight IT. Here the different framing is to be noted: Causing factors implies a negative connotation, which is not the case for lightweight IT and IT Consumerization [1, 3]. Technical accessibility is one of the key aspects of lightweight IT. Not only is it easily available, but also often its deployed directly by users or vendors, bypassing the (heavyweight) IT departments [1]. Issues with the existing heavy-weight IT- be it system shortcomings, organizational slowness or lack of resources - do not appear as explicit drivers for lightweight IT. They are only mentioned as circumstantial, rather the need for a different knowledge regime due to different characteristics is stressed [8]. But there are examples like the lack of interoperability between systems in a Norwegian hospital [18], an EPR (Electronic Patient Record) system provider repeatedly telling his customer to wait for an upgrade to receive new features or functionalities [31], or the lack of resources for local innovation due to a centrally driven mega-program [44]. But the effects of the setup, skills and capabilities of the IT department on lightweight projects does not appear in research. Finally, the cheap underlying technology such as smartphones or tablets contribute to a beneficial cost structure anticipation [1]. Several benefits also over-lap. Productivity gains and the short time to market are also cited as main benefits of lightweight IT solutions [17]. Lightweight IT has been found to foster especially process innovation and thereby lead to an innovation increase [26]. Depending on the established governance regime lightweight IT can lead to a significant agility enhancement and an increase of flexibility [18]. But with these benefits also come related risks like the integration into the existing heavyweight systems architecture and scalability. For example a hospital scheduler solution was not integrated with the EPR system as this was not build for integration and there were data privacy concerns [37]. Depending on the governance concept the lightweight IT approach can also lead to synergy loss and inefficiencies. For example a decentral introduction of RPA lead to optimization of sub-processes without a focus on overall value [22].

(7) **IT Consumerization and Shadow IT.** As the overlap in Fig. 1 shows, interestingly both IT Consumerization and Shadow IT mention more tech savvy staff/ IT user competence, which does not appear as a driver in the lightweight IT literature (yet). Also, the loss of (process) control, which is cited as a risk by IT Consumerization as well as Shadow IT is not mentioned by lightweight IT literature. The reason might be that the lightweight IT concept does not take the perspective of the existing (heavyweight) IT department and its control aspirations [1]. But both assumptions would have to be tested further.

5   Discussion, Outlook and Limitations

This paper contributes to the current IS research along its two research questions: Firstly, the research contributions regarding interplay of heavyweight and lightweight IT and benefits and corresponding risks of lightweight IT in practice were detailed. This allows an overview of the insights gained in the different research streams regarding the different aspects of the lightweight IT concept. On this basis drivers, benefits and risks of lightweight IT could be identified. This leads us to propose that the main benefit of the lightweight IT concept is to enable organizations to fully use the innovation potential outside their IT departments and gives them a toolset to integrate these new solutions with their existing heavyweight IT.

Secondly, these drivers, benefits, and risks of lightweight IT were compared to those drivers, benefits, and risks of the parallel research streams IT Consumerization and Shadow IT. This comparison showed significant overlap, but also conceptual differences. As a result of these discussions we identified six questions for further research which we present along the structure of the chapters in the findings:

Sector and Technologies.

1. For which sectors or types of organizations outside of the healthcare sector is the innovation potential of lightweight IT also interesting? – The literature focuses lightweight IT in healthcare, it would be interesting to also look at other industries.
2. What can be learned from further case studies regarding the value of the lightweight IT concept for other lightweight technologies like RPA or IoT? – The literature review showed that the case studies that developed the concept further focused on whiteboards and mobile technology. It would be helpful to widen the technology focus to test the concepts applicability.

IT Governance

3. What effect have the setups, skills and capabilities of the existing heavyweight IT department on the use of lightweight IT? – It could be helpful to understand for what kind of organization and IT department the lightweight IT concept is helpful. Here, it would be also interesting to assess what effects organizational governance, e.g., business process management governance, has on the use of lightweight IT.
4. How can the lightweight IT concept be developed to serve as a stepping stone into the direction of the convergence of IT and business as envisioned by Urbach and Ahlemann [41]? – The lightweight IT concept calls for a loose coupling of knowledge regimes, this does not yet harness the full potential of IT specialists working directly with business experts in interdisciplinary teams as envisioned.

Comparison to Other Concepts

5. What relevance do practitioners see in the IT Consumerization, Shadow IT and Lightweight IT concepts and what implications do they derive from them? – The comparison with the IT Consumerization and Shadow IT research streams showed theoretical overlaps, but their implications in practice have not been addressed yet.
6. How does the concept of business-managed IT fit into the picture of lightweight IT, IT Consumerization and Shadow IT? – In the context of Shadow IT the notion of business-managed IT (overt use of IT by business entities) has emerged, but was not explored separately here, because the underlying perspective is similar enough to compromise them both in the same framework of drivers, benefits and risks [4]. Nonetheless further research would allow to consolidate insights on governance.

These findings come with several limitations: They are still on the conceptual level and need to be tested regarding their practical value, e.g. through discussions with IT-department representatives for example in an interview or focus group format. Also, certain aspects of the lightweight IT concept like its popularity in healthcare, or its implications for innovation and/or current IT governance concepts were not explored further as this would have exceeded the scope. Nonetheless a more in-depth exploration of these aspects could enhance the understanding of the reception of the concept itself in addition to the identified research questions.

References

1. Bygstad, B.: The coming of lightweight IT. In: European Conference on Information Systems (ECIS) Proceedings (2015)
2. Urbach, N., et al.: The impact of digitalization on the IT department. Bus. Inf. Syst. Eng. **61**(1), 123–131 (2019)
3. Niehaves, B., Köffer, S., Ortbach, K.: IT consumerization - a theory and practice review. In: Americas Conference on Information Systems (AMCIS) Proceedings (2012)
4. Klotz, S., Kopper, A., Westner, M., Strahringer, S.: Causing factors, outcomes, and governance of shadow IT and business-managed IT: a systematic literature review. Int. J. Inf. Syst. Proj. Manag. **7**(1), 15–43 (2018)
5. Behrens, S.: Shadow systems. Commun. ACM **52**(2), 124–129 (2009)
6. Klesel, M., Weber, S., Walsdorff, F., Niehaves, B.: Are employees following the rules? On the effectiveness of IT consumerization policies. In: International Conference on Wirtschaftsinformatik Proceedings (2019)
7. Kopper, A., et al.: Business-managed IT: a conceptual framework and empirical illustration. In: European Conference of Information Systems (ECIS) Proceedings (2018)
8. Bygstad, B.: Generative innovation: a comparison of lightweight and heavyweight IT. J. Inf. Technol. **32**(2), 180–193 (2017)
9. Howard-Grenville, J.A., Carlile, P.R.: The incompatibility of knowledge regimes:. consequences of the material world for cross-domain work. Eur. J. Inf. Syst. **15**, 473–485 (2006)
10. Hallberg, I., Ranerup, A., Bengtsson, U., Kjellgren, K.: Experiences, expectations and challenges of an interactive mobile phone-based system to support self-management of hypertension: patients' and professionals' perspectives. Patient Prefer. Adher. **12**, 467–476 (2018)
11. Stople, A., Steinsund, H., Iden, J., Bygstad, B.: Lightweight IT and the IT function: experiences from robotic process automation in a Norwegian bank. In: Norwegian Conference for IT Use in Organisations (NOKOBIT) (2017)
12. Bygstad, B., Øvrelid, E.: Architectural alignment of process innovation and digital infrastructure in a high-tech hospital. Eur. J. Inf. Syst. **29**(3), 220–237 (2020)
13. vom Brocke, J., Simons, A., Riemer, K., Niehaves, B., Plattfaut, R., Cleven, A.: "Standing on the shoulders of giants: challenges and recommendations of literature search in information systems research. Commun. Assoc. Inf. Syst. **37**, 9 (2015)
14. Schryen, G., Wagner, G., Benlian, A., Paré, G.: A knowledge development perspective on literature reviews: Validation of a new typology in the IS field. Commun. AIS **46**, 134–186 (2020)
15. Linnenluecke, M.K., Marrone, M., Singh, A.K.: Conducting systematic literature reviews and bibliometric analyses. Aust. J. Manag. **45**(2), 175–194 (2020)

16. Bygstad, B., Bergquist, M.: Horizontal affordances for patient centred care in hospitals. In: Hawaii International Conference on System Sciences (HICSS) Proceedings (2018)
17. Bygstad, B., Iden, J.: A Governance Model for Managing Lightweight IT. In: Rocha, Á., Correia, A.M., Adeli, H., Reis, L.P., Costanzo, S. (eds.) WorldCIST 2017. AISC, vol. 569, pp. 384–393. Springer, Cham (2017). https://doi.org/10.1007/978-3-319-56535-4_39
18. Bygstad, B., Hanseth, O., Siebenherz, A., Øvrelid, E.: Process innovation meets digital infrastructure in a high-tech hospital. In: 25th European Conference on Information Systems (ECIS) 2017 Proceedings (2017)
19. Hertzum, M., Simonsen, J.: Configuring information systems and work practices for each other: what competences are needed locally? Int. J. Hum.-Comput. Stud. 122, 242–255 (2018)
20. Hevner, A., Malgonde, O.: Effectual application development on digital platforms. Electron. Mark. 29(3), 407–421 (2019). https://doi.org/10.1007/s12525-019-00334-1
21. Mitrakis, N.: Die Ausrichtung des IT-Service-Managements auf die Digitalisierung. Springer Fachmedien, Wiesbaden (2019)
22. Osmundsen, K., Iden, J., Bygstad, B.: Organizing robotic process automation: balancing loose and tight coupling. In: Hawaii International Conference on System Sciences (HICSS) Proceedings (2019)
23. Øvrelid, E.: Strategic shifts in digital infrastructures: connecting discursive formations and lightweight IT. Series of dissertations submitted to the Faculty of Mathematics and Natural Sciences, University of Oslo No. 2016, Oslo (2018)
24. Øvrelid, E., Bygstad, B.: Extending e-Health Infrastructures with Lightweight IT. In: Lundh Snis, U. (ed.) SCIS 2016. LNBIP, vol. 259, pp. 43–56. Springer, Cham (2016). https://doi.org/10.1007/978-3-319-43597-8_4
25. Øvrelid, E., Bygstad, B.: The role of discourse in transforming digital infrastructures. J. Inf. Technol. 34(3), 221–242 (2019)
26. Øvrelid, E., Halvorsen, M.R.: Process innovation with lightweight IT at an emergency unit. In: Hawaii International Conference on System Sciences (HICSS) Proceedings (2018)
27. Øvrelid, E., Halvorsen, M.R.: Supporting process innovation with lightweight IT at an emergency unit. J. Integr. Des. Process Sci. 22, 27–44 (2019)
28. E. Øvrelid, B. Bygstad, and O. Hanseth: Establishing spaces of interplay: the role of discourse in the growth of information infrastructures. IADIS Int. J. Comput. Sci. Inf. Syst. 11(2) pp. 31–46 (2016)
29. Øvrelid, E., Bygstad, B., Hanseth, O.: Discursive formations and shifting strategies in e-health programmes. In: 25th European Conference on Information Systems (ECIS) 2017 Proceedings (2017)
30. Øvrelid, E., Sanner, T., Siebenherz, A.: From admission to discharge: informating patient flow with "lightweight". In: Norwegian Conference for IT Use in Organisations (NOKOBIT) (2017)
31. Øvrelid, E., Sanner, T., Siebenherz, A.: Creating coordinative paths from admission to discharge: the role of lightweight IT in hospital digital process innovation. In: Hawaii International Conference on System Sciences (HICSS) Proceedings (2018)
32. Øvrelid, E., Kempton, A.M.: From recombination to reconfiguration: affording process innovation in digital infrastructures. In: European Conference on Information Systems (ECIS) Proceedings (2019)
33. Penttinen, E., Henje, K., Asatiani, A.: How to choose between robotic process automation and back-end system automation. In: European Conference of Information Systems (ECIS) Proceedings (2018)
34. Torkilsheyggi, A.M.Á., Hertzum, M.: Incomplete by design. A study of a design-in-use approach to systems implementation. Scand. J. Inf. Syst. 29(2), 35–60 (2017)
35. Urbach, N., Ahlemann, F.: Die IT-organisation im Wandel: Implikationen der Digitalisierung für das IT-Management. HMD Praxis der Wirtschaftsinformatik 54, 300–312 (2017)

36. Lacity, M.C., Willcocks, L.P.: The IT function and robotic process automation. London School of Economics, The Outsourcing Unit Working Research Paper Series Paper 15/05, 2015. http:// eprints.lse.ac.uk/64519/1/OUWRPS_15_05_published.pdf. Accessed 23 Aug 2020
37. Aanestad, M., Vassilakopoulou, P., Øvrelid, E.: Collaborative Innovation in healthcare: boundary resources for peripheral actors. In: International Conference for Information Systems (ICIS) Proceedings (2019)
38. Asatiani, A., Kämäräinen, T., Penttinen, E.: Unexpected Problems associated with the federated IT governance structure in robotic process automation (RPA) deployment. Aalto University Publication Series Business + Economy, Helsinki (2019)
39. Bygstad, B., Hanseth, O.: Transforming digital infrastructures through platformization. In: European Conference of Information Systems (ECIS) Proceedings (2018)
40. Halvorsen, M.R., et al.: Redesigning work with a lightweight approach to coordination technology. Comput. Inform. Nurs. 37(3), 124–132 (2019)
41. Urbach, N., Ahlemann, F.: IT Management im Zeitalter der Digitalisierung. Springer, Heidelberg (2016)
42. von Briel, F., et al.: Researching digital entrepreneurship: current issues and suggestions for future directions. Commun. Assoc. Inf. Syst. (2020, Forthcoming)
43. Lacity, M.C., Willcocks, L.P.: Robotic process automation at Telefonica O2. MIS Q. Executive 15(1) (2015)
44. Øvrelid, E., Bygstad, B., Hanseth, O. (eds.) Discursive Formations and Shifting Stratgies in e-Health Programmes (2017)

Obsolescence in IT Work: Causes, Consequences and Counter-Measures

Lisa Gussek[✉], Lisa Schned, and Manuel Wiesche

Professur Digitale Transformation, Technische Universität Dortmund, Dortmund, Germany
{lisa.gussek,lisa.schned,manuel.wiesche}@tu-dortmund.de

Abstract. The fast-moving nature of information technology is causing frequent obsolescence of technologies and competences. Changes in the environment cause a reduction in the need and demand of old competences. This results in a depreciation of these old competences and a reduction in performance in comparison to individuals with up-to-date competences. Obsolescence is especially relevant for IT professionals because the technologies they work with, and thus the demanded competences, change particularly frequently. However, what effect does that have on the education and development of IT professionals and IT work? To answer that question, we have conducted a systematic literature review. We have analyzed 115 relevant hits and identified key aspects and issues for future research. Causes for obsolescence, consequences of obsolescence, and counter-measures against obsolescence are presented as the three central dimensions of the topic.

Keywords: Obsolescence · IT professionals · IT work · Training · Literature review

1 Introduction

IT professionals are of high demand, given their unique skills in areas such as programming or software design [1]. Therefore, obsolescence is a current and important issue in information technology. When technical or economic skills are obsolete, they are less valuable and the individual is less capable than an individual with more recent skills. This can be problematic for employees and organizations. It is especially relevant for IT professionals because the technologies they work with, and thus the demanded competences, change particularly frequently [2–5].

In April 2020, the US state of New Jersey was looking for COBOL programmers because their unemployment insurance system was overburdened by the many requests resulting from the COVID-19 pandemic. The problem was that hardly any programmers can still use COBOL because the language has been outdated for about 30 years and is no longer taught [6]. This example shows that the obsolescence of systems and skills can have unexpected consequences for various aspects especially for the work of IT professionals. To prevent professional obsolescence, it is necessary to constantly renew one's skills [7, 8]. This makes it interesting to investigate how obsolescence affects the education and further training and learning of IT professionals. For example, continuous training and learning [7, 9–12], and updating [13–16] are necessary to deal with

© The Author(s), under exclusive license to Springer Nature Switzerland AG 2021
F. Ahlemann et al. (Eds.): WI 2021, LNISO 48, pp. 572–586, 2021.
https://doi.org/10.1007/978-3-030-86800-0_40

obsolescence. In addition, a change in the organizational context [17], career pathing and planning [9] or special job design [15, 18, 19] may be required.

Up to now, the topic of obsolescence in research has not been uniformly understood across its various dimensions (e.g. [10, 13–17]). Moreover, there are different perspectives on the topic, especially with regard to the definition of the phenomenon [4, 18, 20–27]. In order to better understand the phenomenon of obsolescence in all its aspects and to find out what causes, consequences and counter-measures exist for obsolescence, we investigate how obsolescence has been conceptualized so far and conduct a structured literature review for this purpose. Therefore, the following research question will be answered: *What are the central characteristics and causes of obsolescence and what are the consequences and possible counter-measures for IT professionals, IT work and organizations?*

The structure of this paper is as follows. The next section reviews the central conceptualizations of obsolescence and highlights differences through an analysis of the definitions. The methodology is then described. The subsequent section presents the three main dimensions of the topic: causes for, consequences of, and counter-measures against obsolescence. Afterward the results are discussed and finally, limitations and issues for future research are described.

2 Theoretical Background

Obsolescence describes that something becomes outdated and therefore loses value [4]. Related to professional competences this means that the once valued competences are not in demand anymore because they do not fit the requirements of the job or the profession and therefore decrease in value and contribute less to performance [4, 18, 20, 21]. Knowledge, skills and abilities are often equated with competencies [22]. There are many different categorizations of skills and abilities, with a division into technical or hard skills and soft skills being common. Soft skills include interpersonal, management and other non-technical skills [23]. In IS research, definitions of obsolescence are not consistent. There are still some differences between the concepts, for example in terms of depth, detail and focus.

In general, obsolescence is frequently not explicitly defined, only a small part of the papers that mention obsolescence in an IS context provide a definition, presumably because obsolescence is part of common language usage. Table 1 lists the most important definitions of obsolescence in an IS context.

The following definitions are based on definitions from other disciplines. While Ferdinand [24] describes obsolescence in engineers and scientists, Dubin [25], Fossum et al. [26] and Kaufman [27] cover obsolescence in professionals in general. Ferdinand [24] and Kaufman [27] both define obsolescence as the lack of up-to-date knowledge. Dubin [25] and Fossum et al. [26] on the other hand describe that obsolescence results from a discrepancy between requirements and competences.

While most of the previous definitions are somewhat similar some notable definitions differ. Shearer and Steger [28] argue that a definition of obsolescence should not be tied to effectiveness because they see no satisfactory way to measure that. They also do not distinguish between obsolescence and incompetence, in contrast to almost all

Table 1. Definitions of obsolescence

Paper	Definition
Blanton, Schambach & Trimmer [18]	"Professional obsolescence represents a deficiency that occurs to the extent a mismatch develops between vocational requirements and abilities possessed by the professional. [...] Professional competency is a broad concept, whereas job competency relates only to ones' ability to perform requirements of their current job or position"
Fu & Chen [20]	"Professional obsolescence refers to the decay or decrease in the value of professional competencies. It occurs when the job incumbent's expertise (which was sufficient to the requirements of the profession previously) is mismatched with current work demands and skill requirements owing to change in the knowledge domain"
Glass [31]	"There will come a time, I realize, when I am no longer able to keep abreast of the states of the art and practice. And I will know I have reached that point because I have just read or heard something about one or both of those states that I am unable to follow, no matter how hard I apply my own personal understanding based on having been there and done that, or studied about it"
Joseph & Ang [4]	"Professional obsolescence is typically defined as the erosion of professional competencies required for successful performance. It is essential that IT professionals possess up-to-date competencies because it affects their employability, career development, and compensation. Therefore, the erosion of competencies constitutes a potential threat to IT professionals, i.e., the threat of not being up-to-date with the rapidly changing technology environment"
Rong & Grover [21]	"Obsolescence examines the discrepancy between the changing rates of job requirements and the rates of acquiring knowledge and skills. In essence, it reflects the extent to which professionals lack in knowledge of up-to-date methods needed to maintain effective performance in their current or near-future job roles"

other definitions, which describe obsolescence as incompetence only in relation to up-to-date competences. However, Pazy [14, 29] emphasizes the importance of exploring individuals' perceptions of obsolescence, which tend to be varied and can therefore not be aggregated. She contrasts this with the prevalent view of obsolescence as simply a deficiency. De Grip, Van Smoorenburg and Borghans [30] describe different kinds of obsolescence, of which obsolescence according to other definitions is only one type, e.g. they also consider wear and tear as one type of obsolescence. But all of these are not specifically related to IS professionals.

Some differences between conceptions are already pointed out in previous research. Pazy [29] categorizes definitions based on whether they focus on the lack of knowledge as a reason for obsolescence or on the consequences, mainly in terms of impaired skills and work performance. Pazy [17] notes that obsolescence is usually defined in relation to the requirements of the workplace or the broader occupational field, but sometimes the reference is a consensually estimated body of knowledge.

Other differences are the inclusion of both obsolescence regarding the current job and obsolescence regarding the general profession (e.g. [24] vs. [20]), the focus on influencing factors or outcomes (e.g. [26] vs. [28]) and whether it is explicitly connected with less effectiveness or performance (e.g. [4] vs. [26]).

Taking all these differences into account, it is difficult to systematize the various definitions, as they are usually based on the same aspects with only minor differences. In all definitions the professional is obsolete because he is not familiar with the competences that are expected of him. In some cases, this is specifically due to new knowledge, sometimes the expectations are specified as job requirements and in some definitions the obsolescence has an explicit impact on performance.

3   Method

In this review, we searched for publications that focus on causes, consequences and countermeasures of obsolescence. We screened relevant outlets according to the guidelines of vom Brocke et al. [32] and then coded the studies with regard to their key findings on the central aspects of obsolescence. We determined the scope of the systematic literature review based on the proposed taxonomy following Cooper [33].

At first, we conducted a search (title, abstract, keywords) with the search term "obsolescence" AND (train* OR learn*) AND (it OR is OR "information technology" OR "information systems" OR cs OR "computer science" OR "programming") in the journals included in the Senior Scholars' Basket of Journals of the Association for Information Systems. However, we have not limited the search to these journals. Hits from other journals and conferences were also included. The following journals were most commonly used (number in brackets): MISQ (5), SIGMIS Database (5), CACM (4), JHRM (4), JISE (4). In addition, the following conferences were used most frequently (number in brackets): ACM SIGMIS CPR (9), AMCIS (6), ICIS (3), HICSS (2). We searched the local university library database, EBSCOhost in Business Source Premier, ERIC, Engineering Source, Education Source, and EconLit, at Scopus and in the ACM Digital Library. The time span was not limited in the literature search. First, we screened the title and then the abstract of all 836 articles and identified 41 relevant publications.

Some articles were excluded by an exclusion procedure based on the following criteria. Articles in which the topic of obsolescence is not mentioned and researched were excluded. In addition, the article should refer to IS professionals and the topic of learning or training should be included in the elaboration. Sometimes articles were included in the analysis that met only one of the criteria, because an interesting aspect is covered.

Then we performed a forward and backward search based on the articles collected so far, looking mainly for theoretical foundations, further new applications and results. This resulted in 38 additional publications. Based on these hits, a second forward and backward search was carried out, which resulted in 50 extra articles. After the exclusion of some hits, the sample consists of 115 articles. Table 2 provides a summary of the literature search process.

Subsequently, we coded the selected publications along three main coding dimensions. The first dimension covers the different causes of obsolescence. Various causes occur in the environmental context (e.g. new technologies) or in the organizational context (e.g. job requirements or organizational development) [26]. The second dimension represents the possible consequences of obsolescence. Obsolescence has different effects on individuals (e.g. emotional consequences), organizations (e.g. worse performance), or the whole environment such as the labor market (e.g. unemployment) [9]. Lastly, the third dimension comprises counter-measures against obsolescence. Various actions can help to combat obsolescence (e.g. updating or job design) [18, 34]. By summarizing the key aspects and findings along the three coding dimensions, we can carve out the focus of existing research and identify issues for future research.

Table 2. Summary of the literature search process

Outlet	Search	Hits	Selected
Scopus	*Obsolescence AND (train* OR learn*)*	193	20
ACM DL	*AND*	37	0
EBSCOhost	*(it OR is OR "information technology"* *OR "information systems" OR cs OR*	66	6
Local university library database	*"computer science" OR* *"programming")*	540	15
	Forward search	-	23
	Backward search	-	15
	Second backward and forward search	-	50
	Excluded		129
			14
	Total	836	115

4   Results

In this section of the paper, we summarize the insights from our literature review on obsolescence in IS following the three main coding dimensions: causes, consequences, and counter-measures of obsolescence. Causes are various conditions or factors that lead to obsolescence. Consequences are conditions or factors that are caused by obsolescence, and counter-measures are actions that can be taken to prevent or mitigate obsolescence. Each dimension is summarized in a separate table. The number of studies identifying the relevant aspects is listed. If more than one aspect is included in the study, it was sometimes counted twice.

4.1   Causes of Obsolescence

Obsolescence occurs when the abilities of the individual no longer match the abilities required by the role. The causes for obsolescence are therefore changes in the role that do not match the changes of the individual. Role changes can be influenced by the environmental context (e.g. new or changed technologies) or by the organizational context (e.g. job requirements or organizational development) [26]. Table 3 summarizes the main causes of obsolescence.

Most articles see the main cause of obsolescence in the technological context, as can be seen in Table 3. Relevant technologies, and thus skills and roles, change over long periods of time [9]. Technological change is often cited as the central driver for role changes and therefore obsolescence (e.g. [35–39]). Existing technologies change and develop over time. Two examples of recent technological changes are the shift from mainframe to client-server (or vice versa) or the move to enterprise resource planning systems [36]. Besides the development of existing technologies, new and innovative technologies also play a major role [21, 40–44]. In addition to technological change or innovation, other factors from the external environmental context can also cause obsolescence. Dubin [25], Blanton et al. [18] and Egan et al. [44] see an impact of globalized markets. In addition, Ang and Slaughter [9] see an influence from IT labor markets, through labor shortages and regional differences.

Another important reason for obsolescence lies in the organizational context. High work and job requirements, overload, a lack of opportunities and support can lead to a continuous failure to keep up to date [46]. Especially in the IT discipline new skills and knowledge are needed due to rapid technological change [7, 8]. Role changes of IT professionals are potential causes of obsolescence [26]. New technology creates the need for new jobs and a broader skills base [23]. More IT professionals work outside the traditional IT department and the tasks of professionals have changed [3]. There are also more IT professionals working as independent contractors [8]. Finally, organizational development can lead to obsolescence, e.g. in consequence of differences between job changes and personal changes [22, 26, 45]. Sørensen and Stuart [47] describe that obsolescence also occurs when the organization's innovations no longer match environmental demand due to technological change.

Table 3. Main causes of obsolescence

Causes for obsolescence		Studies	Total	Example articles
Technology	Existing technologies that are changing or developing	55	71	[35–37]
	New technology and technological innovation	16		[21, 40–42]
Organization-individuum fit	Job requirements (e.g. changes of knowledge and skill requirements)	22	40	[16, 20]
	Change in roles	7		[3, 8]
	Organizational development (e.g. differences between job changes and personal changes)	11		[22, 26, 45]

4.2 Consequences of Obsolescence

The consequences of obsolescence are described below and summarized in Table 4. Different levels are considered: the level of the organization, the individual level, and the macro-environment [9]. The organizational level includes human resources and business results, the individual level covers attitudes and behavior of employees and the macro level describes the aspect of labor markets and the national economy. The results at these levels also influence each other. For example, if individuals are not able to perform high-quality work, this results in the underperformance of companies and thus of the industry as a whole [19].

On the individual level, the emotional consequences of experiencing obsolescence can include dissatisfaction, tension, boredom, pessimism and frustration [29]. Other common negative emotions are helplessness as well as inability and fear for one's reputation. The reason for this can be the forced self-assessment that calls one's own professional identity into question [35, 46]. Obsolescence can also have an impact on stress and psychological strain. Chilton et al. [36], for example, showed mental stress among professionals in transition.

Obsolescence also influences the intention to change the organization or profession ("turnover intention" or "turnaway intention"). Arman et al. [50] as well as Colomo-Palacios et al. [51] identify a strong correlation between the threat of obsolescence and the intention to change the profession or to give up the software career. This is also consistent with the findings of Fu [49] and Fu and Chen [20], which found a correlation between the threat of obsolescence and career commitment among IT professionals. Joseph and Ang [4] note that IT professionals who feel threatened by obsolescence are more likely to want to change their organizations than their careers.

At the organizational level, obsolescence can lead to lower productivity and performance [43, 52, 53]. The lower performance can result from a skills mismatch in the labor market [54]. Lower productivity may also be a reason for lower performance because a

Table 4. Main consequences of obsolescence

Consequences of obsolescence		Studies	Total	Example articles
Individual level	Emotional consequences: stress, strain, work exhaustion, uncertainty	13	24	[29, 35, 36, 46]
	Turnover	3		[4, 48]
	Change of professions or career commitment, turnaway	8		[20, 49–51]
Organizational level	Worse performance or productivity	11	18	[36, 43, 52–54]
	Need for investments or higher costs, legacy systems	7		[29, 55]
Macro level	(Un)employment	3	18	[54, 56]
	Shortage of skilled workers	5		[7, 19]
	Universities: obsolete curricula, obsolete teaching material, outdated courses	10		[39, 57]

lot of learning is needed in transition periods [36]. Obsolescence can also result in information systems becoming "legacy systems", i.e. obsolete systems. This makes them more expensive to maintain [55].

At the macro level, technological change in the labor market can lead to a skills mismatch between supply and demand and thus to higher unemployment [54]. Another emerging problem at the macro level concerns universities. Obsolescence leads to outdated curricula, obsolete courses, and obsolete teaching materials [39, 57].

4.3 Counter-Measures Against Obsolescence

Previous research has not yet brought together what can be done to combat obsolescence. Therefore, this section groups and explains the most important counter-measures against obsolescence. Table 5 summarizes the results. We divided the measures into two categories: Measures relating to the person or the individual and those relating to the task or work of the person.

Measures that start in higher education are mostly about adapting to the needs of the industry. The major problem in curriculum design is the increasing range of skills required by employers [22, 58]. One way to provide this necessary breadth of skills is to offer different courses of study to prepare students for different IT professions [3, 41]. Great flexibility in the composition of courses can also be helpful to allow for different specializations [58]. Another measure against obsolescence is a change in the way teaching is organized, for example, to promote non-technical skills such as communication [38, 39, 63].

Other measures that relate to the individual are aimed at changing the person's skill set. On the one hand, continuous learning and training play an important role. With

Table 5. Main counter-measures against obsolescence

Counter-measures against obsolescence			Studies	Total	Example articles
Related to person	Education	Curriculum design or redesign	24	79	[22, 41, 58]
		Changing the structure of teaching	8		[38, 39, 57]
	Skills set	Training, continuous and lifelong learning	35		[9–12]
		Support updating	12		[13–16]
Related to task	Changing the organisational context		6	17	[21, 59, 60]
	Staffing		4		[23, 26, 61, 62]
	Career pathing and planning		2		[9, 19]
	Job design		6		[15, 18, 19, 63]

rapid changes in IT, it is challenging to maintain a capable workforce [7]. Training is an important part of development measures that can prevent obsolete and stressed employees and staff turnover [7, 9–12]. Training helps employees to acquire the new skills they need to fill new roles [9]. In addition to technical skills, non-technical skills and characteristics such as self-efficacy should be trained [7, 20]. On the other hand, organizations must support updating. Updating can be a reaction to obsolescence [13, 16]. Furthermore, it is a way of coping with obsolescence [13, 14, 17].

Additional measures relate to the work and tasks of individuals. Because the most important learning takes place at work, a supportive climate, work design, and support from supervisors are particularly important in preventing obsolescence [17]. According to Solomon [59], it is important to create an organizational environment where information is shared and to create a culture that sees continuous learning as a core value of the organization. Furthermore, the authors Gallivan et al. [58] and Lentini and Gimenez [52] describe lifelong learning as necessary for IT professionals. Aasheim et al. [41] underline the importance of the willingness of IT graduates to learn. Other research highlights the need to create a basis for lifelong learning [23, 64, 65].

Staffing can also be a way to prevent obsolescence at the organizational level. For organizations, recruitment can be faster than training their own employees [26]. It may also be cheaper to train a graduate than to teach new technologies to a more experienced and thus possibly better-paid employee [23]. Recruitment is also a way for the company to learn. They help older organizations, in particular, to combat obsolescence by creating new areas of knowledge in the company [61].

Additionally, Ang and Slaughter [9] see career pathing and planning as an effective part of professional development. The development of career development plans for individual workers to help to combat obsolescence [19].

Furthermore, the design of the work (job design) determines what kind of work has to be done and how it has to be performed. Challenging tasks and rotation programs can prevent obsolescence [15, 18, 19]. Work design can be used to provide growth opportunities and develop human capital. It also affects job satisfaction and employability [7]. Therefore, job design, for example through job rotation or job enlargement, should be part of development programs [63].

5 Discussion

In this section, we discuss central issues for future research on obsolescence in IS based on the analysis of the existing literature. We discuss three major issues: the importance of obsolescence for IT work research, the need for further research on the counter-measures against obsolescence, and the specialty of the topic for new forms of work like working the gig economy. We suggest that future research on these topics will deepen our understanding of obsolescence in IT and enable us to derive recommendations for dealing with it in practice.

We firstly suggest that obsolescence is especially important in the IT discipline and must be better understood in the future. A constant renewal of the skills and knowledge of IT professionals is necessary, as rapid technological change and other factors mean that old skills are no longer needed and demanded. For example, because of the pressure to adapt to rapidly changing customer requirements and manage increasingly complex IT architectures, many organizations have begun to establish joint cross-functional DevOps teams that integrate tasks, knowledge and skills related to the planning, building and operating of software product activities [66]. At the same time, skills may remain relevant beyond their actual obsolescence if systems based on obsolete technology are not fully replaced [23, 35–37]. This phenomenon should be further investigated in the future.

Especially IT professionals are affected by obsolescence because current technologies and market conditions, and therefore the skills required, change particularly frequently [67]. IT work is driven by rapid technological change, resulting in rapid obsolescence of knowledge and the continuing need for learning, updating and training [68, 69]. The IT discipline has changed more rapidly than other professions. The demands on skills and knowledge of IT professionals have changed significantly and technological change is causing dynamic developments [68]. For this reason, obsolescence is one of the greatest career challenges and a threat to IT professionals [2, 3]. The knowledge and skills of IT professionals are becoming obsolete faster than the skills of other professionals [4].

Despite this described relevance for IT work, the problem of obsolescence has received little attention in previous IS research. It should be investigated more in the future, especially since the topic of obsolescence will become even more important in the future, as new technologies are always being developed, but the old technologies are never completely replaced.

Second, the literature research revealed that there are limitations of current research concerning counter-measures against obsolescence. Although IT professionals are constantly faced with the threat of professional obsolescence, little research has focused on how to deal with it and what counter-measures can be taken. Previous research has not yet brought together what can be done to combat obsolescence.

Several counter-measures were identified in this study, but these will have to be examined more closely in the future. It should be highlighted how the different ways to combat obsolescence affect individuals and organizations. Furthermore, it has not yet been fully investigated how employers and organizations can be motivated to take obsolescence seriously and implement measures to manage it.

The topic is also relevant to universities. In the analysis of this paper, it was emphasized that education has to deal with the consequences of obsolescence, such as obsolete curricula, obsolete teaching material or outdated courses. Due to the special importance of obsolescence in the IS discipline, IT degree programs in particular need to be adapted. Therefore, future research in this area is necessary.

Finally, an analysis of the existing literature revealed a lack of research on the consequences of obsolescence in non-standard employment situations. Papers dealing with updating and obsolescence only consider traditional employment relationships. Although they point out changing roles and labor markets, the focus is usually on employees. Novel work conditions such as those of the gig economy are very different from the working conditions of traditional employees.

Technological change has led to more people working outside strong organizational contexts in a so-called "gig economy", as independent workers loosely linked to organizations or selling directly to the market [70]. Typical characteristics of gig workers, as opposed to traditional employment relationships, are higher financial instability and job insecurity, higher autonomy, career path uncertainty, work transience and psychical and relational separation or loneliness [71]. Self-employed IT professionals such as gig workers must, therefore, take care of measures against obsolescence themselves as they do not receive any support from the organization, their supervisors or colleagues. They cannot shift the responsibility for updating to entire departments and must themselves take the measures that are actually the responsibility of the organization. Also, the motivation of the individual for dealing with obsolescence plays a major role. But the motivation of gig workers may be different from that of traditional employees [72]. Furthermore, the transience of this form of work requires gig workers to constantly apply their skills and expertise to new combinations of tasks when moving between jobs. Thus, many open questions become apparent which can be addressed in future research.

Our study makes several contributions to IS research and practice. First, we provide a broad overview of research on obsolescence in IS and the main aspects of the topic, and we bundle the results in different dimensions. Especially the three result tables help to sort the previous results by developing a structure for embedding obsolescence in the three dimensions. Second, we contribute to the IS literature by expanding the knowledge about the causes of obsolescence, the understanding of the consequences of obsolescence at the individual, organizational and macro levels will be improved and countermeasures against obsolescence will be presented, which are person- or task-related. Third, we identify relevant gaps in research. Fourth, we emphasize the relevance of the topic, especially for IT work. However, it also becomes clear that the results are also relevant for other disciplines such as medicine or mechanical engineering. Finally, this study is relevant to practice by showing the relevance of dealing with obsolescence in organizations. There are several negative consequences if no or the wrong countermeasures are applied.

Despite valuable contributions, our study underlies several limitations. First, the literature search may not cover all relevant studies due to the choice of outlets and keywords. Second, the selection of sources is subjective, despite the systematic approach. Third, there may be other relevant topics for future research that were not identified in this study. These could be discovered by future work.

6 Conclusion

In this paper, we summarized and analyzed recent literature on obsolescence in IT and derived central issues for future research based on the presented results. We analyzed the different definitions and conceptualizations of obsolescence and described differences among these definitions. Furthermore, we identified and presented three main dimensions of the topic: causes for, consequences of, and counter-measures against obsolescence. In doing so, we highlighted three major issues for future research. First, we suggest that obsolescence is very important for IT work and must be better understood in the future. This will become even more important in the future as new technologies are always being developed but the old ones are never completely replaced. Second, the counter-measures against obsolescence need to be examined more closely. Different questions arise, for example how the measures affect different individuals or how employers can be motivated and supported to implement different measures. Third, it is very important, especially for new forms of work such as the gig economy, to investigate the different dimensions of obsolescence, as there is much more self-responsibility among gig workers for their careers and thus also for updating and training.

References

1. Kirwan, E.: Why the demand for IT professionals has increased by 28% (2019). https://www.linkedin.com/pulse/why-demand-professionals-has-increased-28-earlan-kirwan. Accessed 24 Nov 2020
2. Fu, J.-R.: Understanding career commitment of IT professionals: perspectives of push–pull–mooring framework and investment model. Int. J. Inf. Manag. 31, 279–293 (2011)
3. Lee, D.M.S., Trauth, E.M., Farwell, D.: Critical skills and knowledge requirements of is professionals: a joint academic/industry investigation. MISQ. 19, 313–340 (1995)
4. Joseph, D., Ang, S.: The threat-rigidity model of professional obsolescence and its impact on occupational mobility behaviors of IT professionals. In: ICIS 2001 Proceedings, pp. 567–574 (2001)
5. De Grip, A., van Loo, J.: The economics of skills obsolescence: a review. In: Grip, A., de van Loo, J., Mayhew, K. (eds.) The Economics of Skills Obsolescence. Theoretical Innovations and Empirical Applications, Amsterdam, Boston, vol. 21, pp. 1–26. JAI (2002)
6. Steinberg, J.: COVID-19 Response: New Jersey Urgently Needs COBOL Programmers (Yes, You Read That Correctly). https://josephsteinberg.com/covid-19-response-new-jersey-urgently-needs-cobol-programmers-yes-you-read-that-correctly/. Accessed 13 June 2020
7. Bartol, K.M., Martin, D.C.: Managing information systems personnel: a review of the literature and managerial implications. MIS Q. 6, 49–70 (1982)
8. Niederman, F., Sumner, M., Maertz, C.P.: An analysis and synthesis of research related to turnover among IT personnel. In: Shayo, C. (ed.) Proceedings of the 2006 ACM SIGMIS CPR Conference on Computer Personnel Research Forty Four Years of Computer Personnel Research Achievements, Challenges & the Future, pp. 130–136. ACM, New York (2006)

9. Ang, S., Slaughter, S.A.: The missing context of information technology personnel: a review and future directions for research. In: Zmud, R.W., Price, M.F. (eds.) Framing the Domains of IT Management. Projecting the Future Through the Past, Cincinnati, OH, pp. 305–327. Pinnaflex Educational Resources (2000)

10. Biswas, S.B., Chatterjee, S., Mukherjee, A.: Training need in IT sector-focussing on IBM. TCS and CTS. Globsyn Manag. J. **4**, 103–108 (2010)

11. Gaimon, C., Özkan, G.F., Napoleon, K.: Dynamic resource capabilities: managing workforce knowledge with a technology upgrade. Org. Sci. **22**, 1560–1578 (2011)

12. Sethi, V., King, R.C., Quick, J.C.: What causes stress in information system professionals? Commun. ACM **47**, 99–102 (2004)

13. Pazy, A.: The threat of professional obsolescence: how do professionals at different career stages experience it and cope with it? Hum. Resour. Manage. **29**, 251–269 (1990)

14. Pazy, A.: Updating in response to the experience of lacking knowledge. Appl. Psychol. **53**, 436–452 (2004)

15. Chaudhary, P.N., Agrawal, K.G.: Professional obsolescence and the role of continuing education. Ind. J. Ind. Relat. **14**, 19–35 (1978)

16. Joseph, D., Kuan Koh, C.S.: Organization support as a moderator in coping with the threat of professional obsolescence. In: AMCIS 2011 Proceedings - All Submissions, pp. 1–8 (2011)

17. Pazy, A.: Concept and career-stage differentiation in obsolescence research. J. Org. Behav. **17**, 59–78 (1996)

18. Blanton, J.E., Schambach, T., Trimmer, K.J.: Factors affecting professional competence of information technology professionals. SIGCPR Comput. Pers. **19**, 4–19 (1998)

19. Li, H., Driscoll, J.A., Liu, Z.: Obsolescence in Software Engineering Careers. Worcester Polytechnic Institute (2010)

20. Fu, J.-R., Chen, J.H.F.: Career commitment of information technology professionals: the investment model perspective. Information & Management **52**, 537–549 (2015)

21. Rong, G., Grover, V.: Keeping up-to-date with information technology: testing a model of technological knowledge renewal effectiveness for IT professionals. Inf. Manag. **46**, 376–387 (2009)

22. Klimplová, L.: Employers' view on problems related to workforce skills and qualification. J. Competitiveness **4**, 50–66 (2012)

23. Niederman, F., Ferratt, T.W., Trauth, E.M.: On the Co-evolution of information technology and information systems personnel. SIGMIS Datab. **47**, 29–50 (2016)

24. Ferdinand, T.N.: On the Obsolescence of Scientists and Engineers. Am. Sci. **54**, 46–56 (1966)

25. Dubin, S.S.: Maintaining competence through updating. In: Willis, S.L., Dubin, S.S. (eds.) Maintaining Professional Competence. Approaches to Career Enhancement, Vitality, and Success Throughout a Work Life, pp. 9–43. Jossey-Bass, San Francisco (1990)

26. Fossum, J.A., Arvey, R.D., Paradise, C.A., Robbins, N.E.: Modeling the skills obsolescence process: a psychological/economic integration. AMR **11**, 362–374 (1986)

27. Kaufman, H.G.: Obsolescence & Professional Career Development. AMACOM, New York (1974)

28. Shearer, R.L., Steger, J.A.: Manpower obsolescence: a new definition and empirical investigation of personal variables. Acad. Manag. J. **18**, 263–275 (1975)

29. Pazy, A.: Cognitive schemata of professional obsolescence. Hum. Relat. **47**, 1167–1199 (1994)

30. de Grip, A., van Smoorenburg, M., Borghans, L.: The Dutch Observatory on Employment and Training. Research Centre for Education and the Labour Market, Maastricht (1997)

31. Glass, R.L.: On personal technical obsolescence. Commun. ACM **43**, 15 (2000)

32. vom Brocke, J., Simons, A., Niehaves, B., Riemer, K., Plattfaut, R., Cleven, A.: Reconstructing the giant: on the importance of rigour in documenting the literature search process. In: ECIS 2009 Proceedings (2009)

33. Cooper, H.M.: Organizing knowledge syntheses: a taxonomy of literature reviews. Knowl. Soc. **1**, 104–126 (1988)
34. Dubin, S.S.: The psychology of keeping up-to-date. ChemTech **2**, 393–397 (1972)
35. Tsai, H.-Y., Compeau, D., Haggerty, N.: Of races to run and battles to be won: technical skill updating, stress, and coping of IT professionals. Hum. Resour. Manag. **46**, 395–409 (2007)
36. Chilton, M.A., Hardgrave, B.C., Armstrong, D.J.: Performance and strain levels of it workers engaged in rapidly changing environments. SIGMIS Datab. **41**, 8–35 (2010)
37. Wingreen, S.C., Blanton, J.E.: A social cognitive interpretation of person-organization fitting: The maintenance and development of professional technical competency. Hum. Resour. Manage. **46**, 631–650 (2007)
38. Angeli, L., Laconich, J.J.J., Marchese, M.: A constructivist redesign of a graduate-level CS course to address content obsolescence and student motivation. In: Zhang, J., Sherriff, M., Heckman, S., Cutter, P., Monge, A. (eds.) Proceedings of the 51st ACM Technical Symposium on Computer Science Education, pp. 1255–1261. ACM, New York (2020)
39. Bochenina, K., Dukhanov, A., Karpova, M., Shmelev, V.: An approach to hybrid learning resource design for training professionals in computational science. Procedia Comput. Sci. **101**, 439–448 (2016)
40. Nelson, R.R.: Educational needs as perceived by IS and end-user personnel: a survey of knowledge and skill requirements. MIS Q. **15**, 503–525 (1991)
41. Aasheim, C., Shropshire, J., Li, L., Kadlec, C.: Knowledge and skill requirements for entry-level IT workers: a longitudinal study. J. Inf. Syst. Educ. **23**, 193–204 (2012)
42. Tsai, H.P., Compeau, D., Haggerty, N.: A cognitive view of how IT professionals update their technical skills. In: Tanniru, M. (ed.) Proceedings of the 2004 SIGMIS conference on Computer Personnel Research Careers, Culture, and Ethics in a Networked Environment, pp. 70–73. ACM, New York (2004)
43. de Grip, A.: Evaluating Human Capital Obsolescence. Research Centre for Education and the Labour Market, Maastricht (2006)
44. Egan, T.M., Yang, B., Bartlett, K.R.: The effects of organizational learning culture and job satisfaction on motivation to transfer learning and turnover intention. Hum. Resour. Dev. Q. **15**, 279–301 (2004)
45. Kaplan, D.M., Lerouge, C.: Managing on the edge of change: human resource management of information technology employees. Hum. Resour. Manag. **46**, 325–330 (2007)
46. Pazy, A., Goussinsky, R.: Professionals' experience of lack of knowledge: a phenomenological study. J. Soc. Behav. Pers. **10**, 907–922 (1995)
47. Sørensen, J.B., Stuart, T.E.: Aging, obsolescence, and organizational innovation. Adm. Sci. Q. **45**, 81 (2000)
48. Joseph, D., Tan, M.L., Ang, S.: Is updating play or work? Int. J. Soc. Org. Dyn. IT **1**, 37–47 (2011)
49. Fu, J.-R.: Is information technology career unique? Exploring differences in career commitment and its determinants among IT and non-it employees. Int. J. Electron. Bus. Manag. **8**, 272–281 (2010)
50. Arman, M., Mahmud, I., Ramayah, T., Rabaya, T., Rawshon, S.: My knowledge is not enough: An investigation on the impact of threat of professional obsolescence on turn away intention among IT professionals in Bangladesh. In: Proceedings of the 1st International Conference on Business & Management (2017)
51. Colomo-Palacios, R., Casado-Lumbreras, C., Misra, S., Soto-Acosta, P.: Career abandonment intentions among software workers. Hum. Fact. Ergon. Manuf. Serv. Ind. **24**, 641–655 (2014)
52. Lentini, V., Gimenez, G.: Depreciation of human capital: a sectoral analysis in OECD countries. IJM **40**, 1254–1272 (2019)
53. Al-Khatib, W.G., Bukhres, O., Douglas, P.: An empirical study of skills assessment for software practitioners. Inf. Sci. – Appl. 4, 83–118 (1995)

54. Santoso, G.: Technology as a driver of skills obsolescence and skills mismatch: implications for the labour market, society and the economy. ANU Undergraduate Res. J. **7**, 49–62 (2015)
55. Jenab, K., Noori, K., Weinsier, P.D., Khoury, S.: A dynamic model for hardware/software obsolescence. Int. J. Qual. Reliab. Manag. **31**, 588–600 (2014)
56. van Loo, J., de Grip, A., de Steur, M.: Skills obsolescence: causes and cures. IJM **22**, 121–137 (2001)
57. do Rosario, C.A.S., das Rosas, J.A.: Affordable Remote platform for robotics learning in engineering courses. In: Proceedings, IECON 2019 - 45th Annual Conference of the IEEE Industrial Electronics Society. Convention Center, Lisbon, Portugal, 14 - 17 October 2019, pp. 6789–6794. IEEE, Piscataway (2019)
58. Gallivan, M.J., Truex, D.P., Kvasny, L.: Changing patterns in IT skill sets 1988–2003. SIGMIS Datab. **35**, 64–87 (2004)
59. Solomon, C.M.: Continual learning: racing just to keep up. Workforce (10928332) 78, 66 (1999)
60. Kozlowski, S.W.J., Hults, B.M.: An exploration of climates for technical updating and performance. Pers. Psychol. **40**, 539–563 (1987)
61. Jain, A.: Learning by hiring and change to organizational knowledge: countering obsolescence as organizations age. Strat. Manag. J. **37**, 1667–1687 (2016)
62. Boehm, M., Stolze, C., Fuchs, A., Thomas, O.: Enabling IT Professionals to Cope with Technological Change through Skill-based Coaching. Osnabrück (2013)
63. Martins, A., Martins, I., Petiz, O.: Learning and development as cornerstones for sustaining the knowledge economy. Int. J. Learn. **14**, 97–110 (2008)
64. Gallagher, K.P., et al.: A typology of requisite skills for information technology professionals. In: 44th Hawaii International Conference on System Sciences: (HICSS), 4–7 January 2011, Koloa, Kauai, Hawaii, pp. 1–10 (2011)
65. Liu, X.M., Murphy, D.: Tackling an IS educator's dilemma: a holistic model for "when" and "how" to incorporate new technology courses into the IS/IT curriculum. In: SAIS 2012 Proceedings, pp. 176–181 (2012)
66. Wiedemann, A., Wiesche, M., Gewald. H., Krcmar, H.: Understanding how DevOps aligns development and operations: a tripartite model of intra-IT alignment. Eur. J. Inf. Syst. 1–16 (2020)
67. Wiesche, M., Joseph, D., Thatcher, J., Gu, B., Krcmar, H.: IT workforce. MIS Q. Res. Curations (2020). Bush, A., Rai, A. (eds.). http://misq.org/research-curations. Accessed 21 June 2019
68. Zhang, X., Ryan, S.D., Prybutok, V.R., Kappelman, L.: Perceived obsolescence, organizational embeddedness, and turnover of it workers. SIGMIS Datab. **43**, 12–32 (2012)
69. Apfel, I., Pflügler, C., Wiesche, M., Krcmar, H.: IT project member turnover and outsourcing relationship success: an inverted-U effect. In: International Conference on Wirtschaftsinformatik (2020)
70. Petriglieri, G., Ashford, S.J., Wrzesniewski, A.: Agony and Ecstasy in the gig economy: cultivating holding environments for precarious and personalized work identities. Adm. Sci. Q. **64**, 124–170 (2019)
71. Ashford, S.J., Caza, B.B., Reid, E.M.: From surviving to thriving in the Gig economy: a research agenda for individuals in the new world of work. Res. Org. Behav. **38**, 23–41 (2018)
72. Jabagi, N., Croteau, A.M., Audebrand, L.K., Marsan, J.: Gig-workers' motivation: thinking beyond carrots and sticks. J. Manag. Psychol. **34**(4), 192–213 (2019)

Bridging the Gap – An Analysis of Requirements for Performance Measurement Systems in Digital Innovation Units

Thomas Haskamp[✉], Annalena Lorson, Danielly de Paula, and Falk Uebernickel

Chair for Design Thinking and Innovation Research, Hasso Plattner Institute,
University of Potsdam, Potsdam, Germany
{thomas.haskamp,annalena.lorson,danielly.depaula,
falk.uebernickel}@hpi.de

Abstract. Due to a rapidly changing business environment, companies feel under constant pressure to innovate. In response to this challenge, and to accelerate their digital innovation endeavours, many incumbent firms set up Digital Innovation Units. To assess the effectiveness of these units, scholars and practitioners have called for the need to develop adequate means of measuring performance. This paper, therefore, reviews the literature on Performance Measurement Systems for Digital Innovation Units, and derives nine requirements. Conducting five case studies of Digital Innovation Units, we investigate the level of adoption of these requirements and propose three additional ones for a Performance Measurement System for innovation activities in Digital Innovation Units. We discuss these requirements and explain the reasons for their different levels of adoption. Thus, we contribute to literature and practice with a more adequate way of evaluating the performance of Digital Innovation Units, valuable to researchers and managers.

Keywords: Digital Innovation · Digital Innovation Unit · Performance Measurement System (requirements)

1 Introduction

Digital innovation presents a new paradigm and challenges the way we create innovation in firms [1]. One upcoming approach of reorganizing innovation for incumbent firms – which are especially challenged by new market entrants [2] – are Digital Innovation Units (DIU). These are organisational setups intended to initiate and develop digital innovation of various types [3]. While DIUs are gaining increasing attention in both academia [4, 5] and practice [6], there has been no agreement yet on their definition, only on several of their key characteristics. Accordingly, DIUs are dedicated and specialized (digital) units [7], separated from the main organisation in terms of location, mindset, collaboration, and communication. At the same time, they still remain *"connected through the transfer of knowledge, exchange mechanisms, and people moving between the new and 'old' units"* [3]. In this paper, we follow the definition proposed by Barthel et al. [5] which focuses on DIUs as *"organisational units with the overall*

F. Ahlemann et al. (Eds.): WI 2021, LNISO 48, pp. 587–605, 2021.
https://doi.org/10.1007/978-3-030-86800-0_41

goal to foster organisational digital transformation by performing digital innovation activities for existing and novel business areas". Until now, research on the success or performance of DIUs in creating value is rare to non-existent [5]. Conversely, one of the reasons for their failure or abolishment, as identified in a recent study by Raabe et al. [8], is the lack of clarity surrounding the objectives that a DIU has been given. Both the lack of research and the clarity of their objectives underline the need for a Performance Measurement System capable of capturing the value contribution of DIUs. The difficulty here, however, lies in the very nature of the activities of DIUs. By definition, innovation is a very exploratory research area, associated with the early stages of innovation, where projects are subject to high uncertainty [9]. In addition to procedural challenges, the characteristics of digital innovation imply that other forms of measurement are required in addition to those already used by firms [10]. For example, the customer perspective on a specific digital product or service is becoming increasingly important, but has so far not been adequately represented by a key performance indicator [11]. While the literature has already analysed requirements for measuring innovation activities [12], and specifically looked at designing Performance Measurement Systems (PMS) in the context of ambidexterity [13–15], research is limited when it comes to combining the necessity of rethinking measurement efforts for early digital innovation activities [5, 10]. Therefore, this paper aims to investigate the specific requirements of a PMS for innovation activities in DIUs and the current state of awareness and operationalisation in practice. For this purpose, the following research questions are addressed:

- [RQ1] Based on the literature, what are the existing requirements for a PMS relevant to DIUs, and how are these currently adopted in practice?
- [RQ2] What are the specific requirements for a PMS to measure the innovation activities of DIUs?

To answer the first part of RQ1, we review and synthesize the existing literature on PMS, from which we derive a set of requirements relevant to DIUs along three different streams: Requirements for PMS in general (equally applicable to digital innovation and agile performance measurement), requirements for PMS specifically relevant in the area of innovation, and special requirements for PMS for digital innovation and agile working. Subsequently, we use a multiple case study to examine practitioners' awareness of these theoretical requirements and provide initial insights on the status quo of their operationalization – answering the second part of RQ1 – as well as identify three new requirements – answering RQ2. In this way, we aim to contribute to both performance measurement and DIU research by bringing them closer together while focusing on the challenging area of early innovation activities. From the perspective of PMS research, we create the basis for the development of a PMS that can capture the complexity of the early innovation activities and recognize the impact of digital innovation on the measurement process. From a DIU research perspective, we take a first step in the challenging direction of measuring their success, which has already been raised in previous papers [4, 5].

2 Related Work – Measuring Digital Innovation

In today's world, more than ever before, new digital ventures constantly challenge incumbent firms in various industries to keep up the speed and agility of developing customer-centric products and services [2]. To remain competitive, companies need to be able to successfully develop and implement innovations related to digital products, services, processes, and business models – so-called digital innovation [16]. Current research conceptually differentiates between innovation that is enabled by information technology (IT) ('IT-enabled innovation') and digital innovation [16]. IT-enabled innovation refers to the situation where an organisation imports an existing artifact, which it assimilated into the organisational context. Digital innovation – the focus of this paper – has been conceptualised by Yoo et al., for example, as *"the carrying out of new combinations of digital and physical components to produce novel products"* [1]. Managing and effectively orchestrating digital innovation is a complex task, which requires appropriate practices, processes, and principles [17]. In recent years, the digital innovation has increasingly been enabled through the implementation of separate 'fast lanes', often in the form of DIUs [7, 18, 19]. DIUs foster (digital) innovation by bundling a firm's exploration efforts and by adopting special practices such as agile methods (e.g., Scrum) or exploratory methods (e.g., Design Thinking) [3, 7, 8]. With the proliferation of DIUs, research contributions on the topic are also increasing [3–5, 7]. However, the literature still lies in its infancy, and notably the very central question of the efficiency and benefits of DIUs has not yet been addressed. Research already calls for contributions on that topic and Frey et al. [20] and Hund et al. [4], amongst others, raise the specific difficulties of measuring digital innovation outcomes in general and the necessity to deal with this topic [4, 5, 10, 20]. Potential explanations for these difficulties are diverse [21]. Firstly, research has pointed out that, compared to traditional innovation, digital innovation has different characteristics, which requires measurement techniques to be adjusted accordingly [10, 16]. Secondly, due to their exploratory nature, DIUs are often active in the early phases of the innovation process [5, 22], which is also the most uncertain part of that process, covering aspects such as opportunity identification, opportunity analysis, idea genesis, idea selection and concept, and technology development [9]. Attempting to carry out measurement in these contexts is particularly challenging as activities rarely follow predefined processes and therefore metrics are hard to define [23]. Furthermore, the currently low state of maturity of the concept of DIUs might explain why the question of measurement has not yet been addressed [5].

A PMS is usually set up to deal with these challenges. PMSs are information systems that help organisations with the collection, recording, analysis, and presentation of data for control purposes [12]. While the role of such systems – sometimes also termed "management control systems" – has long been seen as detrimental to innovation [14], scholars nowadays have recognized the potential of measurement efforts. Depending on their design, PMSs can facilitate information exchange in teams and align them to their goals [15]. From an Information System's (IS) perspective, research stresses the capacity of IS to reduce the effort of data collection associated with the innovation processes [13]. Beyond this, IS could provide new capabilities for management as *"data become accurate, shareable, and available to different parties without creating the panoptic dream of visibility and action at a distance"* [24]. However, while PMS could add value to the measurement of DIU activities, their role in the context of digital innovation currently remains underexplored and open to discussion [10].

3 Methodology

To answer RQ1, we first conducted a literature review to identify any existing requirements for PMS that are relevant to DIUs. We then used a multiple case study design to examine the awareness and the operationalisation of these requirements in practice. With these case studies we were able to detect three additional requirements for PMS in the context of DIUs that had not yet been considered in the literature – or if so, only insufficiently – thus answering RQ2.

3.1 Literature Review

To investigate the existing requirements, we conducted a literature review, following vom Brocke [25]. Thus, the first step was to define the review of the scope and to conceptualise the topic accordingly. Since DIUs apply agile working practices as an integral part of their innovation endeavours, as mentioned above, we have chosen not only to use the search terms "(digital) innovation" and "PMS", but also to include "agile" as a key word [3, 5]. We then conducted a search looking for a keyword combination of 'Performance Measurement' and 'Agile', 'Performance Measurement' and 'Innovation' as well as 'Performance Measurement' and 'Digital Innovation' in the title, keywords or abstract of the databases EBSCOhost Business Source Complete, Web of Science, Scopus, JSTOR, WISO and AIS eLibrary. In total, we obtained 578 hits after the initial search. In a second step, we filtered all papers with an A +, A or B ranking in the German VHB-JOURQUAL3 and ended up with 58. The subsequent backward search yielded ten more hits, leading to a total of 68 papers that we read in detail, removing those with no clear connection to either (digital) innovation- and/or agile performance measurement. In the final step we analysed the remaining 21 papers and synthesised the requirements for (digital) innovation and agile PMS along three streams: 1) Requirements for PMS in general (equally applicable to digital innovation and agile performance measurement), 2) requirements for PMS specifically relevant in the area of innovation, and 3) special requirements for PMS for digital innovation and agile working.

3.2 Multiple Case Study

In order to determine the requirements for a PMS of DIUs, we have chosen an explorative, qualitative-empirical research approach by carrying out five case studies, which are particularly suitable for more recent phenomena that should be investigated in their real-world context [26]. We decided on a multiple-case design to enable cross- case analysis and to increase the overall robustness of the study [26]. Table 1 provides an overview of the sample. In the selected cases, DIUs have been implemented by German and Swiss companies as part of their organisational digital transformation for at least two years to ensure that the operations of the units extend beyond their conceptualisation. We aimed for diverse cases – particularly in terms of types of industry, size, objective, and scope of the DIU – to generate contrasting results and thereby enhance the study's external validity [26]. Along with the five cases, we conducted 16 interviews between February and August 2020 with DIU employees following a semi-structured interview guide. The interview guide explored issues such as the way in which the DIU actually measures and monitors its progress in specific projects, but also on an overall basis, meaning how the DIU reports progress to the main organisation. Interviews and analysis of company data quickly revealed that many DIUs have a variety of elements for measuring their efforts but a specific PMS is missing, which encouraged us to delve deeper into possible measurement methods. Thus, after initial coding of the first two interviews for cases B and C following Gioia methodology [27], it was decided to use them as training cases to sharpen our interview guide. Here the coding was undertaken by one researcher while another validated the resulting coding table. For the following cases A, D, and E we conducted at least four interviews each used the iterated semi-structured questionnaire to capture different nuances of the application of a PMS in DIUs. We interviewed people with presumably good knowledge of DIU activities, such as the Head of Innovation (Lab), Innovation Managers, Project Managers, etc. The interviews were conducted via telephone in the native language of the participants – as interviewees should be able to express their thoughts in a comfortable way – and lasted 51 min on average. Translation into English took place after coding by researchers with advanced skills in the English language. The results were validated through internal discussions within the research team. All interviews were recorded and transcribed verbatim [28]. For the data triangulation we gathered secondary data including information from firm websites, press releases and internal documents (e.g., management reports, excel sheets with metrics) [26]. We used ATLAS.ti to collect, store, and analyse our data [26, 28].

4   Results

We present our results in three subsections: First, we give an overview of the requirements from literature, presenting them along three streams to lay the foundation for RQ1. Second, we provide an overview of the awareness and the operationalisation of these requirements in the cases, in contribution to the second part of RQ1. Third, we propose three new requirements that have emerged from the data analysis of the five case studies, thus answering RQ2.

4.1   Requirements from Literature Review

From our literature review, we were able to derive requirements based on three streams: 1) Requirements that are relevant to PMS in general, and thus also to (digital) innovation and agile performance measurement, 2) requirements for PMS specifically relevant to innovation, and 3) requirements for PMS specifically relevant to digital innovation and agile working. The first stream comprises four requirements and is based on a total of eight papers. The second stream includes three requirements originating from ten papers. The third stream contains two requirements from seven papers. The results of our literature review are shown in Table 2.

Table 1. Overview of the sample

Case	Size*, industry	DIU size**, founded in	DIU objective and scope***	DIU governance and structure****	Interview partner position (no. interviews)
A	Medium, Consumer Goods	Medium, 2018	1) Primarily internal 2) Existing business 3) Idea generation, Idea selection, Innovation development	1) Balanced 2) Integrated	Head of Innovation Lab (2), Director Business Development (2), Innovation Manager (1)
B	Upper large, insurance	Medium, 2015	1) Primarily internal 2) Existing and novel business 3) Innovation implementation and innovation commercialization	1) Relatively high 2) Integrated	Head of Open Innovation (1)
C	Upper large, mobility	Large, 2014	1) Primarily internal 2) Existing and novel business 3) Idea generation, Idea selection, Innovation development, Innovation implementtation, Innovation commercialization	1) Relatively high 2) Separate legal entity	Venture Developer (1)
D	Medium, real estate	Small, 2018	1) Primarily internal 2) Existing business 3) Idea generation, Idea selection, Innovation development	1) Balanced 2) Separate department	Innovation Manager (1), Head of Innovation (1), Project Manager (3)

(continued)

Table 1. (*continued*)

Case	Size*, industry	DIU size**, founded in	DIU objective and scope***	DIU governance and structure****	Interview partner position (no. interviews)
E	Large, energy	Large, 2017	1) Primarily external 2) Novel business 3) Idea selection, Innovation development, Innovation implementation, Innovation commercialization	1) Relatively high 2) Separate department	Venture Architect (2), UX-Designer (2)

* Size: Small = < 1k FTE & revenue < 100 Mio € Medium = > 1k FTE & revenue < 100 Mio €; Large = > 1k FTE & revenue 1–5B €; Upper Large = > 20k FTE & revenue > 5B €; ** DIU size (number of full time equivalent [FTE]): Small = < 6; Medium = 6 – 15; Large > 15; *** 1) Innovation orientation 2) Market focus of innovation 3) Scope of innovation. Criteria derived from [5, 7]; **** 1) Degree of freedom 2) Embedding. Criteria derived from [3, 7]: the degree of freedom (very low, relatively low, in balance, relatively high, very high), Embedding (integrated, separated department, separate legal entity, virtual)

4.2 Requirements from Literature Found in Cases

Based on the requirements found in the literature, we examined if these were operationalised in the specific company context of DIUs (see Table 3). Here we distinguish between three categories: "Not Mentioned", "Aware, but Not Operationalised" and "Operationalised". The category "Not Mentioned" means that we could not find any reference to this particular requirement in the materials available (e.g., interviews, internal documents). "Aware, Not Operationalised" implies that the interviewees did mention this requirement – and potentially considered it as being important – but have not yet been able to present any concrete approaches for its implementation. "Operationalised" are all those requirements for which proof of detailed implementation is available in the form of specific documents (Excel sheets, reports, etc.) or concrete interview statements. When presenting our results, we specifically focus on the category "Aware, Not Operationalised", as its detailed consideration seems to be most fruitful. "Not Mentioned" is mainly found in cases where the number of interviews was limited and, therefore, we decided to use them as training cases to specific the interview guide. If a requirement is marked as "Operationalised", we are looking at a simple confirmation of knowledge from the literature, which has no real degree of novelty. By looking at "Aware, Not Operationalised" we hope to gain insights into particularities of PMS implementation in the specific context of a DIU.

Requirements Relevant for PMS in General The requirement RE1, was operationalised in one case (E). In three other cases (A, B, D) the requirement was known, but had not yet been implemented. For example, one of the interviewees in Case A

Table 2. Overview of requirements for a PMS in literature

Stream	No	Requirement
1) Requirements relevant to PMS in general	RE1	PMS should allow its user to generate insights for decision-making in innovation projects. This requires the availability of data that can be contextualized (e.g., through benchmarks, targets, etc.) which implies that the user can derive implications for taking action [29–32]
	RE2	PMS should allow high ease of use for different stakeholders and functional groups (main organisation, DIU management, DIU teams) which may have specific expectations towards data and their representation [12, 33, 34]
	RE3	PMS should align the performance criteria with the corporate strategy and select them from its objectives [29, 30]
	RE4	PMS should allow for easy data collection following actual activities that take place in the organisation [12, 35]
2) Requirements for PMS specifically relevant to innovation	RE5	PMS should distinguish between different innovation intentions (e.g., radical vs incremental, process vs product) and their required mode of control [13, 14, 36–39]
	RE6	PMS should allow for the use of different measurement techniques (e.g., focus on input, output, process) and performance dimensions (e.g., Learning and Knowledge, Financial) along with different innovation phases (e.g., idea generation, idea selection, idea development) [34, 35, 39]
	RE7	PMS should contain the opportunity to process both quantitative data (e.g., number of interviews, FTEs employees) and qualitative data (e.g., user insights, Customer Satisfaction) during the innovation process [36, 40, 41]
3) Requirements for PMS for digital innovation and agile working	RE8	PMS should be more closely aligned with the digital innovation process, as the role of IT has changed from measuring an IT department to an integral part of the overall business strategy, which requires greater customer-centricity as well as proximity to market and therefore new metrics [10, 11, 42, 43]

(continued)

Table 2. (*continued*)

Stream	No	Requirement
	RE9	PMS should follow the logic of agile methods (e.g., Scrum) and exploratory methods (e.g., Design Thinking) which rely on shorter cycle times and are more responsive to upcoming changes [21, 44–46]

explicitly mentioned the importance of benchmarking data that could help to contextualise the DIUs efforts and identify implications: *"The benchmark is really exciting. It allows you to measure your own success against others and take concrete measures. The cross comparison would certainly help us. It would support us internally before the management and the board of directors. Externally you can then compare yourself with other companies."* For the second requirement RE2, three cases indicated that they were aware of it but had not yet operationalised it: *"I wonder who this dashboard is talking to. The upper management surely likes dashboards. But for me, the important knowledge is [...] rather qualitative."* (Case E). The quote shows that in actual projects, teams often rely on qualitative expectations, while management looks for quantitatively comparable metrics. The relevance of RE3, was recognised in all five cases and has already been implemented in three (Cases A, B, D). However, the opinions of the interviewees differ to some extent. While one person – whose DIU fulfils RE3 – stated the relevance of this topic: *"When you present the whole thing in front of a board, in addition to these KPIs you need to understand if the project fits into the strategic context."* (Case B), a member from a different DIU – which has not implemented RE3 – seemed much more critical about it considering the early stage of his innovation project: *"In my opinion, measuring strategic goals in the early stages is a waste of time. The founder is there for me to integrate the vision – he has to notice when the vision is not followed."* (Case C). RE4 was found to be implemented twice (Cases A and E), while being on the radar of a third DIU (Case D). The fact that it is still a challenge to collect data with high validity and objectivity – even for DIUs that had already operationalised RE4 – is shown by the following quote: *"I wonder how the data is created in this tool. The numbers must be realistic, so the data should not be entered by a person."* (Case A).

Requirements for PMS Specifically Relevant to Innovation The fifth requirement, specifically addressing different innovation intentions and their required modes of control, was operationalised by two DIUs (Cases A and C). Although Cases D and E are also aware of the need for this requirement, no implementation has taken place so far. Case D, for example, distinguishes between three types of innovation intentions – products, services and internal process improvements: *"[o]ne is actual products [...]. You measure this very differently than a service. The second is ideas for new services. And the third are internal process improvements."* – for which different metrics have not yet been defined. For requirement RE6, we see an implementation in all five DIUs considered. Thus, in all DIUs different dimensions were measured based on a holistic approach, as the following example shows: *"A lab is about bringing together different perspectives; the technological view, the customer's view and the economic view. So, these KPIs are relevant to us."* (Case A). RE7 has not yet been operationalised in cases A and D, although its relevance was recognised. One of the interviewees in Case D for example made a connection between the measurement approach (qualitative/quantitative) and the project intention (type and phase of project): *"[…] we should continue to monitor the projects for five years afterwards. For example, how many offers were sent out as a result, how many orders were actually received and how much money was generated […]. And then […] we had a project; it was really more about finding out what the customers actually want nowadays […]. And there were no orders afterwards. […] That's why there is another side to it. And that's why it was more about the soft facts, like how did the customers react, employee satisfaction, maybe we achieved an image improvement, competence building, etc."*

Table 3. Awareness and operationalization of requirements for a DIU PMS in practice

Stream	No	A	B	C	D	E
1) Requirements relevant for PMS in general	RE1	**Aware, Not Operationalised**	**Aware, Not Operationalised**	Not Mentioned	**Aware, Not Operationalised**	Operationalised
	RE2	**Aware, Not Operationalised**	Not Mentioned	Not Mentioned	**Aware, Not Operationalised**	**Aware, Not Operationalised**
	RE3	Operationalised	Operationalised	**Aware, Not Operationalised**	Operationalised	**Aware, Not Operationalised**
	RE4	Operationalised	Not Mentioned	Not Mentioned	**Aware, Not Operationalised**	Operationalised
2) Requirements for PMS specifically relevant in the area of innovation	RE5	Operationalised	Not Mentioned	Operationalised	**Aware, Not Operationalised**	**Aware, Not Operationalised**
	RE6	Operationalised	Operationalised	Operationalised	Operationalised	Operationalised
	RE7	**Aware, Not Operationalised**	Operationalised	Operationalised	**Aware Not Operationalised**	Operationalised
3) Requirements for PMS for digital innovation and agile working	RE8	**Aware, Not Operationalised**	Operationalised	Not Mentioned	Operationalised	**Aware, Not Operationalised**
	RE9	Operationalised	Not Mentioned	Operationalised	**Aware, Not Operationalised**	**Aware, Not Operationalised**

Requirements for All PMS for Digital Innovation and Agile Working While the necessity of RE8, was recognized by four of the DIUs considered, Cases A and E do not yet implement the requirement. A DIU member from case A reflected on its challenges: *"I realize that in the classical and physical development world certain KPIs and methods* *make sense, and in the digital world other KPIs and methods make sense. As an industry we bring hardware and software together."* (Case A). The ninth and last requirement – RE9 – that we investigate, was also recognised by four of the DIUs considered, however not implemented by Cases D and E. The challenges regarding RE9 in practice were expressed by an interviewee from Case E who regularly works with design sprints and wondered how to set up a PMS that is dynamic enough to change with each sprint: *"My question would be whether this data changes much from sprint to sprint."*

In summary, we found that the DIUs in our case study had already been able to operationalise some of the requirements we derived from literature, but there are still some challenges that not everyone has been able to overcome yet. Especially RE1 and RE2 seem to be difficult to implement. Also, when excluding training cases B and C, the operationalisation of the requirements RE5, RE7, RE8 and RE9 – operationalised by only one of cases A, B or D – also appears to be challenging.

4.3   Requirements for PMS in DIUs

In the course of our interviews, some respondents raised issues that are not yet or insufficiently covered by RE1 to RE9, so we present three additional requirements for PMS in the specific context of DIUs. While some of them still have some connection to the ones identified in the literature, the intention here was to specifically reflect on the role of DIUs in their organisational context. RE3, for example, points out the importance of aligning PMS with corporate strategy, but does not contain any information on how this could be handled in DIUs. For this reason, RE11 takes a closer look at the role of PMS in relation to the idiosyncratic role of DIUs in the corporate context. Overall, the requirements presented here should be considered as an extension/adaptation of the PMS to the specific context of the DIUs. DIU members have often expressed these requirements as wishes, i.e., no implementation has taken place so far. An overview of the data and our coding can be found in Table 4.

RE10 – PMS for DIUs should incentivise employees to experiment and show their learnings (Cases A, B, C, D, E): In our data, we identified both how the desire for a PMS can incentivise employees to experiment more, but also their fear of PMS, as it can also show up failures. One of the fears was that a PMS with more specific metrics could reduce experimentation-prone activities, since failures would also have to be translated into metrics and thus be more clearly visible, which could lead to negative consequences. To address this problem, it would be particularly helpful to develop a PMS that makes both experimentation and failure visible and acknowledges them: *"We also measure the number of pilots and MVPs per year. This shows how much one is trying out. [...]It is also psychologically important to acknowledge the failed projects."* (Case B). Failure must be seen as a learning opportunity, whereby PMS can support "learning from each other" within the DIU and also act as a common database/knowledge base inviting closer communication between employees: *"The platform should therefore not only be a database but also allow personal contact. That way you can learn from each other"* (Case A). However, it is not easy to find appropriate metrics for inputs that do not provide direct financial value as another interviewee from Case A admitted: *"[...] even the things that are not successful have a certain value. Somehow this value must be shown. Even if it doesn't generate financial success, it can still add value in a different way. I find it very difficult to define it as a KPI, but it seems to be a very important point."*

RE11 – PMS should help the DIU and the main organisation to exchange data that allows the DIU to pursue tasks autonomously (Cases A, C, D)*:* Another issue raised during the interviews was the relationship between a DIU and its parent organisation. Depending on whether a DIU operates in proximity to the core business and is more involved in the main organisation's processes or, conversely, is further away from it, the requirements for a PMS are different. One interviewee, for example, explained: *"We have no management guidelines. We formulate hypotheses and these get target values."* (Case C). The DIU in the quote thus appears to be very independent and has set up its own performance measurement – including its own metrics – which is separate from the parent organisation. Another case that has already gone through this phase explains, however: *"In the past, we were rather far removed from our core business and thus had only limited contact with corporate. We want to improve this in the future."* (Case A). This statement could indicate that there may be a learning curve with regard to the cooperation with the main organisation or that this relationship may experience different phases of proximity and distance. Another person working for the same DIU – Case A – explained their learnings and the meaning of the PMS: *"It helps in terms of alignment and allows us a higher degree of freedom. When we agree with each other and we reach the goals, it creates trust. Later on, this gives us more autonomy and a greater degree of freedom."* This view about a PMS is quite interesting because the employee in question obviously understands the use of a PMS as a mechanism that allows a higher degree of freedom for the DIU.

RE12 – PMS data should be credible and meaningful (Cases A, B, E)*:* Although this requirement may seem obvious at first sight, it takes on a new importance in the context of DIUs. Their specific activities – mostly in the early phase of innovation – make it difficult to apply standard metrics, which forces DIUs to identify and collect the relevant data for performance measurement themselves. This poses the challenge that the credibility of the data may be lower, as one respondent mentioned: *"I wonder how the data is created in this tool. The numbers must be realistic, so the data should not be entered by a person. Data validation is also a key point."* (Case A). With regard to the above, another interviewee mentioned the danger of manipulating metrics, so that it is necessary to agree on appropriate metrics and to make their underlying background transparent in each case: *"Especially the internal stakeholders are important for a lab. I then formulated soft hypotheses such as '100 customers in 4 months to confirm the success of the pilot'. But that doesn't really say much either, because it's very easy to influence that via the ads budget."* (Case A). While this may be the case for many metrics used by organisations, the risk may be greater in the context of a DIU with its greater freedom and the desire/need to report favourable metrics to the main organisation.

5   Discussion

We argue that the implementation of a PMS for DIUs offers both the possibility to prevent failure or even its abolishment – by for example addressing the challenge of unclear DIU objectives [8] – and to make their success and thus their value contribution visible to the

Table 4. Sample quotes for new requirements

Second order code	First order code	Representative quote
P-RE10: PMS within the DIU should incentivize employees to experiment and show their learnings	Show and acknowledge experimentation	*"We also measure the number of pilots and MVPs per year. This shows how much we are experimenting. […] It is also psychologically important to us to acknowledge failed projects." (Case B)*
	Hypothesis driven progress reporting	*"Once the target value is reached, we assume that our hypo-thesis been validated positively. If it is not reached, we can see if the target value was set too poorly or if the hypothesis could not be confirmed. If the hypothesis cannot be positively validated, we need to modify the product feature." (Case C)*
	Drive and facilitate personal learning	*"The platform should therefore not only be a database but also allow personal contact. This enables us to learn from each other." (Case A)*
	Incentivize to show how failing projects contribute through learnings	*"[…] even the things that are unsuccessful have a certain value. Somehow this value must be shown. Even if it doesn't generate financial success, it can still add value in a different way. I find it very difficult to define it as a KPI, but it seems to be a very important point." (Case A)*
P-RE11: PMS should help the DIU and main organisation to exchange data that allows the DIU to pursue tasks very autonomously	Closer relationship between lab and mother company	*"It helps for the alignment and allows us a higher degree of freedom. When we agree with each other and reach the set goals, it creates trust. Later on, this gives us more autonomy and a greater degree of freedom." (Case A)*

(continued)

Table 4. (*continued*)

Second order code	First order code	Representative quote
	Independence and Autonomy	*"We have no management guidelines. We formulate hypotheses and target values." (Case C)*
	Create trust that allows for autonomy	*"In the past, we were rather far removed from our core business and thus had only limited contact with corporate. We want to improve this in the future." (Case A)*
P-RE12: PMS data should be credible and meaningful	Metrics should be objective and have a meaning	*"I wonder how the data is created in this tool. The numbers must be realistic, so the data should not be entered by a person. The data validation is also a central point." (Case A)*
	Data Input needs to be credible	*"Especially the internal stakeholders are important for a lab. I formulated soft hypotheses such as "100 customers in 4 months to confirm the success of the pilot". But that doesn't really say much either, because it's very easy to influence that via the ads budget." (Case E)*

main organisation – as already mentioned in previous studies [4, 5]. In order to create the basis for such a system our research is aimed at identifying its requirements in the context of DIUs. We answer RQ1 by giving an overview of the requirements that the literature places on PMS for (digital) innovation and agile working and show how these have been confirmed in practice. However, the actual implementation is very uneven. Furthermore, DIUs have additional requirements for a PMS that are currently not – or only sufficiently – dealt with in the literature, which is why we have proposed three new requirements that relate specifically to DIUs, and thus answer RQ2. In the discussion, we want to reflect three implications on the use of PMS in DIUs, which build on our analysis of these requirements.

PMS and their role in managing autonomy and freedom of DIUs Existing literature on DIUs suggest that the freedom and the autonomy of a DIU depends on its organisational setup [5]. While some DIUs are an integral part of the main organisation, others are set up with much higher degrees of independence regarding their operations and management sometimes even located offsite [5]. As stated by Barthel et al. [5], tight coupling is beneficial for DIUs that focus on internal process improvements while looser coupling is helpful for innovation activities that are further away from the main organisation's core business [5]. Considering our findings, we propose that PMS can be seen as a mechanism to manage the relationship between the DIU and the main organisation. Our data suggest that loosely coupled DIUs, which are more likely to develop completely new innovation, have a learning curve that may bring them closer to the main organisation as they progress. Statements from "younger" DIUs (age two to three years) show that they are given lots of freedom, and employees tend to enjoy this freedom being less concerned with strategic alignment with the main organisation and measuring their activities. This is in line with the findings from Raabe et al. [8] who state that some DIUs lack clear objectives. However, once they have gained experience in their day-to-day work, some DIU might conclude that closer coordination is needed in order to be perceived as valuable by the main organisation (Case A). One of our respondents explained, he sees a PMS as a tool that helps to align with the main organisation's strategy and build trust, which in turn allows the DIU more freedom in its innovation efforts.

Level of PMS adoption in DIUs Our results show that the majority of DUIs considered is aware of the theoretical requirements of a PMS for digital innovation. However, RE1 and RE2 in particular, as well as RE5, RE7, RE8 and RE9 (when excluding training cases B and C) are usually not yet operational, although this is only partly due to a lack of willingness. Most respondents would certainly like to use more metrics than they have done so far and generally have a very positive attitude towards PMS. This is particularly evident in the three new requirements we have introduced. The challenge many of them face, however, is to find the "right" metrics for their sometimes highly exploratory activities. Translating these activities into an understandable meaningful metric has not yet been done sufficiently. Conversely, however, there seems to be a concern that if you measure too much, you are too transparent and the main organisation might misjudge the innovation activities of the DIU. This is already addressed in a previous study which has found that there is a discrepancy between the actions of the DIUs and the way that the main organisation evaluates them [21]. Overall, there seems to be a perception that the current error culture does not allow mistakes to be seen as a normal consequence of innovation, which makes DIU vulnerable to attack by disclosing too many metrics. A third and more pragmatic reason for the lack of operationalised PMS requirements might be the maturity of the DIUs. Two of them existed for roughly two years by the time of data collection and as we mentioned earlier, some DIUs seem to be given more freedom in this initial phase potentially implementing more metrics later on sometimes also in the course of a stronger alignment with the main organisation.

Different measurement approaches of DIU and main organisation Further room for discussion, partly related to the previous section, is provided by the fact that during the data analysis it seemed that the differences in the measurement approaches of DIU and main organisation are a challenge. Our data show that DIUs have already implemented some elements of a PMS, which are partly aligned with the agile practices they base their innovation work on [3]. In some cases, the DIU adopted specific measurements related to those practices such as e.g., tracking the amount of hypothesis validated or counting the number of pilot customers won. The main organisation, on the other hand, continues to work with familiar performance measurement metrics, which means that two different approaches now have to be reconciled. This is anything but trivial as shown by Mayer et al. [21] who found that contact between the DIU and the main organisation can be problematic if, for example, activities of DIUs try to be adopted from the main organisation. This raises the question of governance mechanisms that are capable of increasing the alignment between DIUs and the main organisation, both by developing precise goals for the DIUs and by translating these into concrete fields of action. It is also necessary to ensure that these goals are met, i.e., that the associated process is monitored. Our results indicate that PMS play an important role in this process, but also that their impact is limited if DIUs' objectives are poorly defined.

6   Conclusion

We answer RQ1 by first conducting a literature review and identify the requirements for a PMS for DIU. In a second step, we conduct five case studies with DIUs and analysed whether the requirements from the literature are confirmed and adopted in practice. Regarding RQ2 we propose three new requirements derived from the interviews to broaden the knowledge of PMS for DIUs. We discuss our findings along three implications: The role of PMS in managing autonomy and freedom of DIUs, the level of PMS adoption in DIUs, and the challenges coming from different measurement approaches of DIUs and the main organisation. We see our research both as a starting point to develop more sufficient PMS that help DIUs to measure their activities and as a basis for discussion on quantitative evidence of how successful DIUs are as "fast lanes" for (digital) innovation [5]. Furthermore, we shed light on how to measure the development of digital innovation in general [10]. Due to the increasing customer orientation in their development, research also demands new measuring methods. Our results underline the relevance of agile methods in this context and the need to capture them using a new measurement approach and specific metrics that differ from those previously used in large organisations. Practitioners can use our research to compare their performance measurement with it and consider possible adjustments. In particular, we advise them to clarify objectives early on and translate them into metrics and indicators that can help both the DIU and the main organisation to clearly manage expectations.

Of course, our study is not without limitations. The small sample size and the geographical limitation to companies in Germany and Switzerland does not allow for a generalisation of the results. Future research could extend our results by using a larger sample, specify them by focusing on a particular industry or by highlighting certain demands on PMS according to the different objectives of a DIU e.g., by Fuchs et al. [7]. Furthermore, we have ensured to interview people with different roles within the DIU, both those whose work is to be measured by the PMS (DIU employees) and those who want to measure the performance of the DIU (e.g., head of innovation). Nevertheless, all interview partners had a direct connection to the DIU and are therefore potentially biased. It would be helpful in future studies to also interview people who have a greater distance to the DIU and who potentially evaluate their work/work results differently, such as members of the top management (CEO, CFO, etc.) or representatives of other departments that cooperate with the DIU. The requirements we present could also be investigated specific types of DIUs closer and analyse requirements at this level.

Acknowledgement. We kindly thank Céline Stalder for her support in gathering data and the Hasso Plattner Design Thinking Research Program for funding our research generously.

References

1. Yoo, Y., Henfridsson, O., Lyytinen, K.: Research commentary—the new organizing logic of digital innovation: an agenda for information systems research. Inf. Syst. Res. **21**, 724–735 (2010)
2. Vial, G.: Understanding digital transformation: a review and a research agenda. J. Strateg. Inf. Syst. **28**, 118–144 (2019)
3. Holotiuk, F., Beimborn, D.: Temporal ambidexterity: how digital innovation labs connect exploration and exploitation for digital innovation. In: ICIS 2019 Proceedings, Munich (2019)
4. Hund, A., Holotiuk, F., Wagner, H.-T., Beimborn, D.: Knowledge management in the digital era: how digital innovation labs facilitate knowledge recombination. In: ECIS 2019 Proceedings, Stockholm (2019)
5. Barthel, P., Fuchs, C., Birner, B., Hess, T.: Embedding digital innovations in organizations: a typology for digital innovation units. In: Conference Proceedings, pp. 780–795, Potsdam (2020)
6. Viki, T.: Pirates In The Navy: How Innovators Lead Transformation. Unbound Publishing, London (2020)
7. Fuchs, C., Barthel, P., Herberg, I., Berger, M., Hess, T.: Characterizing approaches to digital transformation: development of a taxonomy of digital units. In: Conference Proceedings, Siegen (2019)
8. Raabe, J.-P., Horlach, B., Schirmer, I., Drews, P.: 'Forewarned is Forearmed': overcoming multifaceted challenges of digital innovation units. In: AMCIS 2020 Proceedings, Virtual (2020)
9. Koen, P., et al.: Providing clarity and a common language to the "fuzzy front end." Res.-Technol. Manage. **44**, 46–55 (2001)

10. Hund, A., Drechsler, K., Reibenspiess, V.A.: The current state and future opportunities of digital innovation: a literature review. In: ECIS 2019 Proceedings, Stockholm (2019)
11. Huang, J., Henfridsson, O., Liu, M.J., Newell, S.: Growing on steroids: rapidly scaling the user base of digital ventures through digital innovation. Miss. Q. **41**, 301–314 (2017)
12. Kerssens-van Drongelen, I.C., Cooke, A.: Design principles for the development of measurement systems for research and development processes. R&D Manage. **27**, 345–357 (1997)
13. Schermann, M., Wiesche, M., Krcmar, H.: The role of information systems in supporting exploitative and exploratory management control activities. J. Manage. Account. Res. **24**, 31–59 (2012)
14. Ylinen, M., Gullkvist, B.: The effects of organic and mechanistic control in exploratory and exploitative innovations. Manage. Account. Res. **25**, 93–112 (2014)
15. Bedford, D.S., Bisbe, J., Sweeney, B.: Performance measurement systems as generators of cognitive conflict in ambidextrous firms. Acc. Organ. Soc. **72**, 21–37 (2019)
16. Kohli, R., Melville, N.P.: Digital innovation: a review and synthesis. Inf. Syst. J. **29**, 200–223 (2019)
17. Nambisan, S., Lyytinen, K., Majchrzak, A., Song, M.: Digital innovation management: reinventing innovation management research in a digital world. MIS Q. **41**, 223–238 (2017)
18. Svahn, F., Mathiassen, L., Lindgren, R.: Embracing digital innovation in incumbent firms: how Volvo cars managed competing concerns. MIS Q. **41**(1), 239–253 (2017). https://doi.org/10.25300/MISQ/2017/41.1.12
19. Gimpel, H., Hosseini, S., Huber, R.X.R., Probst, L., Röglinger, M., Faisst, U.: Structuring digital transformation: a framework of action fields and its application at ZEISS. J. Inf. Technol. Theory Appl. **19**, 3 (2018)
20. Frey, J., Holotiuk, F., Beimborn, D.: Debating digital innovation: a literature review on realizing value from digital innovation. In: Conference Proceedings, Potsdam (2020)
21. Mayer, S., Haskamp, T., de Paula, D.: Measuring what counts: an exploratory study about the key challenges of measuring design thinking activities in digital innovation units. In: Proceedings of the 54nd HICSS 2021, Virutal (2021)
22. Berghaus, S., Back, A.: Disentangling the fuzzy front end of digital transformation: activities and approaches. In: ICIS 2017 Proceedings, pp. 1–17, Seoul (2017)
23. Dziallas, M., Blind, K.: Innovation indicators throughout the innovation process: an extensive literature analysis. Technovation **80–81**, 3–29 (2019)
24. Dechow, N., Mouritsen, J.: Enterprise resource planning systems, management control and the quest for integration. Acc. Organ. Soc. **30**, 691–733 (2005)
25. Vom Brocke, J., et al.: Reconstructing the giant: on the importance of rigour in documenting the literature search process. In: ECIS 2009 Proceedings, pp. 2206–2217, Verona (2009)
26. Yin, R.K.: Case Study Research: Design and Methods. Sage Publications, Thousand oaks (2009)
27. Gioia, D.A., Corley, K.G., Hamilton, A.L.: Seeking qualitative rigor in inductive research: notes on the gioia methodology. Organ. Res. Methods **16**, 15–31 (2013)
28. Miles, M.B., Huberman, A.M., Saldana, M.R.J.: Qualitative Data Analysis. Sage Publications, Christchurch, New Zealand (2013)
29. Globerson, S.: Issues in developing a performance criteria system for an organization. Int. J. Prod. Res. **23**, 639–646 (1985)
30. Neely, A., et al.: Performance measurement system design: developing and testing a process-based approach. Int. J. Oper. Prod. Manage. **20**, 1119–1145 (2000)
31. Lill, P., Wald, A., Munck, J.: In the field of tension between creativity and efficiency: a systematic literature review of management control systems for innovation activities. Eur. J. Innov. Manage. **24**(3), 919–950 (2020). https://doi.org/10.1108/EJIM-11-2019-0329

32. Wiesche, M., Bodner, J., Schermann, M.: Antecedents of IT-enabled organizsational control mechanisms. In: ECIS 2012 Proceedings, Barcelona (2020)
33. Hamilton, S., Chervany, N.L.: Evaluating information system effectiveness - part ii: comparing evaluator viewpoints. Miss. Q. **5**, 79–86 (1981)
34. Henttonen, K., Ojanen, V., Puumalainen, K.: Searching for appropriate performance measures for innovation and development projects. R&D Manage. **46**, 914–927 (2016)
35. Micheli, P., Manzoni, J.-F.: Strategic performance measurement: benefits, limitations and paradoxes. Long Range Plan. **43**, 465–476 (2010)
36. Barros, R.S., da Costa, A.M.D.S.: Bridging management control systems and innovation. Qual. Res. Account. Manage. **16**, 342–372 (2019)
37. Curtis, E., Sweeney, B.: Managing different types of innovation: mutually reinforcing management control systems and the generation of dynamic tension. Account. Bus. Res. **47**, 313–343 (2017)
38. Davila, A., Foster, G., Oyon, D.: Accounting and control, entrepreneurship and innovation: venturing into new research opportunities. Eur. Acc. Rev. **18**, 281–311 (2009)
39. Chiesa, V., Frattini, F., Lamberti, L., Noci, G.: Exploring management control in radical innovation projects. Eur. J. Innov. Manage. **12**, 416–443 (2009)
40. Said, A.A., HassabElnaby, H.R., Wier, B.: An empirical investigation of the performance consequences of nonfinancial measures. J. Manage. Account. Res. **15**, 193–223 (2003)
41. Adams, R., Bessant, J., Phelps, R.: Innovation management measurement: a review. Int. J. Manage. Rev. **8**, 21–47 (2006)
42. Urbach, N., et al.: The impact of digitalization on the IT department. Bus. Inf. Syst. Eng. **61**, 123–131 (2019)
43. Brynjolfsson, E., Oh, J.: The attention economy: measuring the value of free digital services on the internet. In: ICIS 2012 Proceedings, Orlando (2012)
44. Boerman, M.P., Lubsen, Z., Tamburri, D.A., Visser, J.: Measuring and monitoring agile development status. In: 2015 IEEE/ACM 6th International Workshop on Emerging Trends in Software Metrics, pp. 54–62 (2015)
45. Lee, J.Y.H., Hsu, C., Silva, L.: What lies beneath: unraveling the generative mechanisms of smart technology and service design. J. Assoc. Inf. Syst. **21**, 1621–1643 (2020). https://doi.org/10.17705/1jais.00648
46. Basili, V., et al.: Bridging the gap between business strategy and software development. In: ICIS 2007 Proceedings, Montreal & Québec (2007)

Digital Business Strategy and Firm Performance: An Empirical Investigation

Hannes Kurtz[1]([⊠]), Andre Hanelt[2], and Sebastian Firk[3]

[1] Information Management, Georg-August-University Göttingen, Göttingen, Germany
hannes.kurtz01@stud.uni-goettingen.de
[2] Digital Transformation Management, University of Kassel, Kassel, Germany
hanelt@uni-kassel.de
[3] Management Accounting, University of Groningen, Groningen, The Netherlands
s.firk@rug.nl

Abstract. While digital business strategy (DBS) has recently garnered substantial attention, there is still little understanding about different strategy alternatives and their outcomes. However, this is of great importance as different digital business strategy types may utilize different profit mechanisms and thus influence a companies' performance in different ways. We conceptualize four distinct digital business strategy types and examine their influence on firm performance by applying panel fixed effect regression to a longitudinal dataset comprising leading tech companies. We find that not all digital business strategy types achieve to result in a positive impact and derive implications for information systems research and business practice.

Keywords: IS strategy · Performance implications · Panel data regression · Fixed-effect regression · Digital business strategy types

1 Introduction

Digital technologies are fundamentally reshaping conventional wisdom about scope, scale, design and execution of business strategy. Accordingly, we have witnessed a fusion of information technology (IT) and business strategy, which led to the introduction and elaboration of the concept of digital business strategy (DBS). Digital business strategy is defined as "organizational strategy formulated and executed by leveraging digital resources to create differential value" [1]. Given the importance of this topic for contemporary managerial practice, increasingly more researchers have been devoting themselves to the research area of digital business strategy. While some have focused their further theoretical elaboration on the concept [2], others investigated performance implications of digital business strategy [3]. Though valuable advances have undoubtedly been made by these research efforts, we believe that certain gaps remain.

For example, to the best of our knowledge, there is no evidence regarding different strategy types and their implications on firm performance as there is in classical strategy research. Here, researchers assume that strategies consist of a limited number of sets

F. Ahlemann et al. (Eds.): WI 2021, LNISO 48, pp. 606–624, 2021.
https://doi.org/10.1007/978-3-030-86800-0_42

of observable and recurring configurations that can be grouped and generalized into archetypes [4]. There are a multitude of typologies in the realm of strategy research that all relate to different aspects of business strategy [e.g. 5–7]. At the same time, increasing digitalization influences many of these aspects, which calls into question the timeliness of these concepts. For example, digital technologies enable companies to tap into new sources of value creation and capturing [8], which in turn, results in new profit mechanisms [2]. Hence, filling the gap of missing digital business strategy types regarding value creation mechanisms and investigating their effects on firm performance is of importance. Accordingly, we investigate the following research question: *How do different digital business strategy types influence firm performance?*

To provide answers to this research question, we start by systematically and conceptually deriving four types of digital business strategy by using relevant literature and the business model pattern database derived by Remane et al. [9]. Afterwards, we theorize the relationship between the four types of digital business strategy and firm performance. Subsequently, we empirically investigate a longitudinal sample of companies from the NASDAQ 100 over the period from 2007 to 2017 using aforementioned business model patterns to visualize employed digital business strategy types in respective companies. Employing firm fixed-effect regression, we find that not all digital business strategy types positively affect firm performance. While the DBS aimed at the development of IT applications[1] has a negative effect, the intermediation in two-sided markets does not exhibits a significant effect. Emphasizing the DBS aimed at the orchestration of digital business ecosystems and the DBS focusing on the processing of intellectual property, in contrast, positively impact firm performance. Our work provides important contributions to information systems (IS) research on digital business strategy [1]. First, we systematically derive and conceptualize four different types of digital business strategy. Second, we provide insights concerning the influence of different digital business strategy types on a company's performance. Third, on the base of our empirical findings, we discuss the value of the digital business strategy types for IS research and business practice.

2   Theoretical Foundations

Strategy is often defined as a set of committed choices made by management and a contingent plan of actions and activities designed to achieve a particular goal [10]. These choices relate to topics such as resource investments or the set of a firm's dynamic capabilities which are needed to deploy these resources [2]. Even if companies formulate and execute business strategy in response to their individual environment, structure and processes [11] it is possible to detect patterns in this stream of decisions that apply to a large number of companies with different contextual dependencies [12]. These patterns can be generalized and, thus, can be understood as archetypical [4]. Accordingly, different typologies focusing on different aspects of business strategy, exist. One of the most popular typologies is the one developed by Miles and Snow [7] focusing on strategic behavior of companies (i.e. its tendency to innovate, lead, and take risks) [13]. This typology has often been applied in IS research, for instance, in order to classify the

---

[1] We define IT applications according to Ivari [79] as "a system of application software and digital content or a piece of application software – that provides its users with services of affordances.

strategic use of information technology and its implications on firm performance [e.g. 14–16]. However, almost all named articles have in common that they can be dated to the pre-digital era and/or represent and examine the alignment view of business and IT strategy. Simultaneously, digital technologies are fundamentally reshaping the competitive landscape and therefore the business strategy [17–19]. Ongoing digitalization, thus, contributes to a fusion of IT and business strategy. This leads to the emergence of the concept of digital business strategy defined as"organizational strategy formulated and executed by leveraging digital resources to create differential value" [1]. Recently, several studies have been devoted to further develop and enrich the theoretical understanding of digital business strategy and its influence on firm performance. Leischnig et al. [3], for instance, empirically examine the transformation of a firm's digital business strategy into market performance, considering the intervening roles of market intelligence and subsequent value creation and value capture. They conclude that digital business strategy is positively linked to enhanced market intelligence capability, leading to the generation of market-oriented knowledge resources as important inputs for operative and strategic decision making. Mithas and Rust [20], empirically examine how information technology strategy and investments in IT influence firm performance. The results show that the use of digital technologies can influence the performance of a firm in three ways: Firstly, it can reduce a firm's cost by improving its productivity and efficiency. Secondly, it can reduce costs and increase value simultaneously. Lastly, it can increase a firm's revenues by fully exploiting opportunities through existing or by finding and creating new customers, channels and products or services. Drnevich and Croson [2], in contrast, point out ways for an integrated theoretical perspective on information technology and business level strategy and link them to casual profit mechanisms of different theoretical perspectives on strategy.

Taking the aforementioned into account, there are still many gaps when it comes to the topic of digital business strategy. A major shortcoming of all previous and particularly of conceptual studies in information system research is that they treated digital business strategy in an undifferentiated manner. Different digital business strategy types, however, can use different profit mechanisms. Consequently, they influence a company's performance in different ways [2]. Therefore, a more differentiated consideration is needed, shedding light on the influence different digital business strategy types have on a company's performance.

3   Making Digital Business Strategy Tangible via Digital Business Model Patterns

A business model describes the way in which companies create and capture value [21, 22]. Furthermore, the business model in its firm-specific conception allows to describe and design specific components as well as the interactions between those [22]. Therefore, the business model concept is a useful lens for understanding a company's underlying logic [23, 24] and, as a consequence, can be understood as "reflections of the realized strategy" [10]. Business models, on the one hand, translate abstract strategic notions into more concrete configurations of resources and activities, thereby informing about the specific paths that strategies lead to [25]. Business models thus represent a conceptual tool for analyzing business strategies. On the other hand, business models of particular firms are very specific and contextualized. Therefore, in order to systematically learn about business strategies via business models, some abstraction is needed. Such abstraction is provided by business model patterns. Put simply, business model patterns are commonly used and proven successful configurations of specific components of a business model [26], and thus can be used as a systematic tool for analyzing company's business model [28]. Synthesizing the variety of existing business model patterns, Remane et al. [9] built up a database of 182 business model patterns in their study. In the resulting taxonomy, they differentiate, among others, between *purely digital, digitally enabled* and *not necessarily digital* patterns. They also used the dimensions *prototypical*, which addresses patterns describing the general set-up of a company's business model and *solution*, which addresses patterns aiming to change only sub aspects of the business model. In addition, patterns have been classified by four meta-components and related sub-dimensions. The *value proposition*, gives an overall view of a company's products and services. *Value delivery*, describes the customer segments, channels for delivering the value proposition and the company's customer relationship. *Value creation*, explains the key resources, key activities and key partnerships of a company. *Value capture,* specifies the company's revenue streams and cost structure [9]. For the purpose of deriving DBS types, only the 28 business model patterns which are purely digital and prototypical will be considered.

We iterated between the meta-components as well as their corresponding sub-dimensions of the database and contemporary IS and strategy research to extract criteria for the identification of digital business strategy types. In doing so, we were able to identify four digital business strategy types with different profit mechanisms. Using the pattern descriptions contained in the database as well as the corresponding taxonomy we were able to manually assign the 28 patterns to the individual DBS types. Below is a more detailed description of these four DBS types and a brief summary in Table 1.

Digital Business Strategy Type 1 - Development of IT Applications

This digital business strategy type uses the potential of knowledge-based innovation in a digital context by designing unique, digital value propositions to address specific customer needs [29, 30]. Central mechanism of value creation is the development of new digital products and the economic exchange of those [31]. Companies applying this digital business strategy type usually get a payment for licenses or earn a usage fee and, as a consequence, rely on patents and other trade secrets to exploit their innovations effectively [32, 33]. An example are software firms, where new functionality, application concepts, and design patterns that promise the customer more added value, are constantly embedded [24, 30].

Digital Business Strategy Type 2 - Processing of Intellectual Property

The second digital business strategy type takes advantage of the ongoing digitalization of intellectual property [34]. Central mechanism of value creation is the efficient leveraging of own and externally created digital information and content by aggregating, transferring or further processing this data [1]. Companies applying this digital business strategy type, for instance, gain economic value by reutilizing this externally created intellectual property in more useful ways or by analyzing this data [35, 36]. An example are search engines, accumulating available information from the internet and subsequently making it accessible for consumers in a convenient way [24].

Digital Business Strategy Type 3 - Intermediation in Two-Sided Markets
This digital business strategy type uses the multisided-nature of economic exchange to create value. Central value creation mechanism is the efficient design of exchanges by otherwise fragmented parties [31, 37]. In doing so, companies design particular inter-action mechanisms between supplier and customer in a more efficient and convenient way for both sides by, for instance, decreasing search costs, offering a wide selection range or providing symmetric information through a digital platform or a portal [31, 38]. The online restaurant reservation business or job portals are good examples, since they offer easy access to a vast number of offers and considerably facilitate the selection and interaction with these offers [38].

Digital Business Strategy Type 4 - Orchestration of Digital Business Ecosystems
The final digital business strategy type uses complementarities and an ecosystem app-roach [38]. Central value creation mechanism is facilitating and orchestrating of an innovation ecosystem, in which multiple complementors can add their innovations and in doing so, increase the value of the system as a whole [37, 39]. These patterns lead to the creation of lock-in effects resulting from switching-costs and positive network

Table 1. Digital business strategy types, their descriptions and patterns

Strategy name	Description	Corresponding patterns
Development of digital applications	Constant and independent (further) development of new IT applications and their economic exchange	Network utility provider, (Virtual) selling experience, selling online services, selling virtual accessories, software firms, trust services
Processing of intellectual property	Leveraging of intellectual property by aggregating, transferring or further processing it	Content (access) provider, context, horizontal portals, information collection, IP trader, open content, vertical portals
Intermediation in two-sided markets	More efficient design of exchanges by otherwise fragmented parties by decreasing transaction costs	Aggregation, agora, classifieds, demand collection systems, infomediary, online brokers, search agent, transaction service and exchange intermediation, trust intermediary
Orchestration of digital business ecosystems	Facilitation and orchestration of a digital business ecosystem in which multiple parties can participate	Collaborations platforms, E-Mall, marketplace exchange, multi-sided platforms, value chain integrator, virtual community

effects [31]. Examples for such ecosystems is Apple's digital mobile platforms iOS with the corresponding application ecosystems [33, 38].

4 Hypotheses Development

In the competence based perspective, the economic profit mechanism for firms focuses on the balance between value creation and value capture [2]. Digital technologies enable companies to tap into new sources of value creation and capturing [e.g. 1, 8, 40]. In their popular work, Amit and Zott [31], specify *novelty, efficiency, complementarities* and *lock-in* as sources of value creation. Companies can create value based on one of these sources but also have the chance to use a combination of different sources for creating value. *Novelty* refers to new transaction structures, transaction content and participants. *Efficiency* in contrast, is aiming for cost reduction of already existing transactions such as search costs, simplicity and scale economics [41]. *Complementarities* refer to the interdependency between products and services, strategic assets, or several technologies. This means that a bundle of products provides more value than having each of the products separately. *Lock-in* focuses on prevention of migration of customers and strategic partners. Examples for named effect are switching costs of or positive network effects [31]. Our hypotheses base on the assumption that the individual digital business strategy types "trade off efficiency (i.e., maximizing joint profitability through value creation) through the effective use of resources against the distribution of returns from its efforts,[…] (i.e., maximizing producer surplus through value capture)" [2], differently. Ultimately this impacts a company's performance in different ways.

Regarding Amit and Zott's [31] sources of value creation, the first digital business strategy type merely focuses on *novelty*. In an ever more digitally mediated world there is a high market potential for new digital products [42, 43], which favors the digital business strategy type. On the other hand, there are several problems which occur with this DBS. Firstly, companies using this DBS often operate in a hyper-competitive environment, creating substantial pressure on prices [44]. This is reinforced by the fact that customers often show little willingness to pay for digital goods which can also be seen in the trend towards open software [45]. Secondly, companies pursuing this DBS are under pressure to further develop their offerings constantly to keep pace with technological advances and customer preferences, making it an investment-heavy business [8] and a less efficient digital business strategy. As a consequence, we formulate the following hypothesis: *Hypothesis 1: Applying a digital business strategy aimed at the development of IT applications has a negative influence on a firm's performance.*

The second digital business strategy type is based mainly on *efficiency* but to some extent also on *novelty* as sources of value creation. Customers increasingly prefer to consume information and content online [46]. At the same time information goods exhibit fixed costs but almost zero marginal costs for their production and distribution [47]. Additionally, once created, online content often can be used and processed multiple times, allowing to monetize it more than once [19]. Furthermore, social-computing has a positive impact on the companies' costs as the customer can be involved in the value creation process [48, 49]. All together this leads to increased efficiency. At the same time, it is easy for companies pursuing this DBS to fine-tune their activities and develop new offerings, as it is easy for them to identify relevant content on the basis of the customers' engagement and their preferences that can be obtained from data [1]. Accordingly, we present the following hypothesis: *Hypothesis 2: Applying a digital business strategy aimed at the processing of intellectual property has a positive influence on a firm's performance.*

The digital business strategy type aimed at the intermediation in two-sided markets uses *lock-in* as source of value creation. The internet plays a decisive role in a customer's purchasing decision [50]. As a result, there is a high demand for companies providing a digital service that enables interactions between multiple sets of agents [51, 52]. In doing so, the intermediator, pursuing this DBS, tries to generate *lock-ins* by creating value for agents on both sides through the reduction of transaction costs [40]. Since value is created for agents on both sides, the intermediary has the opportunity to generate revenue from both and can thus maximize profit [53]. At the same time, the intermediary has the possibility to be remunerated in numerous ways, e.g. through fees for membership or transaction [52] as well as for listing prices [54] or advertising [51]. Accordingly, we present the following hypothesis: *Hypothesis 3: Applying a digital business strategy aimed at the intermediation in two-sided markets has a positive influence on a firm's performance.*

The fourth digital business strategy type uses all four sources of value creation. These are *novelty, efficiency, complementarities,* and *lock-in.* Ecosystems based on digital platforms are increasingly important in the provision of products and services [55]. These platforms create business value by encouraging participation of customers and complementary third-party innovation of business partners. In doing so, the platform owner is able to exploit indirect network effects [56]. The platform owner benefits in several ways [57], such as by outsourcing the innovation processes and entrepreneurial risk to complementors and subsequently monetizing transactions between these complementors and customers [19, 58, 59] making this DBS more efficient. In addition, through the participation of multiple actors within the innovation process as well as the possibility of direct customer feedback, innovations and novel products often turn out to be more relevant and address customer demands more precisely [60]. We therefore define the following hypothesis: *Hypothesis 4: Applying a digital business strategy aimed at the orchestration of digital business ecosystems has a positive influence on a firm's performance.*

5   Methodology

We investigated a longitudinal sample of tech-savvy companies between 2007 and 2017, focusing on firms in the NASDAQ-100 index and using 2007 as a starting point for our data collection. The NASDAQ-100 lists the largest 100 stocks according to market capitalization traded on the NASDAQ (National Association of Securities Dealers Automated Quotation). We decided to delimit the sample to firms in clearly technological SIC (Standard Industrial Classification) industry groups. Specifically, we focus on SIC groups *(357) Computer and Office Equipment* and *(737) Computer Programming, Data Processing, And Other Computer Related Services.* The reduction to companies from these two industry groups ensures a relatively homogeneous sample, when it comes to industry characteristics and relevance of digital business strategy per se. As a result, 50 companies were excluded. Moreover, we needed to exclude firm-years that did not provide Form 10-K reports required to decode the different business model strategies. Finally, we collected data on firm performance and financial controls for the remaining firm-years from the Datastream database. This process resulted in a final sample consisting of 235 firm-years of 43 firms between 2007 and 2017.

Subsequently, in order to identify the applied digital business strategy of each company within our sample in the respective years, we compared the respective business descriptions within the Form 10-K's with the descriptions of the 28 purely digital and prototypical patterns identified by Remane et al. [9]. By using Form 10-K, we followed previous research [e.g. 61, 62], relying on this source to obtain information about a company's business model. For the sake of verifiability, we marked company statements matching the description of a specific pattern within the Form 10-K with the corresponding designation and within a matrix consisting of the individual companies and the digital business model patterns. Moreover, several rules and guidelines for granting verifiability and avoiding possible mistakes were adhered to by following the established deductive approach of qualitative content analysis [63]. Certain statements open to consideration for several patterns were marked and later discussed among the scholars. Additionally, no more than 30 Form 10-K's were encoded per session and the results of previous sessions were checked in advance of each new session. Furthermore, after half of the data had been analyzed and coded, the results were compared, discrepancies in the coding were discussed as well as corrected and anchor examples were set. The remaining Form 10-K's were encoded by following these anchor examples.

6 Measures

Independent Variable: Digital Business Strategy
The four derived digital business strategy types are used as dummy variables, indicating whether a specific digital business strategy was applied in the respective year. These dummy variables, representing the individual digital business strategy, consist of the corresponding purely digital and prototypical business model patterns applied by the companies within the respective years. Companies might show different patterns representing different digital business strategy and thus may apply several digital business strategy types simultaneously. The mix of strategies applied can therefore be subject to change over time.

Dependent Variable: Performance
We use Tobin's Q to investigate the influence of digital business strategy on firm performance. We chose Tobin's Q as a forward-looking and risk-adjusted measure less susceptible to changes in accounting practices [64]. Moreover, the measure is widely used in information systems research and has been applied in several well-known studies examining the influence of investments in IT and digital technologies on a company's performance [e.g. 20, 65–67]. Our study is therefore in line with a multitude of other studies that use the q ratio to describe the intangible value of a company. Thereby, the

underlying assumption is, that "the long-run equilibrium market value of a firm must be equal to the replacement value of its assets, giving a q value close to unity. Deviations from this relationship (where q is significantly greater than "1") are interpreted as signifying an unmeasured source of value, and generally attributed to the intangible value enjoyed by the firm" [65]. This intangible value also relates to the value and influence of a strategy on the performance of a company. We define Tobin's Q as market value divided by the replacement value of its assets.

6.1   Control Variables

We include a broad set of control variables to allow for other factors that may affect the performance of a company. We use commonly applied controls in empirical studies on innovation outcomes. All data has been obtained from Thomson Reuters Datastream. These measures together with their underlying calculation are listed in the following Table 2.

Table 2. Control variables and corresponding underlying calculations

Variable	Calculation
Firm size	Natural logarithm of firm's net sales
Leverage	Ratio of total debt to total assets
Net profit margin	Measured as net operating profit margin, which equals income divided by net sales. Measured in percent
Growth	One-Year growth of a firm's net sales in percent
Liquidity	Calculated as cash divided by total assets and then multiplied by 100
R&D intensity	Ratio of R&D spending by net sales and then multiplied by 100 (R&D over firm sales, where missing R&D is considered as zero)
Capex	Calculated as capital expenditures divided by net sales and then multiplied by 100
Capital intensity	Natural logarithm of one plus the ratio between property, plant, and equipment and then number of employees

6.2   Model Specifications

To examine the influence of different digital business strategy on a firm's performance, we need to address several empirical challenges. First, firm performance may be influenced by various unobserved factors. To account for this, we exploit our longitudinal design and decide to focus on a firm-fixed effects regression similar to prior research [68, 69]. In such a firm-fixed effects regression, each firm is assigned an individual effect to control for firm-specific unobservable factors, resulting in only time-variant effects within a firm being estimated. In our case, we therefore estimate the influence of changing one of our digital business model strategy variables (e.g., the adoption or abandonment of the respective strategy) on the company's performance. Second, we need to control for exogenous shocks like the financial crisis in 2008 and hence include annual fixed effects in addition to our control variables. Based on this, we use the following model with Tobin's Q as a dependent variable to analyze Hypotheses 1–4 (the item *fixedj* includes the firm-specific effects in the fixed effects regression):

$$Tobins\ Q_{j,+t} = \alpha + \beta_1 (development\ of\ digital\ artefacts)_{j,t} +$$
$$\beta_1 (processing\ of\ intellectual\ capital)_{j,t} + \beta_1 (intermediation\ of\ twosided\ markets)_{j,t} +$$
$$\beta_1 (orchestration\ of\ digital\ business\ ecosystems)_{j,t} + \gamma (controls)_{j,t} + T_t + fixed_j + \mu_{j,t}$$

7 Regression Results

Table 3 displays the means, standard deviations and pairwise correlations of primary variables. Due to partially strong correlation among specific control variables, we investigate variance inflation factors to check for multicollinearity. All resulting values are below critical thresholds (highest $= 2.26$), concluding that our analysis is not constrained by multicollinearity [70].

To test our hypotheses, we investigated a firm-fixed effect regression to calculate the impact of specific digital business strategy on a company's performance while controlling for various confounding effects. We find a highly significant and negative influence on firm performance with regard to the development of IT applications ($p < .01$) supporting our first hypothesis. Regarding the digital business strategy to focus on processing of intellectual property, we find a positive and highly significant ($p < .05$) influence on firm performance. Hence, our results support our second hypothesis. In contrast, we cannot identify any significant influence regarding the strategy on intermediation in two-sided markets. While we find a negative coefficient for the influence on firm performance, as suggested in our third hypothesis, the coefficient turns out to be insignificant. Finally, regarding the orchestration of digital business ecosystems, our results indicate a highly significant ($p < .01$) and positive impact on firm performance supporting our fourth hypothesis. Table 4 displays the results of these regressions.

Table 3. Summary statistics and correlation coefficients

Variable	Mean	Std Dev	1	2	3	4	5	6	7	8	9	10	11	12	13
1. DBS I	0.67	0.47	1												
2. DBS II	0.34	0.47	− 0.43	1											
3. DBS III	0.18	0.38	− 0.15	0.25	1										
4. DBS IV	0.29	0.46	− 0.16	0.47	0.43	1									
5. Tobin's Q*	2.13	1.09	0.03	− 0.15	− 0.07	0.08	1								
6. Size	15.77	1.33	− 0.23	0.23	− 0.08	0.26	0.05	1							
7. Leverage	20.88	19.55	− 0.09	0.10	0.09	− 0.26	0.08	− 0.02	1						
8. Net profit margin	19.06	14.86	0.10	− 0.01	− 0.15	− 0.13	0.36	0.12	0.11	1					
9. Growth*	9.39	13.07	− 0.20	0.05	− 0.03	0.12	0.30	0.19	− 0.15	0.11	1				
10. Liquidity	14.89	12.91	0.02	− 0.02	− 0.11	0.01	0.04	− 0.25	− 0.15	− 0.06	− 0.20	1			
11. R&D intensity	11.88	10.06	0.39	− 0.26	− 0.19	0.06	0.12	− 0.15	− 0.25	− 0.18	− 0.15	0.29	1		
12. Capex	5.16	4.03	0.00	0.14	0.14	0.03	0.02	0.25	0.05	0.08	− 0.03	− 0.03	− 0.08	1	
13. Capital intensity	4.28	1.04	− 0.10	0.30	0.10	0.10	0.02	0.24	0.35	0.09	0.04	− 0.30	− 0.05	0.58	1

* Variables Tobin's Q and Growth are winsorized at level 5% and 95%.

Table 4. Results of fixed effect regressions on a firm's performance

Method	Panel fixed effects	
Dependent variable	Performance: Tobin's Q	
Independent variables		
Strategy 1: Development of Digital Products	− 0.561 (0.005)	***
Strategy 2: Processing of Intellectual Property	0.754 (0.001)	***
Strategy 3: Intermediation in Two-Sided Markets	− 0.125 (0.851)	
Strategy 4: Orchestration of Digital Business Ecosystems	1,995 (0.000)	***
Controls		
Firm size	− 0.005 (0.979)	
Leverage	0.010 (0.161)	
Net profit margin	0.031 (0.001)	***
Growth	0.008 (0.118)	
Liquidity	0.001 (0.945)	
R&D intensity	− 0.033 (0.228)	
Capex	0.048 (0.027)	**
Capital intensity	− 0.598 (0.008)	***
Firm FE	Yes	
Time FE	Yes	
Observations	235	
R-squared	0.5011	

Notes: ***, **, and * indicate significance at the 1%, 5%, and 10% levels (two-tailed), respectively. P-values are reported in parentheses. Standard errors are heteroscedasticity consistent. Dependent variable Tobin's Q and controls are forwarded one year

8 Discussion of Findings

Our findings indicate that there is a negative relationship between the digital business strategy type *development of IT applications* and firm performance. This result suggests that companies do not profit from the development of IT applications on average. A possible reason may be the general problem of profitably commercializing IT applications within a highly competitive environment. This strategy highly depends on a strong protection against imitation via appropriability regimes. With regard to digital technologies, these regimes are often weak since it is easy to decode them and legal protection is inefficient [71, 72]. Besides, in some cases, it is easy for competitors to invent around these patents at modest costs [73, 74]. Finally, digitalization fosters the substitutability of intellectual property, leading to the value of patents to further diminish [72, 75].

Regarding the digital business strategy type *processing of intellectual property*, our findings indicate a positive relationship with firm performance. This result suggests that the performance of a company is positively affected by the processing of intellectual property. Main reasons for this may be the versatile use of generated information and digital content, accompanied by low costs for their production and distribution [47, 76]. Companies applying this approach have the opportunity to monetize the same content multiple times and in different ways. Content, for example, can be delivered for free in order to attract a large number of customers and encourage participation. The actual added value takes place in various downstream businesses, such as data analytics and brokerage or advertising placement [35, 48].

With reference to the relationship between the digital business strategy type *intermediation in two-sided markets* and a company's performance, our results indicate an insignificant influence and do not allow for conclusions about positive or negative correlations between these two. Other reasons could be that positive and negative effects outweigh each other. Profit-maximization is difficult in these businesses, since it will restrict network participation by pricing out some potential participants. Generating profit from both sides is an even greater obstacle, as it prices out yet more potential participants [53]. On the other hand, the technological and market lock-in is weak, making it easy for agents on both sides to migrate to other intermediators [38]. This competition between platforms often leads to openness to attract more customers which, in turn, frequently causes decreases in differentiation and the ability to capture value, since an important source of competitive advantage is the exclusive access to their networks [52, 57].

Findings from our panel data regression show that there is a positive relationship between the digital business strategy type *orchestration of digital business ecosystems* and firm performance. This supports the suggestion of a positive influence on the performance of companies pursuing this digital business strategy type. Possible reasons may be the indirect network effects such ecosystems often create, together with the decisiveness of companies at the center of such ecosystems. The platform owner has the opportunity to control key components inside and outside the ecosystem. This decreases complementors' bargaining power and, at the same time, enables the platform owner to exploit products and services with high margins for himself [77]. As a consequence, companies at the center of ecosystems can appropriate more value from innovations within the ecosystem [38, 58, 72].

8.1 The Value of Digital Business Strategy Types for is Research and Business Practice

Our findings reveal important implications for theory and practice. Firstly, while Leischning et al. [3] state that digital business strategy is positively linked to enhanced market intelligence capability, leading to superior market performance, we can show that this is only valid to a limited extent. Only the derived digital business strategy types, *processing of intellectual property, intermediation in two-sided markets,* and *orchestration of digital business ecosystems* show an enhanced market orientation. Furthermore, only the latter exhibits a positive influence on firm performance. Therefore, the aforementioned findings of Leischnig et al. [3] cannot be generalized.

Secondly, our findings support the perception of strategy as a set of management decisions regarding how to balance the firm's tradeoffs between being efficient and being effective to achieve objectives [2]. Only the two digital business strategy types *processing of intellectual property* and *orchestration of digital business ecosystems* have a positive impact on firm performance. A reason may be that aforementioned two digital business strategy types better balance the tradeoff between being efficient and being effective. Our results thus go in line with findings by Mithas and Rust [20], stating that dual-emphasis firms have stronger profitability relationships than either revenue- or cost-emphasis firms.

With regard to business practice. First of all, companies should take a close look at what types of digital business strategy they are currently pursuing and analyze it in respect of its strengths and weaknesses. In our case, the digital business strategy type *development of IT applications* has a negative impact on the performance of a company but can be a central component of a company's business. If this is the case, companies need to check whether certain mechanisms of other digital business strategy types can be adopted to compensate for the weaknesses of the digital business strategy type they use. For instance, the digital business strategy type *development of IT applications* processes activities mainly in-house and uses internal resources. However, there are solutions such as open content or value co-creation initiatives to involve external actors in the value creation process and thus reduce costs in the development of software by, simultaneously, increasing generativity through the use of external innovation capacity.

Second, and in line with the aforementioned, in digitally fused environments it is key to practitioners to balance the tradeoff between being efficient and being effective in order to stay competitive. This is made possible above all through the establishment of a digital business ecosystem, as demonstrated by the digital business strategy types *processing of intellectual property* and *orchestration of digital business ecosystems*. At the same time, it is difficult to establish these digital business ecosystems due to already existing network and lock-in effects. Therefore, practitioners should carefully consider whether the own market power allows to establish a digital platform business or act as a complementor within an externally hosted digital business ecosystem as both options contain significant risks [19, 38, 76].

8.2 Limitation and Future Research

Our study has some limitations worth noting. Overall we restrict our sample by only including the "NASDAQ 100" index and furthermore merely companies from specific

SIC industry groups included in this index. This procedure was necessary to obtain a homogeneous sample and to guarantee the availability of the Form 10-K as standardized information source. At the same time, however, the generalizability and transferability of our results must be critically questioned. Firstly, we only examined publicly traded companies. Secondly, we only investigated companies listed on the American stock market. Thirdly, we only examined companies from industries characterized by a high digital maturity. In order to gain more generalizable insights, which would also be valid for smaller firms or other industries, further research should repeat the study with a broader focus (e.g. focusing also on small companies or using the MSCI World Information Technology) or include other, more traditional industries, such as the automotive or manufacturing industry. Furthermore, we only record and code fully digital and prototypical business model patterns since we wanted to explore the influence of purely digital strategies on the performance of a company. However, digitally enriched patterns, too, can indicate a digital business strategy. In consequence, we suggest further research to include or focus on digitally enriched business model patterns to gain more insights into digitally enriched strategies. Besides, the identification and characterization of changes of a digital business model is not free from subjectivity, a circumstance our study shares with other studies applying similar approaches [e.g. 62, 78]. In addition, we used the framework derived by Amit and Zott [31] for developing our hypotheses. In doing so, we are in line with several well-known studies using this framework to distinguish between different digital value creation mechanisms. However, it should be noted that the authors, in their initial work, referred to e-business (i.e. business conducted over the Internet). We therefore, are not fully able to guarantee that we cover all value creation mechanisms especially apart from the e-business, which may affects the generalizability of our results. Ultimately, we were not able to investigate contingent events that could have affected the performance of companies within our sample. We would therefore encourage further research to examine digital business strategy types and their performance implications via qualitative interviews or case studies.

References

1. Bharadwaj, A., El Sawy, O.A., Pavlou, P.A., Venkatraman, N.: Digital business strategy: toward a next generation of insights. MIS Q. **37**, 471–482 (2013)
2. Drnevich, P.L., Croson, D.C.: Information technology and business-level strategy: toward an integrated theoretical perspective. MIS Q. **37**, 483–509 (2013)
3. Leischnig, A., Wölfl, S., Ivens, B., Hein, D.: From digital business strategy to market performance: insights into key concepts and processes. In: Thirty Eighth International Conference of Information Systems, Seoul (2017)
4. Galbraith, C., Schendel, D.: An empirical analysis of strategy types. Strateg. Manage. J. **4**, 153–173 (1983)
5. Porter, M.E.: Competitive Strategy: Technicals for Analyzing Industries and Competitors. Free Press, New York (1980)
6. Ansoff, H.I., Stewart, J.M.: Strategies for a technology-based business. Harv. Bus. Rev. **45**, 71–83 (1967)
7. Miles, R., Snow, C.: Organizational strategy, structure, and process. Acad. Manage. Rev. **3**, 546–562 (1978)

8. Woodard, C.J., Ramasubbu, N., Tschang, F.T., Sambamurthy, V.: Design capital and design moves: the logic of digital business strategy. MIS Q. **37**, 537–564 (2013)
9. Remane, G., Hanelt, A., Tesch, J.F., Kolbe, L.M.: The business model pattern database — a tool for systematic business model innovation. Int. J. Innov. Manag. **21**, 1–61 (2017)
10. Casadesus-Masanell, R., Ricart, J.E.: From strategy to business models and onto tactics. Long Range Plann. **43**, 195–215 (2010)
11. Mithas, S., Tafti, A., Mitchell, W.: How a firm's competitive environment and digital strategic posture influence digital business strategy. MIS Q. **37**, 511–536 (2013)
12. Hambrick, D.C.: Some tests of the effectiveness and functional attributes of miles and snow's strategic types. Acad. Manag. J. **26**, 5–26 (1983)
13. Croteau, A.-M., Bergeron, F.: An information technology trilogy: business strategy, technological deployment and organizational performance. J. Strateg. Inf. Syst. **10**, 77–99 (2001)
14. Segars, A.H., Grover, V., Kettinger, W.J.: Strategic users of information technology: a longitudinal analysis of organizational strategy and performanc. J. Strateg. Inf. Syst. **3**, 261–288 (1994)
15. Chan, Y.E., Huff, S.L., Barclay, D.W., Copeland, D.G.: Business strategic orientation, information systems strategic orientation, and strategic alignment. Inf. Syst. Res. **8**, 125–150 (1997)
16. Sabherwal, R., Chan, Y.E.: Alignment between business and is strategies: a study of prospectors, analyzers, and defenders. Inf. Syst. Res. **12**, 11–33 (2011)
17. Barrett, M., Davidson, E., Prabhu, J., Vargo, S.L.: Service innovation in the digital age: key contributions and future directions. MIS Q. **39**, 135–154 (2015)
18. Tiwana, A., Konsynski, B., Bush, A.A.: Platform evolution: coevolution of platform architecture, governance, and environmental dynamics. Inf. Syst. Res. **21**, 675–687 (2010)
19. Yoo, Y., Henfridsson, O., Lyytinen, K.: The new organizing logic of digital innovation: an agenda for information systems research. Inf. Syst. Res. **21**, 724–735 (2010)
20. Mithas, S., Rust, R.T.: How information technology strategy and investments influence firm performance: conjecture and empirical evidence. MIS Q. **40**, 223–245 (2016)
21. Chesbrough, H.: Business model innovation: It's not just about technology anymore. Strateg. Leadersh. **35**, 12–17 (2007)
22. Demil, B., Lecocq, X.: Business model evolution: in search of dynamic consistency. Long Range Plann. **43**(2–3), 227–246 (2010). https://doi.org/10.1016/j.lrp.2010.02.004
23. Osterwalder, A., Pigneur, Y.: Business Model Generation: A Handbook for Visionaries, Game Changers, and Challengers. Wiley, Hoboken, USA (2010)
24. Teece, D.J.: Business models, business strategy and innovation. Long Range Plann. **43**, 172–194 (2010)
25. Al-Debei, M.M., Avison, D.: Developing a unified framework of the business model concept. Eur. J. Inf. Syst. **19**, 359–376 (2010)
26. Lüttgens, D., Diener, K.: Business model patterns used as a tool for creating (new) innovative business models. J. Bus. Model. **4**, 19–36 (2016)
27. Rudtsch, V., Gausemeier, J., Gesing, J., Mittag, T., Peter, S.: Pattern-based business model development for cyber-physical production systems. Procedia CIRP. **25**, 313–319 (2014)
28. Abdelkafi, N., Makhotin, S., Posselt, T.: Business model innovations for electric mobility: What can be learned from existing business model patterns? Int. J. Innov. Manag. **17**, 1–41 (2013)
29. Henfridsson, O., Nandhakumar, J., Scarbrough, H., Panourgias, N.: Recombination in the open-ended value landscape of digital innovation. Inf. Organ. **28**, 89–100 (2018)
30. Lyytinen, K., Rose, G.M.: A Knowledge-based model of radical innovation in small software firms. MIS Q. **36**, 865–895 (2012)

31. Amit, R., Zott, C.: Value creation in E-business. Strateg. Manage. J. **22**, 493–520 (2001)
32. Teece, D.J.: Reflections on "profiting from innovation." Res. Policy. **35**, 1131–1146 (2006)
33. Teece, D.J.: Profiting from technological innovation - Implications for integration, collaboration, licensing and public policy. Res. Policy. **15**, 285–305 (1986)
34. Shivendu, S., Zhang, R.A.: The Impact of Digitization on Content Markets: Prices, Profit, and Social Welfare. MIS Q. (2019, Forthcoming)
35. Günther, W.A., Rezazade Mehrizi, M.H., Huysman, M., Feldberg, F.: Debating big data: a literature review on realizing value from big data. J. Strateg. Inf. Syst. **26**, 191–209 (2017)
36. Loebbecke, C., Picot, A.: Reflections on societal and business model transformation arising from digitization and big data analytics: a research agenda. J. Strateg. Inf. Syst. **24**, 149–157 (2015)
37. Gawer, A.: Bridging differing perspectives on technological platforms: toward an integrative framework. 74. Ann. Meet. Acad. Manage. AOM. **43**, 423–428 (2014)
38. Helfat, C.E., Raubitschek, R.S.: Dynamic and integrative capabilities for profiting from innovation in digital platform-based ecosystems. Res. Policy. **47**, 1391–1399 (2018)
39. Adner, R., Kapoor, R.: Value creation in innovation ecosystems: how the structure of technological interdependence affects firm performance in new technology generations. Strateg. Manag. J. **894**, 306–333 (2010)
40. Pagani, M.: Digital business strategy and value creation: framing the dynamic cycle of control points. MIS Q. Manag. Inf. Syst. **37**, 617–632 (2013)
41. Zott, C., Amit, R.: The fit between product market strategy and business model: implications for firm performance. Strateg. Manage. J. **29**, 1–26 (2008)
42. Garg, R., Telang, R.: Inferring app demand from publicly available data. MIS Q. **37**, 1253–1264 (2013)
43. Tilson, D., Lyytinen, K., Sørensen, C.: Digital infrastructures: the missing IS research agenda. Inf. Syst. Res. **21**, 748–759 (2010)
44. Kapoor, R., Agarwal, S.: Sustaining superior performance in business ecosystems: evidence from application software developers in the iOS and android smartphone ecosystems. Organ. Sci. **28**, 531–551 (2017)
45. Kaltenecker, N., Hess, T., Huesig, S.: Managing potentially disruptive innovations in software companies: transforming from On-premises to the On-demand. J. Strateg. Inf. Syst. **24**, 234–250 (2015)
46. Oh, H., Animesh, A., Pinsonneault, A.: Free versus for-a-fee: the impact of a paywall on the pattern and effectiveness of word-of-mouth via social media. MIS Q. Manage. Inf. Syst. **40**, 31–56 (2016)
47. Shapiro, C., Varian, H.R.: Information Rules. Harvard Business School Press, Boston, USA (1998)
48. Oestreicher-Singer, G., Zalmanson, L.: Content or community? A digital business strategy for content providers in the social age. MIS Q. **37**, 591–616 (2013)
49. Qi Dong, J., Wu, W.: Business value of social media technologies: evidence from online user innovation communities. J. Strateg. Inf. Syst. **24**, 113–127 (2015)
50. Gutt, D., Neumann, J., Zimmermann, S., Kundisch, D., Chen, J.: Design of review systems – a strategic instrument to shape online reviewing behavior and economic outcomes. J. Strateg. Inf. Syst. **28**, 104–117 (2019)
51. Animesh, A., Viswanathan, S., Agarwal, R.: Competing "Creatively" in sponsored search markets: the effect of rank, differentiation strategy, and competition on performance. Inf. Syst. Res. **22**, 153–169 (2011)
52. Mantena, R., Saha, R.: Co-opetition between differentiated platforms in two-sided markets. J. Manage. Inf. Syst. **29**, 109–140 (2012)
53. Bakos, Y., Katsamakas, E.: Design and ownership of two-sided networks: implications for internet platforms. J. Manage. Inf. Syst. **25**, 171–202 (2008)

54. Xu, L., Chen, J., Whinston, A.: Effects of the presence of organic listing in search advertising. Inf. Syst. Res. **23**, 1284–1302 (2012)
55. Han, S.P., Park, S., Oh, W.: Mobile app analytics: a multiple discrete-continuous choice framework. MIS Q. **40**, 983–1008 (2015)
56. Ceccagnoli, M., Forman, C., Huang, P., Wu, D.J.: Co-creation of value in a platform ecosystem - the case of enterprise software. MIS. Q. **36**, 263–290 (2012)
57. Ondrus, J., Gannamaneni, A., Lyytinen, K.: The impact of openness on the market potential of multi-sided platforms: a case study of mobile payment platforms. J. Inf. Technol. **30**, 260–275 (2015)
58. Boudreau, K.: Platform-based organization and boundary choices: "Opening-Up" while still coordinating and orchestrating. In: Entrepreneurship, Innovation, and Platforms, pp. 227–297. Emerald Publishing Limited (2017)
59. Mantena, R., Sankaranarayanan, R., Viswanathan, S.: Platform-based information goods: the economics of exclusivity. Decis. Support Syst. **50**, 79–92 (2010)
60. Ye, H., Kankanhalli, A.: User service innovation on mobile phone platforms: investigating impacts of lead uUerness, toolkit support, and design autonomy. MIS Q. Manage. Inf. rSyst. **42**, 165–187 (2018)
61. Li, C., Peters, G.F., Richardson, V.J.: The consequences of information technology control weaknesses on management information systems: the case of Sarbanes-Oxley internal control reports. MIS Q. **36**, 179–203 (2012)
62. Weill, P., Malone, T.W., D'Urso, V., Herman, G., Woerner, S.: Do some business models perform better than others? A study of the 1000 largest US firms. MIT. Cent. Coord. Sci. Work. Paper. **226**, 1–40 (2004)
63. Mayring, P.: Qualitative Content Analysis: Theoretical Foundation, Basic Procedures and Software Solutions. AAU, Klagenfurt (2014)
64. Montgomery, C.A., Wernerfelt, B.: Diversification, Ricardian rents, and Tobin's q source. RAND J. Econ. **19**, 623–632 (1988)
65. Bharadwaj, A.S., Bharadwaj, S.G., Konsynski, B.R.: Information technology effects on firm performance as measured by Tobin's q. Manage. Sci. **45**, 1008–1024 (1999)
66. Kohli, R., Devaraj, S., Ow, T.T.: Does information technology investment influence a firm's market value? A case of non-publicly traded healthcare firms. MIS Q. Manage. Inf. Syst. **36**, 1145–1164 (2012)
67. Mithas, S., Tafti, A., Bardhan, I., Goh, J.M.: Information technology and firm profitability. MIS Q. **36**, 205–224 (2012)
68. Atasoy, H., Banker, R.D., Pavlou, P.A.: On the longitudinal effects of it use on firm-level employment. Inf. Syst. Res. **27**, 6–26 (2016)
69. Pan, Y., Huang, P., Gopal, A.: Board independence and firm performance in the IT industry: the moderating role of new entry threats. MIS Q. **42**, 979–1000 (2018)
70. Wooldridge, J.M.: Econometric Analysis of Cross Section and Panel Data. MIT Press, Cambridge, MA (2002)
71. Pisano, G.P., Teece, D.J.: How to capture value from innovation: shaping intellectual property and industry architecture. Calif. Manage. Rev. **50**, 278–296 (2007)
72. Teece, D.J.: Profiting from innovation in the digital economy: enabling technologies, standards, and licensing models in the wireless world. Res. Policy. **47**, 1367–1387 (2018)
73. Mansfield, E., Schwartz, M., Wagner, S.: Imitation costs and patents: an empirical study. Econ. J. **91**, 907–918 (1981)
74. Mansfield, E.: How rapidly does new industrial technology leak out? J. Ind. Econ. **34**, 217–223 (1985)
75. Holgersson, M., Granstrand, O., Bogers, M.: The evolution of intellectual property strategy in innovation ecosystems: uncovering complementary and substitute appropriability regimes. Long Range Plann. **51**, 303–319 (2018)

76. Yoo, Y., Boland, R.J., Lyytinen, K., Majchrzak, A.: Organizing for innovation in the digitized world. Organ. Sci. **23**, 1398–1408 (2012)
77. Zhu, F., Liu, Q.: Competing with complementors: an empirical look at Amazon. com. Strateg. Manage. J. **39**, 2618–2642 (2018)
78. Dewan, S., Ren, F.: Risk and return of information technology initiatives: evidence from electronic commerce announcements. Inf. Syst. Res. **18**, 370–394 (2007)
79. Ivari, J.: Information system artefact or information system application: that is the question. Inf. Syst. J. **27**, 753–774 (2017)

Management of Digital Processes and Architectures

Introduction to the WI2021 Track: Management of Digital Processes and Architectures

Stephan Aier, Kazem Haki, and Robert Winter

University of St. Gallen, Institute of Information Management,
St. Gallen, Switzerland
{stephan.aier,kazem.haki,robert.winter}@unisg.ch

1 Track Description

Both business process management and enterprise architecture management have been established in the 1990s. Since then, the interaction between IT and business units has become more differentiated and now comprises perspectives ranging from automation over mutual alignment (co-evolution) to IT-dominated, novel business architectures. Starting from a more local or a more enterprise-wide perspective, both business process management and architecture management also cover broader management perspectives. However, as methodologies they are often criticized for not being able to cope with current dynamics or to imply too much ceremony, and therefore are perceived to be more of a hindrance than a supporter of digital innovations by some.

The aim of this *management of digital processes & architectures* track is to illuminate the many facets of managing digital processes and architectures, to better understand their current and future role, and to discuss streams of development.

This is particularly relevant considering current digitization initiatives. In contrast to the observed effects of automation, which primarily affected the business processes of companies and governmental agencies, current digitization initiatives create considerable and disruptive innovation potential. In agile settings, new IS solutions (or components) are developed, used, and reinvented in ever shorter cycles. The classic differentiation between business and IT areas is increasingly disappearing. Instead, these dynamics create tensions in organizations between local and rather short-term (market, product, project, etc.) perspectives on the one hand, and global, rather long-term perspectives on end-to-end processes on the other. While the former focus on flexibility, speed of innovation, and the customer experience, the latter often focus on efficiency, synergy, and compliance objectives. Both aspects are essential for the long-term success of organizations, so that modern IS management approaches must address this enterprise-wide perspective and related tensions in addition to the established specific local perspectives.

2 Research Articles

Overall, the track received 13 submissions, eight of those being full research papers and five short papers. Two of the submissions received a fast and constructive direct AE reject. All other submissions received three full reviews and an additional AE report.

Based on those reviews and our own reading of the submissions we were able to accept three full research papers and two short papers after one round of revision. Those papers are:

The Status Quo of Process Mining in the Industrial Sector (by Sebastian Dunzer, Sandra Zilker, Emanuel Marx, Valentin Grundler, Martin Matzner): Since process mining can be deployed in different forms for a wide range of purposes, the authors aim at providing guidance by presenting a coherent overview of published cases. They relate production forms and layout to the applied process mining type. Their results indicate that process mining fits best with cellular production layouts for batch or line production processes.

Event-Driven Business Process Management enhancing IoT – a Systematic Literature Review and Development of Research Agenda (by Christoph Stoiber, Stefan Schönig): Event Driven Business Process Management (EDBPM) is discussed as a major lever for dealing with high-frequency data such as IoT generated data. Taking this perspective, the authors provide a literature review on EDBPM. Based on their analysis, the authors present five topical clusters and propose a research agenda that focuses on frameworks, languages, standards, and implemented systems.

How does Enterprise Architecture support the Design and Realization of Data-Driven Business Models? An Empirical Study (by Faisal Rashed, Paul Drews): Data driven business models (DDBM) have generated major economic impact in recent years. However, systematically developing such business models is challenging. Based on empirical data, the authors describe how enterprise architecture (EA) management and modeling is used for the development of DDBM. They systematically show in which activities EA management and modelling may support of the design and realization of DDBM.

BPM Capability Configuration in Times of Crises: How to Adapt Processes when the Virus strikes? (by Vincent Borghoff, Ralf Plattfaut): Triggered by the Covid-19 pandemic, the authors' short paper presents a research design to better understand, which business process management capabilities are crucial for organizations to perform well in times of crisis. Their initial results from a first case interview highlight the importance of an agile, change-open, and employee-centric culture.

Supporting the Development and Implementation of a Digitalization Strategy in SMEs through a Lightweight Architecture-based Method (by Nils Johann Tschoppe, Paul Drews): The ongoing digitalization provides new opportunities and necessities for many organizations. However, for small and medium sized enterprises (SME) it may be challenging to develop and implement a digitalization strategy due to a lack of dedicated roles and expertise. In their short paper the authors present a first version of an architecture-based method for developing and implementing such strategies. They have developed their method in an action design research project with two SMEs. They found the underlying architectural perspective, being enterprise-wide and balancing business and IT aspects, to be beneficial for as-is and to-be analyses as well as for deriving a transformation roadmap.

The Status Quo of Process Mining
in the Industrial Sector

Sebastian Dunzer$^{(\boxtimes)}$, Sandra Zilker, Emanuel Marx, Valentin Grundler,
and Martin Matzner

Lehrstuhl für Digital Industrial Service Systems, Friedrich-Alexander-Universität
Erlangen-Nürnberg, Nürnberg, Germany
{sebastian.dunzer,sandra.zilker,emanuel.marx,valentin.grundler,
martin.matzner}@fau.de

Abstract. Since process mining started to reveal the potential of event logs, it has
been applied in various process settings ranging from healthcare to production.
Every single setting poses its challenges to process analysts who want to apply
process mining. The present paper aims at minimizing such challenges for enterprises in the industrial sector by providing a coherent overview of existing cases.
Our systematic literature review relates each production form and layout from
existing case studies to the applied process mining type. Further, we use Porter's
Value Chain to distinguish operations from other primary and support activities
in production. We present the application of process mining, particularly for the
production process and the primary activities other than the operations. The results
indicate that process mining fits best with cellular production layouts with batch
or line production processes.

Keywords: Process mining · Production · Production form · Production layout

1 Introduction

Recent developments enable companies to use data from information systems to analyze
their operations [1]. One of these developments is process mining. Process mining creates
insights from event logs captured by process-aware information systems (PAIS) [2].
PAIS track all steps that are required to conduct a particular workflow [3]. The range of
existing PAIS includes, e.g., manufacturing execution systems and enterprise resource
planning systems. The resulting event logs must uniquely identify process instances, the
according events, and their respective execution order [4]. With this information, process
mining generates knowledge from event logs by utilizing a combination of data mining
and business process management methods [2].

Process mining can be used for different kinds of processes, such as economic activities. Economic activities can be divided into different sectors based on the activity's
characteristics [5]. Since the *production* processes of tangible goods are at the center of
the *industrial* or secondary *sector*, their optimization has been of particular interest to
researchers and practitioners [6]. The scientific literature contains a multitude of definitions for the term *production*. However, there is a general understanding that *production*

© The Author(s), under exclusive license to Springer Nature Switzerland AG 2021
F. Ahlemann et al. (Eds.): WI 2021, LNISO 48, pp. 629–644, 2021.
https://doi.org/10.1007/978-3-030-86800-0_43

describes the transformation of input, such as raw materials or semi-finished products, combined with immaterial input, such as labor or know-how, into output, like finished goods or services [7]. *Manufacturing,* on the other hand, typically uses raw materials as input. The term *production* is more general than the term *manufacturing* and will be used primarily in this paper. However, both terms are often used interchangeably [8].

In contrast to administrative processes, production processes differ significantly in separate organizations. The variety of production processes ranges from the continuous flow and highly standardized processes [9], e.g., oil refinement, to order-based production with high customization [10], e.g., aircraft. Thus, the production follows distinct paradigms and utilizes different job-shop layouts.

The literature defines several goals for a company's success related to the production processes. These are, e.g., minimizing the throughput time, costs, or downtimes. To realize those goals, e.g., by eliminating bottlenecks, companies must know what their production processes look like [11]. Therefore, process mining, specifically process discovery, aims at generating a process model based on the event log data from a production process. Besides discovering processes, process mining also checks whether a particular process conforms to the to-be process and further enables process enhancement [2, 12]. However, the differences regarding standardization impede recommending general approaches to analyze and optimize production processes.

Recent research evaluated process mining in several settings, e.g., oncology [13], elderly care [14], and health care in general [15, 16]. Even though different views on enterprises, including production firms, have been examined, e.g., the supply chain [17], we find production itself is not at the center of interest [18].

Based on this, we provide a coherent overview of the status quo of process mining in the context of production, i.e., the industrial sector, by answering the following research question:

RQ: *Which type of process mining was applied to the different production layouts and forms?*

We support the general understanding of process mining in production by providing an overview that links the form of production and the production layout to the applied process mining types from existing case studies. Therefore, we follow Webster and Watson's [19] and Kitchenham's [20] guidelines for conducting a systematic literature review. To cover the entire scope of production enterprises' activities, we employ Porter's Value Chain to distinguish between activities [21]. We use a concept-matrix to present the results of the literature review. The matrix classifies existing process mining studies regarding their position in the value chain and their production layout and form. We summarize the identified process mining application shortly to help practitioners find related cases to their own potential process mining use case. As our contribution to academia, we theorize findings from the existing literature and propose future research.

The paper is structured as follows. Section 2 presents the relevant theoretical background on process mining, Porter's Value Chain, and the production setting. Afterward, we present the underlying method. In Sect. 4, we outline the results and roughly summarize the identified process mining studies. The subsequent section discusses the review results, proposes future research for process mining in the industrial sector, and states limitations to this study. The closing section summarizes the paper.

2 Theoretical Background

2.1 Types of Process Mining

Process mining aims to "discover, monitor and improve real-world processes (i.e., not assumed processes) by extracting knowledge from event logs readily available in today's (information) systems" [2, p. 1]. By exploiting this information using different techniques, one can gain insights into processes that would not be possible by following traditional process management approaches. To provide these techniques, process mining is a field of research that sits between data mining as well as business process management. Based on that, the present literature distinguishes three *process mining types* [2]. First, process *discovery* generates process models from an event log. Discovery is useful to gain insights into patterns that may not have been known by process participants. To examine an event log in-depth, analysts filter for specific patterns or data attributes. Second, *conformance checking* reveals whether and how process behavior differs from given models, e.g., process models, organizational models, and policies. Conformance checking can compare planned processes to their respective actual processes, whereby it can unveil errors in the planned and real process. Third, *enhancement* gathers additional information from event logs and adds these to a process model to facilitate process optimization [12].

2.2 Porter's Value Chain

The processes examined with process mining differ significantly regarding complexity, variety, and application areas depending on the company and related activities. We use Porter's [21] value chain to distinguish these activities based on their *value chain positioning*. Porter classifies activities within value chains into two main groups.

First, primary activities reflect the core business of a firm. These consist of "activities associated with transforming inputs into the final product form. In production, these activities comprise machining, packaging, assembly, equipment maintenance, testing, printing, and facility operations" [21]. Therefore, these activities are *in- and outbound logistics, operations, marketing and sales,* and *service* [21]. We further distinguish *operations* from the other primary activities, as it comprises the production itself. The *support activities* increase the effectiveness of at least one primary activity. Porter divides these into procurement, technology development, human resource management, and firm infrastructure [21]. However, we do not focus on support activities in the underlying paper as they are not directly related to the form of production.

2.3 Forms of Production

The existing literature proposes several ways to classify forms of production. For instance, based on the production volume, the variety of produced goods, or the physical organization of machines or workforce. In the following, we characterize the different *production process types* concerning volume, variety, and production-layout.

Production processes differ in variety and volume of produced goods and range from a high level of customization and a low volume to high standardization with a high volume. The four existing archetypes for this range are defined as follows. A *job process* handles a wide variety of produced goods with a high degree of customization and a low production volume, e.g., ships [10]. This type of production process requires a high level of flexibility from both the workforce and machinery [9]. In contrast to job processes, a *batch process* handles high volumes of similar or related products in batches, e.g., bakery goods [22]. When a firm produced the desired number of products from one batch, it reconfigures the production process for the next batch [9]. *Line processes* are geared towards standardized products with high production volumes, e.g., cars. Such processes are at the center of optimizing material handling, automation, and cost savings [9, 23]. Lastly, *continuous flow processes* are highly standardized high-volume processes without any customization, e.g., oil refinement. Raw materials like ores, liquids, or gases flow through such processes. Theoretically, these processes never need to be stopped if enough raw, auxiliary, and operating materials are provided, and machines do not have any outages [9].

In addition to the form of production, we distinguish the *production layout*, i.e., the physical arrangement of operations, facilities, and machines. Overall, there are three types of production layouts, the *job-shop*, the *cellular*, and the *assembly-line* layout. The *job-shop layout* is based on the production process from craftwork. One person is responsible for one item. Hence, the shop floor is designed to enable the free assignment of a producible object to a person or a machine that conducts the complete production process. The flexibility to produce distinct goods is very high but restricts the production volume. Therefore, line processes or continuous-flow processes are considered infeasible in the job-shop layout. Concerning the *cellular layout*, the shop floor comprises independent cells. Each cell, i.e., the assigned machines and workers, is responsible for a specific task. Therefore, the product moves along those cells where each individual step is then performed [24]. Compared to the job-shop layout, cellular layouts are less flexible regarding the produced goods but handle more significant production volumes. In an *assembly line layout,* all materials, machines, and workers are arranged along one line of production. The directed material flow and the resulting fixed order increase the standardization, but job processes become infeasible in an assembly-line layout [24].

3 Method

To answer the research questions, we conduct a systematic literature review following Webster and Watson [19] and Kitchenham [20]. Our overall goal is the presentation of the status quo in a specific area. We analyze the progress and identify potential topics for future research in this area. Thus, our review belongs to the descriptive reviews [25, 26]. The systemic literature review begins with the definition of the review scope [27].

The *focus* of our research is on publications of process mining applications in the industrial sector. The *goal* of our review is to investigate what progress has been made so far in the area mentioned above and how far there is a relationship between the chosen process mining type and the characteristics of the production process. Since we evaluate the current state of research, our review's organization is rather *conceptual* than historical or methodological. Due to the descriptive nature of our review, the *perspective* we take is neutral. Given that we present our findings in this conference paper, our review's *audience* consists of scholars, although it provides guidance for practitioners as well. Regarding coverage, Müller-Bloch and Kranz [28, p. 12] argue that "while it may be argued that literature reviews should always be exhaustive, we reckon that analyzing all prior research is neither always possible nor economical and necessary". Consequently, the *coverage* of our review is representative, as is appropriate for descriptive literature reviews. The literature search was conducted on Scopus, EBSCO, and Proquest to cover a wide range of relevant academic journals and conferences. After Proquest, as the third database consulted, only added one paper that we considered relevant, we see this a proof of high coverage of existing releases. The search string that we used is.

("process mining" OR "workflow mining" OR "trace mining") AND (manufactur* OR production OR factory OR machinery)

In addition to scientific publications, case studies provided by software vendors or companies using process mining are a relevant source of information about industrial applications. For this reason, we consulted a case study database supplied by the "IEEE Task Force on Process Mining" [29] as the second part of our literature search. Within this database, companies and process mining operators publish their use cases by giving information about business problems, implemented process mining techniques, applied tools, and contributions of the analysis to the business processes. The chair of task force founder van der Aalst then checks these papers for completeness and relevance to ensure data quality.

Already cleaned for duplicates, our initial search resulted in 490 hits, from which 290 trace back to Scopus, 103 to EBSCO, 58 to Proquest, and 39 to IEEE. After removing 54 duplicates, we screened these papers' titles and abstracts. Typical causes for exclusion at this stage were: (1) A missing focus on presenting a practical application of process mining. For instance, if a case describes the process mining potential only theoretically or if a case only uses simulated or generated production data. (2) A missing focus on a primary activity in economic production, (3) insufficient assignability to an organizational form of production. In the first round of analysis, 365 papers were removed from the dataset, leaving 71 articles in the review scope. We performed a forward and backward search afterward [19]. Therefore, we looked up the identified papers on Google Scholar and analyzed the titles and abstracts from the identified papers' references and the articles that cited a previously identified paper. Whenever a paper dealt with a process mining application in an industrial setting, we included it in the review. During this process, we added eight papers to our study. Next, we checked the full text of these papers, having the selection criteria mentioned above in mind. After removing 26 irrelevant articles and 13 articles to which we did not get access, the final set comprises 40 articles, including 30 specific applications.

4 Results

To classify the results, we created a concept matrix [19] based on the concepts described in Sect. 2. The first dimension is the value chain positioning, i.e., according to primary and secondary activities suggested by Porter [21]. The second and third dimensions are the production process type and the production layout. Lastly, we distinguish between the process mining type used in each case. Table 1 presents the resulting concept matrix.

4.1 Applications in Operations

We identified 21 applications that apply process mining in production processes. The respective form and layout of production for each of them are depicted in Fig. 1. In general, every case uses process discovery, eight cases utilize conformance checking, and only two cases employ a form of enhancement.

Rozinat et al. [30] outline how a wafer scanner producer conducted a process mining project. Wafer scanners consist of various building blocks. During their production, the scanners are assembled at the plant, then disassembled, shipped to the customer, and finally re-assembled. The authors constructed a process model based on the test logs with process discovery. They found process optimization potential by suggesting performing test activities earlier than usually intended. Park et al. [10] examine analysis techniques from process mining in make-to-order production, such as shipbuilding and aviation. The paper examines process data from Hyundai Heavy Industries Co. The study determines the workload and delay of production processes by comparing the optimized planned process with the actual process. Therefore, they deploy performance- and time-perspective conformance checking in shipbuilding. Ruschel et al. [31] discover Bayesian Networks in a Brazilian automotive company. The Bayesian Networks can estimate the process cycle time based on a defined availability and cost functions. Finally, they optimize the maintenance schedule to improve machine run time.

Lee et al. [32] and Park et al. [33] aim to gain insights into the assembly and the after-assembly block production process of Daewoo Shipbuilding & Marine Engineering. Due to the absence of contextual data in the log, the analysis employs process discovery for identifying undesired process patterns. Pospíšil et al. [34] describe how a Czech door manufacturer uses process mining to predict production times of orders. Their approach employs process discovery to build accurate, evidence-based simulation models to predict performance and recommend future actions.

The coffee machine manufacturer Nuova Simonelli validates and analyses their production process with process mining [39]. The company has six production lines; each of them is divided into stations that serve specific purposes. In this case, the approach is to apply five different discovery algorithms. Subsequently, the analysts use conformance checking to show which of the algorithms leads to the most accurate resulting model. The company could then optimize their process regarding the recommendations derived from the discovered process models.

Meincheim et al. [57] describe how WEG, a Brazilian energy solutions provider and electric motor producer, applies process mining. The company conducts the production planning for each custom control panel. After that, they set up a production route for one batch. The production operators decide which machines take part in the assembling.

Table 1. Overview on applications of process mining by production layout, production process, and their value chain positioning.

	Value chain positioning					Production process type				Production layout			Process mining type		
	Operations	Inbound logistics	Outbound logistics	Marketing & Sales	Services	Job	Batch	Line	Continuous flow	Job shop	Cellular	Assembly line	Discovery	Conformance checking	Enhancement
# of appearances: •	21	5	5	3	3	6	9	4	2	3	10	7	30	8	2
Altan and Birgün [35]	•						•				•		•		
Benayadi et al. [36]; Viale et al. [37, 38]	•							•				•	•	•	
Bettacchi et al. [39]	•					•					•		•	•	
Bhogal and Garg [40]	•							•			•		•		
Brzychczy et al. [41]	•								•			•	•		
Celonis AG [42]		•	•										•		
Celonis AG [43]	•						•					•	•	•	
Denno et al. [44]	•						•					•	•		
Abonyi and Dörgő [45]	•								•				•		
Engel and Bose [46]		•											•		
ER et al. [47, 48]	•	•	•				•				•		•		
Fleig et al. [49]				•									•		
Fluxicon [22, 50]	•	•	•				•				•		•		
Ho and Lau [51]	•						•				•		•		
Ho et al. [52]	•						•				•		•		
Knoll et al. [53]		•	•										•	•	
Koosawad et al. [54]					•								•		
Lee et al. [32, 55]; Park et al. [33, 56]	•					•					•		•		
Meincheim et al. [57]	•							•			•		•		•
Nagy et al. [58, 59]	•							•				•	•		
Park et al. [10]	•					•				•			•	•	
Paszkiewicz [60]			•										•	•	
Pospíšil et al. [34]	•					•					•		•		
QPR Software Plc [61]				•	•								•		
QPR Software Plc [62]				•									•		
Rozinat et al. [30, 63]	•					•				•			•	•	•
Ruschel et al. [31]	•					•				•			•		
Saravanan and Rama Sree [64]					•								•		
Ulsan Institute [65]; Son et al. [66]	•						•					•	•	•	
Viale et al. [67]	•						•					•	•		

D: Discovery
C: Conformance
   checking
E: Enhancement

Production process type
(variety/ volume of produced goods)

		Job process (fully customized; low volume)	**Batch process** (multiple products; low or moderate volume)	**Line process** (few products; higher volume)	**Continuous flow process** (high standardization; high volume)
Production layout *(physical arrangement of operations)*	**Job shop production** (product is flexibly assigned to machine workers)	Wafer scanners D, C, E [30, 63] Ships D, C [10] Maintenance D [31]	*No case study found*	*Not feasible*	*Not feasible*
	Cellular production (product moves along specialized cells/groups)	Ships D [32, 33, 55, 56] Doors D [34] Coffee machine D, C [39]	Control panels D, E [57] Shoe parts D [47, 48] Micro-precision parts D [22, 50] Electronic products D [51] Sliders D [52] Propellers D [35] Maintenance D [40]	*No case study found*	*Not feasible*
	Assembly line production (product moves from workstation to workstation)	*Not feasible*	Computer parts D, C [65, 66] Semiconductors D [67]	Automotive parts D, C [43] Electronic chips D, C [36–38] Automotive assembly D [44] Coils D [58, 59]	Mining machine operation D [41] Oil refinement D [45]

Fig. 1. Distribution of process mining applications in operations by production process type and production layout.

The authors use discovery to analyze the as-is process and afterward enhance the generated models with additional insights from further analysis of the activity frequencies and variants. Thus, this study is the only application that employs enhancement. The authors show that production operators rearrange the shop floor according to currently available resources instead of waiting for the optimal machine assignment. The shoe manufacturer PT. XYZ Indonesia uses process mining to optimize production planning and warehouse management processes [47, 48]. Using discovery, the company identified deviations between their demand prognosis and the actual demand. Such deviations cause errors in production planning and require resource-intensive rescheduling activities. Veco aims to reduce lead time in its production plant for micro-precision parts [22, 50]. The main challenge in their production is that only the finished product can be assessed regarding quality. To get early feedback, the company desires to keep the production cycles short. Veco identified which workstations cause the most delays by visualizing the as-is processes with discovery. The company could improve the flexibility in departments involved in later stages of the production. Ho et al. [52] implemented process discovery with neural networks and fuzzy logic at a slider manufacturer to reduce rework and scrap rates. Ho and Lau [51] implemented real-time process analysis with process discovery from various data sources at a computer electronics producer. The overall objective was to reduce rework. One study uses process discovery with data from a manufacturing system to increase the transparency in propeller production during the implementation of new production technologies [35]. In [40], the authors apply process discovery, including a variant analysis, to examine rework activities and machinery breakdown. To improve future executions, the authors design a new model to-be model from the discovered model.

Son et al. [66] and Ulsan Institute [65] apply process mining at Samsung Electro Mechanics. Although process discovery discloses a high variation in machine utilization, conformance checking only identifies minor deviations between the actual and planned process. Today, Samsung uses the information to balance the machine utilization. STMicroelectronics, a semiconductor producer from Switzerland, utilizes process mining to gain transparency [67]. The production process consists of more than a thousand process variants. Because of the process's complexity, modifying it based on a customer's demand is prone to errors. Therefore, STMicroelectronics wants to discover accurate process models based on event logs from the production processes.

Eissmann, a German automotive supplier, uses process mining to digitize its processes [43]. Especially the purchase-to-pay, the master data management, and the production processes are continuously monitored. Besides, Eissmann can assure quality in labor-intensive process steps by revealing bottlenecks with discovery, e.g., when working with leather whose processing needs to be finished after a fixed amount of time. Denno et al. [44] apply process discovery based on genetic programming to incorporate probabilistic and causal information into the discovered model. In their evaluation, the discovered model is used for scheduling. Nagy et al. [59] apply several process mining techniques in coil manufacturing to find distributions of faulty products in the entire production. In [58], the authors further develop their process mining application for real-time analysis. Three related studies at STMicroelectronics strive to create large-scale process models for electronic chip manufacturing [36–38]. These cases employ different discovery strategies extended by stochastic approaches, time data, and sequence alignment to generate high-quality process models. One study investigates the application of process mining in mining operations to identify opportunities for operational improvement [41]. It describes the first application of process mining to investigate the working process of a roof bolter operating in an underground mine. Abonyi and Dörgő [45] use process mining at an industrial delayed-coker plant to identify frequent operations that lead to alarms. Their objective was to lower the number of alarms raised during production.

4.2 Application in Primary Activities Other than Operations

Nine additional cases show process mining applications in primary activities other than production operations.

Four of these cases employ process mining in logistics processes. Engel et al. [46] analyze the ordering, delivery, and invoicing at a consumer goods producer. The company wanted to identify the items that take the longest until they can be delivered. In this paper, only a subset of the process data was available, which aggravates drawing generalizable conclusions. Neste oil is an oil and gas provider [42]. They analyzed their procurement and logistic processes with discovery and conformance checking to identify deviations. Knoll et al. [53] examine the inbound logistics for the mixed-model assembly line at a German car manufacturer, whereby they discovered unknown process paths and facilitated process transparency. Paszkiewicz [60] examines the inventory management of a mattress producer with an emphasis on conformance checking. The authors checked conformance to a process model as well as policies. Based on the results, the firm organized training for storekeepers and rearranged warehouse management.

Three of the identified case studies examine production-related service processes. MG Motors, a car producer, operates a sales and service unit in India [64]. The authors evaluate fifty troubleshooting methods of motorcycle repair with process mining. The company discovers a process model from data that helps mechanics during process execution. Finally, the authors conclude that unstructured processes pose a challenge to process mining. Vaisala, a producer of measuring instruments and sensors, used discovery to visualize support and repair processes [61]. The gathered insights enable the company to support change management through fast verification of process actions. In another case, the authors apply process mining in the implementation of an enterprise resource planning system in a production setting [49]. They find that process mining can aid in the selection of a process template from process databases such as the SAP Best Practices Explorer.

Additional two cases focused on the application in marketing and sales. QPR Software Plc [61, 62] analyzes the relation between data from opportunity processes and delivery processes in the PAIS of a steel construction company. The case study compares the planned sales to the numbers from the discovered delivery processes. The unveiled deviations led to the adjustment of the planned process. Koosawad [54] shows how process mining can help to improve the efficiency of a car manufacturer's sales process. The company analyzes the participation of each employee in a car sale. An in-depth discovery analysis unveiled that some employees perform better than others. Subsequently, the company established best practices by analyzing the procedures of successful sellers.

5   Discussion

5.1   Findings

We found three main areas of application for production companies that use process mining in their operative processes. First, companies try to gather information about repair and rework steps in the production process. Previous research shows how process mining can identify repair activities as bottlenecks and root-cause for disadvantageous machine disposition. Second, quality assurance as an area of interest for process mining is outlined. Third, the largest proportion of applications concerns machine utilization and workstation efficiency. We conclude that several companies could optimize the performance of these production processes with process mining.

The prevalent production setting for process mining is the batch process with a cellular production layout. In contrast to line and continuous-flow processes, these production forms require resource and workstation allocation relatively often. This hypothesis is supported by the high number of process mining applications that attempt to optimize machine utilization and workstation efficiency. Most of these studies use filtering for data attributes to identify bottlenecks in the production process. Consequently, the firms can redesign the processes based on these insights.

Except for continuous-flow processes, process discovery can identify repair and rework in a similar manner by creating Petri nets or Fuzzy models [45, 51]. Due to the rearrangement of the job shop layout with every production process step, repair and rework becomes a costly problem when temporary solutions need to be installed for reworking a previous process step. Hence, in such settings, users apply process mining to identify potential sources of rework.

Process mining can potentially improve continuous-flow processes [41]. However, both identified case studies had difficulties applying process mining. The event logs contain noise that aggravates process mining [45]. Furthermore, there is no logical termination of the process, processes run for a long time, and the time span between events is longer than in many other business processes. Hence, these studies rather aim at creating process models of their production rather than creating specific opportunities for business improvement. In such settings, the transferability of process mining is not given yet, and the applicability of conformance checking and enhancement are impeded by the absence of existing process models.

Process mining in primary value chain activities other than operations concerns sales and opportunity management [54, 61, 62], support and repair services [61, 64], and logistics [33, 42, 46, 53]. In some of these cases, the companies use process mining in support activities as well. Except for the enterprises that use process mining in logistics, which also use conformance checking, companies tend to apply process discovery exclusively.

Despite the difference in each of the process mining applications, we see a trend regarding the complexity of a production process and the types of process mining. Firms producing complex goods, such as ships, wafer scanners, or cars, are more likely to apply conformance checking or enhancement techniques than companies producing goods in large quantities, e.g., semiconductors, micro-precision parts, propellers. However, this is more of a general trend than a clear observation.

Additionally, Rozinat et al. [30] note that their findings were possibly already out of date because they did not apply to the next product generations. Therefore, such process analysis should be carried out iteratively to provide valuable insights.

5.2 Future Research

Systematic literature reviews should draw implications from previous research for the future, according to Webster and Watson [19]. Therefore, we outline open topics for future research that should be discussed regarding process mining in the industrial sector.

We found that every process mining application includes process discovery, whereas only a few of the identified cases apply other types of process mining. This dominance of discovery indicates that companies perceive it as the most applicable or useful type of process mining. In most cases, the high-level insights generated through discovery seem to satisfy the expectation of process mining users already. Due to the imbalance of process mining types, an in-depth analysis of process mining users' expectations could bear valuable knowledge to create new process mining methods for production processes.

Conformance checking is only rarely represented throughout the process mining cases. Additionally, enhancement is only applied once in the identified case studies. Both conformance checking and enhancement require a process model for their application. We assume the scope of process models for process planning or as workflow instructions differs from the available event logs regarding the level of detail. Perhaps event logs represent a much finer grain of detail than the rather high-level process models which are created by humans. Companies would need to create process models with a similar scope as the event log from production PAIS. This finding is supported by the fact that only two case studies use process models, which were not created during the project itself, i.e., through process discovery. Those two application cases take place in companies with an assembly-line production layout. Due to the design of an assembly line, the process flow rarely changes. Most products pass through similar process steps in a similar order. Thus, firms with an assembly line can create more detailed production process models with reasonable effort. We believe research and practice would profit from studies on existing production process modeling practices. A deeper understanding of the scope of the process in these areas might facilitate more target-oriented process analyses. Furthermore, the difference in the degree of detail in manually modeled processes and existing event logs should be solved by either aggregation techniques regarding events or modeling at the event-level of a process.

Even though the quality and availability of data are presumably higher in assembly-line layouts, companies who apply process mining mostly operate a cellular production layout. We assume that companies want to apply process mining in cases that seem more complex and that can take different paths in a production process. With a cellular layout, it is presumably less likely that the processes are planned as accurately as in assembly-line layouts. Additionally, the production is more standardized than in settings that use the job-shop layout. Consequently, PAIS can protocol process steps within the cells. Still, the finding requires a deeper analysis of the actual reasons.

We believe that for the progress of process mining in production, an analysis of the maturity of the process mining project, the production under examination, and the data quality might provide valuable insights. A descriptive and prescriptive maturity model can support companies and researchers when starting or further developing their process mining projects in a production setting [68].

5.3 Limitations

Although we conducted this research with our best efforts, the paper underlies some limitations. First, while we included the most frequent keywords in the search string, we might have omitted relevant papers or case studies. We further included production-related keywords in the search, which might have caused the omission of articles that do not explicate the area of application. However, we tried to minimize the risk by conducting forward and backward searches. Second, the relatively low number of existing practical reports and case studies aggravates the findings' generalizability. Still, the identified papers cover different industries and can thereby grant some level of generalizability. Third, the process mining studies from practice are mostly provided by process mining vendors, i.e., Celonis AG, Fluxicon, and QPR Software. Thus, these reports are probably handpicked regarding the success of the process mining application. However, since the IEEE Taskforce added the cases to their database, we believe that the studies contain valuable information about where successful process mining applications in the industrial sector were conducted.

6 Conclusion

This paper presents the results of a systematic literature review on applications of process mining in the industrial sector. Therefore, we provide a rough overview of the existing process mining studies. We show that most companies who apply process mining make use of cellular production layouts. Regarding the process mining type, analysts implement discovery in every case, whereas conformance checking was applied only in assembly-line production layouts with process models that existed prior to the process mining project. Only one study applied an enhancement technique to amend a beforehand discovered process model. Further, our findings show that enterprises in the production industry apply process mining in several business areas, i.e., logistics, delivery, quality management, sales, and opportunity management.

References

1. Urbach, N., et al.: The impact of digitalization on the IT department. Bus. Inf. Syst. Eng. **61**, 123–131 (2019)
2. van der Aalst, W., et al.: Process mining manifesto. In: Daniel, F., Barkaoui, K., Dustdar, S. (eds.) BPM 2011. LNBIP, vol. 99, pp. 169–194. Springer, Heidelberg (2012). https://doi.org/10.1007/978-3-642-28108-2_19
3. van der Aalst, W., et al.: Business process mining: an industrial application. Inf. Syst. **32**, 713–732 (2007)
4. Jans, M., Soffer, P., Jouck, T.: Building a valuable event log for process mining: an experimental exploration of a guided process. Enterp. Inf. Syst. **13**, 601–630 (2019)
5. Kenessey, Z.: The primary, secondary, tertiary and quaternary sectors of the economy. Rev. Income Wealth **33**, 359–385 (1987)
6. Alexander, M.: Six sigma: the breakthrough management strategy revolutionizing the world's top corporations. Technometrics **43**, 370 (2001)
7. Bates, J.A., Parkinson, J.R.: Business Economics. Blackwell, Oxford (1971)
8. Kalpakjian, S., Schmid, S.: Manufacturing Engineering and Technology. Prentice Hall, New York (2010)
9. Krajewski, L.J., Malhotra, M.K., Ritzman, L.: Operations Management: Processes and Supply Chains. Pearson, Harlow (2019)
10. Park, M., Song, M., Baek, T.H., Son, S., Ha, S.J., Cho, S.W.: Workload and delay analysis in manufacturing process using process mining. In: Bae, J., Suriadi, S., Wen, L. (eds.) AP-BPM 2015. LNBIP, vol. 219, pp. 138–151. Springer, Cham (2015). https://doi.org/10.1007/978-3-319-19509-4_11

11. Ishaq Bhatti, M., Awan, H.M., Razaq, Z.: The key performance indicators (KPIs) and their impact on overall organizational performance. Qual. Quant. **48**(6), 3127–3143 (2013). https://doi.org/10.1007/s11135-013-9945-y
12. Mannhardt, F.: Multi-perspective process mining. Eindhoven (2018)
13. Kurniati, A.P., Johnson, O., Hogg, D., Hall, G.: Process mining in oncology: a literature review. In: Proceedings of the 6th International Conference on Information Communication and Management (ICICM), pp. 291–297 (2016)
14. Farid, N., de Kamps, M., Johnson, o.: process mining in frail elderly care: a literature review. In: Proceedings of the 12th International Joint Conference on Biomedical Engineering Systems and Technologies, pp. 332–339 (2019)
15. Rojas, E., Munoz-Gama, J., Sepúlveda, M., Capurro, D.: Process mining in healthcare: a literature review. J. Biomed. Inform. **61**, 224–236 (2016)
16. Ghasemi, M., Amyot, D.: Process mining in healthcare: a systematised literature review. Int. J. Electron. Healthc. **9**, 60 (2016)
17. Jokonowo, B., Claes, J., Sarno, R., Rochimah, S.: Process mining in supply chains: a systematic literature review. Int. J. Electr. Comput. Eng. (IJECE) **8**, 4626–4636 (2018)
18. Yahya, B.N.: The development of manufacturing process analysis: lesson learned from process mining. Jurnal Teknik Industri **16**, 95–106 (2014)
19. Webster, J., Watson, R.T.: Analyzing the past to prepare for the future: writing a literature review. MIS Q. **26**, xiii–xxiii (2002)
20. Kitchenham, B.: Procedures for performing systematic reviews, pp. 1–26. Keele University, (2004)
21. Porter, M.E.: Competitive Advantage: Creating and Sustaining Superior Performance. Free Press, New York (1985)
22. Fluxicon BV: Leveraging human process knowledge via process mining (2016)
23. Schuh, G., Schmidt, C. (eds.): Produktionsmanagement. Springer, Heidelberg (2014). https://doi.org/10.1007/978-3-642-54288-6
24. Grabner, T.: Operations Management. Springer, Wiesbaden (2017). https://doi.org/10.1007/978-3-658-14484-5
25. Paré, G., Trudel, M.-C., Jaana, M., Kitsiou, S.: Synthesizing information systems knowledge: a typology of literature reviews. Inf. Manag. **52**, 183–199 (2015)
26. Okoli, C.: A guide to conducting a standalone systematic literature review. Commun. Assoc. Inf. Syst. **37**, 43 (2015)
27. Cooper, H.M.: Organizing knowledge syntheses: a taxonomy of literature reviews. Knowl. Soc. **1**, 104–126 (1988)
28. Müller-Bloch, C., Kranz, J.: A framework for rigorously identifying research gaps in qualitative literature reviews. In: Proceedings of the 23rd European Conference on Information Systems (ECIS) (2015)
29. IEEE CIS Task Force on Process Mining: Process Mining Case Studies. https://www.win.tue.nl/ieeetfpm/doku.php?id=shared:process_mining_case_studies (2019)
30. Rozinat, A., de Jong, I.S.M., Gunther, C.W., van der Aalst, W.M.P.: Process mining applied to the test process of wafer scanners in ASML. IEEE Trans. Syst. Man Cybern. Part C (Appl. Rev.) **39**, 474–479 (2009)
31. Ruschel, E., Santos, E.A.P., de Freitas Rocha Loures, E.: Establishment of maintenance inspection intervals: an application of process mining techniques in manufacturing. J. Intell. Manuf. **467**, 103 (2018)
32. Lee, S.-K., Kim, B., Huh, M., Cho, S., Park, S., Lee, D.: Mining transportation logs for understanding the after-assembly block manufacturing process in the shipbuilding industry. Expert Syst. Appl. **40**, 83–95 (2013)

33. Park, J., Lee, D., Zhu, J.: An integrated approach for ship block manufacturing process performance evaluation: case from a Korean shipbuilding company. Int. J. Prod. Econ. **156**, 214–222 (2014)
34. Pospíšil, M., Mates, V., Hruška, T., Bartík, V.: Process mining in a manufacturing company for predictions and planning. Int. J. Adv. Softw. **6**, 283–297 (2013)
35. Altan, Z., Birgün, S.: Using process mining approach for machining operations. In: Durakbasa, N.M., Gençyılmaz, M.G. (eds.) ISPR -2019. LNME, pp. 452–464. Springer, Cham (2020). https://doi.org/10.1007/978-3-030-31343-2_40
36. Benayadi, N., Le Goc, M., Bouché, P.: Using the stochastic approach framework to model large scale manufacturing processes. In: Proceedings of the Third International Conference on Software and Data Technologies (ICSOFT), pp. 186–191 (2008)
37. Viale, P., Benayadi, N., Le Goc, M., Pinaton, J.: Modeling large scale manufacturing process from timed data - using the TOM4L approach and sequence alignment information for modeling STMicroelectronics' production processes. In: Proceedings of the 12th International Conference on Enterprise Information Systems (ICEIS), pp. 129–138 (2010)
38. Viale, P., Benayadi, N., Le Goc, M., Pinaton, J.: Discovering large scale manufacturing process models from timed data - application to STMicroelectronics' production processes. In: Proceedings of the 5th International Conference on Software and Data Technologies (ICSOFT), pp. 227–235 (2010)
39. Bettacchi, A., Polzonetti, A., Re, B.: Understanding production chain business process using process mining: a case study in the manufacturing scenario. In: Krogstie, J., Mouratidis, H., Su, J. (eds.) CAiSE 2016. LNBIP, vol. 249, pp. 193–203. Springer, Cham (2016). https://doi.org/10.1007/978-3-319-39564-7_19
40. Bhogal, R., Garg, A.: Anomaly detection and fault prediction of breakdown to repair process using mining techniques. In: Proceedings of the International Conference on Intelligent Engineering and Management (ICIEM), pp. 240–245 (2020)
41. Brzychczy, E., Gackowiec, P., Liebetrau, M.: Data analytic approaches for mining process improvement—machinery utilization use case. Resources **9**, 17 (2020)
42. Celonis AG: Big data is the new oil (2017)
43. Celonis AG: Big data-powered tuning for fast and secure processes (2017)
44. Denno, P., Dickerson, C., Harding, J.A.: Dynamic production system identification for smart manufacturing systems. J. Manuf. Syst. **48**, 192–203 (2018)
45. Abonyi, J., Dörgő, G.: Process mining in production systems. In: Proceednings of the 23rd IEEE International Conference on Intelligent Engineering Systems (INES), pp. 267–270 (2019)
46. Engel, R., Bose, R.P.J.C.: A case study on analyzing inter-organizational business processes from EDI messages using physical activity mining. In: Proceedings of the 47th Hawaii International Conference on System Sciences (HICSS), pp. 3858–3867 (2014)
47. Mahendrawathi, E.R., Arsad, N., Astuti, H.M., Kusumawardani, R.P., Utami, R.A.: Analysis of production planning in a global manufacturing company with process mining. J. Enterp. Inf. Manag. **31**, 317–337 (2018)
48. Mahendrawathi, E.R., Astuti, H.M., Wardhani, I.R.K.: Material movement analysis for warehouse business process improvement with process mining: a case study. In: Bae, J., Suriadi, S., Wen, L. (eds.) Asia Pacific Business Process Management AP-BPM 2015. LNBIP, pp. 115–127. Springer, Cham (2015). https://doi.org/10.1007/978-3-319-19509-4_9
49. Fleig, C., Augenstein, D., Mädche, A.: Process mining for business process standardization in ERP implementation projects – an SAP S/4 HANA case study from manufacturing. In: Proceedings of the 16th International Conference on Business Process Management (BPM) (2018)
50. Fluxicon BV: Interview with the logistics manager of the year (2018)

51. Ho, G.T.S., Lau, H.C.W.: Development of an OLAP-fuzzy based process mining system for quality improvement. In: Shi, Z., Shimohara, K., Feng, D. (eds.) IIP 2006. IIFIP, vol. 228, pp. 243–258. Springer, Boston, MA (2006). https://doi.org/10.1007/978-0-387-44641-7_26

52. Ho, G.T.S., Lau, H.C.W., Lee, C.K.M., Ip, A.W.H., Pun, K.F.: An intelligent production workflow mining system for continual quality enhancement. Int. J. Adv. Manuf. Technol. **28**, 792–809 (2006)

53. Knoll, D., Reinhart, G., Prüglmeier, M.: Enabling value stream mapping for internal logistics using multidimensional process mining. Expert Syst. Appl. **124**, 130–142 (2019)

54. Koosawad, K., Saguansakdiyotin, N., Palangsantikul, P., Porouhan, P., Premchaiswadi, W.: Improving sales process of an automotive company with fuzzy miner techniques. In: Proceedings of the 16th International Conference on ICT and Knowledge Engineering (ICT&KE), pp. 1–6 (2018)

55. Lee, D., Park, J., Pulshashi, I.R., Bae, H.: Clustering and operation analysis for assembly blocks using process mining in shipbuilding industry. In: Song, M., Wynn, M.T., Liu, J. (eds.) AP-BPM 2013. LNBIP, vol. 159, pp. 67–80. Springer, Cham (2013). https://doi.org/10.1007/978-3-319-02922-1_5

56. Park, J., Lee, D., Bae, H.: Event-log-data-based method for efficiency evaluation of block assembly processes in shipbuilding industry. ICIC Express Lett. **5**, 157–162 (2014)

57. Meincheim, A., dos Santos Garcia, C., Nievola, J.C., Scalabrin, E.E.: Combining process mining with trace clustering: manufacturing shop floor process - an applied case. In: Proceedings of the 29th International Conference on Tools with Artificial Intelligence (ICTAI), pp. 498–505 (2017)

58. Nagy, Z., Werner-Stark, A., Dulai, T.: Using process mining in real-time to reduce the number of faulty products. In: Welzer, T., Eder, J., Podgorelec, V., Kamišalić Latifić, A. (eds.) ADBIS 2019. LNCS, vol. 11695, pp. 89–104. Springer, Cham (2019). https://doi.org/10.1007/978-3-030-28730-6_6

59. Nagy, Z., Werner-Stark, Á., Dulai, T.: An industrial application using process mining to reduce the number of faulty products. In: Benczúr, A., et al. (eds.) ADBIS 2018. CCIS, vol. 909, pp. 352–363. Springer, Cham (2018). https://doi.org/10.1007/978-3-030-00063-9_33

60. Paszkiewicz, Z.: Process mining techniques in conformance testing of inventory processes: an industrial application. In: Abramowicz, W. (ed.) BIS 2013. LNBIP, vol. 160, pp. 302–313. Springer, Heidelberg (2013). https://doi.org/10.1007/978-3-642-41687-3_28

61. QPR Software Plc: Insight into Vaisala's operations with process mining (2012)

62. QPR Software Plc: From opportunity to delivery, end-to-end process transparency for Ruukki (2013)

63. Rozinat, A., Jong, I., Günther, C., Aalst, W.: Conformance analysis of ASML's test process. In: Mathematics of Computation, vol. 459 (2009)

64. Saravanan, M.S., Rama Sree, R.J.: Application of process mining in automobile: a case study for MG motors. Int. J. Adv. Res. Comput. Sci. **1**, 685–690 (2011)

65. Ulsan Institute: Samsung Electro-Mechanics (2013)

66. Son, S., Yahya, B., Song, M., Choi, S., Hyeon, J.: Process mining for manufacturing process analysis: a case study. In: Proceedings of the 2nd Asia Pacific Conference on Business Process Management (2014)

67. Viale, P., Frydman, C., Pinaton, J.: New methodology for modeling large scale manufacturing process: using process mining methods and experts' knowledge. In: Proceedings of the 9th International Conference on Computer Systems and Applications (AICCSA), pp. 84–89 (2011)

68. Becker, J., Niehaves, B., Poeppelbuss, J., Simons, A.: Maturity models in IS research. In: Proceedings of the 18th European Conference on Information Systems (ECIS) (2010)

Event-Driven Business Process Management Enhancing IoT – A Systematic Literature Review and Development of Research Agenda

Christoph Stoiber[(⊠)] and Stefan Schönig

University of Regensburg, Regensburg, Germany
christoph.stoiber@stud.uni-regensburg.de, stefan.schoenig@ur.de

Abstract. The integration of high frequency event data from Internet of Things (IoT) devices into existing complex and mature Business Process Management Systems (BPMS) constitutes a major hurdle for many organizations. Event-Driven Business Process Management (EDBPM) is a paradigm to tackle this hurdle and to lever the enhancement of industrial IoT applications. Existing literature regarding EDBPM and its underlying technologies and methods form a heterogenous set of approaches, frameworks and applications that lacks standardization and maturity. In this context, the literature review of the work at hand conducts a survey about EDBPM focusing on its capabilities to be a lever for the scale of IoT applications. First, we perform an extensive literature research on EDBPM and related topics. Second, a literature analysis and synthesis are presented by summarizing and clustering the discovered publications. Furthermore, a future research agenda is formulated that addresses the main existing research gaps and challenges of EDBPM.

Keywords: Event-Driven Business Process Management · Internet of Things · Complex Event Processing · Event-Driven Architecture

1 Introduction

The widespread of the Internet of Things (IoT) led to a great variety of different applications in almost each sector of private and professional life [1]. One major focus of applications in the last decade lay on the smart home, smart grid, and smart healthcare market [2]. But especially industrial companies are progressively using IoT technology for efficient management and controlling of industrial processes and assets to increase productivity and reduce operational costs [3]. However, most companies already have matured and sophisticated process landscapes and IT system architectures that often prevent an easy implementation of IoT technologies [4]. One inherent cause for this situation is the need for enterprise IT systems to adapt to the flexible and near real-time continuous data flow that is generated by IoT devices. The high availability of IoT-related business operations data leads to a high scale transmission of event data that needs to be received, correlated, and processed before exploiting it for business processes [5]. A business process is a collection of events, activities, and decisions that involves several

© The Author(s), under exclusive license to Springer Nature Switzerland AG 2021
F. Ahlemann et al. (Eds.): WI 2021, LNISO 48, pp. 645–661, 2021.
https://doi.org/10.1007/978-3-030-86800-0_44

(human) resources [6]. To support processes at an operational level, a Business Process Management System (BPMS) can be used. A BPMS deals, a.o., with the enactment of models that define the interplay between environmental circumstances and activities to be executed. The emergence of IoT is a big challenge for traditional BPMS that are responsible for managing the increasing number of data coming from heterogenous sources. Event-Driven Business Process Management (EDBPM) now constitutes an interesting approach that combines two different disciplines, namely Complex Event Processing (CEP) and Business Process Management (BPM) to tackle the challenges of high-volume event integration. This combination leads to a system that can deal with event-driven behavior and can process real-time data from distributed sources. Having implemented EDBPM into the enterprise IT landscape, a more effective and efficient integration and usage of IoT devices is possible [7].

This paper aims at *(a)* describing the importance of EDBPM for the proliferation of IoT applications, *(b)* synthesizing and interpreting the current state of EDBPM research and *(c)* proposing a possible research agenda. According to Hart [8], through a structured literature review, the current state of research can be systematically reproduced, summarized, and interpreted. In this way, research gaps can be uncovered and new incentives for future research can be created. Especially by synthesizing and interpreting the overall picture, a further gain in knowledge is possible, which is not achievable by only studying a single publication [9]. Therefore, the authors hope to provide a structured entry point, overview, and motivation for further research on EDBPM that paves the way for a larger scale of IoT technologies in process-oriented businesses. The paper is organized as follows. Section 2 provides an overview about the theoretical foundations of EDBPM and related work. In Sect. 3, the applied research methodology is presented. Section 4 presents the results of the literature review by analyzing and synthesizing the considered publications. Section 5 proposes a future research agenda based on the main research gaps, concluding with a summary and outlook in Sect. 6.

2 Theoretical Background and Related Work

2.1 Theoretical Foundation

The research of BPM has already come up with several methods to perform data processing or data analysis. For example, Business Process Intelligence solutions provide tools for the analysis, prediction, monitoring, control, and optimization of business processes [10]. But Business Process Intelligence is mostly used for ex post analysis of process or event data and lacks capabilities of processing enormous amounts of real-time data from heterogenous sources [11]. Business Activity Monitoring (BAM), however, is able to monitor and process event data online in real-time. But traditional BAM does not provide a specific engine to identify rules or create patterns that are essential for the correlation of high-volume event data generated by IoT devices, besides their inflexibility regarding heterogenous data sources [12]. The concept of an Event-Driven Architecture (EDA) constituted an important progress as events turned to a central structural element within the corporate IT environment [5]. Based on this message-driven architecture, further methods like CEP enabled obtaining understandable and usable information on the basis of high-volume event streams generated by heterogenous data sources [13].

EDBPM now comprises and combines several disciplines including CEP and BPM to make use of the acquired data and represents a central paradigm for high volume event integration [14]. A working definition of EDBPM could be the enhancement of traditional BPM by Service Oriented Architecture, EDA, Software as a Service, BAM and CEP to make optimal use of events for process integration [12].

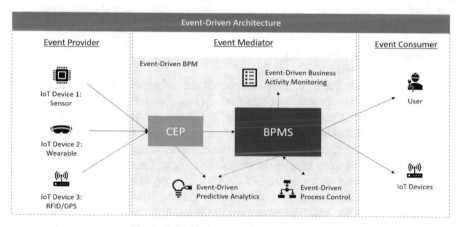

Fig. 1. EDBPM architecture and interfaces

Figure 1 illustrates the main components and interfaces of an EDBPM based on an EDA. An EDBPM serves as an event mediator with its main components CEP and BPMS including interfaces to the event provider and event consumer. Event-Driven Business Activity Monitoring has the capabilities to capture and process events with minimum latency for providing real-time access to business performance indicators. By adding reactive capabilities using Event-Driven Process Control, the system is not mandatory limited to human intervention. Beyond the monitoring and active control of business processes, there is a strongly growing market for further analytics to gain even deeper insights in the operational process data. One of the main interests lies in active, real-time decision support or even predictive tools such as Event-Driven Predictive Analytics.

2.2 Differentiation from Related Work

There are already existing studies on EDBPM and related topics, which mostly focus on various independent aspects including EDA and CEP (see Table 1). However, the few publications performing a comprehensive review on EDBPM are either outdated or pursue a different survey objective. Krumeich et al. [15] for example, investigated the status quo of EDBPM in the year 2014 and proposed a possible research agenda. Yet, in the past six years, the research field of EDBPM has experienced significant growth and needs to be reinvestigated. 25 of the 55 publications presented in Sect. 4 have been published after 2014, confirming the progress of that field of research. Several of the formerly existing challenges have already been solved or at least tackled, as illustrated in Subsect. 5.1. Moreover, the paper at hand underlays EDBPM as a lever to enhance the implementation and scaling of IoT applications and therefore differentiates itself from other similar publications. This mostly becomes apparent both at the formulated clusters of Sect. 4 and the proposed research agenda in Sect. 5 that have a distinct IoT reference. Therefore, the publication focuses on literature that leads to improved EDBPM solutions or EDBPM components with beneficial character for IoT event data processing. Furthermore, the literature review lays a focus on the rather technical aspects of EDBPM without concentration on management or process related publications.

3   Research Methodology

The underlying methodology to survey the current state of research in the field of EDBPM is a structured literature review. Vom Brocke et al. [16] proposed an established procedure that allows a rigorous literature analysis based on a five-step framework. This framework comprises (i) the definition of the review scope, (ii) the conceptualization of the topic, (iii) a literature search, (iv) an extensive literature analysis and synthesis, and (v) the formulation of a research agenda. In combination with the structured taxonomy by Cooper [17], the main characteristics of the review could be concretized. This review mainly focuses on the current state of research regarding EDBPM in the function of a technology enabler for IoT. The main goal is the identification of clusters within the current research contributions and to detect research gaps aiming at the formulation of a research agenda. To cover all important research directions, a neutral perspective needs to be maintained. The coverage can be considered as representative, as an adequate number of publications has been selected in different eminent databases that cover most of the journals and conferences relevant to the topic. The organization of the review follows a conceptual approach and is designated to a specialized scholar.

The literature search itself was conducted according to the Preferred Items for SLRs and Meta-Analysis (PRISMA) statement. The PRISMA statement is a method to help authors to improve the reporting of systematic reviews and includes a structured checklist and flow diagram [18]. Especially the flow diagram is capable of illustrating the procedure and results of the literature search and analysis. Composed of four phases, "Identification", "Screening", "Eligibility", and "Included", the method gradually reduces the number of publications by assessing the eligibility using predefined criteria. Figure 2 shows the resulting four-phase flow diagram including the incorporated databases and number of considered publications. Several fundamental papers about EDBPM have been analyzed by their title, abstract, and keywords to find suitable search terms. Eventually, the search string ("EDBPM" OR "EDA" OR "CEP" OR "BPM") AND ("IoT") as well as the written-out terms have been used for abstract queries in the relevant databases. To incorporate and consider preferably all relevant journals and top conference proceedings of that research area, ACM Direct Library, IEEE Xplore, ScienceDirect, Scopus, Springer Link, and Wiley Online have been queried. According to the PRISMA statement, four criteria have been formulated which a paper needs to achieve to be eligible for this review. The publication must (i) be a peer-reviewed original research paper, (ii) be a full-length paper, (iii) propose novel and relevant scientific findings, and (iv) propose an evaluated solution or method. As criterion (i) and (ii) can be easily and objectively examined for each publication, the assessment of both latter criteria represents a rather subjective procedure based on the authors' capability to estimate the contribution and significance of each publication.

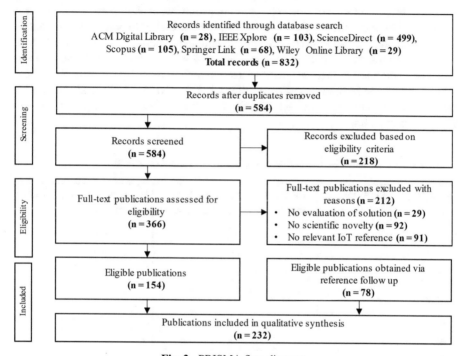

Fig. 2. PRISMA flow diagram

For the initial abstract queries, 832 publications have been found in all utilized databases. After removing duplicates, a first manual review of the remaining 584 records was performed. The authors therefore performed an assessment on title, abstract and keywords based on incongruity with the eligibility criteria. Another 218 papers were discarded based on incongruity with at least one criterion. Eventually, the full texts of 366 articles were analyzed in detail resulting in another discard of 212 articles. Among them, 29 publications did not provide an evaluated solution, 92 could not add significant scientific novelty in comparison with existing contributions, and 91 had no relevant reference to the IoT paradigm. In addition to the 154 remaining publications, 78 further relevant articles were found during forward and backward search or expert recommendations.

4 Literature Analysis and Synthesis

All 232 publications have been analyzed and summarized in detail. Subsequently, the main contribution of each publication could be extracted. These contributions were now used to derive five different clusters that comprise all the relevant research topics of the considered publications. It became evident, that the main topics of EDBPM research focuses on the development of EDBPM architectures, CEP engines and rule identification methods, CEP modeling and the improvement of its usability, advanced predictive CEP capabilities or general applications, and industry use cases.

Table 1 shows a selection of 55 papers representing a minimum viable number to illustrate the current state of research. The publications were chosen by means of significance of the contribution, number of citations, and actuality to hereinafter present the five formed clusters. To translate this into quantitative criteria, publications with more than 50 citations and a publication date after 2014 were preferred. However, if a specific publication is assessed relevant and necessary for describing the state of research, a violation of one or both quantitative criteria is accepted. Each of the stated publications addresses one or several topics of the formulated clusters and can be taken as a representative example.

Table 1. Clustering of publications by main contributions

Reference	EDBPM architecture	CEP engine and rule identification	CEP modeling language and usability	Predictive capabilities	Application
[7, 18–24]	✓	X	X	X	X
[25–31]	✓	X	X	X	✓
[31–33]	✓	✓	X	✓	X
[34–37]	✓	✓	X	X	X
[38]	✓	X	X	✓	✓
[39]	✓	✓	X	✓	✓
[40–47]	✓	✓	X	X	✓
[48]	✓	X	✓	X	✓
[49]	X	✓	X	X	✓
[50–54]	X	✓	X	X	X
[55–59]	X	✓	X	✓	X
[60]	X	✓	X	X	✓
[61]	X	✓	✓	X	X
[62]	X	✓	X	✓	✓
[63–71]	X	X	✓	X	X
[72]	X	X	✓	X	✓

These five clusters are now illustrated and summarized in the following subsections using the 55 publications as representative and current instances.

4.1 Cluster 1: Fundamental EDBPM Architectures and Approaches

The field of EDBPM has been subject of research for several years and resulted in multiple different approaches and architectures. Early reference architectures and concepts for EDBPM mainly focus on monitoring business processes and including performance metrics or similar KPI based systems [20]. With only limited or non-existing reactive capabilities, these approaches are designed to improve the awareness about the business process environment [25, 31]. These systems are often used in combination with IoT technology for tracking and tracing use cases. In addition, there have been several implementations of viable prototypes at major companies that comprise BAM combined with CEP engines [14, 21]. However, there has been an increasing level of advanced EDBPM approaches that feature improved reactiveness and Event-Driven Process Control [22]. Furthermore, there are architectures that enable even case management engines, e.g. Chimera, that are used for knowledge-intensive business process modeling and execution, to incorporate external events [35, 36]. Several approaches are based on reference models and architectures that enable communication between different acting systems or at least have simple rudimental process control features [19, 32, 34, 37]. Recently, more papers emerged that pay more attention to Event-Driven Process Control elements by enhancing CEP to have a more intelligent and collaborative character [23, 24]. Also, the extended integration of edge devices by addressing CEP engines that leverage the edge computing environment is becoming an important challenge, which is tackled by research. By developing collaborative system architectures and providing capabilities to process the events at the edge of the network, the challenge of including data coming together from several heterogenous IoT devices can be faced [24, 39].

4.2 Cluster 2: CEP Engines and Advanced Rule Identification Methods

The main task of CEP is the detection of event patterns in continuous data streams from heterogenous sources such as IoT devices. The core of each CEP system is the CEP engine which is able to operate on a basis of temporal, spatial, or semantic correlation of event data [49]. To detect event patterns, a set of specific rules needs to be predefined which, again, is characterized by several parameters. As the definition of optimal parameter values is very challenging, there are different approaches to automize this task [49]. Early CEP systems are based on a manual detection of event patterns or the predefinition of rules and parameters by experts [50]. Gradually, several semi-automated CEP engines have been presented by researchers including algorithms that perform a prescriptive analysis that consists of detecting event patterns and making automatic decisions [40]. Pielmeier et al. [49] suggested three ways to define rules. They described a manual definition by domain experts and two semi-automated definitions by rule mining or optimization. Other approaches perform an advanced rule definition by rule mining algorithms, clustering, or a Fuzzy Unordered Rule Induction Algorithm [50, 51].

Besides CEP research regarding event pattern detection, some papers directly address the challenge to improve the interfaces between IoT devices and CEP systems. The collection, integration, and appropriate and consistent representation of complex and high frequency sensor data is a rather complex task. Common CEP engines involve various analytical procedures for data fusion and require high computational resources [53]. Still, most of the established CEP systems remain job-specific and are limited to the integration of a few data sources, dependent on specific interface standards. Possible solutions suggest a combination of CEP technologies and stochastic models or semantic annotation processes or adapted CEP system architectures [52, 53]. Advanced CEP systems are therefore able to integrate multiple related sensor data streams coming from distributed sources [55].

4.3   Cluster 3: Usability and Modeling Languages for CEP

As already mentioned, the main task of CEP is to detect relevant events from continuous data streams, process them, and provide the information to further systems or activities, such as Event Processing Workflows. It therefore acts as a major driver for the integration of sensor data from IoT sources and the diffusion of EDBPM. One big challenge for the implementation of CEP is the lack of usability, which is caused by the high complexity of its management [63]. It is a substantial challenge for users to define event patterns and rule sets, especially, when they are non-technical experts [64]. In general, the definition of event patterns and detection of complex events is implemented with a specific Event Processing Language (EPL), which is similar to SQL for databases. There have been several efforts to create a standard for EPLs, such as Esper [63], domain specific languages [65], or other conceptual or graphical modeling approaches [66–69]. Recently, there have been further research activities regarding the integration of CEP elements within the BPMN or BPMN 2.0 representation of business processes [61]. These approaches represent EPL statements through BPMN elements [63, 70] or even map whole EPL syntax elements to existing BPMN artifacts [67, 71]. Besides the representation of CEP, there also exist approaches that try to facilitate programming of whole Wireless Sensor Network by using BPMN artifacts [48]. Alongside BPMN, there has also been a focus on the Event-driven Process Chain standard, which is another widely used process modeling notation [72]. In general, modeling event patterns in an established modeling notation and transforming it into an executable EPL could be a major field of research to decrease the inhibition threshold for using CEP [33, 69]. As most enterprises already have specialists for common business process notation standards, the implementation and integration of CEP and eventually EDBPM would be simplified.

4.4   Cluster 4: CEP with Predictive Capabilities

Current EDBPM approaches and CEP systems provide almost real-time detection and processing of complex event data. However, for specific applications, events should better be anticipated and e.g. proactively prevented before they occur. Examples for such events could be credit card fraud or various issues in the manufacturing industry such as disruption events. There are already several CEP applications in use, that have a predictive character. Krumeich et al. [33] exploited the potentials of CEP in combination with predictive analytics at a steel company and stated the vision of proactive process execution. As a result, process activities can be triggered much sooner as they would have been triggered in traditional BPMS by anticipating events. Another paper introduced an architecture of prescriptive enterprise systems, that is able to predict events from multi-sensor environments and therefore comprises several other systems on a higher-level approach [38]. There are multiple concepts, frameworks, and reference architectures for combining CEP with predictive analytics methods. Besides established prediction methods, such as logical and probabilistic reasoning [55] or Bayesian networks [56], there have been domain specific algorithms [57–59]. These algorithms are particularly designed to predict possible future events by deeply analyzing previous event patterns, that can be predicators for certain occurrences.

4.5 Cluster 5: Applications for IoT Technology Meeting EDBPM

IoT technology meeting EDBPM and CEP systems are already in use in many different areas. Besides of applications in the private sector like smart home technologies and fitness wearables [43, 44], there have been projects in possibly every business sector including manufacturing, logistics, or even agriculture. Using CEP for monitoring complex event data from elders via wearables to create a virtual health profile can relieve the workload of doctors in rural regions [45]. In addition, RFID-enabled hospitals can model surgical events and critical situations via CEP and trigger specific processes [46]. Smart grids are another area of interest, where real-time CEP and Event-Driven Predictive Analytics can e.g. improve the distribution and planning of energy flows [47]. Especially for developing countries with critical air quality situations, novel CEP-based prediction frameworks based on IoT networks can lower people's exposure to pollution [26]. The logistics sector is one of the industrial branches that can benefit most from real-time BAM and the collection and processing of event data [41, 42]. Emmersberger et al. [27] introduced an EDBPM architecture that can be applied for logistics companies and identified several crucial challenges that need to be tackled. While the integration of IoT technology is rather easy for the private sector and small to medium sized logistics companies, it becomes a major challenge for huge corporations in the manufacturing industry with complex operations and processes. For these major enterprises, IoT technology is often used for the whole supply chain including multiple suppliers and customers. This leads to extraordinarily complex environments of IoT devices, IT systems, and interfaces. Several papers address the topic of event processing in the manufacturing industry [28, 60] and describe the status quo and existing hurdles for further scaling of IoT technology [73]. But there have also been publications that propose whole bidirectional communication architectures of IoT systems, which enable an IoT-based BPM with high scalability of devices [29]. These novel use cases show the diverse possibilities of EDBPM and the transferability of current research topics to actual industry applications [30].

5   Findings and Research Agenda

The analysis and synthesis of all relevant publications provided an overview over the major research topics regarding EDBPM. This section now formulates the main findings and research gaps that were identified and proposes a research agenda, which addresses the most relevant identified challenges.

5.1   General Findings and Research Gaps

One main finding of the literature review is, that the publications can be categorized into five distinct clusters which contain specific areas of research. For each of these clusters, relevant scientific progress has been made in the last years that tackled and, in some cases, resolved open challenges formulated by prior publications such as Krumeich et al.

[15]. One major challenge, that was mentioned, is the need for further experiences with EDBPM in industrial applications. However, in recent years, industry-related [29, 30] and domain-specific [41, 47] experiences with integrating IoT technology into business processes based on the EDBPM paradigm have been made. This led to an improved maturity of industrial IoT applications and provided blueprints that can be adapted by other companies. Also, the integration of large amounts of high-volume event data in the context of Big Data was identified as a major challenge for further research. There have been concepts and prototypes by Guo and Huang [53] and Flouris et al. [54] that address this topic and enable a capable handling of massive event data. This improves the integration of IoT devices with high data rates in the context of Big Data and enables more efficient and effective handling of massive event data. In addition, several new methods and tools for the management of CEP rules and systems have been suggested [40, 50, 51], that also improve the usability and therefore acceptance in the industrial context [64]. However, several challenges remain unresolved or lack a mature and practical solution. Early applications almost exclusively focus on pure monitoring of business processes or tracking and tracing of transportable goods. This may be explained by the divergence between existing enterprise software systems and the system architectures required by EDBPM. In addition, the complexity of integrating multiple heterogenous IoT devices into a network and defining rule patterns for the detection and processing of continuous event data is a big hurdle. Most corporates lack specific domain experts for CEP and therefore need solutions which are easy to use and maintain. Also, the focus on EDA is still not quite common in many industries. Just recent research activities show a more advanced use of IoT in combination with EDBPM. As the usability of CEP solutions is improving through the representation of statements by established modeling languages, also the integration of reactive capabilities and predictive analytics is levered. These reactive capabilities and prediction components are rather limited features that still lack an adequate level of automation and often only serve as a basis for a human-centric decision support [42]. Moreover, the sheer bandwidth of different proprietary concepts for EDA, CEP engines, and modeling languages constitute a deterrent for many corporates. As companies have high requirements for the quality and stability of their information systems, most contemporary approaches regarding EDBPM do not have the required maturity, as also mentioned in other publications [73].

5.2 Research Agenda for IoT Meeting EDBPM

Based on the main findings and existing research gaps, a research agenda is provided in this subsection by analyzing the main challenges of each cluster, as seen in Table 2. To guarantee an objective and representative overview of the most important and relevant challenges and opportunities, the research agendas and challenges of the reviewed publications have also been analyzed and incorporated into the following agenda, if still contemporary. The focus of the agenda proposal is the capability of itself to act as a lever for the integration and scaling of IoT technology. Therefore, this paper does possibly not consider all crucial challenges of EDBPM, as they are not considered as a major hurdle for the scaling of IoT applications. For this reason, the provided research agendas are neither prioritized in a certain way nor represent a complete listing. Table 2 states the formulated research agenda and links it to the respective clusters of Sect. 4.

Table 2. Proposed research agenda

No.	Research agenda	Cluster
1	Establishing mature EDA frameworks and CEP reference models	1, 2, 5
2	Automating and simplifying rule pattern definition and modeling languages	2, 3
3	Standardization of interfaces and data formats	3, 5
4	Developing CEP systems with increased reactive and predictive capabilities	2, 4

5.3 Establishing Mature EDA Frameworks and CEP Reference Models

Current EDAs and CEP approaches lack standardization and proven maturity [19, 34]. It is necessary to develop reference architectures and design patterns, that can be easily adopted and broadly scaled. Having mature and proved frameworks and reference models that meet the business requirements and expectations, may have a beneficial influence on the exploration of complex IoT applications. Using architectural blueprints may also reduce the invest and maintenance costs for adapting EDBPM and its components which could also increase the relevance for enterprises.

5.4 Automating and Simplifying Rule Pattern Definition and Modeling Languages

The high complexity of detecting and processing relevant event data from heterogenous IoT devices is a major hurdle for businesses. As most companies do not have specific experts for CEP, the operation and maintenance of related systems needs to be as simple as possible. Future research activities should address the automation of rule pattern definition and examine possibilities for self-improving systems. This incorporates also the standardization and simplification of EPLs which could be done based on existing concepts like Event-Driven Process Chain or BPMN 2.0 [61]. This would lower the inhibition threshold of companies for the technological adoption of IoT applications and improve the general usability of EDBPM related systems.

5.5 Standardization of Interfaces and Data Formats

To fully exploit the benefits of EDBPM, there is a strong need for standardized interfaces to existing information systems [34]. The current systems do not offer sufficient alignment to established formats and interfaces and collectively lack appropriate data formats for events [15]. As major companies are operating heterogenous facilities, IoT devices, and IT systems, the integration and combination of those through flexible interfaces needs to be facilitated. This could also enable a more efficient integration of heterogenous and distributed IoT devices.

5.6 Developing CEP Systems with Increased Reactive and Predictive Capabilities

As the benefits of reactive CEP systems, and therefore process automation, have an enormous value for companies, research on these topics should have a high attention.

Many companies already use passive IoT technology such as RFID tags for pure monitoring tasks and express the desire for a deeper integration of these technologies with the physical world. In addition, the prediction of events could have disruptive effects on businesses and even influence their business models. By avoiding unwanted events through predictions, negative consequences could be prevented. But also, the prediction of minor events can be beneficial, as companies may gain time to prepare for them and therefore reduce uncertainty.

6 Conclusion

This paper gave a representative overview over the current state of research regarding EDBPM and its related technologies and paradigms. The main goal was to identify major challenges and opportunities of EDBPM that have a strong influence on the expansion of IoT technology at businesses. In particular, the authors focused on the recent progress and developments of this research area, as it is gaining importance due to increasing numbers and types of IoT devices and technologies. As the majority of IoT applications require advanced complex data processing systems and proper alignment of the system architecture towards an event-driven paradigm, EDBPM can be an enabling technology. It became evident, that there is a great bandwidth of research activities that address CEP, EDA, EDBPM, and corresponding topics. Some of the once formulated challenges and hurdles have already been tackled and resolved but several are still requiring further effort. There are many concepts, frameworks, and reference models that have a mainly theoretical character and lack maturity and standardization. As the integration of heterogenous data sources in IoT networks requires flexible and stable working systems, the existing and mainly proprietary solutions cannot fulfill the needs of possible users. To cope with this fundamental issue, future research should focus on establishing standards and adaptable real-life applications, that can act as a blueprint for other use cases. Also, improved future approaches with reactive and predictive character could act as a lever for the integration of EDBPM and eventually IoT technologies as they could imply major benefits for enterprises. Further research activities and applications are required to outline the capabilities and possibilities of these systems. By proving the beneficial character of event-orientation and sophisticated EDBPM, companies and other institutions might pay more attention to IoT technologies and the inhibition level could be lowered significantly. This survey may serve as a representative overview, starting point, and motivation for further research activities regarding EDBPM.

References

1. Gubbi, J., Buyya, R., Marusic, S., Palaniswami, M.: Internet of Things (IoT): a vision, architectural elements, and future directions. Future Gener. Comput. Syst. **29**(7), 1645–1660 (2013)
2. Perera, C., Liu, C.H., Jayawardena, S., Chen, M.: A survey on Internet of Things from industrial market perspective. IEEE Access **2**, 1660–1679 (2014)
3. Sisinni, E., Saifullah, A., Han, S., Jennehag, U., Gidlund, M.: Industrial Internet of Things: challenges, opportunities, and directions. IEEE Trans. Ind. Inform. **14**(11), 4724–4734 (2018)

4. Sethi, P., Sarangi, S.: Internet of Things: architectures, protocols, and applications. J. Electr. Comput. Eng. (2017)
5. Bruns, R., Dunkel, J.: Event-Driven Architecture. Softwarearchitektur für ereignisgesteuerte Geschäftsprozesse. Springer, Heidelberg (2010)
6. Lindsay, A., Downs, D., Lunn, K.: Business processes - attempts to find a definition. Inf. Softw. Technol. **45**(15), 1015–1019 (2003)
7. von Ammon, R., Emmersberger, C., Greiner, T., Springer, F., Wolff, C.: Event-driven business process management. In: Second International Conference on Distributed Event-Based Systems (DEBS) (2008)
8. Hart, C.: Doing a Literature Review. Releasing the Social Science Research Imagination. Sage, London (2005)
9. Müller-Bloch, C., Kranz, J.: A framework for rigorously identifying research gaps in qualitative literature reviews. In: International Conference on Information Systems (ICIS 2015), pp. 1–5 (2015)
10. Grigori, D., Casati, F., Castellanos, M., Dayal, U., Sayal, M., Shan, M.-C.: Business process intelligence. Comput. Ind. **53**(3), 321–343 (2004)
11. Matzner, M., Schwegmann, B., Janiesch, C.: A method and tool for predictive event-driven process analytics. In: Proceedings of the 11th International Conference on Wirtschaftsinformatik (WI2013), pp. 721–735 (2013)
12. von Ammon, R., Etzion, O., Ludwig, H., Paschke, A., Stojanovic, N.: Introduction to the second international workshop on event-driven business process management (edBPM09). In: Rinderle-Ma, S., Sadiq, S., Leymann, F. (eds.) BPM 2009. LNBIP, vol. 43, pp. 345–346. Springer, Heidelberg (2010). https://doi.org/10.1007/978-3-642-12186-9_32
13. Buchmann, A., Koldehofe, B.: Complex event processing. Inf. Technol. J. **5**, 241–242 (2009)
14. von Ammon, R., Emmersberger, C., Springer, F., Wolff, C.: Event-driven business process management and its practical application taking the example of DHL. In: 1st International Workshop on Complex Event Processing for the Future Internet, pp. 1–13 (2008)
15. Krumeich, J., Weis, B., Werth, D., Loos, P.: Event-driven business process management: where are we now? A comprehensive synthesis and analysis of literature. Bus. Process Manag. J. **20**(4), 615–633 (2014)
16. vom Brocke, J., Simons, A., Niehaves, B., Riemer, K., Plattfaut, R., Cleven, A.: Reconstructing the giant: on the importance of rigour in documenting the literature search process. In: Newell, S., Whitley, E.A., Pouloudi, N., Wareham, J., Mathiassen, L. (eds.) ECIS, pp. 2206–2217 (2009)
17. Cooper, H.M.: Organizing knowledge syntheses: a taxonomy of literature reviews. Knowl. Soc. **1**, 104–126 (1988)
18. Liberati, A., Altman, D., Tetzlaff, J., Mullrow, C.: The PRISMA statement for reporting systematic reviews and meta-analyses of studies that evaluate healthcare interventions: explanation and elaboration. Br. Med. J. **62**, e1–e34 (2009)
19. Janiesch, C., Matzner, M., Müller, O.: Beyond process monitoring: a proof-of-concept of event-driven business activity management. Bus. Process Manag. J. **18**(4), 625–643 (2012)
20. Costello, C., Molloy, O.: Towards a semantic framework for business activity monitoring and management. In: AAAI Spring Symposium: AI Meets Business Rules and Process Management, pp. 17–27 (2008)
21. Estruch, A., Heredia Álvaro, J.A.: Event-driven manufacturing process management approach. In: Barros, A., Gal, A., Kindler, E. (eds.) BPM 2012. LNCS, vol. 7481, pp. 120–133. Springer, Heidelberg (2012). https://doi.org/10.1007/978-3-642-32885-5_9
22. Grauer, M., Karadgi, S., Metz, D., Schäfer, W.: Online monitoring and control of enterprise processes in manufacturing based on an event-driven architecture. In: zur Muehlen, M., Su, J. (eds.) BPM 2010. LNBIP, vol. 66, pp. 671–682. Springer, Heidelberg (2011). https://doi.org/10.1007/978-3-642-20511-8_61

23. Quaranta, A.G., Raffoni, A., Visani, F.: A multidimensional approach to measuring bank branch efficiency. Eur. J. Oper. Res. **266**(2), 746–760 (2018)
24. He, S., Wang, H., Cao, Y., Zhao, D.: A wide-deep event model for complex event processing in edge and cloud computing environment. In: Proceedings of the ACM Turing Celebration, pp. 1–2. ACM, New York, NY, USA (2019)
25. Magoutas, B., Riemer, D., Apostolou, D., Ma, J., Mentzas, G., Stojanovic, N.: An event-driven system for business awareness management in the logistics domain. In: La Rosa, M., Soffer, P. (eds.) BPM 2012. LNBIP, vol. 132, pp. 402–413. Springer, Heidelberg (2013). https://doi.org/10.1007/978-3-642-36285-9_43
26. Guzel, M., Ozdemir, S.: A new CEP-based air quality prediction framework for fog based IoT. In: The 2019 International Symposium on Networks, Computers and Communications (ISNCC 2019), pp. 1–6. IEEE, Piscataway, NJ (2019)
27. Emmersberger, C., Springer, F., Wolff, C.: Location based logistics services and event driven business process management. In: Tavangarian, D., Kirste, T., Timmermann, D., Lucke, U., Versick, D. (eds.) IMC 2009. CCIS, vol. 53, pp. 167–177. Springer, Heidelberg (2009). https://doi.org/10.1007/978-3-642-10263-9_15
28. Grauer, M., Seeger, B., Metz, D., Karadgi, S., Schneider, M.: About adopting event processing in manufacturing. In: Cezon, M., Wolfsthal, Y. (eds.) ServiceWave 2010. LNCS, vol. 6569, pp. 180–187. Springer, Heidelberg (2011). https://doi.org/10.1007/978-3-642-22760-8_20
29. Schönig, S., Ackermann, L., Jablonski, S., Ermer, A.: IoT meets BPM: a bidirectional communication architecture for IoT-aware process execution. Softw. Syst. Model. **19**(6), 1443–1459 (2020). https://doi.org/10.1007/s10270-020-00785-7
30. Schönig, S., Ackermann, L., Jablonski, S., Ermer, A.: An integrated architecture for IoT-aware business process execution. In: Gulden, J., Reinhartz-Berger, I., Schmidt, R., Guerreiro, S., Guédria, W., Bera, P. (eds.) BPMDS/EMMSAD -2018. LNBIP, vol. 318, pp. 19–34. Springer, Cham (2018). https://doi.org/10.1007/978-3-319-91704-7_2
31. Redlich, D., Gilani, W.: Event-driven process-centric performance prediction via simulation. In: Daniel, F., Barkaoui, K., Dustdar, S. (eds.) BPM 2011. LNBIP, vol. 99, pp. 473–478. Springer, Heidelberg (2012). https://doi.org/10.1007/978-3-642-28108-2_46
32. Fleischmann, A., Schmidt, W., Stary, C., Strecker, F.: Nondeterministic events in business processes. In: La Rosa, M., Soffer, P. (eds.) BPM 2012. LNBIP, vol. 132, pp. 364–377. Springer, Heidelberg (2013). https://doi.org/10.1007/978-3-642-36285-9_40
33. Krumeich, J., Jacobi, S., Werth, D., Loos, P.: Towards planning and control of business processes based on event-based predictions. In: Abramowicz, W., Kokkinaki, A. (eds.) BIS 2014. LNBIP, vol. 176, pp. 38–49. Springer, Cham (2014). https://doi.org/10.1007/978-3-319-06695-0_4
34. Janiesch, C., Matzner, M., Müller, O.: A blueprint for event-driven business activity management. In: Rinderle-Ma, S., Toumani, F., Wolf, K. (eds.) BPM 2011. LNCS, vol. 6896, pp. 17–28. Springer, Heidelberg (2011). https://doi.org/10.1007/978-3-642-23059-2_4
35. Mandal, S., Hewelt, M., Weske, M.: A framework for integrating real-world events and business processes in an IoT environment. In: Panetto, H., et al. (eds.) OTM 2017. LNCS, vol. 10573, pp. 194–212. Springer, Cham (2017). https://doi.org/10.1007/978-3-319-69462-7_13
36. Beyer, J., Kuhn, P., Hewelt, M., Mandal, S., Weske, M.: Unicorn meets chimera: integrating external events into case management. In: Proceedings of the BPM Demo Track Co-located with the 14th International Conference on Business Process Management 2016, pp.67–72, Rio de Janeiro, Brazil (2016)
37. Daum, M., Götz, M., Domaschka, J.: Integrating CEP and BPM. In: Behrend, A. (ed.) Proceedings of the 6th ACM International Conference on Distributed Event-Based Systems, pp. 157–166. ACM, New York, NY (2012)
38. Krumeich, J., Werth, D., Loos, P.: Prescriptive control of business processes. Bus. Inf. Syst. Eng. **58**(4), 261–280 (2015). https://doi.org/10.1007/s12599-015-0412-2

39. Garcia-de-Prado, A., Ortiz, G., Boubeta-Puig, J.: COLLECT: COLLaborativE ConText-aware service-oriented architecture for intelligent decision-making in the Internet of Things. Expert Syst. Appl. **85**, 231–248 (2017)
40. Mazon-Olivo, B., Hernández-Rojas, D., Maza-Salinas, J., Pan, A.: Rules engine and complex event processor in the context of Internet of Things for precision agriculture. Comput. Electron. Agric. **154**, 347–360 (2018)
41. Alias, C., Zahlmann, M., Alarcón Olalla, F.E., Iwersen, H., Noche, B.: Designing smart logistics processes using cyber-physical systems and complex event processing. In: Proff, H. (eds.) Mobilität in Zeiten der Veränderung, pp. 323–336. Springer, Wiesbaden(2019). https://doi.org/10.1007/978-3-658-26107-8_25
42. Schief, M., Kuhn, C., Rösch, P., Stoitsev, T.: Enabling business process integration of iot-events to the benefit of sustainable logistics. Publications of Darmstadt Technical University, Institute for Business Studies (BWL), Darmstadt Technical University (2011)
43. Jarraya, A., Ramoly, N., Bouzeghoub, A., Arour, K., Borgi, A., Finance, B.: A fuzzy semantic CEP model for situation identification in smart homes. In: Proceedings of the Twenty-Second European Conference on Artificial Intelligence, pp. 1678–1679. IOS Press, NLD (2016)
44. Stavropoulos, T.G., Meditskos, G., Andreadis, S., Kompatsiaris, I.: Real-time health monitoring and contextualised alerts using wearables. In: Proceedings of 2015 International Conference on Interactive Mobile Communication Technologies and Learning (IMCL), pp. 358–363. IEEE, Piscataway, NJ (2015)
45. Pérez-Vereda, A., Flores-Martín, D., Canal, C., Murillo, J.M.: Complex event processing for health monitoring. In: García-Alonso, J., Fonseca, C. (eds.) IWoG 2018. CCIS, vol. 1016, pp. 3–14. Springer, Cham (2019). https://doi.org/10.1007/978-3-030-16028-9_1
46. Yao, W., Chu, C.-H., Li, Z.: Leveraging complex event processing for smart hospitals using RFID. J. Netw. Comput. Appl. **34**(3), 799–810 (2011)
47. Liu, G., Zhu, W., Saunders, C., Gao, F., Yu, Y.: Real-time complex event processing and analytics for smart grid. Procedia Comput. Sci. **61**, 113–119 (2015)
48. Sungur, C.T., Spiess, P., Oertel, N., Kopp, O.: Extending BPMN for wireless sensor networks. In: 2013 IEEE 15th Conference on Business Informatics, pp. 109–116. IEEE (2013)
49. Pielmeier, J., Braunreuther, S., Reinhart, G.: Approach for defining rules in the context of complex event processing. Procedia CIRP **67**, 8–12 (2018)
50. Mehdiyev, N., Krumeich, J., Werth, D., Loos, P.: Determination of event patterns for complex event processing using fuzzy unordered rule induction algorithm with multi-objective evolutionary feature subset selection. In: Bui, T.X., Sprague, R.H. (eds.) Proceedings of the 49th Annual Hawaii International Conference on System Sciences, pp. 1719–1728. IEEE, Piscataway, NJ (2016)
51. Simsek, M.U., Ozdemir, S.: CEP rule extraction from unlabeled data in IoT. In: 3rd International Conference on Computer Science and Engineering (UBMK), pp. 429–433. IEEE, Piscataway, NJ (2018)
52. Mahmood, Z. (ed.): Data Science and Big Data Computing. Springer, Cham (2016). https://doi.org/10.1007/978-3-319-31861-5
53. Guo, Q., Huang, J.: A complex event processing-based approach of multi-sensor data fusion in IoT sensing systems. In: Proceedings of 2015 4th International Conference on Computer Science and Network Technology (ICCSNT), pp. 548–551. IEEE, Piscataway, NJ (2015)
54. Flouris, J., Manikaki, V., Giatrakos, N., Deligiannakis, A.: FERARI: a prototype for complex event processing over streaming multi-cloud platforms. In: Proceedings of the 2016 International Conference on Management of Data (SIGMOD), pp. 2093–2096. ACM, New York, NY, USA (2016)
55. Nawaz, F., Janjua, N.K., Hussain, O.K.: PERCEPTUS: predictive complex event processing and reasoning for IoT-enabled supply chain. Knowl.-Based Syst. **180**(15), 133–146 (2019)

56. Wang, Y., Gao, H., Chen, G.: Predictive complex event processing based on evolving Bayesian networks. Pattern Recognit. Lett. **105**, 207–216 (2018)
57. Gillani, S., et al.: Pi-CEP: predictive complex event processing using range queries over historical pattern space. In: Gottumukkala, R. (ed.) 17th IEEE International Conference on Data Mining workshops (ICDMW), pp. 1166–1171. IEEE, Piscataway, NJ (2017)
58. Akbar, A., Carrez, F., Moessner, K., Zoha, A.: Predicting complex events for proactive IoT applications. In: IEEE World Forum on Internet of Things (WF-IoT), pp. 327–332. IEEE, Piscataway, NJ (2015)
59. Christ, M., Krumeich, J., Kempa-Liehr, A.W.: Integrating predictive analytics into complex event processing by using conditional density estimations. In: Dijkman, R., Pires, L.F., Rinderle-Ma, S. (eds.) 2016 IEEE 20th International Enterprise Distributed Object Computing Workshop (EDOCW), pp. 1–8. IEEE, Piscataway, NJ (2016)
60. Ahmad, W., Lobov, A., Lastra, J.L.M.: Formal modelling of complex event processing: a generic algorithm and its application to a manufacturing line. In: 2012 IEEE 10th International Conference on Industrial Informatics (INDIN 2012), pp. 380–385. IEEE, Piscataway, NJ (2012)
61. Appel, S., Frischbier, S., Freudenreich, T., Buchmann, A.: Event stream processing units in business processes. In: Daniel, F., Wang, J., Weber, B. (eds.) BPM 2013. LNCS, vol. 8094, pp. 187–202. Springer, Heidelberg (2013). https://doi.org/10.1007/978-3-642-40176-3_15
62. Krumeich, J., Zapp, M., Mayer, D., Werth, D., Loos, P.: Modeling complex event patterns in EPC-models and transforming them into an executable event pattern language. In: Stelzer, D., Nissen, V., Straßburger, S. (eds.) Tagungsband zur Multikonferenz Wirtschaftsinformatik (MKWI 2016), pp. 81–92. Universitätsverlag Ilmenau (2016)
63. Kunz, S., Fickinger, T., Prescher, J., Spengler, K.: Managing complex event processes with business process modeling notation. In: Mendling, J., Weidlich, M., Weske, M. (eds.) BPMN 2010. LNBIP, vol. 67, pp. 78–90. Springer, Heidelberg (2010). https://doi.org/10.1007/978-3-642-16298-5_8
64. Boubeta-Puig, J., Ortiz, G., Medina-Bulo, I.: ModeL4CEP: graphical domain-specific modeling languages for CEP domains and event patterns. Expert Syst. Appl. **42**(21), 8095–8110 (2015)
65. Mulo, E., Zdun, U., Dustdar, S.: Domain-specific language for event-based compliance monitoring in process-driven SOAs. SOCA **7**, 59–73 (2013)
66. Schimmelpfennig, J., Mayer, D., Walter, P., Seel, C.: Involving business users in the design of complex event processing systems. In: Härder, T., Lehner, W., Mitschang, B., Schöning, H., Schwarz, H. (eds.) Datenbanksysteme für Business, Technologie und Web (BTW), pp. 606–615. Gesellschaft für Informatik e.V, Bonn (2011)
67. Decker, G., Grosskopf, A., Barros, A.: A graphical notation for modeling complex events in business processes. In: 11th IEEE International Enterprise Distributed Object Computing Conference 2007 (EDOC), p. 27. IEEE Computer Society, Los Alamitos, California (2007)
68. Paschke, A.: A semantic design pattern language for complex event processing. In: AAAI Spring Symposium: Intelligent Event Processing (2009)
69. Friedenstab, J.-P., Janiesch, C., Matzner, M., Muller, O.: Extending BPMN for business activity monitoring. In: Sprague, R.H. (ed.) 2012 45th Hawaii International Conference on System Science (HICSS), pp. 4158–4167. IEEE, Piscataway, NJ (2012)
70. Koetter, F., Kochanowski, M.: A model-driven approach for event-based business process monitoring. In: La Rosa, M., Soffer, P. (eds.) BPM 2012. LNBIP, vol. 132, pp. 378–389. Springer, Heidelberg (2013). https://doi.org/10.1007/978-3-642-36285-9_41
71. Patiniotakis, I., Papageorgiou, N., Verginadis, Y., Apostolou, D., Mentzas, G.: An aspect oriented approach for implementing situational driven adaptation of BPMN2.0 workflows. In: La Rosa, M., Soffer, P. (eds.) BPM 2012. LNBIP, vol. 132, pp. 414–425. Springer, Heidelberg (2013). https://doi.org/10.1007/978-3-642-36285-9_44

72. Vidačković, K.: Eine Methode zur Entwicklung dynamischer Geschäftsprozesse auf Basis von Ereignisverarbeitung. Zugl.: Stuttgart, Univ., Diss. 2014. Schriftenreihe zu Arbeitswissenschaft und Technologiemanagement, vol. 15. Fraunhofer-Verl., Stuttgart (2014)
73. Janiesch, C., et al.: The Internet-of-Things meets business process management: mutual benefits and challenges. IEEE Trans. Syst. Man Cybern. Syst. 6(4), 34–44 (2020)

How Does Enterprise Architecture Support the Design and Realization of Data-Driven Business Models? An Empirical Study

Faisal Rashed[1,2(✉)] and Paul Drews[1]

[1] Institute of Information Systems, Leuphana University Lüneburg, Lüneburg, Germany
fr386@cam.ac.uk, paul.drews@leuphana.de
[2] University of Cambridge, Cambridge, UK

Abstract. As part of the data evolution, data-driven business models (DDBMs) have emerged as a phenomenon in great demand for academia and practice. Latest technological advancements such as cloud, internet of things, big data, and machine learning have contributed to the rise of DDBM, along with novel opportunities to monetize data. While enterprise architecture (EA) management and modeling have proven its value for IT-related projects, the support of EA for DDBM is a rather new and unexplored field. Building upon a grounded theory research approach, we shed light on the support of EA for DDBM in practice. We derived four approaches for DDBM design and realization and relate them to the support of EA modeling and management. Our study draws on 16 semi-structured interviews with experts from consulting and industry firms. Our results contribute to a still sparsely researched area with empirical findings and new research avenues. Practitioners gain insights into reference cases and find opportunities to apply EA artifacts in DDBM projects.

Keywords: Data-driven · Business model · Enterprise architecture

1 Introduction

Data has received considerable attention from business and academia. Latest technological advancements such as cloud, internet of things, big data, and machine learning have contributed to the rise of data-driven business models (DDBM) as an emerging phenomenon [1]. DDBMs are characterized by data as a key resource, data processing as a key activity, or both [2, 3]. Novel opportunities appear for organizations to monetize their data. Especially incumbent companies, resting on tremendous amounts of data, are expected to develop new and transform existing business models. However, the failure rate of big data and artificial intelligence projects remains disturbingly high [4].

Considering the high dependency on big data analytics, DDBM deployment implies information system design and implementation, which requires different support in design and realization compared to offline business model innovation [5]. Introducing new DDBM requires deep intervention in the entire organizational structure. The

F. Ahlemann et al. (Eds.): WI 2021, LNISO 48, pp. 662–677, 2021.
https://doi.org/10.1007/978-3-030-86800-0_45

current (as-is) architecture must be well understood and the desired target (to-be) architecture, embedding the DDBM, must be crucially planned. The enterprise architecture (EA) practice is concerned with the aforementioned. EA has proven its potential in many IT-related projects and is deeply rooted in the information system body of knowledge. By providing artifacts such as meta models, frameworks, and management methods, EA supports transparency building on an organization's key components, from business, data, application to the technology level. Furthermore, EA helps to manage the architecture towards common vision [6].

Research on DDBMs is still in its infancy, with most contributions emerging in the past five years [1, 5]. Practitioners face several challenges in DDBM deployment [4, 7], from identifying relevant opportunities, proceeding with evaluation and ultimately implementing the DDBM [5]. Scholars have started to combine the two lenses of EA and DDBM in order to support DDBM deployment [3]. However, existing literature has examined the intersection from a conceptual standpoint. In this paper, we question the underlying assumption of the existing literature about how EA can be beneficial for DDBM design and realization by conducting empirical research. We want to investigate how EA modeling and management supports DDBM design and realization in practice. Accordingly, our study focuses on the following research question: How does enterprise architecture support the design and realization of data-driven business models? To answer this question, we conducted 16 semi-structured interviews with experts from consulting and industry firms working on DDBM projects in North America, Europe, and the Asia Pacific. Based on these interviews and triangulation data from publicly available sources, we collected 19 cases. We derived four approaches for DDBM design and realization and present for each the support from EA modeling and management.

In the next section, we provide an overview of the theoretical background and related work in the intersection of EA and DDBM. We then describe how we conducted the semi-structured interviews. The cases we gathered will be presented before describing the approaches for DDBM deployment and EA support along the process. Ultimately, we discuss our findings and conclude by discussing future research avenues.

2   Background and Related Work

2.1   Big Data Analytics and Data-Driven Business Models

The research on big data is deeply rooted in the information system discipline [7–10]. However, the term under which it was examined has evolved in the past decades from business intelligence, business analytics, and big data to big data analytics (BDA) [11]. In this context, the potential value contribution of data has been researched in three major areas, namely improved decision making, enhanced products and services, and new business models [12]. For the latter, the latest technological advancements have contributed to the urge for new DDBMs. Since 2014, a significant number of papers have been published dealing with the need for DDBM research [1]. Accordingly, several definitions of DDBM have been proposed by scholars. All point out that data has to be an essential component of the business model. For example, Hartmann, Zaki, Feldmann, and Neely [2] define DDBM as "a business model that relies on data as a key resource". Bulger, Taylor, and Schroeder [13, 14] and Brownlow, Zaki, Neely, and Urmetzer [13,

14] similarly highlight the fundamental role of data for DDBMs. Since there is no clear threshold of data utilization for a DDBM, Schüritz and Satzger [15] argue that companies alter from a traditional business model to a DDBM, with increased use of data for the value proposition. In the context of our research, we distinguish between enhancements of existing business models and new DDBMs that are centered on data (data as a key resource and/or data processing as a key activity) [3]. Research on DDBM is thriving but still in an early stage [1]. The latest efforts in academia have focused on extending the most popular business model canvas framework to the special needs of data-driven businesses [2, 16, 17].

2.2 Enterprise Architecture

Research on enterprise architecture can be traced back to the Zachman framework from 1980, which provides an ontology for modeling the fundamental structure of an organization and its information systems [18]. Over the past decades, EA has become essential for many organizations to support technology-driven transformations as it helps maintain an overview of complex sociotechnical systems. The Federation of Enterprise Architecture Organizations defines EA as "a well-defined practice for conducting enterprise analysis, design, planning, and implementation, using a comprehensive approach at all times, for the successful development and execution of strategy" [19]. A more narrowed definition of EA has been provided by the Open Group, which is in line with the ISO/ICE/IEEE Standard 42010 of architecture definition, that is, "the structure of components, their inter-relationships, and the principles and guidelines governing their design and evolution over time" [20]. We acknowledge that researchers and practitioners sometimes refer to EA as the practice and sometimes as the actual architecture of an organization. We use the term EA for the practice comprising the related modeling techniques, frameworks, and management function within an organization (EA management). The actual architecture of an organization is noted as as-is architecture, while planned future states are called to-be architecture [3, 6]. EA has proven its potential in improving information system efficiency and effectiveness. It is a critical component for strategic planning, top management decision making, and project management [21]. EA provides artifacts, such as meta-models, frameworks, tools, guiding principles, and management methods to support the evolution of an organization towards a target state. The key components of an organization and their interdependencies are represented in EA models [22]. The models are based on meta-models and deal with either the current state (as-is) or the desired state (to-be) of the enterprise. The EA management function supports the transition from the as-is to the to-be state through several intermediate architecture stages [3].

2.3 Related Work

To identify the potential relevant related work on the intersection of EA and big data analytics, we conducted a literature review [23]. We queried the following databases with keyword searches: AIS Electronic Library, EBSCO Host Business Source Complete, Google Scholar, IEEE Xplore, JSTOR, Science Direct, and Web of Science. We selected the keywords "enterprise architecture" and "big data". To further extend the literature search, the terms "data-driven" and "analytics," which are associated with "big data" were integrated into the search as well. This led to a total of three strings ("enterprise architecture" and "big data", "enterprise architecture" and "data-driven", "enterprise architecture" and "analytics") for our database queries. We screened all hits based on their title and abstract. Though it limits reproducibility, we included the first 100 search hits from google scholar as an additional source. After reducing irrelevant, duplicate, and non-peer-reviewed articles, a total of 16 articles remained, which we analyzed based on their full text. Additionally, we conducted a backward and forward search (Table 1).

Table 1. Literature search

Database	Hits	Results	Relevant
AIS	10	3	0
EBSCO	5	0	0
Google Scholar	100	6	0
IEEE	35	5	2
JSTOR	0	0	0
Science Direct	13	1	0
Web of Science	14	1	0
		16	2

The results of our literature review revealed a large number of contributions examining EA support for BDA. Scholars have investigated how EA modeling and management can support the design and implementation of BDA [21, 24, 25]. However, with the objective to identify articles focusing on EA support for DDBM, only two contributions remained. First, Vanauer et al. presented a methodology for DDBM design and realization by combining EA and business model canvas techniques. Their theoretical methodology comprises two phases and addresses two different approaches for DDBM deployment. Second, Rashed and Drews have conducted a systematic literature review to illustrate the potential support areas of EA for DDBMs. Furthermore, they have derived 42 DDBM-related EA concerns structured along the business model canvas fields [3]. Both contributions highlight the vast potential of interlinking the rich discipline of EA with the emerging demand of DDBM. However, both articles are purely conceptual with no empirical grounding. We address this research gap an examine EA modeling and management support for DDBM design and realization with a qualitative-empirical study.

3   Methodology

The goal of our study is to empirically examine the support of EA modeling and management for DDBM design and realization. Considering the novelty of DDBM for academia and practice, we planned to conduct an explorative qualitative study. Our approach is to derive theory by building upon the grounded theory approach proposed by Corbin and Strauss [26]. We conducted semi-structured interviews with experts from consulting and industry firms to develop explanatory theory, the second type of theory according to Gregor [27]. Each interviewee has a track record of data monetization projects. The data was analyzed as we proceeded with the data collection. We adjusted the interview guide based on our experience from the first interviews and once again after one third was conducted. Choosing a semi-structured interview approach allowed us to set the direction of our research as we collected the data. Drawing on the recommendations from Myers and Newman allowed us to foresee common pitfalls of qualitative interview research [28].

The unit of our analysis are cases of companies that design and realize DDBMs. To understand how EA modeling and management support DDBM design and realization, we structured our interview questions along two phases, namely DDBM design and realization. These phases have been derived from the literature on DDBM design and realization [29, 30]. We sharpened our questions as we proceeded. In the interviews, we asked the participants about the background and context of the project, the general support from EA, and the DDBM design and implementation phase. We documented their experience along with the case examples.

Between November 2019 and May 2020, we conducted 16 semi-structured expert interviews. All interviews have been recorded, transcribed, and coded by the authors. Except for IP 5, which was a physical meeting, all remaining interviewees have been conducted remotely via internet communication tools. We started with an initial list of interviewees leveraging our professional network, who named well-fitting candidates enjoying expert reputation. Each interviewee has a track record of DDBM projects. This allowed us to get the perspectives of cultural, gender, and regional diverse set of practitioners. Our interviewees have extensive experience in cross-industry firms as well as consulting firms with different specialization. This includes candidates from leading consulting firms, namely McKinsey, Bain, Boston as well as big four companies and large IT consulting firms. We included practitioners from various levels but focused on senior management after the first results demonstrated their broader perspective on the perceived factors (less senior tend to focus on one work package). We acknowledged that our interviewees have different backgrounds and expertise, we adjusted the questions as required. For example, our interviewees had either a stronger business or IT view on the cases they reported. Analyzing the interviewees as we proceeded and asking for further interview candidates allowed us to look for specific experiences, which we might have missed. For example, after the eighth interview, we acknowledged a regional restriction having only European cases collected. We then specifically asked for cases outside of Europe. Similarly, we emphasized the female perspective after taking into account the male dominance. An overview of the candidates' list is illustrated in Table 2.

The interviews were scheduled with a length of 60 min. Depending on the course, the interviewee reported from 1 or 2 cases. We asked for "success" and "failure" cases, referring to the DDBM design and realization. Success constitutes the delivery of the project within time, scope, and budget. In the beginning of each interview, we defined the term DDBM and elaborated on the type of cases we were looking for. At the end of each interview, we asked for project documentation and publicly available data sources for triangulation. Furthermore, we applied internet research to gather additional triangulation data.

To construct a coherent theory based on our gathered data, we drew on grounded theory as proposed by Corbin and Strauss [26]. We applied an open coding approach and selected ATLAS.ti for tool support. Not having a specific framework in mind, we conducted the interviews openly. To uncover relationships among the categories, we reassembled the data that was fractured during open coding. For this, we applied axial coding as described by Corbin and Strauss [26]. Based on the EA support our interviewees described along with the case context and taken steps for DDBM design and realization, we further specified our questions and built theoretical constructs. Dimensions that reached great density within the analysis of the first data were asked specifically for in the following interviews. After the ninth interview, we were able to derive four types of approaches for the collected cases. We used the remaining interviews to test our case cluster with the interviewees.

Table 2. Interview candidates

IP	Role	Organization	Experience
1	Senior Manager	IT Consulting	+8 years
2	Director	IT Consulting	+20 years
3	Senior Manager	IT Consulting	+10 years
4	Director	Insurance Co	+20 years
5	Director	MBB	+12 years
6	Senior Manager	MBB	+10 y/PhD
7	Director	MBB	+20y/PhD
8	Consultant	IT Consulting	+4 years
9	Director	IT Consulting	+15y/PhD
10	Director	IT Consulting	+20 years
11	Director	IT Consulting	+15y/PhD
12	Senior Manager	IT Consulting	+10y/PhD
13	Director	Public Services	+12y/PhD
14	Senior Manager	Financial Services	+10 years
15	Senior Manager	Big four	+8 years
16	Senior Manager	Life Science	+8y/PhD

We acknowledge the threats to validity. Considering the four types of validity as described by Maxwell [31], we put great effort to ensure our interviewees can speak openly and are not in a conflicting situation. The developed concepts were critically assessed by both authors. We triangulated the interview results with project documentation and publicly available data. Furthermore, we discussed our results with four of our interviewees in a second iteration. These interviewees were: IP4, 7, 11, and 13, who reported voluntarily. Their feedback was used to further sharpen our derived design and realization approaches for DDBM. However, we received great support for the developed concepts from these directors and senior managers within industry and consulting firms.

4   Results

In this chapter, we will first present an overview of the cases that were discussed in the interviews. Second, we describe the reported approaches for DDBM design and realization. Third, the support of EA modeling and management is illustrated for the identified approaches.

4.1   Case Overview

Discussing the terms DDBMs and EA at the beginning of our interviews was beneficial for our detailed debates. Furthermore, it gave us an understanding of the divergent interpretation of the term DDBM by practitioners. While some share our view of DDBM as new business model with data as a key resource and/or data processing as a key activity, others interpret the gradual enhancement of the existing business model with data as DDBM as well. Four cases represent DDBMs in line with our interpretation. Our interviewees highlighted the scarcity of latter mentioned cases, as they require a "clear business vision, well understood data and the technological backbone" [IP7]. The remaining cases represent organizational endeavors to gradually enhance technological and analytical capabilities to build the foundation for DDBMs. The term EA was clear to all interviewees. However, in most interviews, we had to emphasize that the EA practice goes beyond the EA department established within an organization. This means, even without the involvement of the mentioned department, EA artifacts can support the DDBM design and realization (Table 3).

The gathered cases reflect organizational endeavors to deploy DDBMs. The companies behind these endeavors are predominantly from the insurance, financial services, and life sciences industry. This may be due to the proximity of the core business to data processing [IP7, 9, 11]. All companies are large size global and local players with origin in Europe, Asia, and the North America. Two of the four DDBM cases comprise European firms and two Asian Pacific firms. The business unit initiating the project was decisive for the expected value and application of the data. For example, the R&D unit of a pharma company seeks maximization of data value for drug development. This might come from shortened clinical trial phases or identification of new drugs [IP9]. Independent from the initiating business unit, CEO sponsorship and support was reported as vital for the cases. Considering the fragmented and isolated data sources throughout the company, timely data access becomes crucial. The majority of the described cases had CEO or CEO-1 level sponsorship. The quantitative analysis as illustrated in Fig. 1. The companies behind all reported cases had an EA department established. However, the duties and impact varied among the companies. For 17 cases our interviewees mentioned that EA must play a vital role in DDBM design and realization. Along all cases

Table 3. Case list

C	IP	Industry	Reg./Glo	HQ	Motivation	Sponsor
1	IP1	Insurance	Local	D	Digital strategy	CDO/CIO
2	IP2	FS	Global	AUT	Digital strategy	CDO/CIO
3	IP2	FS	Global	AUT	Competitive response	CDO/CIO
4	IP3	Insurance	Global	D	Digital strategy	CDO/CIO
5	IP4	Insurance	Global	CH	Competitive response	CDO/CIO
6	IP5	FS	Global	CH	BU vision	Head of M&S and CDO
7	IP5	FS	Global	CH	BU vision	Head of HR
8	IP6	IE	Global	D	Company vision	CEO
9	IP7	Insurance	Global	CHN	Clear business opportunity	CEO
10	IP8	Chemicals	Global	D	Digital strategy	CDO/CIO
11	IP9	LS	Global	CH	BU vision	Head of R&D and CDO
12	IP9	LS	Global	D	BU vision	Head of M&S and CDO
13	IP10	Insurance	Local	US	Digital strategy	CDO/CIO
14	IP11	FS	Global	AUS	Clear business opportunity	CEO
15	IP12	Energy	Local	D	Clear business opportunity	CEO/CIO
16	IP13	PS	Local	D	Digital strategy	CDO/CIO
17	IP14	FS	Global	CH	Digital strategy	CDO/CIO
18	IP15	LS	Global	D	Digital strategy	CDO/CIO
19	IP16	LS	Global	UK	BU vision	Head of R&D and CDO

our interviewees faced EA concerns, regarding transparency of the prevailing architecture, planning of the target architecture and/or managing the transformation from as-is to to-be state. However, for only 10 cases our interviewees stated that EA modeling and management techniques were instrumentalized.

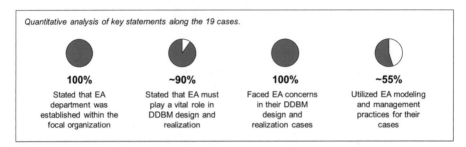

Fig. 1. Key statements

4.2   Approaches for DDBM Design and Realization

The support of EA depends on the company context and the approach taken towards DDBM design and realization. Across the 19 cases we have identified four approaches for DDBM deployment. The companies behind the cases, either take a gradual approach or a direct approach. For the first, they start building technology capabilities first or analyze the existing data to develop use cases for DDBMs. For the latter, they either integrate the new DDBM into the existing organizational structures or establish a new DDBM startup. All companies behind the cases had a dedicated EA management function established. Our interviewees commonly reported that EA must play a vital role for DDBM design and realization, regardless if EA fulfilled the requirements or not. With this critical role, EA can become a "bottleneck" for DDBM design and realization, and the EA management function might be actively excluded from the process. In the following, we will describe the EA support along with the four approaches for DDBM design and realization, referring to Fig. 2.

Technology Centric. Seven cases comprise companies that embark on the journey towards DDBM realization by developing technology capabilities first. Business requirements are blurry and derived from high-level use cases. The process is driven by the IT department and initiated with technology selection efforts. Followed by a proof-of-concept phase and ultimately the implementation. EA supports the technology selection by enabling the development of business and technology capability maps that allow an understanding of the required technologies. These models are used to map technology solutions to the target business capabilities [IP1–3, 14, 15]. Furthermore, EA models were used to grant transparency on the prevailing data and technology landscape [IP1–3, 10, 13]. To proceed after the proof-of-concept phase, a formal sign-off from the architecture board is required. The proposed solution must comply with the prevailing EA principles and overall target architecture [IP2, 3, 13–15]. EA methods and models have been used to cascade from capability domains to technology requirements. The EA management function was actively engaged by providing transparency and guidance. EA frameworks and tools have only been partially mentioned. TOGAF has been used for EA documentations [IP2, 3, 14].

Use Case Centric. Five cases represent companies that begin with the ideation, prioritization, and sequencing of BDA use cases. The use case development is driven by the business units (BUs), followed by a solution architecture development phase. The designed solution is then prototyped and tested via a minimum viable product phase, which results in an implementation in case of success. In two out of the five cases, the EA management function supported the use case development with models to provide transparency on the data and technology landscape [IP5, 16]. Further EA services were required to get sign-offs from architecture boards to proceed with the implementation. EA models were developed for the solution architecture and the implementation roadmap. One consulting firm has applied a self-developed EA method to support the use case and solution architecture development [IP9]. EA frameworks and tools have not been perceived as mentionable.

DDBM Integration. Three cases comprise actual DDBM deployments. The companies behind these cases transformed their existing organizational structure to integrate the new DDBM. The process is initiated with a DDBM design phase, followed by prototyping with a minimum viable product and ultimately implementation. EA models are used to provide transparency over the prevailing data and technology landscape. The models are developed by consulting firms for specific concerns. Standard EA models are only used to derive own models answering the DDBM-related EA concerns. EA models are also developed to envision the solution architecture and guide the implementation. The EA management function is actively excluded from the DDBM design and realization process. The EA services are only required to get formal sign-off from the architecture boards. EA methods, frameworks, and tools have not been perceived as a mentionable component of the design and realization phase [IP6, 11, 12].

DDBM Startup. In contrast to the latter presented path towards DDBM design and realization, the establishment of DDBM through a new company requires a different approach. A new company must be established. The new team moves the DDBM design and realization in a startup way of working forward. The parental company provides the data. EA support is required to access the data via APIs, providing transparency over data and technology landscape. EA services are required to develop models and find solutions for data extraction. However, the EA management function is actively excluded and perceived as a bottleneck that slows down processes. The new company is staffed with technology experts, capable to design and manage the realization of the startup architecture. The importance of rapidly scalable architecture was emphasized by our interviewee [IP7]. Standard EA methods, models, and tools have not been perceived as mentionable along the process.

The highest application of EA artifacts was reported in the technology centric approach for DDBM deployment. EA supports in its traditional role in the integration of new technology, both strategic planning and project realization. The use case centric approach requires a different EA support. The traditional EA models, framework, and tools

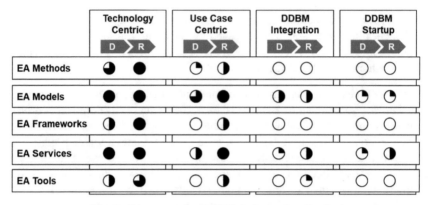

Fig. 2. EA support for DDBM design and realization

are too complex, and technology-focused for business discussions in individual BUs [IP9, 16]. However, our interviewees reported that lightweight models are developed, project-specific together with business users [IP5, 9, 16]. With the DDBM integration and startup approach, EA is facing new challenges. Traditional models, frameworks, and tools are rarely applied. The EA management function with its principles and standards is perceived as a bottleneck and actively excluded [IP6, 7, 11, 12].

4.3 Support Gap of Enterprise Architecture for Data-Driven Business Models

In the previous section, we have described how EA supports the design and realization of DDBMs. The illustration in Fig. 2 implies a gap of support for the DDBM Integration and Startup approach. To demonstrate this gap, we have derived the support potentials of EA for DDBM from our interview results as well as from our literature search. Figure 3 illustrates the potential application areas of EA modeling and management for each of the approaches.

EA finds a higher application in the technology centric approach since the traditional EA capabilities are demanded. Technology selection and implementation are driven by the IT department. The use case centric approach is driven by BUs and requires EA support for use case design and realization. For the DDBM integration approach, EA can be beneficial for ideation, solution sketching, and feasibility testing as well as for the implementation. The DDBM startup approach demands from the EA to support agile teams, rapidly proposing, and developing solutions. In contradiction to its traditional role, EA must adapt to a *fail fast and learn* culture.

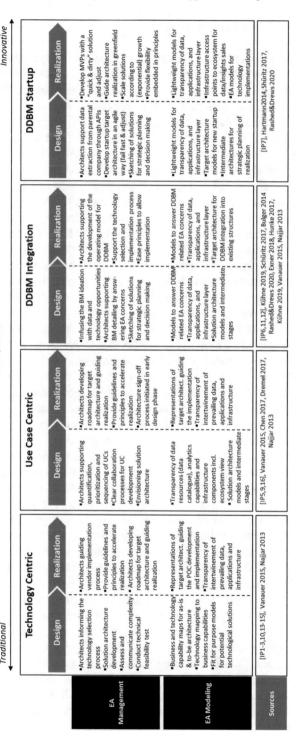

Fig. 3. Potential support of EA for DDBM

5 Conclusion and Future Research

The rise of DDBMs brings unique opportunities to organizations to monetize their data. A considerable number of articles has addressed this topic in the literature [1]. However, most companies struggle to implement DDBM projects [4]. Prevailing methods and tools for the deployment of offline business models do not capture the unique perspectives of data and analytics, that DDBM endeavors require [1, 5]. Even though EA has proven its potential for IT-related projects, the intersection with DDBMs has not been extensively investigated in the literature [3, 29]. First attempts of combining the two lenses of EA and DDBM, imply underlying assumptions about how EA can be beneficial for DDBM deployment. In this study, we questioned these underlying assumptions and examined how EA modeling and management supports DDBM design and realization in practice. To contribute to research, we conducted 16 semi-structured interviews with experts from consulting and industry firms, to empirically investigate the EA – DDBM intersection. We derived four approaches for DDBM design and realization and described for each the support of EA modeling and management. Our results have revealed that EA is a common practice in many companies. Accordingly, is the expectation of EA support for DDBM high. All our interviewees have faced EA concerns along their DDBM journey. However, we found that regardless of the potential support opportunities, many practitioners perceive the EA practice as a bottleneck for innovative project setups like DDBM deployment. Consequently, we have found that EA was utilized high in the technology centric approach, which demands the traditional capabilities of EA and is driven by the IT department. While the more innovative settings like DDBM integration and startup approaches have utilized EA only very rarely. The latter approaches are driven by the business with support from IT. Considering the interview results and the existing literature on the intersection of DDBM and EA, it further comes apparent that EA is not leveraged to its full potential in DDBM design and realization.

The results of our research have implications for academia and practice alike. For academia, our contribution is threefold. First, we have presented 19 international DDBM cases and derived four approaches for DDBM deployment. Along these approaches we demonstrated how EA modeling and management are applied in practice to support DDBMs. Second, we revealed the discrepancies between the underlying assumptions of the literature on EA support for DDBM and the practical manifestation. For example, Rashed and Drews [3] describe EA support along one approach for DDBM design and realization. Our findings demonstrate four different approaches with varying demand on EA support. Furthermore, the literature neglects the perceived value from EA by practitioners [3, 29]. Although a high value potential can be derived from the literature [3], it involves many underlying assumptions that must be questioned when looking into the practical manifestation. Third, by analyzing the literature and conducting empirical research, we have opened new research avenues. Especially for deepened research on EA capabilities to support DDBM design and realization, the role of architects in DDBM endeavors, as well as the perceived value from EA and the negative connotation of a "bottleneck". Future research could investigate the conceptualization of EA as "control point" offering value. For practitioners, the collected cases provide valuable insights into reference projects. The overview of the current literature is beneficial for targeted knowledge development. Additionally, the presented approaches and the respective EA support can be inspiring for EA departments to find new support opportunities.

Our study's results bear some limitations. Drawing upon Maxwell [18], we structure the limitations of our qualitative research along the four proposed types. First, for evaluative limitations, we acknowledge the threat to validity based on the dependency on the individual interpretation of the reported events. Although we have validated the described facts with triangulation data, the threat cannot be completely diminished. Second, for theoretical limitations, we applied a semi-structured interview approach to collect the data open-minded. However, our research was infused by our previous research on the intersection of DDBM and EA. Third, interpretative limitations, the derived approaches are imbued with our interpretation of the data. Although both authors have independently processed the data and the results have been challenged with two directors from management consulting firms, a binding to the interpreter's perspective will remain. Fourth, descriptive limitations, we acknowledge the threat to validity imposed in the description process. In prevention, all results have been written and interpreted by both authors iteratively. The working paper has been sent to two interviewees in order to gather additional feedback. Ultimately, we have to emphasize that the number of conducted interviews and collected cases are limited. However, we analyzed the data as we proceeded with the interviews. After the ninth interview, we were able to derive the approaches. The remaining interviews have been used to test our concepts.

Despite the vast potential of applying EA modeling and management concepts for DDBM design and realization, their utilization is limited in practice. We plan to develop a reference model for the design and realization of DDBM under special consideration of the EA practice. Additionally, we opened new research avenues in the directions of EA capabilities to support DDBM design and realization, the role of architects in DDBM endeavors, as well as the perceived value from EA and the negative connotation of a "bottleneck".

References

1. Wiener, M., Saunders, C., Marabelli, M.: Big-data business models: a critical literature review and multiperspective research framework. J. Inf. Technol. **35**, 66–91 (2020)
2. Hartmann, P.M., Zaki, M., Feldmann, N., Neely, A.: Big data for big business? A taxonomy of data-driven business models used by start-up firms. Cambridge Serv. Alliance 1–29 (2014)
3. Rashed, F., Drews, P.: Supporting the development and realization of data-driven business models with enterprise architecture modeling and management. In: Abramowicz, W., Klein, G. (eds.) BIS 2020. LNBIP, vol. 389, pp. 264–276. Springer, Cham (2020). https://doi.org/10.1007/978-3-030-53337-3_20
4. Redman, T.C.: Do your data scientists know the 'why' behind their work? Harv. Bus. Rev. (2019).
5. Fruhwirth, M., Ropposch, C., Pammer, V.: Supporting data-driven business model innovations: a structured literature review on tools and methods. J. Bus. Model. **8**, 1–19 (2020)
6. Winter, R., Fischer, R.: Essential layers, artifacts, and dependencies of enterprise architecture. J. Enterp. Archit. **3**, 7–18 (2007)
7. Günther, W.A., Rezazade Mehrizi, M.H., Huysman, M., Feldberg, F.: Debating big data: a literature review on realizing value from big data. J. Strateg. Inf. Syst. **26**, 191–209 (2017)

8. Abbasi, A., Sarker, S., Chiang, R.H.L.: Big data research in information systems: toward an inclusive research agenda. J. Assoc. Inf. Syst. **17**, 1–30 (2016)
9. Baesens, B., Bapna, R., Marsden, J.R., Vanthienen, J., Zhao, J.L.: Transformational issues of big data and analytics in networked business. MIS Q. **40**, 807–818 (2016)
10. Sharma, R., Mithas, S., Kankanhalli, A.: Transforming decision-making processes: a research agenda for understanding the impact of business analytics on organisations. Eur. J. Inf. Syst. **23**, 433–441 (2014)
11. Chen, H., Chiang, R.H.L., Storey, V.C.: Business intelligence and analytics: from big data to big impact. MIS Q. **36**, 1165–1188 (2012)
12. Engelbrecht, A., Gerlach, J., Widjaja, T.: Understanding the anatomy of data-driven business models – towards an empirical taxonomy. In: Twenty-Fourth European Conference on Information Systems, İstanbul, pp. 1–15. ECIS (2016)
13. Bulger, M., Taylor, G., Schroeder, R.: Data-driven business models: challenges and opportunities of big data. Oxford Internet Inst. 1–74 (2014)
14. Brownlow, J., Zaki, M., Neely, A., Urmetzer, F.: Data and analytics - data-driven business models : a blueprint for innovation (2015)
15. Schuritz, R., Satzger, G.: Patterns of data-infused business model innovation. In: Proceedings - CBI 2016: 18th IEEE Conference on Business Informatics, Paris, pp. 133–142. IEEE (2016)
16. Kühne, B., Böhmann, T.: Requirements for representing data-driven business models - towards extending the business model canvas. In: Twenty-Fourth Americas Conference on Information Systems, New Orleans, pp. 1–10. AIS (2018)
17. Osterwalder, A., Pigneur, Y.: Business Model Generation: A Handbook for Visionaries, Game Changers and Challengers. Wiley, Hoboken (2010)
18. Zachman, J.A.: Zachman International. https://zachman.com/about-the-zachman-framework. Accessed 12 Nov 2019
19. Federation of EA Professional Organizations: A Common Perspective on Enterprise Architecture (2013)
20. The Open Group: TOGAF. https://www.opengroup.org/togaf. Accessed 06 Oct 2019
21. Burmeister, F., Drews, P., Schirmer, I.: Towards an extended enterprise architecture metamodel for big data – a literature-based approach. In: Twenty-Fourth Americas Conference on Information Systems (AMCIS), New Orleans, pp. 1–10. AIS (2018)
22. Musulin, J., Strahonja, V.: Business model grounds and links: towards enterprise architecture perspective. J. Inf. Organ. Sci. **42**, 241–269 (2018)
23. Vom Brocke, J., Simons, A., Niehaves, B., Reimer, K., Plattfaut, R., Cleven, A.: Reconstructing the giant: on the importance of rigour in documenting the literature search process. In: European Conference on Information Systems, Verona, pp. 2206–2217. ECIS (2009)
24. Kehrer, S., Jugel, D., Zimmermann, A.: Categorizing requirements for enterprise architecture management in big data literature. In: 20th International Enterprise Distributed Object Computing Workshop, Vienna, pp. 98–105. IEEE (2016)
25. Lnenicka, M., Komarkova, J.: Developing a government enterprise architecture framework to support the requirements of big and open linked data with the use of cloud computing. Int. J. Inf. Manage. **46**, 124–141 (2019)
26. Corbin, J.M., Strauss, A.: Grounded theory research: procedures, canons, and evaluative criteria. Qual. Sociol. **13**, 3–21 (1990)
27. Gregor, S.: The nature of theory in information systems. MIS Q. **30**, 611–642 (2006)
28. Myers, M.D., Newman, M.: The qualitative interview in IS research: examining the craft. Inf. Organ. **17**, 2–26 (2007)
29. Vanauer, M., Bohle, C., Hellingrath, B.: Guiding the introduction of big data in organizations: a methodology with business- and data-driven ideation and enterprise architecture management-based implementation. In: 48th Hawaii International Conference on System Science, Hawaii, pp. 908–917. IEEE (2015)

30. Chen, H.-M., Kazman, R., Garbajosa, J., Gonzalez, E.: Big data value engineering for business model innovation. In: 50th Hawaii International Conference on System Sciences, Hawaii, pp. 5921–5930. IEEE (2017)
31. Maxwell, J.A.: Qualitative Research Design: An Interactive Approach. SAGE, Washington (2013)
32. Najjar, M.S., Kettinger, W.J.: Data monetization: lessons from a retailer's journey. MIS Q. Exec. **12**, 21–32 (2013)
33. Dremel, C., Wulf, J.: Towards a capability model for big data analytics. In: 13th International Conference on Wirtschaftsinformatik, St. Gallen, pp. 1141–1155. AIS (2017)
34. Kühne, B., Böhmann, T.: Data-driven business models – building the bridge between data and value. In: 27th European Conference on Information Systems, Stockholm & Uppsala, pp. 1–16. ECIS (2019)
35. Kühne, B., Zolnowski, A., Böhmann, T.: Making data tangible for data-driven innovations in a business model context DSR methodology view project service dominant architecture view project. In: Twenty-Fifth Americas Conference on Information Systems, Cancun, pp. 1–10. AIS (2019).
36. Schüritz, R., Seebacher, S., Dorner, R.: Capturing value from data: revenue models for data-driven services. In: Proceedings of the 50th Hawaii International Conference on System Sciences, Waikoloa, pp. 5348–5357 (2017)
37. Exner, K., Stark, R., Kim, J.Y.: Data-driven business model: a methodology to develop smart services. In: International Conference on Engineering, Technology and Innovation, Madeira Island, pp. 146–154. IEEE (2018)
38. Hunke, F., Seebacher, S., Schuritz, R., Illi, A.: Towards a process model for data-driven business model innovation. In: 19th Conference on Business Informatics, CBI, Thessaloniki, pp. 150–157. IEEE (2017)

BPM Capability Configuration in Times of Crises: How to Adapt Processes When the Virus Strikes?

Vincent Borghoff[(✉)] and Ralf Plattfaut

Process Innovation & Automation Lab, South Westphalia University of Applied Sciences,
Soest, Germany
{borghoff.vincent,plattfaut.ralf}@fh-swf.de

Abstract. With the impact of the Covid-19 pandemic, multiple organizations are experiencing cuts and changes in existing business concepts and face the challenge of adapting to the new circumstances. This short paper discusses preliminary results of a mixed methods based study on business process management capabilities. Using an existing BPM capability framework, we aim to show which configuration of BPM capabilities facilitates organizational survival and processual sustainment during crisis and contribute to both BPM theory and practice.

Keywords: Business process management · Covid-19 · BPM Capabilities

1 Introduction

The Covid-19 crisis has not only changed personal and societal life, it directly affected whole economies as well as individual organizations as it made existing value propositions obsolete and established working routines no longer applicable [1]. In addition, governmental restrictions, as a response to a deepening pandemic, induced a high level of uncertainty into the economic environment [2]. This also manifests on process level, e.g. as social distancing makes an attendance based work culture impossible and forces organizations to quickly adapt and at the same time sustain quality. Organizations differ in their success in adapting to this fast market and environmental changes and their capability to align their business processes.

Business Process Management (BPM) can provide methods and approaches to meet the requirements of the new situation, as it is concerned with managing processes and both internal and external change induced through process drift and exogenous shocks. BPM capabilities depict the ability to successfully develop, monitor and adapt business processes within and between organizations., hence different configurations of those capabilities, inter alia, can form an organizations ability to sustain its business performance throughout a crisis. BPM capabilities in stable and incrementally changing environments are well understood [3–5], whereas there is a lack of insight for exogenous shocks like the Covid-19 crisis. Although there is literature on developing resilience against turbulent environments through BPM [6, 7], there is no specific research concerning required capability configurations.

F. Ahlemann et al. (Eds.): WI 2021, LNISO 48, pp. 678–684, 2021.
https://doi.org/10.1007/978-3-030-86800-0_46

Against this background the presented research-in-progress explores the following research question: *Which configuration of BPM capabilities enables the utmost process performance within the context of a crisis?*

The remainder of this short paper structures as follows: Sect. 2 provides background on BPM and the impact of Covid-19 on business processes. In Sect. 3 the planned research approach is presented, before Sect. 4 points out preliminary results of the study. The paper ends with a concluding discussion in Sect. 5.

2 Background

2.1 Business Process Management

BPM in general tries to ensure consistent outcomes of work and the exploitation of opportunities to improve, by investigating and monitoring how work is performed [8, 9]. It contributes both on overarching (e.g. process culture) and single process level (e.g. process implementation and monitoring) management within process oriented organizations [10, 11]. Through this comprehensive nature, BPM can contribute to overall business success by offering methods and tools for structured process handling [12]. BPM is commonly structured along capability frameworks. One, broadly consented, framework is by de Bruin and Rosemann [13], which has been the basis for multiple studies in the field of BPM [14, 15]. It structures BPM capabilities along the six core elements Strategic alignment, Governance, Methods, Information Technology, People and Culture. The implementation and institutionalization of the included 30 capabilities promotes and enables successful process orientation and therefore efficient business processes [16], as they map both the potential for incremental and radical process change [17, 18] as well as stable business processes [19].

2.2 Covid-19 and Impact on Business Processes

Covid-19, as a globally spreading pandemic, acts like an exogenous shock to businesses all over the world [20]. These shocks are of extreme, unexpected, or unpredictable nature, as they force organizations to quickly respond to their impact [21]. This response involves the adaption of strategies, business logic and business processes to the new circumstances [22]. As existing strategies may become obsolete, even for whole business sectors and within complete value chains [23, 24], upstream and downstream processes, in addition to purely internal ones, must be adapted, e.g. the increase in remote work requires new process models and generates an ascent in IT based workflows to maintain operations [25, 26]. BPM can contribute on the one hand in creating resilient business processes, that are not affected through external and exogenous changes [27], or by fostering agile process adaption and alternation to quickly avoid cuts in efficiency or even exploit emerging opportunities [28]. The best suitable configuration of BPM capabilities for each of these contributions has so far been an underexplored chain within BPM research. While there is knowledge of the methods required for both orientations, there is a lack of insight into the necessary organizational capabilities.

3   (Planned) Research Approach

For our research we follow a sequential, developmental, mixed methods approach (Fig. 1), combining qualitative and quantitative research [29, 30]. On a qualitative theory building phase, follows a quantitative theory testing phase [31]. We focus on the inter-play between BPM capability configurations and business performance and sustainment on the background of an external crisis.

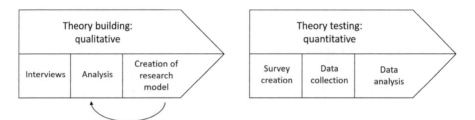

Fig. 1. Schematic depiction of the used research approach

3.1   Qualitative Phase: Theory Building

The qualitative phase aims at developing hypotheses as a basis for further research. For that purpose, we conducted five semi-structured interview with practitioners concerning the impact of the Covid-19 crisis on their organization and their BPM organizational BPM capabilities. All cases were chosen purposive, to achieve a sample of relevant experts and organizations of different sizes, sectors and legal structures [32]. The interview guideline was structured along the BPM core elements framework to determine the state of each core element within each case organization. The process performance prior to and within the crisis, as well as changes induced by the crisis, were specifically addressed. The interviews were transcribed, structured and coded [33], following the BPM core elements and capability areas as a research lens. We identify organizational requirements and actions regarding their representability within the framework and map each aspect to the respective capability area. This should give a first impression of the individual influence of single elements on the overreaching organizational BPM success. We include considerations about the status of each capability, meaning if one specific capability was existent prior to the crisis or developed in course of it. We iterate this process over all transcripts to develop consistent hypotheses and research models as a basis for the following phase [34].

3.2   Quantitative Phase: Theory testing

Based on the qualitative phase we plan to develop a comprehensive survey to test our hypotheses. Therefore we conceptualize our preliminary findings, as well as the BPM capability framework, and process them into a survey with the purpose to verify and generalize our former findings [35]. To reach that goal, we aim at building a measurement model to test the influence of the conceptualized BPM capability areas, as well as a set of context variables, against pre- and in-crisis process performance [36]. For modeling we use a systematic approach utilizing structural equation modeling [37]. We utilize core themes for each capability area from out the literature to make individual configurations measureable. This process is conducted via a systematic literature review. Subsequent to design and pilot testing, the final survey will be sent out and later statistically analyzed [38].

4 Preliminary Results of First Case Interview

Due the ongoing research process, in the following we present our preliminary results, originating from a first interview with the head of human resources of a larger medium-sized manufacturing company, representing findings concerning Covid-19 impact, BPM capabilities, as well as process and organizational change. The data from remaining interviews are currently being evaluated.

Streamlined, Agile Governance Structures. First and foremost, the organization adapted its decision-making processes to the new circumstances. A massive shortening and streamlining of the decision-making structures led to faster adaptation cycles. This gives first hints on how governance-related BPM capabilities need to be configured, highlighting the importance of pace in decision making which is strongly influenced by clearly defined and executed government processes, given in the CE (core element) "process management decision making".

Shortened Strategical Planning Cycles. Due to the large amount of uncertainty, the organization was forced to shorten their strategic scope. Long-term planning is postponed and processes need to align in short notice, which directly affects the strategic alignment core factor, specifically the bidirectional linkage between the overarching organizational strategy and the operated business processes. The organization switched from stable, long running processes to a more flexible process understanding, reweighting the strategic alignment in the short term.

Increased Pace and Willingness to Digitalize. Prior the pandemic the internal drive towards digitalization and the conducted effort towards that goal was seen considerably low, resulting in equally low IT related BPM capabilities. With the changed conditions and need for remote work for a significant part of the workforce, digitalization became a main challenge, which takes up larger parts of the planning and development capacities. Whereas remote IT solutions became a big part of consideration, improvements considering BPM related IT were not part of the organizations efforts.

Shift to a More Change-open Culture. The organization observed a shift of culture towards a more change-open state. Where in the past deviations from routine were considered more as a burden and risk than an opportunity, impeding process change, within the crisis this attitude decreased, reflecting a change in capabilities within the core factor culture, especially concerning the "responsiveness to process change" capability, perceiving change as a potential opportunity.

Employee Centricity. The aforementioned development is accompanied with a more comprehensive employee centricity. The organization stated that with the beginning of the crisis all organizational- and process related changes were adopted by a committee consisting of management and affected employees. The effects and the specific backgrounds were clearly communicated to the workforce. This allowed, as stated, frictionless and broadly accepted process change and emphasizes the importance of the core element people and especially the associated capability area "process collaboration and communication".

5   Concluding Discussion

The preliminary results show that the studied organization is developing towards more agile and therefore more adaptive processes than fostering resilience. This requires capabilities, especially in the area of digital competence, which were previously lacking and are currently being increasingly developed. These rapid, radical changes require clear and integrative decision making and communication in order to implement them, despite an observable change towards an open change culture. This can have a positive influence on the future retention and enhancement of the implemented agile process culture. The crisis can thus also be used as an opportunity to move towards a more agile and more digital way of working, enabling the organization to modernize at a rapid pace and break up existing structures. The faster changing strategic planning may become a risk, as process improvement is made more difficult by volatile conditions.

By means of these and the results of the analysis of the further qualitative data, we plan to achieve a deeper understanding of appropriate organizational capability configurations, which we plan to quantitatively verify in a further step. In addition to the Covid-19 pandemic, the research horizon can be extended and generalized to other exogenous shocks, as the requirements on a capability level are comparable.

The results are limited by the amount of qualitative data analyzed, so generalizability has to be discussed. We hope to overcome this limitation with the conduction of the planned quantitative study.

References

1. Verma, S., Gustafsson, A.: Investigating the emerging COVID-19 research trends in the field of business and management: a bibliometric analysis approach. J. Bus. Res. **118**, 253–261 (2020)
2. Baker, S., Bloom, N., Davis, S., Terry, S.: COVID-Induced Economic Uncertainty. National Bureau of Economic Research, Cambridge, MA (2020)
3. Vom Brocke, J., Rosemann, M. (eds.): Handbook on Business Process Management 1. Introduction, Methods, and Information Systems. Springer Berlin Heidelberg, Berlin, Heidelberg, s.l. (2015)
4. Poeppelbuss, J., Plattfaut, R., Niehaves, B.: How do we progress? An Exploration of Alternate Explanations for BPM Capability Development. CAIS **36** (2015)
5. van Looy, A.: Capabilities for managing business processes: a measurement instrument. Bus. Process Mgmt J. **26**, 287–311 (2020)

6. Trkman, P., McCormack, K.: Supply chain risk in turbulent environments—a conceptual model for managing supply chain network risk. Int. J. Prod. Econ. **119**, 247–258 (2009)
7. Antunes, P., Mourão, H.: Resilient business process management: framework and services. Expert Syst. Appl. **38**, 1241–1254 (2011)
8. Dumas, M., La Rosa, M., Mendling, J., Reijers, H.A.: Fundamentals of Business Process Management. Springer Berlin Heidelberg, Berlin, Heidelberg (2018)
9. Aalst van der, W.M.P.: Business process management: a comprehensive survey. ISRN Softw. Eng. **2013**, 1–37 (2013)
10. de Bruin, T., Doebeli, G.: An organizational approach to BPM: the experience of an Australian transport provider. In: vom Brocke, J., Rosemann, M. (eds.) Handbook on Business Process Management 2. IHIS, pp. 741–759. Springer, Heidelberg (2015). https://doi.org/10.1007/978-3-642-45103-4_31
11. Vom Brocke, J., Zelt, S., Schmiedel, T.: On the role of context in business process management. Int. J. Inf. Manag. **36**, 486–495 (2016)
12. McCormack, K., et al.: A global investigation of key turning points in business process maturity. Bus. Process Mgmt J. **15**, 792–815 (2009)
13. de Bruin, T., Rosemann, M.: Using the Delphi technique to identify BPM capability areas. In: Proceedings of the Australasian Conference on Information Systems (2007)
14. Kerpedzhiev, G.D., König, U.M., Röglinger, M., Rosemann, M.: An exploration into future business process management capabilities in view of digitalization. Bus. Inf. Syst. Eng. **63**(2), 83–96 (2020)
15. van Looy, A., Poels, G., Snoeck, M.: Evaluating business process maturity models. JAIS **18**, 461–486 (2017)
16. Lehnert, M., Linhart, A., Röglinger, M.: Value-based process project portfolio management: integrated planning of BPM capability development and process improvement. Bus. Res. **9**(2), 377–419 (2016). https://doi.org/10.1007/s40685-016-0036-5
17. Schmiedel, T., vom Brocke, J.: Business process management: potentials and challenges of driving innovation. In: vom Brocke, J., Schmiedel, T. (eds.) BPM – Driving Innovation in a Digital World. MP, pp. 3–15. Springer, Cham (2015). https://doi.org/10.1007/978-3-319-14430-6_1
18. Benner, M.J., Tushman, M.L.: Exploitation, exploration, and process management: the productivity dilemma revisited. AMR **28**, 238–256 (2003)
19. Benner, M.J., Tushman, M.: Process management and technological innovation: a longitudinal study of the photography and paint industries. Adm. Sci. Q. **47**, 676 (2002)
20. Papadopoulos, T., Baltas, K.N., Balta, M.E.: The use of digital technologies by small and medium enterprises during COVID-19: Implications for theory and practice. International J. Inf. Manag. **55**, 102192 (2020)
21. Doern, R., Williams, N., Vorley, T.: Special issue on entrepreneurship and crises: business as usual? An introduction and review of the literature. Entrep. Reg. Dev. **31**, 400–412 (2019)
22. Martins, L.L., Rindova, V.P., Greenbaum, B.E.: Unlocking the hidden value of concepts: a cognitive approach to business model innovation. Strateg. Entrep. J. **9**, 99–117 (2015)
23. Verbeke, A.: Will the COVID-19 pandemic really change the governance of global value chains? Brit. J. Manag. **31**, 444–446 (2020)
24. Trkman, P., de Oliveira, M.P.V., McCormack, K.: Value-oriented supply chain risk management: you get what you expect. Ind. Mngmnt Data Syst. **116**, 1061–1083 (2016)
25. Brynjolfsson, E., Horton, J., Ozimek, A., Rock, D., Sharma, G., TuYe, H.-Y.: COVID-19 and Remote Work: An Early Look at US Data. National Bureau of Economic Research, Cambridge, MA (2020)
26. Dwivedi, Y.K., et al.: Impact of COVID-19 pandemic on information management research and practice: Transforming education, work and life. Int. J. Inf. Manag. **55**, 102211 (2020)

27. Linnenluecke, M.K.: Resilience in business and management research: a review of influential publications and a research agenda. Int. J. Manag. Rev. **19**, 4–30 (2017)
28. Badakhshan, P., Conboy, K., Grisold, T., Vom Brocke, J.: Agile business process management. Bus. Process Mgmt J. **26**(6), 1505–1523 (2019)
29. Venkatesh, V., Brown, S.A., Bala, H.: Bridging the qualitative-quantitative divide: guidelines for conducting mixed methods research in information systems. MISQ **37**, 21–54 (2013)
30. Johnson, R.B., Onwuegbuzie, A.J., Turner, L.A.: Toward a definition of mixed methods research. J. Mixed Methods Res. **1**, 112–133 (2007)
31. Teddlie, C., Tashakkori, A.: Foundations of Mixed Methods Research. Integrating Quantitative and Qualitative Approaches in the Social and Behavioral Sciences. SAGE Publ, Los Angeles (2010)
32. Etikan, I.: Comparison of convenience sampling and purposive sampling. AJTAS **5**, 1 (2016)
33. Kaplan, B., Maxwell, J.A.: Qualitative research methods for evaluating computer information systems. In: Anderson, J.G., Aydin, C.E. (eds.) Evaluating the Organizational Impact of Healthcare Information Systems, pp. 30–55. Springer Science+Business Media Inc, New York, NY (2005)
34. Grimsley, M., Meehan, A.: e-Government information systems: evaluation-led design for public value and client trust. Eur. J. Inf. Syst. **16**, 134–148 (2007)
35. Pinsonneault, A., Kraemer, K.: Survey research methodology in management information systems: an assessment. J. Manag. Inf. Syst. **10**, 75–105 (1993)
36. Schmiedel, T., Recker, J., Vom Brocke, J.: The relation between BPM culture, BPM methods, and process performance: evidence from quantitative field studies. Inf. Manag. **57**, 103175 (2020)
37. Urbach, N., Ahlemann, F.: Structural equation modeling in information systems research using partial least squares. J. Inf. Technol. Theory Appl. **11**, 5–40 (2010)
38. Gable, G.G.: Integrating case study and survey research methods: an example in information systems. Eur. J. Inf. Syst. **3**, 112–126 (1994)

Supporting the Development and Implementation of a Digitalization Strategy in SMEs Through a Lightweight Architecture-based Method

Nils J. Tschoppe[✉] and Paul Drews

Institute of Information Systems, Leuphana University of Lüneburg, Lüneburg, Germany
{nils.tschoppe,paul.drews}@leuphana.de

Abstract. Like larger companies, small and medium-sized enterprises (SMEs) need to develop and implement a digitalization strategy. However, they face specific challenges such as a lack of IT know-how, relevant market information and appropriate methods for developing a strategy. Following the Action Design Research method and in cooperation with two medium sized companies, we started to develop a lightweight, architecture-based method for the development and implementation of digitalization strategies in SMEs.

Keywords: Digital entrepreneurship · Enterprise architecture management · Small and medium-sized enterprises · Digitalization strategy · Digital transformation

1 Introduction

The digital transformation as a technology-based change process is not limited to large and established companies. In times of a digital economy, enterprises of all sizes and ages need to rethink their strategy, organization and technology use. This has been referred to as digital entrepreneurship in the literature and it results in manifold change and innovation activities [1–4]. However, most research in this field is based on the assumption that a professional and sufficiently large IT organization with differentiated roles is established in the organization [5, 6]. SMEs, especially away from the conurbations, often face special challenges such as high exploration costs, perceived unbalance of risks and chances for the adoption of innovations and technologies, a lack of relevant market information as well as insufficient digital skills of employees [6–10]. With increasing relevance in practice and research [11, p. 5], the management of enterprise architecture (EA) is considered to be an "essential enabler of the digital transformation" [12, p. 280]. With an enterprise-wide view on organizational and technological artifacts, it supports the alignment of business and IT [11, 13]. It helps to document and analyze the current state and serves as the basis for planning future target states and transformation steps [13–19]. Digital transformation processes may lead to tensions on multiple organizational levels [3]. To anticipate and address these tensions, experts from different departments

F. Ahlemann et al. (Eds.): WI 2021, LNISO 48, pp. 685–691, 2021.
https://doi.org/10.1007/978-3-030-86800-0_47

and levels should be involved in the development process while considering the 'big picture' consisting of strategic objectives, business processes, and IT landscape [20]. In contrast to existing complex frameworks such as TOGAF [21] and FEAF v2 [22], we seek to develop a more lightweight, visualization-oriented and pragmatic approach for SMEs and realize Winter's idea of architectural thinking for this field [23].

Hence, our research question is: How can SMEs develop and implement digitalization strategies using a lightweight, architecture-based method?

2   Research Approach

While this work in progress seeks to contribute to the information systems research discipline by advancing methods of enterprise architecture modelling and management, it also draws upon and contributes to the literature on digital entrepreneurship. In order to develop and evaluate a solution that is both, theory-ingrained and practice-oriented, we employed the Action Design Research (ADR) method according to Sein et al. [24], which focuses on building, intervening and evaluating (BIE) artifacts and allows to co-develop an approach in practice while also supporting the generalization and theorizing.

During the preparation phase, two companies - an online-agency (A) with approximately 100 employees which can be classified as a digital "gazelle" [25] as well as the headquarter of a more senior company (B) selling luxury outdoor furniture with approximately 200 employees - were identified as particularly suitable for the development of a digitalization strategy. The extraordinary growth despite regional restrictions of company A and the advanced maturity, expansion efforts and corporate integration of company B serve as an interesting contrast.

In the problem formulation stage, we diagnosed the lack of an explicit digitalization strategy in both companies. As digitalization describes "the manifold sociotechnical phenomena and processes of adopting and using technologies in broader individual, organizational, and societal contexts" [26, p. 302], a digitalization strategy follows the overall corporate strategy and goes far beyond the mere technology trend; "it constitutes a holistic intention of a company to streamline all activities regarding the digital transformation process to generate competitive advantages through new technologies and methods" [27, p. 670]. With special emphasis on the redesign of the software landscape (A) and the use of new technologies such as virtual and augmented reality (B), the selected BIE form was organization-dominant in both cases as we seek to create a method for developing a digitalization strategy. In the alpha cycle, we iterated and evaluated early designs of the digitalization strategy in workshops with the CEO and the COO (A) and the Head of IT (B). As part of a first as-is analysis, the application of Porter's five competitive forces that determine industry profitability [28, p. 5], amongst others, helped us to develop an understanding of the business ecosystem [29], enterprise systems used therein as well as to reveal potential dependencies. It was accompanied by an analysis of archival material such as industry reports, process descriptions, the organizational chart and a transcript of vision and values as part of the business strategy and supplemented by instruments such as the Gartner Hype Cycle of Emerging Technologies [36] to identify relevant technologies. For identifying inefficiencies and outdated, incompatible software, we mapped existing software to an organization-specific model of Porter's generic value chain [28, p. 37]. This helped us to review the core processes and served as the starting point for discussing which software will be necessary in the future (to-be landscape). In the beta cycle, we took our preliminary findings into a wider organizational setting as our know-how was limited in terms of strategy (B) and software selection (A). By inviting the CEO, the Sales Manager and other experts from the business departments, we were able to enrich our findings in a workshop (B). As Company B's business was more affected by Covid-19, the data collection had to be stopped in March 2020. Nevertheless, we complemented our data by conducting semi-structured interviews (one offline and seven online) on the different levels at company A including the two CEOs & founders, the COO, four department managers as well as a trainee. These interviews lasted between 20 and 90 min depending on experience and responsibility of the interviewee and covered questions ranging from the individual software usage and acceptance to personnel and strategic issues such as digital literacy and the market environment. By analyzing and coding these with MAXQDA [30], we were able to further refine our lightweight, architecture-based method as well as our understanding of the internal structure and external factors. In addition, we conducted a subsequent online workshop across the departments which were likely to be most affected by the transformation to identify internal capabilities and prepare the development of the digitalization strategy and roadmap. To validate and enrich our findings theoretically and practically, intermediate findings regarding the development of the digitalization strategy were mirrored several times with the COO (A) and the Head of IT (B) while reviewing the lightweight, architecture-based method through interdisciplinary discussions in a circle of researchers from different fields such as information systems, strategic management, psychology and organizational science.

3 Results

Based on the findings of the two companies investigated so far, we propose our method for the development of a digitalization strategy in SMEs and its transformation with special attention to a lightweight visualization of the enterprise architecture (Fig. 1).

First of all, an as-is analysis of the internal structure and external factors is beneficial to gain a deeper understanding of the need for necessary changes. Taking into account the business strategy helps to prevent shortsightedness in the development process as it can have a decisive influence on the later design of the digitalization strategy and may additionally provide useful business information. The analysis of the organization and its capabilities as well as the (business) processes linked to the existing software and hardware landscape (1.1) enables a better understanding of potential dependencies in order to reduce medium to long-term costs caused by inefficiencies and wrong IT investments. By doing so, it may be also important to point out interrelations with supplier portals and their interfaces when it comes to selecting, developing or implementing new software. Documents such as organization and capability charts, hardware and software constellations and process descriptions, which may be supplemented by a Business Model Canvas [31] or a Value Proposition Canvas [32], can help to gain a comprehensive picture of the internal structure. As an illustration, it can be advantageous to map the company's software solutions and their dependencies to primary and secondary activities

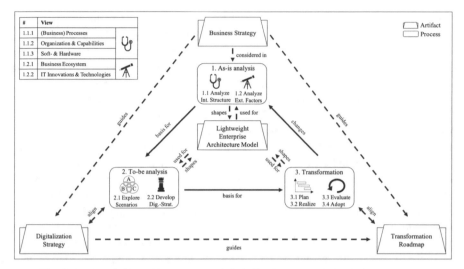

Fig. 1. Lightweight, architecture-based digitalization strategy development method

in Porter's generic value chain [28, p. 37] tailored to the enterprise. The significance of required changes can be pictured, for example, as simple traffic lights (e.g. urgent need for change, needs to be checked, meets requirements). In the case of a multi-divisional organization with several departments, it can also be helpful to represent these as swim lanes and to map existing software to their activities, e.g. ranging from sales generation to invoicing and maintenance. The external view (1.2) comprises the identification of relevant technologies and IT innovations as well as factors of the business ecosystem, which can have a direct (e.g. interlocked supplier processes) or indirect (e.g. competition, customer, partner) impact on the company. One effective tool for this is Porter's five competitive forces that determine industry profitability [28, p. 5] which allows a comprehensive visualization of the market environment and may be supplemented by industry-reports and instruments such as the Gartner Hype Cycle of Emerging Technologies [36]. This perspective can also provide interesting information about which technologies and software the competitors use. After an initial draft of the internal structure and external factors has been prepared by the person or team responsible for the digitalization strategy, further employees from the departments to be transformed should be involved to enrich these findings. This may also help to sensitize employees to technical and organizational changes within the transformation (3).

Secondly, it has proven promising to explore several to-be scenarios of the internal structure under consideration of external factors (2.1) based on the findings of the as-is analysis. This supports prioritization and again sensitizes for the transformation process. After creating a comprehensive overview of the current state and developing a potentially promising scenario, the next step is to develop the business aligned digitalization strategy (2.2). Here, an illustrative presentation of the data compiled in phase 1 and 2.1 should form the basis, coordinated with other stakeholders within the company.

To operationalize the digitalization strategy, a transformation roadmap tailored to the company and its capabilities has to be developed closely coordinated with existing and planned company-wide projects (3.1). For this, it is necessary to allocate resources as well as to determine who is responsible for the realization of the (sub-)projects underlying the transformation (3.2). In some cases, especially when dealing with new technologies or complex software, it can be necessary to draw on external know-how. If this is the case, a selection of possible partners must be made and their advantages and disadvantages in terms of costs, expertise and capacities weighed up. In any case, the transformation process has to be evaluated (3.3) and adjusted (3.4) regularly as changes in 1.1 and 1.2 may occur.

However, we also observed some frictions in this model between theoretical modeling and practical applicability. Despite the lack of an elaborated business strategy (A and B) and without an existing IT department (A), it was nevertheless possible to build on the knowledge of the IT responsible person(s). In smaller companies, such a person with knowledge about the technical properties of IT systems might not be available. While the business strategy is usually anchored in the heads of the management, it is rarely written down in its entirety and communicated to all stakeholders, which may hinder the development of the digitalization strategy and the transformation as it may reveal important insights, e.g. of the business ecosystem, internal processes and technology trends.

4 Conclusion and Outlook

In this paper, we present our research approach and intermediate findings towards the development of a lightweight, architecture-based method for developing and implementing digitalization strategies in SMEs. The method proposes to create coordinated, comprehensive visualizations of relevant views including internal processes and external influences. A structured collection of data and the uncovering of dependencies between IT and business through the enterprise architecture lens helps to set priorities when developing a digitalization strategy while supporting transparency and documentation [13]. The underlying transformation process, however, does not necessarily imply the use of new technologies such as virtual or augmented reality (B), but often also requires basic work like redesigning the software and hardware landscape (A). Besides this, there are manifold reasons why digital transformation projects fail. One of the main reasons is the disconnection between the pure formulation of a strategy and its implementation [33] which has to be addressed through a constant questioning of the status quo. In order to validate and generalize our results, it is necessary to investigate further companies from different industries. We will take a closer look at the phases and evaluate the results at A and B after some time. So far, the consideration of digital technologies has played a subordinate role in entrepreneurial research and its intersection with information systems related research [4, 34, 35]. The investigation of the specific conditions as well as success factors including the selection, evaluation and appropriation of IT innovations in the context of developing a digitalization strategy is still in its infancy and therefore offers a promising field of research.

References

1. Böhmann, T., Drews, P., Meyer-Blankart, C.: Digitale Exzellenz. Eine Bestandsaufnahme zur Digitalisierung deutscher Unternehmen und Behörden. Sopra Steria (2015)
2. Hinings, B., Gegenhuber, T., Greenwood, R.: Digital innovation and transformation: an institutional perspective. Inf. Organ. **28**, 52–61 (2018)
3. Nambisan, S., Wright, M., Feldman, M.: The digital transformation of innovation and entrepreneurship: progress, challenges and key themes. Res. Policy **48**, 1–9 (2019)
4. Nambisan, S.: Digital entrepreneurship: toward a digital technology perspective of entrepreneurship. Entrep. Theory Pract. **41**, 1029–1055 (2017)
5. Horlach, B., Drews, P., Schirmer, I.: Bimodal it: business-it alignment in the age of digital transformation. In: Multikonferenz Wirtschaftsinformatik, pp. 1417–1428. MKWI, Ilmenau (2016)
6. Passerini, K., Tarabishy, A.E., Patten, K.: Information Technology for Small Business. Springer, Dordrecht, Heidelberg, London, New York (2012)
7. Huck-Fries, V., Wiesche, M., Pfluegler, C., Krcmar, H.: The hateful six - factors hindering Adoption of innovation at small and medium sized enterprises. In: 22nd Americas Conference on Information Systems. AMCIS, San Diego (2016)
8. Abel-Koch, J., Al Obaidi, L., El Kasmi, S., Acevedo, M. F., Morin, L., Topczewska, A.: Going Digital The Challenges Facing European SMEs. KfW (2019)
9. Huck-Fries, V., Pflügler, C., Wiesche, M., Krcmar, H.: Innovationshemmnisse für kleine und mittlere Unternehmen. In: Wiesche M., Sauer P., Krimmling J., Krcmar, H. (eds.) Management digitaler Plattformen. Informationsmanagement und digitale Transformation, pp. 297–312. Springer Gabler, Wiesbaden (2018). https://doi.org/10.1007/978-3-658-21214-8_19
10. Zimmermann, V., Thomä, J.: Innovationshemmnisse in KMU - vielfältige Hemmnisse sprechen für eine breit aufgestellte Förderpolitik. KfW (2016)
11. Simon, D., Fischbach, K., Schoder, D.: An exploration of enterprise architecture research. In: Communications of the Association for Information Systems, pp. 1–72. AIS (2013)
12. Hanschke, I.: Digitalisierung und Industrie 4.0 - einfach und effektiv : systematisch und lean die digitale Transformation meistern. Carl Hanser Verlag, München (2018)
13. Aier, S., Winter, R.: Unternehmensarchitektur - Literaturüberblick und Stand der Praxis. Wirtschaftsinformatik **50**, 292–304 (2008)
14. Winter, R., Fischer, R.: Essential layers, artifacts, and dependencies of enterprise architecture. In: 10th IEEE International Enterprise Distributed Object Computing Conference Workshops. IEEE, Hong Kong (2006)
15. Buckl, S.M.: Developing organization-specific enterprise architecture management functions using a method base. Technische Universität München (2011)
16. Petrikina, J., Drews, P., Schirmer, I., Zimmermann, K.: Integrating business models and enterprise architecture. In: 18th International Enterprise Distributed Object Computing Conference Workshops and Demonstrations, pp. 47–56. IEEE, Ulm (2014)
17. Schmidt, J., Drews, P.: Entwicklung und Evaluation eines Metamodells zur Verbesserung der unternehmensweiten Entscheidungsorientierung mithilfe der Unternehmensarchitektur. In: 12th International Conference on Wirtschaftsinformatik, pp. 1814–1828. AIS, Osnabrück (2015)
18. Aier, S., Ahrens, M., Stutz, M., Bub, U.: Deriving SOA evaluation metrics in an enterprise architecture context. In: Di Nitto, E., Ripeanu, M. (eds.) ICSOC 2007. LNCS, vol. 4907, pp. 224–233. Springer, Heidelberg (2009). https://doi.org/10.1007/978-3-540-93851-4_22
19. Keuntje, J.H., Barkow, R., Mannmeusel, T.: Enterprise Architecture Management in der Praxis. Symposion Publishing, Düsseldorf (2010)

20. Horlach, B., Drechsler, A., Schirmer, I., Drews, P.: Everyone's going to be an architect: design principles for architectural thinking in agile organizations. In: 53rd Hawaii International Conference on System Sciences. HICSS, Hawaii (2020)

21. The Open Group: The Open Group Architecture Framework TOGAF. van Haren Publishing, Zaltbommel (2007)

22. Federal government of the United States: Federal Enterprise Architecture Framework Version 2. https://obamawhitehouse.archives.gov/sites/default/files/omb/assets/egov_docs/fea_v2.pdf. Accessed 23 Aug 2020

23. Winter, R.: Architectural thinking. Wirtschaftsinformatik 56(6), 395–398 (2014). https://doi.org/10.1007/s11576-014-0439-x

24. Sein, M.K., Henfridsson, O., Purao, S., Rossi, M., Lindgren, R.: Action design research. MIS Q. 35, 37–56 (2011)

25. Birch, D.G.W.: Job creation in america - how our smallest companies put the most people to work. Univ. Illinois Urbana-Champaign's Acad. Entrep. Leadersh. 27, 1204–1206 (1987)

26. Legner, C., et al.: Digitalization: opportunity and challenge for the business and information systems engineering community. Bus. Inf. Syst. Eng. 59(4), 301–308 (2017). https://doi.org/10.1007/s12599-017-0484-2

27. Pfenning, P., Eigner, M.: A novel procedure model for developing individualized digitalization strategies. Proc. Des. Soc. Des. Conf. 1, 667–676 (2020)

28. Porter, M.E.: Competitive Advantage - Creating and Sustaining Superior Performance. The Free Press, New York (1985)

29. Moore, J.F.: Business ecosystems and the view from the firm. Antitrust Bull. 51, 31–75 (2006)

30. VERBI Software: MAXQDA 2020. VERBI Software, Berlin (2019)

31. Osterwalder, A., Pigneur, Y.: Business Model Generation: A Handbook for Visionaries, Game Changers, and Challengers. Wiley, New York (2010)

32. Osterwalder, A., Pigneur, Y., Bernarda, G., Smith, A.: Value Proposition Design: How to Create Products and Services Customers Want. Wiley, New York (2014)

33. Correani, A., Italia, M., Massis, A. De, Frattini, F., Petruzzelli, A.M., Natalicchio, A.: Implementing a digital strategy: learning from the experience of three digital transformation projects. Calif. Manage. Rev. (2020, in press)

34. Recker, J., von Briel, F.: The future of digital entrepreneurship research: existing and emerging opportunities. In: 40th International Conference on Information Systems, pp. 1–9. ICIS, München (2019)

35. Nambisan, S., Siegel, D., Kenney, M.: On open innovation, platforms, and entrepreneurship. Strateg. Entrep. J. 12, 354–368 (2018)

36. Gartner Inc.: Hype Cycle for Emerging Technologies, Stamford, Connecticut (2020)

Author Index

Printed in the United States
by Baker & Taylor Publisher Services